For many decades *Vine's Expository Dictionary of New Testament Wor* companion for any serious Bible student. The advent of this new ec *Testament Word Pictures*, can only be a cause for rejoicing amongst t the Word more because they understand the Word of the Lord bette

—Dr. Steve Brady, principal, Moorlands College and lecturer in New Testament Greek

The best of Bible dictionaries just got better! Instead of sitting on a shelf, the new *W. E. Vine's New Testament Word Pictures* will be next to your Bible because it is functional. It's genius in motion. Covering every key word in every chapter and verse in the New Testament, *W. E. Vine's New Testament Word Pictures* is a genuine companion to any Bible translation because it's a dictionary, a concise commentary, and a concordance all in one.

—Robert F. Hicks, teacher, preacher, and Bible publisher

Bible students and teachers who want to dig into the meaning of the key words in a verse or Bible passage will find a treasure in *W. E. Vine's New Testament Word Pictures.* I have used *Vine's Expository Dictionary of New Testament Words* for many years, but the format of this new book is much more helpful when leading a Bible study. W. E. Vine's insights on every key word in a passage are in one place where I can see them easily and clearly.

—James F. Couch Jr., executive editor, The Voice Bible translation; reference, curriculum, and Bible publisher, retired; and past executive vice-president, Emmaus Bible College

My dad's copy of *Vine's Expository Dictionary of New Testament Words* sits on the reference shelf next to my study desk. It is often open near at hand as I prepare sermons. What a delight to have a new edition that follows the New Testament text like a commentary! No more searching through an entire entry to find the section relevant to the passage I am studying. The new *W. E. Vine's New Testament Word Pictures* brings the treasures of a classic resource to the minds and hearts and teaching of today's pastor and Bible student.

—Douglas Connelley, pastor, author of seventeen LifeGuide Bible studies and *The Bible for Blockheads*

I first used the famous Vine's Dictionary as a 19-year-old student at Cambridge University, while preparing for a lifetime of Christian ministry. Thomas Nelson Publishers deserves the thanks of Bible students, preachers, and Scripture class leaders worldwide in bringing us this superb new edition of a work that all of us—both advanced and new to God's Word—will want to keep at our sides.

—Richard Bewes O.B.E., former rector of All Souls Church, London, England and current host of international Bible TV programs *Open Home Open Bible*, *Book by Book*, and *The Sermon*

Vine's Expository Dictionary of New Testament Words was an indispensable tool for generations of Bible students, including myself, as it introduced them to the meaning and richness of the vocabulary of the New Testament. This revision and rearrangement makes it even more useful and I hope will introduce it to new generations. Word studies are not all that needs to be done in understanding the New Testament, but they're an essential beginning. There's no better place to start than this improved, comprehensive, and accessible new *W. E. Vine's New Testament Word Pictures.*

—Derek Tidball, former principal, London School of Theology; visiting scholar, Spurgeon's College, London

For heavyweight Bible study, especially by those who do not read Greek, Vine's is the word-explanation book to have. It is great to see it made available to a new generation. In place of the original version's list of words in alphabetical order, this new edition is in verse-by-verse New Testament text order, Matthew to Revelation. This neatly solves the question of what word to look up when using different translations and Bible versions. I commend it to all who wish to do serious study of the basic idea underlying each significant New Testament word.

—C. Peter White, former principal of Glasgow Bible College and minister of Sandyford Henderson Parish Church, Glasgow, Scotland

It is great to see the new format which Martin Manser and his team have given to *Vine's Expository Dictionary of New Testament Words.* In this format this classic will be able to serve new generations of serious readers of the Bible even better.

—Rev. Dr. Pieter J. Lalleman, academic dean and tutor of New Testament, Spurgeon's College, London, England

Vine's has been a seemingly limitless treasure trove of careful theological and linguistic insight for generations of preachers and Bible students, enriching sermons and Christian lives around the world. Now, thanks to Martin Manser and his colleagues, that treasure is accessible in updated form for a new generation to enjoy. The church owes them a huge debt of thanks.

—John P. Bowen, former professor of evangelism, Wycliffe College, Toronto

Any serious study of the Bible involves careful attention to the meaning of words. This imaginative revision of a classic study tool will enable a new generation of readers to engage with the wealth of meaning in each New Testament book.

—Stephen Travis, St. John's College, Nottingham, England

W. E. VINE'S

NEW TESTAMENT WORD PICTURES

HEBREWS TO REVELATION

W. E. VINE'S

NEW TESTAMENT WORD PICTURES

A COMMENTARY DRAWN FROM THE ORIGINAL LANGUAGES

HEBREWS TO REVELATION

EVERY VERSE EXPLAINED

W. E. VINE WITH F. F. BRUCE

Martin H. Manser, editor

Nicola L. Bull, assistant editor

THOMAS NELSON

Since 1798

THOMAS NELSON

W. E. Vine's New Testament Word Pictures: Hebrews to Revelation

Previously published as part of *W. E. Vine's New Testament Word Pictures: Romans to Revelation.*

Published in Nashville, Tennessee, by Thomas Nelson. Thomas Nelson is a registered trademark of HarperCollins Christian Publishing, Inc.

Thomas Nelson titles may be purchased in bulk for educational, business, fundraising, or sales promotional use. For information, please email SpecialMarkets@ThomasNelson.com.

ISBN 978-0-310-15408-2 (softcover)

ISBN 978-0-310-15409-9 (ebook)

Vine's Complete Expository Dictionary of Old and New Testament Words, © 1984, 1996, Thomas Nelson, Inc., Nashville, TN; a compilation work published under an exclusive arrangement with W. E. Vine Copyright Ltd. of Bath, England. First Published in 1985 by Thomas Nelson, Inc., as a compilation of *Vine's Expository Dictionary of New Testament Words*, © 1968, which copyright is now restored by the GATT Treaty to W. E. Vine Copyright Ltd., Bath, England; and *Nelson's Expository Dictionary of the Old Testament*, © 1980, Thomas Nelson, Inc., and Topical Index © 1996, W. E. Vine Copyright Ltd. of Bath, England.

Cover design: James W. Hall
Cover photos: © Carlos Mir; Elliott Photography / Getty Images

Contents

HEBREWS TO REVELATION

Introduction

Welcome to *W. E. Vine's New Testament Word Pictures*.

It's Saturday evening and you have to finish preparing your talk for tomorrow from Matthew's Gospel. You may have used *Vine's Expository Dictionary of New Testament Words* before, but you cannot face the daunting task of looking up every word in each verse of your passage to see if there's a nugget that will set your congregation, class or group alight. Relax – we've done the hard work for you!

We've taken every key word that's in Vine's and re-sorted each one out of its original alphabetical sequence into a handy verse-by-verse order, covering every verse of the New Testament. To make it even more helpful to use, we've also:

- given the text of the KJV to provide the context for the key words
- included the Strong's numbers for the key words
- selected the relevant paragraphs of the entries
- kept W. E. Vine's original comments on alternative readings from the Revised Version
- provided you with inspirational quotations to give your talk that fresh edge.

The text before you is an edited version of the *Expository Dictionary of New Testament Words* by W. E. Vine, originally published in 1940, which has helped countless Bible preachers and teachers to explain the text of the New Testament.

W. E. Vine's original text used the scholarship of Bishop Westcott, W. F. Moulton, A. T. Robertson and James Hastings; forewords were written by the eminent scholars W. Graham Scroggie and F. F. Bruce.

This new reference work makes Vine's material even more accessible, because the edited text has been rearranged in Bible book order and then by chapter and verse. So this means that if you are preparing to give a talk on Matthew chapter 4, you can look up that chapter here and all the words discussed with reference to that chapter in *Vine's Expository Dictionary of New Testament Words* are presented here in a convenient verse-by-verse order. Of course you can still explore the entire riches of the complete *Vine's Expository Dictionary of New Testament Words*.

We are pleased to have worked with Thomas Nelson in producing this text, and you can of course still buy *Vine's Expository Dictionary of New Testament Words* and *Vine's Complete Expository Dictionary of Old and New Testament Words with Topical Index* as books, online, or as Bible software. See www.logos.com.

This unique text contains elements of a Dictionary, Concordance and Commentary, not merely listing the key words of the Bible text, but also explaining the meaning behind them. And because it is keyed to Strong's numbers, you can use it with any version of the Bible.

We trust that this companion will help you explore God's word to discover fresh inspiration you can communicate to others, directing them to God's Word to all humanity, Jesus Christ himself.

Martin Manser
Editor

Thank you, Professor F. F. Bruce

"Give honor to whom honor is due."

Not long after I took on the stewardship of the works of the late W. E. Vine, I was privileged to come to know three of his then-surviving daughters and Mr. Vine's personal Secretary, John Williamson.

Through our conversations, I began to realize the major contribution of Professor F. F. Bruce to the unique book created by Mr. Vine – his *Expository Dictionary of New Testament Words*. Originally published in four volumes, it is now available as a single volume, which is the basis of this book.

Mr. Vine and Prof. Bruce had many things in common academically. They both gained their qualifications by studying the Greek classics, and both were familiar with the many ancient manuscripts that stand behind the Greek New Testament. They were also students of the Greek manuscripts of the Old Testament that were in existence before the first century and which were frequently quoted in the New Testament. In addition to their academic similarity, they both belonged to Brethren assemblies, a group known in the United States as Plymouth Brethren.

Mr. Williamson and Mr. Vine's daughters told me that when Mr. Vine began work on his *Dictionary*, he sent it, section by section, to Prof. Bruce. Interestingly, Mr. Vine's daughter Jeannette manually typed the text. Prof. Bruce then checked the draft script against all reliable sources, making additions and corrections as well as offering suggestions – and these were returned to Mr. Vine.

Mr. Vine incorporated the recommendations into a second draft, which was then sent back to Prof. Bruce. Jeannette informed me that Mr. Vine seldom saw anything in Prof. Bruce's work on which he raised a query.

Prof. Bruce then prepared the text for typesetting, which in those days was a major task. Unusually, Mr. Vine paid for the typesetting himself, rather than having the publisher pay for it, as is more common. The typesetting was then sent to the printer who created a "proof." Prof. Bruce again checked everything on the proof before giving his approval to publish the book.

Martin Manser, who undertook the editorial work for this edition of the *Dictionary*, has told me that there were very few mistakes in the original. This is clear evidence of the professionalism of both Mr. Vine and Prof. Bruce.

While Mr. Vine will always be acknowledged as the originating author of this work, the level of scholarship and assistance that Prof. Bruce contributed means that in today's world he would have been acknowledged alongside Mr. Vine as co-author – as we have done in this edition. Prof. Bruce made significant changes to Mr. Vine's text, effectively rewriting much of the material, bringing his own scholarship to the work. Mr. Vine trusted Prof. Bruce's judgment, allowing Bruce to make changes as necessary without questioning. So, a belated "Thank you" to Professor F. F. Bruce for bringing his significant academic skills to the work of W. E. Vine.

Robert F. Hicks
Publisher

Hebrews

Chapter 1

1:1 God, who at sundry times and in divers manners spake in time past unto the fathers by the prophets,

Sundry times *polumeros* (4181), signifies "in many parts" or "portions," **Heb. 1:1**, RV (KJV, "at sundry times").

Divers manners *polutropos* (4187), means "in many ways" (*polus*, "much," *tropos*, "a manner, way"; Eng., "trope"), "in divers manners," **Heb. 1:1**.

Time *palai* (3819), "long ago, of old," is rendered "of old time" in **Heb. 1:1** (KJV, "in time past").

1:2 Hath in these last days spoken unto us by *his* Son, whom he hath appointed heir of all things, by whom also he made the worlds;

Last In **Heb. 1:2**, RV, "at the end of these days" (KJV, "in these last days"), the reference is to the close of the period of the testimony of the prophets under the Law, terminating with the presence of Christ and His redemptive sacrifice and its effects, the perfect tense "hath spoken" indicating the continued effects of the message embodied in the risen Christ; so in 1 Pet. 1:20, RV, "at the end of the times" (KJV, "in these last times").

Son *The Son of God* In this title the word "Son" is used sometimes (a) of relationship, sometimes (b) of the expression of character. "Thus, e.g., when the disciples so addressed Him, Matt. 14:33; 16:16; John 1:49, when the centurion so spoke of Him, Matt. 27:54, they probably meant that (b) He was a manifestation of God in human form. But in such passages as Luke 1:32, 35; Acts 13:33, which refer to the humanity of the Lord Jesus, ... the word is used in sense (a).

"The Lord Jesus Himself used the full title on occasion, John 5:25; 9:35 [some mss. have 'the Son of Man'; see RV marg.]; 11:4, and on the more frequent occasions on which He spoke of Himself as 'the Son,' the words are to be understood as an abbreviation of 'the Son of God,' not of 'The Son of Man'; this latter He always expressed in full; see Luke 10:22; John 5:19, etc. John uses both the longer and shorter forms of the title in his Gospel, see 3:16-18; 20:31, e.g., and in his Epistles; cf. Rev. 2:18. So does the writer of Hebrews, **1:2**; **4:14**; **6:6**, etc. An eternal relation subsisting between the Son and the Father in the Godhead is to be understood. That is to say, the Son of God, in His eternal relationship with the Father, is not so entitled because He at any time began to derive His being from the Father (in which case He could not be co-eternal with the Father), but because He is and ever has been the expression of what the Father is; cf. John 14:9, 'he that hath seen Me hath seen the Father.' The words of **Heb. 1:3**, 'Who being the effulgence of His (God's) glory, and the very image of His (God's) substance' are a definition of what is meant by 'Son of God.' Thus absolute Godhead, not Godhead in a secondary or derived sense, is intended in the title."

"The Son is the eternal object of the Father's love, John 17:24, and the sole Revealer of the Father's character, John 1:14; **Heb. 1:3**. The words, 'Father' and 'Son,' are never in the NT so used as to suggest that the Father existed before the Son; the Prologue to the Gospel according to John distinctly asserts that the Word existed 'in the beginning,' and that this Word is the Son, Who 'became flesh and dwelt among us.'"

In addressing the Father in His prayer in John 17 He says, "Thou lovedst Me before the foundation of the world." Accordingly in the timeless past the Father and the "Son" existed in that relationship, a relationship of love, as well as of absolute Deity. In this passage the

"Son" gives evidence that there was no more powerful plea in the Father's estimation than that coeternal love existing between the Father and Himself. The declaration "Thou art My Son, this day have I begotten Thee," Ps. 2:7, quoted in Acts 13:33; **Heb. 1:5**; **5:5**, refers to the birth of Christ, not to His resurrection. In Acts 13:33 the verb "raise up" is used of the raising up of a person to occupy a special position in the nation, as of David in verse 22 (so of Christ as a Prophet in 3:22 and 7:37). The word "again" in the KJV in v. 33 represents nothing in the original. The RV rightly omits it. In v. 34 the statement as to the resurrection of Christ receives the greater stress in this respect through the emphatic contrast to that in v. 33 as to His being raised up in the nation, a stress imparted by the added words "from the dead." Accordingly v. 33 speaks of His incarnation, v. 34 of His resurrection. In **Heb. 1:5**, that the declaration refers to the Birth is confirmed by the contrast in verse **6**. Here the word "again" is rightly placed in the RV, "when He again bringeth in the Firstborn into the world." This points on to His second advent, which is set in contrast to His first advent, when God brought His Firstborn into the world the first time. So again in **Heb. 5:5**, where the High Priesthood of Christ is shown to fulfill all that was foreshadowed in the Levitical priesthood, the passage stresses the facts of His humanity, the days of His flesh, His perfect obedience and His sufferings.

Appointed *tithemi* (5087), "to put," is used of "appointment" to any form of service. Christ used it of His followers, John 15:16 (RV, "appointed" for KJV, "ordained"). "I set you" would be more in keeping with the metaphor of grafting. The verb is used by Paul of his service in the ministry of the gospel, 1 Tim. 1:12 (RV, "appointing" for "putting"); 2:7 (RV, "appointed" for "ordained"); and 2 Tim. 1:11 (RV, "appointing" for "putting"); of the overseers, or bishops, in the local church at Ephesus, as those "appointed" by the Holy Ghost, to tend the church of God, Acts 20:28 ("hath made"); of the Son of God, as appointed Heir of all things, **Heb. 1:2**. It is also used of "appointment" to punishment, as of the unfaithful servant, Matt. 24:51; Luke 12:46; of unbelieving Israel, 1 Pet. 2:8. Cf. 2 Pet. 2:6.

Heir *kleronomos* (2818), lit. denotes "one who obtains a lot or portion" (*kleros*, "a lot," *nemomai*, "to possess"), especially of an inheritance. The NT usage may be analyzed as under: "(a) the person to whom property is to pass on the death of the owner, Matt. 21:38; Mark 12:7; Luke 20:14; Gal. 4:1; (b) one to whom something has been assigned by God, on possession of which, however, he has not yet entered, as Abraham, Rom. 4:13, 14; **Heb. 6:17**; Christ, **Heb. 1:2**; the poor saints, Jas. 2:5; (c) believers, inasmuch as they share in the new order of things to be ushered in at the return of Christ, Rom. 8:17; Gal. 3:29; 4:7; Titus 3:7; (d) one who receives something other than by merit, as Noah, **Heb. 11:7**." In the Sept., Judg. 18:7; 2 Sam. 14:7; Jer. 8:10; Mic. 1:15.

Made *poieo* (4160), "to do, to make," is used in the latter sense ... (c) with nouns involving the idea of action (or of something accomplished by action), so as to express the idea of the verb more forcibly (the middle voice is commonly used in this respect, suggesting the action as being of special interest to the doer); for the active voice see, e.g., Mark 2:23, of "making" one's way, where the idea is not that the disciples "made" a path through the standing corn, but simply that they went, the phrase being equivalent to going, "(they began) as they went (to pluck the ears)"; other instances of the active are Rev. 13:13, 14; 16:14; 19:20; for the middle voice (the dynamic or subjective middle), see, e.g., John 14:23, "will make Our abode"; in Acts 20:24, "none of these things move me," lit., "I make account of none of these things"; 25:17, "I made no delay" RV, Rom. 15:26; Eph. 4:16; **Heb. 1:2**; 2 Pet. 1:10; (d) to "make" ready or prepare, e.g., a dinner, Luke 14:12; a supper, John 12:2; (e) to acquire, provide a thing for oneself, Matt. 25:16; Luke 19:18; (f) to render or "make" one or oneself anything, or cause a person or thing to become something, e.g., Matt. 4:19; 12:16, "make (Him known)"; John 5:11, 15, to "make" whole; 16:2, lit., "they shall make (you put out of the synagogue)"; Eph. 2:14; **Heb. 1:7**; to change one thing into another, Matt. 21:13; John 2:16; 4:46; 1 Cor. 6:15; (g) to constitute one anything, e.g., Acts 2:36, (h) to declare one or oneself anything, John 5:18, "making (Himself equal with God)"; 8:53; 10:33; 19:7, 12; 1 John 1:10; 5:10; (i) to "make" one do a thing, e.g., Luke 5:34; John 6:10; Rev. 3:9.

Worlds *aion* (165), "an age, a period of time," marked in the NT usage by spiritual or moral characteristics, is sometimes translated "world"; the RV marg. always has "age." The following are details concerning the world in this respect; its cares, Matt. 13:22; its sons, Luke 16:8; 20:34; its rulers, 1 Cor. 2:6, 8; its wisdom, 1 Cor. 1:20; 2:6; 3:18; its fashion, Rom. 12:2; its character, Gal. 1:4; its god, 2 Cor. 4:4. The phrase "the end of the world" should be rendered "the end of the age," in most places; in 1 Cor. 10:11, KJV, "the ends (*tele*) of the world," RV, "the ends of the ages," probably signifies the fulfillment of the divine purposes concerning the ages in regard to the church. In **Heb 11:3** [lit., "the ages (have been prepared)"] the word indicates all that the successive periods contain; cf. **1:2.** *Aion* is always to be distinguished from *kosmos*, even where the two seem to express the same idea, e.g., 1 Cor. 3:18, *aion*, v. 19, *kosmos;* the two are used together in Eph. 2:2, lit., "the age of this world." For a list of phrases containing *aion*, with their respective meanings.

1:3 Who being the brightness of *his* glory, and the express image of his person, and upholding all things by the word of his power, when he had by himself purged our sins, sat down on the right hand of the Majesty on high;

Brightness *apaugasma* (541), "a shining forth" (*apo*, "from," *auge*, "brightness"), of a light coming from a luminous body, is said of Christ in **Heb. 1:3**, KJV, "brightness," RV, "effulgence," i.e., shining forth (a more probable meaning than reflected brightness).

Glory *doxa* (1391), "glory" (from *dokeo*, "to seem"), primarily signifies an opinion, estimate, and hence, the honor resulting from a good opinion. It is used (I) (a) of the nature and acts of God in self-manifestation, i.e., what He essentially is and does, as exhibited in whatever way he reveals Himself in these respects, and particularly in the person of Christ, in whom essentially His "glory" has ever shone forth and ever will do, John 17:5, 24; **Heb. 1:3**; it was exhibited in the character and acts of Christ in the days of His flesh, John 1:14; John 2:11; at Cana both His grace and His power were manifested, and these constituted His "glory", so also in the resurrection of Lazarus 11:4, 40; the "glory" of God was exhibited in the resurrection of Christ, Rom. 6:4, and in His ascension and exaltation, 1 Pet. 1:21, likewise on the Mount of Transfiguration, 2 Pet. 1:17. In Rom. 1:23 His "everlasting power and Divinity" are spoken of as His "glory," i.e., His attributes and power as revealed through creation; in Rom. 3:23 the word denotes the manifested perfection of His character, especially His righteousness, of which all men fall short; in Col. 1:11 "the might of His glory" signifies the might which is characteristic of His "glory"; in Eph. 1:6, 12, 14, "the praise of the glory of His grace" and "the praise of His glory" signify the due acknowledgement of the exhibition of His attributes and ways; in Eph. 1:17, "the Father of glory" describes Him as the source from whom all divine splendor and perfection proceed in their manifestation, and to whom they belong; (b) of the character and ways of God as exhibited through Christ to and through believers, 2 Cor. 3:18 and 4:6; (c) of the state of blessedness into which believers are to enter hereafter through being brought into the likeness of Christ, e.g., Rom. 8:18, 21; Phil. 3:21 (RV, "the body of His glory"); 1 Pet. 5:1, 10; Rev. 21:11; (d) brightness or splendor, (1) supernatural, emanating from God (as in the *shekinah* "glory," in the pillar of cloud and in the Holy of Holies, e.g., Exod. 16:10; 25:22), Luke 2:9; Acts 22:11; Rom. 9:4; 2 Cor. 3:7; Jas. 2:1; in Titus 2:13 it is used of Christ's return, "the appearing of the glory of our great God and Savior Jesus Christ" (RV); cf. Phil. 3:21, above; (2) natural, as of the heavenly bodies, 1 Cor. 15:40, 41; (II) of good reputation, praise, honor, Luke 14:10 (RV, "glory," for KJV, "worship"); John 5:41 (RV, "glory," for KJV, "honor"); 7:18; 8:50; 12:43 (RV, "glory," for KJV, "praise"); 2 Cor. 6:8 (RV, "glory," for KJV "honor"); Phil. 3:19; **Heb. 3:3**; in 1 Cor. 11:7, of man as representing the authority of God, and of woman as rendering conspicuous the authority of man; in 1 Thess. 2:6, "glory" probably stands, by metonymy, for material gifts, an honorarium, since in human estimation "glory" is usually expressed in things material. The word is used in ascriptions of praise to God, e.g., Luke 17:18; John 9:24, RV, "glory" (KJV, "praise"); Acts 12:23; as in doxologies (lit., "glory-words"), e.g., Luke 2:14; Rom. 11:36; 16:27; Gal. 1:5; Rev. 1:6.

Image *charakter* (5481), denotes, firstly, "a tool for graving" (from *charasso*, "to cut into, to engross"; cf. Eng., "character," "characteristic"); then, "a stamp" or "impress," as on a coin or a seal, in which case the seal or die which makes an impression bears the "image" produced by it, and, *vice versa*, all the features of the "image" correspond respectively with those of the instrument producing it. In the NT it is used metaphorically in **Heb. 1:3**, of the Son of God as "the very image (marg., 'the impress') of His substance," RV. The phrase expresses the fact that the Son "is both personally distinct from, and yet literally equal to, Him of whose essence He is the adequate imprint" (Liddon). The Son of God is not merely his "image" (His *charakter*), He is the "image" or impress of His substance, or essence.

Person *hupostasis* (5287), lit., "a standing under" (*hupo*, "under," *stasis*, "a standing"), "that which stands, or is set, under, a foundation, beginning"; hence, the quality of confidence which leads one to stand under, endure, or undertake anything, 2 Cor. 9:4; 11:17; **Heb. 3:14**. Twice in Heb. it signifies "substance," **1:3** (KJV, "Person") and **11:1**.

Upholding *phero* (5342), "to bear, carry, uphold," is rendered "upholding" in **Heb. 1:3**.

Purged *katharismos* (2512), denotes "cleansing," (a) both the action and its results, in the Levitical sense, Mark 1:44; Luke 2:22, "purification"; 5:14, "cleansing"; John 2:6; 3:25, "purifying"; (b) in the moral sense, from sins, **Heb. 1:3**; 2 Pet. 1:9, RV, "cleansing."

Majesty *megalosune* (3172), from *megas*, "great," denotes "greatness, majesty"; it is used of God the Father, signifying His greatness and dignity, in **Heb. 1:3**, "the Majesty (on high)," and **8:1**, "the Majesty (in the Heavens)"; and in an ascription of praise acknowledging the attributes of God in Jude 25.

High *hupselos* (5308), "high, lofty," is used (a) naturally, of mountains, Matt. 4:8; 17:1; Mark 9:2; Rev. 21:10; of a wall, Rev. 21:12; (b) figuratively, of the arm of God, Acts 13:17; of heaven, "on high," plural, lit., "in high (places)," **Heb. 1:3**; (c) metaphorically, Luke 16:15, RV, "exalted" (KJV, "highly esteemed"); Rom. 11:20, in the best texts, "high-minded" [lit., "mind (not) high things"]; 12:16.

1:4 Being made so much better than the angels, as he hath by inheritance obtained a more excellent name than they.

Much The adjective *tosoutos*, "so great, so much," is translated "so much (bread)," in Matt. 15:33, plural, RV, "so many (loaves)"; in the genitive case, of price, in Acts 5:8, "for so much"; in the dative case, of degree, in **Heb. 1:4**, RV, "by so much" (KJV, "so much"); so in **Heb. 10:25**; in **Heb. 7:22** "by so much" translates the phrase *kata tosouto;* in Rev. 18:7, "so much."

Better *kreisson* (2909), from *kratos*, "strong" (which denotes power in activity and effect), serves as the comparative degree of *agathos*, "good" (good or fair, intrinsically). *Kreisson* is especially characteristic of the Epistle to the Hebrews, where it is used 12 times; it indicates what is (a) advantageous or useful, 1 Cor. 7:9, 38; 11:17; **Heb. 11:40**; **12:24**; 2 Pet. 2:21; Phil. 1:23, where it is coupled with *mallon*, "more," and *pollo*, "much, by far," "very far better" (RV); (b) excellent, **Heb. 1:4**; **6:9**; **7:7, 19, 22**; **8:6**; **9:23**; **10:34**; **11:16, 35**.

Inheritance *kleronomeo* (2816), strictly means "to receive by lot" (*kleros*, "a lot," *nemomai*, "to possess"); then, in a more general sense, "to possess oneself of, to receive as one's own, to obtain." The following list shows how in the NT the idea of inheriting broadens out to include all spiritual good provided through and in Christ, and particularly all that is contained in the hope grounded on the promises of God.

The verb is used of the following objects: "(a) birthright, that into the possession of which one enters in virtue of sonship, not because of a price paid or of a task accomplished, Gal. 4:30; **Heb. 1:4**; **12:17.** (b) that which is received as a gift, in contrast with that which is received as the reward of law-keeping, **Heb. 1:14**; **6:12** ("through," i.e., "through experiences that called for the exercise of faith and patience,' but not 'on the ground of the exercise of faith and patience.') ...

> ***"The Son is the Image of the invisible God. All things that belong to the Father He expresses as the Image; all things that are the Father's He illumines as the splendor of His glory and manifests to us."***
>
> ST. AMBROSE

Obtained For the KJV of **Heb. 1:4**, "He hath by inheritance obtained" (RV, "He hath inherited"), and of Eph. 1:11.

Excellent *diaphoroteros* (1313), comparative degree of *diaphoros*, "excellent," is used twice, in **Heb. 1:4**, "more excellent (name)," and **8:6**, "more excellent (ministry)." For the positive degree see Rom. 12:6; **Heb. 9:10**.

Name *onoma* (3686), is used (I) in general of the "name" by which a person or thing is called, e.g., Mark 3:16, 17, "(He) surnamed," lit., "(He added) the name"; 14:32, lit., "(of which) the name (was)"; Luke 1:63; John 18:10, sometimes translated "named," e.g., Luke 8:5, "named (Zacharias)," lit., "by name"; in the same verse, "named (Elizabeth)," lit., "the name of her," an elliptical phrase, with "was" understood; Acts 8:9, RV, "by name," 10:1; the "name" is put for the reality in Rev. 3:1; in Phil. 2:9, the "Name" represents "the title and dignity" of the Lord, as in Eph. 1:21 and **Heb. 1:4**;

(II) for all that a "name" implies, of authority, character, rank, majesty, power, excellence, etc., of everything that the "name" covers: (a) of the "Name" of God as expressing His attributes, etc., e.g., Matt. 6:9; Luke 1:49; John 12:28; 17:6, 26; Rom. 15:9; 1 Tim. 6:1; **Heb. 13:15**; Rev. 13:6; (b) of the "Name" of Christ, e.g., Matt. 10:22; 19:29; John 1:12; 2:23; 3:18; Acts 26:9; Rom. 1:5; Jas. 2:7; 1 John 3:23; 3 John 7; Rev. 2:13; 3:8; also the phrases rendered "in the name"; these may be analyzed as follows: (1) representing the authority of Christ, e.g., Matt. 18:5 (with *epi*, "on the ground of My authority"); so Matt. 24:5 (falsely) and parallel passages; as substantiated by the Father, John 14:26; 16:23 (last clause), RV; (2) in the power of (with *en*, "in"), e.g., Mark 16:17; Luke 10:17; Acts 3:6; 4:10; 16:18; Jas. 5:14; (3) in acknowledgement or confession of, e.g., Acts 4:12; 8:16; 9:27, 28; (4) in recognition of the authority of (sometimes combined with the thought of relying or resting on), Matt. 18:20; cf. 28:19; Acts 8:16; 9:2 (*eis*, "into"); John 14:13; 15:16; Eph. 5:20; Col. 3:17; (5) owing to the fact that one is called by Christ's "Name" or is identified with Him, e.g. 1 Pet. 4:14 (with *en*, "in"); with *heneken*, "for the sake of," e.g., Matt. 19:29; with *dia*, "on account of," Matt. 10:22; 24:9; Mark 13:13; Luke 21:17; John 15:21; 1 John 2:12; Rev. 2:3.

1:5 For unto which of the angels said he at any time, Thou art my Son, this day have I begotten thee? And again, I will be to him a Father, and he shall be to me a Son?

Son *see* ***Hebrews 1:2***.

This day *semeron* (4594), an adverb (the Attic form is *temeron*), akin to *hemera*, a day, with the prefix *t* originally representing a pronoun. It is used frequently in Matthew, Luke and Acts; in the last it is always rendered "this day"; also in **Heb. 1:5**, and the RV of **5:5** (KJV, "to day") in the same quotation; "today" in **3:7, 13, 15; 4:7** (twice); **13:8**; also Jas. 4:13. The clause containing *semeron* is sometimes introduced by the conjunction *hoti*, "that," e.g., Mark 14:30; Luke 4:21; 19:9; sometimes without the conjunction, e.g., Luke 22:34; 23:43, where "today" is to be attached to the next statement, "shalt thou be with Me"; there are no grammatical reasons for the insistence that the connection must be with the statement "Verily I say unto thee," nor is such an idea necessitated by examples from either the Sept. or the NT; the connection given in the KJV and RV is right. In Rom. 11:8 and 2 Cor. 3:14, 15, the lit. rendering is "unto the today day," the emphasis being brought out by the RV, "unto (until) this very day." In **Heb. 4:7**, the "today" of Ps. 95:7 is evidently designed to extend to the present period of the Christian faith. *See also* **Daily** at ***Hebrews 3:13***.

Begotten *gennao* (1080), "to beget," in the passive voice, "to be born," is chiefly used of men "begetting" children, Matt. 1:2-16; more rarely of women "begetting" children, Luke 1:13, 57, "brought forth"; 23:29; John 16:21, "is delivered of," and of the child, "is born." In Gal. 4:24, it is used allegorically, to contrast Jews under bondage to the Law, and spiritual Israel, KJV, "gendereth," RV, "bearing children," to contrast the natural birth of Ishmael and the supernatural birth of Isaac. In Matt. 1:20 it is used of conception, "that which is conceived in her." It is used of the act of God in the birth of Christ, Acts 13:33; **Heb. 1:5; 5:5**, quoted from Psalm 2:7, none of which indicate that Christ became the Son of God at His birth. It is used metaphorically (a) in the writings of the apostle John, of the gracious act of God in conferring upon those who believe the nature and disposition of "children," imparting to them spiritual life, John 3:3, 5, 7; 1 John 2:29; 3:9; 4:7; 5:1, 4, 18; (b) of one who by means of preaching the gospel becomes the human instrument in the impartation of spiritual life, 1 Cor. 4:15; Philem. 10; (c) in 2 Pet. 2:12, with reference to the evil men whom the apostle is describing, the RV rightly has "born mere animals" (KJV, "natural brute beasts"); (d) in the sense of gendering strife, 2 Tim. 2:23.

Father *pater* (3962), from a root signifying "a nourisher, protector, upholder" (Lat., *pater*, Eng., "father," are akin), is used (a) of the nearest ancestor, e.g., Matt. 2:22; (b) of a more remote ancestor, the progenitor of the people, a "forefather," e.g., Matt. 3:9; 23:30; 1 Cor. 10:1; the patriarchs, 2 Pet. 3:4; (c) one advanced in the knowledge of Christ, 1 John 2:13; (d) metaphorically, of the originator of a family or company of persons animated by the same spirit as himself, as of Abraham, Rom. 4:11, 12, 16, 17, 18, or of Satan, John 8:38, 41, 44; (e) of one who, as a preacher of the gospel and a teacher, stands in a "father's" place, caring for his spiritual children, 1 Cor. 4:15 (not the same as a mere title of honor, which the Lord prohibited, Matt. 23:9); (f) of the members of the Sanhedrin, as of those who exercised religious authority over others, Acts 7:2; 22:1; (g) of God in relation to those who have been born anew (John 1:12,

13), and so are believers, Eph. 2:18; 4:6 (cf. 2 Cor. 6:18), and imitators of their "Father," Matt. 5:45, 48; 6:1, 4, 6, 8, 9, etc. Christ never associated Himself with them by using the personal pronoun "our"; He always used the singular, "My Father," His relationship being unoriginated and essential, whereas theirs is by grace and regeneration, e.g., Matt. 11:27; 25:34; John 20:17; Rev. 2:27; 3:5, 21; so the apostles spoke of God as the "Father" of the Lord Jesus Christ, e.g., Rom. 15:6; 2 Cor. 1:3; 11:31; Eph. 1:3; **Heb. 1:5**; 1 Pet. 1:3; Rev. 1:6; (h) of God, as the "Father" of lights, i.e., the Source or Giver of whatsoever provides illumination, physical and spiritual, Jas. 1:17; of mercies, 2 Cor. 1:3; of glory, Eph. 1:17; (i) of God, as Creator, **Heb. 12:9** (cf. Zech. 12:1).

1:6 And again, when he bringeth in the firstbegotten into the world, he saith, And let all the angels of God worship him.

Firstbegotten *prototokos* (4416), "firstborn" (from *protos*, "first," and *tikto*, "to beget"), is used of Christ as born of the Virgin Mary, Luke 2:7; further, in His relationship to the Father, expressing His priority to, and preeminence over, creation, not in the sense of being the "first" to be born. It is used occasionally of superiority of position in the OT, see Exod. 4:22; Deut. 21:16, 17, the prohibition being against the evil of assigning the privileged position of the "firstborn" to one born subsequently to the "first" child. The five passages in the NT relating to Christ may be set forth chronologically thus: (a) Col. 1:15, where His eternal relationship with the Father is in view, and the clause means both that He was the "Firstborn" before all creation and that He Himself produced creation (the genitive case being objective, as v. 16 makes clear); (b) Col. 1:18 and Rev. 1:5, in reference to His resurrection; (c) Rom. 8:29, His position in relationship to the church; (d) **Heb. 1:6**, RV, His second advent (the RV "when He again bringeth in," puts "again" in the right place, the contrast to His first advent, at His birth, being implied); cf. Ps. 89:27. The word is used in the plural, in **Heb. 11:28**, of the firstborn sons in the families of the Egyptians, and in **12:23**, of the members of the Church.

World *oikoumene* (3625), "the inhabited earth", is used (a) of the whole inhabited world, Matt. 24:14; Luke 4:5; 21:26; Rom. 10:18; **Heb. 1:6**; Rev. 3:10; 16:14; by metonymy, of its inhabitants, Acts 17:31; Rev. 12:9; (b) of the Roman Empire, the world as viewed by the writer or speaker, Luke 2:1; Acts 11:28; 24:5; by metonymy, of its inhabitants, Acts 17:6; 19:27; (c) the inhabited world in a coming age, **Heb. 2:5**.

Worship *proskuneo* (4352), "to make obeisance, do reverence to" (from *pros*, "towards," and *kuneo*, "to kiss"), is the most frequent word rendered "to worship." It is used of an act of homage or reverence (a) to God, e.g., Matt. 4:10; John 4:21-24; 1 Cor. 14:25; Rev. 4:10; 5:14; 7:11; 11:16; 19:10 (2nd part) and 22:9; (b) to Christ, e.g., Matt. 2:2, 8, 11; 8:2; 9:18; 14:33; 15:25; 20:20; 28:9, 17; John 9:38; **Heb. 1:6**, in a quotation from the Sept. of Deut. 32:43, referring to Christ's second advent; (c) to a man, Matt. 18:26; (d) to the Dragon, by men, Rev. 13:4; (e) to the Beast, his human instrument, Rev. 13:4, 8, 12; 14:9, 11; (f) the image of the Beast, 13:15; 14:11; 16:2; (g) to demons, Rev. 9:20; (h) to idols, Acts 7:43.

1:7 And of the angels he saith, Who maketh his angels spirits, and his ministers a flame of fire.

Maketh *see* **Made** at ***Hebrews 1:2***.

Spirits *pneuma* (4151), primarily denotes "the wind" (akin to *pneo*, "to breathe, blow"); also "breath"; then, especially "the spirit," which, like the wind, is invisible, immaterial and powerful. The NT uses of the word may be analyzed approximately as follows:

"(a) the wind, John 3:8 (where marg. is, perhaps, to be preferred); **Heb. 1:7**; cf. Amos 4:13, Sept.; (b) the breath, 2 Thess. 2:8; Rev. 11:11; 13:15; cf. Job 12:10, Sept.; (c) the immaterial, invisible part of man, Luke 8:55; Acts 7:59; 1 Cor. 5:5; Jas. 2:26; cf. Eccl. 12:7, Sept.; (d) the disembodied (or 'unclothed,' or 'naked,' 2 Cor. 5:3, 4) man, Luke 24:37, 39; **Heb. 12:23**; 1 Pet. 4:6; (e) the resurrection body, 1 Cor. 15:45; 1 Tim. 3:16; 1 Pet. 3:18; (f) the sentient element in man, that by which he perceives, reflects, feels, desires, Matt. 5:3; 26:41; Mark 2:8; Luke 1:47, 80; Acts 17:16; 20:22; 1 Cor. 2:11; 5:3, 4; 14:4, 15; 2 Cor. 7:1; cf. Gen. 26:35; Isa. 26:9; Ezek. 13:3; Dan. 7:15; (g) purpose, aim, 2 Cor. 12:18; Phil. 1:27; Eph. 4:23; Rev. 19:10; cf. Ezra 1:5; Ps. 78:8; Dan. 5:12; (h) the equivalent of the personal pronoun, used for emphasis and effect: 1st person, 1 Cor. 16:18; cf. Gen. 6:3; 2nd person, 2 Tim. 4:22; Philem. 25; cf. Ps. 139:7; 3rd person, 2 Cor. 7:13; cf. Isa. 40:13; (i) character, Luke 1:17; Rom. 1:4; cf. Num. 14:24; (j) moral qualities and activities: bad, as of bondage, as of a slave, Rom. 8:15; cf. Isa. 61:3; stupor, Rom. 11:8; cf. Isa. 29:10; timidity, 2 Tim. 1:7; cf. Josh. 5:1; good, as of adoption, i.e., liberty as of a son, Rom. 8:15; cf. Ps. 51:12; meekness, 1 Cor. 4:21; cf. Prov. 16:19; faith, 2 Cor. 4:13; quietness, 1 Pet. 3:4; cf. Prov. 14:29; (k) the Holy Spirit, e.g., Matt. 4:1; Luke 4:18; (l) 'the inward man' (an expression used only of the believer, Rom. 7:22; 2 Cor. 4:16; Eph. 3:16); the new life, Rom. 8:4-6, 10, 16; **Heb. 12:9**; cf. Ps. 51:10; (m) unclean spirits, demons, Matt. 8:16; Luke 4:33; 1 Pet. 3:19; cf. 1 Sam. 18:10; (n) angels, **Heb. 1:14**; cf. Acts 12:15; (o) divine gift for service, 1 Cor. 14:12, 32; (p) by metonymy, those who claim to be depositories of these gifts, 2 Thess. 2:2; 1 John 4:1-3; (q) the significance, as contrasted with the form, of words, or of a rite, John 6:63; Rom. 2:29; 7:6; 2 Cor. 3:6; (r) a vision, Rev. 1:10; 4:2; 17:3; 21:10." *Pneuma* is translated "wind" in John 3:8 (RV, marg., "the Spirit breatheth," the probable meaning); in **Heb. 1:7** the RV has "winds" for KJV, "spirits."

Ministers *leitourgos* (3011), denoted among the Greeks, firstly, "one who discharged a public office at his own expense," then, in general, "a public servant, minister." In the NT it is used (a) of Christ, as a "Minister of the sanctuary" (in the Heavens), **Heb. 8:2**; (b) of angels, **Heb. 1:7** (Ps. 104:4); (c) of the apostle Paul, in his evangelical ministry, fulfilling it as a serving priest, Rom. 15:16; that he used it figuratively and not in an ecclesiastical sense, is obvious from the context; (d) of Epaphroditus, as ministering to Paul's needs on behalf of the church at Philippi, Phil. 2:25; here, representative service is in view; (e) of earthly rulers, who though they do not all act consciously as servants of God, yet discharge functions which are the ordinance of God, Rom. 13:6.

Flame *phlox* (5395), akin to Lat. *fulgeo*, "to shine," is used apart from *pur*, "fire," in Luke 16:24; with *pur*, it signifies "a fiery flame," lit., "a flame of fire," Acts 7:30; 2 Thess. 1:8, where the fire is to be understood as the instrument of divine judgment; **Heb. 1:7**, where the meaning probably is that God makes His angels as active and powerful as a "flame" of fire; in Rev. 1:14; 2:18; 19:12, of the eyes of the Lord Jesus as emblematic of penetrating judgment, searching out evil.

Fire *pur* (4442), (akin to which are *pura*, and *puretos*, "a fever," Eng., "fire," etc.) is used (besides its ordinary natural significance): (a) of the holiness of God, which consumes all that is inconsistent therewith, **Heb. 10:27**; **12:29**; cf. Rev. 1:14; 2:18; 10:1; 15:2; 19:12; similarly of the holy angels as His ministers **Heb. 1:7** in Rev. 3:18 it is symbolic of that which tries the faith of saints, producing what will glorify the Lord. (b) of the divine judgment, testing the deeds of believers, at the judgment seat of Christ 1 Cor. 3:13 and 15. (c) of the fire of divine judgment upon the rejectors of Christ, Matt. 3:11 (where a distinction is to be made between the baptism of the Holy Spirit at Pentecost and the "fire" of divine retribution; Acts 2:3 could not refer to baptism): Luke 3:16 ...

1:8 But unto the Son *he saith*, Thy throne, O God, *is* for ever and ever: a sceptre of righteousness *is* the sceptre of thy kingdom.

Throne *thronos* (2362), "a throne, a seat of authority," is used of the "throne" (a) of God, e.g., **Heb. 4:16**, "the throne of grace," i.e., from which grace proceeds; **8:1**; **12:2**; Rev. 1:4; 3:21 (2nd part); 4:2 (twice); 5:1; frequently in Rev.; in 20:12, in the best texts, "the throne" (some have *Theos*, "God," KJV); cf. 21:3; Matt. 5:34; 23:22; Acts 7:49; (b) of Christ, e.g. **Heb. 1:8**; Rev. 3:21 (1st part); 22:3; His seat of authority in the Millennium, Matt. 19:28 (1st part); (c) by metonymy for angelic powers, Col. 1:16; (d) of the Apostles in millennial authority, Matt. 19:28 (2nd part); Luke 22:30; (e) of the elders in the heavenly vision, Rev. 4:4 (2nd and 3rd parts), RV, "thrones" (KJV, "seats"); so 11:16; (f) of David, Luke 1:32; Acts 2:30; (g) of Satan, Rev. 2:13, RV, "throne" (KJV, "seat"); (h) of "the beast," the final and federal head of the revived Roman Empire, Rev. 13:2; 16:10.

God *theos* (2316), ... the word was appropriated by Jews and retained by Christians to denote "the one true God." In the Sept. *theos* translates (with few exceptions) the Hebrew words *Elohim* and *Jehovah*, the former indicating His power and preeminence, the latter His unoriginated, immutable, eternal and self-sustained existence. In the NT, these and all the other divine attributes are predicated of Him. To Him are ascribed, e.g., His unity, or monism, e.g., Mark 12:29; 1 Tim. 2:5; self-existence, John 5:26; immutability, Jas. 1:17; eternity, Rom. 1:20; universality, Matt. 10:29; Acts 17:26-28; almighty power, Matt. 19:26; infinite knowledge, Acts 2:23; 15:18; Rom. 11:33, creative power, Rom. 11:36; 1 Cor. 8:6; Eph. 3:9; Rev. 4:11; 10:6; absolute holiness, 1 Pet. 1:15; 1 John 1:5; righteousness, John 17:25; faithfulness, 1 Cor. 1:9; 10:13; 1 Thess. 5:24; 2 Thess. 3:3; 1 John 1:9; love, 1 John 4:8, 16; mercy, Rom. 9:15, 18; truthfulness, Titus 1:2; **Heb. 6:18**.

(b) The divine attributes are likewise indicated or definitely predicated of Christ, e.g., Matt. 20:18-19; John 1:1-3; 1:18, RV, marg.; 5:22-29; 8:58; 14:6; 17:22-24; 20:28; Rom. 1:4; 9:5; Phil. 3:21; Col. 1:15; 2:3; Titus 2:13, RV; **Heb. 1:3**; **13:8**; 1 John 5:20; Rev. 22:12, 13.

(c) Also of the Holy Spirit, e.g., Matt. 28:19; Luke 1:35; John 14:16; 15:26; 16:7-14; Rom. 8:9, 26; 1 Cor. 12:11; 2 Cor. 13:14 ...

In the following titles God is described by certain of His

attributes; the God of glory, Acts 7:2; of peace, Rom. 15:33; 16:20; Phil. 4:9; 1 Thess. 5:23; **Heb. 13:20**; of love and peace, 2 Cor. 13:11; of patience and comfort, Rom. 15:5; of all comfort, 2 Cor. 1:3; of hope, Rom. 15:13; of all grace, 1 Pet. 5:10. These describe Him, not as in distinction from other persons, but as the source of all these blessings; hence the employment of the definite article. In such phrases as "the God of a person," e.g., Matt. 22:32, the expression marks the relationship in which the person stands to God and God to him.

(e) In the following the nominative case is used for the vocative, and always with the article; Mark 15:34; Luke 18:11, 13; John 20:28; (Acts 4:24 in some mss.); **Heb. 1:8**; **10:7**.

(f) The phrase "the things of God" (translated literally or otherwise) stands for (1) His interests, Matt. 16:23; Mark 8:33; (2) His counsels, 1 Cor. 2:11; (3) things which are due to Him, Matt. 22:21; Mark 12:17; Luke 20:25. The phrase "things pertaining to God," Rom. 15:17; **Heb. 2:17**; **5:1**, describes, in the Heb. passages, the sacrificial service of the priest; in the Rom. passage the gospel ministry as an offering to God.

Sceptre *rhabdos* (4464), "a staff, rod, scepter," is used (a) of Aaron's "rod," **Heb. 9:4**; (b) a staff used on a journey, Matt. 10:10, RV, "staff" (KJV, "staves"); so Luke 9:3; Mark 6:8, "staff"; **Heb. 11:21**, "staff"; (c) a ruler's staff, a "scepter," **Heb. 1:8** (twice); elsewhere a "rod," Rev. 2:27; 12:5; 19:15; (d) a "rod" for chastisement (figuratively), 1 Cor. 4:21; (e) a measuring rod, Rev. 11:1.

Righteousness *euthutes* (2118), from *euthus*, "straight," is rendered "uprightness" in **Heb. 1:8**, RV, KJV, "righteousness," marg., "rightness," or, "straightness."

1:9 Thou hast loved righteousness, and hated iniquity; therefore God, *even* thy God, hath anointed thee with the oil of gladness above thy fellows.

Hated *miseo* (3404), "to hate," is used especially (a) of malicious and unjustifiable feelings towards others, whether towards the innocent or by mutual animosity, e.g., Matt. 10:22; 24:10; Luke 6:22, 27; 19:14; John 3:20, of "hating" the light (metaphorically); 7:7; 15:18, 19, 23-25; Titus 3:3; 1 John 2:9, 11; 3:13, 15; 4:20; Rev. 18:2, where "hateful" translates the perfect participle passive voice of the verb, lit., "hated," or "having been hated"; (b) of a right feeling of aversion from what is evil; said of wrongdoing, Rom. 7:15; iniquity, **Heb. 1:9**; "the garment (figurative) spotted by the flesh," Jude 23; "the works of the Nicolaitans," Rev. 2:6 (and v. 15, in some mss.; see the KJV); (c) of relative preference for one thing over another, by way of expressing either aversion from, or disregard for, the claims of one person or thing relatively to those of another, Matt. 6:24, and Luke 16:13, as to the impossibility of serving two masters; Luke 14:26, as to the claims of parents relatively to those of Christ; John 12:25, of disregard for one's life relatively to the claims of Christ; Eph. 5:29, negatively, of one's flesh, i.e. of one's own, and therefore a man's wife as one with him.

Iniquity *anomia* (458), lit., "lawlessness" (*a*, negative, *nomos*, "law"), is used in a way which indicates the meaning as being lawlessness or wickedness. Its usual rendering in the NT is "iniquity," which lit. means unrighteousness. It occurs very frequently in the Sept., especially in the Psalms, where it is found about 70 times. It is used (a) of iniquity in general, Matt. 7:23; 13:41; 23:28; 24:12; Rom. 6:19 (twice); 2 Cor. 6:14, RV, "iniquity" (KJV, "unrighteousness"); 2 Thess. 2:3, in some mss.; the KJV and RV follow those which have *hamartia*, "(man of) sin"; 2:7, RV, "lawlessness" (KJV, "iniquity"); Titus 2:14; **Heb. 1:9**; 1 John 3:4 (twice), RV, "(doeth) ... lawlessness" and "lawlessness" (KJV, "transgresseth the law" and "transgression of the law"); (b) in the plural, of acts or manifestations of lawlessness, Rom. 4:7; **Heb. 10:17** (some inferior mss. have it in **8:12**, for the word *hamartia*).

Anointed *chrio* (5548), is confined to "sacred and symbolical anointings"; of Christ as the "Anointed" of God, Luke 4:18; Acts 4:27; 10:38, and **Heb. 1:9**, where it is used metaphorically in connection with "the oil of gladness." The title Christ signifies "The Anointed One," The word (*Christos*) is rendered "(His) Anointed" in Acts 4:26, RV. Once it is said of believers, 2 Cor. 1:21. *Chrio* is very frequent in the Sept., and is used of kings, 1 Sam. 10:1, and priests, Ex. 28:41, and prophets, 1 Kings 19:16. Among the Greeks it was used in other senses than the ceremonial, but in the Scriptures it is not found in connection with secular matters.

Oil *elaion* (1637), "olive oil," is mentioned over 200 times in the Bible. Different kinds were known in Palestine. The "pure," RV (KJV, beaten), mentioned in Exod. 27:20; 29:40; Lev. 24:2; Num. 28:5 (now known as virgin oil), extracted by pressure, without heat, is called "golden" in Zech. 4:12. There were also inferior kinds. In the NT the uses mentioned were (a) for lamps, in which the "oil" is a symbol of the Holy Spirit, Matt. 25:3-4, 8; (b) as a medicinal agent, for healing, Luke 10:34; (c) for anointing at feasts,

Luke 7:46; (d) on festive occasions, **Heb. 1:9**, where the reference is probably to the consecration of kings; (e) as an accompaniment of miraculous power, Mark 6:13, or of the prayer of faith, Jas. 5:14. For its general use in commerce, see Luke 16:6; Rev. 6:6; 18:13.

Gladness *agalliasis* (20), "exultation, exuberant joy," is translated "gladness" in Luke 1:14; Acts 2:6; **Heb. 1:9**; "joy" in Luke 1:44; "exceeding joy" in Jude 24. It indicates a more exultant "joy." In the Sept. this word is found chiefly in the Psalms, where it denotes "joy" in God's redemptive work, e.g., 30:5; 42:4; 45:7, 15.

Fellows *metochos* (3353), properly an adjective, signifying "sharing in, partaking of," is translated "partners" in Luke 5:7; "partakers" in **Heb. 3:1, 14; 6:4; 12:8**; "fellows" in **Heb. 1:9**, of those who share in a heavenly calling, or have held, or will hold, a regal position in relation to the earthly, messianic kingdom. (Cf *summetochos*, "fellow-partakers," in Eph. 3:6, RV).

1:10 And, Thou, Lord, in the beginning hast laid the foundation of the earth; and the heavens are the works of thine hands:

Foundation *themelioo* (2311), "to lay a foundation, to found," is used (a) literally, Matt. 7:25; Luke 6:48; **Heb. 1:10**; (b) metaphorically, Eph. 3:17, "grounded (in love)"; Col. 1:23 (ditto, "in the faith"); 1 Pet. 5:10, KJV, "settle."

Heavens *ouranos* (3772), probably akin to *ornumi*, "to lift, to heave," is used in the NT (a) of "the aerial heavens," e.g., Matt. 6:26; 8:20; Acts 10:12; 11:6 (RV, "heaven," in each place, KJV, "air"); Jas. 5:18; (b) "the sidereal," e.g., Matt. 24:29, 35; Mark 13:25, 31; **Heb. 11:12**, RV, "heaven," KJV, "sky"; Rev. 6:14; 20:11; they, (a) and (b), were created by the Son of God, **Heb. 1:10**, as also by God the Father, Rev. 10:6; (c) "the eternal dwelling place of God," Matt. 5:16; 12 :50; Rev. 3:12; 11:13; 16:11; 20:9. From thence the Son of God descended to become incarnate, John 3:13, 31; 6:38, 42. In His ascension Christ "passed through the heavens," **Heb. 4:14**, RV; He "ascended far above all the heavens," Eph. 4:10, and was "made higher than the heavens," **Heb. 7:26**; He "sat down on the right hand of the throne of the Majesty in the heavens," **Heb. 8:1**; He is "on the right hand of God," having gone into heaven, 1 Pet. 3:22. Since His ascension it is the scene of His present life and activity, e.g., Rom. 8:34; **Heb. 9:24**. From thence the Holy Spirit descended at Pentecost, 1 Pet. 1:12. It is the abode of the angels, e.g., Matt. 18:10; 22:30; cf. Rev. 3:5. Thither Paul was "caught up," whether in the body or out of the body, he knew not, 2 Cor. 12:2. It is to be the eternal dwelling place of the saints in resurrection glory, 2 Cor. 5:1. From thence Christ will descend to the air to receive His saints at the Rapture, 1 Thess. 4:16; Phil. 3:20, 21, and will subsequently come with His saints and with His holy angels at His second advent, Matt. 24:30; 2 Thess. 1:7. In the present life "heaven" is the region of the spiritual citizenship of believers, Phil. 3:20. The present "heavens," with the earth, are to pass away, 2 Pet. 3:10, "being on fire," v. 12 (see v. 7); Rev. 20:11, and new "heavens" and earth are to be created, 2 Pet. 3:13; Rev. 21:1, with Isa. 65:17, e.g.

Works *ergon* (2041), denotes (I) "work, employment, task," e.g., Mark 13:34; John 4:34; 17:4; Acts 13:2; Phil. 2:30; 1 Thess. 5:13; in Acts 5:38 with the idea of enterprise; (II) "a deed, act," (a) of God, e.g., John 6:28, 29; 9:3; 10:37; 14:10; Acts 13:41; Rom. 14:20; **Heb. 1:10; 2:7; 3:9; 4:3, 4, 10**; Rev. 15:3; (b) of Christ, e.g., Matt. 11:2; especially in John, 5:36; 7:3, 21; 10:25, 32, 33, 38; 14:11, 12; 15:24; Rev. 2:26; (c) of believers, e.g., Matt. 5:16; Mark 14:6; Acts 9:36; Rom. 13:3; Col. 1:10; 1 Thess. 1:3, "work of faith," here the initial act of faith at conversion (turning to God, v. 9); in 2 Thess. 1:11, "*every* work of faith," RV, denotes every activity undertaken for Christ's sake; 2:17; 1 Tim. 2:10; 5:10; 6:18; 2 Tim. 2:21; 3:17; Titus 2:7, 14; 3:1, 8, 14; **Heb. 10:24; 13:21**; frequent in James, as the effect of faith [in 1:25, KJV, "(a doer) of the work," RV, "(a doer) that worketh"]; 1 Pet. 2:12; Rev. 2:2 and in several other places in chs. 2 and 3; 14:13; (d) of unbelievers, e.g., Matt. 23:3, 5; John 7:7; Acts 7:41 (for idols); Rom. 13:12; Eph. 5:11; Col. 1:21; Titus 1:16 (1st part); 1 John 3:12; Jude 15, RV; Rev. 2:6, RV; of those who seek justification by works, e.g., Rom. 9:32; Gal. 3:10; Eph. 2:9; described as the works of the law, e.g., Gal. 2:16; 3:2, 5; dead works, **Heb. 6:1; 9:14**; (e) of Babylon, Rev. 18:6; (f) of the Devil, John 8:41; 1 John 3:8.

Hands *cheir* (5495), "the hand" (cf. Eng., "chiropody"), is used, besides its ordinary significance, (a) in the idiomatic phrases, "by the hand of," "at the hand of," etc., to signify "by the agency of," Acts 5:12; 7:35; 17:25; 14:3; Gal. 3:19 (cf. Lev. 26:46); Rev. 19:2; (b) metaphorically, for the power of God, e.g., Luke 1:66; 23:46; John 10:28, 29; Acts 11:21; 13:11; **Heb. 1:10; 2:7; 10:31**; (c) by metonymy, for power, e.g., Matt. 17:22; Luke 24:7; John 10:39; Acts 12:11.

1:11 They shall perish; but thou remainest; and they all shall wax old as doth a garment;

Perish *apollumi* (622), "to destroy," signifies, in the middle voice, "to perish," and is thus used (a) of things, e.g., Matt. 5:29, 30; Luke 5:37; Acts 27:34, RV, "perish" (in some texts *pipto*, "to fall," as KJV); **Heb. 1:11**; 2 Pet. 3:6; Rev. 18:14 (2nd part), RV, "perished" (in some texts *aperchomai*, "to depart," as KJV); (b) of persons, e.g., Matt. 8:25; John 3:15, 16; 10:28; 17:12, RV, "perished" (KJV, "is lost"); Rom. 2:12; 1 Cor. 1:18, lit., "the perishing," where the perfective force of the verb implies the completion of the process of destruction (Moulton, *Proleg.*, p. 114); 8:11; 15:18; 2 Pet. 3:9; Jude 11.

Remainest *diameno* (1265), "to remain throughout," is translated "to remain" in Luke 1:22; **Heb. 1:11**, KJV (RV, "Thou continuest").

Wax old *palaioo* (3822), "to make old" (*palaios*), is translated in **Heb. 8:13**, firstly, "hath made ... old," secondly (passive voice), RV "is becoming old" (KJV, "decayeth"); "wax old," Luke 12:33 and **Heb. 1:11**.

1:12 And as a vesture shalt thou fold them up, and they shall be changed: but thou art the same, and thy years shall not fail.

Vesture *peribolaion* (4018), lit. denotes "something thrown around" (*peri*, "around," *ballo*, "to throw"); hence, "a veil, covering," 1 Cor. 11:15 (marg.), or "a mantle around the body, a vesture," **Heb. 1:12**.

Fold *heilisso*, or *helisso* (1507), "to roll," or "roll up," is used (a) of the "rolling" up of a mantle, illustratively of the heavens, **Heb. 1:12**, RV; (b) of the "rolling" up of a scroll, Rev. 6:14, illustratively of the removing of the heaven.

Changed *allasso* (236), "to make other than it is" (from *allos*, "another"), "to transform, change," is used (a) of the effect of the gospel upon the precepts of the Law, Acts 6:14; (b) of the effect, on the body of a believer, of Christ's return, 1 Cor. 15:51-52; (c) of the final renewal of the material creation, **Heb. 1:12**; (d) of a change in the apostle's mode of speaking (or dealing), Gal. 4:20. In Rom. 1:23 it has its other meaning, "to exchange."

Same *autos* (846), denotes "the same" when preceded by the article, and either with a noun following, e.g., Mark 14:39; Phil. 1:30; 1 Cor. 12:4, or without, e.g., Matt. 5:46, 47; Rom. 2:1; Phil. 2:2; 3:1; **Heb. 1:12; 13:8**. It is thus to be distinguished from uses as a personal and a reflexive pronoun.

Years *etos* (2094), is used (a) to mark a point of time at or from which events take place, e.g., Luke 3:1 (dates were frequently reckoned from the time when a monarch began to reign); in Gal. 3:17 the time of the giving of the Law is stated as 430 "years" after the covenant of promise given to Abraham; there is no real discrepancy between this and Ex. 12:40; the apostle is not concerned with the exact duration of the interval, it certainly was not less than 430 "years"; the point of the argument is that the period was very considerable; Gal. 1:18 and 2:1 mark events in Paul's life; as to the former the point is that three "years" elapsed before he saw any of the apostles; in 2:1 the 14 "years" may date either from his conversion or from his visit to Peter mentioned in 1:18; the latter seems the more natural (for a full discussion of the subject see *Notes on Galatians* by Hogg and Vine, pp. 55ff.); (b) to mark a space of time, e.g., Matt. 9:20; Luke 12:19; 13:11; John 2:20; Acts 7:6, where the 400 "years" mark not merely the time that Israel was in bondage in Egypt, but the time that they sojourned or were strangers there (the RV puts a comma after the word "evil"); the Genevan Version renders Gen. 15:13 "thy posterity shall inhabit a strange land for 400 years"; **Heb. 3:17**; Rev. 20:2-7; (c) to date an event from one's birth, e.g., Mark 5:42; Luke 2:42; 3:23; John 8:57; Acts 4:22; 1 Tim. 5:9; (d) to mark recurring events, Luke 2:41 (with *kata*, used distributively); 13:7; (e) of an unlimited number, **Heb. 1:12**.

Fail *ekleipo* (1587), "to leave out" (*ek*, "out," *leipo*, "to leave"), used intransitively, means "to leave off, cease, fail"; it is said of the cessation of earthly life, Luke 16:9; of faith, 22:32; of the light of the sun, 23:45 (in the best mss.); of the years of Christ, **Heb. 1:12**.

1:13 But to which of the angels said he at any time, Sit on my right hand, until I make thine enemies thy footstool?

Sit *kathemai* (2521), is used (a) of the natural posture, e.g., Matt. 9:9, most frequently in Revelation, some 32 times; frequently in the Gospels and Acts; elsewhere only in 1 Cor. 14:30; Jas. 2:3 (twice); and of Christ's position of authority on the throne of God, Col. 3:1, KJV, "sitteth" (RV, "is, seated"); **Heb. 1:13** (cf. Matt. 22:44; 26:64 and parallel passages in Mark and Luke, and Acts 2:34); often as antecedent or successive to, or accompanying, another act (in no case a superfluous expression), e.g., Matt. 15:29; 27:36; Mark 2:14; 4:1; (b) metaphorically in Matt. 4:16 (twice); Luke 1:79; of inhabiting a place (translated "dwell"), Luke 21:35; Rev. 14:6, RV marg., "sit" (in the best texts: some have *katoikeo*, "to dwell").

Right *dexios* (1188), an adjective, used (a) of "the right" as opposite to the left, e.g., Matt. 5:29, 30; Rev. 10:5, RV, "right hand"; in connection with armor (figuratively), 2 Cor. 6:7; with *en*, followed by the dative plural, Mark 16:5; with *ek*, and the genitive plural, e.g., Matt. 25:33, 34; Luke 1:11; (b) of giving the "right hand" of fellowship, Gal. 2:9, betokening the public expression of approval by leaders at Jerusalem of the course pursued by Paul and Barnabas among the Gentiles; the act was often the sign of a pledge, e.g., 2 Kings 10:15; 1 Chron. 29:24, marg.; Ezra 10:19; Ezek. 17:18; figuratively, Lam. 5:6; it is often so used in the papyri; (c) metaphorically of "power" or "authority," Acts 2:33; with *ek*, signifying "on," followed by the genitive plural, Matt. 26:64; Mark 14:62; **Heb. 1:13**; (d) similarly of "a place of honor in the messianic kingdom," Matt. 20:21; Mark 10:37.

Make *tithemi* (5087), "to put," Matt. 22:44, Mark 12:36; Luke 20:43; Acts 2:35; 1 Cor. 9:18 (of making the gospel without charge); **Heb. 1:13**; **10:13**; 2 Pet. 2:6; Acts 20:28; Rom. 4:17.

Enemies *echthros* (2190), an adjective, primarily denoting "hated" or "hateful" (akin to *echthos*, "hate"; perhaps associated with *ekos*, "outside"), hence, in the active sense, denotes "hating, hostile"; it is used as a noun signifying an "enemy," adversary, and is said (a) of the Devil, Matt. 13:39; Luke 10:19; (b) of death, 1 Cor. 15:26; (c) of the professing believer who would be a friend of the world, thus making himself an enemy of God, Jas. 4:4; (d) of men who are opposed to Christ, Matt. 13:25, 28; 22:44; Mark 12:36; Luke 19:27; 20:43; Acts 2:35; Rom. 11:28; Phil. 3:18; **Heb. 1:13**; **10:13**; or to His servants, Rev. 11:5, 12; to the nation of Israel, Luke 1:71, 74; 19:43; (e) of one who is opposed to righteousness, Acts 13:10; (f) of Israel in its alienation from God, Rom. 11:28; (g) of the unregenerate in their attitude toward God, Rom. 5:10; Col. 1:21; (h) of believers in their former state, 2 Thess. 3:15; (i) of foes, Matt. 5:43-44; 10:36; Luke 6:27, 35; Rom. 12:20; 1 Cor. 15:25; of the apostle Paul because he told converts "the truth," Gal. 4:16. Cf. *echthra*, "enmity".

Footstool *hupopodion* (5286), from *hupo*, "under," and *pous*, "a foot," is used (a) literally in Jas. 2:3, (b) metaphorically, of the earth as God's "footstool," Matt. 5:35; of the foes of the Lord, Matt. 22:44 (in some mss.); Mark 12:36, "underneath" (in some mss.), Luke 20:43; Acts 2:35; 7:49; **Heb. 1:13**; **10:13**. The RV, adhering to the literal rendering, translates the phrase "the footstool of My (Thy, His) feet," for the KJV, "My (etc.) footstool," but in Matt. 22:44, "(till I put Thine enemies) underneath thy feet."

1:14 Are they not all ministering spirits, sent forth to minister for them who shall be heirs of salvation?

Ministering *leitourgikos* (3010), "of or pertaining to service, ministering," is used in **Heb. 1:14**, of angels as "ministering spirits." In the Sept., Exod. 31:10; 39:13; Num. 4:12, 26; 7:5; 2 Chron. 24:14.

Spirits *see Hebrews 1:7*

Sent *apostello* (649), lit., "to send forth" (*apo*, "from"), akin to *apostolos*, "an apostle," denotes (a) "to send on service, or with a commission." (1) of persons; Christ, sent by the Father, Matt. 10:40; 15:24; 21:37; Mark 9:37; 12:6; Luke 4:18, 43; 9:48; 10:16; John 3:17; 5:36, 38; 6:29, 57; 7:29; 8:42; 10:36; 11:42; 17:3, 8, 18 (1st part), 21, 23, 25; 20:21; Acts 3:20 (future); 3:26; 1 John 4:9, 10, 14; the Holy Spirit, Luke 24:49; 1 Pet. 1:12; Rev. 5:6; Moses, Acts 7:35; John the Baptist, John 1:6; 3:28; disciples and apostles, e.g., Matt. 10:16; Mark 11:1; Luke 22:8; John 4:38; 17:18 (2nd part); Acts 26:17; servants, e.g., Matt. 21:34; Luke 20:10; officers and officials, Mark 6:27; John 7:32; Acts 16:35; messengers, e.g., Acts 10:8, 17, 20; 15:27; evangelists, Rom. 10:15; angels, e.g., Matt. 24:31; Mark 13:27; Luke 1:19, 26; **Heb. 1:14**; Rev. 1:1; 22:6; demons, Mark 5:10; (2) of things, e.g., Matt. 21:3; Mark 4:29, RV, marg., "sendeth forth," text, "putteth forth" (KJV, "... in"); Acts 10:36; 11:30; 28:28; (b) "to send away, dismiss," e.g., Mark 8:26; 12:3; Luke 4:18, "to set (at liberty)."

Minister *diakonua* (1248), "the office and work of a *diakonos*", "service, ministry," is used (a) of domestic duties, Luke 10:40; (b) of religious and spiritual "ministration," (1) of apostolic "ministry," e.g., Acts 1:17, 25; 6:4; 12:25; 21:19; Rom. 11:13, RV (KJV, "office"); (2) of the service of believers, e.g., Acts 6:1; Rom. 12:7; 1 Cor. 12:5, RV, "ministrations" (KJV, "administrations"); 1 Cor. 16:15; 2 Cor. 8:4; 9:1, 12, RV, "ministration"; v. 13; Eph. 4:12, RV, "ministering" (KJV, "the ministry," not in the sense of an ecclesiastical function); 2 Tim. 4:11, RV, "(for) ministering"; collectively of a local church, Acts 11:29, "relief" (RV marg. "for ministry"); Rev. 2:19, RV, "ministry" (KJV, "service"); of Paul's service on behalf of poor saints, Rom. 15:31; (3) of the "ministry" of the Holy Spirit in the gospel, 2 Cor. 3:8; (4) of the "ministry" of angels, **Heb. 1:14**, RV, "to do service" (KJV, "to minister"); (5) of the work of the gospel, in general, e.g., 2 Cor. 3:9, "of righteousness;" 5:18, "of reconciliation"; (6) of the general "ministry" of a servant of the Lord in preaching and teaching, Acts 20:24; 2 Cor. 4:1; 6:3; 11:8; 1 Tim. 1:12, RV, "(to His) service"; 2 Tim. 4:5; undefined in Col. 4:17; (7) of the Law, as a "ministration" of death, 2 Cor. 3:7; of condemnation, 3:9.

Shall *mello* (3195), "to be about (to be or do)," is used of purpose, certainty, compulsion or necessity. It is rendered simply by "shall" or "should" (which frequently represent elsewhere part of the future tense of the verb) in the following (the RV sometimes translates differently, as noted): Matt. 16:27 (1st part), lit., "is about to come"; 17:12, 22; 20:22, RV, "am about"; 24:6; Mark 13:4 (2nd part), RV, "are about"; Luke 9:44; 21:7 (2nd part), RV, "are about"; v. 36; Acts 23:3; 24:15; 26:2, RV, "I am (to)"; Rom. 4:24; 8:13 (1st part), RV, "must"; v. 18; 2 Tim. 4:1; **Heb. 1:14**; **10:27**; Jas. 2:12, RV "are to"; 1 Pet. 5:1; Rev. 1:19; 2:10 (1st and 2nd parts), RV, "art about," "is about"; 3:10, RV, "is (to)"; 17:8 (1st part), RV, "is about."

Heirs *kleronomeo* (2816), "to be an heir to, to inherit," is rendered "shall (not) inherit with" in Gal. 4:30, RV, KJV, "shall (not) be heir with"; in **Heb. 1:14**, RV, "shall inherit," KJV, "shall be heirs of." Cf. *kleroomai*, "to be taken as an inheritance," *kleronomia*, "an inheritance," *kleros*, "a lot, an inheritance." See also **Inheritance** at *Hebrews 1:4*.

Salvation *soteria* (4991), denotes "deliverance, preservation, salvation." "Salvation" is used in the NT (a) of material and temporal deliverance from danger and apprehension, (1) national, Luke 1:69, 71; Acts 7:25, RV marg., "salvation" (text, "deliverance"); (2) personal, as from the sea, Acts 27:34; RV, "safety" (KJV, "health"); prison, Phil. 1:19; the flood, **Heb. 11:7**; (b) of the spiritual and eternal deliverance granted immediately by God to those who accept His conditions of repentance and faith in the Lord Jesus, in whom alone it is to be obtained, Acts 4:12, and upon confession of Him as Lord, Rom. 10:10; for this purpose the gospel is the saving instrument, Rom. 1:16; Eph. 1:13; (c) of the present experience of God's power to deliver from the bondage of sin, e.g., Phil. 2:12, where the special, though not the entire, reference is to the maintenance of peace and harmony; 1 Pet. 1:9; this present experience on the part of believers is virtually equivalent to sanctification; for this purpose, God is able to make them wise, 2 Tim. 3:15; they are not to neglect it, **Heb. 2:3**; (d) of the future deliverance of believers at the Parousia of Christ for His saints, a salvation which is the object of their confident hope, e.g., Rom. 13:11; 1 Thess. 5:8, and v. 9, where "salvation" is assured to them, as being deliverance from the wrath of God destined to be executed upon the ungodly at the end of this age (see 1 Thess. 1:10); 2 Thess. 2:13; **Heb. 1:14**; **9:28**; 1 Pet. 1:5; 2 Pet. 3:15; (e) of the deliverance of the nation of Israel at the second advent of Christ at the time of "the epiphany (or shining forth) of His Parousia" (2 Thess. 2:8); Luke 1:71; Rev. 12:10; (f) inclusively, to sum up all the blessings bestowed by God on men in Christ through the Holy Spirit, e.g., 2 Cor. 6:2; **Heb. 5:9**; 1 Pet. 1:9, 10; Jude 3; (g) occasionally, as standing virtually for the Savior, e.g., Luke 19:9; cf. John 4:22; (h) in ascriptions of praise to God, Rev. 7:10, and as that which it is His prerogative to bestow, 19:1 (RV).

Chapter 2

2:1 Therefore we ought to give the more earnest heed to the things which we have heard, lest at any time we should let *them* slip.

Give ... heed *prosecho* (4337), lit., "to hold to," signifies "to turn to, turn one's attention to"; hence, "to give heed"; it is rendered "take heed" in Matt. 6:1; Luke 17:3; 21:34; Acts 5:35; 20:28; 2 Pet. 1:19; to give heed to, in Acts 8:6, 10; in v. 11 (KJV, "had regard to"); 16:14 (KJV, "attended unto"); 1 Tim. 1:4; 4:1, 13 (KJV, "give attendance to"); Titus 1:14; **Heb. 2:1**, lit., "to give heed more earnestly."

Earnest *perissoteros* (4056), means "more abundantly"; in **Heb. 2:1**, lit., "we ought to give heed more abundantly." It is most frequent in 2 Cor. In 11:23, see the RV.

Lest *me pote* (3379), lit., "lest ever," "lest haply," e.g., Luke 14:29, of laying a foundation, with the possibility of being unable to finish the building; Acts 5:39, of the possibility of being found fighting against God; **Heb. 3:2**, RV, "lest haply," of the possibility of having an evil heart of unbelief. The RV usually has "lest haply" (KJV "lest at any time"), e.g., Matt. 4:6; 5:25; 13:15; Mark 4:12; Luke 4:11; 21:34; **Heb. 2:1**; in Matt. 25:9, the RV has "peradventure"; in 2 Tim. 2:25, KJV and RV, have "if peradventure"; in John 7:26 the RV has "Can it be that," for the word "Do" in the KJV.

Time In **Heb. 2:1**, *pote* signifies "at any time"; in 1 Pet. 3:5, "in the old time"; in 2 Pet. 1:21, "in old time." In the following where the KJV has "sometimes" the RV has "once" in Eph. 2:13 and 5:8; "aforetime" in Titus 3:3.

Slip *pararheo* (3901), lit., "to flow past, glide by" (*para,* "by," *rheo,* "to flow"), is used in **Heb. 2:1**, where the significance is to find oneself "flowing" or "passing by," without giving due heed to a thing, here "the things that were heard," or perhaps the salvation of which they spoke; hence the RV, "lest haply we drift away from them," for KJV, "let them slip." The KJV marg. "run out as leaking vessels," does not give the meaning. In the Sept., Prov. 3:21; Isa. 44:4.

2:2 For if the word spoken by angels was stedfast, and every transgression and disobedience received a just recompence of reward;

Was In Luke 10:36, RV, *ginomai,* "to become, come to be," is translated "proved (neighbor)," KJV, "was ..."; so in **Heb. 2:2**.

Stedfast *bebaios* (949), "firm, steadfast," is used of (a) God's promise to Abraham, Rom. 4:16; (b) the believer's hope, **Heb. 6:19**, "steadfast"; (c) the hope of spiritual leaders regarding the welfare of converts, 2 Cor. 1:7, "steadfast"; (d) the glorying of the hope, **Heb. 3:6**, "firm"; (e) the beginning of our confidence, **3:14**, RV, "firm" (KJV, "steadfast"); (f) the Law given at Sinai, **Heb. 2:2**, "steadfast"; (g) the testament (or covenant) fulfilled after a death, **9:17**, "of force"; (h) the calling and election of believers, 2 Pet. 1:10, to be made "sure" by the fulfillment of the injunctions in vv. 5-7; (i) the word of prophecy, "*made* more sure," 2 Pet. 1:19, RV, KJV, "a more sure (word of prophecy)"; what is meant is not a comparison between the prophecies of the OT and NT, but that the former have been confirmed in the person of Christ (vv. 16-18).

Transgression *parabasis* (3847), primarily "a going aside," then, "an overstepping," is used metaphorically to denote "transgression" (always of a breach of law): (a) of Adam, Rom. 5:14; (b) of Eve, 1 Tim. 2:14; (c) negatively, where there is no law, since "transgression" implies the violation of law, none having been enacted between Adam's "transgression" and those under the Law, Rom. 4:15; (d) of "transgressions" of the Law, Gal. 3:19, where the statement "it was added because of transgressions" is best understood according to Rom. 4:15; 5:13 and 5:20; the Law does not make men sinners, but makes them "transgressors"; hence sin becomes "exceeding sinful," Rom. 7:7, 13. Conscience thus had a standard external to itself; by the Law men are taught their inability to yield complete obedience to God, that thereby they may become convinced of their need of a Savior; in Rom. 2:23, RV, "transgression (of the Law)," KJV, "breaking (the Law)"; **Heb. 2:2**; **9:15**.

Disobedience *parakoe* (3876), primarily, "hearing amiss" (*para,* "aside," *akouo,* "to hear"), hence signifies "a refusal to hear"; hence, "an act of disobedience," Rom. 5:19; 2 Cor. 10:6; **Heb. 2:2**. Carelessness in attitude is the precursor of actual "disobedience." In the OT "disobedience" is frequently described as "a refusing to hear," e.g., Jer. 11:10; 35:17; cf. Acts 7:57. See Trench, *Syn.* Sec.lxvi.

Just *endikos* (1738), "just, righteous" (*en,* "in," *dike,* "right"), is said of the condemnation of those who say "Let us do evil, that good may come," Rom. 3:8; of the recompense of reward of transgressions under the Law, **Heb. 2:2**.

Recompence *antimisthia* (489), "a reward, requital" (*anti,* "in return," *misthos,* "wages, hire"), is used (a) in a good sense, 2 Cor. 6:13; (b) in a bad sense, Rom. 1:27.

Reward *misthapodosia* (3405), "a payment of wages," "a recompence," is used (a) of reward, **Heb. 10:35**; **11:26**; (b) of punishment, **Heb. 2:2**. Cf. *misthapodotes,* "a rewarder," **Heb. 11:6**.

2:3 How shall we escape, if we neglect so great salvation; which at the first began to be spoken by the Lord, and was confirmed unto us by them that heard *him*;

Escape *ekpheugo* (1628), "to flee out of a place," is said of the "escape" of prisoners, Acts 16:27; of Sceva's sons, "fleeing" from the demoniac, 19:16; of Paul's escape from Damascus, 2 Cor. 11:33; elsewhere with reference to the judgments of God, Luke 21:36; Rom. 2:3; **Heb. 2:3**; **12:25**; 1 Thess. 5:3.

Neglect *ameleo* (272), denotes (a) "to be careless, not to care" (*a,* negative, *melei,* "it is a care"; from *melo,* "to care, to be a care"), Matt. 22:5, "made light of"; (b) "to be careless of, neglect," 1 Tim. 4:14; **Heb. 2:3**; **8:9**, "I regarded (them) not." In the Sept., Jer. 4:17; 38:32.

Great *telikoutos* (5082), "so great," is used in the NT of things only, a death, 2 Cor. 1:10; salvation, **Heb. 2:3**; ships, Jas. 3:4; an earthquake, Rev. 16:18, KJV, "so mighty," corrected in the RV to "so great."

Salvation *see Hebrews 1:14.*

Began *arche* (746), means "a beginning." The root *arch* primarily indicated what was of worth. Hence the verb *archo* meant "to be first," and *archon* denoted "a ruler." So also arose the idea of "a beginning," the origin, the active cause, whether a person or thing, e.g., Col. 1:18. In **Heb. 2:3** the phrase "having at the first been spoken" is, lit., "having received a beginning to be spoken." In 2 Thess. 2:13 ("God chose you from the beginning"), there is a well supported alternative reading, "chose you as first-fruits" (i.e., *aparchen*, instead of *ap' arches*). In **Heb. 6:1**, where the word is rendered "first principles," the original has "let us leave the word of the beginning of Christ," i.e., the doctrine of the elementary principles relating to Christ. In John 8:25, Christ's reply to the question "Who art Thou?," "Even that which I have spoken unto you from the beginning," does not mean that He had told them before; He declares that He is consistently the unchanging expression of His own teaching and testimony from the first, the immutable embodiment of His doctrine.

Confirmed *bebaioo* (950), "to make firm, establish, make secure" (the connected adjective *bebaios* signifies "stable, fast, firm"), is used of "confirming" a word, Mark 16:20; promises, Rom. 15:8; the testimony of Christ, 1 Cor. 1:6; the saints by the Lord Jesus Christ, 1 Cor. 1:8; the saints by God, 2 Cor. 1:21 ("stablisheth"); in faith, Col. 2:7; the salvation spoken through the Lord and "confirmed" by the apostles, **Heb. 2:3**; the heart by grace, **Heb. 13:9** ("stablished").

2:4 God also bearing *them* witness, both with signs and wonders, and with divers miracles, and gifts of the Holy Ghost, according to his own will?

Witness *sunepimartureo* (4901), denotes "to join in bearing witness with others," **Heb. 2:4**.

Divers *poikilos* (4164), denotes "particolored, variegated" (*poikillo* means "to make gay": the root of the first syllable is *pik-*, found in Eng., "picture"), hence "divers," Matt. 4:24; Mark 1:34; Luke 4:40; 2 Tim. 3:6; Titus 3:3; **Heb. 2:4** (RV, "manifold"), **13:9**; Jas. 1:2 (RV, "manifold"); in 1 Pet. 1:6 and 4:10, "manifold," both KJV and RV.

Miracles *dunamis* (1411), "power, inherent ability," is used of works of a supernatural origin and character, such as could not be produced by natural agents and means. It is translated "miracles" in the RV and KJV in Acts 8:13 (where variant readings give the words in different order); 19:11; 1 Cor. 12:10, 28, 29; Gal. 3:5; KJV only, in Acts 2:22 (RV, "mighty works"); **Heb. 2:4** (RV, "powers"). In Gal. 3:5, the word may be taken in its widest sense, to include "miracles" both physical and moral.

Gifts *merismos* (3311), primarily denotes "a division, partition" (*meros*, "a part"); hence, (a) "a distribution," **Heb. 2:4**, "gifts" (marg. of RV, "distributions"); (b) "a dividing or separation," **Heb. 4:12**, "dividing" (KJV, "dividing asunder"). Some take this in the active sense, "as far as the cleaving asunder or separation of soul and spirit"; others in the passive sense, "as far as the division (i.e., the dividing line) between soul and spirit," i.e., where one differs from the other. The former seems more in keeping with the meaning of the word.

His These translate (a) forms of pronouns under he (a frequent use: in 1 Pet. 2:24, "His own self"); the form *autou*, "his," becomes emphatic when placed between the article and the noun, e.g., 1 Thess. 2:19; Titus 3:5; **Heb. 2:4**; (b) *heautou*, "of himself, his own"; the RV rightly puts "his own," for the KJV, "his," in Luke 11:21; 14:26; Rom. 4:19; 5:8, "His own (love)"; 1 Cor. 7:37; Gal. 6:8; Eph. 5:28, 33; 1 Thess. 2:11, 12; 4:4; in Rev. 10:7 the change has not been made; it should read "his own servants"; (c) *idios*, "one's own," "his own," in the RV, in Matt. 22:5; John 5:18; 2 Pet. 2:16; in Matt. 25:15, it is rendered "his several"; in John 19:27, "his own home," lit., "his own things"; in 1 Tim. 6:15, RV, "its own (times)," referring to the future appearing of Christ; in **Heb. 4:10** (end of verse), both KJV and RV have "his," where it should be "his own"; so in Acts 24:23, for KJV and RV, "his"; in 1 Cor. 7:7, RV, "his own," KJV, "his proper"; (d) in Acts 17:28, the genitive case of the definite article, "His (offspring)," lit., "of the" (i.e., the one referred to, namely, God).

Will *thelesis* (2308), denotes "a willing, a wishing," **Heb. 2:4**.

2:5 For unto the angels hath he not put in subjection the world to come, whereof we speak.

Subjection *hupotasso* (5293), primarily a military term, "to rank under" (*hupo*, "under," *tasso*, "to arrange"), denotes (a) "to put in subjection, to subject," Rom. 8:20 (twice); in the following, the RV, has to subject for KJV, "to put under," 1 Cor. 15:27 (thrice), 28 (3rd clause); Eph. 1:22; **Heb. 2:8** (4th clause); in 1 Cor. 15:28 (1st clause), for KJV "be subdued"; in Phil. 3:21, for KJV, "subdue"; in **Heb. 2:5**, KJV, "hath ... put in subjection"; (b) in the middle or passive voice, to subject oneself, to obey, be subject to, Luke 2:51; 10:17, 20; Rom. 8:7; 10:3, RV, "did (not) subject themselves" [KJV, "have (not) submitted themselves"]; 13:1, 5; 1 Cor. 14:34, RV, "be in subjection" (KJV, "be under obedience"); 15:28 (2nd clause); 16:16 RV, "be in subjection" (KJV, "submit," etc.); so Col. 3:18; Eph. 5:21, RV, "subjecting yourselves" (KJV, "submitting, etc."); v. 22, RV in italics, according to the best texts; v. 24, "is subject"; Titus 2:5, 9, RV, "be in subjection" (KJV, "be obedient"); 3:1, RV, "to be in subjection" (KJV, "to be subject"); **Heb. 12:9**, "be in subjection"; Jas. 4:7, RV, "be subject" (KJV, "submit yourselves"); so 1 Pet. 2:13; v. 18, RV, "be in subjection"; so 3:1, KJV and RV; v. 5, similarly; 3:22, "being made subject"; 5:5, RV, "be subject" (KJV, "submit yourselves"); in some texts in the 2nd part, as KJV.

World *see Hebrews 1:6.*

Come *mello* (3195), "to be about (to do something)," often implying the necessity and therefore the certainty of what is to take place, is frequently rendered "to come," e.g., Matt. 3:7; 11:14; Eph. 1:21; 1 Tim. 4:8; 6:19; **Heb. 2:5**.

2:6 But one in a certain place testified, saying, What is man, that thou art mindful of him? or the son of man, that thou visitest him?

Certain The rendering "certain," is frequently changed in the RV, or omitted, e.g., Luke 5:12; 8:22; Acts 23:17; **Heb. 2:6**; **4:4**.

Place *pou* (4225), a particle, signifies "somewhere" in **Heb. 2:6** and **4:4**, RV (KJV, "in a certain place"); the writer avoids mentioning the place to add stress to his testimony.

Testified *diamarturomai* (1263), "to testify or protest solemnly," an intensive form, is translated "to testify" in Luke 16:28; Acts 2:40; 8:25; 10:42; 18:5; 20:21, 23, 24; 23:11; 28:23; 1 Thess. 4:6; **Heb. 2:6**; "to charge" in 1 Tim. 5:21; 2 Tim. 2:14; 4:8.

Mindful *mimnesko* (5403), the tenses of which are from the older verb *mnaomai*, signifies "to remind"; but in the middle voice, "to remember, to be mindful of," in the sense of caring for, e.g., **Heb. 2:6**, "Thou art mindful"; in **13:3**, "remember"; in 2 Tim. 1:4, RV, "remembering" (KJV, "being mindful of"); so in 2 Pet. 3:2.

Visitest *episkeptomai* (1980), primarily, "to inspect" (a late form of *episkopeo*, "to look upon, care for, exercise oversight"), signifies (a) "to visit" with help, of the act of God, Luke 1:68, 78; 7:16; Acts 15:14; **Heb. 2:6**; (b) "to visit" the sick and afflicted, Matt. 25:36, 43; Jas. 1:27; (c) "to go and see," "pay a visit to," Acts 7:23; 15:36; (d) "to look out" certain men for a purpose, Acts 6:3

2:7 Thou madest him a little lower than the angels; thou crownedst him with glory and honour, and didst set him over the works of thy hands:

Little *brachus* (1024), "short," is used to some extent adverbially of (a) time, with the preposition *meta*, "after," Luke 22:58, "(after) a little while"; in Acts 5:34, without a preposition, RV, "a little while" (KJV, "a little space"); in **Heb. 2:7**, **9**, "a little" (KJV marg. in v. **7**, and RV marg., in both, "a little while"), where the writer transfers to time what the Sept. in Ps. 8:5 says of rank; (b) of quantity, John 6:7; in **Heb. 13:22**, preceded by the preposition *dia*, "by means of," and with *logo*., "words" (genitive plural) understood, "(in) few words"; (c) of distance, Acts 27:28, RV, "a little space" (KJV, "a little further").

Lower *elattoo* (1642), denotes "to make less" (*elatton*, "less"), and is used in the active voice in **Heb. 2:7**, "Thou madest (Him) ... lower," and in the passive in v. **9**, "was made ... lower," and John 3:30, "(I must) decrease," (lit., "be made less").

Angels *angelos* (32), "a messenger" (from *angello*, "to deliver a message"), sent whether by God or by man or by Satan, "is also used of a guardian or representative in Rev. 1:20, cf. Matt. 18:10; Acts 12:15 (where it is better understood as 'ghost'), but most frequently of an order of created beings, superior to man, **Heb. 2:7**; Ps. 8:5, belonging to Heaven, Matt. 24:36; Mark 12:25, and to God, Luke 12:8, and engaged in His service, Ps. 103:20. "Angels" are spirits, **Heb. 1:14**, i.e., they have not material bodies as men have; they are either human in form, or can assume the human form when necessary, cf. Luke 24:4, with v. 23, Acts 10:3 with v. 30.

Crownedst *stephanoo* (4737), "to crown," conforms in meaning to *stephanos;* it is used of the reward of victory in the games, in 2 Tim. 2:5; of the glory and honor bestowed by God upon man in regard to his position in creation, **Heb. 2:7**; of the glory and honor bestowed upon the Lord Jesus in His exaltation, v. **9**.

Honour *time* (5092), primarily "a valuing," hence, objectively, (a) "a price paid or received," e.g., Matt. 27:6, 9; Acts 4:34; 5:2, 3; 7:16, RV, "price" (KJV, "sum"); 19:19; 1 Cor. 6:20; 7:23; (b) of "the preciousness of Christ" unto believers, 1 Pet. 2:7, RV, i.e., the honor and inestimable value of Christ as appropriated by believers, who are joined, as living stones, to Him the cornerstone; (c) in the sense of value, of human ordinances, valueless against the indulgence of the flesh, or, perhaps of no value in attempts at asceticism, Col. 2:23; (d) "honor, esteem," (1) used in ascriptions of worship to God, 1 Tim. 1:17; 6:16; Rev. 4:9, 11; 5:13; 7:12; to Christ, 5:12, 13; (2) bestowed upon Christ by the Father, **Heb. 2:9**; 2 Pet. 1:17; (3) bestowed upon man, **Heb. 2:7**; (4) bestowed upon Aaronic priests, **Heb. 5:4**; (5) to be the reward hereafter of "the proof of faith" on the part of tried saints,

1 Pet. 1:7, RV; (6) used of the believer who as a vessel is "meet for the Master's use," 2 Tim. 2:21; (7) to be the reward of patience in well-doing, Rom. 2:7, and of working good (a perfect life to which man cannot attain, so as to be justified before God thereby), 2:10; (8) to be given to all to whom it is due, Rom. 13:7; (9) as an advantage to be given by believers one to another instead of claiming it for self, Rom. 12:10; (10) to be given to elders that rule well ("double honor"), 1 Tim. 5:17 (here the meaning may be an honorarium); (11) to be given by servants to their master, 1 Tim. 6:1; (12) to be given to wives by husbands, 1 Pet. 3:7; (13) said of the husband's use of the wife, in contrast to the exercise of the passion of lust, 1 Thess. 4:4 (some regard the "vessel" here as the believer's body); (14) of that bestowed upon; parts of the body, 1 Cor. 12:23, 24; (15) of that which belongs to the builder of a house in contrast to the house itself, **Heb. 3:3**; (16) of that which is not enjoyed by a prophet in his own country, John 4:44; (17) of that bestowed by the inhabitants of Melita upon Paul and his fellow-passengers, in gratitude for his benefits of healing, Acts 28:10; (18) of the festive honor to be possessed by nations, and brought into the Holy City, the heavenly Jerusalem, Rev. 21:26 (in some mss., v. 24); (19) of honor bestowed upon things inanimate, a potters' vessel, Rom. 9:21; 2 Tim. 2:20.

Set *kathistemi* (2525), usually signifies "to appoint a person to a position." In this sense the verb is often translated "to make" or "to set," in appointing a person to a place of authority, e.g., a servant over a household, Matt. 24:45, 47; 25:21, 23; Luke 12:42, 44; a judge, Luke 12:14; Acts 7:27, 35; a governor, Acts 7:10; man by God over the work of His hands, **Heb. 2:7**. It is rendered "appoint," with reference to the so-called seven deacons in Acts 6:3. The RV translates it by "appoint" in Titus 1:5, instead of "ordain," of the elders whom Titus was to "appoint" in every city in Crete. Not a formal ecclesiastical ordination is in view, but the "appointment," for the recognition of the churches, of those who had already been raised up and qualified by the Holy Spirit, and had given evidence of this in their life and service. It is used of the priests of old, **Heb. 5:1; 7:28; 8:3** (RV, "appointed").

Works *see Hebrews 1:10*.

Hands *see Hebrews 1:10*.

2:8 Thou hast put all things in subjection under his feet. For in that he put all in subjection under him, he left nothing *that is* not put under him. But now we see not yet all things put under him.

Subjection *see Hebrews 2:5*.

Under *hupokato* (5270), an adverb signifying "under," is used as a preposition and rendered "under" in Mark 6:11; 7:28; Luke 8:16; **Heb. 2:8**; Rev. 5:3, 13; 6:9; 12:1; "underneath" in Matt. 22:44, RV (Mark 12:36 in some mss.); John 1:50, RV (KJV, "under").

Left *aphiemi* (863), *apo*, "from," and *hiemi*, "to send," has three chief meanings, (a) "to send forth, let go, forgive"; (b) "to let, suffer, permit"; (c) "to leave, leave alone, forsake, neglect." It is translated by the verb "to leave" (c), in Matt. 4:11; 4:20, 22, and parallel passages; 5:24; 8:15, and parallel passages; 8:22, RV, "leave (the dead)," KJV, "let," and the parallel passage; 13:36, RV, "left (the multitude)," KJV, "sent ... away"; 18:12; 19:27, and parallel passages, RV, "we have left" (KJV, "we have forsaken"), so v. 29; 22:22, 25; 23:23, RV, "have left undone" (KJV, "have omitted," in the 1st part, "leave undone" in the second); 23:38, and the parallel passage; 24:2, 40, 41, and parallel passages; 26:56, RV, "left"; Mark 1:18, "left"; 1:31; 7:8, RV, "ye leave"; 8:13; 10:28, 29; 12:12, 19-22; 13:34; Luke 10:30; 11:42 (in some mss.); Luke 12:39, RV "have left," KJV "have suffered"; John 4:3, 28, 52; 8:29; 10:12; 14:18, 27; 16:28, 32; Rom. 1:27; 1 Cor. 7:11, RV, "leave" (KJV "put away"); 7:13 (KJV and RV); **Heb. 2:8; 6:1**; Rev. 2:4.

Not put under *anupotaktos* (506), "not subject to rule" (*a*, negative, *n*, euphonic, *hupotasso*, "to put in subjection"), is used (a) of things, **Heb. 2:8**, RV, "not subject" (KJV, "not put under"); (b) of persons, "unruly," 1 Tim. 1:9, RV (KJV, "disobedient"); Titus 1:6, 10.

2:9 But we see Jesus, who was made a little lower than the angels for the suffering of death, crowned with glory and honour; that he by the grace of God should taste death for every man.

Jesus *iesous* (2424), is a transliteration of the Heb. "Joshua," meaning "Jehovah is salvation," i.e., "is the Savior," "a common name among the Jews, e.g., Ex. 17:9; Luke 3:29 (RV); Col. 4:11. It was given to the Son of God in Incarnation as His personal name, in obedience to the command of an angel to Joseph, the husband of His Mother, Mary, shortly before He was born, Matt. 1:21. By it He is spoken of throughout the Gospel narratives generally, but not without exception, as in Mark 16:19, 20; Luke 7:13, and a dozen other places in that Gospel, and a few in John.

"'Jesus Christ' occurs only in Matt. 1:1, 18; 16:21, marg.; Mark 1:1; John 1:17; 17:3. In Acts the name 'Jesus' is found frequently. 'Lord Jesus' is the normal usage, as in Acts 8:16; 19:5, 17; see also the reports of the words of Stephen, 7:59, of Ananias, 9:17, and of Paul, 16:31; though both Peter, 10:36, and Paul, 16:18, also used 'Jesus Christ.' In the Epistles of James, Peter, John and Jude, the personal name is not once found alone, but in Rev. eight times (RV), 1:9; 12:17; 14:12; 17:6; 19:10 (twice); 20:4; 22:16. In the Epistles of Paul 'Jesus' appears alone just thirteen times, and in the Hebrews eight times [**2:9**; **4:8**; **6:20**; **7:22**; **10:19**; **12:2**, **24**; **13:12**]; (in the latter the title 'Lord' is added once only, at **13:20**). In the Epistles of James, Peter, John, and Jude, men who had companied with the Lord in the days of His flesh, 'Jesus Christ' is the invariable order (in the RV) of the Name and Title, for this was the order of their experience; as 'Jesus' they knew Him first, that He was Messiah they learnt finally in His resurrection. But Paul came to know Him first in the glory of heaven, Acts 9:1-6, and his experience being thus the reverse of theirs, the reverse order, 'Christ Jesus,' is of frequent occurrence in his letters, but, with the exception of Acts 24:24, does not occur elsewhere in the RV. In Paul's letters the order is always in harmony with the context. Thus 'Christ Jesus' describes the Exalted One who emptied Himself, Phil. 2:5, and testifies to His pre-existence; 'Jesus Christ' describes the despised and rejected One Who was afterwards glorified, Phil. 2:11, and testifies to His resurrection. 'Christ Jesus' suggests His grace, 'Jesus Christ' suggests His glory."

Little *see Hebrews 2:7.*

Lower *see Hebrews 2:7.*

Suffering *pathema* (3804), from *pathos*, "suffering," signifies "affliction." The word is frequent in Paul's epistles and is found three times in Hebrews, four in 1 Peter; it is used (a) of "afflictions," Rom. 8:18, etc.; of Christ's "sufferings," 1 Pet. 1:11; 5:1; **Heb. 2:9**; of those as shared by believers, 2 Cor. 1:5; Phil. 3:10; 1 Pet. 4:13; 5:1; (b) of "an evil emotion, passion," Rom. 7:5; Gal. 5:24. The connection between the two meanings is that the emotions, whether good or evil, were regarded as consequent upon external influences exerted on the mind (cf. the two meanings of the English "passion"). It is more concrete than *kakopatheia*, and expresses in sense (b) the uncontrolled nature of evil desires, in contrast to *epithumia*, the general and comprehensive term, lit., "what you set your heart upon" (Trench, *Syn.* Sec. lxxxvii). Its concrete character is seen in **Heb. 2:9**.

Crowned *see* **Crownedst** at *Hebrews 2:7.*

Honour *see Hebrews 2:7.*

Taste *geuo* (1089), "to make to taste," is used in the middle voice, signifying "to taste" (a) naturally, Matt. 27:34; Luke 14:24; John 2:9; Col. 2:21; (b) metaphorically, of Christ's "tasting" death, implying His personal experience in voluntarily undergoing death, **Heb. 2:9**; of believers (negatively) as to "tasting" of death, Matt. 16:28; Mark 9:1; Luke 9:27; John 8:52; of "tasting" the heavenly gift (different from receiving it), **Heb. 6:4**; "the good word of God, and the powers of the age to come," **6:5**; "that the Lord is gracious," 1 Pet. 2:3.

2:10 For it became him, for whom *are* all things, and by whom *are* all things, in bringing many sons unto glory, to make the captain of their salvation perfect through sufferings.

Became *prepo* (4241), means "to be conspicuous among a number, to be eminent, distinguished by a thing," hence, "to be becoming, seemly, fit." The adornment of good works "becometh women professing godliness," 1 Tim. 2:10. Those who minister the truth are to speak "the things which befit the sound doctrine," Titus 2:1. Christ, as a High Priest "became us," **Heb. 7:26**. In the impersonal sense, it signifies "it is fitting, it becometh," Matt. 3:15; 1 Cor. 11:13; Eph. 5:3; **Heb. 2:10**.

Bringing *ago* (71), "to lead, to lead along to bring," has the meaning "to bring" (besides its occurrences in the Gospels and Acts) in 1 Thess. 4:14, 2 Tim. 4:11, and **Heb. 2:10**.

Captain *archegos* (747), translated "Prince" in Acts 3:15 (marg., "Author") and 5:31, but "Author" in **Heb. 2:10**, RV, "Captain," RV marg., and KJV, and "Author" in **12:2**, primarily signifies "one who takes a lead in, or provides the first occasion of, anything." In the Sept. it is used of the chief of a tribe or family, Num. 13:2 (RV, prince); of the "heads" of the children of Israel, v. 3; a captain of the whole people, 14:4; in Micah 1:13, of Lachish as the leader of the sin of the daughter of Sion: there, as in **Heb. 2:10**, the word suggests a combination of the meaning of leader with that of the source from whence a thing proceeds. That Christ is the Prince of life signifies, as Chrysostom says, that "the life He had was not from another; the Prince or Author of life must be He who has life from Himself." But the word does not necessarily combine the idea of the source or originating cause with that of leader. In **Heb. 12:2** where Christ is called the "Author and Perfecter of faith," He is represented as the one who takes precedence in faith and is thus the perfect exemplar of it. The pronoun "our" does not correspond to anything in the original, and may well be omitted. Christ in the days of His flesh trod undeviatingly the path of faith, and as the Perfecter has brought it to a perfect end in His own person. Thus He is the leader of all others who tread that path.

Perfect *teleioo* (5048), "to bring to an end by completing or perfecting," is used (I) of "accomplishing"; (II) of "bringing to completeness," (a) of persons: of Christ's assured completion of His earthly course, in the accomplishment of the Father's will, the successive stages culminating in His death, Luke 13:32; **Heb. 2:10**, to make Him "perfect," legally and officially, for all that He would be to His people on the ground of His sacrifice; cf. **5:9**; **7:28**, RV, "perfected" (KJV, "consecrated"); of His saints, John 17:23, RV, "perfected" (KJV, "made perfect"); Phil. 3:12; **Heb. 10:14**; **11:40** (of resurrection glory); **12:23** (of the departed saints); 1 John 4:18, of former priests (negatively), **Heb. 9:9**; similarly of Israelites under the Aaronic priesthood, **10:1**; (b) of things, **Heb. 7:19** (of the ineffectiveness of the Law); Jas. 2:22 (of faith made "perfect" by works); 1 John 2:5, of the love of God operating through him who keeps His word; 4:12, of the love of God in the case of those who love one another; 4:17, of the love of God as "made perfect with" (RV) those who abide in God, giving them to be possessed of the very character of God, by reason of which "as He is, even so are they in this world."

2:11 For both he that sanctifieth and they who are sanctified *are* all of one: for which cause he is not ashamed to call them brethren,

Sanctifieth, Sanctified *hagiazo* (37), "to sanctify," "is used of (a) the gold adorning the Temple and of the gift laid on the altar, Matt. 23:17, 19; (b) food, 1 Tim. 4:5; (c) the unbelieving spouse of a believer, 1 Cor. 7:14; (d) the ceremonial cleansing of the Israelites, **Heb. 9:13**; (e) the Father's Name, Luke 11:2; (f) the consecration of the Son by the Father, John 10:36; (g) the Lord Jesus devoting Himself to the redemption of His people, John 17:19; (h) the setting apart of the believer for God, Acts 20:32; cf. Rom. 15:16; (i) the effect on the believer of the Death of Christ, **Heb. 10:10**, said of God, and **2:11**; **13:12**, said of the Lord Jesus; (j) the separation of the believer from the world in his behavior – by the Father through the Word, John 17:17, 19; (k) the believer who turns away from such things as dishonor God and His gospel, 2 Tim. 2:21; (l) the acknowledgment of the Lordship of Christ, 1 Pet. 3:15.

"Since every believer is sanctified in Christ Jesus, 1 Cor. 1:2, cf. **Heb. 10:10**, a common NT designation of all believers is 'saints,' *hagioi*, i.e., 'sanctified' or 'holy ones.' Thus sainthood, or sanctification, is not an attainment, it is the state into which God, in grace, calls sinful men, and in which they begin their course as Christians, Col. 3:12; **Heb. 3:1**."

For which cause Some phrases introduced by the preposition *dia*, "on account of," *dia touto*, "on account of this," e.g., Matt. 12:31; Rom. 5:12; Eph. 1:15; 3 John 10; *dia hen* (the accusative feminine of *hos*, "who"), "on account of which" (*aitia*, "a cause," being understood), e.g., Acts 10:21 (with *aitia*, expressed, Titus 1:13; **Heb. 2:11**); *dia ti* "on account of what?" (sometimes as one word, *diati*), e.g., Luke 19:23; Rom. 9:32; 2 Cor. 11:11; Rev. 17:7.

Ashamed *epaischunomai* (1870), a strengthened form of *aischuno* (*epi*, "upon," intensive), is used only in the sense "the feeling of shame arising from something that has been done." It is said of being "ashamed" of persons, Mark 8:38; Luke 9:26; the gospel, Rom. 1:16; former evil doing, Rom. 6:21; "the testimony of our Lord," 2 Tim. 1:8; suffering for the gospel, v. 12; rendering assistance and comfort to one who is suffering for the gospel's sake, v. 16. It is used in Heb., of Christ in calling those who are sanctified His brethren, **2:11**, and of God in His not being "ashamed" to be called the God of believers, **11:16**. In the Sept., in Job 34:19; Ps. 119:6; Isa. 1:29.

2:12 Saying, I will declare thy name unto my brethren, in the midst of the church will I sing praise unto thee.

Declare *apangello* (518), signifies "to announce or report from a person or place" (*apo*, "from"); hence, "to declare, publish"; it is rendered "declare" in Luke 8:47; **Heb. 2:12**; 1 John 1:3. It is very frequent in the Gospels and Acts; elsewhere, other than the last two places mentioned, only in 1 Thess. 1:9 and 1 John 1:2.

Church *ekklesia* (1577), is translated "congregation" in **Heb. 2:12**, RV, instead of the usual rendering "church."

Praise *humneo* (5214), denotes (a) transitively, "to sing, to laud, sing to the praise of" (Eng., "hymn"), Acts 16:25, KJV, "sang praises" (RV, "singing hymns"); **Heb. 2:12**, RV, "will I sing (Thy) praise," KJV, "will I sing praise (unto Thee)," lit., "I will hymn Thee"; (b) intransitively, "to sing," Matt. 26:30; Mark 14:26, in both places of the singing of the paschal hymns (Ps. 113-118, and 136), called by Jews the Great Hallel.

2:13 And again, I will put my trust in him. And again, Behold I and the children which God hath given me.

Trust *peitho* (3982), intransitively, in the perfect and pluperfect active, "to have confidence, trust," is rendered "to trust" in Matt. 27:43; Mark 10:24; Luke 11:22; 18:9; 2 Cor. 1:9; 10:7; Phil, 2:24; 3:4, KJV (RV, "to have confidence"); **Heb. 2:13**; in the present middle, **Heb. 13:18**, KJV (RV, "are persuaded").

2:14 Forasmuch then as the children are partakers of flesh and blood, he also himself likewise took part of the same; that through death he might destroy him that had the power of death, that is, the devil;

Partakers *koinoneo* (2841), "to have a share of, to share with, take part in," is translated "to be partaker of" in 1 Tim. 5:22; **Heb. 2:14** (1st part), KJV, "are partakers of," RV, "are sharers in"; 1 Pet. 4:13; 2 John 11, RV, "partaketh in" (KJV, "is partaker of"); in the passive voice in Rom. 15:27.

Blood *haima* (129), (hence Eng., prefix *haem-*), besides its natural meaning, stands, (a) in conjunction with *sarx*, "flesh," "flesh and blood," Matt. 16:17; 1 Cor. 15:50; Gal. 1:16; the original has the opposite order, blood and flesh, in Eph. 6:12 and **Heb. 2:14**; this phrase signifies, by *synecdoche*, "man, human beings." It stresses the limitations of humanity; the two are essential elements in man's physical being; "the life of the flesh is in the blood," Lev. 17:11; (b) for human generation, John 1:13; (c) for "blood" shed by violence, e.g., Matt. 23:35; Rev. 17:6; (d) for the "blood" of sacrificial victims, e.g., **Heb. 9:7**; of the "blood" of Christ, which betokens His death by the shedding of His "blood" in expiatory sacrifice; to drink His "blood" is to appropriate the saving effects of His expiatory death, John 6:53. As "the life of the flesh is in the blood," Lev. 17:11, and was forfeited by sin, life eternal can be imparted only by the expiation made, in the giving up of the life by the sinless Savior.

Likewise *paraplesios* (3898), from *para*, "beside," and the adjective *plesios*, "near" (akin to the adverb *pelas*, "near, hard by"), is used in **Heb. 2:14**, KJV, "likewise" (RV, "in like manner"), expressing the true humanity of Christ in partaking of flesh and blood.

Took part *metecho* (3348), "to partake of, share in" (*meta*, "with," *echo*, "to have"), is translated "of partaking" in 1 Cor. 9:10, RV (KJV, "be partaker of"); "partake of" in 9:12, RV (KJV, "be partakers of"); so in 10:17, 21: in v. 30 "partake"; in **Heb. 2:14**, the KJV "took part of" is awkward; Christ "partook of" flesh and blood, RV; in **Heb. 5:13**, metaphorically, of receiving elementary spiritual teaching, RV, "partaketh of (milk)," KJV, "useth"; in **Heb. 7:13**, it is said of Christ (the antitype of Melchizedek) as "belonging to" (so RV) or "partaking of" (RV marg.) another tribe than that of Levi (KJV, "pertaineth to").

Destroy *katargeo* (2673), is used in 1 Cor. 1:28, "(that) He might bring to nought"; 1 Cor. 2:6 (passive voice in the original); 1 Cor. 6:13, RV, "will bring to nought" (KJV "will destroy"); so 2 Thess. 2:8 and **Heb. 2:14**.

Power *kratos* (2904), is translated "power" in the RV and KJV in 1 Tim. 6:16; **Heb. 2:14**; in Eph. 1:19 (last part); 6:10, KJV, "power" (RV, "strength").

Devil *diabolos* (1228), "an accuser, a slanderer" (from *diaballo*, "to accuse, to malign"), is one of the names of Satan. From it the English word "Devil" is derived, and should be applied only to Satan, as a proper name. *Daimon*, "a demon," is frequently, but wrongly, translated "devil"; it should always be translated "demon," as in the RV margin. There is one "Devil," there are many demons. Being the malignant enemy of God and man, he accuses man to God, Job 1:6-11; 2:1-5; Rev. 12:9, 10, and God to man, Gen. 3. He afflicts men with physical sufferings, Acts 10:38. Being himself sinful, 1 John 3:8, he instigated man to sin, Gen. 3, and tempts man to do evil, Eph. 4:27; 6:11, encouraging him thereto by deception, Eph. 2:2. Death having been brought into the world by sin, the "Devil" had the power of death, but Christ through His own death, has triumphed over him, and will bring him to nought, **Heb. 2:14**; his power over death is intimated in his struggle with Michael over the body of Moses, Jude 9. Judas, who gave himself over to the "Devil," was so identified with him, that the Lord described him as such, John 6:70 (see 13:2). As the "Devil" raised himself in pride against God and fell under condemnation, so believers are warned against similar sin, 1 Tim. 3:6; for them he lays snares, v. 7, seeking to devour them as a roaring lion, 1 Pet. 5:8; those who fall into his snare may be recovered therefrom unto the will of God, 2 Tim. 2:26, "having been taken captive by him (i.e., by the 'Devil')"; "by the Lord's servant" is an alternative, which some regard as confirmed by the use of *zogreo* ("to catch alive") in Luke 5:10; but the general use is that of taking captive in the usual way. If believers resist he will flee from them, Jas. 4:7. His fury and malignity will be especially exercised at the end of the present age, Rev. 12:12. His doom is the lake of fire, Matt. 25:41; Rev. 20:10. The noun is applied to slanderers, false accusers, 1 Tim. 3:11; 2 Tim. 3:3; Titus 2:3.

2:15 And deliver them who through fear of death were all their lifetime subject to bondage.

Deliver *apallasso* (525), lit., "to change from" (*apo*, "from," *allasso*, "to change"), "to free from, release," is translated "might deliver" in **Heb. 2:15**; in Luke 12:58, it is used in a legal sense of being quit of a person, i.e., the opponent being appeased and withdrawing his suit. For its other meaning, "to depart," in Acts 19:12.

Who These are usually the translations of forms of the relative pronoun *hos*, or of the interrogative pronoun *tis;* otherwise of *hostis*, "whoever," usually of a more general subject than *hos*, e.g., Mark 15:7; Luke 23:19; Gal. 2:4; *hosos*, "as many as," **Heb. 2:15**; in Acts 13:7, KJV, *houtos*, "this (man)," is translated "who," RV, "the same."

Fear *phobos* (5401), first had the meaning of "flight," that which is caused by being scared; then, "that which may cause flight," (a) "fear, dread, terror," always with this significance in the four Gospels; also, e.g., in Acts 2:43; 19:17; 1 Cor. 2:3; 1 Tim. 5:20 (lit., "may have fear"); **Heb. 2:15**; 1 John 4:18; Rev. 11:11; 18:10, 15; by metonymy, that which causes "fear," Rom. 13:3; 1 Pet. 3:14, RV, "(their) fear," KJV "(their) terror," an adaptation of the Sept. of Isa. 8:12, "fear not their fear"; hence some take it to mean, as there, "what they fear," but in view of Matt. 10:28, e.g., it seems best to understand it as that which is caused by the intimidation of adversaries; (b) "reverential fear," of God, as a controlling motive of the life, in matters spiritual and moral, not a mere "fear" of His power and righteous retribution, but a wholesome dread of displeasing Him, a "fear" which banishes the terror that shrinks from His presence, Rom. 8:15, and which influences the disposition and attitude of one whose circumstances are guided by trust in God, through the indwelling Spirit of God, Acts 9:31; Rom. 3:18; 2 Cor. 7:1; Eph. 5:21 (RV, "the fear of Christ"); Phil. 2:12; 1 Pet. 1:17 (a comprehensive phrase: the reverential "fear" of God will inspire a constant carefulness in dealing with others in His "fear"); 3:2, 15; the association of "fear and trembling," as, e.g., in Phil. 2:12, has in the Sept. a much sterner import, e.g., Gen. 9:2; Exod. 15:16; Deut. 2:25; 11:25; Ps. 55:5; Isa. 19:16 ...

Death *thanatos* (2288), "death," is used in Scripture of (a) the separation of the soul (the spiritual part of man) from the body (the material part), the latter ceasing to function and turning to dust, e.g., John 11:13; **Heb. 2:15**; **5:7**; **7:23**. In **Heb. 9:15**, the KJV, "by means of death" is inadequate; the RV, "a death having taken place" is in keeping with the subject. In Rev. 13:3, 12, the RV, "death-stroke" (KJV, "deadly wound") is, lit., "the stroke of death." (b) the separation of man from God; Adam died on the day he disobeyed God, Gen. 2:17, and hence all mankind are born in the same spiritual condition, Rom. 5:12, 14, 17, 21, from which, however, those who believe in Christ are delivered, John 5:24; 1 John 3:14. "Death" is the opposite of life; it never denotes nonexistence. As spiritual life is "conscious existence in communion with God," so spiritual "death" is "conscious existence in separation from God."

Lifetime *zao* (2198), "to live, be alive," is used in the NT of "(a) God, Matt. 16:16; John 6:57; Rom. 14:11; (b) the Son in Incarnation, John 6:57; (c) the Son in Resurrection, John 14:19; Acts 1:3; Rom. 6:10; 2 Cor. 13:4; **Heb. 7:8**; (d) spiritual life, John 6:57; Rom. 1:17; 8:13b; Gal. 2:19, 20; **Heb. 12:9**; (e) the present state of departed saints, Luke 20:38; 1 Pet. 4:6; (f) the hope of resurrection, 1 Pet. 1:3; (g) the resurrection of believers, 1 Thess. 5:10; John 5:25; Rev. 20:4, and of unbelievers, v. 5, cf. v. 13; (h) the way of access to God through the Lord Jesus Christ, **Heb. 10:20**; (i) the manifestation of divine power in support of divine authority, 2 Cor. 13:4b; cf. 12:10, and 1 Cor. 5:5; (j) bread, figurative of the Lord Jesus, John 6:51; (k) a stone, figurative of the Lord Jesus, 1 Pet. 2:4; (l) water, figurative of the Holy Spirit, John 4:10; 7:38; (m) a sacrifice, figurative of the believer, Rom. 12:1; (n) stones, figurative of the believer, 1 Pet. 2:5; (o) the oracles, *logion*, Acts 7:38, and word, *logos*, **Heb. 4:12**; 1 Pet. 1:23, of God; (p) the physical life of men, 1 Thess. 4:15; Matt. 27:63; Acts 25:24; Rom. 14:9; Phil. 1:21 (in the infinitive mood used as a noun with the article, 'living'), 22; 1 Pet. 4:5; (q) the maintenance of physical life, Matt. 4:4; 1 Cor. 9:14; (r) the duration of physical life, **Heb. 2:15**; (s) the enjoyment of physical life, 1 Thess. 3:8; (t) the recovery of physical life from the power of disease, Mark 5:23; John 4:50; (u) the recovery of physical life from the power of death, Matt. 9:18; Acts 9:41; Rev. 20:5; (v) the course, conduct, and character of men, (1) good, Acts 26:5; 2 Tim. 3:12; Titus 2:12; (2) evil,

Luke 15:13; Rom. 6:2; 8:13a; 2 Cor. 5:15b; Col. 3:7; (3) undefined, Rom. 7:9; 14:7; Gal. 2:14; (w) restoration after alienation, Luke 15:32."

Subject *enochos* (1777), "held in, bound by," in **Heb. 2:15**, subject to.

Bondage *douleia* (1397), akin to *deo*, "to bind," primarily "the condition of being a slave," came to denote any kind of bondage, as, e.g., of the condition of creation, Rom. 8:21; of that fallen condition of man himself which makes him dread God, v. 15, and fear death, **Heb. 2:15**; of the condition imposed by the Mosaic Law, Gal. 4:24.

2:16 For verily he took not on *him the nature of* angels; but he took on *him* the seed of Abraham.

Verily In **Heb. 2:16**, *depou* (in some texts *de pou*), a particle meaning "of course, we know," is rendered "verily."

Seed *sperma* (4690), akin to *speiro*, "to sow" (Eng., "sperm," "spermatic," etc.), has the following usages, (a) agricultural and botanical, e.g., Matt. 13:24, 27, 32; 1 Cor. 15:38; 2 Cor. 9:10; (b) physiological, **Heb. 11:11**; (c) metaphorical and by metonymy for "offspring, posterity," (1) of natural offspring, e.g., Matt. 22:24, 25, RV, "seed" (KJV, "issue"); John 7:42; 8:33, 37; Acts 3:25; Rom. 1:3; 4:13, 16, 18; 9:7 (twice), 8, 29; 11:1; 2 Cor. 11:22; **Heb. 2:16**; **11:18**; Rev. 12:17; Gal. 3:16, 19, 29; in the 16th v., "He saith not, And to seeds, as of many; but as of one, And to thy seed, which is Christ," quoted from the Sept. of Gen. 13:15 and 17:7, 8, there is especial stress on the word "seed," as referring to an individual (here, Christ) in fulfillment of the promises to Abraham - a unique use of the singular. While the plural form "seeds," neither in Hebrew nor in Greek, would have been natural any more than in English (it is not so used in Scripture of human offspring; its plural occurrence is in 1 Sam. 8:15, of crops), yet if the divine intention had been to refer to Abraham's natural descendants, another word could have been chosen in the plural, such as "children"; all such words were, however, set aside, "seed" being selected as one that could be used in the singular, with the purpose of showing that the "seed" was Messiah. Some of the rabbis had even regarded "seed," e.g., in Gen. 4:25 and Isa. 53:10, as referring to the Coming One. Descendants were given to Abraham by other than natural means, so that through him Messiah might come, and the point of the apostle's argument is that since the fulfillment of the promises of God is secured alone by Christ, they only who are "in Christ" can receive them; (2) of spiritual offspring, Rom. 4:16, 18; 9:8; here "the children of the promise are reckoned for a seed" points, firstly, to Isaac's birth as being not according to the ordinary course of nature but by divine promise, and, secondly, by analogy, to the fact that all believers are children of God by spiritual birth; Gal. 3:29.

2:17 Wherefore in all things it behoved him to be made like unto *his* brethren, that he might be a merciful and faithful high priest in things *pertaining* to God, to make reconciliation for the sins of the people.

Wherefore *hothen* (which denotes "whence," when used of direction or source, e.g., Matt. 12:44), used of cause and denoting "wherefore" in **Heb. 2:17**; **3:1**; **7:25**; **8:3**.

Behoved *opheilo* (3784), "to owe," is once rendered "behove," **Heb. 2:17**; it indicates a necessity, owing to the nature of the matter under consideration; in this instance, the fulfillment of the justice and love of God, voluntarily exhibited in what Christ accomplished, that He might be a merciful and faithful High Priest.

Like unto *homoioo* (3666), "to make like," is used (a) especially in the parables, with the significance of comparing, "likening," or, in the passive voice, "being likened," Matt. 7:24, 26; 11:16; 13:24; 18:23; 22:2 (RV, "likened"); 25:1; Mark 4:30; Luke 7:31; 13:18, RV, "liken" (KJV, "resemble"); v. 20; in several of these instances the point of resemblance is not a specific detail, but the whole circumstances of the parable; (b) of making "like," or, in the passive voice, of being made or becoming "like," Matt. 6:8; Acts 14:11, "in the likeness of (men)," lit., "being made like" (aorist participle, passive); Rom. 9:29; **Heb. 2:17**, of Christ in being "made like" unto His brethren, i.e., in partaking of human nature, apart from sin.

Merciful *eleemon* (1655), "merciful," not simply possessed of pity but actively compassionate, is used of Christ as a High Priest, **Heb. 2:17**, and of those who are like God, Matt. 5:7 (cf. Luke 6:35, 36, where the RV, "sons" is to be read, as representing characteristics resembling those of their Father).

Faithful *pistos* (4103), a verbal adjective, akin to *peitho*, is used in two senses, (a) passive, "faithful, to be trusted, reliable," said of God, e.g., 1 Cor. 1:9; 10:13; 2 Cor. 1:18 (KJV, "true"); 2 Tim. 2:13; **Heb. 10:23**; **11:11**; 1 Pet. 4:19; 1 John 1:9; of Christ, e.g., 2 Thess. 3:3; **Heb. 2:17**; **3:2**; Rev. 1:5; 3:14; 19:11; of the words of God, e.g., Acts 13:34, "sure"; 1 Tim. 1:15; 3:1 (KJV, "true"); 4:9; 2 Tim. 2:11; Titus 1:9; 3:8; Rev. 21:5;

22:6; of servants of the Lord, Matt. 24:45; 25:21, 23; Acts 16:15; 1 Cor. 4:2, 17; 7:25; Eph. 6:21; Col. 1:7; 4:7, 9; 1 Tim. 1:12; 3:11; 2 Tim. 2:2; **Heb. 3:5**; 1 Pet. 5:12; 3 John 5; Rev. 2:13; 17:14; of believers, Eph. 1:1; Col. 1:2; (b) active, signifying "believing, trusting, relying," e.g., Acts 16:1 (feminine); 2 Cor. 6:15; Gal. 3:9 seems best taken in this respect, as the context lays stress upon Abraham's "faith" in God, rather than upon his "faithfulness." In John 20:27 the context requires the active sense, as the Lord is reproaching Thomas for his want of "faith."

High priest *archiereus* (749), designates (a) "the high priests" of the Levitical order, frequently called "chief priests" in the NT, and including "ex-high priests" and members of "high priestly" families, e.g., Matt. 2:4; 16:21; 20:18; 21:15; in the singular, a "high priest," e.g., Abiathar, Mark 2:26; Annas and Caiaphas, Luke 3:2 ... The divine institution of the priesthood culminated in the "high priest," it being his duty to represent the whole people, e.g., Lev. 4:15, 16; ch. 16. The characteristics of the Aaronic "high priests" are enumerated in **Heb. 5:1-4**; **8:3**; **9:7, 25**; in some mss., **10:11** (RV, marg.); **13:11**.

(b) Christ is set forth in this respect in the Ep. to the Hebrews, where He is spoken of as "a high priest," **4:15**; **5:5, 10**; **6:20**; **7:26**; **8:1, 3** (RV); **9:11**; "a great high priest," **4:14**; "a great priest," **10:21**; "a merciful and faithful high priest," **2:17**; "the Apostle and high priest of our confession," **3:1**, RV; "a high priest after the order of Melchizedek," **5:10**. One of the great objects of this Epistle is to set forth the superiority of Christ's High Priesthood as being of an order different from and higher than the Aaronic, in that He is the Son of God (see especially **7:28**), with a priesthood of the Melchizedek order. Seven outstanding features of His priesthood are stressed, (1) its character, **5:6, 10**; (2) His commission, **5:4, 5**; (3) His preparation, **2:17**; **10:5**; (4) His sacrifice, **8:3**; **9:12, 14, 27, 28**; **10:4-12**; (5) His sanctuary, **4:14**; **8:2**; **9:11, 12, 24**; **10:12, 19**; (6) His ministry, **2:18**; **4:15**; **7:25**; **8:6**; **9:15, 24**; (7) its effects, **2:15**; **4:16**; **6:19, 20**; **7:16, 25**; **9:14, 28**; **10:14-17, 22, 39**; **12:1**; **13:13-17**.

Pertaining to In Rom. 15:17, the phrase *ta pros*, lit., "the (things) towards" is translated "things pertaining to," RV (KJV, "those things which pertain to"), in **Heb. 2:17** and **5:1**, RV and KJV, "things pertaining to."

God *see* ***Hebrews 1:8.***

Reconciliation *hilaskomai* (2433), was used amongst the Greeks with the significance "to make the gods propitious, to appease, propitiate," inasmuch as their good will was not conceived as their natural attitude, but something to be earned first. This use of the word is foreign to the Greek Bible, with respect to God whether in the Sept. or in the NT. It is never used of any act whereby man brings God into a favorable attitude or gracious disposition. It is God who is "propitiated" by the vindication of His holy and righteous character, whereby through the provision He has made in the vicarious and expiatory sacrifice of Christ, He has so dealt with sin that He can show mercy to the believing sinner in the removal of his guilt and the remission of his sins. Thus in Luke 18:13 it signifies "to be propitious" or "merciful to" (with the person as the object of the verb), and in **Heb. 2:17** "to expiate, to make propitiation for" (the object of the verb being sins); here the RV, "to make propitiation" is an important correction of the KJV "to make reconciliation." Through the "propitiatory" sacrifice of Christ, he who believes upon Him is by God's own act delivered from justly deserved wrath, and comes under the covenant of grace. Never is God said to be reconciled, a fact itself indicative that the enmity exists on man's part alone, and that it is man who needs to be reconciled to God, and not God to man. God is always the same and, since He is Himself immutable, His relative attitude does change towards those who change. He can act differently towards those who come to Him by faith, and solely on the ground of the "propitiatory" sacrifice of Christ, not because He has changed, but because He ever acts according to His unchanging righteousness. The expiatory work of the Cross is therefore the means whereby the barrier which sin interposes between God and man is broken down. By the giving up of His sinless life sacrificially, Christ annuls the power of sin to separate between God and the believer.

People *laos* (2992), is used of (a) "the people at large," especially of people assembled, e.g., Matt. 27:25; Luke 1:21; 3:15; Acts 4:27; (b) "a people of the same race and language," e.g., Rev. 5:9; in the plural, e.g., Luke 2:31; Rom. 15:11; Rev. 7:9; 11:9; especially of Israel, e.g., Matt. 2:6; 4:23; John 11:50; Acts 4:8; **Heb. 2:17**; in distinction from their rulers and priests, e.g., Matt. 26:5; Luke 20:19; **Heb. 5:3**; in distinction from Gentiles, e.g., Acts 26:17, 23; Rom. 15:10; (c) of Christians as the people of God, e.g., Acts 15:14; Titus 2:14; **Heb. 4:9**; 1 Pet. 2:9.

2:18 For in that he himself hath suffered being tempted, he is able to succour them that are tempted.

Suffered *pascho* (3958), "to suffer," is used (I) of the "sufferings" of Christ (a) at the hands of men, e.g., Matt. 16:21; 17:12; 1 Pet. 2:23; (b) in His expiatory and vicarious sacrifice for sin, **Heb. 9:26**; **13:12**; 1 Pet. 2:21; 3:18; 4:1; (c) including both (a) and (b), Luke 22:15; 24:26, 46; Acts 1:3, "passion"; 3:18; 17:3; **Heb. 5:8**; (d) by the antagonism of the evil one, **Heb. 2:18**; (II) of human "suffering" (a) of followers of Christ, Acts 9:16; 2 Cor. 1:6; Gal. 3:4; Phil. 1:29; 1 Thess. 2:14; 2 Thess. 1:5; 2 Tim. 1:12; 1 Pet. 3:14, 17; 5:10; Rev. 2:10; in identification with Christ in His crucifixion, as the spiritual ideal to be realized, 1 Pet. 4:1; in a wrong way, 4:15; (b) of others, physically, as the result of demoniacal power, Matt. 17:15, RV, "suffereth (grievously)," KJV, "is (sore) vexed"; cf. Mark 5:26; in a dream, Matt. 27:19; through maltreatment, Luke 13:2; 1 Pet. 2:19, 20; by a serpent (negatively), Acts 28:5, RV, "took" (KJV, "felt"); (c) of the effect upon the whole body through the "suffering" of one member, 1 Cor. 12:26, with application to a church.

Tempted *peirazo* (3985), signifies (1) "to try, attempt, assay"; (2) "to test, try, prove," in a good sense, said of Christ and of believers, **Heb. 2:18**, where the context shows that the temptation was the cause of suffering to Him, and only suffering, not a drawing away to sin, so that believers have the sympathy of Christ as their High Priest in the suffering which sin occasions to those who are in the enjoyment of communion with God; so in the similar passage in **4:15**; in all the temptations which Christ endured, there was nothing within Him that answered to sin. There was no sinful infirmity in Him. While He was truly man, and His divine nature was not in any way inconsistent with His Manhood, there was nothing in Him such as is produced in us by the sinful nature which belongs to us; in **Heb. 11:37**, of the testing of OT saints; in 1 Cor. 10:13, where the meaning has a wide scope, the verb is used of "testing" as permitted by God, and of the believer as one who should be in the realization of his own helplessness and his dependence upon God; in a bad sense, "to tempt" (a) of attempts to ensnare Christ in His speech, e.g., Matt. 16:1; 19:3; 22:18, 35, and parallel passages; John 8:6; (b) of temptations to sin, e.g., Gal. 6:1, where one who would restore an erring brother is not to act as his judge, but as being one with him in liability to sin, with the possibility of finding himself in similar circumstances, Jas. 1:13, 14; of temptations mentioned as coming from the Devil, Matt. 4:1; and parallel passages; 1 Cor. 7:5; 1 Thess. 3:5; (c) of trying or challenging God, Acts 15:10; 1 Cor. 10:9 (2nd part); **Heb. 3:9**; the Holy Spirit, Acts 5:9.

Succour *boetheo* (997), "to come to the aid of anyone, to succour," is used in Matt. 15:25; Mark 9:22, 24; Acts 16:9; 21:28; 2 Cor. 6:2, "did I succour"; **Heb. 2:18**, "to succour"; Rev. 12:16.

Chapter 3

3:1 Wherefore, holy brethren, partakers of the heavenly calling, consider the Apostle and High Priest of our profession, Christ Jesus;

Wherefore *see Hebrews 2:17.*

Holy *see* **Sanctifieth, Sanctified** at *Hebrews 2:11.*

Partakers *see* **Fellows** at *Hebrews 1:9.*

Heavenly *epouranios* (2032), "heavenly," what pertains to, or is in, heaven (*epi*, in the sense of "pertaining to," not here, "above") is used (a) of God the Father, Matt. 18:35; (b) of the place where Christ "sitteth at the right hand of God" (i.e., in a position of divine authority), Eph. 1:20; and of the present position of believers in relationship to Christ, Eph 2:6; where they possess "every spiritual blessing," 1:3; (c) of Christ as "the Second Man," and all those who are related to Him spiritually, 1 Cor. 15:48; (d) of those whose sphere of activity or existence is above, or in contrast to that of earth, of "principalities and powers," Eph. 3:10; of "spiritual hosts of wickedness," 6:12, RV, "in heavenly places," for KJV, "in high places"; (e) of the Holy Spirit, **Heb. 6:4**; (f) of "heavenly things," as the subjects of the teaching of Christ, John **3:12**, and as consisting of the spiritual and "heavenly" sanctuary and "true tabernacle" and all that appertains thereto in relation to Christ and His sacrifice as antitypical of the earthly tabernacle and sacrifices under the Law, **Heb. 8:5**; **9:23**; (g) of the "calling" of believers, **Heb. 3:1**; (h) of heaven as the abode of the saints, "a better country" than that of earth, **Heb. 11:16**, and of the spiritual Jerusalem, **12:22**; (i) of the kingdom of Christ in its future manifestation, 2 Tim. 4:18; (j) of all beings and things, animate and inanimate, that are "above the earth," Phil. 2:10; (k) of the resurrection and glorified bodies of believers, 1 Cor. 15:49; (l) of the "heavenly orbs," 1 Cor. 15:40 ("celestial," twice, and so rendered here only).

Calling *klesis* (2821), "a calling," is always used in the NT of that "calling" the origin, nature and destiny of which are heavenly (the idea of invitation being implied); it is used especially of God's invitation to man to accept the benefits of salvation, Rom. 11:29; 1 Cor. 1:26; 7:20 (said there of the condition in which the "calling" finds one); Eph. 1:18, "His calling"; Phil. 3:14, the "high calling"; 2 Thess. 1:11 and 2 Pet. 1:10, "your calling"; 2 Tim. 1:9, a "holy calling"; **Heb. 3:1**, a "heavenly calling"; Eph. 4:1, "the calling wherewith ye were called"; 4:4, "in one hope of your calling."

Consider *katanoeo* (2657), "to perceive clearly" (*kata*, intensive, and *noeo*), "to understand fully, consider closely," is used of not "considering" thoroughly the beam in one's own eye, Matt. 7:3 and Luke 6:41 (KJV, "perceivest"); of carefully "considering" the ravens, Luke 12:24; the lilies, v. 27; of Peter's full "consideration" of his vision, Acts 11:6; of Abraham's careful "consideration" of his own body, and Sarah's womb, as dead, and yet accepting by faith God's promise, Rom. 4:19 (RV); of "considering" fully the Apostle and High Priest of our confession, **Heb. 3:1**; of thoughtfully "considering" one another to provoke unto love and good works, **Heb. 10:24**. It is translated by the verbs "behold," Acts 7:31-32; Jas. 1:23-24; "perceive," Luke 20:23; "discover," Acts 27:39.

Apostle *apostolos* (652), is, lit., "one sent forth" (*apo*, "from," *stello*, "to send"). "The word is used of the Lord Jesus to describe His relation to God, **Heb. 3:1**; see John 17:3. The twelve disciples chosen by the Lord for special training were so called, Luke 6:13; 9:10. Paul, though he had seen the Lord Jesus, 1 Cor. 9:1; 15:8, had not 'companied with' the Twelve 'all the time' of His earthly ministry, and hence was not eligible for a place among them, according to Peter's description of the necessary qualifications, Acts 1:22. Paul was commissioned directly, by the Lord Himself, after His Ascension, to carry the gospel to the Gentiles. The word has also a wider reference. In Acts 14:4, 14, it is used of Barnabas as well as of Paul; in Rom. 16:7 of Andronicus and Junias. In 2 Cor. 8:23 (RV, margin) two unnamed brethren are called 'apostles of the churches'; in Phil. 2:25 (RV, margin) Epaphroditus is referred to as 'your apostle.' It is used in 1 Thess. 2:6 of Paul, Silas and Timothy, to define their relation to Christ."

High priest *see Hebrews 2:17.*

Profession *homologia* (3671), denotes "confession, by acknowledgment of the truth," 2 Cor. 9:13; 1 Tim. 6:12-13; **Heb. 3:1**; **4:14**; **10:23** (KJV, incorrectly, "profession," except in 1 Tim. 6:13).

3:2 Who was faithful to him that appointed him, as also Moses *was faithful* in all his house.

Faithful *see Hebrews 2:17.*

Appointed *poieo* (4160), "to do, to make," is rendered "appointed" in **Heb. 3:2**, of Christ. For Mark 3:14, RV.

House *oikos* (3624), denotes (a) "a house, a dwelling," e.g., Matt. 9:6, 7; 11:8; it is used of the Tabernacle, as the House of God, Matt. 12:4, and the Temple similarly, e.g., Matt. 21:13; Luke 11:51, KJV, "temple," RV, "sanctuary"; John 2:16, 17; called by the Lord "your house" in Matt. 23:38 and Luke 13:35 (some take this as the city of Jerusalem); metaphorically of Israel as God's house, **Heb. 3:2, 5**, where "his house" is not Moses', but God's; of believers, similarly, v. **6**, where Christ is spoken of as "over God's House" (the word "own" is rightly omitted in the RV); **Heb. 10:21**; 1 Pet. 2:5; 4:17; of the body, Matt. 12:44; Luke 11:24; (b) by metonymy, of the members of a household or family, e.g., Luke 10:5; Acts 7:10; 11:14; 1 Tim. 3:4, 5, 12; 2 Tim. 1:16; 4:19, RV (KJV, "household"); Titus 1:11 (plural); of a local church, 1 Tim. 3:15; of the descendants of Jacob (Israel) and David, e.g., Matt. 10:6; Luke 1:27, 33; Acts 2:36; 7:42.

3:3 For this *man* was counted worthy of more glory than Moses, inasmuch as he who hath builded the house hath more honour than the house.

Worthy *axioo* (515), "to think or count worthy," is used (1) of the estimation formed by God (a) favorably, 2 Thess. 1:11, "may count (you) worthy (of your calling)," suggestive of grace (it does not say "may make you worthy"); **Heb. 3:3**, "of more glory," of Christ in comparison with Moses; (b) unfavorably, **10:29**, "of how much sorer punishment"; (2) by a centurion (negatively) concerning himself, Luke 7:7; (3) by a church, regarding its elders, 1 Tim. 5:17, where "honor" stands probably for "honorarium," i.e., "material support."

Glory *see Hebrews 1:3.*

Builded *kataskeuazo* (2680), "to prepare, establish, furnish," is rendered "builded" and "built" in **Heb. 3:3-4**.

More *pleion* (4119), the comparative degree of *polus*, "much," is used (a) as an adjective, e.g., John 15:2; Acts 24:11, RV, "(not) more (than)" (KJV, "yet but"); **Heb. 3:3**; (b) as a noun, or with a noun understood, e.g., Matt. 20:10; Mark 12:43; Acts 19:32 and 27:12, "the more part"; 1 Cor. 9:19; (c) as an adverb, Matt. 5:20, "shall exceed," lit., "(shall abound) more (than)"; 26:53; Luke 9:13.

Honour *see Hebrews 2:7.*

3:4-5 For every house is builded by some *man*; but he that built all things *is* God.

And Moses verily *was* faithful in all his house, as a servant, for a testimony of those things which were to be spoken after;

Verily The particle *men* is rendered "verily," e.g., in 1 Cor. 5:3; 14:17; **Heb. 12:10**; in the KJV, **Heb. 3:5; 7:5, 18**; 1 Pet. 1:20; in Acts 26:9 it is combined with *oun* ("therefore").

Faithful *see Hebrews 2:17.*

House *see Hebrews 3:2.*

Servant *therapon* (2324), akin to *therapeuo*, "to serve, to heal, an attendant, servant," is a term of dignity and freedom, used of Moses in **Heb. 3:5**.

3:6 But Christ as a son over his own house; whose house are we, if we hold fast the confidence and the rejoicing of the hope firm unto the end.

House *see Hebrews 3:2.*

Hold fast *katecho* (2722), "to hold firmly, hold fast," is rendered "hold fast" in 1 Cor. 11:2, RV (KJV, "keep"); 1 Thess. 5:21; **Heb. 3:6, 14** (RV); **10:23**; "hold down," Rom. 1:18, RV, of unrighteous men who restrain the spread of truth by their unrighteousness, or, as RV marg., "who hold the truth in (or with) unrighteousness," contradicting their profession by their conduct (cf. 2:15, RV); in Rom. 7:6, RV, "holden," KJV, "held," of the Law as that which had "held" in bondage those who through faith in Christ were made dead to it as a means of life. *See also* **Stedfast** at ***Hebrews 2:2***.

Confidence *parrhesia* (3954), from *pas*, "all," *rhesis*, "speech," denotes (a), primarily, "freedom of speech, unreservedness of utterance," Acts 4:29, 31; 2 Cor. 3:12; 7:4; Philem. 8; or "to speak without ambiguity, plainly," John 10:24; or "without figures of speech," John 16:25; (b) "the absence of fear in speaking boldly; hence, confidence, cheerful courage, boldness, without any connection necessarily with speech"; the RV has "boldness" in the following; Acts 4:13; Eph. 3:12; 1 Tim. 3:13; **Heb. 3:6; 4:16; 10:19, 35**; 1 John 2:28; 3:21; 4:17; 5:14; (c) the deportment by which one becomes conspicuous, John 7:4; 11:54, acts openly, or secures publicity, Col. 2:15.

Rejoicing *kauchema* (2745), denotes "that in which one glories, a matter or ground of glorying," Rom. 4:2 and Phil. 2:16, RV, "whereof to glory"; in the following the meaning is likewise "a ground of glorying": 1 Cor. 5:6; 9:15, "glorying," 16, "to glory of"; 2 Cor. 1:14 RV; 9:3, RV; Gal. 6:4, RV (KJV, "rejoicing"); Phil. 1:26 (ditto); **Heb. 3:6** (ditto). In 2 Cor. 5:12 and 9:3 the word denotes the boast itself, yet as distinct from the act.

Firm *bebaios* (949), "firm, steadfast, secure" (from *baino*, "to go"), is translated "firm" in **Heb. 3:6**, of the maintenance of the boldness of the believer's hope, and in **3:14**, RV, of "the beginning of our confidence" (KJV, "steadfast").

End The following phrases contain *telos* (the word itself coming under one or other of the above): *eis telos*, "unto the end," e.g., Matt. 10:22; 24:13; Luke 18:5, "continual"; John 13:1; 2 Cor. 3:13, "on the end" (RV); *heos telous*, "unto the end," 1 Cor. 1:8; 2 Cor. 1:13; *achri telous*, "even to the end" (a stronger expression than the preceding); **Heb. 6:11**; Rev. 2:26 (where "even" might well have been added); *mechri telous*, with much the same meaning as *achri telous*, **Heb. 3:6, 14**. S

3:7 Wherefore (as the Holy Ghost saith, To day if ye will hear his voice,

Wherefore *dio = dia ho* (the neuter of the relative pronoun *hos*), "on account of which (thing)," e.g., Matt. 27:8; Acts 15:19; 20:31; 24:26; 25:26; 27:25, 34; Rom. 1:24; 15:7; 1 Cor. 12:3; 2 Cor. 2:8; 5:9; 6:17; Eph. 2:11; 3:13; 4:8, 25; 5:14; Phil. 2:9; 1 Thess. 5:11; Philem. 8; **Heb. 3:7, 10; 10:5; 11:16; 12:12, 28; 13:12**; Jas. 1:21; 4:6; 1 Pet. 1:13; 2 Pet. 1:10, 12; 3:14.

Holy Ghost The "Holy Spirit" is spoken of under various titles in the NT ("Spirit" and "Ghost" are renderings of the same word, *pneuma;* the advantage of the rendering "Spirit" is that it can always be used, whereas "Ghost" always requires the word "Holy" prefixed.) In the following list the omission of the definite article marks its omission in the original (concerning this see below): "Spirit, Matt. 22:43; Eternal Spirit, **Heb. 9:14**; the Spirit, Matt. 4:1; Holy Spirit, Matt. 1:18; the Holy Spirit, Matt. 28:19; the Spirit, the Holy, Matt. 12:32; the Spirit of promise, the Holy, Eph. 1:13; Spirit of God, Rom. 8:9; Spirit of (the) living God, 2 Cor. 3:3; the Spirit of God, 1 Cor. 2:11; the Spirit of our God, 1 Cor. 6:11; the Spirit of God, the Holy, Eph. 4:30; the Spirit of glory and of God, 1 Pet. 4:14; the Spirit of Him that raised up Jesus from the dead (i.e., God), Rom. 8:11; the Spirit of your Father, Matt. 10:20; the Spirit of His Son, Gal. 4:6; Spirit of (the) Lord, Acts 8:39; the Spirit of (the) Lord, Acts 5:9; (the) Lord, (the) Spirit, 2 Cor. 3:18; the Spirit of Jesus, Acts 16:7; Spirit of Christ, Rom. 8:9; the Spirit of Jesus Christ, Phil. 1:19; Spirit of adoption, Rom. 8:15; the Spirit of truth, John 14:17; the Spirit of life, Rom. 8:2; the Spirit of grace, **Heb. 10:29**."

The use or absence of the article in the original where the "Holy Spirit" is spoken of cannot always be decided by grammatical rules, nor can the presence or absence of the article alone determine whether the reference is to the

"Holy Spirit." Examples where the Person is meant when the article is absent are Matt. 22:43 (the article is used in Mark 12:36); Acts 4:25, RV (absent in some texts); 19:2, 6; Rom. 14:17; 1 Cor. 2:4; Gal. 5:25 (twice); 1 Pet. 1:2. Sometimes the absence is to be accounted for by the fact that *Pneuma* (like *Theos*) is substantially a proper name, e.g., in John 7:39. As a general rule the article is present where the subject of the teaching is the Personality of the Holy Spirit, e.g., John 14:26, where He is spoken of in distinction from the Father and the Son. See also 15:26 and cf. Luke 3:22.

The full title with the article before both *pneuma* and *hagios* (the "resumptive" use of the article), lit., "the Spirit the Holy," stresses the character of the Person, e.g., Matt. 12:32; Mark 3:29; 12:36; 13:11; Luke 2:26; 10:21 (RV); John 14:26; Acts 1:16; 5:3; 7:51; 10:44, 47; 13:2; 15:28; 19:6; 20:23, 28; 21:11; 28:25; Eph. 4:30; **Heb. 3:7; 9:8; 10:15**.

The Personality of the Spirit is emphasized at the expense of strict grammatical procedure in John 14:26; 15:26; 16:8, 13, 14, where the emphatic pronoun *ekeinos*, "He," is used of Him in the masculine, whereas the noun *pneuma* is neuter in Greek, while the corresponding word in Aramaic, the language in which our Lord probably spoke, is feminine (*rucha*, cf. Heb. *ruach*). The rendering "itself" in Rom. 8:16, 26, due to the Greek gender, is corrected to "Himself" in the RV.

The subject of the "Holy Spirit" in the NT may be considered as to His divine attributes; His distinct Personality in the Godhead; His operation in connection with the Lord Jesus in His birth, His life, His baptism, His death; His operations in the world; in the church; His having been sent at Pentecost by the Father and by Christ; His operations in the individual believer; in local churches; His operations in the production of Holy Scripture; His work in the world, etc.

To day *see* **This day** at ***Hebrews 1:5***. *See also* **Daily** at ***Hebrews 3:13***.

Voice *phone* (5456), "a sound," is used of the voice (a) of God, Matt. 3:17; John 5:37; 12:28, 30; Acts 7:31; 10:13, 15; 11:7, 9; **Heb. 3:7, 15; 4:7; 12:19, 26**; 2 Pet. 1:17, 18; Rev. 18:4; 21:3; (b) of Christ, (1) in the days of His flesh, Matt. 12:19 (negatively); John 3:29; 5:25; 10:3, 4, 16, 27; 11:43; 18:37; (2) on the cross Matt. 27:46, and parallel passages; (3) from heaven, Acts 9:4, 7; 22:7, 9, 14; 26:14; Rev. 1:10, 12 (here, by metonymy, of the speaker), 15; 3:20; (4) at the resurrection "to life," John 5:28; 1 Thess. 4:16, where "the voice of the archangel" is, lit., "a voice of an archangel," and probably refers to the Lord's voice as being of an archangelic character; (5) at the resurrection to judgment, John 5:28 [not the same event as (4)]; (c) of human beings on earth, e.g., Matt. 2:18; 3:3; Luke 1:42, in some texts, KJV, "voice", and frequently in the Synoptists; (d) of angels, Rev. 5:11, and frequently in Revelation; (e) of the redeemed in heaven, e.g., Rev. 6:10; 18:22; 19:1, 5; (f) of a pagan god, Acts 12:22; (g) of things, e.g., wind, John 3:8, RV, "voice" (KJV, "sound").

3:8 Harden not your hearts, as in the provocation, in the day of temptation in the wilderness:

Harden *skleruno* (4645), "to make dry or hard," is used in Acts 19:9; in Rom. 9:18, illustrated by the case of Pharaoh, who first persistently "hardened" his heart (see the RV marg. of Ex. 7:13, 22; 8:19; text of v. 32 and 9:7), all producing the retributive "hardening" by God, after His much long-suffering, 9:12, etc.; in **Heb. 3:8, 13, 15; 4:7**, warnings against the "hardening" of the heart.

Provocation *parapikrasmos* (3894), from *para*, "amiss" or "from," used intensively, and *pikraino*, "to make bitter" (*pikros*, "sharp, bitter"), "provocation," occurs in **Heb. 3:8, 15**. In the Sept., Ps. 95:8.

Temptation *peirasmos* (3986), is used of (1) "trials" with a beneficial purpose and effect, (a) of "trials" or "temptations," divinely permitted or sent, Luke 22:28; Acts 20:19; Jas. 1:2; 1 Pet. 1:6; 4:12, RV, "to prove," KJV, "to try"; 2 Pet. 2:9 (singular); Rev. 3:10, RV, "trial" (KJV, "temptation"); in Jas. 1:12, "temptation" apparently has meanings (1) and (2) combined and is used in the widest sense; (b) with a good or neutral significance, Gal. 4:14, of Paul's physical infirmity, "a temptation" to the Galatian converts, of such a kind as to arouse feelings of natural repugnance; (c) of "trials" of a varied character, Matt. 6:13 and Luke 11:4, where believers are commanded to pray not to be led into such by forces beyond their own control; Matt. 26:41; Mark 14:38; Luke 22:40, 46, where they are commanded to watch and pray against entering into "temptations" by their own carelessness or disobedience; in all such cases God provides "the way of escape," 1 Cor. 10:13 (where *peirasmos* occurs twice). (2) Of "trial" definitely designed to lead to wrong doing, "temptation," Luke 4:13; 8:13; 1 Tim. 6:9; (3) of "trying" or challenging God, by men, **Heb. 3:8**.

3:9 When your fathers tempted me, proved me, and saw my works forty years.

Tempted *see* ***Hebrews 2:18***.

"Hardening of the heart ages people more quickly than hardening of the arteries."

ANON

Proved *dokimazo* (1381), "to test, prove," with the expectation of approving, is translated "to prove" in Luke 14:19; Rom. 12:2; 1 Cor. 3:13, RV (KJV, "shall try"); 11:28, RV (KJV, "examine"); 2 Cor. 8:8, 22; 13:5; Gal. 6:4; Eph. 5:10; 1 Thess. 2:4 (2nd part), RV (KJV, "trieth"); 5:21; 1 Tim. 3:10; in some mss., **Heb. 3:9** (the most authentic have the noun *dokimasia*, "a proving"); 1 Pet. 1:7, RV (KJV, "tried"); 1 John 4:1, RV (KJV, "try").

Works *see Hebrews 1:10.*

Forty *tessarakonta* (5062), is used in circumstances in Scripture which indicate the number as suggesting probation, separation or judgment, e.g., Matt. 4:2; Acts 1:3; **Heb. 3:9, 17.**

3:10 Wherefore I was grieved with that generation, and said, They do alway err in *their* heart; and they have not known my ways.

Wherefore *see Hebrews 3:7.*

Grieved *prosochthizo* (4360), "to be wroth or displeased with" (*pros*, "toward," or "with," *ochtheo*, "to be sorely vexed"), is used in **Heb. 3:10, 17** (KJV, "grieved"; RV, "displeased"). "Grieved" does not adequately express the righteous anger of God intimated in the passage.

Alway *aei* (104), has two meanings: (a) "perpetually, incessantly," Acts 7:51; 2 Cor. 4:11; 6:10; Titus 1:12; **Heb. 3:10**; (b) "invariably, at any and every time," of successive occurrences, when some thing is to be repeated, according to the circumstances, 1 Pet. 3:15; 2 Pet. 1:12.

Err *planao* (4105), in the active voice, signifies "to cause to wander, lead astray, deceive" (*plane*, "a wandering"; cf. Eng., "planet"); in the passive voice, "to be led astray, to err." It is translated "err," in Matt. 22:29; Mark 12:24, 27; **Heb. 3:10**; Jas. 1:16 (KJV, "do not err," RV, "be not deceived"); 5:19.

Ways *hodos* (3598), denotes (a) "a natural path, road, way," frequent in the Synoptic Gospels; elsewhere, e.g., Acts 8:26; 1 Thess. 3:11; Jas. 2:25; Rev. 16:12; (b) "a traveler's way"; (c) metaphorically, of "a course of conduct," or "way of thinking," e.g., of righteousness, Matt. 21:32; 2 Pet. 2:21; of God, Matt. 22:16, and parallels, i.e., the "way" instructed and approved by God; so Acts 18:26 and **Heb. 3:10**, "My ways" (cf. Rev. 15:3); of the Lord, Acts 18:25; "that leadeth to destruction," Matt. 7:13; "... unto life," 7:14; of peace, Luke 1:79; Rom. 3:17; of Paul's "ways" in Christ, 1 Cor. 4:17 (plural); "more excellent" (of love), 1 Cor. 12:31; of truth, 2 Pet. 2:2; of the right "way," 2:15; of Balaam (*id.*), of Cain, Jude 11; of a "way" consisting in what is from God, e.g., of life, Acts 2:28 (plural); of salvation, Acts 16:17; personified, of Christ as the means of access to the Father, John 14:6; of the course followed and characterized by the followers of Christ, Acts 9:2; 19:9, 23; 24:22.

3:11 So I sware in my wrath, They shall not enter into my rest.)

So *hos*, as, is rendered "so" in **Heb. 3:11** (RV, "as"). For association with other words see , p. 1.

Sware *omnumi or omnuo* (3660), is used of "affirming or denying by an oath," e.g., Matt. 26:74; Mark 6:23; Luke 1:73; **Heb. 3:11, 18; 4:3; 7:21**; accompanied by that by which one swears, e.g., Matt. 5:34, 36; 23:16; **Heb. 6:13, 16**; Jas. 5:12; Rev. 10:6.

Wrath *orge* (3709), originally any "natural impulse, or desire, or disposition," came to signify "anger," as the strongest of all passions. It is used of the wrath of man, Eph. 4:31; Col. 3:8; 1 Tim. 2:8; Jas. 1:19-20; the displeasure of human governments, Rom. 13:4-5; the sufferings of the Jews at the hands of the Gentiles, Luke 21:23; the terrors of the Law, Rom. 4:15; "the anger" of the Lord Jesus, Mark 3:5; God's "anger" with Israel in the wilderness, in a quotation from the OT, **Heb. 3:11; 4:3**; God's present "anger" with the Jews nationally, Rom. 9:22; 1 Thess. 2:16; His present "anger" with those who disobey the Lord Jesus in His gospel, John 3:36; God's purposes in judgment, Matt. 3:7; Luke 3:7; Rom. 1:18; 2:5, 8; 3:5; 5:9; 12:19; Eph. 2:3; 5:6; Col. 3:6; 1 Thess. 1:10; 5:9.

Rest *katapausis* (2663), in classical Greek, denotes "a causing to cease" or "putting to rest"; in the NT, "rest, repose"; it is used (a) of God's "rest," Acts 7:49; **Heb. 3:11, 18; 4:1, 3** (twice), RV (1st part), "that rest" (the KJV, "rest," is ambiguous), **5, 11**; (b) in a general statement, applicable to God and man, **4:10.**

3:12 Take heed, brethren, lest there be in any of you an evil heart of unbelief, in departing from the living God.

Heed *blepo* (991), "to look," see, usually implying more especially an intent, earnest contemplation, is rendered "take heed" in Matt. 24:4; Mark 4:24; 13:5, 9, 23, 33; Luke 8:18;

21:8; 1 Cor. 3:10; 8:9; 10:12; Gal. 5:15; Col. 2:8 (KJV, "beware"); 4:17; **Heb. 3:12**.

Evil *poneros* (4190), akin to *ponos*, "labor, toil," denotes "evil that causes labor, pain, sorrow, malignant evil"; it is used (a) with the meaning bad, worthless, in the physical sense, Matt. 7:17-18; in the moral or ethical sense, "evil," wicked; of persons, e.g., Matt. 7:11; Luke 6:45; Acts 17:5; 2 Thess. 3:2; 2 Tim. 3:13; of "evil" spirits, e.g., Matt. 12:45; Luke 7:21; Acts 19:12-13, 15-16; of a generation, Matt. 12:39, 45; 16:4; Luke 11:29; of things, e.g., Matt. 5:11; 6:23; 20:15; Mark 7:22; Luke 11:34; John 3:19; 7:7; Acts 18:14; Gal. 1:4; Col. 1:21; 1 Tim. 6:4; 2 Tim. 4:18; **Heb. 3:12; 10:22**; Jas. 2:4; 4:16; 1 John 3:12; 2 John 11; 3 John 10; (b) with the meaning toilsome, painful, Eph. 5:16; 6:13; Rev. 16:2. Cf. *poneria*, "iniquity, wickedness."

Heart *kardia* (2588), "the heart" (Eng., "cardiac," etc.), the chief organ of physical life ("for the life of the flesh is in the blood," Lev. 17:11), occupies the most important place in the human system. By an easy transition the word came to stand for man's entire mental and moral activity, both the rational and the emotional elements. In other words, the heart is used figuratively for the hidden springs of the personal life. "The Bible describes human depravity as in the 'heart,' because sin is a principle which has its seat in the center of man's inward life, and then 'defiles' the whole circuit of his action, Matt. 15:19, 20. On the other hand, Scripture regards the heart as the sphere of Divine influence, Rom. 2:15; Acts 15:9... The heart, as lying deep within, contains 'the hidden man,' 1 Pet. 3:4, the real man. It represents the true character but conceals it" (J. Laidlaw, in *Hastings' Bible Dic.*). As to its usage in the NT it denotes (a) the seat of physical life, Acts 14:17; Jas. 5:5; (b) the seat of moral nature and spiritual life, the seat of grief, John 14:1; Rom. 9:2; 2 Cor. 2:4; joy, John 16:22; Eph. 5:19; the desires, Matt. 5:28; 2 Pet. 2:14; the affections, Luke 24:32; Acts 21:13; the perceptions, John 12:40; Eph. 4:18; the thoughts, Matt. 9:4; **Heb. 4:12**; the understanding, Matt. 13:15; Rom. 1:21; the reasoning powers, Mark 2:6; Luke 24:38; the imagination, Luke 1:51; conscience, Acts 2:37; 1 John 3:20; the intentions, **Heb. 4:12**, cf. 1 Pet. 4:1; purpose, Acts 11:23; 2 Cor. 9:7; the will, Rom. 6:17; Col. 3:15; faith, Mark 11:23; Rom. 10:10; **Heb. 3:12**.

Unbelief The negative noun *apistia*, "unbelief," is used twice in Matthew (13:58; 17:20), three times in Mark (6:6; 9:24; 16:14), four times in Romans (3:3; 4:20; 11:20, 23); elsewhere in 1 Tim. 1:13 and **Heb. 3:12, 19**.

Departing *aphistemi* (868), when used intransitively, signifies "to stand off" (*apo*, "from," *histemi*, "to stand"), "to withdraw from"; hence, "to fall away, to apostatize," 1 Tim. 4:1, RV, "shall fall away," for KJV, "shall depart"; **Heb. 3:12**, RV, "falling away."

3:13 But exhort one another daily, while it is called To day; lest any of you be hardened through the deceitfulness of sin.

Daily The following phrases contain the word *hemera*, "day," and are translated "daily" or otherwise: (a) *kath' hemeran*, lit., "according to, or for, (the) day, or throughout the day," "day by day," e.g., Luke 11:3; Acts 3:2; 16:5; 1 Cor. 15:31; **Heb. 7:27**; (b) *hemera kai hemera*, lit., "day and day," "day by day," 2 Cor. 4:16; (c) *hemeran ex hemeras*, lit., "day from day," "from day to day," 2 Pet. 2:8; (d) *semeron*, "this day," or "today," used outside the Synoptists and the Acts, in 2 Cor. 3:14-15, in Hebrews (**1:5; 3:7, 13, 15; 4:7; 5:5; 7:27; 13:8**), and in Jas. 4:13; (e) *tessemeron hemeras*, "(unto) this very day," Rom. 11:8 (RV); (f) *tas hemeras*, Luke 21:37, RV, "every day," for KJV, "in the daytime"; (g) *pasan hemeran*, Acts 5:42, RV, "every day"; preceded by *kata* in Acts 17:17, RV, "every day"; (h) *kath' hekasten hemeran*, lit., "according to each day," **Heb. 3:13**, "day by day," RV.

While In Acts 27:33 and **Heb. 3:13** *achri* (or *achris*) followed by *hou*, the genitive case of the relative pronoun *hos*, lit., "until which," is rendered "while"; cf. *en ho*, in Mark 2:19; Luke 5:34; John 5:7; *en to*, in Luke 1:21, RV, "while"; in **Heb. 3:15**, "while it is said," is, lit., "in the being said" (*en*, with the article and the pres. infin., passive of *lego*); so, e.g., in Matt. 13:25

To day *see* **This day** at *Hebrews 1:5*. *See also* **Daily** at *Hebrews 3:13*.

Hardened *see* **Harden** at *Hebrews 3:8*.

Deceitfulness *apate* (539), "deceit or deceitfulness" (akin to *apatao*, "to cheat, deceive, beguile"), that which gives a false impression, whether by appearance, statement or influence, is said of riches, Matt. 13:22; Mark 4:19; of sin, **Heb. 3:13**. The phrase in Eph. 4:22, "deceitful lusts," KJV, "lusts of deceit," RV, signifies lusts excited by "deceit," of which "deceit" is the source of strength, not lusts "deceitful" in themselves. In 2 Thess. 2:10, "all deceit of unrighteousness," RV, signifies all manner of unscrupulous words and deeds designed to "deceive" (see Rev. 13:13-15).

In Col. 2:8, "vain deceit" suggests that "deceit" is void of anything profitable.

Sin *hamartia* (266), is, lit., "a missing of the mark," but this etymological meaning is largely lost sight of in the NT. It is the most comprehensive term for moral obliquity. It is used of "sin" as (a) a principle or source of action, or an inward element producing acts, e.g., Rom. 3:9; 5:12, 13, 20; 6:1, 2; 7:7 (abstract for concrete); 7:8 (twice), 9, 11, 13, "sin, that it might be shown to be sin," i.e., "sin became death to me, that it might be exposed in its heinous character": in the last clause, "sin might become exceeding sinful," i.e., through the holiness of the Law, the true nature of sin was designed to be manifested to the conscience;

(b) a governing principle or power, e.g., Rom. 6:6, "(the body) of sin," here "sin" is spoken of as an organized power, acting through the members of the body, though the seat of "sin" is in the will (the body is the organic instrument); in the next clause, and in other passages, as follows, this governing principle is personified, e.g., Rom. 5:21; 6:12, 14, 17; 7:11, 14, 17, 20, 23, 25; 8:2; 1 Cor. 15:56; **Heb. 3:13; 11:25; 12:4**; Jas. 1:15 (2nd part);

(c) a generic term (distinct from specific terms yet sometimes inclusive of concrete wrong doing, e.g., John 8:21, 34, 46; 9:41; 15:22, 24; 19:11); in Rom. 8:3, "God, sending His own Son in the likeness of sinful flesh," lit., "flesh of sin," the flesh stands for the body, the instrument of indwelling "sin" [Christ, preexistently the Son of God, assumed human flesh, "of the substance of the Virgin Mary"; the reality of incarnation was His, without taint of sin], and *as an offering* for sin," i.e., "a sin offering" (so the Sept., e.g., in Lev. 4:32; 5:6, 7, 8, 9), "condemned sin in the flesh," i.e., Christ, having taken human nature, "sin" apart (**Heb. 4:15**), and having lived a sinless life, died under the condemnation and judgment due to our "sin"; for the generic sense see further, e.g., **Heb. 9:26; 10:6, 8, 18; 13:11**; 1 John 1:7, 8; 3:4 (1st part; in the 2nd part, "sin" is defined as "lawlessness," RV), 8, 9; in these verses the KJV use of the verb to commit is misleading; not the committal of an act is in view, but a continuous course of "sin," as indicated by the RV, "doeth."

3:14 For we are made partakers of Christ, if we hold the beginning of our confidence stedfast unto the end;

Made *ginomai* (1096), "to become," is sometimes translated by the passive voice of the verb to make, e.g., Matt. 9:16; John 1:3 (three times), 10; 8:33; Rom. 11:9; 1 Cor. 1:30; 3:13; 4:9, 13; Eph. 2:13; 3:7; Phil. 2:7 (but RV marg., "becoming"); Col. 1:23, 25; **Heb. 5:5; 6:4; 7:12, 16, 21, 26; 11:3**; Jas. 3:9; 1 Pet. 2:7. In many places the RV translates otherwise, and chiefly by the verb to become, e.g., Matt. 25:6, "there is"; 27:24, "was arising"; John 1:14, "became"; John 2:9, "become"; Rom. 1:3, "born"; 2:25, "is become"; 10:20, "became"; Gal. 3:13, "having become"; 4:4, "born" (twice); **Heb. 3:14**, "are become", **7:22**, "hath ... become."

Partakers *see* **Fellows** at *Hebrews 1:9*.

Hold *see Hebrews 3:6*.

Confidence *see* **Person** at *Hebrews 1:3*.

Stedfast *see Hebrews 2:2. See also* **Firm** at *Hebrews 3:6*.

End *see Hebrews 3:6*.

3:15 While it is said, To day if ye will hear his voice, harden not your hearts, as in the provocation.

While *see Hebrews 3:13*.

To day *see* **This day** at *Hebrews 1:5. See also* **Daily** at *Hebrews 3:13*.

Voice *see Hebrews 3:7*.

Harden *see Hebrews 3:8*.

Provocation *see Hebrews 3:8*.

3:16 For some, when they had heard, did provoke: howbeit not all that came out of Egypt by Moses.

Provoke *parapikraino* (3893), "to embitter, provoke," occurs in **Heb. 3:16**.

Howbeit *alla* (235), "but," to mark contrast or opposition, is rendered "nay" in Rom. 3:31, RV, "nay" (KJV, "yea"); in 7:7, RV, "howbeit" (KJV, "nay"); 8:37; 1 Cor. 3:2, RV; 6:8; 12:22; in **Heb. 3:16**, RV, "nay" (KJV, "howbeit").

3:17 But with whom was he grieved forty years? *was it* not with them that had sinned, whose carcases fell in the wilderness?

Grieved *see Hebrews 3:10*.

Forty *see Hebrews 3:9*.

Years *see Hebrews 1:12*.

Sinned *hamartano* (264), lit., "to miss the mark," is used in the NT (a) of "sinning" against God, (1) by angels, 2 Pet. 2:4; (2) by man, Matt. 27:4; Luke 15:18, 21 (heaven standing, by metonymy, for God); John 5:14; 8:11; 9:2, 3; Rom. 2:12 (twice); 3:23; 5:12, 14, 16; 6:15; 1 Cor. 7:28 (twice), 36; 15:34; Eph. 4:26; 1 Tim. 5:20; Titus 3:11; **Heb. 3:17; 10:26**; 1 John 1:10; in 2:1 (twice), the aorist tense in each place, referring to an act of "sin"; on the contrary, in 3:6 (twice), 8, 9, the present tense indicates, not the committal of an act, but the continuous practice of "sin"; in 5:16 (twice) the present tense indicates the condition resulting from an act, "unto death" signifying "tending towards death"; (b) against Christ, 1 Cor. 8:12; (c) against man, (1) a brother, Matt. 18:15, RV, "sin" (KJV, "trespass"); v. 21; Luke 17:3, 4, RV, "sin" (KJV, "trespass"); 1 Cor. 8:12; (2) in Luke 15:18, 21, against the father by the Prodigal Son, "in thy sight" being suggestive of befitting reverence; (d) against Jewish law, the Temple, and Caesar, Acts 25:8, RV, "sinned" (KJV, "offended"); (e) against one's own body, by fornication, 1 Cor. 6:18; (f) against earthly masters by servants, 1 Pet. 2:20, RV, "(when) ye sin (and are buffeted for it)," KJV, "(when ye be buffeted) for your faults," lit., "having sinned."

Carcases *kolon* (2966), primarily denotes "a member of a body," especially the external and prominent members, particularly the feet, and so, a dead body (see, e.g., the Sept., in Lev. 26:30; Num. 14:29, 32; Isa. 66:24, etc.). The word is used in **Heb. 3:17**, from Num. 14:29, 32.

3:18 And to whom sware he that they should not enter into his rest, but to them that believed not?

Sware *see Hebrews 3:11.*

Rest *see Hebrews 3:11.*

Believed not *apeitheo* (544), "to refuse to be persuaded, to refuse belief, to be disobedient," is translated "disobedient," or by the verb "to be disobedient," in the RV of Acts 14:2 (KJV, "unbelieving"), and 19:9 (KJV, "believed not"); it is absent from the most authentic mss. in Acts 17:5; in John 3:36 "obeyeth not," RV (KJV, "believeth not"); in Rom. 2:8 "obey not"; in 10:21, "disobedient"; in 11:30, 31, "were disobedient" (KJV, "have not believed"); so in 15:31; **Heb. 3:18**; **11:31**; in 1 Pet. 2:8, "disobedient"; so in 3:20; in 3:1 and 4:17, "obey not." In 2:7 the best mss. have *apisteo*, "to disbelieve."

3:19 So we see that they could not enter in because of unbelief.

So *kai* Sometimes it has the consecutive meaning of "and so": e.g., Matt. 5:15, "and so it shineth"; Phil. 4:7, "and so the peace ... "; **Heb. 3:19**, "and so we see."

Unbelief *see Hebrews 3:12.*

Chapter 4

4:1 Let us therefore fear, lest, a promise being left *us* of entering into his rest, any of you should seem to come short of it.

Promise *epangelia* (1860), primarily a law term, denoting "a summons" (*epi*, "upon," *angello*, "to proclaim, announce"), also meant "an undertaking to do or give something, a promise." Except in Acts 23:21 it is used only of the "promises" of God. It frequently stands for the thing "promised," and so signifies a gift graciously bestowed, not a pledge secured by negotiation; thus, in Gal. 3:14, "the promise of the Spirit" denotes "the promised Spirit": cf. Luke 24:49; Acts 2:33 and Eph. 1:13; so in **Heb. 9:15**, "the promise of the eternal inheritance" is "the promised eternal inheritance." On the other hand, in Acts 1:4, "the promise of the Father," is the "promise" made by the Father. In Gal. 3:16, the plural "promises" is used because the one "promise" to Abraham was variously repeated (Gen. 12:1-3; 13:14-17; 15:18; 17:1-14; 22:15-18), and because it contained the germ of all subsequent "promises"; cf. Rom. 9:4; **Heb. 6:12**; **7:6**; **8:6**; **11:17**; Gal. 3 is occupied with showing that the "promise" was conditional upon faith and not upon the fulfillment of the Law. The Law was later than, and inferior to, the "promise," and did not annul it, v. 21; cf. 4:23, 28. Again, in Eph. 2:12, "the covenants of the promise" does not indicate different covenants, but a covenant often renewed, all centering in Christ as the "promised" Messiah-Redeemer, and comprising the blessings to be bestowed through Him. In 2 Cor. 1:20 the plural is used of every "promise" made by God: cf. **Heb. 11:33**; in **7:6**, of special "promises" mentioned. For other applications of the word, see, e.g., Eph. 6:2; 1 Tim. 4:8; 2 Tim. 1:1; **Heb. 4:1**; 2 Pet. 3:4, 9; in 1 John 1:5 some mss. have this word, instead of *angelia*, "message." The occurrences of the word in relation to Christ and what centers in Him, may be arranged under the headings (1) the contents of the "promise," e.g., Acts 26:6; Rom. 4:20; 1 John 2:25; (2) the heirs, e.g., Rom. 9:8; 15:8; Gal. 3:29; **Heb. 11:9**; (3) the conditions, e.g., Rom. 4:13, 14; Gal. 3:14-22; **Heb. 10:36**.

Rest *see Hebrews 3:11.*

Seem *dokeo* (1380), denotes (a) "to be of opinion" (akin to *doxa*, "opinion"), e.g., Luke 8:18, RV, "thinketh" (KJV, "seemeth"); so 1 Cor. 3:18; to think, suppose, Jas. 1:26, RV, "thinketh himself (KJV, "seem"); (b) "to seem, to be reputed," e.g., Acts 17:18; 1 Cor. 11:16; 12:22; 2 Cor. 10:9; **Heb. 4:1**; **12:11**; (c) impersonally (1) to think, (2) to "seem" good,

Luke 1:3; Acts 15:22, RV, "it seemed good" (KJV, "it pleased"); 15:25, 28 (v. 34 in some mss.); in **Heb. 12:10**, the neuter of the present participle is used with the article, lit., "the (thing) seeming good," RV, "(as) seemed good," KJV, "after (their own) pleasure."

Come short *hustereo* (5302), "to be behind," is translated "to have come short," in **Heb. 4:1**.

4:2 For unto us was the gospel preached, as well as unto them: but the word preached did not profit them, not being mixed with faith in them that heard *it*.

Gospel *euangelizo* (2097), "to bring or announce glad tidings" (Eng., "evangelize"), is used (a) in the active voice in Rev. 10:7 ("declared") and 14:6 ("to proclaim," RV, KJV, "to preach"); (b) in the passive voice, of matters to be proclaimed as "glad tidings," Luke 16:16; Gal. 1:11; 1 Pet. 1:25; of persons to whom the proclamation is made, Matt. 11:5; Luke 7:22; **Heb. 4:2, 6**; 1 Pet. 4:6; (c) in the middle voice, especially of the message of salvation, with a personal object, either of the person preached, e.g., Acts 5:42; 11:20; Gal. 1:16, or, with a preposition, of the persons evangelized, e.g., Acts 13:32, "declare glad tidings"; Rom. 1:15; Gal. 1:8; with an impersonal object, e.g., "the word," Acts 8:4; "good tidings," 8:12; "the word of the Lord," 15:35; "the gospel," 1 Cor. 15:1; 2 Cor. 11:7; "the faith," Gal. 1:23; "peace," Eph. 2:17; "the unsearchable riches of Christ, 3:8.

Preached *euangelizo* (2097), is almost always used of "the good news" concerning the Son of God as proclaimed in the gospel [exceptions are, e.g., Luke 1:19; 1 Thess. 3:6, in which the phrase "to bring (or show) good (or glad) tidings" does not refer to the gospel]; Gal. 1:8 (2nd part). With reference to the gospel the phrase "to bring, or declare, good, or glad, tidings" is used in Acts 13:32; Rom. 10:15; **Heb. 4:2**. In Luke 4:18 the RV "to preach good tidings" gives the correct quotation from Isaiah, rather than the KJV "to preach the gospel." In the Sept. the verb is used of any message intended to cheer the hearers, e.g. 1 Sam. 31:9; 2 Sam. 1:20.

As well as *kathaper* (2509), "even as," with *kai*, is translated "as well as" in **Heb. 4:2**.

Word preached In 1 Cor. 1:18, KJV, *logos*, "a word," is translated "preaching," RV, "the word (of the Cross)," i.e., not the act of "preaching," but the substance of the testimony, all that God has made known concerning the subject. For **Heb. 4:2**, KJV.

Profit *opheleo* (5623), is translated "to profit" in Matt. 15:5; 16:26; Mark 7:11; 8:36; Luke 9:25, RV; John 6:63; Rom. 2:25; 1 Cor. 13:3; 14:6; Gal. 5:2; **Heb. 4:2; 13:9**.

Mixed In **Heb. 4:2**, KJV, *sunkerannumi*, lit., "to mix with" (*sun*, "with," *kerannumi*), is so translated; RV, "were (not) united (by faith) with" [KJV, "(not) being mixed ... in], as said of persons; in 1 Cor. 12:24 "hath tempered."

Heard *akoe* (189), denotes (a) "the sense of hearing," 1 Cor. 12:17; 2 Pet. 2:8; a combination of verb and noun is used in phrases which have been termed Hebraic as they express somewhat literally an OT phraseology, e.g., "By hearing ye shall hear," Matt. 13:14; Acts 28:26, RV, a mode of expression conveying emphasis; (b) "the organ of hearing," Mark 7:35, "ears"; Luke 7:1, RV, "ears," for KJV, "audience"; Acts 17:20; 2 Tim. 4:3, 4; **Heb. 5:11**, "dull of hearing," lit., "dull as to ears"; (c) "a thing heard, a message or teaching," John 12:38, "report"; Rom. 10:16; 1 Thess. 2:13, "the word of the message," lit. "the word of hearing" (KJV, "which ye heard"); **Heb. 4:2**, "the word of hearing," RV, for KJV, "the word preached"; in a somewhat similar sense, "a rumor, report," Matt. 4:24; 14:1; Mark 1:28, KJV, "fame," RV, "report"; Matt. 24:6; Mark 13:7, "rumors (of wars)"; (d) "the receiving of a message," Rom. 10:17, something more than the mere sense of "hearing" [see (a)]; so with the phrase "the hearing of faith," Gal. 3:2, 5, which it seems better to understand so than under (c).

4:3 For we which have believed do enter into rest, as he said, As I have sworn in my wrath, if they shall enter into my rest: although the works were finished from the foundation of the world.

Rest *see Hebrews 3:11*.

Sworn *see* Sware at *Hebrews 3:11*.

Wrath *see Hebrews 3:11*.

Works *see Hebrews 1:10*.

Finished *ginomai* (1096), "to become, to come into existence," is translated "were finished" in **Heb. 4:3**, i.e., were brought to their predestined end.

Foundation *katabole* (2602), lit., "a casting down," is used (a) of "conceiving seed," **Heb. 11:11**; (b) of "a foundation," as that which is laid down, or in the sense of founding; metaphorically, of "the foundation of the world"; in this respect two phrases are used, (1) "from the foundation of the world," Matt. 25:34 (in the most authentic mss. in 13:35 there is no phrase representing "of the world"); Luke 11:50;

Heb. 4:3; **9:26**; Rev. 13:8; 17:8; (2) "before the foundation of the world," John 17:24; Eph. 1:4; 1 Pet. 1:20. The latter phrase looks back to the past eternity.

World *kosmos* (2889), primarily "order, arrangement, ornament, adornment" (1 Pet. 3:3), is used to denote (a) the "earth," e.g., Matt. 13:35; John 21:25; Acts 17:24; Rom. 1:20 (probably here the universe: it had this meaning among the Greeks, owing to the order observable in it); 1 Tim. 6:7; **Heb. 4:3**; **9:26**; (b) the "earth" in contrast with Heaven, 1 John 3:17 (perhaps also Rom. 4:13); (c) by metonymy, the "human race, mankind," e.g., Matt. 5:14; John 1:9 [here "that cometh (RV, 'coming') into the world" is said of Christ, not of "every man"; by His coming into the world He was the light for all men]; v. 10; 3:16, 17 (thrice), 19; 4:42, and frequently in Rom., 1 Cor. and 1 John; (d) "Gentiles" as distinguished from Jews, e.g., Rom. 11:12, 15, where the meaning is that all who will may be reconciled (cf. 2 Cor. 5:19); (e) the "present condition of human affairs," in alienation from and opposition to God, e.g., John 7:7; 8:23; 14:30; 1 Cor. 2:12; Gal. 4:3; 6:14; Col. 2:8; Jas. 1:27; 1 John 4:5 (thrice); 5:19; (f) the "sum of temporal possessions," Matt. 16:26; 1 Cor. 7:31 (1st part); (g) metaphorically, of the "tongue" as "a world (of iniquity)," Jas. 3:6, expressive of magnitude and variety.

4:4 For he spake in a certain place of the seventh *day* on this wise, And God did rest the seventh day from all his works.

Certain *see* ***Hebrews 2:6.***

Place *see* ***Hebrews 2:6.***

Seventh *hebdomos* (1442), occurs in John 4:52; **Heb. 4:4** (twice); Jude 14; Rev. 8:1; 10:7; 11:15; 16:17; 21:20.

On this wise *houtos* or *houto* (3779), "in this way, so, thus," is used (a) with reference to what precedes, e.g., Luke 1:25; 2:48; (b) with reference to what follows, e.g., Luke 19:31, rendered "on this wise," in Matt. 1:18; John 21:1, and before quotations, Acts 7:6; 13:34; Rom. 10:6, KJV (RV, "thus"); **Heb. 4:4**; (c) marking intensity, rendered "so," e.g., Gal. 1:6; **Heb. 12:21**; Rev. 16:18; (d) in comparisons, rendered "so," e.g., Luke 11:30; Rom. 5:15.

Rest *katapauo* (2664), used transitively, signifies "to cause to cease, restrain," Acts 14:18; "to cause to rest," **Heb. 4:8**; intransitively, "to rest," **Heb. 4:4, 10**.

Works *see* ***Hebrews 1:10.***

4:5 And in this *place* again, If they shall enter into my rest.

This In Acts 17:32 the RV rightly omits "*matter*"; in **Heb. 4:5** "*place*" is italicized; it is frequently rendered "this man," e.g., Matt. 9:3; John 6:52; "of this sort," 2 Tim. 3:6, KJV (RV, "of these"); (b) as an adjective with a noun, either with the article and before it, e.g., Matt. 12:32, or after the noun (which is preceded by the article), e.g., Matt. 3:9 and 4:3, "these stones"; or without the article often forming a predicate, e.g., John 2:11; 2 Cor. 13:1.

Place In **Heb. 4:5** in this place" is, lit., "in this," i.e., "in this (passage)."

Rest *see* ***Hebrews 3:11.***

4:6 Seeing therefore it remaineth that some must enter therein, and they to whom it was first preached entered not in because of unbelief:

Remaineth *apoleipo* (620), in the passive voice, "to be reserved, to remain," is translated "remaineth" in **Heb. 4:6, 9**; **10:26**.

Must Sometimes the infinitive mood of a verb, with or without the article, is necessarily rendered by a phrase involving the word "must," e.g., 1 Pet. 4:17, KJV, "must (begin)"; or "should," **Heb. 4:6**, RV, "should" (KJV "must").

First *proteron* (4386), the comparative of *pro*, "before, aforetime," as being definitely antecedent to something else, is more emphatic than *pote* in this respect. See, e.g., John 6:62; 7:50; 9:8; 2 Cor. 1:13; Gal. 4:13; 1 Tim. 1:13; **Heb. 4:6**; **7:27**; **10:32**; 1 Pet. 1:14.

Preached *see* ***Hebrews 4:2.***

Unbelief *apeitheia* (543), lit., "the condition of being unpersuadable" (*a*, negative, *peitho*, "to persuade"), denotes "obstinacy, obstinate rejection of the will of God"; hence, "disobedience"; Eph. 2:2; 5:6; Col. 3:6, and in the RV of Rom. 11:30, 32 and **Heb. 4:6, 11** (for KJV, "unbelief"), speaking of Israel, past and present.

4:7 Again, he limiteth a certain day, saying in David, To day, after so long a time; as it is said, To day if ye will hear his voice, harden not your hearts.

Limiteth *horizo* (3724), denotes "to bound, to set a boundary" (Eng., "horizon"); hence, "to mark out definitely, determine"; it is translated "to determine" in Luke 22:22, of the foreordained pathway of Christ; Acts 11:29, of a "determination" to send relief; 17:26, where it is used of fixing the bounds of seasons. In Acts 2:23 the verb is translated "determinate," with reference to counsel. Here the verbal form might have been adhered to by the translation "determined"; that is to say, in the sense of "settled." In Rom. 1:4 it is translated "declared," where the meaning is that Christ was marked out as the

Son of God by His resurrection and that of others. In Acts 10:42 and 17:31 it has its other meaning of "ordain," that is, "to appoint by determined counsel." In **Heb. 4:7**, it is translated "limiteth," but preferably in the RV, "defineth," with reference to a certain period; here again it approaches its primary meaning of marking out the bounds of.

To day *see* **This day** at *Hebrews 1:5. See also* **Daily** at *Hebrews 3:13.*

Long *tosoutos* (5118), "so long," is used with *chronos* in John 14:9 and **Heb. 4:7.**

Voice *see Hebrews 3:7.*

Harden *see Hebrews 3:8.*

4:8 For if Jesus had given them rest, then would he not afterward have spoken of another day.

Jesus *see Hebrews 2:9.*

Rest *see Hebrews 4:4.*

4:9 There remaineth therefore a rest to the people of God.

Remaineth *see Hebrews 4:6.*

Rest *sabbatismos* (4520), "a Sabbath-keeping," is used in **Heb. 4:9**, RV, "a sabbath rest," KJV marg., "a keeping of a sabbath" (akin to *sabbatizo*, "to keep the Sabbath," used, e.g., in Exod. 16:30, not in the NT); here the sabbath-keeping is the perpetual sabbath "rest" to be enjoyed uninterruptedly by believers in their fellowship with the Father and the Son, in contrast to the weekly Sabbath under the Law. Because this sabbath "rest" is the "rest" of God Himself, 4:10, its full fruition is yet future, though believers now enter into it. In whatever way they enter into divine "rest," that which they enjoy is involved in an indissoluble relation with God.

People *see Hebrews 2:17.*

4:10 For he that is entered into his rest, he also hath ceased from his own works, as God *did* from his.

His *see Hebrews 2:4.*

Rest *see Hebrews 3:11.*

Ceased *katapauo* (2664), "to rest," is so translated in **Heb. 4:10**, for the KJV "hath ceased."

Works *see Hebrews 1:10.*

4:11 Let us labour therefore to enter into that rest, lest any man fall after the same example of unbelief.

Labour *spoudazo* (4704), signifies "to hasten to do a thing, to exert oneself, endeavor, give diligence"; in Gal. 2:10, of remembering the poor, KJV, "was forward," RV, "was zealous"; in Eph. 4:3, of keeping the unity of the Spirit, KJV "endeavoring," RV, "giving diligence"; in 1 Thess. 2:17, of going to see friends, "endeavored"; in 2 Tim. 4:9; 4:21, "do thy diligence"; in the following the RV uses the verb "to give diligence": 2 Tim. 2:15, KJV, "study"; Titus 3:12, KJV, "be diligent"; **Heb. 4:11**, of keeping continuous Sabbath rest, KJV, "let us labor"; in 2 Pet. 1:10, of making our calling and election sure; in 2 Pet. 1:15, of enabling believers to call Scripture truth to remembrance, KJV, "endeavour"; in 2 Pet. 3:14, of being found in peace without fault and blameless, when the Lord comes, KJV, "be diligent."

Rest *see Hebrews 3:11.*

Example *hupodeigma* (5262), lit., "that which is shown" (from *hupo*, "under," and *deiknumi*, "to show"), hence, (a) "a figure, copy," **Heb. 8:5**, RV, "copy," for KJV, "example"; **9:23**; (b) "an example," whether for imitation, John 13:15; Jas. 5:10, or for warning, **Heb. 4:11**; 2 Pet. 2:6, RV, example.

Unbelief *see Hebrews 4:6.*

4:12 For the word of God *is* quick, and powerful, and sharper than any two-edged sword, piercing even to the dividing asunder of soul and spirit, and of the joints and marrow, and *is* a discerner of the thoughts and intents of the heart.

Word *logos* (3056), denotes ... "the expression of thought" – not the mere name of an object – (a) as embodying a conception or idea, e.g., Luke 7:7; 1 Cor. 14:9, 19; (b) a saying or statement, (1) by God, e.g., John 15:25; Rom. 9:9; 9:28, RV, "word" (KJV, "work"); Gal. 5:14; **Heb. 4:12**; (2) by Christ, e.g., Matt. 24:35 (plur.); John 2:22; 4:41; 14:23 (plur.); 15:20. In connection with (1) and (2) the phrase "the word of the Lord," i.e., the revealed will of God (very frequent in the OT), is used of a direct revelation given by Christ, 1 Thess. 4:15; of the gospel, Acts 8:25; 13:49; 15:35, 36; 16:32; 19:10; 1 Thess. 1:8; 2 Thess. 3:1; in this respect it is the message from the Lord, delivered with His authority and made effective by His power (cf. Acts 10:36); for other instances relating to the gospel see Acts 13:26; 14:3; 15:7; 1 Cor. 1:18, RV; 2 Cor. 2:17; 4:2; 5:19; 6:7; Gal. 6:6; Eph. 1:13; Phil. 2:16; Col. 1:5; **Heb. 5:13**; sometimes it is used as the sum of God's utterances, e.g., Mark 7:13; John 10:35; Rev. 1:2, 9; (c) discourse, speech, of instruction, etc., e.g., Acts 2:40; 1 Cor. 2:13; 12:8; 2 Cor. 1:18; 1 Thess. 1:5; 2 Thess. 2:15; **Heb. 6:1**, RV, marg.; doctrine, e.g., Matt. 13:20; Col. 3:16; 1 Tim. 4:6; 2 Tim. 1:13; Titus 1:9; 1 John 2:7.

Quick *zao* is translated "quick" (i.e., "living") in Acts 10:42; 2 Tim. 4:1; 1 Pet. 4:5; in **Heb. 4:12**, KJV (RV, "living"). *See also* **Lifetime** at *Hebrews 2:15*.

Powerful *energes* (1756), lit., "in work" (cf. Eng., "energetic"), is used (a) of the Word of God, **Heb. 4:12** (RV, "active," KJV, "powerful"); (b) of a door for the gospel, 1 Cor. 16:9, "effectual"; (c) of faith, Philem. 6, "effectual." Cf. the synonymous words *dunatos* and *ischuros*.

Sharper *tomos* (5114), akin to *temno*, "to cut" [Eng., "(ana)tomy," etc.], is used metaphorically in the comparative degree, *tomoteros*, in **Heb. 4:12**, of the Word of God.

Two-edged *distomos* (1366), lit., "two-mouthed" (*dis*, and *stoma*, "a mouth"), was used of rivers and branching roads; in the NT of swords, **Heb. 4:12**; Rev. 1:16; 2:12, RV, "two-edged" (KJV, "with two edges"). In the Sept., Judg. 3:16; Ps. 149:6; Prov. 5:4.

Sword *machaira* (3162), "a short sword or dagger," e.g., Matt. 26:47, 51, 52 and parallel passages; Luke 21:24; 22:38, possibly "a knife" (Field, *Notes on the Translation of the NT*); **Heb. 4:12**; metaphorically and by metonymy, (a) for ordinary violence, or dissensions, that destroy peace, Matt. 10:34; (b) as the instrument of a magistrate or judge, e.g., Rom. 13:4; (c) of the Word of God, "the sword of the Spirit," probing the conscience, subduing the impulses to sin, Eph. 6:17.

Piercing *diikneomai* (1338), "to go through, penetrate" (*dia*, "through," *ikneomai*, "to go"), is used of the power of the Word of God, in **Heb. 4:12**, "piercing." In the Sept., Ex. 26:28.

Dividing *see* **Gifts** at *Hebrews 2:4*.

Soul *psuche* (5590), denotes "the breath, the breath of life," then "the soul," in its various meanings. The NT uses "may be analyzed approximately as follows: (a) the natural life of the body, Matt. 2:20; Luke 12:22; Acts 20:10; Rev. 8:9; 12:11; cf. Lev. 17:11; 2 Sam. 14:7; Esth. 8:11; (b) the immaterial, invisible part of man, Matt. 10:28; Acts 2:27; cf. 1 Kings 17:21; (c) the disembodied (or "unclothed" or "naked," 2 Cor. 5:3, 4) man, Rev. 6:9; (d) the seat of personality, Luke 9:24, explained as = "own self," v. 25; **Heb. 6:19**; **10:39**; cf. Isa. 53:10 with 1 Tim. 2:6; (e) the seat of the sentient element in man, that by which he perceives, reflects, feels, desires, Matt. 11:29; Luke 1:46; 2:35; Acts 14:2, 22; cf. Ps. 84:2; 139:14; Isa. 26:9; (f) the seat of will and purpose, Matt. 22:37; Acts 4:32; Eph. 6:6; Phil. 1:27; **Heb. 12:3**; cf. Num. 21:4; Deut. 11:13; (g) the seat of appetite, Rev. 18:14; cf. Ps. 107:9; Prov. 6:30; Isa. 5:14 ("desire"); 29:8; (h) persons, individuals, Acts 2:41, 43; Rom. 2:9; Jas. 5:20; 1 Pet. 3:20; 2 Pet. 2:14; cf. Gen. 12:5; 14:21 ("persons"); Lev. 4:2 ('any one');Ezek. 27:13; of dead bodies, Num. 6:6, lit., "dead soul"; and of animals, Lev. 24:18, lit., "soul for soul"; (i) the equivalent of the personal pronoun, used for emphasis and effect: 1st person, John 10:24 ("us"); **Heb. 10:38**; cf. Gen. 12:13; Num. 23:10; Jud. 16:30; Ps. 120:2 ("me"); 2nd person, 2 Cor. 12:15; **Heb. 13:17**; Jas. 1:21; 1 Pet. 1:9; 2:25; cf. Lev. 17:11; 26:15; 1 Sam. 1:26; 3rd person, 1 Pet. 4:19; 2 Pet. 2:8; cf. Exod. 30:12; Job 32:2, Heb. "soul," Sept. "self"; (j) an animate creature, human or other, 1 Cor. 15:45; Rev. 16:3; cf. Gen. 1:24; 2:7, 19; (k) "the inward man," the seat of the new life, Luke 21:19 (cf. Matt. 10:39); 1 Pet. 2:11; 3 John 2 ....

"The language of **Heb. 4:12** suggests the extreme difficulty of distinguishing between the soul and the spirit, alike in their nature and in their activities. Generally speaking the spirit is the higher, the soul the lower element. The spirit may be recognized as the life principle bestowed on man by God, the soul as the resulting life constituted in the individual, the body being the material organism animated by soul and spirit ..."

Joints *harmos* (719), "a joining, joint" (akin to *harmozo*, "to fit, join"), is found in **Heb. 4:12**, figuratively (with the word "marrow") of the inward moral and spiritual being of man, as just previously expressed literally in the phrase "soul and spirit."

Marrow *muelos* (3452), "marrow," occurs in **Heb. 4:12**, where, by a natural metaphor, the phraseology changes from the material to the spiritual.

Discerner *kritikos* (2924), signifies "that which relates to judging (*krino*, "to judge"), fit for, or skilled in, judging" (Eng., "critical"), found in **Heb. 4:12**, of the Word of God as "quick to discern the thoughts and intents of the heart," (lit., "critical of, etc."), i.e., discriminating and passing judgment on the thoughts and feelings.

Thoughts *enthumesis* (1761), "a cogitation, an inward reasoning" (generally, evil surmising or supposition), is formed from *en*, "in," and *thumos*, "strong feeling, passion" (cf. *thumoo*, in the middle voice, "to be wroth, furious"); Eng., "fume" is akin; the root, *thu*, signifies "to rush, rage." The word is translated "device" in Acts 17:29, of man's production of images; elsewhere, "thoughts," Matt. 9:4; 12:25; **Heb. 4:12**, where the accompanying word *ennoia* denotes inward intentions.

Intents *ennoia* (1771), primarily "a thinking, idea, consideration," denotes "purpose, intention, design" (*en*, in, *nous*, mind); it is rendered "intents" in **Heb. 4:12**; "mind," in 1 Pet. 4:1 (RV, marg., "thought"). Cf. *Enthumesis*, "thought".

Heart *see Hebrews 3:12.*

4:13 Neither is there any creature that is not manifest in his sight: but all things *are* naked and opened unto the eyes of him with whom we have to do.

Manifest *aphanes* (852), denotes "unseen, hidden," **Heb. 4:13**, "not manifest" (*a*, negative and *phaino*). In the Sept., Neh. 4:8; Job 24:20.

Naked *gumnos* (1131), signifies (a) "unclothed," Mark 14:52; in v. 51 it is used as a noun ("*his*" and "*body*" being italicized); (b) "scantily or poorly clad," Matt. 25:36, 38, 43, 44; Acts 19:16 (with torn garments); Jas. 2:15; (c) "clad in the undergarment only" (the outer being laid aside), John 21:7; (d) metaphorically, (1) of "a bare seed," 1 Cor. 15:37; (2) of "the soul without the body," 2 Cor. 5:3; (3) of "things exposed to the allseeing eye of God," **Heb. 4:13**; (4) of "the carnal condition of a local church," Rev. 3:17; (5) of "the similar state of an individual," 16:15; (6) of "the desolation of religious Babylon," 17:16.

Eyes *ophthalmos* (3788), akin to *opsis*, "sight," probably from a root signifying "penetration, sharpness" (Curtius, Gk. Etym.) (cf. Eng., "ophthalmia," etc.), is used (a) of the physical organ, e.g., Matt. 5:38; of restoring sight, e.g., Matt. 20:33; of God's power of vision, **Heb. 4:13**; 1 Pet. 3:12; of Christ in vision, Rev. 1:14; 2:18; 19:12; of the Holy Spirit in the unity of Godhood with Christ, Rev. 5:6; (b) metaphorically, of ethical qualities, evil, Matt. 6:23; Mark 7:22 (by metonymy, for envy); singleness of motive, Matt. 6:22; Luke 11:34; as the instrument of evil desire, "the principal avenue of temptation," 1 John 2:16; of adultery, 2 Pet. 2:14; (c) metaphorically, of mental vision, Matt. 13:15; John 12:40; Rom. 11:8; Gal. 3:1, where the metaphor of the "evil eye" is altered to a different sense from that of bewitching (the posting up or placarding of an "eye" was used as a charm, to prevent mischief); by gospel-preaching Christ had been, so to speak, placarded before their "eyes"; the question may be paraphrased, "What evil teachers have been malignly fascinating you?"; Eph. 1:18, of the "eyes of the heart," as a means of knowledge.

Opened *trachelizo* (5136), "to seize and twist the neck" (from *trachelos*, "the throat"), was used of wrestlers, in the sense of taking by the throat. The word is found in **Heb. 4:13**, "laid open," RV (KJV, "opened"). The literal sense of the word seems to be "with the head thrown back and the throat exposed." Various suggestions have been made as to the precise significance of the word in this passage. Some have considered that the metaphor is from the manner of treating victims about to be sacrificed. Little help, however, can be derived from these considerations. The context serves to explain the meaning and the RV rendering is satisfactory.

Do In **Heb. 4:13** the phrase *hemin ho logos*, rendered "(with whom) we have to do," is, lit., "(with whom is) the account to us."

4:14 Seeing then that we have a great high priest, that is passed into the heavens, Jesus the Son of God, let us hold fast *our* profession.

High priest *see Hebrews 2:17.*

Passed *dierchomai* (1330), denotes "to pass through or over," (a) of persons, e.g., Matt. 12:43, RV, "passeth (KJV, walketh) through"; Mark 4:35, KJV, "pass (RV, go) over"; Luke 19:1, 4; **Heb. 4:14**, RV, "passed through" (KJV "into"); Christ "passed through" the created heavens to the throne of God; (b) of things, e.g., Matt. 19:24, "to go through"; Luke 2:35, "shall pierce through" (metaphorically of a sword).

Heavens *see Hebrews 1:10.*

Son *see Hebrews 1:2.*

Hold *krateo* (2902), "to be strong, mighty, to prevail," (1) is most frequently rendered "to lay or take hold on" (a) literally, e.g., Matt. 12:11; 14:3; 18:28 and 21:46, RV (KJV, "laid hands on"); 22:6, RV (KJV, "took"); 26:55, KJV (RV, "took"); 28:9, RV, "took hold of" (KJV, "held by"); Mark 3:21; 6:17; 12:12; 14:51; Act 24:6, RV (KJV, "took"); Rev. 20:2; (b) metaphorically, of "laying hold of the hope of the Lord's return," **Heb. 6:18**; (2) also signifies "to hold" or "hold fast," i.e., firmly, (a), literally, Matt. 26:48, KJV (RV, "take"); Acts 3:11; Rev. 2:1; (b) metaphorically, of "holding fast a tradition or teaching," in an evil sense, Mark 7:3, 4, 8; Rev. 2:14, 15; in a good sense, 2 Thess. 2:15; Rev. 2:25; 3:11; of "holding" Christ, i.e., practically apprehending Him, as the head of His church, Col. 2:19; a confession, **Heb. 4:14**; the name of Christ, i.e., abiding by all that His name implies, Rev. 2:13; of restraint, Luke 24:16, "(their eyes) were holden"; of the winds, Rev. 7:1; of the impossibility of Christ's being "holden" of death, Acts 2:24.

Profession *see Hebrews 3:1.*

4:15 For we have not an high priest which cannot be touched with the feeling of our infirmities; but was in all points tempted like as *we are, yet* without sin.

Priest *see* ***Hebrews 2:17.***

Touched *sumpatheo* (4834), is rendered "be touched with" in **Heb. 4:15**.

Feeling *sumpatheo* (4834), "to have a fellow-feeling for or with," is rendered "touched with the feeling of" in **Heb. 4:15**; "have compassion" in **10:34**.

Points In **Heb. 4:15**, "in all points" represents the phrase *kata* with the neuter plural of *pas*, "all," lit., "according to all (things)."

Tempted *see* ***Hebrews 2:18.***

Like In **Heb. 4:15**, the phrase *kath'homoioteta* (*kata*, "according to," *homoiotes*, "a likeness," i.e., "after the similitude"), is rendered "like as," in the statement that Christ has been tempted in all points "like as we are, yet without sin"; this may mean either "according to the likeness of our temptations," or "in accordance with His likeness to us."

Without *choris*, "apart from," frequently used as a preposition, especially in Hebrews [**4:15**; **7:7, 20, 21**; **9:7, 18, 22, 28**; **11:6**; in **11:40**, RV, "apart from" (KJV, "without"); **12:8, 14**].

Sin Christ is predicated as having been without "sin" in every respect, e.g., (a), (b), (c) above, 2 Cor. 5:21 (1st part); 1 John 3:5; John 14:30; (d) John 8:46; **Heb. 4:15**; 1 Pet. 2:22. *See also* ***Hebrews 3:13.***

4:16 Let us therefore come boldly unto the throne of grace, that we may obtain mercy, and find grace to help in time of need.

Come ... unto *proserchomai* (4334), is translated "draw near" in **Heb. 4:16**; **7:25**, RV, and **10:22**, KJV and RV; in Acts 7:31, "drew near."

Boldly *see* **Confidence** at ***Hebrews 3:6.***

Throne *see* ***Hebrews 1:8.***

Obtain *lambano* (2983), "to take, to receive," is translated by the verb "to obtain" in 1 Cor. 9:25; Phil. 3:12, RV, "(not that) I have (already) obtained" (contrast *katantao*, "to attain," v. 11); Moule translates it "not that I have already received," i.e., the prize; the verb does not signify "to attain"; **Heb. 4:16**, KJV, "obtain."

Mercy *eleos* (1656), "is the outward manifestation of pity; it assumes need on the part of him who receives it, and resources adequate to meet the need on the part of him who shows it. It is used (a) of God, who is rich in mercy, Eph. 2:4, and who has provided salvation for all men, Titus 3:5, for Jews, Luke 1:72, and Gentiles, Rom. 15:9. He is merciful to those who fear him, Luke 1:50, for they also are compassed with infirmity, and He alone can succor them. Hence they are to pray boldly for mercy, **Heb. 4:16**, and if for themselves, it is seemly that they should ask for mercy for one another, Gal. 6:16; 1 Tim. 1:2. When God brings His salvation to its issue at the Coming of Christ, His people will obtain His mercy, 2 Tim. 1:16; Jude 21; (b) of men; for since God is merciful to them, He would have them show mercy to one another, Matt. 9:13; 12:7; 23:23; Luke 10:37; Jas. 2:13."

Help *boetheia* (996), from *boe*, "a shout," and *theo*, "to run," denotes "help, succour," **Heb. 4:16**, lit., "(grace) unto (timely) help"; in Acts 27:17, where the plural is used, the term is nautical, "frapping."

> *"Talk to him in prayer of all your wants, your troubles, even of the weariness you feel in serving him. You cannot speak too freely, too trustfully, of him."*
>
> FRANÇOIS DE LA MOTHE FÉNELON

Time of need *eukairos* (2121), lit., "well-timed" (*eu*, "well," *kairos*, "a time, season"), hence signifies "timely, opportune, convenient"; it is said of a certain day, Mark 6:21; elsewhere, **Heb. 4:16**, "in time of need." Cf. *eukairia*, "opportunity," Matt. 26:16; Luke 22:6; *eukaireo*, "to have opportunity," Mark 6:31; Acts 17:21 ("they spent their time," marg. "had leisure for nothing else"); 1 Cor. 16:12.

Chapter 5

5:1 For every high priest taken from among men is ordained for men in things *pertaining* to God, that he may offer both gifts and sacrifices for sins:

High priest *see* ***Hebrews 2:17.***

Ordained *kathistemi* (2525), from *kata*, "down," or "over against," and *histemi*, "to cause to stand, to set," is translated "to ordain" in the KJV of Titus 1:5; **Heb. 5:1**; **8:3**. *See also* **Set** at ***Hebrews 2:7.***

Pertaining to *see Hebrews 2:17.*

God *see Hebrews 1:8.*

Offer *prosphero* (4374), primarily, "to bring to" (*pros,* "to," *phero,* "to bring"), also denotes "to offer," (a) of the sacrifice of Christ Himself, **Heb. 8:3**; of Christ in virtue of his High Priesthood (RV, "this *high priest*"; KJV, "this man"); **9:14, 25** (negative), **28**; **10:12**; (b) of offerings under, or according to, the Law, e.g., Matt. 8:4; Mark 1:44; Acts 7:42; 21:26; **Heb. 5:1, 3; 8:3; 9:7, 9; 10:1-2, 8, 11**; (c) of "offerings" previous to the Law, **Heb. 11:4, 17** (of Isaac by Abraham); (d) of gifts "offered" to Christ, Matt. 2:11, RV, "offered" (KJV, "presented unto"); (e) of prayers "offered" by Christ, **Heb. 5:7**; (f) of the vinegar "offered" to Him in mockery by the soldiers at the cross, Luke 23:36; (g) of the slaughter of disciples by persecutors, who think they are "offering" service to God, John 16:2, RV (KJV, "doeth"); (h) of money "offered" by Simon the sorcerer, Acts 8:18.

Gifts *doron* (1435), akin to *didomi,* "to give," is used (a) of "gifts" presented as an expression of honor, Matt. 2:11; (b) of "gifts" for the support of the temple and the needs of the poor, Matt. 15:5; Mark 7:11; Luke 21:1, 4; (c) of "gifts" offered to God, Matt. 5:23, 24; 8:4; 23:18, 19; **Heb. 5:1; 8:3, 4; 9:9; 11:4**; (d) of salvation by grace as the "gift" of God, Eph. 2:8; (e) of "presents" for mutual celebration of an occasion, Rev. 11:10.

Sacrifices *thusia* (2378), primarily denotes "the act of offering"; then, objectively, "that which is offered" (a) of idolatrous "sacrifice," Acts 7:41; (b) of animal or other "sacrifices," as offered under the Law, Matt. 9:13; 12:7; Mark 9:49; 12:33; Luke 2:24; 13:1; Acts 7:42; 1 Cor. 10:18; **Heb. 5:1; 7:27** (RV, plural); **8:3; 9:9; 10:1, 5, 8** (RV, plural), **11:4**; (c) of Christ, in His "sacrifice" on the cross, Eph. 5:2; **Heb. 9:23**, where the plural antitypically comprehends the various forms of Levitical "sacrifices" in their typical character; **9:26; 10:12, 26**; (d) metaphorically, (1) of the body of the believer, presented to God as a living "sacrifice," Rom. 12:1; (2) of faith, Phil. 2:17; (3) of material assistance rendered to servants of God, Phil. 4:18; (4) of praise, Heb, **13:15**; (5) of doing good to others and communicating with their needs, **Heb. 13:16**; (6) of spiritual "sacrifices" in general, offered by believers as a holy priesthood, 1 Pet. 2:5.

5:2 Who can have compassion on the ignorant, and on them that are out of the way; for that he himself also is compassed with infirmity.

Compassion *metriopatheo* (3356), is rendered "have compassion," in **Heb. 5:2**, KJV.

Ignorant *agnoeo* (50), signifies (a) "to be ignorant, not to know," either intransitively, 1 Cor. 14:38 (in the 2nd occurrence in this verse, the RV text translates the active voice, the margin the passive); 1 Tim. 1:13, lit., "being ignorant (I did it)"; **Heb. 5:2**, "ignorant"; or transitively, 2 Pet. 2:12, KJV, "understand not," RV, "are ignorant (of)"; Acts 13:27, "knew (Him) not"; 17:23, RV, "(what ye worship) in ignorance," for KJV, "(whom ye) ignorantly (worship)," lit., "(what) not knowing (ye worship"; also rendered by the verb "to be ignorant that," or "to be ignorant of," Rom. 1:13; 10:3; 11:25; 1 Cor. 10:1; 12:1; 2 Cor. 1:8; 2:11; 1 Thess. 4:13; to know not, Rom. 2:4; 6:3; 7:1; to be unknown (passive voice), 2 Cor. 6:9; Gal. 1:22; (b) "not to understand," Mark 9:32; Luke 9:45.

Way In **Heb. 5:2**, KJV, *planao,* middle voice, "to wander," is rendered "(them) that are out of the way," RV, "(the) erring."

Compassed *perikeimai* (4029), lit., "to lie around" (*peri,* "around," *keimai,* "to lie"), "to be compassed," is used of binding fetters around a person, Acts 28:20; in Mark 9:42, and Luke 17:2, to hang about a person's neck; in **Heb. 5:2**, to compass about, metaphorically of infirmities; in **12:1**, of those who have witness borne to their faith.

5:3 And by reason hereof he ought, as for the people, so also for himself, to offer for sins.

Hereof In **Heb. 5:3**, KJV, *dia tauten,* lit., "by reason of (*dia*) this" (i.e., this infirmity), is rendered "hereof"; the best texts have *auten,* RV, "thereof."

Ought *opheilo* (3784), "to owe," is translated "ought," with various personal pronouns, in John 13:14; 19:7; Acts 17:29; Rom. 15:1; **Heb. 5:3**, KJV (RV, "he is bound"); **5:12**; 1 John 3:16; 4:11; 3 John 8; with other subjects in 1 Cor. 11:7, 10; 2 Cor. 12:14; Eph. 5:28; 1 John 2:6.

People *see Hebrews 2:17.*

Offer *see Hebrews 5:1.*

5:4 And no man taketh this honour unto himself, but he that is called of God, as *was* Aaron.

No man In some mss. the negative *me* and the indefinite pronoun *tis,* "some one, anyone," appear as one word, *metis* (always separated in the best mss.), e.g., Matt. 8:28, "no man"; so in 1 Cor. 16:11; 2 Cor. 11:16; 2 Thess. 2:3. The words are separated also in Matt. 24:4; 2 Cor. 8:20 (RV, "any man," after "avoiding"); Rev. 13:17. These instances represent either impossibility or prohibition; contrast *ouch* (i.e., *ou*) ... *tis* in **Heb. 5:4**, "no man (taketh)," where a direct negative statement is made.

Honour *see Hebrews 2:7*.

5:5 So also Christ glorified not himself to be made an high priest; but he that said unto him, Thou art my Son, to day have I begotten thee.

Made *see Hebrews 3:14*.

High priest *see Hebrews 2:17*.

Said *laleo* (2980), "to speak," is sometimes translated "to say"; in the following where the KJV renders it thus, the RV alters it to the verb "to speak," e.g., John 8:25 (3rd part), 26; 16:6; 18:20 (2nd part), 21 (1st part); Acts 3:22 (2nd part); 1 Cor. 9:8 (1st part); **Heb. 5:5**; in the following the RV uses the verb "to say," John 16:18; Acts 23:18 (2nd part); 26:22 (2nd part); **Heb. 11:18**.

Son *see Hebrews 1:2*.

To day *see* **This day** at *Hebrews 1:5*. *See also* **Daily** at *Hebrews 3:13*.

Begotten *see Hebrews 1:5*.

5:6 As he saith also in another *place*, Thou *art* a priest for ever after the order of Melchisedec.

Priest *hiereus* (2409), "one who offers sacrifice and has the charge of things pertaining thereto," is used (a) of a "priest" of the pagan god Zeus, Acts 14:13; (b) of Jewish "priests," e.g., Matt. 8:4; 12:4, 5; Luke 1:5, where allusion is made to the 24 courses of "priests" appointed for service in the Temple (cf. 1 Chron. 24:4ff.); John 1:19; **Heb. 8:4**; (c) of believers, Rev. 1:6; 5:10; 20:6. Israel was primarily designed as a nation to be a kingdom of "priests," offering service to God, e.g., Ex. 19:6, the Israelites having renounced their obligations, Ex. 20:19, the Aaronic priesthood was selected for the purpose, till Christ came to fulfil His ministry in offering up Himself; since then the Jewish priesthood has been abrogated, to be resumed nationally, on behalf of Gentiles, in the millennial kingdom, Is. 61:6; 66:21. Meanwhile all believers, from Jews and Gentiles, are constituted "a kingdom of priests," Rev. 1:6, "a holy priesthood," 1 Pet. 2:5, and "royal," v. 9. The NT knows nothing of a sacerdotal class in contrast to the laity; all believers are commanded to offer the sacrifices mentioned in Rom. 12:1; Phil. 2:17; 4:18; **Heb. 13:15, 16**; 1 Pet. 2:5; (d) of Christ, **Heb. 5:6**; **7:11, 15, 17, 21**; **8:4** (negatively); (e) of Melchizedek, as the foreshadower of Christ, **Heb. 7:1, 3**. *See also* **High priest** at *Hebrews 2:17*.

Ever *aion* (165), "an age, era" (to be connected with *aei*, "ever," rather than with *ao*, "to breathe"), signifies a period of indefinite duration, or time viewed in relation to what takes place in the period. The force attaching to the word is not so much that of the actual length of a period, but that of a period marked by spiritual or moral characteristics. This is illustrated in the use of the adjective in the phrase "life eternal," in John 17:3, in respect of the increasing knowledge of God. The phrases containing this word should not be rendered literally, but consistently with its sense of indefinite duration. Thus *eis ton aiona* does not mean "unto the age" but "for ever" (see, e.g., **Heb. 5:6**). The Greeks contrasted that which came to an end with that which was expressed by this phrase, which shows that they conceived of it as expressing interminable duration. The word occurs most frequently in the Gospel of John, the Hebrews and Revelation. It is sometimes wrongly rendered "world." It is a characteristic word of John's Gospel.

Order *taxis* (5010), "an arranging, arrangement, order" (akin to *tasso*, "to arrange, draw up in order"), is used in Luke 1:8 of the fixed succession of the course of the priests; of due "order," in contrast to confusion, in the gatherings of a local church, 1 Cor. 14:40; of the general condition of such, Col. 2:5 (some give it a military significance here); of the divinely appointed character or nature of a priesthood, of Melchizedek, as foreshadowing that of Christ, **Heb. 5:6, 10**; **6:20**; **7:11** (where also the character of the Aaronic priesthood is set in contrast); **7:17** (in some mss., v. **21**).

5:7 Who in the days of his flesh, when he had offered up prayers and supplications with strong crying and tears unto him that was able to save him from death, and was heard in thathe feared;

Flesh *sarx* (4561) ... Its uses in the NT may be analyzed as follows:

"(a) "the substance of the body," whether of beasts or of men, 1 Cor. 15:39; (b) "the human body," 2 Cor. 10:3a; Gal. 2:20; Phil. 1:22; (c) by synecdoche, of "mankind," in the totality of all that is essential to manhood, i.e., spirit, soul, and body, Matt. 24:22; John 1:13; Rom. 3:20; (d) by synecdoche, of "the holy humanity" of the Lord Jesus, in the totality of all that is essential to manhood, i.e., spirit, soul, and body John 1:14; 1 Tim. 3:16; 1 John 4:2; 2 John 7, in **Heb. 5:7**, "the days of His flesh," i.e., His past life on earth in distinction from His present life in resurrection; (e) by synecdoche, for "the complete person," John 6:51-57; 2 Cor. 7:5;

Jas. 5:3; (f) "the weaker element in human nature," Matt. 26:41; Rom. 6:19; 8:3a; (g) "the unregenerate state of men," Rom. 7:5; 8:8, 9; (h) "the seat of sin in man" (but this is not the same thing as in the body), 2 Pet. 2:18; 1 John 2:16; (i) "the lower and temporary element in the Christian," Gal. 3:3; 6:8, and in religious ordinances, **Heb. 9:10**; (j) "the natural attainments of men," 1 Cor. 1:26; 2 Cor. 10:2, 3b; (k) "circumstances," 1 Cor. 7:28; the externals of life, 2 Cor. 7:1; Eph. 6:5; **Heb. 9:13**; (l) by metonymy, "the outward and seeming," as contrasted with the spirit, the inward and real, John 6:63; 2 Cor. 5:16; (m) "natural relationship, consanguine," 1 Cor. 10:18; Gal. 4:23, or marital, Matt. 19:5."

Offered *see* **Offer** at *Hebrews 5:1*.

Prayers *deesis* (1162), primarily "a wanting, a need," then, "an asking, entreaty, supplication," in the NT is always addressed to God and always rendered "supplication" or "supplications" in the RV; in the KJV "prayer," or "prayers," in Luke 1:13; 2:37; 5:33; Rom. 10:1; 2 Cor. 1:11; 9:14; Phil. 1:4 (in the 2nd part, "request"); 1:19; 2 Tim. 1:3; **Heb. 5:7**; Jas. 5:16; 1 Pet. 3:12.

Supplications *hiketeria* (2428), is the feminine form of the adjective *hiketerios*, denoting "of a suppliant," and used as a noun, formerly "an olive branch" carried by a suppliant (*hiketes*), then later, "a supplication," used in **Heb. 5:7**. In the Sept., Job 40:22 (Eng. Vers. 41:3).

Strong *ichuros* (2478), "strong, mighty," is used of (a) persons: (1) God, Rev. 18:8; (2) angels, Rev. 5:2; 10:1; 18:21; (3) men, Matt. 12:29 (twice) and parallel passages; **Heb. 11:34**, KJV, "valiant" (RV, "mighty"); Rev. 6:15 (in the best texts); 19:18, "mighty"; metaphorically, (4) the church at Corinth, 1 Cor. 4:10, where the apostle reproaches them ironically with their unspiritual and self-complacent condition; (5) of young men in Christ spiritually strong, through the Word of God, to overcome the evil one, 1 John 2:14; of (b) things: (1) wind, Matt. 14:30 (in some mss.), "boisterous"; (2) famine, Luke 15:14; (3) things in the mere human estimate, 1 Cor. 1:27; (4) Paul's letters, 2 Cor. 10:10; (5) the Lord's crying and tears, **Heb. 5:7**; (6) consolation, **6:18**; (7) the voice of an angel, Rev. 18:2 (in the best texts; some have *megas*, "great"); (8) Babylon, Rev. 18:10; (9) thunderings, Rev. 19:6.

Crying *krauge* (2906), an onomatopoeic word, is used in Matt. 25:6; Luke 1:42 (some mss. have *phone*); Acts 23:9, RV, "clamor"; Eph. 4:31, "clamor"; **Heb. 5:7**; Rev. 21:4, "crying." Some mss. have it in Rev. 14:18 (the most authentic have *phone*).

Tears *dakruon* or *dakru* (1144), akin to *dakruo*, "to weep," is used in the plural, Mark 9:24; Luke 7:38, 44 (with the sense of washing therewith the Lord's feet); Acts 20:19, 31; 2 Cor. 2:4; 2 Tim. 1:4; **Heb. 5:7**; **12:17**; Rev. 7:17; 21:4.

Death *see Hebrews 2:15*.

Heard *eisakouo* (1522), "to listen to," has two meanings, (a) "to hear and to obey," 1 Cor. 14:21, "they will not hear"; (b) "to hear so as to answer," of God's answer to prayer, Matt. 6:7; Luke 1:13; Acts 10:31; **Heb. 5:7**.

Feared *eulabeia* (2124), signifies, firstly, "caution"; then, "reverence, godly fear," **Heb. 5:7**; **12:28**, in best mss., "reverence"; in general, "apprehension, but especially holy fear," "that mingled fear and love which, combined, constitute the piety of man toward God; the OT places its emphasis on the fear, the NT ... on the love, though there was love in the fear of God's saints then, as there must be fear in their love now" (Trench, *Syn.* Sec.xlviii). In the Sept., Josh. 22:24; Prov. 28:14.

5:8 Though he were a Son, yet learned he obedience by the things which he suffered;

Learned *manthano* (3129), denotes (a) "to learn" (akin to *mathetes*, "a disciple"), "to increase one's knowledge," or "be increased in knowledge," frequently "to learn by inquiry, or observation," e.g., Matt. 9:13; 11:29; 24:32; Mark 13:28; John 7:15; Rom. 16:17; 1 Cor. 4:6; 14:35; Phil. 4:9; 2 Tim. 3:14; Rev. 14:3; said of "learning" Christ, Eph. 4:20, not simply the doctrine of Christ, but Christ Himself, a process not merely of getting to know the person but of so applying the knowledge as to walk differently from the rest of the Gentiles; (b) "to ascertain," Acts 23:27, RV, "learned" (KJV, "understood"); Gal. 3:2, "This only would I learn from you," perhaps with a tinge of irony in the enquiry, the answer to which would settle the question of the validity of the new Judaistic gospel they were receiving; (c) "to learn by use and practice, to acquire the habit of, be accustomed to," e.g., Phil. 4:11; 1 Tim. 5:4, 13; Titus 3:14; **Heb. 5:8**.

Obedience *hupakoe* (5218), "obedience" (*hupo*, "under," *akouo*, "to hear"), is used (a) in general, Rom. 6:16 (1st part), RV, "(unto) obedience," KJV, "(to) obey"; here "obedience" is not personified, as in the next part of the verse, "servants ... of obedience" [see (c)], but is simply shown to be the effect of the presentation mentioned; (b) of the fulfillment of apostolic counsels, 2 Cor. 7:15; 10:6; Philem.

21; (c) of the fulfillment of God's claims or commands, Rom. 1:5 and 16:26, "obedience of faith," which grammatically might be objective, to the faith (marg.), or subjective, as in the text. Since faith is one of the main subjects of the Epistle, and is the initial act of obedience in the new life, as well as an essential characteristic thereof, the text rendering is to be preferred; Rom. 6:16 (2nd part); 15:18, RV "(for) the obedience," KJV, "(to make) obedient"; 16:19; 1 Pet. 1:2, 14, RV, "(children of) obedience," i.e., characterized by "obedience," KJV, "obedient (children)"; v. 22, RV, "obedience (to the truth)," KJV, "obeying (the truth)"; (d) of "obedience" to Christ (objective), 2 Cor. 10:5; (e) of Christ's "obedience," Rom. 5:19 (referring to His death; cf. Phil. 2:8); **Heb. 5:8**, which refers to His delighted experience in constant "obedience" to the Father's will (not to be understood in the sense that He learned to obey).

Suffered *see Hebrews 2:18.*

5:9 And being made perfect, he became the author of eternal salvation unto all them that obey him;

Perfect *see Hebrews 2:10.*

Author *aitios* (159), an adjective (cf. *aitia*, a cause), denotes "that which causes something." *Aitios*, in **Heb. 5:9**, describes Christ as the "Author of eternal salvation unto all them that obey Him," signifying that Christ, exalted and glorified as our High Priest, on the ground of His finished work on earth, has become the personal mediating cause (RV, margin) of eternal salvation. It is difficult to find an adequate English equivalent to express the meaning here. Christ is not the merely formal cause of our salvation. He is the concrete and active cause of it. He has not merely caused or effected it, He is, as His name, "Jesus," implies, our salvation itself, Luke 2:30; 3:6.

Eternal *aionios* (166), "describes duration, either undefined but not endless, as in Rom. 16:25; 2 Tim. 1:9; Titus 1:2; or undefined because endless as in Rom. 16:26, and the other sixty-six places in the NT. The predominant meaning of *aionios*, that in which it is used everywhere in the NT, save the places noted above, may be seen in 2 Cor. 4:18, where it is set in contrast with *proskairos*, lit., 'for a season,' and in Philem. 15, where only in the NT it is used without a noun. Moreover it is used of persons and things which are in their nature endless, as, e.g., of God, Rom. 16:26; of His power, 1 Tim. 6:16, and of His glory, 1 Pet. 5:10; of the Holy Spirit, **Heb. 9:14**; of the redemption effected by Christ, **Heb. 9:12**, and of the consequent salvation of men, **5:9**, as well as of His future rule, 2 Pet. 1:11, which is elsewhere declared to be without end, Luke 1:33; of the life received by those who believe in Christ, John 3:16, concerning whom He said, 'they shall never perish,' 10:28, and of the resurrection body, 2 Cor. 5:1, elsewhere said to be 'immortal,' 1 Cor. 15:53, in which that life will be finally realized, Matt. 25:46; Titus 1:2. *Aionios* is also used of the sin that 'hath never forgiveness,' Mark 3:29, and of the judgment of God, from which there is no appeal, **Heb. 6:2**, and of the fire, which is one of its instruments, Matt. 18:8; 25:41; Jude 7, and which is elsewhere said to be 'unquenchable,' Mark 9:43. The use of *aionios* here shows that the punishment referred to in 2 Thess. 1:9, is not temporary, but final, and, accordingly, the phraseology shows that its purpose is not remedial but retributive."

Salvation *see Hebrews 1:14.*

Obey *hupakouo* (5219), "to listen, attend" (as in Acts 12:13), and so, "to submit, to obey," is used of "obedience" (a) to God, **Heb. 5:9; 11:8**; (b) to Christ, by natural elements, Matt. 8:27; Mark 1:27; 4:41; Luke 8:25; (c) to disciples of Christ, Luke 17:6; (d) to the faith, Acts 6:7; the gospel, Rom. 10:16; 2 Thess. 1:8; Christian doctrine, Rom. 6:17 (as to a form or mold of teaching); (e) to apostolic injunctions, Phil. 2:12; 2 Thess. 3:14; (f) to Abraham by Sarah, 1 Pet. 3:6; (g) to parents by children, Eph. 6:1; Col. 3:20; (h) to masters by servants, Eph. 6:5; Col. 3:22; (i) to sin, Rom. 6:12; (j) in general, Rom. 6:16.

5:10 Called of God an high priest after the order of Melchisedec.

Called *prosagoreuo* (4316), primarily denotes "to address, greet, salute"; hence, "to call by name," **Heb. 5:10**, RV, "named (of God a High Priest)" (KJV, "called"), expressing the formal ascription of the title to Him whose it is; "called" does not adequately express the significance. Some suggest the meaning "addressed," but this is doubtful. The reference is to Ps. 110:4, a prophecy confirmed at the Ascension. In the Sept., Deut. 23:6.

High priest *see Hebrews 2:17.*

Order *see Hebrews 5:6.*

5:11 Of whom we have many things to say, and hard to be uttered, seeing ye are dull of hearing.

Say In **Heb. 5:11**, "we have many things to say" is, lit., "much (*polus*) is the word (or discourse, *logos*) for us."

Uttered In **Heb. 5:11**, KJV, *dusermeneutos*, followed by *lego*, "to speak," [translated "hard of interpretation" (RV), *dus* (whence "dys-" in Eng., "dyspeptic," etc.), a prefix like Eng., "un-," or "mis-," and *hermeneuo*, "to interpret"], is rendered "hard to be uttered."

Dull *nothros* (3576), "slow, sluggish, indolent, dull" (the etymology is uncertain), is translated "dull" in **Heb. 5:11** (in connection with *akoe*, "hearing"; lit., "in hearings"); "sluggish," in **6:12**. In the Sept., Prov. 22:29. Cf. *nothrokardios*, "slow of heart" (*kardia*, "the heart), Prov. 12:8.

Hearing *see* **Heard** at *Hebrews 4:2*.

5:12 For when for the time ye ought to be teachers, ye have need that one teach you again which *be* the first principles of the oracles of God; and are become such as have need of milk, and not of strong meat.

Ought *see Hebrews 5:3*.

Teachers *didaskalos* (1320), is rendered "teacher" or "teachers" in Matt. 23:8, by Christ, of Himself; in John 3:2 of Christ; of Nicodemus in Israel, 3:10, RV; of "teachers" of the truth in the churches, Acts 13:1; 1 Cor. 12:28, 29; Eph. 4:11; **Heb. 5:12**; Jas. 3:1, RV; by Paul of his work among the churches, 1 Tim. 2:7; 2 Tim. 1:11; of "teachers," wrongfully chosen by those who have "itching ears," 2 Tim. 4:3.

First *arche* (746), "a beginning," is translated "first" in **Heb. 5:12**, "of the first (principles of the oracles of God)," lit. "(the principles) of the beginning (of the oracles of God)"; in **6:1** "the first (principles) of Christ," lit., "(the account) of the beginning of Christ," i.e., the elementary teaching concerning Christ. In Acts 26:4, where the word is preceded by *apo*, "from," the KJV has "at the first," the RV, "from the beginning."

Principles *stoicheion* (4747), used in the plural, primarily signifies any first things from which others in a series, or a composite whole take their rise; the word denotes "an element, first principle" (from *stoichos*, "a row, rank, series"; cf. the verb *stoicheo*, "to walk or march in rank"); it was used of the letters of the alphabet, as elements of speech. In the NT it is used of (a) the substance of the material world, 2 Pet. 3:10, 12; (b) the delusive speculations of gentile cults and of Jewish theories, treated as elementary principles, "the rudiments of the world," Col. 2:8, spoken of as "philosophy and vain deceit"; these were presented as superior to faith in Christ; at Colosse the worship of angels, mentioned in v. 18, is explicable by the supposition, held by both Jews and Gentiles in that district, that the constellations were either themselves animated heavenly beings, or were governed by them; (c) the rudimentary principles of religion, Jewish or Gentile, also described as "the rudiments of the world," Col. 2:20, and as "weak and beggarly rudiments," Gal. 4:3, 9, RV, constituting a yoke of bondage; (d) the "elementary" principles (the A.B.C.) of the OT, as a revelation from God, **Heb. 5:12**, RV, "rudiments," lit., "the rudiments of the beginning of the oracles of God," such as are taught to spiritual babes.

Oracles *logion* (3051), a diminutive of *logos*, "a word, narrative, statement," denotes "a divine response or utterance, an oracle"; it is used of (a) the contents of the Mosaic Law, Acts 7:38; (b) all the written utterances of God through OT writers, Rom. 3:2; (c) the substance of Christian doctrine, **Heb. 5:12**; (d) the utterances of God through Christian teachers, 1 Pet. 4:11.

Milk *gala* (1051), is used (a) literally, 1 Cor. 9:7; (b) metaphorically, of rudimentary spiritual teaching, 1 Cor. 3:2; **Heb. 5:12, 13**; 1 Pet. 2:2; here the meaning largely depends upon the significance of the word *logikos*, which the KJV renders "of the word," RV "spiritual." While *logos* denotes "a word," the adjective *logikos* is never used with the meaning assigned to it in the KJV, nor does the context in 1:23 compel this meaning. While it is true that the Word of God, like "milk," nourishes the soul, and this is involved in the exhortation, the only other occurrence in the NT is Rom. 12:1, where it is translated "reasonable," i.e., rational, intelligent (service), in contrast to the offering of an irrational animal; so here the nourishment may be understood as of that spiritually rational nature which, acting through the regenerate mind, develops spiritual growth. God's Word is not given so that it is impossible to understand it, or that it requires a special class of men to interpret it; its character is such that the Holy Spirit who gave it can unfold its truths even to the young convert. Cf. 1 John 2:27.

Strong *stereos* (4731), has the meaning "solid" in **Heb. 5:12, 14**, of food (KJV, "strong"). As "solid" food requires more powerful digestive organs than are possessed by a babe, so a fuller knowledge of Christ (especially here with reference to His Melchizedek priesthood) required that exercise of spiritual intelligence which is derived from the practical appropriation of what had already been received.

Meat *trophe* (5160), denotes "nourishment, food" (akin to *trepho*, "to rear, nourish, feed"); it is used literally, in the Gospels, Acts and Jas. 2:15; metaphorically, in **Heb. 5:12, 14**, RV, "(solid) food," KJV, "(strong) meat," i.e., deeper subjects of the faith than that of elementary instruction. The word is always rendered "food" in the RV, where the KJV has "meat"; e.g., Matt. 3:4; 6:25; 10:10; 24:45; Luke 12:23; John 4:8; Acts 2:46, "did take their food," RV (KJV, "did eat their meat"); 9:19, "took food"; 27:33, 34, 36. The KJV also has "food" in Acts 14:17 and Jas. 2:15.

5:13 For every one that useth milk *is* unskilful in the word of righteousness: for he is a babe.

Useth *see* **Took part** at *Hebrews 2:14*.

Milk *see Hebrews 5:12*.

Unskilful *apeiros* (552), "without experience" (*a*, negative, *peira*, "a trial, experiment") is used in **Heb. 5:13**, RV, "without experience," KJV, "unskillful," with reference to "the word of righteousness." In the Sept., Num. 14:23, of youths; Jer. 2:6, of a land, "untried"; Zech. 11:15, of a shepherd.

Word *see Hebrews 4:12*.

Righteousness *dikaiosune* (1343), is "the character or quality of being right or just"; it was formerly spelled "rightwiseness," which clearly expresses the meaning. It is used to denote an attribute of God, e.g., Rom. 3:5, the context of which shows that "the righteousness of God" means essentially the same as His faithfulness, or truthfulness, that which is consistent with His own nature and promises; Rom. 3:25, 26 speaks of His "righteousness" as exhibited in the death of Christ, which is sufficient to show men that God is neither indifferent to sin nor regards it lightly. On the contrary, it demonstrates that quality of holiness in Him which must find expression in His condemnation of sin.

"*Dikaiosune* is found in the sayings of the Lord Jesus, (a) of whatever is right or just in itself, whatever conforms to the revealed will of God, Matt. 5:6, 10, 20; John 16:8, 10; (b) whatever has been appointed by God to be acknowledged and obeyed by man, Matt. 3:15; 21:32; (c) the sum total of the requirements of God, Matt. 6:33; (d) religious duties, Matt. 6:1 (distinguished as almsgiving, man's duty to his neighbor, vv. 2-4, prayer, his duty to God, vv. 5-15, fasting, the duty of self-control, vv. 16–18). In the preaching of the apostles recorded in Acts the word has the same general meaning. So also in Jas. 1:20, 3:18, in both Epp. of Peter, 1st John and the Revelation. In 2 Pet. 1:1, 'the righteousness of our God and Savior Jesus Christ,' is the righteous dealing of God with sin and with sinners on the ground of the death of Christ. 'Word of righteousness,' **Heb. 5:13**, is probably the gospel, and the Scriptures as containing the gospel, wherein is declared the righteousness of God in all its aspects."

Babe *nepios* (3516), lit., "without the power of speech," denotes "a little child," the literal meaning having been lost in the general use of the word. It is used (a) of "infants," Matt. 21:16; (b) metaphorically, of the unsophisticated in mind and trustful in disposition, Matt. 11:25 and Luke 10:21, where it stands in contrast to the wise; of those who are possessed merely of natural knowledge, Rom. 2:20; of those who are carnal, and have not grown, as they should have done, in spiritual understanding and power, the spiritually immature, 1 Cor. 3:1, those who are so to speak partakers of milk, and "without experience of the word of righteousness," **Heb. 5:13**; of the Jews, who, while the Law was in force, were in a state corresponding to that of childhood, or minority, just as the word "infant" is used of a minor, in English law, Gal. 4:3, "children"; of believers in an immature condition, impressionable and liable to be imposed upon instead of being in a state of spiritual maturity, Eph. 4:14, "children." "Immaturity" is always associated with this word.

5:14 But strong meat belongeth to them that are of full age, *even* those who by reason of use have their senses exercised to discern both good and evil.

Strong *see Hebrews 5:12*.

Meat *see Hebrews 5:12*.

Belongeth This word represents (a) a phrase consisting of *eimi*, "to be," with or without a preposition and a noun, and usually best rendered, as in the RV, by the verb "to be," Mark 9:41, lit., "ye are of Christ"; Luke 23:7 and **Heb. 5:14**; cf. Rom. 12:19, "belongeth unto Me," RV; (b) a phrase consisting of the neuter plural of the definite article, either with the preposition *pros*, "unto," as in Luke 19:42, where the phrase "the things which belong unto peace" (RV) is, lit., "the (things) unto peace," or with the genitive case of the noun, as in 1 Cor. 7:32, KJV, "the things that belong to the Lord," RV, suitably, "the things of the Lord"; (c) a distinct verb, e.g., *metecho*, "to partake of, share in," **Heb. 7:13** RV, "belongeth to (another tribe)," KJV, "pertaineth to."

Full *teleios* (5049), signifies "having reached its end" (*telos*), "finished, complete perfect." It is used (I) of persons, (a) primarily of physical development, then, with ethical import, "fully grown, mature," 1 Cor. 2:6; 14:20 ("men"; marg., "of full age"); Eph. 4:13; Phil. 3:15; Col. 1:28; 4:12; in **Heb. 5:14**, RV, "fullgrown" (marg., "perfect"), KJV, "of full age" (marg., "perfect"); (b) "complete," conveying the idea of goodness without necessary reference to maturity or what is expressed under (a) Matt. 5:48; 19:21; Jas. 1:4 (2nd part); 3:2. It is used thus of God in Matt. 5:48; (II) of "things, complete, perfect," Rom. 12:2; 1 Cor. 13:10 (referring to the complete revelation of God's will and ways, whether in the completed Scriptures or in the hereafter); Jas. 1:4 (of the work of patience); v. 25; 1 John 4:18.

Age *teleios* (5046), "complete, perfect," from *telos*, "an end," is translated "of full age" in **Heb. 5:14**, KJV (RV, "fullgrown man").

Use *hexis* (1838), akin to *echo*, "to have," denotes "habit, experience," "use," **Heb. 5:14**.

Senses *aistheterion* (145), "sense, the faculty of perception, the organ of sense" (akin to *aisthanomai*, "to perceive"), is used in **Heb. 5:14**, "senses," the capacities for spiritual apprehension. In the Sept., Jer. 4:19, "(I am pained ... in the) sensitive powers (of my heart)."

Exercised *gumnazo* (1128), primarily signifies "to exercise naked" (from *gumnos*, "naked"); then, generally, "to exercise, to train the body or mind" (Eng., "gymnastic"), 1 Tim. 4:7, with a view to godliness; **Heb. 5:14**, of the senses, so as to discern good and evil; **12:11**, of the effect of chastening, the spiritual "exercise producing the fruit of righteousness"; 2 Pet. 2:14, of certain evil teachers with hearts "exercised in covetousness," RV.

Discern *diakrisis* (1253), "a distinguishing," and so "a decision," signifies "discerning" in 1 Cor. 12:10; **Heb. 5:14**, lit., "unto a discerning of good and evil" (translated "to discern"); in Rom. 14:1, "not to (doubtful) disputations" is more literally rendered in the margin "not for decisions (of doubts)."

Evil *kakon* (2556), is used with the article, as a noun, e.g., Acts 23:9; Rom. 7:21; **Heb. 5:14**; in the plural, "evil things," e.g., 1 Cor. 10:6; 1 Tim. 6:10, "all kinds of evil," RV.

Chapter 6

6:1 Therefore leaving the principles of the doctrine of Christ, let us go on unto perfection; not laying again the foundation of repentance from dead works, and of faith toward God,

Leaving *aphiemi* (863), "to let go," is translated "let us cease to" in **Heb. 6:1**, RV (marg., "leave") for KJV, "leaving." *See also* **Left** at *Hebrews 2:8*.

Principles *arche* (746), "beginning," is used in **Heb. 6:1**, in its relative significance, of the beginning of the thing spoken of; here "the first principles of Christ," lit., "the account (or word) of the beginning of Christ," denotes the teaching relating to the elementary facts concerning Christ. *See also* **First** at *Hebrews 5:12*.

Doctrine In **Heb. 6:1**, *logos*, "a word," is translated "doctrine," KJV; the RV margin gives the lit. rendering, "the word (of the beginning of Christ)," and, in the text, "the (first) principles (of Christ)." *See also* **Word** at *Hebrews 4:12*.

Go *phero* (5342), "to bear, carry," is used in the passive voice in **Heb. 6:1**, "let us ... press on," RV, lit., "let us be borne on" (KJV, "go on").

Perfection *teleiotes* (5047), stresses perhaps the actual accomplishment of the end in view, Col. 3:14, "perfectness"; **Heb. 6:1**, "perfection." In the Sept., Judg. 9:16, 19; Prov. 11:3; Jer. 2:2.

Laying *kataballo* (2598), "to cast down" (*kata*), is used metaphorically in **Heb. 6:1**, in the middle voice, negatively, "of laying" a foundation of certain doctrines.

Foundation *themelios*, or *themelion* (2310), is properly an adjective denoting "belonging to a foundation" (connected with *tithemi*, "to place"). It is used (1) as a noun, with *lithos*, "a stone," understood, in Luke 6:48, 49; 14:29; **Heb. 11:10**; Rev. 21:14, 19; (2) as a neuter noun in Acts 16:26, and metaphorically, (a) of "the ministry of the gospel and the doctrines of the faith," Rom. 15:20; 1 Cor. 3:10, 11, 12; Eph. 2:20, where the "of" is not subjective (i.e., consisting of the apostles and prophets), but objective (i.e., laid by the apostles, etc.); so in 2 Tim. 2:19, where "the foundation of God" is "the foundation laid by God," – not the Church (which is not a "foundation"), but Christ Himself, upon whom the saints are built; **Heb. 6:1**; (b) "of good works," 1 Tim. 6:19.

Dead *nekros* (3498), is used of (a) the death of the body, cf. Jas. 2:26, its most frequent sense: (b) the actual spiritual condition of unsaved men, Matt. 8:22; John 5:25; Eph. 2:1, 5; 5:14; Phil. 3:11; Col. 2:13; cf. Luke 15:24: (c) the ideal spiritual condition of believers in regard to sin, Rom. 6:11: (d) a church in declension, inasmuch as in that state it is inactive and barren, Rev. 3:1: (e) sin, which apart from law cannot produce a sense of guilt, Rom. 7:8: (f) the body of the believer in contrast to his spirit, Rom. 8:10: (g) the works of the Law, inasmuch as, however good in themselves, Rom. 7:13, they cannot produce life, **Heb. 6:1**; **9:14**: (h) the faith that does not produce works, Jas. 2:17, 26; cf. v. 20.

Works *see Hebrews 1:10.*

6:2 Of the doctrine of baptisms, and of laying on of hands, and of resurrection of the dead, and of eternal judgment.

Baptisms *baptismos* (909), as distinct from *baptisma* (the ordinance), is used of the "ceremonial washing of articles," Mark 7:4, 8, in some texts; **Heb. 9:10**; once in a general sense, **Heb. 6:2**.

Laying on *epithesis* (1936), "a laying on" (*epi*, "on," *tithemi*, "to put"), is used in the NT (a) of the "laying" on of hands by the apostles accompanied by the impartation of the Holy Spirit in outward demonstration, in the cases of those in Samaria who had believed, Acts 8:18; such supernatural manifestations were signs especially intended to give witness to Jews as to the facts of Christ and the faith, they were thus temporary; there is no record of their continuance after the time and circumstances narrated in Acts 19 (in v. 6 of which the corresponding verb *epitithemi* is used), nor was the gift delegated by the apostles to others; (b) of the similar act by the elders of a church on occasions when a member of a church was set apart for a particular work, having given evidence of qualifications necessary for it, as in the case of Timothy, 1 Tim. 4:14; of the impartation of a spiritual gift through the laying on of the hands of the apostle Paul, 2 Tim. 1:6, RV, "laying" (KJV, "putting"); cf. the verb *epitithemi* in Acts 6:6, on the appointment of the seven, and in the case of Barnabas and Saul, 13:3, also in 19:6, (c) in **Heb. 6:2**, the doctrine of the "laying" on of hands refers to the act enjoined upon an Israelite in connection, e.g., with the peace offerings, Lev. 3:2, 8, 13; 4:29, 33; upon the priests in connection with the sin offering, 4:4; 16:21; upon the elders, 4:15; upon a ruler, 4:24. The principle underlying the act was that of identification on the part of him who did it with the animal or person upon whom the hands were laid. In the Sept., 2 Chron. 25:27; Ezek. 23:11.

Resurrection *anastasis* (386), denotes (I) "a raising up," or "rising" (*ana*, "up," and *histemi*, "to cause to stand"), Luke 2:34, "the rising up"; the KJV "again" obscures the meaning; the Child would be like a stone against which many in Israel would stumble while many others would find in its strength and firmness a means of their salvation and spiritual life; (II) of "resurrection" from the dead, (a) of Christ, Acts 1:22; 2:31; 4:33; Rom. 1:4; 6:5; Phil. 3:10; 1 Pet. 1:3; 3:21; by metonymy, of Christ as the Author of "resurrection," John 11:25; (b) of those who are Christ's at His Parousia, Luke 14:14, "the resurrection of the just"; Luke 20:33, 35, 36; John 5:29 (1st part), "the resurrection of life"; 11:24; Acts 23:6; 24:15 (1st part); 1 Cor. 15:21, 42; 2 Tim. 2:18; **Heb. 11:35** (2nd part); Rev. 20:5, "the first resurrection"; hence the insertion of "is" stands for the completion of this "resurrection," of which Christ was "the firstfruits"; 20:6; (c) of "the rest of the dead," after the Millennium (cf. Rev. 20:5); John 5:29 (2nd part), "the resurrection of judgment"; Acts 24:15 (2nd part), "of the unjust"; (d) of those who were raised in more immediate connection with Christ's "resurrection," and thus had part already in the first "resurrection," Acts 26:23 and Rom. 1:4 (in each of which "dead" is plural; see Matt. 27:52); (e) of the "resurrection" spoken of in general terms, Matt. 22:23; Mark 12:18; Luke 20:27; Acts 4:2; 17:18; 23:8; 24:21; 1 Cor. 15:12, 13; **Heb. 6:2**; (f) of those who were raised in OT times, to die again, **Heb. 11:35** (1st part), lit., "out of resurrection."

Eternal *see Hebrews 5:9.*

Judgment *krima* (2917), denotes the result of the action signified by the verb *krino*, "to judge"; it is used (a) of a decision passed on the faults of others, Matt. 7:2; (b) of "judgment" by man upon Christ, Luke 24:20; (c) of God's "judgment" upon men, e.g., Rom. 2:2, 3; 3:8; 5:16; 11:33; 13:2; 1 Cor. 11:29; Gal. 5:10; **Heb. 6:2**; Jas. 3:1; through Christ, e.g., John 9:39; (d) of the right of "judgment," Rev. 20:4; (e) of a lawsuit, 1 Cor. 6:7.

6:3 And this will we do, if God permit.

Permit *epitrepo* (2010), lit., "to turn to" (*epi*, "to," *trepo*, "to turn"), "to entrust," signifies "to permit," Acts 26:1; 1 Cor. 14:34; 1 Cor. 16:7; 1 Tim. 2:12, RV "permit" (KJV, "suffer"); **Heb. 6:3**.

6:4 For *it is* impossible for those who were once enlightened, and have tasted of the heavenly gift, and were made partakers of the Holy Ghost,

Impossible *adunatos* (102), from *a*, negative, and *dunatos*, "able, strong," is used (a) of persons, Acts 14:8, "impotent"; figuratively, Rom. 15:1, "weak"; (b) of things, "impossible," Matt. 19:26; Mark 10:27; Luke 18:27; **Heb. 6:4**, **18**; **10:4**; **11:6**; in Rom. 8:3, "for what the Law could not do," is, more lit., "the inability of the law"; the meaning may be either "the weakness of the Law," or "that which was impossible for the Law"; the latter is perhaps preferable; literalism is ruled out here, but the sense is that the Law could neither justify nor impart life.

Once *hapax* (530), denotes (a) "once, one time," 2 Cor. 11:25; **Heb. 9:7, 26-27**; **12:26-27**; in the phrase "once and again," lit., "once and twice," Phil. 4:16; 1 Thess. 2:18; (b) "once for all," of what is of perpetual validity, not requiring repetition, **Heb. 6:4**; **9:28**; **10:2**; 1 Pet. 3:18; Jude 3, RV, "once for all" (KJV, "once"); v. 5 (ditto); in some mss. 1 Pet. 3:20 (so the KJV).

Enlightened *photizo* (5461), from *phos*, "light," (a), used intransitively, signifies "to give light, shine," Rev. 22:5; (b), used transitively, "to enlighten, illumine," is rendered "enlighten" in Eph. 1:18, metaphorically of spiritual "enlightenment"; so John 1:9, i.e., "lighting every man" (by reason of His coming); Eph. 3:9, "to make (all men) see" (RV marg., "to bring to light"); **Heb. 6:4**, "were enlightened"; **10:32**, RV, "enlightened," KJV, "illuminated." Cf. *photismos*, "light," and *photeinos*, "full of light."

Tasted *see* Taste at *Hebrews 2:9*.

Heavenly *see Hebrews 3:1*.

Gift *dorea* (1431), denotes "a free gift," stressing its gratuitous character; it is always used in the NT of a spiritual or supernatural gift, John 4:10; Acts 8:20; 11:17; Rom. 5:15; 2 Cor. 9:15; Eph. 3:7; **Heb. 6:4**; in Eph. 4:7, "according to the measure of the gift of Christ," the "gift" is that given by Christ; in Acts 2:28, "the gift of the Holy Ghost," the clause is epexegetical, the "gift" being the Holy Ghost Himself; cf. 10:45; 11:17, and the phrase, "the gift of righteousness," Rom. 5:17.

Made *see Hebrews 3:14*.

Partakers *see* Fellows at *Hebrews 1:9*.

6:5 And have tasted the good word of God, and the powers of the world to come,

Tasted *see* Taste at *Hebrews 2:9*.

6:6 If they shall fall away, to renew them again unto repentance; seeing they crucify to themselves the Son of God afresh, and put *him* to an open shame.

Fall *parapipto* (3895), properly, "to fall in one's way" (*para*, "by"), signifies "to fall away" (from adherence to the realities and facts of the faith), **Heb. 6:6**.

Renew *anakainizo* (340), used in **Heb. 6:6**, of the impossibility of "renewing" to repentance those Jews who professedly adhered to the Christian faith, if, after their experiences of it (not actual possession of its regenerating effects), they apostatized into their former Judaism. In the Sept., 2 Chron. 15:8; Ps. 39:2; 103:5; 104:30; Lam. 5:21.

Crucify *anastauroo* (388), (*ana*, again) is used in **Heb. 6:6** of Hebrew apostates, who as merely nominal Christians, in turning back to Judaism, were thereby virtually guilty of "crucifying" Christ again.

Son *see Hebrews 1:2*.

Shame *paradeigmatizo* (3856), signifies "to set forth as an example" (*para*, "beside," *deiknumi*, "to show"), and is used in **Heb. 6:6** of those Jews, who, though attracted to, and closely associated with, the Christian faith, without having experienced more than a tasting of the heavenly gift and partaking of the Holy Ghost (not actually receiving Him), were tempted to apostatize to Judaism, and, thereby crucifying the Son of God a second time, would "put Him to an open shame." So were criminals exposed. In the Sept., Num. 25:4; Jer. 13:22; Ezek. 28:17.

6:7 For the earth which drinketh in the rain that cometh oft upon it, and bringeth forth herbs meet for them by whom it is dressed, receiveth blessing from God:

Drinketh *pino* (4095), "to drink," is used chiefly in the Gospels and in 1 Cor., whether literally (most frequently), or figuratively, (a) of "drinking" of the blood of Christ, in the sense of receiving eternal life, through His death, John 6:53-54, 56; (b) of "receiving" spiritually that which refreshes, strengthens and nourishes the soul, John 7:37; (c) of "deriving" spiritual life from Christ, John 4:14, as Israel did typically, 1 Cor. 10:4; (d) of "sharing" in the sufferings of Christ humanly inflicted, Matt. 20:22-23; Mark 10:38-39; (e) of "participating" in the abominations imparted by the corrupt religious and commercial systems emanating from Babylon, Rev. 18:3; (f) of "receiving" divine judgment, through partaking unworthily of the Lord's Supper, 1 Cor. 11:29; (g) of "experiencing" the wrath of God, Rev. 14:10; 16:6; (h) of the earth's "receiving" the benefits of rain, **Heb. 6:7**.

Rain *huetos* (5205), from *huo*, "to rain," is used especially, but not entirely, of "showers," and is found in Acts 14:17; 28:2; **Heb. 6:7**; Jas. 5:7; 5:18; Rev. 11:6.

Herbs *botane* (1008), denotes "grass, fodder, herbs" (from *bosko*, "to feed"; cf. Eng., "botany"), **Heb. 6:7**.

Meet *euthetos* (2111), "ready for use, fit, well adapted," lit., "well placed" (*eu*, "well," *tithemi*, "to place"), is used

(a) of persons, Luke 9:62, negatively, of one who is not fit for the kingdom of God; (b) of things, Luke 14:35, of salt that has lost its savor; rendered "meet" in **Heb. 6:7**, of herbs.

Dressed *georgeo* (1090), "to till the ground," is used in the passive voice in **Heb. 6:7**, RV, "it is tilled" (KJV, "... dressed"). Moulton and Milligan point out that, agriculture being the principal industry in Egypt, this word and its cognates are very common in the papyri with reference to the cultivation of private allotments and the crown lands.

Receiveth *metalambano* (3335), "to have or get a share of, partake of" (*meta*, with), is rendered "receiveth" in **Heb. 6:7**. In the Sept., Esth. 5:1.

Blessing *eulogia* (2129), lit., "good speaking, praise," is used of (a) God and Christ, Rev. 5:12-13; 7:12; (b) the invocation of blessings, benediction, **Heb. 12:17**; Jas. 3:10; (c) the giving of thanks, 1 Cor. 10:16; (d) a blessing, a benefit bestowed, Rom. 15:29; Gal. 3:14; Eph. 1:3; **Heb. 6:7**; of a monetary gift sent to needy believers, 2 Cor. 9:5-6; (e) in a bad sense, of fair speech, Rom. 16:18, RV, where it is joined with *chrestologia*, "smooth speech," the latter relating to the substance, *eulogia* to the expression.

6:8 But that which beareth thorns and briers *is* rejected, and *is* nigh unto cursing; whose end *is* to be burned.

Beareth *ekphero* (1627), is used, literally, "of carrying something forth, or out," e.g., a garment, Luke 15:22; sick folk, Acts 5:15; a corpse, Acts 5:6; 9-10; of the impossibility of "carrying" anything out from this world at death, 1 Tim. 6:7. The most authentic mss. have this word in Mark 8:23, of the blind man, whom the Lord brought out of the village (RV). It is also used of the earth, in "bringing forth" produce, **Heb. 6:8**.

Thorns *akantha* (173), "a brier, a thorn" (from *ake*, "a point"), is always used in the plural in the NT, Matt. 7:16 and parallel passage in Luke 6:44; Matt. 13:7 (twice), 22 and parallels in Mark and Luke; in Matt. 27:29 and John 19:2, of the crown of "thorns" placed on Christ's head in mock imitation of the garlands worn by emperors. They were the effects of the divine curse on the ground (Gen. 3:18; contrast Isa. 55:13). The "thorns" of the crown plaited by the soldiers, are usually identified with those of the *Zizyphus spina Christi*, some 20 feet high or more, fringing the Jordan and abundant in Palestine; its twigs are flexible. Another species, however, the Arabian *qundaul*, crowns of which are plaited and sold in Jerusalem as representatives of Christ's crown, seems likely to be the one referred to. The branches are easily woven and adapted to the torture intended. The word *akantha* occurs also in **Heb. 6:8**.

Briers *tribolos* (5146), occurs in Matt. 7:16 and **Heb. 6:8** (KJV, "briers"). In the Sept., Gen. 3:18; 2 Sam. 12:31; Prov. 22:5; Hos. 10:8.

Rejected *adokimos* (96), "not standing the test", is translated "rejected" in 1 Cor. 9:27, RV; **Heb. 6:8**, KJV and RV.

Nigh *engus* (1451), "near, nigh," is used (a) of place, e.g., Luke 19:11, "nigh"; John 3:23; 11:54, "near"; 6:19, 23, "nigh"; metaphorically in Rom. 10:8; Eph. 2:13, 17, "nigh"; (b) of time, e.g., Matt. 24:32-33, "nigh"; so Luke 21:30-31; as a preposition, **Heb. 6:8**, "nigh unto (a curse)," and **8:13**, "nigh unto (vanishing away)."

Cursing *katara* (2671), denotes an "execration, imprecation, curse," uttered out of malevolence, Jas. 3:10; 2 Pet. 2:14; or pronounced by God in His righteous judgment, as upon a land doomed to barrenness, **Heb. 6:8**; upon those who seek for justification by obedience, in part or completely, to the Law, Gal. 3:10, 13; in this 13th verse it is used concretely of Christ, as having "become a curse" for us, i.e., by voluntarily undergoing on the cross the appointed penalty of the "curse." He thus was identified, on our behalf, with the doom of sin. Here, not the verb in the Sept. of Deut. 21:23 is used, but the concrete noun.

End *telos* (5056), signifies (a) "the limit," either at which a person or thing ceases to be what he or it was up to that point, or at which previous activities were ceased, 2 Cor. 3:13; 1 Pet. 4:7; (b) "the final issue or result" of a state or process, e.g., Luke 1:33; in Rom. 10:4, Christ is described as "the end of the Law unto righteousness to everyone that believeth"; this is best explained by Gal. 3:23-26; cf. Jas. 5:11; the following more especially point to the issue or fate of a thing, Matt. 26:58; Rom. 6:21; 2 Cor. 11:15; Phil. 3:19; **Heb. 6:8**; 1 Pet. 1:9; (c) "a fulfillment," Luke 22:37, KJV, "(have) an end"; (d) "the utmost degree" of an act, as of the love of Christ towards His disciples, John 13:1; (e) "the aim or purpose" of a thing, 1 Tim. 1:5; (f) "the last" in a succession or series Rev. 1:8 (KJV, only, "ending"); 21:6; 22:13.

Burned *kausis* (2740), (Eng., "caustic"), is found in **Heb. 6:8**, lit. "whose end is unto burning."

6:9 But, beloved, we are persuaded better things of you, and things that accompany salvation, though we thus speak.

Persuaded *peitho* (3982), in the active voice, signifies "to apply persuasion, to prevail upon or win over, to persuade," bringing about a change of mind by the influence of reason or moral considerations, e.g., in Matt. 27:20; 28:14; Acts 13:43; 19:8; in the passive voice, "to be persuaded, believe," e.g., Luke 16:31; 20:6; Acts 17:4, RV (KJV, "believed"); 21:14; 26:26; Rom. 8:38; 14:14; 15:14; 2 Tim. 1:5, 12; **Heb. 6:9**; **11:13**, in some mss.; **13:18**, RV (KJV, "trust").

Better *see Hebrews 1:4*.

Accompany *echo* (2192), "to have," is rendered "accompany," in **Heb. 6:9**, "things that accompany salvation." The margin gives perhaps the better sense, "things that are near to salvation."

6:10 For God *is* not unrighteous to forget your work and labour of love, which ye have shewed toward his name, in that ye have ministered to the saints, and do minister.

Unrighteous *adikos* (94), not conforming to *dike*, "right," is translated "unrighteous" in Luke 16:10 (twice), RV, 11; Rom. 3:5; 1 Cor. 6:1, RV; 6:9; **Heb. 6:10**; 1 Pet. 3:18, RV; 2 Pet. 2:9, RV.

Forget *epilanthanomai* (1950), "to forget, or neglect," is said (a) negatively of God, indicating His remembrance of sparrows, Luke 12:6, and of the work and labor of love of His saints, **Heb. 6:10**; (b) of the disciples regarding taking bread, Matt. 16:5: Mark 8:14; (c) of Paul regarding "the things which are behind," Phil. 3:13; (d) of believers, as to showing love to strangers, **Heb. 13:2**, RV, and as to doing good and communicating, v. **16**; (e) of a person who after looking at himself in a mirror, forgets what kind of person he is, Jas. 1:24.

Labour *kopos* (2873), primarily denotes "a striking, beating" (akin to *kopto*, "to strike, cut"), then, "toil resulting in weariness, laborious toil, trouble"; it is translated "labor" or "labors" in John 4:38; 1 Cor. 3:8; 15:58; 2 Cor. 6:5; 10:15; 11:23, 27, RV, "labor" (KJV, "weariness"); 1 Thess. 1:3; 2:9; 3:5; 2 Thess. 3:8; (in some mss., **Heb. 6:10**); Rev. 2:2 (RV "toil"); 14:13. In the following the noun is used as the object of the verb *parecho*, "to afford, give, cause," the phrase being rendered "to trouble," lit., "to cause toil or trouble," to embarrass a person by giving occasion for anxiety, as some disciples did to the woman with the ointment, perturbing her spirit by their criticisms, Matt. 26:10; Mark 14:6; or by distracting attention or disturbing a person's rest, as the importunate friend did, Luke 11:7; 18:5; in Gal. 6:17, "let no man trouble me," the apostle refuses, in the form of a peremptory prohibition, to allow himself to be distracted further by the Judaizers, through their proclamation of a false gospel and by their malicious attacks upon himself.

Shewed *endeiknumi* (1731), signifies (1) "to show forth, prove" (middle voice), said (a) of God as to His power, Rom. 9:17; His wrath, 9:22; the exceeding riches of His grace, Eph. 2:7; (b) of Christ, as to His longsuffering, 1 Tim. 1:16; (c) of Gentiles, as to "the work of the Law written in their hearts," Rom. 2:15; (d) of believers, as to the proof of their love, 2 Cor. 8:24; all good fidelity, Titus 2:10; meekness, 3:2; love toward God's Name, **Heb. 6:10**; diligence in ministering to the saints, v. **11**; (2) "to manifest by evil acts," 2 Tim. 4:14, "did (me much evil)," marg., "showed."

Minister *diakoneo* (1247), signifies "to be a servant, attendant, to serve, wait upon, minister." In the following it is translated "to minister," except where "to serve" is mentioned: it is used (a) with a general significance, e.g., Matt. 4:11; 20:28; Mark 1:13; 10:45; John 12:26 ("serve," twice); Acts 19:22; Philem. 13; (b) of waiting at table, "ministering" to the guests, Matt. 8:15; Luke 4:39; 8:3; 12:37; 17:8, "serve"; 22:26, "serve," v. 27, "serveth," twice; the 2nd instance, concerning the Lord, may come under (a); so of women preparing food, etc., Mark 1:31; Luke 10:40, "serve"; John 12:2, "served"; (c) of relieving one's necessities, supplying the necessaries of life, Matt. 25:44; 27:55; Mark 15:41; Acts 6:2, "serve"; Rom. 15:25; **Heb. 6:10**; more definitely in connection with such service in a local church, 1 Tim. 3:10, 13 [there is nothing in the original representing the word "office"; RV, "let them serve as deacons," "they that have served (well) as deacons"]; (d) of attending, in a more general way, to anything that may serve another's interests, as of the work of an amanuensis, 2 Cor. 3:3 (metaphorical): of the conveyance of material gifts for assisting the needy, 2 Cor. 8:19, 20, RV, "is ministered" (KJV, "is administered"); of a variety of forms of service, 2 Tim. 1:18; of the testimony of the OT prophets, 1 Pet. 1:12; of the ministry of believers one to another in various ways, 1 Pet. 4:10, 11 (not here of discharging ecclesiastical functions).

6:11 And we desire that every one of you do shew the same diligence to the full assurance of hope unto the end:

Desire *epithumeo* (1937), "to desire earnestly," stresses the inward impulse rather than the object desired. It is translated "to desire" in Luke 16:21; 17:22; 22:15; 1 Tim. 3:1; **Heb. 6:11**; 1 Pet. 1:12; Rev. 9:6.

Shew *see* **Shewed** at *Hebrews 6:10*.

Diligence *spoude* (4710), "earnestness, zeal," or sometimes "the haste accompanying this," Mark 6:25; Luke 1:39, is translated "diligence" in Rom. 12:8; in v. 11, KJV, "business" (RV, "diligence"); in 2 Cor. 8:7, KJV, "diligence," RV, "earnestness"; both have "diligence" in **Heb. 6:11**; 2 Pet. 1:5; Jude 3; in 2 Cor. 7:11, 12, RV, "earnest care," KJV, "carefulness," and "care."

Assurance *plerophoria* (4136), "a fullness, abundance," also means "full assurance, entire confidence"; lit., a "full-carrying" (*pleros*, "full," *phero*, "to carry"). Some explain it as full fruitfulness (cf. RV, "fullness" in **Heb. 6:11**). In 1 Thess. 1:5 it describes the willingness and freedom of spirit enjoyed by those who brought the gospel to Thessalonica; in Col. 2:2, the freedom of mind and confidence resulting from an understanding in Christ; in **Heb. 6:11** (KJV, "full assurance," RV, "fullness"), the engrossing effect of the expectation of the fulfillment of God's promises; in **Heb. 10:22**, the character of the faith by which we are to draw near to God.

Hope *elpis* (1680), in the NT, "favorable and confident expectation" (contrast the Sept. in Isa. 28:19, "an evil hope"). It has to do with the unseen and the future, Rom. 8:24, 25. "Hope" describes (a) the happy anticipation of good (the most frequent significance), e.g., Titus 1:2; 1 Pet. 1:21; (b) the ground upon which "hope" is based, Acts 16:19; Col. 1:27, "Christ in you the hope of glory"; (c) the object upon which the "hope" is fixed, e.g., 1 Tim. 1:1. Various phrases are used with the word "hope," in Paul's epistles and speeches: (1) Acts 23:6, "the hope and resurrection of the dead"; this has been regarded as a hendiadys (one by means of two), i.e., the "hope" of the resurrection; but the *kai*, "and," is epexegetic, defining the "hope," namely, the resurrection; (2) Acts 26:6, 7, "the hope of the promise (i.e., the fulfillment of the promise) made unto the fathers"; (3) Gal. 5:5, "the hope of righteousness"; i.e., the believer's complete conformity to God's will, at the coming of Christ; (4) Col. 1:23, "the hope of the gospel," i.e., the "hope" of the fulfillment of all the promises presented in the gospel; cf. 1:5; (5) Rom. 5:2, "(the) hope of the glory of God," i.e., as in Titus 2:13, "the blessed hope and appearing of the glory of our great God and Savior Jesus Christ"; cf. Col. 1:27; (6) 1 Thess. 5:8, "the hope of salvation," i.e., of the rapture of believers, to take place at the opening of the Parousia of Christ; (7) Eph. 1:18, "the hope of His (God's) calling," i.e., the prospect before those who respond to His call in the gospel; (8) Eph. 4:4, "the hope of your calling," the same as (7), but regarded from the point of view of the called; (9) Titus 1:2, and 3:7, "the hope of eternal life," i.e., the full manifestation and realization of that life which is already the believer's possession; (10) Acts 28:20, "the hope of Israel," i.e., the expectation of the coming of the Messiah. In Eph. 1:18; 2:12 and 4:4, the "hope" is objective. The objective and subjective use of the word need to be distinguished, in Rom. 15:4, e.g., the use is subjective. In the NT three adjectives are descriptive of "hope": "good," 2 Thess. 2:16; "blessed," Titus 2:13; "living," 1 Pet. 1:3. To these may be added **Heb. 7:19**, "a better hope," i.e., additional to the commandment, which became disannulled (v. **18**), a hope centered in a new priesthood. In Rom. 15:13 God is spoken of as "the God of hope," i.e., He is the author, not the subject, of it. "Hope" is a factor in salvation, Rom. 8:24; it finds its expression in endurance under trial, which is the effect of waiting for the coming of Christ, 1 Thess. 1:3; it is "an anchor of the soul," staying it amidst the storms of this life, **Heb. 6:18, 19**; it is a purifying power, "every one that hath this hope set on Him (Christ) purifieth himself, even as He is pure," 1 John 3:3, RV (the apostle John's one mention of "hope"). The phrase "fullness of hope," **Heb. 6:11**, RV, expresses the completeness of its activity in the soul; cf. "fullness of faith," **10:22**, and "of understanding," Col. 2:2 (RV, marg.).

End *see* ***Hebrews 3:6.***

6:12 That ye be not slothful, but followers of them who through faith and patience inherit the promises.

Slothful *nothros* (3576), "indolent, sluggish," is rendered "slothful" in **Heb. 6:12**, KJV. *See also* **Dull** at ***Hebrews 5:11.***

Followers *mimetes* (3402), "an imitator," so the RV for KJV, "follower," is always used in a good sense in the NT. In 1 Cor. 4:16; 11:1; Eph. 5:1; **Heb. 6:12**, it is used in exhortations, accompanied by the verb *ginomai*, "to be, become," and in the continuous tense except in **Heb. 6:12**, where the aorist or momentary tense indicates a decisive act with permanent results; in 1 Thess. 1:6; 2:14, the accompanying verb is in the aorist tense, referring to the definite act of conversion in the past. These instances, coupled with the continuous tenses referred to, teach that what we became at conversion we must diligently continue to be thereafter.

Patience *makrothumia* (3115), "forbearance, patience, longsuffering" (*makros*, "long," *thumos*, "temper"), is usually rendered "longsuffering," Rom. 2:4; 9:22; 2 Cor. 6:6; Gal. 5:22;

Eph. 4:2; Col. 1:11; 3:12; 1 Tim. 1:16; 2 Tim. 3:10; 4:2; 1 Pet. 3:20; 2 Pet. 3:15; "patience" in **Heb. 6:12** and Jas. 5:10.

Inherit *see* Inheritance at *Hebrews 1:4*.

Promise *see Hebrews 4:1*.

6:13 For when God made promise to Abraham, because he could swear by no greater, he sware by himself,

Promise *epangello* (1861), "to announce, proclaim," has in the NT the two meanings "to profess" and "to promise," each used in the middle voice; "to promise" (a) of "promises" of God, Acts 7:5; Rom. 4:21; in Gal. 3:19, passive voice; Titus 1:2; **Heb. 6:13**; **10:23**; **11:11**; **12:26**; Jas. 1:12; 2:5; 1 John 2:25; (b) made by men, Mark 14:11; 2 Pet. 2:19.

Could *echo* (2192), "to have," is translated "could" in Mark 14:8, lit., "she hath done what she had", in Luke 14:14, for the KJV, "cannot," the RV has "they have not wherewith"; in Acts 4:14, "could say nothing against" is, lit., "had nothing to say against"; in **Heb. 6:13**, "he could swear" is, lit., "He had (by none greater) to swear."

Sware *see Hebrews 3:11*.

6:14 Saying, Surely blessing I will bless thee, and multiplying I will multiply thee.

Surely *men* (3303), a conjunctive particle (in **Heb. 6:14**, "surely" represents the phrase *ei men* [so the best texts; some have *e men*].) Usually related to an adversative conjunction or particle, like *de*, in the following clause, which is placed in opposition to it. Frequently it is untranslatable; sometimes it is rendered "indeed," e.g., Matt. 3:11; 13:32; 17:11, RV (KJV, "truly"); 20:23; 26:41; (some mss. have it in Mark 1:8); Mark 9:12, RV (KJV, "verily").

Multiplying, Multiply *plethuno* (4129), used (a) transitively, denotes "to cause to increase, to multiply," 2 Cor. 9:10; **Heb. 6:14** (twice); in the passive voice, "to be multiplied," Matt. 24:12, RV, "(iniquity) shall be multiplied" (KJV, "shall abound"); Acts 6:7; 7:17; 9:31; 12:24; 1 Pet. 1:2; 2 Pet. 1:2; Jude 2; (b) intransitively it denotes "to be multiplying," Acts 6:1, RV, "was multiplying" (KJV, "was multiplied").

6:15 And so, after he had patiently endured, he obtained the promise.

Patiently *makrothumeo* (3114), is translated "to have patience," or "to be patient," in Matt. 18:26, 29; 1 Thess. 5:14, KJV (RV, "be longsuffering"); Jas. 5:7 (1st part, "be patient"; 2nd part, RV, "being patient," KJV, "hath long patience"); in **Heb. 6:15**, RV, "having (KJV, after he had) patiently endured."

Obtained *epitunchano* (2013), primarily, "to light upon," denotes "to obtain," Rom. 11:7 (twice); **Heb. 6:15**; **11:33**; Jas. 4:2.

6:16 For men verily swear by the greater: and an oath for confirmation *is* to them an end of all strife.

Swear *see* Sware at *Hebrews 3:11*.

Oath *horkos* (3727), is primarily equivalent to *herkos*, "a fence, an enclosure, that which restrains a person"; hence, "an oath." The Lord's command in Matt. 5:33 was a condemnation of the minute and arbitrary restrictions imposed by the scribes and Pharisees in the matter of adjurations, by which God's Name was profaned. The injunction is repeated in Jas. 5:12. The language of the apostle Paul, e.g., in Gal. 1:20 and 1 Thess. 5:27 was not inconsistent with Christ's prohibition, read in the light of its context. Contrast the "oaths" mentioned in Matt. 14:7, 9; 26:72; Mark 6:26. **Heb. 6:16** refers to the confirmation of a compact among men, guaranteeing the discharge of liabilities; in their disputes "the oath is final for confirmation." This is referred to in order to illustrate the greater subject of God's "oath" to Abraham, confirming His promise; cf. Luke 1:73; Acts 2:30.

Confirmation *bebaiosis* (951), is used in two senses (a) "of firmness, establishment," said of the "confirmation" of the gospel, Phil. 1:7; (b) "of authoritative validity imparted," said of the settlement of a dispute by an oath to produce confidence, **Heb. 6:16**. The word is found frequently in the papyri of the settlement of a business transaction.

End *peras* (4009), "a limit, boundary" (from *pera*, "beyond"), is used (a) of space, chiefly in the plural, Matt. 12:42, RV, "ends," for KJV, "uttermost parts"; so Luke 11:31 (KJV, "utmost"); Rom. 10:18 (KJV and RV, "ends"); (b) of the termination of something occurring in a period, **Heb. 6:16**, RV, "final," for KJV, "an end," said of strife.

Strife *antilogia* (485), *antilogia* (485), denotes "a gainsaying, contradiction" (*anti*, "against," *lego*, "to speak"), **Heb. 6:16** (KJV, "strife," RV, "dispute,"); **7:7**, "a gainsaying" (RV, "dispute"; KJV, "contradiction"); **12:3** (RV, "gainsaying"; KJV, "contradiction"), Jude 11 ("gainsaying").

6:17 Wherein God, willing more abundantly to shew unto the heirs of promise the immutability of his counsel, confirmed *it* by an oath:

Willing *boulomai* (1014), "to wish, will, desire, purpose" (akin to *boule*, "counsel, purpose"), is translated "was minded" in Matt. 1:19; Acts 15:37, RV (KJV, "determined"); 18:27, RV (KJV, "was disposed"); 19:30, RV (KJV, "would have"); 5:33, RV, "were minded" (KJV, "took counsel"); 18:15, RV, "I am (not) minded (to be)," KJV, "I will (be no)"; **Heb. 6:17**, "being minded," RV (KJV, "willing"), said of God.

Shew *epideiknumi* (1925), signifies (a) "to exhibit, display," Matt. 16:1; 22:19; 24:1; Luke 17:14 (in some mss. 24:40); in the middle voice, "to display," with a special interest in one's own action, Acts 9:39; (b) "to point out, prove, demonstrate," Acts 18:28; **Heb. 6:17**.

Heirs *see* **Heir** at ***Hebrews 1:2***.

Immutability *ametathetos* (276), an adjective signifying "immutable" (*a*, negative, *metatithemi*, "to change"), **Heb. 6:18**, where the "two immutable things" are the promise and the oath. In v. **17** the word is used in the neuter with the article, as a noun, denoting "the immutability," with reference to God's counsel. Examples from the papyri show that the word was used as a technical term in connection with wills, "The connotation adds considerably to the force of **Heb. 6:17** (and foll.)" (Moulton and Milligan).

Counsel *boule* (1012), from a root meaning "a will," hence "a counsel, a piece of advice," is to be distinguished from *gnome; boule* is the result of determination, *gnome* is the result of knowledge. *Boule* is everywhere rendered by "counsel" in the RV except in Acts 27:12, "advised," lit., "gave counsel." In Acts 13:36 the KJV wrongly has "by the will of God fell on sleep"; the RV, "after he had served the counsel of God, fell on sleep." The word is used of the counsel of God, in Luke 7:30; Acts 2:23; 4:28; 13:36; 20:27; Eph. 1:11; **Heb. 6:17**; in other passages, of the counsel of men, Luke 23:51; Acts 27:12, 42; 1 Cor. 4:5.

Confirmed *mesiteuo* (3315), "to act as a mediator, to interpose," is rendered "confirmed," in the KJV of **Heb. 6:17** (marg., and RV, "interposed").

6:18 That by two immutable things, in which *it was* impossible for God to lie, we might have a strong consolation, who have fled for refuge to lay hold upon the hope set before us:

Immutable *see* **Immutability** at ***Hebrews 6:17***.

Things *pragma* (4229), is translated thing in Matt. 18:19, as part of the word "anything," lit., "every thing"; Luke 1:1, KJV only; Acts 5:4; in **Heb. 6:18**; **10:1**, and **11:1**, "things."

Impossible *see* ***Hebrews 6:4***.

God *see* ***Hebrews 1:8***.

Lie *pseudo* (5574), "to deceive by lies" (always in the middle voice in the NT), is used (a) absolutely, in Matt. 5:11, "falsely," lit., "lying" (v, marg.); Rom. 9:1; 2 Cor. 11:31; Gal. 1:20; Col. 3:9 (where the verb is followed by the preposition *eis*, "to"); 1 Tim. 2:7; **Heb. 6:18**; Jas. 3:14 (where it is followed by the preposition *kata*, "against"); 1 John 1:6; Rev. 3:9; (b) transitively, with a direct object (without a preposition following), Acts 5:3 (with the accusative case) "to lie to (the Holy Ghost)," RV marg., "deceive"; v. 4 (with the dative case) "thou hast (not) lied (unto men, but unto God)."

Strong *ischuros* denotes "strong, mighty"; in an active sense, "mighty," in having inherent and moral power, e.g., Matt. 12:29; 1 Cor. 4:10; **Heb. 6:18**. *See also* ***Hebrews 5:7***.

Consolation *paraklesis* (3874), is translated "consolation," in both KJV and RV, in Luke 2:25; 6:24; Acts 15:31; in 1 Cor. 14:3, KJV, "exhortation," RV, "comfort"; in the following the KJV has "consolation," the RV, "comfort," Rom. 15:5; 2 Cor. 1:6-7; 7:7; Phil. 2:1; 2 Thess. 2:16; Philem. 7; in Acts 4:36, RV, "exhortation"; in **Heb. 6:18**, RV, "encouragement."

Fled *katapheugo* (2703), "to flee for refuge," is used (a) literally in Acts 14:6; (b) metaphorically in **Heb. 6:18**, of "fleeing" for refuge to lay hold upon hope.

Hold *see* ***Hebrews 4:14***.

Hope *see* ***Hebrews 6:11***.

Set before *prokeimai* (4295), signifies (a) "to be set before," and is so rendered in **Heb. 6:18** of the hope of the believer; **12:1**, of the Christian race; v. **2**, of the joy "set" before Christ in the days of His flesh and at His death; (b) "to be set forth," said of Sodom and Gomorrah, in Jude 7. It is used elsewhere in 2 Cor. 8:12, "to lie beforehand."

6:19 Which *hope* we have as an anchor of the soul, both sure and stedfast, and which entereth into that within the veil;

Hope *see* ***Hebrews 6:11***.

Anchor *ankura* (45), (Eng., "anchor"), was so called because of its curved form (*ankos*, "a curve"), Acts 27:29-30, 40; **Heb. 6:19**. In Acts 27:13 the verb *airo*, "to lift," signifies "to lift anchor" (the noun being understood), RV, "they weighed anchor" (KJV, "loosing thence").

Soul *see* ***Hebrews 4:12***.

Sure *asphales* (804), safe, is translated "certainty," Acts 21:34; 22:30; "certain," Acts 25:26; "safe," Phil. 3:1; "sure," **Heb. 6:19**.

Stedfast *see Hebrews 2:2.*

Within *esoteros* (2082), denotes "inner," Acts 16:24 (of a prison); **Heb. 6:19**, with the article, and practically as a noun, "that which is within (the veil)," lit., "the inner (of the veil)." Cf. Eng., esoteric.

Veil *katapetasma* (2665), lit., "that which is spread out" (*petannumi*) "before" (*kata*), hence, "a veil," is used (a) of the inner "veil" of the tabernacle, **Heb. 6:19**; **9:3**; (b) of the corresponding "veil" in the Temple, Matt. 27:51; Mark 15:38; Luke 23:45; (c) metaphorically of the "flesh" of Christ, **Heb. 10:20**, i.e., His body which He gave up to be crucified, thus by His expiatory death providing a means of the spiritual access of believers, the "new and living way," into the presence of God. *See also* **High priest** at *Hebrews 2:17.*

6:20 Whither the forerunner is for us entered, *even* Jesus, made an high priest for ever after the order of Melchisedec.

Forerunner *prodromos* (4274), an adjective signifying "running forward, going in advance," is used as a noun, of "those who were sent before to take observations," acting as scouts, especially in military matters; or of "one sent before a king" to see that the way was prepared, Isa. 40:3; (cf. Luke 9:52; and, of John the Baptist, Matt. 11:10, etc.). In the NT it is said of Christ in **Heb. 6:20**, as going in advance of His followers who are to be where He is, when He comes to receive them to Himself. In the Sept., Num. 13:21, "forerunners (of the grape)"; Isa. 28:4, "an early (fig)."

Jesus *see Hebrews 2:9.*

High priest *see Hebrews 2:17.*

Order *see Hebrews 5:6.*

Chapter 7

7:1 For this Melchisedec, king of Salem, priest of the most high God, who met Abraham returning from the slaughter of the kings, and blessed him;

King *basileus* (935), "a king" (cf. Eng., "Basil"), e.g., Matt. 1:6, is used of the Roman emperor in 1 Pet. 2:13, 17 (a command of general application); this reference to the emperor is illustrated frequently in the *Koine*; of Herod the Tetrarch (used by courtesy), Matt. 14:9; of Christ, as the "King" of the Jews, e.g., Matt, 2:2; 27:11, 29, 37; as the "King" of Israel, Mark 15:32; John 1:49; 12:13; as "King of kings," Rev. 17:14; 19:16; as "the King" in judging nations and men at the establishment of the millennial kingdom, Matt. 25:34, 40; of God, "the great King," Matt. 5:35; "the King eternal, incorruptible, invisible," 1 Tim. 1:17; "King of kings," 1 Tim. 6:15; "King of the ages," Rev. 15:3, RV (KJV, "saints"). Christ's "kingship" was predicted in the OT, e.g., Ps. 2:6, and in the NT, e.g., Luke 1:32, 33; He came as such, e.g., Matt. 2:2; John 18:37; was rejected and died as such, Luke 19:14; Matt. 27:37; is now a "King" Priest, after the order of Melchizedek, **Heb. 5:6**; **7:1**, **17**; and will reign for ever and ever, Rev. 11:15.

Priest *see Hebrews 5:6.*

Most high *hupsistos* (5310), "most high," is a superlative degree, the positive not being in use; it is used of God in Luke 1:32, 35, 76; 6:35, in each of which the RV has "the most High," for KJV, "the highest", KJV and RV in Mark 5:7; Luke 8:28; Acts 7:48; 16:17; **Heb. 7:1**.

Met *sunantao* (4876), "to meet with," lit., "to meet together with," is used in Luke 9:37 (in v. 18, in some mss.); 22:10; Acts 10:25; **Heb. 7:1**, **10**; metaphorically in Acts 20:22 ("shall befall").

Returning *hupostrepho* (5290), "to turn behind," or "back" (*hupo*, "under"), is translated "to return" (in some texts in Mark 14:40) in Luke 1:56; 2:20, 43; v. 45, RV (KJV, "turned back again"), 4:1, 14; 7:10; 8:37; 10:17; 11:24, KJV (RV, "I will turn back"); 17:18; 19:12; 23:48, 56; Acts 1:12; 12:25; 13:13; 13:34; 20:3; 21:6; 22:17, RV (KJV, "was come again"); 23:32; Gal. 1:17; **Heb. 7:1**.

Slaughter *kope* (2871), "a stroke" (akin to *kopto*, "to strike, to cut"), signifies "a smiting in battle," in **Heb. 7:1**. In the Sept., Gen. 14:17; Deut. 28:25; Josh. 10:20.

7:2 To whom also Abraham gave a tenth part of all; first being by interpretation King of righteousness, and after that also King of Salem, which is, King of peace;

Gave For *merizo*, "to divide into parts," rendered "gave a part" (RV, "divided") in **Heb. 7:2**.

Tenth *dekate* (1181), grammatically the feminine form of *dekatos*, with *meris*, "a part," understood, is used as a noun, translated "a tenth part" in **Heb. 7:2**, "a tenth," v. **4**; "tithes" in vv. **8**, **9**.

Part *merizo* (3307), "to divide, to distribute" is translated "divided (KJV, gave) a ... part" in **Heb. 7:2**, RV.

First *proton* (4412), the neuter of the adjective *protos* (the superlative degree of *pro*, "before"), signifies "first, or at the first," (a) in order of time, e.g., Luke 10:5; John 18:13; 1 Cor. 15:46; 1 Thess. 4:16; 1 Tim. 3:10; (b) in enumerating various particulars, e.g., Rom. 3:2; 1 Cor. 11:18; 12:28; **Heb. 7:2**; Jas. 3:17. It is translated "before" in John 15:18.

Interpretation *hermeneuo* (2059), (cf. *Hermes*, the Greek name of the pagan god Mercury, who was regarded as the messenger of the gods), denotes "to explain, interpret" (Eng., "hermeneutics"), and is used of explaining the meaning of words in a different language, John 1:38 (in some mss.); 9:7 ("Siloam," interpreted as "sent"); **Heb. 7:2** (Melchizedec, "by interpretation," lit., "being interpreted," King of righteousness).

After that *epeita* (1899), "thereupon, thereafter," then (in some texts, Mark 7:5; *kai*, "and," in the best); Luke 16:7; John 11:7; 1 Cor. 12:28, RV, "then" (KJV, "after that"); 15:6 and 7 (ditto); v. 23, RV, KJV, "afterward"; v. 46 (ditto); Gal. 1:18; v. 21, RV (KJV, "afterwards"), 2:1; 1 Thess. 4:17; **Heb. 7:2**, RV (KJV, "after that"); v. **27**; Jas. 3:17; 4:14.

7:3 Without father, without mother, without descent, having neither beginning of days, nor end of life; but made like unto the Son of God; abideth a priest continually.

Father *apator* (540), "without father" (*a*, negative, and *pater*), signifies, in **Heb. 7:3**, with no recorded genealogy.

Mother *ametor* (282), "without a mother," is used in **Heb. 7:3**, of the Genesis record of Melchizedek, certain details concerning him being purposely omitted, in order to conform the description to facts about Christ as the Son of God. The word has been found in this sense in the writings of Euripides the dramatist and Herodotus the historian.

Descent *agenealogetos* (35), denoting "without recorded pedigree," is rendered "without genealogy" in **Heb. 7:3**. The narrative in Gen. 14 is so framed in facts and omissions as to foreshadow the person of Christ.

Like unto *aphomoioo* (871), "to make like," is used in **Heb. 7:3**, of Melchizedek as "made like" the Son of God, i.e., in the facts related and withheld in the Genesis record.

Priest *see Hebrews 5:6.*

Continually The adjective *dienekes*, "unbroken, continuous," is used in a phrase with *eis*, "unto," and the article, signifying "perpetually, for ever," **Heb. 7:3; 10:1, 12, 14**.

7:4 Now consider how great this man *was*, unto whom even the patriarch Abraham gave the tenth of the spoils.

Consider *theoreo* (2334), from *theoros*, "a spectator," is used of one who looks at a thing with interest and for a purpose, usually indicating the careful observation of details; see, e.g., Mark 15:47; Luke 10:18; 23:35; John 20:6 (RV, "beholdeth," for KJV, "seeth"); so in verses 12 and 14; "consider," in **Heb. 7:4**. It is used of experience, in the sense of partaking of, in John 8:51; 17:24. Cf. *theoria*, "sight," Luke 23:48, only.

Great *pelikos* (4080), primarily a direct interrogative, "how large? how great?" is used in exclamations, indicating magnitude, in Gal. 6:11, of letter characters; in **Heb. 7:4**, metaphorically, of the distinguished character of Melchizedek.

Patriarch *patriarches* (3966), from *patria*, "a family," and *archo*, "to rule," is found in Acts 2:29; 7:8, 9; **Heb. 7:4**. In the Sept., 1 Chron. 24:31; 27:22; 2 Chron. 19:8; 23:20; 26:12.

Tenth *see Hebrews 7:2.*

Spoils *akrothinion* (205), primarily "the top of a heap" (*akros*, "highest, top," and *this*, "a heap"), hence "first-fruit offerings," and in war "the choicest spoils," **Heb. 7:4**.

7:5 And verily they that are of the sons of Levi, who receive the office of the priesthood, have a commandment to take tithes of the people according to the law, that is, of their brethren, though they come out of the loins of Abraham:

Verily *see Hebrews 3:5.*

Office *hieroteia* (2405), or *hieratia*, denotes "a priests's office," Luke 1:9; **Heb. 7:5**, RV, "priest's office" (KJV "office of the priesthood").

Priesthood *hierateia* (2405), "a priesthood," denotes the priest's office, Luke 1:9; **Heb. 7:5**, RV, "priest's office."

Tithes *apodekatoo* (586), denotes (a) "to tithe" (*apo*, "from," *dekatos*, "tenth"), Matt. 23:23 (KJV, "pay tithe of"); Luke 11:42; in Luke 18:12 (where the best texts have the alternative form *apodekateuo*), "I give tithes"; (b) "to exact tithes" from **Heb. 7:5**.

Brethren *adelphos* (80), denotes "a brother, or near kinsman"; in the plural, "a community based on identity of origin or life." It is used of male descendants of the same parents, Acts 7:23, 26; **Heb. 7:5**.

Loins *osphus* (3751), is used (a) in the natural sense in Matt. 3:4; Mark 1:6; (b) as "the seat of generative power," **Heb. 7:5, 10**; metaphorically in Acts 2:30; (c) metaphorically, (1) of girding the "loins" in readiness for active service for the Lord, Luke 12:35; (2) the same, with truth, Eph. 6:14, i.e., bracing up oneself so as to maintain perfect sincerity and reality as the counteractive in Christian character against hypocrisy and falsehood; (3) of girding the "loins" of the mind, 1 Pet. 1:13, RV, "girding," suggestive of the alertness necessary for sobriety and for setting one's hope perfectly on "the grace to be brought ... at the revelation of Jesus Christ" (the present participle, "girding," is introductory to the rest of the verse).

7:6 But he whose descent is not counted from them received tithes of Abraham, and blessed him that had the promises.

Descent *genealogeo* (1075), "to reckon or trace a genealogy" (from *genea*, "a race," and *lego*, "to choose, pick out"), is used, in the passive voice, of Melchizedek in **Heb. 7:6**, RV, "whose genealogy (KJV, 'descent') is not counted." *See also* ***Hebrews 7:3.***

Received For "received (RV, 'hath taken') tithes," **Heb. 7:6**.

Tithes *dekatoo* (1183), from *dekatos*, "tenth", in the active voice denotes "to take tithes of," **Heb. 7:6**, RV, "hath taken (KJV, received) tithes"; in the passive, "to pay tithes," **7:9**, RV, "hath paid (KJV, 'payed') tithes." In the Sept., Neh. 10:37.

Promises *see* **Promise** at ***Hebrews 4:1.***

7:7 And without all contradiction the less is blessed of the better.

Without *see* ***Hebrews 4:15.***

Contradiction *antilogia* (485), is translated "contradiction" in the KJV of **Heb. 7:7**; **12:3**, "dispute," and "gainsaying." *See also* **Strife** at ***Hebrews 6:16.***

Less *elasson* (1640), serves as a comparative degree of *mikros*, "little", and denotes "less" in (a) quality, as of wine, John 2:10, "worse;" (b) age, Rom. 9:12, "younger"; 1 Tim. 5:9, "under" (neuter, adverbially); (c) rank, **Heb. 7:7**.

Better *see* ***Hebrews 1:4.***

7:8 And here men that die receive tithes; but there he *receiveth them*, of whom it is witnessed that he liveth.

Tithes *see* **Tenth** at ***Hebrews 7:2.***

Witnessed *martureo* (3140), denotes (I) "to be a *martus*," or "to bear witness to," sometimes rendered "to testify"; it is used of the witness (a) of God the Father to Christ, John 5:32, 37; 8:18 (2nd part); 1 John 5:9, 10; to others, Acts 13:22; 15:8; **Heb. 11:2, 4** (twice), 5, 39; (b) of Christ, John 3:11, 32; 4:44; 5:31; 7:7; 8:13, 14, 18 (1st part); 13:21; 18:37; Acts 14:3; 1 Tim. 6:13; Rev. 22:18, 20; of the Holy Spirit, to Christ, John 15:26; **Heb. 10:15**; 1 John 5:7, 8, RV, which rightly omits the latter part of v. 7 (it was a marginal gloss which crept into the original text); it finds no support in Scripture; (c) of the Scriptures, to Christ, John 5:39; **Heb. 7:8, 17**; (d) of the works of Christ, to Himself, and of the circumstances connected with His death, John 5:36; 10:25; 1 John 5:8; (e) of prophets and apostles, to the righteousness of God, Rom. 3:21; to Christ, John 1:7, 8, 15, 32, 34; 3:26; 5:33, RV; 15:27; 19:35; 21:24; Acts 10:43; 23:11; 1 Cor. 15:15; 1 John 1:2; 4:14; Rev. 1:2; to doctrine, Acts 26:22 (in some texts, so KJV); to the Word of God, Rev. 1:2; (f) of others, concerning Christ, Luke 4:22; John 4:39; 12:17; (g) of believers to one another, John 3:28; 2 Cor. 8:3; Gal. 4:15; Col. 4:13; 1 Thess. 2:11; 3 John 3, 6, 12 (2nd part); (h) of the apostle Paul concerning Israel, Rom. 10:2; (i) of an angel, to the churches, Rev. 22:16; (j) of unbelievers, concerning themselves, Matt. 23:31; concerning Christ, John 18:23; concerning others, John 2:25; Acts 22:5; 26:5; (II) "to give a good report, to approve of," Acts 6:3; 10:22; 16:2; 22:12; 1 Tim. 5:10; 3 John 12 (1st part); some would put Luke 4:22 here.

Liveth *see* **Lifetime** at ***Hebrews 2:15.***

7:9 And as I may so say, Levi also, who receiveth tithes, payed tithes in Abraham.

May In **Heb. 7:9** the phrase *hos* ("so") *epos* ("a word") *eipein* ("to say"), i.e., lit., "so to say a word" is an idiom, translated in the RV, "so to say" (KJV, "if I may so say"); the Eng. equivalent is "one might almost say."

So In **Heb. 7:9** *epos*, "a word," is used in a phrase rendered "so to say."

Tithes *see* ***Hebrews 7:6.*** *See also* **Tenth** at ***Hebrews 7:2.***

Payed In **Heb. 7:9**, *dekatoo* (passive voice), "to pay tithe," is translated "hath paid tithes," RV (perfect tense).

7:10 For he was yet in the loins of his father, when Melchisedec met him.

Loins *see* ***Hebrews 7:5.***

Met *see* ***Hebrews 7:1.***

7:11 If therefore perfection were by the Levitical priesthood, (for under it the people received the law,) what further need *was there* that another priest should rise after the order of Melchisedec, and not be called after the order of Aaron?

Perfection *teleiosis* (5050), denotes "a fulfillment, completion, perfection, an end accomplished as the effect of a process," **Heb. 7:11**; in Luke 1:45, RV, "fulfillment" (KJV, "performance").

Priesthood *hierosune* (2420), "a priesthood," signifies the office, quality, rank and ministry of "a priest," **Heb. 7:11, 12, 24**, where the contrasts between the Levitical "priesthood" and that of Christ are set forth. In the Sept., 1 Chron. 29:22.

Under The preposition *epi*, "upon," is rendered "under" in **Heb. 7:11; 9:15; 10:28**, KJV (RV, "*on the word of*").

Received the law *nomotheteo* (3549), (a) used intransitively, signifies "to make laws"; in the passive voice, "to be furnished with laws," **Heb. 7:11**, "received the law," lit., "was furnished with (the) law"; (b) used transitively, it signifies "to ordain by law, to enact"; in the passive voice, **Heb. 8:6**.

Further *eti* (2089), "yet, still, further," is used (a) of time, most usually translated "yet," e.g., Matt. 12:46; or negatively, "any more," "no more," e.g., **Heb. 8:12**; (b) of degree, translated "further," or "any further," Matt. 26:65; Mark 5:35; 14:63; Luke 22:71; **Heb. 7:11** in Acts 21:28, RV, "moreover" (KJV, "further").

Priest *see Hebrews 5:6*.

Rise *anistemi* (450), "to stand up or to make to stand up," according as its use is intransitive or transitive (*ana*, "up," *histemi*, "to stand"), is used (a) of a physical change of position, e.g., of "rising" from sleep, Mark 1:35; from a meeting in a synagogue, Luke 4:29; of the illegal "rising" of the high priest in the tribunal in Matt. 26:62; of an invalid "rising" from his couch, Luke 5:25; the "rising" up of a disciple from his vocation to follow Christ, Luke 5:28; cf. John 11:31; "rising" up from prayer, Luke 22:45; of a whole company, Acts 26:30; 1 Cor. 10:7; (b) metaphorically, of "rising" up antagonistically against persons, e.g. of officials against people, Acts 5:17; of a seditious leader, 5:36, of the "rising" up of Satan, Mark 3:26; of false teachers, Acts 20:30; (c) of "rising" to a position of preeminence or power; e.g., of Christ as a prophet, Acts 3:22; 7:37; as God's servant in the midst of the nation of Israel, Acts 3:26; as the Son of God in the midst of the nation, 13:33 (not here of resurrection, but with reference to the Incarnation: the KJV "again" has nothing corresponding to it in the original, it was added as a misinterpretation: the mention of His resurrection is in the next verse, in which it is stressed by way of contrast and by the addition, "from the dead"); as a priest, **Heb. 7:11, 15**; as king over the nations, Rom. 15:12; (d) of a spiritual awakening from lethargy, Eph. 5:14; (e) of resurrection from the dead: (1) of the resurrection of Christ, Matt. 17:9; 20:19; Mark 8:31; 9:9-10, 31; 10:34; Luke 18:33; 24:7, 46; John 20:9; Acts 2:24, 32; 10:41; 13:34; 17:3, 31; 1 Thess. 4:14; (2) of believers, John 6:39-40, 44, 54; 11:24; 1 Thess. 4:16; of unbelievers, Matt. 12:41.

Order *see Hebrews 5:6*.

Called *lego* (3004), "to say, speak," also has the meaning "to gather, reckon, account," used in this sense in **Heb. 7:11**, RV, "be reckoned" (KJV, "be called").

7:12 For the priesthood being changed, there is made of necessity a change also of the law.

Priesthood *see Hebrews 7:11*.

Changed, Change *metathesis* (3331), "a transposition, or a transference from one place to another" (from *meta*, implying "change," and *tithemi* "to put"), has the meaning of "change" in **Heb. 7:12**, in connection with the necessity of a "change" of the Law (or, as margin, law), if the priesthood is changed. It is rendered "translation" in **11:5**, "removing" in **12:27**.

Made *see Hebrews 3:14*.

Necessity *ananke* (318), signifies (a) "a necessity," what must needs be, translated "necessity" (in some mss. in Luke 23:17) in 1 Cor. 7:37; 9:16; 2 Cor. 9:7 (with *ek* "out of"); Philem. 14 (with *kata*, "according to"); **Heb. 7:12**; **9:16**; (b) "distress, pain," translated "necessities" in 2 Cor. 6:4; 12:10.

7:13 For he of whom these things are spoken pertaineth to another tribe, of which no man gave attendance at the altar.

Pertaineth to *metecho* (3348), **Heb. 7:13**, KJV. *See also* **Took part** at *Hebrews 2:14*; **Belongeth** at *Hebrews 5:14*.

Tribe *phule* (5443), "a company of people united by kinship or habitation, a clan, tribe," is used (a) of the peoples of the earth, Matt. 24:30; in the following the RV has "tribe(-s)" for KJV, "kindred(-s)," Rev. 1:7; 5:9; 7:9; 11:9; 13:7; 14:6; (b) of the "tribes" of Israel, Matt. 19:28; Luke 2:36; 22:30; Acts 13:21; Rom. 11:1; Phil. 3:5; **Heb. 7:13, 14**; Jas. 1:1; Rev. 5:5; 7:4-8; 21:12.

Attendance *prosecho* (4337), "to take heed, give heed," is said of the priests who "gave attendance at the altar," **Heb. 7:13**. It suggests devotion of thought and effort to a thing. In 1 Tim. 4:13 (in the exhortation regarding the public reading of the Scriptures), the RV translates it "give heed," for the KJV, "give attendance." In Acts 16:14, "to give heed" (for KJV, "attended").

Altar *naos* (3485), "a shrine or sanctuary," was used (a) among the heathen, to denote the shrine containing the idol, Acts 17:24; 19:24 (in the latter, miniatures); (b) among the Jews, the sanctuary in the "Temple," into which only the priests could lawfully enter, e.g., Luke 1:9, 21, 22; Christ, as being of the tribe of Judah, and thus not being a priest while upon the earth (**Heb. 7:13, 14; 8:4**), did not enter the *naos*; (c) by Christ metaphorically, of His own physical body, John 2:19, 21; (d) in apostolic teaching, metaphorically, (1) of the church, the mystical body of Christ, Eph. 2:21; (2) of a local church, 1 Cor. 3:16, 17; 2 Cor. 6:16; (3) of the present body of the individual believer, 1 Cor. 6:19; (4) of the "Temple" seen in visions in Revelation, 3:12; 7:15; 11:19; 14:15, 17; 15:5, 6, 8; 16:1, 17; (5) of the Lord God Almighty and the Lamb, as the "Temple" of the new and heavenly Jerusalem, Rev. 21:22.

7:14 For *it is* evident that our Lord sprang out of Juda; of which tribe Moses spake nothing concerning priesthood.

Evident *prodelos* (4271), "manifest beforehand," is used in **Heb. 7:14** in the sense of "clearly evident." So in 1 Tim. 5:24-25, RV, "evident," for KJV, "open beforehand," and "manifest beforehand." The *pro* is somewhat intensive.

Sprang *anatello* (393), "to arise," is used especially of things in the natural creation, e.g., "the rising" of the sun, moon and stars; metaphorically, of light, in Matt. 4:16, "did spring up"; of the sun, Matt. 5:45; 13:6 (RV); Mark 4:6; Jas. 1:11; in Mark 16:2 the RV has "when the sun was risen," keeping to the verb form, for the KJV, "at the rising of"; of a cloud, Luke 12:54; of the day-star, 2 Pet. 1:19; in **Heb. 7:14** metaphorically, of the Incarnation of Christ: "Our Lord hath sprung out of Judah," more lit., "Our Lord hath arisen out of Judah," as of the rising of the light of the sun.

Tribe *see* ***Hebrews 7:13.***

7:15 And it is yet far more evident: for that after the similitude of Melchisedec there ariseth another priest,

Far In **Heb. 7:15** the KJV "far more" translates *perissoteron*, RV, "more abundantly".

More *perissoteron* (4054), the neuter of the comparative degree of *perissos*, "more abundant," is used as an adverb, "more," e.g., Luke 12:4; 2 Cor. 10:8, KJV (RV, "abundantly"); **Heb. 7:15**, RV, "more abundantly" (KJV, "far more").

Evident *katadelos* (2612), a strengthened form of *delos*, "quite manifest, evident," is used in **Heb. 7:15** (KJV, "more evident"). See also ***Hebrews 7:14.***

Similitude *homoiotes* (3665), is translated "likeness" in **Heb. 7:15**, RV (KJV, "similitude").

Ariseth *see* **Rise** at ***Hebrews 7:11.***

Priest *see* ***Hebrews 5:6.***

7:16 Who is made, not after the law of a carnal commandment, but after the power of an endless life.

Made *see* ***Hebrews 3:14.***

Law *nomos* (3551) In the NT it is used ... of the Mosaic Law, the "law" of Sinai, (1) with the definite article, e.g., Matt. 5:18; John 1:17; Rom. 2:15, 18, 20, 26, 27; 3:19; 4:15; 7:4, 7, 14, 16, 22; 8:3, 4, 7; Gal. 3:10, 12, 19, 21, 24; 5:3; Eph. 2:15; Phil. 3:6; 1 Tim. 1:8; **Heb. 7:19**; Jas. 2:9; (2) without the article, thus stressing the Mosaic Law in its quality as "law," e.g., Rom. 2:14 (1st part); 5:20; 7:9, where the stress in the quality lies in this, that "the commandment which was unto (i.e., which he thought would be a means of) life," he found to be "unto (i.e., to have the effect of revealing his actual state of) death"; 10:4; 1 Cor. 9:20; Gal. 2:16, 19, 21; 3:2, 5, 10 (1st part), 11, 18, 23; 4:4, 5, 21 (1st part); 5:4, 18; 6:13; Phil. 3:5, 9; **Heb. 7:16; 9:19**; Jas. 2:11; 4:11; (in regard to the statement in Gal. 2:16, that "a man is not justified by the works of the Law," the absence of the article before *nomos* indicates the assertion of a principle, "by obedience to law," but evidently the Mosaic Law is in view. Here the apostle is maintaining that submission to circumcision entails the obligation to do the whole "Law." Circumcision belongs to the ceremonial part of the "Law," but, while the Mosaic Law is actually divisible into the ceremonial and the moral, no such distinction is made or even assumed in Scripture. The statement maintains the freedom of the believer from the "law" of Moses in its totality as a means of justification);

The following phrases specify "laws" of various kinds: ... (i) "the law of a carnal commandment," **Heb. 7:16**, i.e., the "law" respecting the Aaronic priesthood, which appointed men conditioned by the circumstances and limitations of the flesh. In the Epistle to the Hebrews the "Law" is treated of especially in regard to the contrast between the Priesthood of Christ and that established under the "law" of Moses, and in regard to access to God and to worship. In these respects the "Law" "made nothing perfect," **7:19**. There was "a disannulling of a foregoing commandment ... and a bringing in of a better hope." This is established under the "new Covenant," a covenant instituted on the basis of "better promises," **8:6**.

Carnal *sarkinos* (4560), (a) "consisting of flesh," 2 Cor. 3:3, "tables that are hearts of flesh" (KJV, "fleshy tables of the heart"); (b) "pertaining to the natural, transient life of the body," **Heb. 7:16**, "a carnal commandment"; (c) given up to the flesh, i.e., with almost the same significance as *sarkikos*, above, Rom. 7:14, "I am carnal sold under sin"; 1 Cor. 3:1 (some texts have *sarkikos*, in both these places, and in those in (a) and (b), but textual evidence is against it). It is difficult to discriminate between *sarkikos* and *sarkinos* in some passages. In regard to 1 Pet. 2:11, Trench (*Syn.* Sec.lxxi, lxxii) says that *sarkikos* describes the lusts which have their source in man's corrupt and fallen nature, and the man is *sarkikos* who allows to the flesh a place which does not belong to it of right; in 1 Cor. 3:1 *sarkinos* is an accusation far less grave than *sarkikos* would have been. The Corinthian saints were making no progress, but they were not anti-spiritual in respect of the particular point with which the apostle was there dealing. In vv. 3-4, they are charged with being *sarkikos*.

Endless *akatalutos* (179), denotes indissoluble (from *a*, negative, *kata*, "down," *luo*, "to loose"), **Heb. 7:16**, "endless"; see the RV, marg., i.e., a life which makes its possessor the holder of His priestly office for evermore.

7:17 For he testifieth, Thou *art* a priest for ever after the order of Melchisedec.

Testifieth *martureo* (3140), is frequently rendered "to bear witness, to witness," in the RV, where KJV renders it "to testify," John 2:25; 3:11, 32; 5:39; 15:26; 21:24; 1 Cor. 15:15; **Heb. 7:17**; **11:4**; 1 John 4:14; 5:9; 3 John 3. In the following, however, the RV, like the KJV, has the rendering "to testify," John 4:39, 44; 7:7; 13:21; Acts 26:5; Rev. 22:16, 18, 20. *See also* **Witnessed** at ***Hebrews 7:8***.

Priest *see* ***Hebrews 5:6***.

Order *see* ***Hebrews 5:6***.

7:18 For there is verily a disannulling of the commandment going before for the weakness and unprofitableness thereof.

Verily *see* ***Hebrews 3:5***.

Disannulling *athetesis* (115), is translated "disannulling" in **Heb. 7:18**, with reference to a commandment; in **9:26** "to put away," with reference to sin, lit., "for a putting away."

Commandment *diatheke* (1242) ... "The NT uses of the word may be analyzed as follows: (a) a promise or undertaking, human or divine, Gal. 3:15; (b) a promise or undertaking on the part of God, Luke 1:72; Acts 3:25; Rom. 9:4; 11:27; Gal. 3:17; Eph. 2:12; **Heb. 7:22**; **8:6, 8, 10**; **10:16**; (c) an agreement, a mutual undertaking, between God and Israel, see Deut. 29-30 (described as a 'commandment,' **Heb. 7:18**, cf. v. **22**); **Heb. 8:9**; **9:20**; (d) by metonymy, the token of the covenant, or promise, made to Abraham, Acts 7:8, (e) by metonymy, the record of the covenant, 2 Cor. 3:14; **Heb. 9:4**; cf. Rev. 11:19; (f) the basis, established by the death of Christ, on which the salvation of men is secured, Matt. 26:28; Mark 14:24; Luke 22:20; 1 Cor. 11:25; 2 Cor. 3:6; **Heb. 10:29**; **12:24**; **13:20**. This covenant is called the 'new,' **Heb. 9:15**, the 'second,' **8:7**, the 'better,' **7:22**. In **Heb. 9:16-17**, the translation is much disputed. There does not seem to be any sufficient reason for departing in these verses from the word used everywhere else. The English word 'Testament' is taken from the titles prefixed to the Latin Versions."

Going before *proago* (4254), when used intransitively, signifies either to "lead the way," or "to go before, precede"; in **Heb. 7:18**, it is used of the commandment of the Law (v. **16**), as preceding the bringing in of "a better hope" (RV, "foregoing"). *See also* **Hope** at ***Hebrews 6:11***.

Weakness *asthenes* (772), lit., "strengthless", is translated "weak," (a) of physical "weakness," Matt. 26:41; Mark 14:38; 1 Cor. 1:27; 4:10; 11:30 (a judgment upon spiritual laxity in a church); 2 Cor. 10:10; 1 Pet. 3:7 (comparative degree); (b) in the spiritual sense, said of the rudiments of Jewish religion, in their inability to justify anyone, Gal. 4:9; of the Law, **Heb. 7:18**; in Rom. 5:6, RV, "weak" (KJV, "without strength"), of the inability of man to accomplish his salvation; (c) morally or ethically, 1 Cor. 8:7, 10; 9:22; (d) rhetorically, of God's actions according to the human estimate, 1 Cor. 1:25, "weakness," lit., "the weak things of God."

Unprofitableness *anopheles* (512), "not beneficial or serviceable" (*a*, negative, *n*, euphonic, *opheleo*, "to do good, to benefit"), is rendered "unprofitable" in Titus 3:9; in the neuter, used as a noun, "unprofitableness," **Heb. 7:18**, said of the Law as not accomplishing that which the "better hope" could alone bring. In the Sept., Prov. 28:3; Isa. 44:10; Jer. 2:8.

7:19 For the law made nothing perfect, but the bringing in of a better hope *did*; by the which we draw nigh unto God.

Law *see* ***Hebrews 7:16***.

Perfect *see* ***Hebrews 2:10***.

Bringing *epeisagoge* (1898), lit., "a bringing in besides," is translated "a bringing in thereupon" in **Heb. 7:19**.

Better *see* ***Hebrews 1:4***.

Hope *see* ***Hebrews 6:11***.

Draw nigh *engizo* (1448), "to draw near, to approach," from *engus*, "near," is used (a) of place and position, literally and physically, Matt. 21:1; Mark 11:1; Luke 12:33; 15:25; figuratively, of drawing near to God, Matt. 15:8; **Heb. 7:19**; Jas. 4:8; (b) of time, with reference to things that are imminent, as the kingdom of heaven, Matt. 3:2; 4:17; 10:7; the kingdom of God, Mark 1:15; Luke 10:9, 11; the time of fruit, Matt. 21:34; the desolation of Jerusalem, Luke 21:8; redemption, 21:28; the fulfillment of a promise, Acts 7:17; the Day of Christ in contrast to the present night of the world's spiritual darkness, Rom. 13:12; **Heb. 10:25**; the coming of the Lord, Jas. 5:8; the end of all things, 1 Pet. 4:7. It is also said of one who was drawing near to death, Phil. 2:30.

7:20 And inasmuch as not without an oath *he was made priest*:

Without *see Hebrews 4:15.*

Oath *horkomosia* (3728), denotes "an affirmation on oath." This is used in **Heb. 7:20-21** (twice), **28**, of the establishment of the Priesthood of Christ, the Son of God, appointed a Priest after the order of Melchizedek, and "perfected for evermore." In the Sept., Ezek. 17:18, 19.

7:21 (For those priests were made without an oath; but this with an oath by him that said unto him, The Lord sware and will not repent, Thou *art* a priest for ever after the order of Melchisedec:)

Those In **Heb. 7:21**, KJV, "those" translates the article, which requires the RV, "they."

Priests, Priest *see* **Priest** at *Hebrews 5:6.*

Made *see Hebrews 3:14.*

Without *see Hebrews 4:15.*

Sware *see Hebrews 3:11.*

Repent *metamelomai* (3338), is used in the passive voice with middle voice sense, signifying "to regret, to repent oneself," Matt. 21:29, RV, "repented himself"; v. 32, RV, "ye did (not) repent yourselves" (KJV, "ye repented not"); 27:3, "repented himself"; 2 Cor. 7:8 (twice), RV, "regret" in each case; **Heb. 7:21**, where alone in the NT it is said (negatively) of God.

Order *see Hebrews 5:6.*

7:22 By so much was Jesus made a surety of a better testament.

Much *see Hebrews 1:4.*

Jesus *see Hebrews 2:9.*

Made *see Hebrews 3:14.*

Surety *enguos* (1450), primarily signifies "bail," the bail who personally answers for anyone, whether with his life or his property (to be distinguished from *mesites*, "a mediator"); it is used in **Heb. 7:22**, "(by so much also hath Jesus become) the Surety (of a better covenant)," referring to the abiding and unchanging character of His Melchizedek priesthood, by reason of which His suretyship is established by God's oath (vv. **20**, **21**). As the Surety, He is the personal guarantee of the terms of the new and better covenant, secured on the ground of His perfect sacrifice (v. **27**).

Better *see Hebrews 1:4.*

Testament *see* **Commandment** at *Hebrews 7:18.*

7:23 And they truly were many priests, because they were not suffered to continue by reason of death:

Many *pleion* (4119), "more, greater," the comparative, is translated "many" in Acts 2:40; 13:31; 21:10; 24:17; 25:14; 27:20; 28:23 (KJV; RV, "in great number"); with the article, "most," RV (or rather, "the more part") Acts 19:32; 1 Cor. 10:5, and Phil. 1:14 (for KJV, "many," an important change); in 2 Cor. 2:6, RV, "the many" (marg., "the more"); so 4:15; in 9:2, "very many" (marg., "the more part"); in **Heb. 7:23**, RV, "many in number" (KJV "many").

Suffered *koluo* (2967), "to hinder, forbid, restrain," is translated "to hinder" in Luke 11:52; Acts 8:36; Rom. 1:13, RV (KJV, "was let"); **Heb. 7:23**, RV (KJV, "were not suffered").

Continue *parameno* (3887), "to remain beside" (para, "beside"), "to continue near," came to signify simply "to continue," e.g., negatively, of the Levitical priests, **Heb. 7:23**. In Phil. 1:25, the apostle uses both the simple verb *meno* and the compound *parameno* (some mss. have *sumparameno*), to express his confidence that he will "abide," and "continue to abide," with the saints. In 1 Cor. 16:6 some mss. have this word. In Jas. 1:25, of steadfast continuance in the law of liberty.

Death *see Hebrews 2:15.*

7:24 But this *man*, because he continueth ever, hath an unchangeable priesthood.

Continueth *meno* (3306), used (a) of place, e.g., Matt. 10:11, metaphorically 1 John 2:19, is said of God, 1 John 4:15; Christ, John 6:56; 15:4, etc.; the Holy Spirit, John 1:32-33; 14:17; believers, John 6:56; 15:4; 1 John 4:15, etc.; the Word of God, 1 John 2:14; the truth, 2 John 2, etc.; (b) of time; it is said of believers, John 21:22-23; Phil. 1:25; 1 John 2:17; Christ, John 12:34; **Heb. 7:24**; the Word of God, 1 Pet. 1:23; sin,

John 9:41; cities, Matt. 11:23; **Heb. 13:14**; bonds and afflictions, Acts 20:23; (c) of qualities; faith, hope, love, 1 Cor. 13:13; Christ's love, John 15:10; afflictions, Acts 20:23; brotherly love, **Heb. 13:1**; the love of God, 1 John 3:17; the truth, 2 John 2. The RV usually translates it by "abide," but "continue" in 1 Tim. 2:15; in the following, the RV substitutes "to abide" for the KJV, "to continue," John 2:12; 8:31; 15:9; 2 Tim. 3:14; **Heb. 7:24**; **13:14**; 1 John 2:24.

Unchangeable *aparabatos* (531), is used of the priesthood of Christ, in **Heb. 7:24**, "unchangeable," "unalterable, inviolable," RV, marg. (a meaning found in the papyri); the more literal meaning in KJV and RV margins, "that doth not pass from one to another," is not to be preferred. This active meaning is not only untenable, and contrary to the constant usage of the word, but does not adequately fit with either the preceding or the succeeding context.

Priesthood *see Hebrews 7:11.*

7:25 Wherefore he is able also to save them to the uttermost that come unto God by him, seeing he ever liveth to make intercession for them.

Wherefore *see Hebrews 2:17.*

Save *sozo* (4982), "to save," is used (as with the noun *soteria*, "salvation") (a) of material and temporal deliverance from danger, suffering, etc., e.g., Matt. 8:25; Mark 13:20; Luke 23:35; John 12:27; 1 Tim. 2:15; 2 Tim. 4:18 (KJV, "preserve"); Jude 5; from sickness, Matt. 9:22, "made ... whole" (RV, marg., "saved"); so Mark 5:34; Luke 8:48; Jas. 5:15; (b) of the spiritual and eternal salvation granted immediately by God to those who believe on the Lord Jesus Christ, e.g., Acts 2:47, RV "(those that) were being saved"; 16:31; Rom. 8:24, RV, "were we saved"; Eph. 2:5, 8; 1 Tim. 2:4; 2 Tim. 1:9; Titus 3:5; of human agency in this, Rom. 11:14; 1 Cor. 7:16; 9:22; (c) of the present experiences of God's power to deliver from the bondage of sin, e.g., Matt. 1:21; Rom. 5:10; 1 Cor. 15:2; **Heb. 7:25**; Jas. 1:21; 1 Pet. 3:21; of human agency in this, 1 Tim. 4:16; (d) of the future deliverance of believers at the second coming of Christ for His saints, being deliverance from the wrath of God to be executed upon the ungodly at the close of this age and from eternal doom, e.g., Rom. 5:9; (e) of the deliverance of the nation of Israel at the second advent of Christ, e.g., Rom. 11:26; (f) inclusively for all the blessings bestowed by God on men in Christ, e.g., Luke 19:10; John 10:9; 1 Cor. 10:33; 1 Tim. 1:15; (g) of those who endure to the end of the time of the Great Tribulation, Matt. 10:22; Mark 13:13; (h) of the individual believer, who, though losing his reward at the judgment seat of Christ hereafter, will not lose his salvation, 1 Cor. 3:15; 5:5; (i) of the deliverance of the nations at the Millennium, Rev. 21:24 (in some mss.).

Uttermost *panteles* (3838), the neuter of the adjective *panteles*, "complete, perfect," used with *eis to* ("unto the"), is translated "to the uttermost" in **Heb. 7:25**, where the meaning may be "finally"; in Luke 13:11 (negatively), "in no wise."

Come unto *see* **Come ... unto** at *Hebrews 4:16.*

Ever *pantote* (3842), "at all times, always" (akin to *pas*, "all"), is translated "ever" in Luke 15:31; John 18:20; 1 Thess. 4:17; 5:15; 2 Tim. 3:7; **Heb. 7:25**; "evermore" in John 6:34; in 1 Thess. 5:16, RV, "alway," for KJV, "evermore." It there means "on all occasions," as, e.g., in 1 Thess. 1:2; 3:6; 5:15; 2 Thess. 1:3, 11; 2:13.

"If I could hear Christ praying for me in the next room, I would not fear a million enemies. Yet the distance makes no difference; he is praying for me!"

ROBERT MURRAY M'CHEYNE

Intercession *entunchano* (1793), primarily "to fall in with, meet with in order to converse"; then, "to make petition," especially "to make intercession, plead with a person," either for or against others; (a) against, Acts 25:24, "made suit to (me)," RV [KJV, "have dealt with (me)"], i.e., against Paul; in Rom. 11:2, of Elijah in "pleading" with God, RV (KJV, "maketh intercession to"), against Israel; (b) for, in Rom. 8:27, of the intercessory work of the Holy Spirit for the saints; v. 34, of the similar intercessory work of Christ; so **Heb. 7:25**.

7:26 For such an high priest became us, *who is* holy, harmless, undefiled, separate from sinners, and made higher than the heavens;

High priest *see Hebrews 2:17.*

Became *see Hebrews 2:10.*

Holy *hosios* (3741), signifies "religiously right, holy," as opposed to what is unrighteous or polluted. It is commonly associated with righteousness. It is used "of God, Rev. 15:4; 16:5; and of the body of the Lord Jesus, Acts 2:27; 13:35, citations from Ps. 16:10, Sept.; **Heb. 7:26**; and of certain promises made to David, which could be fulfilled only in the resurrection of the Lord Jesus, Acts 13:34. In 1 Tim. 2:8 and Titus 1:8, it is used of the character of Christians.... In the Sept., *hosios* frequently represents the Hebrew word *chasid*, which varies in meaning between 'holy' and 'gracious,' or 'merciful;' cf. Ps. 16:10 with 145:17."

Harmless *akakos* (172), the negative of *kakos*, "void of evil," is rendered "harmless" in **Heb. 7:26** (RV, "guileless"), of the character of Christ as a High Priest; in Rom. 16:18, RV, "innocent," KJV, "simple."

Undefiled *amiantos* (283), "undefiled, free from contamination" (*a*, negative, *miaino*, "to defile"), is used (a) of Christ, **Heb. 7:26**; (b) of pure religion, Jas. 1:27; (c) of the eternal inheritance of believers, 1 Pet. 1:4; (d) of the marriage bed as requiring to be free from unlawful sexual intercourse, **Heb. 13:4**.

Separate *chorizo* (5563), "to put asunder, separate," is translated "to separate" in Rom. 8:35, 39; in the middle voice, "to separate oneself, depart"; in the passive voice in **Heb. 7:26**, RV, "separated" (KJV, "separate"), the verb here relates to the resurrection of Christ, not, as KJV indicates, to the fact of His holiness in the days of His flesh; the list is progressive in this respect that the first three qualities apply to His sinlessness, the next to His resurrection, the last to His ascension.

Made *see Hebrews 3:14.*

Heavens *see Hebrews 1:10.*

7:27 Who needeth not daily, as those high priests, to offer up sacrifice, first for his own sins, and then for the people's: for this he did once, when he offered up himself.

Daily *see Hebrews 3:13.*

Offer, Offered *anaphero* (399), primarily, "to lead" or "carry up" (*ana*), also denotes "to offer," (a) of Christ's sacrifice, **Heb. 7:27**; (b) of sacrifices under the Law, **Heb. 7:27**; (c) of such previous to the Law, Jas. 2:21 (of Isaac by Abraham); (d) of praise, **Heb. 13:15**; (e) of spiritual sacrifices in general, 1 Pet. 2:5.

Sacrifice *see* **Sacrifices** at *Hebrews 5:1*. *See also* **Surety** at *Hebrews 7:22.*

First *proteron* (4386), the neuter of *proteros*, the comparative degree of *pro*, is always used of time, and signifies "aforetime before," e.g., John 6:62; 9:8; 2 Cor. 1:15; **Heb. 7:27**; in Gal. 4:13, "the first time" (RV), lit., "the former time," i.e., the former of two previous visits; in **Heb. 10:32** it is placed between the article and the noun, "the former days"; so in 1 Pet. 1:14, "the former lusts," i.e., the lusts formerly indulged. *See also Hebrews 4:6.*

Then *see* **After that** at *Hebrews 7:2.*

Once *ephapax* (2178), a strengthened form, signifies (a) "once for all," Rom. 6:10; **Heb. 7:27**, RV (KJV, "once"); **9:12** (ditto); **10:10**; (b) "at once," 1 Cor. 15:6.

7:28 For the law maketh men high priests which have infirmity; but the word of the oath, which was since the law, *maketh* the Son, who is consecrated for evermore.

Maketh *kathistemi* (2525), "to set down, set in order, appoint," is used in Acts 7:10, 27, 35; **Heb. 7:28**, KJV (RV, "appointeth"), and in Rom. 5:19 (twice). *See also* **Set** at *Hebrews 2:7.*

High priests *see* **High priest** at *Hebrews 2:15.*

Oath *see Hebrews 7:20.*

Consecrated In **Heb. 7:28** the verb *teleioo* is translated "perfected" in the RV, for KJV, "consecrated"; so in **9:18** and **10:20**, *enkainizo*, RV, dedicated. *See also* **Perfect** at *Hebrews 2:10.*

Chapter 8

8:1 Now of the things which we have spoken *this is* the sum: We have such an high priest, who is set on the right hand of the throne of the Majesty in the heavens;

Spoken A characteristic of *lego* is that it refers to the purport or sentiment of what is said as well as the connection of the words; this is illustrated in **Heb. 8:1**, RV, "(in the things which) we are saying," KJV, "(which) we have spoken." In comparison with *laleo*, *lego* refers especially to the substance of what is "said," *laleo*, to the words conveying the utterance; see, e.g., John 12:49, "what I should say (*lego*, in the 2nd aorist subjunctive form *eipo*), and what I should speak (laleo)"; v. 50, "even as the Father hath said (*lego*, in the perfect form *eireke*) unto Me, so I speak" (*laleo*); cf. 1 Cor. 14:34, "saith (*lego*) the law"; v. 35, "to speak" (*laleo*). Sometimes *laleo* signifies the utterance, as opposed to silence, *lego* declares what is "said"; e.g., Rom. 3:19, "what things soever the law saith (*lego*), it speaketh (*laleo*) to them that are under the law"; see also Mark 6:50; Luke 24:6. In the NT *laleo* never has the meaning "to chatter."

Sum *kephalaion* (2774), the neuter of the adjective *kephalaios*, "of the head," is used as a noun, signifying (a) "a sum, amount, of money," Acts 22:28; (b) "a chief point," **Heb. 8:1**, not the summing up of the subject, as the KJV suggests, for the subject was far from being finished in the Epistle; on the contrary, in all that was being set forth by the writer "the chief point" consisted in the fact that believers have "a High Priest" of the character already described.

High priest *see Hebrews 2:17.*

Set In **Heb. 8:1**, *kathizo* is used intransitively, RV, "sat down" (KJV, "is set"); so in **12:2**, RV, "hath sat down" (KJV, "is set down"); Rev. 3:21, RV, "I ... sat down" (KJV, "am set down"). So *epikathizo* in Matt. 21:7 (last part), RV, "He sat" [some mss. have the plural in a transitive sense, KJV, "they set (Him)]."

Throne *see Hebrews 1:8.*

Majesty *see Hebrews 1:3.*

Heavens *see Hebrews 1:10.*

8:2 A minister of the sanctuary, and of the true tabernacle, which the Lord pitched, and not man.

Minister *see* **Ministers** at **Hebrews** *1:7. See also* **High priest** at *Hebrews 2:17.*

Sanctuary *hagion* (39), the neuter of the adjective *hagios*, "holy," is used of those structures which are set apart to God, (a) of "the tabernacle" in the wilderness, **Heb. 9:1**, RV, "its sanctuary, a *sanctuary* of this world" (KJV, "a worldly sanctuary"); in v. **2** the outer part is called "the Holy place," RV (KJV, "the sanctuary"); here the neuter plural *hagia* is used, as in v. **3**. Speaking of the absence of the article, Westcott says "The anarthrous form *Agia* (literally *Holies*) in this sense appears to be unique, as also *agia agiwa* below, if indeed the reading is correct. Perhaps it is chosen to fix attention on the character of the sanctuary as in other cases. The plural suggests the idea of the sanctuary with all its parts: cf. Moulton-Winer, p. 220." In their margin, Westcott and Hort prefix the article *ta* to *hagia* in vv. **2** and **3**. In v. **3** the inner part is called "the Holy of holies," RV (KJV, "the holiest of all"); in v. 8, "the holy place" (KJV, "the holiest of all"), lit., "(the way) of the holiest"; in v. **24** "a holy place," RV (KJV, "the holy places"), neuter plural; so in v. **25**, "the holy place" (KJV and RV), and in **13:11**, RV, "the holy place" (KJV, "the sanctuary"); in all these there is no separate word *topos*, "place," as of the Temple in Matt. 24:15; (b) of "Heaven itself," i.e., the immediate presence of God and His throne, **Heb. 8:2**, "the sanctuary" (RV, marg., "holy things"); the neut. plur. with the article points to the text as being right, in view of **9:24, 25** and **13:11** (see above), exegetically designated "the true tabernacle"; neut. plur. in **9:12**, "the holy place"; so **10:19**, RV (KJV, "the holiest"; there are no separate compartments in the antitypical and heavenly sanctuary), into which believers have "boldness to enter" by faith.

True *alethinos* (228), denotes "true" in the sense of real, ideal, genuine; it is used (a) of God, John 7:28; 17:3; 1 Thess. 1:9; Rev. 6:10; these declare that God fulfills the meaning of His Name; He is "very God," in distinction from all other gods, false gods (*alethes*, see John 3:33, signifies that He is veracious, "true" to His utterances, He cannot lie); (b) of Christ, John 1:9; 6:32; 15:1; 1 John 2:8; 5:20 (thrice); Rev. 3:7, 14; 19:11; His judgment, John 8:16; (c) God's words, John 4:37; Rev. 19:9, 21:5; 22:6; (d) His ways, Rev. 15:3; (e) His judgments, Rev. 16:7; 19:2; (f) to His riches, Luke 16:11; (g) His worshipers, John 4:23; (h) their hearts, **Heb. 10:22**; (i) the witness of the apostle John, John 19:35; (j) the spiritual, antitypical tabernacle, **Heb. 8:2**; **9:24**, not that the wilderness tabernacle was false, but that it was a weak and earthly copy of the heavenly.

Tabernacle *skene* (4633), "a tent, booth, tabernacle," is used of (a) tents as dwellings, Matt. 17:4; Mark 9:5; Luke 9:33; **Heb. 11:9**, KJV, "tabernacles" (RV, "tents"); (b) the Mosaic tabernacle, Acts 7:44; **Heb. 8:5**; **9:1** (in some mss.); **9:8, 21**, termed "the tent of meeting," RV (i.e., where the people were called to meet God), a preferable description to "the tabernacle of the congregation," as in the KJV in the OT; the outer part **9:2, 6**; the inner sanctuary, **9:3**; (c) the heavenly prototype, **Heb. 8:2**; **9:11**; Rev. 13:6; 15:5; 21:3 (of its future descent); (d) the eternal abodes of the saints, Luke 16:9, RV, "tabernacles" (KJV, "habitations"); (e) the Temple in Jerusalem, as continuing the service of the tabernacle, **Heb. 13:10**; (f) the house of David, i.e., metaphorically of his people, Acts 15:16; (g) the portable shrine of the god Moloch, Acts 7:43.

Pitched *pegnumi* (4078), "to make fast, to fix" (cf. *prospegnumi*, Acts 2:23, of crucifixion), is used of "pitching" a tent; in **Heb. 8:2**, of the "true tabernacle," the heavenly and spiritual, which "the Lord pitched."

8:3 For every high priest is ordained to offer gifts and sacrifices: wherefore *it is* of necessity that this man have somewhat also to offer.

High priest *see Hebrews 2:17.*

Ordained *see Hebrews 5:1. See also* **Set** at *Hebrews 2:7.*

Offer *see Hebrews 5:1.*

Gifts *see Hebrews 5:1.*

Sacrifices *see Hebrews 5:1.*

Wherefore *see Hebrews 2:17.*

Necessity *anankaios* (316), "necessary" (from *ananke*, "necessity"), is so rendered in Acts 13:46; 1 Cor. 12:22; 2 Cor. 9:5; Phil. 2:25; Titus 3:14; **Heb. 8:3**, RV (KJV, "of necessity"); for Acts 10:24, "near friends."

Somewhat The indefinite pronoun *tis* in its singular or plural forms, frequently means "some," "some one" (translated "some man," in the KJV, e.g., of Acts 8:31; 1 Cor. 15:35), or "somebody," Luke 8:46; the neuter plural denotes "some things" in 2 Pet. 3:16; the singular denotes "something," e.g., Luke 11:54; John 13:29 (2nd part); Acts 3:5; 23:18; Gal. 6:3, where the meaning is "anything," as in 2:6, "somewhat." It is translated "somewhat," in the more indefinite sense, in Luke 7:40; Acts 23:20; 25:26; 2 Cor. 10:8; **Heb. 8:3**.

8:4 For if he were on earth, he should not be a priest, seeing that there are priests that offer gifts according to the law:

Priest, Priests *see* Priest at *Hebrews 5:6.*

Gifts *see Hebrews 5:1.*

8:5 Who serve unto the example and shadow of heavenly things, as Moses was admonished of God when he was about to make the tabernacle: for, See, saith he, *that* thou make all things according to the pattern shewed to thee in the mount.

Serve *latreuo* (3000), primarily "to work for hire" (akin to *latris*, "a hired servant"), signifies (1) to worship, (2) to "serve"; in the latter sense it is used of service (a) to God, Matt. 4:10; Luke 1:74 ("without fear"); 4:8; Acts 7:7; 24:14, RV, "serve" (KJV, "worship"); 26:7; 27:23; Rom. 1:9 ("with my spirit"); 2 Tim. 1:3; **Heb. 9:14; 12:28**, KJV, "we may serve," RV, "we may offer service"; Rev. 7:15; (b) to God and Christ ("the Lamb"), Rev. 22:3; (c) in the tabernacle, **Heb. 8:5**, RV; **13:10**; (d) to "the host of heaven," Acts 7:42, RV, "to serve" (KJV, "to worship"); (e) to "the creature," instead of the Creator, Rom. 1:25, of idolatry.

Example *see Hebrews 4:11.*

Shadow *skia* (4639), is used (a) of "a shadow," caused by the interception of light, Mark 4:32; Acts 5:15; metaphorically of the darkness and spiritual death of ignorance, Matt. 4:16; Luke 1:79; (b) of "the image" or "outline" cast by an object, Col. 2:17, of ceremonies under the Law; of the tabernacle and its appurtenances and offerings, **Heb. 8:5**; of these as appointed under the Law, **Heb. 10:1**.

Heavenly *see Hebrews 3:1.*

Admonished *chrematizo* (5537), primarily, "to transact business," then, "to give advice to enquirers" (especially of official pronouncements of magistrates), or "a response to those consulting an oracle," came to signify the giving of a divine "admonition" or instruction or warning, in a general way; "admonished" in **Heb. 8:5**, KJV (RV, "warned"). Elsewhere it is translated by the verb "to warn." The word is derived from *chrema*, "an affair, business." Names were given to men from the nature of their business (see the same word in Acts 11:26; Rom. 7:3); hence, the idea of dealing with a person and receiving instruction. In the case of oracular responses, the word is derived from *chresmos*, "an oracle."

About *mello* (3195), signifies (a) "of intention, to be about to do something," e.g., Acts 3:3; 18:14; 20:3; **Heb. 8:5**; (b) "of certainty, compulsion or necessity, to be certain to act," e.g., John 6:71.

Make *epiteleo* (2005), is a strengthened form of that verb, in the sense of "accomplishing." The fuller meaning is "to accomplish perfectly"; in Rom. 15:28, RV, "accomplish"; "perfecting" in 2 Cor. 7:1; "complete" in 8:6 and 11; "completion" in the latter part of this 11th verse, which is better than "performance"; "perfected" in Gal. 3:3; "perfect" in Phil. 1:6. In **Heb. 8:5** the margin rightly has "complete" instead of "make," with regard to the tabernacle. In **Heb. 9:6** it is translated "accomplish" and in 1 Pet. 5:9.

Tabernacle *see Hebrews 8:2.*

Pattern *tupos* (5179), primarily denoted "a blow" (from a root *tup-*, seen also in *tupto*, "to strike"), hence, (a) an impression, the mark of a "blow," John 20:25; (b) the "impress" of a seal, the stamp made by a die, a figure, image, Acts 7:43; (c) a "form" or mold, Rom. 6:17 (see RV); (d) the sense or substance of a letter, Acts 23:25; (e) "an ensample," pattern, Acts 7:44; **Heb. 8:5**, "pattern"; in an ethical sense, 1 Cor. 10:6; Phil. 3:17; 1 Thess. 1:7; 2 Thess. 3:9; 1 Tim. 4:12, RV, "ensample"; Titus 2:7, RV, "ensample," for KJV, "pattern"; 1 Pet. 5:3; in a doctrinal sense, a type, Rom. 5:14.

Mount *oros* (3735), is used (a) without specification, e.g., Luke 3:5 (distinct from *bounos*, "a hill"); John 4:20; (b) of "the Mount of Transfiguration," Matt. 17:1, 9; Mark 9:2, 9; Luke 9:28, 37 (KJV, "hill"); 2 Pet. 1:18; (c) of "Zion," **Heb. 12:22**; Rev. 14:1; (d) of "Sinai," Acts 7:30, 38; Gal. 4:24, 25; **Heb. 8:5; 12:20**; (e) of "the Mount of Olives," Matt. 21:1; 24:3; Mark 11:1; 13:3; Luke 19:29, 37; 22:39; John 8:1; Acts 1:12; (f) of "the hill districts as distinct from the lowlands," especially of the hills above the Sea of Galilee, e.g., Matt. 5:1; 8:1; 18:12; Mark 5:5; (g) of "the mountains on the east of Jordan" and "those in the land of Ammon" and "the region of Petra," etc., Matt. 24:16; Mark 13:14; Luke 21:21; (h) proverbially, "of overcoming difficulties, or accomplishing great things," 1 Cor. 13:2; cf. Matt. 17:20; 21:21; Mark 11:23; (i) symbolically, of "a series of the imperial potentates of the Roman dominion, past and future," Rev. 17:9.

8:6 But now hath he obtained a more excellent ministry, by how much also he is the mediator of a better covenant, which was established upon better promises.

Obtained *tunchano* (5177), "to meet with, light upon," also signifies "to obtain, attain to, reach, get" (with regard to things), translated "to obtain" in Acts 26:22, of "the help that is from God"; 2 Tim. 2:10, of "the salvation which is in Christ Jesus with eternal glory"; **Heb. 8:6**, of the ministry obtained by Christ; **11:35**, of "a better resurrection."

Excellent *see* ***Hebrews 1:4.***

Ministry *leitourgia* (3009), akin to *leitourgos*, to which the meanings of *leitourgia* correspond, is used in the NT of "sacred ministrations," (a) priestly, Luke 1:23; **Heb. 8:6; 9:21**; (b) figuratively, of the practical faith of the members of the church at Philippi regarded as priestly sacrifice, upon which the apostle's lifeblood might be poured out as a libation, Phil. 2:17; (c) of the "ministration" of believers one to another, regarded as priestly service, 2 Cor. 9:12; Phil. 2:30.

Mediator *mesites* (3316), lit., "a go-between" (from *mesos*, "middle," and *eimi*, "to go"), is used in two ways in the NT, (a) "one who mediates" between two parties with a view to producing peace, as in 1 Tim. 2:5, though more than mere "mediatorship" is in view, for the salvation of men necessitated that the Mediator should Himself possess the nature and attributes of Him towards whom He acts, and should likewise participate in the nature of those for whom He acts (sin apart); only by being possessed both of deity and humanity could He comprehend the claims of the one and the needs of the other; further, the claims and the needs could be met only by One who, Himself being proved sinless, would offer Himself an expiatory sacrifice on behalf of men; (b) "one who acts as a guarantee" so as to secure something which otherwise would not be obtained. Thus in **Heb. 8:6; 9:15; 12:24** Christ is the Surety of "the better covenant," "the new covenant," guaranteeing its terms for His people. In Gal. 3:19 Moses is spoken of as a "mediator," and the statement is made that "a mediator is not a mediator of one," v. 20, that is, of one party. Here the contrast is between the promise given to Abraham and the giving of the Law. The Law was a covenant enacted between God and the Jewish people, requiring fulfillment by both parties. But with the promise to Abraham, all the obligations were assumed by God, which is implied in the statement, "but God is one." In the Sept., Job 9:33, daysman.

Better *see* ***Hebrews 1:4.***

Covenant *see* **Commandment** at ***Hebrews 7:18.***

Established *see* **Received the law** at ***Hebrews 7:11.***

Promises *see* **Promise** at ***Hebrews 4:1.***

8:7 For if that first *covenant* had been faultless, then should no place have been sought for the second.

Covenant *see* **Commandment** at ***Hebrews 7:18.***

Faultless *amemptos* (273), "without blame," is rendered "faultless," in **Heb. 8:7**.

8:8 For finding fault with them, he saith, Behold, the days come, saith the Lord, when I will make a new covenant with the house of Israel and with the house of Judah:

Fault *memphomai* (3201), "to blame," is translated "to find fault" in Rom. 9:19 and **Heb. 8:8**. Some mss. have the verb in Mark 7:2.

Make *sunteleo* (4931), "to end, fulfilled" is translated "I will make" in **Heb. 8:8**, said of the New Covenant.

New *neos* (3501), signifies "new" in respect of time, that which is recent; it is used of the young, and so translated, especially the comparative degree "younger"; accordingly what is *neos* may be a reproduction of the old in quality or character. *Neos* and *kainos* are sometimes used of the same thing, but there is a difference, as already indicated. Thus the "new man" in Eph. 2:15 (*kainos*) is "new" in differing in character; so in 4:24; but the "new man" in Col. 3:10 (*neos*) stresses the fact of the believer's "new" experience, recently begun, and still proceeding. "The old man in him ... dates as far back as Adam; a new man has been born, who therefore is fitly so called" [i.e., *neos*], Trench, *Syn.* Sec.lx. The "New" Covenant in **Heb. 12:24** is "new" (*neos*) compared with the Mosaic, nearly fifteen hundred years before; it is "new" (*kainos*) compared with the Mosaic, which is old in character, ineffective, **8:8, 13; 9:15.**

Covenant *see* **Commandment** at *Hebrews 7:18.*

8:9 Not according to the covenant that I made with their fathers in the day when I took them by the hand to lead them out of the land of Egypt; because they continued not in my covenant, and I regarded them not, saith the Lord.

Covenant *see* **Commandment** at *Hebrews 7:18.*

Took *epilambano* (1949), in the middle voice, "to lay hold of, take hold of," is used literally, e.g., Mark 8:23; Luke 9:47; 14:4; metaphorically, e.g., **Heb. 8:9**, "(I) took them (by the hand)": for other instances in each respect.

Lead *exago* (1806), "to lead out," is rendered by the verb "to lead, out or forth," in Mark 15:20 (in some mss. in 8:23, the best have *ekphero*, "to bring out)"; Luke 24:50; John 10:3; Acts 7:36, 40 (KJV "brought"), and 13:17, RV; Acts 21:38; **Heb. 8:9.**

Continued *emmeno* (1696), "to remain in" (*en*, "in"), is used of "abiding in a house," Acts 28:30 (in the best mss.); of "continuing" in the faith, Acts 14:22; in the Law, Gal. 3:10; in God's covenant, **Heb. 8:9.**

Regarded ... not *ameleo* (272), "not to care," is translated "I regarded ... not" in **Heb. 8:9.** *See also* **Neglect** at *Hebrews 2:3.*

8:10 For this *is* the covenant that I will make with the house of Israel after those days, saith the Lord; I will put my laws into their mind, and write them in their hearts: and I will be to them a God, and they shall be to me a people:

Covenant *see* **Commandment** at *Hebrews 7:18.*

Make *diatithemi* (1303), "to arrange, dispose," is used only in the middle voice in the NT; in **Heb. 9:16, 17**, the present participle with the article, lit., "the (one) making a testament (or covenant)," virtually a noun, "the testator" (the covenanting one); it is used of "making a covenant" in **8:10** and **10:16** and Acts 3:25. In "covenant-making," the sacrifice of a victim was customary (Gen. 15:10; Jer. 34:18, 19). He who "made a covenant" did so at the cost of a life. While the terminology in **Heb. 9:16, 17** has the appearance of being appropriate to the circumstances of making a will, there is excellent reason for adhering to the meaning "covenant-making." The rendering "the death of the testator" would make Christ a Testator, which He was not. He did not die simply that the terms of a testamentary disposition might be fulfilled for the heirs. Here He who is "the Mediator of a new covenant" (v. **15**) is Himself the Victim whose death was necessary. The idea of "making a will" destroys the argument of v. **18.** In spite of various advocacies of the idea of a will, the weight of evidence is confirmatory of what Hatch, in *Essays in Biblical Greek*, p. 48, says: "There can be little doubt that the word (*diatheke*) must be invariably taken in this sense of 'covenant' in the NT, and especially in a book ... so impregnated with the language of the Sept. as the Epistle to the Hebrews" (see also Westcott, and W. F. Moulton). We may render somewhat literally thus: 'For where a covenant (is), a death (is) necessary to be brought in of the one covenanting; for a covenant over dead ones (victims) is sure, since never has it force when the one covenanting lives' [Christ being especially in view]. The writer is speaking from a Jewish point of view, not from that of the Greeks. "To adduce the fact that in the case of wills the death of the testator is the condition of validity, is, of course, no proof at all that a death is necessary to make a covenant valid.... To support his argument, proving the necessity of Christ's death, the writer adduces the general law that he who makes a covenant does so at the expense of life" (Marcus Dods).

Put *didomi* (1325), "to give," is rendered "to put" in Luke 15:22, of the ring on the returned Prodigal's finger; 2 Cor. 8:16 and Rev. 17:17, of "putting" into the heart by God; **Heb. 8:10**, of laws into the mind (KJV, marg., "give"); **10:16**, of laws on (RV; KJV, "into") the heart.

Mind *dianoia* (1271), lit. "a thinking through, or over, a meditation, reflecting," signifies (a) "the faculty of knowing, understanding, or moral reflection," (1) with an evil significance, a consciousness characterized by a perverted moral impulse, Eph. 2:3 (plural); 4:18; (2) with a good significance, the faculty renewed by the Holy Spirit, Matt. 22:37; Mark 12:30; Luke 10:27; **Heb. 8:10; 10:16;** 1 Pet. 1:13; 1 John 5:20; (b) "sentiment, disposition" (not as a function but as a product); (1) in an evil sense, Luke 1:51, "imagination"; Col. 1:21; (2) in a good sense, 2 Pet. 3:1.

Write *epigrapho* (1924), is rendered "to write over or upon" (*epi*) in Mark 15:26; figuratively, on the heart, **Heb. 8:10; 10:16;** on the gates of the heavenly Jerusalem, Rev. 21:12.

Hearts In **Heb. 8:10** and **10:16**, the KJV has "in their hearts" and "into their hearts"; RV, "on their heart."

8:11 And they shall not teach every man his neighbour, and every man his brother, saying,

Know the Lord: for all shall know me, from the least to the greatest.

Neighbour *plesion* (4139), the neuter of the adjective *plesios* (from *pelas*, "near"), is used as an adverb accompanied by the article, lit., "the (one) near"; hence, one's "neighbor." There were no farmhouses scattered over the agricultural areas of Palestine; the populations, gathered in villages, went to and fro to their toil. Hence domestic life was touched at every point by a wide circle of neighborhood. The terms for neighbor were therefore of a very comprehensive scope. This may be seen from the chief characteristics of the privileges and duties of neighborhood as set forth in Scripture, (a) its helpfulness, e.g., Prov. 27:10; Luke 10:36; (b) its intimacy, e.g., Luke 15:6, 9; **Heb. 8:11**; (c) its sincerity and sanctity, e.g., Ex. 22:7, 10; Prov. 3:29; 14:21; Rom. 13:10; 15:2; Eph. 4:25; Jas. 4:12. The NT quotes and expands the command in Lev. 19:18, "to love one's neighbor as oneself"; see, e.g., Matt. 5:43; 19:19; 22:39; Mark 12:31, 33; Luke 10:27; Gal. 5:14; Jas. 2:8. See also Acts 7:27.

polites (4177), "a member of a city or state, or the inhabitant of a country or district," Luke 15:15, is used elsewhere in Luke 19:14; Acts 21:39, and, in the most authentic mss., in **Heb. 8:11** (where some texts have *plesion*, "a neighbor"). Apart from **Heb. 8:11**, the word occurs only in the writings of Luke (himself a Greek).

Least *mikros* (3398), "small, little," is translated "the least" in Acts 8:10 and **Heb. 8:11**, with reference to rank or influence.

Greatest *megas* (3173), is translated "the greatest," in Acts 8:10 and **Heb. 8:11**. The whole phrase, lit., "from small to great," is equivalent to the Eng. idiom "one and all." It is used in the Sept., e.g., in 1 Sam. 5:9: "God smote the people of Gath from the least to the greatest," ("both small and great"). So 1 Sam. 30:19; 2 Chron. 34:30, etc.

8:12 For I will be merciful to their unrighteousness, and their sins and their iniquities will I remember no more.

Merciful *hileos* (2436), "propitious, merciful," was used in profane Greek just as in the case of the verb (which see). There is nothing of this in the use of the word in Scripture. The quality expressed by it there essentially appertains to God, though man is undeserving of it. It is used only of God, **Heb. 8:12**; in Matt. 16:22, "Be it far from Thee" (Peter's word to Christ) may have the meaning given in the RV marg., "(God) have mercy on Thee," lit., "propitious to Thee" (KJV marg., "Pity Thyself") Cf. the Sept., 2 Sam. 20:20; 23:17.

Unrighteousness *adikia* (93), denotes (a) "injustice," Luke 18:6, lit., "the judge of injustice"; Rom. 9:14; (b) "unrighteousness, iniquity," e.g., Luke 16:8, lit., "the steward of unrighteousness," RV marg., i.e., characterized by "unrighteousness"; Rom. 1:18, 29; 2:8; 3:5; 6:13; 1 Cor. 13:6, RV, "unrighteousness"; 2 Thess. 2:10, "[with all (lit., 'in every) deceit'] of unrighteousness," i.e., deceit such as "unrighteousness" uses, and that in every variety; Antichrist and his ministers will not be restrained by any scruple from words or deeds calculated to deceive; 2 Thess. 2:12, of those who have pleasure in it, not an intellectual but a moral evil; distaste for truth is the precursor of the rejection of it; 2 Tim. 2:19, RV; 1 John 1:9, which includes (c); (c) "a deed or deeds violating law and justice" (virtually the same as *adikema*, "an unrighteous act"), e.g., Luke 13:27, "iniquity"; 2 Cor. 12:13, "wrong," the wrong of depriving another of what is his own, here ironically of a favor; **Heb. 8:12**, 1st clause, "iniquities," lit., "unrighteousnesses" (plural, not as KJV); 2 Pet. 2:13, 15, RV, "wrongdoing," KJV, "unrighteousness"; 1 John 5:17.

> *"Thy nature, gracious Lord, impart; / Come quickly from above; / Write thy new name upon my heart, / Thy new, best name of Love."*
>
> CHARLES WESLEY

Iniquities *see* **Iniquity** at *Hebrews 1:9*.

No more *eti* (2089), the double negative *ou me*, "by no means, in no wise," followed by *eti*, "longer, still, yet," is rendered "no more" in **Heb. 8:12**; **10:17**; Rev. 3:12; "(will I remember no) more"; **10:2**, "(no) more (conscience)"; **11:32**, "(what shall I) more (say)?" Rev. 3:12, "(he shall go out thence no) more"; 7:16, "(no) more" and "any more;" 9:12, KJV "more" (RV, "hereafter"); 18:21-23, "(no) more" "any more" (5 times); 20:3, "(no) more"; 21:1, 4 (twice); 22:3. *See also* **Further** at *Hebrews 7:11*.

8:13 In that he saith, A new *covenant*, he hath made the first old. Now that which decayeth and waxeth old *is* ready to vanish away.

New *see Hebrews 8:8.*

Old *gerasko* (1095), from *geras*, "old age," signifies "to grow old," John 21:18 ("when thou shalt be old") and **Heb. 8:13** (RV, "that which ... waxeth aged," KJV, "old"). *See also* **Wax old** at *Hebrews 1:11.*

Decayeth *see* **Wax old** at *Hebrews 1:11.*

Ready In **Heb. 8:13**, KJV, *engus*, "near," is translated "ready" (RV, "nigh"). *See also* **Nigh** at *Hebrews 6:8.*

Vanish *aphanismos* (854), *a*, negative, *phaino*, "to cause to appear," occurs in **Heb. 8:13**, RV, "(nigh unto) vanishing away"; the word is suggestive of abolition.

Chapter 9

9:1 Then verily the first *covenant* had also ordinances of divine service, and a worldly sanctuary.

Ordinances *dikaioma* (1345), has three distinct meanings, and seems best described comprehensively as "a concrete expression of righteousness"; it is a declaration that a person or thing is righteous, and hence, broadly speaking, it represents the expression and effect of *dikaiosis*. It signifies (a) "an ordinance," Luke 1:6; Rom. 1:32, RV, "ordinance," i.e., what God has declared to be right, referring to His decree of retribution (KJV, "judgment"); Rom. 2:26, RV, "ordinances of the Law" (i.e., righteous requirements enjoined by the Law); so 8:4, "ordinance of the Law," i.e., collectively, the precepts of the Law, all that it demands as right; in **Heb. 9:1, 10**, ordinances connected with the tabernacle ritual; (b) "a sentence of acquittal," by which God acquits men of their guilt, on the conditions (1) of His grace in Christ, through His expiatory sacrifice, (2) the acceptance of Christ by faith, Rom. 5:16; (c) "a righteous act," Rom. 5:18, "(through one) act of righteousness," RV, not the act of "justification," nor the righteous character of Christ (as suggested by the KJV: *dikaioma* does not signify character, as does *dikaiosune*, righteousness), but the death of Christ, as an act accomplished consistently with God's character and counsels; this is clear as being in antithesis to the "one trespass" in the preceding statement. Some take the word here as meaning a decree of righteousness, as in v. 16; the death of Christ could indeed be regarded as fulfilling such a decree, but as the apostle's argument proceeds, the word, as is frequently the case, passes from one shade of meaning to another, and here stands not for a decree, but an act; so in Rev. 15:4, RV, "righteous acts" (KJV, "judgments"), and 19:8, "righteous acts (of the saints)" (KJV, "righteousness").

Divine service *latreia* (2999), akin to *latreuo*, primarily "hired service," is used (a) of the "service" *of God* in connection with the tabernacle, Rom. 9:4; **Heb. 9:1**, "divine service"; v. **6**, plural, RV, "services" (KJV, "service", and, in italics, "of God"); (b) of the intelligent "service" of believers in presenting their bodies to God, a living sacrifice, Rom. 12:1, RV marg., "worship"; (c) of imagined "service" to God by persecutors of Christ's followers, John 16:2.

Worldly *kosmikos* (2886), "pertaining to this world," is used (a) in **Heb. 9:1**, of the tabernacle, KJV, "worldly," RV, "of this world" (i.e., made of mundane materials, adapted to this visible world, local and transitory); (b) in Titus 2:12, ethically, of "worldly lusts," or desires.

Sanctuary *see* **Tabernacle** at *Hebrews 8:2.*

9:2 For there was a tabernacle made; the first, wherein *was* the candlestick, and the table, and the shewbread; which is called the sanctuary.

Tabernacle *see Hebrews 8:2.*

Made *kataskeuazo* (2680), "to prepare, make ready" (*kata*, used intensively, *skeue*, "equipment"), is so translated in Matt. 11:10; Mark 1:2; Luke 1:17; 7:27; **Heb. 9:2**, RV (KJV, "made"); **9:6**, RV (KJV, "were ... ordained"); **11:7**; 1 Pet. 3:20.

Candlestick *luchnia* (3087), is mistranslated "candlestick" in every occurrence in the KJV and in certain places in the RV; the RV has "stand" in Matt. 5:15; Mark 4:21; Luke 8:16; 11:33; "candlestick" in **Heb. 9:2**; Rev. 1:12, 13, 20 (twice); 2:1, 5; 11:4; the RV marg., gives "lampstands" in the passages in Rev., but not in **Heb. 9:2**.

Table *trapeza* (5132), is used of (a) "a dining table," Matt. 15:27; Mark 7:28; Luke 16:21; 22:21, 30; (b) "the table of shewbread," **Heb. 9:2**; (c) by metonymy, of "what is provided on the table" (the word being used of that with which it is associated), Acts 16:34; Rom. 11:9 (figurative of the special privileges granted to Israel and centering in Christ); 1 Cor. 10:21 (twice), "the Lord's table," denoting all that is provided for believers in Christ on the ground of His death (and thus expressing something more comprehensive than the Lord's Supper); "the table of demons," denoting all that is partaken of by idolaters as the result of the influence of demons in connection with their sacrifices; (d) "a moneychanger's table," Matt. 21:12; Mark 11:15; John 2:15; (e) "a bank," Luke 19:23

(cf. *trapezites*); (f) by metonymy for "the distribution of money," Acts 6:2.

Shewbread The phrase rendered "the shewbread" is formed by the combination of the nouns *prothesis*, "a setting forth" (*pro*, "before," *tithemi*, "to place") and *artos*, "a loaf" (in the plural), each with the article, Matt. 12:4; Mark 2:26 and Luke 6:4, lit., "the loaves of the setting forth"; in **Heb. 9:2**, lit., "the setting forth of the loaves." The corresponding OT phrases are lit., "bread of the face," Exod. 25:30, i.e., the presence, referring to the Presence of God (cf. Isa. 63:9 with Exod. 33:14, 15); "the bread of ordering," 1 Chron. 9:32, marg. In Num. 4:7 it is called "the continual bread"; in 1 Sam. 21:4, 6, "holy bread" (KJV, "hallowed"). In the Sept. of 1 Kings 7:48, it is called "the bread of the offering" (*prosphora*, "a bearing towards"). The twelve loaves, representing the tribes of Israel, were set in order every Sabbath day before the Lord, "on the behalf of the children," Lev. 24:8, RV (marg., and KJV, "from"), "an everlasting covenant." The loaves symbolized the fact that on the basis of the sacrificial atonement of the Cross, believers are accepted before God, and nourished by Him in the person of Christ. The showbread was partaken of by the priests, as representatives of the nation. Priesthood now being coextensive with all who belong to Christ, 1 Pet. 2:5, 9, He, the Living Bread, is the nourishment of all, and where He is, there, representatively, they are.

9:3 And after the second veil, the tabernacle which is called the Holiest of all;

Veil *see* ***Hebrews 6:19.***

Tabernacle *see* ***Hebrews 8:2.***

Holiest *hagios* (40), which are from the same root as *hagnos* (found in *hazo*, "to venerate"), fundamentally signifies "separated" (among the Greeks, dedicated to the gods), and hence, in Scripture in its moral and spiritual significance, separated from sin and therefore consecrated to God, sacred.

(a) It is predicated of God (as the absolutely "Holy" One, in His purity, majesty and glory): of the Father, e.g., Luke 1:49; John 17:11; 1 Pet. 1:15, 16; Rev. 4:8; 6:10; of the Son, e.g., Luke 1:35; Acts 3:14; 4:27, 30; 1 John 2:20; of the Spirit, e.g., Matt. 1:18 and frequently in all the Gospels, Acts, Romans, 1 and 2 Cor., Eph., 1 Thess.; also in 2 Tim. 1:14; Titus 3:5; 1 Pet. 1:12; 2 Pet. 1:21; Jude 20.

(b) It is used of men and things in so far as they are devoted to God. Indeed the quality, as attributed to God, is often presented in a way which involves divine demands upon the conduct of believers. These are called *hagioi*, "saints," i.e., "sanctified" or "holy" ones ...

"It is evident that *hagios* and its kindred words ... express something more and higher than *hieros*, sacred, outwardly associated with God; ... something more than *semnos*, worthy, honorable; something more than *hagnos*, pure, free from defilement. *Hagios* is ... more comprehensive.... It is characteristically godlikeness" (G. B. Stevens, in *Hastings' Bib. Dic.*).

The adjective is also used of the outer part of the tabernacle, **Heb. 9:2** (RV, "the holy place"); of the inner sanctuary, **9:3**, RV, "the Holy of Holies"; **9:4**, "a holy place," RV; v. **25** (plural), of the presence of God in heaven, where there are not two compartments as in the tabernacle, all being "the holy place"; **9:8**, **12** (neuter plural); **10:19**, "the holy place," RV (KJV, "the holiest," neut. plural); of the city of Jerusalem. Rev. 11:2; its temple, Acts 6:13; of the faith. Jude 20; of the greetings of saints, 1 Cor. 16:20; of angels, e.g., Mark 8:38; of apostles and prophets, Eph. 3:5; of the future heavenly Jerusalem, Rev. 21:2, 10; 22:19.

9:4 Which had the golden censer, and the ark of the covenant overlaid round about with gold, wherein *was* the golden pot that had manna, and Aaron's rod that budded, and the tables of the covenant;

Golden *chruseos* (5552), denotes "golden," i.e., made of, or overlaid with, gold, 2 Tim. 2:20; **Heb. 9:4**, and fifteen times in Revelation.

Censer *thumiaterion* (2369), "a vessel for burning incense" (2 Chron. 26:19; Ezek. 8:11), is found in **Heb. 9:4.**

Ark *kibotos* (2787), "a wooden box, a chest," is used of (a) Noah's vessel, Matt. 24:38; Luke 17:27; **Heb. 11:7**; 1 Pet. 3:20; (b) the "ark" of the covenant in the tabernacle, **Heb. 9:4**; (c) the "ark" seen in vision in the heavenly temple, Rev. 11:19.

Covenant *see* **Commandment** at ***Hebrews 7:18.***

Overlaid *perikalupto* (4028), denotes "to cover around, cover up or over"; it is translated "overlaid" in **Heb. 9:4**.

Round about *pantothen* (3840), "on all sides" (from *pas*, "all"), is translated "round about" in **Heb. 9:4**.

Gold *chrusion* (5553), is used (a) of "coin," Acts 3:6; 20:33; 1 Pet. 1:18; (b) of "ornaments," 1 Pet. 3:3, and the following, 1 Tim. 2:9; Rev. 17:4; 18:16; (c) of "the metal in general," **Heb. 9:4**; 1 Pet. 1:7; Rev. 21:18, 21; metaphorically, (d) of "sound doctrine and its effects," 1 Cor. 3:12; (e) of "righteousness of life and conduct," Rev. 3:18.

Pot *stamnos* (4713), primarily "an earthen jar" for racking off wine, hence, "any kind of jar," occurs in **Heb. 9:4**.

Manna *manna* (3131), the supernaturally provided food for Israel during their wilderness journey (for details see Exod. 16 and Num. 11). The Hebrew equivalent is given in Exod. 16:15, RV marg., "*man hu.*" The translations are, RV, "what is it?"; KJV and RV marg., "it is manna." It is described in Ps. 78:24, 25 as "the corn of heaven" and "the bread of the mighty," RV text and KJV marg. ("angels' food," KJV text), and in 1 Cor. 10:3, as "spiritual meat." The vessel appointed to contain it as a perpetual memorial, was of gold, **Heb. 9:4**, with Exod. 16:33. The Lord speaks of it as being typical of Himself, the true Bread from Heaven, imparting eternal life and sustenance to those who by faith partake spiritually of Him, John 6:31-35. The "hidden manna" is promised as one of the rewards of the overcomer, Rev. 2:17; it is thus suggestive of the moral excellence of Christ in His life on earth, hid from the eyes of men, by whom He was "despised and rejected"; the path of the overcomer is a reflex of His life. None of the natural substances called "manna" is to be identified with that which God provided for Israel.

Rod *see* **Sceptre** at **Hebrews** *1:8*.

Tables *plax* (4109), primarily denotes "anything flat and broad," hence, "a flat stone, a tablet," 2 Cor. 3:3 (twice); **Heb. 9:4**.

9:5 And over it the cherubims of glory shadowing the mercy-seat; of which we cannot now speak particularly.

Cherubims *cheroubim* (5502), are regarded by some as the ideal representatives of redeemed animate creation. In the tabernacle and Temple they were represented by the two golden figures of two-winged living creatures. They were all of one piece with the golden lid of the ark of the covenant in the Holy of Holies signifying that the prospect of redeemed and glorified creatures was bound up with the sacrifice of Christ. This in itself would indicate that they represent redeemed human beings in union with Christ, a union seen, figuratively, proceeding out of the mercy seat. Their faces were towards this mercy seat, suggesting a consciousness of the means whereby union with Christ has been produced. The first reference to the "cherubim" is in Gen. 3:24, which should read "... at the East of the Garden of Eden He caused to dwell in a tabernacle the cherubim, and the flaming sword which turned itself to keep the way of the Tree of Life." This was not simply to keep fallen human beings out; the presence of the "cherubim" suggests that redeemed men, restored to God on God's conditions, would have access to the Tree of Life. (See Rev. 22:14). Certain other references in the OT give clear indication that angelic beings are upon occasion in view, e.g., Ps. 18:10; Ezek. 28:4. So with the vision of the cherubim in Ezek. 10:1-20; 11:22. In the NT the word is found in **Heb. 9:5**, where the reference is to the ark in the tabernacle, and the thought is suggested of those who minister to the manifestation of the glory of God. We may perhaps conclude, therefore, that, inasmuch as in the past and in the present angelic beings have functioned and do function administratively in the service of God, and that redeemed man in the future is to act administratively in fellowship with Him, the "cherubim" in Scripture represent one or other of these two groups of created beings according to what is set forth in the various passages relating to them.

Shadowing *kataskiazo* (2683), lit., "to shadow down," is used of the "overshadowing" (RV) of the cherubim of glory above the mercy seat, **Heb. 9:5** (KJV, "shadowing").

Mercyseat *hilasterion* (2435), "the lid or cover of the ark of the covenant," signifies the Propitiatory, so called on account of the expiation made once a year on the great Day of Atonement, **Heb. 9:5**. For the formation see Exod. 25:17-21. The Heb. word is *kapporeth*, "the cover," a meaning connected with the covering or removal of sin (Ps. 32:1) by means of expiatory sacrifice. This mercy seat, together with the ark, is spoken of as the footstool of God, 1 Chron. 28:2; cf. Ps. 99:5; 132:7. The Lord promised to be present upon it and to commune with Moses "from above the mercy seat, from between the two cherubim," Exod. 25:22. In the Sept. the word *epithema*, which itself means "a cover," is added to *hilasterion; epithema* was simply a translation of *kapporeth;* accordingly, *hilasterion*, not having this meaning, and being essentially connected with propitiation, was added. Eventually *hilasterion* stood for both. In 1 Chron. 28:11 the Holy of Holies is called "the House of the Kapporeth" (see RV, marg.). Through His voluntary expiatory sacrifice in the shedding of His blood, under divine judgment upon sin, and through His resurrection, Christ has become the Mercy Seat for His people.

Cannot *esti* (1510), meaning "it is," is translated "we cannot," in **Heb. 9:5**, lit., "it is not possible (now to speak)"; so in 1 Cor. 11:20; see margin.

Now *mepo*, "not yet," Rom. 9:11; **Heb. 9:5**.

Particularly *meros* is used with certain prepositions in adverbial phrases, (a) with *ana*, used distributively, 1 Cor. 14:27, "in turn," RV, KJV, "by course"; (b) with *kata*, "according to," **Heb. 9:5**, RV, "severally" (KJV, "particularly"); (c) with *apo*, "from," "in part," Rom. 11:25; 2 Cor. 1:14; 2:5; (d) with *ek*, "from," 1 Cor. 13:9, 10, 12; in 1 Cor. 12:27, RV, "severally," marg., "each in his part" (KJV, "in particular").

9:6 Now when these things were thus ordained, the priests went always into the first tabernacle, accomplishing the service *of God*.

Ordained In **Heb. 9:6**, KJV, *kataskeuazo*, "to prepare" (so RV), is translated "were ... ordained." *See also* **Made** at *Hebrews 9:2*.

Went ... into *eiseimi* (1524), "to go into" (*eis*, "into," *eimi*, "to go"), Acts 3:3; 21:18, 26, KJV, "entered"; **Heb. 9:6**, RV, "go in," for KJV, "went into."

Always *diapantos* (1275), is, lit., "through all," i.e., through all time, (*dia*, "through," *pas*, "all"). In the best texts the words are separated. The phrase, which is used of the time throughout which a thing is done, is sometimes rendered "continually," sometimes "always"; "always" or "alway" in Mark 5:5; Acts 10:2; 24:16; Rom. 11:10; "continually" in Luke 24:53; **Heb. 9:6**; **13:15**, the idea being that of a continuous practice carried on without being abandoned.

Tabernacle *see Hebrews 8:2*.

Accomplishing *see* **Make** at *Hebrews 8:5*.

Service of God *see* **Divine service** at *Hebrews 9:1*.

9:7 But into the second *went* the high priest alone once every year, not without blood, which he offered for himself, and *for* the errors of the people:

High priest *see Hebrews 2:17*.

Once *see Hebrews 6:4*.

Year *eniautos* (1763), originally "a cycle of time," is used (a) of a particular time marked by an event, e.g., Luke 4:19; John 11:49, 51; 18:13; Gal. 4:10; Rev. 9:15; (b) to mark a space of time, Acts 11:26; 18:11; Jas. 4:13; 5:17; (c) of that which takes place every year, **Heb. 9:7**; with *kata*, **Heb. 9:25**; **10:1**, 3.

Without *see Hebrews 4:15*.

Blood *see Hebrews 2:14*.

Offered *see* **Offer** at *Hebrews 5:1*.

Errors *agnoema* (51), "a sin of ignorance" (cf. *agnoia*, "ignorance," and *agnoeo*, "to be ignorant"), is used in the plural in **Heb. 9:7**. *See also* **Ignorant** at *Hebrews 5:2*.

9:8 The Holy Ghost this signifying, that the way into the holiest of all was not yet made manifest, while as the first tabernacle was yet standing:

Holy Ghost *see Hebrews 3:7*.

Signifying *deloo* (1213), "to make plain" (*delos*, "evident"), is translated "to signify" in 1 Cor. 1:11, RV, "it hath been signified" (KJV, "declared"); **Heb. 9:8**; **12:27**; 1 Pet. 1:11, KJV (RV, "point unto"); 2 Pet. 1:14, RV, "signified" (KJV, "hath showed").

Holiest of all *see* **Sanctuary** at *Hebrews 8:2*.

Tabernacle *see Hebrews 8:2*.

Standing *stasis* (4714), akin to *histemi*, "to stand," denotes (a) "a standing, stability," **Heb. 9:8**, "(while as the first tabernacle) is yet standing"; (b) "an insurrection, uproar," Mark 15:7; Luke 23:19, 25; Acts 19:40; 24:5; (c) "a dissension, Acts 15:2; 23:7, 10.

9:9 Which *was* a figure for the time then present, in which were offered both gifts and sacrifices, that could not make him that did the service perfect, as pertaining to the conscience;

Figure *parabole* (3850), "a casting or placing side by side" (*para*, "beside," *ballo*, "to throw") with a view to comparison or resemblance, a parable, is translated "figure" in the KJV of **Heb. 9:9** (RV, "a parable for the time now present") and **11:19**, where the return of Isaac was (parabolically, in the lit. sense of the term) figurative of resurrection (RV, "parable").

Present *enistemi* (1764), "to set in," or, in the middle voice and perfect tense of the active voice, "to stand in, be present," is used of the present in contrast with the past, **Heb. 9:9**, where the RV correctly has "(for the time) *now* present" (for the incorrect KJV, "then present"); in contrast to the future, Rom. 8:38; 1 Cor. 3:22; Gal. 1:4, "present"; 1 Cor. 7:26, where "the present distress" is set in contrast to both the past and the future; 2 Thess. 2:2, where the RV, "is *now* present" gives the correct meaning (KJV, incorrectly, "is at hand"); the saints at Thessalonica, owing to their heavy afflictions were possessed of the idea that "the day of the Lord," RV (not as KJV, "the day of Christ"), had begun; this mistake the apostle corrects; 2 Tim. 3:1, "shall come."

Offered *see* **Offer** at *Hebrews 5:1*.

Gifts *see Hebrews 5:1*.

Sacrifices *see Hebrews 5:1*.

Perfect *see Hebrews 2:10*.

Conscience *suneidesis* (4893), lit., "a knowing with" (*sun*, "with," *oida*, "to know"), i.e., "a co-knowledge (with oneself), the witness borne to one's conduct by conscience, that faculty by which we apprehend the will of God, as that which is designed to govern our lives"; hence (a) the sense of guiltiness before God; **Heb. 10:2**; (b) that process of thought which distinguishes what it considers morally good or bad, commending the good, condemning the bad, and so prompting to do the former, and avoid the latter; Rom. 2:15 (bearing witness with God's law); 9:1; 2 Cor. 1:12; acting in a certain way because "conscience" requires it, Rom. 13:5; so as not to cause scruples of "conscience" in another, 1 Cor. 10:28-29; not calling a thing in question unnecessarily, as if conscience demanded it, 1 Cor. 10:25, 27; "commending oneself to every man's conscience," 2 Cor. 4:2; cf. 5:11. There may be a "conscience" not strong enough to distinguish clearly between the lawful and the unlawful, 1 Cor. 8:7, 10, 12 (some regard consciousness as the meaning here). The phrase "conscience toward God," in 1 Pet. 2:19, signifies a "conscience" (or perhaps here, a consciousness) so controlled by the apprehension of God's presence, that the person realizes that griefs are to be borne in accordance with His will. **Heb. 9:9** teaches that sacrifices under the Law could not so perfect a person that he could regard himself as free from guilt. For various descriptions of "conscience" see Acts 23:1; 24:16; 1 Cor. 8:7; 1 Tim. 1:5, 19; 3:9; 4:2; 2 Tim. 1:3; Titus 1:15; **Heb. 9:14**; **10:22**; **13:18**; 1 Pet. 3:16, 2l.

9:10 *Which stood* only in meats and drinks, and divers washings, and carnal ordinances, imposed *on them* until the time of reformation.

Meats *broma* (1033), "food" (akin to *bibrosko*, "to eat," John 6:13), solid food in contrast to milk, is translated "food" in Matt. 14:15, RV (KJV, "victuals"); "meats," Mark 7:19; 1 Cor. 6:13 (twice); 1 Tim. 4:3; **Heb. 9:10**; **13:9**; "meat," John 4:34; Rom. 14:15 (twice), 20; 1 Cor. 3:2; 8:8, 13; 10:3; "food," RV, for KJV, "meat," Luke 3:11; 9:13.

Drinks *poma* (4188), denotes "the thing drunk" (from a root *po-*, found in the Eng., "potion"; it is connected with the root *pi-*), 1 Cor. 10:4; **Heb. 9:10**.

Divers *diaphoros* (1313), signifies "varying in kind, different, diverse." It is used of spiritual gifts, Rom. 12:6; of ceremonial washings, **Heb. 9:10** ("divers").

Washings *see* **Baptisms** at ***Hebrews 6:2***.

Carnal *see* **Flesh** at ***Hebrews 5:7***.

Ordinances *see* ***Hebrews 9:1***.

Imposed *epikeimai* (1945), denotes "to be placed on, to lie on," (a) literally, as of the stone on the sepulchre of Lazarus, John 11:38; of the fish on the fire of coals, 21:9; (b) figuratively, of a tempest (to press upon), Acts 27:20; of a necessity laid upon the apostle Paul, 1 Cor. 9:16; of the pressure of the multitude upon Christ to hear Him, Luke 5:1, "pressed upon"; of the insistence of the chief priests, rulers and people that Christ should be crucified, Luke 23:23, "were instant"; of carnal ordinances "imposed" under the Law until a time of reformation, brought in through the High Priesthood of Christ, **Heb. 9:10**.

Reformation *diorthosis* (1357), properly, "a making straight" (*dia*, "through," *orthos*, "straight"; cf. *diorthoma* in Acts 24:2), denotes a "reformation" or reforming, **Heb. 9:10**; the word has the meaning either (a) of a right arrangement, right ordering, or, more usually, (b) of restoration, amendment, bringing right again; what is here indicated is a time when the imperfect, the inadequate, would be superseded by a better order of things, and hence the meaning (a) seems to be the right one; it is thus to be distinguished from that of Acts 24:2, mentioned above. The word is used in the papyri in the other sense of the rectification of things, whether by payments or manner of life.

9:11 But Christ being come an high priest of good things to come, by a greater and more perfect tabernacle, not made with hands, that is to say, not of this building;

High priest *see* ***Hebrews 2:17***.

Good *agathos* (18), describes that which, being "good" in its character or constitution, is beneficial in its effect; it is used (a) of things physical, e.g., a tree, Matt. 7:17; ground, Luke 8:8; (b) in a moral sense, frequently of persons and things. God is essentially, absolutely and consummately "good," Matt. 19:17; Mark 10:18; Luke 18:19. To certain persons the word is applied in Matt. 20:15; 25:21, 23; Luke 19:17; 23:50; John 7:12; Acts 11:24; Titus 2:5; in a general application, Matt. 5:45; 12:35; Luke 6:45; Rom. 5:7; 1 Pet. 2:18. The neuter of the adjective with the definite article signifies that which is "good," lit., "the good," as being morally honorable, pleasing to God, and therefore beneficial. Christians are to prove it, Rom. 12:2; to cleave to it, 12:9; to do it, 13:3; Gal. 6:10; 1 Pet. 3:11 (here, and here only, the article is absent); John 5:29 (here, the neuter plural is used, "the good things");

to work it, Rom. 2:10; Eph. 4:28; 6:8; to follow after it, 1 Thess. 5:15; to be zealous of it, 1 Pet. 3:13; to imitate it, 3 John 11; to overcome evil with it, Rom. 12:21. Governmental authorities are ministers of "good," i.e., that which is salutary, suited to the course of human affairs, Rom. 13:4. In Philem. 14, "thy goodness," RV (lit., "thy good"), means "thy benefit." As to Matt. 19:17, "why askest thou Me concerning that which is good?" the RV follows the most ancient mss. The neuter plural is also used of material "goods," riches, etc., Luke 1:53; 12:18, 19; 16:25; Gal. 6:6 (of temporal supplies); in Rom. 10:15; **Heb. 9:11**; **10:1**, the "good" things are the benefits provided through the sacrifice of Christ, in regard both to those conferred through the gospel and to those of the coming messianic kingdom.

Tabernacle *see Hebrews 8:2*.

Perfect *teleioteros* (5046), the comparative degree, is used in **Heb. 9:11**, of the very presence of God.

Hands *cheiropoietos* (5499), "made by hand," of human handiwork (*cheir*, and *poieo*, "to make"), is said of the temple in Jerusalem, Mark 14:58; temples in general, Acts 7:48 (RV, "houses"); 17:24; negatively, of the heavenly and spiritual tabernacle, **Heb. 9:11**; of the holy place in the earthly tabernacle, v. **24**; of circumcision, Eph. 2:11. In the Sept., of idols, Lev. 26:1, 30; Isa. 2:18; 10:11; 16:12; 19:1; 21:9; 31:7; 46:6.

Say The phrase *tout' esti* (i.e., *touto esti*), "that is," is so translated in Matt. 27:46, RV (KJV, "that is to say"); so Acts 1:19; in **Heb. 9:11** and **10:20**, KJV and RV, "that is to say"; in Mark 7:11 the phrase is *ho esti*, lit., "which is"; the phrase *ho legetai*, lit., "which is said," John 1:38 and 20:16, is rendered "which is to say."

Building *ktisis* (2937), "a creation," is so translated in the RV of **Heb. 9:11** (KJV "building").

9:12 Neither by the blood of goats and calves, but by his own blood he entered in once into the holy place, having obtained eternal redemption *for us*.

Goats *tragos* (5131), denotes "a hegoat," **Heb. 9:12, 13, 19; 10:4**, the male prefiguring the strength by which Christ laid down His own life in expiatory sacrifice.

Calves *moschos* (3448), primarily denotes "anything young," whether plants or the offspring of men or animals, the idea being that which is tender and delicate; hence "a calf, young bull, heifer," Luke 15:23, 27, 30; **Heb. 9:12, 19**; Rev. 4:7.

Once *see Hebrews 7:27*.

Holy *see* **Holiest** at *Hebrews 9:2*.

Holy place *see* **Sanctuary** at *Hebrews 8:2*.

Obtained *heurisko* (2147), denotes "to find"; in the middle voice, "to find for oneself, to procure, get, obtain," with the suggestion of accomplishing the end which had been in view; so in **Heb. 9:12**, "having obtained (eternal redemption)."

Eternal *see Hebrews 5:9*.

Redemption *lutrosis* (30), "a redemption," is used (a) in the general sense of "deliverance," of the nation of Israel, Luke 1:68 RV, "wrought redemption"; 2:38; (b) of "the redemptive work" of Christ, **Heb. 9:12**, bringing deliverance through His death, from the guilt and power of sin. In the Sept., Lev. 25:29, 48; Num. 18:16; Judg. 1:15; Ps. 49:8; 111:9; 130:7; Isa. 63:4.

9:13 For if the blood of bulls and of goats, and the ashes of an heifer sprinkling the unclean, sanctifieth to the purifying of the flesh:

Bulls *tauros* (5022), Latin *taurus*, is translated "oxen" in Matt. 22:4 and Acts 14:13; "bulls" in **Heb. 9:13** and **10:4**.

Goats *see Hebrews 9:12*.

Ashes *spodos* (4700), "ashes", is found three times, twice in association with sackcloth, Matt. 11:21 and Luke 10:13, as tokens of grief (cf. Esth. 4:1, 3; Isa. 58:5; 61:3; Jer. 6:26; Jonah 3:6); of the ashes resulting from animal sacrifices, **Heb. 9:13**; in the OT, metaphorically, of one who describes himself as dust and "ashes," Gen. 18:27, etc.

Heifer *damalis* (1151), etymologically "one of fit age to be tamed to the yoke" (*damao*, "to tame"), occurs in **Heb. 9:13**, with reference to the "red heifer" of Num. 19.

Sprinkling *rhantizo* (4472), "to sprinkle" (a later form of *rhaino*), is used in the active voice in **Heb. 9:13**, of "sprinkling" with blood the unclean, a token of the efficacy of the expiatory sacrifice of Christ, His blood signifying the giving up of His life in the shedding of His blood (cf. **9:22**) under divine judgment upon sin (the voluntary act to be distinguished from that which took place after His death in the piercing of His side); so again in vv. **19, 21**; in **Heb. 10:22**, passive voice, of the purging (on the ground of the same efficacy) of the hearts of believers from an evil conscience. This application of the blood of Christ is necessary for believers, in respect of their committal of sins, which on that ground receive forgiveness, 1 John 1:9. In Mark 7:4, the verb is found in the middle voice "in some ancient authorities" (RV marg.) instead of *baptizo*.

In Rev. 19:13, the RV, "sprinkled" follows those texts which have *rhantizo* (marg., "some anc. auth. read 'dipped in.'" *bapto*; so Nestle's text).

Unclean *koinoo* (2840), to make *koinos*, "to defile," is translated "unclean" in **Heb. 9:13**, KJV, where the perfect participle, passive, is used with the article, hence the RV, "them that have been defiled."

Sanctifieth *see Hebrews 2:11.*

Purifying *katharotes* (2514), "cleansing," **Heb. 9:13**.

Flesh *see Hebrews 5:7.*

9:14 How much more shall the blood of Christ, who through the eternal Spirit offered himself without spot to God, purge your conscience from dead works to serve the living God?

Eternal *see Hebrews 5:9.*

Spirit *see* Holy Ghost at *Hebrews 3:7.*

Offered *see* Offer at *Hebrews 5:1.*

Spot *amomos* (299), "without blemish"; is always so rendered in the RV, Eph. 1:4; 5:27; Phil. 2:15; Col. 1:22; **Heb. 9:14**; 1 Pet. 1:19; Jude 24; Rev. 14:5. This meaning is to be preferred to the various KJV renderings, "without blame," Eph. 1:4, "unblameable," Col. 1:22, "faultless," Jude 24, "without fault," Rev. 14:5. The most authentic mss. have *amomos*, "without blemish," in Phil. 2:15, for *amometos*, "without rebuke." In the Sept., in reference to sacrifices, especially in Lev. and Num., the Psalms and Ezek., "of blamelessness in character and conduct."

Purge *katharizo* (2511), signifies (1) "to make clean, to cleanse" (a) from physical stains and dirt, as in the case of utensils, Matt. 23:25 (figuratively in verse 26); from disease, as of leprosy, Matt. 8:2; (b) in a moral sense, from the defilement of sin, Acts 15:9; 2 Cor. 7:1; **Heb. 9:14**; Jas. 4:8, "cleanse" from the guilt of sin, Eph. 5:26; 1 John 1:7; (2) "to pronounce clean in a Levitical sense," Mark 7:19, RV; Acts 10:15; 11:9; "to consecrate by cleansings," **Heb. 9:22, 23; 10:2.**

Conscience *see Hebrews 9:9.*

Dead *see Hebrews 6:1.*

Works *see Hebrews 1:10.*

Serve *see Hebrews 8:5.*

9:15 And for this cause he is the mediator of the new testament, that by means of death, for the redemption of the transgressions *that were* under the first testament, they which are called might receive the promise of eternal inheritance.

Mediator *see Hebrews 8:6.*

New *see Hebrews 8:8.*

Testament *see* Commandment at *Hebrews 7:18.*

Means *ginomai* (1096), "to become, take place," is translated "(a death) having taken place" in **Heb. 9:15**, RV, KJV, "by means of (death)," referring, not to the circumstances of a testamentary disposition, but to the sacrifice of Christ as the basis of the New Covenant.

Death *see Hebrews 2:15.*

Redemption *apolutrosis* (629), a strengthened form, lit., "a releasing, for (i.e., on payment of) a ransom." It is used of (a) "deliverance" from physical torture, **Heb. 11:35**; (b) the deliverance of the people of God at the coming of Christ with His glorified saints, "in a cloud with power and great glory," Luke 21:28, a "redemption" to be accomplished at the "outshining of His Parousia," 2 Thess. 2:8, i.e., at His second advent; (c) forgiveness and justification, "redemption" as the result of expiation, deliverance from the guilt of sins, Rom. 3:24, "through the redemption that is in Christ Jesus"; Eph. 1:7, defined as "the forgiveness of our trespasses," RV; so Col. 1:14, "the forgiveness of our sins," indicating both the liberation from the guilt and doom of sin and the introduction into a life of liberty, "newness of life" (Rom. 6:4); **Heb. 9:15**, "for the redemption of the transgressions that were under the first covenant," RV, here "redemption of" is equivalent to "redemption from," the genitive case being used of the object from which the "redemption" is effected, not from the consequence of the transgressions, but from the transgressions themselves; (d) the deliverance of the believer from the presence and power of sin, and of his body from bondage to corruption, at the coming (the Parousia in its inception) of the Lord Jesus, Rom. 8:23; 1 Cor. 1:30; Eph. 1:4; 4:30.

Transgressions *see* Transgression at *Hebrews 2:2.*

Under *see Hebrews 7:11.*

Called *kaleo* (2564), derived from the root *kal-*, whence Eng. "call" and "clamor," is used (a) with a personal object, "to call anyone, invite, summon," e.g., Matt. 20:8; 25:14; it is used particularly of the divine call to partake of the blessings of redemption, e.g., Rom. 8:30; 1 Cor. 1:9; 1 Thess. 2:12; **Heb. 9:15**; (b) of nomenclature or vocation, "to call by a name, to name"; in the passive voice, "to be called by a name, to bear a name." Thus it suggests either vocation or destination; the context determines which, e.g., Rom. 9:25-26; "surname," in Acts 15:37, KJV, is incorrect (RV, "was called").

Promise *see Hebrews 4:1.*

Inheritance *kleronomia* (2817), "a lot," properly "an inherited property, an inheritance." "It is always rendered inheritance in NT, but only in a few cases in the Gospels has it the meaning ordinarily attached to that word in English, i.e., that into possession of which the heir enters only on the death of an ancestor. The NT usage may be set out as follows: (a) that property in real estate which in ordinary course passes from father to son on the death of the former, Matt. 21:38; Mark 12:7; Luke 12:13; 20:14; (b) a portion of an estate made the substance of a gift, Acts 7:5; Gal. 3:18, which also is to be included under (c); (c) the prospective condition and possessions of the believer in the new order of things to be ushered in at the return of Christ, Acts 20:32; Eph. 1:14; 5:5; Col. 3:24; **Heb. 9:15**; 1 Pet. 1:4; (d) what the believer will be to God in that age, Eph. 1:18."

9:16 For where a testament *is*, there must also of necessity be the death of the testator.

Testament *see* **Commandment** at *Hebrews 7:18.*

Necessity *see Hebrews 7:12.*

Testator *see* **Make** at *Hebrews 8:10.*

9:17 For a testament *is* of force after men are dead: otherwise it is of no strength at all while the testator liveth.

Force *bebaios* (949), "firm, secure," is translated "of force" (present usage would translate it "in force") in **Heb. 9:17**, of a testament, or covenant, in relation to a death. *See also* **Stedfast** at *Hebrews 2:2.*

Otherwise *epei* (1893), when used of time, means "since" or "when"; used of cause, it means "since, because"; used elliptically it means "otherwise" or "else"; "otherwise" in Rom. 11:6 (the 2nd part of the v. is absent from the most authentic mss.); v. 22; in **Heb. 9:17**, KJV, "otherwise (it is of no strength at all)," RV, "for (doth it ever avail?)."

Strength *ischuo* (2480), signifies (a) "to be strong in body, to be robust, in sound health," Matt. 9:12; Mark 2:17; (b) "to have power," as of the gospel, Acts 19:20; to prevail against, said of spiritual enemies, Rev. 12:8; of an evil spirit against exorcists, Acts 19:16; (c) "to be of force, to be effective, capable of producing results," Matt. 5:13 ("it is good for nothing"; lit., "it availeth nothing"); Gal. 5:6; in **Heb. 9:17** it apparently has the meaning "to be valid" (RV, "for doth it ever avail ...?", for KJV, "it is of no strength"). It is translated "avail" with reference to prayer, in Jas. 5:16; cf. the strengthened form *exischuo* in Eph. 3:18.

While *hote*, "when," is rendered "while" in John 17:12; **Heb. 9:17**.

Testator *see* **Make** at *Hebrews 8:10.*

9:18 Whereupon neither the first *testament* was dedicated without blood.

Dedicated *enkainizo* (1457), primarily means "to make new, to renew" (*en*, "in," *kainos*, "new"), as in the Sept. of 2 Chron. 15:8; then, to initiate or "dedicate," **Heb. 9:18**, with reference to the first covenant, as not "dedicated" without blood; in **10:20**, of Christ's "dedication" of the new and living way (KJV, "consecrated"; RV, "dedicated"). In the Sept. it has this meaning in Deut. 20:5; 2 Chron. 7:5; Isa. 16:11; 41:1; 45:16, "keep feast (to Me)." *See also* **Consecrated** at *Hebrews 7:28.*

Without *see Hebrews 4:15.*

9:19 For when Moses had spoken every precept to all the people according to the law, he took the blood of calves and of goats, with water, and scarlet wool, and hyssop, and sprinkled both the book, and all the people,

Precept *entole* (1785), "a commandment," is translated "precept" in Mark 10:5 (RV, "commandment"); so **Heb. 9:19**.

Law *see Hebrews 7:16.*

Calves *see Hebrews 9:12.*

Goats *see Hebrews 9:12.*

Water *hudor* (5204), whence Eng. prefix, "hydro-," is used (a) of the natural element, frequently in the Gospels; in the plural especially in Revelation; elsewhere, e.g., **Heb. 9:19**; Jas. 3:12; in 1 John 5:6, that Christ "came by water and blood," may refer either (1) to the elements that flowed from His side on the cross after His death, or, in view of the order of the words and the prepositions here used, (2) to His baptism in Jordan and His death on the cross. As to (1), the "water" would symbolize the moral and practical cleansing effected by the removal of defilement by our taking heed to the Word of God in heart, life and habit; cf. Lev. 14, as to the cleansing of the leper.

Scarlet *kokkinos* (2847), is derived from *kokkos*, used of the "berries" (clusters of the eggs of an insect) collected from the *ilex coccifera;* the color, however, is obtained from the cochineal insect, which attaches itself to the leaves and twigs of the coccifera oak; another species is raised on the leaves of the *cactus ficus*. The Arabic name for this insect is *qirmiz*, whence the word "crimson." It is used (a) of "scarlet" wool, **Heb. 9:19**; cf. in connection with the cleansing of a leper, Lev. 14:4, 6, "scarlet"; with the offering of the red heifer, Num. 19:6; (b) of the robe put on Christ by the soldiers, Matt. 27:28; (c) of the "beast" seen in symbolic vision in Rev. 17:3, "scarlet-colored"; (d) of the clothing of the "woman" as seen sitting on the "beast," 17:4; (e) of part of the merchandise of Babylon, 18:12; (f) figuratively, of the glory of the city itself, 18:16; the neuter is used in the last three instances.

Wool *erion* (2053), occurs in **Heb. 9:19**; Rev. 1:14.

Hyssop *hussopos* (5301), a bunch of which was used in ritual sprinklings, is found in **Heb. 9:19**; in John 19:29 the reference is apparently to a branch or rod of "hyssop," upon which a sponge was put and offered to the Lord on the cross. The suggestion has been made that the word in the original may have been *hussos*, "a javelin"; there seems to be no valid reason for the supposition.

Sprinkled *see* **Sprinkling** at *Hebrews 9:13*.

Book *biblion* (975), had in Hellenistic Greek almost lost its diminutive force and was ousting *biblos* in ordinary use; it denotes "a scroll or a small book." It is used in Luke 4:17, 20, of the "book" of Isaiah; in John 20:30, of the Gospel of John; in Gal. 3:10 and **Heb. 10:7**, of the whole of the OT; in **Heb. 9:19**, of the "book" of Exodus; in Rev. 1:11; 22:7, 9-10, 18 (twice), 19, of the Apocalypse; in John 21:25 and 2 Tim. 4:13, of "books" in general; in Rev. 13:8; 17:8; 20:12; 21:27, of the "Book" of Life; in Rev. 20:12, of other "books" to be opened in the Day of Judgment, containing, it would seem, the record of human deeds. In Rev. 5:1- 9 the "Book" represents the revelation of God's purposes and counsels concerning the world. So with the "little book" in Rev. 10:8. In 6:14 it is used of a scroll, the rolling up of which illustrates the removal of the heaven. In Matt. 19:7 and Mark 10:4 the word is used of a bill of divorcement.

9:20 Saying, This *is* the blood of the testament which God hath enjoined unto you.

Testament *see* **Commandment** at *Hebrews 7:18*.

Enjoined *entello* (1781), signifies "to enjoin upon, to charge with"; it is used in the Middle Voice in the sense of commanding, Matt. 19:7; 28:20; Mark 10:3; 13:34; John 8:5; 15:14, 17; Acts 13:47; **Heb. 9:20**; **11:22**, "gave commandment."

9:21 Moreover he sprinkled with blood both the tabernacle, and all the vessels of the ministry.

Moreover *homoios* (3668), akin to the adjective *homoios*, "like," signifies in "like manner, equally"; in the following the RV has "in like manner" for KJV, "likewise"; Matt. 27:41; Mark 4:16; Luke 10:32; 13:3; 16:25; John 5:19; (**Heb. 9:21**); Jas. 2:25; 1 Pet. 3:1, 7; Rev. 8:12; in Rev. 2:15 the KJV "which thing I hate" translates a variant reading (*ho miso*).

Sprinkled *see* **Sprinkling** at *Hebrews 9:13*.

Tabernacle *see* ***Hebrews 8:2***.

Vessels *skeuos* (4632), is used (a) of "a vessel or implement" of various kinds, Mark 11:16; Luke 8:16; John 19:29; Acts 10:11, 16; 11:5; 27:17 (a sail); Rom. 9:21; 2 Tim. 2:20; **Heb. 9:21**; Rev. 2:27; 18:12; (b) of "goods or household stuff," Matt. 12:29 and Mark 3:27, "goods"; Luke 17:31, RV, "goods" (KJV, "stuff"); (c) of "persons," (1) for the service of God, Acts 9:15, "a (chosen) vessel"; 2 Tim. 2:21, "a vessel (unto honor)"; (2) the "subjects" of divine wrath, Rom. 9:22; (3) the "subjects" of divine mercy, Rom. 9:23; (4) the human frame, 2 Cor. 4:7; perhaps 1 Thess. 4:4; (5) a husband and wife, 1 Pet. 3:7; of the wife, probably, 1 Thess. 4:4; while the exhortation to each one "to possess himself of his own vessel in sanctification and honor" is regarded by some as referring to the believer's body [cf. Rom. 6:13; 1 Cor. 9:27], the view that the "vessel" signifies the wife, and that the reference is to the sanctified maintenance of the married state, is supported by the facts that in 1 Pet. 3:7 the same word *time*, "honor," is used with regard to the wife, again in **Heb. 13:4**, *timios*, "honorable" (RV, "in honor") is used in regard to marriage; further, the preceding command in 1 Thess. 4 is against fornication, and the succeeding one (v. 6) is against adultery. In Ruth 4:10, Sept., *ktaomai*, "to possess," is used of a wife.

Ministry *see* ***Hebrews 8:6***.

9:22 And almost all things are by the law purged with blood; and without shedding of blood is no remission.

Almost *schedon* (4975), is used either (a) of locality, Acts 19:26, or (b) of degree, Acts 13:44; **Heb. 9:22**.

Purged *see* **Purge** at *Hebrews 9:14*.

Without *choris* (5565), is used both as an adverb and as a preposition. As an adverb it signifies "separately, by itself," John 20:7, of the napkin which had been around the Lord's head in the tomb; as a preposition (its more frequent use), "apart from, without, separate from." It is rendered "apart from" in the RV of John 15:5; Rom. 3:21, 28; 4:6; 2 Cor. 12:3; **Heb. 9:22, 28; 11:40**; Jas. 2:18, 20, 26. *See also* ***Hebrews 4:15***.

Blood *haimatekchusia* (130), denotes "shedding of blood," **Heb. 9:22** (*haima*, "blood," *ekchuno*, "to pour out, shed").

Remission *aphesis* (859), "a dismissal, release" (from *aphiemi*), is used of the forgiveness of sins and translated "remission" in Matt. 26:28; Mark 1:4; Luke 1:77; 3:3; 24:47; Acts 2:38; 5:31 (KJV, "forgiveness"); 10:43; 13:38, RV (KJV, "forgiveness"); 26:18 (ditto); **Heb. 9:22; 10:18.**

9:23 *It was* therefore necessary that the patterns of things in the heavens should be purified with these; but the heavenly things themselves with better sacrifices than these.

Necessary *ananke* (318), "a necessity", is rendered "(it was) necessary" in **Heb. 9:23**, lit., "it was a necessity."

Patterns *hupodeigma* (5262), is translated "patterns" in **Heb. 9:23**, KJV. *See also* Example at *Hebrews 4:11.*

Heavens *see* Heavenly at *Hebrews 3:1.*

Purified *katharizo* (2511), "to cleanse, make free from admixture," is translated "to purify" in Acts 15:9, KJV (RV, "cleansing"); Titus 2:14; **Heb. 9:23**, KJV (RV, "cleansed"). *See also* Purge at *Hebrews 9:14.*

Better *see Hebrews 1:4.*

Sacrifices *see Hebrews 5:1.*

9:24 For Christ is not entered into the holy places made with hands, *which are* the figures of the true; but into heaven itself, now to appear in the presence of God for us:

Holy places *see* Sanctuary at *Hebrews 8:2.*

Hands *see Hebrews 9:11.*

Figures *antitupos* (499), an adjective, used as a noun, denotes, lit., "a striking back"; metaphorically, "resisting, adverse"; then, in a passive sense, "struck back"; in the NT metaphorically, "corresponding to," (a) a copy of an archetype, i.e., the event or person or circumstance corresponding to the type, **Heb. 9:24**, RV, "like in pattern" (KJV, "the figure of"), of the tabernacle, which, with its structure and appurtenances, was a pattern of that "holy place," "Heaven itself," "the true," into which Christ entered, "to appear before the face of God for us." The earthly tabernacle anticipatively represented what is now made good in Christ; it was a "figure" or "parable" (**9:9**), "for the time now present," RV, i.e., pointing to the present time, not "then present," KJV; (b) "a corresponding type," 1 Pet. 3:21, said of baptism; the circumstances of the flood, the ark and its occupants, formed a type, and baptism forms "a corresponding type" (not an antitype), each setting forth the spiritual realities of the death, burial, and resurrection of believers in their identification with Christ. It is not a case of type and antitype, but of two types, that in Genesis, the type, and baptism, the corresponding type.

True *see Hebrews 8:2.*

Heaven *see* Heavens at *Hebrews 1:10.*

Appear *emphanizo* (1718), from *en*, "in," intensive, and *phaino*, "to shine," is used, either of "physical manifestation," Matt. 27:53; **Heb. 9:24**; cf. John 14:22, or, metaphorically, of "the manifestation of Christ" by the Holy Spirit in the spiritual experience of believers who abide in His love, John 14:21. It has another, secondary meaning, "to make known, signify, inform." This is confined to the Acts, where it is used five times, 23:15, 22; 24:1; 25:2, 15. There is perhaps a combination of the two meanings in **Heb. 11:14**, i.e., to declare by oral testimony and to "manifest" by the witness of the life.

> *"Bearing shame and scoffing rude, / In my place condemned He stood; / Sealed my pardon with His blood: / Hallelujah, what a Savior!"*
>
> PHILIPP PAUL BLISS

9:25 Nor yet that he should offer himself often, as the high priest entereth into the holy place every year with blood of others;

Offer *see Hebrews 5:1.*

High priest *see Hebrews 2:17.*

Holy place *see* Sanctuary at *Hebrews 8:2.*

Every The preposition *kata*, "down," is sometimes found governing a noun, in the sense of "every," e.g., Luke 2:41, "every year"; 16:19, "every day"; **Heb. 9:25**, "every year" (RV, "year by year"); so **10:3**. This construction sometimes signifies "in every ... ," e.g., Acts 14:23, "in every church"; 15:21, "in every city"; so 20:23; Titus 1:5; Acts 22:19, "in every synagogue" (plural); Acts 8:3 "(into) every house." In Luke 8:1 the phrase means "throughout every city," as in the KJV; in v. 4 "of every city," RV. In Acts 5:42 the RV renders *kat' oikon* "at home," for KJV, "in every house"; in 2:46, for KJV, "from house to house" (marg., "at home"). In Acts 15:21 (last part) the adjective *pas*, "all," is placed between the preposition and the noun for the sake of emphasis. In Acts 26:11, *kata*, followed by the plural of *pas* and the article before the noun, is rendered "in all the synagogues," RV, for KJV, "in every synagogue." The presence of the article confirms the RV.

Year *see Hebrews 9:7.*

Others *allotrios* (245), "belonging to another, not one's own," is translated "other men's" in 2 Cor. 10:15; 1 Tim. 5:22; in **Heb. 9:25**, RV, "not his own" (KJV, "of others").

9:26 For then must he often have suffered since the foundation of the world: but now once in the end of the world hath he appeared to put away sin by the sacrifice of himself.

Then *epei* (1893), a conjunction, when used of cause, meaning "since," "otherwise," "for then," "because"; in an ellipsis, "else," as in 1 Cor. 7:14, where the ellipsis would be "if the unbelieving husband were not sanctified in the wife, your children would be unclean"; cf. Rom. 11:6, 22; 1 Cor. 5:10; **Heb. 9:26**. Sometimes it introduces a question, as in Rom. 3:6; 1. Cor. 14:16; 15:29; **Heb. 10:2**. It is translated "else" in 1 Cor. 14:16 and in the RV in **Heb. 9:26** and **10:2**, for KJV, "for then."

Must *dei* (1163), an impersonal verb, signifying "it is necessary" or "one must," "one ought," is found most frequently in the Gospels, Acts and Revelation, and is used (a) of a necessity lying in the nature of the case, e.g., John 3:30; 2 Tim. 2:6; (b) of necessity brought about by circumstances, e.g., Matt. 26:35, RV, "must," KJV, "should"; John 4:4; Acts 27:21, "should"; 2 Cor. 11:30; in the case of Christ, by reason of the Father's will, e.g., Luke 2:49; 19:5; (c) of necessity as to what is required that something may be brought about, e.g., Luke 12:12, "ought"; John 3:7; Acts 9:6; 1 Cor. 11:19; **Heb. 9:26**; (d) of a necessity of law, duty, equity, e.g., Matt. 18:33, "shouldest"; 23:23, "ought"; Luke 15:32, "it was meet"; Acts 15:5, "it is needful" (RV); Rom. 1:27, RV, "was due," KJV, "was meet" (of a recompense due by the law of God); frequently requiring the rendering "ought," e.g., Rom. 8:26; 12:3; 1 Cor. 8:2; (e) of necessity arising from the determinate will and counsel of God, e.g., Matt. 17:10; 24:6; 26:54; 1 Cor. 15:53, especially regarding the salvation of men through the death, resurrection and ascension of Christ, e.g., John 3:14; Acts 3:21; 4:12.

Suffered *see Hebrews 2:18.*

Foundation *see Hebrews 4:3.*

World *see Hebrews 4:3.*

Once *see Hebrews 6:4.*

End *sunteleia* (4930), signifies "a bringing to completion together" (*sun* "with," *teleo*, "to complete"), marking the "completion" or consummation of the various parts of a scheme. In Matt. 13:39-40, 49; 24:3; 28:20, the rendering "the end of the world" (KJV and RV, text) is misleading; the RV marg., "the consummation of the age," is correct. The word does not denote a termination, but the heading up of events to the appointed climax. *Aion* is not the world, but a period or epoch or era in which events take place. In **Heb. 9:26**, the word translated "world" (KJV) is in the plural, and the phrase is "the consummation of the ages." It was at the heading up of all the various epochs appointed by divine counsels that Christ was manifested (i.e., in His Incarnation) "to put away sin by the sacrifice of Himself."

Appeared *phaneroo* (5319), signifies, in the active voice, "to manifest"; in the passive voice, "to be manifested"; so, regularly, in the RV, instead of "to appear." See 2 Cor. 7:12; Col. 3:4; **Heb. 9:26**; 1 Pet. 5:4; 1 John 2:28; 3:2; Rev. 3:18. To be manifested, in the Scriptural sense of the word, is more than to "appear." A person may "appear" in a false guise or without a disclosure of what he truly is; to be manifested is to be revealed in one's true character; this is especially the meaning of *phaneroo*, see, e.g., John 3:21; 1 Cor. 4:5; 2 Cor. 5:10-11; Eph. 5:13.

Put For *athetesis*, "a putting away," translated "to put away" in **Heb. 9:26**, lit., "(unto) a setting aside." *See also* **Disannulling** at *Hebrews 7:18.*

Sin *see Hebrews 3:13.*

Sacrifice *see* Sacrifices at *Hebrews 5:1.*

9:27 And as it is appointed unto men once to die, but after this the judgment:

Appointed *apokeimai* (606), *apo*, "from," and *keimai*, signifies "to be laid, reserved," Luke 19:20; Col. 1:5; 2 Tim. 4:8; "appointed," in **Heb. 9:27**, where it is said of death and the judgment following (RV, marg., "laid up").

9:28 So Christ was once offered to bear the sins of many; and unto them that look for him shall he appear the second time without sin unto salvation.

Once *see Hebrews 6:4.*

Offered *see* Offer at *Hebrews 5:1.*

Bear *anaphero* (399), is used of "leading persons up to a higher place," and, in this respect, of the Lord's ascension, Luke 24:51. It is used twice of the Lord's propitiatory sacrifice, in His bearing sins on the cross, **Heb. 9:28** and 1 Pet. 2:24; the KJV margin, "to the tree," is to be rejected. The KJV text, "on," and the RV "upon" express the phrase rightly.

Look for *opekdechomai* (553), "to await or expect eagerly," is rendered "to wait for" in Rom. 8:19, 23, 25; 1 Cor. 1:7; Gal. 5:5; Phil. 3:20, RV (KJV, "look for"); **Heb. 9:28**, RV (KJV, "look for"), here "them that wait" represents believers in general, not a section of them; 1 Pet. 3:20 (in the best texts).

Appear *optomai* (3700), "to see" (from *ops*, "the eye"; cf. Eng. "optical," etc.), in the passive sense, "to be seen, to appear," is used (a) objectively, with reference to the person or thing seen, e.g., 1 Cor. 15:5-8, RV "appeared," for KJV, "was seen"; (b) subjectively, with reference to an inward impression or a spiritual experience, John 3:36, or a mental occupation, Acts 18:15, "look to it"; cf. Matt. 27:4, 24, "see (thou) to it," "see (ye) to it," throwing responsibility on others. *Optomai* is to be found in dictionaries under the word *horao*, "to see"; it supplies some forms that are lacking in that verb. These last three words, *emphanizo*, *phaneroo* and *optomai* are used with reference to the "appearances" of Christ in the closing verses of **Heb. 9**; *emphanizo* in v. **24**, of His presence before the face of God for us; *phaneroo* in v. **26**, of His past manifestation for "the sacrifice of Himself"; *optomai* in v. **28**, of His future "appearance" for His saints.

Second *deuteros* (1208), denotes "second in order" with or without the idea of time, e.g., Matt. 22:26, 39; 2 Cor. 1:15; Rev. 2:11; in Rev. 14:8, RV only ("a second angel"); it is used in the neuter, *deuteron*, adverbially, signifying a "second" time, e.g., John 3:4; 21:16; Acts 7:13; Rev. 19:3, RV (KJV, "again"); Jude 5, "afterward" (RV, marg., "the second time"); used with *ek* ("of") idiomatically, the preposition signifying "for (the second time)," Mark 14:72; John 9:24 and Acts 11:9, RV (KJV, "again"); **Heb. 9:28**; in 1 Cor. 12:28, KJV, "secondarily," RV, "secondly."

Without *see Hebrews 9:22. See also Hebrews 4:15.*

Sin In **Heb. 9:28** (2nd part) the reference is to a "sin" offering.

Salvation *see Hebrews 1:14.*

Chapter 10

10:1 For the law having a shadow of good things to come, *and* not the very image of the things, can never with those sacrifices which they offered year by year continually make the comers thereunto perfect.

Shadow *see Hebrews 8:5.*

Good *see Hebrews 9:11.*

Things *see Hebrews 6:18.*

Come *proserchomai* (4334), denotes "to come or go near to" (*pros*, "near to"), e.g., Matt. 4:3; **Heb. 10:1**, KJV, "comers," RV, them that draw nigh.

Very Occasionally one of the forms of the pronoun *autos*, "self, same," is translated "very"; the RV rendering is sometimes "himself," etc., e.g., 1 Thess. 5:23, "(The God of peace) Himself"; see, however, John 14:11, "(the) very (works)"; Rom. 13:6 and Phil. 1:6, "(this) very (thing)"; **Heb. 10:1**, "(the) very (image)"; and the RV, "very" (KJV, "same") in Luke 12:12; 20:19; 24:13, 33; Acts 16:18; Rom. 9:17; Eph. 6:22.

Image *eikon* (1504), denotes "an image"; the word involves the two ideas of representation and manifestation. "The idea of perfection does not lie in the word itself, but must be sought from the context" (Lightfoot); the following instances clearly show any distinction between the imperfect and the perfect likeness. The word is used (1) of an "image" or a coin (not a mere likeness), Matt. 22:20; Mark 12:16; Luke 20:24; so of a statue or similar representation (more than a resemblance), Rom. 1:23; Rev. 13:14, 15 (thrice); 14:9, 11; 15:2; 16:2; 19:20; 20:4; of the descendants of Adam as bearing his image, 1 Cor. 15:49, each a representation derived from the prototype; (2) of subjects relative to things spiritual, **Heb. 10:1**, negatively of the Law as having "a shadow of the good things to come, not the very image of the things," i.e., not the essential and substantial form of them; the contrast has been likened to the difference between a statue and the shadow cast by it ...

Never *oudepote* (3763), from *oude*, "not even," and *pote*, "at any time," is used in definite negative statements, e.g., Matt. 7:23; 1 Cor. 13:8; **Heb. 10:1**, **11**, or questions, e.g., Matt. 21:16, 42; in Luke 15:29 (1st part), RV, "never" (KJV, "neither ... at any time"); KJV and RV, "never" (2nd part).

Sacrifices *see Hebrews 5:1.*

Offered *see* **Offer** at *Hebrews 5:1.*

Year *see Hebrews 9:7.*

Continually *see Hebrews 7:3.*

Perfect *see Hebrews 2:10.*

10:2 For then would they not have ceased to be offered? because that the worshippers once purged should have had no more conscience of sins.

Ceased *pauo* (3973), "to stop, to make an end," is used chiefly in the middle voice in the NT, signifying "to come to an end, to take one's rest, a willing cessation" (in contrast to the passive voice which denotes a forced cessation), Luke 5:4, of a discourse; 8:24, of a storm, 11:1, of Christ's prayer; Acts 5:42, of teaching and preaching; 6:13, of speaking against; 13:10, of evil doing; 20:1, of an uproar; 20:31, of admonition; 21:32, of a scourging; 1 Cor. 13:8, of tongues; Eph. 1:16, of giving thanks; Col. 1:9, of prayer; **Heb. 10:2**, of sacrifices; 1 Pet. 4:1, of "ceasing" from sin. It is used in the active voice in 1 Pet. 3:10, "let him cause his tongue to cease from evil."

Because *see* Then at *Hebrews 9:26*.

Worshippers *latreuo* (3000), "to serve, to render religious service or homage," is translated "to worship" in Phil. 3:3, "(who) worship (by the Spirit of God)," RV, KJV, "(which) worship (God in the spirit)"; the RV renders it "to serve" (for KJV, "to worship") in Acts 7:42; 24:14; KJV and RV, "(the) worshipers" in **Heb. 10:2**, present participle, lit., "(the ones) worshiping."

Once *see Hebrews 6:4*.

Purged *see* Purge at *Hebrews 9:14*.

More *see Hebrews 8:12*.

Conscience *see Hebrews 9:9*.

10:3 But in those *sacrifices there is* a remembrance again *made* of sins every year.

Remembrance *anamnesis* (364), "a remembrance," is used (a) in Christ's command in the institution of the Lord's Supper, Luke 22:19; 1 Cor. 11:24, 25, not "in memory of" but in an affectionate calling of the Person Himself to mind; (b) of the "remembrance" of sins, **Heb. 10:3**, RV, "a remembrance" (KJV, "a remembrance again"; but the prefix *ana* does not here signify "again"); what is indicated, in regard to the sacrifices under the Law, is not simply an external bringing to "remembrance," but an awakening of mind. In the Sept., Lev. 24:7; Num. 10:10; Pss. 38 and 70, Titles.

Every *see Hebrews 9:25*.

Year *see Hebrews 9:7*.

10:4 For *it is* not possible that the blood of bulls and of goats should take away sins.

Not possible *see* **Impossible** at *Hebrews 6:4*.

Bulls *see Hebrews 9:13*.

Goats *see Hebrews 9:12*.

Take *aphaireo* (851), "to take away" (*apo*), is used with this meaning in Luke 1:25; 10:42; 16:3; Rom. 11:27, of the "removal" of the sins of Israel; **Heb. 10:4**, of the impossibility of the "removal" of sins by offerings under the Law; in Rev. 22:19 (twice).

10:5 Wherefore when he cometh into the world, he saith, Sacrifice and offering thou wouldest not, but a body hast thou prepared me:

Wherefore *see Hebrews 3:7*.

Sacrifice *see* Sacrifices at *Hebrews 5:1*.

Offering *prosphora* (4376), lit., "a bringing to," hence an "offering," in the NT a sacrificial "offering," (a) of Christ's sacrifice, Eph. 5:2; **Heb. 10:10** (of His body); **10:14**; negatively, of there being no repetition, **10:18**; (b) of "offerings" under, or according to, the Law, Acts 21:26; **Heb. 10:5**, **8**; (c) of gifts in kind conveyed to needy Jews, Acts 24:17; (d) of the presentation of believers themselves (saved from among the Gentiles) to God, Rom. 15:16.

Prepared *katartizo* (2675), "to render fit, complete" (*artios*), "is used of mending nets, Matt. 4:21; Mark 1:19, and is translated 'restore' in Gal. 6:1. It does not necessarily imply, however, that that to which it is applied has been damaged, though it may do so, as in these passages; it signifies, rather, right ordering and arrangement, **Heb. 11:3**, 'framed;' it points out the path of progress, as in Matt. 21:16; Luke 6:40; cf. 2 Cor. 13:9; Eph. 4:12, where corresponding nouns occur. It indicates the close relationship between character and destiny, Rom. 9:22, 'fitted.' It expresses the pastor's desire for the flock, in prayer, **Heb. 13:21**, and in exhortation, 1 Cor. 1:10, RV, 'perfected' (KJV, 'perfectly joined'); 2 Cor. 13:11, as well as his conviction of God's purpose for them, 1 Pet. 5:10. It is used of the Incarnation of the Word in **Heb. 10:5**, 'prepare,' quoted from Ps. 40:6 (Sept.), where it is apparently intended to describe the unique creative act involved in the Virgin Birth, Luke 1:35. In 1 Thess. 3:10 it means to supply what is necessary, as the succeeding words show."

10:6 In burnt offerings and *sacrifices* for sin thou hast had no pleasure.

Burnt offerings *holokautoma* (3646), denotes "a whole burnt offering" (*holos*, "whole," *kautos*, for *kaustos*, a verbal adjective from *kaio*, "to burn"), i.e., "a victim," the whole of which is burned, as in Ex. 30:20; Lev. 5:12; 23:8, 25, 27. It is used in Mark 12:33, by the scribe who questioned the Lord as to the first commandment in the Law and in **Heb. 10:6**, **8**, RV "whole burnt offerings."

Sin *see Hebrews 3:13.*

Pleasure *eudokeo* (2106), signifies (a) "to be well pleased, to think it good," not merely an understanding of what is right and good as in *dokeo*, but stressing the willingness and freedom of an intention or resolve regarding what is good, e.g., Luke 12:32, "it is (your Father's) good pleasure"; so Rom. 15:26, 27, RV; 1 Cor. 1:21; Gal. 1:15; Col. 1:19; 1 Thess. 2:8, RV, "we were well pleased" (KJV, "we were willing"); this meaning is frequently found in the papyri in legal documents; (b) "to be well pleased with," or "take pleasure in," e.g., Matt. 3:17; 12:18; 17:5; 1 Cor. 10:5; 2 Cor. 12:10; 2 Thess. 2:12; **Heb. 10:6, 8, 38**; 2 Pet. 1:17.

10:7 Then said I, Lo, I come (in the volume of the book it is written of me,) to do thy will, O God.

Volume *kephalis* (2777), lit., "a little head" (a diminutive of *kephale*, "a head"; Lat., *capitulum*, a diminutive of *caput*), hence, "a capital of a column," then, "a roll" (of a book), occurs in **Heb. 10:7**, RV, "in the roll" (KJV, "in the volume"), lit., "in the heading of the scroll" (from Ps. 40:7).

Book *see Hebrews 9:19.*

Will *thelema* (2307), signifies (a) objectively, "that which is willed, of the will of God," e.g., Matt. 18:14; Mark 3:35, the fulfilling being a sign of spiritual relationship to the Lord, John 4:34; 5:30; 6:39, 40; Acts 13:22, plural, "my desires"; Rom. 2:18; 12:2, lit., "the will of God, the good and perfect and acceptable"; here the repeated article is probably resumptive, the adjectives describing the will, as in the Eng. versions; Gal. 1:4; Eph. 1:9; 5:17, "of the Lord"; Col. 1:9; 4:12; 1 Thess. 4:3; 5:18, where it means "the gracious design," rather than "the determined resolve"; 2 Tim. 2:26, which should read "which have been taken captive by him" [(*autou*), i.e., by the Devil; the RV, "by the Lord's servant" is an interpretation; it does not correspond to the Greek] unto His (*ekeinou*) will" (i.e., "God's will"; the different pronoun refers back to the subject of the sentence, viz., God); **Heb. 10:10**; Rev. 4:11, RV, "because of Thy will"; of human will, e.g., 1 Cor. 7:37; (b) subjectively, the "will" being spoken of as the emotion of being desirous, rather than as the thing "willed"; of the "will" of God, e.g., Rom. 1:10; 1 Cor. 1:1; 2 Cor. 1:1; 8:5; Eph. 1:1, 5, 11; Col. 1:1; 2 Tim. 1:1; **Heb. 10:7, 9, 36**; 1 John 2:17; 5:14; of human "will," e.g., John 1:13; Eph. 2:3, "the desires of the flesh"; 1 Pet. 4:3 (in some texts); 2 Pet. 1:21.

God *see Hebrews 1:8.*

10:8 Above when he said, Sacrifice and offering and burnt offerings and *offering* for sin thou wouldest not, neither hadst pleasure *therein*; which are offered by the law;

Above *anoteron* (511), the comparative degree, is the neuter of the adjective *anoteros*. It is used (a) of motion to a higher place, "higher," Luke 14:10; (b) of location in a higher place, i.e., in the preceding part of a passage, "above" **Heb. 10:8**.

Sacrifice *see* **Sacrifices** at *Hebrews 5:1.*

Offering *see* **Offer** at *Hebrews 5:1.*

Burnt offerings *see Hebrews 10:6.*

Sin *see Hebrews 3:13.*

Pleasure *see Hebrews 10:6.*

10:9 Then said he, Lo, I come to do thy will, O God. He taketh away the first, that he may establish the second.

Come *erchomai* (2064), the most frequent verb, denoting either "to come, or to go," signifies the act, in contrast with *heko*, which stresses the arrival, as, e.g., "I am come and am here," John 8:42 and **Heb. 10:9**.

Will *see Hebrews 10:7.*

Taketh *anaireo* (337), "to take up" (*ana*, "up," and *haireo*, "to take"), is used of Pharaoh's daughter in "taking up" the infant Moses, Acts 7:21; of God's act in "taking away" the typical animal sacrifices under the Law, **Heb. 10:9**.

First *protos* (4413), the superlative degree of *pro*, "before," is used (I) "of time or place," (a) as a noun, e.g., Luke 14:18; Rev. 1:17; opposite to "the last," in the neuter plural, Matt. 12:45; Luke 11:26; 2 Pet. 2:20; in the neuter singular, opposite to "the second," **Heb. 10:9**; in 1 Cor. 15:3, *en protois*, lit., "in the first (things, or matters)" denotes "first of all"; (b) as an adjective, e.g., Mark 16:9, used with "day" understood, lit., "the first (day) of (i.e., after) the Sabbath," in which phrase the "of" is objective, not including the Sabbath, but following it; in John 20:4, 8; Rom. 10:19, e.g., equivalent to an English adverb; in John 1:15, lit., "first of me," i.e., "before me" (of superiority).

Establish *histemi* (2476), "to cause to stand," is translated "establish" in Rom. 3:31; 10:3; **Heb. 10:9**.

10:10 By the which will we are sanctified through the offering of the body of Jesus Christ once *for all*.

Will *see Hebrews 10:7.*

Sanctified *hagiasmos* (38), "sanctification," is used of (a) separation to God, 1 Cor. 1:30; 2 Thess. 2:13; 1 Pet. 1:2; (b) the course of life befitting those so separated, 1 Thess. 4:3, 4, 7; Rom. 6:19, 22; 1 Tim. 2:15; **Heb.**

12:14. "Sanctification is that relationship with God into which men enter by faith in Christ, Acts 26:18; 1 Cor. 6:11, and to which their sole title is the death of Christ, Eph. 5:25, 26; Col. 1:22; **Heb. 10:10, 29; 13:12**.

"Sanctification is also used in NT of the separation of the believer from evil things and ways. This sanctification is God's will for the believer, 1 Thess. 4:3, and His purpose in calling him by the gospel, v. 7; it must be learned from God, v. 4, as He teaches it by His Word, John 17:17, 19, cf. Ps. 17:4; 119:9, and it must be pursued by the believer, earnestly and undeviatingly, 1 Tim. 2:15; **Heb. 12:14**. For the holy character, *hagiosune*, 1 Thess. 3:13, is not vicarious, i.e., it cannot be transferred or imputed, it is an individual possession, built up, little by little, as the result of obedience to the Word of God, and of following the example of Christ, Matt. 11:29; John 13:15; Eph. 4:20; Phil. 2:5, in the power of the Holy Spirit, Rom. 8:13; Eph. 3:16. The Holy Spirit is the Agent in sanctification, Rom. 15:16; 2 Thess. 2:13; 1 Pet. 1:2; cf. 1 Cor. 6:11... The sanctification of the Spirit is associated with the choice, or election, of God; it is a Divine act preceding the acceptance of the Gospel by the individual." *See also* **Sanctifieth, Sanctified** at *Hebrews 2:11*.

Offering *see Hebrews 10:5*.

Once *see Hebrews 7:27*.

10:11 And every priest standeth daily ministering and offering oftentimes the same sacrifices, which can never take away sins:

Priest *see* **High priest** at *Hebrews 2:17*.

Ministering *leitourgeo* (3008), in classical Greek, signified at Athens "to supply public offices at one's own cost, to render public service to the State"; hence, generally, "to do service," said, e.g., of service to the gods. In the NT it is used (a) of the prophets and teachers in the church at Antioch, who "ministered to the Lord," Acts 13:2; (b) of the duty of churches of the Gentiles to "minister" in "carnal things" to the poor Jewish saints at Jerusalem, in view of the fact that the former had "been made partakers" of the "spiritual things" of the latter, Rom. 15:27; (c) of the official service of priests and Levites under the Law, **Heb. 10:11** (in the Sept., e.g., Exod. 29:30; Num. 16:9).

Offering *see* **Offer** at *Hebrews 5:1*.

Sacrifices *see Hebrews 5:1*.

Never *see Hebrews 10:1*.

Take *periaireo* (4014), "to take away that which surrounds" (*peri*, "around"), is used (a) literally, of "casting off" anchors, Acts 27:40, RV (KJV, "having taken up"); 28:13 in some texts, for *perierchomai*, "to make a circuit"; (b) metaphorically, of "taking away" the veil off the hearts of Israel, 2 Cor. 3:16; of hope of rescue, Acts 27:20; of sins (negatively), **Heb. 10:11**.

10:12 But this man, after he had offered one sacrifice for sins for ever, sat down on the right hand of God;

Offered *see* **Offer** at *Hebrews 5:1*.

Sacrifice *see* **Sacrifices** at *Hebrews 5:1*.

Ever *see* **Continually** at *Hebrews 7:3*.

10:13 From henceforth expecting till his enemies be made his footstool.

Henceforth Positively, "henceforth" stands for the following: (a) *ap' arti* (i.e., *apo arti*), lit., "from now," e.g., Matt. 26:64; Luke 22:69; John 13:19, RV, and KJV marg., "from henceforth"; Rev. 14:13 (where *aparti* is found as one word in the best mss.); (b) *to loipon*, lit., "(for) the remaining (time)," **Heb. 10:13**; *tou loipou*, Gal. 6:17; (c) *apo tou nun*, lit., "from the now," e.g., Luke 1:48; 5:10; 12:52; Acts 18:6; 2 Cor. 5:16 (1st part).

Expecting *ekdechomai* (1551), lit. and primarily, "to take or receive from" (*ek*, "from," *dechomai*, "to receive"), hence denotes "to await, expect," the only sense of the word in the NT; it suggests a reaching out in readiness to receive something; "expecting," **Heb. 10:13**; "expect," 1 Cor. 16:11, RV (KJV, "look for"); to wait for, John 5:3 (KJV only); Acts 17:16; 1 Cor. 11:33, RV (KJV, "tarry for"); Jas. 5:7; to wait, 1 Pet. 3:20 in some mss.; "looked for," **Heb. 11:10**.

Enemies *see Hebrews 1:13*.

Made *see* **Make** at *Hebrews 1:13*.

Footstool *see Hebrews 1:13*.

10:14 For by one offering he hath perfected for ever them that are sanctified.

Offering *see Hebrews 10:5*.

Perfected *see* **Perfect** at *Hebrews 2:10*.

Ever *see* **Continually** at *Hebrews 7:3*.

10:15 *Whereof* the Holy Ghost also is a witness to us: for after that he had said before,

Holy Ghost *see Hebrews 3:7*.

Witness *see* Witnessed at Hebrews *7:8*.

Said before *prolego* (4302), with the aorist form *proeipon*, and a perfect form *proeireka* (from *proereo*), signifies (1) "to declare openly" or "plainly," or "to say" or "tell beforehand" (*pro*, "before," *lego*, "to say"), translated in 2 Cor. 13:2 (in the first sentence), RV, "I have said beforehand," KJV, "I told ... before", in the next sentence, KJV, "I foretell," RV, "I do say beforehand" (marg., "plainly"); not prophecy is here in view, but a warning given before and repeated; (2) "to speak before, of prophecy," as "foretelling" the future, Mark 13:23, KJV, "have foretold," RV, "have told ... beforehand"; Acts 1:16 (of the prophecy concerning Judas); Rom. 9:29; 2 Pet. 3:2; Jude 17; some inferior mss. have it in **Heb. 10:15**.

10:16 This *is* the covenant that I will make with them after those days, saith the Lord, I will put my laws into their hearts, and in their minds will I write them;

Covenant *see* Commandment at *Hebrews 7:18*.

Make *see Hebrews 8:10*.

Put *see Hebrews 8:10*.

Hearts *see Hebrews 8:10*.

Minds *see* Mind at *Hebrews 8:10*.

Write *see Hebrews 8:10*.

10:17 And their sins and iniquities will I remember no more.

Iniquities *see* Iniquity at *Hebrews 1:9*.

No more *see Hebrews 8:12*.

10:18 Now where remission of these *is, there is* no more offering for sin.

Remission *see Hebrews 9:22*.

Offering *see Hebrews 10:5*.

Sin *see Hebrews 3:13*.

10:19 Having therefore, brethren, boldness to enter into the holiest by the blood of Jesus,

Boldness *see* Confidence at *Hebrews 3:6*.

Enter *eisodos* (1529), lit., "a way in" (*eis*, "in," *hodos*, "a way"), "an entrance," is used (a) of the "coming" of Christ into the midst of the Jewish nation, Acts 13:24, RV marg., "entering in"; (b) of "entrance" upon gospel work in a locality, 1 Thess. 1:9; 2:1; (c) of the present "access" of believers into God's presence, **Heb. 10:19**, lit., "for entrance into"; (d) of their "entrance" into Christ's eternal Kingdom, 2 Pet. 1:11.

Holiest *see* Sanctuary at *Hebrews 8:2*.

Jesus *see Hebrews 2:9*.

10:20 By a new and living way, which he hath consecrated for us, through the veil, that is to say, his flesh;

New *prosphatos* (4732), originally signifying "freshly slain," acquired the general sense of "new," as applied to flowers, oil, misfortune, etc. It is used in **Heb. 10:20** of the "living way" which Christ "dedicated for us ... through the veil ... His flesh" (which stands for His expiatory death by the offering of His body, v. **10**). In the Sept., Num. 6:3; Deut. 32:17; Ps. 81:9; Eccl. 1:9. Cf. the adverb *prosphatos*, "lately, recently," Acts 18:2.

Living *see* Lifetime at *Hebrews 2:15*.

Consecrated *see Hebrews 7:28*. *See also* Dedicated at *Hebrews 9:18*.

Veil *see Hebrews 6:19*.

Say *see Hebrews 9:11*.

10:21 And *having* an high priest over the house of God;

High priest *see Hebrews 2:17*.

House *see Hebrews 3:2*.

10:22 Let us draw near with a true heart in full assurance of faith, having our hearts sprinkled from an evil conscience, and our bodies washed with pure water.

Draw *see* Come ... unto at *Hebrews 4:16*.

Near *proserchomai* (4334), "to come to, go to," is translated "drew near" in Acts 7:31 and **Heb. 10:22**.

True *see Hebrews 8:2*.

Assurance *see Hebrews 6:11*.

Sprinkled *see* Sprinkling at *Hebrews 9:13*.

Evil *see Hebrews 3:12*.

Conscience *see Hebrews 9:9*.

Washed *louo* (3068), signifies "to bathe, to wash the body," (a) active voice, Acts 9:37; 16:33; (b) passive voice, John 13:10, RV, "bathed" (KJV, "washed"); **Heb. 10:22**, lit., "having been washed as to the body," metaphorical of the effect of the Word of God upon the activities of the believer; (c) middle voice, 2 Pet. 2:22. Some inferior mss. have it instead of *luo*, "to loose," in Rev. 1:5 (see RV).

Pure *katharos* (2513), "pure," as being cleansed, e.g., Matt. 5:8; 1 Tim. 1:5; 3:9; 2 Tim. 1:3; 2:22; Titus 1:15; **Heb. 10:22**; Jas. 1:27; 1 Pet. 1:22; Rev. 15:6; 21:18; 22:1 (in some mss.).

10:23 Let us hold fast the profession of *our* faith without wavering; (for he *is* faithful that promised;)

Hold *see Hebrews 3:6*.

Profession *see Hebrews 3:1*.

Faith In **Heb. 10:23**, *elpis*, "hope," is mistranslated "faith" in the KJV (RV, "hope").

Wavering *aklines* (186), "without bending" (*a*, negative, *klino*, "to bend"), occurs in **Heb. 10:23**, KJV, "without wavering," RV, "that it waver not."

Faithful *see Hebrews 2:17*.

Promised *see* Promise at *Hebrews 6:13*.

10:24 And let us consider one another to provoke unto love and to good works:

Consider *see Hebrews 3:1.*

Provoke *paroxusmos* (3948), denotes "a stimulation" (Eng., "paroxysm"): in **Heb. 10:24**, "to provoke," lit., "unto a stimulation (of love)."

Good *kalos* (2570), denotes that which is intrinsically "good," and so, "goodly, fair, beautiful," as (a) of that which is well adapted to its circumstances or ends, e.g., fruit, Matt. 3:10; a tree, 12:33; ground, 13:8, 23; fish, 13:48; the Law, Rom. 7:16; 1 Tim. 1:8; every creature of God, 1 Tim. 4:4; a faithful minister of Christ and the doctrine he teaches, 4:6; (b) of that which is ethically good, right, noble, honorable, e.g., Gal. 4:18; 1 Tim. 5:10, 25; 6:18; Titus 2:7, 14; 3:8, 14. The word does not occur in Revelation, nor indeed after 1 Peter. Christians are to "take thought for things honorable" (*kalos*), 2 Cor. 8:21, RV; to do that which is honorable, 13:7; not to be weary in well doing, Gal. 6:9; to hold fast "that which is good," 1 Thess. 5:21; to be zealous of good works, Titus 2:14; to maintain them, 3:8; to provoke to them, **Heb. 10:24**; to bear testimony by them, 1 Pet. 2:12.

Works *see Hebrews 1:10.*

10:25 Not forsaking the assembling of ourselves together, as the manner of some *is*; but exhorting *one another*: and so much the more, as ye see the day approaching.

Forsaking *enkataleipo* (1459), denotes (a) "to leave behind, among, leave surviving," Rom. 9:29; (b) "to forsake, abandon, leave in straits, or helpless," said by, or of, Christ, Matt. 27:46; Mark 15:34; Acts 2:27, 31; of men, 2 Cor. 4:9; 2 Tim. 4:10, 16; by God, **Heb. 13:5**; of things, by Christians (negatively), **Heb. 10:25**.

Assembling *episunagoge* (1997), "a gathering together," is used in 2 Thess. 2:1, of the "rapture" of the saints; for **Heb. 10:25**.

Manner *ethos* (1485), "a habit, custom" (akin to the verb *etho*, "to be accustomed"), is always translated "custom" in the RV ("manner" in the KJV of John 19:40; Acts 15:1; 25:16; **Heb. 10:25**).

One another In **Heb. 10:25**, "*one another*" is necessarily added in English to complete the sense of *parakaleo*, "to exhort."

Much *see Hebrews 1:4.*

More *mallon* (3123), the comparative degree of *mala*, "very, very much," is used (a) of increase, "more," with qualifying words, with *pollo*, "much," e.g., Mark 10:48, "the more (a great deal)"; Rom. 5:15, 17, "(much) more"; Phil. 2:12 (ditto); with *poso*, "how much," e.g., Luke 12:24; Rom. 11:12; with *tosouto*, "by so much," **Heb. 10:25**; (b) without a qualifying word, by way of comparison, "the more," e.g., Luke 5:15, "so much the more"; John 5:18, "the more"; Acts 5:14 (ditto); Phil. 1:9; 1 Thess. 4:1, 10, "more and more"; 2 Pet. 1:10, RV, "the more" (KJV, "the rather"); in Acts 20:35, by a periphrasis, it is translated "more (blessed)"; in Gal. 4:27, "more (than)," lit., "rather (than)"; (c) with qualifying words, similarly to (a), e.g., Mark 7:36.

Approaching *engizo* (1448), "to come near draw nigh" (akin to *engus*, "near"), is translated by the verb "draw near or nigh," in the RV, Luke 12:33, KJV, "approacheth"; **Heb. 10:25**, KJV, "approaching"; Luke 18:35; 19:29, 37; Acts 22:6, KJV, "was come nigh"; Luke 7:12 "came nigh"; Acts 9:3, "came near." *See also* **Draw nigh** at *Hebrews 7:19.*

10:26 For if we sin wilfully after that we have received the knowledge of the truth, there remaineth no more sacrifice for sins,

Sin *see* **Sinned** at **Hebrews** *3:17.*

Wilfully *hekousios* (1596), denotes "voluntarily, willingly," **Heb. 10:26**, (of sinning) "willfully"; in 1 Pet. 5:2, "willingly" (of exercising oversight over the flock of God).

Knowledge *epignosis* (1922), denotes "exact or full knowledge, discernment, recognition," and is a strengthened form of *gnosis*, expressing a fuller or a full "knowledge," a greater participation by the "knower" in the object "known," thus more powerfully influencing him. It is not found in the Gospels and Acts. Paul uses it 15 times (16 if **Heb. 10:26** is included) out of the 20 occurrences; Peter 4 times, all in his 2nd Epistle. Contrast Rom. 1:28 (*epignosis*) with the simple verb in v. 21. "In all the four Epistles of the first Roman captivity it is an element in the Apostle's opening prayer for his correspondents' well-being, Phil. 1:9; Eph. 1:17; Col. 1:9; Philem. 6" (Lightfoot). It is used with reference to God in Rom. 1:28; 10:2; Eph. 1:17; Col. 1:10; 2 Pet. 1:3; God and Christ, 2 Pet. 1:2; Christ, Eph. 4:13; 2 Pet. 1:8; 2:20; the will of the Lord, Col. 1:9; every good thing, Philem. 6, RV (KJV, "acknowledging"); the truth, 1 Tim. 2:4; 2 Tim. 2:25, RV; 3:7; Titus 1:1, RV; the mystery of God. Col. 2:2, RV, "(that they) may know" (KJV, "to the acknowledgment of"), lit., "into a full knowledge." It is used without the mention of an object in Phil. 1:9; Col. 3:10, RV, "(renewed) unto knowledge."

Remaineth *see Hebrews 4:6.*

Sacrifice *see* **Sacrifices** at *Hebrews 5:1.*

10:27 But a certain fearful looking for of judgment and fiery indignation, which shall devour the adversaries.

Fearful *phoberos* (5398), "fearful," is used only in the active sense in the NT, i.e., causing "fear," terrible, **Heb. 10:27, 31; 12:21**, RV, "fearful," for KJV, "terrible."

Looking for *ekdoche* (1561), is translated "looking for" in **Heb. 10:27**, KJV.

Fiery *zelos* (2205), "zeal, jealousy," is rendered "fierceness" in **Heb. 10:27**, RV (of fire). *See also* **Fire** at *Hebrews 1:7.*

Indignation In Acts 5:17, the KJV translates *zelos* by "indignation" (RV "jealousy"); in **Heb. 10:27**, KJV, "indignation" (RV, "fierceness"; marg., "jealousy").

Shall *see Hebrews 1:14.*

Devour *esthio* (2068), is a strengthened form of an old verb *edo*, from the root *ed-*, whence Lat., *edo*, Eng., "eat." The form *ephagon*, used as the 2nd aorist tense of this verb, is from the root *phag-*, "to eat up." It is translated "devour" in **Heb. 10:27**; elsewhere, by the verb "to eat."

Adversaries *hupenantios* (5227), "contrary, opposed," is a strengthened form of *enantios* (*en*, "in," and *antios*, "set against"). The intensive force is due to the preposition *hupo*. It is translated "contrary to," in Col. 2:14, of ordinances; in **Heb. 10:27**, "adversaries." In each place a more violent form of opposition is suggested than in the case of *enantios*

10:28 He that despised Moses' law died without mercy under two or three witnesses:

He The indefinite pronoun *tis*, "anyone, any man," is rendered "he" in Acts 4:35, KJV (RV, rightly, "any one"); in **Heb. 10:28**, RV, "a man."

Despised *atheteo* (114), "to set aside, reject," is translated "set at nought" in **Heb. 10:28**, RV (KJV, "despised"); so Jude 8.

Died *apothnesko* (599), lit., "to die off or out," is used (a) of the separation of the soul from the body, i.e., the natural "death" of human beings, e.g., Matt. 9:24; Rom. 7:2; by reason of descent from Adam, 1 Cor. 15:22; or of violent "death," whether of men or animals; with regard to the latter it is once translated "perished," Matt. 8:32; of vegetation, Jude 12; of seeds, John 12:24; 1 Cor. 15:36; it is used of "death" as a punishment in Israel under the Law, in **Heb. 10:28**; (b) of the separation of man from God, all who are descended from Adam not only "die" physically, owing to sin, see (a) above, but are naturally in the state of separation from God, 2 Cor. 5:14. From this believers are freed both now and eternally, John 6:50; 11:26, through the "death" of Christ, Rom. 5:8, e.g.; unbelievers, who "die" physically as such, remain in eternal separation from God, John 8:24. Believers have spiritually "died" to the Law as a means of life, Gal. 2:19; Col. 2:20; to sin, Rom. 6:2, and in general to all spiritual association with the world and with that which pertained to their unregenerate state, Col. 3:3, because of their identification with the "death" of Christ, Rom. 6:8. As life never means mere existence, so "death," the opposite of life, never means nonexistence.

Without mercy *oiktirmos* (3628), is used in **Heb. 10:28** with *choris*, "without," (lit., "without compassions"). It is translated "mercies" in Rom. 12:1 and 2 Cor. 1:3.

Under *see Hebrews 7:11.*

Three *treis* (5143), is regarded by many as a number sometimes symbolically indicating fullness of testimony or manifestation, as in the three persons in the Godhead, cf. 1 Tim. 5:19; **Heb. 10:28**; the mention in 1 John 5:7 is in a verse which forms no part of the original; no Greek ms. earlier than the 14th century contained it; no version earlier than the 5th cent. in any other language contains it, nor is it quoted by any of the Greek or Latin "Fathers" in their writings on the Trinity. That there are those who bear witness in Heaven is not borne out by any other Scripture. It must be regarded as the interpolation of a copyist. In Mark 9:31 and 10:34 the best texts have *meta treis hemeras*, "after three days," which idiomatically expresses the same thing as *te tritehemera*, "on the third day," which some texts have here, as, e.g., the phrase "the third day" in Matt. 17:23; 20:19; Luke 9:22; 18:33, where the repetition of the article lends stress to the number, lit., "the day the third"; 24:7, 46; Acts 10:40.

Witnesses *martus* or *martur* (3144), (whence Eng., "martyr," one who bears "witness" by his death) denotes "one who can or does after what he has seen or heard or knows"; it is used (a) of God, Rom. 1:9; 2 Cor. 1:23; Phil. 1:8; 1 Thess. 2:5, 10 (2nd part); (b) of Christ, Rev. 1:5; 3:14; (c) of those who "witness" for Christ by their death, Acts 22:20; Rev. 2:13; Rev. 17:6; (d) of the interpreters of God's counsels, yet to "witness" in Jerusalem in the times of the Antichrist, Rev. 11:3; (e) in a forensic sense, Matt. 18:16; 26:65; Mark 14:63; Acts 6:13; 7:58; 2 Cor. 13:1; 1 Tim. 5:19; **Heb. 10:28**; (f) in a historical sense, Luke 11:48; 24:48; Acts 1:8, 22; 2:32; 3:15; 5:32; 10:39, 41; 13:31; 22:15; 26:16; 1 Thess. 2:10

(1st part); 1 Tim. 6:12; 2 Tim. 2:2; **Heb. 12:1**, "(a cloud) of witnesses," here of those mentioned in **ch. 11**, those whose lives and actions testified to the worth and effect of faith, and whose faith received "witness" in Scripture; 1 Pet. 5:1.

10:29 Of how much sorer punishment, suppose ye, shall he be thought worthy, who hath trodden under foot the Son of God, and hath counted the blood of the covenant, wherewith he was sanctified, an unholy thing, and hath done despite unto the Spirit of grace?

Sorer *cheiron* (5501), used as the comparative degree of *kakos*, "evil," describes (a) the condition of certain men, Matt. 12:45; Luke 11:26; 2 Pet. 2:20; (b) evil men themselves and seducers, 2 Tim. 3:13; (c) indolent men who refuse to provide for their own households, and are worse than unbelievers, 1 Tim. 5:8, RV; (d) a rent in a garment, Matt. 9:16; Mark 2:21; (e) an error, Matt. 27:64; (f) a person suffering from a malady, Mark 5:26; (g) a possible physical affliction, John 5:14; (h) a punishment, **Heb. 10:29**, "sorer."

Punishment *timoria* (5098), primarily "help", denotes "vengeance, punishment," **Heb. 10:29**.

Suppose *dokeo* (1380), "to be of opinion," is translated "to suppose" in Mark 6:49; Luke 24:37; John 20:15; Acts 27:13; in the following, KJV "suppose," RV, "think," Luke 12:51; 13:2; **Heb. 10:29**. It is most frequently rendered "to think," always in Matthew; always in John, except 11:31, "supposing," RV [where the best texts have this verb (for *lego*, KJV, "saying")], and 20:15.

Worthy *see* ***Hebrews 3:3***.

Trodden *katapateo* (2662), "to tread down, trample under foot," is used (a) literally, Matt. 5:13; 7:6; Luke 8:5; 12:1; (b) metaphorically, of "treading under foot" the Son of God, **Heb. 10:29**, i.e., turning away from Him, to indulge in willful sin.

Counted *hegeomai* (2233), primarily, "to lead the way"; hence, "to lead before the mind, account," is found with this meaning in Phil. 2:3, RV (KJV, "esteem"); 2:6, RV (KJV, "thought"); 2:25 (KJV, "supposed"); Phil. 3:7-8; 2 Thess. 3:15; 1 Tim. 1:12; 6:1; **Heb. 10:29**; Jas. 1:2; **Heb. 11:11** (KJV, "judged"); 2 Pet. 2:13; 3:9.

Covenant *see* **Commandment** at ***Hebrews 7:18***.

Sanctified *see* ***Hebrews 10:10***.

Unholy *koinon* (2839), the neut. of *koinos*, "common," is translated "an unholy thing" in **Heb. 10:29**.

Despite *enubrizo* (1796), "to treat insultingly, with contumely" (*en*, intensive, *hubrizo*, "to insult"; some connect it with *huper*, "above, over," Lat. *super*, which suggests the insulting disdain of one who considers himself superior), is translated "hath done despite" in **Heb. 10:29**.

Spirit *see* **Holy Ghost** at ***Hebrews 3:7***.

10:30 For we know him that hath said, Vengeance *belongeth* unto me, I will recompense, saith the Lord. And again, The Lord shall judge his people.

Vengeance *ekdikesis* (1557), vengeance," is used with the verb *poieo*, "to make," i.e., to avenge, in Luke 18:7-8; Acts 7:24; twice it is used in statements that "vengeance" belongs to God, Rom. 12:19; **Heb. 10:30**. In 2 Thess. 1:8 it is said of the act of divine justice which will be meted out to those who know not God and obey not the gospel, when the Lord comes in flaming fire at His second advent. In the divine exercise of judgment there is no element of vindictiveness, nothing by way of taking revenge. In Luke 21:22, it is used of the "days of vengeance" upon the Jewish people; in 1 Pet. 2:14, of civil governors as those who are sent of God "for vengeance on evildoers" (KJV, "punishment"); in 2 Cor. 7:11, of the "self-avenging" of believers, in their godly sorrow for wrong doing, RV, "avenging," for KJV, revenge.

Recompense *antapodidomi* (467), "to give back as an equivalent, to requite, recompense" (the *anti* expressing the idea of a complete return), is translated "render" in 1 Thess. 3:9, here only in the NT of thanksgiving to God (cf. the Sept. of Ps. 116:12); elsewhere it is used of "recompense," "whether between men (but in that case only of good, not of evil, 1 Thess. 5:15), Luke 14:14*a*, cf. the corresponding noun in v. 12; or between God and evil-doers, Rom. 12:19, RV (KJV, "repay"); **Heb. 10:30**, cf. the noun in Rom. 11:9; or between God and those who do well, Luke 14:14 *b*; Rom. 11:35, cf. the noun in Col. 3:24; in 2 Thess. 1:6 both reward and retribution are in view."

Judge *krites* (2923), "a judge," is used (a) of God, **Heb. 12:23**, where the order in the original is "to a Judge who is God of all"; this is really the significance; it suggests that He who is the Judge of His people is at the same time their God; that is the order in **10:30**; the word is also used of God in Jas. 4:12, RV; (b) of Christ, Acts 10:42; 2 Tim. 4:8; Jas. 5:9; (c) of a ruler in Israel in the times of the Judges, Acts 13:20; (d) of a Roman procurator, Acts 24:10; (e) of those whose conduct provides a standard of "judging," Matt. 12:27; Luke 11:19; (f) in the forensic sense, of one who tries and decides a case, Matt. 5:25 (twice); Luke 12:14; 12:58 (twice); 18:2; 18:6 (lit., "the judge of unrighteousness," expressing subjectively his character); Acts 18:15; (g) of one who passes, or arrogates to himself, judgment on anything, Jas. 2:4 (see the RV); 4:11.

10:31 *It is* a fearful thing to fall into the hands of the living God.

Fearful *see Hebrews 10:27.*

Hands *see Hebrews 1:10.*

10:32 But call to remembrance the former days, in which, after ye were illuminated, ye endured a great fight of afflictions;

Remembrance *anamimnesko* (363), *ana*, "back," and *mimnesko*, signifies in the active voice "to remind, call to one's mind," 1 Cor. 4:17, "put (KJV, bring) ... into remembrance"; so 2 Tim. 1:6; in the passive voice, "to remember, call to (one's own) mind," Mark 11:21, "calling to remembrance"; 14:72, "called to mind"; 2 Cor. 7:15, "remembereth"; **Heb. 10:32**, "call to remembrance."

Former *proteros* (4387), "before, former," is translated "former" in Eph. 4:22; **Heb. 10:32**; 1 Pet. 1:14. *See also* **First** at *Hebrews 4:6; 7:27.*

Illuminated *see* **Enlightened** at *Hebrews 6:4.*

Endured *hupomeno* (5278), a strengthened form, denotes "to abide under, to bear up courageously" (under suffering), Matt. 10:22; 24:13; Mark 13:13; Rom. 12:12, translated "patient"; 1 Cor. 13:7; 2 Tim. 2:10, 12 (KJV, "suffer"); **Heb. 10:32; 12:2-3, 7**; Jas. 1:12; 5:11; 1 Pet. 2:20, "ye shall take it patiently." It has its other significance, "to tarry, wait for, await," in Luke 2:43; Acts 17:14 (in some mss., Rom. 8:24). Cf. *makrothumeo*, "to be longsuffering".

Fight *athlesis* (119), denotes "a combat, contest of athletes"; hence, "a struggle, fight," **Heb. 10:32**, with reference to affliction. Cf. *athleo*, "to strive," 2 Tim. 2:5 (twice).

Afflictions *pathema* (3804), is rendered "sufferings" in the RV (KJV, "afflictions") in 2 Tim. 3:11; **Heb. 10:32**; 1 Pet. 5:9; in Gal. 5:24, "passions (KJV, "affections").

10:33 Partly, whilst ye were made a gazingstock both by reproaches and afflictions; and partly, whilst ye became companions of them that were so used.

Partly In **Heb. 10:33**, "partly ... partly" is a translation of the antithetic phrases "*touto men*," ("this indeed,") and "*touto de*," ("but this,"), i.e., "on the one hand ... and on the other hand."

Whilst In **Heb. 10:33**, AV., "whilst ye were made," partly translating the present participle of *theatrizomai*, "to become a gazing-stock," RV, "being made"; in the 2nd part, *ginomai*, "to become," is translated "whilst ye became," KJV (RV, "becoming").

Gazingstock *theatrizo* (2301), signifies "to make a spectacle" (from *theatron*, "a theater, spectacle, show"); it is used in the passive voice in **Heb. 10:33**, "being made a gazingstock."

Reproaches *oneidismos* (3680), "a reproach, defamation," is used in Rom. 15:3; 1 Tim. 3:7; **Heb. 10:33; 11:26; 13:13.**

Afflictions *thlipsis* (2347), primarily means "a pressing, pressure," anything which burdens the spirit. In two passages in Paul's Epistles it is used of future retribution, in the way of "affliction," Rom. 2:9; 2 Thess. 1:6. In Matt. 24:9, the KJV renders it as a verb, "to be afflicted," (RV, "unto tribulation"). It is coupled with *stenochoria*, "anguish," in Rom. 2:9; 8:35; with *ananke*, "distress," 1 Thess. 3:7; with *diogmos*, "persecution," Matt. 13:21; Mark 4:17; 2 Thess. 1:4. It is used of the calamities of war, Matt. 24:21, 29; Mark 13:19, 24; of want, 2 Cor. 8:13, lit., "distress for you"; Phil. 4:14 (cf. 1:16); Jas. 1:27; of the distress of woman in childbirth, John 16:21; of persecution, Acts 11:19; 14:22; 20:23; 1 Thess. 3:3, 7; **Heb. 10:33**; Rev. 2:10; 7:14; of the "afflictions" of Christ, from which (His vicarious sufferings apart) his followers must not shrink, whether sufferings of body or mind, Col. 1:24; of sufferings in general, 1 Cor. 7:28; 1 Thess. 1:6, etc.

Companions *koinonos* (2844), is rendered "companions" in the KJV of **Heb. 10:33** (RV "partakers"). So *sunkoinonos* in Rev. 1:9, KJV, "companion"; RV, "partaker with you."

Used *anastrepho* (390), chiefly denotes "to behave, to live in a certain manner," rendered "(were so) used" in **Heb. 10:33** (passive voice); the verb, however, does not mean "to treat or use"; here it has the significance of "living amidst sufferings, reproaches," etc.

10:34 For ye had compassion of me in my bonds, and took joyfully the spoiling of your goods, knowing in yourselves that ye have in heaven a better and an enduring substance.

Compassion *see* **Feeling** at *Hebrews 4:15.*

Bonds *desmos* (1199), from *deo*, "to bind", is usually found in the plural, either masculine or neuter; (a) it stands thus for the actual "bonds" which bind a prisoner, as in Luke 8:29; Acts 16:26; 20:23 (the only three places where the neuter plural is used); 22:30; (b) the masculine plural stands frequently in a figurative sense for "a condition of imprisonment," Phil. 1:7, 13, i.e., "so that my captivity became manifest as appointed for the cause of Christ"; verses 14, 16; Col. 4:18; 2 Tim. 2:9; Philem. 10, 13; **Heb. 10:34**. In Mark 7:35 "the bond (KJV, string)" stands metaphorically for "the infirmity which caused an impediment in his speech." So in Luke 13:16, of the infirmity of the woman who was bowed together.

Took *prosdechomai* (4327), "to receive favorably," is rendered "took" in **Heb. 10:34**.

Joyfully In **Heb. 12:11**, "joyous" represents the phrase *meta*, "with," followed by *chara*, lit., "with joy." So in **10:34**, "joyfully"; in 2 Cor. 7:4 the noun is used with the middle voice of *huperperisseuo*, "to abound more exceedingly," and translated "(I overflow) with joy," RV (KJV, "I am exceeding joyful").

Spoiling *harpage* (724), "pillage," is rendered "spoiling" in **Heb. 10:34**.

Goods *huparcho* (5225), "to be in existence," and, in a secondary sense, "to belong to," is used with this meaning in the neuter plural of the present participle with the article signifying one's "possessions," "the things which he possesseth," Luke 12:15; Acts 4:32; in **Heb. 10:34**, RV, "possessions" (KJV, "goods").

Knowing *ginosko* (1097), signifies "to be taking in knowledge, to come to know, recognize, understand," or "to understand completely," e.g., Mark 13:28, 29; John 13:12; 15:18; 21:17; 2 Cor. 8:9; **Heb. 10:34**; 1 John 2:5; 4:2, 6 (twice), 7, 13; 5:2, 20; in its past tenses it frequently means "to know in the sense of realizing," the aorist or point tense usually indicating definiteness, Matt. 13:11; Mark 7:24; John 7:26; in 10:38 "that ye may know (aorist tense) and understand, (present tense)"; 19:4; Acts 1:7; 17:19; Rom. 1:21; 1 Cor. 2:11 (2nd part), 14; 2 Cor. 2:4; Eph. 3:19; 6:22; Phil. 2:19; 3:10; 1 Thess. 3:5; 2 Tim. 2:19; Jas. 2:20; 1 John 2:13 (twice), 14; 3:6; 4:8; 2 John 1; Rev. 2:24; 3:3, 9. In the passive voice, it often signifies "to become known," e.g., Matt. 10:26; Phil. 4:5. In the sense of complete and absolute understanding on God's part, it is used, e.g., in Luke 16:15; John 10:15 (of the Son as well as the Father); 1 Cor. 3:20 ...

Better *see Hebrews 1:4.*

Enduring *meno* (3306), "to abide," is rendered "to endure" in the KJV of John 6:27 and 1 Pet. 1:25 (RV, "abideth"); **Heb. 10:34**, KJV, "enduring (substance)," RV, "abiding."

Substance *huparxis* (5223), primarily "subsistence," later denoted "substance, property, possession" in **Heb. 10:34**, RV (KJV, substance).

10:35 Cast not away therefore your confidence, which hath great recompence of reward.

Cast *apoballo* (577), "to throw off from, to lay aside, to cast away," Mark 10:50; **Heb. 10:35**.

Confidence *see Hebrews 3:6.*

Recompence *see Hebrews 2:2.*

10:36 For ye have need of patience, that, after ye have done the will of God, ye might receive the promise.

Will *see Hebrews 10:7.*

Receive *komizo* (2865), denotes "to bear, carry," e.g., Luke 7:37; in the middle voice, "to bear for oneself," hence (a) "to receive," **Heb. 10:36**; **11:13** (in the best texts; some have *lambano*, "to take" or "to receive"), **39**; 1 Pet. 1:9; 5:4; in some texts in 2 Pet. 2:13 (in the best mss. *adikeomai*, "suffering wrong," RV); (b) "to receive back, recover," Matt. 25:27; **Heb. 11:19**; metaphorically, of requital, 2 Cor. 5:10; Col. 3:25, of "receiving back again" by the believer at the judgment seat of Christ hereafter, for wrong done in this life; Eph. 6:8, of "receiving," on the same occasion, "whatsoever good thing each one doeth," RV.

Promise *see Hebrews 4:1.*

10:37 For yet a little while, and he that shall come will come, and will not tarry.

Little *mikron* (3397), is used adverbially (a) of distance, Matt. 26:39; Mark 14:35; (b) of quantity, 2 Cor. 11:1, 16; (c) of time, Matt. 26:73, "a while"; Mark 14:70; John 13:33, "a little while", 14:19; 16:16-9; **Heb. 10:37**, with the repeated *hoson*, "how very," lit., "a little while, how little, how little."

Tarry *chronizo* (5549), from *chronos*, "time," lit. means "to while away time," i.e., by way of lingering, tarrying, "delaying"; "delayeth," Matt. 24:48; Luke 12:45, "tarried" Matt. 25:5; "tarried so long," Luke 1:21; "will (not) tarry," **Heb. 10:37**.

10:38 Now the just shall live by faith: but if *any man* draw back, my soul shall have no pleasure in him.

Just *dikaios* (1342), signifies "just," without prejudice or partiality, e.g., of the judgment of God, 2 Thess. 1:5, 6; of His judgments, Rev. 16:7; 19:2; of His character as Judge, 2 Tim. 4:8; Rev. 16:5; of His ways and doings, Rev. 15:3. In the following the RV substitutes "righteous" for the KJV "just"; Matt. 1:19; 13:49; 27:19, 24; Mark 6:20; Luke 2:25; 15:7; 20:20; 23:50; John 5:30; Acts 3:14; 7:52; 10:22; 22:14; Rom. 1:17; 7:12; Gal. 3:11; **Heb. 10:38**; Jas. 5:6; 1 Pet. 3:18; 2 Pet. 2:7; 1 John 1:9; Rev. 15:3.

Draw *hupostello* (5288), "to draw back, withdraw," perhaps a metaphor from lowering a sail and so slackening the course, and hence of being remiss in holding the truth; in the active voice, rendered "drew back" in Gal. 2:12, RV (KJV, "withdrew"); in the middle, in **Heb. 10:38**, "shrink back" RV (KJV, "draw back"); the prefix *hupo*, "underneath," is here suggestive of stealth. In v. **39** the corresponding noun, *hupostole*, is translated "of them that shrink back," RV; KJV, "draw back" (lit., "of shrinking back"). In Acts 20:20, 27, "shrank," RV.

Soul *see Hebrews 4:12.*

Pleasure *see Hebrews 10:6.*

10:39 But we are not of them who draw back unto perdition; but of them that believe to the saving of the soul.

Draw *see Hebrews 10:38.*

Perdition *apoleia* (684), indicating "loss of well-being, not of being," is used (a) of things, signifying their waste, or ruin; of ointment, Matt. 26:8; Mark 14:4; of money, Acts 8:20 ("perish"); (b) of persons, signifying their spiritual and eternal perdition, Matt. 7:13; John 17:12; 2 Thess. 2:3, where "son of perdition" signifies the proper destiny of the person mentioned; metaphorically of men persistent in evil, Rom. 9:22, where "fitted" is in the middle voice, indicating that the vessels of wrath fitted themselves for "destruction", of the adversaries of the Lord's people, Phil. 1:28 ("perdition"); of professing Christians, really enemies of the cross of Christ, Phil. 3:19 (RV, "perdition"); of those who are subjects of foolish and hurtful lusts, 1 Tim. 6:9; of professing Hebrew adherents who shrink back into unbelief, **Heb. 10:39**; of false teachers, 2 Pet. 2:1, 3; of ungodly men, 3:7; of those who wrest the Scriptures, 3:16; of the Beast, the final head of the revived Roman Empire, Rev. 17:8, 11; (c) of impersonal subjects, as heresies, 2 Pet. 2:1, where "destructive heresies" (RV; KJV, "damnable") is, lit., "heresies of destruction" (marg., "sects of perdition"); in v. 2 the most authentic mss. have *aselgeiais*, "lascivious," instead of *apoleiais*.

Saving *peripoiesis* (4047), (a) "preservation," (b) "acquiring or gaining something," is used in this latter sense in **Heb. 10:39**, translated "saving" (RV marg., "gaining"); the reference here is to salvation in its completeness.

Soul *see Hebrews 4:12.*

Chapter 11

11:1 Now faith is the substance of things hoped for, the evidence of things not seen.

Substance *hupostasis* (5287), lit., "a standing under, support" (*hupo*, "under," *histemi*, "to stand"), hence, an "assurance," is so rendered in **Heb. 11:1**, RV, for KJV, "substance." It here may signify a title-deed, as giving a guarantee, or reality. *See also* **Person** at *Hebrews 1:3.*

Things *see Hebrews 6:18.*

11:2 For by it the elders obtained a good report.

Elders *presbuteros* (4245), an adjective, the comparative degree of *presbus*, "an old man, an elder," is used (a) of age, whether of the "elder" of two persons, Luke 15:25, or more, John 8:9, "the eldest", or of a person advanced in life, a senior, Acts 2:17; in **Heb. 11:2**, the "elders" are the forefathers in Israel so in Matt. 15:2; Mark 7:3, 5 the feminine of the adjective is used of "elder" women in the churches, 1 Tim. 5:2, not in respect of position but in seniority of age; (b) of rank or positions of responsibility, (1) among Gentiles, as in the Sept. of Gen. 50:7; Num. 22:7, (2) in the Jewish nation, firstly, those who were the heads or leaders of the tribes and families, as of the seventy who assisted Moses, Num. 11:16; Deut. 27:1, and those assembled by Solomon; secondly, members of the Sanhedrin, consisting of the chief priests, "elders" and scribes, learned in Jewish law, e.g., Matt. 16:21; 26:47; thirdly, those who managed public affairs in the various cities, Luke 7:3; (3) in the Christian churches those who, being raised up and qualified by the work of the Holy Spirit, were appointed to have the spiritual care of, and to exercise oversight over, the churches. To these the term "bishops," *episkopoi*, or "overseers," is applied (see Acts 20, v. 17 with v. 28, and Titus 1:5 and 7), the latter term indicating the nature of their work *presbuteroi* their maturity of spiritual experience. The divine arrangement seen throughout

"Faith is to believe, on the word of God, what we do not see, and its reward is to see and enjoy what we believe."

ST. AUGUSTINE

the NT was for a plurality of these to be appointed in each church, Acts 14:23; 20:17; Phil. 1:1; 1 Tim. 5:17; Titus 1:5. The duty of "elders" is described by the verb *episkopeo*. They were appointed according as they had given evidence of fulfilling the divine qualifications, Titus 1:6 to 9; cf. 1 Tim. 3:1-7 and 1 Pet. 5:2; (4) the twenty-four "elders" enthroned in heaven around the throne of God, Rev. 4:4, 10; 5:5-14; 7:11, 13; 11:16; 14:3; 19:4. The number twenty-four is representative of earthly conditions. The word "elder" is nowhere applied to angels.

Obtained In **Heb. 11:2, 4, 39**, KJV, *martureo*, "to bear witness," and in the passive voice, "to have witness borne to one," is translated "to obtain" a good report, or "to obtain" witness (RV, "had witness borne").

Report *martureo* (3140), "to be a witness, bear witness, testify," signifies, in the passive voice, "to be well testified of, to have a good report," Acts 6:3, "of good (KJV, honest) report," lit., "being well testified of"; 10:22; 16:2; 22:12; 1 Tim. 5:10; in **Heb. 11:2, 39**, KJV, "obtained a good report" (RV, "had witness borne to them"); in 3 John 12, KJV "hath good report" (RV, "hath the witness"), lit., "witness hath been borne." *See also* **Witnessed** at *Hebrews 7:8*.

11:3 Through faith we understand that the worlds were framed by the word of God, so that things which are seen were not made of things which do appear.

Understand *noeo* (3539), "to perceive with the mind," as distinct from perception by feeling, is so used in Matt. 15:17, KJV, "understand," RV, "perceive"; 16:9, 11; 24:15 (here rather perhaps in the sense of considering) and parallels in Mark (not in Luke); John 12:40; Rom. 1:20; 1 Tim. 1:7; **Heb. 11:3**; in Eph. 3:4, KJV, "may understand" (RV, "can perceive"); 3:20, "think"; 2 Tim. 2:7, "consider."

Worlds *see Hebrews 1:2*.

Framed *katartizo* (2675), "to fit, to render complete," is translated "have been framed" in **Heb. 11:3**, of the worlds or ages. *See also* **Prepared** at *Hebrews 10:5*.

Word *rhema* (4487), denotes "that which is spoken, what is uttered in speech or writing"; in the singular, "a word," e.g., Matt. 12:36; 27:14; 2 Cor. 12:4; 13:1; **Heb. 12:19**; in the plural, speech, discourse, e.g., John 3:34; 8:20; Acts 2:14; 6:11, 13; 11:14; 13:42; 26:25; Rom. 10:18; 2 Pet. 3:2; Jude 17; it is used of the gospel in Rom. 10:8 (twice), 17, RV, "the word of Christ" (i.e., the "word" which preaches Christ); 10:18; 1 Pet. 1:25 (twice); of a statement, command, instruction, e.g., Matt. 26:75; Luke 1:37, RV, "(no) word (from God shall be void of power)", v. 38; Acts 11:16; **Heb. 11:3**. The significance of *rhema* (as distinct from *logos*) is exemplified in the injunction to take "the sword of the Spirit, which is the word of God," Eph. 6:17; here the reference is not to the whole Bible as such, but to the individual Scripture which the Spirit brings to our remembrance for use in time of need, a prerequisite being the regular storing of the mind with Scripture.

Made *see Hebrews 3:14*.

Appear *phaino* (5316), signifies, in the active voice, "to shine"; in the passive, "to be brought forth into light, to become evident, to appear." In Rom. 7:13, concerning sin, the RV has "might be shewn to be," for KJV, "appear." It is used of the "appearance" of Christ to the disciples, Mark 16:9; of His future "appearing" in glory as the Son of Man, spoken of as a sign to the world, Matt. 24:30; there the genitive is subjective, the sign being the "appearing" of Christ Himself; of Christ as the light, John 1:5; of John the Baptist, 5:35; of the "appearing" of an angel of the Lord, either visibly, Matt. 1:20, or in a dream, 2:13; of a star, 2:7; of men who make an outward show, Matt. 6:5; 6:18 (see the RV); 23:27-28; 2 Cor. 13:7; of tares, Matt. 13:26; of a vapor, Jas. 4:14; of things physical in general, **Heb. 11:3**; used impersonally in Matt. 9:33, "it was never so seen"; also of what appears to the mind, and so in the sense of to think, Mark 14:64, or to seem, Luke 24:11 (RV, appeared).

11:4 By faith Abel offered unto God a more excellent sacrifice than Cain, by which he obtained witness that he was righteous, God testifying of his gifts: and by it he being dead yet speaketh.

Offered *see* **Offer** at *Hebrews 5:1*.

Sacrifice *see* **Sacrifices** at *Hebrews 5:1*.

Obtained *see Hebrews 11:2*.

Witness *see* **Witnessed** at Hebrews *7:8*.

Testifying *see* **Testifieth** at *Hebrews 7:17*.

Gifts *see Hebrews 5:1*.

11:5 By faith Enoch was translated that he should not see death; and was not found, because God had translated him: for before his translation he had this testimony, that he pleased God.

Translated *metatithemi* (3346), "to transfer to another place" (*meta,* implying "change," *tithemi,* "to put"), is rendered "to translate" in **Heb. 11:5** (twice).

See *horao* (3708), with its aorist form *eidon,* "to see" (in a few places the KJV uses the verb "to behold"), is said (a) of bodily vision, e.g., Mark 6:38; John 1:18, 46; (b) of mental perception, e.g., Rom. 15:21; Col. 2:18; (c) of taking heed, e.g., Matt. 8:4; 1 Thess. 5:15; (d) of experience, as of death, Luke 2:26; **Heb. 11:5**; life, John 3:36; corruption, Acts 2:27; (e) of caring for, Matt. 27:4; Acts 18:15 (here the form *opsomai* is used).

Found *heurisko* (2147), denotes (a) "to find," either with previous search, e.g., Matt. 7:7, 8, or without, e.g., Matt. 27:32; in the passive voice, of Enoch's disappearance, **Heb. 11:5**; of mountains, Rev. 16:20; of Babylon and its occupants, 18:21, 22; (b) metaphorically, "to find out by enquiry," or "to learn, discover," e.g., Luke 19:48; John 18:38; 19:4, 6; Acts 4:21; 13:28; Rom. 7:10; Gal. 2:17, which indicates "the surprise of the Jew" who learned for the first time that before God he had no moral superiority over the Gentiles whom he superciliously dubbed "sinners," while he esteemed himself to be "righteous"; 1 Pet. 1:7; Rev. 5:4; (c) in the middle voice, "to find for oneself, gain, procure, obtain," e.g. Matt. 10:39; 11:29, "ye shall find (rest)"; Luke 1:30; Acts 7:46; 2 Tim. 1:18.

Translation *metathesis* (3331), "a change of position," is rendered "translation" in **Heb. 11:5**. *See also* **Changed, Change** at *Hebrews 7:12.*

Pleased *euaresteo* (2100), signifies "to be well-pleasing"; in the active voice, **Heb. 11:5**, RV, "he had been "well-pleasing" (unto God)," KJV, "he pleased"; so v. **6**; in the passive voice **Heb. 13:16**.

11:6 But without faith *it is* impossible to please *him*: for he that cometh to God must believe that he is, and *that* he is a rewarder of them that diligently seek him.

Without *see Hebrews 4:15.*

Impossible *see Hebrews 6:4.*

Please *see* **Pleased** at *Hebrews 11:5.*

Rewarder *misthapodotes* (3406), "one who pays wages" (*misthos,* "wages," *apo,* "back," *didomi,* "to give"), is used by metonymy in **Heb. 11:6**, of God, as the "Rewarder" of those who "seek after Him" (RV). Cf. *misthapodosia,* "recompence." *See also* **Recompence** at *Hebrews 2:2.*

Seek *ekzeteo* (1567), signifies (a) "to seek out (*ek*) or after, to search for"; e.g., God Rom. 3:11; the Lord, Acts 15:17; in **Heb. 11:6**, RV, "seek after" (KJV, "diligently seek"); **12:17**, RV, "sought diligently" (KJV, "sought carefully"); 1 Pet. 1:10, RV, "sought" (KJV, "have inquired"), followed by *exeraunao,* "to search diligently", (b) "to require or demand," Luke 11:50, 51.

11:7 By faith Noah, being warned of God of things not seen as yet, moved with fear, prepared an ark to the saving of his house; by the which he condemned the world, and became heir of the righteousness which is by faith.

Warned *see* **Admonished** at *Hebrews 8:5.*

Fear *eulbeomai* (2125), "to be cautious, to beware," signifies to act with the reverence produced by holy "fear," **Heb. 11:7**, "moved with godly fear."

Prepared *see* **Made** at *Hebrews 9:2.*

Ark *see Hebrews 9:4.*

Saving *see* **Salvation** at *Hebrews 1:14.*

Condemned *katakrino* (2632), a strengthened form, signifies "to give judgment against, pass sentence upon"; hence, "to condemn," implying (a) the fact of a crime, e.g., Rom. 2:1; 14:23; 2 Pet. 2:6; some mss. have it in Jas. 5:9; (b) the imputation of a crime, as in the "condemnation" of Christ by the Jews, Matt. 20:18; Mark 14:64. It is used metaphorically of "condemning" by a good example, Matt. 12:41-42; Luke 11:31-32; **Heb. 11:7**. In Rom. 8:3, God's "condemnation" of sin is set forth in that Christ, His own Son, sent by Him to partake of human nature (sin apart) and to become an offering for sin, died under the judgment due to our sin.

Heir *see Hebrews 1:2.*

11:8 By faith Abraham, when he was called to go out into a place which he should after receive for an inheritance, obeyed; and he went out, not knowing whither he went.

Obeyed *see* **Obey** at *Hebrews 5:9.*

Knowing *epistamai* (1987), "to know, know of, understand" (probably an old middle voice form of *ephistemi,* "to set over"), is used in Mark 14:68, "understand," which follows *oida* "I (neither) know"; most frequently in the Acts, 10:28; 15:7; 18:25; 19:15, 25; 20:18; 22:19; 24:10; 26:26; elsewhere, 1 Tim. 6:4; **Heb. 11:8**; Jas. 4:14; Jude 10.

11:9 By faith he sojourned in the land of promise, as *in* a strange country, dwelling in tabernacles with Isaac and Jacob, the heirs with him of the same promise:

Sojourned *paroikeo* (3939), denotes "to dwell beside, among or by" (*para,* "beside," *oikeo,* "to dwell"); then, "to dwell in a place as a *paroikos*, a stranger," Luke 24:18, RV, "Dost thou (alone) sojourn ...?" [marg., "Dost thou sojourn (alone)" is preferable], KJV, "art thou (only) a stranger?" (*monos*, "alone," is an adjective, not an adverb); in **Heb. 11:9**, RV, "he became a sojourner" (KJV, "he sojourned"), the RV gives the force of the aorist tense.

Land *ge* (1093), in one of its usages, denotes (a) "land" as distinct from sea or other water, e.g., Mark 4:1; 6:47; Luke 5:3; John 6:21; (b) "land" as subject to cultivation, e.g., Luke 14:35; (c) "land" as describing a country or region, e.g., Matt. 2:20, 21; 4:15; Luke 4:25; in 23:44, RV, "(the whole) land," KJV, "(all the) earth"; Acts 7:29; **Heb. 11:9**, RV, "a land (not his own)," KJV "a (strange) country;" Jude 5. In Acts 7:11 the KJV follows a reading of the noun with the definite article which necessitates the insertion of "land."

Promise *see Hebrews 4:1.*

Strange *allotrios* (245), denotes (a) "belonging to another" (*allos*); (b) "alien, foreign, strange," Acts 7:6; **Heb. 11:9, 34** KJV, RV, "(a land) not his own."

Tabernacles *see* **Tabernacle** at *Hebrews 8:2.*

Heirs *sunkleronomos* (4789), "a joint-heir, co-inheritor," "is used of Isaac and Jacob as participants with Abraham in the promises of God, **Heb. 11:9**; of husband and wife who are also united in Christ, 1 Pet. 3:7; of Gentiles who believe, as participants in the gospel with Jews who believe, Eph. 3:6; and of all believers as prospective participants with Christ in His glory, as recompense for their participation in His sufferings, Rom. 8:17."

11:10 For he looked for a city which hath foundations, whose builder and maker *is* God.

Looked for *ekdechomai* (1551), primarily "to receive from another," hence, "to expect, to await," is translated "he looked for" in **Heb. 11:10**; in 1 Cor. 16:11, KJV, "I look for" (RV, "I expect"). *See also* **Expecting** at *Hebrews 10:13.*

City *polis* (4172), primarily "a town enclosed with a wall" (perhaps from a root *ple-*, signifying "fullness," whence also the Latin *pleo*, "to fill," Eng., "polite, polish, politic, etc."), is used also of the heavenly Jerusalem, the abode and community of the redeemed, **Heb. 11:10, 16; 12:22; 13:14.** In Revelation it signifies the visible capital of the heavenly kingdom, as destined to descend to earth in a coming age, e.g., Rev. 3:12; 21:2, 14, 19. By metonymy the word stands for the inhabitants, as in the English use, e.g., Matt. 8:34; 12:25; 21:10; Mark 1:33; Acts 13:44.

Foundations *see* **Foundation** at *Hebrews 6:1.*

Builder *technites* (5079), "an artificer, one who does a thing by rules of art," is rendered "builder" in **Heb. 11:10**, marg., "architect," which gives the necessary contrast between this and the next noun in the verse.

Maker *demiourgos* (1217), lit., "one who works for the people" (from *demos*, "people," *ergon*, "work"; an ancient inscription speaks of the magistrates of Tarsus as *demiourgoi*: the word was formerly used thus regarding several towns in Greece; it is also found used of an artist), came to denote, in general usage, a builder or "maker," and is used of God as the "Maker" of the heavenly city, **Heb. 11:10.** In that passage the first word of the two, *technites*, denotes "an architect, designer," the second, *demiourgos*, is the actual Framer, the city is the archetype of the earthly one which God chose for His earthly people. Cf. *ktistes*, "creator."

11:11 Through faith also Sara herself received strength to conceive seed, and was delivered of a child when she was past age, because she judged him faithful who had promised.

Strength *dunamis* (1411), is rendered "strength" in the RV and KJV of Rev. 1:16; elsewhere the RV gives the word its more appropriate meaning "power," for KJV, "strength," 1 Cor. 15:56; 2 Cor. 1:8; 12:9; **Heb. 11:11**; Rev. 3:8; 12:10.

Conceive The phrase *eis katabolen*, lit., "for a casting down, or in," is used of conception in **Heb. 11:11.** *See also* **Foundation** at *Hebrews 4:3.*

Seed *see Hebrews 2:16.*

Age *helikia* (2244), primarily "an age," as a certain length of life, came to mean (a) "a particular time of life," as when a person is said to be "of age," John 9:21, 23, or beyond a certain stage of life, **Heb. 11:11**; (b) elsewhere only "of stature," e.g., Matt. 6:27; Luke 2:52; 12:25; 19:3; Eph. 4:13. Some regard Matt. 6:27 and Luke 12:25 as coming under (a). It is to be distinguished from *aion* and *genea*, since it has to do simply with matters relating to an individual, either his time of life or his height.

Judged In **Heb. 11:11**, the verb *hegeomai*, "to consider, think, account," is rendered "she judged (Him faithful)," KJV (RV, "she counted"). *See also* **Counted** at *Hebrews 10:29.*

Faithful *see Hebrews 2:17.*

Promised *see* **Promise** at *Hebrews 6:13.*

11:12 Therefore sprang there even of one, and him as good as dead, *so many* as the stars of the sky in multitude, and as the sand which is by the sea shore innumerable.

Sprang *ginomai* (1096), "to become," is used in the best texts in **Heb. 11:12**, "sprang" (some have *gennao*, in the passive voice, rendered in the same way).

Dead *nekroo* (3499), "to put to death," is used in the active voice in the sense of destroying the strength of, depriving of power, with reference to the evil desires which work in the body, Col. 3:5. In the passive voice it is used of Abraham's body as being "as good as dead," Rom. 4:19 with **Heb. 11:12**.

Stars *astron* (798), is used (a) in the sing. in Acts 7:43, "the star of the god Rephan," RV, the symbol or "figure," probably of Saturn, worshiped as a god, apparently the same as Chiun in Amos 5:26 (Rephan being the Egyptian deity corresponding to Saturn, Chiun the Assyrian); (b) in the plur., Luke 21:25; Acts 27:20; **Heb. 11:12**.

Sky *see* **Heavens** at *Hebrews 1:10*.

Multitude *plethos* (4128), lit., "a fullness," hence, "a large company, a multitude," is used (a) of things: of fish, Luke 5:6; John 21:6; of sticks ("bundle"), Acts 28:3; of stars and of sand, **Heb. 11:12**; of sins, Jas. 5:20; 1 Pet. 4:8; (b) of persons, (1) a "multitude": of people, e.g., Mark 3:7, 8; Luke 6:17; John 5:3; Acts 14:1; of angels, Luke 2:13; (2) with the article, the whole number, the "multitude," the populace, e.g., Luke 1:10; 8:37; Acts 5:16; 19:9; 23:7; a particular company, e.g., of disciples, Luke 19:37; Acts 4:32; 6:2, 5; 15:30; of elders, priests, and scribes, 23:7; of the apostles and the elders of the Church in Jerusalem, Acts 15:12.

Sand *ammos* (285), "sand" or "sandy ground," describes (a) an insecure foundation, Matt. 7:26; (b) numberlessness, vastness, Rom. 9:27; **Heb. 11:12**; Rev. 20:8; (c) symbolically in Rev. 13:1, RV, the position taken up by the Dragon (not, as in the KJV, by John), in view of the rising of the Beast out of the sea (emblematic of the restless condition of nations).

Shore *cheilos* (5491), is used (a) of the organ of speech, Matt. 15:8 and Mark 7:6, where "honoring with the lips," besides meaning empty words, may have reference to a Jewish custom of putting to the mouth the tassel of the tallith (the woollen scarf wound round the head and neck during prayer), as a sign of acceptance of the Law from the heart; Rom. 3:13; 1 Cor. 14:21 (from Isa. 28:11, 12, speaking of the Assyrian foe as God's message to disobedient Israel); **Heb. 13:15**; 1 Pet. 3:10; (b) metaphorically, of "the brink or edge of things," as of the sea shore, **Heb. 11:12**, lit., "the shore (of the sea)."

Innumerable *anarithmetos* (382), *a*, negative, *n*, euphonic, *arithmeo*, "to number," is used in **Heb. 11:12**.

11:13 These all died in faith, not having received the promises, but having seen them afar off, and were persuaded of *them*, and embraced *them*, and confessed that they were strangers and pilgrims on the earth.

Received *see* **Receive** at *Hebrews 10:36*.

Afar *porrothen* (4207), "afar off," from *porro*, "at a distance, a great way off," is found in Luke 17:12 and **Heb. 11:13**.

Persuaded *see Hebrews 6:9*.

Embraced *aspazomai* (782), signifies "to greet welcome," or "salute." In the KJV it is chiefly rendered by either of the verbs "to greet" or "to salute." "There is little doubt that the revisers have done wisely in giving 'salute' ... in the passages where KJV has 'greet.' For the cursory reader is sure to imagine a difference of Greek and of meaning when he finds, e.g., in Phil. 4:21, 'Salute every saint in Christ Jesus. The brethren which are with me greet you,' or in 3 John 14, 'Our friends salute thee. Greet the friends by name'" (*Hastings' Bible Dic.*). In Acts 25:13 the meaning virtually is "to pay his respects to." In two passages the renderings vary otherwise; in Acts 20:1, of bidding farewell, KJV, "embraced them," RV, "took leave of them," or, as Ramsay translates it, "bade them farewell"; in **Heb. 11:13**, of welcoming promises, KJV, "embraced," RV, "greeted." The verb is used as a technical term for conveying "greetings" at the close of a letter, often by an amanuensis, e.g., Rom. 16:22, the only instance of the use of the first person in this respect in the NT; see also 1 Cor. 16:19, 20; 2 Cor. 13:13; Phil. 4:22; Col. 4:10-15; 1 Thess. 5:26; 2 Tim. 4:21; Titus 3:15; Philem. 23; **Heb. 13:24**; 1 Pet. 5:13, 14; 2 John 13. This special use is largely illustrated in the papyri, one example of this showing how keenly the absence of the greeting was felt. The papyri also illustrate the use of the addition "by name," when several persons are included in the greeting, as in 3 John 14 (Moulton and Milligan, *Vocab*).

Confessed *homologeo* (3670), lit., "to speak the same thing" (*homos*, "same," *lego*, "to speak"), "to assent, accord, agree with," denotes, (a) "to confess, declare, admit," John 1:20; e.g., Acts 24:14; **Heb. 11:13**; (b) "to confess by way of admitting oneself guilty of what one is accused of, the result of inward conviction," 1 John 1:9; (c) "to declare openly by way of speaking out freely, such confession being the effect of deep conviction of facts," Matt. 7:23; 10:32 (twice) and Luke 12:8 (see next par.); John 9:22; 12:42; Acts 23:8; Rom. 10:9-10 ("confession is made"); 1 Tim. 6:12 (RV); Titus 1:16; 1 John 2:23; 4:2, 15; 2 John 7 (in John's epistle it is the necessary antithesis to Gnostic doceticism); Rev. 3:5, in the best mss.; (d) "to confess by way of celebrating with praise," **Heb. 13:15**; (e) "to promise," Matt. 14:7. In Matt. 10:32 and Luke 12:8 the construction of this verb with *en*, "in," followed by the dative case of the personal pronoun, has a special significance, namely, to "confess" in a person's name, the nature of the "confession" being determined by the context, the suggestion being to make a public "confession." Thus the statement, "every one ... who shall confess Me (lit. "in Me," i.e., in My case) before men, him (lit., "in him," i.e., in his case) will I also confess before My Father ... ," conveys the thought of "confessing" allegiance to Christ as one's Master and Lord, and, on the other hand, of acknowledgment, on His part, of the faithful one as being His worshipper and servant, His loyal follower; this is appropriate to the original idea in *homologeo* of being identified in thought or language.

Strangers *xenos* (3581), "strange", denotes "a stranger, foreigner," Matt. 25:35, 38, 43, 44; 27:7; Acts 17:21; Eph. 2:12, 19; **Heb. 11:13**; 3 John 5.

Pilgrims *parepidemos* (3927), an adjective signifying "sojourning in a strange place, away from one's own people" (*para*, "from," expressing a contrary condition, and *epidemeo*, "to sojourn"; *demos*, "a people"), is used of OT saints, **Heb. 11:13**, "pilgrims" (coupled with *xenos*, "a foreigner"); of Christians, 1 Pet. 1:1, "sojourners (of the Dispersion)," RV; 2:11, "pilgrims" (coupled with *paroikos*, "an alien, sojourner"); the word is thus used metaphorically of those to whom Heaven is their own country, and who are sojourners on earth.

Earth *ge* (1093), denotes (a) "earth as arable land," e.g., Matt. 13:5, 8, 23; in 1 Cor. 15:47 it is said of the "earthly" material of which "the first man" was made, suggestive of frailty; (b) "the earth as a whole, the world," in contrast, whether to the heavens, e.g., Matt. 5:18, 35, or to heaven, the abode of God, e.g., Matt. 6:19, where the context suggests the "earth" as a place characterized by mutability and weakness; in Col. 3:2 the same contrast is presented by the word "above"; in John 3:31 (RV, "of the earth," for KJV, "earthly") it describes one whose origin and nature are "earthly" and whose speech is characterized thereby, in contrast with Christ as the One from heaven; in Col. 3:5 the physical members are said to be "upon the earth," as a sphere where, as potential instruments of moral evils, they are, by metonymy, spoken of as the evils themselves; (c) "the inhabited earth," e.g., Luke 21:35; Acts 1:8; 8:33; 10:12; 11:6; 17:26; 22:22; **Heb. 11:13**; Rev. 13:8. In the following the phrase "on the earth" signifies "among men," Luke 12:49; 18:8; John 17:4, (d) "a country, territory," e.g. Luke 4:25; John 3:22; (e) "the ground," e.g., Matt. 10:29; Mark 4:26, RV, "(upon the) earth," for KJV, "(into the) ground"; (f) "land," e.g., Mark 4:1; John 21:8-9, 11. Cf. Eng. words beginning with *ge-*, e.g., "geodetic," "geodesy," "geology," "geometry," "geography."

11:14 For they that say such things declare plainly that they seek a country.

Declare plainly *emphanizo* (1718), is translated "to manifest, make manifest," in John 14:21, 22; **Heb. 11:14**, RV. *See also* **Appear** at ***Hebrews 9:24***.

Seek *epizeteo* (1934), "to seek after" (directive, *epi*, "towards") is always rendered in the RV, by some form of the verb "to seek," Acts 13:7, "sought" (KJV, "desired"); 19:39, "seek" (KJV, "inquire"); Phil. 4:17, "seek for" (KJV, "desire"), twice; elsewhere, Matt. 6:32; 12:39; 16:4; Mark 8:12 (in some texts); Luke 12:30; Acts 12:19; Rom. 11:7; **Heb. 11:14**; **13:14**.

Country *patris* (3968), primarily signifies "one's fatherland, native country, of one's own town," Matt. 13:54, 57; Mark 6:1, 4; Luke 4:23-24; John 4:44; **Heb. 11:14**.

11:15 And truly, if they had been mindful of that *country* from whence they came out, they might have had opportunity to have returned.

Mindful of *mnemoneuo* (3421), signifies "to call to mind, remember"; it is used absolutely in Mark 8:18; everywhere else it has an object, (a) persons, Luke 17:32; Gal. 2:10; 2 Tim. 2:8, where the RV rightly has "remember Jesus Christ, risen from the dead"; Paul was not reminding Timothy (nor did he need to) that Christ was raised from the dead (KJV), what was needful for him was to "remember" (to keep in mind) the One who rose, the Source and Supplier of all his requirements; (b) things, e.g., Matt. 16:9; John 15:20; 16:21; Acts 20:35; Col. 4:18; 1 Thess. 1:3; 2:9; **Heb. 11:15**, "had been mindful of"; **13:7**; Rev. 18:5; (c) a clause, representing a circumstance, etc., John 16:4; Acts 20:31; Eph. 2:11; 2 Thess. 2:5; Rev. 2:5; 3:3; in **Heb. 11:22** it signifies "to make mention of."

Came *ekbaino* (1543a), "to come or go out," appears in the best mss. in **Heb. 11:15**; KJV, "came out," RV, "went out."

Opportunity *kairos* (2540), primarily, "a due measure," is used of "a fixed and definite period, a time, season," and is translated "opportunity" in Gal. 6:10 and **Heb. 11:15**.

Returned *anakampto* (344), "to turn or bend back," occurs in Matt. 2:12; Luke 10:6 (i.e., as if it was unsaid); Acts 18:21; **Heb. 11:15**.

11:16 But now they desire a better *country*, that is, an heavenly: wherefore God is not ashamed to be called their God: for he hath prepared for them a city.

Desire *orego* (3713), "to reach or stretch out," is used only in the middle voice, signifying the mental effort of stretching oneself out for a thing, of longing after it, with stress upon the object desired; it is translated "desire" in **Heb. 11:16**; in 1 Tim. 3:1, RV, "seeketh," for KJV, "desireth"; in 1 Tim. 6:10, RV, "reached after," for KJV, "coveted after." In **Heb. 11:16**, a suitable rendering would be "reach after." Cf. *orexis*, lust, Rom. 1:27.

Better *see Hebrews 1:4.*

Heavenly *see Hebrews 3:1.*

Wherefore *see Hebrews 3:7.*

Ashamed *see Hebrews 2:11.*

Prepared *hetoimazo* (2090), "to prepare, make ready," is used (I) absolutely, e.g., Mark 14:15; Luke 9:52; (II) with an object, e.g., (a) of those things which are ordained (1) by God, such as future positions of authority, Matt. 20:23; the coming Kingdom, 25:34; salvation personified in Christ, Luke 2:31; future blessings, 1 Cor. 2:9; a city, **Heb. 11:16**; a place of refuge for the Jewish remnant, Rev. 12:6; Divine judgments on the world, Rev. 8:6; 9:7, 15; 16:12; eternal fire, for the Devil and his angels, Matt. 25:41; (2) by Christ: a place in Heaven for His followers, John 14:2, 3; (b) of human "preparation" for the Lord, e.g., Matt. 3:3; 26:17, 19; Luke 1:17 ("make ready"), 76; 3:4, KJV (RV, "make ye ready"); 9:52 ("to make ready"); 23:56; Rev. 19:7; 21:2; in 2 Tim. 2:21, of "preparation" of oneself for "every good work"; (c) of human "preparations" for human objects, e.g., Luke 12:20, RV, "thou hast prepared" (KJV, "provided"); Acts 23:23; Philem. 22.

City *see Hebrews 11:10.*

11:17 By faith Abraham, when he was tried, offered up Isaac: and he that had received the promises offered up his only begotten *son*,

Tried *peirazo* (3985), is rendered "to try" in **Heb. 11:17**; Rev. 2:2, 10; 3:10. In Acts 16:7 it is rendered "assayed"; in 24:6, RV, "assayed" (KJV, "hath gone about").

Offered *see* **Offer** at *Hebrews 5:1.*

Received *anadechomai* (324), "to receive gladly," is used in Acts 28:7, of the reception by Publius of the shipwrecked company in Melita; in **Heb. 11:17**, of Abraham's reception of God's promises, RV, "gladly (*ana*, "up," regarded as intensive) received." Moulton and Milligan point out the frequency of this verb in the papyri in the legal sense of taking the responsibility of something, becoming security for, undertaking, and say "The predominance of this meaning suggests its application in **Heb. 11:17**. The statement that Abraham had 'undertaken,' 'assumed the responsibility of,' the promises, would not perhaps be alien to the thought." The responsibility would surely be that of his faith in "receiving" the promises. In Classical Greek it had the meaning of "receiving," and it is a little difficult to attach any other sense to the circumstances, save perhaps that Abraham's faith undertook to exercise the assurance of the fulfillment of the promises.

Promises *see* **Promise** at *Hebrews 4:1.*

Only begotten *monogenes* (3439), "only begotten," has the meaning "only," of human offspring, in Luke 7:12; 8:42; 9:38; the term is one of endearment, as well as of singleness. Used in **Heb. 11:17** to describe the relationship of Isaac to Abraham.

11:18 Of whom it was said, That in Isaac shall thy seed be called:

Said *see Hebrews 5:5.*

Seed *see Hebrews 2:16.*

11:19 Accounting that God *was* able to raise *him* up, even from the dead; from whence also he received him in a figure.

Accounting *logizomai* (3049), primarily signifies "to reckon," whether by calculation or imputation, e.g., Gal. 3:6 (RV, "reckoned"); then, to deliberate, and so to suppose, "account," Rom. 8:36; 14:14 (KJV, "esteemeth"); John 11:50; 1 Cor. 4:1; **Heb. 11:19**; (KJV, "consider"); Acts 19:27 ("made of no account"; KJV, "despised"); 1 Pet. 5:12 (KJV, "suppose"). It is used of love in 1 Cor. 13:5, as not taking "account" of evil, RV (KJV, "thinketh"). In 2 Cor. 3:5 the apostle uses it in repudiation of the idea that he and fellow-servants of God are so selfsufficient as to "account anything" (RV) as from themselves (KJV, "think"), i.e., as to attribute anything to themselves. Cf. 12:6. In

2 Tim. 4:16 it is used of laying to a person's "account" (RV) as a charge against him (KJV, "charge").

Raise *egeiro* (1453), is used (a) of "raising" the dead, active and passive voices, e.g. of the resurrection of Christ, Matt. 16:21; 17:23; 20:19, RV; 26:32, RV, "(after) I am raised up" (KJV, "... risen again"); Luke 9:22; 20:37; John 2:19; Acts 3:15; 4:10 [not 5:30, see (c) below]; 10:40 [not 13:23 in the best texts]; 13:30, 37; Rom. 4:24, 25; 6:4, 9; 7:4; 8:11 (twice); 8:34, RV; 10:9; 1 Cor. 6:14 (1st part); 15:13, 14, RV; 15:15 (twice), 16, 17; 15:20, RV; 2 Cor. 4:14; Gal. 1:1; Eph. 1:20; Col. 2:12; 1 Thess. 1:10; 1 Pet. 1:21; in 2 Tim. 2:8, RV, "risen"; (b) of the resurrection of human beings, Matt. 10:8; 11:5; Matt. 27:52. RV (KJV, "arose"); Mark 12:26, RV; Luke 7:22; John 5:21; 12:1, 9, 17; Acts 26:8; 1 Cor. 15:29 and 32, RV; 15:35, 42, 43 (twice), 44, 52; 2 Cor. 1:9; 4:14; **Heb. 11:19**; (c) of "raising" up a person to occupy a place in the midst of a people, said of Christ, Acts 5:30; in 13:23, KJV only (the best texts have *ago*, to bring, RV, "hath ... brought"); of David, Acts 13:22; (d) metaphorically, of a horn of salvation, Luke 1:69; (e) of children, from stones, by creative power, Luke 3:8; (f) of the Temple, as the Jews thought, John 2:20, RV, "wilt Thou raise (it) Up" (KJV, "rear"); (g) of "lifting" up a person, from physical infirmity, Mark 1:31, RV, "raised ... up" (KJV, "lifted"); so 9:27; Acts 3:7; 10:26, RV (KJV, "took"); Jas. 5:15, "shall raise ... up"; (h) metaphorically, of "raising" up affliction, Phil. 1:17, RV (in the best texts; the KJV, v. 16, following those which have *epiphero*, has "to add").

Received *see* ***Hebrews 10:36***.

Figure *see* ***Hebrews 9:9***.

11:20-21 By faith Isaac blessed Jacob and Esau concerning things to come.

By faith Jacob, when he was a dying, blessed both the sons of Joseph; and worshipped, *leaning* upon the top of his staff.

Top *akron* (206), is used of Jacob's staff, **Heb. 11:21**.

Staff *rhabdos* (4464), rendered "staff" or "staves" in Matt. 10:10, parallel passages, and **Heb. 11:21**. *See also* **Sceptre** at ***Hebrews 1:8***.

11:22 By faith Joseph, when he died, made mention of the departing of the children of Israel; and gave commandment concerning his bones.

Died *teleutao* (5053), "to end" (from *telos*, "an end"), hence, "to end one's life," is used (a) of the "death" of the body, Matt. 2:19; 9:18; 15:4, where "die the death" means "surely die," RV, marg., lit., "let him end by death"; Mark 7:10; Matt. 22:25, "deceased"; Luke 7:2; John 11:39; Acts 2:29; 7:15; **Heb. 11:22** (RV, "his end was nigh"); (b) of the gnawings of conscience in self reproach, under the symbol of a worm, Mark 9:48 (vv. 44 and 46, KJV).

Made mention *see* **Mindful of** at ***Hebrews 11:15***.

Mention *mnemoneuo* (3421), which most usually means "to call to mind, remember," signifies "to make mention of," in **Heb. 11:22**.

Gave commandment *see* **Enjoined** at ***Hebrews 9:20***.

Bones *osteon* (3747), probably from a word signifying strength, or firmness, sometimes denotes "hard substances other than bones," e.g., the stone or kernel of fruit. In the NT it always denotes "bones," Matt. 23:27; Luke 24:39; John 19:36; **Heb. 11:22**.

11:23 By faith Moses, when he was born, was hid three months of his parents, because they saw *he was* a proper child; and they were not afraid of the king's commandment.

Months *trimenos* (5150), an adjective, denoting "of three months," is used as a noun, a space of three "months," in **Heb. 11:23**.

Parents *pater* (3962), "a father," is used in **Heb. 11:23**, in the plural, of both father and mother, the "parents" of Moses.

Proper *asteios* (791), lit., "of the city" (from *astu*, "a city"; like Lat. *urbanus*, from *urbs*, "a city"; Eng., "urbane"; similarly, "polite," from *polis*, "a town"), hence, "fair, elegant" (used in the papyri writings of clothing), is said of the external form of a child, Acts 7:20, of Moses "(exceeding) fair," lit., "fair to God"; **Heb. 11:23** (RV, "goodly," KJV, "proper").

Child *paidion* (3813), a diminutive of *pais*, signifies "a little or young child"; it is used of an infant just born, John 16:21, of a male child recently born, e.g., Matt. 2:8; **Heb. 11:23**; of a more advanced child, Mark 9:24; of a son, John 4:49; of a girl, Mark 5:39, 40, 41; in the plural, of "children," e.g., Matt. 14:21. It is used metaphorically of believers who are deficient in spiritual understanding, 1 Cor. 14:20, and in affectionate and familiar address by the Lord to His disciples, almost like the Eng., "lads," John 21:5; by the apostle John to the youngest believers in the family of God, 1 John 2:13, 18; there it is to be distinguished from *teknia*, which term he uses in addressing all his readers (vv. 1, 12, 28).

Commandment *diatagma* (1297), signifies "that which is imposed by decree or law," **Heb. 11:23**. It stresses the concrete character of the "commandment" more than *epitage.*

11:24 By faith Moses, when he was come to years, refused to be called the son of Pharaoh's daughter;

Come to years In **Heb. 11:24**, KJV, *ginomai,* "to become," with *megas,* "great," is rendered "when he was come to years" (RV, "when he was grown up").

Refused *arneomai* (720), signifies (a) "to say ... not, to contradict," e.g., Mark 14:70; John 1:20; 18:25, 27; 1 John 2:22; (b) "to deny" by way of disowning a person, as, e.g., the Lord Jesus as master, e.g., Matt. 10:33; Luke 12:9; John 13:38 (in the best mss.); 2 Tim. 2:12; or, on the other hand, of Christ Himself, "denying" that a person is His follower, Matt. 10:33; 2 Tim. 2:12; or to "deny" the Father and the Son, by apostatizing and by disseminating pernicious teachings, to "deny" Jesus Christ as master and Lord by immorality under a cloak of religion, 2 Pet. 2:1; Jude 4; (c) "to deny oneself," either in a good sense, by disregarding one's own interests, Luke 9:23, or in a bad sense, to prove false to oneself, to act quite unlike oneself, 2 Tim. 2:13; (d) to "abrogate, forsake, or renounce a thing," whether evil, Titus 2:12, or good, 1 Tim. 5:8; 2 Tim. 3:5; Rev. 2:13; 3:8; (e) "not to accept, to reject" something offered, Acts 3:14; 7:35, "refused"; **Heb. 11:24** "refused."

11:25 Choosing rather to suffer affliction with the people of God, than to enjoy the pleasures of sin for a season;

Choosing *haireo* (138), "to take," is used in the middle voice only, in the sense of taking for oneself, choosing, 2 Thess. 2:13, of a "choice" made by God (as in Deut. 7:6-7; 26:18, Sept.); in Phil. 1:22 and **Heb. 11:25**, of human "choice." Its special significance is to select rather by the act of taking, than by showing preference or favor.

Suffer affliction *sunkakoucheomai* (4778), "to endure adversity with," is used in **Heb. 11:25**, RV, "to be evil entreated with," KJV, "to suffer affliction with."

Enjoy *apolausis* (619), "enjoyment" (from *apolauo,* "to take hold of, enjoy a thing"), suggests the advantage or pleasure to be obtained from a thing (from a root, *lab-* seen in *lambano,* "to obtain"); it is used with the preposition *eis,* in 1 Tim. 6:17, lit., "unto enjoyment," rendered "to enjoy"; with *echo,* "to have," in **Heb. 11:25**, lit., "to have pleasure (of sin)," translated "to enjoy the pleasures."

Pleasures *apolausis* (619), "enjoyment," is used with *echo,* "to have," and rendered "enjoy the pleasures" (lit., "pleasure") in **Heb. 11:25.**

Sin *see* ***Hebrews 3:13.***

Season *proskairos* (4340), "temporary, transient," is rendered "for a season" in **Heb. 11:25.**

11:26 Esteeming the reproach of Christ greater riches than the treasures in Egypt: for he had respect unto the recompence of the reward.

Esteeming *hegeomai* (2233), signifies "to lead"; then, "to lead before the mind, to suppose, consider, esteem"; translated "esteem" in Phil. 2:3, KJV, RV, "counting"; in 1 Thess. 5:13, "esteem"; in **Heb. 11:26**, KJV, "esteeming," RV, "accounting."

Reproach *see* **Reproaches** at ***Hebrews 10:33.***

Riches *ploutos* (4149), is used in the singular (I) of material "riches," used evilly, Matt. 13:22: Mark 4:19; Luke 8:14; 1 Tim. 6:17; Jas. 5:2; Rev. 18:17; (II) of spiritual and moral "riches," (a) possessed by God and exercised towards men, Rom. 2:4, "of His goodness and forbearance and longsuffering"; 9:23 and Eph. 3:16, "of His glory" (i.e., of its manifestation in grace towards believers); Rom. 11:33, of His wisdom and knowledge; Eph. 1:7 and 2:7, "of His grace"; 1:18, "of the glory of His inheritance in the saints"; 3:8, "of Christ"; Phil. 4:19, "in glory in Christ Jesus," RV; Col. 1:27, "of the glory of this mystery ... Christ in you, the hope of glory"; (b) to be ascribed to Christ, Rev. 5:12; (c) of the effects of the gospel upon the Gentiles, Rom. 11:12 (twice); (d) of the full assurance of understanding in regard to the mystery of God, even Christ, Col. 2:2, RV; (e) of the liberality of the churches of Macedonia, 2 Cor. 8:2 (where "the riches" stands for the spiritual and moral value of their liberality); (f) of "the reproach of Christ" in contrast to this world's treasures, **Heb. 11:26.**

Treasures *thesauros* (2344), denotes (1) "a place of safe keeping" (possibly akin to *tithemi,* "to put"), (a) "a casket," Matt. 2:11; (b) "a storehouse," Matt. 13:52; used metaphorically of the heart, Matt. 12:35, twice (RV, "out of his treasure"); Luke 6:45; (2) "a treasure," Matt. 6:19, 20, 21; 13:44; Luke 12:33, 34; **Heb. 11:26**; "treasure" (in heaven or the heavens), Matt. 19:21; Mark 10:21; Luke 18:22; in these expressions (which are virtually equivalent to that in Matt. 6:1, "with your Father which is in Heaven") the promise does not simply refer to the present life, but looks likewise to the hereafter; in 2 Cor. 4:7 it is used of "the light of the knowledge

"Faith tells us of things we have never seen, and cannot come to know by our natural senses."

ST. JOHN OF THE CROSS

of the glory of God in the face of Jesus Christ," descriptive of the gospel, as deposited in the earthen vessels of the persons who proclaim it (cf. v. 4); in Col. 2:3, of the wisdom and knowledge hidden in Christ.

Respect *apoblepo* (578), "to look away from all else at one object" (*apo*, "from"), hence, "to look steadfastly," is translated "he had respect" in **Heb. 11:26**, KJV (RV, "looked").

Recompence *see Hebrews 2:2*.

11:27 By faith he forsook Egypt, not fearing the wrath of the king: for he endured, as seeing him who is invisible.

Forsook *kataleipo* (2641), a strengthened form of *leipo*, "to leave," signifies (a) "to leave, to leave behind," e.g., Matt. 4:13; (b) "to leave remaining, reserve," e.g., Luke 10:40; (c) "to forsake," in the sense of abandoning, translated "to forsake" in the RV of Luke 5:28 and Acts 6:2; in **Heb. 11:27** and 2 Pet. 2:15, KJV and RV. In this sense it is translated "to leave," in Mark 10:7; 14:52; Luke 15:4; Eph. 5:31.

Wrath *thumos* (2372), "hot anger, passion," is translated "wrath" in Luke 4:28; Acts 19:28; Rom. 2:8, RV; Gal. 5:20; Eph. 4:31; Col. 3:8; **Heb. 11:27**; Rev. 12:12; 14:8, 10, 19; 15:1, 7; 16:1; 18:3; "wraths" in 2 Cor. 12:20; "fierceness" in Rev. 16:19; 19:15.

Endured *kartereo* (2594), "to be steadfast, patient," is used in **Heb. 11:27**, "endured," of Moses in relation to Egypt. In the Sept., Job 2:9; Isa. 42:14.

Invisible *aoratos* (517), lit., "unseen" (*a*, negative, *horao*, "to see"), is translated "invisible" in Rom. 1:20, of the power and divinity of God; of God Himself, Col. 1:15; 1 Tim. 1:17; **Heb. 11:27**; of things unseen, Col. 1:16. In the Sept., Gen. 1:2; Isa. 45:3, "unseen (treasures)."

11:28 Through faith he kept the passover, and the sprinkling of blood, lest he that destroyed the firstborn should touch them.

Passover *pascha* (3957), the Greek spelling of the Aramaic word for the Passover, from the Hebrew *pasach*, "to pass over, to spare," a feast instituted by God in commemoration of the deliverance of Israel from Egypt, and anticipatory of the expiatory sacrifice of Christ. The word signifies (I) "the Passover Feast," e.g., Matt. 26:2; John 2:13, 23; 6:4; 11:55; 12:1; 13:1; 18:39; 19:14; Acts 12:4; **Heb. 11:28**; (II) by metonymy, (a) "the Paschal Supper," Matt. 26:18, 19; Mark 14:16; Luke 22:8, 13; (b) "the Paschal lamb," e.g., Mark 14:12 (cf. Exod. 12:21); Luke 22:7; (c) "Christ Himself," 1 Cor. 5:7.

Sprinkling *proschusis* (4378), "a pouring or sprinkling upon," occurs in **Heb. 11:28**, of the "sprinkling" of the blood of the Passover lamb.

Destroyed *olothreuo* (3645), "to destroy," especially in the sense of slaying, is found in **Heb. 11:28**, where the RV translates the present participle with the article by the noun "destroyer." The verb occurs frequently in the Sept., e.g., Ex. 12:23; Josh. 3:10; 7:25; Jer. 2:30; 5:6; 22:7.

Firstborn *see* **Firstbegotten** at *Hebrews 1:6*.

Touch *thingano* (2345), signifies (a) "to touch, to handle" (though "to handle" is rather stronger than the actual significance). In Col. 2:21 the RV renders it "touch," and the first verb (*hapto*, "to lay hold of") "handle," i.e., "handle not, nor taste, nor touch"; "touch" is the appropriate rendering; in **Heb. 12:20** it is said of a beast's touching Mount Sinai; (b) "to touch by way of injuring," **Heb. 11:28**. In the Sept., Exod. 19:12.

11:29 By faith they passed through the Red sea as by dry *land*: which the Egyptians assaying to do were drowned.

Passed *diabaino* (1224), "to step across, cross over," is translated "to pass" in Luke 16:26 (of "passing" across the fixed gulf); in **Heb. 11:29**, "passed through."

Red *eruthros* (2063), denotes "red" (the ordinary color); the root *rudh-* is seen, e.g., in the Latin *rufus*, Eng., "ruby," "ruddy," "rust," etc. It is applied to the Red Sea, Acts 7:36; **Heb. 11:29**. The origin of the name is uncertain; it has been regarded as due, e.g., to the color of the corals which cover the Red Sea bed or line its shores, or to the tinge of the mountains which border it, or to the light of the sky upon its waters.

Sea *thalassa* (2281), is used (a) chiefly literally, e.g., "the Red Sea," Acts 7:36; 1 Cor. 10:1; **Heb. 11:29**; the "sea" of Galilee or Tiberias, Matt. 4:18; 15:29; Mark 6:48, 49, where the acts of Christ testified to His deity; John 6:1; 21:1; in general, e.g., Luke 17:2; Acts 4:24; Rom. 9:27; Rev. 16:3; 18:17; 20:8, 13; 21:1; (b) metaphorically, of "the ungodly men" described in Jude 13 (cf. Isa. 57:20); (c) symbolically, in the apocalyptic vision of "a glassy sea like unto crystal," Rev. 4:6, emblematic of the fixed purity and holiness of all that appertains to the authority and judicial dealings of God; in 15:2, the same, "mingled with fire," and, standing by it (RV) or on it (KJV and RV marg.), those who had "come victorious from the beast" (ch. 13); of the wild and restless condition of nations, Rev. 13:1 (see 17:1, 15), where "he stood" (RV) refers to the dragon, not John (KJV); from the midst of this state arises the beast, symbolic of the final gentile power dominating the federated nations of the Roman world (see Dan., chs. 2, 7, etc.).

Dry *xeros* (3584), is used (a) naturally, of "dry" land, **Heb. 11:29**; or of land in general, Matt. 23:15, "land"; or of physical infirmity, "withered," Matt. 12:10; Mark 3:3; Luke 6:6, 8; John 5:3; (b) figuratively, in Luke 23:31, with reference to the spiritual "barrenness" of the Jews, in contrast to the character of the Lord. Cf. Ps. 1:3; Isa. 56:3; Ezek. 17:24; 20:47.

Land *xeros* (3584), "dry," "dry land," Matt. 23:15 (*ge*, "land," being understood); **Heb. 11:29**.

Assaying *peira* (3984), "a making trial, an experiment," is used with *lambano*, "to receive or take," in **Heb. 11:29**, rendered "assaying," and v. **36**, in the sense of "having experience of" (akin to *peirao*, "to assay, to try"), "had trial." In the Sept., Deut. 28:56.

Drowned *katapino* (2666), lit., "to drink down" (*pino*, "to drink," prefixed by *kata*, "down"), signifies "to swallow up" (RV, in **Heb. 11:29**, for KJV, "were drowned"). It is elsewhere translated by the verb "to swallow, or swallow up," except in 1 Pet. 5:8, "devour."

11:30 By faith the walls of Jericho fell down, after they were compassed about seven days.

Walls *teichos* (5038), "a wall," especially one around a town, is used (a) literally, Acts 9:25; 2 Cor. 11:33; **Heb. 11:30**; (b) figuratively, of the "wall" of the heavenly city, Rev. 21:12, 14, 15, 17, 18, 19.

Fell *pipto* (4098), "to fall," is used (a) of descent, to "fall" down from, e.g., Matt. 10:29; 13:4; (b) of a lot, Acts 1:26; (c) of "falling" under judgment, Jas. 5:12 (cf. Rev. 18:2, RV); (d) of persons in the act of prostration, to prostrate oneself, e.g., Matt. 17:6; John 18:6; Rev. 1:17; in homage and worship, e.g., Matt. 2:11; Mark 5:22; Rev. 5:14; 19:4; (e) of things, "falling" into ruin, or failing, e.g., Matt. 7:25; Luke 16:17, RV, "fall," for KJV, "fail"; **Heb. 11:30**; (f), of "falling" in judgment upon persons, as of the sun's heat, Rev. 7:16, RV, "strike," KJV, "light"; of a mist and darkness, Acts 13:11 (some mss. have *epipipto*); (g) of persons, in "falling" morally or spiritually, Rom. 14:4; 1 Cor. 10:8, 12; Rev. 2:5.

Compassed *kukloo* (2944), (cf. Eng., cycle"), signifies "to move in a circle, to compass about," as of a city "encompassed" by armies, Luke 21:20; **Heb. 11:30**; in Acts 14:20, "stood round about.

Seven *hepta* (2033), whence Eng. words beginning with "hept-," corresponds to the Heb. *sheba'* (which is akin to *saba'*, signifying "to be full, abundant"), sometimes used as an expression of fullness, e.g., Ruth 4:15: it generally expresses completeness, and is used most frequently in Revelation; it is not found in the Gospel of John, nor between the Acts and Revelation, except in **Heb. 11:30** (in Rom. 11:4 the numeral is *heptakischilioi*, "seven thousand"); in Matt. 22:26 it is translated "seventh" (marg., "seven").

11:31 By faith the harlot Rahab perished not with them that believed not, when she had received the spies with peace.

Harlot *porne* (4204), "a prostitute, harlot" (from *pernemi*, "to sell"), is used (a) literally, in Matt. 21:31, 32, of those who were the objects of the mercy shown by Christ; in Luke 15:30, of the life of the Prodigal; in 1 Cor. 6:15, 16, in a warning to the Corinthian church against the prevailing licentiousness which had made Corinth a byword; in **Heb. 11:31** and Jas. 2:25, of Rahab; (b) metaphorically, of mystic Babylon, Rev. 17:1, 5 (KJV, "harlots"), 15, 16; 19:2, RV, for KJV, "whore."

Perished *sunapollumi* (4881), in the middle voice, denotes "to perish together," **Heb. 11:31**.

Believed not *see Hebrews 3:18*.

Received *dechomai* (1209), "to receive by deliberate and ready reception of what is offered," is used of (a) taking with the hand, taking hold, taking hold of or up, e.g., Luke 2:28, RV, "he received (Him)," KJV, "took he (Him) up"; 16:6, 7; 22:17; Eph. 6:17; (b) "receiving," said of a place "receiving" a person, of Christ into the Heavens, Acts 3:21; or of persons in giving access to someone as a visitor, e.g., John 4:45; 2 Cor. 7:15; Gal. 4:14; Col. 4:10; by way of giving hospitality, etc., e.g., Matt. 10:14, 40 (four times), 41 (twice); 18:5; Mark 6:11; 9:37; Luke 9:5, 48, 53; 10:8, 10; 16:4; v. 9, of reception, "into the eternal tabernacles," said of followers of Christ who have used "the mammon of unrighteousness" to render assistance to ("make ... friends of") others; of Rahab's reception of the spies, **Heb. 11:31**; of the reception, by the Lord, of the spirit of a departing believer, Acts 7:59; of "receiving" a gift, 2 Cor. 8:4 (in some mss.; RV follows those which omit it); of the favorable reception of testimony and teaching, etc., Luke 8:13; Acts 8:14; 11:1; 17:11; 1 Cor. 2:14; 2 Cor. 8:17; 1 Thess. 1:6; 2:13, where *paralambano* is used in the 1st part, "ye received," *dechomai* in the 2nd part, "ye accepted," RV (KJV, "received"), the former refers to the ear, the latter, adding the idea of appropriation, to the heart; Jas. 1:21; in 2 Thess. 2:10, "the love of the truth," i.e., love for the truth; cf. Matt. 11:14, "if ye are willing to receive it," an elliptical construction frequent in Greek writings; of "receiving," by way of bearing with, enduring, 2 Cor. 11:16; of "receiving" by way of getting, Acts 22:5; 28:21, of becoming partaker of benefits, Mark 10:15; Luke 18:17; Acts 7:38; 2 Cor. 6:1; 11:4 (last clause "did accept": cf. *lambano* in previous clauses); Phil. 4:18.

Spies *kataskopos* (2685), denotes "a spy" (*kata*, "down," signifying "closely," and *skopeo*, "to view"), **Heb. 11:31**.

Peace *eirene* (1515), "occurs in each of the books of the NT, save 1 John and save in Acts 7:26 ['(at) one again'] it is translated "peace" in the RV. It describes (a) harmonious relationships between men, Matt. 10:34; Rom. 14:19; (b) between nations, Luke 14:32; Acts 12:20; Rev. 6:4; (c) friendliness, Acts 15:33; 1 Cor. 16:11; **Heb. 11:31**; (d) freedom from molestation, Luke 11:21; 19:42; Acts 9:31 (RV, 'peace,' KJV, 'rest'); 16:36; (e) order, in the State, Acts 24:2 (RV, 'peace,' KJV, 'quietness'); in the churches, 1 Cor. 14:33; (f) the harmonized relationships between God and man, accomplished through the gospel, Acts 10:36; Eph. 2:17; (g) the sense of rest and contentment consequent thereon, Matt. 10:13; Mark 5:34; Luke 1:79; 2:29; John 14:27; Rom. 1:7; 3:17; 8:6; in certain passages this idea is not distinguishable from the last, Rom. 5:1."

"The God of peace" is a title used in Rom. 15:33; 16:20; Phil. 4:9; 1 Thess. 5:23; **Heb. 13:20**; cf. 1 Cor. 14:33; 2 Cor. 13:11. The corresponding Heb. word *shalom* primarily signifies "wholeness": see its use in Josh. 8:31, "unhewn"; Ruth 2:12, "full"; Neh. 6:15, "finished"; Isa. 42:19, marg., "made perfect." Hence there is a close connection between the title in 1 Thess. 5:23 and the word *holokleros*, "entire," in that verse. In the Sept. *shalom* is often rendered by *soteria*, "salvation, e.g., Gen. 26:31; 41:16; hence the "peace-offering" is called the "salvation offering." Cf. Luke 7:50; 8:48. In 2 Thess. 3:16, the title "the Lord of peace" is best understood as referring to the Lord Jesus. In Acts 7:26, "would have set them at one" is, lit., "was reconciling them (conative imperfect tense, expressing an earnest effort) into peace."

11:32 And what shall I more say? for the time would fail me to tell of Gedeon, and *of* Barak, and *of* Samson, and *of* Jephthae; *of* David also, and Samuel, and *of* the prophets:

More *see Hebrews 8:12*.

Fail *epileipo* (1952), "not to suffice for a purpose" (*epi*, over), is said of insufficient time, in **Heb. 11:32**.

Tell *diegeomai* (1334), is rendered "to tell," in the KJV and RV, in Mark 9:9; **Heb. 11:32**.

11:33 Who through faith subdued kingdoms, wrought righteousness, obtained promises, stopped the mouths of lions,

Subdued *katagonizomai* (2610), primarily, "to struggle against" (*kata*, "against," *agon*, "a contest"), came to signify "to conquer," **Heb. 11:33**, "subdued."

Wrought *ergazomai* (2038), is used (I) intransitively, e.g., Matt. 21:28; John 5:17; 9:4 (2nd part); Rom. 4:4, 5; 1 Cor. 4:12; 9:6; 1 Thess. 2:9; 4:11; 2 Thess. 3:8, 10-12; (II) transitively, (a) "to work something, produce, perform," e.g., Matt. 26:10, "she hath wrought"; John 6:28, 30; 9:4 (1st part); Acts 10:35; 13:41; Rom. 2:10; 13:10; 1 Cor. 16:10; 2 Cor. 7:10a; Gal. 6:10, RV, "let us work"; Eph. 4:28; **Heb. 11:33**; 2 John 8; (b) "to earn by working, work for," John 6:27, RV, "work" (KJV, "labor").

Obtained *see Hebrews 6:15*.

Promises *see* **Promise** at *Hebrews 4:1*.

Stopped *phrasso* (5420), "to fence in" (akin to *phragmos*, "a fence"), "close, stop," is used (a) metaphorically, in Rom. 3:19, of "preventing" all excuse from Jew and Gentile, as sinners; in 2 Cor. 11:10, lit., "this boasting shall not be stopped to me"; passive voice in both; (b) physically, of the mouths of lions, **Heb. 11:33** (active voice).

Mouths *stoma* (4750), akin to *stomachos* (which originally meant "a throat, gullet"), is used (a) of "the mouth" of man, e.g., Matt. 15:11; of animals, e.g., Matt. 17:27; 2 Tim. 4:17 (figurative); **Heb. 11:33**; Jas. 3:3; Rev. 13:2 (2nd occurrence); (b) figuratively of "inanimate things," of the "edge" of a sword, Luke 21:24; **Heb. 11:34**; of the earth, Rev. 12:16; (c) figuratively, of the "mouth," as the organ of speech,

(1) of Christ's words, e.g., Matt. 13:35; Luke 11:54; Acts 8:32; 22:14; 1 Pet. 2:22; (2) of human, e.g., Matt. 18:16; 21:16; Luke 1:64; Rev. 14:5; as emanating from the heart, Matt. 12:34; Rom. 10:8, 9; of prophetic ministry through the Holy Spirit, Luke 1:70; Acts 1:16; 3:18; 4:25; of the destructive policy of two world potentates at the end of this age, Rev. 13:2, 5, 6; 16:13 (twice); of shameful speaking, Eph. 4:29 and Col. 3:8; (3) of the Devil speaking as a dragon or serpent, Rev. 12:15, 16; 16:13; (d) figuratively, in the phrase "face to face" (lit., "mouth to mouth"), 2 John 12; 3 John 14; (e) metaphorically, of "the utterances of the Lord, in judgment," 2 Thess. 2:8; Rev. 1:16; 2:16; 19:15, 21; of His judgment upon a local church for its lukewarmness, Rev. 3:16; (f) by metonymy, for "speech," Matt. 18:16; Luke 19:22; 21:15; 2 Cor. 13:1.

Lions *leon* (3023), occurs in 2 Tim. 4:17, probably figurative of the imminent peril of death, the figure being represented by the whole phrase, not by the word "lion" alone; some suppose the reference to be to the lions of the amphitheater; the Greek commentators regarded the "lion" as Nero; others understand it to be Satan. The language not improbably recalls that of Ps. 22:21, and Dan. 6:20. The word is used metaphorically, too, in Rev. 5:5, where Christ is called "the Lion of the tribe of Judah." Elsewhere it has the literal meaning, **Heb. 11:33**; 1 Pet. 5:8; Rev. 4:7; 9:8, 17; 10:3; 13:2. Taking the OT and NT occurrences the allusions are to the three great features of the "lion," (1) its majesty and strength, indicative of royalty, e.g., Prov. 30:30, (2) its courage, e.g., Prov. 28:1, (3) its cruelty, e.g., Ps. 22:13.

11:34 Quenched the violence of fire, escaped the edge of the sword, out of weakness were made strong, waxed valiant in fight, turned to flight the armies of the aliens.

Quenched *sbennumi* (4570), is used (a) of "quenching" fire or things on fire, Matt. 12:20, quoted from Isa. 42:3, figurative of the condition of the feeble; **Heb. 11:34**; in the passive voice, Matt. 25:8, of torches, RV, "are going out," lit., "are being quenched"; of the retributive doom hereafter of sin unrepented of and unremitted in this life, Mark 9:48 (in some mss. in vv. 44, 46); (b) metaphorically, of "quenching" the fire-tipped darts of the evil one, Eph. 6:16; of "quenching" the Spirit, by hindering His operations in oral testimony in the church gatherings of believers, 1 Thess. 5:19. "The peace, order, and edification of the saints were evidence of the ministry of the Spirit among them, 1 Cor. 14:26, 32, 33, 40, but if, through ignorance of His ways, or through failure to recognize, or refusal to submit to, them, or through impatience with the ignorance or self-will of others, the Spirit were quenched, these happy results would be absent. For there was always the danger that the impulses of the flesh might usurp the place of the energy of the Spirit in the assembly, and the endeavor to restrain this evil by natural means would have the effect of hindering His ministry also. Apparently then, this injunction was intended to warn believers against the substitution of a mechanical order for the restraints of the Spirit." Cf. Song of Sol. 8:7.

Violence In **Heb. 11:34**, KJV, *dunamis*, "power" (RV), is rendered "violence."

Escaped *pheugo* (5343), "to flee" (Lat., *fuga*, "flight," etc.; cf. Eng., "fugitive, subterfuge"), is rendered "escape" in Matt. 23:33; **Heb. 11:34**.

Edge *stoma* (4750), the mouth (cf. Eng., "stomach," from *stomachos*, 1 Tim. 5:23), has a secondary and figurative meaning in reference to the "edge of a sharp instrument, as of a sword," Luke 21:24; **Heb. 11:34** (cf. the Sept., e.g., Gen. 34:26; Judg. 18:27). *See also* **Mouths** at ***Hebrews 11:33***.

Weakness *astheneia* (769), is rendered "weakness," of the body, 1 Cor. 2:3; 15:43; 2 Cor. 11:30, RV; 12:5 (plural, RV), 9, 10, RV; **Heb. 11:34**; in 2 Cor. 13:4, "He was crucified through weakness" is said in respect of the physical sufferings to which Christ voluntarily submitted in giving Himself up to the death of the cross.

Made strong *endunamoo* (1743), "to make strong" (*en*, "in," *dunamis*, "power"), "to strengthen," is rendered "waxed strong" in Rom. 4:20, RV (KJV, "was strong"); "be strong," Eph. 6:10; "were made strong," **Heb. 11:34**. *See also* **Strong** at ***Hebrews 5:7***.

Waxed *ginomai* (1096), "to become," is translated "waxed" in Luke 13:19, KJV (RV, "became"); in **Heb. 11:34**, KJV and RV, "waxed".

Valiant *ischuros* (2478), "strong, mighty," is usually translated "strong"; "mighty" in Luke 15:14 (of a famine); Rev. 19:6 (of thunders); 19:18 (of men): in the following, where the KJV has "mighty," the RV substitutes "strong," 1 Cor. 1:27; Rev. 6:15 (KJV, "mighty men"); 18:10, 21; **Heb. 11:34**, RV, "(waxed) mighty" (KJV, "valiant").

Fight *polemos* (4171), "war," is so translated in the RV, for KJV, "battle," 1 Cor. 14:8; Rev. 9:7, 9; 16:14; 20:8; for KJV, "fight," **Heb. 11:34**; KJV and RV in Jas. 4:1, hyperbolically of private "quarrels"; elsewhere, literally, e.g., Matt. 24:6; Rev. 11:7.

Turned to flight *klino* (2827), "to make to bend," is translated "turned to flight" in **Heb. 11:34**.

Armies *parembole* (3925), lit., "a casting in among, an insertion" (*para*, "among," *ballo*, "to throw"), in the Macedonian dialect, was a military term. In the NT it denotes the distribution of troops in army formation, "armies," **Heb. 11:34**; a camp, as of the Israelites, Exod. 19:17; 29:14; 32:17; hence, in **Heb. 13:11, 13**, of Jerusalem, since the city was to the Jews what the camp in the wilderness had been to the Israelites; in Rev. 20:9, the "armies" or camp of the saints, at the close of the Millennium. It also denoted a castle or barracks, Acts 21:34, 37; 22:24; 23:10, 16, 32.

Aliens *allotrios* (245), primarily, "belonging to another" (the opposite to *idios*, "one's own"), came to mean "foreign, strange, not of one's own family, alien, an enemy"; "aliens" in, **Heb. 11:34**, elsewhere "strange," etc. *See also* **Strange** at *Hebrews 11:9*.

11:35 Women received their dead raised to life again: and others were tortured, not accepting deliverance; that they might obtain a better resurrection:

Raised In **Heb. 11:35**, KJV, the noun *anastasis*, a resurrection, preceded by *ex* (i.e., *ek*), "out of, or by," instrumental, is translated "raised to life again" (a paraphrase), RV, "by a resurrection."

Tortured *tumpanizo* (5178), primarily denotes "to beat a drum" (*tumpanon*, "a kettledrum," Eng., "tympanal," "tympanitis," "tympanum"), hence, "to torture by beating, to beat to death," **Heb. 11:35**. In the Sept., 1 Sam. 21:13, "(David) drummed (upon the doors of the city)." The tympanum as an instrument of "torture" seems to have been a wheel-shaped frame upon which criminals were stretched and beaten with clubs or thongs.

Accepting *prosdechomai* (4327), "to accept favorably, or receive to oneself," is used of things future, in the sense of expecting; with the meaning of "accepting," it is used negatively in **Heb. 11:35**, "not accepting their deliverance"; of receiving, e.g., Luke 15:2; Rom. 16:2; Phil. 2:29.

Deliverance *apolutrosis* (629), denotes "redemption" (*apo*, "from," *lutron*, "a price of release"). In **Heb. 11:35** it is translated "deliverance"; usually the release is effected by the payment of a ransom, or the required price, the *lutron* (ransom). *See also* **Redemption** at *Hebrews 9:15*.

Obtain *see* **Obtained** at *Hebrews 8:6*.

Better *see Hebrews 1:4*.

Resurrection *see Hebrews 6:2*.

11:36 And others had trial of *cruel* mockings and scourgings, yea, moreover of bonds and imprisonment:

Had In Mark 12:22, in some mss., *lambano*, "to take" or "receive," is translated "had," in the statement "the seven had her"; in Acts 25:16, RV, "have had" (KJV, "have"); in **Heb. 11:36**, "had."

Trial *see* **Assaying** at *Hebrews 11:29*.

Mockings *empaigmos* (1701), the act of the *empaiktes*, "a mocking," is used in **Heb. 11:36**, "mockings." In the Sept., Ps. 38:7; Ezek. 22:4.

Scourgings *mastix* (3148), "a whip, scourge," is used (a) with the meaning "scourging," in Acts 22:24, of the Roman method, (b) in **Heb. 11:36**, of the "sufferings" of saints in the OT times. Among the Hebrews the usual mode, legal and domestic, was that of beating with a rod (see 2 Cor. 11:25); (c) metaphorically, of "disease" or "suffering".

Moreover *eti* (2089), "yet, as yet, still," is translated "moreover" in Acts 2:26; in 21:28, RV (KJV, "further"); **Heb. 11:36**.

Imprisonment *phulake* (5438), denotes a "prison," e.g., Matt. 14:10; Mark 6:17; Acts 5:19; 2 Cor. 11:23; in 2 Cor. 6:5 and **Heb. 11:36** it stands for the condition of imprisonment; in Rev. 2:10; 18:2, "hold" (twice, RV, marg., "prison"; in the 2nd case, KJV, "cage"); 20:7.

11:37 They were stoned, they were sawn asunder, were tempted, were slain with the sword: they wandered about in sheepskins and goatskins; being destitute, afflicted, tormented;

Stoned *lithazo* (3034), "to stone," not stressing the casting, occurs in John 8:5 (in the most authentic mss.); 10:31-33; 11:8; Acts 5:26; 14:19; 2 Cor. 11:25; **Heb. 11:37**.

Sawn asunder *prizo* or *prio* (4249), "to saw asunder," occurs in **Heb. 11:37**. Some have seen here a reference to the tradition of Isaiah's martyrdom under Manasseh. In the Sept., Amos 1:3. Cf. *diaprio*, "to cut to the heart" Acts 5:33; 7:54.

Tempted *see Hebrews 2:18*.

Slain *phonos* (5408), is used (a) of a special act, Mark 15:7; Luke 23:19, 25; (b) in the plural, of "murders" in general, Matt. 15:19; Mark 7:21 (Gal. 5:21, in some inferior mss.); Rev. 9:21; in the singular, Rom. 1:29; (c) in the sense of "slaughter," **Heb. 11:37**, "they were slain with the sword," lit., "(they died by) slaughter (of the sword)"; in Acts 9:1, "slaughter."

Wandered *perierchomai* (4022), "to go around, or about," is translated "going about" in 1 Tim. 5:13, RV (KJV, "wandering about"); "went about" in **Heb. 11:37**, RV (KJV, "wandered about").

Sheepskins *melote* (3374), from *melon*, "a sheep or goat," occurs in **Heb. 11:37**. In the Sept., 1 Kings 19:13, 19; 2 Kings 2:8, 13, 14.

Goatskins The adjective *aigeios* signifies "belonging to a goat" (from *aix*, "a goat"); it is used with *derma*, "a skin," in **Heb. 11:37**.

Destitute *hustereo* (5302), primarily, "to be behind, to be last," hence, "to lack, fail of, come short of," is translated "being destitute" in **Heb. 11:37**.

Afflicted *thlibo* (2346), "to suffer affliction, to be troubled," has reference to sufferings due to the pressure of circumstances, or the antagonism of persons, 1 Thess. 3:4; 2 Thess. 1:6-7; "straitened," in Matt. 7:14 (RV); "throng," Mark 3:9; "afflicted," 2 Cor. 1:6; 7:5 (RV); 1 Tim. 5:10; **Heb. 11:37**; "pressed," 2 Cor. 4:8. Both the verb and the noun, when used of the present experience of believers, refer almost invariably to that which comes upon them from without.

Tormented *kakoucheo* (2558), from *kakos*, "evil," and *echo*, "to have," signifies, in the passive voice, "to suffer ill, to be maltreated, tormented," **Heb. 11:37** (KJV, "tormented," RV, "afflicted"); **13:3**, KJV, "suffer adversity," RV, evil entreated. In the Sept., 1 Kings, 2:26; 11:39.

11:38 (Of whom the world was not worthy:) they wandered in deserts, and *in* mountains, and *in* dens and caves of the earth.

Worthy *axios* (514), "of weight, worth, worthy," is said of persons and their deeds: (a) in a good sense, e.g., Matt. 10:10, 11, 13 (twice), 37 (twice), 38; 22:8; Luke 7:4; 10:7; 15:19, 21; John 1:27; Acts 13:25; 1 Tim. 5:18; 6:1; **Heb. 11:38**; Rev. 3:4; 4:11; 5:2, 4, 9, 12; (b) in a bad sense, Luke 12:48; 23:15; Acts 23:29; 25:11, 25; 26:31; Rom. 1:32; Rev. 16:6.

Wandered *planao* (4105), (Eng., "planet"), in the passive form sometimes means "to go astray, wander," Matt. 18:12; 1 Pet. 2:25; **Heb. 11:38**; frequently active, "to deceive, by leading into error, to seduce," e.g., Matt. 24:4, 5, 11, 24; John 7:12, "leadeth astray," RV (cf. 1 John 3:7). In Rev. 12:9 the present participle is used with the definite article, as a title of the Devil, "the Deceiver," lit., "the deceiving one." Often it has the sense of "deceiving oneself," e.g., 1 Cor. 6:9; 15:33; Gal. 6:7; Jas. 1:16, "be not deceived," RV, "do not err," KJV.

Deserts *eremia* (2047), primarily "a solitude, an uninhabited place," in contrast to a town or village, is translated "deserts" in **Heb. 11:38**; "the wilderness" in Matt. 15:33, KJV, "a desert place," RV; so in Mark 8:4; "wilderness" in 2 Cor. 11:26. It does not always denote a barren region, void of vegetation; it is often used of a place uncultivated, but fit for pasturage.

Dens *spelaion* (4693), "a grotto, cavern, den" (Lat., *spelunca*), "cave," John 11:38, is said of the grave of Lazarus; in the RV in **Heb. 11:38** and Rev. 6:15 (KJV, "dens"); in the Lord's rebuke concerning the defilement of the Temple, Matt. 21:13; Mark 11:17; Luke 19:46, "den" is used.

Caves *ope* (3692), perhaps from *ops*, "sight," denotes "a hole, an opening," such as a fissure in a rock, **Heb. 11:38**. In Jas. 3:11, the RV has "opening," of the orifice of a fountain (KJV, "place").

"Faith is a living and unshakeable confidence, a belief in the grace of God so assured that a man would die a thousand deaths for its sake."

MARTIN LUTHER

11:39 And these all, having obtained a good report through faith, received not the promise:

Obtained *see Hebrews 11:2.*

Report *see Hebrews 11:2.*

Received *see Hebrews 10:36.*

11:40 God having provided some better thing for us, that they without us should not be made perfect.

Provided *problepo* (4265), from *pro*, "before," and *blepo*, "to see, perceive," is translated "having provided" in **Heb. 11:40** (middle voice), marg., "foreseen," which is the lit. meaning of the verb, as with Eng. "provide." In the Sept., Ps. 37:13.

Better *see Hebrews 1:4.*

Without *see Hebrews 4:15. See also Hebrews 9:22.*

Perfect *see Hebrews 2:10.*

Chapter 12

12:1 Wherefore seeing we also are compassed about with so great a cloud of witnesses, let us lay aside every weight, and the sin which doth so easily beset *us*, and let us run with patience the race that is set before us,

Wherefore *toigaroun*, "therefore," rendered "wherefore" in **Heb. 12:1**, KJV.

Compassed *see Hebrews 5:2.*

Great *tosoutos* (5118), "so great, so many, so much," of quantity, size, etc., is rendered "so great," in Matt. 8:10, and Luke 7:9, of faith; Matt. 15:33, of a multitude; **Heb. 12:1**, of a cloud of witnesses; Rev. 18:17, of riches.

Cloud *nephos* (3509), denotes "a cloudy, shapeless mass covering the heavens." Hence, metaphorically, of "a dense multitude, a throng," **Heb. 12:1**.

Witnesses *see Hebrews 10:28.*

Lay *apotithemi* (659), "to put off from oneself," always in the middle voice in the NT, is used metaphorically in **Heb. 12:1**, "laying aside (every weight);" in Jas. 1:21, KJV, "lay apart," RV, "putting away"; in Acts 7:58 of "laying" down garments, after taking them off, for the purpose of stoning Stephen.

Weight *onkos* (3591), denotes "a bulk or mass"; hence, metaphorically, "an encumbrance, weight," **Heb. 12:1**.

Easily The adverb "easily" is included in the translation of *euperistatos* in **Heb. 12:1**, "easily beset," lit., "the easily besetting sin," probably a figure from a garment, "easily surrounding," and therefore easily entangling.

Beset *euperistatos* (2139), used in **Heb. 12:1**, and translated "which doth so easily beset," lit. signifies "standing well (i.e., easily) around" (*eu*, "well," *peri*, "around," *statos*, "standing," i.e., easily encompassing). It describes sin as having advantage in favor of its prevailing.

Run *trecho* (5143), "to run," is used (a) literally, e.g., Matt. 27:48 (*dramon*, an aorist participle, from an obsolete verb *dramo*, but supplying certain forms absent from *trecho*, lit., "having run, running," expressive of the decisiveness of the act); the same form in the indicative mood is used, e.g., in Matt. 28:8; in the Gospels the literal meaning alone is used; elsewhere in 1 Cor. 9:24 (twice in 1st part); Rev. 9:9, KJV, "running" (RV, "rushing"); (b) metaphorically, from the illustration of "runners" in a race, of either swiftness or effort to attain an end, Rom. 9:16, indicating that salvation is not due to human effort, but to God's sovereign right to exercise mercy; 1 Cor. 9:24 (2nd part), and v. 26, of persevering activity in the Christian course with a view to obtaining the reward; so **Heb. 12:1**; in Gal. 2:2 (1st part), RV, "(lest) I should be running," continuous present tense referring to the activity of the special service of his mission to Jerusalem; (2nd part), "had run," aorist tense, expressive of the continuous past, referring to the activity of his antagonism to the Judaizing teachers at Antioch, and his consent to submit the case to the judgment of the church in Jerusalem; in 5:7 of the erstwhile faithful course doctrinally of the Galatian believers; in Phil. 2:16, of the apostle's manner of life among the Philippian believers; in 2 Thess. 3:1, of the free and rapid progress of "the word of the Lord."

Patience *hupomone* (5281), lit., "an abiding under" (*hupo*, "under," *meno*, "to abide"), is almost invariably rendered "patience." "Patience, which grows only in trial, Jas. 1:3 may be passive, i.e. = "endurance," as, (a) in trials, generally, Luke 21:19 (which is to be understood by Matt. 24:13), cf. Rom. 12:12; Jas. 1:12; (b) in trials incident to service in the gospel, 2 Cor. 6:4; 12:12; 2 Tim. 3:10; (c) under chastisement, which is trial viewed as coming from the hand of God our Father, **Heb. 12:7**; (d) under undeserved affliction, 1 Pet. 2:20; or active, i.e. = "persistence, perseverance," as (e) in well doing, Rom. 2:7 (KJV, "patient continuance"); (f) in fruit bearing, Luke 8:15; (g) in running the appointed race, **Heb. 12:1**.

"Patience perfects Christian character, Jas. 1:4, and fellowship in the patience of Christ is therefore the condition upon which believers are to be admitted to reign with Him, 2 Tim. 2:12; Rev. 1:9. For this patience believers are 'strengthened with all power,' Col. 1:11, 'through His Spirit in the inward man,' Eph. 3:16. In 2 Thess. 3:5, the phrase 'the patience of Christ,' RV, is possible of three interpretations, (a) the patient waiting for Christ, so KJV paraphrases the words, (b) that they might be patient in their sufferings as Christ was in His, see **Heb. 12:2**, (c) that since Christ is 'expecting till His enemies be made the footstool of His feet,' **Heb. 10:13**, so they might be patient also in their hopes of His triumph and their deliverance. While a too rigid exegesis is to be avoided it may, perhaps, be permissible to paraphrase: 'the Lord teach and enable you to love as God loves, and to be patient as Christ is patient.'"

Race *agon* (73), from *ago*, "to lead," signifies (a) "a place of assembly," especially the place where the Greeks assembled for the Olympic and Pythian games; (b) "a contest of athletes," metaphorically, 1 Tim. 6:12; 2 Tim. 4:7, "fight"; **Heb. 12:1**, "race"; hence, (c) "the inward conflict of the soul"; inward "conflict" is often the result, or the accompaniment, of outward "conflict," Phil. 1:30; 1 Thess. 2:2, implying a contest against spiritual foes, as well as human adversaries; so Col. 2:1, "conflict," KJV; RV, "(how greatly) I strive," lit., "how great a conflict I have." Cf. *agonizomai* (Eng., "agonize"), 1 Cor. 9:25, etc.

Set *see* ***Hebrews 6:18.***

12:2 Looking unto Jesus the author and finisher of *our* faith; who for the joy that was set before him endured the cross, despising the shame, and is set down at the right hand of the throne of God.

Looking *aphorao* (872), "to look away from one thing so as to see another," "to concentrate the gaze upon," occurs in Phil. 2:23, "I shall see;" **Heb. 12:2**, "looking."

Jesus *see* ***Hebrews 2:9.***

Author *see* **Captain** at ***Hebrews 2:10.***

Finisher In **Heb. 12:2** the RV suitably translates *teleiotes* "perfecter," for KJV, "finisher."

Joy *chara* (5479), "joy, delight" (akin to *chairo*, "to rejoice"), is found frequently in Matthew and Luke, and especially in John, once in Mark (4:16, RV, "joy," KJV, "gladness"); it is absent from 1 Cor. (though the verb is used three times), but is frequent in 2 Cor., where the noun is used five times, and the verb eight times, suggestive of the apostle's relief in comparison with the circumstances of the Should be 1st. Epistle; in Col. 1:11, KJV, "joyfulness," RV, "joy." The word is sometimes used, by metonymy, of the occasion or cause of "joy," Luke 2:10 (lit., "I announce to you a great joy"); in 2 Cor. 1:15, in some mss., for *charis*, "benefit"; Phil. 4:1, where the readers are called the apostle's "joy"; so 1 Thess. 2:19, 20; **Heb. 12:2**, of the object of Christ's "joy"; Jas. 1:2, where it is connected with falling into trials; perhaps also in Matt. 25:21, 23, where some regard it as signifying, concretely, the circumstances attending cooperation in the authority of the Lord.

Set *see* ***Hebrews 8:1.***

Endured *hupomeno* (5278), lit., "to abide under" (*hupo*, "under"), signifies "to remain in a place instead of leaving it, to stay behind," e.g., Luke 2:43; Acts 17:14; or "to persevere," Matt. 10:22; 24:13; Mark 13:13; in each of which latter it is used with the phrase "unto the end"; or "to endure bravely and trustfully," e.g., **Heb. 12:2-3, 7**, suggesting endurance under what would be burdensome. See also Jas. 1:12; 5:11; 1 Pet. 2:20. Cf., *makrothumeo*, "to be longsuffering." *See also* ***Hebrews 10:32.***

Despising *kataphroneo* (2706), lit., "to think down upon or against anyone" (*kata*, "down," *phren*, "the mind"), hence signifies "to think slightly of, to despise," Matt. 6:24; 18:10; Luke 16:13; Rom. 2:4; 1 Cor. 11:22; 1 Tim. 4:12; 6:2; **Heb. 12:2**; 2 Pet. 2:10.

Shame *aischune* (152), "shame," so the RV in 2 Cor. 4:2 (for KJV, "dishonesty"), is elsewhere rendered "shame," Luke 14:9; Phil. 3:19; **Heb. 12:2**; Jude 13; Rev. 3:18.

Throne *see* ***Hebrews 1:8.***

12:3 For consider him that endured such contradiction of sinners against himself, lest ye be wearied and faint in your minds.

Consider *analogizomai* (357), "to consider," occurs in **Heb. 12:3**.

> *"There is no detour to holiness. Jesus came to the resurrection through the cross, not around it."*
>
> LEIGHTON FORD

Endured *see* ***Hebrews 12:2.***

Contradiction *see* ***Hebrews 7:7.*** *See also* **Strife** at ***Hebrews 6:16.***

Wearied *kamno* (2577), primarily signified "to work"; then, as the effect of continued labor, "to be weary"; it is used in **Heb. 12:3**, of becoming "weary," RV, "wax not weary"; in Jas. 5:15, of sickness; some mss. have it in Rev. 2:3, KJV, "hast (not) fainted," RV, "grown weary."

Faint *ekluo* (1590), denotes (a) "to loose, release" (*ek*, "out," *luo*, "to loose"); (b) "to unloose," as a bowstring, "to relax," and so, "to enfeeble," and is used in the passive voice with the significance "to be faint, grow weary," (1) of the body, Matt. 15:32; (some mss. have it in 9:36); Mark 8:3; (2) of the soul, Gal. 6:9 (last clause), in discharging responsibilities in obedience to the Lord; in **Heb. 12:3**, of becoming weary in the strife against sin; in v. **5**, under the chastening hand of God. It expresses the opposite of *anazonnumi*, "to gird up," 1 Pet. 1:13.

Minds In three places, Acts 14:2; Phil. 1:27; **Heb. 12:3**, the KJV translates *psuche*, "the soul," by "mind" (RV, "soul"). *See also* **Soul** at ***Hebrews 4:12.***

12:4 Ye have not yet resisted unto blood, striving against sin.

Resisted *antikathistemi* (478), "to stand firm against" (*anti*, "against," *kathistemi*, "to set down," *kata*), is translated "ye have (not) resisted" in **Heb. 12:4**. In the Sept., Deut. 31:21; Josh. 5:7; Mic. 2:8.

Striving *antagonizomai* (464), "to struggle against" (*anti*), is used in **Heb. 12:4**, "striving against."

Sin *see Hebrews 3:13.*

12:5 And ye have forgotten the exhortation which speaketh unto you as unto children, My son, despise not thou the chastening of the Lord, nor faint when thou art rebuked of him:

Forgotten *eklanthanomai* (1585), "to forget utterly" (*ek*, "out," intensive), is used in the middle voice in **Heb. 12:5**, of "forgetting" an exhortation.

Speaketh *dialegomai* (1256), "to think different things with oneself, to ponder," then, "to dispute with others," is translated "to reason" in Acts 17:2, KJV and RV; 17:17, RV; 18:4, 19, KJV and RV; 19:8, 9, RV; 24:25, KJV and RV; **Heb. 12:5**, RV, "reasoneth (with you)," KJV, "speaketh (unto you)."

Despise *oligoreo* (3643), denotes "to think little of" (*oligos*, "little," *ora*, "care"), "to regard lightly," **Heb. 12:5**, RV (KJV, "despise").

Chastening *paideia* (3809), denotes "the training of a child, including instruction"; hence, "discipline, correction," "chastening," Eph. 6:4, RV (KJV, "nurture"), suggesting the Christian discipline that regulates character; so in **Heb. 12:5, 7, 8** (in v. **8**, KJV, "chastisement," the RV corrects to "chastening"); in 2 Tim. 3:16, "instruction.

Lord *kurios* (2962), properly an adjective, signifying "having power" (*kuros*) or "authority," is used as a noun, variously translated in the NT, " 'Lord,' 'master,' 'Master,' 'owner,' 'Sir,' a title of wide significance, occurring in each book of the NT save Titus and the Epistles of John. "... *kurios* is the Sept. and NT representative of Heb. Jehovah ('LORD' in Eng. versions), see Matt. 4:7; Jas. 5:11, e.g., of *adon*, Lord, Matt. 22:44, and of *Adonay*, Lord, 1:22; it also occurs for *Elohim*, God, 1 Pet. 1:25 ... Christ Himself assumed the title, Matt. 7:21, 22; 9:38; 22:41-45; Mark 5:19 (cf. Ps. 66:16; the parallel passage, Luke 8:39, has 'God'); Luke 19:31; John 13:13, apparently intending it in the higher senses of its current use, and at the same time suggesting its OT associations. His purpose did not become clear to the disciples until after His resurrection, and the revelation of His Deity consequent thereon. Thomas, when he realized the significance of the presence of a mortal wound in the body of a living man, immediately joined with it the absolute title of Deity, saying, 'My Lord and my God,' John 20:28. Thereafter, except in Acts 10:4 and Rev. 7:14, there is no record that *kurios* was ever again used by believers in addressing any save God and the Lord Jesus; cf Acts 2:47 with 4:29, 30. How soon and how completely the lower meaning had been superseded is seen in Peter's declaration in his first sermon after the resurrection, 'God hath made Him – Lord,' Acts 2:36, and that in the house of Cornelius, 'He is Lord of all,' 10:36, cf. Deut. 10:14; Matt. 11:25; Acts 17:24. In his writings the implications of his early teaching are confirmed and developed. Thus Ps. 34:8, 'O taste and see that Jehovah is good,' is applied to the Lord Jesus, 1 Pet. 2:3, and 'Jehovah of Hosts, Him shall ye sanctify,' Isa. 8:13, becomes 'sanctify in your hearts Christ as Lord,' 3:15. So also James who uses *kurios* alike of God, 1:7 (cf. v. 5); 3:9; 4:15; 5:4, 10, 11, and of the Lord Jesus, 1:1 (where the possibility that *kai* is intended epexegetically, i.e. = even, cf. 1 Thess. 3:11, should not be overlooked); 2:1 (lit., 'our Lord Jesus Christ of glory,' cf. Ps. 24:7; 29:3; Acts 7:2; 1 Cor. 2:8); 5:7, 8, while the language of 4:10; 5:15, is equally applicable to either. Jude, v. 4, speaks of 'our only – Lord, Jesus Christ,' and immediately, v. 5, uses 'Lord' of God (see the remarkable marg. here), as he does later, vv. 9, 14. Paul ordinarily uses *kurios* of the Lord Jesus, 1 Cor. 1:3, e.g., but also on occasion, of God, in quotations from the OT, 1 Cor. 3:20, e.g., and in his own words, 1 Cor. 3:5, cf. v. 10. It is equally appropriate to either in 1 Cor. 7:25; 2 Cor. 3:16; 8:21; 1 Thess. 4:6, and if 1 Cor. 11:32 is to be interpreted by 10:21, 22, the Lord Jesus is intended, but if by **Heb. 12:5-9**, then *kurios* here also = God. 1 Tim. 6:15, 16 is probably to be understood of the Lord Jesus, cf. Rev. 17:14."

Faint *see Hebrews 12:3.*

Rebuked *elencho* (1651), "to convict, refute, reprove," is translated "to rebuke" in the KJV of the following (the RV always has the verb "to reprove"): 1 Tim. 5:20; Titus 1:13; 2:15; **Heb. 12:5**; Rev. 3:19.

12:6 For whom the Lord loveth he chasteneth, and scourgeth every son whom he receiveth.

Chasteneth *paideuo* (3811), primarily denotes "to train children," suggesting the broad idea of education (*pais*, "a child"), Acts 7:22; 22:3; see also Titus 2:12, "instructing" (RV), here of a training gracious and firm; grace, which brings salvation, employs means to give us full possession of it, hence, "to chastise," this being part of the training, whether (a) by correcting with words, reproving, and admonishing, 1 Tim. 1:20 (RV, "be taught"); 2 Tim. 2:25, or (b) by "chastening" by the infliction of evils and calamities, 1 Cor. 11:32; 2 Cor. 6:9; **Heb. 12:6-7, 10**; Rev. 3:19. The verb also has the meaning "to chastise with blows, to scourge," said of the command of a judge, Luke 23:16, 22.

Scourgeth *mastigoo* (3146), akin to *mastix*, is used of Jewish "scourgings," Matt. 10:17 and 23:34; and metaphorically, in **Heb. 12:6**, of the "chastening" by the Lord administered in love to His spiritual sons.

Receiveth *paradechomai* (3858), "to receive or admit with approval" (*para*, "beside"), is used (a) of persons, Acts 15:4; **Heb. 12:6**; (b) of things, Mark 4:20, KJV, "receive" (RV, "accept"); Acts 16:21; 22:18; 1 Tim. 5:9. In the Sept., Ex. 23:1; Prov. 3:12.

12:7 If ye endure chastening, God dealeth with you as with sons; for what son is he whom the father chasteneth not?

Endure *see* **Endured** at *Hebrews 10:32*. *See also* **Endured** at *Hebrews 12:2*.

Chastening *see Hebrews 12:5*.

Dealeth with *prosphero* (4374), "to bring or bear to" (*pros*, "to," *phero*, "to bear"), signifies, in the middle voice, to bear oneself towards any one, to deal with anyone in a certain manner, **Heb. 12:7**, "God dealeth with you."

Chasteneth *see Hebrews 12:6*.

12:8 But if ye be without chastisement, whereof all are partakers, then are ye bastards, and not sons.

Without *see Hebrews 4:15*.

Chastisement *see* **Chastening** at *Hebrews 12:5*.

Partakers *see* **Fellows** at *Hebrews 1:9*.

Bastards *nothos* (3541), denotes "an illegitimate child, one born out of lawful wedlock," **Heb. 12:8**.

Sons *huios* (5207), primarily signifies the relation of offspring to parent (see John 9:18-20; Gal. 4:30). It is often used metaphorically of prominent moral characteristics. "It is used in the NT of (a) male offspring, Gal. 4:30; (b) legitimate, as opposed to illegitimate offspring, **Heb. 12:8** ...

12:9 Furthermore we have had fathers of our flesh which corrected *us*, and we gave *them* reverence: shall we not much rather be in subjection unto the Father of spirits, and live?

Furthermore *eita* (1534), denotes sequence (a) "of time, then, next," Mark 4:17, RV, "then"; 4:28, in some texts; 8:25, RV, "then" (KJV, "after that"); Luke 8:12; John 13:5; 19:27; 20:27; in some texts in 1 Cor. 12:28; 1 Cor. 15:5, 7, 24; 1 Tim. 2:13; 3:10; Jas. 1:15; (b) In argument, **Heb. 12:9**, "furthermore."

Fathers, Father *see* **Father** at *Hebrews 1:5*.

Corrected *paideutes* (3810), has two meanings, corresponding to the two meanings of the verb *paideuo* from which it is derived, (a) "a teacher, preceptor, corrector," Rom. 2:20 (KJV, "instructor"), (b) "a chastiser," **Heb. 12:9**, rendered "to chasten" (KJV, "which corrected"; lit., "chastisers").

Reverence *entrepo* (1788), lit., "to turn in" (i.e., upon oneself), "to put to shame," denotes, when used in the passive voice, "to feel respect for, to show deference to, to reverence," Matt. 21:37; Mark 12:6; Luke 20:13; **Heb. 12:9**.

Subjection *see Hebrews 2:5*.

Spirits *see Hebrews 1:7*.

Live *see* **Lifetime** at *Hebrews 2:15*.

12:10 For they verily for a few days chastened *us* after their own pleasure; but he for *our* profit, that *we* might be partakers of his holiness.

Verily *see Hebrews 3:5*.

Chastened *see* **Chasteneth** at *Hebrews 12:6*.

Pleasure In Acts 15:22, KJV, *dokeo*, "to seem good to" (RV), is translated "it pleased" (in some mss., v. 34); in **Heb. 12:10**, KJV, "(after their own) pleasure," RV, "(as) seemed good (to them)." *See also* **Seem** at *Hebrews 4:1*.

Profit *sumpheron* (4851), the neuter form of the present participle of *sumphero*, is used as a noun with the article in **Heb. 12:10**, "(for our) profit"; in some mss. in 1 Cor. 7:35 and 10:33; in 1 Cor. 12:7, preceded by *pros*, "with a view to, towards," translated "to profit withal," lit., "towards the profiting."

Might "May," "might," sometimes translate the prepositional phrase *eis*, "unto," with the definite article, followed by the infinitive mood of some verb, expressing purpose, e.g., Acts 3:19, "may be blotted out," lit., "unto the blotting out of"; Rom. 3:26, "that he might be," lit., "unto his being"; so 8:29; 2 Cor. 1:4, "that we may be able," lit., "unto our being able"; Eph. 1:18, "that ye may know," lit., "unto your knowing"; Acts 7:19; Rom. 1:11; 4:16; 12:2; 15:13; Phil. 1:10; 1 Thess. 3:10, 13; 2 Thess. 1:5; 2:6, 10; **Heb. 12:10**. In Luke 20:20 the best mss. have *hoste*, "so as to," RV, as, e.g., in 1 Pet. 1:21. Sometimes the article with the infinitive mood without a preceding preposition, expresses result, e.g., Luke 21:22; Acts 26:18 (twice), "that they may turn," RV; cf. Rom. 6:6; 11:10; 1 Cor. 10:13; Phil. 3:10, "that I may know"; Jas. 5:17.

Partakers *metalambano* (3335), "to have, or get, a share of," is translated "to be partaker (or partakers) of" in 2 Tim. 2:6 and **Heb. 12:10**.

Holiness *hagiotes* (41), "sanctity," the abstract quality of "holiness," is used (a) of God, **Heb. 12:10**; (b) of the manifestation of it in the conduct of the apostle Paul and his fellowlaborers, 2 Cor. 1:12 (in the best mss., for *haplotes*).

12:11 Now no chastening for the present seemeth to be joyous, but grievous: nevertheless afterward it yieldeth the peaceable fruit of righteousness unto them which are exercised thereby.

Present *pareimi* (3918), signifies (a) "to be by, at hand or present," of persons, e.g., Luke 13:1; Acts 10:33; 24:19; 1 Cor. 5:3; 2 Cor. 10:2, 11; Gal. 4:18, 20; of things, John 7:6, of a particular season in the Lord's life on earth, "is (not yet) come," or "is not yet at hand"; **Heb. 12:11**, of chastening "(for the) present" (the neuter of the present participle, used as a noun); in **13:5** "such things as ye have" is, lit., "the things that are present"; 2 Pet. 1:12, of the truth "(which) is with (you)" (not as KJV, "the present truth," as if of special doctrines applicable to a particular time); in v. 9 "he that lacketh" is lit., "to whom are not present"; (b) "to have arrived or come," Matt. 26:50, "thou art come," RV; John 11:28; Acts 10:21; Col. 1:6.

Seemeth *see* **Seem** at ***Hebrews 4:1***.

Joyous *see* **Joyfully** at ***Hebrews 10:34***.

Grievous *lupe* (3077), signifies "pain," of body or mind; it is used in the plural in 1 Pet. 2:19 only, RV, "griefs" (KJV, "grief"); here, however, it stands, by metonymy, for "things that cause sorrow, grievances"; hence Tyndale's rendering, "grief," for Wycliffe's "sorews"; everywhere else it is rendered "sorrow," except in **Heb. 12:11**, where it is translated "grievous" (lit., "of grief").

Afterwards *husteron* (5305), "afterwards," with the suggestion of at length, is found in Matt. 4:2; 21:29, 32, 37 (KJV, "last of all"); 22:27; 25:11; 26:60 (KJV, "at the last"), Mark 16:14; Luke 4:2; 20:32 (KJV, "last"), John 13:36; **Heb. 12:11**.

Yieldeth *apodidomi* (591), "to give up or back," is translated "to yield" in **Heb. 12:11**; Rev. 22:2 (in each case, of bearing fruit).

Peaceable *eirenikos* (1516), denotes "peaceful." It is used (a) of the fruit of righteousness, **Heb. 12:11**, "peaceable" (or "peaceful") because it is produced in communion with God the Father, through His chastening; (b) of "the wisdom that is from above," Jas. 3:17.

Fruit *karpos* (2590), "fruit," is used (I) of the fruit of trees, fields, the earth, that which is produced by the inherent energy of a living organism, e.g., Matt. 7:17; Jas. 5:7, 18; plural, e.g., in Luke 12:17 and 2 Tim. 2:6; of the human body, Luke 1:42; Acts 2:30; (II) metaphorically, (a) of works or deeds, "fruit" being the visible expression of power working inwardly and invisibly, the character of the "fruit" being evidence of the character of the power producing it, Matt. 7:16. As the visible expressions of hidden lusts are the works of the flesh, so the invisible power of the Holy Spirit in those who are brought into living union with Christ (John 15:2-8, 16) produces "the fruit of the Spirit," Gal. 5:22, the singular form suggesting the unity of the character of the Lord as reproduced in them, namely, "love, joy, peace, longsuffering, kindness, goodness, faithfulness, meekness, temperance," all in contrast with the confused and often mutually antagonistic "works of the flesh." So in Phil. 1:11, marg., "fruit of righteousness." In **Heb. 12:11**, "the fruit of righteousness" is described as "peaceable fruit," the outward effect of divine chastening; "the fruit of righteousness is sown in peace," Jas. 3:18, i.e., the seed contains the fruit; those who make peace, produce a harvest of righteousness; in Eph. 5:9, "the fruit of the light" (RV, and see context) is seen in "goodness and righteousness and truth," as the expression of the union of the Christian with God (Father, Son and Holy Spirit); for God is good, Mark 10:18, the Son is "the righteous One," Acts 7:52, the Spirit is "the Spirit of truth," John 16:13; (b) of advantage, profit, consisting (1) of converts as the result of evangelistic ministry, John 4:36; Rom. 1:13; Phil. 1:22; (2) of sanctification, through deliverance from a life of sin and through service to God, Rom. 6:22, in contrast to (3) the absence of anything regarded as advantageous as the result of former sins, v. 21; (4) of the reward for ministration to servants of God, Phil. 4:17; (5) of the effect of making confession to God's Name by the sacrifice of praise, **Heb. 13:15**.

Exercised *see* ***Hebrews 5:14***.

Thereby *di'autes* occurs in Matt. 7:13; John 11:4; **Heb. 12:11**.

12:12 Wherefore lift up the hands which hang down, and the feeble knees;

Wherefore *see Hebrews 3:7.*

Lift *anorthoo* (461), "to set upright" (*ana*, "up," *orthos*, "straight"), is used of "lifting" up "hands that hang down," **Heb. 12:12**; of setting up a building, restoring ruins, Acts 15:16 (cf, e.g., 2 Sam. 7:13, 16; 1 Chron. 17:12; Jer. 10:12; often so used in the papyri); of the healing of the woman with a spirit of infirmity, Luke 13:13, "was made straight."

Hang *pariemi* (3935), signifies (a) "to disregard, leave alone, leave undone," Luke 11:42 (some mss. have *aphiemi*, here); (b) "to relax, loosen," and, in the passive voice, "to be relaxed, exhausted," said of hands that "hang" down in weakness, **Heb. 12:12**.

Feeble *paraluo* (3886), lit., "to loose from the side," hence, "to set free," is used in the passive voice of "being enfeebled by a paralytic stroke, palsied," Luke 5:18, RV, "palsied" (KJV, "taken with a palsy"); 5:24 (ditto), in the best mss.; Acts 8:7 (ditto); 9:33, RV, "he was palsied" (KJV, "was sick of the palsy"); **Heb. 12:12**, RV, "palsied (knees)," KJV, "feeble."

Knees *gonu* (1119), "a knee" (Latin, *genu*), is used (a) metaphorically in **Heb. 12:12**, where the duty enjoined is that of "courageous self-recovery in God's strength;" (b) literally, of the attitude of a suppliant, Luke 5:8; Eph. 3:14; of veneration, Rom. 11:4; 14:11; Phil. 2:10; in mockery, Mark 15:19.

12:13 And make straight paths for your feet, lest that which is lame be turned out of the way; but let it rather be healed.

Straight *orthos* (3717), used of height, denotes "upright," Acts 14:10; of line of direction, figuratively, said of paths of righteousness, **Heb. 12:13**.

Paths *trochia* (5163), "the track of a wheel" (*trochos*, "a wheel"; *trecho*, "to run") hence, "a track, path," is used figuratively in **Heb. 12:13**. In the Sept., Prov. 2:15; 4:11, 26, 27; 5:6, 21; in some texts, Ezek. 27:19.

Feet *pous* (4228), besides its literal meaning, is used, by metonymy, of "a person in motion," Luke 1:79; Acts 5:9; Rom. 3:15; 10:15; **Heb. 12:13**. It is used in phrases expressing subjection, 1 Cor. 15:27, RV; of the humility and receptivity of discipleship, Luke 10:39; Acts 22:3; of obeisance and worship, e.g., Matt. 28:9; of scornful rejection, Matt. 10:14; Acts 13:51. Washing the "feet" of another betokened the humility of the service and the comfort of the guest, and was a feature of hospitality, Luke 7:38; John 13:5; 1 Tim. 5:10 (here figuratively).

Lame *cholos* (5560), "lame," is translated "halt" in Matt. 18:8; Mark 9:45; John 5:3, in Acts 14:8, "cripple"; in Luke 14:21, KJV, "halt," RV, "lame"; elsewhere, "lame," Matt. 11:5; 15:30, 31; 21:14: Luke 7:22; 14:13; Acts 3:2; 8:7; **Heb. 12:13**; some mss. have it in Acts 3:11 (KJV, "the lame man"), RV, "he," translating *autou*, as in the best texts.

Turned *ektrepo* (1624), lit., "to turn or twist out," is used in the passive voice in **Heb. 12:13**, "that which is lame be not turned out of the way" (or rather, "put out of joint"); in the sense of the middle voice (though passive in form) of turning aside, or turning away from, 2 Tim. 4:4 (KJV, "shall be turned unto fables," RV, "shall turn aside"); in 1 Tim. 1:6, of those who, having swerved from the faith, have turned aside unto vain talking; in 5:15, of those who have turned aside after Satan; in 6:20, RV, of "turning away from (KJV, 'avoiding') profane babblings and oppositions of the knowledge which is falsely so called." In the Sept., Amos 5:8.

Healed *iaomai* (4390), "to heal," is used (a) of physical treatment 22 times; in Matt. 5:28, KJV, "made whole," RV, "healed"; so in Acts 9:34; (b) figuratively, of spiritual "healing," Matt. 13:15; John 12:40; Acts 28:27; **Heb. 12:13**; 1 Pet. 2:24; possibly, Jas. 5:16 includes both (a) and (b); some mss. have the word, with sense (b), in Luke 4:18. Apart from this last, Luke, the physician, uses the word fifteen times.

12:14 Follow peace with all *men*, and holiness, without which no man shall see the Lord:

Follow *dioko* (1377), denotes (a) "to drive away," Matt. 23:34; (b) "to pursue without hostility, to follow, follow after," said of righteousness, Rom. 9:30; the Law, 9:31; 12:13, hospitality ("given to") lit., "pursuing" (as one would a calling), the things which make for peace, 14:19; love, 1 Cor. 14:1; that which is good, 1 Thess. 5:15; righteousness, godliness, faith, love, patience, meekness, 1 Tim. 6:11; righteousness, faith, love, peace, 2 Tim. 2:22; peace and sanctification, **Heb. 12:14**; peace, 1 Pet. 3:11; (c) "to follow on" (used intransitively), Phil. 3:12, 14, RV, "I press on"; "follow after," is an inadequate meaning.

Holiness *hagiasmos* (38), translated "holiness" in the KJV of Rom. 6:19, 22; 1 Thess. 4:7; 1 Tim. 2:15; **Heb. 12:14**, is always rendered "sanctification" in the RV. It signifies (a) separation to God, 1 Cor. 1:30; 2 Thess. 2:13; 1 Pet. 1:2; (b) the resultant state, the conduct befitting those so separated, 1 Thess. 4:3, 4, 7, and the four other places mentioned above. "Sanctification" is thus the state predetermined by God for believers, into which in grace He calls them, and in which they begin their Christian course and so pursue it. Hence they are called "saints" (*hagioi*). *See also* **Sanctified** at *Hebrews 10:10*.

Without *see Hebrews 4:15*.

12:15 Looking diligently lest any man fail of the grace of God; lest any root of bitterness springing up trouble *you*, and thereby many be defiled;

Looking diligently *episkopeo* (1983), lit., "to look upon," is rendered "looking carefully" in **Heb. 12:15**, RV (KJV, "looking diligently"), *epi* being probably intensive here; in 1 Pet. 5:2, "to exercise the oversight, to visit, care for."

Fail *hustereo* (5302), "to come late, to be last, behind, inferior," is translated "falleth short" in **Heb. 12:15**, RV, for KJV, "fail," and "fall short" in Rom. 3:23, for KJV, "come short," which, in view of the preceding "have," is ambiguous, and might be taken as a past tense.

Root *rhiza* (4491), is used (a) in the natural sense, Matt. 3:10; 13:6, 21; Mark 4:6, 17, 11:20; Luke 3:9; 8:13; (b) metaphorically (1) of "cause, origin, source," said of persons, ancestors, Rom. 11:16, 17, 18 (twice); of things, evils, 1 Tim. 6:10, RV, of the love of money as a "root" of all "kinds of evil" (marg., "evils", KJV, "evil"); bitterness, **Heb. 12:15**; (2) of that which springs from a "root," a shoot, said of offspring, Rom. 15:12; Rev. 5:5; 22:16.

Bitterness *pikria* (4088), denotes "bitterness." It is used in Acts 8:23, metaphorically, of a condition of extreme wickedness, "gall of bitterness" or "bitter gall"; in Rom. 3:14, of evil speaking; in Eph. 4:31, of "bitter" hatred; in **Heb. 12:15**, in the same sense, metaphorically, of a root of "bitterness," producing "bitter" fruit.

Springing *phuo* (5453), used transitively, "to bring forth, produce," denotes, in the passive voice, "to spring up, grow," of seed, Luke 8:6, 8, KJV, "was sprung up" and "sprang up" (RV, "grew"); in the active voice, intransitively, in **Heb. 12:15**, of a root of bitterness.

Up *ano* (507), denotes "above, in a higher place," Acts 2:19 (the opposite to *kato*, "below"). With the article it means "that which is above," Gal. 4:26; Phil. 3:14, "the high calling" (RV marg., "upward"); with the plural article, "the things above," John 8:23, lit., "from the things above"; Col. 3:1-2. With *heos*, "as far as," it is translated "up to the brim," in John 2:7. It has the meaning "upwards" in John 11:41 and **Heb. 12:15**.

Trouble *enochleo* (1776), from *en*, "in," *ochlos*, "a throng, crowd," is used in **Heb. 12:15** of a root of bitterness; in Luke 6:18 (in the best texts; some have *ochleo*), RV, "were troubled" (KJV, "were vexed").

Thereby *dia tautes*, "by means of this, thereby," occurs in **Heb. 12:15; 13:2**.

Defiled *miaino* (3392), primarily, "to stain, to tinge or dye with another color," as in the staining of a glass, hence, "to pollute, contaminate, soil, defile," is used (a) of "ceremonial defilement," John 18:28; so in the Sept., in Lev. 22:5, 8; Num. 19:13, 20, etc.; (b) of "moral defilement," Titus 1:15 (twice); **Heb. 12:15**; "of moral and physical defilement," Jude 8.

12:16 Lest there *be* any fornicator, or profane person, as Esau, who for one morsel of meat sold his birthright.

Fornicator *pornos* (4205), denotes "a man who indulges in fornication, a fornicator," 1 Cor. 5:9, 10, 11; 6:9; Eph. 5:5, RV; 1 Tim. 1:10, RV; **Heb. 12:16; 13:4**, RV; Rev. 21:8 and 22:15, RV (KJV, "whoremonger").

Profane *bebelos* (952), primarily, "permitted to be trodden, accessible" (from *baino*, "to go," whence *belos*, "a threshold"), hence, "unhallowed, profane" (opposite to *hieros*, "sacred"), is used of (a) persons, 1 Tim. 1:9; **Heb. 12:16**; (b) things, 1 Tim. 4:7; 6:20; 2 Tim. 2:16. "The natural antagonism between the profane and the holy or divine grew into a moral antagonism.... Accordingly *bebelos* is that which lacks all relationship or affinity to God" (Cremer, who compares *koinos*, "common," in the sense of ritual uncleanness).

Meat *brosis* (1035), denotes (a) "the act of eating," 1 Cor. 8:4; (b) "food," translated "meat" in John 4:32; 6:27 (twice, the second time metaphorically, of spiritual food); 6:55, RV, marg., "(true) meat"; Rom. 14:17, KJV, "meat," RV, "eating"; Col. 2:16; in **Heb. 12:16**, RV, "mess of meat," KJV, "morsel of meat"; in 2 Cor. 9:10, "food"; in Matt. 6:19, 20, "rust."

Sold *apodidomi* (591), signifies "to give up or back, to restore, return, render what is due, to pay, give an account," e.g., of an account. Matt. 5:26; 12:36; Luke 16:2; Acts. 19:40; **Heb. 13:17**; 1 Pet. 4:5; of wages, etc., e.g., Matt. 18:25-34; 20:8; of conjugal duty, 1 Cor. 7:3; of a witness, Acts 4:33; frequently of recompensing or rewarding, 1 Tim. 5:4; 2 Tim. 4:8, 14; 1 Pet. 3:9; Rev. 18:6; 22:12. In the middle voice it is used of "giving" up what is one's own; hence, "to sell," Acts 5:8; 7:9; **Heb. 12:16**.

Birthright *prototokia* (4415), a birthright" (from *protos*, "first," *tikto*, "to beget"), is found in **Heb. 12:16**, with reference to Esau (cf. *prototokos*, firstborn). The "birthright" involved preeminence and authority, Gen. 27:29; 49:3. Another right was that of the double portion, Deut. 21:17; 1 Chron. 5:1-2. Connected with the "birthright" was the progenitorship of the Messiah. Esau transferred his "birthright" to Jacob for a paltry mess of pottage, profanely despising this last spiritual privilege, Gen. 25 and 27. In the history of the nation God occasionally set aside the "birthright," to show that the objects of His choice depended not on the will of the flesh, but on His own authority. Thus Isaac was preferred to Ishmael, Jacob to Esau, Joseph to Reuben, David to his elder brethren, Solomon to Adonijah.

12:17 For ye know how that afterward, when he would have inherited the blessing, he was rejected: for he found no place of repentance, though he sought it carefully with tears.

Afterward *metepeita* (3347), "afterwards," without necessarily indicating an order of events, is found in **Heb. 12:17**.

Would *thelo* (2309), "to will, to wish," implying volition and purpose, frequently a determination, is most usually rendered "to will." It is translated "to desire" in the RV of the following: Matt. 9:13; 12:7; Mark 6:19; Luke 10:29; 14:28; 23:20; Acts 24:27; 25:9; Gal. 4:17; 1 Tim. 5:11; **Heb. 12:17**; **13:18**.

Inherited *see* **Inheritance** at *Hebrews 1:4*.

Blessing *see Hebrews 6:7*.

Rejected *apodokimazo* (593), "to reject" as the result of examination and disapproval (*apo*, "away from," *dokimazo*, "to approve"), is used (a) of the "rejection" of Christ by the elders and chief priests of the Jews, Matt. 21:42; Mark 8:31; 12:10; Luke 9:22; 20:17; 1 Pet. 2:4, 7 (KJV, "disallowed"); by the Jewish people, Luke 17:25; (b) of the "rejection" of Esau from inheriting "the blessing," **Heb. 12:17**. Cf. and contrast *exoutheneo*, Acts 4:11.

Place In **Heb. 12:17**, *topos*, "a place," is rendered in KJV marg., "way (to change his mind)."

Repentance *metanoia* (3341), "afterthought, change of mind, repentance," is used of "repentance" from sin or evil, except in **Heb. 12:17**, where the word "repentance" seems to mean, not simply a change of Isaac's mind, but such a change as would reverse the effects of his own previous state of mind. Esau's birthright-bargain could not be recalled; it involved an irretrievable loss. As regards "repentance" from sin, (a) the requirement by God on man's part is set forth, e.g., in Matt. 3:8; Luke 3:8; Acts 20:21; 26:20; (b) the mercy of God in giving "repentance" or leading men to it is set forth, e.g., in Acts 5:31; 11:18; Rom. 2:4; 2 Tim. 2:25. The most authentic mss. omit the word in Matt. 9:13 and Mark 2:17, as in the RV.

Sought *see* **Seek** at *Hebrews 11:6*.

Tears *see Hebrews 5:7*.

12:18 For ye are not come unto the mount that might be touched, and that burned with fire, nor unto blackness, and darkness, and tempest,

Touched *pselaphao* (5584), "to feel, to handle," is rendered "that might be touched" in **Heb. 12:18**.

Burned *kaio* (2545), "to set fire to, to light"; in the passive voice, "to be lighted, to burn," Matt. 5:15; John 15:6; **Heb. 12:18**; Rev. 4:5; 8:8, 10; 19:20; 21:8; 1 Cor. 13:3, is used metaphorically of the heart, Luke 24:32; of spiritual light, Luke 12:35; John 5:35.

Blackness *gnophos* (1105), **Heb. 12:18**, "blackness, gloom," seems to have been associated with the idea of a tempest. It is related to *skotos*, "darkness," in that passage, and in the Sept. of Exod. 10:22; Deut. 4:11; Zeph. 1:15.

Darkness *zophos* (2217), denotes "the gloom of the nether world", hence, "thick darkness, darkness that may be felt"; it is rendered "darkness" in **Heb. 12:18**; 2 Pet. 2:4 and Jude 6; in 2 Pet. 2:17, RV, "blackness," KJV, "mists"; in Jude 13, RV and KJV, blackness. *skotos* (4655), an older form, grammatically masculine, is found in some mss. in **Heb. 12:18**.

Tempest *thuella* (2366), "a hurricane, cyclone, whirlwind" (akin to *thuo*, "to slay," and *thumos*, "wrath"), is used in **Heb. 12:18**. In the Sept., Ex. 10:22; Deut. 4:11; 5:22.

12:19 And the sound of a trumpet, and the voice of words; which *voice* they that heard intreated that the word should not be spoken to them any more:

Sound *echos* (2279), "a noise, a sound of any sort" (Eng., "echo"), is translated "sound" in Acts 2:2; **Heb. 12:19**.

Trumpet *salpinx* (4536), is used (1) of the natural instrument, 1 Cor. 14:8; (2) of the supernatural accompaniment of divine interpositions, (a) at Sinai, **Heb. 12:19**; (b) of the acts of angels at the second advent of Christ, Matt. 24:31; (c) of their acts in the period of divine judgments preceding this, Rev. 8:2, 6, 13; 9:14; (d) of a summons to John to the presence of God, Rev. 1:10; 4:1; (e) of the act of the Lord in raising from the dead the saints who have fallen asleep and changing the bodies of those who are living, at the Rapture of all to meet Him in the air, 1 Cor. 15:52, where "the last trump" is a military allusion, familiar to Greek readers, and has no connection with the series in Rev. 8:6 to 11:15; there is a possible allusion to Num. 10:2-6, with reference to the same event, 1 Thess. 4:16, "the (lit., a) trump of God" (the absence of the article suggests the meaning "a trumpet such as is used in God's service").

Voice *see* ***Hebrews 3:7.***

Words *see* **Word** at ***Hebrews 11:3.***

Intreated *paraiteomai* (3868), lit., "to ask aside" (*para*, "aside," *aiteo*, "to ask"), signifies (a) "to beg of (or from) another," Mark 15:6, in the most authentic mss.; (b) "to deprecate," (1) "to entreat (that) not," **Heb. 12:19**; (2) "to refuse, decline, avoid," 1 Tim. 4:7; 5:11; 2 Tim. 2:23; Titus 3:10; **Heb. 12:25**; (c) "to beg off, ask to be excused," Luke 14:18-19 (some would put **Heb. 12:25** here).

Spoken *prostithemi* (4369), "to put to" (*pros*, "to," *tithemi*, "to put"), "to add, or to place beside" (the primary meaning), in Luke 17:5 is translated "increase," in the request "increase our faith"; in Luke 20:11-12, "he sent yet" (KJV, "again he sent"), lit., "he added and sent," as in 19:11, "He added and spake." In Acts 12:3, RV, "proceeded," KJV, "proceeded further" (of repeating or continuing the action mentioned by the following verb); in Acts 13:36, "was laid unto"; in **Heb. 12:19**, "more ... be spoken," (lit., "that no word should be added"). In Gal. 3:19, "What then is the law? It was "added" because of transgressions, there is no contradiction of what is said in v. 15, where the word is *epidiatasso*, for there the latter word conveys the idea of supplementing an agreement already made; here in v. 19 the meaning is not that something had been 'added' to the promise with a view to complete it, which the apostle denies, but that something had been given "in addition" to the promise, as in Rom. 5:20, "The law came in beside."

12:20 (For they could not endure that which was commanded, And if so much as a beast touch the mountain, it shall be stoned, or thrust through with a dart:

Endure *phero* (5342), "to bear," is translated "endured" in Rom. 9:22 and **Heb. 12:20**.

Commanded *diastellomai* (1291), lit., "to draw asunder" (*dia*, "asunder," *stello*, "to draw"), signifies "to admonish, order, charge," Matt. 16:20; Mark 5:43; 7:36 (twice); 8:15; 9:9. In Acts 15:24 it is translated "gave commandment"; in **Heb. 12:20**, KJV, "commanded," RV, "enjoined."

Much as In **Heb. 12:20**, KJV, *kai ean* (contracted to *k'an*), "if even" (RV), is translated "and if so much as."

Beast *therion* (2342), to be distinguished from *zoon*, almost invariably denotes "a wild beast." In Acts 28:4, "venomous beast" is used of the viper which fastened on Paul's hand. *Zoon* stresses the vital element, *therion* the bestial. The idea of a "beast" of prey is not always present. Once, in **Heb. 12:20**, it is used of the animals in the camp of Israel, such, e.g., as were appointed for sacrifice: But in the Sept. *therion* is never used of sacrificial animals; the word *ktenos* is reserved for these. *Therion*, in the sense of wild "beast," is used in Revelation for the two antichristian potentates who are destined to control the affairs of the nations with Satanic power in the closing period of the present era, 11:7; 13:1-18; 14:9, 11; 15:2; 16:2, 10, 13; 17:3-17; 19:19-20; 20:4, 10.

Touch *see* ***Hebrews 11:28.***

Mountain *see* **Mount** at ***Hebrews 8:5.***

Stoned *lithoboleo* (3036), "to pelt with stones," "to stone to death," occurs in Matt. 21:35; 23:37; Luke 13:34 (John 8:5 in some mss.); Acts 7:58, 59; 14:5; **Heb. 12:20**.

Thrust *katatoxeuo* (2700), "to strike down with an arrow, shoot dead," occurs in **Heb. 12:20** in some mss. (in a quotation from Ex. 19:13, Sept.).

Dart The noun *bolis*, "a dart," is found in some texts in **Heb. 12:20**.

12:21 And so terrible was the sight, *that* Moses said, I exceedingly fear and quake:)

So *see* **On this wise** at ***Hebrews 4:4.***

Sight *phantazo* (5324), "to make visible," is used in its participial form (middle voice), with the neuter article, as equivalent to a noun, and is translated "appearance," RV, for KJV, "sight," **Heb. 12:21**.

Fear *ekphobos* (1630), signifies "frightened outright," **Heb. 12:21** (with *eimi*, "I am"), "I exceedingly fear"; Mark 9:6, "sore afraid." *See also* **Fearful** at ***Hebrews 10:27.***

Quake *entromos* (1790), an adjective signifying "trembling with fear" (*en*, "in," *tremo*, "to tremble"), is used with *eimi*, "to be," in **Heb. 12:21** (some mss. have *ektromos*, with the same meaning), "I quake," lit.,

"I am trembling." It is used with *ginomai*, "to become," in Acts 7:32, "trembled," lit., "became trembling," and 16:29, RV, "trembling for fear" (KJV, "came trembling").

12:22 But ye are come unto mount Sion, and unto the city of the living God, the heavenly Jerusalem, and to an innumerable company of angels,

Mount *see Hebrews 8:5.*

City *see Hebrews 11:10.*

Heavenly *see Hebrews 3:1.*

Innumerable company *murias* (3461), denotes either "ten thousand," or, "indefinitely, a myriad, a numberless host," in the plural, Acts 19:19; lit. "five ten-thousands," Rev. 5:11; 9:16; in the following, used of vast numbers, Luke 12:1, KJV, "an innumerable multitude," RV, "the many thousands" (RV marg., "the myriads"); Acts 21:20, "thousands"; **Heb. 12:22**, "innumerable hosts"; Jude 14, "ten thousands" (RV, marg., in each place, "myriads"). Cf. the adjective *murios*, "ten thousand," Matt. 18:24; 1 Cor. 4:15; 14:19.

12:23 To the general assembly and church of the firstborn, which are written in heaven, and to God the Judge of all, and to the spirits of just men made perfect,

Assembly *paneguris* (3831), from *pan*, "all," and *agora*, "any kind of assembly," denoted, among the Greeks, an assembly of the people in contrast to the council of national leaders, or a "gathering" of the people in honor of a god, or for some public festival, such as the Olympic games. The word is used in **Heb. 12:23**, coupled with the word "church," as applied to all believers who form the body of Christ.

Firstborn *see* **Firstbegotten** at *Hebrews 1:6.*

Written *apographo* (583), primarily signifies "to write out, to copy"; then, "to enroll, to inscribe," as in a register. It is used of a census, Luke 2:1, RV, "be enrolled," for KJV, "be taxed"; in the middle voice, vv. 3, 5, to enroll oneself, KJV, "be taxed." Confirmation that this census (not taxation) was taken in the dominions of the Roman Empire is given by the historians Tacitus and Suetonius. Augustus himself drew up a sort of Roman Doomsday Book, a rationarium, afterwards epitomized into a breviarium, to include the allied kingdoms, appointing twenty commissioners to draw up the lists. In **Heb. 12:23** the members of the church of the firstborn are said to be "enrolled," RV.

Judge *see Hebrews 10:30.*

Spirits *see Hebrews 1:7.*

Perfect *see Hebrews 2:10.*

12:24 And to Jesus the mediator of the new covenant, and to the blood of sprinkling, that speaketh better things than *that of* Abel.

Jesus *see Hebrews 2:9.*

Mediator *see Hebrews 8:6.*

New *see Hebrews 8:8.*

Covenant *see* **Commandment** at *Hebrews 7:18.*

Sprinkling *rhantismos* (4473), "sprinkling," is used of the "sprinkling" of the blood of Christ, in **Heb. 12:24** and 1 Pet. 1:2, an allusion to the use of the blood of sacrifices, appointed for Israel, typical of the sacrifice of Christ.

Better *see Hebrews 1:4.*

12:25 See that ye refuse not him that speaketh. For if they escaped not who refused him that spake on earth, much more *shall not* we *escape*, if we turn away from him that *speaketh* from heaven:

Refuse, Refused *paraiteo mai* (3868), denotes "to refuse" in Acts 25:11; 1 Tim. 4:7; 5:11; 2 Tim. 2:23, RV (KJV, "avoid"); Titus 3:10, RV (marg., "avoid"; KJV, "reject"); **Heb. 12:25** (twice), perhaps in the sense of "begging off." *See also* **Intreated** at *Hebrews 12:19.*

Escaped, Escape *ekpheugo* (1628), "to flee away, escape," is translated "fled" in Acts 16:27 (KJV only); 19:16. In **Heb. 12:25** the best mss. have this verb. *See also* **Escape** at *Hebrews 2:3.*

Spake In **Heb. 12:25**, KJV *chrematizo*, "to warn, instruct," is translated "spake" (RV, "warned"). *See also* **Admonished** at *Hebrews 8:5.*

Turn *apostrepho* (654), denotes (a) "to cause to turn away (*apo*), to remove," Rom. 11:26; 2 Tim. 4:4 (1st clause); metaphorically, "to turn away from allegiance, pervert," Luke 23:14; (b) "to make to return, put back," Matt. 26:52, (c) in the passive voice, used reflexively, "to turn oneself away from," Matt. 5:42; 2 Tim. 1:15; Titus 1:14; **Heb. 12:25**; in the active voice, Acts 3:26.

12:26 Whose voice then shook the earth: but now he hath promised, saying, Yet once more I shake not the earth only, but also heaven.

Voice *see Hebrews 3:7.*

Shook *saleuo* (4531), "to agitate, shake," primarily of the action of stormy winds, waves, etc., is used (a) literally, of a reed, Matt. 11:7; Luke 7:24; a vessel, "shaken" in filling, Luke

"There is a danger of forgetting that the Bible reveals, not first the love of God, but the intense, blazing holiness of God, with his love as the centre of that holiness."

OSWALD CHAMBERS

6:38; a building, Luke 6:48; Acts 4:31; 16:26; the natural forces of the heavens and heavenly bodies, Matt. 24:29; Mark 13:25; Luke 21:26; the earth, **Heb. 12:26**, "shook"; (b) metaphorically, (1) of "shaking" so as to make insecure, **Heb. 12:27** (twice); (2) of casting down from a sense of security, Acts 2:25, "I should (not) be moved"; (3) to stir up (a crowd), Acts 17:13; (4) to unsettle, 2 Thess. 2:2, "(to the end that) ye be not (quickly) shaken (from your mind)," i.e., from their settled conviction and the purpose of heart begotten by it, as to the return of Christ before the Day of the Lord begins; the metaphor may be taken from the loosening of a ship from its moorings by a storm.

Promised *see* **Promise** at *Hebrews 6:13.*

Yet The adverb *eti*, implying addition or duration, e.g., Matt. 12:40; Rom. 3:7; 5:6, 8; 9:19; in **Heb. 12:26, 27**, "yet ... more".

Once *see Hebrews 6:4.*

Shake *seio* (4579), "to shake to and fro," is rendered "to shake" in Matt. 28:4, KJV; **Heb. 12:26**, KJV; Rev. 6:13, KJV and RV.

12:27 And this *word*, Yet once more, signifieth the removing of those things that are shaken, as of things that are made, that those things which cannot be shaken may remain.

Yet *see Hebrews 12:26.*

Signifieth *see* **Signifying** at *Hebrews 9:8.*

Removing *see* **Changed, Change** at *Hebrews 7:12.*

Those The article *ho*, Matt. 21:21 (*to*, the neuter), KJV (RV, "what"); in Rom. 13:9 (1st part); Gal. 5:14; **Heb. 12:27**, the article *to* is virtually equivalent to "the following."

Shaken *see* **Shook** at *Hebrews 12:26.*

Remain *meno* (3306), "to stay, abide," is frequently rendered "to remain," e.g., Matt. 11:23; Luke 10:7; John 1:33, KJV (RV, "abiding"); 9:41 (in 15:11, the best texts have the verb to be, see RV); 15:16, KJV (RV, "abide"); 19:31; Acts 5:4 (twice), RV, "whiles it remained, did it (not) remain (thine own)?"; 27:41; 1 Cor. 7:11; 15:6; 2 Cor. 3:11, 14; 9:9, KJV (RV, "abideth"); **Heb. 12:27**; 1 John 3:9.

12:28 Wherefore we receiving a kingdom which cannot be moved, let us have grace, whereby we may serve God acceptably with reverence and godly fear:

Wherefore *see Hebrews 3:7.*

Receiving *paralambano* (3880), "to receive from another" (*para*, "from beside"), or "to take," signifies "to receive," e.g., in Mark 7:4; John 1:11; 14:3; 1 Cor. 11:23; 15:1, 3; Gal. 1:9, 12; Phil. 4:9; Col. 2:6; 4:17; 1 Thess. 2:13 (1st part); 4:1; 2 Thess. 3:6; **Heb. 12:28.**

Moved *asaleutos* (761), "unmoved, immoveable," is translated "unmoveable" in Acts 27:41; "which cannot be moved" in **Heb. 12:28**, KJV (RV, "that cannot be shaken"). In the Sept., Exod. 13:16; Deut. 6:8; 11:18.

Serve *see Hebrews 8:5.*

Acceptably *euarestos* (2102), is used in **Heb. 12:28**, "so as to please."

Reverence *eulabeia* (2124), "caution, reverence," is translated "reverence" in **Heb. 12:28** (1st part in the best mss.; some have *aidos* (127), "a sense of shame, modesty," which is used regarding the demeanor of women in the church, 1 Tim. 2:9).

Fear *see* **Feared** at *Hebrews 5:7.*

12:29 For our God *is* a consuming fire.

Consuming *katanalisko* (2654), "to consume utterly, wholly" (*kata*, intensive), is said, in **Heb. 12:29**, of God as "a consuming fire."

Fire *see Hebrews 1:7.*

Chapter 13

13:1 Let brotherly love continue.

Brotherly Associated words are *adelphotes*, primarily, "a brotherly relation," and so, the community possessed of this relation, "a brotherhood," 1 Pet. 2:17 (see 5:9, marg.).; *philadelphos*, (*phileo*, "to love," and *adelphos*), "fond of one's brethren," 1 Pet. 3:8; "loving as brethren," RV.; *philadelphia*, "brotherly love," Rom. 12:10; 1 Thess. 4:9; **Heb. 13:1**; "love of the brethren," 1 Pet. 1:22 and 2 Pet. 1:7, RV.; *pseudadelphos*, "false brethren," 2 Cor. 11:26; Gal. 2:4.

Continue *see* **Continueth** at *Hebrews 7:24.*

13:2 Be not forgetful to

entertain strangers: for thereby some have entertained angels unawares.

Forgetful *see* **Forget** at ***Hebrews 6:10.***

Entertain strangers *philoxenia* (5381), "love of strangers" (*philos*, "loving," *xenos*, "a stranger"), is used in Rom. 12:13; **Heb. 13:2**, lit. "(be not forgetful of) hospitality."

Thereby *see* ***Hebrews 12:15.***

Entertained *xenizo* (3579), signifies (a) "to receive as a guest" (*xenos*, "a guest") rendered "entertained" in Acts 28:7, RV, for KJV, "lodged"; in **Heb. 13:2**, "have entertained"; (b) "to be astonished by the strangeness of a thing," Acts 17:20; 1 Pet. 4:4, 12.

Unawares In **Heb. 13:2**, *lanthano*, "to escape notice," is used with the aorist participle of *xenizo*, "to entertain," signifying "entertained ... unawares" (an idiomatic usage common in classical Greek).

13:3 Remember them that are in bonds, as bound with them; *and* them which suffer adversity, as being yourselves also in the body.

Remember *see* **Mindful** at ***Hebrews 2:6.***

Bonds *desmios* (1198), "a binding," denotes "a prisoner," e.g., Acts 25:14, RV, for the KJV, "in bonds"; **Heb. 13:3**, "them that are in bonds." Paul speaks of himself as a prisoner of Christ, Eph. 3:1; 2 Tim. 1:8; Philem. 1, 9; "in the Lord," Eph. 4:1. *See also* ***Hebrews 10:34.***

Bound *sundeo* (4887), "to bind together," implying association, is used in **Heb. 13:3** of those bound together in confinement.

Suffer *see* **Afflicted** at ***Hebrews 11:37.***

Yourselves The addition of *autoi*, "yourselves," to the pronoun marks especial emphasis, e.g., Mark 6:31; John 3:28; 1 Cor. 11:13; 1 Thess. 4:9. Sometimes *autoi* is used without the pronoun, e.g., Luke 11:46, 52; Acts 2:22; 20:34; 1 Thess. 2:1; 3:3; 5:2; 2 Thess. 3:7; **Heb. 13:3**.

13:4 Marriage *is* honourable in all, and the bed undefiled: but whoremongers and adulterers God will judge.

Marriage *gamos* (1062), "a marriage, wedding," or "wedding feast," is used to denote (a) the ceremony and its proceedings, including the "marriage feast," John 2:1, 2; of the "marriage ceremony" only, figuratively, Rev. 19:7, as distinct from the "marriage feast" (v. 9); (b) "the marriage feast," RV in Matt. 22:2-4, 9; in v. 8, 10, "wedding;" in 25:10, RV "marriage feast;" so Luke 12:36; 14:8; in Matt. 22:11, 12, the "wedding garment" is, lit., "a garment of a wedding." In Rev. 19, where, under the figure of a "marriage," the union of Christ, as the Lamb of God, with His heavenly bride is so described, the marriage itself takes place in heaven during the Parousia, v. 7 (the aorist or point tense indicating an accomplished fact; the bride is called "His wife"); the "marriage feast" or supper is to take place on earth, after the Second Advent, v. 9. That Christ is spoken of as the Lamb points to His atoning sacrifice as the ground upon which the spiritual union takes place. The background of the phraseology lies in the OT description of the relation of God to Israel, e.g., Isa. 54:4ff.; Ezek. 16:7ff.; Hos. 2:19; (c) "marriage" in general, including the "married" state, which is to be "had in honor," **Heb. 13:4**, RV.

Honourable *timios* (5093), "precious, valuable, honorable," is used of marriage in **Heb. 13:4**, KJV, as a statement, "(marriage) is honorable (in all)," RV, as an exhortation, "let (marriage) be had in honor (among all)." *See also* **Vessels** at ***Hebrews 9:21.***

Bed *koite* (2845), primarily "a place for lying down" (connected with *keimai*, "to lie"), denotes a "bed," Luke 11:7; the marriage "bed," **Heb. 13:4**; in Rom. 13:13, it is used of sexual intercourse. By metonymy, the cause standing for the effect, it denotes conception, Rom. 9:10.

Undefiled *see* ***Hebrews 7:26.***

Whoremongers *see* **Fornicator** at ***Hebrews 12:16.***

Adulterers *moichos* (3432), denotes one "who has unlawful intercourse with the spouse of another," Luke 18:11; 1 Cor. 6:9; **Heb. 13:4**.

13:5 *Let your* conversation *be* without covetousness; *and be* content with such things as ye have: for he hath said, I will never leave thee, nor forsake thee.

Conversation *tropos* (5158), "a turning, a manner," is translated simply "be ye," RV in **Heb. 13:5**, instead of "let your conversation be."

Covetousness *aphilarguros* (866), is translated "without covetousness" in **Heb. 13:5**, KJV; RV, "free from the love of money." In 1 Tim. 3:3, the KJV has "not covetous," the RV, "no lover of money."

Content *arkeo* (174), primarily signifies "to be sufficient, to be possessed of sufficient strength, to be strong, to be enough for a thing"; hence, "to defend, ward off"; in the middle voice, "to be satisfied, contented with," Luke 3:14, with wages; 1 Tim. 6:8, with food and raiment; **Heb. 13:5**, with "such things as ye have"; negatively of Diotrephes, in 3 John 10, "not content therewith."

Such In **Heb. 13:5**, "such things as ye have" represents the phrase *ta paronta*, "the (things) present" (present participle of *pareimi*).

Have In **Heb. 13:5**, "such things as ye have" is, lit., "the (things) present." *See also* **Present** at *Hebrews 12:11*.

Leave *aniemi* (447), *ana*, "back" and *hiemi*, "to send," denotes "to let go, loosen, forbear"; it is translated "I will (never) leave (thee)" in **Heb. 13:5**.

Forsake *see* **Forsaking** at *Hebrews 10:25*.

13:6 So that we may boldly say, The Lord *is* my helper, and I will not fear what man shall do unto me.

Boldly *tharreo* (2292), a later form of *tharseo*, is connected with *thero*, "to be warm" (warmth of temperament being associated with confidence); hence, "to be confident, bold, courageous"; RV, invariably, "to be of good courage"; 2 Cor. 5:6, 8 (KJV, "to be confident"); 7:16 (KJV, "to have confidence"); 10:1-2 (KJV, "to be bold"); **Heb. 13:6**, KJV, "boldly"; RV, "with good courage" (lit., "being courageous").

Helper *boethos* (998), an adjective, signifying "helping," is used as a noun in **Heb. 13:6**, of God as the helper of His saints.

13:7 Remember them which have the rule over you, who have spoken unto you the word of God: whose faith follow, considering the end of *their* conversation.

Remember *see* **Mindful** at *Hebrews 11:15*.

Rule *hegeomai* (2233), "to lead," is translated "to rule" in **Heb. 13:7, 17, 24** (KJV marg., in the first two, "are the guides" and "guide."

Follow *mimeomai* (3401), "a mimic, an actor" (Eng., "mime," etc.), is always translated "to imitate" in the RV, for KJV, "to follow," (a) of imitating the conduct of missionaries, 2 Thess. 3:7, 9; the faith of spiritual guides, **Heb. 13:7**; (b) that which is good, 3 John 11. The verb is always used in exhortations, and always in the continuous tense, suggesting a constant habit or practice.

Considering *anatheoreo* (333), "to observe carefully, consider well" (*ana*, "up," intensive, and *theoreo*, "to behold"), is used in Acts 17:23, RV, "observed" (of Paul's notice of the objects of Athenian worship), and **Heb. 13:7**, "considering."

End *ekbasis* (1545), "a way out," "way of escape," 1 Cor. 10:13 (*ek*, "out," *baino*, "to go"), is rendered "issue" in **Heb. 13:7**, RV, for KJV, "end," regarding the manner of life of deceased spiritual guides.

Conversation, *anastrophe* (391), lit., "a turning back" is translated "manner of life," "living," etc. in the RV, for KJV, "conversation," Gal. 1:13; Eph. 4:22; 1 Tim. 4:12; **Heb. 13:7**; Jas. 3:13; 1 Pet. 1:15, 18; 2:1 ("behavior"); 3:1, 2, 16 (ditto); 2 Pet. 2:7; 3:11.

13:8 Jesus Christ the same yesterday, and to day, and for ever.

Same *see* *Hebrews 1:12*.

Yesterday *echthes* or *chthes* (5504), occurs in John 4:52; Acts 7:28; **Heb. 13:8**.

To day *see* **This day** at *Hebrews 1:5*. *See also* **Daily** at *Hebrews 3:13*.

13:9 Be not carried about with divers and strange doctrines. For *it is* a good thing that the heart be established with grace; not with meats, which have not profited them that have been occupied therein.

Carried about *periphero* (4064), signifies "to carry about, or bear about," and is used literally, of carrying the sick Mark 6:55, or of physical sufferings endured in fellowship with Christ, 2 Cor. 4:10; metaphorically, of being "carried" about by different evil doctrines, Eph. 4:14; **Heb. 13:9**; Jude 12.

Divers *see* *Hebrews 2:4*.

Strange *xenos* (3581), denotes (a) "foreign, alien," Acts 17:18, of gods; **Heb. 13:9**, of doctrines; (b) "unusual," 1 Pet. 4:12, 2nd part, of the fiery trial of persecution.

Established *bebaioo* (950), "to confirm," is rendered "stablish," 2 Cor. 1:21; "stablished," Col. 2:7; "be established," **Heb. 13:9**. *See also* **Confirmed** at *Hebrews 2:3*.

Meats *see* *Hebrews 9:10*.

Profited *see* **Profit** at *Hebrews 4:2*.

Occupied *peripateo* (4043), "to walk," is sometimes used of the state in which one is living, or of that to which a person is given, e.g., **Heb. 13:9**, "(meats, wherein they that) occupied themselves," RV (marg., "walked"; KJV, "have been occupied"), i.e., exercising themselves about different kinds of food, regarding some as lawful, others as unlawful (referring especially to matters of the ceremonial details of the law).

13:10 We have an altar, whereof they have no right to eat which serve the tabernacle.

Right *exousia* (1849), "authority, power," is translated "right" in the RV, for KJV, "power," in John 1:12; Rom. 9:21; 1 Cor. 9:4, 5, 6, 12 (twice), 18; 2 Thess. 3:9, where the "right" is that of being maintained by those among whom the ministers of the gospel had labored, a "right" possessed in virtue of the "authority" given them by Christ, **Heb. 13:10**; Rev. 22:14.

Serve *see Hebrews 8:5.*

Tabernacle *see Hebrews 8:2.*

13:11 For the bodies of those beasts, whose blood is brought into the sanctuary by the high priest for sin, are burned without the camp.

Beasts *zoon* (2226), primarily denotes "a living being" (*zoe*, "life"). The Eng., "animal," is the equivalent, stressing the fact of life as the characteristic feature. In **Heb. 13:11** the KJV and the RV translate it "beasts" ("animals" would be quite suitable). In 2 Pet. 2:12 and Jude 10, the KJV has "beasts," the RV "creatures." In Revelation, where the word is found some 20 times, and always of those beings which stand before the throne of God, who give glory and honor and thanks to Him, 4:6, and act in perfect harmony with His counsels, 5:14; 6:1-7, e.g., the word "beasts" is most unsuitable; the RV, "living creatures," should always be used; it gives to *zoon* its appropriate significance.

Brought *eisphero* (1533), denotes "to bring to," Acts 17:20; "to bring into," Luke 5:18, 19; 1 Tim. 6:7; **Heb. 13:11**.

Sanctuary *see Hebrews 8:2.*

High priest *see Hebrews 2:17.*

Sin *see Hebrews 3:13.*

Burned *katakaio* (2618), signifies "to burn up, burn utterly," as of chaff, Matt. 3:12; Luke 3:17; tares, Matt. 13:30, 40; the earth and its works, 2 Pet. 3:10; trees and grass, Rev. 8:7. This form should be noted in Acts 19:19; 1 Cor. 3:15; **Heb. 13:11**, Rev. 17:16. In each place the full rendering "burn utterly" might be used, as in Rev. 18:8.

Without *see Hebrews 4:15.*

Camp *see* **Armies** *at Hebrews 11:34.*

13:12 Wherefore Jesus also, that he might sanctify the people with his own blood, suffered without the gate.

Wherefore *see Hebrews 3:7.*

Jesus *see Hebrews 2:9.*

Sanctify *see* **Sanctified** at *Hebrews 10:10.*

Suffered *see Hebrews 2:18.*

Gate *pule* (4439), is used (a) literally, for a larger sort of "gate," in the wall either of a city or palace or temple, Luke 7:12, of Nain (burying places were outside the "gates" of cities); Acts 3:10; 9:24; 12:10; **Heb. 13:12**; (b) metaphorically, of the "gates" at the entrances of the ways leading to life and to destruction, Matt. 7:13, 14; some mss. have *pule*, for *thura*, "a door," in Luke 13:24 (see the RV); of the "gates" of Hades, Matt. 16:18, than which nothing was regarded as stronger. The importance and strength of "gates" made them viewed as synonymous with power. By metonymy, the "gates" stood for those who held government and administered justice there.

13:13 Let us go forth therefore unto him without the camp, bearing his reproach.

Camp *see* **Armies** at *Hebrews 11:34.*

Bearing *phero* (5342), "to bring or bear," is translated in the RV by the latter verb in Luke 23:26; John 2:8 (twice); 12:24; 15:2 (twice); **Heb. 13:13**.

Reproach *see* **Reproaches** at *Hebrews 10:33.*

13:14 For here have we no continuing city, but we seek one to come.

Continuing *see* **Continueth** at *Hebrews 7:24.*

City *see Hebrews 11:10.*

Seek *see Hebrews 11:14.*

13:15 By him therefore let us offer the sacrifice of praise to God continually, that is, the fruit of *our* lips giving thanks to his name.

Offer *see Hebrews 7:27.*

Sacrifice *see* **Sacrifices** at *Hebrews 5:1.*

Praise *ainesis* (133), "praise," is found in **Heb. 13:15**, where it is metaphorically represented as a sacrificial offering.

Continually *see* **Always** at *Hebrews 9:6.*

Fruit *see Hebrews 12:11.*

Lips *see* **Shore** at *Hebrews 11:12.*

Thanks *homologeo* (3670), rendered "giving thanks" in **Heb. 13:15** (RV, "make confession"). *See also* **Confessed** at *Hebrews 11:13.*

Name *see Hebrews 1:4.*

13:16 But to do good and to communicate forget not: for with such sacrifices God is well pleased.

Good *eupoiia* (2140), "beneficence, doing good" (*eu*, "well," *poieo*, "to do"), is translated as a verb in **Heb. 13:16**, "to do good."

Communicate *koinonia* (2842), is translated in **Heb. 13:16** "to communicate," lit., "be not forgetful of good deed and of fellowship"; "fellowship" (KJV, "communication") in Philem. 6, RV.

Forget *see Hebrews 6:10.*

Sacrifices *see Hebrews 5:1.*

Pleased *see Hebrews 11:5.*

13:17 Obey them that have the rule over you, and submit yourselves: for they watch for your souls, as they that must give account, that they may do it with joy, and not with grief: for that *is* unprofitable for you.

Obey *peitho* (3982), "to persuade, to win over," in the passive and middle voices, "to be persuaded, to listen to, to obey," is so used with this meaning, in the middle voice, e.g., in Acts 5:36-37 (in v. 40, passive voice, "they agreed"); Rom. 2:8; Gal. 5:7; **Heb. 13:17**; Jas. 3:3. The "obedience" suggested is not by submission to authority, but resulting from persuasion.

Rule *see Hebrews 13:7.*

Submit *hupeiko* (5226), "to retire, withdraw" (*hupo*, under, *eiko*, "to yield"), hence, "to yield, submit," is used metaphorically in **Heb. 13:17**, of "submitting" to spiritual guides in the churches.

Watch *agrupneo* (69), "to be sleepless" (from *agreuo*, "to chase," and *hupnos*, "sleep"), is used metaphorically, "to be watchful," in Mark 13:33; Luke 21:36; Eph. 6:18; **Heb. 13:17**. The word expresses not mere wakefulness, but the "watchfulness" of those who are intent upon a thing.

Souls *see* **Soul** at *Hebrews 4:12*.

Must give In **Heb. 13:17**, KJV, the future participle of *apodidomi*, "to give," is translated "they that must give" (RV, "they that shall give"). *See also* **Sold** at *Hebrews 12:16*.

Account *logos* (3056), "a word or saying," also means "an account which one gives by word of mouth," Matt. 12:36; Matt. 18:23, RV, "reckoning"; 16:2; Acts 19:40; 20:24 (KJV, "count"); Rom. 14:12; Phil. 4:17; **Heb. 13:17**; 1 Pet. 4:5.

Grief *stenazo* (4727), "to groan" (of an inward, unexpressed feeling of sorrow), is translated "with grief" in **Heb. 13:17** (marg. "groaning"). It is rendered "sighed" in Mark 7:34; "groan," in Rom. 8:23; 2 Cor. 5:2, 4; "murmur," in Jas. 5:9, RV (KJV, "grudge").

Unprofitable *alusiteles* (255), "not advantageous, not making good the expense involved" (*lusiteles*, "useful") occurs in **Heb. 13:17**.

13:18 Pray for us: for we trust we have a good conscience, in all things willing to live honestly.

Pray *proseuchomai* (4336), "to pray," is always used of "prayer" to God, and is the most frequent word in this respect, especially in the Synoptists and Acts, once in Romans, 8:26; in Ephesians, 6:18; in Philippians, 1:9; in 1 Timothy, 2:8; in Hebrews, **13:18**; in Jude, v. 20. For the injunction in 1 Thess. 5:17.

Trust *peitho* (3982), "to persuade," in the middle and passive voices signifies "to suffer oneself to be persuaded," e.g., Luke 16:31; **Heb. 13:18**; it is sometimes translated "believe" in the RV, but not in Acts 17:4, RV, "were persuaded," and 27:11, "gave (more) heed"; in Acts 28:24, "believed. *See also Hebrews 2:13. See also* **Persuaded** at *Hebrews 6:9*.

Conscience *see Hebrews 9:9*.

Willing *see* **Would** at *Hebrews 12:17*.

Live *anastrepho* (390), used metaphorically, in the middle voice, "to conduct oneself, behave, live," is translated "to live," in **Heb. 13:18** ("honestly"); in 2 Pet. 2:18 ("in error").

Honestly *kalos* (2573), is used in **Heb. 13:18**, "honestly," i.e., honorably.

13:19 But I beseech *you* the rather to do this, that I may be restored to you the sooner.

Beseech *parakaleo* (3870), primarily, "to call to a person" (*para*, "to the side," *kaleo*, "to call"), denotes (a) "to call on, entreat"; (b) to admonish, exhort, to urge one to pursue some course of conduct (always prospective, looking to the future, in contrast to the meaning to comfort, which is retrospective, having to do with trial experienced), translated "exhort" in the RV of Phil. 4:2; 1 Thess. 4:10; **Heb. 13:19**, **22**, for KJV, "beseech"; in 1 Tim. 5:1, for KJV, "intreat"; in 1 Thess. 5:11, for KJV, "comfort"; "exhorted" in 2 Cor. 8:6 and 12:18, for KJV, "desired"; in 1 Tim. 1:3, for KJV, "besought.

Rather In **Heb. 13:19**, KJV, *perissoteros*, "the more exceedingly" (RV), is translated "the rather."

Restored *apokathistemi* or the alternative form *apokathistano* (600), is used (a) of "restoration" to a former condition of health Matt. 12:13; Mark 3:5; 8:25; Luke 6:10; (b) of the divine "restoration" of Israel and conditions affected by it, including the renewal of the covenant broken by them, Matt. 17:11; Mark 9:12; Acts 1:6; (c) of "giving" or "bringing" a person back, **Heb. 13:19**. In the papyri it is used of financial restitution, of making good the breaking of a stone by a workman by his substituting another, of the reclamation of land, etc. (Moulton and Milligan).

Sooner *tacheion* (5032), the comparative degree, is translated "quickly" in John 13:27; "out(ran)" in 20:4, RV, lit., "(ran before) more quickly (than Peter)"; "shortly" in 1 Tim. 3:14 and **Heb. 13:23**; in **13:19**, "(the) sooner."

13:20 Now the God of peace, that brought again from the dead our Lord Jesus, that great shepherd of the sheep, through the blood of the everlasting covenant,

God *see* ***Hebrews 1:8.***

Peace *see* ***Hebrews 11:31.***

Brought *anago* (321), "to lead or bring up to," Luke 2:22; Acts 9:39, etc.; "to bring forth," Acts 12:4; "to bring again," **Heb. 13:20**; "to bring up again," Rom. 10:7.

Lord Jesus *see* ***Hebrews 2:9.***

Shepherd *poimen* (4166), is used (a) in its natural significance, Matt. 9:36; 25:32; Mark 6:34; Luke 2:8, 15, 18, 20; John 10:2, 12; (b) metaphorically of Christ, Matt. 26:31; Mark 14:27; John 10:11, 14, 16; **Heb. 13:20**; 1 Pet. 2:25; (c) metaphorically of those who act as pastors in the churches, Eph. 4:11.

Sheep *probaton* (4263), from *probaino*, "to go forward," i.e., of the movement of quadrupeds, was used among the Greeks of small cattle, sheep and goats; in the NT, of "sheep" only (a) naturally, e.g., Matt. 12:11, 12; (b) metaphorically, of those who belong to the Lord, the lost ones of the house of Israel, Matt. 10:6; of those who are under the care of the Good Shepherd, e.g., Matt. 26:31; John 10:1, lit., "the fold of the sheep," and vv. 2-27; 21:16, 17 in some texts; **Heb. 13:20**; of those who in a future day, at the introduction of the millennial kingdom, have shown kindness to His persecuted earthly people in their great tribulation, Matt. 25:33; of the clothing of false shepherds, Matt. 7:15; (c) figuratively, by way of simile, of Christ, Acts 8:32; of the disciples, e.g., Matt. 10:16; of true followers of Christ in general, Rom. 8:36; of the former wayward condition of those who had come under His Shepherd care, 1 Pet. 2:25; of the multitudes who sought the help of Christ in the days of His flesh, Matt. 9:36; Mark 6:34.

Covenant *see* **Commandment** at *Hebrews 7:18.*

13:21 Make you perfect in every good work to do his will, working in you that which is wellpleasing in his sight, through Jesus Christ; to whom *be* glory for ever and ever. Amen.

Perfect *see* **Prepared** at ***Hebrews 10:5.***

Work *see* **Works** at ***Hebrews 1:10.***

Working *poieo* (4160), "to do," is rendered "to work" in Matt. 20:12, KJV (RV, "spent"); Acts 15:12, "had wrought"; 19:11; 21:19; **Heb. 13:21**; Rev. 16:14; 19:20; 21:27, KJV (RV, "maketh"; marg., "doeth").

Wellpleasing *euarestos* (2101), is used in Rom. 12:1, 2, translated "acceptable (RV marg., "well-pleasing"); in the following the RV has "well-pleasing," Rom. 14:18; 2 Cor. 5:9; Eph. 5:10; in Phil. 4:18 and Col. 3:20 (RV and KJV); in Titus 2:9, RV, "well-pleasing" (KJV, "please ... well"); in **Heb. 13:21**, RV and KJV.

13:22 And I beseech you, brethren, suffer the word of exhortation: for I have written a letter unto you in few words.

Beseech, Exhortation *see* **Beseech** at ***Hebrews 13:19.***

Suffer *anechomai* (430), signifies "to hold up against a thing and so to bear with" (*ana*, "up," and *echomai*, the middle voice of *echo*, "to have, to hold"), e.g., Matt. 17:7; 1 Cor. 4:12; 2 Cor. 11:1, 4, 19-20; **Heb. 13:22**, etc.

Written *epistello* (1989), denotes "to send a message by letter, to write word" (*stello*, "to send"; Eng., "epistle"), Acts 15:20; 21:25 (some mss. have *apostello*, "to send"); **Heb. 13:22.**

Few *see* **Little** at ***Hebrews 2:7.***

13:23 Know ye that *our* brother Timothy is set at liberty; with whom, if he come shortly, I will see you.

Liberty *apoluo* (630), is translated "to set at liberty" in Acts 26:32 and **Heb. 13:23.**

Shortly *see* **Sooner** at ***Hebrews 13:19.***

13:24-25 Salute all them that have the rule over you, and all the saints. They of Italy salute you.
Grace *be* with you all. Amen.

Salute *see* **Embraced** at *Hebrews 11:13.*

Rule *see* ***Hebrews 13:7.***

They Sometimes the plural of the article is rendered "they," e.g., Phil. 4:22; **Heb. 13:24**; in 1 Cor. 11:19, "they which are (approved)" is, lit., "the approved"; in Gal. 2:6, "they ... (who were of repute)," RV.

James

Chapter 1

1:1 James, a servant of God and of the Lord Jesus Christ, to the twelve tribes which are scattered abroad, greeting.

Servant *doulos* (1401), an adjective, signifying "in bondage," Rom. 6:19 (neuter plural, agreeing with *mele*, "members"), is used as a noun, and as the most common and general word for "servant," frequently indicating subjection without the idea of bondage; it is used (a) of natural conditions, e.g., Matt. 8:9; 1 Cor. 7:21, 22 (1st part); Eph. 6:5; Col. 4:1; 1 Tim. 6:1; frequently in the four Gospels; (b) metaphorically of spiritual, moral and ethical conditions: "servants" (1) of God, e.g., Acts 16:17; Titus 1:1; 1 Pet. 2:16; Rev. 7:3; 15:3; the perfect example being Christ Himself, Phil. 2:7; (2) of Christ, e.g., Rom. 1:1; 1 Cor. 7:22 (2nd part); Gal. 1:10; Eph. 6:6; Phil. 1:1; Col. 4:12; **Jas. 1:1**; 2 Pet. 1:1; Jude 1; (3) of sin, John 8:34 (RV, "bondservants"); Rom. 6:17, 20; (4) of corruption, 2 Pet. 2:19 (RV, "bondservants"); cf. the verb *douloo*.

Lord *kurios* (2962), properly an adjective, signifying "having power" (*kuros*) or "authority," is used as a noun, variously translated in the NT, "'Lord,' 'master,' 'Master,' 'owner,' 'Sir,' a title of wide significance, occurring in each book of the NT save Titus and the Epistles of John. It is used (a) of an owner, as in Luke 19:33, cf. Matt. 20:8; Acts 16:16; Gal. 4:1; or of one who has the disposal of anything, as the Sabbath, Matt. 12:8; (b) of a master, i.e., one to whom service is due on any ground, Matt. 6:24; 24:50; Eph. 6:5; (c) of an Emperor or King, Acts 25:26; Rev. 17:14; (d) of idols, ironically, 1 Cor. 8:5, cf. Isa. 26:13; (e) as a title of respect addressed to a father, Matt. 21:30, a husband, 1 Pet. 3:6, a master, Matt. 13:27; Luke 13:8, a ruler, Matt. 27:63, an angel, Acts 10:4; Rev. 7:14; (f) as a title of courtesy addressed to a stranger, John 12:21; 20:15; Acts 16:30; from the outset of His ministry this was a common form of address to the Lord Jesus, alike by the people, Matt. 8:2; John 4:11, and by His disciples, Matt. 8:25; Luke 5:8; John 6:68; (g) *kurios* is the Sept. and NT representative of Heb. Jehovah ('LORD' in Eng. versions), see Matt. 4:7; **Jas. 5:11**, e.g., of *adon*, Lord, Matt. 22:44, and of *Adonay*, Lord, 1:22; it also occurs for *Elohim*, God, 1 Pet. 1:25.

"Thus the usage of the word in the NT follows two main lines: one, *a-f*, customary and general, the other, *g*, peculiar to the Jews, and drawn from the Greek translation of the OT. Christ Himself assumed the title, Matt. 7:21, 22; 9:38; 22:41-45; Mark 5:19 (cf. Ps. 66:16; the parallel passage, Luke 8:39, has 'God'); Luke 19:31; John 13:13, apparently intending it in the higher senses of its current use, and at the same time suggesting its OT associations. His purpose did not become clear to the disciples until after His resurrection, and the revelation of His Deity consequent thereon. Thomas, when he realized the significance of the presence of a mortal wound in the body of a living man, immediately joined with it the absolute title of Deity, saying, 'My Lord and my God,' John 20:28. Thereafter, except in Acts 10:4 and Rev. 7:14, there is no record that *kurios* was ever again used by believers in addressing any save God and the Lord Jesus; cf Acts 2:47 with 4:29, 30. How soon and how completely the lower meaning had been superseded is seen in Peter's declaration in his first sermon after the resurrection, 'God hath made Him – Lord,' Acts 2:36, and that in the house of Cornelius, 'He is Lord of all,' 10:36, cf. Deut. 10:14; Matt. 11:25; Acts 17:24. In his writings the implications of his early teaching are confirmed and developed. Thus Ps. 34:8, 'O taste and see that Jehovah is good,' is applied to the Lord Jesus, 1 Pet. 2:3, and 'Jehovah of Hosts, Him shall ye sanctify,' Isa. 8:13, becomes 'sanctify in your hearts Christ as Lord,' 3:15. So also James who uses *kurios* alike of God, **1:7** (cf. v. **5**); **3:9; 4:15; 5:4, 10, 11**, and of the Lord Jesus, **1:1** (where the possibility that *kai* is intended epexegetically, i.e. = even, cf. 1 Thess. 3:11, should not be overlooked); **2:1** (lit., 'our Lord Jesus Christ of glory,' cf. Ps. 24:7; 29:3; Acts 7:2; 1 Cor. 2:8); **5:7, 8**, while the language of **4:10; 5:15**, is equally applicable to either."

Twelve *dodeka* (1427), is used frequently in the Gospels for the twelve apostles, and in Acts 6:2; 1 Cor. 15:5; Rev. 21:14b; of the tribes of Israel, Matt. 19:28; Luke 22:30; **Jas. 1:1**; Rev. 21:12c (cf. 7:5-8; 12:1); in various details relating to the heavenly Jerusalem, Rev. 21:12-21; 22:2. The number in general is regarded as suggestive of divine administration.

Tribes *phule* (5443), "a company of people united by kinship or habitation, a clan, tribe," is used (a) of the peoples of the earth, Matt. 24:30; in the following the RV has "tribe(-s)" for KJV, "kindred(-s)," Rev. 1:7; 5:9; 7:9; 11:9; 13:7; 14:6; (b) of the "tribes" of Israel, Matt. 19:28; Luke 2:36; 22:30; Acts 13:21; Rom. 11:1; Phil. 3:5; Heb. 7:13, 14; **Jas. 1:1**; Rev. 5:5; 7:4-8; 21:12.

Scattered *diaspora* (1290), "a dispersion," is rendered "scattered abroad" in **Jas. 1:1**, KJV; "scattered" in 1 Pet. 1:1, KJV.

Greeting *chairo* (5463), "to rejoice," is thrice used as a formula of salutation in Acts 15:23, KJV, "send greeting," RV, "greeting"; so 23:26; **Jas. 1:1**. In 2 John 10, 11, the RV substitutes the phrase (to give) "greeting," for the KJV (to bid) "God speed." *Charis* (5485), has various uses, in an... objective sense, the effect of "grace," the spiritual state of those who have experienced its exercise, whether (1) a state of "grace," e.g., Rom. 5:2; 1 Pet. 5:12; 2 Pet. 3:18, or (2) a proof thereof in practical effects, deeds of "grace," e.g., 1 Cor. 16:3, RV, "bounty" (KJV, "liberality"); 2 Cor. 8:6, 19 (in 2 Cor. 9:8 it means the sum of earthly blessings); the power and equipment for ministry, e.g., Rom. 1:5; 12:6; 15:15; 1 Cor. 3:10; Gal. 2:9; Eph. 3:2, 7. To be in favor with is to find "grace" with, e.g., Acts 2:47; hence it appears in this sense at the beginning and the end of several epistles, where the writer desires "grace" from God for the readers, e.g., Rom. 1:7; 1 Cor. 1:3; in this respect it is connected with the imperative mood of the word *chairo*, "to rejoice," a mode of greeting among Greeks, e.g., Acts 15:23; **Jas. 1:1** (marg.); 2 John 10, 11, RV, "greeting" (KJV, "God speed"). The fact that "grace" is received both from God the Father, 2 Cor. 1:12, and from Christ, Gal. 1:6; Rom. 5:15 (where both are mentioned), is a testimony to the deity of Christ. See also 2 Thess. 1:12, where the phrase "according to the grace of our God and the Lord Jesus Christ" is to be taken with each of the preceding clauses, "in you," "and ye in Him." In **Jas. 4:6**, "But He giveth more grace" (Greek, "a greater grace," RV, marg.), the statement is to be taken in connection with the preceding verse, which contains two remonstrating, rhetorical questions, "Think ye that the Scripture speaketh in vain?" and "Doth the Spirit (the Holy Spirit) which He made to dwell in us long unto envying?" (see the RV). The implied answer to each is "it cannot be so." Accordingly, if those who are acting so flagrantly, as if it were so, will listen to the Scripture instead of letting it speak in vain, and will act so that the Holy Spirit may have His way within, God will give even "a greater grace," namely, all that follows from humbleness and from turning away from the world.

1:2 My brethren, count it all joy when ye fall into divers temptations;

Count *hegeomai* (2233), primarily, "to lead the way"; hence, "to lead before the mind, account," is found with this meaning in Phil. 2:3, RV (KJV, "esteem"); 2:6, RV (KJV, "thought"); 2:25 (KJV, "supposed"); Phil. 3:7-8; 2 Thess. 3:15; 1 Tim. 1:12; 6:1; Heb. 10:29; **Jas. 1:2**; Heb. 11:11 (KJV, "judged"); 2 Pet. 2:13; 3:9.

Joy *chara* (5479), "joy, delight" (akin to *chairo*, "to rejoice"), is found frequently in Matthew and Luke, and especially in John, once in Mark (4:16, RV, "joy," KJV, "gladness"); it is absent from 1 Cor. (though the verb is used three times), but is frequent in 2 Cor., where the noun is used five times, and the verb eight times, suggestive of the apostle's relief in comparison with the circumstances of the 1st Epistle; in Col. 1:11, KJV, "joyfulness," RV, "joy." The word is sometimes used, by metonymy, of the occasion or cause of "joy," Luke 2:10 (lit., "I announce to you a great joy"); in 2 Cor. 1:15, in some mss., for *charis*, "benefit"; Phil. 4:1, where the readers are called the apostle's "joy"; so 1 Thess. 2:19, 20; Heb. 12:2, of the object of Christ's "joy"; **Jas. 1:2**, where it is connected with falling into trials; perhaps also in Matt. 25:21, 23, where some regard it as signifying, concretely, the circumstances attending cooperation in the authority of the Lord.

Fall *peripipto* (4045), "to fall around" (*peri*, "around"), hence signifies to "fall" in with, or among, to light upon, come across, Luke 10:30, "among (robbers)"; Acts 27:41, KJV, "falling into," RV, "lighting upon," a part of a shore; **Jas. 1:2**, into temptation (i.e., trials).

Divers *poikilos* (4164), denotes "particolored, variegated" (*poikillo* means "to make gay": the root of the first syllable is *pik*-, found in Eng., "picture"), hence "divers," Matt. 4:24; Mark 1:34; Luke 4:40; 2 Tim. 3:6; Titus 3:3; Heb. 2:4 (RV, "manifold"), 13:9; **Jas. 1:2** (RV, "manifold"); in 1 Pet. 1:6 and 4:10, "manifold," both KJV and RV.

Temptations *peirasmos* (3986), is used of (1) "trials" with a beneficial purpose and effect, (a) of "trials" or "temptations," divinely permitted or sent, Luke 22:28; Acts 20:19; **Jas. 1:2**; 1 Pet. 1:6; 4:12, RV, "to prove," KJV, "to try"; 2 Pet. 2:9 (singular); Rev. 3:10, RV, "trial" (KJV, "temptation"); in **Jas. 1:12**, "temptation" apparently has meanings (1) and (2) combined, and is used in the widest sense; (b) with a good or neutral significance, Gal. 4:14, of Paul's physical infirmity, "a temptation" to the Galatian converts, of such a kind as to arouse feelings of natural repugnance; (c) of "trials" of a varied character, Matt. 6:13 and Luke 11:4, where believers are commanded to pray not to be led into such by forces beyond their own control; Matt. 26:41; Mark 14:38; Luke 22:40, 46, where they are commanded to watch and pray against entering into "temptations" by their own carelessness or disobedience; in all such cases God provides "the way of escape," 1 Cor. 10:13 (where *peirasmos* occurs twice). (2) Of "trial" definitely designed to lead to wrong doing, "temptation," Luke 4:13; 8:13; 1 Tim. 6:9; (3) of "trying" or challenging God, by men, Heb. 3:8.

1:3 Knowing *this*, that the trying of your faith worketh patience.

Trying *dokimion* (1383), "a test, a proof," is rendered "proof" in **Jas. 1:3**, RV (KJV, "trying"); it is regarded by some as equivalent to *dokimeion*, "a crucible, a test"; it is the neuter form of the adjective *dokimios*, used as a noun, which has been taken to denote the means by which a man is tested and "proved" (Mayor), in the same sense as *dokime* in 2 Cor. 8:2; the same phrase is used in 1 Pet. 1:7, RV, "the proof (of your faith)," KJV, "the trial"; where the meaning probably is "that which is approved [i.e., as genuine] in your faith"; this interpretation, which was suggested by Hort, and may hold good for **Jas. 1:3**, has been confirmed from the papyri by Deissmann (*Bible Studies*, p. 259ff.). Moulton and Milligan (*Vocab.*) give additional instances.

Worketh *katergazomai* (2716), an emphatic form, signifies "to work out, achieve, effect by toil," rendered "to work" (past tense, "wrought") in Rom. 1:27; 2:9, RV; 4:15 (the Law brings men under condemnation and so renders them subject to divine wrath); 5:3; 7:8, 13; 15:18; 2 Cor. 4:17; 5:5; 7:10, 11; 12:12; Phil. 2:12, where "your own salvation" refers especially to freedom from strife and vainglory; **Jas. 1:3, 20**; 1 Pet. 4:3.

Patience *hupomone* (5281), lit., "an abiding under" (*hupo*, "under," *meno*, "to abide"), is almost invariably rendered "patience." Patience, which grows only in trial, **Jas. 1:3** may be passive, i.e., = "endurance," as, (a) in trials, generally, Luke 21:19 (which is to be understood by Matt. 24:13), cf. Rom. 12:12; **Jas. 1:12**; (b) in trials incident to service in the gospel, 2 Cor. 6:4; 12:12; 2 Tim. 3:10; (c) under chastisement, which is trial viewed as coming from the hand of God our Father, Heb. 12:7; (d) under undeserved affliction, 1 Pet. 2:20; or active, i.e. = "persistence, perseverance," as (e) in well doing, Rom. 2:7 (KJV, "patient continuance"); (f) in fruit bearing, Luke 8:15; (g) in running the appointed race, Heb. 12:1.

Patience perfects Christian character, **Jas. 1:4**, and fellowship in the patience of Christ is therefore the condition upon which believers are to be admitted to reign with Him, 2 Tim. 2:12; Rev. 1:9. For this patience believers are 'strengthened with all power,' Col. 1:11, 'through His Spirit in the inward man,' Eph. 3:16.

1:4 But let patience have *her* perfect work, that ye may be perfect and entire, wanting nothing.

Patience *see James 1:3.*

Have *echo* (2192), the usual verb for "to have," is used with the following meanings: (a) "to hold, in the hand," etc., e.g., Rev. 1:16; 5:8; (b) "to hold fast, keep," Luke 19:20; metaphorically, of the mind and conduct, e.g., Mark 16:8; John 14:21; Rom. 1:28; 1 Tim. 3:9; 2 Tim. 1:13; (c) "to hold on, cling to, be next to," e.g., of accompaniment, Heb. 6:9, "things that accompany (salvation)," lit., "the things holding themselves of salvation" (RV, marg., "are near to"); of place, Mark 1:38, "next (towns)," lit., "towns holding nigh"; of time, e.g., Luke 13:33, "(the day) following," lit., "the holding (day)"; Acts 13:44; 20:15; 21:26; (d) "to hold, to count, consider, regard," e.g., Matt. 14:5; 21:46; Mark 11:32; Luke 14:18; Philem. 17; (e) "to involve," Heb. 10:35; **Jas. 1:4**; 1 John 4:18; (f) "to wear," of clothing, arms, etc., e.g., Matt. 3:4; 22:12; John 18:10; (g) "to be with child," of a woman, Mark 13:17; Rom. 9:10 (lit., "having conception"); (h) "to possess," the most frequent use, e.g., Matt. 8:20; 19:22;

Acts 9:14; 1 Thess. 3:6; (i) of complaints, disputes, Matt. 5:23; Mark 11:25; Acts 24:19; Rev. 2:4, 20; (j) of ability, power, e.g., Luke 12:4; Acts 4:14 (lit., "had nothing to say"); (k) of necessity, e.g., Luke 12:50; Acts 23:17-19; (l) "to be in a certain condition," as of readiness, Acts 21:12 (lit., "I have readily"); of illness, Matt. 4:24, "all that were sick" (lit., "that had themselves sickly"); Mark 5:23, "lieth (lit., "hath herself") at the point of death"; Mark 16:18 "they shall recover" (lit., "shall have themselves well"), John 4:52, "he began to amend" (lit., "he had himself better"); of evil works, 1 Tim. 5:25, "they that are otherwise," (lit., "the things having otherwise"); to be so, e.g., Acts 7:1, "are these things so?" (lit., "have these things thus?"), of time, Acts 24:25, "for this time" (lit., "the thing having now").

Perfect *teleios* (5049), signifies "having reached its end" (*telos*), "finished, complete perfect." It is used (I) of persons, (a) primarily of physical development, then, with ethical import, "fully grown, mature," 1 Cor. 2:6; 14:20 ("men"; marg., "of full age"); Eph. 4:13; Phil. 3:15; Col. 1:28; 4:12; in Heb. 5:14, RV, "fullgrown" (marg., "perfect"), KJV, "of full age" (marg., "perfect"); (b) "complete," conveying the idea of goodness without necessary reference to maturity or what is expressed under (a) Matt. 5:48; 19:21; **Jas. 1:4** (2nd part); **3:2**. It is used thus of God in Matt. 5:48; (II) of "things, complete, perfect," Rom. 12:2; 1 Cor. 13:10 (referring to the complete revelation of God's will and ways, whether in the completed Scriptures or in the hereafter); **Jas. 1:4** (of the work of patience); v. **25**; 1 John 4:18.

Entire *holokleros* (3648), "complete, sound in every part" (*holos*, "whole," *kleros*, "a lot," i.e., with all that has fallen by lot), is used ethically in 1 Thess. 5:23, indicating that every grace present in Christ should be manifested in the believer; so **Jas. 1:4**. In the Sept. the word is used, e.g., of a "full" week, Lev. 23:15; of altar stones unhewn, Deut. 27:6 and Josh. 8:31; of a "full-grown" vine tree, useless for work, Ezek. 15:5; of the "sound" condition of a sheep, Zech. 11:16. The corresponding noun *holokleria* is used in Acts 3:16, "perfect soundness." The synonymous word *teleios*, used also in **Jas. 1:4**, "perfect," indicates the development of every grace into maturity. The Heb. *shalom*, "peace," is derived from a root meaning "wholeness." See, e.g., Isa. 42:19, marg., "made perfect," for text, "at peace"; cf. 26:3. Cf. also Col. 1:28 with 2 Pet. 3:14.

Wanting *leipo* (3007), "to leave," denotes (a) transitively, in the passive voice, "to be left behind, to lack," **Jas. 1:4**, "ye may be lacking in (nothing)," RV (KJV, "wanting"); v. **5**, "lacketh" (KJV, "lack"); **2:15**, RV, "be ... in lack," (KJV, "be ... destitute"); (b) intransitively, active voice, Luke 18:22, "(one thing thou) lackest," is, lit., "(one thing) is lacking (to thee)"; Titus 1:5, "(the things) that were wanting"; 3:13, "(that nothing) be wanting."

1:5 If any of you lack wisdom, let him ask of God, that giveth to all *men* liberally, and upbraideth not; and it shall be given him.

Lack *see* **Wanting** at *James 1:4*.

Wisdom *sophia* (4678), is used with reference to (a) God, Rom. 11:33; 1 Cor. 1:21, 24; 2:7; Eph. 3:10; Rev. 7:12; (b) Christ, Matt. 13:54; Mark 6:2; Luke 2:40, 52; 1 Cor. 1:30; Col. 2:3; Rev. 5:12; (c) "wisdom" personified, Matt. 11:19; Luke 7:35; 11:49; (d) human "wisdom" (1) in spiritual things, Luke 21:15; Acts 6:3, 10; 7:10; 1 Cor. 2:6 (1st part); 12:8; Eph. 1:8, 17; Col. 1:9, RV, "(spiritual) wisdom," 28; 3:16; 4:5; **Jas. 1:5**; **3:13**, **17**; 2 Pet. 3:15; Rev. 13:18; 17:9; (2) in the natural sphere, Matt. 12:42; Luke 11:31; Acts 7:22; 1 Cor. 1:17, 19, 20, 21 (twice), 22; 2:1, 4, 5, 6 (2nd part), 13; 3:19; 2 Cor. 1:12; Col. 2:23; (3) in its most debased form, **Jas. 3:15**, "earthly, sensual, devilish" (marg., "demoniacal").

Ask *aiteo* (154), "to ask," frequently suggests the attitude of a suppliant, the petition of one who is lesser in position than he to whom the petition is made; e.g., in the case of men in asking something from God, Matt. 7:7; a child from a parent, Matt. 7:9-10; a subject from a king, Acts 12:20; priests and people from Pilate, Luke 23:23 (RV, "asking," for KJV, "requiring"); a beggar from a passer by, Acts 3:2. With reference to petitioning God, this verb is found in Paul's epistles in Eph. 3:20 and Col. 1:9; in James four times, **1:5-6**; **4:2-3**; in 1 John, five times, 3:22; 5:14, 15 (twice), 16.

God *see* **Lord** at *James 1:1*.

Liberally *haplos* (574), "liberally, with singleness of heart," is used in **Jas. 1:5** of God as the gracious and "liberal" Giver. The word may be taken either (a) in a logical sense, signifying unconditionally, simply, or (b) in a moral sense, generously. On this passage Hort writes as follows: "Later writers comprehend under the one word the whole magnanimous and honorable type of character in which singleness of mind is the central feature."

Upbraideth *oneidizo* (3679), (a), in the active voice, "to reproach, upbraid," Matt. 5:11, RV, "shall reproach" (KJV, "shall revile"); 11:20, "to upbraid";

27:44, RV, "cast ... reproach" [KJV, "cast ... in (His) teeth"]; Mark 15:32 RV, "reproached" (KJV, "reviled"); 16:14 "upbraided"; Luke 6:22 "shall reproach", Rom. 15:3; **Jas. 1:5**, "upbraideth"; (b) in the passive voice, "to suffer reproach, be reproached," 1 Tim. 4:10 (in some mss. in the 2nd part); 1 Pet. 4:14.

1:6 But let him ask in faith, nothing wavering. For he that wavereth is like a wave of the sea driven with the wind and tossed.

Ask *see James 1:5.*

Wavering, Wavereth *diakrino* (1252), is rendered "to waver" in Rom. 4:20, RV (KJV, "staggered"); in **Jas. 1:6** (twice).

Like *eoika* (1503), a perfect tense with a present meaning (from an obsolete present, *eiko*), denotes "to be like, to resemble," **Jas. 1:6, 23.** In the Sept., Job 6:3, 25.

Wave *kludon* (2830), "a billow," is translated "wave" in **Jas. 1:6**, KJV (RV, "surge"); in Luke 8:24 it is translated "raging (of the water)."

Driven *anemizo* (416), "to drive by the wind" (*anemos*, "wind"), is used in **Jas. 1:6**.

Wind For *anemizo*, **Jas. 1:6**, "driven by the wind."

Tossed *rhipizo* (4494), primarily "to fan a fire" (*rhipis*, "a fan," cf. *rhipe*, "twinkling"), then, "to make a breeze," is used in the passive voice in **Jas. 1:6**, "tossed," of the raising of waves by the wind.

1:7 For let not that man think that he shall receive any thing of the Lord.

Think *oiomai* or *oimai* (3633), "to imagine," is rendered "I suppose" in John 21:25; "thinking" in Phil. 1:17, RV (v. 16, KJV, "supposing"); "let (not that man) think," **Jas. 1:7**.

Lord *see James 1:1.*

1:8 A double minded man *is* unstable in all his ways.

Double minded *dipsuchos* (1374), lit. means "twosouled" (*dis*, "twice," *psuche*, "a soul"), hence, "double-minded," **Jas. 1:8; 4:8**.

Unstable *akatastatos* (182), "unsettled, unstable, disorderly" (*a*, negative, *kathistemi*, "to set in order"), is translated "unstable" in **Jas. 1:8**; "restless" in **3:8**, RV [in the latter, the KJV "unruly" represents the word *akataschetos*, signifying "that cannot be restrained" (*a*, negative, *katecho*, "to hold down, restrain"). In the Sept., Job 31:11.]. In the Sept., Isa. 54:11.

1:9 Let the brother of low degree rejoice in that he is exalted:

Low degree *tapeinos* (5011), primarily "that which is low, and does not rise far from the ground," as in the Sept. of Ezek. 17:24, hence, metaphorically, signifies "lowly, of no degree." So the RV in 2 Cor. 10:1. Cf. Luke 1:52 and **Jas. 1:9**, "of low degree." Cf. *tapeinophrosune*, "lowliness of mind," and *tapeinoo*, "to humble."

Rejoice *kauchaomai* (2744), "to boast or glory," is always translated in the RV by the verb "to glory," where the KJV uses the verb "to boast" (see, e.g., Rom. 2:17, 23; 2 Cor. 7:14; 9:2; 10:8, 13, 15, 16); it is used (a) of "vainglorying," e.g., 1 Cor. 1:29; 3:21; 4:7; 2 Cor. 5:12; 11:12, 18; Eph. 2:9; (b) of "valid glorying," e.g., Rom. 5:2, "rejoice"; 5:3, 11 (RV, "rejoice"); 1 Cor. 1:31; 2 Cor. 9:2; 10:8, 12:9; Gal. 6:14; Phil. 3:3 and **Jas. 1:9**, RV, "glory" (KJV, "rejoice").

Exalted *hupsos* (5311), signifying "height," is rendered "(in his) high estate," **Jas. 1:9**, RV, for KJV, "in that he is exalted"; "on high," Luke 1:78; 24:49; Eph. 4:8; "height," Eph. 3:18; Rev. 21:16.

1:10 But the rich, in that he is made low: because as the flower of the grass he shall pass away.

Rich *plousios* (4145), "rich, wealthy," is used (I) literally, (a) adjectivally (with a noun expressed separately) in Matt. 27:57; Luke 12:16; 14:12; 16:1, 19; (without a noun), 18:23; 19:2; (b) as a noun, singular, a "rich" man (the noun not being expressed), Matt. 19:23, 24; Mark 10:25; 12:41; Luke 16:21, 22; 18:25; **Jas. 1:10, 11**, "the rich," "the rich (man)"; plural, Mark 12:41, lit., "rich (ones)"; Luke 6:24 (ditto); 21:1; 1 Tim. 6:17, "(them that are) rich," lit., "(the) rich"; **Jas. 2:6**, RV, "the rich"; **5:1**, RV, "ye rich"; Rev. 6:15 and 13:16, RV, "the rich"; (II) metaphorically, of God, Eph. 2:4 ("in mercy"); of Christ, 2 Cor. 8:9; of believers, **Jas. 2:5**, RV, "(*to be*) rich (in faith)"; Rev. 2:9, of spiritual "enrichment" generally; 3:17, of a false sense of "enrichment."

Low *tapeinosis* (5014), "abasement, humiliation, low estate," is translated "low estate" in Luke 1:48; in **Jas. 1:10**, "that he is made low," lit., "in his abasement."

Flower *anthos* (438), "a blossom, flower" (used in certain names of flowers), occurs in **Jas. 1:10, 11**; 1 Pet. 1:24 (twice).

Grass *chortos* (5528), primarily denoted "a feeding enclosure" (whence Latin *hortus*, "a garden"; Eng.. "yard," and "garden"); then, "food," especially grass for feeding cattle; it is translated "grass" in Matt. 6:30; 14:19; Mark 6:39 (where "the green grass" is the first evidence of early spring); Luke 12:28; John 6:10; **Jas. 1:10, 11**; 1 Pet. 1:24; Rev. 8:7; 9:4; "blade" in Matt. 13:26; Mark 4:28; "hay" in 1 Cor. 3:12, used figuratively. In Palestine or Syria there are 90 genera and 243 species of grass.

Pass *parerchomai* (3928), from *para*, "by," *erchomai*, "to come" or "go," denotes (I) literally, "to pass, pass by," (a) of persons, Matt. 8:28; Mark 6:48; Luke 18:37; Acts 16:8; (b) of things, Matt. 26:39, 42; of time, Matt. 14:15; Mark 14:35; Acts 27:9, KJV, "past" (RV, "gone by"); 1 Pet. 4:3; (II) metaphorically, (a) "to pass away, to perish," Matt. 5:18; 24:34, 35; Mark 13:30, 31; Luke 16:17; 21:32, 33; 2 Cor. 5:17; **Jas. 1:10**; 2 Pet. 3:10; (b) "to pass by, disregard, neglect, pass over," Luke 11:42; 15:29, "transgressed." For the meaning "to come forth or come," see Luke 12:37; 17:7, RV (Acts 24:7 in some mss.).

1:11 For the sun is no sooner risen with a burning heat, but it withereth the grass, and the flower thereof falleth, and the grace of the fashion of it perisheth: so also shall the rich man fade away in his ways.

Sun *helios* (2246), whence Eng. prefix "helio–," is used (a) as a means of the natural benefits of light and heat, e.g., Matt. 5:45, and power, Rev. 1:16; (b) of its qualities of brightness and glory, e.g., Matt. 13:43; 17:2; Acts 26:13; 1 Cor. 15:41; Rev. 10:1; 12:1; (c) as a means of destruction, e.g., Matt. 13:6; **Jas. 1:11**; of physical misery, Rev. 7:16; (d) as a means of judgment, e.g., Matt. 24:29; Mark 13:24; Luke 21:25; 23:45; Acts 2:20; Rev. 6:12; 8:12; 9:2; 16:8.

Risen *anatello* (393), "to arise," is used especially of things in the natural creation, e.g., "the rising" of the sun, moon and stars; metaphorically, of light, in Matt. 4:16, "did spring up"; of the sun, Matt. 5:45; 13:6 (RV); Mark 4:6; **Jas. 1:11**; in Mark 16:2 the RV has "when the sun was risen," keeping to the verb form, for the KJV, "at the rising of"; of a cloud, Luke 12:54; of the day-star, 2 Pet. 1:19; in Heb. 7:14 metaphorically, of the Incarnation of Christ: "Our Lord hath sprung out of Judah," more lit., "Our Lord hath arisen out of Judah," as of the rising of the light of the sun.

Burning *kauson* (2742), "burning heat" (akin to *kaio*, "to burn"), is translated "scorching heat" in Matt. 20:12 (KJV, "heat"); Luke 12:55 (ditto); in **Jas. 1:11**, RV, "scorching wind" (KJV, "burning heat"), here the reference is to a hot wind from the east (cf. Job 1:19). In the Sept., Job 27:21; Jer. 18:17; 51:1; Ezek. 17:10; 19:12; Hos. 12:1; 13:15; Jonah 4:8.

Heat *kauson* (2742), denotes "a burning heat" (from *kaio*, "to burn"; cf. Eng., "caustic," "cauterize"), Matt. 20:12; Luke 12:55 (KJV, "heat"), RV, in each place, "scorching heat" (marg. "hot wind"); in **Jas. 1:11**, "a burning heat," KJV, RV, "the scorching wind" like the sirocco. Cf. Amos 4:9, where the Sept. has *purosis*, "burning" (*pur*, "fire").

Withereth *xeraino* (3583), "to dry up, parch, wither," is translated "to wither," (a) of plants, Matt. 13:6; 21:19, 20; Mark 4:6; 11:20, RV (KJV, "dried up"), 21; Luke 8:6; John 15:6; **Jas. 1:11**; 1 Pet. 1:24; (b) of members of the body, Mark 3:1, and, in some texts, 3.

Grass *see James 1:10.*

Flower *see James 1:10.*

Falleth *ekpipto* (1601), "to fall out of," "is used in the NT, literally, of flowers that wither in the course of nature, **Jas. 1:11**; 1 Pet. 1:24; of a ship not under control, Acts 27:17, 26, 29, 32; of shackles loosed from a prisoner's wrist, 12:7; figuratively, of the Word of God (the expression of His purpose), which cannot "fall" away from the end to which it is set, Rom. 9:6; of the believer who is warned lest he "fall" away from the course in which he has been confirmed by the Word of God, 2 Pet. 3:17." So of those who seek to be justified by law, Gal. 5:4, "ye are fallen away from grace." Some mss. have this verb in Mark 13:25; so in Rev. 2:5.

Grace *euprepeia* (2143), "comeliness, goodly appearance," is said of the outward appearance of the flower of the grass, **Jas. 1:11**.

Fashion *prosopon* (4383), "the face, countenance," is translated "fashion" in **Jas. 1:11**, of the flower of grass. Cf. v. **24**, "what manner of man," which translates *hopoios*, "of what sort."

Rich *see James 1:10.*

Fade *maraino* (3133), was used (a) to signify "to quench a fire," and in the passive voice, of the "dying out of a fire"; hence (b) in various relations, in the active voice, "to quench, waste, wear out"; in the passive, "to waste away," **Jas. 1:11**, of the "fading" away of a rich man, as illustrated by the flower of the field. In the Sept., Job 15:30; 24:24.

Ways In Luke 13:22 the noun *poreia*, "a journey, a going," is used with the verb *poieo*, "to make," with the meaning "to journey," lit., "making (for Himself, middle voice) a way", "journeying." In **Jas. 1:11**, "ways."

1:12 Blessed *is* the man that endureth temptation: for when he is tried, he shall receive the crown of life, which the Lord hath promised to them that love him.

Endureth *hupomeno* (5278), a strengthened form, denotes "to abide under, to bear up courageously" (under suffering), Matt. 10:22; 24:13; Mark 13:13; Rom. 12:12, translated "patient"; 1 Cor. 13:7; 2 Tim. 2:10, 12 (KJV, "suffer"); Heb. 10:32; 12:2-3, 7; **Jas. 1:12; 5:11**; 1 Pet. 2:20, "ye shall take it patiently." It has its other significance, "to tarry, wait for, await," in Luke 2:43; Acts 17:14 (in some mss., Rom. 8:24). Cf. *makrothumeo*, to be longsuffering". *See also* **Patience** at *James 1:3*.

Temptation *see* **Temptations** at *James 1:2*.

Tried *dokimos* (1384), akin to *dechomai*, "to receive," always signifies "approved"; so the RV everywhere, e.g., in **Jas. 1:12** for KJV, "when he is tried." The word is used of coins and metals in the Sept.; in Gen. 23:16, "four hundred didrachms of silver approved with merchants"; in Zech. 11:13, in regard to the 30 pieces of silver, "Cast them into a furnace and I will see if it is good (approved) metal."

Crown *stephanos* (4735), primarily, "that which surrounds, as a wall or crowd" (from *stepho*, "to encircle"), denotes (a) "the victor's crown," the symbol of triumph in the games or some such contest; hence, by metonymy, a reward or prize; (b) "a token of public honor" for distinguished service, military prowess, etc., or of nuptial joy, or festal gladness, especially at the parousia of kings. It was woven as a garland of oak, ivy, parsley, myrtle, or olive, or in imitation of these in gold. In some passages the reference to the games is clear, 1 Cor. 9:25; 2 Tim. 4:8 ("crown of righteousness"); it may be so in 1 Pet. 5:4, where the fadeless character of "the crown of glory" is set in contrast to the garlands of earth. In other passages it stands as an emblem of life, joy, reward and glory, Phil. 4:1; 1 Thess. 2:19; **Jas. 1:12** ("crown of life "); Rev. 2:10 (ditto); 3:11; 4:4, 10: of triumph, 6:2; 9:7; 12:1; 14:14. It is used of "the crown of thorns" which the soldiers plaited and put on Christ's head, Matt. 27:29; Mark 15:17; John 19:2, 5. At first sight this might be taken as an alternative for *diadema*, "a kingly crown," but considering the blasphemous character of that masquerade, and the materials used, obviously *diadema* would be quite unfitting and the only alternative was *stephanos* (see Trench *Syn*. Sec.xxxii).

Promised *epangello* (1861), "to announce, proclaim," has in the NT the two meanings "to profess" and "to promise," each used in the middle voice; "to promise" (a) of "promises" of God, Acts 7:5; Rom. 4:21; in Gal. 3:19, passive voice; Titus 1:2; Heb. 6:13; 10:23; 11:11; 12:26; **Jas. 1:12; 2:5**; 1 John 2:25; (b) made by men, Mark 14:11; 2 Pet. 2:19.

1:13 Let no man say when he is tempted, I am tempted of God: for God cannot be tempted with evil, neither tempteth he any man:

Tempted, Tempteth *peirazo* (3985), signifies (1) "to try, attempt, assay"; (2) "to test, try, prove," in a good sense, said of Christ and of believers, Heb. 2:18, where the context shows that the temptation was the cause of suffering to Him, and only suffering, not a drawing away to sin, so that believers have the sympathy of Christ as their High Priest in the suffering which sin occasions to those who are in the enjoyment of communion with God; so in the similar passage in 4:15; in all the temptations which Christ endured, there was nothing within Him that answered to sin. There was no sinful infirmity in Him. While He was truly man, and His divine nature was not in any way inconsistent with His Manhood, there was nothing in Him such as is produced in us by the sinful nature which belongs to us; in Heb. 11:37, of the testing of OT saints; in 1 Cor. 10:13, where the meaning has a wide scope, the verb is used of "testing" as permitted by God, and of the believer as one who should be in the realization of his own helplessness and his dependence upon God; in a bad sense, "to tempt" (a) of attempts to ensnare Christ in His speech, e.g., Matt. 16:1; 19:3; 22:18, 35, and parallel passages; John 8:6; (b) of temptations to sin, e.g., Gal. 6:1, where one who would restore an erring brother is not to act as his judge, but as being one with him in liability to sin, with the possibility of finding himself in similar circumstances, **Jas. 1:13, 14**; of temptations mentioned as coming from the Devil, Matt. 4:1; and parallel passages; 1 Cor. 7:5; 1 Thess. 3:5; (c) of trying or challenging God, Acts 15:10; 1 Cor. 10:9 (2nd part); Heb. 3:9; the Holy Spirit, Acts 5:9.

James 1:13-15 seems to contradict other statements of Scripture in two respects, saying (a) that 'God cannot be tempted with evil,' and (b) that 'He Himself tempteth no man.' But God tempted, or tried, Abraham, Heb. 11:17, and the Israelites tempted, or tried, God, 1 Cor. 10:9. V. 14, however, makes it plain that, whereas in these cases the temptation, or trial, came from without, James refers to temptation, or trial, arising within, from uncontrolled appetites and from evil passions, cf. Mark 7:20-23. But though such temptation does not proceed from God, yet does God regard His people while they endure it, and by it tests and approves them."

Cannot be tempted *apeirastos* (551), "untempted, untried," occurs in **Jas. 1:13**, with *eimi*, "to be," "cannot be tempted," "untemptable" (Mayor).

1:14 But every man is tempted, when he is drawn away of his own lust, and enticed.

Tempted *see* **Tempted, Tempteth** at **James** *1:13*.

Drawn *exelko* (1828), "to draw away, or lure forth," is used metaphorically in **Jas. 1:14**, of being "drawn away" by lust. As in hunting or fishing the game is "lured" from its haunt, so man's lust "allures" him from the safety of his self-restraint.

Lust *epithumia* (1939), denotes "strong desire" of any kind, the various kinds being frequently specified by some adjective. The word is used of a good desire in Luke 22:15; Phil. 1:23, and 1 Thess. 2:17 only. Everywhere else it has a bad sense. In Rom. 6:12 the injunction against letting sin reign in our mortal body to obey the "lust" thereof, refers to those evil desires which are ready to express themselves in bodily activity. They are equally the "lusts" of the flesh, Rom. 13:14; Gal. 5:16, 24; Eph. 2:3; 2 Pet. 2:18; 1 John 2:16, a phrase which describes the emotions of the soul, the natural tendency towards things evil. Such "lusts" are not necessarily base and immoral, they may be refined in character, but are evil if inconsistent with the will of God. Other descriptions besides those already mentioned are: "of the mind," Eph. 2:3; "evil (desire)," Col. 3:5; "the passion of," 1 Thess. 4:5, RV; "foolish and hurtful," 1 Tim. 6:9; "youthful," 2 Tim. 2:22; "divers," 2 Tim. 3:6 and Titus 3:3; "their own," 2 Tim. 4:3; 2 Pet. 3:3; Jude 16; "worldly," Titus 2:12; "his own," **Jas. 1:14**; "your former," 1 Pet. 1:14, RV; "fleshly," 2:11; "of men," 4:2; "of defilement," 2 Pet. 2:10; "of the eyes," 1 John 2:16; of the world ("thereof"), v. 17; "their own ungodly," Jude 18. In Rev. 18:14 "(the fruits) which thy soul lusted after" is, lit., "of thy soul's lust."

Enticed *deleazo* (1185), primarily, "to lure by a bait" (from *delear*, "a bait"), is used metaphorically in **Jas. 1:14**, of the "enticement" of lust; in 2 Pet. 2:14, of seducers, RV, "enticing," for KJV, "beguiling"; in v. 18, RV, "entice (in)," for KJV, "allure (through)."

1:15 Then when lust hath conceived, it bringeth forth sin: and sin, when it is finished, bringeth forth death.

Then *eita* (1534), denotes sequence (a) "of time, then, next," Mark 4:17, RV, "then"; 4:28, in some texts; 8:25, RV, "then" (KJV, "after that"); Luke 8:12; John 13:5; 19:27; 20:27; in some texts in 1 Cor. 12:28; 1 Cor. 15:5, 7, 24; 1 Tim. 2:13; 3:10; **Jas. 1:15**; (b) In argument, Heb. 12:9, "furthermore."

Conceived *sullambano* (4815), lit., "to take together" (*sun*, "with," *lambano*, "to take or receive"), is used (a) of a woman, to "conceive," Luke 1:24, 31, 36; in the passive voice. Luke 2:21; (b) metaphorically, of the impulse of lust in the human heart, enticing to sin, **Jas. 1:15**. For its other meanings

Bringeth forth *tikto* (5088), "to beget, bring forth," Matt. 1:21, 23, 25; **Jas. 1:15** (first part of verse, according to the best mss.); Rev. 12:5 (RV, "was delivered of").

Sin *hamartia* (266), is, lit., "a missing of the mark," but this etymological meaning is largely lost sight of in the NT. It is the most comprehensive term for moral obliquity. It is used of "sin" as (a) a principle or source of action, or an inward element producing acts, e.g., Rom. 3:9; 5:12, 13, 20; 6:1, 2; 7:7 (abstract for concrete); 7:8 (twice), 9, 11, 13, "sin, that it might be shown to be sin," i.e., "sin became death to me, that it might be exposed in its heinous character": in the last clause, "sin might become exceeding sinful," i.e., through the holiness of the Law, the true nature of sin was designed to be manifested to the conscience.

(b) a governing principle or power, e.g., Rom. 6:6, "(the body) of sin," here "sin" is spoken of as an organized power, acting through the members of the body, though the seat of "sin" is in the will (the body is the organic instrument); in the next clause, and in other passages, as follows, this governing principle is personified, e.g., Rom. 5:21; 6:12, 14, 17; 7:11, 14, 17, 20, 23, 25; 8:2; 1 Cor. 15:56; Heb. 3:13; 11:25; 12:4; **Jas. 1:15** (2nd part).

(c) a generic term; in Rom. 8:3, "God, sending His own Son in the likeness of sinful flesh," lit., "flesh of sin," the flesh stands for the body, the instrument of indwelling "sin," and *as an offering* for sin," i.e., "a sin offering," "condemned sin in the flesh," i.e., Christ, having taken human nature, "sin" apart (Heb. 4:15), and having lived a sinless life, died under the condemnation and judgment due to our "sin"; for the generic sense see further, e.g.,

> *"Temptation is not a sin; it is a call to battle."*
>
> ERWIN W. LUTZER

Heb. 9:26; 10:6, 8, 18; 13:11; 1 John 1:7, 8; 3:4, 8, 9 ...

(d) a sinful deed, an act of "sin," e.g., Matt. 12:31; Acts 7:60; **Jas. 1:15** (1st part); **2:9; 4:17; 5:15, 20**; 1 John 5:16 (1st part).

Finished *apoteleo* (658), "to bring to an end, accomplish," is translated "I perform" in Luke 13:32, RV (KJV, "I do"); in **Jas. 1:15**, it is used of sin, "fullgrown" RV (KJV, "finished").

Bringeth forth *apokueo* (616), "to bear young," "bringeth forth" in **Jas. 1:15** (end of verse) and "brought forth," v. **18** (KJV, "begat").

1:16 Do not err, my beloved brethren.

Err *planao* (4105), in the active voice, signifies "to cause to wander, lead astray, deceive" (*plane*, "a wandering"; cf. Eng., "planet"); in the passive voice, "to be led astray, to err." It is translated "err," in Matt. 22:29; Mark 12:24, 27; Heb. 3:10; **Jas. 1:16** (KJV, "do not err," RV, "be not deceived"); **5:19**.

1:17 Every good gift and every perfect gift is from above, and cometh down from the Father of lights, with whom is no variableness, neither shadow of turning.

Gift *dosis* (1394), denotes, properly, "the act of giving," Phil. 4:15, euphemistically referring to "gifts" as a matter of debt and credit accounts; then, objectively, "a gift," **Jas. 1:17** (1st mention).

Gift *dorerna* (1434), translated "boon" in **Jas. 1:17**, RV, is thus distinguished, as the thing given, from the preceding word in the verse, *dosis*, "the act of giving" (KJV, "gift" in each case); elsewhere in Rom. 5:16. It is to be distinguished also from *doron*, the usual word for a gift.

Above *anothen* (509), "from above," is used of place, (a) with the meaning "from the top," Matt. 27:51; Mark 15:38, of the temple veil; in John 19:23, of the garment of Christ, lit., "from the upper parts" (plural); (b) of things which come from heaven, or from God in Heaven, John 3:31; 19:11; **Jas. 1:17; 3:15, 17**. It is also used in the sense of "again."

Father *pater* (3962), from a root signifying "a nourisher, protector, upholder" (Lat., *pater*, Eng., "father," are akin), is used (a) of the nearest ancestor, e.g., Matt. 2:22; (b) of a more remote ancestor, the progenitor of the people, a "forefather," e.g., Matt. 3:9; 23:30; 1 Cor. 10:1; the patriarchs, 2 Pet. 3:4; (c) one advanced in the knowledge of Christ, 1 John 2:13; (d) metaphorically, of the originator of a family or company of persons animated by the same spirit as himself, as of Abraham, Rom. 4:11, 12, 16, 17, 18, or of Satan, John 8:38, 41, 44; (e) of one who, as a preacher of the gospel and a teacher, stands in a "father's" place, caring for his spiritual children, 1 Cor. 4:15 (not the same as a mere title of honor, which the Lord prohibited, Matt. 23:9); (f) of the members of the Sanhedrin, as of those who exercised religious authority over others, Acts 7:2; 22:1; (g) of God in relation to those who have been born anew (John 1:12, 13), and so are believers, Eph. 2:18; 4:6 (cf. 2 Cor. 6:18), and imitators of their "Father," Matt. 5:45, 48; 6:1, 4, 6, 8, 9, etc. Christ never associated Himself with them by using the personal pronoun "our"; He always used the singular, "My Father," His relationship being unoriginated and essential, whereas theirs is by grace and regeneration, e.g., Matt. 11:27; 25:34; John 20:17; Rev. 2:27; 3:5, 21; so the apostles spoke of God as the "Father" of the Lord Jesus Christ, e.g., Rom. 15:6; 2 Cor. 1:3; 11:31; Eph. 1:3; Heb. 1:5; 1 Pet. 1:3; Rev. 1:6; (h) of God, as the "Father" of lights, i.e., the Source or Giver of whatsoever provides illumination, physical and spiritual, **Jas. 1:17**; of mercies, 2 Cor. 1:3; of glory, Eph. 1:17; (i) of God, as Creator, Heb. 12:9 (cf. Zech. 12:1).

Lights *phos* (5457), akin to *phao*, "to give light" (from roots *pha-* and *phan-*, expressing "light as seen by the eye," and, metaphorically, as "reaching the mind," whence *phaino*, "to make to appear," *phaneros*, "evident," etc.); cf. Eng., "phosphorus" (lit., "light-bearing"). "Primarily light is a luminous emanation, probably of force, from certain bodies, which enables the eye to discern form and color. Light requires an organ adapted for its reception (Matt. 6:22). Where the eye is absent, or where it has become impaired from any cause, light is useless. Man, naturally, is incapable of receiving spiritual light inasmuch as he lacks the capacity for spiritual things, 1 Cor. 2:14. Hence believers are called 'sons of light,' Luke 16:8, not merely because they have received a revelation from God, but because in the New Birth they have received the spiritual capacity for it.

"Apart from natural phenomena, light is used in Scripture of (a) the glory of God's dwellingplace, 1 Tim. 6:16; (b) the nature of God, 1 John 1:5; (c) the impartiality of God, **Jas. 1:17**; (d) the favor of God, Ps. 4:6; of the King, Prov. 16:15; of an influential man, Job 29:24; (e) God, as the illuminator of His people, Isa. 60:19, 20; (f) the Lord Jesus as the illuminator of men, John 1:4, 5, 9; 3:19; 8:12; 9:5; 12:35, 36, 46; Acts 13:47; (g) the illuminating power of the Scriptures, Ps. 119:105; and of the judgments and commandments of

God, Isa. 51:4; Prov. 6:23, cf. Ps. 43:3; (h) the guidance of God Job 29:3; Ps. 112:4; Isa. 58:10; and, ironically, of the guidance of man, Rom. 2:19; (i) salvation, 1 Pet. 2:9; (j) righteousness, Rom. 13:12; 2 Cor. 11:14, 15; 1 John 2:9, 10; (k) witness for God, Matt. 5:14, 16; John 5:35; (1) prosperity and general well-being, Esth. 8:16; Job 18:18; Isa. 58:8-10."

Variableness *parallage* (3883), denotes, in general, "a change" (Eng., "parallax," the difference between the directions of a body as seen from two different points), "a transmission" from one condition to another; it occurs in **Jas. 1:17**, RV, "variation" (KJV, "variableness"); the reference may be to the sun, which "varies" its position in the sky. In the Sept., 2 Kings 9:20.

Shadow *aposkiasma* (644), "a shadow," is rendered "shadow that is cast" in **Jas. 1:17**, RV; the KJV makes no distinction between this and *skia* (4639). The probable significance of this word is "overshadowing" or "shadowing-over" (which *apo* may indicate), and this with the genitive case of *trope*, "turning," yields the meaning "shadowing-over of mutability" implying an alternation of "shadow" and light; of this there are two alternative explanations, namely, "overshadowing" (1) not caused by mutability in God, or (2) caused by change in others, i.e., "no changes in this lower world can cast a shadow on the unchanging Fount of light" [Mayor, who further remarks, "The meaning of the passage will then be, 'God is alike incapable of change (*parallage*) and incapable of being changed by the action of others'"].

Turning *trope* (5157), used especially of the revolution of the heavenly orbs (akin to *trepo*, "to turn"), occurs in **Jas. 1:17**, "(neither shadow) that is cast by turning," RV (KJV, "of turning").

1:18 Of his own will begat he us with the word of truth, that we should be a kind of firstfruits of his creatures.

Will *boulomai* (1014), usually expresses the deliberate exercise of volition, and is rendered as follows in the RV, where the KJV has "will": Matt. 11:27 and Luke 10:22, "willeth"; **Jas. 4:4**, "would"; in **Jas. 3:4**, RV, "willeth" (KJV, "listeth"). In **Jas. 1:18** the perfect participle is translated "of His own will," lit. "having willed."

Begat *see* **Bringeth forth** at *James 1:15*.

Kind The indefinite pronoun *tis*, "some, a certain, one," is used adjectively with the noun *aparche*, "firstfruits," in **Jas. 1:18**, "a kind of."

Firstfruits *aparche* (536), denotes, primarily, "an offering of firstfruits" (akin to *aparchomai*, "to make a beginning"; in sacrifices, "to offer firstfruits"). "Though the English word is plural in each of its occurrences save Rom. 11:16, the Greek word is always singular. Two Hebrew words are thus translated, one meaning the "chief" or "principal part," e.g., Num. 18:12; Prov. 3:9; the other, "the earliest ripe of the crop or of the tree," e.g., Exod. 23:16; Neh. 10:35; they are found together, e.g., in Exod. 23:19, "the first of the firstfruits."

"The term is applied in things spiritual, (a) to the presence of the Holy Spirit with the believer as the firstfruits of the full harvest of the Cross, Rom. 8:23; (b) to Christ Himself in resurrection in relation to all believers who have fallen asleep, 1 Cor. 15:20, 23; (c) to the earliest believers in a country in relation to those of their countrymen subsequently converted, Rom. 16:5; 1 Cor. 16:15; (d) to the believers of this age in relation to the whole of the redeemed, 2 Thess. 2:13 and **Jas. 1:18**. Cf. Rev. 14:4.

Creatures *ktistma* (2938), has the concrete sense, "the created thing, the creature, the product of the creative act," 1 Tim. 4:4; **Jas. 1:18**; Rev. 5:13; 8:9.

1:19 Wherefore, my beloved brethren, let every man be swift to hear, slow to speak, slow to wrath:

Man *anthropos* (444), is used (a) generally, of "a human being, male or female," without reference to sex or nationality, e.g., Matt. 4:4; 12:35; John 2:25; (b) in distinction from God, e.g., Matt. 19:6; John 10:33; Gal. 1:11; Col. 3:23; (c) in distinction from animals, etc., e.g., Luke 5:10; (d) sometimes, in the plural, of "men and women," people, e.g., Matt. 5:13, 16; in Mark 11:2 and 1 Tim. 6:16, lit., "no one of men"; (e) in some instances with a suggestion of human frailty and imperfection e.g., 1 Cor. 2:5; Acts 14:15 (2nd part); (f) in the phrase translated "after man," "after the manner of men," "as a man" (KJV), lit. "according to (*kata*) man," is used only by the apostle Paul, of "(1) the practices of fallen humanity 1 Cor. 3:3; (2) anything of human origin, Gal. 1:11; (3) the laws that govern the administration of justice among men, Rom. 3:5; (4) the standard generally accepted among men, Gal. 3:15; (5) an illustration not drawn from Scripture, 1 Cor. 9:8; (6) probably = 'to use a figurative expression' (see KJV, marg.), i.e., to speak evil of men with whom he had contended at Ephesus as 'beasts' (cf. 1 Cor. 4:6), 1 Cor. 15:32; Lightfoot prefers 'from worldly motives'; but the other interpretation seems to make better sense" ... (j) as equivalent simply to "a person," or "one," whether "man" or woman, e.g., Acts 19:16; Rom. 3:28; Gal. 2:16; **Jas. 1:19**; **2:24**; **3:8** (like the pronoun *tis*, "someone"; *tis* is rendered "man" in Matt. 8:28); or, again (as *tis* sometimes signifies), "a man," e.g., Matt. 17:14; Luke 13:19.

Swift *tachus* (5036), "swift, speedy," is used in **Jas. 1:19**. Cf. *tacheos, tachu* and *tacheion*, "quickly," *tachos*, "quickness, speed."

Slow *bradus* (1021), is used twice in **Jas. 1:19**, in an exhortation to "be slow to speak" and "slow to wrath"; in Luke 24:25, metaphorically of the understanding.

Wrath *orge* (3709), originally any "natural impulse, or desire, or disposition," came to signify "anger," as the strongest of all passions. It is used of the wrath of man, Eph. 4:31; Col. 3:8; 1 Tim. 2:8; **Jas. 1:19-20**; the displeasure of human governments, Rom. 13:4-5; the sufferings of the Jews at the hands of the Gentiles, Luke 21:23; the terrors of the Law, Rom. 4:15; "the anger" of the Lord Jesus, Mark 3:5; God's "anger" with Israel in the wilderness, in a quotation from the OT, Heb. 3:11; 4:3; God's present "anger" with the Jews nationally, Rom. 9:22; 1 Thess. 2:16; His present "anger" with those who disobey the Lord Jesus in His gospel, John 3:36; God's purposes in judgment, Matt. 3:7; Luke 3:7; Rom. 1:18; 2:5, 8; 3:5; 5:9; 12:19; Eph. 2:3; 5:6; Col. 3:6; 1 Thess. 1:10; 5:9.

1:20 For the wrath of man worketh not the righteousness of God.

Worketh *see James 1:3.*

Righteousness *dikaiosune* (1343), is "the character or quality of being right or just"; it was formerly spelled "rightwiseness," which clearly expresses the meaning. It is used to denote an attribute of God, e.g., Rom. 3:5, the context of which shows that "the righteousness of God" means essentially the same as His faithfulness, or truthfulness, that which is consistent with His own nature and promises; Rom. 3:25, 26 speaks of His "righteousness" as exhibited in the death of Christ, which is sufficient to show men that God is neither indifferent to sin nor regards it lightly. On the contrary, it demonstrates that quality of holiness in Him which must find expression in His condemnation of sin.

"*Dikaiosune* is found in the sayings of the Lord Jesus, (a) of whatever is right or just in itself, whatever conforms to the revealed will of God, Matt. 5:6, 10, 20; John 16:8, 10; (b) whatever has been appointed by God to be acknowledged and obeyed by man, Matt. 3:15; 21:32; (c) the sum total of the requirements of God, Matt. 6:33; (d) religious duties, Matt. 6:1 (distinguished as almsgiving, man's duty to his neighbor, vv. 2-4, prayer, his duty to God, vv. 5-15, fasting, the duty of self-control, vv. 16–18). In the preaching of the apostles recorded in Acts the word has the same general meaning. So also in **Jas. 1:20**, **3:18** ..."

1:21 Wherefore lay apart all filthiness and superfluity of naughtiness, and receive with meekness the engrafted word, which is able to save your souls.

Wherefore *dio = dia ho* (the neuter of the relative pronoun *hos*), "on account of which (thing)," e.g., Matt. 27:8; Acts 15:19; 20:31; 24:26; 25:26; 27:25, 34; Rom. 1:24; 15:7; 1 Cor. 12:3; 2 Cor. 2:8; 5:9; 6:17; Eph. 2:11; 3:13; 4:8, 25; 5:14; Phil. 2:9; 1 Thess. 5:11; Philem. 8; Heb. 3:7, 10; 10:5; 11:16; 12:12, 28; 13:12; **Jas. 1:21**; **4:6**; 1 Pet. 1:13; 2 Pet. 1:10, 12; 3:14.

Lay *apotithemi* (659), "to put off from oneself," always in the middle voice in the NT, is used metaphorically in Heb. 12:1, "laying aside (every weight);" in **Jas. 1:21**, KJV, "lay apart," RV, "putting away"; in Acts 7:58 of "laying" down garments, after taking them off, for the purpose of stoning Stephen.

Filthiness *rhuparia* (4507), denotes "dirt, filth," and is used metaphorically of moral "defilement" in **Jas. 1:21**.

Superfluity *perisseia* (4050), "an exceeding measure, something above the ordinary," is used four times; Rom. 5:17, "of abundance of grace"; 2 Cor. 8:2, "of abundance of joy"; 2 Cor. 10:15, of the extension of the apostle's sphere of service through the practical fellowship of the saints at Corinth; in **Jas. 1:21** it is rendered, metaphorically, "overflowing," KJV "superfluity," with reference to wickedness. Some would render it "residuum," or "what remains."

Naughtiness *kakia* (2549), "evil," is rendered "wickedness" in Acts 8:22; RV in **Jas. 1:21**, KJV, "naughtiness."

Receive *dechomai* (1209), "to receive by deliberate and ready reception of what is offered," is used of (a) taking with the hand, taking hold, taking hold of or up, e.g., Luke 2:28, RV, "he received (Him)," KJV, "took he (Him) up"; 16:6, 7; 22:17; Eph. 6:17; (b) "receiving," said of a place "receiving" a person, of Christ into the Heavens, Acts 3:21; or of persons in giving access to someone as a visitor, e.g., John 4:45; 2 Cor. 7:15; Gal. 4:14; Col. 4:10; by way of giving hospitality, etc., e.g., Matt. 10:14, 40 (four times), 41 (twice); 18:5; Mark 6:11; 9:37; Luke 9:5, 48, 53; 10:8, 10; 16:4; v. 9, of reception, "into the eternal tabernacles," said of followers of Christ who have used "the mammon of unrighteousness" to render assistance to ("make ... friends of") others; of Rahab's reception of the spies, Heb. 11:31; of the reception, by the Lord, of the spirit of a departing believer, Acts 7:59; of "receiving" a gift, 2 Cor. 8:4 (in some mss.; RV follows those which omit it); of the favorable reception of testimony and teaching, etc., Luke 8:13; Acts 8:14; 11:1; 17:11; 1 Cor. 2:14; 2 Cor. 8:17; 1 Thess. 1:6; 2:13, where *paralambano* is used in the 1st part, "ye received," *dechomai* in the 2nd part, "ye accepted," RV (KJV, "received"), the former refers to the ear, the latter, adding the idea of appropriation, to the heart; **Jas. 1:21**; in 2 Thess. 2:10, "the love of the truth," i.e., love for the truth; cf. Matt. 11:14, "if ye are willing to receive it," an elliptical construction frequent in Greek writings; of "receiving," by way of bearing with, enduring, 2 Cor. 11:16; of "receiving" by way of getting, Acts 22:5; 28:21, of becoming partaker of benefits, Mark 10:15; Luke 18:17; Acts 7:38; 2 Cor. 6:1; 11:4 (last clause "did accept": cf. *lambano* in previous clauses); Phil. 4:18.

Meekness *prautes, or praotes,* an earlier form, (4240), denotes "meekness." In its use in Scripture, in which it has a fuller, deeper significance than in nonscriptural Greek writings, it consists not in a person's "outward behavior only; nor yet in his relations to his fellow-men; as little in his mere natural disposition. Rather it is an inwrought grace of the soul; and the exercises of it are first and chiefly towards God. It is that temper of spirit in which we accept His dealings with us as good, and therefore without disputing or resisting; it is closely linked with the word *tapeinophrosune* [humility], and follows directly upon it, Eph. 4:2; Col. 3:12; cf. the adjectives in the Sept. of Zeph. 3:12, "meek and lowly"; ... it is only the humble heart which is also the meek, and which, as such, does not fight against God and more or less struggle and contend with Him. This meekness, however, being first of all a meekness before God, is also such in the face of men, even of evil men, out of a sense that these, with the insults and injuries which they may inflict, are permitted and employed by Him for the chastening and purifying of His elect" (Trench, *Syn.* Sec.xlii). In Gal. 5:23 it is associated with *enkrateia,* "self-control." The meaning of *prautes* "is not readily expressed in English, for the terms meekness, mildness, commonly used, suggest weakness and pusillanimity to a greater or less extent, whereas *prautes* does nothing of the kind. Nevertheless, it is difficult to find a rendering less open to objection than 'meekness'; 'gentleness' has been suggested, but as *prautes* describes a condition of mind and heart, and as 'gentleness' is appropriate rather to actions, this word is no better than that used in both English Versions. It must be clearly understood, therefore, that the meekness manifested by the Lord and commended to the believer is the fruit of power. The common assumption is that when a man is meek it is because he cannot help himself; but the Lord was 'meek' because he had the infinite resources of God at His command. Described negatively, meekness is the opposite to self-assertiveness and self-interest; it is equanimity of spirit that is neither elated nor cast down, simply because it is not occupied with self at all.

"In 2 Cor. 10:1 the apostle appeals to the 'meekness ... of Christ.' Christians are charged to show 'all meekness toward all men,' Titus 3:2, for meekness becomes 'God's elect,' Col. 3:12. To this virtue the 'man of God' is urged; he is to 'follow after meekness' for his own sake, 1 Tim. 6:11, and in his service, and more especially in his dealings with the 'ignorant and erring,' he is to exhibit 'a spirit of meekness,' 1 Cor. 4:21, and Gal. 6:1; even 'they that oppose themselves' are to be corrected in meekness, 2 Tim. 2:25. James exhorts his 'beloved brethren' to 'receive with meekness the implanted word,' **1:21.** Peter enjoins 'meekness' in setting forth the grounds of the Christian hope, 3:15."

Engrafted *emphutos* (1721), "implanted," or "rooted" (from *emphuo,* "to implant"), is used in **Jas. 1:21**, RV, "implanted," for KJV, "engrafted," of the Word of God, as the "rooted word," i.e., a word whose property it is to root itself like a seed in the heart. "The KJV seems to identify it with *emphuteuton,* which however would be out of place here, since the word is sown, not grafted, in the heart" (Mayor).

Save *sozo* (4982), "to save," is used (as with the noun *soteria,* "salvation") (a) of material and temporal deliverance from danger, suffering, etc., e.g., Matt. 8:25; Mark 13:20; Luke 23:35; John 12:27; 1 Tim. 2:15; 2 Tim. 4:18 (KJV, "preserve"); Jude 5; from sickness, Matt. 9:22, "made ... whole" (RV, marg., "saved"); so Mark 5:34; Luke 8:48; **Jas. 5:15**; (b) of the spiritual and eternal salvation granted immediately by God to those who believe on the Lord Jesus Christ, e.g., Acts 2:47, RV "(those that) were being saved"; 16:31; Rom. 8:24, RV, "were we saved"; Eph. 2:5, 8; 1 Tim. 2:4; 2 Tim. 1:9; Titus 3:5; of human agency in this, Rom. 11:14; 1 Cor. 7:16; 9:22; (c) of the present experiences of God's power to deliver from the bondage of sin, e.g., Matt. 1:21; Rom. 5:10; 1 Cor. 15:2; Heb. 7:25; **Jas. 1:21**; 1 Pet. 3:21; of human agency in this, 1 Tim. 4:16; (d) of the future deliverance of believers at the second coming of Christ for His saints, being deliverance from the wrath of God to be executed upon the ungodly at the close of this age and from eternal doom, e.g., Rom. 5:9; (e) of the deliverance of the nation of Israel at the second advent of Christ, e.g., Rom. 11:26; (f) inclusively for all the blessings bestowed by God on men in Christ, e.g., Luke 19:10; John 10:9; 1 Cor. 10:33; 1 Tim. 1:15; (g) of those who endure to the end of the time of the Great Tribulation, Matt. 10:22; Mark 13:13; (h) of the individual believer, who, though losing his reward at the judgment seat of Christ hereafter, will not lose his salvation, 1 Cor. 3:15; 5:5; (i) of the deliverance of the nations at the Millennium, Rev. 21:24 (in some mss.).

Souls *psuche* (5590), denotes "the breath, the breath of life," then "the soul," in its various meanings. The NT uses "may be analyzed approximately as follows: (a) the natural life of the body, Matt. 2:20; Luke 12:22; Acts 20:10; Rev. 8:9; 12:11; cf. Lev. 17:11; 2 Sam. 14:7; Esth. 8:11; (b) the immaterial, invisible part of man, Matt. 10:28; Acts 2:27; cf. 1 Kings 17:21; (c) the disembodied (or "unclothed" or "naked," 2 Cor. 5:3, 4) man, Rev. 6:9; (d) the seat of personality, Luke 9:24, explained as = "own self," v. 25; Heb. 6:19; 10:39; cf. Isa. 53:10 with 1 Tim. 2:6; (e) the seat of the sentient element in man, that by which he perceives, reflects, feels, desires, Matt. 11:29; Luke 1:46; 2:35; Acts 14:2, 22; cf. Ps. 84:2; 139:14; Isa. 26:9; (f) the seat of will and purpose, Matt. 22:37; Acts 4:32; Eph. 6:6; Phil. 1:27; Heb. 12:3; cf. Num. 21:4; Deut. 11:13; (g) the seat of appetite, Rev. 18:14; cf. Ps. 107:9; Prov. 6:30; Isa. 5:14 ("desire"); 29:8; (h) persons, individuals, Acts 2:41, 43; Rom. 2:9; **Jas. 5:20**; 1 Pet. 3:20; 2 Pet. 2:14; cf. Gen. 12:5; 14:21 ("persons"); Lev. 4:2 ('any one'); Ezek. 27:13; of dead bodies, Num. 6:6, lit., "dead soul"; and of animals, Lev. 24:18, lit., "soul for soul"; (i) the equivalent of the personal pronoun, used for emphasis and effect: 1st person, John 10:24 ("us"); Heb. 10:38; cf. Gen. 12:13; Num. 23:10; Jud. 16:30; Ps. 120:2 ("me"); 2nd person, 2 Cor. 12:15; Heb. 13:17; **Jas. 1:21**; 1 Pet. 1:9; 2:25; cf. Lev. 17:11; 26:15; 1 Sam. 1:26; 3rd person, 1 Pet. 4:19; 2 Pet. 2:8; cf. Exod. 30:12; Job 32:2, Heb. "soul," Sept. "self"; (j) an animate creature, human or other, 1 Cor. 15:45; Rev. 16:3; cf. Gen. 1:24; 2:7, 19; (k) "the inward man," the seat of the new life, Luke 21:19 (cf. Matt. 10:39); 1 Pet. 2:11; 3 John 2.

"Body and soul are the constituents of the man according to Matt. 6:25; 10:28; Luke 12:20; Acts 20:10; body and spirit according to Luke 8:55; 1 Cor. 5:3; 7:34; **Jas. 2:26** ... Apparently, then, the relationships may be thus summed up '*Soma*, body, and *pneuma*, spirit, may be separated, *pneuma* and *psuche*, soul, can only be distinguished' (Cremer)."

1:22 But be ye doers of the word, and not hearers only, deceiving your own selves.

Doers *poiētes* (4163), akin to *poieo*, signifies "a doer," Rom. 2:13; **Jas. 1:22-23, 25; 4:11**. Its meaning "poet" is found in Acts 17:28.

Hearers *akroates* (202), from *akroaomai*, "to listen," is used in Rom. 2:13, "of a law"; **Jas. 1:22, 23**, "of the word"; v. **25**, "a (forgetful) hearer."

Deceiving *paralogizomai* (3884), lit. and primarily, "to reckon wrong," hence means "to reason falsely" (*para*, "from, amiss," *logizomai*, "to reason") or "to deceive by false reasoning"; translated "delude" in Col. 2:4, RV (KJV, "beguile") and **Jas. 1:22** (KJV, "deceive").

1:23 For if any be a hearer of the word, and not a doer, he is like unto a man beholding his natural face in a glass:

Hearer *see* **Hearers** at *James 1:22*.

Like unto *see* **Like** at *James 1:6*.

Beholding *katanoeo* (2657), a strengthened form of *noeo*, "to perceive," (*kata*, intensive), denotes "the action of the mind in apprehending certain facts about a thing"; hence, "to consider"; "behold," Acts 7:31-32; **Jas. 1:23-24**.

Natural *genesis* (1078), "birth," is used in **Jas. 1:23**, of the "natural face," lit., "the face of his birth," "what God made him to be" (Hort).

Glass *esoptron* (2072), rendered "glass" in the KJV, is used of any surface sufficiently smooth and regular to reflect rays of light uniformly, and thus produce images of objects which actually in front of it appear to the eye as if they were behind it. "Mirrors" in Biblical times were, it seems, metallic; hence the RV adopts the more general term "mirror"; in 1 Cor. 13:12, spiritual knowledge in this life is represented metaphorically as an image dimly perceived in a "mirror"; in **Jas. 1:23**, the "law of liberty" is figuratively compared to a "mirror"; the hearer who obeys not is like a person who, having looked into the "mirror," forgets the reflected image after turning away; he who obeys is like one who gazes into the "mirror" and retains in his soul the image of what he should be.

1:24 For he beholdeth himself, and goeth his way, and straightway forgetteth what manner of man he was.

Way *aperchomai*, "to go away," is rendered "to go one's way," e.g., Matt. 13:25; 20:4; Mark 11:4; 12:12; Luke 19:32; John 11:46; Acts 9:17; **Jas. 1:24**.

Forgetteth *epilanthanomai* (1950), "to forget, or neglect," is said (a) negatively of God, indicating His remembrance of sparrows, Luke 12:6, and of the work and labor of love of His saints, Heb. 6:10; (b) of the disciples regarding taking bread, Matt. 16:5: Mark 8:14; (c) of Paul regarding "the things which are behind," Phil. 3:13; (d) of believers, as to showing love to strangers, Heb. 13:2, RV, and as to doing good and communicating, v. 16; (e) of a person who after looking at himself in a mirror, forgets what kind of person he is, **Jas. 1:24**.

Manner *hopoios* (3697), is rendered "what manner of" in 1 Thess. 1:9; **Jas. 1:24**. *See also* **Fashion** at *James 1:11*.

1:25 But whoso looketh into the perfect law of liberty, and continueth *therein*, he being not a forgetful hearer, but a doer of the work, this man shall be blessed in his deed.

Looketh *parakupto* (3879), lit. and primarily, "to stoop sideways" *para*, "aside," *kupto*, "to bend forward," denotes "to stoop to look into," Luke 24:12, "stooping and looking in" (KJV, "stooping down"), John 20:5, 11; metaphorically in **Jas. 1:25**, of "looking" into the perfect law of liberty; in 1 Pet. 1:12 of things which the angels desire "to look into."

Perfect *see James 1:4*.

Law *nomos* (3551), akin to *nemo*, "to divide out, distribute," primarily meant "that which is assigned"; hence, "usage, custom," and then, "law, law as prescribed by custom, or by statute"; the word *ethos*, "custom," was retained for unwritten "law," while *nomos* became the established name for "law" as decreed by a state and set up as the standard for the administration of justice. In the NT it is used ... (c) of the Mosaic Law, the "law" of Sinai, (1) with the definite article, e.g., Matt. 5:18; John 1:17; Rom. 2:15, 18, 20, 26, 27; 3:19; 4:15; 7:4, 7, 14, 16, 22; 8:3, 4, 7; Gal. 3:10, 12, 19, 21, 24; 5:3; Eph. 2:15; Phil. 3:6; 1 Tim. 1:8; Heb. 7:19; **Jas. 2:9**; (2) without the article, thus stressing the Mosaic Law in its quality as "law," e.g., Rom. 2:14 (1st part); 5:20; 7:9, where the stress in the quality lies in this, that "the commandment which was unto (i.e., which he thought would be a means of) life," he found to be "unto (i.e., to have the effect of revealing his actual state of) death"; 10:4; 1 Cor. 9:20; Gal. 2:16, 19, 21; 3:2, 5, 10 (1st part), 11, 18, 23; 4:4, 5, 21 (1st part); 5:4, 18; 6:13; Phil. 3:5, 9; Heb. 7:16; 9:19; **Jas. 2:11**; **4:11**; (in regard to the statement in Gal. 2:16, that "a man is not justified by the works of the Law," the absence of the article before *nomos* indicates the assertion of a principle, "by obedience to law," but evidently the Mosaic Law is in view. Here the apostle is maintaining that submission to circumcision entails the obligation to do the whole "Law." Circumcision belongs to the ceremonial part of the "Law," but, while the Mosaic Law is actually divisible into the ceremonial and the moral, no such distinction is made or even assumed in Scripture. The statement maintains the freedom of the believer from the "law" of Moses in its totality as a means of justification)...

The following phrases specify "laws" of various kinds; (a) "the law of Christ," Gal. 6:2, i.e., either given by Him (as in the Sermon on the Mount and in John 13:14, 15; 15:4), or the "law" or principle by which Christ Himself lived (Matt. 20:28; John 13:1); these are not actual alternatives, for the "law" imposed by Christ was always that by which He Himself lived in the "days of His flesh." He confirmed the "Law" as being of divine authority (cf. Matt. 5:18); yet He presented a higher standard of life than perfunctory obedience to the current legal rendering of the "Law," a standard which, without annulling the "Law," He embodied in His own character and life (see, e.g., Matt. 5:21-48; this breach with legalism is especially seen in regard to the ritual or ceremonial part of the "Law" in its wide scope); He showed Himself superior to all human interpretations of it; (b) "a law of faith," Rom. 3:27, i.e., a principle which demands only faith on man's part; (c) "the law of my mind," Rom. 7:23, that principle which governs the new nature in virtue of the new birth; (d) "the law of sin," Rom. 7:23, the principle by which sin exerts its influence and power despite the desire to do what is right; "of sin and death," 8:2, death being the effect; (e) "the law of liberty," **Jas. 1:25**; **2:12**, a term comprehensive of all the Scriptures, not a "law" of compulsion enforced from without, but meeting with ready obedience through the desire and delight of the renewed being who is subject to it; into it he looks, and in its teaching he delights; he is "under law (*ennomos*, "in law," implying union and subjection) to Christ," 1 Cor. 9:21; cf, e.g., Ps. 119:32, 45, 97; 2 Cor. 3:17; (f) "the royal law," **Jas. 2:8**, i.e., the "law" of love, royal in the majesty of its power, the "law" upon which all others hang, Matt. 22:34-40; Rom. 13:8; Gal. 5:14 ...

Continueth *parameno* (3887), "to remain by or near" (*para*, "beside," and *meno*), hence, "to continue or persevere in anything," is used of the inability of Levitical priests to "continue," Heb. 7:23; of persevering in the law of liberty, **Jas. 1:25**; it is translated "abide" in Phil. 1:25 (2nd clause, in the best mss.), RV, and in 1 Cor. 16:6

He *houtos* (3778), "this, this person here," is always emphatic; it is used with this meaning, sometimes to refer to what precedes, e.g., Matt. 5:19, "he (shall be called great)"; John 6:46, "he (hath seen)"; often rendered "this," e.g., Rom. 9:9, or "this man," e.g., Matt. 27:58, RV; **Jas. 1:25**; "the same," e.g., Luke 9:48.

Forgetful *epilesmone* (1953), "forgetfulness," is used in **Jas. 1:25**, "a forgetful hearer," RV, "a hearer that forgetteth," lit., "a hearer of forgetfulness," i.e., a hearer characterized by "forgetfulness."

Hearer *see* **Hearers** at *James 1:22*.

Doer *see* **Doers** at *James 1:22*.

Work *ergon* (2041), denotes "a work" (Eng., "work" is etymologically akin), "deed, act." When used in the sense of a "deed or act," the idea of "working" is stressed, e.g., Rom. 15:18; it frequently occurs in an ethical sense of human actions, good or bad, e.g., Matt. 23:3; 26:10; John 3:20-21; Rom. 2:7, 15; 1 Thess. 1:3; 2 Thess. 1:11, etc.; sometimes in a less concrete sense, e.g., Titus 1:16; **Jas. 1:25** (RV that worketh, lit., of work).

Deed *poiesis* (4162), "a doing" (akin to *poieo*, "to do"), is translated "deed" in **Jas. 1:25**, KJV (RV, "doing").

1:26 If any man among you seem to be religious, and bridleth not his tongue, but deceiveth his own heart, this man's religion *is* vain.

Seem *dokeo* (1380), denotes (a) "to be of opinion" (akin to *doxa*, "opinion"), e.g., Luke 8:18, RV, "thinketh" (KJV, "seemeth"); so 1 Cor. 3:18; to think, suppose, **Jas. 1:26**, RV, "thinketh himself (KJV, "seem"); (b) "to seem, to be reputed," e.g., Acts 17:18; 1 Cor. 11:16; 12:22; 2 Cor. 10:9; Heb. 4:1; 12:11; for Gal. 2:2, 6, 9; (c) impersonally (1) to think, (2) to "seem" good, Luke 1:3; Acts 15:22, RV, "it seemed good" (KJV, "it pleased"); 15:25, 28 (v. 34 in some mss.); in Heb. 12:10, the neuter of the present participle is used with the article, lit., "the (thing) seeming good," RV, "(as) seemed good," KJV, "after (their own) pleasure."

Religious *threskos* (2357), "religious, careful of the externals of divine service," akin to *threskeia*, is used in **Jas. 1:26**.

Bridleth *chalinagogeo* (5468), from *chalinos* and *ago*, "to lead," signifies "to lead by a bridle, to bridle, to hold in check, restrain"; it is used metaphorically of the tongue and of the body in **Jas. 1:26** and **3:2**.

Tongue *glossa* (1100), is used of (1) the "tongues ... like as of fire" which appeared at Pentecost; (2) "the tongue," as an organ of speech, e.g., Mark 7:33; Rom. 3:13; 14:11; 1 Cor. 14:9; Phil. 2:11; **Jas. 1:26**; **3:5, 6, 8**; 1 Pet. 3:10; 1 John 3:18; Rev. 16:10; (3) (a) "a language," coupled with *phule*, "a tribe," *laos*, "a people," *ethnos*, "a nation," seven times in Revelation, 5:9; 7:9; 10:11; 11:9; 13:7; 14:6; 17:15 ...

Deceiveth *apatao* (538), "to beguile, deceive," is used (a) of those who "deceive" "with empty words," belittling the true character of the sins mentioned, Eph. 5:6; (b) of the fact that Adam was "not beguiled," 1 Tim. 2:14, RV (cf. what is said of Eve); (c) of the "self-deceit" of him who thinks himself religious, but bridles not his tongue, **Jas. 1:26**.

Religion *threskeia* (2356), signifies "religion" in its external aspect (akin to *threskos*), "religious worship," especially the ceremonial service of "religion"; it is used of the "religion" of the Jews, Acts 26:5; of the "worshiping" of angels, Col. 2:18, which they themselves repudiate (Rev. 22:8, 9); "there was an officious parade of humility in selecting these lower beings as intercessors rather than appealing directly to the Throne of Grace" (Lightfoot); in **Jas. 1:26, 27** the writer purposely uses the word to set in contrast that which is unreal and deceptive, and the "pure religion" which consists in visiting "the fatherless and widows in their affliction," and in keeping oneself "unspotted from the world." He is "not herein affirming ... these offices to be the sum total, nor yet the great essentials, of true religion, but declares them to be the body, the *threskeia*, of which godliness, or the love of God, is the informing soul" (Trench).

Vain *mataios* (3152), "void of result," is used of (a) idolatrous practices, Acts 14:15, RV, "vain things" (KJV, "vanities"); (b) the thoughts of the wise, 1 Cor. 3:20; (c) faith, if Christ is not risen, 1 Cor. 15:17; (d) questionings, strifes, etc., Titus 3:9; (e) religion, with an unbridled tongue, **Jas. 1:26**; (f) manner of life, 1 Pet. 1:18.

1:27 Pure religion and undefiled before God and the Father is this, To visit the fatherless and widows in their affliction, *and* to keep himself unspotted from the world.

Pure *katharos* (2513), "pure," as being cleansed, e.g., Matt. 5:8; 1 Tim. 1:5; 3:9; 2 Tim. 1:3; 2:22; Titus 1:15; Heb. 10:22; **Jas. 1:27**; 1 Pet. 1:22; Rev. 15:6; 21:18; 22:1 (in some mss.).

Religion *see James 1:26.*

Undefiled *amiantos* (283), "undefiled, free from contamination" (*a*, negative, *miaino*, "to defile"), is used (a) of Christ, Heb. 7:26; (b) of pure religion, **Jas. 1:27**; (c) of the eternal inheritance of believers, 1 Pet. 1:4; (d) of the marriage bed as requiring to be free from unlawful sexual intercourse, Heb. 13:4.

Visit *episkeptomai* (1980), primarily, "to inspect" (a late form of *episkopeo*, "to look upon, care for, exercise oversight"), signifies (a) "to visit" with help, of the act of God, Luke 1:68, 78; 7:16; Acts 15:14; Heb. 2:6; (b) "to visit" the sick and afflicted, Matt. 25:36, 43; **Jas. 1:27**; (c) "to go and see," "pay a visit to," Acts 7:23; 15:36; (d) "to look out" certain men for a purpose, Acts 6:3

Fatherless *orphanos* (3737), properly, "an orphan," is rendered "fatherless" in **Jas. 1:27**; "desolate" in John 14:18, for KJV, "comfortless."

Widows *chera* (5503), Matt. 28:13 (in some texts); Mark 12:40, 42, 43; Luke 2:37; 4:25, 26, lit., "a woman a widow"; 7:12; 18:3, 5; 20:47; 21:2, 3; Acts 6:1; 9:39, 41; 1 Tim. 5:3 (twice), 4, 5, 11, 16 (twice); **Jas. 1:27**; 1 Tim. 5:9 refers to elderly "widows" (not an ecclesiastical "order"), recognized, for relief or maintenance by the church (cf. vv. 3, 16), as those who had fulfilled the conditions mentioned; where relief could be ministered by those who had relatives that were "widows" (a likely circumstance in large families), the church was not to be responsible; there is an intimation of the tendency to shelve individual responsibility at the expense of church funds. In Rev. 18:7, it is used figuratively of a city forsaken.

Affliction *thlipsis* (2347), primarily means "a pressing, pressure," anything which burdens the spirit. In two passages in Paul's Epistles it is used of future retribution, in the way of "affliction," Rom. 2:9; 2 Thess. 1:6. In Matt. 24:9, the KJV renders it as a verb, "to be afflicted," (RV, "unto tribulation"). It is coupled with *stenochoria*, "anguish," in Rom. 2:9; 8:35; with *ananke*, "distress," 1 Thess. 3:7; with *diogmos*, "persecution," Matt. 13:21; Mark 4:17; 2 Thess. 1:4. It is used of the calamities of war, Matt. 24:21, 29; Mark 13:19, 24; of want, 2 Cor. 8:13, lit., "distress for you"; Phil. 4:14 (cf. 1:16); **Jas. 1:27**; of the distress of woman in childbirth, John 16:21; of persecution, Acts 11:19; 14:22; 20:23; 1 Thess. 3:3, 7; Heb. 10:33; Rev. 2:10; 7:14; of the "afflictions" of Christ, from which (His vicarious sufferings apart) his followers must not shrink, whether sufferings of body or mind, Col. 1:24; of sufferings in general, 1 Cor. 7:28; 1 Thess. 1:6, etc.

Keep *tereo* (5083), denotes (a) "to watch over, preserve, keep, watch," e.g., Acts 12:5, 6; 16:23; in 25:21, RV (1st part), "kept" (KJV, "reserved"); the present participle is translated "keepers" in Matt. 28:4, lit. "the keeping (ones)"; it is used of the "keeping" power of God the Father and Christ, exercised over His people, John 17:11, 12, 15; 1 Thess. 5:23, "preserved"; 1 John 5:18, where "He that was begotten of God," RV, is said of Christ as the Keeper ("keepeth him," RV, for KJV, "keepeth himself"); Jude 1, RV, "kept for Jesus Christ" (KJV, "preserved in Jesus Christ"), Rev. 3:10; of their inheritance, 1 Pet. 1:4 ("reserved"); of judicial reservation by God in view of future doom, 2 Pet. 2:4, 9, 17; 3:7; Jude 6, 13; of "keeping" the faith, 2 Tim. 4:7; the unity of the Spirit, Eph. 4:3; oneself, 2 Cor. 11:9; 1 Tim. 5:22; **Jas. 1:27**; figuratively, one's garments, Rev. 16:15; (b) "to observe, to give heed to," as of keeping commandments, etc., e.g., Matt. 19:17; John 14:15; 15:10; 17:6; **Jas. 2:10**; 1 John 2:3, 4, 5; 3:22, 24; 5:2 (in some mss.), 3; Rev. 1:3; 2:26; 3:8, 10; 12:17; 14:12; 22:7, 9.

Unspotted *aspilos* (784), "unspotted, unstained," is used of a lamb, 1 Pet. 1:19; metaphorically, of keeping a commandment without alteration and in the fulfillment of it, 1 Tim. 6:14; of the believer in regard to the world, **Jas. 1:27**, and free from all defilement in the sight of God, 2 Pet. 3:14.

World *kosmos* (2889), primarily "order, arrangement, ornament, adornment," is used to denote (a) the "earth," e.g., Matt. 13:35; John 21:25; Acts 17:24; Rom. 1:20 (probably here the universe: it had this meaning among the Greeks, owing to the order observable in it); 1 Tim. 6:7; Heb. 4:3; 9:26; (b) the "earth" in contrast with Heaven, 1 John 3:17 (perhaps also Rom. 4:13); (c) by metonymy, the "human race, mankind," e.g., Matt. 5:14; John 1:9 [here "that cometh (RV, 'coming') into the world" is said of Christ, not of "every man"; by His coming into the world He was the light for all men]; v. 10; 3:16, 17 (thrice), 19; 4:42, and frequently in Rom., 1 Cor. and 1 John; (d) "Gentiles" as distinguished from Jews, e.g., Rom. 11:12, 15, where the meaning is that all who will may be reconciled (cf. 2 Cor. 5:19); (e) the "present condition of human affairs," in alienation from and opposition to God, e.g., John 7:7; 8:23; 14:30; 1 Cor. 2:12; Gal. 4:3; 6:14; Col. 2:8; **Jas. 1:27**; 1 John 4:5 (thrice); 5:19; (f) the "sum of temporal possessions," Matt. 16:26; 1 Cor.

7:31 (1st part); (g) metaphorically, of the "tongue" as "a world (of iniquity)," **Jas. 3:6**, expressive of magnitude and variety.

Chapter 2

2:1 My brethren, have not the faith of our Lord Jesus Christ, *the Lord* of glory, with respect of persons.

Lord *see James 1:1.*

Glory *doxa* (1391), "glory" (from *dokeo*, "to seem"), primarily signifies an opinion, estimate, and hence, the honor resulting from a good opinion. It is used (a) of the nature and acts of God in self-manifestation, i.e., what He essentially is and does, as exhibited in whatever way he reveals Himself in these respects, and particularly in the person of Christ, in whom essentially His "glory" has ever shone forth and ever will do, John 17:5, 24; Heb. 1:3; it was exhibited in the character and acts of Christ in the days of His flesh, John 1:14; John 2:11; at Cana both His grace and His power were manifested, and these constituted His "glory", so also in the resurrection of Lazarus 11:4, 40; the "glory" of God was exhibited in the resurrection of Christ, Rom. 6:4, and in His ascension and exaltation, 1 Pet. 1:21, likewise on the Mount of Transfiguration, 2 Pet. 1:17. In Rom. 1:23 His "everlasting power and Divinity" are spoken of as His "glory," i.e., His attributes and power as revealed through creation; in Rom. 3:23 the word denotes the manifested perfection of His character, especially His righteousness, of which all men fall short; in Col. 1:11 "the might of His glory" signifies the might which is characteristic of His "glory"; in Eph. 1:6, 12, 14, "the praise of the glory of His grace" and "the praise of His glory" signify the due acknowledgement of the exhibition of His attributes and ways; in Eph. 1:17, "the Father of glory" describes Him as the source from whom all divine splendor and perfection proceed in their manifestation, and to whom they belong; (b) of the character and ways of God as exhibited through Christ to and through believers, 2 Cor. 3:18 and 4:6; (c) of the state of blessedness into which believers are to enter hereafter through being brought into the likeness of Christ, e.g., Rom. 8:18, 21; Phil. 3:21 (RV, "the body of His glory"); 1 Pet. 5:1, 10; Rev. 21:11; (d) brightness or splendor, (1) supernatural, emanating from God (as in the *shekinah* "glory," in the pillar of cloud and in the Holy of Holies, e.g., Exod. 16:10; 25:22), Luke 2:9; Acts 22:11; Rom. 9:4; 2 Cor. 3:7; **Jas. 2:1**; in Titus 2:13 it is used of Christ's return, "the appearing of the glory of our great God and Savior Jesus Christ" (RV); cf. Phil. 3:21, above; (2) natural, as of the heavenly bodies, 1 Cor. 15:40, 41 ...

Respect of persons *prosopolempsia* (in inferior texts without the letter *m*) (4382), denotes "respect of persons, partiality," the fault of one who, when responsible to give judgment, has respect to the position, rank, popularity, or circumstances of men, instead of their intrinsic conditions, preferring the rich and powerful to those who are not so, Rom. 2:11; Eph. 6:9; Col. 3:25; **Jas. 2:1**.

2:2 For if there come unto your assembly a man with a gold ring, in goodly apparel, and there come in also a poor man in vile raiment;

Assembly *sunagoge* (4864), properly "a bringing together" (*sun*, "together," *ago*, "to bring"), denoted (a) "a gathering of things, a collection," then, of "persons, an assembling, of Jewish religious gatherings," e.g., Acts 9:2; an assembly of Christian Jews, **Jas. 2:2**, RV, "synagogue" (KJV, marg.; text, "assembly"); a company dominated by the power and activity of Satan, Rev. 2:9; 3:9; (b) by metonymy, "the building" in which the gathering is held, e.g. Matt. 6:2; Mark 1:21. The origin of the Jewish "synagogue" is probably to be assigned to the time of the Babylonian exile. Having no temple, the Jews assembled on the Sabbath to hear the Law read, and the practice continued in various buildings after the return. Cf. Ps. 74:8.

Gold ring *chrusodaktulios* (5554), an adjective denoting "with a gold ring" (*daktulos*, "a finger"), occurs in **Jas. 2:2**.

Apparel *esthes* (2066), and *esthesis* (2067), connected with *hennumi*, "to clothe" means "clothing, raiment," usually suggesting the ornate, the goodly. The former is found in Luke 23:11, RV, "apparel" (KJV, "robe"); 24:4 (KJV, "garments"); Acts 10:30 (KJV, "clothing"); 12:21; **Jas. 2:2** (RV, clothing," twice; KJV, "apparel" and "raiment"); **2:3** ("clothing"). *Esthesis* is used in Acts 1:10, "apparel."

Poor *ptochos* (4434), has the broad sense of "poor," (a) literally, e.g., Matt. 11:5; 26:9, 11; Luke 21:3 (with stress on the word, "a conspicuously poor widow"); John 12:5, 6, 8; 13:29; **Jas. 2:2, 3, 6**; the "poor" are constantly the subjects of injunctions to assist them, Matt. 19:21; Mark 10:21; Luke 14:13, 21; 18:22; Rom. 15:26; Gal. 2:10; (b) metaphorically, Matt. 5:3; Luke 6:20; Rev. 3:17.

Vile *rhuparos* (4508), "filthy dirty," is used (a) literally, of old shabby clothing, **Jas. 2:2**, "vile"; (b) metaphorically, of moral defilement, Rev. 22:11 (in the best texts). In the Sept., Zech. 3:3, 4.

Raiment For *himation*, rendered "raiment" in Matt. 17:2, KJV (RV, "garments"), so Matt. 27:31; Mark 9:3; Luke 23:34; John 19:24; Acts 22:20; Rev. 3:5, 18; 4:4; KJV and RV, Acts 18:6. *Himatismos* is rendered "raiment" in Luke 9:29; *enduma* in Matt. 3:4; 6:25, 28; 28:3 and Luke 12:23. For *esthes*, translated "raiment" in **Jas. 2:2** (2nd part), KJV.

2:3 And ye have respect to him that weareth the gay clothing, and say unto him, Sit thou here in a good place; and say to the poor, Stand thou there, or sit here under my footstool:

Respect *epiblepo* (1914), "to look upon" (*epi*, "upon," and *blepo* "to behold, look, perceive, see"), in the NT "to look on with favor," is used in Luke 1:48, KJV, "hath regarded" (RV, "hath looked upon"); in **Jas. 2:3**, RV, "ye have regard to" (KJV, "ye have respect to").

Weareth *phoreo* (5409), a frequentative form of *phero*, "to bear," and denoting "repeated or habitual action," is chiefly used of clothing, weapons, etc., of soft raiment, Matt. 11:8; fine clothing, **Jas. 2:3**; the crown of thorns, John 19:5.

Clothing *see* **Apparel** at *James 2:2*.

Sit *kathemai* (2521), is used (a) of the natural posture, e.g., Matt. 9:9, most frequently in Revelation, some 32 times; frequently in the Gospels and Acts; elsewhere only in 1 Cor. 14:30; **Jas. 2:3** (twice); and of Christ's position of authority on the throne of God, Col. 3:1, KJV, "sitteth" (RV, "is, seated"); Heb. 1:13 (cf. Matt. 22:44; 26:64 and parallel passages in Mark and Luke, and Acts 2:34); often as antecedent or successive to, or accompanying, another act (in no case a superfluous expression), e.g., Matt. 15:29; 27:36; Mark 2:14; 4:1; (b) metaphorically in Matt. 4:16 (twice); Luke 1:79; of inhabiting a place (translated "dwell"), Luke 21:35; Rev. 14:6, RV marg., "sit" (in the best texts: some have *katoikeo*, "to dwell").

Good *kalos* (2573), "well, finely," is used in some mss. in Matt. 5:44, with *poieo*, "to do," and translated "do good." In **Jas. 2:3** it is rendered "in a good place" (KJV marg., "well" or "seemly").

Poor *see James 2:2*.

Footstool *hupopodion* (5286), from *hupo*, "under," and *pous*, "a foot," is used (a) literally in **Jas. 2:3**, (b) metaphorically, of the earth as God's "footstool," Matt. 5:35; of the foes of the Lord, Matt. 22:44 (in some mss.); Mark 12:36, "underneath" (in some mss.), Luke 20:43; Acts 2:35; 7:49; Heb. 1:13; 10:13. The RV, adhering to the literal rendering, translates the phrase "the footstool of My (Thy, His) feet," for the KJV, "My (etc.) footstool," but in Matt. 22:44, "(till I put Thine enemies) underneath thy feet."

2:4 Are ye not then partial in yourselves, and are become judges of evil thoughts?

Partial *diakrino* (1252), "to separate," discriminate, hence, "to be at variance with oneself, to be divided in one's mind," is rendered "divided" in **Jas. 2:4**, RV; KJV, "partial."

Judges *krites* (2923), "a judge," is used (a) of God, Heb. 12:23, where the order in the original is "to a Judge who is God of all"; this is really the significance; it suggests that He who is the Judge of His people is at the same time their God; that is the order in 10:30; the word is also used of God in **Jas. 4:12**, RV; (b) of Christ, Acts 10:42; 2 Tim. 4:8; **Jas. 5:9**; (c) of a ruler in Israel in the times of the Judges, Acts 13:20; (d) of a Roman procurator, Acts 24:10; (e) of those whose conduct provides a standard of "judging," Matt. 12:27; Luke 11:19; (f) in the forensic sense, of one who tries and decides a case, Matt. 5:25 (twice); Luke 12:14; 12:58 (twice); 18:2; 18:6 (lit., "the judge of unrighteousness," expressing subjectively his character); Acts 18:15; (g) of one who passes, or arrogates to himself, judgment on anything, **Jas. 2:4** (see the RV); **4:11**.

Evil *poneros* (4190), akin to *ponos*, "labor, toil," denotes "evil that causes labor, pain, sorrow, malignant evil"; it is used (a) with the meaning bad, worthless, in the physical sense, Matt. 7:17-18; in the moral or ethical sense, "evil," wicked; of persons, e.g., Matt. 7:11; Luke 6:45; Acts 17:5; 2 Thess. 3:2; 2 Tim. 3:13; of "evil" spirits, e.g., Matt. 12:45; Luke 7:21; Acts 19:12-13, 15-16; of a generation, Matt. 12:39, 45; 16:4; Luke 11:29; of things, e.g., Matt. 5:11; 6:23; 20:15; Mark 7:22; Luke 11:34; John 3:19; 7:7; Acts 18:14; Gal. 1:4; Col. 1:21; 1 Tim. 6:4; 2 Tim. 4:18; Heb. 3:12; 10:22; **Jas. 2:4**; **4:16**; 1 John 3:12; 2 John 11; 3 John 10; (b) with the meaning toilsome, painful, Eph. 5:16; 6:13; Rev. 16:2. Cf. *poneria*, "iniquity, wickedness."

Thoughts *dialogismos* (1261), "reasoning," is translated "thoughts" in Matt. 15:19; Mark 7:21; Luke 2:35; 6:8; in 5:22, KJV, RV, "reasonings"; in 9:47, KJV, RV, "reasoning," and 24:38, KJV, RV, "reasonings"; so 1 Cor. 3:20; in Luke 9:46, KJV and RV, "reasoning"; "thoughts" in **Jas. 2:4**, KJV and RV.

2:5 Hearken, my beloved brethren, Hath not God chosen the poor of this world rich in faith, and heirs of the kingdom which he hath promised to them that love him?

Hearken *akouo* (191), "to hear," is rendered "hearken" in the KJV and RV, in Mark 4:3; Acts 4:19; 7:2; 15:13; **Jas. 2:5**; in the RV only, in Acts 3:22, 23; 13:16 (KJV, "give audience"); 15:12, "hearkened" (KJV "gave audience").

Chosen *eklego* (1586), "to pick out, select," means, in the middle voice, "to choose for oneself," not necessarily implying the rejection of what is not chosen, but "choosing" with the subsidiary ideas of kindness or favor or love, Mark 13:20; Luke 6:13; 9:35 (RV); 10:42; 14:7; John 6:70; 13:18; 15:16, 19; Acts 1:2, 24; 6:5; 13:17; 15:22, 25; in 15:7 it is rendered "made choice"; 1 Cor. 1:27-28; Eph. 1:4; **Jas. 2:5**.

Rich *see James 1:10.*

Heirs *kleronomos* (2818), lit. denotes "one who obtains a lot or portion" (*kleros*, "a lot," *nemomai*, "to possess"), especially of an inheritance. The NT usage may be analyzed as under: "(a) the person to whom property is to pass on the death of the owner, Matt. 21:38; Mark 12:7; Luke 20:14; Gal. 4:1; (b) one to whom something has been assigned by God, on possession of which, however, he has not yet entered, as Abraham, Rom. 4:13, 14; Heb. 6:17; Christ, Heb. 1:2; the poor saints, **Jas. 2:5**; (c) believers, inasmuch as they share in the new order of things to be ushered in at the return of Christ, Rom. 8:17; Gal. 3:29; 4:7; Titus 3:7; (d) one who receives something other than by merit, as Noah, Heb. 11:7." In the Sept., Judg. 18:7; 2 Sam. 14:7; Jer. 8:10; Mic. 1:15.

Promised *see James 1:12.*

2:6 But ye have despised the poor. Do not rich men oppress you, and draw you before the judgment seats?

Despised *atimazo* (818), signifies "to dishonour, treat shamefully, insult," whether in word, John 8:49, or deed, Mark 12:4; Luke 20:11, RV "handled (him) shamefully," (RV "entreated ... shamefully"); Rom. 1:24; 2:23, "dishonorest;" **Jas. 2:6**, RV, "ye have dishonored (the poor)," (KJV, "despised"); in the passive voice, to suffer dishonor, Acts 5:41 (KJV, "suffer shame").

Poor *see James 2:2.*

Rich *see James 1:10.*

Oppress *katadunasteuo* (2616), "to exercise power over" (*kata*, "down," *dunastes*, "a potentate": *dunamai* "to have power"), "to oppress," is used, in the passive voice, in Acts 10:38; in the active, in **Jas. 2:6**.

Draw *helko* (1670), is translated "to draw" in the KJV, of Acts 21:30 and **Jas. 2:6**.

Judgment seats *kriterion* (2922), primarily "a means of judging" (akin to *krino*, "to judge": Eng., "criterion"), then, a tribunal, law court, or "lawsuit," 1 Cor. 6:2 (last clause); 6:4; **Jas. 2:6**.

2:7 Do not they blaspheme that worthy name by the which ye are called?

Worthy In **Jas. 2:7**, KJV, *kalos*, "good, fair," is translated "worthy" (RV, "honorable").

Name *onoma* (3686), is used ... for all that a "name" implies, of authority, character, rank, majesty, power, excellence, etc., of everything that the "name" covers: (a) of the "Name" of God as expressing His attributes, etc., e.g., Matt. 6:9; Luke 1:49; John 12:28; 17:6, 26; Rom. 15:9; 1 Tim. 6:1; Heb. 13:15; Rev. 13:6; (b) of the "Name" of Christ, e.g., Matt. 10:22; 19:29; John 1:12; 2:23; 3:18; Acts 26:9; Rom. 1:5; **Jas. 2:7**; 1 John 3:23; 3 John 7; Rev. 2:13; 3:8; also the phrases rendered "in the name"; these may be analyzed as follows: (1) representing the authority of Christ, e.g., Matt. 18:5 (with *epi*, "on the ground of My authority"); so Matt. 24:5 (falsely) and parallel passages; as substantiated by the Father, John 14:26; 16:23 (last clause), RV; (2) in the power of (with *en*, "in"), e.g., Mark 16:17; Luke 10:17; Acts 3:6; 4:10; 16:18; **Jas. 5:14**; (3) in acknowledgement or confession of, e.g., Acts 4:12; 8:16; 9:27, 28; (4) in recognition of the authority of (sometimes combined with the thought of relying or resting on), Matt. 18:20; cf. 28:19; Acts 8:16; 9:2 (*eis*, "into"); John 14:13; 15:16; Eph. 5:20; Col. 3:17; (5) owing to the fact that one is called by Christ's "Name" or is identified with Him, e.g. 1 Pet. 4:14 (with *en*, "in"); with *heneken*, "for the sake of," e.g., Matt. 19:29; with *dia*, "on account of," Matt. 10:22; 24:9; Mark 13:13; Luke 21:17; John 15:21; 1 John 2:12; Rev. 2:3.

Called *epikaleo* (1941), denotes (a) "to surname"; (b) "to be called by a person's name"; hence it is used of being declared to be dedicated to a person, as to the Lord, Acts 15:17 (from Amos 9:12); **Jas. 2:7**; (c) "to call a person by a name by charging him with an offense," as the Pharisees charged Christ with doing His works by the help of Beelzebub, Matt. 10:25 (the most authentic reading has *epikaleo*, for *kaleo*); (d) "to call upon, invoke"; in the middle voice, "to call upon for oneself" (i.e., on one's behalf), Acts 7:59, or "to call upon a person as a witness," 2 Cor. 1:23, or to appeal to an authority, Acts 25:11, etc.; (e)"to call upon by way of adoration, making use of the Name of the Lord," Acts 2:21; Rom. 10:12-14; 2 Tim. 2:22.

2:8 If ye fulfil the royal law according to the scripture, Thou shalt love thy neighbour as thyself, ye do well:

Fulfil *teleo* (5055), "to end" (akin to *telos*, "an end"), signifies, among its various meanings, "to give effect to," and is translated "fulfill," of the Law, intentionally, **Jas. 2:8**, or unconsciously, Rom. 2:27; of the prophetic Scriptures concerning the death of Christ, Acts 13:29; prohibitively, of the lust of the flesh, Gal. 5:16.

Royal *basilikos* (937), "belonging to a king," is translated "royal" in Acts 12:21; **Jas. 2:8**.

Law *see James 1:25.*

Neighbour *plesion* (4139), the neuter of the adjective *plesios* (from *pelas*, "near"), is used as an adverb accompanied by the article, lit., "the (one) near"; hence, one's "neighbor"; see refs. below. This has a wider range of meaning than that of the Eng. word "neighbor." There were no farmhouses scattered over the agricultural areas of Palestine; the populations, gathered in villages, went to and fro to their toil. Hence domestic life was touched at every point by a wide circle of neighborhood. The terms for neighbor were therefore of a very comprehensive scope. This may be seen from the chief characteristics of the privileges and duties of neighborhood as set forth in Scripture, (a) its helpfulness, e.g., Prov. 27:10; Luke 10:36; (b) its intimacy, e.g., Luke 15:6, 9; Heb. 8:11; (c) its sincerity and sanctity, e.g., Ex. 22:7, 10; Prov. 3:29; 14:21; Rom. 13:10; 15:2; Eph. 4:25; **Jas. 4:12**. The NT quotes and expands the command in Lev. 19:18, "to love one's neighbor as oneself"; see, e.g., Matt. 5:43; 19:19; 22:39; Mark 12:31, 33; Luke 10:27; Gal. 5:14; **Jas. 2:8**. See also Acts 7:27.

2:9 But if ye have respect to persons, ye commit sin, and are convinced of the law as transgressors.

Respect to persons *prosopolempteo* (4380), "to have respect of persons," occurs in **Jas. 2:9**. *See also* **Respect of persons** at *James 2:1*.

Commit *ergazomai* (2038), to work, is translated by the verb "to commit" (of committing sin), in **Jas. 2:9**. This is a stronger expression than *poieo*, "to do," or *prasso*, "to practice."

Sin *see James 1:15.*

Convinced *elencho* (1651), signifies (a) "to convict, confute, refute," usually with the suggestion of putting the convicted person to shame; see Matt. 18:15, where more than telling the offender his fault is in view; it is used of "convicting" of sin, John 8:46; 16:8; gainsayers in regard to the faith, Titus 1:9; transgressors of the Law, **Jas. 2:9**; some texts have the verb in John 8:9; (b) "to reprove," 1 Cor. 14:24, RV (for KJV, "convince"), for the unbeliever is there viewed as being reproved for, or "convicted" of, his sinful state; so in Luke 3:19; it is used of reproving works, John 3:20; Eph. 5:11, 13; 1 Tim. 5:20; 2 Tim. 4:2; Titus 1:13; 2:15; all these speak of reproof by word of mouth. In Heb. 12:5 and Rev. 3:19, the word is used of reproving by action.

Law *see James 1:25.*

Transgressors *parabates* (3848), lit. and primarily, "one who stands beside," then, "one who oversteps the prescribed limit, a transgressor" (akin to *parabaino*, "to transgress"); so Rom. 2:25, RV (KJV, "a breaker"); v. 27, RV, "a transgressor" (KJV, "dost transgress"); Gal. 2:18; **Jas. 2:9, 11**.

2:10 For whosoever shall keep the whole law, and yet offend in one *point*, he is guilty of all.

Keep *see James 1:27.*

Offend *ptaio* (4417), "to cause to stumble," signifies, intransitively, "to stumble," used metaphorically in Rom. 11:11 and with moral significance in **Jas. 2:10** and **3:2** (twice), RV, "stumble" (KJV, "offend"); in 2 Pet. 1:10, RV, "stumble" (KJV, "fall").

Point In **Jas. 2:10**, *en heni* (the dative case of *heis*, "one"), lit., "in one," is rendered "in one point."

2:11 For he that said, Do not commit adultery, said also, Do not kill. Now if thou commit no adultery, yet if thou kill, thou art become a transgressor of the law.

Adultery *moicheuo* (3431), is used in Matt. 5:27-28, 32; 19:18; Mark 10:19; Luke 16:18; 18:20; John 8:4; Rom. 2:22; 13:9; **Jas. 2:11**; in Rev. 2:22, metaphorically, of those who are by a Jezebel's solicitations drawn away to idolatry.

Kill *phoneuo* (5407), "to murder," akin to *phoneus*, "a murderer," is always rendered by the verb "to kill"

> *"Because the law of God is ... a unity, even one sin results in the law as a whole being broken."*
>
> JOHN BLANCHARD

(except in Matt. 19:18, KJV, "do ... murder," and in Matt. 23:35, KJV and RV, "ye slew"); Matt. 5:21 (twice); 23:31; Mark 10:19; Luke 18:20; Rom. 13:9; **Jas. 2:11** (twice); **4:2; 5:6.**

Transgressor *see* **Transgressors** at *James 2:9.*

Law *see James 1:25.*

2:12 So speak ye, and so do, as they that shall be judged by the law of liberty.

Shall *mello* (3195), "to be about (to be or do)," is used of purpose, certainty, compulsion or necessity. It is rendered simply by "shall" or "should" (which frequently represent elsewhere part of the future tense of the verb) in the following (the RV sometimes translates differently, as noted): Matt. 16:27 (1st part), lit., "is about to come"; 17:12, 22; 20:22, RV, "am about"; 24:6; Mark 13:4 (2nd part), RV, "are about"; Luke 9:44; 21:7 (2nd part), RV, "are about"; v. 36; Acts 23:3; 24:15; 26:2, RV, "I am (to)"; Rom. 4:24; 8:13 (1st part), RV, "must"; v. 18; 2 Tim. 4:1; Heb. 1:14; 10:27; **Jas. 2:12**, RV "are to"; 1 Pet. 5:1; Rev. 1:19; 2:10 (1st and 2nd parts), RV, "art about," "is about"; 3:10, RV, "is (to)"; 17:8 (1st part), RV, "is about."

Judged *krino* (2919), primarily denotes "to separate, select, choose"; hence, "to determine," and so "to judge, pronounce judgment." "The uses of this verb in the NT may be analyzed as follows: (a) to assume the office of a judge, Matt. 7:1; John 3:17; (b) to undergo process of trial, John 3:18; 16:11; 18:31; **Jas. 2:12**; (c) to give sentence, Acts 15:19; 16:4; 21:25; (d) to condemn, John 12:48; Acts 13:27; Rom. 2:27; (e) to execute judgment upon, 2 Thess. 2:12; Acts 7:7; (f) to be involved in a lawsuit, whether as plaintiff, Matt. 5:40; 1 Cor. 6:1; or as defendant, Acts 23:6; (g) to administer affairs, to govern, Matt. 19:28; cf. Judg. 3:10; (h) to form an opinion, Luke 7:43; John 7:24; Acts 4:19; Rom. 14:5; (i) to make a resolve, Acts 3:13; 20:16; 1 Cor. 2:2."

Law *see James 1:25.*

2:13 For he shall have judgment without mercy, that hath shewed no mercy; and mercy rejoiceth against judgment.

Judgment *krisis* (2920), (a) denotes "the process of investigation, the act of distinguishing and separating"; hence "a judging, a passing of judgment upon a person or thing"; it has a variety of meanings, such as judicial authority, John 5:22, 27; justice, Acts 8:33; **Jas. 2:13**; a tribunal, Matt. 5:21-22; a trial, John 5:24; 2 Pet. 2:4; a judgment, 2 Pet. 2:11; Jude 9; by metonymy, the standard of judgment, just dealing, Matt. 12:18, 20; 23:23; Luke 11:42; divine judgment executed, 2 Thess. 1:5; Rev. 16:7; (b) sometimes it has the meaning "condemnation," and is virtually equivalent to *krima* (a); see Matt. 23:33; John 3:19; **Jas. 5:12**, *hupo krisin*, "under judgment."

Without mercy *aneleos* or *anileos* (448), "unmerciful, merciless," occurs in **Jas. 2:13**, said of judgment on him who shows no mercy.

Shewed *poieo* (4160), "to make, to do," is translated, "He hath showed" in Luke 1:51; "to show (mercy)," v. 72, RV (KJV, "perform"); "showed (mercy)," 10:37; John 6:30, KJV, "showest Thou," RV, "doest Thou (for a sign)"; Acts 7:36, KJV, "showed," RV, "wrought"; **Jas. 2:13**, "showed (no mercy)"; in Mark 13:22 in the best texts (some have *didomi*), "shall show (signs)."

Mercy *eleos* (1656), "is the outward manifestation of pity; it assumes need on the part of him who receives it, and resources adequate to meet the need on the part of him who shows it. It is used (a) of God, who is rich in mercy, Eph. 2:4, and who has provided salvation for all men, Titus 3:5, for Jews, Luke 1:72, and Gentiles, Rom. 15:9. He is merciful to those who fear him, Luke 1:50, for they also are compassed with infirmity, and He alone can succor them. Hence they are to pray boldly for mercy, Heb. 4:16, and if for themselves, it is seemly that they should ask for mercy for one another, Gal. 6:16; 1 Tim. 1:2. When God brings His salvation to its issue at the Coming of Christ, His people will obtain His mercy, 2 Tim. 1:16; Jude 21; (b) of men; for since God is merciful to them, He would have them show mercy to one another, Matt. 9:13; 12:7; 23:23; Luke 10:37; **Jas. 2:13**."

Rejoiceth *katakauchaomai* (2620), a strengthened form, signifies "to boast against, exult over," Rom. 11:18, RV, "glory" (KJV, "boast"); **Jas. 2:13**, RV, "glorieth" (KJV, "rejoiceth"); **3:14**, "glory (not)."

2:14 What *doth it* profit, my brethren, though a man say he hath faith, and have not works? can faith save him?

Profit *ophelos* (3786), akin to *ophello*, "to increase," comes from a root signifying "to increase"; hence, "advantage, profit"; it is rendered as a verb in its three occurrences, 1 Cor. 15:32 (KJV, "advantageth"; RV, "doth it profit"); **Jas. 2:14, 16**, lit., "What (is) the profit?" In the Sept., Job 15:3.

Man *tis* (5100), "some one, a certain one," is rendered "a man," "a certain man," e.g., in Matt. 22:24; Mark 8:4, KJV (RV, "one"); 12:19; John 3:3, 5; 6:50; 14:23; 15:6, 13; Acts 13:41, KJV (RV, "one"); 1 Cor. 4:2; 1 Tim. 1:8; 2 Tim. 2:5, 21; **Jas. 2:14, 18**; 1 Pet. 2:19; 1 John 4:20.

2:15 If a brother or sister be naked, and destitute of daily food,

Brother Believers, with *aner*, "male," prefixed, and with "or sister" added, 1 Cor. 7:14 (RV), 15; **Jas. 2:15**, male as distinct from female, Acts 1:16; 15:7, 13, but not 6:3.

Sister *adelphe* (79), is used (a) of natural relationship, e.g., Matt. 19:29; of the "sisters" of Christ, the children of Joseph and Mary after the virgin birth of Christ, e.g., Matt. 13:56; (b) of "spiritual kinship" with Christ, an affinity marked by the fulfillment of the will of the Father, Matt. 12:50; Mark 3:35; of spiritual relationship based upon faith in Christ, Rom. 16:1; 1 Cor. 7:15; 9:5, KJV and RV marg.; **Jas. 2:15**; Philem. 2, RV.

Naked *gumnos* (1131), signifies (a) "unclothed," Mark 14:52; in v. 51 it is used as a noun ("*his*" and "*body*" being italicized); (b) "scantily or poorly clad," Matt. 25:36, 38, 43, 44; Acts 19:16 (with torn garments); **Jas. 2:15**; (c) "clad in the undergarment only" (the outer being laid aside), John 21:7; (d) metaphorically, (1) of "a bare seed," 1 Cor. 15:37; (2) of "the soul without the body," 2 Cor. 5:3; (3) of "things exposed to the allseeing eye of God," Heb. 4:13; (4) of "the carnal condition of a local church," Rev. 3:17; (5) of "the similar state of an individual," 16:15; (6) of "the desolation of religious Babylon," 17:16.

Destitute *leipo* (3007), signifies "to leave, forsake"; in the passive voice, "to be left, forsaken, destitute"; in **Jas. 2:15**, KJV, "destitute," RV, "be in lack." *See also* **Wanting** at *James 1:4*.

Daily *ephemeros* (2184), signifies "for the day" (*epi* "upon, or for," *hemera*, "a day," Eng., "ephemeral"), **Jas. 2:15**.

Food *trophe* (5160), denotes "nourishment, food" (akin to *trepho*, "to rear, nourish, feed"); it is used literally, in the Gospels, Acts and **Jas. 2:15**; metaphorically, in Heb. 5:12, 14, RV, "(solid) food," KJV, "(strong) meat," i.e., deeper subjects of the faith than that of elementary instruction. The word is always rendered "food" in the RV, where the KJV has "meat"; e.g., Matt. 3:4; 6:25; 10:10; 24:45; Luke 12:23; John 4:8; Acts 2:46, "did take their food," RV (KJV, "did eat their meat"); 9:19, "took food"; 27:33, 34, 36. The KJV also has "food" in Acts 14:17 and **Jas. 2:15**.

2:16 And one of you say unto them, Depart in peace, be *ye* warmed and filled; notwithstanding ye give them not those things which are needful to the body; what *doth it* profit?

Depart *hupago* (5217), "to go," translated "depart" in **Jas. 2:16**, KJV, primarily and lit. meant "to lead under" (*hupo*, "under"); in its later use, it implied a "going," without noise or notice, or by stealth. In this passage the idea is perhaps that of a polite dismissal, "Go your ways."

Warmed *thermaino* (2328), "to warm, heat" (Eng. "thermal," etc.), when used in the middle voice, signifies "to warm oneself," Mark 14:54, 67; John 18:18 (twice), 25; **Jas. 2:16**.

Needful *epitedeios* (2006), primarily, "suitable, convenient," then, "useful, necessary," is translated "needful" in **Jas. 2:16**, neuter plural, "necessaries." In the Sept., 1 Chron. 28:2, "suitable."

Profit *see James 2:14*.

2:17 Even so faith, if it hath not works, is dead, being alone.

Dead *nekros* (3498), is used of (a) the death of the body, cf. **Jas. 2:26**, its most frequent sense: (b) the actual spiritual condition of unsaved men, Matt. 8:22; John 5:25; Eph. 2:1, 5; 5:14; Phil. 3:11; Col. 2:13; cf. Luke 15:24: (c) the ideal spiritual condition of believers in regard to sin, Rom. 6:11: (d) a church in declension, inasmuch as in that state it is inactive and barren, Rev. 3:1: (e) sin, which apart from law cannot produce a sense of guilt, Rom. 7:8: (f) the body of the believer in contrast to his spirit, Rom. 8:10: (g) the works of the Law, inasmuch as, however good in themselves, Rom. 7:13, they cannot produce life, Heb. 6:1; 9:14: (h) the faith that does not produce works, **Jas. 2:17, 26**; cf. v. 20.

Alone The phrase *kath' heauten* means "by (or in) itself," **Jas. 2:17**, RV, for KJV, "being alone" (see KJV, marg.).

2:18 Yea, a man may say, Thou hast faith, and I have works: shew me thy faith without thy works, and I will shew thee my faith by my works.

Yea *alla* (235), "but," is translated "yea" in John 16:2; Rom. 3:31, KJV (RV, "nay"); 1 Cor. 4:3; 2 Cor. 7:11 (six times); Gal. 4:17, KJV (RV, "nay"); Phil. 1:18; 2:17; 3:8; **Jas. 2:18**.

Man *see James 2:14*.

Say *eiro* (3004), an obsolete verb, has the future tense *ereo*, used, e.g., in Matt. 7:4; Luke 4:23 (2nd part); 13:25 (last part); Rom. 3:5; 4:1; 6:1; 7:7 (1st part); 8:31; 9:14, 19, 20, 30; 11:19; 1 Cor. 15:35; 2 Cor. 12:6; **Jas. 2:18**. The perfect is used, e.g., in John 12:50. The 1st aorist passive, "it was said," is used in Rom. 9:12, 26; Rev. 6:11.

Shew *deiknumi*, or *deiknuo*, (1166), denotes (a) "to show, exhibit," e.g., Matt. 4:8; 8:4; John 5:20; 20:20; 1 Tim. 6:15; (b) "to show by making known," Matt. 16:21; Luke 24:40;

John 14:8, 9; Acts 10:28; 1 Cor. 12:31; Rev. 1:1; 4:1; 22:6; (c) "to show by way of proving," **Jas. 2:18; 3:13**.

Without *choris* (5565), is used both as an adverb and as a preposition. As an adverb it signifies "separately, by itself," John 20:7, of the napkin which had been around the Lord's head in the tomb; as a preposition (its more frequent use), "apart from, without, separate from." It is rendered "apart from" in the RV of John 15:5; Rom. 3:21, 28; 4:6; 2 Cor. 12:3; Heb. 9:22, 28; 11:40; **Jas. 2:18, 20, 26**.

2:19 Thou believest that there is one God; thou doest well: the devils also believe, and tremble.

Devils *daimonion* (1140), not a diminutive of *daimon*, but the neuter of the adjective *daimonios*, pertaining to a demon, is also mistranslated "devil," "devils." In Acts 17:18, it denotes an inferior pagan deity. "Demons" are the spiritual agents acting in all idolatry. The idol itself is nothing, but every idol has a "demon" associated with it who induces idolatry, with its worship and sacrifices, 1 Cor. 10:20-21; Rev. 9:20; cf. Deut. 32:17; Isa. 13:21; 34:14; 65:3, 11. They disseminate errors among men, and seek to seduce believers, 1 Tim. 4:1. As seducing spirits they deceive men into the supposition that through mediums (those who have "familiar spirits," Lev. 20:6, 27, e.g.) they can converse with deceased human beings. Hence the destructive deception of spiritism, forbidden in Scripture, Lev. 19:31; Deut. 18:11; Isa. 8:19. "Demons" tremble before God, **Jas. 2:19**; they recognized Christ as Lord and as their future Judge, Matt. 8:29; Luke 4:41. Christ cast them out of human beings by His own power. His disciples did so in His name, and by exercising faith, e.g., Matt. 17:20. Acting under Satan (cf. Rev. 16:13-14), "demons" are permitted to afflict with bodily disease, Luke 13:16. Being unclean they tempt human beings with unclean thoughts, Matt. 10:1; Mark 5:2; 7:25; Luke 8:27-29; Rev. 16:13; 18:2, e.g. They differ in degrees of wickedness, Matt. 12:45. They will instigate the rulers of the nations at the end of this age to make war against God and His Christ, Rev. 16:14.

Tremble *phrisso* (5425), primarily, "to be rough, to bristle," then, "to shiver, shudder, tremble," is said of demons, **Jas. 2:19**, RV, "shudder" (KJV, "tremble"). Cf. Matt. 8:29, indicating a cognizance of their appointed doom.

2:20 But wilt thou know, O vain man, that faith without works is dead?

Know *ginosko* (1097), signifies "to be taking in knowledge, to come to know, recognize, understand," or "to understand completely," e.g., Mark 13:28, 29; John 13:12; 15:18; 21:17; 2 Cor. 8:9; Heb. 10:34; 1 John 2:5; 4:2, 6 (twice), 7, 13; 5:2, 20; in its past tenses it frequently means "to know in the sense of realizing," the aorist or point tense usually indicating definiteness, Matt. 13:11; Mark 7:24; John 7:26; in 10:38 "that ye may know (aorist tense) and understand, (present tense)"; 19:4; Acts 1:7; 17:19; Rom. 1:21; 1 Cor. 2:11 (2nd part), 14; 2 Cor. 2:4; Eph. 3:19; 6:22; Phil. 2:19; 3:10; 1 Thess. 3:5; 2 Tim. 2:19; **Jas. 2:20**; 1 John 2:13 (twice), 14; 3:6; 4:8; 2 John 1; Rev. 2:24; 3:3, 9. In the passive voice, it often signifies "to become known," e.g., Matt. 10:26; Phil. 4:5. In the sense of complete and absolute understanding on God's part, it is used, e.g., in Luke 16:15; John 10:15 (of the Son as well as the Father); 1 Cor. 3:20 ...

Vain *kenos* (2756), "empty," with special reference to quality, is translated "vain" (as an adjective) in Acts 4:25; 1 Cor. 15:10, 14 (twice); Eph. 5:6; Col. 2:8; **Jas. 2:20**; in the following the neuter, *kenon*, follows the preposition *eis*, "in," and denotes "in vain," 2 Cor. 6:1; Gal. 2:2; Phil. 2:16 (twice); 1 Thess. 3:5. *Raka* (4469), is an Aramaic word akin to the Heb. *req*, "empty," the first *a* being due to a Galilean change. In the KJV of 1611 it was spelled *racha*; in the edition of 1638, *raca*. It was a word of utter contempt, signifying "empty," intellectually rather than morally, "empty-headed," like Abimelech's hirelings, Judg. 9:4, and the "vain" man of **Jas. 2:20**. As condemned by Christ, Matt. 5:22, it was worse than being angry, inasmuch as an outrageous utterance is worse than a feeling unexpressed or somewhat controlled in expression; it does not indicate such a loss of self-control as the word rendered "fool," a godless, moral reprobate. *See also **James 1:26**.*

Without *see **James 2:18**.*

Dead *argos* (692), denotes "inactive, idle, unfruitful, barren" (*a*, negative, and *ergon*, "work"; cf. the verb *katargeo*, "to reduce to inactivity"); it is used (a) literally, Matt. 20:3, 6; 1 Tim. 5:13 (twice); Titus 1:12, RV, "idle (gluttons); 2 Pet. 1:8, RV, "idle," KJV, "barren"; (b) metaphorically in the sense of "ineffective, worthless," as of a word, Matt. 12:36; of faith unaccompanied by works, **Jas. 2:20** (some mss. have *nekra*, "dead"). *See also **James 2:17**.*

2:21 Was not Abraham our father justified by works, when he had offered Isaac his son upon the altar?

Justified *dikaioo* (1344), primarily "to deem to be right," signifies, in the NT, (a) "to show to be right or righteous"; in the passive voice, to be justified, Matt. 11:19; Luke 7:35; Rom. 3:4; 1 Tim. 3:16; (b) "to declare to be righteous, to pronounce righteous," (1) by man, concerning God, Luke 7:29 (see Rom. 3:4, above); concerning himself, Luke 10:29; 16:15; (2) by God concerning men, who are declared to be righteous before Him on certain conditions laid down by Him. Ideally the complete fulfillment of the law of God would provide a basis of "justification" in His sight, Rom. 2:13. But no such case has occurred in mere human experience, and therefore no one can be "justified" on this ground, Rom. 3:9-20; Gal. 2:16; 3:10, 11; 5:4. From this negative presentation in Rom. 3, the apostle proceeds to show that, consistently with God's own righteous character, and with a view to its manifestation, He is, through Christ, as "a propitiation ... by (*en*, "instrumental") His blood," 3:25, RV, "the Justifier of him that hath faith in Jesus" (v. 26), "justification" being the legal and formal acquittal from guilt by God as Judge, the pronouncement of the sinner as righteous, who believes on the Lord Jesus Christ. In v. 24, "being justified" is in the present continuous tense, indicating the constant process of "justification" in the succession of those who believe and are "justified." In 5:1, "being justified" is in the aorist, or point, tense, indicating the definite time at which each person, upon the exercise of faith, was justified. In 8:1, "justification" is presented as "no condemnation." That "justification" is in view here is confirmed by the preceding chapters and by verse 34. In 3:26, the word rendered "Justifier" is the present participle of the verb, lit., "justifying"; similarly in 8:33 (where the artide is used), "God that justifieth," is, more lit., "God is the (One) justifying," with stress upon the word "God." "Justification" is primarily and gratuitously by faith, subsequently and evidentially by works. In regard to "justification" by works, the so-called contradiction between James and the apostle Paul is only apparent. There is harmony in the different views of the subject. Paul has in mind Abraham's attitude toward God, his acceptance of God's word. This was a matter known only to God. The Romans epistle is occupied with the effect of this Godward attitude, not upon Abraham's character or actions, but upon the contrast between faith and the lack of it, namely, unbelief, cf. Rom. 11:20. James (**2:21-26**) is occupied with the contrast between faith that is real and faith that is false, a faith barren and dead, which is not faith at all. Again, the two writers have before them different epochs in Abraham's life – Paul, the event recorded in Gen. 15, James, that in Gen. 22. Contrast the words "believed" in Gen. 15:6 and "obeyed" in 22:18. Further, the two writers use the words "faith" and "works" in somewhat different senses. With Paul, faith is acceptance of God's word; with James, it is acceptance of the truth of certain statements about God, (v. 19), which may fail to affect one's conduct. Faith, as dealt with by Paul, results in acceptance with God, i.e., "justification," and is bound to manifest itself. If not, as James says "Can that faith save him?" (v. 14). With Paul, works are dead works, with James they are life works. The works of which Paul speaks could be quite independent of faith: those referred to by James can be wrought only where faith is real, and they will attest its reality. So with righteousness, or "justification": Paul is occupied with a right relationship with God, James, with right conduct. Paul testifies that the ungodly can be "justified" by faith, James that only the rightdoer is "justified."

Offered *anaphero* (399), primarily, "to lead" or "carry up" (*ana*), also denotes "to offer," (a) of Christ's sacrifice, Heb. 7:27; (b) of sacrifices under the Law, Heb. 7:27; (c) of such previous to the Law, **Jas. 2:21** (of Isaac by Abraham); (d) of praise, Heb. 13:15; (e) of spiritual sacrifices in general, 1 Pet. 2:5.

2:22 Seest thou how faith wrought with his works, and by works was faith made perfect?

Wrought *sunergeo* (4903), "to work with or together" (*sun*), occurs in Mark 16:20; Rom. 8:28, "work together"; 1 Cor. 16:16, "helpeth with"; 2 Cor. 6:1, "workers together," present participle, "working together"; the "*with Him*" represents nothing in the Greek; **Jas. 2:22**, "wrought with."

Perfect *teleioo* (5048), "to bring to an end by completing or perfecting," is used (I) of "accomplishing"; (II) of "bringing to completeness," (a) of persons: of Christ's assured completion of His earthly course, in the accomplishment of the Father's will, the successive stages culminating in His death, Luke 13:32; Heb. 2:10, to make Him "perfect," legally and officially, for all that He would be to His people on the ground of His sacrifice; cf. 5:9; 7:28, RV, "perfected" (KJV, "consecrated"); of His saints, John 17:23, RV, "perfected" (KJV, "made perfect"); Phil. 3:12; Heb. 10:14; 11:40 (of resurrection glory); 12:23 (of the departed

"It is faith alone that justifies, but the faith that justifies is not alone."

JOHN CALVIN

saints); 1 John 4:18, of former priests (negatively), Heb. 9:9; similarly of Israelites under the Aaronic priesthood, 10:1; (b) of things, Heb. 7:19 (of the ineffectiveness of the Law); **Jas. 2:22** (of faith made "perfect" by works); 1 John 2:5, of the love of God operating through him who keeps His word; 4:12, of the love of God in the case of those who love one another; 4:17, of the love of God as "made perfect with" (RV) those who abide in God, giving them to be possessed of the very character of God, by reason of which "as He is, even so are they in this world."

2:23 And the scripture was fulfilled which saith, Abraham believed God, and it was imputed unto him for righteousness: and he was called the Friend of God.

Fulfilled *pleroo* (4137), signifies (1) "to fill"; (2) "to fulfill, complete," (a) of time, e.g., Mark 1:15; Luke 21:24; John 7:8 (KJV, "full come"); Acts 7:23, RV, "he was wellnigh forty years old" (KJV, "was full," etc.), lit., "the time of forty years was fulfilled to him"; v. 30, KJV, "were expired"; 9:23; 24:27 (KJV, "after two years"; RV, "when two years were fulfilled"); (b) of number, Rev. 6:11; (c) of good pleasure, 2 Thess. 1:11; (d) of joy, Phil. 2:2; in the passive voice, "to be fulfilled," John 3:29 and 17:13; in the following the verb is rendered "fulfilled" in the RV, for the KJV, "full," John 15:11; 16:24; 1 John 1:4; 2 John 12; (e) of obedience, 2 Cor. 10:6; (f) of works, Rev. 3:2; (g) of the future Passover, Luke 22:16; (h) of sayings, prophecies, etc., e.g., Matt. 1:22 (twelve times in Matt., two in Mark, four in Luke, eight in John, two in Acts); **Jas. 2:23**; in Col. 1:25 the word signifies to preach "fully," to complete the ministry of the gospel appointed.

Imputed *logizomai* (3049), "to reckon, take into account," or, metaphorically, "to put down to a person's account," is never rendered in the RV by the verb "to impute." In the following, where the KJV has that rendering, the RV uses the verb "to reckon," which is far more suitable, Rom. 4:6, 8, 11, 22, 23, 24; 2 Cor. 5:19; **Jas. 2:23**.

Friend *philos* (5384), primarily an adjective, denoting "loved, dear, or friendly," became used as a noun, (a) masculine, Matt. 11:19; fourteen times in Luke (once feminine, 15:9); six in John; three in Acts; two in James, **2:23**, "the friend of God"; **4:4**, "a friend of the world"; 3 John 14 (twice); (b) feminine, Luke 15:9, "her friends."

2:24 Ye see then how that by works a man is justified, and not by faith only.

Then In **James 2:24**, where in some texts the inferential particle *toinun*, "therefore," occurs, the KJV renders it by "then" (RV follows the superior mss. which omit it).

Man *see James 1:19.*

2:25 Likewise also was not Rahab the harlot justified by works, when she had received the messengers, and had sent *them* out another way?

Likewise *homoios* (3668), "in like manner" (from the adjective *homoios*), is rendered "likewise" in the KJV of Matt. 22:26; 27:41, Luke 10:32; 16:25; John 5:19; **Jas. 2:25**; 1 Pet. 3:1, 7; Jude 8; Rev. 8:12 (in all these the RV has "in like manner"); in the following, KJV and RV have "likewise"; Matt. 26:35; Luke 5:33; 6:31; 10:37; 17:28, 31; 22:36; John 6:11; 21:13; Rom. 1:27; 1 Pet. 5:5.

Harlot *porne* (4204), "a prostitute, harlot" (from *pernemi*, "to sell"), is used (a) literally, in Matt. 21:31, 32, of those who were the objects of the mercy shown by Christ; in Luke 15:30, of the life of the Prodigal; in 1 Cor. 6:15, 16, in a warning to the Corinthian church against the prevailing licentiousness which had made Corinth a byword; in Heb. 11:31 and **Jas. 2:25**, of Rahab; (b) metaphorically, of mystic Babylon, Rev. 17:1, 5 (KJV, "harlots"), 15, 16; 19:2, RV, for KJV, "whore."

Received *hupodechomai* (5264), denotes "to receive under one's roof" (*hupo*, "under"), "receive as a guest, entertain hospitably," Luke 10:38; 19:6; Acts 17:7; **Jas. 2:25**.

Messengers *angelos* (32), "a messenger, an angel, one sent," is translated "messenger," of John the Baptist, Matt. 11:10; Mark 1:2; Luke 7:27; in the plural, of John's "messengers," 7:24; of those whom Christ sent before Him when on His journey to Jerusalem, 9:52; of Paul's "thorn in the flesh," "a messenger of Satan," 2 Cor. 12:7; of the spies as received by Rahab, **Jas. 2:25**.

Sent *ekballo* (1544), "to cast out," or "send out," is translated "sent out" in Mark 1:43, RV (KJV, "sent away"), and in KJV and RV in **Jas. 2:25**.

Way *hodos* (3598), denotes (a) "a natural path, road, way," frequent in the Synoptic Gospels;

elsewhere, e.g., Acts 8:26; 1 Thess. 3:11; **Jas. 2:25**; Rev. 16:12; (b) "a traveler's way"; (c) metaphorically, of "a course of conduct," or "way of thinking," e.g., of righteousness, Matt. 21:32; 2 Pet. 2:21; of God, Matt. 22:16, and parallels, i.e., the "way" instructed and approved by God; so Acts 18:26 and Heb. 3:10, "My ways" (cf. Rev. 15:3); of the Lord, Acts 18:25; "that leadeth to destruction," Matt. 7:13; "... unto life," 7:14; of peace, Luke 1:79; Rom. 3:17; of Paul's "ways" in Christ, 1 Cor. 4:17 (plural); "more excellent" (of love), 1 Cor. 12:31; of truth, 2 Pet. 2:2; of the right "way," 2:15; of Balaam (*id.*), of Cain, Jude 11; of a "way" consisting in what is from God, e.g., of life, Acts 2:28 (plural); of salvation, Acts 16:17; personified, of Christ as the means of access to the Father, John 14:6; of the course followed and characterized by the followers of Christ, Acts 9:2; 19:9, 23; 24:22.

2:26 For as the body without the spirit is dead, so faith without works is dead also.

Without *see James 2:18*.

Spirit *pneuma* (4151), primarily denotes "the wind" (akin to *pneo*, "to breathe, blow"); also "breath"; then, especially "the spirit," which, like the wind, is invisible, immaterial and powerful. The NT uses of the word may be analyzed approximately as follows: "(a) the wind, John 3:8 (where marg. is, perhaps, to be preferred); Heb. 1:7; cf. Amos 4:13, Sept.; (b) the breath, 2 Thess. 2:8; Rev. 11:11; 13:15; cf. Job 12:10, Sept.; (c) the immaterial, invisible part of man, Luke 8:55; Acts 7:59; 1 Cor. 5:5; **Jas. 2:26**; cf. Eccl. 12:7, Sept.; (d) the disembodied (or 'unclothed,' or 'naked,' 2 Cor. 5:3, 4) man, Luke 24:37, 39; Heb. 12:23; 1 Pet. 4:6; (e) the resurrection body, 1 Cor. 15:45; 1 Tim. 3:16; 1 Pet. 3:18; (f) the sentient element in man, that by which he perceives, reflects, feels, desires, Matt. 5:3; 26:41; Mark 2:8; Luke 1:47, 80; Acts 17:16; 20:22; 1 Cor. 2:11; 5:3, 4; 14:4, 15; 2 Cor. 7:1; cf. Gen. 26:35; Isa. 26:9; Ezek. 13:3; Dan. 7:15 ...

Dead *see James 2:17*.

Chapter 3

3:1 My brethren, be not many masters, knowing that we shall receive the greater condemnation.

Masters *didaskalos* (1320), "a teacher" (from *didasko*, "to teach"), is frequently rendered "Master" in the four Gospels, as a title of address to Christ, e.g., Matt. 8:19; Mark 4:38 (there are more instances in Luke than in the other Gospels); John 1:38, where it interprets "Rabbi"; 20:16, where it interprets "Rabboni." It is used by Christ of Himself in Matt. 23:8 and John 13:13-14; by others concerning Him, Matt. 17:24; 26:18; Mark 5:35; 14:14; Luke 8:49; 22:11; John 11:28. In John 3:10, the Lord uses it in addressing Nicodemus, RV, "the teacher" (KJV, "a master"), where the article does not specify a particular "teacher," but designates the member of a class; for the class see Luke 2:46, "the doctors" (RV, marg., "teachers"). It is used of the relation of a disciple to his "master," in Matt. 10:24, 25; Luke 6:40. It is not translated "masters" in the rest of the NT, save in the KJV of **Jas. 3:1** "(be not many) masters," where obviously the RV "teachers" is the meaning.

Greater *meizon* (3187), is the comparative degree of *megas*, e.g., Matt. 11:11; in Matt. 13:32, the RV rightly has "greater than" (KJV, "the greatest among"); 23:17; in Luke 22:26, RV, "the greater (among you)" (KJV, "greatest"); in **Jas. 3:1**, RV, "the heavier (marg., greater) judgment" (KJV, "the greater condemnation"); it is used in the neuter plural in John 1:50, "greater things"; in 14:12, "greater works" (lit., "greater things"); in 1 Cor. 12:31, RV, "the greater," KJV, "the best".

Condemnation *krima* (2917), denotes (a) "the sentence pronounced, a verdict, a condemnation, the decision resulting from an investigation," e.g., Mark 12:40; Luke 23:40; 1 Tim. 3:6; Jude 4; (b) "the process of judgment leading to a decision," 1 Pet. 4:17 ("judgment"), where *krisis* might be expected. In Luke 24:20, "to be condemned" translates the phrase *eis krima*, "unto condemnation" (i.e., unto the pronouncement of the sentence of "condemnation"). For the rendering "judgment," see,

"Teaching is a partnership with God. You are not molding iron nor chiseling marble; you are working with the Creator of the universe in shaping human character and determining destiny."

RUTH VAUGHN

e.g., Rom. 11:33; 1 Cor. 11:34; Gal. 5:10; **Jas. 3:1**. In these (a) the process leading to a decision and (b) the pronouncement of the decision, the verdict, are to be distinguished. In 1 Cor. 6:7 the word means a matter for judgment, a lawsuit.

3:2 For in many things we offend all. If any man offend not in word, the same *is* a perfect man, *and* able also to bridle the whole body.

Offend *see James 2:10.*

Same *houtos* (3778), "this" (person or thing), or "he" (and the feminine and neuter forms), is sometimes translated "the same," e.g., John 3:2, 26; 7:18; **Jas. 3:2**; sometimes the RV translates it by "this" or "these," e.g., John 12:21, "these" (KJV, "the same"); 2 Cor. 8:6, "this" (KJV, "the same").

Perfect *see James 1:4.*

Bridle *see* **Bridleth** at *James 1:26.*

3:3 Behold, we put bits in the horses' mouths, that they may obey us; and we turn about their whole body.

Put *ballo* (906), "to throw, cast, put," is translated "to put," in Matt. 9:17 (twice); 25:27; 27:6; Mark 2:22; 7:33; Luke 5:37; John 5:7; 12:6; 13:2 (of "putting" into the heart by the Devil); 18:11 (of "putting" up a sword); 20:25 (RV twice, KJV, "put" and "thrust"); v. 27, RV; Jas, **3:3**; Rev. 2:24 (RV, "cast").

Bits *chalinos* (5469), "a bridle," is used in **Jas. 3:3** (KJV, "bits"), and Rev. 14:20. "The primitive bridle was simply a loop on the halter-cord passed round the lower jaw of the horse. Hence in Ps. 32:9 the meaning is bridle and halter" (*Hastings' Bib. Dic.*).

Horses *hippos* (2462), apart from the fifteen occurrences in Revelation, occurs only in **Jas. 3:3**; in Revelation "horses" are seen in visions in 6:2, 4, 5, 8; 9:7, 9, 17 (twice); 14:20; 19:11, 14, 19, 21; otherwise in 18:13; 19:18.

Mouths *stoma* (4750), akin to *stomachos* (which originally meant "a throat, gullet"), is used (a) of "the mouth" of man, e.g., Matt. 15:11; of animals, e.g., Matt. 17:27; 2 Tim. 4:17 (figurative); Heb. 11:33; **Jas. 3:3**; Rev. 13:2 (2nd occurrence); (b) figuratively of "inanimate things," of the "edge" of a sword, Luke 21:24; Heb. 11:34; of the earth, Rev. 12:16; (c) figuratively, of the "mouth," as the organ of speech, (1) of Christ's words, e.g., Matt. 13:35; Luke 11:54; Acts 8:32; 22:14; 1 Pet. 2:22; (2) of human, e.g., Matt. 18:16; 21:16; Luke 1:64; Rev. 14:5; as emanating from the heart, Matt. 12:34; Rom. 10:8, 9; of prophetic ministry through the Holy Spirit, Luke 1:70; Acts 1:16; 3:18; 4:25; of the destructive policy of two world potentates at the end of this age, Rev. 13:2, 5, 6; 16:13 (twice); of shameful speaking, Eph. 4:29 and Col. 3:8; (3) of the Devil speaking as a dragon or serpent, Rev. 12:15, 16; 16:13; (d) figuratively, in the phrase "face to face" (lit., "mouth to mouth"), 2 John 12; 3 John 14; (e) metaphorically, of "the utterances of the Lord, in judgment," 2 Thess. 2:8; Rev. 1:16; 2:16; 19:15, 21; of His judgment upon a local church for its lukewarmness, Rev. 3:16; (f) by metonymy, for "speech," Matt. 18:16; Luke 19:22; 21:15; 2 Cor. 13:1.

Obey *peitho* (3982), "to persuade, to win over," in the passive and middle voices, "to be persuaded, to listen to, to obey," is so used with this meaning, in the middle voice, e.g., in Acts 5:36-37 (in v. 40, passive voice, "they agreed"); Rom. 2:8; Gal. 5:7; Heb. 13:17; **Jas. 3:3**. The "obedience" suggested is not by submission to authority, but resulting from persuasion.

"*Peitho* and *pisteuo*, 'to trust,' are closely related etymologically; the difference in meaning is that the former implies the obedience that is produced by the latter, cf. Heb. 3:18-19, where the disobedience of the Israelites is said to be the evidence of their unbelief Faith is of the heart, invisible to men; obedience is of the conduct and may be observed. When a man obeys God he gives the only possible evidence that in his heart he believes God. Of course it is persuasion of the truth that results in faith (we believe because we are persuaded that the thing is true, a thing does not become true because it is believed), but *peitho*, in NT suggests an actual and outward result of the inward persuasion and consequent faith."

Turn *metago* (3329), "to move from one side to another," is rendered "to turn about" in **Jas. 3:3, 4**.

3:4 Behold also the ships, which though *they be* so great, and *are* driven of fierce winds, yet are they turned about with a very small helm, whithersoever the governor listeth.

Ships *ploion* (4143), KJV, "ship," is preferably translated "boat" (RV) in the Gospels, where it is of frequent use; it is found 18 times in Acts, where, as in **Jas. 3:4**; Rev. 8:9; 18:19, it signifies a ship.

Great *telikoutos* (5082), "so great," is used in the NT of things only, a death, 2 Cor. 1:10; salvation, Heb. 2:3; ships, **Jas. 3:4**; an earthquake, Rev. 16:18, KJV, "so mighty," corrected in the RV to "so great."

Driven *elauno* (1643), signifies "to drive, impel, urge on." It is used of "rowing," Mark 6:48 and John

6:19; of the act of a demon upon a man, Luke 8:29; of the power of winds upon ships, **Jas. 3:4**; and of storms upon mists, 2 Pet. 2:17, KJV, "carried," RV, "driven."

Fierce In **Jas. 3:4**, *skleros*, "hard, rough, violent," is said of winds, RV, "rough," for KJV, "fierce."

Turned *see* **Turn** at *James 3:3*.

Small *elachistos* (1646), "least," is a superlative degree formed from the word *elachus*, "little," the place of which was taken by *mikros* (the comparative degree being *elasson*, "less"); it is used of (a) size, **Jas. 3:4**; (b) amount; of the management of affairs, Luke 16:10 (twice), 19:17, "very little"; (c) importance, 1 Cor. 6:2, "smallest (matters)"; (d) authority: of commandments, Matt. 5:19; (e) estimation, as to persons, Matt. 5:19 (2nd part); 25:40, 45; 1 Cor. 15:9; as to a town, Matt. 2:6; as to activities or operations, Luke 12:26; 1 Cor. 4:3, "a very small thing."

Helm *pedalion* (4079), "a rudder" (akin to *pedos*, "the blade of an oar"), occurs in **Jas. 3:4**, RV, "rudder" (KJV, "helm"), and Acts 27:40, plural, RV, "(the bands of) the rudders," KJV, "the rudder (bands)." The *pedalia* were actually steering paddles, two of which were used as "rudders" in ancient ships.

Governor In **Jas. 3:4**, the verb *euthuno*, "to make or guide straight," is used in the present participle, as a noun, denoting the "steersman" (RV) or pilot of a vessel, KJV, "governor."

Listeth *boulomai* (1014), "to will, be minded," is translated "listeth" in **Jas. 3:4** (RV, "willeth"). *See also* **Will** at *James 1:18*.

3:5 Even so the tongue is a little member, and boasteth great things. Behold, how great a matter a little fire kindleth!

Tongue *see James 1:26*.

Little *mikros* (3398), "little, small" (the opposite of *megos*, "great"), is used (a) of persons, with regard to (1) station, or age, in the singular, Mark 15:40, of James "the less" (RV marg., "little"), possibly referring to age; Luke 19:3; in the plural, "little" ones, Matt. 18:6, 10, 14; Mark 9:42; (2) rank or influence, e.g., Matt. 10:42 (see context); Acts 8:10; 26:22, "small," as in Rev. 11:18; 13:16; 19:5, 18; 20:12; (b) of things, with regard to (1) size, e.g., **Jas. 3:5**; (2) quantity, Luke 12:32; 1 Cor. 5:6; Gal. 5:9; Rev. 3:8; (3) time, John 7:33; 12:35; Rev. 6:11; 20:3.

Member *melos* (3196), "a limb of the body," is used (a) literally, Matt. 5:29-30; Rom. 6:13 (twice), 19 (twice); 7:5, 23 (twice); 12:4 (twice); 1 Cor. 12:12 (twice), 14, 18-20, 22, 25-26 (twice); **Jas. 3:5, 6; 4:1**; in Col. 3:5, "mortify therefore your members which are upon the earth"; since our bodies and their "members" belong to the earth, and are the instruments of sin, they are referred to as such (cf. Matt. 5:29-30; Rom. 7:5, 23, mentioned above); the putting to death is not physical, but ethical; as the physical "members" have distinct individualities, so those evils, of which the physical "members" are agents, are by analogy regarded as examples of the way in which the "members" work if not put to death; this is not precisely the same as "the old man," v. 9, i.e., the old nature, though there is a connection; (b) metaphorically, "of believers as members of Christ," 1 Cor. 6:15 (1st part); of one another, Rom. 12:5 (as with the natural illustration, so with the spiritual analogy, there is not only vital unity, and harmony in operation, but diversity, all being essential to effectivity; the unity is not due to external organization but to common and vital union in Christ); there is stress in v. 5 upon "many" and "in Christ" and "members;" 1 Cor. 12:27 (of the "members" of a local church as a body); Eph. 4:25 (of the "members" of the whole Church as the mystical body of Christ); in 1 Cor. 6:15 (2nd part), of one who practices fornication.

Boasteth *megalaucheo* (3166), from *megala*, "great things," and *aucheo*, "to lift up the neck," hence, "to boast," is found in some texts of **Jas. 3:5**. The most authentic mss. have the two words separated. It indicates any kind of haughty speech which stirs up strife or provokes others.

Great *helikos* (2245), primarily denotes "as big as, as old as" (akin to *helikia*, "an age"); then, as an indirect interrogation, "what, what size, how great, how small" (the context determines the meaning), said of a spiritual conflict, Col. 2:1, KJV, "what great (conflict) I have"; RV, "how greatly (I strive)"; of much wood as kindled by a little fire, **Jas. 3:5** (twice in the best mss.), "how much (wood is kindled by) how small (a fire)," RV, said metaphorically of the use of the tongue.

Matter *hule* (5208), denotes "a wood, a forest." In **Jas. 3:5**, KJV, *hule*, "a wood, forest," is translated "a matter" (RV, and KJV marg., "wood"). In older English the word "matter" actually meant "wood" (like its Latin original, *materia*).

Kindleth *anapto* (381), "to light up" (*ana*, "up," and *hapto*), is used (a) literally, in **Jas. 3:5**, "kindleth"; (b) metaphorically, in the passive voice, in Luke 12:49, of the "kindling" of the fire of hostility.

3:6 And the tongue *is* a fire, a world of iniquity: so is the tongue among our members, that it defileth the whole body,

and setteth on fire the course of nature; and it is set on fire of hell.

Tongue *see James 1:26.*

Fire *pur* (4442), (akin to which are *pura*, and *puretos*, "a fever," Eng., "fire," etc.) is used (besides its ordinary natural significance): ... as illustrative of retributive judgment upon the luxurious and tyrannical rich, **Jas. 5:3** ... of the tongue, as governed by a "fiery" disposition and as exercising a destructive influence over others, **Jas. 3:6**.

World *see James 1:27.*

Iniquity *adikia* (93), denotes "unrighteousness," lit., "unrightness" (*a*, negative, *dike*, "right"), a condition of not being right, whether with God, according to the standard of His holiness and righteousness, or with man, according to the standard of what man knows to be right by his conscience. In Luke 16:8 and 18:6, the phrases lit. are, "the steward of unrighteousness" and "the judge of injustice," the subjective genitive describing their character; in 18:6 the meaning is "injustice" and so perhaps in Rom. 9:14. The word is usually translated "unrighteousness," but is rendered "iniquity" in Luke 13:27; Acts 1:18; 8:23; 1 Cor. 13:6, KJV (RV, "unrighteousness"); so in 2 Tim. 2:19; **Jas. 3:6**.

Members *see* **Member** at *James 3:5.*

Defileth *spiloo* (4695), "to make a stain or spot," and so "to defile," is used in **Jas. 3:6** of the "defiling" effects of an evil use of the tongue; in Jude 23, "spotted," with reference to moral "defilement."

Body *soma* (4983), is "the body as a whole, the instrument of life," whether of man living, e.g., Matt. 6:22, or dead, Matt. 27:52; or in resurrection, 1 Cor. 15:44; or of beasts, Heb. 13:11; of grain, 1 Cor. 15:37-38; of the heavenly hosts, 1 Cor. 15:40. In Rev. 18:13 it is translated "slaves." In its figurative uses the essential idea is preserved. Sometimes the word stands, by *synecdoche*, for "the complete man," Matt. 5:29; 6:22; Rom. 12:1; **Jas. 3:6**; Rev. 18:13. Sometimes the person is identified with his or her "body," Acts 9:37; 13:36, and this is so even of the Lord Jesus, John 19:40 with 42. The "body" is not the man, for he himself can exist apart from his "body," 2 Cor. 12:2-3. The "body" is an essential part of the man and therefore the redeemed are not perfected till the resurrection, Heb. 11:40; no man in his final state will be without his "body," John 5:28-29; Rev. 20:13. The word is also used for physical nature, as distinct from *pneuma*, "the spiritual nature," e.g., 1 Cor. 5:3, and from *psuche*, "the soul," e.g., 1 Thess. 5:23. "*Soma*, 'body,' and *pneuma*, 'spirit,' may be separated; *pneuma* and *psuche*, 'soul,' can only be distinguished" (Cremer). It is also used metaphorically, of the mystic body of Christ, with reference to the whole church, e.g., Eph. 1:23; Col. 1:18, 22, 24; also of a local church, 1 Cor. 12:27.

Setteth on fire, Set on fire *phlogizo* (5394), "to set on fire, burn up," is used figuratively, in both active and passive voices, in **Jas. 3:6**, of the tongue, firstly of its disastrous effects upon the whole round of the circumstances of life; secondly, of satanic agency in using the tongue for this purpose.

Course *trochos* (5164), "a wheel," is translated "wheel" in **Jas. 3:6**, RV, with metaphorical reference to the round of human activity (KJV, "course"), as a glowing axle would set on fire the whole wooden wheel.

Nature *genesis* (1078), is used in the phrase in **Jas. 3:6**, "the wheel of nature," RV (marg., "birth"). Some regard this as the course of birth or of creation, or the course of man's "nature" according to its original divine purpose; Mayor (on the Ep. of James) regards *trochos* here as a wheel, "which, catching fire from the glowing axle, is compared to the widespreading mischief done by the tongue," and shows that "the fully developed meaning" of genesis denotes "the incessant change of life ... the sphere of this earthly life, meaning all that is contained in our life." The significance, then, would appear to be the whole round of human life and activity. Moulton and Milligan illustrate it in this sense from the papyri.

Hell *geenna* (1067), represents the Hebrew Ge-Hinnom (the valley of Tophet) and a corresponding Aramaic word; it is found twelve times in the NT, eleven of which are in the Synoptists, in every instance as uttered by the Lord Himself. He who says to his brother, Thou fool, will be in danger of "the hell of fire," Matt. 5:22; it is better to pluck out (a metaphorical description of irrevocable law) an eye that causes its possessor to stumble, than that his "whole body be cast into hell," v. 29; similarly with the hand, v. 30; in Matt. 18:8, 9, the admonitions are repeated, with an additional mention of the foot; here, too, the warning concerns the person himself (for which obviously the "body" stands in chapt. 5); in v. 8, "the eternal fire" is mentioned as the doom, the character of the region standing for the region itself, the two being combined in the phrase "the hell of fire," v. 9. To the passage in Matt. 18, that in Mark 9:43-47, is parallel; here to the word "hell" are applied the extended descriptions "the unquenchable fire" and "where their worm dieth not and the fire is not quenched." That God, "after He hath killed, hath power to cast into hell," is assigned as a reason why He should be feared with the fear that keeps from evil doing, Luke 12:5; the parallel passage to this in Matt. 10:28 declares, not the casting in, but the doom which follows, namely, the destruction (not the loss of being, but of wellbeing) of "both soul and body." In Matt. 23 the Lord denounces the scribes and Pharisees, who in proselytizing a person "make him two-fold more a son of hell" than themselves (v. 15), the phrase here being expressive of moral characteristics, and declares the impossibility of their escaping "the judgment of hell," v. 33. In **Jas. 3:6** "hell" is described as the source of the evil done by misuse of the tongue; here the word stands for the powers of darkness, whose characteristics and destiny are those of "hell." For terms descriptive of "hell," see e.g., Matt. 13:42; 25:46; Phil. 3:19; 2 Thess. 1:9; Heb. 10:39; 2 Pet. 2:17; Jude 13; Rev. 2:11; 19:20; 20:6, 10, 14; 21:8.

3:7 For every kind of beasts, and of birds, and of serpents, and of things in the sea, is tamed, and hath been tamed of mankind:

Kind *phusis* (5449), among its various meanings denotes "the nature, the natural constitution or power of a person or thing," and is translated "kind" in **Jas. 3:7** (twice), "kind" (of beasts, etc.), and "(man)kind," lit., "human kind."

Serpents *herpeton* (2062), "a creeping thing" (from *herpo*, "to creep"), "a reptile," is rendered "serpents" in **Jas. 3:7**, KJV (RV, "creeping things," as elsewhere).

Sea *enalios* (1724), "in the sea," lit., "of, or belonging to, the salt water" (from *hals*, "salt"), occurs in **Jas. 3:7**.

Tamed *damazo* (1150), "to subdue, tame," is used (a) naturally in Mark 5:4 and **Jas. 3:7** (twice); (b) metaphorically, of the tongue, in **Jas. 3:8**. In the Sept., Dan. 2:40.

Mankind *anthropinos* (442), "human, belonging to man" (from *anthropos*), is used (a) of man's wisdom, in 1 Cor. 2:13 (some mss. have it in v. 4, where indeed it is implied; see, however, the RV); (b) of "man's judgement," 1 Cor. 4:3 (marg., "day"); (c) of "mankind," **Jas. 3:7**, lit., "the human nature," RV marg. (KJV marg., "nature of man"); (d) of human ordinance, 1 Pet. 2:13; Moulton and Milligan show from the papyri how strongly antithetic to the divine the use of the word is in this respect; (e) of temptation, 1 Cor. 10:13, RV, "such as man can bear" (KJV, "such as is common to man"), i.e., such as must and does come to "men"; (f) of "men's" hands, Acts 17:25; (g) in the phrase "after the manner of men," Rom. 6:19.

3:8 But the tongue can no man tame; *it is* an unruly evil, full of deadly poison.

Tongue *see James 1:26.*

Man *see James 1:19.*

Tame *see* **Tamed** at *James 3:7.*

Unruly In **Jas. 3:8**, some texts have *akataschetos*, "that cannot be restrained," KJV, "unruly". *See also* **Unstable** at *James 1:8.*

Evil *kakos* (2556), indicates the lack in a person or thing of those qualities which should be possessed; it means "bad in character" (a) morally, by way of thinking, feeling or acting, e.g., Mark 7:21, "thoughts"; 1 Cor. 15:33, "company"; Col. 3:5, "desire"; 1 Tim. 6:10, "all kinds of evil"; 1 Pet. 3:9, "evil for evil"; (b) in the sense of what is injurious or baneful, e.g., the tongue as "a restless evil," **Jas. 3:8**; "evil beasts," Titus 1:12; "harm," Acts 16:28; once it is translated "bad," 2 Cor. 5:10. It is the opposite of *agathos*, "good."

> *"When you have nothing to say, say nothing."*
>
> CHARLES CALEB COLTON

Full *mestos* (3324), probably akin to a root signifying "to measure," hence conveys the sense of "having full measure," (a) of material things, a vessel, John 19:29; a net, 21:11; (b) metaphorically, of thoughts and feelings, exercised (1) in evil things, hypocrisy, Matt. 23:28; envy, murder, strife, deceit, malignity, Rom. 1:29; the utterances of the tongue, **Jas. 3:8**; adultery, 2 Pet. 2:14; (2) in virtues, goodness, Rom. 15:14; mercy, etc., **Jas. 3:17**.

Deadly *thanatephoros* (2287), lit., "death-bearing, deadly" (*thanatos*, "death," *phero*, "to bear"), is used in **Jas. 3:8**. In the Sept., Num. 18:22; Job 33:23.

Poison *ios* (2447), denotes "something active" as (a) "rust," as acting on metals, affecting their nature, **Jas. 5:3**; (b) "poison," as of asps, acting destructively on living tissues, figuratively of the evil use of the lips as the organs of speech, Rom. 3:13; so of the tongue, **Jas. 3:8**.

3:9 Therewith bless we God, even the Father; and therewith curse we men, which are made after the similitude of God.

Bless *eulogeo* (2127), lit., "to speak well of" (*eu*, "well," *logos*, "a word"), signifies, (a) "to praise, to celebrate with praises," of that which is addressed to God, acknowledging His goodness, with desire for His glory, Luke 1:64; 2:28; 24:51, 53; **Jas. 3:9**; (b) "to invoke blessings upon a person," e.g., Luke 6:28; Rom. 12:14. The present participle passive, "blessed, praised," is especially used of Christ in Matt. 21:9; 23:39, and the parallel passages; also in John 12:13; (c) "to consecrate a thing with solemn prayers, to ask God's blessing on a thing," e.g., Luke 9:16; 1 Cor. 10:16; (d) "to cause to prosper, to make happy, to bestow blessings on," said of God, e.g., in Acts 3:26; Gal. 3:9; Eph. 1:3. Cf. the synonym *aineo*, "to praise."

God *see* **Lord** at *James 1:1*.

Curse *kataraomai* (2672), primarily signifies "to pray against, to wish evil against a person or thing"; hence "to curse," Matt. 25:41; Mark 11:21; Luke 6:28; Rom. 12:14; Jas. 3:9. Some mss. have it in Matt. 5:44.

Made *ginomai* (1096), "to become," is sometimes translated by the passive voice of the verb to make, e.g., Matt. 9:16; John 1:3 (three times), 10; 8:33; Rom. 11:9; 1 Cor. 1:30; 3:13; 4:9, 13; Eph. 2:13; 3:7; Phil. 2:7 (but RV marg., "becoming"); Col. 1:23, 25; Heb. 5:5; 6:4; 7:12, 16, 21, 26; 11:3; **Jas. 3:9**; 1 Pet. 2:7. In many places the RV translates otherwise, and chiefly by the verb to become, e.g., Matt. 25:6, "there is"; 27:24, "was arising"; John 1:14, "became"; John 2:9, "become"; Rom. 1:3, "born"; 2:25, "is become"; 10:20, "became"; Gal. 3:13, "having become"; 4:4, "born" (twice); Heb. 3:14, "are become", 7:22, "hath ... become."

Similitude *homoiosis* (3669), "a making like," is translated "likeness" in **Jas. 3:9**, RV (KJV, "similitude").

3:10 Out of the same mouth proceedeth blessing and cursing. My brethren, these things ought not so to be.

Proceedeth *exerchomai* (1831), is translated "proceed" in Matt. 15:19, KJV (RV, "come forth"); John 8:42, RV, "came forth"; **Jas. 3:10**. The verb "to proceed" is not so suitable.

Blessing *eulogia* (2129), lit., "good speaking, praise," is used of (a) God and Christ, Rev. 5:12-13; 7:12; (b) the invocation of blessings, benediction, Heb. 12:17; **Jas. 3:10**; (c) the giving of thanks, 1 Cor. 10:16; (d) a blessing, a benefit bestowed, Rom. 15:29; Gal. 3:14; Eph. 1:3; Heb. 6:7; of a monetary gift sent to needy believers, 2 Cor. 9:5-6; (e) in a bad sense, of fair speech, Rom. 16:18, RV, where it is joined with *chrestologia*, "smooth speech," the latter relating to the substance, *eulogia* to the expression.

Cursing *katara* (2671), denotes an "execration, imprecation, curse," uttered out of malevolence, **Jas. 3:10**; 2 Pet. 2:14; or pronounced by God in His righteous judgment, as upon a land doomed to barrenness, Heb. 6:8; upon those who seek for justification by obedience, in part or completely, to the Law, Gal. 3:10, 13; in this 13th verse it is used concretely of Christ, as having "become a curse" for us, i.e., by voluntarily undergoing on the cross the appointed penalty of the "curse." He thus was identified, on our behalf, with the doom of sin. Here, not the verb in the Sept. of Deut. 21:23 is used, but the concrete noun.

Ought *chre* (5534), an impersonal verb (akin to *chraomai*, "to use"), occurs in **Jas. 3:10**, "(these things) ought (not so to be)," lit., "it is not befitting, these things so to be."

3:11 Doth a fountain send forth at the same place sweet *water* and bitter?

Fountain *pege* (4077), "a spring or fountain," is used of (a) "an artificial well," fed by a spring, John 4:6; (b) metaphorically (in contrast to such a well), "the indwelling Spirit of God," 4:14; (c) "springs," metaphorically in 2 Pet. 2:17, RV, for KJV, "wells"; (d) "natural fountains or springs," **Jas. 3:11, 12**; Rev. 8:10; 14:7; 16:4; (e) metaphorically, "eternal life and the future blessings accruing from it," Rev. 7:17; 21:6; (f) "a flow of blood," Mark 5:29.

Send *bruo* (1032), "to be full to bursting," was used of the earth in producing vegetation, of plants in putting forth buds; in **Jas. 3:11** it is said of springs gushing with water, "(doth the fountain) send forth ...."

Place *ope* (3692), perhaps from *ops*, "sight," denotes "a hole, an opening," such as a fissure in a rock, Heb. 11:38. In **Jas. 3:11**, the RV has "opening," of the orifice of a fountain (KJV, "place").

Sweet *glukus* (1099), (cf. Eng., "glycerine," "glucose"), occurs in **Jas. 3:11, 12** (KJV, "fresh" in this verse); Rev. 10:9, 10.

Bitter *pikros* (4089), from a root *pik-*, meaning "to cut, to prick," hence, lit., "pointed, sharp, keen, pungent to the sense of taste, smell, etc.," is found in **Jas. 3:11, 14**. In v. **11** it has its natural sense, with reference to water; in v. **14** it is used metaphorically of jealousy, RV.

3:12 Can the fig tree, my brethren, bear olive berries? either a vine, figs? so *can* no fountain both yield salt water and fresh.

Fig tree *suke* or *sukea* (4808), "a fig tree," is found in Matt. 21:19, 20, 21; 24:32; Mark 11:13, 20, 21; 13:28; Luke 13:6, 7; 21:29; John 1:48, 50, **Jas. 3:12**; Rev. 6:13.

Bear, Yield *poieo* (4160), "to do," sometimes means "to produce, bear," Luke 8:8; 13:9; **Jas. 3:12** (KJV, "bear," RV, "yield"); Rev. 22:2.

Olive berries *elaia* (1636), denotes (a) "an olive tree," Rom. 11:17, 24; Rev. 11:4 (plural); the Mount of Olives was so called from the numerous olive trees there, and indicates the importance attached to such; the Mount is mentioned in the NT in connection only with the Lord's life on earth, Matt. 21:1; 24:3; 26:30; Mark 11:1; 13:3; 14:26; Luke 19:37; 22:39; John 8:1; (b) "an olive," **Jas. 3:12**, RV (KJV, "olive berries").

Either *e* (2228), is a disjunctive particle. One of its uses is to distinguish things which exclude each other, or one of which can take the place of another. It is translated "either" in Matt. 6:24; 12:33; Luke 16:13; Acts 17:21; 1 Cor. 14:6. The RV rightly omits it in Luke 6:42, and translates it by "or" in Luke 15:8; Phil. 3:12 and **Jas. 3:12**.

Vine *ampelos* (288), is used (a) lit., e.g., Matt. 26:29 and parallel passages; **Jas. 3:12**; (b) figuratively, (1) of Christ, John 15:1, 4, 5; (2) of His enemies, Rev. 14:18, 19, "the vine of the earth" (RV, "vintage" in v. 19), probably figurative of the remaining mass of apostate Christendom.

Figs *sukon* (4810), denotes "the ripe fruit of a *suke*, a fig-tree," Matt. 7:16; Mark 11:13; Luke 6:44; **Jas. 3:12**.

Fountain *see James 3:11.*

Salt *halukos* (252), occurs in **Jas. 3:12**, "salt (water)."

Water *hudor* (5204), whence Eng. prefix, "hydro-," is used (a) of the natural element, frequently in the Gospels; in the plural especially in Revelation; elsewhere, e.g., Heb. 9:19; **Jas. 3:12**; in 1 John 5:6, that Christ "came by water and blood," may refer either (1) to the elements that flowed from His side on the cross after His death, or, in view of the order of the words and the prepositions here used, (2) to His baptism in Jordan and His death on the cross ...

Fresh *see* **Sweet** at *James 3:11.*

3:13 Who *is* a wise man and endued with knowledge among you? let him shew out of a good conversation his works with meekness of wisdom.

Wise *sophos* (4680), is used of (a) God, Rom. 16:27; in 1 Tim. 1:17 and Jude 25 *sophos* is absent, in the best mss. (see the RV), the comparative degree, *sophoteros*, occurs in 1 Cor. 1:25, where "foolishness" is simply in the human estimate; (b) spiritual teachers in Israel, Matt. 23:34; (c) believers endowed with spiritual and practical wisdom, Rom. 16:19; 1 Cor. 3:10; 6:5; Eph. 5:15; **Jas. 3:13**; (d) Jewish teachers in the time of Christ, Matt. 11:25; Luke 10:21; (e) the naturally learned, Rom. 1:14, 22; 1 Cor. 1:19, 20, 26, 27; 3:15-20.

Endued In **Jas. 3:13** the adjective *epistemon*, "knowing, skilled," is translated "endued with knowledge," KJV, RV, "understanding."

Knowledge *epistemon* (1990), "knowing, skilled," is used in **Jas. 3:13**, KJV, "endued with knowledge" (RV "understanding").

Shew *see James 2:18.*

Conversation *anastrophe* (391), lit., "a turning back," is translated "manner of life," "living," etc., in the RV, for KJV, "conversation," Gal. 1:13; Eph. 4:22; 1 Tim. 4:12; Heb. 13:7; **Jas. 3:13**; 1 Pet. 1:15, 18; 2:1 ("behavior"); 3:1, 2, 16 (ditto); 2 Pet. 2:7; 3:11.

Wisdom *see James 1:5.*

3:14 But if ye have bitter envying and strife in your hearts, glory not, and lie not against the truth.

Bitter *see James 3:11.*

Envying *zelos* (2205), "zeal, jealousy," is rendered "jealousy" in the RV (KJV, "envying") in Rom. 13:13; 1 Cor. 3:3; **Jas. 3:14, 16**; in 2 Cor. 12:20 (KJV, "envyings"); in Gal. 5:20, RV "jealousies" (KJV, "emulations"); in Acts 5:17 (KJV, "indignation"); in 13:45 (KJV, "envy"); in 2 Cor. 11:2 it is used in the phrase "with a godly jealousy," lit., "with a jealousy of God" (RV, marg.).

Strife *erithia* (or *-eia*) (2052), denotes "ambition, self-seeking, rivalry," self-will being an underlying idea in the word; hence it denotes "party-making." It is derived, not from *eris*, "strife," but from *erithos*, "a hireling"; hence the meaning of "seeking to win followers," "factions," so rendered in the RV of 2 Cor. 12:20, KJV, "strifes"; not improbably the meaning here is rivalries, or base ambitions (all the other words in the list express abstract ideas rather than factions); Gal. 5:20 (ditto); Phil. 1:17 (RV; KJV, v. 16, "contention"); 2:3 (KJV, "strife"); **Jas. 3:14, 16** (ditto); in Rom. 2:8 it is translated as an adjective, "factious" (KJV, "contentious"). The order "strife, jealousy, wrath, faction," is the same in 2 Cor. 12:20 and Gal. 5:20. "Faction" is the fruit of jealousy. Cf. the synonymous adjective *hairetikos*, Titus 3:10, causing division (marg., "factious"), not necessarily "heretical," in the sense of holding false doctrine.

Glory *see* **Rejoiceth** at *James 2:13.*

Lie *pseudo* (5574), "to deceive by lies" (always in the middle voice in the NT), is used (a) absolutely, in Matt. 5:11, "falsely," lit., "lying" (v, marg.); Rom. 9:1; 2 Cor. 11:31; Gal. 1:20; Col. 3:9 (where the verb is followed by the preposition *eis*, "to"); 1 Tim. 2:7; Heb. 6:18; **Jas. 3:14** (where it is followed by the preposition *kata*, "against"); 1 John 1:6; Rev. 3:9; (b) transitively, with a direct object (without a preposition following), Acts 5:3 (with the accusative case) "to lie to (the Holy Ghost)," RV marg., "deceive"; v. 4 (with the dative case) "thou hast (not) lied (unto men, but unto God)."

3:15 This wisdom descendeth not from above, but *is* earthly, sensual, devilish.

Wisdom *see James 1:5.*

Descendeth *katetchomai* (2718), "to come or go down," is translated "descendeth," in **Jas. 3:15**, KJV; RV, "cometh down."

Above *see James 1:17.*

Earthly *epigeios* (1919), "on earth" (*epi*, "on," *ge*, "the earth"), is rendered "earthly" in John 3:12; 2 Cor. 5:1; Phil. 3:19; **Jas. 3:15**; in Phil. 2:10, "on earth," RV; "terrestrial" in 1 Cor. 15:40 (twice).

Sensual *psuchikos* (5591), "belonging to the *psuche*, soul" (as the lower part of the immaterial in man), "natural, physical," describes the man in Adam and what pertains to him (set in contrast to *pneumatikos* "spiritual"), 1 Cor. 2:14; 15:44 (twice), 46 (in the latter used as a noun); **Jas. 3:15**, "sensual" (RV marg., "natural" or "animal"), here relating perhaps more especially to the mind, a wisdom in accordance with, or springing from, the corrupt desires and affections; so in Jude 19.

Devilish *daimoniodes* (1141), signifies "proceeding from, or resembling, a demon, demoniacal"; see marg. of **Jas. 3:15**, RV (text, "devilish").

3:16 For where envying and strife *is*, there *is* confusion and every evil work.

Envying *see James 3:14.*

Strife *see James 3:14.*

Confusion *akatastasia* (181), "instability," (*a*, negative, *kata*, "down," *stasis*, "a standing"), denotes "a state of disorder, disturbance, confusion, tumult," 1 Cor. 14:33; **Jas. 3:16**, "revolution or anarchy"; translated "tumults" in Luke 21:9 (KJV, "commotions"); 2 Cor. 6:5; 12:20.

Evil *phaulos* (5337), primarily denotes "slight, trivial, blown about by every wind"; then, "mean, common, bad," in the sense of being worthless, paltry or contemptible, belonging to a low order of things; in John 5:29, those who have practiced "evil" things, RV, "ill" (*phaula*), are set in contrast to those who have done good things (*agatha*); the same contrast is presented in Rom. 9:11 and 2 Cor. 5:10, in each of which the most authentic mss. have *phaulos* for *kakos*; he who practices "evil" things (RV, "ill") hates the light, John 3:20; jealousy and strife are accompanied by "every vile deed," **Jas. 3:16**. It is used as a noun in Titus 2:8.

Work For *pragma*, **Jas. 3:16**, rendered "work" in KJV, the RV has "deed."

3:17 But the wisdom that is from above is first pure, then peaceable, gentle, *and* easy to be intreated, full of mercy and good fruits, without partiality, and without hypocrisy.

Wisdom *see James 1:5.*

Above *see James 1:17.*

First *proton* (4412), the neuter of the adjective *protos* (the superlative degree of *pro*, "before"), signifies "first, or at the first," (a) in order of time, e.g., Luke 10:5; John 18:13; 1 Cor. 15:46; 1 Thess. 4:16; 1 Tim. 3:10; (b) in enumerating various particulars, e.g., Rom. 3:2; 1 Cor. 11:18; 12:28; Heb. 7:2; **Jas. 3:17**. It is translated "before" in John 15:18.

Pure *hagnos* (53), "pure from defilement, not contaminated" (from the same root as *hagios*, "holy"), is rendered "pure" in Phil. 4:8; 1 Tim. 5:22; **Jas. 3:17**; 1 John 3:3.

Then *epeita* (1899), "thereupon, thereafter," then (in some texts, Mark 7:5; *kai*, "and," in the best); Luke 16:7; John 11:7; 1 Cor. 12:28, RV, "then" (KJV, "after that"); 15:6 and 7 (ditto); v. 23, RV, KJV, "afterward"; v. 46; Gal. 1:18; v. 21, RV (KJV, "afterwards"), 2:1; 1 Thess. 4:17; Heb. 7:2, RV (KJV, "after that"); v. 27; **Jas. 3:17; 4:14**.

Peaceable *eirenikos* (1516), denotes "peaceful." It is used (a) of the fruit of righteousness, Heb. 12:11, "peaceable" (or "peaceful") because it is produced in communion with God the Father, through His chastening; (b) of "the wisdom that is from above," **Jas. 3:17**.

Gentle *epieikes* (1933), from *epi*, "unto," and *eikos*, "likely," denotes "seemly, fitting"; hence, "equitable, fair, moderate, forbearing, not insisting on the letter of the law"; it expresses that considerateness that looks "humanely and reasonably at the facts of a case"; it is rendered "gentle" in 1 Tim. 3:3, RV (KJV, "patient"), in contrast to contentiousness; in Titus 3:2, "gentle," in association with meekness, in **Jas. 3:17**, as a quality of the wisdom from above, in 1 Pet. 2:18, in association with the good. In the Sept., Esth. 8:13; Ps. 86:5.

Intreated *eupeithes* (2138), "ready to obey" (*eu*, "well," *peithomai*, "to obey, to be persuaded"), "compliant," is translated "easy to be intreated" in **Jas. 3:17**, said of the wisdom that is from above.

Full *see James 3:8.*

Partiality *adiakritos* (87), primarily signifies "not to be parted," hence, "without uncertainty," or "indecision," **Jas. 3:17**, KJV, "without partiality" (marg. "wrangling"), RV, "without variance" (marg., "or, doubtfulness; or, partiality"). In the Sept., Prov. 25:1.

Without hypocrisy *anupokritos* (505), from *a*, negative, *n*, euphonic, and an adjectival form corresponding to *hupokrisis*, signifies "unfeigned"; it is said of love, 2 Cor. 6:6; 1 Pet. 1:22; Rom. 12:9, KJV, "without dissimulation," RV, "without hypocrisy"; of faith, 1 Tim. 1:5; 2 Tim. 1:5, "unfeigned"; of the wisdom that is from above, **Jas. 3:17**, "without hypocrisy."

3:18 And the fruit of righteousness is sown in peace of them that make peace.

Fruit *karpos* (2590), "fruit," is used (I) of the fruit of trees, fields, the earth, that which is produced by the inherent energy of a living organism, e.g., Matt. 7:17; **Jas. 5:7, 18**; plural, e.g., in Luke 12:17 and 2 Tim. 2:6; of the human body, Luke 1:42; Acts 2:30; (II) metaphorically, (a) of works or deeds, "fruit" being the visible expression of power working inwardly and invisibly, the character of the "fruit" being evidence of the character of the power producing it, Matt. 7:16. As the visible expressions of hidden lusts are the works of the flesh, so the invisible power of the Holy Spirit in those who are brought into living union with Christ (John 15:2-8, 16) produces "the fruit of the Spirit," Gal. 5:22, the singular form suggesting the unity of the character of the Lord as reproduced in them, namely, "love, joy, peace, longsuffering, kindness, goodness, faithfulness, meekness, temperance," all in contrast with the confused and often mutually antagonistic "works of the flesh." So in Phil. 1:11, marg., "fruit of righteousness." In Heb. 12:11, "the fruit of righteousness" is described as "peaceable fruit," the outward effect of divine chastening; "the fruit of righteousness is sown in peace," **Jas. 3:18**, i.e., the seed contains the fruit; those who make peace, produce a harvest of righteousness; in Eph. 5:9, "the fruit of the light" (RV, and see context) is seen in "goodness and righteousness and truth," as the expression of the union of the Christian with God (Father, Son and Holy Spirit); for God is good, Mark 10:18, the Son is "the righteous One," Acts 7:52, the Spirit is "the Spirit of truth," John 16:13; (b) of advantage, profit, consisting (1) of converts as the result of evangelistic ministry, John 4:36; Rom. 1:13; Phil. 1:22; (2) of sanctification, through deliverance from a life of sin and through service to God, Rom. 6:22, in contrast to (3) the absence of anything regarded as advantageous as the result of former sins, v. 21; (4) of the reward for ministration to servants of God, Phil. 4:17; (5) of the effect of making confession to God's Name by the sacrifice of praise, Heb. 13:15.

Righteousness *see James 1:20.*

Sown *speiro* (4687), "to sow seed," is used (1) literally, especially in the Synoptic Gospels; elsewhere, 1 Cor. 15:36, 37; 2 Cor. 9:10, "the sower", (2) metaphorically, (a) in proverbial sayings, e.g., Matt. 13:3, 4; Luke 19:21, 22; John 4:37; 2 Cor. 9:6; (b) in the interpretation of parables, e.g., Matt. 13:19-23 (in these vv., RV, "was sown," for KJV, "received seed"); (c) otherwise as follows: of "sowing" spiritual things in preaching and teaching, 1 Cor. 9:11; of the interment of the bodies of deceased believers, 1 Cor. 15:42-44; of ministering to the necessities of others in things temporal (the harvest being proportionate to the "sowing"), 2 Cor. 9:6, 10; of "sowing" to the flesh, Gal. 6:7, 8 ("that" in v. 7 is emphatic, "that and that only," what was actually "sown"); in v. 8, *eis*, "unto," signifies "in the interests of"; of the "fruit of righteousness" by peacemakers, **Jas. 3:18**.

"Modesty is the badge of wisdom."

MATTHEW HENRY

Make *poieo* (4160), "to do, to make," is used in the latter sense (a) of constructing or producing anything, of the creative acts of God, e.g., Matt. 19:4 (2nd part); Acts 17:24; of the acts of human beings, e.g., Matt. 17:4; Acts 9:39; (b) with nouns denoting a state or condition, to be the author of, to cause, e.g., peace, Eph. 2:15; **Jas. 3:18**; stumbling blocks, Rom. 16:17; (c) with nouns involving the idea of action (or of something accomplished by action), so as to express the idea of the verb more forcibly (the middle voice is commonly used in this respect, suggesting the action as being of special interest to the doer); for the active voice see, e.g., Mark 2:23, of "making" one's way, where the idea is not that the disciples "made" a path through the standing corn, but simply that they went, the phrase being equivalent to going, "(they began) as they went (to pluck the ears)"; other instances of the active are Rev. 13:13, 14; 16:14; 19:20; for the middle voice (the dynamic or subjective middle), see, e.g., John 14:23, "will make Our abode"; in Acts 20:24, "none of these things move me," lit., "I make account of none of these things"; 25:17, "I made no delay" RV, Rom. 15:26; Eph. 4:16; Heb. 1:2; 2 Pet. 1:10; (d) to "make" ready or prepare, e.g., a dinner, Luke 14:12; a supper, John 12:2; (e) to acquire, provide a thing for oneself, Matt. 25:16; Luke 19:18; (f) to render or "make" one or oneself anything, or cause a person or thing to become something, e.g., Matt. 4:19; 12:16, "make (Him known)"; John 5:11, 15, to "make" whole; 16:2, lit., "they shall make (you put out of the synagogue)"; Eph. 2:14; Heb. 1:7; to change one thing into another, Matt. 21:13; John 2:16; 4:46; 1 Cor. 6:15; (g) to constitute one anything, e.g., Acts 2:36, (h) to declare one or oneself anything, John 5:18, "making (Himself equal with God)"; 8:53; 10:33; 19:7, 12; 1 John 1:10; 5:10; (i) to "make" one do a thing, e.g., Luke 5:34; John 6:10; Rev. 3:9.

Chapter 4

4:1 From whence *come* wars and fightings among you? *come they* not hence, *even* of your lusts that war in your members?

Wars *polemos* (4171), "war," is so translated in the RV, for KJV, "battle," 1 Cor. 14:8; Rev. 9:7, 9; 16:14; 20:8; for KJV, "fight," Heb. 11:34; KJV and RV in **Jas. 4:1**, hyperbolically of private "quarrels"; elsewhere, literally, e.g., Matt. 24:6; Rev. 11:7.

Fightings *mache* (3163), "a fight, strife," is always used in the plural in the NT, and translated "fightings" in 2 Cor. 7:5; **Jas. 4:1**; and Titus 3:9, RV (for KJV, "strivings"); "strifes" in 2 Tim. 2:23.

Hence *enteuthen* (1782), is used (a) of place, "hence," or "from hence," Luke 4:9; 13:31; John 2:16; 7:3; 14:31; 18:36; in John 19:18, "on either side (one)," lit., "hence and hence"; in Rev. 22:2, it is contrasted with *ekeithen*, "thence," RV, "on this side ... on that" (KJV, "on either side"), lit. "hence ... thence"; (b) causal; **Jas. 4:1**, "(come they not) hence," i.e., "owing to."

Of The following are instances in which "of" translates *ek*, or *ex*, "out of, from," Matt. 21:25 (RV, "from"); 1 Cor. 1:30; 15:6; 2 Cor. 5:1 (RV, "from"); **Jas. 4:1**.

Lusts *hedone* (2237), "pleasure," is translated "lusts," in the KJV of **Jas. 4:1, 3** (RV, "pleasures").

War *strateuo* (4754), used in the middle voice, "to make war" (from *stratos*, "an encamped army"), is translated "to war" in 2 Cor. 10:3; metaphorically, of spiritual "conflict," 1 Tim. 1:18; 2 Tim. 2:3, KJV; **Jas. 4:1**; 1 Pet. 2:11.

Members *see* **Member** at *James 3:5*.

4:2 Ye lust, and have not: ye kill, and desire to have, and cannot obtain: ye fight and war, yet ye have not, because ye ask not.

Lust *epithumeo* (1937), has the same twofold meaning as the noun, namely (a) "to desire," used of the Holy Spirit against the flesh, Gal. 5:17; of the Lord Jesus, Luke 22:15, "I have desired;" of the holy angels, 1 Pet. 1:12; of good men, for good things, Matt. 13:17; 1 Tim. 3:1; Heb. 6:11; of men, for things without moral quality, Luke 15:16; 16:21; 17:22; Rev. 9:6; (b) of "evil desires," in respect of which it is translated "to lust" in Matt. 5:28; 1 Cor. 10:6; Gal. 5:17 (1st part); **Jas. 4:2**; to covet, Acts 20:23; Rom. 7:7; 13:9.

Kill *see James 2:11*.

Desire *zeloo* (2206), "to have a zeal for, to be zealous towards," whether in a good or evil sense, the former in 1 Cor. 14:1, concerning spiritual gifts RV, "desire earnestly," KJV, "desire"; in an evil sense, in **Jas. 4:2**, RV, "covet," for KJV, "desire to have."

Obtain *epitunchano* (2013), primarily, "to light upon," denotes "to obtain," Rom. 11:7 (twice); Heb. 6:15; 11:33; **Jas. 4:2**.

Fight *machomai* (3164), "to fight," is so rendered in **Jas. 4:2** and translated "strive" in 2 Tim. 2:24; "strove" in John 6:52; Acts 7:26.

War *polemeo* (4170), (Eng., "polemics"), "to fight, to make war," is used (a) literally, Rev. 12:7 (twice), RV; 13:4; 17:14; 19:11; (b) metaphorically, Rev. 2:16, RV; (c) hyperbolically, **Jas. 4:2**.

Ask *see James 1:5*.

4:3 Ye ask, and receive not, because ye ask amiss, that ye may consume *it* upon your lusts.

Ask *see James 1:5*.

Amiss *kakos* (2560), akin to *kakos*, "evil," is translated "amiss" in **Jas. 4:3**; elsewhere in various ways.

Consume *dapanao* (1159), denotes (a) "to expend, spend," Mark 5:26; 2 Cor. 12:15 (1st part); (b) "to consume, squander," Luke 15:14; **Jas. 4:3**.

Lusts *see James 4:1*.

4:4 Ye adulterers and adulteresses, know ye not that the friendship of the world is enmity with God? whosoever therefore will be a friend of the world is the enemy of God.

Adulterers *moichos* (3432), denotes one "who has unlawful intercourse with the spouse of another," Luke 18:11; 1 Cor. 6:9; Heb. 13:4. As to **Jas. 4:4**, see **Adultereresses** at *James 4:4*.

Adultereresses *moichalis* (3428), "an adulteress," is used (a) in the natural sense, 2 Pet. 2:14; Rom. 7:3; (b) in the spiritual sense, **Jas. 4:4**; here the RV rightly omits the word "adulterers." It was added by a copyist. As in Israel the breach of their relationship with God through their idolatry, was described as "adultery" or "harlotry" (e.g., Ezek. 16:15, etc.; 23:43), so believers who cultivate friendship with the world, thus breaking their spiritual union with Christ, are spiritual "adulteresses," having been spiritually united to Him as wife to husband, Rom. 7:4. It is used adjectivally to describe the Jewish people in transferring their affections from God, Matt. 12:39; 16:4; Mark 8:38. In 2 Pet. 2:14, the lit. translation is "full of an adulteress" (RV, marg.).

Friendship *philia* (5373), akin to *philos*, "a friend," is rendered in **Jas. 4:4**, "the friendship (of the world)." It involves "the idea of loving as well as being loved" (Mayor); cf. the verb in John 15:19.

Enmity *echthra* (2189), from the adjective *echthros* is rendered "enmity" in Luke 23:12; Rom. 8:7; Eph. 2:15-16; **Jas. 4:4**; "enmities," Gal. 5:20, RV, for KJV, "hatred." It is the opposite of *agape*, "love."

Will *see James 1:18.*

Friend *see James 2:23.*

Enemy *echthros* (2190), an adjective, primarily denoting "hated" or "hateful" (akin to *echthos*, "hate"; perhaps associated with *ekos*, "outside"), hence, in the active sense, denotes "hating, hostile"; it is used as a noun signifying an "enemy," adversary, and is said (a) of the Devil, Matt. 13:39; Luke 10:19; (b) of death, 1 Cor. 15:26; (c) of the professing believer who would be a friend of the world, thus making himself an enemy of God, **Jas. 4:4**; (d) of men who are opposed to Christ, Matt. 13:25, 28; 22:44; Mark 12:36; Luke 19:27; 20:43; Acts 2:35; Rom. 11:28; Phil. 3:18; Heb. 1:13; 10:13; or to His servants, Rev. 11:5, 12; to the nation of Israel, Luke 1:71, 74; 19:43; (e) of one who is opposed to righteousness, Acts 13:10; (f) of Israel in its alienation from God, Rom. 11:28; (g) of the unregenerate in their attitude toward God, Rom. 5:10; Col. 1:21; (h) of believers in their former state, 2 Thess. 3:15; (i) of foes, Matt. 5:43-44; 10:36; Luke 6:27, 35; Rom. 12:20; 1 Cor. 15:25; of the apostle Paul because he told converts "the truth," Gal. 4:16. Cf. *echthra*, "enmity".

4:5 Do ye think that the scripture saith in vain, The spirit that dwelleth in us lusteth to envy?

Scripture *graphe* (1124), akin to *grapho*, "to write" (Eng., "graph," "graphic," etc.), primarily denotes "a drawing, painting"; then "a writing," (a) of the OT Scriptures, (1) in the plural, the whole, e.g., Matt. 21:42; 22:29; John 5:39; Acts 17:11; 18:24; Rom. 1:2, where "the prophets" comprises the OT writers in general; 15:4; 16:26, lit., "prophetic writings," expressing the character of all the Scriptures; (2) in the singular in reference to a particular passage, e.g., Mark 12:10; Luke 4:21; John 2:22; 10:35 (though applicable to all); 19:24, 28, 36, 37; 20:9; Acts 1:16; 8:32, 35; Rom. 4:3; 9:17; 10:11; 11:2; Gal. 3:8, 22; 4:30; 1 Tim. 5:18, where the 2nd quotation is from Luke 10:7, from which it may be inferred that the apostle included Luke's Gospel as "Scripture" alike with Deuteronomy, from which the first quotation is taken; in reference to the whole, e.g. **Jas. 4:5** (see RV, a separate rhetorical question from the one which follows); in 2 Pet. 1:20, "no prophecy of Scripture," a description of all, with special application to the OT in the next verse; (b) of the OT Scriptures (those accepted by the Jews as canonical) and all those of the NT which were to be accepted by Christians as authoritative, 2 Tim. 3:16; these latter were to be discriminated from the many forged epistles and other religious "writings" already produced and circulated in Timothy's time. Such discrimination would be directed by the fact that "every Scripture," characterized by inspiration of God, would be profitable for the purposes mentioned; so the RV. The KJV states truth concerning the completed canon of Scripture, but that was not complete when the apostle wrote to Timothy. The Scriptures are frequently personified by the NT writers (as by the Jews, John 7:42), (a) as speaking with divine authority, e.g., John 19:37; Rom. 4:3; 9:17, where the Scripture is said to speak to Pharaoh, giving the message actually sent previously by God to him through Moses; **Jas. 4:5**; (b) as possessed of the sentient quality of foresight, and the active power of preaching, Gal. 3:8, where the Scripture mentioned was written more than four centuries after the words were spoken. The Scripture, in such a case, stands for its divine Author with an intimation that it remains perpetually characterized as the living voice of God. This divine agency is again illustrated in Gal. 3:22 (cf. v. 10 and Matt. 11:13).

Vain *see James 1:26.*

Dwelleth *katoikizo* (2730), "to cause to dwell," is said of the act of God concerning the Holy Spirit in **Jas. 4:5**, RV (some mss. have *katoikeo*).

Lusteth *epipotheo* (1971), "to long for greatly" (a strengthened form of *potheo*, "to long for," not found in the NT), is translated "I long," in Rom. 1:11; in 2 Cor. 5:2, RV, "longing" (KJV, "earnestly desiring"); in 1 Thess. 3:6 and 2 Tim. 1:4, RV, "longing" (KJV, "desiring greatly"); to long after, in 2 Cor. 9:14; Phil. 1:8; 2:26; to long for, in 1 Pet. 2:2, RV (KJV, "desire"); **Jas. 4:5**, RV, "long."

Envy *phthonos* (5355), "envy," is the feeling of displeasure produced by witnessing or hearing of the advantage or prosperity of others; this evil sense always attaches to this word, Matt. 27:18; Mark 15:10; Rom. 1:29; Gal. 5:21; Phil. 1:15; 1 Tim. 6:4; Titus 3:3; 1 Pet. 2:1; so in **Jas. 4:5**, where the question is rhetorical and strongly remonstrative, signifying that the Spirit (or spirit) which God made to dwell in us was certainly not so bestowed that we should be guilty of "envy."

4:6 But he giveth more grace. Wherefore he saith, God resisteth the proud, but giveth grace unto the humble.

More In **Jas. 4:6**, KJV, the adjective *meizon*, "greater," is translated "more (grace)" (RV marg. "a greater grace").

Grace *see* **Greeting** at *James 1:1*.

Wherefore *see James 1:21*.

Resisteth *antitasso* (498), *anti*, "against," *tasso*, "to arrange," originally a military term, "to range in battle against," and frequently so found in the papyri, is used in the middle voice signifying "to set oneself against, resist," (a) of men, Acts 18:6, "opposed themselves"; elsewhere "to resist," of resisting human potentates, Rom. 13:2; (b) of God, **Jas. 4:6**; **5:6**, negatively, of leaving persistent evildoers to pursue their self-determined course, with eventual retribution; 1 Pet. 5:5.

Proud *huperephanos* (5244), signifies "showing oneself above others, preeminent" (*huper*, "above," *phainomai*, "to appear, be manifest"); it is always used in Scripture in the bad sense of "arrogant, disdainful, proud," Luke 1:51; Rom. 1:30; 2 Tim. 3:2; **Jas. 4:6**; 1 Pet. 5:5.

Humble *see* **Low degree** at *James 1:9*.

4:7 Submit yourselves therefore to God. Resist the devil, and he will flee from you.

Submit *hupotasso* (5293), primarily a military term, "to rank under" (*hupo*, "under," *tasso*, "to arrange"), denotes (a) "to put in subjection, to subject," Rom. 8:20 (twice); in the following, the RV, has to subject for KJV, "to put under," 1 Cor. 15:27 (thrice), 28 (3rd clause); Eph. 1:22; Heb. 2:8 (4th clause); in 1 Cor. 15:28 (1st clause), for KJV "be subdued"; in Phil. 3:21, for KJV, "subdue"; in Heb. 2:5, KJV, "hath ... put in subjection"; (b) in the middle or passive voice, to subject oneself, to obey, be subject to, Luke 2:51; 10:17, 20; Rom. 8:7; 10:3, RV, "did (not) subject themselves" [KJV, "have (not) submitted themselves"]; 13:1, 5; 1 Cor. 14:34, RV, "be in subjection" (KJV, "be under obedience"); 15:28 (2nd clause); 16:16 RV, "be in subjection" (KJV, "submit, etc."); so Col. 3:18; Eph. 5:21, RV, "subjecting yourselves" (KJV, "submitting, etc."); v. 22, RV in italics, according to the best texts; v. 24, "is subject"; Titus 2:5, 9, RV, "be in subjection" (KJV, "be obedient"); 3:1, RV, "to be in subjection" (KJV, "to be subject"); Heb. 12:9, "be in subjection"; **Jas. 4:7**, RV, "be subject" (KJV, "submit yourselves"); so 1 Pet. 2:13; v. 18, RV, "be in subjection"; so 3:1, KJV and RV; v. 5, similarly; 3:22, "being made subject"; 5:5, RV, "be subject" (KJV, "submit yourselves"); in some texts in the 2nd part, as KJV.

Resist *anthistemi* (436), "to set against" (*anti*, "against," *histemi*, "to cause to stand"), used in the middle (or passive) voice and in the intransitive 2nd aorist and perfect active, signifying "to withstand, oppose, resist," is translated "to resist" in Matt. 5:39; Acts 6:10, KJV (RV, withstand); Rom. 9:19, KJV (RV, "withstandeth"); 13:2 (2nd and 3rd parts), KJV (RV, "withstandeth" and "withstand"); Gal. 2:11, RV (KJV, "withstood"); 2 Tim. 3:8 (2nd part), KJV (RV, "withstand"); **Jas. 4:7**; 1 Pet. 5:9, KJV (RV, "withstand"); "to withstand" in Acts 13:8; Eph. 6:13; 2 Tim. 3:8 (1st part); 4:15.

Devil *diabolos* (1228), "an accuser, a slanderer" (from *diaballo*, "to accuse, to malign"), is one of the names of Satan. From it the English word "Devil" is derived, and should be applied only to Satan, as a proper name. *Daimon*, "a demon," is frequently, but wrongly, translated "devil"; it should always be translated "demon," as in the RV margin. There is one "Devil," there are many demons. Being the malignant enemy of God and man, he accuses man to God, Job 1:6-11; 2:1-5; Rev. 12:9, 10, and God to man, Gen. 3. He afflicts men with physical sufferings, Acts 10:38. Being himself sinful, 1 John 3:8, he instigated man to sin, Gen. 3, and tempts man to do evil, Eph. 4:27; 6:11, encouraging him thereto by deception, Eph. 2:2. Death having been brought into the world by sin, the "Devil" had the power of death, but Christ through His own death, has triumphed over him, and will bring him to nought, Heb. 2:14; his power over death is intimated in his struggle with Michael over the body of Moses, Jude 9. Judas, who gave himself over to the "Devil," was so identified with him, that the Lord described him as such, John 6:70 (see 13:2). As the "Devil" raised himself in pride against God and fell under condemnation, so believers are warned against similar sin, 1 Tim. 3:6; for them he lays snares, v. 7, seeking to devour them as a roaring lion, 1 Pet. 5:8; those who fall into his snare may be recovered therefrom unto the will of God, 2 Tim. 2:26, "having been taken captive by him (i.e., by the 'Devil')"; "by the Lord's servant" is an alternative, which some regard as confirmed by the use of *zogreo* ("to catch alive") in Luke 5:10; but the general use is that of taking captive in the usual way. If believers resist he will flee from them, **Jas. 4:7**. His fury and malignity will be especially exercised at the end of the present age, Rev. 12:12. His doom is the lake of fire, Matt. 25:41; Rev. 20:10. The noun is applied to slanderers, false accusers, 1 Tim. 3:11; 2 Tim. 3:3; Titus 2:3.

4:8 Draw nigh to God, and he will draw nigh to you. Cleanse *your* hands, *ye* sinners; and purify *your* hearts, *ye* double minded.

Draw nigh *engizo* (1448), "to draw near, to approach," from *engus*, "near," is used (a) of place and position, literally and physically, Matt. 21:1; Mark 11:1; Luke 12:33; 15:25; figuratively, of drawing near to God, Matt. 15:8; Heb. 7:19; **Jas. 4:8**; (b) of time, with reference to things that are imminent, as the kingdom of heaven, Matt. 3:2; 4:17; 10:7; the kingdom of God, Mark 1:15; Luke 10:9, 11; the time of fruit, Matt. 21:34; the desolation of Jerusalem, Luke 21:8; redemption, 21:28; the fulfillment of a promise, Acts 7:17; the Day of Christ in contrast to the present night of the world's spiritual darkness, Rom. 13:12; Heb. 10:25; the coming of the Lord, **Jas. 5:8**; the end of all things, 1 Pet. 4:7. It is also said of one who was drawing near to death, Phil. 2:30.

Cleanse *katharizo* (2511), signifies (1) "to make clean, to cleanse" (a) from physical stains and dirt, as in the case of utensils, Matt. 23:25 (figuratively in verse 26); from disease, as of leprosy, Matt. 8:2; (b) in a moral sense, from the defilement of sin, Acts 15:9; 2 Cor. 7:1; Heb. 9:14; **Jas. 4:8**, "cleanse" from the guilt of sin, Eph. 5:26; 1 John 1:7; (2) "to pronounce clean in a Levitical sense," Mark 7:19, RV; Acts 10:15; 11:9; "to consecrate by cleansings," Heb. 9:22, 23; 10:2.

Purify *hagnizo* (48), akin to *hagnos*, "pure", "to purify, cleanse from defilement," is used of "purifying" (a) ceremonially, John 11:55; Acts 21:24, 26; 24:18; (b) morally, the heart, **Jas. 4:8**; the soul, 1 Pet. 1:22; oneself, 1 John 3:3.

Double minded *see James 1:8.*

4:9 Be afflicted, and mourn, and weep: let your laughter be turned to mourning, and *your* joy to heaviness.

Afflicted *talaiporia* (5004), "hardship, suffering, distress" (akin to *talaiporos*, "wretched," Rom. 7:24; Rev. 3:17, and to *talaiporeo*, in the middle voice, "to afflict oneself," in **Jas. 4:9**, "be afflicted"), is used as an abstract noun, "misery," in Rom. 3:16; as a concrete noun, "miseries," in **Jas. 5:1**.

Mourn *pentheo* (3996), "to mourn for, lament," is used (a) of mourning in general, Matt. 5:4; 9:15; Luke 6:25; (b) of sorrow for the death of a loved one, Mark 16:10; (c) of "mourning" for the overthrow of Babylon and the Babylonish system, Rev. 18:11, 15, RV, "mourning" (KJV, "wailing"); v. 19 (ditto); (d) of sorrow for sin or for condoning it, **Jas. 4:9**; 1 Cor. 5:2; (e) of grief for those in a local church who show no repentance for evil committed, 2 Cor. 12:21, RV, "mourn" (KJV, "bewail").

Weep *klaio* (2799), is used of "any loud expression of grief," especially in mourning for the dead, Matt. 2:18; Mark 5:38, 39; 16:10; Luke 7:13; 8:52 (twice); John 11:31, 33 (twice); 20:11 (twice), 13, 15; Acts 9:39; otherwise, e.g., in exhortations, Luke 23:28; Rom. 12:15; **Jas. 4:9; 5:1**; negatively, "weep not," Luke 7:13; 8:52; 23:28; Rev. 5:5 (cf. Acts 21:13); in 18:9, RV, "shall weep" (KJV, "bewail").

Laughter *gelos* (1071), denotes "laughter," **Jas. 4:9**. This corresponds to the kind of "laughter" mentioned above.

Turned *metastrepho* (3344), signifies, in the passive voice, "to be turned" (of a change into something different, *meta*) in Acts 2:20 and **Jas. 4:9**.

Mourning *penthos* (3997), "mourning," is used in **Jas. 4:9**; Rev. 18:7 (twice), RV, "mourning" (KJV, "sorrow"); v. 8, "mourning"; 21:4, RV, "mourning" (KJV, "sorrow").

Heaviness *katepheia* (2726), probably denotes a downcast look, expressive of sorrow; hence, "dejection, heaviness"; it is used in **Jas. 4:9**.

4:10 Humble yourselves in the sight of the Lord, and he shall lift you up.

Humble *tapeinoo* (5013), signifies "to make low," (a) literally, "of mountains and hills," Luke 3:5 (passive voice); (b) metaphorically, in the active voice, Matt. 18:4; 23:12 (2nd part); Luke 14:11 (2nd part); 18:14 (2nd part); 2 Cor. 11:7 ("abasing"); 12:21; Phil. 2:8; in the passive voice, Matt. 23:12 (1st part), RV, "shall be humbled," KJV, "shall be abased"; Luke 14:11 (ditto); 18:14 (ditto); Phil. 4:12, "to be abased"; in the passive, with middle voice sense, **Jas. 4:10**, "humble yourselves"; 1 Pet. 5:6 (ditto).

In the sight of *enopion* (1799), from *en*, "in," and *ops*, "the eye," is the neuter of the adjective *enopios*, and is used prepositionally, (a) of place, that which is before or opposite a person, "towards which he turns his eyes," e.g., Luke 1:19; Acts 4:10; 6:6; Rev. 1:4; 4-10; 7:15; (b) in metaphorical phrases after verbs of motion, Luke 1:17; 12:9; Acts 9:15, etc.; signifying "in the mind or soul of persons," Luke 12:6; Acts 10:31; Rev. 16:19; (c) "in one's sight or hearing," Luke 24:43; John 20:30; 1 Tim. 6:12; metaphorically, Rom. 14:22; especially in Gal. 1:20; 1 Tim. 5:21; 6:13; 2 Tim. 2:14; 4:1; before, as "having a person present to the mind," Acts 2:25; **Jas. 4:10**; "in the judgment of a person," Luke 16:15; 24:11, RV, "in their sight," for KJV, "to"; Acts 4:19; Rom. 3:20; 12:17; 2 Cor. 8:21; 1 Tim. 2:3; "in the approving sight of God," Luke 1:75; Acts 7:46; 10:33; 2 Cor. 4:2; 7:12.

Lord *see* ***James 1:1.***

Lift *hupsoo* (5312), "to lift or raise up" (akin to *hupsos*, "height"), is rendered by the verb "to lift up" in John 3:14, of the brazen serpent; of Christ in crucifixion (*id.*), and 8:28; 12:32, 34; metaphorically, "to exalt, lift up," e.g., **Jas. 4:10**, KJV, "shall lift ... up," RV, "shall exalt."

4:11 Speak not evil one of another, brethren. He that speaketh evil of *his* brother, and judgeth his brother, speaketh evil of the law, and judgeth the law: but if thou judge the law, thou art not a doer of the law, but a judge.

Speak ... evil, Speaketh evil The verb *katalaleo* the RV translates "speak against," in its five occurrences, **Jas. 4:11** (three times); 1 Pet. 2:12, and 3:16; v, "speak evil," in all the passages except 1 Pet. 2:12.

Judgeth *see* **Judges** at ***James 2:4.***

Law *see* ***James 1:25.***

Doer *see* **Doers** at ***James 1:22.***

4:12 There is one lawgiver, who is able to save and to destroy: who art thou that judgest another?

One In Mark 2:7, KJV, *heis*, "one" (so RV), is translated "only"; in **Jas. 4:12**, RV, "one only" (KJV, "one").

Lawgiver *nomothetes* (3550), "a lawgiver," occurs in **Jas. 4:12**, of God, as the sole "Lawgiver"; therefore, to criticize the Law is to presume to take His place, with the presumption of enacting a better law.

Destroy *apollumi* (622), a strengthened form of *ollumi*, signifies "to destroy utterly"; in middle voice, "to perish." The idea is not extinction but ruin, loss, not of being, but of wellbeing. This is clear from its use, as, e.g., of the marring of wine skins, Luke 5:37; of lost sheep, i.e., lost to the shepherd, metaphorical of spiritual destitution, Luke 15:4, 6, etc.; the lost son, 15:24; of the perishing of food, John 6:27; of gold, 1 Pet. 1:7. So of persons, Matt. 2:13, "destroy"; 8:25, "perish"; 22:7; 27:20; of the loss of well-being in the case of the unsaved hereafter, Matt. 10:28; Luke 13:3, 5; John 3:16 (v. 15 in some mss.); 10:28; 17:12; Rom. 2:12; 1 Cor. 15:18; 2 Cor. 2:15, "are perishing"; 4:3; 2 Thess. 2:10; **Jas. 4:12**; 2 Pet. 3:9.

Judgest *see* **Judges** at ***James 2:4.***

Another *see* **Neighbour** at ***James 2:8.***

4:13 Go to now, ye that say, To day or to morrow we will go into such a city, and continue there a year, and buy and sell, and get gain:

To day *semeron* (4594), an adverb (the Attic form is *temeron*), akin to *hemera*, a day, with the prefix *t* originally representing a pronoun. It is used frequently in Matthew, Luke and Acts; in the last it is always rendered "this day"; also in Heb. 1:5, and the RV of 5:5 (KJV, "to day") in the same quotation; "today" in 3:7, 13, 15; 4:7 (twice); 13:8; also **Jas. 4:13**. The clause containing *semeron* is sometimes introduced by the conjunction *hoti*, "that," e.g., Mark 14:30; Luke 4:21; 19:9; sometimes without the conjunction, e.g., Luke 22:34; 23:43, where "today" is to be attached to the next statement, "shalt thou be with Me"; there are no grammatical reasons for the insistence that the connection must be with the statement "Verily I say unto thee," nor is such an idea necessitated by examples from either the Sept. or the NT; the connection given in the KJV and RV is right. In Rom. 11:8 and 2 Cor. 3:14, 15, the lit. rendering is "unto the today day," the emphasis being brought out by the RV, "unto (until) this very day." In Heb. 4:7, the "today" of Ps. 95:7 is evidently designed to extend to the present period of the Christian faith.

To morrow *aurion* (839), is used either without the article, e.g., Matt. 6:30; 1 Cor. 15:32; **Jas. 4:13**; or with the article in the feminine form, to agree with *hemera*, "day," e.g., Matt. 6:34; Acts 4:3, RV, "the morrow" (KJV, "next day"); **Jas. 4:14**; preceded by *epi*, "on," e.g., Luke 10:35; Acts 4:5.

Continue *poieo* (4160), "to do, make," is used of spending a time or tarrying, in a place, Acts 15:33; 20:3; in 2 Cor. 11:25 it is rendered "I have been (a night and a day)"; a preferable translation is "I have spent," as in **Jas. 4:13**, "spend a year" (RV). So in Matt. 20:12. Cf., the English idiom "did one hour"; in Rev. 13:5 "continue" is perhaps the best rendering.

Year *eniautos* (1763), originally "a cycle of time," is used (a) of a particular time marked by an event, e.g., Luke 4:19; John 11:49, 51; 18:13; Gal. 4:10; Rev. 9:15; (b) to mark a space of time, Acts 11:26; 18:11; **Jas. 4:13**; **5:17**; (c) of that which takes place every year, Heb. 9:7; with *kata*, Heb. 9:25; 10:1, 3.

Buy and sell *emporeuomai* (1710), primarily signifies "to travel," especially for business; then, "to traffic, trade," **Jas. 4:13**; then, "to make a gain of, make merchandise of," 2 Pet. 2:3.

Get gain *kerdaino* (2770), "to gain," is rendered "have gotten" in Acts 27:21, RV (of injury and loss); the word is there used metaphorically, however, of avoiding, or saving oneself from. For the meaning, "to get gain," **Jas. 4:13**.

4:14 Whereas ye know not what *shall be* on the morrow. For what *is* your life? It is even a vapour, that appeareth for a little time, and then vanisheth away.

Know *epistamai* (1987), "to know, know of, understand" (probably an old middle voice form of *ephistemi*, "to set over"), is used in Mark 14:68, "understand," which follows *oida* "I (neither) know"; most frequently in the Acts, 10:28; 15:7; 18:25; 19:15, 25; 20:18; 22:19; 24:10; 26:26; elsewhere, 1 Tim. 6:4; Heb. 11:8; **Jas. 4:14**; Jude 10.

What *poios*, "what sort of," e.g., Matt. 21:23, 24, 27; 24:42, 43; Luke 5:19; 6:32-34; 20:2, 8; 24:19; John 12:33, "what manner of"; so in 18:32; 21:19; Rom. 3:27; 1 Cor. 15:35; in **Jas. 4:14**, "what"; 1 Pet. 2:20 and Rev. 3:3 (ditto); 1 Pet. 1:11, "what manner of."

Morrow *see* **To morrow** at *James 4:13*.

Vapour *atmis* (822), is used of "smoke," Acts 2:19; figuratively of human life, **Jas. 4:14**.

Appeareth *phaino* (5316), signifies, in the active voice, "to shine"; in the passive, "to be brought forth into light, to become evident, to appear." In Rom. 7:13, concerning sin, the RV has "might be shewn to be," for KJV, "appear." It is used of the "appearance" of Christ to the disciples, Mark 16:9; of His future "appearing" in glory as the Son of Man, spoken of as a sign to the world, Matt. 24:30; there the genitive is subjective, the sign being the "appearing" of Christ Himself; of Christ as the light, John 1:5; of John the Baptist, 5:35; of the "appearing" of an angel of the Lord, either visibly, Matt. 1:20, or in a dream, 2:13; of a star, 2:7; of men who make an outward show, Matt. 6:5; 6:18 (see the RV); 23:27-28; 2 Cor. 13:7; of tares, Matt. 13:26; of a vapor, **Jas. 4:14**; of things physical in general, Heb. 11:3; used impersonally in Matt. 9:33, "it was never so seen"; also of what appears to the mind, and so in the sense of to think, Mark 14:64, or to seem, Luke 24:11 (RV, appeared).

Then *see James 3:17*.

Vanisheth *aphanizo* (853), "to render unseen," is translated "vanisheth away" in **Jas. 4:14** (passive voice, lit., "is made to disappear").

4:15 For that ye *ought* to say, If the Lord will, we shall live, and do this, or that.

Lord *see James 1:1*.

4:16 But now ye rejoice in your boastings: all such rejoicing is evil.

Rejoice *kauchesis* (2746), denotes "the act of boasting," Rom. 3:27; 15:17, RV, "(my) glorying" (KJV, "whereof I may glory"); 1 Cor. 15:31, RV, "glorying"; 2 Cor. 1:12 (ditto); 7:4, 14 (KJV, "boasting"); 8:24; 11:10, and 17 (ditto); 1 Thess. 2:19 (KJV, "rejoicing"); **Jas. 4:16** (ditto). The distinction between this and *kauchema* is to be observed in 2 Cor. 8:24, speaking of the apostle's act of "glorying" in the liberality of the Corinthians, while in 9:3 he exhorts them not to rob him of the ground of his "glorying". *See also James 1:9*.

Boastings *alazoneia*, or *-ia* (212), denotes "boastfulness, vaunting," translated "vainglory" in 1 John 2:16, RV (KlV, "pride"); in **Jas. 4:16**, RV, "vauntings" (KJV, "boastings"). Cf. *alazon*, "a boaster."

Rejoicing The nouns *kauchema, kauchesis*, signifying "glorying, boasting," are always so rendered in the RV, where the KJV has "rejoicing," the former in 2 Cor. 1:14; Gal. 6:4; Phil. 1:26; 2:16; Heb. 3:6; the latter in 1 Cor. 15:31; 2 Cor. 1:12; 1 Thess. 2:19; **Jas. 4:16**.

Evil *see James 2:4*.

4:17 Therefore to him that knoweth to do good, and doeth *it* not, to him it is sin.

Do good *kalopoieo* (2569), "to do well, excellently, act honorably" (*kalos*, "good," *poieo*, "to do"), occurs in 2 Thess. 3:13. The two parts of the word occur separately in Rom. 7:21; 2 Cor. 13:7; Gal. 6:9; **Jas. 4:17**.

Sin *see James 1:15*.

Chapter 5

5:1 Go to now, *ye* rich men, weep and howl for your miseries that shall come upon *you*.

Rich *see James 1:10*.

Weep *see James 4:9*.

Howl *ololuzo* (3649), an onomatopoeic verb (expressing its significance in its sound), "to cry aloud" (the Sept. uses it to translate the Heb. *ualal*, e.g., Isa. 13:6; 15:3; Jer. 4:8; Ezek. 21:12; Lat., *ululare*, and Eng., howl are akin) was primarily used of crying aloud to the gods; it is found in **Jas. 5:1** in an exhortation to the godless rich.

Miseries *see* Afflicted at *James 4:9*.

5:2 Your riches are corrupted, and your garments are motheaten.

Riches *ploutos* (4149), is used in the singular (I) of material "riches," used evilly, Matt. 13:22: Mark 4:19; Luke 8:14; 1 Tim. 6:17; **Jas. 5:2**; Rev. 18:17; (II) of spiritual and moral "riches," (a) possessed by God and exercised towards men, Rom. 2:4, "of His goodness and forbearance and longsuffering"; 9:23 and Eph. 3:16, "of His glory" (i.e., of its manifestation in grace towards believers); Rom. 11:33, of His wisdom and knowledge; Eph. 1:7 and 2:7, "of His grace"; 1:18, "of the glory of His inheritance in the saints"; 3:8, "of Christ"; Phil. 4:19, "in glory in Christ Jesus," RV; Col. 1:27, "of the glory of this mystery ... Christ in you, the hope of glory"; (b) to be ascribed to Christ, Rev. 5:12; (c) of the effects of the gospel upon the Gentiles, Rom. 11:12 (twice); (d) of the full assurance of understanding in regard to the mystery of God, even Christ, Col. 2:2, RV; (e) of the liberality of the churches of Macedonia, 2 Cor. 8:2 (where "the riches" stands for the spiritual and moral value of their liberality); (f) of "the reproach of Christ" in contrast to this world's treasures, Heb. 11:26.

> *"It is not the fact that a man has riches which keeps him from the kingdom of heaven, but the fact that riches have him."*
>
> JOHN CAIRD

Corrupted *sepo* (4595), signifies "to make corrupt, to destroy"; in the passive voice with middle sense, "to become corrupt or rotten, to perish," said of riches, **Jas. 5:2**, of the gold and silver of the luxurious rich who have ground down their laborers. The verb is derived from a root signifying "to rot off, drop to pieces."

Motheaten *setobrotos* (4598), from *ses*, "a moth," and *bibrosko*, "to eat," is used in **Jas. 5:2**. In the Sept. Job 13:28.

5:3 Your gold and silver is cankered; and the rust of them shall be a witness against you, and shall eat your flesh as it were fire. Ye have heaped treasure together for the last days.

Gold *chrusos* (5557), is used (a) of "coin," Matt. 10:9; **Jas. 5:3**; (b) of "ornaments," Matt. 23:16, 17; **Jas. 5:3** (perhaps both coin and ornaments); Rev. 18:12; some mss. have it in 1 Cor. 3:12; (c) of "images," Acts 17:29; (d) of "the metal in general," Matt. 2:11; Rev. 9:7 (some mss. have it in Rev. 18:16).

Silver *arguros* (696), akin to *argos*, "shining," denotes "silver." In each occurrence in the NT it follows the mention of gold, Matt. 10:9; Acts 17:29; **Jas. 5:3**; Rev. 18:12.

Cankered *katioo* (2728), an intensive form of *ioo*, "to poison," strengthened by *kata*, "down," "to rust over," and in the passive voice, "to become rusted over," occurs in **Jas. 5:3**, RV, "are rusted" (KJV, "are cankered"). Cf. *gangraina*, "a gangrene," 2 Tim. 2:17, RV.

Rust *ios* (2447), "poison," denotes "rust" in **Jas. 5:3**. *See also* **Poison** at *James 3:8*.

Witness *marturion* (3142), "a testimony, witness," is almost entirely translated "testimony" in both KJV and RV. The only place where both have "witness" is Acts 4:33. In Acts 7:44 and **Jas. 5:3**, the RV has "testimony" (KJV, "witness").

Flesh *sarx* (4561), has a wider range of meaning in the NT than in the OT. Its uses in the NT may be analyzed as follows: "(a) "the substance of the body," whether of beasts or of men, 1 Cor. 15:39; (b) "the human body," 2 Cor. 10:3a; Gal. 2:20; Phil. 1:22; (c) by synecdoche, of "mankind," in the totality of all that is essential to manhood, i.e., spirit, soul, and body, Matt. 24:22; John 1:13; Rom. 3:20; (d) by synecdoche, of "the holy humanity" of the Lord Jesus, in the totality of all that is essential to manhood, i.e., spirit, soul, and body John 1:14; 1 Tim. 3:16; 1 John 4:2; 2 John 7, in Heb. 5:7, "the days of His flesh," i.e., His past life on earth in distinction from His present life in resurrection; (e) by synecdoche, for "the complete person," John 6:51-57; 2 Cor. 7:5; **Jas. 5:3** ...

Fire *see James 3:6.*

Heaped *thesaurizo* (2343), "to lay up, store up" (akin to *thesauros*, "a treasury, a storehouse, a treasure"), is used of "laying" up treasures, on earth, Matt. 6:19; in Heaven, v. 20; in the last days, **Jas. 5:3**, RV, "ye have laid up your treasure" (KJV, "ye have heaped treasure together"); in Luke 12:21, "that layeth up treasure (for himself)"; in 1 Cor. 16:2, of money for needy ones (here the present participle is translated "in store," lit. "treasuring" or "storing," the "laying by" translating the preceding verb *tithemi*); in 2 Cor. 12:14, negatively, of children for parents; metaphorically, of "laying" up wrath, Rom. 2:5, "treasurest up." In 2 Pet. 3:7 the passive voice is used of the heavens and earth as "stored up" for fire, RV (marg., "stored" with fire), KJV, "kept in store."

Last *eschatos* (2078), "last, utmost, extreme," is used (a) of place, e.g., Luke 14:9, 10, "lowest;" Acts 1:8 and 13:47, "uttermost part;" (b) of rank, e.g., Mark 9:35; (c) of time, relating either to persons or things, e.g., Matt. 5:26, "the last (farthing)," RV (KJV, "uttermost"); Matt. 20:8, 12, 14; Mark 12:6, 22; 1 Cor. 4:9, of apostles as "last" in the program of a spectacular display; 1 Cor. 15:45, "the last Adam"; Rev. 2:19; of the "last" state of persons, Matt. 12:45, neuter plural, lit., "the last (things)"; so Luke 11:26; 2 Pet. 2:20, RV, "the last state" (KJV, "the latter end"); of Christ as the Eternal One, Rev. 1:17 (in some mss. v. 11); 2:8; 22:13; in eschatological phrases as follows: (a) "the last day," a comprehensive term including both the time of the resurrection of the redeemed, John 6:39, 40, 44, 54 and 11:24, and the ulterior time of the judgment of the unregenerate, at the Great White Throne, John 12:48; (b) "the last days," Acts 2:17, a period relative to the supernatural manifestation of the Holy Spirit at Pentecost and the resumption of the divine interpositions in the affairs of the world at the end of the present age, before "the great and notable Day of the Lord," which will usher in the messianic kingdom; (c) in 2 Tim. 3:1, "the last days" refers to the close of the present age of world conditions; (d) in **Jas. 5:3**, the phrase "in the last days" (RV) refers both to the period preceding the Roman overthrow of the city and the land in AD 70, and to the closing part of the age in consummating acts of gentile persecution including "the time of Jacob's trouble" (cf. verses **7**, **8**); (e) in 1 Pet. 1:5, "the last time" refers to the time of the Lord's second advent; (f) in 1 John 2:18, "the last hour" (RV) and, in Jude 18, "the last time" signify the present age previous to the Second Advent.

5:4 Behold, the hire of the labourers who have reaped down your fields, which is of you kept back by fraud, crieth: and the cries of them which have reaped are entered into the ears of the Lord of sabaoth.

Hire *misthos* (3408), denotes (a) "wages, hire," Matt. 20:8; Luke 10:7; **Jas. 5:4**; in 1 Tim. 5:18; 2 Pet. 2:13; Jude 11, RV, "hire" (KJV, "reward"); in 2 Pet. 2:15, RV, "hire" (KJV, "wages").

Labourers *ergates* (2040), akin to *ergazomai*, "to work," and *ergon*, "work," denotes (a) "a field laborer, a husbandman," Matt. 9:37, 38; 20:1, 2, 8; Luke 10:2 (twice); **Jas. 5:4**; (b) "a workman, laborer," in a general sense, Matt. 10:10; Luke 10:7; Acts 19:25; 1 Tim. 5:18; it is used (c) of false apostles and evil teachers, 2 Cor. 11:13; Phil. 3:2, (d) of a servant of Christ, 2 Tim. 2:15; (e) of evildoers, Luke 13:27.

Reaped down *amao* (270), "to mow," is translated "mowed" in **Jas. 5:4**, RV (KJV, "have reaped down"). "The cognate words seem to show that the sense of cutting or mowing was original, and that of gathering-in secondary" (Liddell and Scott, *Lex.*).

Fields *chora* (5561), (a) "a space, place," then, (b) "land, country, region," is translated "fields" in John 4:35; **Jas. 5:4**.

Fraud *aphustereo* (575 and 5302), "to keep back, deprive" (*apo*, "from," *hustereo*, "to be lacking"), is used in **Jas. 5:4**, "is kept back by fraud" (some mss. have *apostereo*, "to defraud"). The word is found in a papyrus writing of AD 42, of a bath insufficiently warmed (Moulton and Milligan, *Vocab.*). The Law required the prompt payment of the laborer, Deut. 24:15. *apostereo* (650), signifies "to rob, despoil, defraud," Mark 10:19; 1 Cor. 6:8; 7:5 (of that which is due to the condition of natural relationship of husband and wife); in the middle voice, "to allow oneself to be defrauded," 1 Cor. 6:7; in the passive voice, "bereft," 1 Tim. 6:5, RV, with reference to the truth, with the suggestion of being retributively "robbed" of the truth, through the corrupt condition of the mind. Some mss. have this verb in **Jas. 5:4** for *aphustereo*, "to keep back by fraud." In the Sept., Exod. 21:10; in some mss., Deut. 24:14.

Crieth *krazo* (2896), "to cry out," an onomatopoeic word, used especially of the "cry" of the raven; then, of any inarticulate cries, from fear, pain, etc.; of the "cry" of a Canaanitish woman, Matt. 15:22 (so the best mss., instead of *kraugazo*); of the shouts of the children in the Temple, Matt. 21:15; of the people who shouted for Christ to be crucified, 27:23; Mark 15:13-14; of the "cry" of Christ on the Cross at the close of His sufferings, Matt. 27:50; Mark 15:39. In John's Gospel it is used three times, out of the six, of Christ's utterances, 7:28, 37; 12:44. In the Acts it is not used of "cries" of distress, but chiefly of the shouts of opponents; in Revelation, chiefly of the utterances of heavenly beings concerning earthly matters; in Rom. 8:15 and Gal. 4:6, of the appeal of believers to God the Father; in Rom. 9:27, of a prophecy concerning Israel; in **Jas. 5:4**, metaphorically, of hire kept back by fraud.

Cries *boe* (995), especially "a cry for help," an onomatopoeic word (cf. Eng., "boo"), connected with *boao*, is found in **Jas. 5:4**.

Reaped *therizo* (2325), "to reap" (akin to *theros*, "summer, harvest"), is used (a) literally, Matt. 6:26; 25:24, 26; Luke 12:24; 19:21, 22; **Jas. 5:4** (2nd part), KJV, "have reaped"; (b) figuratively or in proverbial expressions, John 4:36 (twice), 37, 38, with immediate reference to bringing Samaritans into the kingdom of God, in regard to which the disciples would enjoy the fruits of what Christ Himself had been doing in Samaria; the Lord's words are, however, of a general application in respect of such service; in 1 Cor. 9:11, with reference to the right of the apostle and his fellow missionaries to receive material assistance from the church, a right which he forbore to exercise; in 2 Cor. 9:6 (twice), with reference to rendering material help to the needy, either "sparingly" or "bountifully," the "reaping" being proportionate to the sowing; in Gal. 6:7, 8 (twice), of "reaping" corruption, with special reference, according to the context, to that which is naturally shortlived transient (though the statement applies to every form of sowing to the flesh), and of "reaping" eternal life (characteristics and moral qualities being in view), as a result of sowing "to the Spirit," the reference probably being to the new nature of the believer, which is, however, under the controlling power of the Holy Spirit, v. 9, the "reaping" (the effect of well doing) being accomplished, to a limited extent, in this life, but in complete fulfillment at and beyond the judgment seat of Christ; diligence or laxity here will then produce proportionate results; in Rev. 14:15 (twice), 16, figurative of the discriminating judgment divinely to be fulfilled at the close of this age, when the wheat will be separated from the tares (see Matt. 13:30).

Ears *ous* (3775), Latin *auris*, is used (a) of the physical organ, e.g., Luke 4:21; Acts 7:57; in Acts 11:22, in the plural with *akouo*, "to hear," lit., "was heard into the ears of someone," i.e., came to the knowledge of, similarly, in the singular, Matt. 10:27, in familiar private conversation; in **Jas. 5:4** the phrase is used with *eiserchomai*, "to enter into"; in Luke 1:44, with *ginomai*, "to become, to come"; in Luke 12:3, with *lalein*, "to speak" and *pros*, "to", (b) metaphorically, of the faculty of perceiving with the mind, understanding and knowing, Matt. 13:16; frequently with *akouo*, "to hear," e.g., Matt. 11:15; 13:9, 43; Rev. 2 and 3, at the close of each of the messages to the churches, in Matt. 13:15 and Acts 28:27, with *bareos*, "heavily," of being slow to understand and obey; with a negative in Mark 8:18; Rom. 11:8; in Luke 9:44 the lit. meaning is "put those words into your ears," i.e., take them into your mind and keep them there, in Acts 7:51 it is used with *aperitmetos*, "uncircumcised." As seeing is metaphorically associated with conviction, so hearing is with obedience (*hupakoe*, lit., "hearing under"; the Eng., "obedience" is etymologically "hearing over against," i.e., with response in the hearer).

Lord *see* ***James 1:1***.

Sabaoth *sabaoth* (4519), is the transliteration of a Hebrew word which denotes "hosts" or "armies," Rom. 9:29; **Jas. 5:4**. While the word "hosts" probably had special reference to angels, the title "the LORD of hosts" became used to designate Him as the One who is supreme over all the innumerable hosts of spiritual agencies, or of what are described as "the armies of heaven." Eventually it was used as equivalent to "the LORD all-sovereign." In the prophetical books of the OT the Sept. sometimes has *Kurios Sabaoth* as the equivalent of "the LORD of hosts," sometimes *Kurios Pantokrator*, in Job, it uses *Pantokrator* to render the Hebrew divine title *Shadday*.

5:5 Ye have lived in pleasure on the earth, and been wanton; ye have nourished your hearts, as in a day of slaughter.

Pleasure *truphao* (5171), from *thrupto*, "to enervate," signifies "to lead a voluptuous life, to give oneself up to pleasure," **Jas. 5:5**, RV, "ye have lived delicately"; KJV, "ye have lived in pleasure."

Wanton *spatalao* (4684), "to live riotously," is translated "giveth herself to pleasure" in 1 Tim. 5:6, RV (KJV, "liveth in pleasure"); "taken your pleasure" in **Jas. 5:5**, KJV, "been wanton."

Nourished *trepho* (5142), "to rear, feed, nourish," is translated by the verb "to nourish" in **Jas. 5:5** (of luxurious living); Rev. 12:14 (of God's care for

Israel against its enemies); so v. 6, RV (KJV, feed); in Acts 12:20, RV, "was fed" (KJV, "was nourished").

Hearts *kardia* (2588), "the heart" (Eng., "cardiac," etc.), the chief organ of physical life ("for the life of the flesh is in the blood," Lev. 17:11), occupies the most important place in the human system. By an easy transition the word came to stand for man's entire mental and moral activity, both the rational and the emotional elements. In other words, the heart is used figuratively for the hidden springs of the personal life. "The Bible describes human depravity as in the 'heart,' because sin is a principle which has its seat in the center of man's inward life, and then 'defiles' the whole circuit of his action, Matt. 15:19, 20. On the other hand, Scripture regards the heart as the sphere of Divine influence, Rom. 2:15; Acts 15:9... The heart, as lying deep within, contains 'the hidden man,' 1 Pet. 3:4, the real man. It represents the true character but conceals it" (J. Laidlaw, in *Hastings' Bible Dic.*). As to its usage in the NT it denotes (a) the seat of physical life, Acts 14:17; **Jas. 5:5**; (b) the seat of moral nature and spiritual life, the seat of grief, John 14:1; Rom. 9:2; 2 Cor. 2:4; joy, John 16:22; Eph. 5:19; the desires, Matt. 5:28; 2 Pet. 2:14; the affections, Luke 24:32; Acts 21:13; the perceptions, John 12:40; Eph. 4:18; the thoughts, Matt. 9:4; Heb. 4:12; the understanding, Matt. 13:15; Rom. 1:21; the reasoning powers, Mark 2:6; Luke 24:38; the imagination, Luke 1:51; conscience, Acts 2:37; 1 John 3:20; the intentions, Heb. 4:12, cf. 1 Pet. 4:1; purpose, Acts 11:23; 2 Cor. 9:7; the will, Rom. 6:17; Col. 3:15; faith, Mark 11:23; Rom. 10:10; Heb. 3:12. The heart, in its moral significance in the OT, includes the emotions, the reason and the will.

Slaughter *sphage* (4967), is used in two quotations from the Sept., Acts 8:32 from Isa. 53:7, and Rom. 8:36 from Ps. 44:22; in the latter the quotation is set in a strain of triumph, the passage quoted being an utterance of sorrow. In **Jas. 5:5** there is an allusion to Jer. 12:3, the luxurious rich, getting wealth by injustice, spending it on their pleasures, are "fattening themselves like sheep unconscious of their doom."

5:6 Ye have condemned *and* killed the just; *and* he doth not resist you.

Condemned *katadikazo* (2613), signifies "to exercise right or law against anyone"; hence, "to pronounce judgment, to condemn" (*kata*, "down, or against," *dike*, "justice"), Matt. 12:7, 37; Luke 6:37; **Jas. 5:6**.

Killed *see* **Kill** at *James 2:11*.

Just *dikaios* (1342), signifies "just," without prejudice or partiality, e.g., of the judgment of God, 2 Thess. 1:5, 6; of His judgments, Rev. 16:7; 19:2; of His character as Judge, 2 Tim. 4:8; Rev. 16:5; of His ways and doings, Rev. 15:3. In the following the RV substitutes "righteous" for the KJV "just": Matt. 1:19; 13:49; 27:19, 24; Mark 6:20; Luke 2:25; 15:7; 20:20; 23:50; John 5:30; Acts 3:14; 7:52; 10:22; 22:14; Rom. 1:17; 7:12; Gal. 3:11; Heb. 10:38; **Jas. 5:6**; 1 Pet. 3:18; 2 Pet. 2:7; 1 John 1:9; Rev. 15:3.

Resist *see* **Resisteth** at *James 4:6*.

5:7 Be patient therefore, brethren, unto the coming of the Lord. Behold, the husbandman waiteth for the precious fruit of the earth, and hath long patience for it, until he receive the early and latter rain.

Patient, Patience *makrothumeo* (3114), "to be long-tempered," is translated "to have patience," or "to be patient," in Matt. 18:26, 29; 1 Thess. 5:14, KJV (RV, "be longsuffering"); **Jas. 5:7** (1st part, "be patient"; 2nd part, RV, "being patient," KJV, "hath long patience"); in Heb. 6:15, RV, "having (KJV, after he had) patiently endured"; so in **Jas. 5:7, 8**; in 2 Pet. 3:9, KJV and RV, "is longsuffering."

Coming *parousia* (3952), lit., "a presence," *para*, "with," and *ousia*, "being" (from *eimi*, "to be"), denotes both an "arrival" and a consequent "presence with." For instance, in a papyrus letter a lady speaks of the necessity of her parousia in a place in order to attend to matters relating to her property there. Paul speaks of his *parousia* in Philippi, Phil. 2:12 (in contrast to his *apousia*, "his absence"). Other words denote "the arrival." *Parousia* is used to describe the presence of Christ with His disciples on the Mount of Transfiguration, 2 Pet. 1:16. When used of the return of Christ, at the rapture of the church, it signifies, not merely His momentary "coming" for His saints, but His presence with them from that moment until His revelation and manifestation to the world. In some passages the word gives prominence to the beginning of that period, the course of the period being implied, 1 Cor. 15:23; 1 Thess. 4:15; 5:23; 2 Thess. 2:1; **Jas. 5:7-8**; 2 Pet. 3:4. In some, the course is prominent, Matt. 24:3, 37; 1 Thess. 3:13; 1 John 2:28; in others the conclusion of the period, Matt. 24:27; 2 Thess. 2:8. The word is also used of the Lawless One, the Man of Sin, his access to power and his doings in the world during his *parousia*, 2 Thess. 2:9. In addition to Phil. 2:12 (above), it is used in the same way of the apostle, or his companions, in 1 Cor. 16:17; 2 Cor. 7:6-7; 10:10; Phil. 1:26; of the Day of God, 2 Pet. 3:12.

Husbandman *georgos* (1092), from *ge*, "land, ground," and *ergo* (or *erdo*), "to do" (Eng., "George"), denotes (a) "a husbandman," a tiller of the ground, 2 Tim. 2:6; **Jas. 5:7**; (b) "a vinedresser," Matt. 21:33-35, 38, 40, 41; Mark 12:1, 2, 7, 9; Luke 20:9, 10, 14, 16; John 15:1, where Christ speaks of the Father as the "Husbandman," Himself as the Vine, His disciples as the branches, the object being to bear much fruit, life in Christ producing the fruit of the Spirit, i.e., character and ways in conformity to Christ.

Waiteth *ekdechomai* (1551), lit. and primarily, "to take or receive from" (*ek*, "from," *dechomai*, "to receive"), hence denotes "to await, expect," the only sense of the word in the NT; it suggests a reaching out in readiness to receive something; "expecting," Heb. 10:13; "expect," 1 Cor. 16:11, RV (KJV, "look for"); to wait for, John 5:3 (KJV only); Acts 17:16; 1 Cor. 11:33, RV (KJV, "tarry for"); **Jas. 5:7**; to wait, 1 Pet. 3:20 in some mss.; "looked for," Heb. 11:10.

Precious *timios* (5093), from *time*, "honor, price," signifies (a), primarily, "accounted as of great price, precious, costly," 1 Cor. 3:12; Rev. 17:4; 18:12, 16; 21:19, and in the superlative degree, 18:12; 21:11; the comparative degree is found in 1 Pet. 1:7 (*polutimoteros*, in the most authentic mss., "much more precious"); (b) in the metaphorical sense, "held in honor, esteemed, very dear," Acts 5:34, "had in honor," RV (KJV, "had in reputation"); so in Heb. 13:4, RV, "let marriage be had in honor"; KJV, "is honorable"; Acts 20:24, "dear," negatively of Paul's estimate of his life; **Jas. 5:7**, "precious" (of fruit); 1 Pet. 1:19, "precious" (of the blood of Christ); 2 Pet. 1:4 (of God's promises). Cf. *timiotes*, preciousness, Rev. 18:19.

Fruit *see James 3:18.*

Early *proimos* (4406), or *proimos*, a longer and later form of *proios*, pertaining to the "morning," is formed from *pro*, "before" (cf. *protos*, "first"), and used in **Jas. 5:7**, of the early rain.

Latter *opsimos* (3797), akin to *opse* and *opsios*, denotes "late," or "latter," and is used of "the latter rain" in **Jas. 5:7** (the most authentic mss. omit *huetos*, "rain"; some have *karpos*, "fruit"); this rain falls in March and April, just before the harvest, in contrast to the early rain, in October. In the Sept., Deut. 11:14; Prov. 16:15; Jer. 5:24; Hos. 6:3; Joel 2:23; Zech. 10:1. *See also* **Last** at *James 5:3.*

Rain *huetos* (5205), from *huo*, "to rain," is used especially, but not entirely, of "showers," and is found in Acts 14:17; 28:2; Heb. 6:7; **Jas. 5:7**; **5:18**; Rev. 11:6.

5:8 Be ye also patient; stablish your hearts: for the coming of the Lord draweth nigh.

Ye These are most frequently the translations of various inflections of a verb; sometimes of the article before a nominative used as a vocative, e.g., Rev. 18:20, "ye saints, and ye apostles, and ye prophets" (lit., "the saints, etc."). When the 2nd person plural pronouns are used separately from a verb, they are usually one or other of the forms of *humeis*, the plural of *su*, "thou," and are frequently emphatic, especially when they are subjects of the verb, an emphasis always to be noticed, e.g., Matt. 5:13, 14, 48; 6:9, 19, 20; Mark 6:31, 37; John 15:27a; Rom. 1:6; 1 Cor. 3:17, 23; Gal. 3:28, 29a; Eph. 1:13a; 2:8; 2:11, 13; Phil. 2:18; Col. 3:4, 7a; 4:1; 1 Thess. 1:6; 2:10, 19, 20; 3:8; 2 Thess. 3:13; **Jas. 5:8**; 1 Pet. 2:9a; 1 John 2:20, 24 (1st and 3rd occurrences), 27a; 4:4; Jude 17, 20.

Patient *see* **Patient, Patience** at *James 5:7.*

Stablish *sterizo* (4741), "to fix, make fast, to set" (from *sterix*, "a prop"), is used of "establishing" or "stablishing" (i.e., the confirmation) of persons; the apostle Peter was called by the Lord to "establish" his brethren, Luke 22:32, translated "strengthen"; Paul desired to visit Rome that the saints might be "established," Rom. 1:11; cf. Acts 8:23; so with Timothy at Thessalonica, 1 Thess. 3:2; the "confirmation" of the saints is the work of God, Rom. 16:25, "to stablish (you)"; 1 Thess. 3:13, "stablish (your hearts)"; 2 Thess. 2:17, "stablish them (in every good work and word)"; 1 Pet. 5:10, "stablish"; the means used to effect the "confirmation" is the ministry of the Word of God, 2 Pet. 1:12, "are established (in the truth which is with you)"; James exhorts Christians to "stablish" their hearts, **Jas. 5:8**; cf. Rev. 3:2, RV.

Coming *see* **Last** at *James 5:3.*

Nigh *engus* (1451), "near, nigh," frequently rendered "at hand," is used (a) of place, e.g., of the Lord's sepulchre, John 19:42, "nigh at hand"; (b) of time, e.g., Matt. 26:18; Luke 21:30, 31, RV, "nigh," KJV, "nigh at hand"; in Phil. 4:5, "the Lord is at hand," it is possible to regard the meaning as that either of (a) or (b); the following reasons may point to (b): (1) the subject of the preceding context has been the return of Christ, 3:20, 21; (2) the phrase is a translation of the Aramaic "Maranatha," 1 Cor. 16:22, a Christian watchword, and the use of the title "the Lord" is appropriate; (3) the similar use of the adverb in Rev. 1:3 and 22:10; (4) the similar use of the corresponding verb in Rom. 13:12; Heb. 10:25, "drawing nigh," RV; **Jas. 5:8**; cf. 1 Pet. 4:7. *See also* **Draw nigh** at *James 4:8*.

5:9 Grudge not one against another, brethren, lest ye be condemned: behold, the judge standeth before the door.

Grudge *stenazo* (4727), "to groan" (of an inward, unexpressed feeling of sorrow), is translated "with grief" in Heb. 13:17 (marg. "groaning"). It is rendered "sighed" in Mark 7:34; "groan," in Rom. 8:23; 2 Cor. 5:2, 4; "murmur," in **Jas. 5:9**, RV (KJV, "grudge").

Condemned *krino* (2919), "to distinguish, choose, give an opinion upon, judge," sometimes denotes "to condemn," e.g., Acts 13:27; Rom. 2:27; **Jas. 5:9** (in the best mss.). *katakrino* (2632), a strengthened form, signifies "to give judgment against, pass sentence upon"; hence, "to condemn," implying (a) the fact of a crime, e.g., Rom. 2:1; 14:23; 2 Pet. 2:6; some mss. have it in **Jas. 5:9**; (b) the imputation of a crime, as in the "condemnation" of Christ by the Jews, Matt. 20:18; Mark 14:64. It is used metaphorically of "condemning" by a good example, Matt. 12:41-42; Luke 11:31-32; Heb. 11:7. In Rom. 8:3, God's "condemnation" of sin is set forth in that Christ, His own Son, sent by Him to partake of human nature (sin apart) and to become an offering for sin, died under the judgment due to our sin.

Judge *see* **Judges** at *James 2:4*.

Door *thura* (2374), "a door, gate" (Eng., "door" is connected), is used (a) literally, e.g., Matt. 6:6; 27:60; (b) metaphorically, of Christ, John 10:7, 9; of faith, by acceptance of the gospel, Acts 14:27; of "openings" for preaching and teaching the Word of God, 1 Cor. 16:9; 2 Cor. 2:12; Col. 4:3; Rev. 3:8; of "entrance" into the Kingdom of God, Matt. 25:10; Luke 13:24-25; of Christ's "entrance" into a repentant believer's heart, Rev. 3:20; of the nearness of Christ's second advent, Matt. 24:33; Mark 13:29; cf. **Jas. 5:9**; of "access" to behold visions relative to the purposes of God, Rev. 4:1.

5:10 Take, my brethren, the prophets, who have spoken in the name of the Lord, for an example of suffering affliction, and of patience.

Take *lambano* (2983), "to take, lay hold of," besides its literal sense, e.g., Matt. 5:40; 26:26, 27, is used metaphorically, of fear, in "taking" hold of people, Luke 7:16, RV (KJV, "came ... on"); of sin in "finding (occasion)," RV (KJV, "taking"), Rom. 7:8, 11, where sin is viewed as the corrupt source of action, an inward element using the commandment to produce evil effects; of the power of temptation, 1 Cor. 10:13; of "taking" an example, **Jas. 5:10**; of "taking" peace from the earth, Rev. 6:4; of Christ in "taking" the form of a servant, Phil. 2:7; of "taking" rightful power (by the Lord, hereafter), Rev. 11:17.

Lord *see James 1:1*.

Example *hupodeigma* (5262), lit., "that which is shown" (from *hupo*, "under," and *deiknumi*, "to show"), hence, (a) "a figure, copy," Heb. 8:5, RV, "copy," for KJV, "example"; 9:23; (b) "an example," whether for imitation, John 13:15; **Jas. 5:10**, or for warning, Heb. 4:11; 2 Pet. 2:6, RV, example.

Affliction *kakopatheia* (2552), from *kakos*, "evil," and *pascho*, "to suffer" is rendered "suffering" in **Jas. 5:10**, RV (KJV, "suffering affliction"). In Sept., Mal. 1:13.

Patience *makrothumia* (3115), "forbearance, patience, longsuffering" (*makros*, "long," *thumos*, "temper"), is usually rendered "longsuffering," Rom. 2:4; 9:22; 2 Cor. 6:6; Gal. 5:22; Eph. 4:2; Col. 1:11; 3:12; 1 Tim. 1:16; 2 Tim. 3:10; 4:2; 1 Pet. 3:20; 2 Pet. 3:15; "patience" in Heb. 6:12 and **Jas. 5:10**.

5:11 Behold, we count them happy which endure. Ye have heard of the patience of Job, and have seen the end of the Lord; that the Lord is very pitiful, and of tender mercy.

Count ... happy *makarizo* (3106), "to call blessed," Luke 1:48, is rendered "we count ... happy" in **Jas. 5:11**.

Endure *see* **Endureth** at *James 1:12*.

End *telos* (5056), signifies (a) "the limit," either at which a person or thing ceases to be what he or it was up to that point, or at which previous activities were ceased, 2 Cor. 3:13; 1 Pet. 4:7; (b) "the final issue or result" of a state or process, e.g., Luke 1:33; in Rom. 10:4, Christ is described as "the end of the Law unto righteousness to everyone that believeth"; this is best explained by Gal. 3:23-26; cf. **Jas. 5:11**; the following more especially point to the issue or fate of a thing, Matt. 26:58; Rom. 6:21; 2 Cor. 11:15; Phil. 3:19; Heb. 6:8; 1 Pet. 1:9; (c) "a fulfillment," Luke 22:37, KJV, "(have) an end"; (d) "the utmost degree" of an act, as of the love of Christ towards His disciples, John 13:1; (e) "the aim or purpose" of a thing, 1 Tim. 1:5; (f) "the last" in a succession or series Rev. 1:8 (KJV, only, "ending"); 21:6; 22:13.

Lord *see James 1:1*.

Pitiful *polusplanchnos* (4184), denotes "very pitiful" or "full of pity" (*polus*, "much," *splanchnon*, "the heart"; in the plural, "the affections"), occurs in **Jas. 5:11**, RV, "full of pity."

Mercy *oiktirmon* (3629), "pitiful, compassionate for the ills of others," is used twice in Luke 6:36, "merciful" (of the character of God, to be expressed in His people); **Jas. 5:11**, RV, "merciful," KJV, "of tender mercy."

5:12 But above all things, my brethren, swear not, neither by heaven, neither by the earth, neither by any other oath: but let your yea be yea; and *your* nay, nay; lest ye fall into condemnation.

Swear *omnumi* or *omnuo* (3660), is used of "affirming or denying by an oath," e.g., Matt. 26:74; Mark 6:23; Luke 1:73; Heb. 3:11, 18; 4:3; 7:21; accompanied by that by which one swears, e.g., Matt. 5:34, 36; 23:16; Heb. 6:13, 16; **Jas. 5:12**; Rev. 10:6.

Oath *horkos* (3727), is primarily equivalent to *herkos*, "a fence, an enclosure, that which restrains a person"; hence, "an oath." The Lord's command in Matt. 5:33 was a condemnation of the minute and arbitrary restrictions imposed by the scribes and Pharisees in the matter of adjurations, by which God's Name was profaned. The injunction is repeated in **Jas. 5:12**. The language of the apostle Paul, e.g., in Gal. 1:20 and 1 Thess. 5:27 was not inconsistent with Christ's prohibition, read in the light of its context. Contrast the "oaths" mentioned in Matt. 14:7, 9; 26:72; Mark 6:26. Heb. 6:16 refers to the confirmation of a compact among men, guaranteeing the discharge of liabilities; in their disputes "the oath is final for confirmation." This is referred to in order to illustrate the greater subject of God's "oath" to Abraham, confirming His promise; cf. Luke 1:73; Acts 2:30. Cf. the verbs *horkizo*, and *exorkizo*.

Yea *nai* (3483), a particle of affirmation, is used (a) in answer to a question, Matt. 9:28; 11:9; 13:51; 17:25; 21:16; Luke 7:26; John 11:27; 21:15, 16; Acts 5:8; 22:27; Rom. 3:29; (b) in assent to an assertion, Matt. 15:27, RV (KJV, "truth"); Mark 7:28; Rev. 14:13; 16:7, RV (KJV, "even so"); (c) in confirmation of an assertion, Matt. 11:26 and Luke 10:21, RV (KJV, "even so"); Luke 11:51, RV (KJV, "verily"); 12:5; Phil. 4:3 (in the best texts); Philem. 20; (d) in solemn asseveration, Rev. 1:7 (KJV and RV, "even so"); 22:20, RV (KJV, "surely"); (e) in repetition for emphasis, Matt. 5:37; 2 Cor. 1:17; **Jas. 5:12**; (f) singly in contrast to *ou*, "nay," 2 Cor. 1:18, 19 (twice), 20, "(the) yea," RV.

Nay *ou* (3756), "no, not," expressing a negation absolutely, is rendered "nay," e.g., in Matt. 5:37; 13:29; John 7:12, KJV (RV, "not so"); Acts 16:37; 2 Cor. 1:17-19; **Jas. 5:12**.

Fall *pipto* (4098), "to fall," is used (a) of descent, to "fall" down from, e.g., Matt. 10:29; 13:4; (b) of a lot, Acts 1:26; (c) of "falling" under judgment, **Jas. 5:12** (cf. Rev. 18:2, RV); (d) of persons in the act of prostration, to prostrate oneself, e.g., Matt. 17:6; John 18:6; Rev. 1:17; in homage and worship, e.g., Matt. 2:11; Mark 5:22; Rev. 5:14; 19:4; (e) of things, "falling" into ruin, or failing, e.g., Matt. 7:25; Luke 16:17, RV, "fall," for KJV, "fail"; Heb. 11:30; (f), of "falling" in judgment upon persons, as of the sun's heat, Rev. 7:16, RV, "strike," KJV, "light"; of a mist and darkness, Acts 13:11 (some mss. have *epipipto*); (g) of persons, in "falling" morally or spiritually, Rom. 14:4; 1 Cor. 10:8, 12; Rev. 2:5.

Condemnation *see* **Judgment** at *James 2:13*.

5:13 Is any among you afflicted? let him pray. Is any merry? let him sing psalms.

Afflicted *kakopatheo* (2553), from *kakos*, "evil," *pathos*, "suffering," signifies "to suffer hardship." So the RV in 2 Tim. 2:9; and 4:5; in **Jas. 5:13**, "suffer" (KJV, "afflicted").

Merry *euthumeo* (2114), from *eu*, "well," and *thumos*, "the soul," as the principle of feeling, especially strong feeling, signifies "to make cheerful"; it is used intransitively in the NT, "to be of good cheer," Acts 27:22, 25; in **Jas. 5:13**, RV, "is (any) cheerful?" (KJV, "... merry?").

Sing psalms *psallo* (5567), primarily, "to twitch" or "twang" (as a bowstring, etc.), then, "to play" (a stringed instrument with the fingers), in the Sept., to sing psalms, denotes, in the NT, to sing a hymn, sing "praise"; in **Jas. 5:13**, RV, "sing praise" (KJV, "sing psalms").

5:14 Is any sick among you? let him call for the elders of the church; and let them pray over him, anointing him with oil in the name of the Lord:

Sick *astheneo* (770), lit., "to be weak, feeble" (*a*, negative, *sthenos*, "strength"), is translated "to be sick," e.g., in Matt. 10:8, "(the) sick"; 25:36; v. 39 in the best texts; Mark 6:56; Luke 4:40; 7:10 (RV omits the word); 9:2; John 4:46; 5:3, RV (KJV, "impotent folk"); v. 7; 6:2, RV (KJV, "were diseased"); 11:1-3, 6; Acts 9:37; 19:12; Phil. 2:26, 27; 2 Tim. 4:20; **Jas. 5:14**.

Call *proskaleo* (4341), signifies (a) "to call to oneself, to bid to come"; it is used only in the middle voice, e.g., Matt. 10:1; Acts 5:40; **Jas. 5:14**; (b)

"God's call to Gentiles through the gospel," Acts 2:39; (c) the divine call in entrusting men with the preaching of the gospel," Acts 13:2; 16:10.

Elders *presbuteros,* "an elder," is another term for the same person as bishop or overseer. See Acts 20:17 with verse 28. The term "elder" indicates the mature spiritual experience and understanding of those so described; the term "bishop," or "overseer," indicates the character of the work undertaken. According to the divine will and appointment, as in the NT, there were to be "bishops" in every local church, Acts 14:23; 20:17; Phil. 1:1; Titus 1:5; **Jas. 5:14**. Where the singular is used, the passage is describing what a "bishop" should be, 1 Tim. 3:2; Titus 1:7. Christ Himself is spoken of as "the ... Bishop of our souls," 1 Pet. 2:25.

Anointing *aleipho* (218), is a general term used for "an anointing" of any kind, whether of physical refreshment after washing, e.g., in the Sept. of Ruth 3:3; 2 Sam. 12:20; Dan. 10:3; Micah 6:15; in the NT, Matt. 6:17; Luke 7:38, 46; John 11:2; 12:3; or of the sick, Mark 6:13; **Jas. 5:14**; or a dead body, Mark 16:1. The material used was either oil, or ointment, as in Luke 7:38, 46. In the Sept. it is also used of "anointing" a pillar, Gen. 31:13, or captives, 2 Chron. 28:15, or of daubing a wall with mortar, Ezek. 13:10-12, 14-15; and, in the sacred sense, of "anointing" priests, in Exod. 40:15 (twice), and Num. 3:3.

Oil *elaion* (1637), "olive oil," is mentioned over 200 times in the Bible. Different kinds were known in Palestine. The "pure," RV (KJV, beaten), mentioned in Exod. 27:20; 29:40; Lev. 24:2; Num. 28:5 (now known as virgin oil), extracted by pressure, without heat, is called "golden" in Zech. 4:12. There were also inferior kinds. In the NT the uses mentioned were (a) for lamps, in which the "oil" is a symbol of the Holy Spirit, Matt. 25:3-4, 8; (b) as a medicinal agent, for healing, Luke 10:34; (c) for anointing at feasts, Luke 7:46; (d) on festive occasions, Heb. 1:9, where the reference is probably to the consecration of kings; (e) as an accompaniment of miraculous power, Mark 6:13, or of the prayer of faith, **Jas. 5:14**. For its general use in commerce, see Luke 16:6; Rev. 6:6; 18:13.

Name *see James 2:7.*

5:15 And the prayer of faith shall save the sick, and the Lord shall raise him up; and if he have committed sins, they shall be forgiven him.

Prayer *euche* (2171), denotes "a prayer," **Jas. 5:15**; "a vow," Acts 18:18 and 21:23.

Save *see James 1:21.*

Sick *kamno* (2577), primarily, "to work," hence, from the effect of constant work, "to be weary," Heb. 12:3, is rendered "(him) that is sick," in **Jas. 5:15**, RV, KJV "(the) sick." The choice of this verb instead of the repetition of *astheneo* (v. **14**), is suggestive of the common accompaniment of "sickness," weariness of mind (which is the meaning of this verb), which not infrequently hinders physical recovery; hence this special cause is here intimated in the general idea of "sickness." In some mss. it occurs in Rev. 2:3. In the Sept., Job 10:1; 17:2. *See also James 5:14.*

Lord *see James 1:1.*

Raise *egeiro* (1453), is frequently used in the NT in the sense of "raising" (active voice), or "rising" (middle and passive voices): (a) from sitting, lying, sickness, e.g., Matt. 2:14; 9:5, 7, 19; **Jas. 5:15**; Rev. 11:1; (b) of causing to appear, or, in the passive, appearing, or raising up so as to occupy a place in the midst of people, Matt. 3:9; 11:11; Mark 13:22; Acts 13:22. It is thus said of Christ in Acts 13:23; (c) of rousing, stirring up, or "rising" against, Matt. 24:7; Mark 13:8; (d) of "raising buildings," John 2:19-20; (e) of "raising or rising" from the dead; (1) of Christ, Matt. 16:21; and frequently elsewhere (but not in Phil., 2 Thess., 1 Tim., Titus, Jas., 2 Pet., 1, 2, 3 John, and Jude); (2) of Christ's "raising" the dead, Matt. 11:5; Mark 5:41; Luke 7:14; John 12:1, 9, 17; (3) of the act of the disciples, Matt. 10:8; (4) of the resurrection of believers, Matt. 27:52; John 5:21; 1 Cor. 15:15-16, 29, 32, 35, 42-44 52; 2 Cor. 1:9; 4:14; of unbelievers, Matt. 12:42. *Egeiro* stands in contrast to *anistemi* (when used with reference to resurrection) in this respect, that *egeiro* is frequently used both in the transitive sense of "raising up" and the intransitive of "rising," whereas *anistemi* is comparatively infrequent in the transitive use.

Committed *poieo* (4160), "to do, cause, etc.," sometimes signifies "to commit, of any act, as of murder," Mark 15:7; sin, John 8:34; 2 Cor. 11:7; **Jas. 5:15**.

Sins *see* **Sin** at *James 1:15.*

Forgiven *aphiemi* (863), primarily, "to send forth, send away" (*apo,* "from," *hiemi,* "to send"), denotes, besides its other meanings, "to remit or forgive" (a) debts, Matt. 6:12; 18:27, 32, these being completely cancelled; (b) sins, e.g., Matt. 9:2, 5, 6; 12:31, 32; Acts 8:22 ("the thought of thine heart"); Rom. 4:7; **Jas. 5:15**; 1 John 1:9; 2:12. In this latter respect the verb, like its corresponding noun (below), firstly signifies the remission of the punishment due to sinful conduct, the deliverance of the sinner from the penalty divinely, and therefore righteously, imposed; secondly, it involves the complete removal of the cause of offense; such remission is based upon the vicarious and propitiatory sacrifice of Christ. In the OT atoning sacrifice and "forgiveness" are often associated, e.g., Lev. 4:20, 26. The verb is used in the NT with reference to trespasses (*paraptoma*), e.g., Matt. 6:14, 15; sins (*hamartia*), e.g., Luke 5:20; debts (*opheilema*), Matt. 6:12; (*opheile*), 18:32; (*daneion*), 18:27; the thought (*dianoia*) of the heart, Acts 8:22. Cf. *kalupto*, "to cover," 1 Pet. 4:8; **Jas. 5:20**; and *epikalupto*, "to cover over," Rom. 4:7, representing the Hebrew words for "atonement." Human "forgiveness" is to be strictly analogous to divine "forgiveness," e.g., Matt. 6:12. If certain conditions are fulfilled, there is no limitation to Christ's law of "forgiveness," Matt. 18:21, 22. The conditions are repentance and confession, Matt. 18:15-17; Luke 17:3. As to limits to the possibility of divine "forgiveness," see Matt. 12:32, 2nd part and 1 John 5:16.

5:16 Confess *your* faults one to another, and pray one for another, that ye may be healed. The effectual fervent prayer of a righteous man availeth much.

Confess *exomologeo* (1843), is used (a) "of a public acknowledgment or confession of sins," Matt. 3:6; Mark 1:5; Acts 19:18; **Jas. 5:16**; (b) "to profess or acknowledge openly," Matt. 11:25 (translated "thank," but indicating the fuller idea); Phil. 2:11 (some mss. have it in Rev. 3:5); (c) "to confess by way of celebrating, giving praise," Rom. 14:11; 15:9. In Luke 10:21, it is translated "I thank," the true meaning being "I gladly acknowledge." In Luke 22:6 it signifies to consent (RV), for KJV, "promised."

Faults *paraptoma* (3900), "a false step, a trespass," translated "fault" in Gal. 6:1, KJV, and "faults" in **Jas. 5:16**, KJV.

Pray *euchomai* (2172), "to pray (to God)," is used with this meaning in 2 Cor. 13:7; v. 9, RV, "pray" (KJV, "wish"); **Jas. 5:16**; 3 John 2, RV, "pray" (KJV, wish). Even when the RV and KJV translate by "I would," Acts 26:29, or "wished for," Acts 27:29 (RV, marg., "prayed"), or "could wish," Rom. 9:3 (RV, marg., "could pray"), the indication is that "prayer" is involved. *See also* **Ask** at *James 1:5*.

Healed *iaomai* (4390), "to heal," is used (a) of physical treatment 22 times; in Matt. 5:28, KJV, "made whole," RV, "healed"; so in Acts 9:34; (b) figuratively, of spiritual "healing," Matt. 13:15; John 12:40; Acts 28:27; Heb. 12:13; 1 Pet. 2:24; possibly, **Jas. 5:16** includes both (a) and (b); some mss. have the word, with sense (b), in Luke 4:18. Apart from this last, Luke, the physician, uses the word fifteen times.

Effectual *energeo* (1754), "to put forth power, be operative, to work" (its usual meaning), is rendered by the verb "to work effectually," or "to be effectual," in the KJV of 2 Cor. 1:6; Gal. 2:8 and 1 Thess. 2:13; in each case the RV translates it by the simple verb "to work" (past tense, "wrought"). In **Jas. 5:16** the RV omits the superfluous word "effectual," and translates the sentence "the supplication of a righteous man availeth much in its working," the verb being in the present participial form. Here the meaning may be "in its inworking," i.e., in the effect produced in the praying man, bringing him into line with the will of God, as in the case of Elijah.

Fervent In **Jas. 5:17**, "he prayed fervently" (KJV, "earnestly") translates the noun *proseuche*, followed by the corresponding verb, lit., "he prayed with prayer." In v. **16** *deesis*, "supplication," is so translated in the RV, for the KJV, "effectual fervent prayer." There is nothing in the original corresponding to the word "effectual." The phrase, including the verb *energeomai*, "to work in," is, lit., "the inworking supplication," suggesting a supplication consistent with inward conformity to the mind of God.

Prayer *deesis* (1162), primarily "a wanting, a need," then, "an asking, entreaty, supplication," in the NT is always addressed to God and always rendered "supplication" or "supplications" in the RV; in the KJV "prayer," or "prayers," in Luke 1:13; 2:37; 5:33; Rom. 10:1; 2 Cor. 1:11; 9:14; Phil. 1:4 (in the 2nd part, "request"); 1:19; 2 Tim. 1:3; Heb. 5:7; **Jas. 5:16**; 1 Pet. 3:12.

Availeth *ischuo* (2480), signifies (a) "to be strong in body, to be robust, in sound health," Matt. 9:12; Mark 2:17; (b) "to have power," as of the gospel, Acts 19:20; to prevail against, said of spiritual enemies, Rev. 12:8; of an evil spirit against exorcists, Acts 19:16; (c) "to be of force, to be effective, capable of producing results," Matt. 5:13 ("it is good for nothing"; lit., "it availeth nothing"); Gal. 5:6; in Heb. 9:17 it apparently has the meaning "to be valid" (RV, "for doth it ever avail ...?", for KJV, "it is of no strength"). It is translated "avail" with reference to prayer, in **Jas. 5:16**; cf. the strengthened form *exischuo* in Eph. 3:18.

Much *polus* (4183), is used (a) as an adjective of degree, e.g., Matt. 13:5, "much (earth)"; Acts 26:24, "much (learning)"; in v. 29, in the answer to Agrippa's "with but little persuasion," some texts have *pollo* (some *megalo*, "with great"), RV, "(whether with little or) with much"; of number, e.g., Mark 5:24, RV, "a great (multitude)," KJV, "much (people)"; so Luke 7:11; John 12:12; Rev. 19:1, etc.; (b) in the neuter singular form (*polu*), as a noun, e.g., Luke 16:10 (twice); in the plural (*polla*), e.g., Rom. 16:6, 12, "(labored) much," lit., "many things"; (c) adverbially, in the neuter singular, e.g., Acts 18:27; **James 5:16**; Matt. 26:9 (a genitive of price); in the plural, e.g., Mark 5:43, RV, "much" (KJV, "straitly"); Mark 9:26, RV, "much" (KJV, "sore"); John 14:30; and with the article, Acts 26:24; Rom. 15:22; 1 Cor. 16:19; Rev. 5:4.

5:17 Elias was a man subject to like passions as we are, and he prayed earnestly that it might not rain: and it rained not on the earth by the space of three years and six months.

Passions *homoiopathes* (3663), "of like feelings or affections" (Eng., "homeopathy"), is rendered "of like passions" in Acts 14:15 (RV marg., "nature"); in **Jas. 5:17**, RV, ditto (KJV, "subject to like passions").

Prayed *proseuche* (4335), denotes (a) "prayer" (to God), the most frequent term, e.g., Matt. 21:22; Luke 6:12, where the phrase is not to be taken literally as if it meant, "the prayer of God" (subjective genitive), but objectively, "prayer to God." In **Jas. 5:17**, "He prayed fervently," RV, is, lit., "he prayed with prayer" (a Hebraistic form); in the following the word is used with *deesis*, (primarily "a wanting, a need" ... then, "an asking, entreaty, supplication" Eph. 6:18; Phil. 4:6; 1 Tim. 2:1; 5:5; (b) "a place of prayer," Acts 16:13, 16, a place outside the city wall, RV.

Earnestly *see* **Fervent** at *James 5:16.*

Might "May," "might," sometimes translate the prepositional phrase *eis*, "unto," with the definite article, followed by the infinitive mood of some verb, expressing purpose, e.g., Acts 3:19, "may be blotted out," lit., "unto the blotting out of"; Rom. 3:26, "that he might be," lit., "unto his being"; so 8:29; 2 Cor. 1:4, "that we may be able," lit., "unto our being able"; Eph. 1:18, "that ye may know," lit., "unto your knowing"; Acts 7:19; Rom. 1:11; 4:16; 12:2; 15:13; Phil. 1:10; 1 Thess. 3:10, 13; 2 Thess. 1:5; 2:6, 10; Heb. 12:10. In Luke 20:20 the best mss. have *hoste*, "so as to," RV, as, e.g., in 1 Pet. 1:21. Sometimes the article with the infinitive mood without a preceding preposition, expresses result, e.g., Luke 21:22; Acts 26:18 (twice), "that they may turn," RV; cf. Rom. 6:6; 11:10; 1 Cor. 10:13; Phil. 3:10, "that I may know"; **Jas. 5:17**.

Rain, Rained *brecho* (1026), signifies (a) "to wet," Luke 7:38, 44, RV (KJV, to wash); (b) "to send rain," Matt. 5:45; to rain, Luke 17:29 (of fire and brimstone); **Jas. 5:17**, used impersonally (twice); Rev. 11:6, where *huetos* is used as the subject, lit., "(that) rain rain (not)."

Space In **Jas. 5:17** there is no word in the original representing the phrase "by the space of," KJV (RV, "for").

Years *see* **Year** at *James 4:13.*

Six *hex* (1803), whence Eng. prefix, "hex"-, is used separately from other numerals in Matt. 17:1; Mark 9:2; Luke 4:25; 13:14; John 2:6; 12:1; Acts 11:12; 18:11; **Jas. 5:17**; Rev. 4:8. It sometimes suggests incompleteness, in comparison with the perfect number seven.

"We talk about heaven being so far away. It is within speaking distance to those who belong there."

D. L. MOODY

Months *men* (3376), connected with *mene*, "the moon," akin to a Sanskrit root *ma-*, "to measure" (the Sanskrit *masa* denotes both moon and month, cf, e.g., Lat. *mensis*, Eng., "moon" and "month," the moon being in early times the measure of the "month"). The interval between the 17th day of the second "month" (Gen. 7:11) and the 17th day of the seventh "month," is said to be 150 days (8:3, 4), i.e., five months of 30 days each; hence the year would be 360 days (cf. Dan. 7:25; 9:27; 12:7 with Rev. 11:2-3; 12:6, 14; 13:5; whence we conclude that 3 ½ years or 42 months = 1260 days, i.e., one year = 60 days); this was the length of the old Egyptian year; later, five days were added to correspond to the solar year. The Hebrew year was as nearly solar as was compatible with its commencement, coinciding with the new moon, or first day of the "month." This was a regular feast day, Num. 10:10; 28:11-14; the Passover coincided with the full moon (the 14th of the month Abib). Except in Gal. 4:10; **Jas. 5:17**; Rev. 9:5, 10, 15; 11:2; 13:5; 22:2, the word is found only in Luke's writings, Luke 1:24, 26, 36, 56; 4:25; Acts 7:20; 18:11; 19:8; 20:3; 28:11, examples of Luke's care as to accuracy of detail.

5:18 And he prayed again, and the heaven gave rain, and the earth brought forth her fruit.

Heaven *ouranos* (3772), probably akin to *ornumi*, "to lift, to heave," is used in the NT (a) of "the aerial heavens," e.g., Matt. 6:26; 8:20; Acts 10:12; 11:6 (RV, "heaven," in each place, KJV, "air"); **Jas. 5:18**; (b) "the sidereal," e.g., Matt. 24:29, 35; Mark 13:25, 31; Heb. 11:12, RV, "heaven," KJV, "sky"; Rev. 6:14; 20:11; they, (a) and (b), were created by the Son of God, Heb. 1:10, as also by God the Father, Rev. 10:6; (c) "the eternal dwelling place of God," Matt. 5:16; 12 :50; Rev. 3:12; 11:13; 16:11; 20:9. From thence the Son of God descended to become incarnate, John 3:13, 31; 6:38, 42. In His ascension Christ "passed through the heavens," Heb. 4:14, RV; He "ascended far above all the heavens," Eph. 4:10, and was "made higher than the heavens," Heb. 7:26; He "sat down on the right hand of the throne of the Majesty in the heavens," Heb. 8:1; He is "on the right hand of God," having gone into heaven, 1 Pet. 3:22. Since His ascension it is the scene of His present life and activity, e.g., Rom. 8:34; Heb. 9:24. From thence the Holy Spirit descended at Pentecost, 1 Pet. 1:12. It is the abode of the angels, e.g., Matt. 18:10; 22:30; cf. Rev. 3:5. Thither Paul was "caught up," whether in the body or out of the body, he knew not, 2 Cor. 12:2. It is to be the eternal dwelling place of the saints in resurrection glory, 2 Cor. 5:1. From thence Christ will descend to the air to receive His saints at the Rapture, 1 Thess. 4:16; Phil. 3:20, 21, and will subsequently come with His saints and with His holy angels at His second advent, Matt. 24:30; 2 Thess. 1:7. In the present life "heaven" is the region of the spiritual citizenship of believers, Phil. 3:20. The present "heavens," with the earth, are to pass away, 2 Pet. 3:10, "being on fire," v. 12 (see v. 7); Rev. 20:11, and new "heavens" and earth are to be created, 2 Pet. 3:13; Rev. 21:1, with Isa. 65:17, e.g. In Luke 15:18, 21, "heaven" is used, by metonymy, for God.

Rain *see* **James** *5:7*. *See also* **Rain, Rained** at *James 5:17*.

Brought *blastano* (985), "to bud, spring up," translated "brought forth" (i.e., "caused to produce"), in **Jas. 5:18**.

Fruit *see James 3:18*.

5:19 Brethren, if any of you do err from the truth, and one convert him;

Err *see James 1:16*.

Convert *epistrepho* (1994), "to turn about, turn towards" (*epi*, "towards" and *strepho*, "to turn"), is used transitively, and so rendered "convert" (of causing a person to turn) in **Jas. 5:19-20**. Elsewhere, where the KJV translates this verb, either in the middle voice and intransitive use, or the passive, the RV adheres to the middle voice significance, and translates by "turn again," Matt. 13:15; Mark 4:12; Luke 22:32; Acts 3:19; 28:27.

5:20 Let him know, that he which converteth the sinner from the error of his way shall save a soul from death, and shall hide a multitude of sins.

Converteth *see* **Convert** at *James 5:19*.

Error *plane* (4106), akin to *planao*, "a wandering, a forsaking of the right path," see **Jas. 5:20**, whether in doctrine, 2 Pet. 3:17; 1 John 4:6, or in morals, Rom. 1:27; 2 Pet. 2:18; Jude 11, though, in Scripture, doctrine and morals are never divided by any sharp line. See also Matt. 27:64, where it is equivalent to 'fraud.'" "Errors" in doctrine are not infrequently the effect of relaxed morality, and vice versa. In Eph. 4:14 the RV has "wiles of error," for KJV, "they lie in wait to deceive"; in 1 Thess. 2:3, RV, "error," for KJV, "deceit"; in 2 Thess. 2:11, RV, "a working of error," for KJV, "strong delusion." Cf. *planetes*, "a wandering," Jude 13, and the adjective *planos*, "leading astray, deceiving, a deceiver."

Soul *see* **Souls** at *James 1:21*.

Hide *kalupto* (2572), signifies "to cover, conceal," so that no trace of it can be seen: it is not translated "to hide" in the RV; in 2 Cor. 4:3 it is rendered "veiled," suitably continuing the subject of 3:13-18; in **Jas. 5:20**, "shall hide," KJV (RV, "shall cover"). *See also* **Forgiven** at *James 5:15*.

Multitude *plethos* (4128), lit., "a fullness," hence, "a large company, a multitude," is used (a) of things: of fish, Luke 5:6; John 21:6; of sticks ("bundle"), Acts 28:3; of stars and of sand, Heb. 11:12; of sins, **Jas. 5:20**; 1 Pet. 4:8; (b) of persons, (1) a "multitude": of people, e.g., Mark 3:7, 8; Luke 6:17; John 5:3; Acts 14:1; of angels, Luke 2:13; (2) with the article, the whole number, the "multitude," the populace, e.g., Luke 1:10; 8:37; Acts 5:16; 19:9; 23:7; a particular company, e.g., of disciples, Luke 19:37; Acts 4:32; 6:2, 5; 15:30; of elders, priests, and scribes, 23:7; of the apostles and the elders of the Church in Jerusalem, Acts 15:12.

Sins *see* **Sin** at *James 1:15*.

1 Peter

Chapter 1

1:1 Peter, an apostle of Jesus Christ, to the strangers scattered throughout Pontus, Galatia, Cappadocia, Asia, and Bithynia,

Strangers *parepidemos* (3927), an adjective signifying "sojourning in a strange place, away from one's own people" (*para*, "from," expressing a contrary condition, and *epidemeo*, "to sojourn"; *demos*, "a people"), is used of OT saints, Heb. 11:13, "pilgrims" (coupled with *xenos*, "a foreigner"); of Christians, **1 Pet. 1:1**, "sojourners (of the Dispersion)," RV; **2:11**, "pilgrims" (coupled with *paroikos*, "an alien, sojourner"); the word is thus used metaphorically of those to whom Heaven is their own country, and who are sojourners on earth.

Scattered *diaspora* (1290), "a scattering, a dispersion," was used of the Jews who from time to time had been scattered among the Gentiles, John 7:35; later with reference to Jews, so "scattered," who had professed, or actually embraced, the Christian faith, "the Dispersion," Jas. 1:1, RV; especially of believers who were converts from Judaism and "scattered" throughout certain districts, "sojourners of the Dispersion," **1 Pet. 1:1**, RV. In the Sept., of Israelites, "scattered" and exiled, e.g., Deut. 28:25; 30:4; Neh. 1:9.

1:2 Elect according to the foreknowledge of God the Father, through sanctification of the Spirit, unto obedience and sprinkling of the blood of Jesus Christ: Grace unto you, and peace, be multiplied.

Foreknowledge *prognosis* (4268), "a foreknowledge," is used only of divine "foreknowledge," Acts 2:23; **1 Pet. 1:2**. "Foreknowledge" is one aspect of omniscience; it is implied in God's warnings, promises and predictions. See Acts 15:18. God's "foreknowledge" involves His electing grace, but this does not preclude human will. He "foreknows" the exercise of faith which brings salvation. The apostle Paul stresses especially the actual purposes of God rather than the ground of the purposes, see, e.g., Gal. 1:16; Eph. 1:5, 11. The divine counsels will ever be unthwartable.

Sanctification *hagiasmos* (38), translated "holiness" in the KJV of Rom. 6:19, 22; 1 Thess. 4:7; 1 Tim. 2:15; Heb. 12:14, is always rendered "sanctification" in the RV. It signifies (a) separation to God, 1 Cor. 1:30; 2 Thess. 2:13; **1 Pet. 1:2**; (b) the resultant state, the conduct befitting those so separated, 1 Thess. 4:3, 4, 7, and the four other places mentioned above. "Sanctification" is thus the state predetermined by God for believers, into which in grace He calls them, and in which they begin their Christian course and so pursue it. Hence they are called "saints" (*hagioi*).

Spirit The "Holy Spirit" is spoken of under various titles in the NT ("Spirit" and "Ghost" are renderings of the same word, *pneuma;* the advantage of the rendering "Spirit" is that it can always be used, whereas "Ghost" always requires the word "Holy" prefixed.) In the following list the omission of the definite article marks its omission in the original (concerning this see below): "Spirit, Matt. 22:43; Eternal Spirit, Heb. 9:14; the Spirit, Matt. 4:1; Holy Spirit, Matt. 1:18; the Holy Spirit, Matt. 28:19; the Spirit, the Holy, Matt. 12:32; the Spirit of promise, the Holy, Eph. 1:13; Spirit of God, Rom. 8:9; Spirit of (the) living God, 2 Cor. 3:3; the Spirit of God, 1 Cor. 2:11; the Spirit of our God, 1 Cor. 6:11; the Spirit of God, the Holy, Eph. 4:30; the Spirit of glory and of God, **1 Pet. 4:14**; the Spirit of Him that raised up Jesus from the dead (i.e., God), Rom. 8:11; the Spirit of your Father, Matt. 10:20; the Spirit of His Son, Gal. 4:6; Spirit of (the) Lord, Acts 8:39; the Spirit of (the) Lord, Acts 5:9; (the) Lord, (the) Spirit, 2 Cor. 3:18; the Spirit of Jesus, Acts 16:7; Spirit of Christ, Rom. 8:9; the Spirit of Jesus

Christ, Phil. 1:19; Spirit of adoption, Rom. 8:15; the Spirit of truth, John 14:17; the Spirit of life, Rom. 8:2; the Spirit of grace, Heb. 10:29."

The use or absence of the article in the original where the "Holy Spirit" is spoken of cannot always be decided by grammatical rules, nor can the presence or absence of the article alone determine whether the reference is to the "Holy Spirit." Examples where the Person is meant when the article is absent are Matt. 22:43 (the article is used in Mark 12:36); Acts 4:25, RV (absent in some texts); 19:2, 6; Rom. 14:17; 1 Cor. 2:4; Gal. 5:25 (twice); **1 Pet. 1:2**. Sometimes the absence is to be accounted for by the fact that *Pneuma* (like *Theos*) is substantially a proper name, e.g., in John 7:39. As a general rule the article is present where the subject of the teaching is the Personality of the Holy Spirit, e.g., John 14:26, where He is spoken of in distinction from the Father and the Son ...

Obedience *hupakoe* (5218), "obedience" (*hupo*, "under," *akouo*, "to hear"), is used (a) in general, Rom. 6:16 (1st part), RV, "(unto) obedience," KJV, "(to) obey"; here "obedience" is not personified, as in the next part of the verse, "servants ... of obedience" [see (c)], but is simply shown to be the effect of the presentation mentioned; (b) of the fulfillment of apostolic counsels, 2 Cor. 7:15; 10:6; Philem. 21; (c) of the fulfillment of God's claims or commands, Rom. 1:5 and 16:26, "obedience of faith," which grammatically might be objective, to the faith (marg.), or subjective, as in the text. Since faith is one of the main subjects of the Epistle, and is the initial act of obedience in the new life, as well as an essential characteristic thereof, the text rendering is to be preferred; Rom. 6:16 (2nd part); 15:18, RV "(for) the obedience," KJV, "(to make) obedient"; 16:19; **1 Pet. 1:2, 14**, RV, "(children of) obedience," i.e., characterized by "obedience," KJV, "obedient (children)"; v. **22**, RV, "obedience (to the truth)," KJV, "obeying (the truth)"; (d) of "obedience" to Christ (objective), 2 Cor. 10:5; (e) of Christ's "obedience," Rom. 5:19 (referring to His death; cf. Phil. 2:8); Heb. 5:8, which refers to His delighted experience in constant "obedience" to the Father's will (not to be understood in the sense that He learned to obey).

Sprinkling *rhantismos* (4473), "sprinkling," is used of the "sprinkling" of the blood of Christ, in Heb. 12:24 and **1 Pet. 1:2**, an allusion to the use of the blood of sacrifices, appointed for Israel, typical of the sacrifice of Christ.

Multiplied *plethuno* (4129), used (a) transitively, denotes "to cause to increase, to multiply," 2 Cor. 9:10; Heb. 6:14 (twice); in the passive voice, "to be multiplied," Matt. 24:12, RV, "(iniquity) shall be multiplied" (KJV, "shall abound"); Acts 6:7; 7:17; 9:31; 12:24; **1 Pet. 1:2**; 2 Pet. 1:2; Jude 2; (b) intransitively it denotes "to be multiplying," Acts 6:1, RV, "was multiplying" (KJV, "was multiplied").

1:3 Blessed *be* the God and Father of our Lord Jesus Christ, which according to his abundant mercy hath begotten us again unto a lively hope by the resurrection of Jesus Christ from the dead,

Blessed *eulogetos* (2128), means "blessed, praised"; it is applied only to God, Mark 14:61; Luke 1:68; Rom. 1:25; 9:5; 2 Cor. 1:3; 11:31; Eph. 1:3; **1 Pet. 1:3**. In the Sept. it is also applied to man, e.g., in Gen. 24:31; 26:29; Deut. 7:14; Judg. 17:2; Ruth 2:20; 1 Sam. 15:13.

Father *pater* (3962), from a root signifying "a nourisher, protector, upholder" (Lat., *pater*, Eng., "father," are akin), is used (a) of the nearest ancestor, e.g., Matt. 2:22; (b) of a more remote ancestor, the progenitor of the people, a "forefather," e.g., Matt. 3:9; 23:30; 1 Cor. 10:1; the patriarchs, 2 Pet. 3:4; (c) one advanced in the knowledge of Christ, 1 John 2:13; (d) metaphorically, of the originator of a family or company of persons animated by the same spirit as himself, as of Abraham, Rom. 4:11, 12, 16, 17, 18, or of Satan, John 8:38, 41, 44; (e) of one who, as a preacher of the gospel and a teacher, stands in a "father's" place, caring for his spiritual children, 1 Cor. 4:15 (not the same as a mere title of honor, which the Lord prohibited, Matt. 23:9); (f) of the members of the Sanhedrin, as of those who exercised religious authority over others, Acts 7:2; 22:1; (g) of God in relation to those who have been born anew (John 1:12, 13), and so are believers, Eph. 2:18; 4:6 (cf. 2 Cor. 6:18), and imitators of their "Father," Matt. 5:45, 48; 6:1, 4, 6, 8, 9, etc. Christ never associated Himself with them by using the personal pronoun "our"; He always used the singular, "My Father," His relationship being unoriginated and essential, whereas theirs is by grace and regeneration, e.g., Matt. 11:27; 25:34; John 20:17; Rev. 2:27; 3:5, 21; so the apostles spoke of God as the "Father" of the Lord Jesus Christ, e.g., Rom. 15:6; 2 Cor. 1:3; 11:31; Eph. 1:3; Heb. 1:5; **1 Pet. 1:3**; Rev. 1:6; (h) of God, as the "Father" of lights, i.e., the Source or Giver of whatsoever provides illumination, physical and spiritual, Jas. 1:17; of mercies, 2 Cor. 1:3; of glory, Eph. 1:17; (i) of God, as Creator, Heb. 12:9 (cf. Zech. 12:1).

Abundant *polus* (4183), "much, many, great," is used of number, e.g., Luke 5:6; Acts 11:21; degree, e.g., of harvest, Matt. 9:37 [See *Note* (8)]; mercy, **1 Pet. 1:3**, RV "great" (KJV, "abundant"); glory, Matt. 24:30; joy, Philem. 7, RV, "much" (KJV, "great"); peace, Acts 24:2. The best mss. have it in Acts 8:8 (RV, "much"), of joy.

Begotten *anagennao* (313), is found in **1 Pet. 1:3, 23.**

Lively *zao* (2198), "to live, be alive," is used in the NT of "(a) God, Matt. 16:16; John 6:57; Rom. 14:11; (b) the Son in Incarnation, John 6:57; (c) the Son in Resurrection, John 14:19; Acts 1:3; Rom. 6:10; 2 Cor. 13:4; Heb. 7:8; (d) spiritual life, John 6:57; Rom. 1:17; 8:13b; Gal. 2:19, 20; Heb. 12:9; (e) the present state of departed saints, Luke 20:38; **1 Pet. 4:6**; (f) the hope of resurrection, **1 Pet. 1:3**; (g) the resurrection of believers, 1 Thess. 5:10; John 5:25; Rev. 20:4, and of unbelievers, v. 5, cf. v. 13; (h) the way of access to God through the Lord Jesus Christ, Heb. 10:20; (i) the manifestation of divine power in support of divine authority, 2 Cor. 13:4b; cf. 12:10, and 1 Cor. 5:5; (j) bread, figurative of the Lord Jesus, John 6:51; (k) a stone, figurative of the Lord Jesus, **1 Pet. 2:4**; (l) water, figurative of the Holy Spirit, John 4:10; 7:38; (m) a sacrifice, figurative of the believer, Rom. 12:1; (n) stones, figurative of the believer, **1 Pet. 2:5**; (o) the oracles, *logion*, Acts 7:38, and word, *logos*, Heb. 4:12; **1 Pet. 1:23**, of God; (p) the physical life of men, 1 Thess. 4:15; Matt. 27:63; Acts 25:24; Rom. 14:9; Phil. 1:21 (in the infinitive mood used as a noun with the article, 'living'), 22; **1 Pet. 4:5**; (q) the maintenance of physical life, Matt. 4:4; 1 Cor. 9:14; (r) the duration of physical life, Heb. 2:15; (s) the enjoyment of physical life, 1 Thess. 3:8; (t) the recovery of physical life from the power of disease, Mark 5:23; John 4:50; (u) the recovery of physical life from the power of death, Matt. 9:18; Acts 9:41; Rev. 20:5; (v) the course, conduct, and character of men, (1) good, Acts 26:5; 2 Tim. 3:12; Titus 2:12; (2) evil, Luke 15:13; Rom. 6:2; 8:13a; 2 Cor. 5:15b; Col. 3:7; (3) undefined, Rom. 7:9; 14:7; Gal. 2:14; (w) restoration after alienation, Luke 15:32."

Hope *elpis* (1680), in the NT, "favorable and confident expectation" (contrast the Sept. in Isa. 28:19, "an evil hope"). It has to do with the unseen and the future, Rom. 8:24, 25. "Hope" describes (a) the happy anticipation of good (the most frequent significance), e.g., Titus 1:2; **1 Pet. 1:21**; (b) the ground upon which "hope" is based, Acts 16:19; Col. 1:27, "Christ in you the hope of glory"; (c) the object upon which the "hope" is fixed, e.g., 1 Tim. 1:1. Various phrases are used with the word "hope," in Paul's epistles and speeches: (1) Acts 23:6, "the hope and resurrection of the dead"; this has been regarded as a hendiadys (one by means of two), i.e., the "hope" of the resurrection; but the *kai*, "and," is epexegetic, defining the "hope," namely, the resurrection; (2) Acts 26:6, 7, "the hope of the promise (i.e., the fulfillment of the promise) made unto the fathers"; (3) Gal. 5:5, "the hope of righteousness"; i.e., the believer's complete conformity to God's will, at the coming of Christ; (4) Col. 1:23, "the hope of the gospel," i.e., the "hope" of the fulfillment of all the promises presented in the gospel; cf. 1:5; (5) Rom. 5:2, "(the) hope of the glory of God," i.e., as in Titus 2:13, "the blessed hope and appearing of the glory of our great God and Savior Jesus Christ"; cf. Col. 1:27; (6) 1 Thess. 5:8, "the hope of salvation," i.e., of the rapture of believers, to take place at the opening of the Parousia of Christ; (7) Eph. 1:18, "the hope of His (God's) calling," i.e., the prospect before those who respond to His call in the gospel; (8) Eph. 4:4, "the hope of your calling," the same as (7), but regarded from the point of view of the called; (9) Titus 1:2, and 3:7, "the hope of eternal life," i.e., the full manifestation and realization of that life which is already the believer's possession; (10) Acts 28:20, "the hope of Israel," i.e., the expectation of the coming of the Messiah. In Eph. 1:18; 2:12 and 4:4, the "hope" is objective. The objective and subjective use of the word need to be distinguished, in Rom. 15:4, e.g., the use is subjective. In the NT three adjectives are descriptive of "hope": "good," 2 Thess. 2:16; "blessed," Titus 2:13; "living," **1 Pet. 1:3**. To these may be added Heb. 7:19, "a better hope," i.e., additional to the commandment, which became disannulled (v. 18), a hope centered in a new priesthood. In Rom. 15:13 God is spoken of as "the God of hope," i.e., He is the author, not the subject, of it. "Hope" is a factor in salvation, Rom. 8:24; it finds its expression in endurance under trial, which is the effect of waiting for the coming of Christ, 1 Thess. 1:3; it is "an anchor of the soul," staying it amidst the storms of this life, Heb. 6:18, 19; it is a purifying power, "every one that hath this hope set on Him (Christ) purifieth himself, even as He is pure," 1 John 3:3, RV (the apostle John's one mention of "hope"). The phrase "fullness of hope," Heb. 6:11, RV, expresses the completeness of its activity in the soul; cf. "fullness of faith," 10:22, and "of understanding," Col. 2:2 (RV, marg.).

Resurrection *anastasis* (386), denotes (I) "a raising up," or "rising" (*ana*, "up," and *histemi*, "to cause to stand"), Luke 2:34, "the rising up"; the KJV "again" obscures the meaning; the Child would be like a stone against which many in Israel would stumble while many others would find in its strength and firmness a means of their salvation and spiritual life; (II) of "resurrection" from the dead, (a) of Christ, Acts 1:22; 2:31; 4:33; Rom. 1:4; 6:5; Phil. 3:10; **1 Pet. 1:3**; **3:21**; by metonymy, of Christ as the Author of "resurrection," John 11:25; (b) of those who are Christ's at His Parousia, Luke 14:14, "the resurrection of the just"; Luke 20:33, 35, 36; John 5:29 (1st part), "the resurrection of life"; 11:24; Acts 23:6; 24:15 (1st part); 1 Cor. 15:21, 42; 2 Tim. 2:18; Heb. 11:35 (2nd part); Rev. 20:5, "the first resurrection"; hence the insertion of "is" stands for the completion of this "resurrection," of which Christ was "the firstfruits"; 20:6; (c) of "the rest of the dead," after the Millennium (cf. Rev. 20:5); John 5:29 (2nd part), "the resurrection of judgment"; Acts 24:15 (2nd part), "of the unjust"; (d) of those who were raised in more immediate connection with Christ's "resurrection," and thus had part already in the first "resurrection," Acts 26:23 and Rom. 1:4 (in each of which "dead" is plural; see Matt. 27:52); (e) of the "resurrection" spoken of in general terms, Matt. 22:23; Mark 12:18; Luke 20:27; Acts 4:2; 17:18; 23:8; 24:21; 1 Cor. 15:12, 13; Heb. 6:2; (f) of those who were raised in OT times, to die again, Heb. 11:35 (1st part), lit., "out of resurrection."

1:4 To an inheritance incorruptible, and undefiled, and that fadeth not away, reserved in heaven for you,

Inheritance *kleronomia* (2817), "a lot," properly "an inherited property, an inheritance." "It is always rendered inheritance in NT, but only in a few cases in the Gospels has it the meaning ordinarily attached to that word in English, i.e., that into possession of which the heir enters only on the death of an ancestor. The NT usage may be set out as follows: (a) that property in real estate which in ordinary course passes from father to son on the death of the former, Matt. 21:38; Mark 12:7; Luke 12:13; 20:14; (b) a portion of an estate made the substance of a gift, Acts 7:5; Gal. 3:18, which also is to be included under (c); (c) the prospective condition and possessions of the believer in the new order of things to be ushered in at the return of Christ, Acts 20:32; Eph. 1:14; 5:5; Col. 3:24; Heb. 9:15; **1 Pet. 1:4**; (d) what the believer will be to God in that age, Eph. 1:18."

Incorruptible *apthartos* (862), "not liable to corruption or decay, incorruptible," is used of (a) God, Rom. 1:23; 1 Tim. 1:17 (KJV, "immortal"); (b) the raised dead, 1 Cor. 15:52; (c) rewards given to the saints hereafter, metaphorically described as a "crown," 1 Cor. 9:25; (d) the eternal inheritance of the saints, **1 Pet. 1:4**; (e) the Word of God, as "incorruptible" seed, **1 Pet. 1:23**; (f) a meek and quiet spirit, metaphorically spoken of as "incorruptible" apparel, **1 Pet. 3:4**.

Undefiled *amiantos* (283), "undefiled, free from contamination" (*a*, negative, *miaino*, "to defile"), is used (a) of Christ, Heb. 7:26; (b) of pure religion, Jas. 1:27; (c) of the eternal inheritance of believers, **1 Pet. 1:4**; (d) of the marriage bed as requiring to be free from unlawful sexual intercourse, Heb. 13:4.

Fadeth not *amarantos* (263), "unfading," whence the "amaranth," an unfading flower, a symbol of perpetuity (see *Paradise Lost*, iii. 353), is used in **1 Pet. 1:4** of the believer's inheritance, "that fadeth not away." It is found in various writings in the language of the *Koine*, e.g., on a gladiator's tomb; and as a proper name (Moulton and Milligan, Vocab.).

Reserved *tereo* (5083), "to guard, keep, preserve, give heed to," is translated "to reserve," (a) with a happy issue, **1 Pet. 1:4**; (b) with a retributive issue, 2 Pet. 2:4; v. 9, KJV (RV, "keep"); 2:17; 3:7; Jude 6, KJV (RV, "hath kept"); v. 13; and referenced (c) the possibility either of deliverance or execution, Acts 25:21, KJV (RV, kept).

1:5 Who are kept by the power of God through faith unto salvation ready to be revealed in the last time.

Kept *phroureo* (5432), a military term, "to keep by guarding, to keep under guard," as with a garrison (*phrouros*, "a guard, or garrison"), is used, (a) of blocking up every way of escape, as in a siege; (b) of providing protection against the enemy, as a garrison does; see 2 Cor. 11:32, "guarded." KJV, "kept," i.e., kept the city, "with a garrison." It is used of the security of the Christian until the end, **1 Pet. 1:5**, RV, "are guarded," and of the sense of that security that is his when he puts all his matters into the hand of God, Phil. 4:7, RV, "shall guard." In these passages the idea is not merely that of protection, but of inward garrisoning as by the Holy Spirit; in Gal. 3:23 ("were kept in ward"), it means rather a benevolent custody and watchful guardianship in view of worldwide idolatry (cf. Isa. 5:2).

Salvation *soteria* (4991), denotes "deliverance, preservation, salvation." "Salvation" is used in the NT (a) of material and temporal deliverance from danger and apprehension, (1) national, Luke 1:69, 71; Acts 7:25, RV marg., "salvation" (text, "deliverance"); (2) personal, as from the sea, Acts 27:34; RV, "safety" (KJV, "health"); prison, Phil. 1:19; the flood, Heb. 11:7; (b) of the spiritual and eternal deliverance granted immediately by God to those who accept His conditions of repentance and faith in the Lord Jesus, in whom alone it is to be obtained, Acts 4:12, and upon confession of Him as Lord, Rom. 10:10; for this purpose the gospel is the saving instrument, Rom. 1:16; Eph. 1:13; (c) of the present experience of God's power to deliver from the bondage of sin, e.g., Phil. 2:12, where the special, though not the entire, reference is to the maintenance of peace and harmony; **1 Pet. 1:9**; this present experience on the part of believers is virtually equivalent to sanctification; for this purpose, God is able to make them wise, 2 Tim. 3:15; they are not to neglect it, Heb. 2:3; (d) of the future deliverance of believers at the Parousia of Christ for His saints, a salvation which is the object of their confident hope, e.g., Rom. 13:11; 1 Thess. 5:8, and v. 9, where "salvation" is assured to them, as being deliverance from the wrath of God destined to be executed upon the ungodly at the end of this age (see 1 Thess. 1:10); 2 Thess. 2:13; Heb. 1:14; 9:28; **1 Pet. 1:5**; 2 Pet. 3:15; (e) of the deliverance of the nation of Israel at the second advent of Christ at the time of "the epiphany (or shining forth) of His Parousia" (2 Thess. 2:8); Luke 1:71; Rev. 12:10; (f) inclusively, to sum up all the blessings bestowed by God on men in Christ through the Holy Spirit, e.g., 2 Cor. 6:2; Heb. 5:9; **1 Pet. 1:9, 10**; Jude 3; (g) occasionally, as standing virtually for the Savior, e.g., Luke 19:9; cf. John 4:22; (h) in ascriptions of praise to God, Rev. 7:10, and as that which it is His prerogative to bestow, 19:1 (RV).

Ready *hetoimos* (2092), "prepared, ready" (akin to *hetoimasia*, "preparation"), is used (a) of persons, Matt. 24:44; 25:10; Luke 12:40; 22:33; Acts 23:15, 21; Titus 3:1; **1 Pet. 3:15**; (b) of things, Matt. 22:4 (2nd part), 8; Mark 14:15, RV, "ready" (KJV, "prepared"); Luke 14:17; John 7:6; 2 Cor. 9:5; 10:16, RV, "things ready" (KJV, "things made ready"); **1 Pet. 1:5**.

Revealed *apokalupto* (601), signifies "to uncover, unveil" (*apo*, "from," *kalupto*, "to cover"); both verbs are used in Matt. 10:26; in Luke 12:2, *apokalupto* is set in contrast to *sunkalupto*, "to cover up, cover completely." "The NT occurrences of this word fall under two heads, subjective and objective. The subjective use is that in which something is presented to the mind directly, as, (a) the meaning of the acts of God, Matt. 11:25; Luke 10:21; (b) the secret of the Person of the Lord Jesus, Matt. 16:17; John 12:38; (c) the character of God as Father, Matt. 11:27; Luke 10:22; (d) the will of God for the conduct of His children, Phil. 3:15; (e) the mind of God to the prophets of Israel, **1 Pet. 1:12**, and of the Church, 1 Cor. 14:30; Eph. 3:5.

"The objective use is that in which something is presented to the senses, sight or hearing, as, referring to the past, (f) the truth declared to men in the gospel, Rom. 1:17; 1 Cor. 2:10; Gal. 3:23; (g) the Person of Christ to Paul on the way to Damascus, Gal. 1:16; (h) thoughts before hidden in the heart, Luke 2:35; referring to the future, (i) the coming in glory of the Lord Jesus, Luke 17:30; (j) the salvation and glory that await the believer, Rom. 8:18; **1 Pet. 1:5; 5:1**; (k) the true value of service, 1 Cor. 3:13; (l) the wrath of God (at the Cross, against sin, and, at the revelation of the Lord Jesus, against the sinner), Rom. 1:18; (m) the Lawless One, 2 Thess. 2:3, 6, 8.

Last *eschatos* (2078), "last, utmost, extreme," is used (a) of place, e.g., Luke 14:9, 10, "lowest;" Acts 1:8 and 13:47, "uttermost part;" (b) of rank, e.g., Mark 9:35; (c) of time, relating either to persons or things, e.g., Matt. 5:26, "the last (farthing)," RV (KJV, "uttermost"); Matt. 20:8, 12, 14; Mark 12:6, 22; 1 Cor. 4:9, of apostles as "last" in the program of a spectacular display; 1 Cor. 15:45, "the last Adam"; Rev. 2:19; of the "last" state of persons, Matt. 12:45, neuter plural, lit., "the last (things)"; so Luke 11:26; 2 Pet. 2:20, RV, "the last state" (KJV, "the latter end"); of Christ as the Eternal One, Rev. 1:17 (in some mss. v. 11); 2:8; 22:13; in eschatological phrases as follows: (a) "the last day," a comprehensive term including both the time of the resurrection of the redeemed, John 6:39, 40, 44, 54 and 11:24, and the ulterior time of the judgment of the unregenerate, at the Great White Throne, John 12:48; (b) "the last days," Acts 2:17, a period relative to the supernatural manifestation of the Holy Spirit at Pentecost and the resumption of the divine interpositions in the affairs of the world at the end of the present age, before "the great and notable Day of the Lord," which will usher in the messianic kingdom; (c) in 2 Tim. 3:1, "the last days" refers to the close of the present age of world conditions; (d) in Jas. 5:3, the phrase "in the last days" (RV) refers both to the period preceding the Roman overthrow of the city and the land in AD 70, and to the closing part of the age in consummating acts of gentile persecution including "the time of Jacob's trouble" (cf. verses 7, 8); (e) in **1 Pet. 1:5**, "the last time" refers to the time of the Lord's second advent; (f) in 1 John 2:18, "the last hour" (RV) and, in Jude 18, "the last time" signify the present age previous to the Second Advent.

1:6 Wherein ye greatly rejoice, though now for a season, if need be, ye are in heaviness through manifold temptations:

Rejoice *agalliao* (21), "to rejoice greatly, to exult," is used, (I) in the active voice, of "rejoicing" in God, Luke 1:47; in faith in Christ, **1 Pet. 1:8**, RV (middle voice in some mss.), "ye rejoice greatly"; in the event of the marriage of the Lamb, Rev. 19:7, "be exceeding glad," RV; (II) in the middle voice, (a) of "rejoicing" in persecutions, Matt. 5:12 (2nd part); in the light of testimony for God, John 5:35; in salvation received through the gospel, Acts 16:34, "he rejoiced greatly," RV; in salvation ready to be revealed, **1 Pet. 1:6**; at the revelation of His glory, **1 Pet. 4:13**, "with exeeding joy," lit., "ye may rejoice exulting"; (b) of Christ's "rejoicing" (greatly) "in the Holy Spirit," Luke 10:21, RV; said of His praise, as foretold in Ps. 16:9, quoted in Acts 2:26 (which follows the Sept., "My tongue"); (c) of Abraham's "rejoicing," by faith, to see Christ's day, John 8:56.

Now *arti* (737), expressing "coincidence," and denoting "strictly present time," signifies "just now, this moment," in contrast (a) to the past, e.g., Matt. 11:12; John 2:10; 9:19, 25; 13:33; Gal. 1:9-10; (b) to the future, e.g., John 13:37; 16:12, 31; 1 Cor. 13:12; 2 Thess. 2:7; **1 Pet. 1:6, 8**; (c) sometimes without necessary reference to either, e.g., Matt. 3:15; 9:18; 26:53; Gal. 4:20; Rev. 12:10.

Season *oligon* (3641), is used adverbially of (a) time, Mark 6:31, "a while;" **1 Pet. 1:6**, RV, "a little while (KJV, "a season"); **5:10**, RV, "a little while" (KJV, "a while"); Rev. 17:10, RV, "a little while" (KJV, "a short space"); (b) space, Mark 1:19; Luke 5:3; (c) extent, with the preposition *pros*, "for," in 1 Tim. 4:8, RV, "(for) a little" (KJV, and RV marg., "little"), where, while the phrase might refer to duration (as KJV marg.), yet the antithesis "for all things" clearly indicates extent, i.e., "physical training is profitable towards few objects in life."

Need *deon* (1163), is used as a noun, signifying "that which is needful, due, proper," in **1 Pet. 1:6**, with the meaning "need," "(if) need (be)," with the verb to be understood.

Heaviness *lupeo* (3076), "to distress, grieve," is rendered "are in heaviness" in **1 Pet. 1:6**, KJV (RV, "have been put to grief"); here, as frequently, it is in the passive voice.

Manifold *poikilos* (4164), "varied," is translated "manifold" in **1 Pet. 1:6**; **4:10** and in Jas. 1:2, RV (KJV, "divers").

Temptations *peirasmos* (3986), is used of (1) "trials" with a beneficial purpose and effect, (a) of "trials" or "temptations," divinely permitted or sent, Luke 22:28; Acts 20:19; Jas. 1:2; **1 Pet. 1:6**; **4:12**, RV, "to prove," KJV, "to try"; 2 Pet. 2:9 (singular); Rev. 3:10, RV, "trial" (KJV, "temptation"); in Jas. 1:12, "temptation" apparently has meanings (1) and (2) combined and is used in the widest sense; (b) with a good or neutral significance, Gal. 4:14, of Paul's physical infirmity, "a temptation" to the Galatian converts, of such a kind as to arouse feelings of natural repugnance; (c) of "trials" of a varied character, Matt. 6:13 and Luke 11:4, where believers are commanded to pray not to be led into such by forces beyond their own control; Matt. 26:41; Mark 14:38; Luke 22:40, 46, where they are commanded to watch and pray against entering into "temptations" by their own carelessness or disobedience; in all such cases God provides "the way of escape," 1 Cor. 10:13 (where *peirasmos* occurs twice). (2) Of "trial" definitely designed to lead to wrong doing, "temptation," Luke 4:13; 8:13; 1 Tim. 6:9; (3) of "trying" or challenging God, by men, Heb. 3:8.

1:7 That the trial of your faith, being much more precious than of gold that perisheth, though it be tried with fire, might be found unto praise and honour and glory at the appearing of Jesus Christ:

Trial *dokimion* (1383), "a test, a proof," is rendered "proof" in Jas. 1:3, RV (KJV, "trying"); it is regarded by some as equivalent to *dokimeion*, "a crucible, a test"; it is the neuter form of the adjective *dokimios*, used as a noun, which has been taken to denote the means by which a man is tested and "proved" (Mayor), in the same sense as *dokime* in 2 Cor. 8:2; the same phrase is used in **1 Pet. 1:7**, RV, "the proof (of your faith)," KJV, "the trial"; where the meaning probably is "that which is approved [i.e., as genuine] in your faith"; this interpretation, which was suggested by Hort, and may hold good for Jas. 1:3, has been confirmed from the papyri by Deissmann (*Bible Studies*, p. 259ff.).

Precious *timios* (5093), from *time*, "honor, price," signifies (a), primarily, "accounted as of great price, precious, costly," 1 Cor. 3:12; Rev. 17:4; 18:12, 16; 21:19, and in the superlative degree, 18:12; 21:11; the comparative degree is found in **1 Pet. 1:7** (*polutimoteros*, in the most authentic mss., "much more precious"); (b) in the metaphorical sense, "held in honor, esteemed, very dear," Acts 5:34, "had in honor," RV (KJV, "had in reputation"); so in Heb. 13:4, RV, "let marriage be had in honor"; KJV, "is honorable"; Acts 20:24, "dear," negatively of Paul's estimate of his life; Jas. 5:7, "precious" (of fruit); **1 Pet. 1:19**, "precious" (of the blood of Christ); 2 Pet. 1:4 (of God's promises); of Christ, as a precious stone, **1 Pet. 2:4**, **6** (RV marg., "honorable").

Gold *chrusion* (5553), a diminutive, is used (a) of "coin," Acts 3:6; 20:33; **1 Pet. 1:18**; (b) of "ornaments," **1 Pet. 3:3**, 1 Tim. 2:9; Rev. 17:4; 18:16; (c) of "the metal in general," Heb. 9:4; **1 Pet. 1:7**; Rev. 21:18, 21; metaphorically, (d) of "sound doctrine and its effects," 1 Cor. 3:12; (e) of "righteousness of life and conduct," Rev. 3:18.

Perisheth *apollumi* (622), a strengthened form of *ollumi*, signifies "to destroy utterly"; in middle voice, "to perish." The idea is not extinction but ruin, loss, not of being, but of wellbeing. This is clear from its use, as, e.g., of the marring of wine skins, Luke 5:37; of lost sheep, i.e., lost to the shepherd, metaphorical of spiritual destitution, Luke 15:4, 6, etc.; the lost son, 15:24; of the perishing of food, John 6:27; of gold, **1 Pet. 1:7**. So of persons, Matt. 2:13, "destroy"; 8:25, "perish"; 22:7; 27:20; of the loss of well-being in the case of the unsaved hereafter, Matt. 10:28; Luke 13:3, 5; John 3:16 (v. 15 in some mss.); 10:28; 17:12; Rom. 2:12; 1 Cor. 15:18; 2 Cor. 2:15, "are perishing"; 4:3; 2 Thess. 2:10; Jas. 4:12; 2 Pet. 3:9.

Tried *dokimazo* (1381), is rendered "to try" in the KJV in 1 Cor. 3:13; 1 Thess. 2:4; **1 Pet. 1:7**; 1 John 4:1.

Found *heurisko* (2147), denotes (a) "to find," either with previous search, e.g., Matt. 7:7, 8, or without, e.g., Matt. 27:32; in the passive voice, of Enoch's disappearance, Heb. 11:5; of mountains, Rev. 16:20; of Babylon and its occupants, 18:21, 22; (b) metaphorically, "to find out by enquiry," or "to learn, discover," e.g., Luke 19:48; John 18:38; 19:4, 6; Acts 4:21; 13:28; Rom. 7:10; Gal. 2:17, which indicates "the surprise of the Jew" who learned for the first time that before God he had no moral superiority over the Gentiles whom he superciliously dubbed "sinners," while he esteemed himself to be "righteous"; **1 Pet. 1:7**; Rev. 5:4; (c) in the middle voice, "to find for oneself, gain, procure, obtain," e.g. Matt. 10:39; 11:29, "ye shall find (rest)"; Luke 1:30; Acts 7:46; 2 Tim. 1:18.

Praise *epainos* (1868), a strengthened form, denotes "approbation, commendation, praise"; it is used (a) of those on account of, and by reason of, whom as God's heritage, "praise" is to be ascribed to God, in respect of His glory (the exhibition of His character and operations), Eph. 1:12 in v. 14, of the whole company, the church, viewed as "*God's* own possession" (RV); in v. 6, with particular reference to the glory of His grace towards them; in Phil. 1:11, as the result of "the fruits of righteousness" manifested in them through the power of Christ; (b) of "praise" bestowed by God, upon the Jew spiritually (Judah = "praise"), Rom. 2:29; bestowed upon believers hereafter at the judgment seat of Christ, 1 Cor. 4:5 (where the definite article indicates that the "praise" will be exactly in accordance with each person's actions); as the issue of present trials, "at the revelation of Jesus Christ," **1 Pet. 1:7**; (c) of whatsoever is "praiseworthy," Phil. 4:8; (d) of the approbation by churches of those who labor faithfully in the ministry of the gospel, 2 Cor. 8:18; (e) of the approbation of well-doers by human rulers, Rom. 13:3; **1 Pet. 2:14**.

Honour *time* (5092), primarily "a valuing," hence, objectively, (a) "a price paid or received," e.g., Matt. 27:6, 9; Acts 4:34; 5:2, 3; 7:16, RV, "price" (KJV, "sum"); 19:19; 1 Cor. 6:20; 7:23; (b) of "the preciousness of Christ" unto believers, **1 Pet. 2:7**, RV, i.e., the honor and inestimable value of Christ as appropriated by believers, who are joined, as living stones, to Him the cornerstone; (c) in the sense of value, of human ordinances, valueless against the indulgence of the flesh, or, perhaps of no value in attempts at asceticism, Col. 2:23; (d) "honor, esteem," (1) used in ascriptions of worship to God, 1 Tim. 1:17; 6:16; Rev. 4:9, 11; 5:13; 7:12; to Christ, 5:12, 13; (2) bestowed upon Christ by the Father, Heb. 2:9; 2 Pet. 1:17; (3) bestowed upon man, Heb. 2:7; (4) bestowed upon Aaronic priests, Heb. 5:4; (5) to be the reward hereafter of "the proof of faith" on the part of tried saints, **1 Pet. 1:7**, RV; (6) used of the believer who as a vessel is "meet for the Master's use," 2 Tim. 2:21; (7) to be the reward of patience in well-doing, Rom. 2:7, and of working good (a perfect life to which man cannot attain, so as to be justified before God thereby), 2:10; (8) to be given to all to whom it is due, Rom. 13:7 (see **1 Pet. 2:17**); (9) as an advantage to be given by believers one to another instead of claiming it for self, Rom. 12:10; (10) to be given to elders that rule well ("double honor"), 1 Tim. 5:17 (here the meaning may be an honorarium); (11) to be given by servants to their master, 1 Tim. 6:1; (12) to be given to wives by husbands, **1 Pet. 3:7**; (13) said of the husband's use of the wife, in contrast to the exercise of the passion of lust, 1 Thess. 4:4 (some regard the "vessel" here as the believer's body); (14) of that bestowed upon; parts of the body, 1 Cor. 12:23, 24; (15) of that which belongs to the builder of a house in contrast to the house itself, Heb. 3:3; (16) of that which is not enjoyed by a prophet in his own country, John 4:44; (17) of that bestowed by the inhabitants of Melita upon Paul and his fellow-passengers, in gratitude for his benefits of healing, Acts 28:10; (18) of the festive honor to be possessed by nations, and brought into the Holy City, the heavenly Jerusalem, Rev. 21:26 (in some mss., v. 24); (19) of honor bestowed upon things inanimate, a potters' vessel, Rom. 9:21; 2 Tim. 2:20.

Appearing *apokalupsis* (602), "an uncovering" (akin to *apokalupto*, "to uncover, unveil"), "is used in the NT of (a) the drawing away by Christ of the veil of darkness covering the Gentiles, Luke 2:32; cf. Isa. 25:7; (b) 'the mystery,' the purpose of God in this age, Rom. 16:25; Eph. 3:3; (c) the communication of the knowledge of God to the soul, Eph. 1:17; (d) an expression of the mind of God for the instruction of the church, 1 Cor. 14:6, 26, for the instruction of the Apostle Paul, 2 Cor. 12:1, 7; Gal. 1:12, and for his guidance, Gal. 2:2; (e) the Lord Jesus Christ, to the saints at His Parousia, 1 Cor. 1:7, RV (KJV, 'coming'); **1 Pet. 1:7**, RV (KJV, 'appearing'), **13**; **4:13**; (f) the Lord Jesus Christ when He comes to dispense the judgments of God, 2 Thess. 1:7; cf. Rom. 2:5; (g) the saints, to the creation, in association with Christ in His glorious reign, Rom. 8:19, RV, 'revealing' (KJV, 'manifestation'); (h) the symbolic forecast of the final judgments of God, Rev. 1:1 (hence the Greek title of the book, transliterated 'Apocalypse' and translated 'Revelation')."

1:8 Whom having not seen, ye love; in whom, though now ye see *him* not, yet believing, ye rejoice with joy unspeakable and full of glory:

Love *phileo* (5368), is to be distinguished from *agapao* in this, that *phileo* more nearly represents "tender affection." The two words are used for the "love" of the Father for the Son, John 3:35 (*agapao*), and 5:20 (*phileo*); for the believer, 14:21 (*agapao*) and 16:27 (*phileo*); both, of Christ's "love" for a certain disciple, 13:23 (*agapao*), and 20:2 (*phileo*). Yet the distinction between the two verbs remains, and they are never used indiscriminately in the same passage; if each is used with reference to the same objects, as just mentioned, each word retains its distinctive and essential character. *Phileo* is never used in a command to men to "love" God; it is, however, used as a warning in 1 Cor. 16:22; *agapao* is used instead, e.g., Matt. 22:37; Luke 10:27; Rom. 8:28; 1 Cor. 8:3; **1 Pet. 1:8**; 1 John 4:21. The distinction between the two verbs finds a conspicuous instance in the narrative of John 21:15-17. The context itself indicates that *agapao* in the first two questions suggests the "love" that values and esteems (cf. Rev. 12:11). It is an unselfish "love," ready to serve. The use of *phileo* in Peter's answers and the Lord's third question, conveys the thought of cherishing the Object above all else, of manifesting an affection characterized by constancy, from the motive of the highest veneration. See also Trench, *Syn.*, Sec.xii. Again, to "love" (*phileo*) life, from an undue desire to preserve it, forgetful of the real object of living, meets with the Lord's reproof, John 12:25. On the contrary, to "love" life (*agapao*) as used in **1 Pet. 3:10**, is to consult the true interests of living. Here the word *phileo* would be quite inappropriate.

Now *see 1 Peter 1:6*.

Rejoice *see 1 Peter 1:6*.

Unspeakable *aneklaletos* (412), denotes "unable to be told out" (*eklaleo*, "to speak out"), **1 Pet. 1:8**, of the believer joy.

Glory *doxazo* (1392), primarily denotes "to suppose" (from *doxa*, "an opinion"); in the NT (a) "to magnify, extol, praise" (see *doxa* below), especially of "glorifying"; God, i.e., ascribing honor to Him, acknowledging Him as to His being, attributes and acts, i.e., His glory, e.g., Matt. 5:16; 9:8; 15:31; Rom. 15:6, 9; Gal. 1:24; **1 Pet. 4:16**; the Word of the Lord, Acts 13:48; the Name of the Lord, Rev. 15:4; also of "glorifying" oneself, John 8:54; Rev. 18:7; (b) "to do honor to, to make glorious," e.g., Rom. 8:30; 2 Cor. 3:10; **1 Pet. 1:8**, "full of glory," passive voice (lit., "glorified"); said of Christ, e.g., John 7:39; 8:54, RV, "glorifieth," for KJV, "honor" and "honoreth" (which would translate *timao*, "to honor"); of the Father, e.g., John 13:31, 32; 21:19; **1 Pet. 4:11**; of "glorifying" one's ministry, Rom. 11:13, RV, "glorify" (KJV, "magnify"); of a member of the body, 1 Cor. 12:26, "be honored" (RV marg., "be glorified").

"As the glory of God is the revelation and manifestation of all that He has and is ..., it is said of a Self-revelation in which God manifests all the goodness that is His, John 12:28. So far as it is Christ through whom this is made manifest, He is said to glorify the Father, John 17:1, 4; or the Father is glorified in Him, 13:31; 14:13; and Christ's meaning is analogous when He says to His disciples, 'Herein is My Father glorified, that ye bear much fruit; and so shall ye be My disciples,' John 15:8. When *doxazo* is predicated of Christ ..., it means simply that His innate glory is brought to light, is made manifest; cf. 11:4. So 7:39; 12:16, 23; 13:31; 17:1, 5. It is an act of God the Father in Him.... As the revelation of the Holy Spirit is connected with the glorification of Christ, Christ says regarding Him, 'He shall glorify Me,' 16:14" (Cremer).

1:9 Receiving the end of your faith, *even* the salvation of *your* souls.

Receiving *komizo* (2865), denotes "to bear, carry," e.g., Luke 7:37; in the middle voice, "to bear for oneself," hence (a) "to receive," Heb. 10:36; 11:13 (in the best texts; some have *lambano*), 39; **1 Pet. 1:9; 5:4**; in some texts in 2 Pet. 2:13 (in the best mss. *adikeomai*, "suffering wrong," RV); (b) "to receive back, recover," Matt. 25:27; Heb. 11:19; metaphorically, of requital, 2 Cor. 5:10; Col. 3:25, of "receiving back again" by the believer at the judgment seat of Christ hereafter, for wrong done in this life; Eph. 6:8, of "receiving," on the same occasion, "whatsoever good thing each one doeth," RV.

End *telos* (5056), signifies (a) "the limit," either at which a person or thing ceases to be what he or it was up to that point, or at which previous activities were ceased, 2 Cor. 3:13; **1 Pet. 4:7**; (b) "the final issue or result" of a state or process, e.g., Luke 1:33; in Rom. 10:4, Christ is described as "the end of the Law unto righteousness to everyone that believeth"; this is best explained by Gal. 3:23-26; cf. Jas. 5:11; the following more especially point to the issue or fate of a thing, Matt. 26:58; Rom. 6:21; 2 Cor. 11:15; Phil. 3:19; Heb. 6:8; **1 Pet. 1:9**; (c) "a fulfillment," Luke 22:37, KJV, "(have) an end"; (d) "the utmost degree" of an act, as of the love of Christ towards His disciples, John 13:1; (e) "the aim or purpose" of a thing, 1 Tim. 1:5; (f) "the last" in a succession or series, Rev. 1:8 (KJV, only, "ending"); 21:6; 22:13.

Salvation *see 1 Peter 1:5.*

Souls *psuche* (5590), denotes "the breath, the breath of life," then "the soul," in its various meanings. The NT uses "may be analyzed approximately as follows:

"(a) the natural life of the body, Matt. 2:20; Luke 12:22; Acts 20:10; Rev. 8:9; 12:11; cf. Lev. 17:11; 2 Sam. 14:7; Esth. 8:11; (b) the immaterial, invisible part of man, Matt. 10:28; Acts 2:27; cf. 1 Kings 17:21; (c) the disembodied (or "unclothed" or "naked," 2 Cor. 5:3, 4) man, Rev. 6:9; (d) the seat of personality, Luke 9:24, explained as = "own self," v. 25; Heb. 6:19; 10:39; cf. Isa. 53:10 with 1 Tim. 2:6; (e) the seat of the sentient element in man, that by which he perceives, reflects, feels, desires, Matt. 11:29; Luke 1:46; 2:35; Acts 14:2, 22; cf. Ps. 84:2; 139:14; Isa. 26:9; (f) the seat of will and purpose, Matt. 22:37; Acts 4:32; Eph. 6:6; Phil. 1:27; Heb. 12:3; cf. Num. 21:4; Deut. 11:13; (g) the seat of appetite, Rev. 18:14; cf. Ps. 107:9; Prov. 6:30; Isa. 5:14 ("desire"); 29:8; (h) persons, individuals, Acts 2:41, 43; Rom. 2:9; Jas. 5:20; **1 Pet. 3:20**; 2 Pet. 2:14; cf. Gen. 12:5; 14:21 ("persons"); Lev. 4:2 ('any one'); Ezek. 27:13; of dead bodies, Num. 6:6, lit., "dead soul"; and of animals, Lev. 24:18, lit., "soul for soul"; (i) the equivalent of the personal pronoun, used for emphasis and effect:—1st person, John 10:24 ("us"); Heb. 10:38; cf. Gen. 12:13; Num. 23:10; Jud. 16:30; Ps. 120:2 ("me"); 2nd person, 2 Cor. 12:15; Heb. 13:17; Jas. 1:21; **1 Pet. 1:9; 2:25**; cf. Lev. 17:11; 26:15; 1 Sam. 1:26; 3rd person, **1 Pet. 4:19**; 2 Pet. 2:8; cf. Exod. 30:12; Job 32:2, Heb. "soul," Sept. "self"; (j) an animate creature, human or other, 1 Cor. 15:45; Rev. 16:3; cf. Gen. 1:24; 2:7, 19; (k) "the inward man," the seat of the new life, Luke 21:19 (cf. Matt. 10:39); **1 Pet. 2:11**; 3 John 2."

1:10 Of which salvation the prophets have enquired and searched diligently, who prophesied of the grace *that should come* unto you:

Salvation *see 1 Peter 1:5.*

Enquired *ekzeteo*, "to seek out, search after," is rendered "have inquired" in **1 Pet. 1:10**, KJV (RV, "sought").

Searched *exeraunao* (1830), a strengthened form (*ek*, or *ex*, "out"), "to search out," is used in **1 Pet. 1:10**, "searched diligently."

Prophesied *propheteuo* (4395), "to be a prophet, to prophesy," is used (a) with the primary meaning of telling forth the divine counsels, e.g., Matt. 7:22; 26:68; 1 Cor. 11:4, 5; 13:9; 14:1, 3-5, 24, 31, 39; Rev. 11:3; (b) of foretelling the future, e.g., Matt. 15:7; John 11:51; **1 Pet. 1:10**; Jude 14.

1:11 Searching what, or what manner of time the Spirit of Christ which was in them did signify, when it testified

beforehand the sufferings of Christ, and the glory that should follow.

Searching *eraunao* or *ereunao*, an earlier form, (2045), "to search, examine," is used (a) of God, as "searching" the heart, Rom. 8:27; (b) of Christ, similarly, Rev. 2:23; (c) of the Holy Spirit, as "searching" all things, 1 Cor. 2:10, acting in the spirit of the believer; (d) of the OT prophets, as "searching" their own writings concerning matters foretold of Christ, testified by the Spirit of Christ in them, **1 Pet. 1:11**; (e) of the Jews, as commanded by the Lord to "search" the Scriptures, John 5:39, KJV, and RV marg., "search," RV text, "ye search," either is possible grammatically; (f) of Nicodemus as commanded similarly by the chief priests and Pharisees, John 7:52.

What *poios*, "what sort of," e.g., Matt. 21:23, 24, 27; 24:42, 43; Luke 5:19; 6:32-34; 20:2, 8; 24:19; John 12:33, "what manner of"; so in 18:32; 21:19; Rom. 3:27; 1 Cor. 15:35; in Jas. 4:14, "what"; **1 Pet. 2:20** and Rev. 3:3 (ditto); **1 Pet. 1:11**, "what manner of."

Time *kairos* (2540), primarily, "due measure, fitness, proportion," is used in the NT to signify "a season, a time, a period" possessed of certain characteristics, frequently rendered "time" or "times"; in the following the RV substitutes "season" for the KJV "time," thus distinguishing the meaning from *chronos*: Matt. 11:25; 12:1; 14:1; 21:34; Mark 11:13; Acts 3:19; 7:20; 17:26; Rom. 3:26; 5:6; 9:9; 13:11; 1 Cor. 7:5; Gal. 4:10; 1 Thess. 2:17, lit., "for a season (of an hour)", 2 Thess. 2:6; in Eph. 6:18, "at all seasons" (KJV, "always"); in Titus 1:3, "His own seasons" (marg., "its"; KJV, "in due times"); in the preceding clause *chronos* is used. The characteristics of a period are exemplified in the use of the term with regard, e.g. to harvest, Matt. 13:30; reaping, Gal. 6:9; punishment, Matt. 8:29; discharging duties, Luke 12:42; opportunity for doing anything, whether good, e.g., Matt. 26:18; Gal. 6:10 ("opportunity"); Eph. 5:16; or evil, e.g., Rev. 12:12; the fulfillment of prophecy, Luke 1:20; Acts 3:19; **1 Pet. 1:11**; a time suitable for a purpose, Luke 4:13, lit., "until a season"; 2 Cor. 6:2.

Signify *deloo* (1213), "to make plain" (*delos*, "evident"), is translated "to signify" in 1 Cor. 1:11, RV, "it hath been signified" (KJV, "declared"); Heb. 9:8; 12:27; **1 Pet. 1:11**, KJV (RV, "point unto"); 2 Pet. 1:14, RV, "signified" (KJV, "hath showed").

Testified *promarturomai* (4303), "to testify beforehand," occurs in **1 Pet. 1:11**, where the pronoun "it" should be "He" (the "it" being due to the grammatically neuter form of *pneuma;* the personality of the Holy Spirit requires the masculine pronoun).

Sufferings *pathema* (3804), from *pathos*, "suffering," signifies "affliction." The word is frequent in Paul's epistles and is found three times in Hebrews, four in 1 Peter; it is used (a) of "afflictions," Rom. 8:18, etc.; of Christ's "sufferings," **1 Pet. 1:11; 5:1**; Heb. 2:9; of those as shared by believers, 2 Cor. 1:5; Phil. 3:10; **1 Pet. 4:13; 5:1**; (b) of "an evil emotion, passion," Rom. 7:5; Gal. 5:24. The connection between the two meanings is that the emotions, whether good or evil, were regarded as consequent upon external influences exerted on the mind (cf. the two meanings of the English "passion").

Follow In **1 Pet. 1:11**, the phrase *meta tauta*, lit., "after these things," is translated "that should follow," said of glories after the sufferings of Christ.

1:12 Unto whom it was revealed, that not unto themselves, but unto us they did minister the things, which are now reported unto you by them that have preached the gospel unto you with the Holy Ghost sent down from heaven; which things the angels desire to look into.

Revealed *see* ***1 Peter 1:5***.

Minister *diakoneo* (1247), signifies "to be a servant, attendant, to serve, wait upon, minister." In the following it is translated "to minister," except where "to serve" is mentioned: it is used (a) with a general significance, e.g., Matt. 4:11; 20:28; Mark 1:13; 10:45; John 12:26 ("serve," twice); Acts 19:22; Philem. 13; (b) of waiting at table, "ministering" to the guests, Matt. 8:15; Luke 4:39; 8:3; 12:37; 17:8, "serve"; 22:26, "serve," v. 27, "serveth," twice; the 2nd instance, concerning the Lord, may come under (a); so of women preparing food, etc., Mark 1:31; Luke 10:40, "serve"; John 12:2, "served"; (c) of relieving one's necessities, supplying the necessaries of life, Matt. 25:44; 27:55; Mark 15:41; Acts 6:2, "serve"; Rom. 15:25; Heb. 6:10; more definitely in connection with such service in a local church, 1 Tim. 3:10, 13 [there is nothing in the original representing the word "office"; RV, "let them serve as deacons," "they that have served (well) as deacons"]; (d) of attending, in a more general way, to anything that may serve another's interests, as of the work of an amanuensis, 2 Cor. 3:3 (metaphorical): of the conveyance of material gifts for assisting the needy, 2 Cor. 8:19, 20, RV, "is ministered" (KJV, "is administered"); of a variety of forms of service, 2 Tim. 1:18; of the testimony of the OT prophets, **1 Pet. 1:12**; of the ministry of believers one to another in various ways, **1 Pet. 4:10, 11** (not here of discharging ecclesiastical functions).

Reported *anangello* (312), "to declare, announce" (*ana*, "up," *angello*, "to report"), is used especially of heavenly messages, and is translated "announced" in the RV of **1 Pet. 1:12**, for KJV "reported," and in 1 John 1:5, RV, "announce," for KJV, "declare."

Holy *hagios* (40), fundamentally signifies "separated" (among the Greeks, dedicated to the gods), and hence, in Scripture in its moral and spiritual significance, separated from sin and therefore consecrated to God, sacred.

(a) It is predicated of God (as the absolutely "Holy" One, in His purity, majesty and glory): of the Father, e.g., Luke 1:49; John 17:11; **1 Pet. 1:15, 16**; Rev. 4:8; 6:10; of the Son, e.g., Luke 1:35; Acts 3:14; 4:27, 30; 1 John 2:20; of the Spirit, e.g., Matt. 1:18 and frequently in all the Gospels, Acts, Romans, 1 and 2 Cor., Eph., 1 Thess.; also in 2 Tim. 1:14; Titus 3:5; **1 Pet. 1:12**; 2 Pet. 1:21; Jude 20.

(b) It is used of men and things in so far as they are devoted to God. Indeed the quality, as attributed to God, is often presented in a way which involves divine demands upon the conduct of believers. These are called *hagioi*, "saints," i.e., "sanctified" or "holy" ones.

This sainthood is not an attainment, it is a state into which God in grace calls men; yet believers are called to sanctify themselves (consistently with their calling, 2 Tim. 1:9), cleansing themselves from all defilement, forsaking sin, living a "holy" manner of life, **1 Pet. 1:15**; 2 Pet. 3:11, and experiencing fellowship with God in His holiness. The saints are thus figuratively spoken of as "a holy temple", 1 Cor. 3:17 (a local church); Eph. 2:21 (the whole Church), cp. 5:27; "a holy priesthood," **1 Pet. 2:5**; "a holy nation," **2:9**.

Sent *apostello* (649), lit., "to send forth" (*apo*, "from"), akin to *apostolos*, "an apostle," denotes (a) "to send on service, or with a commission." (1) of persons; Christ, sent by the Father, Matt. 10:40; 15:24; 21:37; Mark 9:37; 12:6; Luke 4:18, 43; 9:48; 10:16; John 3:17; 5:36, 38; 6:29, 57; 7:29; 8:42; 10:36; 11:42; 17:3, 8, 18 (1st part), 21, 23, 25; 20:21; Acts 3:20 (future); 3:26; 1 John 4:9, 10, 14; the Holy Spirit, Luke 24:49; **1 Pet. 1:12**; Rev. 5:6; Moses, Acts 7:35; John the Baptist, John 1:6; 3:28; disciples and apostles, e.g., Matt. 10:16; Mark 11:1; Luke 22:8; John 4:38; 17:18 (2nd part); Acts 26:17; servants, e.g., Matt. 21:34; Luke 20:10; officers and officials, Mark 6:27; John 7:32; Acts 16:35; messengers, e.g., Acts 10:8, 17, 20; 15:27; evangelists, Rom. 10:15; angels, e.g., Matt. 24:31; Mark 13:27; Luke 1:19, 26; Heb. 1:14; Rev. 1:1; 22:6; demons, Mark 5:10; (2) of things, e.g., Matt. 21:3; Mark 4:29, RV, marg., "sendeth forth," text, "putteth forth" (KJV, "... in"); Acts 10:36; 11:30; 28:28; (b) "to send away, dismiss," e.g., Mark 8:26; 12:3; Luke 4:18, "to set (at liberty)."

Heaven *ouranos* (3772), probably akin to *ornumi*, "to lift, to heave," is used in the NT (a) of "the aerial heavens," e.g., Matt. 6:26; 8:20; Acts 10:12; 11:6 (RV, "heaven," in each place, KJV, "air"); Jas. 5:18; (b) "the sidereal," e.g., Matt. 24:29, 35; Mark 13:25, 31; Heb. 11:12, RV, "heaven," KJV, "sky"; Rev. 6:14; 20:11; they, (a) and (b), were created by the Son of God, Heb. 1:10, as also by God the Father, Rev. 10:6; (c) "the eternal dwelling place of God," Matt. 5:16; 12 :50; Rev. 3:12; 11:13; 16:11; 20:9. From thence the Son of God descended to become incarnate, John 3:13, 31; 6:38, 42. In His ascension Christ "passed through the heavens," Heb. 4:14, RV; He "ascended far above all the heavens," Eph. 4:10, and was "made higher than the heavens," Heb. 7:26; He "sat down on the right hand of the throne of the Majesty in the heavens," Heb. 8:1; He is "on the right hand of God," having gone into heaven, **1 Pet. 3:22**. Since His ascension it is the scene of His present life and activity, e.g., Rom. 8:34; Heb. 9:24. From thence the Holy Spirit descended at Pentecost, **1 Pet. 1:12**. It is the abode of the angels, e.g., Matt. 18:10; 22:30; cf. Rev. 3:5. Thither Paul was "caught up," whether in the body or out of the body, he knew not, 2 Cor. 12:2. It is to be the eternal dwelling place of the saints in resurrection glory, 2 Cor. 5:1. From thence Christ will descend to the air to receive His saints at the Rapture, 1 Thess. 4:16; Phil. 3:20, 21, and will subsequently come with His saints and with His holy angels at His second advent, Matt. 24:30; 2 Thess. 1:7. In the present life "heaven" is the region of the spiritual citizenship of believers, Phil. 3:20. The present "heavens," with the earth, are to pass away, 2 Pet. 3:10, "being on fire," v. 12 (see v. 7); Rev. 20:11, and new "heavens" and earth are to be created, 2 Pet. 3:13; Rev. 21:1, with Isa. 65:17, e.g.

Desire *epithumeo* (1937), "to desire earnestly," stresses the inward impulse rather than the object desired. It is translated "to desire" in Luke 16:21; 17:22; 22:15; 1 Tim. 3:1; Heb. 6:11; **1 Pet. 1:12**; Rev. 9:6.

Look *parakupto* (3879), lit. and primarily, "to stoop sideways" *para*, "aside," *kupto*, "to bend forward"), denotes "to stoop to look into," Luke 24:12, "stooping and looking in" (KJV, "stooping down"), John 20:5,

11; metaphorically in Jas. 1:25, of "looking" into the perfect law of liberty; in **1 Pet. 1:12** of things which the angels desire "to look into.

1:13 Wherefore gird up the loins of your mind, be sober, and hope to the end for the grace that is to be brought unto you at the revelation of Jesus Christ;

Wherefore *dio* = *dia ho* (the neuter of the relative pronoun *hos*), "on account of which (thing)," e.g., Matt. 27:8; Acts 15:19; 20:31; 24:26; 25:26; 27:25, 34; Rom. 1:24; 15:7; 1 Cor. 12:3; 2 Cor. 2:8; 5:9; 6:17; Eph. 2:11; 3:13; 4:8, 25; 5:14; Phil. 2:9; 1 Thess. 5:11; Philem. 8; Heb. 3:7, 10; 10:5; 11:16; 12:12, 28; 13:12; Jas. 1:21; 4:6; **1 Pet. 1:13**; 2 Pet. 1:10, 12; 3:14.

Gird *anazonnumi* (328), "to gird up," is used metaphorically of the loins of the mind, **1 Pet. 1:13**; cf. Luke 12:35. The figure is taken from the circumstances of the Israelites as they ate the Passover in readiness for their journey, Exod. 12:11; the Christian is to have his mental powers alert in expectation of Christ's coming. The verb is in the middle voice, indicating the special interest the believer is to take in so doing.

Loins *osphus* (3751), is used (a) in the natural sense in Matt. 3:4; Mark 1:6; (b) as "the seat of generative power," Heb. 7:5, 10; metaphorically in Acts 2:30; (c) metaphorically, (1) of girding the "loins" in readiness for active service for the Lord, Luke 12:35; (2) the same, with truth, Eph. 6:14, i.e., bracing up oneself so as to maintain perfect sincerity and reality as the counteractive in Christian character against hypocrisy and falsehood; (3) of girding the "loins" of the mind, **1 Pet. 1:13**, RV, "girding," suggestive of the alertness necessary for sobriety and for setting one's hope perfectly on "the grace to be brought ... at the revelation of Jesus Christ" (the present participle, "girding," is introductory to the rest of the verse).

Mind *dianoia* (1271), lit. "a thinking through, or over, a meditation, reflecting," signifies (a) "the faculty of knowing, understanding, or moral reflection," (1) with an evil significance, a consciousness characterized by a perverted moral impulse, Eph. 2:3 (plural); 4:18; (2) with a good significance, the faculty renewed by the Holy Spirit, Matt. 22:37; Mark 12:30; Luke 10:27; Heb. 8:10; 10:16; **1 Pet. 1:13**; 1 John 5:20; (b) "sentiment, disposition" (not as a function but as a product); (1) in an evil sense, Luke 1:51, "imagination"; Col. 1:21; (2) in a good sense, 2 Pet. 3:1.

Sober *nepho* (3525), signifies "to be free from the influence of intoxicants"; in the NT, metaphorically, it does not in itself imply watchfulness, but is used in association with it, 1 Thess. 5:6, 8; 2 Tim. 4:5; **1 Pet. 1:13; 4:7**, RV (KJV, "watch"); **5:8.**

End *teleios* (5049), "perfectly," is so translated in **1 Pet. 1:13**, RV (KJV, "to the end"), of setting one's hope on coming grace.

Revelation *see* **Appearing** at *1 Peter 1:7.*

1:14 As obedient children, not fashioning yourselves according to the former lusts in your ignorance:

Obedient *see* **Obedience** at *1 Peter 1:2.*

Children *teknon* (5043), "a child" (akin to *tikto*, "to beget, bear"), is used in both the natural and the figurative senses. In contrast to *huios*, "son," it gives prominence to the fact of birth, whereas *huios* stresses the dignity and character of the relationship. Figuratively, *teknon* is used of "children" of (a) God, John 1:12; (b) light, Eph. 5:8; (c) obedience, **1 Pet. 1:14**; (d) a promise, Rom. 9:8; Gal. 4:28; (e) the Devil, 1 John 3:10; (f) wrath, Eph. 2:3; (g) cursing, 2 Pet. 2:14; (h) spiritual relationship, 2 Tim. 2:1; Philem. 10.

Fashioning *suschematizo* (4964), "to fashion or shape one thing like another," is translated "conformed" in Rom. 12:2, KJV; RV, "fashioned"; "fashioning" in **1 Pet. 1:14**. This verb has more especial reference to that which is transitory, changeable, unstable; *summorphizo*, to that which is essential in character and thus complete or durable, not merely a form or outline. *Suschematizo* could not be used of inward transformation.

Former *proteros* (4387), "before, former," is translated "former" in Eph. 4:22; Heb. 10:32; **1 Pet. 1:14**.

Lusts *epithumia* (1939), denotes "strong desire" of any kind, the various kinds being frequently specified by some adjective. The word is used of a good desire in Luke 22:15; Phil. 1:23, and 1 Thess. 2:17 only. Everywhere else it has a bad sense. In Rom. 6:12 the injunction against letting sin reign in our mortal body to obey the "lust" thereof, refers to those evil desires which are ready to express themselves in bodily activity. They are equally the "lusts" of the flesh, Rom. 13:14; Gal. 5:16, 24; Eph. 2:3; 2 Pet. 2:18; 1 John 2:16, a phrase which describes the emotions of the soul, the natural tendency towards things evil. Such "lusts" are not necessarily base and immoral, they may be refined in character, but are evil if inconsistent with the will of God. Other descriptions besides those already mentioned are: "of the mind," Eph. 2:3; "evil (desire)," Col. 3:5; "the passion of," 1 Thess. 4:5, RV; "foolish and hurtful," 1 Tim. 6:9; "youthful," 2 Tim. 2:22; "divers," 2 Tim. 3:6 and Titus 3:3; "their own," 2 Tim. 4:3; 2 Pet. 3:3; Jude 16; "worldly," Titus 2:12; "his own," Jas. 1:14; "your former," **1 Pet. 1:14**, RV; "fleshly," **2:11**; "of men," **4:2**; "of defilement," 2 Pet. 2:10; "of the eyes," 1 John 2:16; of the world ("thereof"), v. 17; "their own ungodly," Jude 18. In Rev. 18:14 "(the fruits) which thy soul lusted after" is, lit., "of thy soul's lust."

Ignorance *agnoia* (52), lit., "want of knowledge or perception" (akin to *agnoeo*, "to be ignorant"), denotes "ignorance" on the part of the Jews regarding Christ, Acts 3:17; of Gentiles in regard to God, 17:30; Eph. 4:18 (here including the idea of willful blindness: see Rom. 1:28, not the "ignorance" which mitigates guilt); **1 Pet. 1:14**, of the former unregenerate condition of those who became believers (RV, "in *the time of* your ignorance").

1:15 But as he which hath called you is holy, so be ye holy in all manner of conversation;

Holy *see 1 Peter 1:12. See also* **God** at *1 Peter 5:10.*

Conversation *anastrophe* (391), lit., "a turning back," is translated "manner of life," "living," etc. in the RV, for KJV, "conversation," Gal. 1:13; Eph. 4:22; 1 Tim. 4:12; Heb. 13:7; Jas. 3:13; **1 Pet. 1:15**, **18**; **2:1** ("behavior"); **3:1**, **2**, **16** (ditto); 2 Pet. 2:7; 3:11.

1:16 Because it is written, Be ye holy; for I am holy.

Holy *see 1 Peter 1:12.*

1:17 And if ye call on the Father, who without respect of persons judgeth according to every man's work, pass the time of your sojourning *here* in fear:

Without respect of persons *aprosopolemptos* (678), "without respect of persons, impartially" (*a*, negative), occurs in **1 Pet. 1:17**.

Pass *anastrepho* (390), lit., "to turn back" (*ana*, "back," *strepho*, "to turn"), in the middle voice, "to conduct oneself, behave, live," is translated "pass (the time)" in **1 Pet. 1:17**.

Sojourning *paroikia* (3940), "a sojourning," occurs in Acts 13:17, rendered "they sojourned," RV, KJV, "dwelt as strangers," lit., "in the sojourning"; in **1 Pet. 1:17**, "sojourning."

Fear *phobos* (5401), first had the meaning of "flight," that which is caused by being scared; then, "that which may cause flight," (a) "fear, dread, terror," always with this significance in the four Gospels; also e.g., in Acts 2:43; 19:17; 1 Cor. 2:3; 1 Tim. 5:20 (lit., "may have fear"); Heb. 2:15; 1 John 4:18; Rev. 11:11; 18:10, 15; by metonymy, that which causes "fear," Rom. 13:3; **1 Pet. 3:14**, RV, "(their) fear," KJV "(their) terror," an adaptation of the Sept. of Isa. 8:12, "fear not their fear"; hence some take it to mean, as there, "what they fear," but in view of Matt. 10:28, e.g., it seems best to understand it as that which is caused by the intimidation of adversaries; (b) "reverential fear," (1) of God, as a controlling motive of the life, in matters spiritual and moral, not a mere "fear" of His power and righteous retribution, but a wholesome dread of displeasing Him, a "fear" which banishes the terror that shrinks from His presence, Rom. 8:15, and which influences the disposition and attitude of one whose circumstances are guided by trust in God, through the indwelling Spirit of God, Acts 9:31; Rom. 3:18; 2 Cor. 7:1; Eph. 5:21 (RV, "the fear of Christ"); Phil. 2:12; **1 Pet. 1:17** (a comprehensive phrase: the reverential "fear" of God will inspire a constant carefulness in dealing with others in His "fear"); **3:2**, **15**; the association of "fear and trembling," as, e.g., in Phil. 2:12, has in the Sept. a much sterner import, e.g., Gen. 9:2; Exod. 15:16; Deut. 2:25; 11:25; Ps. 55:5; Isa. 19:16; (2) of superiors, e.g., Rom. 13:7; **1 Pet. 2:18**.

1:18 Forasmuch as ye know that ye were not redeemed with corruptible things, *as* silver and gold, from your vain conversation *received* by tradition from your fathers;

Redeemed *lutroo* (3084), "to release on receipt of ransom" (akin to *lutron*, "a ransom"), is used in the middle voice, signifying "to release by paying a ransom price, to redeem" (a) in the natural sense of delivering, Luke 24:21, of setting Israel free from the Roman yoke; (b) in a spiritual sense, Titus 2:14, of the work of Christ in "redeeming" men "from all iniquity" (*anomia*, "lawlessness," the bondage of self-will which rejects the will of God); **1 Pet. 1:18** (passive voice), "ye were redeemed," from a vain manner of life, i.e., from bondage to tradition. In both instances the death of Christ is stated as the means of "redemption."

Corruptible *phthartos* (5349), "corruptible," is used (a) of man as being mortal, liable to decay (in contrast to God), Rom. 1:23; (b) of man's body as death-doomed, 1 Cor. 15:53-54; (c) of a crown of reward at the Greek games, 1 Cor.

9:25; (d) of silver and gold, as specimens or "corruptible" things, **1 Pet. 1:18**; (e) of natural seed, **1 Pet. 1:23**.

Silver *argurion* (694), is rendered "silver" in Acts 3:6; 8:20, RV (KJV, "money"); 20:33; 1 Cor. 3:12 (metaphorical); **1 Pet. 1:18**.

Gold *see **1 Peter 1:7**.*

Vain *mataios* (3152), "void of result," is used of (a) idolatrous practices, Acts 14:15, RV, "vain things" (KJV, "vanities"); (b) the thoughts of the wise, 1 Cor. 3:20; (c) faith, if Christ is not risen, 1 Cor. 15:17; (d) questionings, strifes, etc., Titus 3:9; (e) religion, with an unbridled tongue, Jas. 1:26; (f) manner of life, **1 Pet. 1:18**.

Conversation *see **1 Peter 1:15**.*

Received *patroparadotos* (3970), an adjective, denoting "handed down from one's fathers," is used in **1 Pet. 1:18**, RV, for KJV, "*received* by tradition from your fathers" (from *pater*, "a father," and *paradidomi*, "to hand down").

Fathers *patroparadotos* (3970), "handed down from one's fathers" (*pater*, and *paradidomi*, "to hand down"), is used in **1 Pet. 1:18**.

1:19 But with the precious blood of Christ, as of a lamb without blemish and without spot:

Precious *timios* (5093), translated "precious," e.g., in Jas. 5:7; **1 Pet. 1:19**; 2 Pet. 1:4; in 1 Cor. 3:12, KJV (RV, "costly"). *See also **1 Peter 1:7**.*

Lamb *amnos* (286), "a lamb," is used figuratively of Christ, in John 1:29, 36, with the article, pointing Him out as the expected One, the One to be well known as the personal fulfillment and embodiment of all that had been indicated in the OT, the One by whose sacrifice deliverance from divine judgment was to be obtained; in Acts 8:32 (from the Sept. of Is. 53:7) and **1 Pet. 1:19**, the absence of the article stresses the nature and character of His sacrifice as set forth in the symbolism. The reference in each case is to the lamb of God's providing, Gen. 22:8, and the Paschal lamb of God's appointment for sacrifice in Israel, e.g., Ex. 12:5, 14, 27 (cf. 1 Cor. 5:7).

Blemish *amomos* (299), "without blemish"; is always so rendered in the RV, Eph. 1:4; 5:27; Phil. 2:15; Col. 1:22; Heb. 9:14; **1 Pet. 1:19**; Jude 24; Rev. 14:5. This meaning is to be preferred to the various KJV renderings, "without blame," Eph. 1:4, "unblameable," Col. 1:22, "faultless," Jude 24, "without fault," Rev. 14:5. The most authentic mss. have *amomos*, "without blemish," in Phil. 2:15, for *amometos*, "without rebuke." In the Sept., in reference to sacrifices, especially in Lev. and Num., the Psalms and Ezek., "of blamelessness in character and conduct."

Spot *aspilos* (784), "unspotted, unstained," is used of a lamb, **1 Pet. 1:19**; metaphorically, of keeping a commandment without alteration and in the fulfillment of it, 1 Tim. 6:14; of the believer in regard to the world, Jas. 1:27, and free from all defilement in the sight of God, 2 Pet. 3:14.

1:20 Who verily was foreordained before the foundation of the world, but was manifest in these last times for you,

Verily The particle *men* is rendered "verily," e.g., in 1 Cor. 5:3; 14:17; Heb. 12:10; in the KJV, Heb. 3:5; 7:5, 18; **1 Pet. 1:20**; in Acts 26:9 it is combined with *oun* ("therefore").

Foreordained *proginosko* (4267), "to know before" (*pro*, "before," *ginosko*, "to know"), is used (a) of divine knowledge, concerning (1) Christ, **1 Pet. 1:20**, RV, "foreknown" (KJV, "foreordained"); (2) Israel as God's earthly people, Rom. 11:2; (3) believers, Rom. 8:29; "the foreknowledge" of God is the basis of His foreordaining counsels; (b) of human knowledge, (1) of persons, Acts 26:5; (2) of facts, 2 Pet. 3:17.

Foundation *katabole* (2602), lit., "a casting down," is used (a) of "conceiving seed," Heb. 11:11; (b) of "a foundation," as that which is laid down, or in the sense of founding; metaphorically, of "the foundation of the world"; in this respect two phrases are used, (1) "from the foundation of the world," Matt. 25:34 (in the most authentic mss. in 13:35 there is no phrase representing "of the world"); Luke 11:50; Heb. 4:3; 9:26; Rev. 13:8; 17:8; (2) "before the foundation of the world," John 17:24; Eph. 1:4; **1 Pet. 1:20**. The latter phrase looks back to the past eternity.

Manifest *phaneroo* (5319), "to make visible, clear, manifest, known," is used especially in the writings of the apostles John and Paul, occurring 9 times in the Gospel, 9 times in 1 John, 2 in Rev.; in the Pauline Epistles (including Heb.) 24 times; in the other Gospels, only in Mark, 3 times; elsewhere in **1 Pet. 1:20**; **5:4**. The true meaning is "to uncover, lay bare reveal." The following are variations in the rendering, which should be noted: Mark 16:12, 14 (RV, "was manifested," KJV, "appeared"); John 21:1 (RV, "manifested," KJV, "shewed"; cf. v. 14); Rom. 1:19 (RV, "manifested," KJV, "hath shewed"); 2 Cor. 3:3 (RV, "being made manifest," KJV, "are manifestly declared"); 2 Cor. 5:10; 7:12 and Rev. 3:18 (RV, "be made manifest," KJV, "appear"); 2 Cor. 11:6 (RV, "we have made it manifest," KJV, "we have been throughly made manifest"); Col. 1:26 (RV "hath it been manifested," KJV, "is made manifest"); 3:4 (RV, "be manifested," KJV, "appear"; so **1 Pet. 5:4**); 1 Tim. 3:16 (RV, "was manifested," KJV, "was manifest"); 2 Tim. 1:10 (RV, "hath ... been manifested," KJV, "is ... made manifest"; cf. Rom. 16:26, 2 Cor. 4:10, 11; **1 Pet. 1:20**); Heb. 9:26 (RV, "hath He been manifested," KJV, "hath He appeared"); 1 John 2:28; 3:2 (RV, "is ... made manifest," KJV, "doth appear").

Last *eschatos* (2078), "last, utmost, extreme," is used as a noun (a) of time, rendered "end" in Heb. 1:2, RV, "at the "end" of these days," i.e., at the "end" of the period under the Law, for KJV, "in these last days"; so in **1 Pet. 1:20**, "at the end of the times." In 2 Pet. 2:20, the plural, *ta eschata*, lit., "the last things," is rendered "the latter end," KJV, (RV, "the last state"); the same phrase is used in Matt. 12:45; Luke 11:26; (b) of place, Acts 13:47, KJV, "ends (of the earth)," RV, "uttermost part.

1:21 Who by him do believe in God, that raised him up from the dead, and gave him glory; that your faith and hope might be in God.

Believe *pistos* (4103), (a) in the active sense means "believing, trusting"; (b) in the passive sense, "trusty, faithful, trustworthy." It is translated "believer" in 2 Cor. 6:15; "them that believe" in 1 Tim. 4:12, RV (KJV, "believers"); in 1 Tim. 5:16, "if any woman that believeth," lit. "if any believing woman." So in 6:2, "believing masters." In **1 Pet. 1:21** the RV, following the most authentic mss., gives the noun form, "are believers in God" (KJV, "do believe in God"). In John 20:27 it is translated "believing." It is best understood with significance (a), above, e.g., in Gal. 3:9; Acts 16:1; 2 Cor. 6:15; Titus 1:6; it has significance (b), e.g., in 1 Thess. 5:24; 2 Thess. 3:3 (see *Notes on Thess.* p. 211, and *Gal.* p. 126, by Hogg and Vine).

Raised *egeiro* (1453), is used (a) of "raising" the dead, active and passive voices, e.g. of the resurrection of Christ, Matt. 16:21; 17:23; 20:19, RV; 26:32, RV, "(after) I am raised up" (KJV, "... risen again"); Luke 9:22; 20:37; John 2:19; Acts 3:15; 4:10 [not 5:30, see (c) below]; 10:40 [not 13:23 in the best texts, see (c) below]; 13:30, 37; Rom. 4:24, 25; 6:4, 9; 7:4; 8:11 (twice); 8:34, RV; 10:9; 1 Cor. 6:14 (1st part); 15:13, 14, RV; 15:15 (twice), 16, 17; 15:20, RV; 2 Cor. 4:14; Gal. 1:1; Eph. 1:20; Col. 2:12; 1 Thess. 1:10; **1 Pet. 1:21**; in 2 Tim. 2:8, RV, "risen"; (b) of the resurrection of human beings, Matt. 10:8; 11:5; Matt. 27:52. RV (KJV, "arose"); Mark 12:26, RV; Luke 7:22; John 5:21; 12:1, 9, 17; Acts 26:8; 1 Cor. 15:29 and 32, RV; 15:35, 42, 43 (twice), 44, 52; 2 Cor. 1:9; 4:14; Heb. 11:19; (c) of "raising" up a person to occupy a place in the midst of a people, said of Christ, Acts 5:30; in 13:23, KJV only (the best texts have *ago*, to bring, RV, "hath ... brought"); of David, Acts 13:22; (d) metaphorically, of a horn of salvation, Luke 1:69; (e) of children, from stones, by creative power, Luke 3:8; (f) of the Temple, as the Jews thought, John 2:20, RV, "wilt Thou raise (it) Up" (KJV, "rear"); (g) of "lifting" up a person, from physical infirmity, Mark 1:31, RV, "raised ... up" (KJV, "lifted"); so 9:27; Acts 3:7; 10:26, RV (KJV, "took"); Jas. 5:15, "shall raise ... up"; (h) metaphorically, of "raising" up affliction, Phil. 1:17, RV (in the best texts; the KJV, v. 16, following those which have *epiphero*, has "to add").

Glory *doxa* (1391), "glory" (from *dokeo*, "to seem"), primarily signifies an opinion, estimate, and hence, the honor resulting from a good opinion. It is used (I) (a) of the nature and acts of God in self-manifestation, i.e., what He essentially is and does, as exhibited in whatever way he reveals Himself in these respects, and particularly in the person of Christ, in whom essentially His "glory" has ever shone forth and ever will do, John 17:5, 24; Heb. 1:3; it was exhibited in the character and acts of Christ in the days of His flesh, John 1:14; John 2:11; at Cana both His grace and His power were manifested, and these constituted His "glory", so also in the resurrection of Lazarus 11:4, 40; the "glory" of God was exhibited in the resurrection of Christ, Rom. 6:4, and in His ascension and exaltation, **1 Pet. 1:21**, likewise on the Mount of Transfiguration, 2 Pet. 1:17. In Rom. 1:23 His "everlasting power and Divinity" are spoken of as His "glory," i.e., His attributes and power as revealed through creation; in Rom. 3:23 the word denotes the manifested perfection of His character, especially His righteousness, of which all men fall short; in Col. 1:11 "the might of His glory" signifies the might which is characteristic of His "glory"; in Eph. 1:6, 12, 14, "the praise of the glory of His grace" and "the praise of His glory" signify the due acknowledgement of the exhibition of His attributes and ways; in Eph. 1:17, "the Father of glory" describes Him as the source from whom all divine splendor and perfection proceed in their manifestation, and to whom they belong; (b) of the character and ways of God as exhibited through Christ to and through believers, 2 Cor. 3:18 and 4:6; (c) of the state of blessedness into which believers are to enter hereafter through being brought into the likeness of Christ, e.g., Rom. 8:18, 21; Phil. 3:21 (RV, "the body of His glory"); **1 Pet. 5:1, 10**; Rev. 21:11; (d) brightness or splendor, (1) supernatural, emanating from God (as in the *shekinah* "glory," in the pillar of cloud and in the Holy of Holies, e.g., Exod. 16:10; 25:22), Luke 2:9; Acts 22:11; Rom. 9:4; 2 Cor. 3:7; Jas. 2:1; in Titus 2:13 it is used of Christ's return, "the appearing of the glory of our great God and Savior Jesus Christ" (RV); cf. Phil. 3:21, above; (2) natural, as of the heavenly bodies, 1 Cor. 15:40, 41; (II) of good reputation, praise, honor, Luke 14:10 (RV, "glory," for KJV, "worship"); John 5:41 (RV, "glory," for KJV, "honor"); 7:18; 8:50; 12:43 (RV, "glory," for KJV, "praise"); 2 Cor. 6:8 (RV, "glory," for KJV "honor"); Phil. 3:19; Heb. 3:3; in 1 Cor. 11:7, of man as representing the authority of God, and of woman as rendering conspicuous the authority of man; in 1 Thess. 2:6, "glory" probably stands, by metonymy, for material gifts, an honorarium, since in human estimation "glory" is usually expressed in things material. The word is used in ascriptions of praise to God, e.g., Luke 17:18; John 9:24, RV, "glory" (KJV, "praise"); Acts 12:23; as in doxologies (lit., "glory-words"), e.g., Luke 2:14; Rom. 11:36; 16:27; Gal. 1:5; Rev. 1:6.

Hope *see 1 Peter 1:3*.

Might "May," "might," sometimes translate the prepositional phrase *eis*, "unto," with the definite article, followed by the infinitive mood of some verb, expressing purpose, e.g., Acts 3:19, "may be blotted out," lit., "unto the blotting out of"; Rom. 3:26, "that he might be," lit., "unto his being"; so 8:29; 2 Cor. 1:4, "that we may be able," lit., "unto our being able"; Eph. 1:18, "that ye may know," lit., "unto your knowing"; Acts 7:19; Rom. 1:11; 4:16; 12:2; 15:13; Phil. 1:10; 1 Thess. 3:10, 13; 2 Thess. 1:5; 2:6, 10; Heb. 12:10. In Luke 20:20 the best mss. have *hoste*, "so as to," RV, as, e.g., in **1 Pet. 1:21**. Sometimes the article with the infinitive mood without a preceding preposition, expresses result, e.g., Luke 21:22; Acts 26:18 (twice), "that they may turn," RV; cf. Rom. 6:6; 11:10; 1 Cor. 10:13; Phil. 3:10, "that I may know"; Jas. 5:17.

1:22 Seeing ye have purified your souls in obeying the truth through the Spirit unto unfeigned love of the brethren, *see that ye* love one another with a pure heart fervently:

Purified *hagnizo* (48), akin to *hagnos*, "pure", "to purify, cleanse from defilement," is used of "purifying" (a) ceremonially, John 11:55; Acts 21:24, 26; 24:18; (b) morally, the heart, Jas. 4:8; the soul, **1 Pet. 1:22**; oneself, 1 John 3:3.

Obeying *see* **Obedience** at *1 Peter 1:2*.

Unfeigned *anupokritos* (505), signifies "unfeigned"; it is said of love, 2 Cor. 6:6; **1 Pet. 1:22**; Rom. 12:9, KJV, "without dissimulation," RV, "without hypocrisy"; of faith, 1 Tim. 1:5; 2 Tim. 1:5, "unfeigned"; of the wisdom that is from above, Jas. 3:17, "without hypocrisy."

Brethren Associated words are *adelphotes*, primarily, "a brotherly relation," and so, the community possessed of this relation, "a brotherhood," **1 Pet. 2:17** (see **5:9**, marg.).; *philadelphos*, (*phileo*, "to love," and *adelphos*), "fond of one's brethren," **1 Pet. 3:8**; "loving as brethren," RV.; *philadelphia*, "brotherly love," Rom. 12:10; 1 Thess. 4:9; Heb. 13:1; "love of the brethren," **1 Pet. 1:22** and 2 Pet. 1:7, RV.; *pseudadelphos*, "false brethren," 2 Cor. 11:26; Gal. 2:4.

Pure *katharos* (2513), "pure," as being cleansed, e.g., Matt. 5:8; 1 Tim. 1:5; 3:9; 2 Tim. 1:3; 2:22; Titus 1:15; Heb. 10:22; Jas. 1:27; **1 Pet. 1:22**; Rev. 15:6; 21:18; 22:1 (in some mss.).

Fervently *ektenos* (1619), "fervently," is said of love, in **1 Pet. 1:22**; of prayer, in some mss., Acts 12:5; for the comparative degree in Luke 22:44.

1:23 Being born again, not of corruptible seed, but of incorruptible, by the word of God, which liveth and abideth for ever.

Born *see* **Begotten** at *1 Peter 1:3*.

Corruptible *see 1 Peter 1:18*.

Seed *spora* (4701), denotes "seed sown," **1 Pet. 1:23**, of human offspring. In the Sept., 2 Kings 19:29.

Liveth *see* **Lively** at *1 Peter 1:3*.

Abideth *meno* (3306), used (a) of place, e.g., Matt. 10:11, metaphorically 1 John 2:19, is said of God, 1 John 4:15; Christ, John 6:56; 15:4, etc.; the Holy Spirit, John 1:32-33; 14:17; believers, John 6:56; 15:4; 1 John 4:15, etc.; the Word of God, 1 John 2:14; the truth, 2 John 2, etc.; (b) of time; it is said of believers, John 21:22-23; Phil. 1:25; 1 John 2:17; Christ, John 12:34; Heb. 7:24; the Word of God, **1 Pet. 1:23**; sin, John 9:41; cities, Matt. 11:23; Heb. 13:14; bonds and afflictions, Acts 20:23; (c) of qualities; faith, hope, love, 1 Cor. 13:13; Christ's love, John 15:10; afflictions, Acts 20:23; brotherly love, Heb. 13:1; the love of God, 1 John 3:17; the truth, 2 John 2. The RV usually translates it by "abide," but "continue" in 1 Tim. 2:15; in the following, the RV substitutes "to abide" for the KJV, "to continue," John 2:12; 8:31; 15:9; 2 Tim. 3:14; Heb. 7:24; 13:14; 1 John 2:24.

1:24 For all flesh *is* as grass, and all the glory of man as the flower of grass. The grass withereth, and the flower thereof falleth away:

Grass *chortos* (5528), primarily denoted "a feeding enclosure" (whence Latin *hortus*, "a garden";

Eng.. "yard," and "garden"); then, "food," especially grass for feeding cattle; it is translated "grass" in Matt. 6:30; 14:19; Mark 6:39 (where "the green grass" is the first evidence of early spring); Luke 12:28; John 6:10; Jas. 1:10, 11; **1 Pet. 1:24**; Rev. 8:7; 9:4; "blade" in Matt. 13:26; Mark 4:28; "hay" in 1 Cor. 3:12, used figuratively. In Palestine or Syria there are 90 genera and 243 species of grass.

Flower *anthos* (438), "a blossom, flower" (used in certain names of flowers), occurs in Jas. 1:10, 11; **1 Pet. 1:24** (twice).

Withereth *xeraino* (3583), "to dry up, parch, wither," is translated "to wither," (a) of plants, Matt. 13:6; 21:19, 20; Mark 4:6; 11:20, RV (KJV, "dried up"), 21; Luke 8:6; John 15:6; Jas. 1:11; **1 Pet. 1:24**; (b) of members of the body, Mark 3:1, and, in some texts, 3.

Falleth *ekpipto* (1601), "to fall out of," "is used in the NT, literally, of flowers that wither in the course of nature, Jas. 1:11; **1 Pet. 1:24**; of a ship not under control, Acts 27:17, 26, 29, 32; of shackles loosed from a prisoner's wrist, 12:7; figuratively, of the Word of God (the expression of His purpose), which cannot "fall" away from the end to which it is set, Rom. 9:6; of the believer who is warned lest he "fall" away from the course in which he has been confirmed by the Word of God, 2 Pet. 3:17." So of those who seek to be justified by law, Gal. 5:4, "ye are fallen away from grace."

1:25 But the word of the Lord endureth for ever. And this is the word which by the gospel is preached unto you.

Word *rhema* (4487), denotes "that which is spoken, what is uttered in speech or writing"; in the singular, "a word," e.g., Matt. 12:36; 27:14; 2 Cor. 12:4; 13:1; Heb. 12:19; in the plural, speech, discourse, e.g., John 3:34; 8:20; Acts 2:14; 6:11, 13; 11:14; 13:42; 26:25; Rom. 10:18; 2 Pet. 3:2; Jude 17; it is used of the gospel in Rom. 10:8 (twice), 17, RV, "the word of Christ" (i.e., the "word" which preaches Christ); 10:18; **1 Pet. 1:25** (twice); of a statement, command, instruction, e.g., Matt. 26:75; Luke 1:37, RV, "(no) word (from God shall be void of power)", v. 38; Acts 11:16; Heb. 11:3. The significance of *rhema* (as distinct from *logos*) is exemplified in the injunction to take "the sword of the Spirit, which is the word of God," Eph. 6:17; here the reference is not to the whole Bible as such, but to the individual scripture which the Spirit brings to our remembrance for use in time of need, a prerequisite being the regular storing of the mind with Scripture.

Lord *kurios* (2962), properly an adjective, signifying "having power" (*kuros*) or "authority," is used as a noun, variously translated in the NT, " 'Lord,' 'master,' 'Master,' 'owner,' 'Sir,' a title of wide significance, occurring in each book of the NT save Titus and the Epistles of John. It is used (a) of an owner, as in Luke 19:33, cf. Matt. 20:8; Acts 16:16; Gal. 4:1; or of one who has the disposal of anything, as the Sabbath, Matt. 12:8; (b) of a master, i.e., one to whom service is due on any ground, Matt. 6:24; 24:50; Eph. 6:5; (c) of an Emperor or King, Acts 25:26; Rev. 17:14; (d) of idols, ironically, 1 Cor. 8:5, cf. Isa. 26:13; (e) as a title of respect addressed to a father, Matt. 21:30, a husband, **1 Pet. 3:6**, a master, Matt. 13:27; Luke 13:8, a ruler, Matt. 27:63, an angel, Acts 10:4; Rev. 7:14; (f) as a title of courtesy addressed to a stranger, John 12:21; 20:15; Acts 16:30; from the outset of His ministry this was a common form of address to the Lord Jesus, alike by the people, Matt. 8:2; John 4:11, and by His disciples, Matt. 8:25; Luke 5:8; John 6:68; (g) *kurios* is the Sept. and NT representative of Heb. Jehovah ('LORD' in Eng. versions), see Matt. 4:7; Jas. 5:11, e.g., of *adon*, Lord, Matt. 22:44, and of *Adonay*, Lord, 1:22; it also occurs for *Elohim*, God, **1 Pet. 1:25**.

"Thus the usage of the word in the NT follows two main lines: one, *a–f*, customary and general, the other, *g*, peculiar to the Jews, and drawn from the Greek translation of the OT.

"Christ Himself assumed the title, Matt. 7:21, 22; 9:38; 22:41-45; Mark 5:19 (cf. Ps. 66:16; the parallel passage, Luke 8:39, has 'God'); Luke 19:31; John 13:13, apparently intending it in the higher senses of its current use, and at the same time suggesting its OT associations. His purpose did not become clear to the disciples until after His resurrection, and the revelation of His Deity consequent thereon. Thomas, when he realized the significance of the presence of a mortal wound in the body of a living man, immediately joined with it the absolute title of Deity, saying, 'My Lord and my God,' John 20:28. Thereafter, except in Acts 10:4 and Rev. 7:14, there is no record that *kurios* was ever again used by believers in addressing any save God and the Lord Jesus; cf Acts 2:47 with 4:29, 30. How soon and how completely the lower meaning had been superseded is seen in Peter's declaration in his first sermon after the resurrection, 'God hath made Him – Lord,' Acts 2:36, and that in the house of Cornelius, 'He is Lord of all,' 10:36, cf. Deut. 10:14; Matt. 11:25; Acts 17:24. In his writings the implications of his early teaching are confirmed and developed. Thus Ps. 34:8, 'O taste and see that Jehovah is good,' is applied to the

Lord Jesus, **1 Pet. 2:3**, and 'Jehovah of Hosts, Him shall ye sanctify,' Isa. 8:13, becomes 'sanctify in your hearts Christ as Lord,' 3:15 ..."

Endureth *meno* (3306), "to abide," is rendered "to endure" in the KJV of John 6:27 and **1 Pet. 1:25** (RV, "abideth"); Heb. 10:34, KJV, "enduring (substance)," RV, "abiding."

Gospel *euangelizo* (2097), "to bring or announce glad tidings" (Eng., "evangelize"), is used (a) in the active voice in Rev. 10:7 ("declared") and 14:6 ("to proclaim," RV, KJV, "to preach"); (b) in the passive voice, of matters to be proclaimed as "glad tidings," Luke 16:16; Gal. 1:11; **1 Pet. 1:25**; of persons to whom the proclamation is made, Matt. 11:5; Luke 7:22; Heb. 4:2, 6; **1 Pet. 4:6**; (c) in the middle voice, especially of the message of salvation, with a personal object, either of the person preached, e.g., Acts 5:42; 11:20; Gal. 1:16, or, with a preposition, of the persons evangelized, e.g., Acts 13:32, "declare glad tidings"; Rom. 1:15; Gal. 1:8; with an impersonal object, e.g., "the word," Acts 8:4; "good tidings," 8:12; "the word of the Lord," 15:35; "the gospel," 1 Cor. 15:1; 2 Cor. 11:7; "the faith," Gal. 1:23; "peace," Eph. 2:17; "the unsearchable riches of Christ, 3:8.

Chapter 2

2:1 Wherefore laying aside all malice, and all guile, and hypocrisies, and envies, and all evil speakings,

Laying aside *apotithemi* (659), always in the middle voice in the NT, "to put off (*apo*) from oneself," is rendered "to put away" in the RV in the following: Eph. 4:22 (KJV, "put off"); Col. 3:8 (KJV, ditto); Eph. 4:25; Jas. 1:21 (KJV, "laying apart"); **1 Pet. 2:1** (KJV, "laying aside").

Malice *kakia* (2549), "badness in quality" (the opposite of *arete*, "excellence"), "the vicious character generally" (Lightfoot), is translated "malice" in 1 Cor. 5:8; 14:20; Eph. 4:31; Col. 3:8; Titus 3:3; **1 Pet. 2:1**, KJV (RV, "wickedness"; marg., "malice"); "maliciousness" in Rom. 1:29; in **1 Pet. 2:16**, KJV (RV, "wickedness"; marg., "malice"). Elsewhere, Matt. 6:34; Acts 8:22; Jas. 1:21 (RV marg., "malice").

Guile *dolos* (1388), "a bait, snare, deceit," is rendered "guile" in John 1:47, negatively of Nathanael; Acts 13:10, RV, KJV, "subtlety" (of Bar-Jesus); 2 Cor. 12:16, in a charge made against Paul by his detractors, of catching the Corinthian converts by "guile" (the apostle is apparently quoting the language of his critics); 1 Thess. 2:3, negatively, of the teaching of the apostle and his fellow missionaries; **1 Pet. 2:1**, of that from which Christians are to be free; **2:22**, of the guileless speech of Christ; **3:10**, of the necessity that the speech of Christians should be guileless. See also Matt. 26:4; Mark 7:22; 14:1.

Hypocrisies *hupokrisis* (5272), primarily denotes "a reply, an answer" (akin to *hupokrinomai*, "to answer"); then, "play-acting," as the actors spoke in dialogue; hence, "pretence, hypocrisy"; it is translated "hypocrisy" in Matt. 23:28; Mark 12:15; Luke 12:1; 1 Tim. 4:2; the plural in **1 Pet. 2:1**. For Gal. 2:13 and *anupokritos*, "without hypocrisy," in Jas. 3:17.

Envies *phthonos* (5355), "envy," is the feeling of displeasure produced by witnessing or hearing of the advantage or prosperity of others; this evil sense always attaches to this word, Matt. 27:18; Mark 15:10; Rom. 1:29; Gal. 5:21; Phil. 1:15; 1 Tim. 6:4; Titus 3:3; **1 Pet. 2:1**; so in Jas. 4:5, where the question is rhetorical and strongly remonstrative, signifying that the Spirit (or spirit) which God made to dwell in us was certainly not so bestowed that we should be guilty of "envy."

Evil speakings *katalalia* (2636), "evil speaking," **1 Pet. 2:1**.

2:2 As newborn babes, desire the sincere milk of the word, that ye may grow thereby:

Newborn *artigennetos* (738), "newborn," is used in **1 Pet. 2:2**.

Babes *brephos* (1025), denotes (a) "an unborn child," as in Luke 1:41, 44; (b) "a newborn child, or an infant still older," Luke 2:12, 16; 18:15; Acts 7:19; 2 Tim. 3:15; **1 Pet. 2:2**.

Desire *epipotheo*, "to long after, to lust"; in 2 Cor. 5:2, RV, "longing"; in 1 Thess. 3:6 and 2 Tim. 1:4, RV, "longing"; in **1 Pet. 2:2**, RV, "long for."

Sincere *adolos* (97), "guileless, pure," is translated "sincere" in **1 Pet. 2:2**, KJV, "without guile," RV.

Milk *gala* (1051), is used (a) literally, 1 Cor. 9:7; (b) metaphorically, of rudimentary spiritual teaching, 1 Cor. 3:2; Heb. 5:12, 13; **1 Pet. 2:2**; here the meaning largely depends upon the significance of the word *logikos*, which the KJV renders "of the word," RV "spiritual." While *logos* denotes "a word," the adjective *logikos* is never used with the meaning assigned to it in the KJV, nor does the context in **1:23** compel this meaning. While it is true that the Word of God, like "milk," nourishes the soul, and this is involved in the exhortation, the only other occurrence in the NT is Rom. 12:1, where it is translated "reasonable," i.e., rational, intelligent (service), in contrast to the offering of an irrational animal; so here the nourishment may be understood as of that spiritually rational nature which, acting through the regenerate mind, develops spiritual growth. God's Word is not given so that it is impossible to understand it, or that it requires a special class of men to interpret it; its character is such that the Holy Spirit who gave it can unfold its truths even to the young convert. Cf. 1 John 2:27.

Word For *logikos*, **1 Pet. 2:2** (RV, "spiritual"), rendered "of the word," KJV.

Grow *auxano* (837), "to grow or increase," of the growth of that which lives, naturally or spiritually, is used (a) transitively, signifying to make to increase, said of giving the increase, 1 Cor. 3:6, 7; 2 Cor. 9:10, the effect of the work of God, according to the analogy of His operations in nature; "to grow, become greater," e.g. of plants and fruit, Matt. 6:28; used in the passive voice in 13:32 and Mark 4:8, "increase"; in the active in Luke 12:27; 13:19; of the body, Luke 1:80; 2:40; of Christ, John 3:30, "increase"; of the work of the gospel of God, Acts 6:7, "increased"; 12:24; 19:20; of people, Acts 7:17; of faith, 2 Cor. 10:15 (passive voice), RV, "groweth" (KJV, "is increased"); of believers individually, Eph. 4:15; Col. 1:6, RV, 10 (passive voice), "increasing"; **1 Pet. 2:2**; 2 Pet. 3:18; of the church, Col. 2:19; of churches, Eph. 2:21.

Thereby *en aute*, "in, or by, it," is rendered "thereby" in Rom. 10:5; *en auto* in Eph. 2:16 (some texts have *en heauto*, "in Himself"); **1 Pet. 2:2**.

2:3 If so be ye have tasted that the Lord *is* gracious.

Tasted *geuo* (1089), "to make to taste," is used in the middle voice, signifying "to taste" (a) naturally, Matt. 27:34; Luke 14:24; John 2:9; Col. 2:21; (b) metaphorically, of Christ's "tasting" death, implying His personal experience in voluntarily undergoing death, Heb. 2:9; of believers (negatively) as to "tasting" of death, Matt. 16:28; Mark 9:1; Luke 9:27; John 8:52; of "tasting" the heavenly gift (different from receiving it), Heb. 6:4; "the good word of God, and the powers of the age to come," 6:5; "that the Lord is gracious," **1 Pet. 2:3**.

Lord *see* ***1 Peter 1:25.***

Gracious *chrestos* (5543), primarily signifies "fit for use, able to be used" (akin to *chraomai*, "to use"), hence, "good, virtuous, mild, pleasant" (in contrast to what is hard, harsh, sharp, bitter). It is said (a) of the character of God as "kind, gracious," Luke 6:35; **1 Pet. 2:3**; "good," Rom. 2:4, where the neuter of the adjective is used as a noun, "the goodness" (cf. the corresponding noun *chrestotes*, "goodness," in the same verse); of the yoke of Christ, Matt. 11:30, "easy" (a suitable rendering would be "kindly"); (c) of believers, Eph. 4:32; (d) of things, as wine, Luke 5:39, RV, "good," for KJV, "better" (cf. Jer. 24:3, 5, of figs); (e) ethically, of manners, 1 Cor. 15:33.

2:4 To whom coming, *as unto* a living stone, disallowed indeed of men, but chosen of God, *and* precious,

Living *see* **Lively** at ***1 Peter 1:3.***

Stone *lithos* (3037), is used (I) literally, of (a) the "stones" of the ground, e.g., Matt. 4:3, 6; 7:9; (b) "tombstones," e.g., Matt. 27:60, 66; (c) "building stones," e.g., Matt. 21:42; (d) "a millstone," Luke 17:2; cf. Rev. 18:21; (e) the "tables (or tablets)" of the Law, 2 Cor. 3:7; (f) "idol images," Acts 17:29; (g) the "treasures" of commercial Babylon, Rev. 18:12, 16; (II) metaphorically, of (a) Christ, Rom. 9:33; **1 Pet. 2:4, 6, 8**; (b) believers, **1 Pet. 2:5**; (c) spiritual edification by scriptural teaching, 1 Cor. 3:12; (d) the adornment of the foundations of the wall of the spiritual and heavenly Jerusalem, Rev. 21:19; (e) the adornment of the seven angels in Rev. 15:6, RV (so the best texts; some have *linon*, "linen," KJV); (f) the adornment of religious Babylon, Rev. 17:4; (III) figuratively, of Christ, Rev. 4:3; 21:11, where "light" stands for "Light-giver" (*phoster*).

Disallowed *apodokimazo* (593), "to reject as the result of disapproval" (*apo*, "away from," *dokimazo*, "to approve"), is always translated "to reject," except in the KJV of **1 Pet. 2:4** and **7**.

Chosen *eklektos* (1588), lit. signifies "picked out, chosen" (*ek*, "from," *lego*, "to gather, pick out"), and is used of (a) Christ, the "chosen" of God, as the Messiah, Luke 23:35, and metaphorically as a "living Stone," "a chief corner Stone," **1 Pet. 2:4, 6**; some mss. have it in John 1:34, instead of *huios*, "Son"; (b) angels, 1 Tim. 5:21, as "chosen" to be of especially high rank in administrative association with God, or as His messengers to human beings, doubtless in contrast to fallen angels (see 2 Pet. 2:4 and Jude 6); (c) believers (Jews or Gentiles), Matt. 24:22, 24, 31; Mark 13:20, 22, 27; Luke 18:7; Rom. 8:33; Col. 3:12; 2 Tim. 2:10; Titus 1:1; **1 Pet. 2:9** (as a spiritual race); Matt. 20:16; 22:14 and Rev. 17:14, "chosen"; individual believers are so mentioned in Rom. 16:13; 2 John 1, 13. Believers were "chosen" "before the foundation of the world" (cf. "before times eternal," 2 Tim. 1:9), in Christ, Eph. 1:4, to adoption, Eph. 1:5; good works, 2:10; conformity to Christ, Rom. 8:29; salvation from the delusions of the Antichrist and the doom of the deluded, 2 Thess. 2:13; eternal glory, Rom. 9:23. The source of their "election" is God's grace, not human will, Eph. 1:4, 5; Rom. 9:11; 11:5. They are given by God the Father to Christ as the fruit of His death, all being foreknown and foreseen by God, John 17:6 and Rom. 8:29. While Christ's death was sufficient for all men, and is effective in the case of the "elect," yet men are treated as responsible, being capable of the will and power to choose. For the rendering "being chosen as firstfruits," an alternative reading in 2 Thess. 2:13.

Precious *entimos* (1784), "held in honor, precious, dear," is found in Luke 7:2, of the centurion's servant; 14:8, "more honorable"; Phil. 2:29, "honor" (KJV, "reputation"), of devoted servants of Christ, in **1 Pet. 2:4, 6**, "precious," of stones, metaphorically. *See also **1 Peter 1:7.***

2:5 Ye also, as lively stones, are built up a spiritual house, an holy priesthood, to offer up spiritual sacrifices, acceptable to God by Jesus Christ.

Lively *see **1 Peter 1:3.***

Stones *see* **Stone** at ***1 Peter 2:4.***

Spiritual *pneumatikos* (4152), "always connotes the ideas of invisibility and of power. It does not occur in the Sept. nor in the Gospels; it is in fact an after-Pentecost word. In the NT it is used as follows: (a) the angelic hosts, lower than God but higher in the scale of being than man in his natural state, are 'spiritual hosts,' Eph. 6:12; (b) things that have their origin with God, and which, therefore, are in harmony with His character, as His law is, are 'spiritual,' Rom. 7:14; (c) 'spiritual' is prefixed to the material type in order to indicate that what the type sets forth, not the type itself, is intended, 1 Cor. 10:3, 4; (d) the purposes of God revealed in the gospel by the Holy Spirit, 1 Cor. 2:13a, and the words in which that revelation is expressed, are 'spiritual,' 13b, matching, or combining, spiritual things with spiritual words [or, alternatively, 'interpreting spiritual things to spiritual men,' see (e) below]; 'spiritual songs' are songs of which the burden is the things revealed by the Spirit, Eph. 5:19; Col. 3:16; 'spiritual wisdom and understanding' is wisdom in, and understanding of, those things, Col. 1:9; (e) men in Christ who walk so as to please God are 'spiritual,' Gal. 6:1; 1 Cor. 2:13b [but see (d) above], 15; 3:1; 14:37; (f) the whole company of those who believe in Christ is a 'spiritual house,' **1 Pet. 2:5a**; (g) the blessings that accrue to regenerate men at this present time are called 'spiritualities,' Rom. 15:27; 1 Cor. 9:11; 'spiritual blessings,' Eph. 1:3; 'spiritual gifts,' Rom. 1:11; (h) the activities Godward of regenerate men are 'spiritual sacrifices,' **1 Pet. 2:5b**; their appointed activities in the churches are also called 'spiritual gifts,' lit., 'spiritualities,' 1 Cor. 12:1; 14:1; (i) the resurrection body of the dead in Christ is 'spiritual,' i.e., such as is suited to the heavenly environment, 1 Cor. 15:44; (j) all that is produced and maintained among men by the operations of the Spirit of God is 'spiritual,' 1 Cor. 15:46 ..."

House *oikos* (3624), denotes (a) "a house, a dwelling," e.g., Matt. 9:6, 7; 11:8; it is used of the Tabernacle, as the House of God, Matt. 12:4, and the Temple similarly, e.g., Matt. 21:13; Luke 11:51, KJV, "temple," RV, "sanctuary"; John 2:16, 17; called by the Lord "your house" in Matt. 23:38 and Luke 13:35 (some take this as the city of Jerusalem); metaphorically of Israel as God's house, Heb. 3:2, 5, where "his house" is not Moses', but God's; of believers, similarly, v. 6, where Christ is spoken of as "over God's House" (the word "own" is rightly omitted in the RV); Heb. 10:21; **1 Pet. 2:5**; **4:17**; of the body, Matt. 12:44; Luke 11:24; (b) by metonymy, of the members of a household or family, e.g., Luke 10:5; Acts 7:10; 11:14; 1 Tim. 3:4, 5, 12; 2 Tim. 1:16; 4:19, RV (KJV, "household"); Titus 1:11 (plural); of a local church, 1 Tim. 3:15; of the descendants of Jacob (Israel) and David, e.g., Matt. 10:6; Luke 1:27, 33; Acts 2:36; 7:42.

Holy *see **1 Peter 1:12.***

Priesthood *hierateuma* (2406), denotes "a priesthood," "a body of priests," consisting of all believers, the whole church (not a special order from among them), called "a holy priesthood," **1 Pet. 2:5**; "a royal priesthood," v. **9**; the former term is associated with offering spiritual sacrifices, the latter with the royal dignity of showing forth the Lord's excellencies (RV). In the Sept., Exod. 19:6; 23:22.

Offer *anaphero* (399), primarily, "to lead" or "carry up" (*ana*), also denotes "to offer," (a) of Christ's sacrifice, Heb. 7:27; (b) of sacrifices under the Law, Heb. 7:27; (c) of such previous to the Law, Jas. 2:21 (of Isaac by Abraham); (d) of praise, Heb. 13:15; (e) of spiritual sacrifices in general, **1 Pet. 2:5**.

Sacrifices *thusia* (2378), primarily denotes "the act of offering"; then, objectively, "that which is offered" (a) of idolatrous "sacrifice," Acts 7:41; (b) of animal or other "sacrifices," as offered under the Law, Matt. 9:13; 12:7; Mark 9:49; 12:33; Luke 2:24; 13:1; Acts 7:42; 1 Cor. 10:18; Heb. 5:1; 7:27 (RV, plural);

8:3; 9:9; 10:1, 5, 8 (RV, plural), 11; 11:4; (c) of Christ, in His "sacrifice" on the cross, Eph. 5:2; Heb. 9:23, where the plural antitypically comprehends the various forms of Levitical "sacrifices" in their typical character; 9:26; 10:12, 26; (d) metaphorically, (1) of the body of the believer, presented to God as a living "sacrifice," Rom. 12:1; (2) of faith, Phil. 2:17; (3) of material assistance rendered to servants of God, Phil. 4:18; (4) of praise, Heb. 13:15; (5) of doing good to others and communicating with their needs, Heb. 13:16; (6) of spiritual "sacrifices" in general, offered by believers as a holy priesthood, **1 Pet. 2:5**.

Acceptable *euprosdektos* (2144), a still stronger form of *dektos*, signifies a "very favorable acceptance" (*eu*, "well," *pros*, "towards," *dektos*, "a person or thing who has been regarded favorably"), Rom. 15:16, 31; 2 Cor. 6:2; 8:12; **1 Pet. 2:5**.

2:6 Wherefore also it is contained in the scripture, Behold, I lay in Sion a chief corner stone, elect, precious: and he that believeth on him shall not be confounded.

Contained *periecho* (4023), lit., "to have round" (*peri*, "around," *echo*, "to have"), means "to encompass, enclose, contain," as a writing contains details, **1 Pet. 2:6**. Some mss. have it in Acts 23:25, lit., "having this form" (the most authentic have *echo*, "to have"). For the secondary meaning, "amazed" (KJV, "astonished"), Luke 5:9 (lit., "amazement encompassed," i.e., seized, him).

Chief corner stone *akrogoniaios* (204), denotes "a chief corner-stone" (from *akros*, "highest, extreme," *gonia*, "a corner, angle"), Eph. 2:20 and **1 Pet. 2:6**. In the Sept., Isa. 28:16. *See also* **Stone** at *1 Peter 2:4*.

Elect *see* **Chosen** at *1 Peter 2:4*.

Precious *see 1 Peter 2:4. See also 1 Peter 1:7.*

Confounded *kataischuno* (2617), another strengthened form (*kata*, "down," intensive), is used (a) in the active voice, "to put to shame," e.g., Rom. 5:5; 1 Cor. 1:27 (KJV, "confound"); 11:4-5 ("dishonoreth"), and v. 22; (b) in the passive voice, Rom. 9:33; 10:11; 2 Cor. 7:14; **1 Pet. 2:6; 3:16**.

2:7 Unto you therefore which believe *he is* precious: but unto them which be disobedient, the stone which the builders disallowed, the same is made the head of the corner,

Precious In **1 Pet. 2:7**, KJV, the noun *time*, is translated "precious" (RV, "preciousness"). *See also 1 Peter 1:7.*

Disobedient *apeitheo* (544), "to refuse to be persuaded, to refuse belief, to be disobedient," is translated "disobedient," or by the verb "to be disobedient," in the RV of Acts 14:2 (KJV, "unbelieving"), and 19:9 (KJV, "believed not"); it is absent from the most authentic mss. in Acts 17:5; in John 3:36 "obeyeth not," RV (KJV, "believeth not"); in Rom. 2:8 "obey not"; in 10:21, "disobedient"; in 11:30, 31, "were disobedient" (KJV, "have not believed"); so in 15:31; Heb. 3:18; 11:31; in **1 Pet. 2:8**, "disobedient"; so in **3:20**; in **3:1** and **4:17**, "obey not." In **2:7** the best mss. have *apisteo*, "to disbelieve."

apisteo (569), "to be unbelieving" (*a*, negative, *pistis*, "faith"; cf. *apistos*, "unbelieving"), is translated "believed not," etc., in the KJV (except in **1 Pet. 2:7**, "be disobedient"); "disbelieve" (or "disbelieved") in the RV, in Mark 16:11, 16; Luke 24:11, 41; Acts 28:24; "disbelieve" is the best rendering, implying that the unbeliever has had a full opportunity of believing and has rejected it; some mss. have *apeitheo*, "to be disobedient," in **1 Pet. 2:7**; Rom. 3:3, RV, "were without faith"; 2 Tim. 2:13, RV, "are faithless."

Builders *oikodomeo* (3618), lit., "to build a house" (*oikos*, "a house," *domeo*, "to build"), hence, to build anything, e.g., Matt. 7:24; Luke 4:29; 6:48, RV, "well builded" (last clause of verse); John 2:20; is frequently used figuratively, e.g., Acts 20:32; Gal. 2:18; especially of edifying, Acts 9:31; Rom. 15:20; 1 Cor. 10:23; 14:4; 1 Thess. 5:11 (RV). In 1 Cor. 8:10 it is translated "emboldened" (marg., "builded up"). The participle with the article (equivalent to a noun) is rendered "builder," Matt. 21:42; Acts 4:11; **1 Pet. 2:7**.

Disallowed *see 1 Peter 2:4.*

Made *ginomai* (1096), "to become," is sometimes translated by the passive voice of the verb to make, e.g., Matt. 9:16; John 1:3 (three times), 10; 8:33; Rom. 11:9; 1 Cor. 1:30; 3:13; 4:9, 13; Eph. 2:13; 3:7; Phil. 2:7 (but RV marg., "becoming"); Col. 1:23, 25; Heb. 5:5; 6:4; 7:12, 16, 21, 26; 11:3; Jas. 3:9; **1 Pet. 2:7**. In many places the RV translates otherwise, and chiefly by the verb to become, e.g., Matt. 25:6, "there is"; 27:24, "was arising"; John 1:14, "became"; John 2:9, "become"; Rom. 1:3, "born"; 2:25, "is become"; 10:20, "became"; Gal. 3:13, "having become"; 4:4, "born" (twice); Heb. 3:14, "are become", 7:22, "hath ... become."

Corner *gonia* (1137), "an angle" (Eng., "coign"), signifies (a) "an external angle," as of the "corner" of a street, Matt. 6:5; or of a building, 21:42; Mark 12:10; Luke 20:17; Acts 4:11;

1 Pet. 2:7, "the corner stone or head-stone of the corner"; or the four extreme limits of the earth, Rev. 7:1; 20:8; (b) "an internal corner," a secret place, Acts 26:26.

2:8 And a stone of stumbling, and a rock of offence, *even to them* which stumble at the word, being disobedient: whereunto also they were appointed.

Stone of stumbling *proskomma* (4348), "an obstacle against which one may dash his foot" (akin to *proskopto*, "to stumble" or "cause to stumble"; *pros*, "to or against," *kopto*, "to strike"), is translated "offense" in Rom. 14:20, in v. 13, "a stumbling-block," of the spiritual hindrance to another by a selfish use of liberty; so in 1 Cor. 8:9. It is used of Christ, in Rom. 9:32-33, RV, "(a stone) of stumbling," and **1 Pet. 2:8**, where the KJV also has this rendering. Cf. the Sept. in Ex. 23:33, "these (the gods of the Canaanites) will be an offense (stumblingblock) unto thee." *See also* **Stone** at *1 Peter 2:4.*

Rock *petra* (4073), denotes "a mass of rock," as distinct from *petros*, "a detached stone or boulder," or a stone that might be thrown or easily moved. For the nature of *petra*, see Matt. 7:24, 25; 27:51, 60; Mark 15:46; Luke 6:48 (twice), a type of a sure foundation (here the true reading is as in the RV, "because it had been well builded"); Rev. 6:15, 16 (cf. Isa. 2:19ff.; Hos. 10:8); Luke 8:6, 13, used illustratively; 1 Cor. 10:4 (twice), figuratively, of Christ; in Rom. 9:33 and **1 Pet. 2:8**, metaphorically, of Christ; in Matt. 16:18, metaphorically, of Christ and the testimony concerning Him; here the distinction between *petra*, concerning the Lord Himself, and *Petros*, the apostle, is clear.

Offence *skandalon* (4625), originally was "the name of the part of a trap to which the bait is attached, hence, the trap or snare itself, as in Rom. 11:9, RV, 'stumblingblock,' quoted from Psa. 69:22, and in Rev. 2:14, for Balaam's device was rather a trap for Israel than a stumblingblock to them, and in Matt. 16:23, for in Peter's words the Lord perceived a snare laid for Him by Satan.

"In NT *skandalon* is always used metaphorically, and ordinarily of anything that arouses prejudice, or becomes a hindrance to others, or causes them to fall by the way. Sometimes the hindrance is in itself good, and those stumbled by it are the wicked."

Thus it is used (a) of Christ in Rom. 9:33, "(a rock) of offense"; so **1 Pet. 2:8**; 1 Cor. 1:23 (KJV and RV, "stumblingblock"), and of His cross, Gal. 5:11 (RV, ditto); of the "table" provided by God for Israel, Rom. 11:9; (b) of that which is evil, e.g., Matt. 13:41, RV, "things that cause stumbling" (KJV, "things that offend"), lit., "all stumblingblocks"; 18:7, RV, "occasions of stumbling" and "occasion"; Luke 17:1 (ditto); Rom. 14:13, RV, "an occasion of falling" (KJV, "an occasion to fall"), said of such a use of Christian liberty as proves a hindrance to another; 16:17, RV, "occasions of stumbling," said of the teaching of things contrary to sound doctrine; 1 John 2:10, "occasion of stumbling," of the absence of this in the case of one who loves his brother and thereby abides in the light. Love, then, is the best safeguard against the woes pronounced by the Lord upon those who cause others to stumble. Cf. the Sept. in Hos. 4:17, "Ephraim partaking with idols hath laid stumbling-blocks in his own path."

Stumble *proskopto* (4350), "to strike against," is used of "stumbling," (a) physically, John 11:9, 10; (b) metaphorically, (1) of Israel in regard to Christ, whose Person, teaching, and atoning death, and the gospel relating thereto, were contrary to all their ideas as to the means of righteousness before God, Rom. 9:32; **1 Pet. 2:8**; (2) of a brother in the Lord in acting against the dictates of his conscience, Rom. 14:21.

Disobedient *see 1 Peter 2:7.*

Appointed *tithemi* (5087), "to put," is used of "appointment" to any form of service. Christ used it of His followers, John 15:16 (RV, "appointed" for KJV, "ordained"). "I set you" would be more in keeping with the metaphor of grafting. The verb is used by Paul of his service in the ministry of the gospel, 1 Tim. 1:12 (RV, "appointing" for "putting"); 2:7 (RV, "appointed" for "ordained"); and 2 Tim. 1:11 (RV, "appointing" for "putting"); of the overseers, or bishops, in the local church at Ephesus, as those "appointed" by the Holy Ghost, to tend the church of God, Acts 20:28 ("hath made"); of the Son of God, as appointed Heir of all things, Heb. 1:2. It is also used of "appointment" to punishment, as of the unfaithful servant, Matt. 24:51; Luke 12:46; of unbelieving Israel, **1 Pet. 2:8**. Cf. 2 Pet. 2:6.

2:9 But ye *are* a chosen generation, a royal priesthood, an holy nation, a peculiar people; that ye should shew forth the praises of him who hath called you out of darkness into his marvellous light:

Ye These are most frequently the translations of various inflections of a verb; sometimes of the article before a nominative used as a vocative, e.g., Rev. 18:20, "ye saints, and ye apostles, and ye prophets" (lit., "the saints, etc."). When the 2nd person plural pronouns are used separately from a verb, they are usually one or other of the forms of *humeis*, the plural of *su*, "thou," and are frequently emphatic, especially when they are subjects of the verb, an emphasis always to be noticed, e.g., Matt. 5:13, 14, 48; 6:9, 19, 20; Mark 6:31, 37; John 15:27a; Rom. 1:6; 1 Cor. 3:17, 23; Gal. 3:28, 29a; Eph. 1:13a; 2:8; 2:11, 13; Phil. 2:18; Col. 3:4, 7a; 4:1; 1 Thess. 1:6; 2:10, 19, 20; 3:8; 2 Thess. 3:13; Jas. 5:8; **1 Pet. 2:9a**; 1 John 2:20, 24 (1st and 3rd occurrences), 27a; 4:4; Jude 17, 20.

Chosen *see 1 Peter 2:4.*

Generation For *genos*, translated "generation" in **1 Pet. 2:9**, KJV.

Royal *basileios* (934), from *basileus*, "a king," is used in **1 Pet. 2:9** of the priesthood consisting of all believers. In the Sept., Ex. 19:6; 23:22; Deut. 3:10.

Priesthood *see 1 Peter 2:5.*

Holy *see 1 Peter 1:12.*

Nation *genos* (1085), akin to *ginomai*, "to become," denotes (a) "a family," Acts 4:6, "kindred;" 7:13, RV, "race" (KJV, "kindred"); 13:26, "stock"; (b) "an offspring," Acts 17:28; Rev. 22:16; (c) "a nation, a race," Mark 7:26, RV, "race" (KJV, "nation"); Acts 4:36, RV "(a man of Cyprus) by race," KJV, "of the country (of Cyprus);" *genos* does not mean "a country;" the word here signifies "parentage" (Jews had settled in Cyprus from, or even before, the reign of Alexander the Great); 7:19, RV, "race" (KJV, "kindred"); 18:2, 24, RV, "by race" (KJV, "born"); 2 Cor. 11:26, "countrymen"; Gal. 1:14, RV, "countrymen" (KJV, "nation"); Phil. 3:5, "stock"; **1 Pet. 2:9**, RV, "race" (KJV, "generation"); (d) "a kind, sort, class," Matt. 13:47, "kind"; in some mss. in 17:21, KJV, "kind;" Mark 9:29, "kind"; 1 Cor. 12:10, 28, "kinds" (KJV, "diversities"); 14:10 (ditto).

Peculiar *peripoiesis* (4047), lit., "a making around" (*peri*, "around," *poieo*, "to do or make"), denotes (a) "the act of obtaining" anything, as of salvation in its completeness 1 Thess. 5:9; 2 Thess. 2:14; (b) "a thing acquired, an acquisition, possession," Eph. 1:14, RV, "(*God's* own) possession" [some would put this under (a)]; so **1 Pet. 2:9**, RV, KJV, "a peculiar (people);" cf. Isa. 43:21; (c) preservation, this may be the meaning in Heb. 10:39, "saving" (RV marg., "gaining"); cf. the corresponding verb in Luke 17:33 (in the best texts), "preserve." In the Sept. the noun has the meaning (b) in Hag. 2:10 and Mal. 3:17, (c) in 2 Chron. 14:13.

People *laos* (2992), is used of (a) "the people at large," especially of people assembled, e.g., Matt. 27:25; Luke 1:21; 3:15; Acts 4:27; (b) "a people of the same race and language," e.g., Rev. 5:9; in the plural, e.g., Luke 2:31; Rom. 15:11; Rev. 7:9; 11:9; especially of Israel, e.g., Matt. 2:6; 4:23; John 11:50; Acts 4:8; Heb. 2:17; in distinction from their rulers and priests, e.g., Matt. 26:5; Luke 20:19; Heb. 5:3; in distinction from Gentiles, e.g., Acts 26:17, 23; Rom. 15:10; (c) of Christians as the people of God, e.g., Acts 15:14; Titus 2:14; Heb. 4:9; **1 Pet. 2:9**.

Shew *exangello* (1804), "to tell out, proclaim abroad, to publish completely" (*ek*, or *ex*, "out," *angello*, "to proclaim"), is rendered "show forth" in **1 Pet. 2:9**; it indicates a complete proclamation (verbs compounded with *ek* often suggest what is to be done fully).

Praises *arete* (703), properly denotes whatever procures preeminent estimation for a person or thing; hence, "intrinsic eminence, moral goodness, virtue," (a) of God, **1 Pet. 2:9**, "excellencies" (KJV, "praises"); here the original and general sense seems to be blended with the impression made on others, i.e., renown, excellence or praise (Hort); in 2 Pet. 1:3, "(by His own glory and) virtue," RV (instrumental dative), i.e., the manifestation of His divine power; this significance is frequently illustrated in the papyri and was evidently common in current Greek speech; (b) of any particular moral excellence, Phil. 4:8; 2 Pet. 1:5 (twice), where virtue is enjoined as an essential quality in the exercise of faith, RV, "(in your faith supply) virtue."

Darkness *skotos* (4655), a neuter noun frequent in the Sept., is used in the NT as the equivalent of (a) of "physical darkness," Matt. 27:45; 2 Cor. 4:6; (b) of "intellectual darkness," Rom. 2:19; (c) of "blindness," Acts 13:11; (d) by metonymy, of the "place of punishment," e.g., Matt. 8:12; 2 Pet. 2:17; Jude 13; (e) metaphorically, of "moral and spiritual darkness," e.g., Matt. 6:23; Luke 1:79; 11:35; John 3:19; Acts 26:18; 2 Cor. 6:14; Eph. 6:12; Col. 1:13; 1 Thess. 5:4-5; **1 Pet. 2:9**; 1 John 1:6; (f) by metonymy, of "those who are in moral or spiritual darkness," Eph. 5:8; (g) of "evil works," Rom. 13:12; Eph. 5:11, (h) of the "evil powers that dominate the world," Luke 22:53; (i) "of secrecy." While *skotos* is used more than twice as many times as *skotia* in the NT, the apostle John uses *skotos* only once, 1 John 1:6, but *skotia* 15 times out of the 18.

"With the exception of the significance of secrecy, darkness is always used in a bad sense. Moreover the different forms of darkness are so closely allied, being either cause and effect, or else concurrent effects of the same cause, that they cannot always be distinguished; 1 John 1:5; 2:8, e.g., are passages in which both spiritual and moral darkness are intended."

"Salvation is worth working for. It is worth a man's going round the world on his hands and knees, climbing its mountains, crossing its valleys, swimming its rivers, going through all manner of hardship in order to attain it. But we do not get it in that way. It is to him who believes."

D. L. MOODY

Marvellous *thaumastos* (2298), "marvellous," is said (a) of the Lord's doing in making the rejected Stone the Head of the corner, Matt. 21:42; Mark 12:11; (b) of the erstwhile blind man's astonishment that the Pharisees knew not from whence Christ had come, and yet He had given him sight, John 9:30, RV, "the marvel," KJV, "a marvellous thing"; (c) of the spiritual light into which believers are brought, **1 Pet. 2:9**; (d) of the vision of the seven angels having the seven last plagues, Rev. 15:1; (e) of the works of God, 15:3.

Light *phos* (5457), akin to *phao*, "to give light" (from roots *pha-* and *phan-*, expressing "light as seen by the eye," and, metaphorically, as "reaching the mind," whence *phaino*, "to make to appear," *phaneros*, "evident," etc.); cf. Eng., "phosphorus" (lit., "light-bearing"). "Primarily light is a luminous emanation, probably of force, from certain bodies, which enables the eye to discern form and color. Light requires an organ adapted for its reception (Matt. 6:22). Where the eye is absent, or where it has become impaired from any cause, light is useless. Man, naturally, is incapable of receiving spiritual light inasmuch as he lacks the capacity for spiritual things, 1 Cor. 2:14. Hence believers are called 'sons of light,' Luke 16:8, not merely because they have received a revelation from God, but because in the New Birth they have received the spiritual capacity for it.

"Apart from natural phenomena, light is used in Scripture of (a) the glory of God's dwellingplace, 1 Tim. 6:16; (b) the nature of God, 1 John 1:5; (c) the impartiality of God, Jas. 1:17; (d) the favor of God, Ps. 4:6; of the King, Prov. 16:15; of an influential man, Job 29:24; (e) God, as the illuminator of His people, Isa. 60:19, 20; (f) the Lord Jesus as the illuminator of men, John 1:4, 5, 9; 3:19; 8:12; 9:5; 12:35, 36, 46; Acts 13:47; (g) the illuminating power of the Scriptures, Ps. 119:105; and of the judgments and commandments of God, Isa. 51:4; Prov. 6:23, cf. Ps. 43:3; (h) the guidance of God Job 29:3; Ps. 112:4; Isa. 58:10; and, ironically, of the guidance of man, Rom. 2:19; (i) salvation, **1 Pet. 2:9**; (j) righteousness, Rom. 13:12; 2 Cor. 11:14, 15; 1 John 2:9, 10; (k) witness for God, Matt. 5:14, 16; John 5:35; (l) prosperity and general well-being, Esth. 8:16; Job 18:18; Isa. 58:8-10."

2:10 Which in time past *were* not a people, but *are* now the people of God: which had not obtained mercy, but now have obtained mercy.

Past *pote* (4218), "once, formerly, sometime," is translated "in time (or times) past," in Rom. 11:30; Gal. 1:13;Ga 1:23, KJV (RV, "once"); Eph. 2:2, 11 (RV, "aforetime"); v. 3 (RV, "once"); Philem. 11 (RV, "aforetime"); **1 Pet. 2:10**.

Obtained For the phrase "to obtain mercy," the passive voice of *eleeo* in Matt. 5:7; Rom. 11:30-31; 1 Cor. 7:25; 2 Cor. 4:1 (RV); 1 Tim. 1:13, 16; **1 Pet. 2:10** (twice).

Mercy *eleeo* (1653), signifies, in general, "to feel sympathy with the misery of another," and especially sympathy manifested in act, (a) in the active voice, "to have pity or mercy on, to show mercy" to, e.g., Matt. 9:27; 15:22; 17:15; 18:33; 20:30, 31 (three times in Mark, four in Luke); Rom. 9:15, 16, 18; 11:32; 12:8; Phil. 2:27; Jude 22, 23; (b) in the passive voice, "to have pity or mercy shown one, to obtain mercy," Matt. 5:7; Rom. 11:30, 31; 1 Cor. 7:25; 2 Cor. 4:1; 1 Tim. 1:13, 16; **1 Pet. 2:10**.

2:11 Dearly beloved, I beseech *you* as strangers and pilgrims, abstain from fleshly lusts, which war against the soul;

Strangers *paroikos* (3941), an adjective, lit., "dwelling near," then, "foreign, alien" (found with this meaning in inscriptions), hence, as a noun, "a sojourner," is used with *eimi*, "to be," in Acts 7:6, "should sojourn," lit., "should be a sojourner"; in 7:29, RV, "sojourner" (KJV, "stranger"); in Eph. 2:19, RV, "sojourners" (KJV, "foreigners"), the preceding word rendered "strangers" is *xenos;* in **1 Pet. 2:11**, RV, ditto (KJV, "strangers").

Pilgrims *see* **Strangers** at ***1 Peter 1:1.***

Abstain *apecho* (568), "to hold oneself from" (*apo*, "from," *echomai*, the middle voice of *echo*, "to have," i.e., to keep oneself from), in the NT, invariably refers to evil practices, moral and ceremonial, Acts 15:20, 29; 1 Thess. 4:3; 5:22; 1 Tim. 4:3; **1 Pet. 2:11**; so in the Sept. in Job 1:1; 2:3.

Fleshly *sarkikos* (4559), from *sarx*, "flesh," signifies (a) "having the nature of flesh," i.e., sensual, controlled by animal appetites, governed by human nature, instead of by the Spirit of God, 1 Cor. 3:3; having its seat in the animal nature, or excited by it, **1 Pet. 2:11**, "fleshly"; or as the equivalent of "human," with the added idea of weakness, figuratively of the weapons of spiritual warfare, "of the flesh" (KJV, "carnal"), 2 Cor. 10:4; or with the idea of unspirituality, of human wisdom, "fleshly," 2 Cor. 1:12; (b) "pertaining to the flesh" (i.e., the body), Rom. 15:27; 1 Cor. 9:11.

Lusts *see* ***1 Peter 1:14.***

War *strateuo* (4754), used in the middle voice, "to make war" (from *stratos*, "an encamped army"), is translated "to war" in 2 Cor. 10:3; metaphorically, of spiritual "conflict," 1 Tim. 1:18; 2 Tim. 2:3, KJV; Jas. 4:1; **1 Pet. 2:11**.

Soul *see* **Souls** at ***1 Peter 1:9.***

2:12 Having your conversation honest among the Gentiles: that, whereas they speak against you as evildoers, they may by *your* good works, which they shall behold, glorify God in the day of visitation.

Honest *kalos* (2570), "good, admirable, becoming," has also the ethical meaning of what is "fair, right, honorable, of such conduct as deserves esteem"; it is translated "honest" [cf. Latin *honestus* (from *honos*, "honor")], which has the same double meaning as "honest" in the KJV, namely, regarded with honor, honorable, and bringing honor, becoming; in Luke 8:15 (KJV, and RV), "an honest and good (*agathos*) heart"; Rom. 12:17; 2 Cor. 8:21 and 13:7, RV, "honorable" (KJV, "honest"), of things which are regarded with esteem; in **1 Pet. 2:12**, of behavior, RV, "seemly," KJV, "honest" (i.e., becoming).

Gentiles When, under the new order of things introduced by the gospel the mystery of the church was made known, the word *ethnos* was often used in contrast to the local church, 1 Cor. 5:1; 10:20; 12:2; 1 Thess. 4:5; **1 Pet. 2:12**.

Evildoers *kakopoios* (2555), properly the masculine gender of the adjective, denotes an "evil-doer" (*kakon*, "evil," *poieo*, "to do"), **1 Pet. 2:12, 14; 4:15**; in some mss. in **3:16** and John 18:30 (so the KJV). In the Sept., Prov. 12:4; 24:19.

Good *kalos* (2570), denotes that which is intrinsically "good," and so, "goodly, fair, beautiful," as (a) of that which is well adapted to its circumstances or ends, e.g., fruit, Matt. 3:10; a tree, 12:33; ground, 13:8, 23; fish, 13:48; the Law, Rom. 7:16; 1 Tim. 1:8; every creature of God, 1 Tim. 4:4; a faithful minister of Christ and the doctrine he teaches, 4:6; (b) of that which is ethically good, right, noble, honorable e.g., Gal. 4:18; 1 Tim. 5:10, 25; 6:18; Titus 2:7, 14; 3:8, 14. The word does not occur in Revelation, nor indeed after 1 Peter. Christians are to "take thought for things honorable" (*kalos*), 2 Cor. 8:21, RV; to do that which is honorable, 13:7; not to be weary in well doing, Gal. 6:9; to hold fast "that which is good," 1 Thess. 5:21; to be zealous of good works, Titus 2:14; to maintain them, 3:8; to provoke to them, Heb. 10:24; to bear testimony by them, **1 Pet. 2:12**.

Kalos and *agathos* occur together in Luke 8:15, an "honest" (*kalos*) heart, i.e., the attitude of which is right towards God; a "good" (*agathos*) heart, i.e., one that, instead of working ill to a neighbor, acts beneficially towards him. In Rom. 7:18, "in me ... dwelleth no good thing" (*agathos*) signifies that in him is nothing capable of doing "good," and hence he lacks the power "to do that which is good" (*kalos*). In 1 Thess. 5:15, "follow after that which is good" (*agathos*), the "good" is that which is beneficial; in v. 21, "hold fast that which is good (*kalos*)," the "good" describes the intrinsic value of the teaching.

Works *ergon* (2041), denotes (I) "work, employment, task," e.g., Mark 13:34; John 4:34; 17:4; Acts 13:2; Phil. 2:30; 1 Thess. 5:13; in Acts 5:38 with the idea of enterprise; (II) "a deed, act," (a) of God, e.g., John 6:28, 29; 9:3; 10:37; 14:10; Acts 13:41; Rom. 14:20; Heb. 1:10; 2:7; 3:9; 4:3, 4, 10; Rev. 15:3; (b) of Christ, e.g., Matt. 11:2; especially in John, 5:36; 7:3, 21; 10:25, 32, 33, 38; 14:11, 12; 15:24; Rev. 2:26; (c) of believers, e.g., Matt. 5:16; Mark 14:6; Acts 9:36; Rom. 13:3; Col. 1:10; 1 Thess. 1:3, "work of faith," here the initial act of faith at conversion (turning to God, v. 9); in 2 Thess. 1:11, "*every* work of faith," RV, denotes every activity undertaken for Christ's sake; 2:17; 1 Tim. 2:10; 5:10; 6:18; 2 Tim. 2:21; 3:17; Titus 2:7, 14; 3:1, 8, 14; Heb. 10:24; 13:21; frequent in James, as the effect of faith [in 1:25,

KJV, "(a doer) of the work," RV, "(a doer) that worketh"]; **1 Pet. 2:12**; Rev. 2:2 and in several other places in chs. 2 and 3; 14:13; (d) of unbelievers, e.g., Matt. 23:3, 5; John 7:7; Acts 7:41 (for idols); Rom. 13:12; Eph. 5:11; Col. 1:21; Titus 1:16 (1st part); 1 John 3:12; Jude 15, RV; Rev. 2:6, RV; of those who seek justification by works, e.g., Rom. 9:32; Gal. 3:10; Eph. 2:9; described as the works of the law, e.g., Gal. 2:16; 3:2, 5; dead works, Heb. 6:1; 9:14; (e) of Babylon, Rev. 18:6; (f) of the Devil, John 8:41; 1 John 3:8.

Behold *epopteuo* (2029), from *epi*, "upon," and a form of *horao*, "to see," is used of "witnessing as a spectator, or overseer," **1 Pet. 2:12; 3:2.**

Visitation *episkope* (1984), besides its meaning, "visitation," e.g., **1 Pet. 2:12** (cf. the Sept. of Exod. 3:16; Isa. 10:3; Jer. 10:15), is rendered "office," in Acts 1:20, RV (KJV, "bishoprick"); in 1 Tim. 3:1 "the office of a bishop," lit., "(if any one seeketh) overseership," there is no word representing office.

2:13 Submit yourselves to every ordinance of man for the Lord's sake: whether it be to the king, as supreme;

Submit *hupotasso* (5293), primarily a military term, "to rank under" (*hupo*, "under," *tasso*, "to arrange"), denotes (a) "to put in subjection, to subject," Rom. 8:20 (twice); in the following, the RV, has to subject for KJV, "to put under," 1 Cor. 15:27 (thrice), 28 (3rd clause); Eph. 1:22; Heb. 2:8 (4th clause); in 1 Cor. 15:28 (1st clause), for KJV "be subdued"; in Phil. 3:21, for KJV, "subdue"; in Heb. 2:5, KJV, "hath ... put in subjection"; (b) in the middle or passive voice, to subject oneself, to obey, be subject to, Luke 2:51; 10:17, 20; Rom. 8:7; 10:3, RV, "did (not) subject themselves" [KJV, "have (not) submitted themselves"]; 13:1, 5; 1 Cor. 14:34, RV, "be in subjection" (KJV, "be under obedience"); 15:28 (2nd clause); 16:16 RV, "be in subjection" (KJV, "submit, etc."); so Col. 3:18; Eph. 5:21, RV, "subjecting yourselves" (KJV, "submitting, etc."); v. 22, RV in italics, according to the best texts; v. 24, "is subject"; Titus 2:5, 9, RV, "be in subjection" (KJV, "be obedient"); 3:1, RV, "to be in subjection" (KJV, "to be subject"); Heb. 12:9, "be in subjection"; Jas. 4:7, RV, "be subject" (KJV, "submit yourselves"); so **1 Pet. 2:13**; v. **18**, RV, "be in subjection"; so **3:1**, KJV and RV; v. **5**, similarly; **3:22**, "being made subject"; **5:5**, RV, "be subject" (KJV, "submit yourselves"); in some texts in the 2nd part, as KJV.

Ordinance *ktisis* (2937), "a creation, creature," is translated "ordinance" in **1 Pet. 2:13**. In 1 Cor. 11:2, KJV, *paradosis*, "a tradition" (marg., and RV, "traditions"), is translated "ordinances."

Man *anthropinos* (442), "human, belonging to man" (from *anthropos*), is used (a) of man's wisdom, in 1 Cor. 2:13 (some mss. have it in v. 4, where indeed it is implied; see, however, the RV); (b) of "man's judgement," 1 Cor. 4:3 (marg., "day"); (c) of "mankind," Jas. 3:7, lit., "the human nature," RV marg. (KJV marg., "nature of man"); (d) of human ordinance, **1 Pet. 2:13**; Moulton and Milligan show from the papyri how strongly antithetic to the divine the use of the word is in this respect; (e) of temptation, 1 Cor. 10:13, RV, "such as man can bear" (KJV, "such as is common to man"), i.e., such as must and does come to "men"; (f) of "men's" hands, Acts 17:25; (g) in the phrase "after the manner of men," Rom. 6:19.

King *basileus* (935), "a king" (cf. Eng., "Basil"), e.g., Matt. 1:6, is used of the Roman emperor in **1 Pet. 2:13, 17** (a command of general application); this reference to the emperor is illustrated frequently in the *Koine* (see Preface to this volume); of Herod the Tetrarch (used by courtesy), Matt. 14:9; of Christ, as the "King" of the Jews, e.g., Matt. 2:2; 27:11, 29, 37; as the "King" of Israel, Mark 15:32; John 1:49; 12:13; as "King of kings," Rev. 17:14; 19:16; as "the King" in judging nations and men at the establishment of the millennial kingdom, Matt. 25:34, 40; of God, "the great King," Matt. 5:35; "the King eternal, incorruptible, invisible," 1 Tim. 1:17; "King of kings," 1 Tim. 6:15, see *Note* (2) below; "King of the ages," Rev. 15:3, RV (KJV, "saints"). Christ's "kingship" was predicted in the OT, e.g., Ps. 2:6, and in the NT, e.g., Luke 1:32, 33; He came as such e.g., Matt. 2:2; John 18:37; was rejected and died as such, Luke 19:14; Matt. 27:37; is now a "King" Priest, after the order of Melchizedek, Heb. 5:6; 7:1, 17; and will reign for ever and ever, Rev. 11:15.

Supreme *huperecho* (5242), "to be superior, to excel," is translated "supreme" in **1 Pet. 2:13**.

2:14 Or unto governors, as unto them that are sent by him for the punishment of evildoers, and for the praise of them that do well.

Governors *hegemon* (2232), is a term used (a) for "rulers" generally, Mark 13:9; **1 Pet. 2:14**; translated "princes" (i.e., leaders) in Matt. 2:6; (b) for the Roman procurators, referring, in the Gospels to Pontius Pilate, e.g., Matt. 27:2; Luke 20:20 (so designated by Tacitus, *Annals*, xv. 44); to Felix, Acts 23:26. Technically the procurator was a financial official under a proconsul or propretor, for collecting the imperial revenues, but entrusted also with magisterial powers for decisions of questions relative to the revenues. In certain provinces, of which Judea was one (the procurator of which was dependent on the legate of Syria), he was the general administrator and supreme judge, with sole power of life and death. Such a governor was a person of high social standing. Felix, however, was an ex-slave, a freedman, and his appointment to Judea could not but be regarded by the Jews as an insult to the nation. The headquarters of the governor of Judea was Caesarea, which was made a garrison town.

Sent *pempo* (3992), "to send," is used (a) of persons: Christ, by the Father, Luke 20:13; John 4:34; 5:23, 24, 30, 37; 6:38, 39, (40), 44; 7:16, 18, 28, 33; 8:16, 18, 26, 29; 9:4; 12:44, 45, 49; 13:20 (2nd part); 14:24; 15:21; 16:5; Rom. 8:3; the Holy Spirit, John 14:26; 15:26; 16:7; Elijah, Luke 4:26; John the Baptist, John 1:33; disciples and apostles, e.g., Matt. 11:2; John 20:21; servants, e.g., Luke 20:11, 12; officials, Matt. 14:10; messengers, e.g., Acts 10:5, 32, 33; 15:22, 25; 2 Cor. 9:3, Eph. 6:22; Phil. 2:19, 23, 25; 1 Thess. 3:2, 5; Titus 3:12; a prisoner, Acts 25:25, 27; potentates, by God, **1 Pet. 2:14**; an angel, Rev. 22:16, demons, Mark 5:12; (b) of things, Acts 11:29; Phil. 4:16; 2 Thess. 2:11; Rev. 1:11; 11:10; 14:15, 18, RV, "send forth" (KJV, "thrust in").

Punishment *ekdikesis* (1557), vengeance," is used with the verb *poieo*, "to make," i.e., to avenge, in Luke 18:7-8; Acts 7:24; twice it is used in statements that "vengeance" belongs to God, Rom. 12:19; Heb. 10:30. In 2 Thess. 1:8 it is said of the act of divine justice which will be meted out to those who know not God and obey not the gospel, when the Lord comes in flaming fire at His second advent. In the divine exercise of judgment there is no element of vindictiveness, nothing by way of taking revenge. In Luke 21:22, it is used of the "days of vengeance" upon the Jewish people; in **1 Pet. 2:14**, of civil governors as those who are sent of God "for vengeance on evildoers" (KJV, "punishment"); in 2 Cor. 7:11, of the "self-avenging" of believers, in their godly sorrow for wrong doing, RV, "avenging," for KJV, revenge.

Evildoers *see 1 Peter 2:12.*

Praise *see 1 Peter 1:7.*

Well *agathopoieo* (15), "to do," is used (a) in a general way, "to do well," **1 Pet. 2:15, 20; 3:6, 17**; 3 John 11; (b) with pointed reference "to the benefit of another," Luke 6:9, 33, 35; in Mark 3:4 the parts of the word are separated in some mss. Some mss. have it in Acts 14:17. Cf. the noun *agathopoiia*, "well-doing," **1 Pet. 4:19**, and the adjective *agathopoios* (17), "doing good, beneficent," is translated "them that do well" in **1 Pet. 2:14**, lit., "well-doing (ones)."

2:15 For so is the will of God, that with well doing ye may put to silence the ignorance of foolish men:

Well doing *agathopoieo* (15), "to do good" (*agathos*, "good," *poieo*, "to do"), is used (a) of such activity in general, **1 Pet. 2:15**, "well-doing"; v. **20**, "do well"; **3:6, 17**; 3 John 11, "doeth good"; (b) of "acting for another's benefit," Mark 3:4; Luke 6:9, 33, 35. *See also* **Well** at *1 Peter 2:14.*

Silence *phimoo* (5392), "to close the mouth with a muzzle" (*phimos*), is used (a) of "muzzling" the ox when it treads out the corn, 1 Cor. 9:9, KJV, "muzzle the mouth of," RV, "muzzle," and 1 Tim. 5:18, with the lesson that those upon whom spiritual labor is bestowed should not refrain from ministering to the material needs of those who labor on their behalf; (b) metaphorically, of putting to silence, or subduing to stillness, Matt. 22:12, 34; Mark 1:25; 4:39; Luke 4:35; **1 Pet. 2:15**.

Ignorance *agnosia* (56), denotes "ignorance" as directly opposed to *gnosis*, which signifies "knowledge" as a result of observation and experience (*a*, negative, *ginosko*, "to know"; cf. Eng., "agnostic"); 1 Cor. 15:34 ("no knowledge"); **1 Pet. 2:15**. In both these passages reprehensible "ignorance" is suggested.

Foolish *aphron* (878), signifies "without reason" (*a*, negative, *phren*, "the mind"), "want of mental sanity and sobriety, a reckless and inconsiderate habit of mind" (Hort), or "the lack of commonsense perception of the reality of things natural and spiritual ... or the imprudent ordering of one's life in regard to salvation" (G. Vos, in *Hastings' Bible Dic.*); it is mostly translated "foolish" or "foolish ones" in the RV; Luke 11:40; 12:20; Rom. 2:20; 1 Cor. 15:36; 2 Cor. 11:16 (twice), 19 (contrasted with *phronimos*, "prudent"); 12:6, 11; Eph. 5:17; **1 Pet. 2:15**.

2:16 As free, and not using *your* liberty for a cloke of maliciousness, but as the servants of God.

Free *eleutheros* (1658), primarily of "freedom to go wherever one likes," is used (a) of "freedom from restraint and obligation" in general, Matt. 17:26; Rom. 7:3; 1 Cor. 7:39, RV, "free," of the second marriage of a woman; 9:1, 19; **1 Pet. 2:16**; from the Law, Gal. 4:26;

from sin, John 8:36; with regard to righteousness, Rom. 6:20 (i.e., righteousness laid no sort of bond upon them, they had no relation to it); (b) in a civil sense, "free" from bondage or slavery, John 8:33; 1 Cor. 7:21, 22, 2nd part; 12:13; Gal. 3:28; Eph. 6:8; Rev. 13:16; 19:18; as a noun, "freeman," Col. 3:11, RV; Rev. 6:15; "freewoman," Gal. 4:22, 23, 30, and v. 31, RV.

Using *echo* (2192), "to have," is rendered "using" in **1 Pet. 2:16** (marg., "having").

Liberty *eleutheria* (1657), "liberty," is rendered "freedom" in Gal. 5:1, "with freedom did Christ set us free." The combination of the noun with the verb stresses the completeness of the act, the aorist (or point) tense indicating both its momentary and comprehensive character; it was done once for all. The RV margin "for freedom" gives perhaps the preferable meaning, i.e., "not to bring us into another form of bondage did Christ liberate us from that in which we were born, but in order to make us free from bondage."

The word is twice rendered "freedom" in the RV of Gal. 5:13 (KJV, "liberty"). The phraseology is that of manumission from slavery, which among the Greeks was effected by a legal fiction, according to which the manumitted slave was purchased by a god; as the slave could not provide the money, the master paid it into the temple treasury in the presence of the slave, a document being drawn up containing the words "for freedom." No one could enslave him again, as he was the property of the god. Hence the word *apeleutheros*. The word is also translated "freedom" in **1 Pet. 2:16**, RV. In 2 Cor. 3:17 the word denotes "freedom" of access to the presence of God.

Cloke *epikalumma* (1942), is "a covering, a means of hiding" (*epi*, "upon," *kalupto*, "to cover"); hence, "a pretext, a cloke, for wickedness," **1 Pet. 2:16**. In the Sept. it is used in Ex. 26:14; 39:21, "coverings"; 2 Sam. 17:19; Job 19:29, "deceit."

Maliciousness *see* **Malice** at *1 Peter 2:1*.

Servants *doulos* (1401), an adjective, signifying "in bondage," Rom. 6:19 (neuter plural, agreeing with *mele*, "members"), is used as a noun, and as the most common and general word for "servant," frequently indicating subjection without the idea of bondage; it is used (a) of natural conditions, e.g., Matt. 8:9; 1 Cor. 7:21, 22 (1st part); Eph. 6:5; Col. 4:1; 1 Tim. 6:1; frequently in the four Gospels; (b) metaphorically of spiritual, moral and ethical conditions: "servants" (1) of God, e.g., Acts 16:17; Titus 1:1; **1 Pet. 2:16**; Rev. 7:3; 15:3; the perfect example being Christ Himself, Phil. 2:7; (2) of Christ, e.g., Rom. 1:1; 1 Cor. 7:22 (2nd part); Gal. 1:10; Eph. 6:6; Phil. 1:1; Col. 4:12; Jas. 1:1; 2 Pet. 1:1; Jude 1; (3) of sin, John 8:34 (RV, "bondservants"); Rom. 6:17, 20; (4) of corruption, 2 Pet. 2:19 (RV, "bondservants"); cf. the verb *douloo*.

2:17 Honour all *men*. Love the brotherhood. Fear God. Honour the king.

Honour *timao* (5091), "to honor," is used of (a) valuing Christ at a price, Matt. 27:9; (b) "honoring" a person: (1) the "honor" done by Christ to the Father, John 8:49; (2) "honor" bestowed by the Father upon him who serves Christ, John 12:26; (3) the duty of all to "honor" the Son equally with the Father, 5:23; (4) the duty of children to "honor" their parents, Matt. 15:4; 19:19; Mark 7:10; 10:19; Luke 18:20; Eph. 6:2; (5) the duty of Christians to "honor" the king, and all men, **1 Pet. 2:17**; (6) the respect and material assistance to be given to widows "that are widows indeed," 1 Tim. 5:3; (7) the "honor" done to Paul and his companions by the inhabitants of Melita, Acts 28:10; (8) mere lip profession of "honor" to God, Matt. 15:8: Mark 7:6. *See also 1 Peter 1:7.*

Brotherhood *see* **Brethren** at *1 Peter 1:22*.

Fear *phobeo* (5399), in earlier Greek, "to put to flight," in the NT is always in the passive voice, with the meanings either (a) "to fear, be afraid," its most frequent use, e.g., Acts 23:10, according to the best mss.; or (b) "to show reverential fear," (1) of men, Mark 6:20; Eph. 5:33, RV, "fear," for KJV, "reverence"; (2) of God, e.g., Acts 10:2, 22; 13:16, 26; Col. 3:22 (RV, "the Lord"); **1 Pet. 2:17**; Rev. 14:7; 15:4; 19:5; (a) and (b) are combined in Luke 12:4, 5, where Christ warns His followers not to be afraid of men, but to "fear" God.

King *see 1 Peter 2:13.*

2:18 Servants, *be* subject to *your* masters with all fear; not only to the good and gentle, but also to the froward.

Servants *oiketes* (3610), "a house servant" (*oikeo*, "to dwell," *oikos*, "a house"), is translated "servant" in Luke 16:13 (RV marg., "household servant"); so Rom. 14:4 and **1 Pet. 2:18**; in Acts 10:7, KJV and RV, "household servants."

Subject *see* **Submit** at *1 Peter 2:13*.

Gentle *epieikes* (1933), from *epi*, "unto," and *eikos*, "likely," denotes "seemly, fitting"; hence, "equitable, fair, moderate, forbearing, not insisting on the letter of the law";

it expresses that considerateness that looks "humanely and reasonably at the facts of a case"; it is rendered "gentle" in 1 Tim. 3:3, RV (KJV, "patient"), in contrast to contentiousness; in Titus 3:2, "gentle," in association with meekness, in Jas. 3:17, as a quality of the wisdom from above, in **1 Pet. 2:18**, in association with the good. In the Sept., Esth. 8:13; Ps. 86:5.

Fear *see 1 Peter 1:17.*

Good *agathos* (18), describes that which, being "good" in its character or constitution, is beneficial in its effect; it is used (a) of things physical, e.g., a tree, Matt. 7:17; ground, Luke 8:8; (b) in a moral sense, frequently of persons and things. God is essentially, absolutely and consummately "good," Matt. 19:17; Mark 10:18; Luke 18:19. To certain persons the word is applied in Matt. 20:15; 25:21, 23; Luke 19:17; 23:50; John 7:12; Acts 11:24; Titus 2:5; in a general application, Matt. 5:45; 12:35; Luke 6:45; Rom. 5:7; **1 Pet. 2:18**. The neuter of the adjective with the definite article signifies that which is "good," lit., "the good," as being morally honorable, pleasing to God, and therefore beneficial. Christians are to prove it, Rom. 12:2; to cleave to it, 12:9; to do it, 13:3; Gal. 6:10; **1 Pet. 3:11** (here, and here only, the article is absent); John 5:29 (here, the neuter plural is used, "the good things"); to work it, Rom. 2:10; Eph. 4:28; 6:8; to follow after it, 1 Thess. 5:15; to be zealous of it, **1 Pet. 3:13**; to imitate it, 3 John 11; to overcome evil with it, Rom. 12:21. Governmental authorities are ministers of "good," i.e., that which is salutary, suited to the course of human affairs, Rom. 13:4. In Philem. 14, "thy goodness," RV (lit., "thy good"), means "thy benefit." As to Matt. 19:17, "why askest thou Me concerning that which is good?" the RV follows the most ancient mss. The neuter plural is also used of material "goods," riches, etc., Luke 1:53; 12:18, 19; 16:25; Gal. 6:6 (of temporal supplies); in Rom. 10:15; Heb. 9:11; 10:1, the "good" things are the benefits provided through the sacrifice of Christ, in regard both to those conferred through the gospel and to those of the coming messianic kingdom.

Masters *despotes* (1203), one who has "absolute ownership and uncontrolled power," is translated "masters" in 1 Tim. 6:1, 2; Titus 2:9; **1 Pet. 2:18**; of Christ, 2 Tim. 2:21; 2 Pet. 2:1, RV (for KJV, Lord); in Jude 4, RV, it is applied to Christ "(our only) Master (and Lord, Jesus Christ)," KJV "(the only) Lord (God)"; in Rev. 6:10, RV, in an address to God, "O Master" (KJV, "O Lord"). It is rendered "Lord" in Luke 2:29 and Acts 4:24.

Froward *skolios* (4646), "curved, crooked," was especially used (a) of a way, Luke 3:5, with spiritual import (see Prov. 28:18, Sept.); it is set in contrast to *orthos* and *euthus*, "straight"; (b) metaphorically, of what is morally "crooked," perverse, froward, of people belonging to a particular generation, Acts 2:40 (KJV, "untoward"); Phil. 2:15; of tyrannical or unjust masters, **1 Pet. 2:18**, "froward"; in this sense it is set in contrast to *agathos*, "good."

2:19 For this *is* thankworthy, if a man for conscience toward God endure grief, suffering wrongfully.

Thankworthy *charis* (5485), is rendered "thank" in Luke 6:32, 33, 34; in 17:9, "doth he thank" is lit., "hath he thanks to"; it is rendered "thanks (be to God)" in Rom. 6:17, RV (KJV, "God be thanked"); "thanks" in 1 Cor. 15:57; in 1 Tim. 1:12 and 2 Tim. 1:3, "I thank" is, lit., "I have thanks"; "thankworthy," **1 Pet. 2:19**, KJV (RV, "acceptable").

Man *tis* (5100), "some one, a certain one," is rendered "a man," "a certain man," e.g., in Matt. 22:24; Mark 8:4, KJV (RV, "one"); 12:19; John 3:3, 5; 6:50; 14:23; 15:6, 13; Acts 13:41, KJV (RV, "one"); 1 Cor. 4:2; 1 Tim. 1:8; 2 Tim. 2:5, 21; Jas. 2:14, 18; **1 Pet. 2:19**; 1 John 4:20.

Conscience *suneidesis* (4893), lit., "a knowing with" (*sun*, "with," *oida*, "to know"), i.e., "a co-knowledge (with oneself), the witness borne to one's conduct by conscience, that faculty by which we apprehend the will of God, as that which is designed to govern our lives"; hence (a) the sense of guiltiness before God; Heb. 10:2; (b) that process of thought which distinguishes what it considers morally good or bad, commending the good, condemning the bad, and so prompting to do the former, and avoid the latter; Rom. 2:15 (bearing witness with God's law); 9:1; 2 Cor. 1:12; acting in a certain way because "conscience" requires it, Rom. 13:5; so as not to cause scruples of "conscience" in another, 1 Cor. 10:28-29; not calling a thing in question unnecessarily, as if conscience demanded it, 1 Cor. 10:25, 27; "commending oneself to every man's conscience," 2 Cor. 4:2; cf. 5:11. There may be a "conscience" not strong enough to distinguish clearly between the lawful and the unlawful, 1 Cor. 8:7, 10, 12 (some regard consciousness as the meaning here). The phrase "conscience toward God," in **1 Pet. 2:19**, signifies a "conscience" (or perhaps here, a consciousness) so controlled by the apprehension of God's presence, that the person realizes that griefs are to be borne in accordance with His will. Heb.

9:9 teaches that sacrifices under the Law could not so perfect a person that he could regard himself as free from guilt. For various descriptions of "conscience" see Acts 23:1; 24:16; 1 Cor. 8:7; 1 Tim. 1:5, 19; 3:9; 4:2; 2 Tim. 1:3; Titus 1:15; Heb. 9:14; 10:22; 13:18; **1 Pet. 3:16, 21.**

Endure *hupophero* (5297), a strengthened form, "to bear or carry," by being under, is said metaphorically of "enduring" temptation, 1 Cor. 10:13, KJV, "bear"; persecutions, 2 Tim. 3:11; griefs, **1 Pet. 2:19**.

Grief *lupe* (3077), signifies "pain," of body or mind; it is used in the plural in **1 Pet. 2:19** only, RV, "griefs" (KJV, "grief"); here, however, it stands, by metonymy, for "things that cause sorrow, grievances"; hence Tyndale's rendering, "grief," for Wycliffe's "sorews"; everywhere else it is rendered "sorrow," except in Heb. 12:11, where it is translated "grievous" (lit., "of grief").

Suffering *pascho* (3958), "to suffer," is used (I) of the "sufferings" of Christ (a) at the hands of men, e.g., Matt. 16:21; 17:12; **1 Pet. 2:23**; (b) in His expiatory and vicarious sacrifice for sin, Heb. 9:26; 13:12; **1 Pet. 2:21; 3:18; 4:1**; (c) including both (a) and (b), Luke 22:15; 24:26, 46; Acts 1:3, "passion"; 3:18; 17:3; Heb. 5:8; (d) by the antagonism of the evil one, Heb. 2:18; (II) of human "suffering" (a) of followers of Christ, Acts 9:16; 2 Cor. 1:6; Gal. 3:4; Phil. 1:29; 1 Thess. 2:14; 2 Thess. 1:5; 2 Tim. 1:12; **1 Pet. 3:14, 17; 5:10**; Rev. 2:10; in identification with Christ in His crucifixion, as the spiritual ideal to be realized, **1 Pet. 4:1**; in a wrong way, **4:15**; (b) of others, physically, as the result of demoniacal power, Matt. 17:15, RV, "suffereth (grievously)," KJV, "is (sore) vexed"; cf. Mark 5:26; in a dream, Matt. 27:19; through maltreatment, Luke 13:2; **1 Pet. 2:19, 20**; by a serpent (negatively), Acts 28:5, RV, "took" (KJV, "felt"); (c) of the effect upon the whole body through the "suffering" of one member, 1 Cor. 12:26, with application to a church.

Wrongfully *adikos* (95), akin to the above, occurs in **1 Pet. 2:19**.

2:20 For what glory *is it*, if, when ye be buffeted for your faults, ye shall take it patiently? but if, when ye do well, and suffer *for it*, ye take it patiently, this *is* acceptable with God.

What *see 1 Peter 1:11.*

Glory *kleos* (2811), "good report, fame, renown," is used in **1 Pet. 2:20**. The word is derived from a root signifying "hearing"; hence, the meaning "reputation."

Buffeted *kolaphizo* (2852), signifies "to strike with clenched hands, to buffet with the fist" (*kolaphos*, "a fist"), Matt. 26:67; Mark 14:65; 1 Cor. 4:11; 2 Cor. 12:7; **1 Pet. 2:20**.

Faults *hamartano* (264), lit., "to miss the mark," is used in the NT (a) of "sinning" against God, (1) by angels, 2 Pet. 2:4; (2) by man, Matt. 27:4; Luke 15:18, 21 (heaven standing, by metonymy, for God); John 5:14; 8:11; 9:2, 3; Rom. 2:12 (twice); 3:23; 5:12, 14, 16; 6:15; 1 Cor. 7:28 (twice), 36; 15:34; Eph. 4:26; 1 Tim. 5:20; Titus 3:11; Heb. 3:17; 10:26; 1 John 1:10; in 2:1 (twice), the aorist tense in each place, referring to an act of "sin"; on the contrary, in 3:6 (twice), 8, 9, the present tense indicates, not the committal of an act, but the continuous practice of "sin"; in 5:16 (twice) the present tense indicates the condition resulting from an act, "unto death" signifying "tending towards death"; (b) against Christ, 1 Cor. 8:12; (c) against man, (1) a brother, Matt. 18:15, RV, "sin" (KJV, "trespass"); v. 21; Luke 17:3, 4, RV, "sin" (KJV, "trespass"); 1 Cor. 8:12; (2) in Luke 15:18, 21, against the father by the Prodigal Son, "in thy sight" being suggestive of befitting reverence; (d) against Jewish law, the Temple, and Caesar, Acts 25:8, RV, "sinned" (KJV, "offended"); (e) against one's own body, by fornication, 1 Cor. 6:18; (f) against earthly masters by servants, **1 Pet. 2:20**, RV, "(when) ye sin (and are buffeted for it)," KJV, "(when ye be buffeted) for your faults," lit., "having sinned."

Well *see 1 Peter 2:14. See also* **Well doing** at *1 Peter 2:15.*

Take ... patiently *hupomone* (5281), lit., "an abiding under" (*hupo*, "under," *meno*, "to abide"), is almost invariably rendered "patience." "Patience, which grows only in trial, Jas. 1:3 may be passive, i.e., = "endurance," as, (a) in trials, generally, Luke 21:19 (which is to be understood by Matt. 24:13), cf. Rom. 12:12; Jas. 1:12; (b) in trials incident to service in the gospel, 2 Cor. 6:4; 12:12; 2 Tim. 3:10; (c) under chastisement, which is trial viewed as coming from the hand of God our Father, Heb. 12:7; (d) under undeserved affliction, **1 Pet. 2:20**; or active, i.e. = "persistence, perseverance," as (e) in well doing, Rom. 2:7 (KJV, "patient continuance"); (f) in fruit bearing, Luke 8:15; (g) in running the appointed race, Heb. 12:1.

"Patience perfects Christian character, Jas. 1:4, and fellowship in the patience of Christ is therefore the condition upon which believers are to be admitted to reign with Him, 2 Tim. 2:12; Rev. 1:9. For this patience believers are 'strengthened with all power,' Col. 1:11, 'through His Spirit in the inward man,' Eph. 3:16. In 2 Thess. 3:5, the phrase 'the patience of Christ,' RV, is possible of three interpretations, (a) the patient waiting for Christ, so KJV paraphrases the words, (b) that they might be patient in their sufferings as Christ was in His, see Heb. 12:2, (c) that since Christ is 'expecting till His enemies be made the footstool of His feet,' Heb. 10:13, so they might be patient also in their hopes of His triumph and their deliverance. While a too rigid exegesis is to be avoided it may, perhaps, be permissible to paraphrase: 'the Lord teach and enable you to love as God loves, and to be patient as Christ is patient.'"

Suffer *see* **Suffering** at *1 Peter 2:19.*

2:21 For even hereunto were ye called: because Christ also suffered for us, leaving us an example, that ye should follow his steps:

Hereunto This translates the phrase *eis touto,* lit., "unto this," in **1 Pet. 2:21**.

Suffered *see* **Suffering** at *1 Peter 2:19.*

Leaving *hupolimpano* (5277), *limpano* being a late form for *leipo,* "to leave," is used in **1 Pet. 2:21**, "leaving (us an example)."

Example *hupogrammos* (5261), lit., "an under-writing" (from *hupographo,* "to write under, to trace letters" for copying by scholars); hence, "a writing-copy, an example," **1 Pet. 2:21**, said of what Christ left for believers, by His sufferings (not expiatory, but exemplary), that they might "follow His steps."

Follow *epakoloutheo* (1872), "to follow after, close upon," is used of signs "following" the preaching of the gospel. Mark 16:20; of "following" good works, 1 Tim. 5:10; of sins "following" after those who are guilty of them, 5:24; of "following" the steps of Christ, **1 Pet. 2:21**.

Steps *ichnos* (2487), "a footstep, a track," is used metaphorically of the "steps" (a) of Christ's conduct, **1 Pet. 2:21**; (b) of Abraham's faith, Rom. 4:12; (c) of identical conduct in carrying on the work of the gospel, 2 Cor. 12:18.

2:22 Who did no sin, neither was guile found in his mouth:

Sin Christ is predicated as having been without "sin" in every respect, e.g., (a), (b), (c) above, 2 Cor. 5:21 (1st part); 1 John 3:5; John 14:30; (d) John 8:46; Heb. 4:15; **1 Pet. 2:22**.

Guile *see 1 Peter 2:1.*

Mouth *stoma* (4750), akin to *stomachos* (which originally meant "a throat, gullet"), is used (a) of "the mouth" of man, e.g., Matt. 15:11; of animals, e.g., Matt. 17:27; 2 Tim. 4:17 (figurative); Heb. 11:33; Jas. 3:3; Rev. 13:2 (2nd occurrence); (b) figuratively of "inanimate things," of the "edge" of a sword, Luke 21:24; Heb. 11:34; of the earth, Rev. 12:16; (c) figuratively, of the "mouth," as the organ of speech, (1) of Christ's words, e.g., Matt. 13:35; Luke 11:54; Acts 8:32; 22:14; **1 Pet. 2:22**; (2) of human, e.g., Matt. 18:16; 21:16; Luke 1:64; Rev. 14:5; as emanating from the heart, Matt. 12:34; Rom. 10:8, 9; of prophetic ministry through the Holy Spirit, Luke 1:70; Acts 1:16; 3:18; 4:25; of the destructive policy of two world potentates at the end of this age, Rev. 13:2, 5, 6; 16:13 (twice); of shameful speaking, Eph. 4:29 and Col. 3:8; (3) of the Devil speaking as a dragon or serpent, Rev. 12:15, 16; 16:13; (d) figuratively, in the phrase "face to face" (lit., "mouth to mouth"), 2 John 12; 3 John 14; (e) metaphorically, of "the utterances of the Lord, in judgment," 2 Thess. 2:8; Rev. 1:16; 2:16; 19:15, 21; of His judgment upon a local church for its lukewarmness, Rev. 3:16; (f) by metonymy, for "speech," Matt. 18:16; Luke 19:22; 21:15; 2 Cor. 13:1.

2:23 Who, when he was reviled, reviled not again; when he suffered, he threatened not; but committed *himself* to him that judgeth righteously:

Reviled *loidoreo* (3058), denotes "to abuse, revile," John 9:28; Acts 23:4; 1 Cor. 4:12; **1 Pet. 2:23** (1st clause).

Reviled ... again *antiloidoreo* (486), "to revile back or again," is found in **1 Pet. 2:23** (2nd clause).

Suffered *see* **Suffering** at *1 Peter 2:19.*

Threatened *apeileo* (546), is used of Christ, negatively, in **1 Pet. 2:23**; in the middle voice, Acts 4:17, where some texts have the noun *apeile* in addition, hence the KJV, "let us straitly threaten," lit., "let us threaten ... with threatening.

Committed *paradidomi* (3860), "to give over," is often rendered by the verb "to commit," e.g., to prison, Acts 8:3; to the grace of God, Acts 14:26; to God, **1 Pet. 2:23**; by God to pits of darkness, 2 Pet. 2:4.

Righteously *dikaios* (1346), is translated "righteously" in 1 Cor. 15:34, RV "(awake up) righteously," KJV, "(awake to) righteousness"; 1 Thess. 2:10, RV (KJV, "justly"); Titus 2:12; **1 Pet. 2:23**.

2:24 Who his own self bare our sins in his own body on the tree, that we, being dead to sins, should live unto righteousness: by whose stripes ye were healed.

His own self Forms of pronouns under *autos* (846), (a frequent use: in **1 Pet. 2:24**, "His own self"); the form *autou,* "his," becomes emphatic when placed between the article and the noun, e.g., 1 Thess. 2:19; Titus 3:5; Heb. 2:4; also under *ekeinos* (1565), (in which "his" is emphasized), e.g., John 5:47; 9:28; 1 Cor. 10:28; 2 Cor. 8:9; 2 Tim. 2:26; Titus 3:7; 2 Pet. 1:16; (b) *heautou*, "of himself, his own"; the RV rightly puts "his own," for the KJV, "his," in Luke 11:21; 14:26; Rom. 4:19; 5:8, "His own (love)"; 1 Cor. 7:37; Gal. 6:8; Eph. 5:28, 33; 1 Thess. 2:11, 12; 4:4; in Rev. 10:7 the change has not been made; it should read "his own servants"; (c) *idios*, "one's own," "his own," in the RV, in Matt. 22:5; John 5:18; 2 Pet. 2:16; in Matt. 25:15, it is rendered "his several"; in John 19:27, "his own home," lit., "his own things"; in 1 Tim. 6:15, RV, "its own (times)," referring to the future appearing of Christ; in Heb. 4:10 (end of verse), both KJV and RV have "his," where it should be "his own"; so in Acts 24:23, for KJV and RV, "his"; in 1 Cor. 7:7, RV, "his own," KJV, "his proper"; (d) in Acts 17:28, the genitive case of the definite article, "His (offspring)," lit., "of the" (i.e., the one referred to, namely, God).

Bare *anaphero* (399), is used of "leading persons up to a higher place," and, in this respect, of the Lord's ascension, Luke 24:51. It is used twice of the Lord's propitiatory sacrifice, in His bearing sins on the cross, Heb. 9:28 and **1 Pet. 2:24**; the KJV margin, "to the tree," is to be rejected. The KJV text, "on," and the RV "upon" express the phrase rightly.

Tree *xulon* (3586), "wood, a piece of wood, anything made of wood", is used, with the rendering "tree," (a) in Luke 23:31, where "the green tree" refers either to Christ, figuratively of all His living power and excellencies, or to the life of the Jewish people while still inhabiting their land, in contrast to "the dry," a figure fulfilled in the horrors of the Roman massacre and devastation in AD 70 (cf. the Lord's parable in Luke 13:6–9; see Ezek. 20:47, and cf. 21:3); (b) of "the cross," the tree being the *stauros*, the upright pale or stake to which Romans nailed those who were thus to be executed, Acts 5:30; 10:39; 13:29; Gal. 3:13; **1 Pet. 2:24**; (c) of "the tree of life," Rev. 2:7; 22:2 (twice), 14, 19, RV, KJV, "book."

Dead *apoginomai* (581), lit., "to be away from" (*apo*, "from," *ginomai*, "to be, become"; *apo* here signifies "separation"), is used in **1 Pet. 2:24** of the believer's attitude towards sin as the result of Christ's having borne our sins in His body on the tree; RV, "having died unto sins," the aorist or momentary tense, expressing an event in the past.

Stripes *molops* (3468), "a bruise, a wound from a stripe," is used in **1 Pet. 2:24** (from the Sept. of Isa. 53:5), lit., in the original, "by whose bruise," not referring to Christ's scourging, but figurative of the stroke of divine judgment administered vicariously to Him on the cross (a comforting reminder to these Christian servants, who were not infrequently buffeted, v. **20**, by their masters).

Healed *iaomai* (4390), "to heal," is used (a) of physical treatment 22 times; in Matt. 5:28, KJV, "made whole," RV, "healed"; so in Acts 9:34; (b) figuratively, of spiritual "healing," Matt. 13:15; John 12:40; Acts 28:27; Heb. 12:13; **1 Pet. 2:24**; possibly, Jas. 5:16 includes both (a) and (b); some mss. have the word, with sense (b), in Luke 4:18. Apart from this last, Luke, the physician, uses the word fifteen times.

2:25 For ye were as sheep going astray; but are now returned unto the Shepherd and Bishop of your souls.

Sheep *probaton* (4263), from *probaino*, "to go forward," i.e., of the movement of quadrupeds, was used among the Greeks of small cattle, sheep and goats; in the NT, of "sheep" only (a) naturally, e.g., Matt. 12:11, 12; (b) metaphorically, of those who belong to the Lord, the lost ones of the house of Israel, Matt. 10:6; of those who are under the care of the Good Shepherd, e.g., Matt. 26:31; John 10:1, lit., "the fold of the sheep," and vv. 2-27; 21:16, 17 in some texts; Heb. 13:20; of those who in a future day, at the introduction of the millennial kingdom, have shown kindness to His persecuted earthly people in their great tribulation, Matt. 25:33; of the clothing of false shepherds, Matt. 7:15; (c) figuratively, by way of simile, of Christ, Acts 8:32; of the disciples, e.g., Matt. 10:16; of true followers of Christ in general, Rom. 8:36; of the former wayward condition of those who had come under His Shepherd care, **1 Pet. 2:25**; of the multitudes who sought the help of Christ in the days of His flesh, Matt. 9:36; Mark 6:34.

Astray *planao* (4105), (Eng., "planet"), in the passive form sometimes means "to go astray, wander," Matt. 18:12; **1 Pet. 2:25**; Heb. 11:38; frequently active, "to deceive, by leading into error, to seduce," e.g., Matt. 24:4, 5, 11, 24; John 7:12, "leadeth astray," RV (cf. 1 John 3:7). In Rev. 12:9 the present participle is used with the definite article, as a title of the Devil, "the Deceiver," lit., "the deceiving one." Often it has the sense of "deceiving oneself," e.g., 1 Cor. 6:9; 15:33; Gal. 6:7; Jas. 1:16, "be not deceived," RV, "do not err," KJV.

Shepherd *poimen* (4166), is used (a) in its natural significance, Matt. 9:36; 25:32; Mark 6:34; Luke 2:8, 15, 18, 20; John 10:2, 12; (b) metaphorically of Christ, Matt. 26:31;

Mark 14:27; John 10:11, 14, 16; Heb. 13:20; **1 Pet. 2:25**; (c) metaphorically of those who act as pastors in the churches, Eph. 4:11.

Bishop *episkopos* (1985), lit., an overseer" (*epi*, "over," *skopeo*, "to look or watch"), whence Eng. "bishop," which has precisely the same meaning, is found in Acts 20:28; Phil. 1:1; 1 Tim. 3:2; Titus 1:7; **1 Pet. 2:25**.

presbuteros, "an elder," is another term for the same person as bishop or overseer. See Acts 20:17 with verse 28. The term "elder" indicates the mature spiritual experience and understanding of those so described; the term "bishop," or "overseer," indicates the character of the work undertaken. According to the divine will and appointment, as in the NT, there were to be "bishops" in every local church, Acts 14:23; 20:17; Phil. 1:1; Titus 1:5; Jas. 5:14. Where the singular is used, the passage is describing what a "bishop" should be, 1 Tim. 3:2; Titus 1:7. Christ Himself is spoken of as "the ... Bishop of our souls," **1 Pet. 2:25**.

Souls *see 1 Peter 1:9.*

Chapter 3

3:1 Likewise, ye wives, *be* in subjection to your own husbands; that, if any obey not the word, they also may without the word be won by the conversation of the wives;

Likewise *homoios* (3668), "in like manner" (from the adjective *homoios*), is rendered "likewise" in the KJV of Matt. 22:26; 27:41, Luke 10:32; 16:25; John 5:19; Jas. 2:25; **1 Pet. 3:1**, **7**; Jude 8; Rev. 8:12 (in all these the RV has "in like manner"); in the following, KJV and RV have "likewise"; Matt. 26:35; Luke 5:33; 6:31; 10:37; 17:28, 31; 22:36; John 6:11; 21:13; Rom. 1:27; **1 Pet. 5:5**.

Subjection *see* **Submit** at *1 Peter 2:13*.

Obey not *apeitheo* (544), "to disobey, be disobedient," is translated "obey not" in Rom. 2:8; **1 Pet. 3:1**; **4:17**. *See also* **Disobedient** at *1 Peter 2:7*.

Also *kai* The *ascensive* use. This is somewhat similar to the epexegetic significance. It represents, however, an advance in thought upon what precedes and has the meaning "even." The context alone can determine the occurrences of this use. The following are some instances. In Matt. 5:46, 47, the phrases "even the publicans" and "even the Gentiles" represent an extension of thought in regard to the manner of reciprocity exhibited by those referred to, in comparison with those who, like the Pharisees, were considered superior to them. In Mark 1:27, "even the unclean spirits" represents an advance in the minds of the people concerning Christ's miraculous power, in comparison with the authority exercised by the Lord in less remarkable ways. So in Luke 10:17. In Acts 10:45, the *kai*, rendered "also," in the phrase "on the Gentiles also," seems necessary to be regarded in the same way, in view of the amazement manifested by those of the circumcision, and thus the rendering will be "even on the Gentiles was poured out the gift"; cf. 11:1. In Rom. 13:5, the clause "but also for conscience sake" should probably be taken in this sense. In Gal. 2:13, the phrase "even Barnabas" represents an advance of thought in comparison with the waywardness of others; as much as to say, "the Apostle's closest associate, from whom something different might be expected, was surprisingly carried away." In Phil. 4:16 there are three occurrences of *kai*, the first ascensive, "even"; the second (untranslated) meaning "both," before the word "once"; the third meaning "and." In 1 Thess. 1:5, in the cause "and in the Holy Ghost," the *kai* rendered "and," is ascensive, conveying an extension of thought beyond "power"; that is to say, "power indeed, but the power of the Holy Spirit." In **1 Pet. 4:14** "the Spirit of God" is "the Spirit of glory." Here there is an advance in idea from the abstract to the personal. The phrase "the Spirit of God" does more than define "the Spirit of glory"; it is explanatory but ascensive also. When preceded or followed by the conjunction *ei*, "if," the phrase signifies "even if," or "if even," e.g., Mark 14:29; Phil. 2:17; **1 Pet. 3:1**.

Without The opposite of *choris* is *sun*, "with." A synonymous preposition, *aneu*, denotes "without," Matt. 10:29; **1 Pet. 3:1** and **4:9**.

Won *kerdaino* (2770), signifies (I) literally, (a) "to gain something," Matt. 16:26; 25:16 (in the best mss.), 17, 20, 22; Mark 8:36; Luke 9:25; (b) "to get gain, make a profit," Jas. 4:13; (II) metaphorically, (a) "to win persons," said (1) of "gaining" an offending brother who by being told privately of his offense, and by accepting the representations, is won from alienation and from the consequences of his fault, Matt. 18:15; (2) of winning souls into the kingdom of God by the gospel, 1 Cor. 9:19, 20 (twice), 21, 22, or by godly conduct, **1 Pet. 3:1** (RV, "gained"); (3) of so practically appropriating Christ to oneself that He becomes the dominating power in and over one's whole being and circumstances, Phil. 3:8 (RV, "gain"); (b) "to gain things," said of getting injury and loss, Acts 27:21, RV, "gotten."

Conversation *see 1 Peter 1:15.*

3:2 While they behold your chaste conversation *coupled* with fear.

Behold *see 1 Peter 2:12.*

Chaste *hagnos* (53), signifies (a) "pure from every fault, immaculate," 2 Cor. 7:11 (KJV, "clear"); Phil. 4:8; 1 Tim. 5:22; Jas. 3:17; 1 John 3:3 (in all which the RV rendering is "pure"), and **1 Pet. 3:2**, "chaste"; (b) "pure from carnality, modest," 2 Cor. 11:2, RV, "pure"; Titus 2:5, chaste.

Conversation *see 1 Peter 1:15.*

Coupled The word "coupled" is inserted in italics in **1 Pet. 3:2**, the more adequately to express the original, which is, lit., "your chaste behavior in fear."

Fear *see 1 Peter 1:17.*

3:3 Whose adorning let it not be that outward *adorning* of plaiting the hair, and of wearing of gold, or of putting on of apparel;

Adorning *kosmos* (2889), "a harmonious arrangement or order," then, "adornment, decoration," came to denote "the world, or the universe, as that which is divinely arranged." The meaning "adorning" is found in **1 Pet. 3:3**. Elsewhere it signifies "the world." Cf. *kosmios*, decent, modest, 1 Tim. 2:9; 3:2.

Outward *exothen* (1855), is translated "outward" in Matt. 23:27 (RV, "outwardly"); it is used with the article, adjectivally, in **1 Pet. 3:3**, of "outward" adorning.

Plaiting Cf. *emploke*, **1 Pet. 3:3**, "plaiting," i.e., intertwining the hair in ornament.

Hair *thrix* (2359), denotes the "hair," whether of beast, as of the camel's "hair" which formed the raiment of John the Baptist, Matt. 3:4; Mark 1:6; or of man. Regarding the latter (a) it is used to signify the minutest detail, as that which illustrates the exceeding care and protection bestowed by God upon His children, Matt. 10:30; Luke 12:7; 21:18; Acts 27:34; (b) as the Jews swore by the "hair," the Lord used the natural inability to make one "hair" white or black, as one of the reasons for abstinence from oaths, Matt. 5:36; (c) while long "hair" is a glory to a woman, and to wear it loose or dishevelled is a dishonor, yet the woman who wiped Christ's feet with her "hair" (in place of the towel which Simon the Pharisee omitted to provide), despised the shame in her penitent devotion to the Lord (slaves were accustomed to wipe their masters' feet), Luke 7:38, 44 (RV, "hair"); see also John 11:2; 12:3; (d) the dazzling whiteness of the head and "hair" of the Son of Man in the vision of Rev. 1 (v. 14) is suggestive of the holiness and wisdom of "the Ancient of Days"; (e) the long "hair" of the spirit-beings described as locusts in Rev. 9:8 is perhaps indicative of their subjection to their satanic master (cf. 1 Cor. 11:10, RV); (f) Christian women are exhorted to refrain from adorning their "hair" for outward show, **1 Pet. 3:3**.

Wearing *perithesis* (4025), "a putting around or on" (*peri*, "around," *tithemi*, "to put"), is used in **1 Pet. 3:3** of "wearing" jewels of gold (RV).

Gold *see 1 Peter 1:7.*

Putting on *endusis* (745), "a putting on" (akin to *enduo*), is used of apparel, **1 Pet. 3:3**. In the Sept., Esth. 5:1; Job 41:4.

Apparel *himation* (2440), a diminutive of *heima*, "a robe," was used especially of an outer cloak or mantle, and in general of raiment, "apparel" in **1 Pet. 3:3**. The word is not in the original in the next verse, but is supplied in English to complete the sentence.

3:4 But *let it be* the hidden man of the heart, in that which is not corruptible, *even the ornament* of a meek and quiet spirit, which is in the sight of God of great price.

Hidden *kruptos* (2927), "hidden, secret," is translated "hid" in Matt. 10:26; Mark 4:22; Luke 8:17, RV, for KJV, "secret"; 12:2 (last part); in 1 Cor. 4:5, "hidden (things of darkness)"; 2 Cor. 4:2, "hidden (things of shame)"; **1 Pet. 3:4**, "hidden (man of the heart)."

Man *anthropos* (444), is used (a) generally, of "a human being, male or female," without reference to sex or nationality, e.g., Matt. 4:4; 12:35; John 2:25; (b) in distinction from God, e.g., Matt. 19:6; John 10:33; Gal. 1:11; Col. 3:23; (c) in distinction from animals, etc., e.g., Luke 5:10; (d) sometimes, in the plural, of "men and women," people, e.g., Matt. 5:13, 16; in Mark 11:2 and 1 Tim. 6:16, lit., "no one of men"; (e) in some instances with a suggestion of human frailty and imperfection e.g., 1 Cor. 2:5; Acts 14:15 (2nd part); (f) in the phrase translated "after man," "after the manner of men," "as a man" (KJV), lit. "according to (*kata*) man," is used only by the apostle Paul, of "(1) the practices of fallen humanity 1 Cor. 3:3; (2) anything of human origin, Gal. 1:11; (3) the laws that govern the administration of justice among men, Rom. 3:5; (4) the standard generally accepted among men, Gal. 3:15; (5) an illustration not drawn from Scripture, 1 Cor. 9:8; (6) probably = 'to use a figurative expression' (see KJV, marg.), i.e., to speak evil of men with whom he had contended at Ephesus as 'beasts' (cf. 1 Cor. 4:6), 1 Cor. 15:32; Lightfoot prefers 'from worldly motives'; but the other interpretation, No. (4), seems to make better sense. See also Rom. 6:19, where, however, the Greek is slightly different, anthropinos, 'pertaining to mankind'; the meaning is as Nos. (5) and (6)."

(g) in the phrase "the inward man," the regenerate person's spiritual nature personified, the inner self of the believer, Rom. 7:22, as approving of the law of God; in Eph. 3:16, as the sphere of the renewing power of the Holy Spirit; in 2 Cor. 4:16 (where *anthropos* is not repeated), in contrast to "the outward man," the physical frame, the "man" as cognizable by the senses; the "inward" man is identical with "the hidden man of the heart," **1 Pet. 3:4** ...

Heart *kardia* (2588), "the heart" (Eng., "cardiac," etc.), the chief organ of physical life ("for the life of the flesh is in the blood," Lev. 17:11), occupies the most important place in the human system. By an easy transition the word came to stand for man's entire mental and moral activity, both the rational and the emotional elements. In other words, the heart is used figuratively for the hidden springs of the personal life. "The Bible describes human depravity as in the 'heart,' because sin is a principle which has its seat in the center of man's inward life, and then 'defiles' the whole circuit of his action, Matt. 15:19, 20. On the other hand, Scripture regards the heart as the sphere of Divine influence, Rom. 2:15; Acts 15:9.... The heart, as lying deep within, contains 'the hidden man,' **1 Pet. 3:4**, the real man. It represents the true character but conceals it" (J. Laidlaw, in *Hastings' Bible Dic.*). As to its usage in the NT it denotes (a) the seat of physical life, Acts 14:17; Jas. 5:5; (b) the seat of moral nature and spiritual life, the seat of grief, John 14:1; Rom. 9:2; 2 Cor. 2:4; joy, John 16:22; Eph. 5:19; the desires, Matt. 5:28; 2 Pet. 2:14; the affections, Luke 24:32; Acts 21:13; the perceptions, John 12:40; Eph. 4:18; the thoughts, Matt. 9:4; Heb. 4:12; the understanding, Matt. 13:15; Rom. 1:21; the reasoning powers, Mark 2:6; Luke 24:38; the imagination, Luke 1:51; conscience, Acts 2:37; 1 John 3:20; the intentions, Heb. 4:12, cf. **1 Pet. 4:1**; purpose, Acts 11:23; 2 Cor. 9:7; the will, Rom. 6:17; Col. 3:15; faith, Mark 11:23; Rom. 10:10; Heb. 3:12. The heart, in its moral significance in the OT, includes the emotions, the reason and the will.

Corruptible *see* **Incorruptible** at *1 Peter 1:4*.

Meek *praus* or *praos* (4239), denotes "gentle, mild, meek." Christ uses it of His own disposition, Matt. 11:29; He gives it in the third of His Beatitudes, 5:5; it is said of Him as the King Messiah, 21:5, from Zech. 9:9; it is an adornment of the Christian profession, **1 Pet. 3:4**. Cf. *epios*, "gentle, of a soothing disposition," 1 Thess. 2:7; 2 Tim. 2:24.

Quiet *hesuchios* (2272), indicates "tranquillity arising from within," causing no disturbance to others. It is translated "quiet" in 1 Tim. 2:2, RV (KJV, "peaceable"); "quiet" in **1 Pet. 3:4**, where it is associated with "meek," and is to characterize the spirit or disposition.

Spirit *pneuma* (4151), primarily denotes "the wind" (akin to *pneo*, "to breathe, blow"); also "breath"; then, especially "the spirit," which, like the wind, is invisible, immaterial and powerful. The NT uses of the word may be analyzed approximately as follows:

"(a) the wind, John 3:8 (where marg. is, perhaps, to be preferred); Heb. 1:7; cf. Amos 4:13, Sept.; (b) the breath, 2 Thess. 2:8; Rev. 11:11; 13:15; cf. Job 12:10, Sept.; (c) the immaterial, invisible part of man, Luke 8:55; Acts 7:59; 1 Cor. 5:5; Jas. 2:26; cf. Eccl. 12:7, Sept.; (d) the disembodied (or 'unclothed,' or 'naked,' 2 Cor. 5:3, 4) man, Luke 24:37, 39; Heb. 12:23; **1 Pet. 4:6**; (e) the resurrection body, 1 Cor. 15:45; 1 Tim. 3:16; **1 Pet. 3:18**; (f) the sentient element in man, that by which he perceives, reflects, feels, desires, Matt. 5:3; 26:41; Mark 2:8; Luke 1:47, 80; Acts 17:16; 20:22; 1 Cor. 2:11; 5:3, 4; 14:4, 15; 2 Cor. 7:1; cf. Gen. 26:35; Isa. 26:9; Ezek. 13:3; Dan. 7:15; (g) purpose, aim, 2 Cor. 12:18; Phil. 1:27; Eph. 4:23; Rev. 19:10; cf. Ezra 1:5; Ps. 78:8; Dan. 5:12; (h) the equivalent of the personal pronoun, used for emphasis and effect: 1st person, 1 Cor. 16:18; cf. Gen. 6:3; 2nd person, 2 Tim. 4:22; Philem. 25; cf. Ps. 139:7; 3rd person, 2 Cor. 7:13; cf. Isa. 40:13; (i) character, Luke 1:17; Rom. 1:4; cf. Num. 14:24; (j) moral qualities and activities: bad, as of bondage, as of a slave, Rom. 8:15; cf. Isa. 61:3; stupor, Rom. 11:8; cf. Isa. 29:10; timidity, 2 Tim. 1:7; cf. Josh. 5:1; good, as of adoption, i.e., liberty as of a son, Rom. 8:15; cf. Ps. 51:12; meekness, 1 Cor. 4:21; cf. Prov. 16:19; faith, 2 Cor. 4:13; quietness, **1 Pet. 3:4**; cf. Prov. 14:29; (k) the Holy Spirit, e.g., Matt. 4:1; Luke 4:18; (l) 'the inward man' (an expression used only of the believer, Rom. 7:22; 2 Cor. 4:16; Eph. 3:16); the new life, Rom. 8:4-6, 10, 16; Heb. 12:9; cf. Ps. 51:10; (m) unclean spirits, demons, Matt. 8:16; Luke 4:33; **1 Pet. 3:19**; cf. 1 Sam. 18:10; (n) angels, Heb. 1:14; cf. Acts 12:15; (o) divine gift for service, 1 Cor. 14:12, 32; (p) by metonymy, those who claim to be depositories of these gifts, 2 Thess. 2:2; 1 John

4:1-3; (q) the significance, as contrasted with the form, of words, or of a rite, John 6:63; Rom. 2:29; 7:6; 2 Cor. 3:6; (r) a vision, Rev. 1:10; 4:2; 17:3; 21:10."

Price *poluteles* (4185), primarily, "the very end or limit" (from *polus*, "much," *telos*, "revenue"), with reference to price, of highest "cost," very expensive, is said of spikenard, Mark 14:3; raiment, 1 Tim. 2:9; metaphorically, of a meek and quiet spirit, **1 Pet. 3:4**, "of great price."

3:5 For after this manner in the old time the holy women also, who trusted in God, adorned themselves, being in subjection unto their own husbands:

Manner *houtos* or *houto* (3779), "thus, in this way," is rendered "after this manner" in Matt. 6:9; **1 Pet. 3:5**; Rev. 11:5.

Old time *pote* (4218), signifies "once, at some time," John 9:13 (cf. *proteron*, in v. 8); Eph. 2:2, 11; Col. 3:7; Titus 3:3; Philem. 11; 1 Pet. **3:5, 20**. In all these the RV translates it "aforetime." The KJV varies it with "in time past," "some time," "sometimes," "in the old time."

Trusted *elpizo* (1679), "to hope," is not infrequently translated in the KJV, by the verb "to trust"; the RV adheres to some form of the verb "to hope," e.g., John 5:45, "Moses, on whom ye have set your hope"; 2 Cor. 1:10, "on whom we have set our hope"; so in 1 Tim. 4:10; 5:5; 6:17; see also, e.g., Matt. 12:21; Luke 24:21; Rom. 15:12, 24. The verb is followed by three prepositions: (1) *eis*, rendered "on" in John 5:45 (as above); the meaning is really "in" as in **1 Pet. 3:5**, "who hoped in God"; the "hope" is thus said to be directed to, and to center in, a person; (2) *epi*, "on," Rom. 15:12, "On Him shall the Gentiles hope," RV; so 1 Tim. 4:10; 5:5 (in the best mss.); 6:17, RV; this expresses the ground upon which "hope" rests; (3) *en*, "in," 1 Cor. 15:19, "we have hoped in Christ," RV, more lit., "we are (men) that have hoped in Christ," the preposition expresses that Christ is not simply the ground upon whom, but the sphere and element in whom, the "hope" is placed. The form of the verb (the perfect participle with the verb to be, lit., "are having hoped") stresses the character of those who "hope," more than the action; "hope" characterizes them, showing what sort of persons they are.

Adorned *kosmeo* (2885), primarily "to arrange, to put in order" (Eng., "cosmetic"), is used of furnishing a room, Matt. 12:44; Luke 11:25, and of trimming lamps, Matt. 25:7. Hence, "to adorn, to ornament," as of garnishing tombs, Matt. 23:29; buildings, Luke 21:5; Rev. 21:19; one's person, 1 Tim. 2:9; **1 Pet. 3:5**; Rev. 21:2; metaphorically, of "adorning" a doctrine, Titus 2:10.

Subjection *see* **Submit** at *1 Peter 2:13*.

3:6 Even as Sara obeyed Abraham, calling him lord: whose daughters ye are, as long as ye do well, and are not afraid with any amazement.

Even as *hos* (5613), "as," in comparative sentences, is sometimes translated "even as," Matt. 15:28; Mark 4:36; Eph. 5:33; **1 Pet. 3:6** (KJV only); Jude 7.

Obeyed *hupakouo* (5219), "to listen, attend" (as in Acts 12:13), and so, "to submit, to obey," is used of "obedience" (a) to God, Heb. 5:9; 11:8; (b) to Christ, by natural elements, Matt. 8:27; Mark 1:27; 4:41; Luke 8:25; (c) to disciples of Christ, Luke 17:6; (d) to the faith, Acts 6:7; the gospel, Rom. 10:16; 2 Thess. 1:8; Christian doctrine, Rom. 6:17 (as to a form or mold of teaching); (e) to apostolic injunctions, Phil. 2:12; 2 Thess. 3:14; (f) to Abraham by Sarah, **1 Pet. 3:6**; (g) to parents by children, Eph. 6:1; Col. 3:20; (h) to masters by servants, Eph. 6:5; Col. 3:22; (i) to sin, Rom. 6:12; (j) in general, Rom. 6:16.

Lord *see 1 Peter 1:25*.

Daughters In **1 Pet. 3:6**, *teknon*, "a child," is translated "daughters" (KJV), "children" (RV).

Well *see 1 Peter 2:14*. *See also* **Well doing** at *1 Peter 2:15*.

Amazement *ptoesis* signifies "terror," not "amazement," **1 Pet. 3:6**, RV.

3:7 Likewise, ye husbands, dwell with *them* according to knowledge, giving honour unto the wife, as unto the weaker vessel, and as being heirs together of the grace of life; that your prayers be not hindered.

Likewise *see 1 Peter 3:1*.

Dwell *sunoikeo* (4924), "to dwell with," is used in **1 Pet. 3:7**.

Knowledge *gnosis* (1108), primarily "a seeking to know, an enquiry, investigation," denotes, in the NT, "knowledge," especially of spiritual truth; it is used (a) absolutely, in Luke 11:52; Rom. 2:20; 15:14; 1 Cor. 1:5; 8:1 (twice), 7, 10, 11; 13:2, 8; 14:6; 2 Cor. 6:6; 8:7; 11:6; Eph. 3:19; Col. 2:3; **1 Pet. 3:7**; 2 Pet. 1:5, 6; (b) with an object: in respect of (1) God, 2 Cor. 2:14; 10:5; (2) the glory of God, 2 Cor. 4:6; (3) Christ Jesus, Phil. 3:8; 2 Pet. 3:18; (4) salvation, Luke 1:77; (c) subjectively, of God's "knowledge," Rom. 11:33; the word of "knowledge," 1 Cor. 12:8; "knowledge" falsely so called, 1 Tim. 6:20.

Giving *aponemo* (632), "to assign, apportion" (*apo*, "away," *nemo*, "to distribute"), is rendered "giving" in **1 Pet. 3:7**, of giving honor to the wife. In the papyri writings it is said of a prefect who "gives" to all their dues. In the Sept., Deut. 4:19.

Honour *see 1 Peter 1:7.*

Wife *gunaikeios* (1134), an adjective denoting "womanly, female," is used as a noun in **1 Pet. 3:7**, KJV, "wife," RV, "woman."

Weaker *asthenes* (772), lit., "strengthless", is translated "weak," (a) of physical "weakness," Matt. 26:41; Mark 14:38; 1 Cor. 1:27; 4:10; 11:30 (a judgment upon spiritual laxity in a church); 2 Cor. 10:10; **1 Pet. 3:7** (comparative degree); (b) in the spiritual sense, said of the rudiments of Jewish religion, in their inability to justify anyone, Gal. 4:9; of the Law, Heb. 7:18; in Rom. 5:6, RV, "weak" (KJV, "without strength"), of the inability of man to accomplish his salvation; (c) morally or ethically, 1 Cor. 8:7, 10; 9:22; (d) rhetorically, of God's actions according to the human estimate, 1 Cor. 1:25, "weakness," lit., "the weak things of God."

Vessel *skeuos* (4632), is used (a) of "a vessel or implement" of various kinds, Mark 11:16; Luke 8:16; John 19:29; Acts 10:11, 16; 11:5; 27:17 (a sail); Rom. 9:21; 2 Tim. 2:20; Heb. 9:21; Rev. 2:27; 18:12; (b) of "goods or household stuff," Matt. 12:29 and Mark 3:27, "goods"; Luke 17:31, RV, "goods" (KJV, "stuff"); (c) of "persons," (1) for the service of God, Acts 9:15, "a (chosen) vessel"; 2 Tim. 2:21, "a vessel (unto honor)"; (2) the "subjects" of divine wrath, Rom. 9:22; (3) the "subjects" of divine mercy, Rom. 9:23; (4) the human frame, 2 Cor. 4:7; perhaps 1 Thess. 4:4; (5) a husband and wife, **1 Pet. 3:7**; of the wife, probably, 1 Thess. 4:4; while the exhortation to each one "to possess himself of his own vessel in sanctification and honor" is regarded by some as referring to the believer's body [cf. Rom. 6:13; 1 Cor. 9:27], the view that the "vessel" signifies the wife, and that the reference is to the sanctified maintenance of the married state, is supported by the facts that in **1 Pet. 3:7** the same word *time*, "honor," is used with regard to the wife, again in Heb. 13:4, *timios*, "honorable" (RV, "in honor") is used in regard to marriage; further, the preceding command in 1 Thess. 4 is against fornication, and the succeeding one (v. 6) is against adultery. In Ruth 4:10, Sept., *ktaomai*, "to possess," is used of a wife.

Heirs together *sunkleronomos* (4789), "a joint-heir, co-inheritor," "is used of Isaac and Jacob as participants with Abraham in the promises of God, Heb. 11:9; of husband and wife who are also united in Christ, **1 Pet. 3:7**; of Gentiles who believe, as participants in the gospel with Jews who believe, Eph. 3:6; and of all believers as prospective participants with Christ in His glory, as recompense for their participation in His sufferings, Rom. 8:17."

That *eis*, "unto," followed by the article and the infinitive mood of a verb, signifies "to the end that ..." marking the aim of an action, Acts 7:19; Rom. 1:11; 4:16, 18; Eph. 1:12; 1 Thess. 3:13; 2 Thess. 1:5; 2:2, 6; **1 Pet. 3:7**. In Luke 18:1, *pros*, "to," has the same construction and meaning.

Hindered *enkopto* (1465), lit., "to cut into" (*en*, "in," *kopto*, "to cut"), was used of "impeding" persons by breaking up the road, or by placing an obstacle sharply in the path; hence, metaphorically, of "detaining" a person unnecessarily, Acts 24:4, of "hindrances" in the way of reaching others, Rom. 15:22; or returning to them, 1 Thess. 2:18; of "hindering" progress in the Christian life, Gal. 5:7 (*anakopto* in some mss.), where the significance virtually is "who broke up the road along which you were travelling so well?"; of "hindrances" to the prayers of husband and wife, through low standards of marital conduct, **1 Pet. 3:7** (*ekkopto*, "to cut out, repulse," in some mss.).

"A happy marriage is the union of two good forgivers."

ROBERT QUILLEN

3:8 Finally, *be ye* all of one mind, having compassion one of another, love as brethren, *be* pitiful, *be* courteous:

Finally *telos* (5056), "an end," most frequently of the termination of something, is used with the article adverbially, meaning "finally" or "as to the end," i.e., as to the last detail, **1 Pet. 3:8**.

Of one mind *homophron* (3675), "agreeing, of one mind" (*homos*, "same," *phren*, "the mind"), is used in **1 Pet. 3:8**.

Compassion *sumpathes* (4835), denotes suffering with, "compassionate," **1 Pet. 3:8**, RV (KJV, "having compassion").

One ... another In **1 Pet. 3:8**, KJV, "one of another" represents nothing in the original (the RV, "compassionate" sufficiently translates the adjective *sumpathes*."

Brethren *see 1 Peter 1:22.*

Pitiful *eusplanchnos* (2155), "compassionate, tenderhearted," lit., "of good heartedness" (*eu*, "well," and *splanchnon*), is translated "pitiful" in **1 Pet. 3:8**, KJV, RV, "tenderhearted," as in Eph. 4:32.

Courteous Some mss. have the corresponding adjective *philophron*, "courteous," in **1 Pet. 3:8**; the most authentic mss. have *tapeinophron*, "humble-minded."

3:9 Not rendering evil for evil, or railing for railing: but contrariwise blessing; knowing that ye are thereunto called, that ye should inherit a blessing.

Rendering *apodidomi* (591), signifies "to give up or back, to restore, return, render what is due, to pay, give an account," e.g., of an account. Matt. 5:26; 12:36; Luke 16:2; Acts. 19:40; Heb. 13:17; **1 Pet. 4:5**; of wages, etc., e.g., Matt. 18:25-34; 20:8; of conjugal duty, 1 Cor. 7:3; of a witness, Acts 4:33; frequently of recompensing or rewarding, 1 Tim. 5:4; 2 Tim. 4:8, 14; **1 Pet. 3:9**; Rev. 18:6; 22:12. In the middle voice it is used of "giving" up what is one's own; hence, "to sell," Acts 5:8; 7:9; Heb. 12:16.

Evil *kakos* (2556), stands for "whatever is evil in character, base," in distinction (wherever the distinction is observable) from *poneros*, which indicates "what is evil in influence and effect, malignant." *Kakos* is the wider term and often covers the meaning of *poneros*. *Kakos* is antithetic to *kalos*, "fair, advisable, good in character," and to *agathos*, "beneficial, useful, good in act"; hence it denotes what is useless, incapable, bad; *poneros* is essentially antithetic to *chrestos*, "kind, gracious, serviceable"; hence it denotes what is destructive, injurious, evil. As evidence that *poneros* and *kakos* have much in common, though still not interchangeable, each is used of thoughts, cf. Matt. 15:19 with Mark 7:21; of speech, Matt. 5:11 with **1 Pet. 3:10**; of actions, 2 Tim. 4:18 with 1 Thess. 5:15; of man, Matt. 18:32 with 24:48. The use of *kakos* may be broadly divided as follows: (a) of what is morally or ethically "evil," whether of persons, e.g., Matt. 21:41; 24:48; Phil. 3:2; Rev. 2:2, or qualities, emotions, passions, deeds, e.g., Mark 7:21; John 18:23, 30; Rom. 1:30; 3:8; 7:19, 21; 13:4; 14:20; 16:19; 1 Cor. 13:5; 2 Cor. 13:7; 1 Thess. 5:15; 1 Tim. 6:10; 2 Tim. 4:14; **1 Pet. 3:9, 12**; (b) of what is injurious, destructive, baneful, pernicious, e.g., Luke 16:25; Acts 16:28; 28:5; Titus 1:12; Jas. 3:8; Rev. 16:2, where *kakos* and *poneros* come in that order, "noisome and grievous."

Railing *loidoria* (3059), "abuse, railing, reviling," is rendered "reviling" in the RV, **1 Pet. 3:9** (twice); in 1 Tim. 5:14, KJV marg., "for their reviling."

Contrariwise *t'ounantion* (5121), for *to enantion*, "the contrary, on the contrary or contrariwise," is used in 2 Cor. 2:7; Gal. 2:7; **1 Pet. 3:9**.

Inherit *kleronomeo* (2816), strictly means "to receive by lot" (*kleros*, "a lot," *nemomai*, "to possess"); then, in a more general sense, "to possess oneself of, to receive as one's own, to obtain." The following list shows how in the NT the idea of inheriting broadens out to include all spiritual good provided through and in Christ, and particularly all that is contained in the hope grounded on the promises of God. The verb is used of the following objects: "(a) birthright, that into the possession of which one enters in virtue of sonship, not because of a price paid or of a task accomplished, Gal. 4:30; Heb. 1:4; 12:17. (b) that which is received as a gift, in contrast with that which is received as the reward of law-keeping, Heb. 1:14; 6:12 ("through," i.e., "through experiences that called for the exercise of faith and patience,' but not 'on the ground of the exercise of faith and patience.'). (c) that which is received on condition of obedience to certain precepts, **1 Pet. 3:9**, and of faithfulness to God amidst opposition, Rev. 21:7 ..."

3:10 For he that will love life, and see good days, let him refrain his tongue from evil, and his lips that they speak no guile:

Will *thelo* (2309), usually expresses "desire" or "design"; it is most frequently translated by "will" or "would"; see especially Rom. 7:15, 16, 18-21. In 1 Tim. 2:4, RV, "willeth" signifies the gracious "desire" of God for all men to be saved; not all are "willing" to accept His condition, depriving themselves either by the self-established criterion of their perverted reason, or because of their self-indulgent preference for sin. In John 6:21, the KJV renders the verb "willingly" (RV, "they were willing"); in 2 Pet. 3:5, KJV, the present participle is translated "willingly" (RV, "wilfully"). The following are RV renderings for the KJV, "will": Matt. 16:24, 25, "would"; "wouldest," 19:21 and 20:21; "would," 20:26, 27; Mark 8:34, 35; 10:43, 44; "would fain," Luke 13:31; "would," John 6:67; "willeth," 7:17; in 8:44, "it is your will (to do)"; "wouldest," Rom. 13:3; "would," 1 Cor. 14:35 and **1 Pet. 3:10**.

Love *see 1 Peter 1:8.*

Life *zoe* (2222), (Eng., "zoo," "zoology") is used in the NT "of life as a principle, life in the absolute sense, life as God has it, that which the Father has in Himself, and which He gave to the Incarnate Son to have in Himself, John 5:26, and which the Son manifested in the world, 1 John 1:2. From this life man has become alienated in consequence of the Fall, Eph. 4:18, and of this life men become partakers through faith in the Lord Jesus Christ, John 3:15, who becomes its Author to all such as trust in Him, Acts 3:15, and who is therefore said to be 'the life' of the believer, Col. 3:4, for the life that He gives He maintains, John 6:35, 63. Eternal life is the present actual possession of the believer because of his relationship with Christ, John 5:24; 1 John 3:14, and that it will one day extend its domain to the sphere of the body is assured by the Resurrection of Christ, 2 Cor. 5:4; 2 Tim. 1:10. This life is not merely a principle of power and mobility, however, for it has moral associations which are inseparable from it, as of holiness and righteousness. Death and sin, life and holiness, are frequently contrasted in the Scriptures.

"*Zoe* is also used of that which is the common possession of all animals and men by nature, Acts 17:25; 1 John 5:16, and of the present sojourn of man upon the earth with reference to its duration, Luke 16:25; 1 Cor. 15:19; 1 Tim. 4:8; **1 Pet. 3:10**. 'This life' is a term equivalent to 'the gospel,' 'the faith,' 'Christianity,' Acts 5:20."

Death came through sin, Rom. 5:12, which is rebellion against God. Sin thus involved the forfeiting of the "life." "The life of the flesh is in the blood," Lev. 17:11. Therefore the impartation of "life" to the sinner must be by a death caused by the shedding of that element which is the life of the flesh. "It is the blood that maketh atonement by reason of the life" (*id.* RV). The separation from God caused by the forfeiting of the "life" could be removed only by a sacrifice in which the victim and the offerer became identified. This which was appointed in the typical offerings in Israel received its full accomplishment in the voluntary sacrifice of Christ. The shedding of the blood in the language of Scripture involves the taking or the giving of the "life." Since Christ had no sins of his own to die for, His death was voluntary and vicarious, John 10:15 with Isa. 53:5, 10, 12; 2 Cor. 5:21. In His sacrifice He endured the divine judgment due to man's sin. By this means the believer becomes identified with Him in His deathless "life," through His resurrection, and enjoys conscious and eternal fellowship with God.

Refrain *pauo* (3973), "to stop, to make an end," is used chiefly in the middle voice in the NT, signifying "to come to an end, to take one's rest, a willing cessation" (in contrast to the passive voice which denotes a forced cessation), Luke 5:4, of a discourse; 8:24, of a storm, 11:1, of Christ's prayer; Acts 5:42, of teaching and preaching; 6:13, of speaking against; 13:10, of evil doing; 20:1, of an uproar; 20:31, of admonition; 21:32, of a scourging; 1 Cor. 13:8, of tongues; Eph. 1:16, of giving thanks; Col. 1:9, of prayer; Heb. 10:2, of sacrifices; **1 Pet. 4:1**, of "ceasing" from sin. It is used in the active voice in **1 Pet. 3:10**, "let him cause his tongue to cease from evil."

Tongue *glossa* (1100), is used of (1) the "tongues ... like as of fire" which appeared at Pentecost; (2) "the tongue," as an organ of speech, e.g., Mark 7:33; Rom. 3:13; 14:11; 1 Cor. 14:9; Phil. 2:11; Jas. 1:26; 3:5, 6, 8; **1 Pet. 3:10**; 1 John 3:18; Rev. 16:10; (3) (a) "a language," coupled with *phule*, "a tribe," *laos*, "a people," *ethnos*, "a nation," seven times in Revelation, 5:9; 7:9; 10:11; 11:9; 13:7; 14:6; 17:15; (b) "the supernatural gift of speaking in another language without its having been learnt"; in Acts 2:4-13 the circumstances are recorded from the viewpoint of the hearers; to those in whose language the utterances were made it appeared as a supernatural phenomenon; to others, the stammering of drunkards; what was uttered was not addressed primarily to the audience but consisted in recounting "the mighty works of God"; cf. 2:46; in 1 Cor., chapters 12 and 14, the use of the gift of "tongues" is mentioned as exercised in the gatherings of local churches; 12:10 speaks of the gift in general terms, and couples with it that of "the interpretation of tongues"; chapt. 14 gives instruction concerning the use of the gift, the paramount object being the edification of the church ...

Evil *poneros* (4190), connected with *ponos*, "labor," expresses especially the "active form of evil." It is used, e.g., of thoughts, Matt. 15:19 (cf. *kakos*, in Mark 7:21); of speech, Matt. 5:11 (cf. *kakos*, in **1 Pet. 3:10**); of acts 2 Tim. 4:18. Where *kakos* and *poneros* are put together, *kakos* is always put first and signifies "bad in character, base," *poneros*, "bad in effect, malignant": see 1 Cor. 5:8, and Rev. 16:2. *Kakos* has a wider meaning, *poneros* a stronger meaning. *Poneros* alone is used of Satan and might well be translated "the malignant one," e.g., Matt. 5:37 and five times in 1 John (2:13-14; 3:12; 5:18-19, RV); of demons, e.g., Luke 7:21. Once it is translated bad, Matt. 22:10. *See also **1 Peter 3:9**.*

Lips *cheilos* (5491), is used (a) of the organ of speech, Matt. 15:8 and Mark 7:6, where "honoring with the lips," besides meaning empty words, may have reference to a Jewish custom of putting to the mouth the tassel of the tallith (the woollen scarf wound round the head and neck during prayer), as a sign of acceptance of the Law from the heart; Rom. 3:13; 1 Cor. 14:21 (from Isa. 28:11, 12, speaking of the Assyrian foe as God's message to disobedient Israel); Heb. 13:15; **1 Pet. 3:10**; (b) metaphorically, of "the brink or edge of things," as of the sea shore, Heb. 11:12, lit., "the shore (of the sea)."

Guile *see 1 Peter 2:1.*

3:11 Let him eschew evil, and do good; let him seek peace, and ensue it.

Eschew *ekklino* (1578), "to turn aside" (*ek*, "from," *klino*, "to turn, bend"), is used metaphorically (a) of leaving the right path, Rom. 3:12, RV, "turned aside," for KJV, "gone out of the way"; (b) of turning away from divisionmakers, and errorists, 16:17, RV, "turn away from"; (c) of turning away from evil, **1 Pet. 3:11**, RV, "turn away from," KJV, "eschew." In the Sept. the verb is frequently used of declining or swerving from God's ways, e.g., Job 23:11; Ps. 44:18; 119:51, 157.

Good *see 1 Peter 2:18.*

Seek *zeteo* (2212), signifies (a) "to seek, to seek for," e.g., Matt. 7:7, 8; 13:45; Luke 24:5; John 6:24; of plotting against a person's life, Matt. 2:20; Acts 21:31; Rom. 11:3; metaphorically, to "seek" by thinking, to "seek" how to do something, or what to obtain, e.g., Mark 11:18; Luke 12:29; to "seek" to ascertain a meaning, John 16:19, "do ye inquire"; to "seek" God, Acts 17:27, RV; Rom. 10:20; (b) "to seek or strive after, endeavor, to desire," e.g., Matt. 12:46, 47, RV, "seeking" (KJV, "desiring"); Luke 9:9, RV, "sought" (KJV, "desired"); John 7:19, RV, "seek ye" (KJV, "go ye about"); so v. 20; Rom. 10:3, RV, "seeking" (KJV, "going about"); of "seeking" the kingdom of God and His righteousness, in the sense of coveting earnestly, striving after, Matt. 6:33; "the things that are above," Col. 3:1; peace, **1 Pet. 3:11**; (c) "to require or demand," e.g., Mark 8:12; Luke 11:29; 1 Cor. 4:2, "it is required"; 2 Cor. 13:3, "ye seek."

Ensue *dioko* (1377), "to put to flight, pursue, persecute," is rendered "to pursue" in 2 Cor. 4:9, RV (KJV, "persecute"), and is used metaphorically of "seeking eagerly" after peace in **1 Pet. 3:11**, RV (KJV, "ensue").

3:12 For the eyes of the Lord *are* over the righteous, and his ears *are open* unto their prayers: but the face of the Lord *is* against them that do evil.

Eyes *ophthalmos* (3788), akin to *opsis*, "sight," probably from a root signifying "penetration, sharpness" (Curtius, Gk. Etym.) (cf. Eng., "ophthalmia," etc.). is used (a) of the physical organ, e.g., Matt. 5:38; of restoring sight, e.g., Matt. 20:33; of God's power of vision, Heb. 4:13; **1 Pet. 3:12**; of Christ in vision, Rev. 1:14; 2:18; 19:12; of the Holy Spirit in the unity of Godhood with Christ, Rev. 5:6; (b) metaphorically, of ethical qualities, evil, Matt. 6:23; Mark 7:22 (by metonymy, for envy); singleness of motive, Matt. 6:22; Luke 11:34; as the instrument of evil desire, "the principal avenue of temptation," 1 John 2:16; of adultery, 2 Pet. 2:14; (c) metaphorically, of mental vision, Matt. 13:15; John 12:40; Rom. 11:8; Gal. 3:1, where the metaphor of the "evil eye" is altered to a different sense from that of bewitching (the posting up or placarding of an "eye" was used as a charm, to prevent mischief); by gospel-preaching Christ had been, so to speak, placarded before their "eyes"; the question may be paraphrased, "What evil teachers have been malignly fascinating you?"; Eph. 1:18, of the "eyes of the heart," as a means of knowledge.

Prayers *deesis* (1162), primarily "a wanting, a need," then, "an asking, entreaty, supplication," in the NT is always addressed to God and always rendered "supplication" or "supplications" in the RV; in the KJV "prayer," or "prayers," in Luke 1:13; 2:37; 5:33; Rom. 10:1; 2 Cor. 1:11; 9:14; Phil. 1:4 (in the 2nd part, "request"); 1:19; 2 Tim. 1:3; Heb. 5:7; Jas. 5:16; **1 Pet. 3:12**.

Face *prosopon* (4383), denotes "the countenance," lit., "the part towards the eyes" (from *pros*, "towards," *ops*, "the eye"), and is used (a) of the "face," Matt. 6:16-17; 2 Cor. 3:7, 2nd part (KJV, "countenance"); in 2 Cor. 10:7, in the RV, "things that are before your face" (KJV, "outward appearance"), the phrase is figurative of superficial judgment; (b) of the look, i.e., the "face," which by its various movements affords an index of inward thoughts and feelings. e g., Luke 9:51, 53; **1 Pet. 3:12**; (c) the presence of a person, the "face" being the noblest part, e.g., Acts 3:13, RV, "before the face of," KJV, "in the presence of"; 5:41, "presence"; 2 Cor. 2:10, "person"; 1 Thess. 2:17 (first part), "presence"; 2 Thess. 1:9, RV, "face," KJV, "presence"; Rev. 12:14, "face"; (d) the person himself, e.g., Gal. 1:22; 1 Thess. 2:17 (second part); (e) the appearance one presents by his wealth or poverty, his position or state, Matt. 22:16; Mark 12:14; Gal. 2:6; Jude 16; (f) the outward appearance of inanimate things, Matt. 16:3; Luke 12:56; 21:35; Acts 17:26. "To spit in a person's face" was an expression of the utmost scorn and aversion, e.g., Matt. 26:67 (cf. 27:30; Mark 10:34; Luke 18:32).

Evil *see 1 Peter 3:9.*

3:13 And who *is* he that will harm you, if ye be followers of that which is good?

Harm *kakoo* (2559), "to do evil to a person," is rendered "harm" in **1 Pet. 3:13**, and in the RV of Acts 18:10 (KJV, "hurt").

Good *see 1 Peter 2:18.*

3:14 But and if ye suffer for righteousness' sake, happy *are ye*: and be not afraid of their terror, neither be troubled;

Suffer *see* **Suffering** at *1 Peter 2:19.*

Happy *makarios* (3107), "blessed, happy," is rendered "happy" in the RV, in two places only, as in the KJV, Acts 26:2 and Rom. 14:22 (where "blessed" would have done); also the comparative "happier" in 1 Cor. 7:40. Elsewhere the RV uses "blessed" for KJV "happy," e.g., John 13:17; **1 Pet. 3:14; 4:14.**

Afraid *see* **Fear** at *1 Peter 1:17.*

Terror *phobos* (5401), "fear," is rendered "terror" in Rom. 13:3; in 2 Cor. 5:11 and **1 Pet. 3:14**, KJV (RV, "fear").

Troubled *tarosso* (5015), akin to *tarache*, is used (1) in a physical sense, John 5:7 (in some mss. v. 4), (2) metaphorically, (a) of the soul and spirit of the Lord, John 11:33, where the true rendering is "He troubled Himself"; (b) of the hearts of disciples, 14:1, 27; (c) of the minds of those in fear or perplexity, Matt. 2:3; 14:26; Mark 6:50; Luke 1:12; 24:38; **1 Pet. 3:14**; (d) of subverting the souls of believers, by evil doctrine, Acts 15:24; Gal. 1:7; 5:10; (e) of stirring up a crowd, Acts 17:8; v. 13 in the best texts, "troubling (the multitudes)," RV.

3:15 But sanctify the Lord God in your hearts: and *be* ready always to *give* an answer to every man that asketh you a reason of the hope that is in you with meekness and fear:

Sanctify *hagiazo* (37), "to sanctify," "is used of (a) the gold adorning the Temple and of the gift laid on the altar, Matt. 23:17, 19; (b) food, 1 Tim. 4:5; (c) the unbelieving spouse of a believer, 1 Cor. 7:14; (d) the ceremonial cleansing of the Israelites, Heb. 9:13; (e) the Father's Name, Luke 11:2; (f) the consecration of the Son by the Father, John 10:36; (g) the Lord Jesus devoting Himself to the redemption of His people, John 17:19; (h) the setting apart of the believer for God, Acts 20:32; cf. Rom. 15:16; (i) the effect on the believer of the Death of Christ, Heb. 10:10, said of God, and 2:11; 13:12, said of the Lord Jesus; (j) the separation of the believer from the world in his behavior – by the Father through the Word, John 17:17, 19; (k) the believer who turns away from such things as dishonor God and His gospel, 2 Tim. 2:21; (l) the acknowledgment of the Lordship of Christ, **1 Pet. 3:15.**

"Since every believer is sanctified in Christ Jesus, 1 Cor. 1:2, cf. Heb. 10:10, a common NT designation of all believers is 'saints,' *hagioi*, i.e., 'sanctified' or 'holy ones.' Thus sainthood, or sanctification, is not an attainment, it is the state into which God, in grace, calls sinful men, and in which they begin their course as Christians, Col. 3:12; Heb. 3:1."

Ready *see 1 Peter 1:5.*

Always *aei* (104), has two meanings: (a) "perpetually, incessantly," Acts 7:51; 2 Cor. 4:11; 6:10; Titus 1:12; Heb. 3:10; (b) "invariably, at any and every time," of successive occurrences, when some thing is to be repeated, according to the circumstances, **1 Pet. 3:15**; 2 Pet. 1:12.

Answer *apologia* (627), a "verbal defense, a speech in defense," is sometimes translated "answer," in the KJV, Acts 25:16; 1 Cor. 9:3; 2 Tim. 4:16, all which the RV corrects to "defense." See Acts 22:1; Phil. 1:7, 16; 2 Cor. 7:11, "clearing." Once it signifies an "answer," **1 Pet. 3:15.**

Reason *logos* (3056), "a word," etc., has also the significance of "the inward thought itself, a reckoning, a regard, a reason," translated "reason" in Acts 18:14, in the phrase "reason would," *kata logon*, lit., "according to reason (I would bear with you)"; in **1 Pet. 3:15**, "a reason (concerning the hope that is in you)."

Meekness *prautes*, or *praotes*, an earlier form, (4240), denotes "meekness." In its use in Scripture, in which it has a fuller, deeper significance than in nonscriptural Greek writings, it consists not in a person's "outward behavior only; nor yet in his relations to his fellow-men; as little in his mere natural disposition. Rather it is an inwrought grace of the soul; and the exercises of it are first and chiefly towards God. It is that temper of spirit in which we accept His dealings with us as good, and therefore without disputing or resisting; it is closely linked with the word *tapeinophrosune* [humility], and follows directly upon it, Eph. 4:2; Col. 3:12; cf. the adjectives in the Sept. of Zeph. 3:12, "meek and lowly"; ... it is only the humble heart which is also the meek, and which, as such, does not fight against God and more or less struggle and contend with Him. This meekness, however, being first of all a meekness before God, is also such in the face of men, even of evil men, out of a sense that these, with the insults and injuries which they may inflict, are permitted and employed by Him for the chastening and purifying of His elect" (Trench, *Syn.* Sec.xlii). In Gal. 5:23 it is associated with *enkrateia*, "self-control."

The meaning of *prautes* "is not readily expressed in English, for the terms meekness, mildness, commonly used, suggest weakness and pusillanimity to a greater or less extent, whereas *prautes* does nothing of the kind. Nevertheless, it is difficult to find a rendering less open to objection than 'meekness'; 'gentleness' has been suggested, but as *prautes* describes a condition of mind and heart, and as 'gentleness' is appropriate rather to actions, this word is no better than that used in both English Versions. It must be clearly understood, therefore, that the meekness manifested by the Lord and commended to the believer is the fruit of power. The common assumption is that when a man is meek it is because he cannot help himself; but the Lord was 'meek' because he had the infinite resources of God at His command. Described negatively, meekness is the opposite to self-assertiveness and self-interest; it is equanimity of spirit that is neither elated nor cast down, simply because it is not occupied with self at all.

"In 2 Cor. 10:1 the apostle appeals to the 'meekness ... of Christ.' Christians are charged to show 'all meekness toward all men,' Titus 3:2, for meekness becomes 'God's elect,' Col. 3:12. To this virtue the 'man of God' is urged; he is to 'follow after meekness' for his own sake, 1 Tim. 6:11, and in his service, and more especially in his dealings with the 'ignorant and erring,' he is to exhibit 'a spirit of meekness,' 1 Cor. 4:21, and Gal. 6:1; even 'they that oppose themselves' are to be corrected in meekness, 2 Tim. 2:25. James exhorts his 'beloved brethren' to 'receive with meekness the implanted word,' 1:21. Peter enjoins 'meekness' in setting forth the grounds of the Christian hope, **3:15**."

Fear *see 1 Peter 1:17.*

3:16 Having a good conscience; that, whereas they speak evil of you, as of evildoers, they may be ashamed that falsely accuse your good conversation in Christ.

Conscience *see 1 Peter 2:19.*

Evildoers *see 1 Peter 2:12.*

Ashamed *see* **Confounded** at **1** *Peter 2:6.*

Accuse *epereazo* (1908), besides its more ordinary meaning, "to insult, treat abusively, despitefully," Luke 6:28, has the forensic significance "to accuse falsely," and is used with this meaning in **1 Pet. 3:16**, RV, "revile."

Conversation *see 1 Peter 1:15.*

3:17 For *it is* better, if the will of God be so, that ye suffer for well doing, than for evil doing.

So In **1 Pet. 3:17**, *thelo*, "to will," is translated "should so will," lit., "willeth."

Suffer *see* **Suffering** at *1 Peter 2:19.*

Well doing *see 1 Peter 2:15. See also* **Well** at *1 Peter 2:14.*

Evil *kakopoieo* (2554), signifies "to do evil," Mark 3:4 (RV, "to do harm"); so, Luke 6:9; in 3 John 11, "doeth evil"; in **1 Pet. 3:17**, "evil doing."

3:18 For Christ also hath once suffered for sins, the just for the unjust, that he might bring us to God, being put to death in the flesh, but quickened by the Spirit:

Once *hapax* (530), denotes (a) "once, one time," 2 Cor. 11:25; Heb. 9:7, 26-27; 12:26-27; in the phrase "once and again," lit., "once and twice," Phil. 4:16; 1 Thess. 2:18; (b) "once for all," of what is of perpetual validity, not requiring repetition, Heb. 6:4; 9:28; 10:2; **1 Pet. 3:18**; Jude 3, RV, "once for all" (KJV, "once"); v. 5 (ditto); in some mss. **1 Pet. 3:20** (so the KJV)

Suffered *see* **Suffering** at *1 Peter 2:19.*

Just *dikaios* (1342), was first used of persons observant of *dike*, "custom, rule, right," especially in the fulfillment of duties towards gods and men, and of things that were in accordance with right. The Eng. word "righteous" was formerly spelt "rightwise," i.e., (in a) straight way. In the NT it denotes "righteous," a state of being right, or right conduct, judged whether by the divine standard, or according to human standards, of what is right. Said of God, it designates the perfect agreement between His nature and His acts (in which He is the standard for all men). It is used (1) in the broad sense, of persons: (a) of God, e.g., John 17:25; Rom. 3:26; 1 John 1:9; 2:29; 3:7; (b) of Christ, e.g., Acts 3:14; 7:52; 22:14; 2 Tim. 4:8; **1 Pet. 3:18**; 1 John 2:1; (c) of men, Matt. 1:19; Luke 1:6; Rom. 1:17; 2:13; 5:7. (2) of things; blood (metaphorical), Matt. 23:35; Christ's judgment, John 5:30; any circumstance, fact or deed, Matt. 20:4 (v. 7, in some mss.); Luke 12:57; Acts 4:19; Eph. 6:1; Phil. 1:7; 4:8; Col. 4:1; 2 Thess. 1:6; "the commandment" (the Law), Rom. 7:12; works, 1 John 3:12, the ways of God, Rev. 15:3.

Unjust *adikos* (94), not conforming to *dike*, "right," is translated "unrighteous" in Luke 16:10 (twice), RV, 11; Rom. 3:5; 1 Cor. 6:1, RV; 6:9; Heb. 6:10; **1 Pet. 3:18**, RV; 2 Pet. 2:9, RV.

Bring *prosago* (4317), is used (a) transitively, "to bring," Acts 16:20; **1 Pet. 3:18**; (b) intransitively, "to draw near," in the latter sense in Acts 27:27.

Death *thanatoo* (2289), "to put to death," in Matt. 10:21; Mark 13:12; Luke 21:16, is translated "shall ... cause (them) to be put to death," lit., "shall put (them) to death" (RV marg.). It is used of the death of Christ in Matt. 26:59; 27:1; Mark 14:55 and **1 Pet. 3:18**. In Rom. 7:4 (passive voice) it is translated "ye ... were made dead," RV (for KJV, "are become"), with reference to the change from bondage to the Law to union with Christ; in 8:13, "mortify" (marg., "make to die"), of the act of the believer in regard to the deeds of the body; in 8:36, "are killed"; so in 2 Cor. 6:9.

Quickened *zoopoieo* (2227), "to make alive, cause to live, quicken" (from *zoe*, "life," and *poieo*, "to make"), is used as follows: "(a) of God as the bestower of every kind of life in the universe, 1 Tim. 6:13 (*zoogoneo*, to preserve alive, is the alternative reading adopted by most editors), and, particularly, of resurrection life, John 5:21; Rom. 4:17; (b) of Christ, who also is the bestower of resurrection life, John 5:21 (2nd part); 1 Cor. 15:45; cf. v. 22; (c) of the resurrection of Christ in "the body of His glory," **1 Pet. 3:18**; (d) of the power of reproduction inherent in seed, which presents a certain analogy with resurrection, 1 Cor. 15:36; (e) of the 'changing,' or 'fashioning anew,' of the bodies of the living, which corresponds with, and takes place at the same time as, the resurrection of the dead in Christ, Rom. 8:11; (f) of the impartation of spiritual life, and the communication of spiritual sustenance generally, John 6:63; 2 Cor. 3:6; Gal. 3:21."

Spirit *see 1 Peter 3:4.*

3:19 By which also he went and preached unto the spirits in prison;

Preached *kerusso* (2784), signities (a) "to be a herald," or, in general, "to proclaim," e.g., Matt. 3:1; Mark 1:45, "publish"; in Luke 4:18, RV, "to proclaim," KJV, "to preach"; so verse 19; Luke 12:3; Acts 10:37; Rom. 2:21; Rev. 5:2. In **1 Pet. 3:19** the probable reference is, not to glad tidings (which there is no real evidence that Noah preached, nor is there evidence that the spirits of antediluvian people are actually "in prison"), but to the act of Christ after His resurrection in proclaiming His victory to fallen angelic spirits; (b) "to preach the gospel as a herald," e.g., Matt. 24:14; Mark 13:10, RV, "be preached" (KJV, "be published"); 14:9; 16:15, 20; Luke 8:1; 9:2; 24:47; Acts 8:5; 19:13; 28:31; Rom. 10:14, present participle, lit., "(one) preaching," "a preacher"; 10:15 (1st part); 1 Cor. 1:23; 15:11, 12; 2 Cor. 1:19; 4:5; 11:4; Gal. 2:2; Phil. 1:15; Col. 1:23; 1 Thess. 2:9; 1 Tim. 3:16; (c) "to preach the word," 2 Tim. 4:2 (of the ministry of the Scriptures, with special reference to the gospel).

Spirits *see* **Spirit** at *1 Peter 3:4.*

3:20 Which sometime were disobedient, when once the longsuffering of God waited in the days of Noah, while the ark was a preparing, wherein few, that is, eight souls were saved by water.

Sometime *see* **Old time** at *1 Peter 3:5.*

Disobedient *see 1 Peter 2:7.*

Once *see 1 Peter 3:18.*

Longsuffering *makrothumia* (3115), "forbearance, patience, longsuffering" (*makros*, "long," *thumos*, "temper"), is usually rendered "longsuffering," Rom. 2:4; 9:22; 2 Cor. 6:6; Gal. 5:22; Eph. 4:2; Col. 1:11; 3:12; 1 Tim. 1:16; 2 Tim. 3:10; 4:2; **1 Pet. 3:20**; 2 Pet. 3:15; "patience" in Heb. 6:12 and Jas. 5:10.

Waited *opekdechomai* (553), "to await or expect eagerly," is rendered "to wait for" in Rom. 8:19, 23, 25; 1 Cor. 1:7; Gal. 5:5; Phil. 3:20, RV (KJV, "look for"); Heb. 9:28, RV (KJV, "look for"), here "them that wait" represents believers in general, not a section of them; **1 Pet. 3:20** (in the best texts).

Ark *kibotos* (2787), "a wooden box, a chest," is used of (a) Noah's vessel, Matt. 24:38; Luke 17:27; Heb. 11:7; **1 Pet. 3:20**; (b) the "ark" of the covenant in the tabernacle, Heb. 9:4; (c) the "ark" seen in vision in the heavenly temple, Rev. 11:19.

Preparing *kataskeuazo* (2680), "to prepare, make ready" (*kata*, used intensively, *skeue*, "equipment"), is so translated in Matt. 11:10; Mark 1:2; Luke 1:17; 7:27; Heb. 9:2, RV (KJV, "made"); 9:6, RV (KJV, "were ... ordained"); 11:7; **1 Pet. 3:20**.

Eight *okto* (3638), "eight" (Lat., *octo, octavus;* cf. Eng., "octagon," "octave," "octavo," "October," etc.), is used in Luke 2:21; 9:28; John 20:26; Acts 9:33; 25:6; **1 Pet. 3:20**; in composition with other numerals, *okto kai deka*, lit., "eight and ten, eighteen," Luke 13:4, 11, 16; *triakonta kai okto*, "thirty and eight," John 5:5.

Souls *see 1 Peter 1:9.*

Saved *diasozo* (1295), "to bring safely through," is used (a) of the healing of the sick by the Lord, Matt. 14:36, RV, "were made whole" (KJV adds "perfectly"); Luke 7:3; (b) of bringing "safe" to a destination, Acts 23:24; (c) of keeping a person "safe," 27:43; (d) of escaping through the perils of shipwreck, 27:44; 28:1, 4, passive voice; (e) through the Flood, **1 Pet. 3:20**. *Note:* In 2 Pet. 2:5, KJV, *phulasso*, "to guard, keep, preserve," is translated "saved" (RV, "preserved"). In Luke 17:33 some mss. have *sozo* (KJV, "save"), for the RV. For "save alive," Luke 17:33, RV.

3:21 The like figure whereunto *even* baptism doth also now save us (not the putting away of the filth of the flesh, but the answer of a good conscience toward God,) by the resurrection of Jesus Christ:

Figure *antitupos* (499), an adjective, used as a noun, denotes, lit., "a striking back"; metaphorically, "resisting, adverse"; then, in a passive sense, "struck back"; in the NT metaphorically, "corresponding to," (a) a copy of an archetype (*anti*, "corresponding to," and *tupos*, "a type, figure, pattern"), i.e., the event or person or circumstance corresponding to the type, Heb. 9:24, RV, "like in pattern" (KJV, "the figure of"), of the tabernacle, which, with its structure and appurtenances, was a pattern of that "holy place," "Heaven itself," "the true," into which Christ entered, "to appear before the face of God for us." The earthly tabernacle anticipatively represented what is now made good in Christ; it was a "figure" or "parable" (9:9), "for the time now present," RV, i.e., pointing to the present time, not "then present," KJV; (b) "a corresponding type," **1 Pet. 3:21**, said of baptism; the circumstances of the flood, the ark and its occupants, formed a type, and baptism forms "a corresponding type" (not an antitype), each setting forth the spiritual realities of the death, burial, and resurrection of believers in their identification with Christ. It is not a case of type and antitype, but of two types, that in Genesis, the type, and baptism, the corresponding type.

Baptism *baptizo* (907), "to baptize," primarily a frequentative form of *bapto*, "to dip," was used among the Greeks to signify the dyeing of a garment, or the drawing of water by dipping a vessel into another, etc. Plutarchus uses it of the drawing of wine by dipping the cup into the bowl (*Alexis*, 67) and Plato, metaphorically, of being overwhelmed with questions (*Euthydemus*, 277 D). It is used in the NT in Luke 11:38 of washing oneself (as in 2 Kings 5:14, "dipped himself," Sept.); see also Isa. 21:4, lit., "lawlessness overwhelms me." In the early chapters of the four Gospels and in Acts 1:5; 11:16; 19:4, it is used of the rite performed by John the Baptist who called upon the people to repent that they might receive remission of sins. Those who obeyed came "confessing their sins," thus acknowledging their unfitness to be in the Messiah's coming kingdom. Distinct from this is the "baptism" enjoined by Christ, Matt. 28:19, a "baptism" to be undergone by believers, thus witnessing to their identification with Him in death, burial and resurrection, e.g., Acts 19:5; Rom. 6:3-4; 1 Cor. 1:13-17; 12:13; Gal. 3:27; Col. 2:12. The phrase in Matt. 28:19, "baptizing them into the Name" (RV; cf. Acts 8:16, RV), would indicate that the "baptized" person was closely bound to, or became the property of, the one into whose name he was "baptized." In Acts 22:16 it is used in the middle voice, in the command given to Saul of Tarsus, "arise and be baptized," the significance of the middle voice form being "get thyself baptized." The experience of those who were in the ark at the time of the Flood was a figure or type of the facts of spiritual death, burial, and resurrection, Christian "baptism" being an *antitupon*, "a corresponding type," a "like figure," **1 Pet. 3:21**. Likewise the nation of Israel was figuratively baptized when made to pass through the Red Sea under the cloud, 1 Cor. 10:2. The verb is used metaphorically also in two distinct senses: firstly, of "baptism" by the Holy Spirit, which took place on the Day of Pentecost; secondly, of the calamity which would come upon the nation of the Jews, a "baptism" of the fire of divine judgment for rejection of the will and word of God, Matt. 3:11; Luke 3:16.

Save *sozo* (4982), "to save," is used (as with the noun *soteria*, "salvation") (a) of material and temporal deliverance from danger, suffering, etc., e.g., Matt. 8:25; Mark 13:20; Luke 23:35; John 12:27; 1 Tim. 2:15; 2 Tim. 4:18 (KJV, "preserve"); Jude 5; from sickness, Matt. 9:22, "made ... whole" (RV, marg., "saved"); so Mark 5:34; Luke 8:48; Jas. 5:15; (b) of the spiritual and eternal salvation granted immediately by God to those who believe on the Lord Jesus Christ, e.g., Acts 2:47, RV "(those that) were being saved"; 16:31; Rom. 8:24, RV, "were we saved"; Eph. 2:5, 8; 1 Tim. 2:4; 2 Tim. 1:9; Titus 3:5; of human agency in this, Rom. 11:14; 1 Cor. 7:16; 9:22; (c) of the present experiences of God's power to deliver from the bondage of sin, e.g., Matt. 1:21; Rom. 5:10; 1 Cor. 15:2; Heb. 7:25; Jas. 1:21; **1 Pet. 3:21**; of human agency in this, 1 Tim. 4:16; (d) of the future deliverance of believers at the second coming of Christ for His saints, being deliverance from the wrath of God to be executed upon the ungodly at the close of this age and from eternal doom, e.g., Rom. 5:9; (e) of the deliverance of the nation of Israel at the second advent of Christ, e.g., Rom. 11:26; (f) inclusively for all the blessings bestowed by God on men in Christ, e.g., Luke 19:10; John 10:9; 1 Cor. 10:33; 1 Tim. 1:15; (g) of those who endure to the end of the time of the Great Tribulation, Matt. 10:22; Mark 13:13; (h) of the individual believer, who, though losing his reward at the judgment seat of Christ hereafter, will not lose his salvation, 1 Cor. 3:15; 5:5; (i) of the deliverance of the nations at the Millennium, Rev. 21:24 (in some mss.).

Putting *apothesis* (595), "a putting off or away," is used metaphorically in **1 Pet. 3:21**, of the "putting" away of the filth of the flesh; in 2 Pet. 1:14, RV, of "the putting off" of the body (as a tabernacle) at death (KJV, "I must put off").

Filth *rhupos* (4509), denotes "dirt, filth," **1 Pet. 3:21**. Cf. *rhuparia*, "filthiness"); *rhuparos*, "vile," Jas. 2:2; Rev. 22:11, in the best mss.; *rhupoo*, "to make filthy," Rev. 22:11; *rhupaino*.

Answer *eperotema* (1906), primarily a question or inquiry, denotes "a demand or appeal"; it is found in **1 Pet. 3:21**, RV, "interrogation" (KJV, "answer"). Some take the word to indicate that baptism affords a good conscience, an appeal against the accuser.

Resurrection *see* *1 Peter 1:3*.

3:22 Who is gone into heaven, and is on the right hand of God; angels and authorities and powers being made subject unto him.

Heaven *see* *1 Peter 1:12*.

Authorities *exousia* (1849), denotes "authority" (from the impersonal verb *exesti*, "it is lawful"). From the meaning of "leave or permission," or liberty of doing as one pleases, it passed to that of "the ability or strength with which one is endued," then to that of the "power of authority," the right to exercise power, e.g., Matt. 9:6; 21:23; 2 Cor. 10:8; or "the power of rule or government," the power of one whose will and commands must be obeyed by others, e.g., Matt. 28:18; John 17:2; Jude 25; Rev. 12:10; 17:13; more specifically of apostolic "authority," 2 Cor. 10:8; 13:10; the "power" of judicial decision, John 19:10; of "managing domestic affairs," Mark 13:34. By metonymy, or name-change (the substitution of a suggestive word for the name of the thing meant), it stands for "that which is subject to authority or rule," Luke 4:6 (RV, "authority," for the KJV "power"); or, as with the English "authority," "one who possesses authority, a ruler, magistrate," Rom. 13:1-3; Luke 12:11; Titus 3:1; or "a spiritual potentate," e.g., Eph. 3:10; 6:12; Col. 1:16; 2:10, 15; **1 Pet. 3:22**. The RV usually translates it "authority." In 1 Cor. 11:10 it is used of the veil with which a woman is required to cover herself in an assembly or church, as a sign of the Lord's "authority" over the church.

Powers *dunamis* (1411), is sometimes used, by metonymy, of persons and things, e.g., (a) of God, Matt. 26:64; Mark 14:62; (b) of angels, e.g., perhaps in Eph. 1:21, RV, "power," KJV, "might" (cf. Rom. 8:38; **1 Pet. 3:22**); (c) of that which manifests God's "power": Christ, 1 Cor. 1:24; the gospel, Rom. 1:16; (d) of mighty works (RV, marg., "power" or "powers"), e.g., Mark 6:5, "mighty work"; so 9:39, RV (KJV, "miracle"); Acts 2:22 (ditto); 8:13, "miracles"; 2 Cor. 12:12, RV, "mighty works" (KJV, "mighty deeds").

Subject *see* **Submit** at *1 Peter 2:13*.

Chapter 4

4:1 Forasmuch then as Christ hath suffered for us in the flesh, arm yourselves likewise with the same mind: for he that hath suffered in the flesh hath ceased from sin;

Suffered *see* **Suffering** at *1 Peter 2:19*.

Arm *hoplizo* (3695), "to arm oneself," is used in **1 Pet. 4:1**, in an exhortation "to arm" ourselves with the same mind as that of Christ in regard to His sufferings.

Likewise *kai* (2532), "and, even," is translated "likewise" in the KJV and RV of Matt. 20:10 (last *kai* in the verse), more lit., "even they"; elsewhere the RV has "also," for the KJV, "likewise," Matt. 18:35; 24:33; Luke 3:14; 17:10; 19:19; 21:31; Acts 3:24; 1 Cor. 14:9; Col. 4:16; **1 Pet. 4:1**; in Matt. 21:24, the KJV has "in like wise" (RV, "likewise").

Mind *ennoia* (1771), primarily "a thinking, idea, consideration," denotes "purpose, intention, design" (*en*, in, *nous*, mind); it is rendered "intents" in Heb. 4:12; "mind," in **1 Pet. 4:1** (RV, marg., "thought"). Cf. *enthumesis*, "thought".

Ceased *see* **Refrain** at *1 Peter 3:10*.

Sin *hamartia* (266), is, lit., "a missing of the mark," but this etymological meaning is largely lost sight of in the NT. It is the most comprehensive term for moral obliquity. It is used of "sin" as (a) a principle or source of action, or an inward element producing acts, e.g., Rom. 3:9; 5:12, 13, 20; 6:1, 2; 7:7 (abstract for concrete); 7:8 (twice), 9, 11, 13, "sin, that it might be shown to be sin," i.e., "sin became death to me, that it might be exposed in its heinous character": in the last clause, "sin might become exceeding sinful," i.e., through the holiness of the Law, the true nature of sin was designed to be manifested to the conscience;

(b) a governing principle or power, e.g., Rom. 6:6 ...

(c) a generic term (distinct from specific terms yet sometimes inclusive of concrete wrong doing, e.g., John 8:21, 34, 46; 9:41; 15:22, 24; 19:11); in Rom. 8:3, "God, sending His own Son in the likeness of sinful flesh," lit., "flesh of sin," the flesh stands for the body, the instrument of indwelling "sin" [Christ, preexistently the Son of God, assumed human flesh, "of the substance of the Virgin Mary"; the reality of incarnation was His, without taint of sin], and *as an offering* for sin," i.e., "a sin offering" (so the Sept., e.g., in Lev. 4:32; 5:6, 7, 8, 9), "condemned sin in the flesh," i.e., Christ, having taken human nature, "sin" apart (Heb. 4:15), and having lived a sinless life, died under the condemnation and judgment due to our "sin"; for the generic sense see further, e.g., Heb. 9:26; 10:6, 8, 18; 13:11; 1 John 1:7, 8; 3:4 (1st part; in the 2nd part, "sin" is defined as "lawlessness," RV), 8, 9; in these verses the KJV use of the verb to commit is misleading; not the committal of an act is in view, but a continuous course of "sin," as indicated by the RV, "doeth." The apostle's use of the present tense of *poieo*, "to do," virtually expresses the meaning of *prasso*, "to practice," which John does not use (it is not infrequent in this sense in Paul's Epp., e.g., Rom. 1:32, RV; 2:1; Gal. 5:21; Phil. 4:9); **1 Pet. 4:1** (singular in the best texts), lit., "has been made to cease from sin," i.e., as a result of suffering in the flesh, the mortifying of our members, and of obedience to a Savior who suffered in flesh. Such no longer lives in the flesh, "to the lusts of men, but to the will of God"; sometimes the word is used as virtually equivalent to a condition of "sin," e.g., John 1:29, "the sin (not sins) of the world"; 1 Cor. 15:17; or a course of "sin," characterized by continuous acts, e.g., 1 Thess. 2:16; in 1 John 5:16 (2nd part) the RV marg., is probably to be preferred, "there is sin unto death," not a special act of "sin," but the state or condition producing acts; in v. 17, "all unrighteousness is sin" is not a definition of "sin" (as in 3:4), it gives a specification of the term in its generic sense.

4:2 That he no longer should live the rest of *his* time in the flesh to the lusts of men, but to the will of God.

No longer *meketi* (3371), generally expressing a prohibition, e.g., Matt. 21:19; John 5:14; Rom. 14:13; Eph. 4:28; 1 Tim. 5:23; **1 Pet. 4:2**; indicating some condition expressed or implied e.g., 1 Thess. 3:5; or nonexistence, when the existence might have been possible under certain conditions, e.g., Mark 1:45; 2:2, RV, "no longer" (KJV, "no").

Live *bioo* (980), "to spend life, to pass one's life," is used in **1 Pet. 4:2**.

Rest *epiloipos* (1954), signifying "still left, left over," is used in the neuter with the article in **1 Pet. 4:2**, "the rest (of your time)."

Lusts *see 1 Peter 1:14.*

4:3 For the time past of *our* life may suffice us to have wrought the will of the Gentiles, when we walked in lasciviousness, lusts, excess of wine, revellings, banquetings, and abominable idolatries:

Past *parerchomai* (3928), from *para*, "by," *erchomai*, "to come" or "go," denotes (I) literally, "to pass, pass by," (a) of persons, Matt. 8:28; Mark 6:48; Luke 18:37; Acts 16:8; (b) of things, Matt. 26:39, 42; of time, Matt. 14:15; Mark 14:35; Acts 27:9, KJV, "past" (RV, "gone by"); **1 Pet. 4:3**; (II) metaphorically, (a) "to pass away, to perish," Matt. 5:18; 24:34, 35; Mark 13:30, 31; Luke 16:17; 21:32, 33; 2 Cor. 5:17; Jas. 1:10; 2 Pet. 3:10; (b) "to pass by, disregard, neglect, pass over," Luke 11:42; 15:29, "transgressed." For the meaning "to come forth or come," see Luke 12:37; 17:7, RV (Acts 24:7 in some mss.).

Life *bios* (979), (cf. Eng. words beginning with *bio*), is used in three respects (a) of "the period or duration of life," e.g., in the KJV of **1 Pet. 4:3**, "the time past of our life" (the RV follows the mss. which omit "of our life"); Luke 8:14; 2 Tim. 2:4; (b) of "the manner of life, life in regard to its moral conduct," 1 Tim. 2:2; 1 John 2:16; (c) of "the means of life, livelihood, maintenance, living," Mark 12:44; Luke 8:43; 15:12, 30; 21:4; 1 John 3:17, "goods," RV (KJV, "good").

Suffice *arketos* (713), "to be," is translated "may suffice" in **1 Pet. 4:3**.

Wrought *katergazomai* (2716), an emphatic form, signifies "to work out, achieve, effect by toil," rendered "to work" (past tense, "wrought") in Rom. 1:27; 2:9, RV; 4:15 (the Law brings men under condemnation and so renders them subject to divine wrath); 5:3; 7:8, 13; 15:18; 2 Cor. 4:17; 5:5; 7:10, 11; 12:12; Phil. 2:12, where "your own salvation" refers especially to freedom from strife and vainglory; Jas. 1:3, 20; **1 Pet. 4:3**.

Will *boulema* (1013), "a deliberate design, that which is purposed," Rom. 9:19; **1 Pet. 4:3** (in the best texts). *thelema* (2307), signifies (a) objectively, "that which is willed, of the will of God," e.g., Matt. 18:14; Mark 3:35, the fulfilling being a sign of spiritual relationship to the Lord, John 4:34; 5:30; 6:39, 40; Acts 13:22, plural, "my desires"; Rom. 2:18; 12:2, lit., "the will of God, the good and perfect and acceptable"; here the repeated article is probably resumptive, the adjectives describing the will, as in the Eng. versions; Gal. 1:4; Eph. 1:9; 5:17, "of the Lord"; Col. 1:9; 4:12; 1 Thess. 4:3; 5:18, where it means "the gracious design," rather than "the determined resolve"; 2 Tim. 2:26, which should read "which have been taken captive by him" [(*autou*), i.e., by the Devil; the RV, "by the Lord's servant" is an interpretation; it does not correspond to the Greek] unto His (*ekeinou*) will" (i.e., "God's will"; the different pronoun refers back to the subject of the sentence, viz., God); Heb. 10:10; Rev. 4:11, RV, "because of Thy will"; of human will, e.g., 1 Cor. 7:37; (b) subjectively, the "will" being spoken of as the emotion of being desirous, rather than as the thing "willed"; of the "will" of God, e.g., Rom. 1:10; 1 Cor. 1:1; 2 Cor. 1:1; 8:5; Eph. 1:1, 5, 11; Col. 1:1; 2 Tim. 1:1; Heb. 10:7, 9, 36; 1 John 2:17; 5:14; of human "will," e.g., John 1:13; Eph. 2:3, "the desires of the flesh"; **1 Pet. 4:3** (in some texts); 2 Pet. 1:21.

Walked *poreuo* (4198), is used in the middle voice and rendered "to walk" in Luke 1:6, of the general activities of life; so in Luke 13:33, KJV, "walk" (RV, "go on My way"); Acts 9:31; 14:16; **1 Pet. 4:3**; 2 Pet. 2:10; Jude 16, 18.

Lasciviousness *aselgeia* (766), denotes "excess, licentiousness, absence of restraint, indecency, wantonness"; "lasciviousness" in Mark 7:22, one of the evils that proceed from the heart; in 2 Cor. 12:21, one of the evils of which some in the church at Corinth had been guilty; in Gal. 5:19, classed among the works of the flesh; in Eph. 4:19, among the sins of the unregenerate who are "past feeling"; so in **1 Pet. 4:3**; in Jude 4, of that into which the grace of God had been turned by ungodly men; it is translated "wantonness" in Rom. 13:13, one of the sins against which believers are warned; in 2 Pet. 2:2, according to the best mss., "lascivious (doings)," RV (the KJV "pernicious ways" follows those texts which have *apoleiais*); in v. 7, RV, "lascivious (life)," KJV, "filthy (conversation)," of the people of Sodom and Gomorrah; in 2:18, RV, "lasciviousness" (KJV, "wantonness"), practiced by the same persons as mentioned in Jude. The prominent idea is shameless conduct. Some have derived the word from *a*, negative, and *selge*, "a city in Pisidia." Others, with similar improbability, trace it to *a*, negative, and *selgo*, or *thelgo*, "to charm."

Excess of wine In **1 Pet. 4:3**, *oinophlugia*, "drunkenness, debauchery" (*oinos*, "wine," *phluo*, "to bubble up, overflow"), is rendered "excess of wine," KJV (RV, "winebibbings").

Revellings *komos* (2970), "a revel, carousal," the concomitant and consequence of drunkenness, is used in the plural, Rom. 13:13, translated by the singular, RV, "reveling" (KJV, "rioting"); Gal. 5:21 and **1 Pet. 4:3**, "revelings."

Banquetings *potos* (4224), lit., "a drinking," signifies not simply a banquet but "a drinking bout, a carousal," **1 Pet. 4:3** (RV, "carousings," KJV, "banquetings"). Synonymous is *kraipale*, "surfeiting," Luke 21:34.

Abominable *athemitos* (111), a late form for *athemistos* (*themis*, "custom, right"; in classical Greek "divine law"), "contrary to what is right," is rendered "an unlawful thing" (neuter) in Acts 10:28; in **1 Pet. 4:3**, "abominable."

Idolatries *eidololatria* (or *-eia*) (1495), whence Eng., "idolatry," (from *eidolon*, and *latreia*, "service"), is found in 1 Cor. 10:14; Gal. 5:20; Col. 3:5; and, in the plural, in **1 Pet. 4:3**.

Heathen sacrifices were sacrificed to demons, 1 Cor. 10:19; there was a dire reality in the cup and table of demons and in the involved communion with demons. In Rom. 1:22-25, "idolatry," the sin of the mind against God (Eph. 2:3), and immorality, sins of the flesh, are associated, and are traced to lack of the acknowledgment of God and of gratitude to Him. An "idolater" is a slave to the depraved ideas his idols represent, Gal. 4:8, 9; and thereby, to divers lusts, Titus 3:3 (see *Notes on Thess.* by Hogg and Vine, p. 44).

4:4 Wherein they think it strange that ye run not with *them* to the same excess of riot, speaking evil of *you*:

Strange *xenizo* (3579), denotes "to think something strange," **1 Pet. 4:4, 12**, passive voice, i.e., "they are surprised," and "be (not) surprised"; in Acts 17:20, the present participle, active, is rendered "strange," i.e., "surprising."

Run *suntrecho* (4936), "to run together with" (*sun*, "with"), is used (a) literally, Mark 6:33; Acts 3:11; (b) metaphorically, **1 Pet. 4:4**, of "running" a course of evil with others. In the Sept., Ps. 50:18.

Excess *anachusis* (401), lit., "a pouring out, overflowing" (akin to *anacheo*, "to pour out"), is used metaphorically in **1 Pet. 4:4**, "excess," said of the riotous conduct described in v. **3**.

Riot *asotia* (810), "prodigality, a wastefulness, profligacy" (*a*, negative, *sozo*, "to save"), is rendered "riot" in Eph. 5:18, RV (KJV, "excess"); Titus 1:6 and **1 Pet. 4:4** (KJV and RV, "riot"). The corresponding verb is found in a papyrus writing, telling of "riotous living" (like the adverb *asotos*). In the Sept., Prov. 28:7. Cf. the synonymous word *aselgeia*.

Speaking evil *blasphemeo* (987), "to blaspheme, rail at or revile," is used (a) in a general way, of any contumelious speech, reviling, calumniating, railing at, etc., as of those who railed at Christ, e.g., Matt. 27:39; Mark 15:29; Luke 22:65 (RV, "reviling"); 23:39; (b) of those who speak contemptuously of God or of sacred things, e.g., Matt. 9:3; Mark 3:28; Rom. 2:24; 1 Tim. 1:20; 6:1; Rev. 13:6; 16:9, 11, 21; "hath spoken blasphemy," Matt. 26:65; "rail at," 2 Pet. 2:10; Jude 8, 10; "railing," 2 Pet. 2:12; "slanderously reported," Rom. 3:8; "be evil spoken of," Rom. 14:16; 1 Cor. 10:30; 2 Pet. 2:2; "speak evil of," Titus 3:2; **1 Pet. 4:4**; "being defamed," 1 Cor. 4:13. The verb (in the present participial form) is translated "blasphemers" in Acts 19:37; in Mark 2:7, "blasphemeth," RV, for KJV, "speaketh blasphemies." There is no noun in the original representing the English "blasphemer." This is expressed either by the verb, or by the adjective *blasphemos*.

4:5 Who shall give account to him that is ready to judge the quick and the dead.

Give *see* **Rendering** at *1 Peter 3:9*.

Account *logos* (3056), "a word or saying," also means "an account which one gives by word of mouth," Matt. 12:36; Matt. 18:23, RV, "reckoning"; 16:2; Acts 19:40; 20:24 (KJV, "count"); Rom. 14:12; Phil. 4:17; Heb. 13:17; **1 Pet. 4:5**.

Ready *hetoimos* (2093), "readily," is used with *echo*, "to have," lit., "to have readily," ie, "to be in readiness, to be ready," Acts 21:13; 2 Cor. 12:14; **1 Pet. 4:5**.

Quick *zao* is translated "quick" (i.e., "living") in Acts 10:42; 2 Tim. 4:1; **1 Pet. 4:5**; in Heb. 4:12, KJV (RV, "living"). *See also* **Lively** at *1 Peter 1:3*.

4:6 For for this cause was the gospel preached also to them that are dead, that they might be judged according to men in the flesh, but live according to God in the spirit.

For this cause The phrase *eis touto*, lit., "unto this," signifies "to this end," John 18:37, RV (twice; KJV, "for this cause," in the second clause); so Mark 1:38; Acts 26:16; Rom. 14:9; 2 Cor. 2:9; 1 Tim. 4:10 (KJV, "therefore"); **1 Pet. 4:6**; 1 John 3:8 (KJV, "for this purpose").

Gospel *see 1 Peter 1:25*.

Live *see* **Lively** at *1 Peter 1:3*.

Spirit *see 1 Peter 3:4*.

4:7 But the end of all things is at hand: be ye therefore sober, and watch unto prayer.

End *see 1 Peter 1:9*.

At hand *engus* (1451), "near, nigh," frequently rendered "at hand," is used (a) of place, e.g., of the Lord's sepulchre, John 19:42, "nigh at hand"; (b) of time, e.g., Matt. 26:18; Luke 21:30, 31, RV, "nigh," KJV, "nigh at hand"; in Phil. 4:5, "the Lord is at hand," it is possible to regard the meaning as that either of (a) or (b); the following reasons may point to (b): (1) the subject of the preceding context has been the return of Christ, 3:20, 21; (2) the phrase is a translation of the Aramaic "Maranatha," 1 Cor. 16:22, a Christian watchword, and the use of the title "the Lord" is appropriate; (3) the similar use of the adverb in Rev. 1:3 and 22:10; (4) the similar use of the corresponding verb in Rom. 13:12; Heb. 10:25, "drawing nigh," RV; Jas. 5:8; cf. **1 Pet. 4:7**.

Sober *sophroneo* (4993), signifies (a) "to be of sound mind," or "in one's right mind, sober-minded" (*sozo*, "to save," *phren*, "the mind"), Mark 5:15 and Luke 8:35, "in his right mind"; 2 Cor. 5:13, RV, "we are of sober mind" (KJV, "we be sober"); (b) "to be temperate, self-controlled," Titus 2:6, "to be sober-minded"; **1 Pet. 4:7**, RV, "be ye ... of sound mind" (KJV, "be ye sober"). See also Rom. 12:3. *See also 1 Peter 1:13*.

4:8 And above all things have fervent charity among yourselves: for charity shall cover the multitude of sins.

Fervent *ektenes* (1618), denotes "strained, stretched" (*ek*, "out," *teino*, "to stretch"); hence, metaphorically, "fervent," **1 Pet. 4:8**. Some mss. have it in Acts 12:5. Cf. *ekteneia* (with *en*), "intently, strenuously," in Acts 26:7, KJV, "instantly," RV, "earnestly."

Yourselves The reflexive pronoun "yourselves" represents the various plural forms of the reflexive pronoun *heautou* (frequently governed by some preposition), e.g., Matt. 3:9; 16:8; 23:31; 25:9; Mark 9:50; Luke 3:8; 12:33, 57; 16:9; 21:30, "of your own selves"; 21:34; Acts 5:35; in Rom. 11:25, "in your own (conceits)," lit., "in (*en;* some texts have *para*, 'among') yourselves"; so 12:16 (with *para*); **1 Pet. 4:8**; Jude 20, 21; in Eph. 5:19, RV, "one to another" (KJV, and RV marg., "to yourselves"). In 1 Thess. 5:11, KJV, *allelous*, "one another" (RV), is rendered "yourselves together."

Cover *kalupto* (2572), signifies "to cover," Matt. 8:24; 10:26; Luke 8:16; 23:30; Jas. 5:20 (RV); **1 Pet. 4:8**; to veil, in 2 Cor. 4:3 (RV; KJV, "hid").

Multitude *plethos* (4128), lit., "a fullness," hence, "a large company, a multitude," is used (a) of things: of fish, Luke 5:6; John 21:6; of sticks ("bundle"), Acts 28:3; of stars and of sand, Heb. 11:12; of sins, Jas. 5:20; **1 Pet. 4:8**; (b) of persons, (1) a "multitude": of people, e.g., Mark 3:7, 8; Luke 6:17; John 5:3; Acts 14:1; of angels, Luke 2:13; (2) with the article, the whole number, the "multitude," the populace, e.g., Luke 1:10; 8:37; Acts 5:16; 19:9; 23:7; a particular company, e.g., of disciples, Luke 19:37; Acts 4:32; 6:2, 5; 15:30; of elders, priests, and scribes, 23:7; of the apostles and the elders of the Church in Jerusalem, Acts 15:12.

4:9 Use hospitality one to another without grudging.

Hospitality *philoxenos* (5382), "loving strangers" (*xenia*, "hospitality"), translated "a lover of hospitality" in Titus 1:8, KJV (RV, "given to h."); elsewhere, in 1 Tim. 3:2; **1 Pet. 4:9**.

Without *see 1 Peter 3:1.*

Grudging *gongusmos* (1112), "a murmuring, muttering," is used (a) in the sense of secret debate among people, John 7:12 (as with the verb in v. 32); (b) of displeasure or complaining (more privately than in public), said of Grecian Jewish converts against Hebrews, Acts 6:1; in general admonitions, Phil. 2:14; **1 Pet. 4:9**, RV, "murmuring" (KJV "grudging").

4:10 As every man hath received the gift, *even so* minister the same one to another, as good stewards of the manifold grace of God.

Gift *charisma* (5486), "a gift of grace, a gift involving grace" (*charis*) on the part of God as the donor, is used (a) of His free bestowments upon sinners, Rom. 5:15, 16; 6:23; 11:29; (b) of His endowments upon believers by the operation of the Holy Spirit in the churches, Rom. 12:6; 1 Cor. 1:7; 12:4, 9, 28, 30, 31; 1 Tim. 4:14; 2 Tim. 1:6; **1 Pet. 4:10**; (c) of that which is imparted through human instruction, Rom. 1:11; (d) of the natural "gift" of continence, consequent upon the grace of God as Creator, 1 Cor. 7:7; (e) of gracious deliverances granted in answer to the prayers of fellow believers, 2 Cor. 1:11.

Minister *see 1 Peter 1:12.*

Stewards *oikonomos* (3623), primarily denoted "the manager of a household or estate" (*oikos*, "a house," *nemo*, "to arrange"), "a steward" (such were usually slaves or freedmen), Luke 12:42; 16:1, 3, 8; 1 Cor. 4:2; Gal. 4:2, RV (KJV, "governors"); in Rom. 16:23, the "treasurer" (RV) of a city; it is used metaphorically, in the wider sense, of a "steward" in general, (a) of preachers of the gospel and teachers of the Word of God, 1 Cor. 4:1; (b) of elders or bishops in churches, Titus 1:7; (c) of believers generally, **1 Pet. 4:10**.

Manifold *see 1 Peter 1:6.*

4:11 If any man speak, *let him speak* as the oracles of God; if any man minister, *let him do it* as of the ability which God giveth: that God in all things may be glorified through Jesus Christ, to whom be praise and dominion for ever and ever. Amen.

Oracles *logion* (3051), a diminutive of *logos*, "a word, narrative, statement," denotes "a divine response or utterance, an oracle"; it is used of (a) the contents of the Mosaic Law, Acts 7:38; (b) all the written utterances of God through OT writers, Rom. 3:2; (c) the substance of Christian doctrine, Heb. 5:12; (d) the utterances of God through Christian teachers, **1 Pet. 4:11**.

Minister *see 1 Peter 1:12.*

Ability *ischus* (2479), connected with *ischo* and *echo*, "to have, to hold" (from the root *ech-*, signifying "holding"), denotes "ability, force, strength"; "ability" in **1 Pet. 4:11**, KJV (RV, "strength"). In Eph. 1:19 and 6:10, it is said of the strength of God bestowed upon believers, the phrase "the power of His might" indicating strength afforded by power. In 2 Thess. 1:9, "the glory of His might" signifies the visible expression of the inherent personal power of the Lord Jesus. It is said of angels in 2 Pet. 2:11 (cf., Rev. 18:2, KJV, "mightily"). It is ascribed to God in Rev. 5:12 and 7:12. In Mark 12:30, 33, and Luke 10:27 it describes the full extent of the power wherewith we are to love God.

Giveth *choregeo* (5524), primarily, among the Greeks, signified "to lead a stage chorus or dance" (*choros*, and *hegeomai*, "to lead"), then, "to defray the expenses of a chorus"; hence, later, metaphorically, "to supply," 2 Cor. 9:10 (2nd part), RV, "supply" (KJV "minister"); **1 Pet. 4:11**, RV, "supplieth" (KJV, "giveth").

Glorified *see* Glory at *1 Peter 1:8.*

Praise In the following the KJV translates *doxa*, "glory," by "praise" (RV, "glory"); John 9:24, where "give glory to God" signifies "confess thy sins" (cf. Josh. 7:19, indicating the genuine confession of facts in one's life which gives glory to God); 12:43 (twice); **1 Pet. 4:11**.

Dominion *kratos* (2904), "force, strength, might," more especially "manifested power," is derived from a root *kra-*, "to perfect, to complete": "creator" is probably connected. It also signifies "dominion," and is so rendered frequently in doxologies, **1 Pet. 4:11**; **5:11**; Jude 25; Rev. 1:6; 5:13 (RV); in 1 Tim. 6:16, and Heb. 2:14 it is translated "power."

4:12 Beloved, think it not strange concerning the fiery trial which is to try you, as though some strange thing happened unto you:

Think *see 1 Peter 4:4.*

Strange *xenos* (3581), denotes (a) "foreign, alien," Acts 17:18, of gods; Heb. 13:9, of doctrines; (b) "unusual," **1 Pet. 4:12**, 2nd part, of the fiery trial of persecution.

Fiery trial *purosis* (4451), akin to *puroo*, "to set on fire," signifies (a) "a burning"; (b) "a refining," metaphorically in **1 Pet. 4:12**, "fiery trial," or rather "trial by fire," referring to the refining of gold.

Try *peirasmos* (3986), (a) "a trying, testing," (b) "a temptation," is used in sense (a) in **1 Pet. 4:12**, with the preposition *pros*, "towards" or "with a view to," RV, "to prove" (KJV, "to try"), lit., "for a testing." *See also* **Temptations** at *1 Peter 1:6*.

Happened *sumbaino* (4819), lit., "to go or come together" (*sun*, "with," *baino*, "to go"), signifies "to happen together," of things or events, Mark 10:32; Luke 24:14; Acts 3:10; 1 Cor. 10:11; **1 Pet. 4:12**; 2 Pet. 2:22; "befell" in Acts 20:19; in Acts 21:35, "so it was."

4:13 But rejoice, inasmuch as ye are partakers of Christ's sufferings; that, when his glory shall be revealed, ye may be glad also with exceeding joy.

Rejoice, Be glad *chairo* (5463), "to rejoice," is most frequently so translated. As to this verb, the following are grounds and occasions for "rejoicing," on the part of believers: in the Lord, Phil. 3:1; 4:4; His incarnation, Luke 1:14; His power, Luke 13:17; His presence with the Father, John 14:28; His presence with them, John 16:22; 20:20; His ultimate triumph, 8:56; hearing the gospel, Acts 13:48; their salvation, Acts 8:39; receiving the Lord, Luke 19:6; their enrollment in Heaven, Luke 10:20; their liberty in Christ, Acts 15:31; their hope, Rom. 12:12 (cf. Rom. 5:2; Rev. 19:7); their prospect of reward, Matt. 5:12; the obedience and godly conduct of fellow believers, Rom. 16:19, RV, "I rejoice" (KJV, "I am glad"); 2 Cor. 7:7, 9; 13:9; Col. 2:5; 1 Thess. 3:9; 2 John 4; 3 John 3; the proclamation of Christ, Phil. 1:18; the gospel harvest, John 4:36; suffering with Christ, Acts 5:41; **1 Pet. 4:13**; suffering in the cause of the gospel, 2 Cor. 13:9 (1st part); Phil. 2:17 (1st part); Col. 1:24; in persecutions, trials and afflictions, Matt. 5:12; Luke 6:23; 2 Cor. 6:10; the manifestation of grace, Acts 11:23; meeting with fellow believers, 1 Cor. 16:17, RV, "I rejoice"; Phil. 2:28; receiving tokens of love and fellowship, Phil. 4:10; the "rejoicing" of others, Rom. 12:15; 2 Cor. 7:13; learning of the well-being of others, 2 Cor. 7:16. *See also* **Rejoice** at *1 Peter 1:6*.

Inasmuch as *katho* (2526), lit., "according to what" (*kata*, "according to," and *ho*, the neuter of the relative pronoun), is translated "inasmuch as" in **1 Pet. 4:13**, KJV (RV, "insomuch as"); in Rom. 8:26, "as (we ought)"; in 2 Cor. 8:12, RV, "according as" (KJV, "according to that").

Partakers *koinoneo* (2841), "to have a share of, to share with, take part in," is translated "to be partaker of" in 1 Tim. 5:22; Heb. 2:14 (1st part), KJV, "are partakers of," RV, "are sharers in"; **1 Pet. 4:13**; 2 John 11, RV, "partaketh in" (KJV, "is partaker of"); in the passive voice in Rom. 15:27.

Sufferings *see 1 Peter 1:11.*

Revealed *see* **Appearing** at *1 Peter 1:7*.

Joy *agalliao* (21), "to exult, rejoice greatly," is translated "with exceeding joy" in **1 Pet. 4:13** (middle voice), lit., "(ye rejoice, *chairo*) exulting."

4:14 If ye be reproached for the name of Christ, happy *are ye*; for the spirit of glory and of God resteth upon you: on their part he is evil spoken of, but on your part he is glorified.

Reproached *oneidizo* (3679), signifies (a), in the active voice, "to reproach, upbraid," Matt. 5:11, RV, "shall reproach" (KJV, "shall revile"); 11:20, "to upbraid"; 27:44, RV, "cast ... reproach" [KJV, "cast ... in (His) teeth"]; Mark 15:32 RV, "reproached" (KJV, "reviled"); 16:14 "upbraided"; Luke 6:22 "shall reproach", Rom. 15:3; Jas. 1:5, "upbraideth"; (b) in the passive voice, "to suffer reproach, be reproached," 1 Tim. 4:10 (in some mss. in the 2nd part); **1 Pet. 4:14**.

Name *onoma* (3686), is used (I) in general of the "name" by which a person or thing is called, e.g., Mark 3:16, 17 ... (II) for all that a "name" implies, of authority, character, rank, majesty, power, excellence, etc., of everything that the "name" covers: (a) of the "Name" of God as expressing His attributes, etc., e.g., Matt. 6:9; Luke 1:49; John 12:28; 17:6, 26; Rom. 15:9; 1 Tim. 6:1; Heb. 13:15; Rev. 13:6; (b) of the "Name" of Christ, e.g., Matt. 10:22; 19:29; John 1:12; 2:23; 3:18; Acts 26:9; Rom. 1:5; Jas. 2:7; 1 John 3:23; 3 John 7; Rev.

2:13; 3:8; also the phrases rendered "in the name"; these may be analyzed as follows: (1) representing the authority of Christ, e.g., Matt. 18:5 (with *epi*, "on the ground of My authority"); so Matt. 24:5 (falsely) and parallel passages; as substantiated by the Father, John 14:26; 16:23 (last clause), RV; (2) in the power of (with *en*, "in"), e.g., Mark 16:17; Luke 10:17; Acts 3:6; 4:10; 16:18; Jas. 5:14; (3) in acknowledgement or confession of, e.g., Acts 4:12; 8:16; 9:27, 28; (4) in recognition of the authority of (sometimes combined with the thought of relying or resting on), Matt. 18:20; cf. 28:19; Acts 8:16; 9:2 (*eis*, "into"); John 14:13; 15:16; Eph. 5:20; Col. 3:17; (5) owing to the fact that one is called by Christ's "Name" or is identified with Him, e.g. **1 Pet. 4:14** (with *en*, "in"); with *heneken*, "for the sake of," e.g., Matt. 19:29; with *dia*, "on account of," Matt. 10:22; 24:9; Mark 13:13; Luke 21:17; John 15:21; 1 John 2:12; Rev. 2:3;

Happy *see 1 Peter 3:14*.

Spirit *see 1 Peter 1:2*. *See also* **Also** at *1 Peter 3:1*.

Resteth *anapauo* (373), in the active voice, signifies "to give intermission from labor, to give rest, to refresh," Matt. 11:28; 1 Cor. 16:18, "have refreshed"; Philem. 20, "refresh"; passive voice, "to be rested, refreshed," 2 Cor. 7:13, "was refreshed"; Philem. 7, "are refreshed"; in the middle voice, "to take or enjoy rest," Matt. 26:45; Mark 6:31; 14:41; Luke 12:19, "take thine ease"; **1 Pet. 4:14**; Rev. 6:11; 14:13. In the papyri it is found as an agricultural term, e.g., of giving land "rest" by sowing light crops upon it. In inscriptions it is found on gravestones of Christians, followed by the date of death (Moulton and Milligan).

Part In **1 Pet. 4:14**, KJV, "on (their) part," "on (your) part," represents the preposition *kata*, "according to," followed by the personal pronouns; the statements are not found in the most authentic mss.

4:15 But let none of you suffer as a murderer, or *as* a thief, or *as* an evildoer, or as a busybody in other men's matters.

Suffer *see* **Suffering** at **1** *Peter 2:19*.

Murderer *phoneus* (5406), akin to *phoneuo* and *phonos*, is used (a) in a general sense, in the singular, **1 Pet. 4:15**; in the plural, Rev. 21:8; 22:15; (b) of those guilty of particular acts, Matt. 22:7; Acts 3:14, lit. "a man (*aner*), a murderer"; 7:52; 28:4.

Thief *kleptes* (2812), is used (a) literally, Matt. 6:19, 20; 24:43; Luke 12:33, 39; John 10:1, 10; 12:6; 1 Cor. 6:10; **1 Pet. 4:15**; (b) metaphorically of "false teachers," John 10:8; (c) figuratively, (1) of the personal coming of Christ, in a warning to a local church, with most of its members possessed of mere outward profession and defiled by the world, Rev. 3:3; in retributive intervention to overthrow the foes of God, 16:15; (2) of the Day of the Lord, in divine judgment upon the world, 2 Pet. 3:10 and 1 Thess. 5:2, 4; in v. 2, according to the order in the original "the word 'night' is not to be read with 'the day of the Lord,' but with 'thief,' i.e., there is no reference to the time of the coming, only to the manner of it. To avoid ambiguity the phrase may be paraphrased, 'so comes as a thief in the night comes.' The use of the present tense instead of the future emphasizes the certainty of the coming.... The unexpectedness of the coming of the thief, and the unpreparedness of those to whom he comes, are the essential elements in the figure; cf. the entirely different figure used in Matt. 25:1-13."

Evildoer *see* **Evildoers** at *1 Peter 2:12*.

Busybody *allotrioepiskopos* (244), from *allotrios*, "belonging to another person," and *episkopos*, "an overseer," translated "busybody" in the KJV of **1 Pet. 4:15**, "meddler," RV, was a legal term for a charge brought against Christians as being hostile to civilized society, their purpose being to make Gentiles conform to Christian standards. Some explain it as a pryer into others' affairs.

4:16 Yet if *any man suffer* as a Christian, let him not be ashamed; but let him glorify God on this behalf.

Christian *christianos* (5546), "Christian," a word formed after the Roman style, signifying an adherent of Jesus, was first applied to such by the Gentiles and is found in Acts 11:26; 26:28; **1 Pet. 4:16**. Though the word rendered "were called" in Acts 11:26 might be used of a name adopted by oneself or given by others, the "Christians" do not seem to have adopted it for themselves in the times of the apostles. In **1 Pet. 4:16**, the apostle is speaking from the point of view of the persecutor, cf. "as a thief," "as a murderer." Nor is it likely that the appellation was given by Jews. As applied by Gentiles there was no doubt an implication of scorn, as in Agrippa's statement in Acts 26:28. Tacitus, writing near the end of the first century, says, "The vulgar call them Christians. The author or origin of this denomination, Christus, had, in the reign of Tiberius, been executed by the procurator, Pontius Pilate" (Annals xv. 44). From the second century onward the term was accepted by believers as a title of honor.

"Pain can either make us better or bitter."

TIM HANSEL

Ashamed *aischuno* (153), from *aischos*, "shame," always used in the passive voice, signifies (a) "to have a feeling of fear or shame which prevents a person from doing a thing," e.g., Luke 16:3; (b) "the feeling of shame arising from something that has been done," e.g., 2 Cor. 10:8; Phil. 1:20; 1 John 2:28, of the possibility of being "ashamed" before the Lord Jesus at His judgment seat in His Parousia with His saints; in **1 Pet. 4:16**, of being ashamed of suffering as a Christian.

Glorify *see* **Glory** at **1** *Peter 1:8.*

Behalf *meros* (3313), "a part," is translated "behalf" in the KJV of 2 Cor. 9:3 (RV, "respect") and **1 Pet. 4:16**; here the most authentic texts have *onoma*, "a name"; hence RV, "in this name." *See also* **Name** at *1 Peter 4:14.*

4:17 For the time *is come* that judgment must begin at the house of God: and if *it* first *begin* at us, what shall the end *be* of them that obey not the gospel of God?

Judgment *krima* (2917), denotes (a) "the sentence pronounced, a verdict, a condemnation, the decision resulting from an investigation," e.g., Mark 12:40; Luke 23:40; 1 Tim. 3:6; Jude 4; (b) "the process of judgment leading to a decision," **1 Pet. 4:17** ("judgment"), where *krisis* ("the process of investigation, the act of distinguishing and separating ... hence "a judging, a passing of judgment upon a person or thing") might be expected. In Luke 24:20, "to be condemned" translates the phrase *eis krima*, "unto condemnation" (i.e., unto the pronouncement of the sentence of "condemnation"). For the rendering "judgment," see, e.g., Rom. 11:33; 1 Cor. 11:34; Gal. 5:10; Jas. 3:1. In these (a) the process leading to a decision and (b) the pronouncement of the decision, the verdict, are to be distinguished. In 1 Cor. 6:7 the word means a matter for judgment, a lawsuit.

Must Sometimes the infinitive mood of a verb, with or without the article, is necessarily rendered by a phrase involving the word "must," e.g., **1 Pet. 4:17**, KJV, "must (begin)"; or "should," Heb. 4:6, RV, "should" (KJV "must").

House *see 1 Peter 2:5.*

Obey not *see 1 Peter 3:1. See also* **Disobedient** at *1 Peter 2:7.*

Gospel *euangelion* (2098), originally denoted a reward for good tidings; later, the idea of reward dropped, and the word stood for "the good news" itself. The Eng. word "gospel," i.e. "good message," is the equivalent of *euangelion* (Eng., "evangel"). In the NT it denotes the "good tidings" of the kingdom of God and of salvation through Christ, to be received by faith, on the basis of His expiatory death, His burial, resurrection, and ascension, e.g., Acts 15:7; 20:24; **1 Pet. 4:17**. Apart from those references and those in the Gospels of Matthew and Mark, and Rev. 14:6, the noun is confined to Paul's epistles. The apostle uses it of two associated yet distinct things, (a) of the basic facts of the death, burial and resurrection of Christ, e.g., 1 Cor. 15:1-3; (b) of the interpretation of these facts, e.g., Rom. 2:16; Gal. 1:7, 11; 2:2; in (a) the "gospel" is viewed historically, in (b) doctrinally, with reference to the interpretation of the facts, as is sometimes indicated by the context. The following phrases describe the subjects or nature or purport of the message; it is the "gospel" of God, Mark 1:14; Rom. 1:1; 15:16; 2 Cor. 11:7; 1 Thess. 2:2, 9; **1 Pet. 4:17**; God, concerning His Son, Rom. 1:1-3; His Son, Rom. 1:9; Jesus Christ, the Son of God, Mark 1:1; our Lord Jesus, 2 Thess. 1:8; Christ, Rom. 15:19, etc.; the glory of Christ, 2 Cor. 4:4; the grace of God, Acts 20:24; the glory of the blessed God, 1 Tim. 1:11; your salvation, Eph. 1:13; peace, Eph. 6:15. Cf. also "the gospel of the Kingdom," Matt. 4:23; 9:35; 24:14; "an eternal gospel," Rev. 14:6.

4:18 And if the righteous scarcely be saved, where shall the ungodly and the sinner appear?

Scarcely *molis* (3433), signifies "with difficulty, hardly" (from *molos*, "toil"). In Luke 9:39, it is rendered "hardly," of the "difficulty" in the departure of a demon. In Acts 27:7, 8, 16, where the KJV has three different renderings, "scarce," "hardly," and "much work," respectively, the RV has "with difficulty" in each place. For its other meanings, "scarce, scarcely," see Acts 14:18; Rom. 5:7 **1 Pet. 4:18**.

Ungodly *asebes* (765), "impious, ungodly," "without reverence for God," not merely irreligious, but acting in contravention of God's demands, Rom. 4:5; 5:6; 1 Tim. 1:9; **1 Pet. 4:18**; 2 Pet. 2:5 (v. 6 in some mss.); 3:7; Jude 4, 15 (twice).

4:19 Wherefore let them that suffer according to the will of God commit the keeping of their souls *to him* in well doing, as unto a faithful Creator.

Wherefore *hoste,* "so that," "wherefore," e.g., Rom. 7:12, 13; 1 Cor. 10:12; 11:27, 33; 14:22, 39; 2 Cor. 5:16; Gal. 3:24; 4:7; Phil. 4:1; 1 Thess. 4:18; **1 Pet. 4:19**.

Commit *paratithemi* (3908), signifies "to entrust, commit to one's charge," e.g., in Luke 12:48; 1 Tim. 1:18; 2 Tim. 2:2; **1 Pet. 4:19** (KJV, "commit the keeping").

Keeping *paratithemi* is rendered "commit the keeping" in **1 Pet. 4:19**, KJV.

Souls *see 1 Peter 1:9.*

Well doing *agathopoiia* (16), "well-doing," occurs in **1 Pet. 4:19**. *See also* **Well** at *1 Peter 2:14.*

Faithful *pistos* (4103), a verbal adjective, akin to *peitho,* is used in two senses, (a) passive, "faithful, to be trusted, reliable," said of God, e.g., 1 Cor. 1:9; 10:13; 2 Cor. 1:18 (KJV, "true"); 2 Tim. 2:13; Heb. 10:23; 11:11; **1 Pet. 4:19**; 1 John 1:9; of Christ, e.g., 2 Thess. 3:3; Heb. 2:17; 3:2; Rev. 1:5; 3:14; 19:11; of the words of God, e.g., Acts 13:34, "sure"; 1 Tim. 1:15; 3:1 (KJV, "true"); 4:9; 2 Tim. 2:11; Titus 1:9; 3:8; Rev. 21:5; 22:6; of servants of the Lord, Matt. 24:45; 25:21, 23; Acts 16:15; 1 Cor. 4:2, 17; 7:25; Eph. 6:21; Col. 1:7; 4:7, 9; 1 Tim. 1:12; 3:11; 2 Tim. 2:2; Heb. 3:5; **1 Pet. 5:12**; 3 John 5; Rev. 2:13; 17:14; of believers, Eph. 1:1; Col. 1:2; (b) active, signifying "believing, trusting, relying," e.g., Acts 16:1 (feminine); 2 Cor. 6:15; Gal. 3:9 seems best taken in this respect, as the context lays stress upon Abraham's "faith" in God, rather than upon his "faithfulness." In John 20:27 the context requires the active sense, as the Lord is reproaching Thomas for his want of "faith." With regard to believers, they are spoken of sometimes in the active sense, sometimes in the passive, i.e., sometimes as believers, sometimes as "faithful." See Lightfoot on Galatians, p. 155.

Creator (2939), among the Greeks, the founder of a city, etc., denotes in Scripture "the Creator," **1 Pet. 4:19** (cf. Rom. 1:20).

Chapter 5

5:1 The elders which are among you I exhort, who am also an elder, and a witness of the sufferings of Christ, and also a partaker of the glory that shall be revealed:

Elders, Elder *sumpresbuteros* (4850), "a fellow-elder" (*sun,* "with"), is used in **1 Pet. 5:1**.

Witness *martus or martur* (3144), (whence Eng., "martyr," one who bears "witness" by his death) denotes "one who can or does aver what he has seen or heard or knows"; it is used (a) of God, Rom. 1:9; 2 Cor. 1:23; Phil. 1:8; 1 Thess. 2:5, 10 (2nd part); (b) of Christ, Rev. 1:5; 3:14; (c) of those who "witness" for Christ by their death, Acts 22:20; Rev. 2:13; Rev. 17:6; (d) of the interpreters of God's counsels, yet to "witness" in Jerusalem in the times of the Antichrist, Rev. 11:3; (e) in a forensic sense, Matt. 18:16; 26:65; Mark 14:63; Acts 6:13; 7:58; 2 Cor. 13:1; 1 Tim. 5:19; Heb. 10:28; (f) in a historical sense, Luke 11:48; 24:48; Acts 1:8, 22; 2:32; 3:15; 5:32; 10:39, 41; 13:31; 22:15; 26:16; 1 Thess. 2:10 (1st part); 1 Tim. 6:12; 2 Tim. 2:2; Heb. 12:1, "(a cloud) of witnesses," here of those mentioned in ch. 11, those whose lives and actions testified to the worth and effect of faith, and whose faith received "witness" in Scripture; **1 Pet. 5:1**.

Sufferings *see 1 Peter 1:11.*

Partaker *koinonos* (2844), an adjective, signifying "having in common" (*koinos,* "common"), is used as a noun, denoting "a companion, partner, partaker," translated "partakers" in Matt. 23:30; 1 Cor. 10:18, KJV; 2 Cor. 1:7; Heb. 10:33, RV; 2 Pet. 1:4; "partaker" in **1 Pet. 5:1**.

Glory *see 1 Peter 1:21.*

Shall *mello* (3195), "to be about (to be or do)," is used of purpose, certainty, compulsion or necessity. It is rendered simply by "shall" or "should" (which frequently represent elsewhere part of the future tense of the verb) in the following (the RV sometimes translates differently, as noted): Matt. 16:27 (1st part), lit., "is about to come"; 17:12, 22; 20:22, RV, "am about"; 24:6; Mark 13:4 (2nd part), RV, "are about"; Luke 9:44; 21:7 (2nd part), RV, "are about"; v. 36; Acts 23:3; 24:15; 26:2, RV, "I am (to)"; Rom. 4:24; 8:13 (1st part), RV, "must"; v. 18; 2 Tim. 4:1; Heb. 1:14; 10:27; Jas. 2:12, RV "are to"; **1 Pet. 5:1**; Rev. 1:19; 2:10 (1st and 2nd parts), RV, "art about," "is about"; 3:10, RV, "is (to)"; 17:8 (1st part), RV, "is about."

Revealed *see 1 Peter 1:5.*

5:2 Feed the flock of God which is among you, taking the oversight *thereof*, not by constraint, but willingly; not for filthy lucre, but of a ready mind;

Feed *poimaino* (4165), "to act as a shepherd" (from *poimen,* "a shepherd"), is used (a) literally, Luke 17:7, RV, "keeping sheep," for KJV, "feeding cattle"; 1 Cor. 9:7, (b) metaphorically, "to tend, to shepherd"; said of Christ Matt. 2:6, RV, "shall be Shepherd of" (for KJV, "shall rule"); of those who act as spiritual shepherds under Him, John 21:16, RV, "tend" (for KJV "feed"), so **1 Pet. 5:2**;

Acts 20:28, "to feed" ("to tend" would have been a consistent rendering; a shepherd does not only "feed" his flock); of base shepherds, Jude 12.

Flock *poimnion* (4168), is used in the NT only metaphorically, of a group of Christ's disciples, Luke 12:32; of local churches cared for by elders, Acts 20:28, 29; **1 Pet. 5:2, 3**.

Among In Rom. 1:15, the phrase *to kat' eme*, lit., "the (thing) according to me," signifies "as much as in me is"; cf. the KJV marg. in **1 Pet. 5:2** [lit., "the (extent) in, or among, you"; the text takes the word "flock" as understood, the marg. regards the phrase as adverbially idiomatic]; in Rom. 12:18 "as much as in you lieth" translates a similar phrase, lit., "the (extent) out of you."

Oversight *episkopeo* (1983), lit., "to look upon" (*epi*, "upon," *skopeo*, "to look at, contemplate"), is found in **1 Pet. 5:2** (some ancient authorities omit it), "exercising the oversight," RV (KJV, "taking ..."); "exercising" is the right rendering; the word does not imply the entrance upon such responsibility, but the fulfillment of it. It is not a matter of assuming a position, but of the discharge of the duties. The word is found elsewhere in Heb. 12:15, "looking carefully," RV. Cf. *episkope* in 1 Tim. 3:1.

presbuteros (4245), an adjective, the comparative degree of *presbus*, "an old man, an elder," is used (a) of age, whether of the "elder" of two persons, Luke 15:25, or more, John 8:9, "the eldest", or of a person advanced in life, a senior, Acts 2:17; in Heb. 11:2, the "elders" are the forefathers in Israel so in Matt. 15:2; Mark 7:3, 5 the feminine of the adjective is used of "elder" women in the churches, 1 Tim. 5:2, not in respect of position but in seniority of age; (b) of rank or positions of responsibility, (1) among Gentiles, as in the Sept. of Gen. 50:7; Num. 22:7, (2) in the Jewish nation, firstly, those who were the heads or leaders of the tribes and families, as of the seventy who assisted Moses, Num. 11:16; Deut. 27:1, and those assembled by Solomon; secondly, members of the Sanhedrin, consisting of the chief priests, "elders" and scribes, learned in Jewish law, e.g., Matt. 16:21; 26:47; thirdly, those who managed public affairs in the various cities, Luke 7:3; (3) in the Christian churches those who, being raised up and qualified by the work of the Holy Spirit, were appointed to have the spiritual care of, and to exercise oversight over, the churches. To these the term "bishops," *episkopoi*, or "overseers," is applied (see Acts 20, v. 17 with v. 28, and Titus 1:5 and 7), the latter term indicating the nature of their work *presbuteroi* their maturity of spiritual experience. The divine arrangement seen throughout the NT was for a plurality of these to be appointed in each church, Acts 14:23; 20:17; Phil. 1:1; 1 Tim. 5:17; Titus 1:5. The duty of "elders" is described by the verb *episkopeo*. They were appointed according as they had given evidence of fulfilling the divine qualifications, Titus 1:6 to 9; cf. 1 Tim. 3:1-7 and **1 Pet. 5:2**; (4) the twenty-four "elders" enthroned in heaven around the throne of God, Rev. 4:4, 10; 5:5-14; 7:11, 13; 11:16; 14:3; 19:4. The number twenty-four is representative of earthly conditions. The word "elder" is nowhere applied to angels.

Constraint *anankastos* (317), "by force, unwillingly, by constraint," is used in **1 Pet. 5:2**.

Willingly *hekousios* (1596), denotes "voluntarily, willingly," Heb. 10:26, (of sinning) "willfully"; in **1 Pet. 5:2**, "willingly" (of exercising oversight over the flock of God).

Filthy lucre *aischrokerdos* (147), "eagerness for base gain," is used in **1 Pet. 5:2**, "for filthy lucre."

Ready In **1 Pet. 5:2** *prothumos*, "willingly, with alacrity," is rendered "of a ready mind."

5:3 Neither as being lords over *God's* heritage, but being ensamples to the flock.

Lords *katakurieuo* (2634), "to exercise, or gain, dominion over, to lord it over," is used of (a) the "lordship" of gentile rulers, Matt. 20:25, KJV, "exercise dominion," RV, "lord it", Mark 10:42, KJV, "exercise lordship," RV, "lord it"; (b) the power of demons over men, Acts 19:16, KJV, "overcame," RV, "mastered"; (c) of the evil of elders in "lording" it over the saints under their spiritual care, **1 Pet. 5:3**.

Heritage *kleros* (2819), (whence Eng., "clergy"), denotes (a) "a lot," given or cast (the latter as a means of obtaining divine direction), Matt. 27:35; Mark 15:24; Luke 23:24; John 19:24; Acts 1:26; (b) "a person's share" in anything, Acts 1:17, RV, "portion" (KJV, "part"); 8:21, "lot"; (c) "a charge" (lit., "charges") "allotted," to elders, **1 Pet. 5:3**, RV [KJV, "(God's) heritage"]; the figure is from portions of lands allotted to be cultivated; (d) "an inheritance"; Acts 26:18; Col. 1:12.

Ensamples *tupos* (5179), primarily denoted "a blow" (from a root *tup-*, seen also in *tupto*, "to strike"), hence, (a) an impression, the mark of a "blow," John 20:25; (b) the "impress" of a seal, the stamp made by a die, a figure, image, Acts 7:43; (c) a "form" or mold, Rom. 6:17 (see RV); (d) the sense or substance of a letter, Acts 23:25; (e) "an ensample," pattern, Acts 7:44; Heb. 8:5, "pattern"; in an ethical sense, 1 Cor. 10:6; Phil. 3:17; 1 Thess. 1:7; 2 Thess.

3:9; 1 Tim. 4:12, RV, "ensample"; Titus 2:7, RV, "ensample," for KJV, "pattern"; **1 Pet. 5:3**; in a doctrinal sense, a type, Rom. 5:14.

Flock *see 1 Peter 5:2.*

5:4 And when the chief Shepherd shall appear, ye shall receive a crown of glory that fadeth not away.

Chief *archipoimen* (750), "a chief shepherd" (*arche*, "chief," *poimen*, "a shepherd"), is said of Christ only, **1 Pet. 5:4**. Modern Greeks use it of tribal chiefs.

Appear *phaneroo* (5319), signifies, in the active voice, "to manifest"; in the passive voice, "to be manifested"; so, regularly, in the RV, instead of "to appear." See 2 Cor. 7:12; Col. 3:4; Heb. 9:26; **1 Pet. 5:4**; 1 John 2:28; 3:2; Rev. 3:18. To be manifested, in the Scriptural sense of the word, is more than to "appear." A person may "appear" in a false guise or without a disclosure of what he truly is; to be manifested is to be revealed in one's true character; this is especially the meaning of *phaneroo*, see, e.g., John 3:21; 1 Cor. 4:5; 2 Cor. 5:10-11; Eph. 5:13. *See also* **Manifest** at *1 Peter 1:20.*

Receive *see* **Receiving** at *1 Peter 1:9.*

Crown *stephanos* (4735), primarily, "that which surrounds, as a wall or crowd" (from *stepho*, "to encircle"), denotes (a) "the victor's crown," the symbol of triumph in the games or some such contest; hence, by metonymy, a reward or prize; (b) "a token of public honor" for distinguished service, military prowess, etc., or of nuptial joy, or festal gladness, especially at the parousia of kings. It was woven as a garland of oak, ivy, parsley, myrtle, or olive, or in imitation of these in gold. In some passages the reference to the games is clear, 1 Cor. 9:25; 2 Tim. 4:8 ("crown of righteousness"); it may be so in **1 Pet. 5:4**, where the fadeless character of "the crown of glory" is set in contrast to the garlands of earth. In other passages it stands as an emblem of life, joy, reward and glory, Phil. 4:1; 1 Thess. 2:19; Jas. 1:12 ("crown of life "); Rev. 2:10 (ditto); 3:11; 4:4, 10: of triumph, 6:2; 9:7; 12:1; 14:14. It is used of "the crown of thorns" which the soldiers plaited and put on Christ's head, Matt. 27:29; Mark 15:17; John 19:2, 5. At first sight this might be taken as an alternative for *diadema*, "a kingly crown," but considering the blasphemous character of that masquerade, and the materials used, obviously *diadema* would be quite unfitting and the only alternative was *stephanos* (see Trench *Syn.* Sec.xxxii).

Fadeth not *amarantinos* (262), primarily signifies "composed of amaranth"; hence, "unfading," **1 Pet. 5:4**, of the crown of glory promised to faithful elders. Cf. *rhodinos*, "made of roses" (*rhodon*, "a rose"). *See also* **Incorruptible** at *1 Peter 1:4.*

5:5 Likewise, ye younger, submit yourselves unto the elder. Yea, all *of you* be subject one to another, and be clothed with humility: for God resisteth the proud, and giveth grace to the humble.

Likewise *see 1 Peter 3:1.*

Younger *neoteros* (3501), occurs in Luke 15:12, 13; 22:26; 1 Tim. 5:1 ("younger men"); 5:2, feminine; v. 11, "younger (widows)"; v. 14, "younger (*widows*)," RV, marg. and KJV, "younger (women)"; **1 Pet. 5:5**.

Submit *see 1 Peter 2:13.*

Clothed The verb *enkomboomai*, "to gird oneself with a thing," in **1 Pet. 5:5**, is rendered in the KJV, "be clothed with."

Humility *tapeinophrosune* (5012), "lowliness of mind" (*tapeinos* and *phren*, "the mind"), is rendered "humility of mind" in Acts 20:19, KJV (RV, "lowliness of mind"); in Eph. 4:2, "lowliness"; in Phil. 2:3, "lowliness of mind"; in Col. 2:18, 23, of a false "humility"; in Col. 3:12, KJV, "humbleness of mind," RV, "humility"; **1 Pet. 5:5**, "humility."

Resisteth *antitasso* (498), *anti*, "against," *tasso*, "to arrange," originally a military term, "to range in battle against," and frequently so found in the papyri, is used in the middle voice signifying "to set oneself against, resist," (a) of men, Acts 18:6, "opposed themselves"; elsewhere "to resist," of resisting human potentates, Rom. 13:2; (b) of God, Jas. 4:6; 5:6, negatively, of leaving persistent evildoers to pursue their self-determined course, with eventual retribution; **1 Pet. 5:5**.

Proud *huperephanos* (5244), "showing oneself above others" (*huper*, "over," *phainomai*, "to appear"), though often denoting preeminent, is always used in the NT in the evil sense of "arrogant, disdainful, haughty"; it is rendered "haughty" in Rom. 1:30 and 2 Tim. 3:2, RV, KJV, "proud," but "proud" in both versions in Luke 1:51; Jas. 4:6, and **1 Pet. 5:5**; in the last two it is set in opposition to *tapeinos*, "humble, lowly." Cf. the noun *huperephania*, Mark 7:22, "pride".

Humble *tapeinos* (5011), primarily signifies "low-lying." It is used always in a good sense in the NT, metaphorically, to denote (a) "of low degree, brought low," Luke 1:52; Rom. 12:16, KJV, "(men) of low estate," RV, "(things that are) lowly" (i.e., of low degree); 2 Cor. 7:6, KJV, "cast down," RV, "lowly"; the preceding context shows that this occurrence belongs to (a); Jas. 1:9, "of low degree"; (b) humble in spirit, Matt. 11:29; 2 Cor. 10:1, RV, "lowly," KJV "base"; Jas. 4:6; **1 Pet. 5:5**.

5:6 Humble yourselves therefore under the mighty hand of God, that he may exalt you in due time:

Humble *tapeinoo* (5013), signifies "to make low," (a) literally, "of mountains and hills," Luke 3:5 (passive voice); (b) metaphorically, in the active voice, Matt. 18:4; 23:12 (2nd part); Luke 14:11 (2nd part); 18:14 (2nd part); 2 Cor. 11:7 ("abasing"); 12:21; Phil. 2:8; in the passive voice, Matt. 23:12 (1st part), RV, "shall be humbled," KJV, "shall be abased"; Luke 14:11 (ditto); 18:14 (ditto); Phil. 4:12, "to be abased"; in the passive, with middle voice sense, Jas. 4:10, "humble yourselves"; **1 Pet. 5:6** (ditto).

Mighty *krataios* (2900), "strong, mighty" (akin to *kratos*, "strength," relative and manifested power), is found in **1 Pet. 5:6**, of the "mighty" hand of God.

"In submission we are free to value other people. Their dreams and plans become important to us. We have entered into a new, wonderful, glorious freedom, the freedom to give up our own rights for the good of others."

RICHARD J. FOSTER

Exalt *hupsoo* (5312), "to lift up" (akin to *hupsos*, "height"), is used (a) literally of the "lifting" up of Christ in His crucifixion, John 3:14; 8:28; 12:32, 34; illustratively, of the serpent of brass, John 3:14; (b) figuratively, of spiritual privileges bestowed on a city, Matt. 11:23; Luke 10:15; of "raising" to dignity and happiness, Luke 1:52; Acts 13:17; of haughty self-exaltation, and, contrastingly, of being "raised" to honor, as a result of self-humbling, Matt. 23:12; Luke 14:11; 18:14; of spiritual "uplifting" and revival, Jas. 4:10; **1 Pet. 5:6**; of bringing into the blessings of salvation through the gospel, 2 Cor. 11:7; (c) with a combination of the literal and metaphorical, of the "exaltation" of Christ by God the Father, Acts 2:33; 5:31.

Due In the phrases "in due season" in Matt. 24:45; Luke 12:42; Rom. 5:6 (lit., "according to time"), and "in due time," **1 Pet. 5:6**, there is no word representing "due" in the original, and the phrases are, lit., "in season," "in time."

5:7 Casting all your care upon him; for he careth for you.

Casting *epiripto* (1977), "to cast upon," (a) lit., "of casting garments on a colt," Luke 19:35; (b) figuratively, "of casting care upon God," **1 Pet. 5:7**.

Care *merimna* (3308), probably connected with *merizo*, "to draw in different directions, distract," hence signifies "that which causes this, a care, especially an anxious care," Matt. 13:22; Mark 4:19; Luke 8:14; 21:34; 2 Cor. 11:28 (RV, "anxiety for"), **1 Pet. 5:7** (RV, "anxiety").

Careth *melei* (3199), the third person sing. of *melo*, used impersonally, signifies that "something is an object of care," especially the care of forethought and interest, rather than anxiety, Matt. 22:16; Mark 4:38; 12:14; Luke 10:40; John 10:13; 12:6; Acts 18:17; 1 Cor. 9:9 (RV, "Is it for the oxen that God careth?" The KJV seriously misses the point. God does "care" for oxen, but there was a divinely designed significance in the OT passage, relating to the service of preachers of the gospel); 7:21; **1 Pet. 5:7**.

5:8 Be sober, be vigilant; because your adversary the devil, as a roaring lion, walketh about, seeking whom he may devour:

Sober *see 1 Peter 1:13*.

Vigilant *gregoreo* (1127), "to watch," is used (a) of "keeping awake," e.g., Matt. 24:43; 26:38, 40, 41; (b) of "spiritual alertness," e.g., Acts 20:31; 1 Cor. 16:13; Col. 4:2; 1 Thess. 5:6, 10; **1 Pet. 5:8**, RV, "be watchful" (KJV, "be vigilant"); Rev. 3:2, 3; 16:15.

Adversary *antidikos* (476), firstly, "an opponent in a lawsuit," Matt. 5:25 (twice); Luke 12:58; 18:3, is also used to denote "an adversary or an enemy," without reference to legal affairs, and this is perhaps its meaning in **1 Pet. 5:8**, where it is used of the Devil. Some would regard the word as there used in a legal sense, since the Devil accuses men before God.

Devil *diabolos* (1228), "an accuser, a slanderer" (from *diaballo*, "to accuse, to malign"), is one of the names of Satan. From it the English word "Devil" is derived, and should be applied only to Satan, as a proper name. *Daimon*, "a demon," is frequently, but wrongly, translated "devil"; it should always be translated "demon," as in the RV margin.

There is one "Devil," there are many demons. Being the malignant enemy of God and man, he accuses man to God, Job 1:6-11; 2:1-5; Rev. 12:9, 10, and God to man, Gen. 3. He afflicts men with physical sufferings, Acts 10:38. Being himself sinful, 1 John 3:8, he instigated man to sin, Gen. 3, and tempts man to do evil, Eph. 4:27; 6:11, encouraging him thereto by deception, Eph. 2:2. Death having been brought into the world by sin, the "Devil" had the power of death, but Christ through His own death, has triumphed over him, and will bring him to nought, Heb. 2:14; his power over death is intimated in his struggle with Michael over the body of Moses, Jude 9. Judas, who gave himself over to the "Devil," was so identified with him, that the Lord described him as such, John 6:70 (see 13:2). As the "Devil" raised himself in pride against God and fell under condemnation, so believers are warned against similar sin, 1 Tim. 3:6; for them he lays snares, v. 7, seeking to devour them as a roaring lion, **1 Pet. 5:8**; those who fall into his snare may be recovered therefrom unto the will of God, 2 Tim. 2:26, "having been taken captive by him (i.e., by the 'Devil')"; "by the Lord's servant" is an alternative, which some regard as confirmed by the use of *zogreo* ("to catch alive") in Luke 5:10; but the general use is that of taking captive in the usual way. If believers resist he will flee from them, Jas. 4:7. His fury and malignity will be especially exercised at the end of the present age, Rev. 12:12. His doom is the lake of fire, Matt. 25:41; Rev. 20:10. The noun is applied to slanderers, false accusers, 1 Tim. 3:11; 2 Tim. 3:3; Titus 2:3.

Roaring *oruomai* (5612), "to howl" or "roar," onomatopoeic, of animals or men, is used of a lion, **1 Pet. 5:8**, as a simile of Satan.

Lion *leon* (3023), occurs in 2 Tim. 4:17, probably figurative of the imminent peril of death, the figure being represented by the whole phrase, not by the word "lion" alone; some suppose the reference to be to the lions of the amphitheater; the Greek commentators regarded the "lion" as Nero; others understand it to be Satan. The language not improbably recalls that of Ps. 22:21, and Dan. 6:20. The word is used metaphorically, too, in Rev. 5:5, where Christ is called "the Lion of the tribe of Judah." Elsewhere it has the literal meaning, Heb. 11:33; **1 Pet. 5:8**; Rev. 4:7; 9:8, 17; 10:3; 13:2. Taking the OT and NT occurrences the allusions are to the three great features of the "lion," (1) its majesty and strength, indicative of royalty, e.g., Prov. 30:30, (2) its courage, e.g., Prov. 28:1, (3) its cruelty, e.g., Ps. 22:13.

Devour *katapino* (2666), from *kato*, "down," intensive, *pino*, "to drink," in **1 Pet. 5:8** is translated "devour," of Satan's activities against believers. The meaning "to swallow" is found in Matt. 23:24; 1 Cor. 15:54; 2 Cor. 2:7; 5:4; Heb. 11:29, RV (for KJV, "drowned"); Rev. 12:16.

5:9 Whom resist stedfast in the faith, knowing that the same afflictions are accomplished in your brethren that are in the world.

Resist *anthistemi* (436), "to set against" (*anti*, "against," *histemi*, "to cause to stand"), used in the middle (or passive) voice and in the intransitive 2nd aorist and perfect active, signifying "to withstand, oppose, resist," is translated "to resist" in Matt. 5:39; Acts 6:10, KJV (RV, withstand); Rom. 9:19, KJV (RV, "withstandeth"); 13:2 (2nd and 3rd parts), KJV (RV, "withstandeth" and "withstand"); Gal. 2:11, RV (KJV, "withstood"); 2 Tim. 3:8 (2nd part), KJV (RV, "withstand"); Jas. 4:7; **1 Pet. 5:9**, KJV (RV, "withstand"); "to withstand" in Acts 13:8; Eph. 6:13; 2 Tim. 3:8 (1st part); 4:15.

Stedfast *stereos* (4731), "solid, hard, stiff," is translated "firm" in 2 Tim. 2:19, RV, "the firm (foundation of God)," KJV, "(standeth) sure"; *stereos* is not part of the predicate; "solid (food)" in Heb. 5:12, 14, RV; "stedfast" in **1 Pet. 5:9**.

Afflictions *pathema* (3804), is rendered "sufferings" in the RV (KJV, "afflictions") in 2 Tim. 3:11; Heb. 10:32; **1 Pet. 5:9**; in Gal. 5:24, "passions (KJV, "affections").

Accomplished *epiteleo* (2005), is a strengthened form of that verb, in the sense of "accomplishing." The fuller meaning is "to accomplish perfectly"; in Rom. 15:28, RV, "accomplish"; "perfecting" in 2 Cor. 7:1; "complete" in 8:6 and 11; "completion" in the latter part of this 11th verse, which is better than "performance"; "perfected" in Gal. 3:3; "perfect" in Phil. 1:6. In Heb. 8:5 the margin rightly has "complete" instead of "make," with regard to the tabernacle. In Heb. 9:6 it is translated "accomplish" and in 1 Pet. 5:9.

Brethren *see 1 Peter 1:22.*

5:10 But the God of all grace, who hath called us unto his eternal glory by Christ Jesus, after that ye have suffered a while, make you perfect, stablish, strengthen, settle *you*.

God *theos* (2316 ... (a) ... the word was appropriated by Jews and retained by Christians to denote "the one true God." In the Sept. *theos* translates (with few exceptions) the Hebrew words *Elohim* and *Jehovah*, the former indicating His power and preeminence, the latter His unoriginated, immutable, eternal and self-sustained existence. In the NT, these and all the other divine attributes are predicated of Him. To Him are ascribed, e.g., His unity, or monism, e.g., Mark 12:29; 1 Tim. 2:5; self-existence, John 5:26; immutability, Jas. 1:17; eternity, Rom. 1:20; universality, Matt. 10:29; Acts 17:26-28; almighty power Matt. 19:26; infinite knowledge, Acts 2:23; 15:18; Rom. 11:33, creative power, Rom. 11:36; 1 Cor. 8:6; Eph. 3:9; Rev. 4:11; 10:6; absolute holiness, **1 Pet. 1:15**; 1 John 1:5; righteousness, John 17:25; faithfulness, 1 Cor. 1:9; 10:13; 1 Thess. 5:24; 2 Thess. 3:3; 1 John 1:9; love, 1 John 4:8, 16; mercy, Rom. 9:15, 18; truthfulness, Titus 1:2; Heb. 6:18.

(b) The divine attributes are likewise indicated or definitely predicated of Christ, e.g., Matt. 20:18-19; John 1:1-3; 1:18, RV, marg.; 5:22-29; 8:58; 14:6; 17:22-24; 20:28; Rom. 1:4; 9:5; Phil. 3:21; Col. 1:15; 2:3; Titus 2:13, RV; Heb. 1:3; 13:8; 1 John 5:20; Rev. 22:12, 13.

(c) Also of the Holy Spirit, e.g., Matt. 28:19; Luke 1:35; John 14:16; 15:26; 16:7-14; Rom. 8:9, 26; 1 Cor. 12:11; 2 Cor. 13:14.

(d) *Theos* is used (1) with the definite article, (2) without (i.e., as an anarthrous noun). "The English may or may not have need of the article in translation. But that point cuts no figure in the Greek idiom. Thus in Acts 27:23 ('the God whose I am,' RV) the article points out the special God whose Paul is, and is to be preserved in English. In the very next verse (*ho theos*) we in English do not need the article" (A. T. Robertson, *Gram. of Greek, NT*, p. 758). As to this latter it is usual to employ the article with a proper name, when mentioned a second time. There are, of course, exceptions to this, as when the absence of the article serves to lay stress upon, or give precision to, the character or nature of what is expressed in the noun. A notable instance of this is in John 1:1, "and the Word was God"; here a double stress is on *theos*, by the absence of the article and by the emphatic position. To translate it literally, "a god was the Word," is entirely misleading. Moreover, that "the Word" is the subject of the sentence, exemplifies the rule that the subject is to be determined by its having the article when the predicate is anarthrous (without the article). In Rom. 7:22, in the phrase "the law of God," both nouns have the article; in v. 25, neither has the article. This is in accordance with a general rule that if two nouns are united by the genitive case (the "of" case), either both have the article, or both are without. Here, in the first instance, both nouns, "God" and "the law" are definite, whereas in v. 25 the word "God" is not simply titular; the absence of the article stresses His character as lawgiver. Where two or more epithets are applied to the same person or thing, one article usually serves for both (the exceptions being when a second article lays stress upon different aspects of the same person or subject, e.g., Rev. 1:17). In Titus 2:13 the RV correctly has "our great God and Savior Jesus Christ." Moulton (*Prol.*, p. 84) shows, from papyri writings of the early Christian era, that among Greek-speaking Christians this was "a current formula" as applied to Christ. So in 2 Pet. 1:1 (cf. 1:11; 3:18). In the following titles God is described by certain of His attributes; the God of glory, Acts 7:2; of peace, Rom. 15:33; 16:20; Phil. 4:9; 1 Thess. 5:23; Heb. 13:20; of love and peace, 2 Cor. 13:11; of patience and comfort, Rom. 15:5; of all comfort, 2 Cor. 1:3; of hope, Rom. 15:13; of all grace, **1 Pet. 5:10**. These describe Him, not as in distinction from other persons, but as the source of all these blessings; hence the employment of the definite article. In such phrases as "the God of a person," e.g., Matt. 22:32, the expression marks the relationship in which the person stands to God and God to him.

Eternal *aionios* (166), "describes duration, either undefined but not endless, as in Rom. 16:25; 2 Tim. 1:9; Titus 1:2; or undefined because endless as in Rom. 16:26, and the other sixty-six places in the NT.

"The predominant meaning of *aionios*, that in which it is used everywhere in the NT, save the places noted above, may be seen in 2 Cor. 4:18, where it is set in contrast with *proskairos*, lit., 'for a season,' and in Philem. 15, where only in the NT it is used without a noun. Moreover it is used of persons and things which are in their nature endless, as, e.g., of God, Rom. 16:26; of His power, 1 Tim. 6:16, and of His glory, **1 Pet. 5:10**; of the Holy Spirit, Heb. 9:14; of the redemption effected by Christ, Heb. 9:12, and of the consequent salvation of men, 5:9, as well as of His future rule, 2 Pet. 1:11, which is elsewhere declared to be without end, Luke 1:33; of the life received by those who believe in Christ, John 3:16, concerning whom He said, 'they shall never perish,' 10:28, and of the resurrection body, 2 Cor. 5:1, elsewhere said to be 'immortal,' 1 Cor. 15:53, in which that life will be finally realized, Matt. 25:46; Titus 1:2. *Aionios* is also used of the sin that 'hath never forgiveness,' Mark 3:29, and of the judgment of God, from which there is no appeal, Heb. 6:2, and of the fire, which is one of its instruments, Matt. 18:8; 25:41; Jude 7, and which is elsewhere said to be 'unquenchable,' Mark

9:43. The use of *aionios* here shows that the punishment referred to in 2 Thess. 1:9, is not temporary, but final, and, accordingly, the phraseology shows that its purpose is not remedial but retributive."

Glory *see 1 Peter 1:21.*

Suffered *see* **Suffering** at *1 Peter 2:19.*

While *see* **Season** at *1 Peter 1:6.*

Make ... perfect *katartizo* (2675), "to render fit, complete" (*artios*), "is used of mending nets, Matt. 4:21; Mark 1:19, and is translated 'restore' in Gal. 6:1. It does not necessarily imply, however, that that to which it is applied has been damaged, though it may do so, as in these passages; it signifies, rather, right ordering and arrangement, Heb. 11:3, 'framed;' it points out the path of progress, as in Matt. 21:16; Luke 6:40; cf. 2 Cor. 13:9; Eph. 4:12, where corresponding nouns occur. It indicates the close relationship between character and destiny, Rom. 9:22, 'fitted.' It expresses the pastor's desire for the flock, in prayer, Heb. 13:21, and in exhortation, 1 Cor. 1:10, RV, 'perfected' (KJV, 'perfectly joined'); 2 Cor. 13:11, as well as his conviction of God's purpose for them, **1 Pet. 5:10.** It is used of the Incarnation of the Word in Heb. 10:5, 'prepare,' quoted from Ps. 40:6 (Sept.), where it is apparently intended to describe the unique creative act involved in the Virgin Birth, Luke 1:35. In 1 Thess. 3:10 it means to supply what is necessary, as the succeeding words show."

Stablish *sterizo* (4741), "to fix, make fast, to set" (from *sterix*, "a prop"), is used of "establishing" or "stablishing" (i.e., the confirmation) of persons; the apostle Peter was called by the Lord to "establish" his brethren, Luke 22:32, translated "strengthen"; Paul desired to visit Rome that the saints might be "established," Rom. 1:11; cf. Acts 8:23; so with Timothy at Thessalonica, 1 Thess. 3:2; the "confirmation" of the saints is the work of God, Rom. 16:25, "to stablish (you)"; 1 Thess. 3:13, "stablish (your hearts)"; 2 Thess. 2:17, "stablish them (in every good work and word)"; **1 Pet. 5:10**, "stablish"; the means used to effect the "confirmation" is the ministry of the Word of God, 2 Pet. 1:12, "are established (in the truth which is with you)"; James exhorts Christians to "stablish" their hearts, Jas. 5:8; cf. Rev. 3:2, RV. The character of this "confirmation" may be learned from its use in Luke 9:51, "steadfastly set"; 16:26, "fixed," and in the Sept. in Exod. 17:12, "stayed up" (also from its strengthened form *episterizo*, "to confirm," in Acts 14:22; 15:32, 41; in some mss. "to strengthen," in 18:23). Neither the laying on of hands nor the impartation of the Holy Spirit is mentioned in the NT in connection with either of these words, or with the synonymous verb *bebaioo* (see 1 Cor. 1:8; 2 Cor. 1:21, etc.).

Strengthen *sthenoo* (4599), from *sthenos*, "strength," occurs in **1 Pet. 5:10**, in a series of future tenses, according to the best texts, thus constituting divine promises.

Settle *themelioo* (2311), "to lay a foundation, to found," is used (a) literally, Matt. 7:25; Luke 6:48; Heb. 1:10; (b) metaphorically, Eph. 3:17, "grounded (in love)"; Col. 1:23 (ditto, "in the faith"); **1 Pet. 5:10**, KJV, "settle."

5:11 To him *be* glory and dominion for ever and ever. Amen.

Dominion *see 1 Peter 4:11.*

5:12 By Silvanus, a faithful brother unto you, as I suppose, I have written briefly, exhorting, and testifying that this is the true grace of God wherein ye stand.

Faithful *see 1 Peter 4:19.*

Suppose *logizomai* (3049), primarily signifies "to reckon," whether by calculation or imputation, e.g., Gal. 3:6 (RV, "reckoned"); then, to deliberate, and so to suppose, "account," Rom. 8:36; 14:14 (KJV, "esteemeth"); John 11:50; 1 Cor. 4:1; Heb. 11:19; (KJV, "consider"); Acts 19:27 ("made of no account"; KJV, "despised"); **1 Pet. 5:12** (KJV, "suppose"). It is used of love in **1 Cor.** 13:5, as not taking "account" of evil, RV (KJV, "thinketh"). In 2 Cor. 3:5 the apostle uses it in repudiation of the idea that he and fellow-servants of God are so selfsufficient as to "account anything" (RV) as from themselves (KJV, "think"), i.e., as to attribute anything to themselves. Cf. 12:6. In 2 Tim. 4:16 it is used of laying to a person's "account" (RV) as a charge against him (KJV, "charge").

Testifying *epimartureo* (1957), "to bear witness to" (a strengthened form), is rendered "testifying" in **1 Pet. 5:12.**

True *alethes* (227), primarily, "unconcealed, manifest" (*a*, negative, *letho*, "to forget," = *lanthano*, "to escape notice"), hence, actual, "true to fact," is used (a) of persons, "truthful," Matt. 22:16; Mark 12:14; John 3:33; 7:18; 8:26; Rom. 3:4; 2 Cor. 6:8; (b) of things, "true," conforming to reality, John 4:18, "truly," lit., "true"; 5:31, 32; in the best texts, 6:55 (twice), "indeed"; 8:13, 14 (v. 16 in some texts), 17; 10:41; 19:35; 21:24; Acts 12:9; Phil. 4:8; Titus 1:13; **1 Pet. 5:12**; 2 Pet. 2:22; 1 John 2:8, 27; 3 John 1:2.

Grace *charis* (5485), has various uses, (a) objective, that which bestows or occasions pleasure, delight, or causes favorable regard; it is applied, e.g., to beauty, or gracefulness of person, Luke 2:40; act, 2 Cor. 8:6, or speech, Luke 4:22, RV, "words of grace" (KJV, "gracious words"); Col. 4:6; (b) subjective, (1) on the part of the bestower, the friendly disposition from which the kindly act proceeds, graciousness, loving-kindness, goodwill generally, e.g., Acts 7:10; especially with reference to the divine favor or "grace," e.g., Acts 14:26; in this respect there is stress on its freeness and universality, its spontaneous character, as in the case of God's redemptive mercy, and the pleasure or joy He designs for the recipient; thus it is set in contrast with debt, Rom. 4:4, 16, with works, 11:6, and with law, John 1:17; see also, e.g., Rom. 6:14, 15; Gal. 5:4; (2) on the part of the receiver, a sense of the favor bestowed, a feeling of gratitude, e.g., Rom. 6:17 ("thanks"); in this respect it sometimes signifies "to be thankful," e.g., Luke 17:9 ("doth he thank the servant?" lit., "hath he thanks to"); 1 Tim. 1:12; (c) in another objective sense, the effect of "grace," the spiritual state of those who have experienced its exercise, whether (1) a state of "grace," e.g., Rom. 5:2; **1 Pet. 5:12**; 2 Pet. 3:18, or (2) a proof thereof in practical effects, deeds of "grace," e.g., 1 Cor. 16:3, RV, "bounty" (KJV, "liberality"); 2 Cor. 8:6, 19 (in 2 Cor. 9:8 it means the sum of earthly blessings); the power and equipment for ministry, e.g., Rom. 1:5; 12:6; 15:15; 1 Cor. 3:10; Gal. 2:9; Eph. 3:2, 7. To be in favor with is to find "grace" with, e.g., Acts 2:47; hence it appears in this sense at the beginning and the end of several epistles, where the writer desires "grace" from God for the readers, e.g., Rom. 1:7; 1 Cor. 1:3 ...

5:13 The *church that is* at Babylon, elected together with *you*, saluteth you; and *so doth* Marcus my son.

Elected *suneklektos* (4899), means "elect together with," **1 Pet. 5:13**.

Saluteth *aspazomai* (782), signifies "to greet welcome," or "salute." In the KJV it is chiefly rendered by either of the verbs "to greet" or "to salute." "There is little doubt that the revisers have done wisely in giving 'salute' ... in the passages where KJV has 'greet.' For the cursory reader is sure to imagine a difference of Greek and of meaning when he finds, e.g., in Phil. 4:21, 'Salute every saint in Christ Jesus. The brethren which are with me greet you,' or in 3 John 14, 'Our friends salute thee. Greet the friends by name'" (*Hastings' Bible Dic.*). In Acts 25:13 the meaning virtually is "to pay his respects to." In two passages the renderings vary otherwise; in Acts 20:1, of bidding farewell, KJV, "embraced them," RV, "took leave of them," or, as Ramsay translates it, "bade them farewell"; in Heb. 11:13, of welcoming promises, KJV, "embraced," RV, "greeted." The verb is used as a technical term for conveying "greetings" at the close of a letter, often by an amanuensis, e.g., Rom. 16:22, the only instance of the use of the first person in this respect in the NT; see also 1 Cor. 16:19, 20; 2 Cor. 13:13; Phil. 4:22; Col. 4:10-15; 1 Thess. 5:26; 2 Tim. 4:21; Titus 3:15; Philem. 23; Heb. 13:24; **1 Pet. 5:13, 14**; 2 John 13. This special use is largely illustrated in the papyri, one example of this showing how keenly the absence of the greeting was felt. The papyri also illustrate the use of the addition "by name," when several persons are included in the greeting, as in 3 John 14 (Moulton and Milligan, *Vocab*).

5:14 Greet ye one another with a kiss of charity. Peace *be* with you all that are in Christ Jesus. Amen.

Greet *see* **Saluteth** at *1 Peter 5:13*.

Kiss *philema* (5370), "a kiss," Luke 7:45; 22:48, was a token of Christian brotherhood, whether by way of welcome or farewell, "a holy kiss," Rom. 16:16; 1 Cor. 16:20; 2 Cor. 13:12; 1 Thess. 5:26, "holy" (*hagios*), as free from anything inconsistent with their calling as saints (*hagioi*); "a kiss of love," **1 Pet. 5:14**. There was to be an absence of formality and hypocrisy, a freedom from prejudice arising from social distinctions, from discrimination against the poor, from partiality towards the well-to-do. In the churches masters and servants would thus salute one another without any attitude of condescension on the one part or disrespect on the other. The "kiss" took place thus between persons of the same sex. In the "Apostolic Constitutions," a writing compiled in the 4th century, AD, there is a reference to the custom whereby men sat on one side of the room where a meeting was held and women on the other side of the room (as is frequently the case still in parts of Europe and Asia), and the men are bidden to salute the men, and the women the women, with "the kiss of the Lord."

2 Peter

Chapter 1

1:1 Simon Peter, a servant and an apostle of Jesus Christ, to them that have obtained like precious faith with us through the righteousness of God and our Saviour Jesus Christ:

Servant *doulos* (1401), an adjective, signifying "in bondage," Rom. 6:19 (neuter plural, agreeing with *mele*, "members"), is used as a noun, and as the most common and general word for "servant," frequently indicating subjection without the idea of bondage; it is used (a) of natural conditions, e.g., Matt. 8:9; 1 Cor. 7:21, 22 (1st part); Eph. 6:5; Col. 4:1; 1 Tim. 6:1; frequently in the four Gospels; (b) metaphorically of spiritual, moral and ethical conditions: "servants" (1) of God, e.g., Acts 16:17; Titus 1:1; 1 Pet. 2:16; Rev. 7:3; 15:3; the perfect example being Christ Himself, Phil. 2:7; (2) of Christ, e.g., Rom. 1:1; 1 Cor. 7:22 (2nd part); Gal. 1:10; Eph. 6:6; Phil. 1:1; Col. 4:12; Jas. 1:1; **2 Pet. 1:1**; Jude 1; (3) of sin, John 8:34 (RV, "bondservants"); Rom. 6:17, 20; (4) of corruption, **2 Pet. 2:19** (RV, "bondservants"); cf. the verb *douloo*.

Obtained *lanchano* (2975), "to obtain by lot," is translated "that have obtained" in **2 Pet. 1:1**; in Acts 1:17, KJV, "had obtained" (RV, "received"), with *kleros*, "a lot" or "portion."

Like precious *isotimos* (2472), "of equal value, held in equal honor" (*isos*, "equal," and *time*, is used in **2 Pet. 1:1**, "a like precious (faith)," RV (marg., "an equally precious").

Righteousness *dikaiosune* (1343), is "the character or quality of being right or just"; it was formerly spelled "rightwiseness," which clearly expresses the meaning. It is used to denote an attribute of God, e.g., Rom. 3:5, the context of which shows that "the righteousness of God" means essentially the same as His faithfulness, or truthfulness, that which is consistent with His own nature and promises; Rom. 3:25, 26 speaks of His "righteousness" as exhibited in the death of Christ, which is sufficient to show men that God is neither indifferent to sin nor regards it lightly. On the contrary, it demonstrates that quality of holiness in Him which must find expression in His condemnation of sin.

"*Dikaiosune* is found in the sayings of the Lord Jesus, (a) of whatever is right or just in itself, whatever conforms to the revealed will of God, Matt. 5:6, 10, 20; John 16:8, 10; (b) whatever has been appointed by God to be acknowledged and obeyed by man, Matt. 3:15; 21:32; (c) the sum total of the requirements of God, Matt. 6:33; (d) religious duties, Matt. 6:1 (distinguished as almsgiving, man's duty to his neighbor, vv. 2-4, prayer, his duty to God, vv. 5-15, fasting, the duty of self-control, vv. 16–18). In the preaching of the apostles recorded in Acts the word has the same general meaning. So also in Jas. 1:20, 3:18, in both Epp. of Peter, 1st John and the Revelation. In **2 Pet. 1:1**, 'the righteousness of our God and Savior Jesus Christ,' is the righteous dealing of God with sin and with sinners on the ground of the death of Christ. 'Word of righteousness,' Heb. 5:13, is probably the gospel, and the Scriptures as containing the gospel, wherein is declared the righteousness of God in all its aspects. This meaning of *dikaiosune*, right action, is frequent also in Paul's writings, as in all five of its occurrences in Rom. 6; Eph. 6:14, etc. But for the most part he uses it of that gracious gift of God to men whereby all who believe on the Lord Jesus Christ are brought into right relationship with God. This righteousness is unattainable by obedience to any law, or by any merit of man's own, or any other condition than that of faith in Christ.... The man who trusts in Christ becomes 'the righteousness of God in Him,' 2 Cor. 5:21, i.e., becomes in Christ all that God requires a man to be, all that he could never be in himself Because

Abraham accepted the Word of God, making it his own by that act of the mind and spirit which is called faith, and, as the sequel showed, submitting himself to its control, therefore God accepted him as one who fulfilled the whole of His requirements, Rom. 4:3 ..."

God *theos* (2316) ...*Theos* is used (1) with the definite article, (2) without (i.e., as an anarthrous noun). "The English may or may not have need of the article in translation. But that point cuts no figure in the Greek idiom. Thus in Acts 27:23 ('the God whose I am,' RV) the article points out the special God whose Paul is, and is to be preserved in English. In the very next verse (*ho theos*) we in English do not need the article" (A. T. Robertson, *Gram. of Greek, NT*, p. 758). As to this latter it is usual to employ the article with a proper name, when mentioned a second time. There are, of course, exceptions to this, as when the absence of the article serves to lay stress upon, or give precision to, the character or nature of what is expressed in the noun. A notable instance of this is in John 1:1, "and the Word was God"; here a double stress is on *theos*, by the absence of the article and by the emphatic position. To translate it literally, "a god was the Word," is entirely misleading. Moreover, that "the Word" is the subject of the sentence, exemplifies the rule that the subject is to be determined by its having the article when the predicate is anarthrous (without the article). In Rom. 7:22, in the phrase "the law of God," both nouns have the article; in v. 25, neither has the article. This is in accordance with a general rule that if two nouns are united by the genitive case (the "of" case), either both have the article, or both are without. Here, in the first instance, both nouns, "God" and "the law" are definite, whereas in v. 25 the word "God" is not simply titular; the absence of the article stresses His character as lawgiver. Where two or more epithets are applied to the same person or thing, one article usually serves for both (the exceptions being when a second article lays stress upon different aspects of the same person or subject, e.g., Rev. 1:17). In Titus 2:13 the RV correctly has "our great God and Savior Jesus Christ." Moulton (*Prol.*, p. 84) shows, from papyri writings of the early Christian era, that among Greek-speaking Christians this was "a current formula" as applied to Christ. So in **2 Pet. 1:1** (cf. **1:11**; **3:18**). In the following titles God is described by certain of His attributes; the God of glory, Acts 7:2; of peace, Rom. 15:33; 16:20; Phil. 4:9; 1 Thess. 5:23; Heb. 13:20; of love and peace, 2 Cor. 13:11; of patience and comfort, Rom. 15:5; of all comfort, 2 Cor. 1:3; of hope, Rom. 15:13; of all grace, 1 Pet. 5:10. These describe Him, not as in distinction from other persons, but as the source of all these blessings; hence the employment of the definite article. In such phrases as "the God of a person," e.g., Matt. 22:32, the expression marks the relationship in which the person stands to God and God to him.

Saviour *soter* (4990), "a savior, deliverer, preserver," is used (a) of God, Luke 1:47; 1 Tim. 1:1; 2:3; 4:10 (in the sense of "preserver," since He gives "to all life and breath and all things"); Titus 1:3; 2:10; 3:4; Jude 25; (b) of Christ, Luke 2:11; John 4:42; Acts 5:31; 13:23 (of Israel); Eph. 5:23 (the sustainer and preserver of the church, His "body"); Phil. 3:20 (at His return to receive the Church to Himself); 2 Tim. 1:10 (with reference to His incarnation, "the days of His flesh"); Titus 1:4 (a title shared, in the context, with God the Father); 2:13, RV, "our great God and Savior Jesus Christ," the pronoun "our," at the beginning of the whole clause, includes all the titles; Titus 3:6; **2 Pet. 1:1**, "our God and Savior Jesus Christ; RV, where the pronoun "our," coming immediately in connection with "God," involves the inclusion of both titles as referring to Christ, just as in the parallel in v. **11**, "our Lord and Savior Jesus Christ" (KJV and RV); these passages are therefore a testimony to His deity; **2 Pet. 2:20**; **3:2**, **18**; 1 John 4:14.

1:2 Grace and peace be multiplied unto you through the knowledge of God, and of Jesus our Lord,

Multiplied *plethuno* (4129), used (a) transitively, denotes "to cause to increase, to multiply," 2 Cor. 9:10; Heb. 6:14 (twice); in the passive voice, "to be multiplied," Matt. 24:12, RV, "(iniquity) shall be multiplied" (KJV, "shall abound"); Acts 6:7; 7:17; 9:31; 12:24; 1 Pet. 1:2; **2 Pet. 1:2**; Jude 2; (b) intransitively it denotes "to be multiplying," Acts 6:1, RV, "was multiplying" (KJV, "was multiplied").

Knowledge *epignosis* (1922), denotes "exact or full knowledge, discernment, recognition," and is a strengthened form of *gnosis*, expressing a fuller or a full "knowledge," a greater participation by the "knower" in the object "known," thus more powerfully influencing him. It is not found in the Gospels and Acts. Paul uses it 15 times (16 if Heb. 10:26 is included) out of the 20 occurrences; Peter 4 times, all in his 2nd Epistle. Contrast Rom. 1:28 (*epignosis*) with the simple verb in v. 21. "In all the four Epistles of the first Roman captivity it is an element in the Apostle's opening prayer for his correspondents' well-being, Phil. 1:9; Eph. 1:17; Col. 1:9; Philem. 6" (Lightfoot). It is used with reference to God in Rom. 1:28; 10:2; Eph. 1:17; Col. 1:10; **2 Pet. 1:3**; God and Christ, **2 Pet. 1:2**; Christ, Eph. 4:13; **2 Pet. 1:8**; **2:20**; the will of the Lord, Col. 1:9; every good thing, Philem. 6, RV (KJV, "acknowledging"); the truth, 1 Tim. 2:4; 2 Tim. 2:25, RV; 3:7; Titus 1:1, RV; the mystery of God. Col. 2:2, RV, "(that they) may know" (KJV, "to the acknowledgment of"), lit., "into a full knowledge." It is used without the mention of an object in Phil. 1:9; Col. 3:10, RV, "(renewed) unto knowledge."

1:3 According as his divine power hath given unto us all things that *pertain* unto life and godliness, through the knowledge of him that hath called us to glory and virtue:

According as *hos* (5613), is sometimes rendered "according as," e.g., Rev. 22:12; in **2 Pet. 1:3**, the RV has "seeing that," for the KJV "according as."

Divine *theios* (2304), "divine" (from *theos*, "God"), is used of the power of God, **2 Pet. 1:3**, and of His nature, v. **4**, in each place, as that which proceeds from Himself. In Acts 17:29 it is used as a noun with the definite article, to denote "the Godhead," the Deity (i.e., the one true God). This word, instead of *theos*, was purposely used by the apostle in speaking to Greeks on Mars Hill, as in accordance with Greek usage. In the Sept., Exod. 31:3; 35:31; Job 27:3; 33:4; Prov. 2:17.

Given *doreo* (143), used in the middle voice, "to bestow, make a gift of," is translated in the RV by the verb "to grant," instead of the KJV, "to give," Mark 15:45; **2 Pet. 1:3**, **4**.

Godliness *eusebeia* (2150), from *eu*, "well," and *sebomai*, "to be devout," denotes that piety which, characterized by a Godward attitude, does that which is well-pleasing to Him. This and the corresponding verb and adverb are frequent in the Pastoral Epistles, but do not occur in previous epistles of Paul. The apostle Peter has the noun four times in his 2nd Epistle, **1:3**, **6**, **7**; **3:11**. Elsewhere it occurs in Acts 3:12; 1 Tim. 2:2; 3:16; 4:7, 8; 6:3, 5, 6, 11; 2 Tim. 3:5; Titus 1:1. In 1 Tim. 6:3 "the doctrine which is according to godliness" signifies that which is consistent with "godliness," in contrast to false teachings; in Titus 1:1, "the truth which is according to godliness" is that which is productive of "godliness"; in 1 Tim. 3:16, "the mystery of godliness" is "godliness" as embodied in, and communicated through, the truths of the faith concerning Christ; in **2 Pet. 3:11**, the word is in the plural, signifying acts of "godliness."

Knowledge *see 2 Peter 1:2.*

Virtue *arete* (703), properly denotes whatever procures preeminent estimation for a person or thing; hence, "intrinsic eminence, moral goodness, virtue," (a) of God, 1 Pet. 2:9, "excellencies" (KJV, "praises"); here the original and general sense seems to be blended with the impression made on others, i.e., renown, excellence or praise (Hort); in **2 Pet. 1:3**, "(by His own glory and) virtue," RV (instrumental dative), i.e., the manifestation of His divine power; this significance is frequently illustrated in the papyri and was evidently common in current Greek speech; (b) of any particular moral excellence, Phil. 4:8; **2 Pet. 1:5** (twice), where virtue is enjoined as an essential quality in the exercise of faith, RV, "(in your faith supply) virtue."

1:4 Whereby are given unto us exceeding great and precious promises: that by these ye might be partakers of the divine nature, having escaped the corruption that is in the world through lust.

Given *see 2 Peter 1:3.*

Great In **2 Pet. 1:4**, *megistos*, the superlative of *megas*, said of the promises of God, is rendered "exceeding great."

Precious *timios* (5093), from *time*, "honor, price," signifies (a), primarily, "accounted as of great price, precious, costly," 1 Cor. 3:12; Rev. 17:4; 18:12, 16; 21:19, and in the superlative degree, 18:12; 21:11; the comparative degree is found in 1 Pet. 1:7 (*polutimoteros*, in the most authentic mss., "much more precious"); (b) in the metaphorical sense, "held in honor, esteemed, very dear," Acts 5:34, "had in honor," RV (KJV, "had in reputation"); so in Heb. 13:4, RV, "let marriage be had in honor"; KJV, "is honorable"; Acts 20:24, "dear," negatively of Paul's estimate of his life; Jas. 5:7, "precious" (of fruit); 1 Pet. 1:19, "precious" (of the blood of Christ); **2 Pet. 1:4** (of God's promises). Cf. *timiotes*, preciousness, Rev. 18:19.

Promises *epangelma* (1862), denotes "a promise made," **2 Pet. 1:4**; **3:13**.

Partakers *koinonos* (2844), an adjective, signifying "having in common" (*koinos*, "common"), is used as a noun, denoting "a companion, partner, partaker," translated "partakers" in Matt. 23:30; 1 Cor. 10:18, KJV; 2 Cor. 1:7; Heb. 10:33, RV; **2 Pet. 1:4**; "partaker" in 1 Pet. 5:1.

Divine *see 2 Peter 1:3.*

Nature *phusis* (5449), from *phuo*, "to bring forth, produce," signifies (a) "the nature" (i.e., the natural

"The work of God is held back not by bad men and women, but by good ones who have stopped growing."

M. P. HORBAN

powers or constitution) of a person or thing, Eph. 2:3; Jas. 3:7 ("kind"); **2 Pet. 1:4**; (b) "origin, birth," Rom. 2:27, one who by birth is a Gentile, uncircumcised, in contrast to one who, though circumcised, has become spiritually uncircumcised by his iniquity; Gal. 2:15; (c) "the regular law or order of nature," Rom. 1:26, against "nature" (*para*, "against"); 2:14, adverbially, "by nature"; 1 Cor. 11:14; Gal. 4:8, "by nature (are no gods)," here "nature" is the emphatic word, and the phrase includes demons, men regarded as deified, and idols; these are gods only in name (the negative, *me*, denies not simply that they were gods, but the possibility that they could be).

Escaped *apopheugo* (668), "to flee away from," is used in **2 Pet. 1:4**; **2:18, 20**.

Corruption *phthora* (5356), connected with *phtheiro*, signifies "a bringing or being brought into an inferior or worse condition, a destruction or corruption." It is used (a) physically, (1) of the condition of creation, as under bondage, Rom. 8:21; (2) of the effect of the withdrawal of life, and so of the condition of the human body in burial, 1 Cor. 15:42; (3) by metonymy, of anything which is liable to "corruption," 1 Cor. 15:50; (4) of the physical effects of merely gratifying the natural desires and ministering to one's own needs or lusts, Gal. 6:8, to the flesh in contrast to the Spirit, "corruption" being antithetic to "eternal life"; (5) of that which is naturally short-lived and transient, Col. 2:22, "perish"; (b) of the death and decay of beasts, **2 Pet. 2:12**, RV, "destroyed" (first part of verse; lit., "unto ... destruction"); (c) ethically, with a moral significance, (1) of the effect of lusts, **2 Pet. 1:4**; (2) of the effect upon themselves of the work of false and immoral teachers, **2 Pet. 2:12**, RV, "destroying"; KJV, "corruption," and verse **19**.

1:5 And beside this, giving all diligence, add to your faith virtue; and to virtue knowledge;

Beside In **2 Pet. 1:5**, the phrase, wrongly translated in the KJV, "beside this," means "for this very cause" (RV).

Giving For *pareisphero*, "to add," rendered "giving" in **2 Pet. 1:5**, KJV.

Diligence *spoude* (4710), "earnestness, zeal," or sometimes "the haste accompanying this," Mark 6:25; Luke 1:39, is translated "diligence" in Rom. 12:8; in v. 11, KJV, "business" (RV, "diligence"); in 2 Cor. 8:7, KJV, "diligence," RV, "earnestness"; both have "diligence" in Heb. 6:11; **2 Pet. 1:5**; Jude 3; in 2 Cor. 7:11, 12, RV, "earnest care," KJV, "carefulness," and "care."

Add *epichoregeo* (2023), "to supply fully, abundantly" (a strengthened form), is rendered "to supply" in the RV of 2 Cor. 9:10 (1st part) and Gal. 3:5 (for KJV, "to minister"), where the present continuous tense speaks of the work of the Holy Spirit in all His ministrations to believers individually and collectively; in Col. 2:19, RV, "being supplied" (KJV, "having nourishment ministered"), of the work of Christ as the Head of the church His body, in **2 Pet. 1:5**, "supply" (KJV, "add"); in v. **11**, "shall be ... supplied" (KJV, "shall be ministered"), of the reward hereafter which those are to receive, in regard to positions in the kingdom of God, for their fulfillment here of the conditions mentioned.

Virtue *see 2 Peter 1:3.*

Knowledge *gnosis* (1108), primarily "a seeking to know, an enquiry, investigation," denotes, in the NT, "knowledge," especially of spiritual truth; it is used (a) absolutely, in Luke 11:52; Rom. 2:20; 15:14; 1 Cor. 1:5; 8:1 (twice), 7, 10, 11; 13:2, 8; 14:6; 2 Cor. 6:6; 8:7; 11:6; Eph. 3:19; Col. 2:3; 1 Pet. 3:7; **2 Pet. 1:5, 6**; (b) with an object: in respect of (1) God, 2 Cor. 2:14; 10:5; (2) the glory of God, 2 Cor. 4:6; (3) Christ Jesus, Phil. 3:8; **2 Pet. 3:18**; (4) salvation, Luke 1:77; (c) subjectively, of God's "knowledge," Rom. 11:33; the word of "knowledge," 1 Cor. 12:8; "knowledge" falsely so called, 1 Tim. 6:20.

1:6 And to knowledge temperance; and to temperance patience; and to patience godliness;

Knowledge *see 2 Peter 1:5.*

Temperance *enkrateia* (1466), from *kratos*, "strength," occurs in Acts 24:25; Gal. 5:23; **2 Pet. 1:6** (twice), in all of which it is rendered "temperance"; the RV marg., "self-control" is the preferable rendering, as "temperance" is now limited to one form of self-control; the various powers bestowed by God upon man are capable of abuse; the right use demands the controlling power of the will under the operation of the Spirit of God; in Acts 24:25 the word follows "righteousness," which represents God's claims, self-control being man's response thereto; in **2 Pet. 1:6**, it follows "knowledge," suggesting that what is learned requires to be put into practice.

Godliness *see 2 Peter 1:3.*

1:7 And to godliness brotherly kindness; and to brotherly kindness charity.

Godliness *see 2 Peter 1:3.*

Brotherly Associated words are *adelphotes*, primarily, "a brotherly relation," and so, the community possessed of this relation, "a brotherhood," 1 Pet. 2:17 (see 5:9, marg.).; *philadelphos*, (*phileo*, "to love," and *adelphos*), "fond of one's brethren," 1 Pet. 3:8; "loving as brethren," RV; *philadelphia*, "brotherly love," Rom. 12:10; 1 Thess. 4:9; Heb. 13:1; "love of the brethren," 1 Pet. 1:22 and **2 Pet. 1:7**, RV; *pseudadelphos*, "false brethren," 2 Cor. 11:26; Gal. 2:4. **Charity** *agapao* (25), and the corresponding noun *agape* present "the characteristic word of Christianity, and since the Spirit of revelation has used it to express ideas previously unknown, inquiry into its use, whether in Greek literature or in the Septuagint, throws but little light upon its distinctive meaning in the NT. Cf, however, Lev. 19:18; Deut. 6:5.

"*Agape* and *agapao* are used in the NT (a) to describe the attitude of God toward His Son, John 17:26; the human race, generally, John 3:16; Rom. 5:8, and to such as believe on the Lord Jesus Christ particularly John 14:21; (b) to convey His will to His children concerning their attitude one toward another, John 13:34, and toward all men, 1 Thess. 3:12; 1 Cor. 16:14; **2 Pet. 1:7**; (c) to express the essential nature of God, 1 John 4:8. Love can be known only from the actions it prompts. God's love is seen in the gift of His Son, 1 John 4:9, 10. But obviously this is not the love of complacency, or affection, that is, it was not drawn out by any excellency in its objects, Rom. 5:8. It was an exercise of the divine will in deliberate choice, made without assignable cause save that which lies in the nature of God Himself, Cf. Deut. 7:7, 8. Love had its perfect expression among men in the Lord Jesus Christ, 2 Cor. 5:14; Eph. 2:4; 3:19; 5:2; Christian love is the fruit of His Spirit in the Christian, Gal. 5:22. Christian love has God for its primary object, and expresses itself first of all in implicit obedience to His commandments, John 14:15, 21, 23; 15:10; 1 John 2:5; 5:3; 2 John 6. Selfwill, that is, self-pleasing, is the negation of love to God. Christian love, whether exercised toward the brethren, or toward men generally, is not an impulse from the feelings, it does not always run with the natural inclinations, nor does it spend itself only upon those for whom some affinity is discovered. Love seeks the welfare of all, Rom. 15:2, and works no ill to any, 13:8-10; love seeks opportunity to do good to 'all men, and especially toward them that are of the household of the faith,' Gal. 6:10. See further 1 Cor. 13 and Col. 3:12-14."

1:8 For if these things be in you, and abound, they make *you that ye shall* neither *be* barren nor unfruitful in the knowledge of our Lord Jesus Christ.

Abound *pleonazo* (4121), from *pleion*, or *pleon*, "more" (greater in quantity), akin to *pleo*, "to fill," signifies, (a) intransitively, "to superabound," of a trespass or sin, Rom. 5:20; of grace, Rom. 6:1; 2 Cor. 4:15; of spiritual fruit, Phil. 4:17; of love, 2 Thess. 1:3; of various fruits, **2 Pet. 1:8**; of the gathering of the manna, 2 Cor. 8:15, "had ... over"; (b) transitively, "to make to increase," 1 Thess. 3:12.

Barren *argos* (692), denoting "idle, barren, yielding no return, because of inactivity," is found in the best mss. in Jas. 2:20 (RV, "barren"); it is rendered "barren" in **2 Pet. 1:8**, KJV, (RV, "idle"). In Matt. 12:36, the "idle word" means the word that is thoughtless or profitless.

Unfruitful *akarpos* (175), "unfruitful," is used figuratively (a) of "the word of the Kingdom," rendered "unfruitful" in the case of those influenced by the cares of the world and the deceitfulness of riches, Matt. 13:22; Mark 4:19; (b) of the understanding of one praying with a "tongue," which effected no profit to the church without an interpretation of it, 1 Cor. 14:14; (c) of the works of darkness, Eph. 5:11; (d) of believers who fail "to maintain good works," indicating the earning of one's living so as to do good works to others, Titus 3:14; of the effects of failing to supply in one's faith the qualities of virtue, knowledge, temperance, patience, godliness, love of the brethren, and love, **2 Pet. 1:8**. In Jude 12 it is rendered "without fruit," of ungodly men, who oppose the gospel while pretending to uphold it, depicted as "autumn trees." In the Sept., Jer. 2:6.

Knowledge *see 2 Peter 1:2.*

1:9 But he that lacketh these things is blind, and cannot see afar off, and hath forgotten that he was purged from his old sins.

Lacketh In **2 Pet. 1:9**, "he that lacketh" translates a phrase the lit. rendering of which is "(he to whom these things) are not present" (*pareimi*, "to be present").

Blind *tuphlos* (5185), "blind," is used both physically and metaphorically, chiefly in the Gospels; elsewhere four times; physically, Acts 13:11; metaphorically, Rom. 2:19; **2 Pet. 1:9**; Rev. 3:17. The word is frequently used as a noun, signifying "a blind man."

See *muopazo* (3467), "to be shortsighted" (*muo*, "to shut," *ops*, "the eye"; cf. Eng., "myopy," "myopic": the root *mu* signifies a sound made with closed lips, e.g., in the words "mutter," "mute"), occurs in **2 Pet. 1:9**, RV, "seeing only what is near" (KJV, "and cannot see afar oft"); this does not contradict the preceding word "blind," it qualifies it; he of whom it is true is blind in that he cannot discern spiritual things, he is near-sighted in that he is occupied in regarding worldly affairs.

Afar In **2 Pet. 1:9**, *muopazo*, "to be shortsighted," is translated "cannot see afar off" (KJV); RV, "seeing only what is near."

Forgotten *lethe* (3024), "forgetfulness" (from *letho*, "to forget," an old form of *lanthano*; cf. Eng. "lethal," "lethargy," and the mythical river "Lethe," which was supposed to cause forgetfulness of the past to those who drank of it), is used with *lambano*, "to take," in **2 Pet. 1:9**, "having forgotten," lit., "having taken forgetfulness" (cf. 2 Tim. 1:5, lit., "having taken reminder"), a periphrastic expression for a single verb.

Purged *katharismos* (2512), denotes "cleansing," (a) both the action and its results, in the Levitical sense, Mark 1:44; Luke 2:22, "purification"; 5:14, "cleansing"; John 2:6; 3:25, "purifying"; (b) in the moral sense, from sins, Heb. 1:3; **2 Pet. 1:9**, RV, "cleansing.

Old *palai* (3819), denotes "long ago, of old," Heb. 1:1, RV, "of old time" (KJV, "in time past"); in Jude 4, "of old"; it is used as an adjective in **2 Pet. 1:9**, "(his) old (sins)," lit., "his sins of old."

Sins *hamartema* (265), denotes "an act of disobedience to divine law"; plural in Mark 3:28; Rom. 3:25; **2 Pet. 1:9**, in some texts; sing. in Mark 3:29 (some mss. have *krisis*, KJV, "damnation"); 1 Cor. 6:18.

1:10 Wherefore the rather, brethren, give diligence to make your calling and election sure: for if ye do these things, ye shall never fall:

Wherefore *dio* = *dia ho* (the neuter of the relative pronoun *hos*), "on account of which (thing)," e.g., Matt. 27:8; Acts 15:19; 20:31; 24:26; 25:26; 27:25, 34; Rom. 1:24; 15:7; 1 Cor. 12:3; 2 Cor. 2:8; 5:9; 6:17; Eph. 2:11; 3:13; 4:8, 25; 5:14; Phil. 2:9; 1 Thess. 5:11; Philem. 8; Heb. 3:7, 10; 10:5; 11:16; 12:12, 28; 13:12; Jas. 1:21; 4:6; 1 Pet. 1:13; **2 Pet. 1:10, 12; 3:14**.

Rather *mallon* (3123), the comparative degree of *mala*, "very, very much," is frequently translated "rather," e.g., Matt. 10:6, 28; 1 Cor. 14:1, 5; sometimes followed by "than," with a connecting particle, e.g., Matt. 18:13 ("more than"); or without, e.g., John 3:19; Acts 4:19, RV (KJV, "more"); in 1 Cor. 9:12, KJV, "rather" (RV, "yet more"); 12:22, RV, "rather" (KJV, "more"); 2 Cor. 3:9 (ditto); Philem. 16 (ditto); in **2 Pet. 1:10**, KJV, "the rather" (RV, "the more").

Diligence *spoudazo* (4704) ... signifies "to hasten to do a thing, to exert oneself, endeavor, give diligence"; in Gal. 2:10, of remembering the poor, KJV, "was forward," RV, "was zealous"; in Eph. 4:3, of keeping the unity of the Spirit, KJV "endeavoring," RV, "giving diligence"; in 1 Thess. 2:17, of going to see friends, "endeavored"; in 2 Tim. 4:9; 4:21, "do thy diligence"; in the following the RV uses the verb "to give diligence": 2 Tim. 2:15, KJV, "study"; Titus 3:12, KJV, "be diligent"; Heb. 4:11, of keeping continuous Sabbath rest, KJV, "let us labor"; in **2 Pet. 1:10**, of making our calling and election sure; in **2 Pet. 1:15**, of enabling believers to call Scripture truth to remembrance, KJV, "endeavour"; in **2 Pet. 3:14**, of being found in peace without fault and blameless, when the Lord comes, KJV, "be diligent."

Make *poieo* (4160), "to do, to make," is used in the latter sense (a) of constructing or producing anything, of the creative acts of God, e.g., Matt. 19:4 (2nd part); Acts 17:24; of the acts of human beings, e.g., Matt. 17:4; Acts 9:39; (b) with nouns denoting a state or condition, to be the author of, to cause, e.g., peace, Eph. 2:15; Jas. 3:18; stumbling blocks, Rom. 16:17; (c) with nouns involving the idea of action (or of something accomplished by action), so as to express the idea of the verb more forcibly (the middle voice is commonly used in this respect, suggesting the action as being of special interest to the doer); for the active voice see, e.g., Mark 2:23, of "making" one's way, where the idea is not that the disciples "made" a path through the standing corn, but simply that they went, the phrase being equivalent to going, "(they began) as they went (to pluck the ears)"; other instances of the active are Rev. 13:13, 14; 16:14; 19:20; for the middle voice (the dynamic or subjective middle), see, e.g., John 14:23, "will make Our abode"; in Acts 20:24, "none of these things move me," lit., "I make account of none of these things"; 25:17, "I made no delay" RV, Rom. 15:26; Eph. 4:16; Heb. 1:2; **2 Pet. 1:10**; (d) to "make" ready or prepare, e.g., a dinner, Luke 14:12; a supper, John 12:2; (e) to acquire, provide a thing for oneself, Matt. 25:16; Luke 19:18; (f) to render or "make" one or oneself anything, or cause a person or thing to become something, e.g., Matt. 4:19; 12:16, "make (Him known)"; John 5:11, 15, to "make" whole; 16:2, lit., "they shall make (you put out of the synagogue)"; Eph. 2:14; Heb. 1:7; to change one thing into another, Matt. 21:13; John 2:16; 4:46; 1 Cor. 6:15; (g) to constitute one anything, e.g., Acts 2:36, (h) to declare one or oneself anything, John 5:18, "making (Himself equal with God)"; 8:53; 10:33; 19:7, 12; 1 John 1:10; 5:10; (i) to "make" one do a thing, e.g., Luke 5:34; John 6:10; Rev. 3:9.

Calling *klesis* (2821), "a calling," is always used in the NT of that "calling" the origin, nature and destiny of which are heavenly (the idea of invitation being implied); it is used especially of God's invitation to man to accept the benefits of salvation, Rom. 11:29; 1 Cor. 1:26; 7:20 (said there of the condition in which the "calling" finds one); Eph. 1:18, "His calling"; Phil. 3:14, the "high calling"; 2 Thess. 1:11 and **2 Pet. 1:10**, "your calling"; 2 Tim. 1:9, a "holy calling"; Heb. 3:1, a "heavenly calling"; Eph. 4:1, "the calling wherewith ye were called"; 4:4, "in one hope of your calling."

Election *ekloge* (1589), denotes "a picking out, selection" (Eng., "eclogue"), then, "that which is chosen"; in Acts 9:15, said of the "choice" of God of Saul of Tarsus, the phrase is, lit., "a vessel of choice." It is used four times in Romans; in 9:11, of Esau and Jacob, where the phrase "the purpose ... according to election" is virtually equivalent to "the electing purpose"; in 11:5, the "remnant according to the election of grace" refers to believing Jews, saved from among the unbelieving nation; so in v. 7; in v. 28, "the election" may mean either the "act of choosing" or the "chosen" ones; the context, speaking of the fathers, points to the former, the choice of the nation according to the covenant of promise. In 1 Thess. 1:4, "your election" refers not to the church collectively, but to the individuals constituting it; the apostle's assurance of their "election" gives the reason for his thanksgiving. Believers are to give "the more diligence to make their calling and election sure," by the exercise of the qualities and graces which make them fruitful in the knowledge of God, **2 Pet. 1:10**.

Sure *bebaios* (949), "firm, steadfast," is used of (a) God's promise to Abraham, Rom. 4:16; (b) the believer's hope, Heb. 6:19, "steadfast"; (c) the hope of spiritual leaders regarding the welfare of converts, 2 Cor. 1:7, "steadfast"; (d) the glorying of the hope, Heb. 3:6, "firm"; (e) the beginning of our confidence, 3:14, RV, "firm" (KJV, "steadfast"); (f) the Law given at Sinai, Heb. 2:2, "steadfast"; (g) the testament (or covenant) fulfilled after a death, 9:17, "of force"; (h) the calling and election of believers, **2 Pet. 1:10**, to be made "sure" by the fulfillment of the injunctions in vv. **5-7**; (i) the word of prophecy, "*made* more sure," **2 Pet. 1:19**, RV, KJV, "a more sure (word of prophecy)"; what is meant is not a comparison between the prophecies of the OT and NT, but that the former have been confirmed in the person of Christ (vv. **16-18**).

Never In **2 Pet. 1:10**, "never" is the translation of *ou me pote*, i.e., "by no means ever"; so with the double negative followed by the extended word *popote*, i.e., "by no means not even at any time," John 6:35 (2nd part).

Fall *ptaio* (4417), "to cause to stumble," signifies, intransitively, "to stumble," used metaphorically in Rom. 11:11 ...; with moral significance in Jas. 2:10 and 3:2 (twice), RV, "stumble" (KJV, "offend"); in **2 Pet. 1:10**, RV, "stumble" (KJV, "fall").

1:11 For so an entrance shall be ministered unto you abundantly into the everlasting kingdom of our Lord and Saviour Jesus Christ.

Entrance *eisodos* (1529), lit., "a way in" (*eis*, "in," *hodos*, "a way"), "an entrance," is used (a) of the "coming" of Christ into the midst of the Jewish nation, Acts 13:24, RV marg., "entering in"; (b) of "entrance" upon gospel work in a locality, 1 Thess. 1:9; 2:1; (c) of the present "access" of believers into God's presence, Heb. 10:19, lit., "for entrance into"; (d) of their "entrance" into Christ's eternal Kingdom, **2 Pet. 1:11**.

Ministered *see* **Giving** at *2 Peter 1:5*.

Abundantly *plousios* (4146), connected with *ploutos*, "riches," is rendered "abundantly," Titus 3:6 and **2 Pet. 1:11**; "richly," Col. 3:16 and 1 Tim. 6:17. It is used of (a) the gift of the Holy Spirit; (b) entrance into the coming kingdom; (c) the indwelling of the Word of Christ; (d) material benefits.

Everlasting *aionios* (166), "describes duration, either undefined but not endless, as in Rom. 16:25; 2 Tim. 1:9; Titus 1:2; or undefined because endless as in Rom. 16:26, and the other sixty-six places in the NT.

"The predominant meaning

of *aionios*, that in which it is used everywhere in the NT, save the places noted above, may be seen in 2 Cor. 4:18, where it is set in contrast with *proskairos*, lit., 'for a season,' and in Philem. 15, where only in the NT it is used without a noun. Moreover it is used of persons and things which are in their nature endless, as, e.g., of God, Rom. 16:26; of His power, 1 Tim. 6:16, and of His glory, 1 Pet. 5:10; of the Holy Spirit, Heb. 9:14; of the redemption effected by Christ, Heb. 9:12, and of the consequent salvation of men, 5:9, as well as of His future rule, **2 Pet. 1:11**, which is elsewhere declared to be without end, Luke 1:33; of the life received by those who believe in Christ, John 3:16, concerning whom He said, 'they shall never perish,' 10:28, and of the resurrection body, 2 Cor. 5:1, elsewhere said to be 'immortal,' 1 Cor. 15:53, in which that life will be finally realized, Matt. 25:46; Titus 1:2. *Aionios* is also used of the sin that 'hath never forgiveness,' Mark 3:29, and of the judgment of God, from which there is no appeal, Heb. 6:2, and of the fire, which is one of its instruments, Matt. 18:8; 25:41; Jude 7, and which is elsewhere said to be 'unquenchable,' Mark 9:43. The use of *aionios* here shows that the punishment referred to in 2 Thess. 1:9, is not temporary, but final, and, accordingly, the phraseology shows that its purpose is not remedial but retributive."

Kingdom *basileia* (932), is primarily an abstract noun, denoting "sovereignty, royal power, dominion." It is used especially of the "kingdom" of God and of Christ.

"The Kingdom of God is (a) the sphere of God's rule, Ps. 22:28; 145:13; Dan. 4:25; Luke 1:52; Rom. 13:1, 2. Since, however, this earth is the scene of universal rebellion against God, e.g., Luke 4:5, 6; 1 John 5:19; Rev. 11:15-18, the "kingdom" of God is (b) the sphere in which, at any given time, His rule is acknowledged. God has not relinquished His sovereignty in the face of rebellion, demoniac and human, but has declared His purpose to establish it, Dan. 2:44; 7:14; 1 Cor. 15:24, 25. Meantime, seeking willing obedience, He gave His law to a nation and appointed kings to administer His "kingdom" over it, 1 Chron. 28:5. Israel, however, though declaring still a nominal allegiance shared in the common rebellion, Isa. 1:2-4, and, after they had rejected the Son of God, John 1:11 (cf. Matt. 21:33-43), were "cast away," Rom. 11:15, 20, 25. Henceforth God calls upon men everywhere, without distinction of race or nationality, to submit voluntarily to His rule. Thus the "kingdom" is said to be "in mystery" now, Mark 4:11, that is, it does not come within the range of the natural powers of observation, Luke 17:20, but is spiritually discerned, John 3:3 (cf. 1 Cor. 2:14). When, hereafter, God asserts His rule universally, then the "kingdom" will be in glory, that is, it will be manifest to all; cf. Matt. 25:31-34; Phil. 2:9-11; 2 Tim. 4:1, 18. Thus, speaking generally, references to the Kingdom fall into two classes, the first, in which it is viewed as present and involving suffering for those who enter it, 2 Thess. 1:5; the second, in which it is viewed as future and is associated with reward, Matt. 25:34, and glory, 13:43. See also Acts 14:22. The fundamental principle of the Kingdom is declared in the words of the Lord spoken in the midst of a company of Pharisees, "the Kingdom of God is in the midst of you," Luke 17:21, marg., that is, where the King is, there is the Kingdom. Thus at the present time and so far as this earth is concerned, where the King is and where His rule is acknowledged, is, first, in the heart of the individual believer, Acts 4:19; Eph. 3:17; 1 Pet. 3:15; and then in the churches of God, 1 Cor. 12:3, 5, 11; 14:37; cf. Col. 1:27, where for "in" read "among." Now, the King and His rule being refused, those who enter the Kingdom of God are brought into conflict with all who disown its allegiance, as well as with the desire for ease, and the dislike of suffering and unpopularity, natural to all. On the other hand, subjects of the Kingdom are the objects of the care of God, Matt. 6:33, and of the rejected King, Heb. 13:5. Entrance into the Kingdom of God is by the new birth, Matt. 18:3; John 3:5, for nothing that a man may be by nature, or can attain to by any form of self-culture, avails in the spiritual realm. And as the new nature, received in the new birth, is made evident by obedience, it is further said that only such as do the will of God shall enter into His Kingdom, Matt. 7:21, where, however, the context shows that the reference is to the future, as in **2 Pet. 1:10, 11**. Cf. also 1 Cor. 6:9, 10; Gal. 5:21; Eph. 5:5. The expression 'Kingdom of God' occurs four times in Matthew, 'Kingdom of the Heavens' usually taking its place. The latter (cf. Dan. 4:26) does not occur elsewhere in NT, but see 2 Tim. 4:18, "His heavenly Kingdom." ... This Kingdom is identical with the Kingdom of the Father (cf. Matt. 26:29 with Mark 14:25), and with the Kingdom of the Son (cf. Luke 22:30). Thus there is but one Kingdom, variously described: of the Son of Man, Matt. 13:41; of Jesus, Rev. 1:9; of Christ Jesus, 2 Tim. 4:1; "of Christ and God," Eph. 5:5; "of our Lord, and of

His Christ," Rev. 11:15; "of our God, and the authority of His Christ," 12:10; "of the Son of His love," Col. 1:13. Concerning the future, the Lord taught His disciples to pray, "Thy Kingdom come," Matt. 6:10, where the verb is in the point tense, precluding the notion of gradual progress and development, and implying a sudden catastrophe as declared in 2 Thess. 2:8."

Saviour *see 2 Peter 1:1.*

1:12 Wherefore I will not be negligent to put you always in remembrance of these things, though ye know *them*, and be established in the present truth.

Wherefore *see 2 Peter 1:10.*

Negligent *mello* (3195), "to be about to," is translated "to be ready" in **2 Pet. 1:12**, RV, where the future indicates that the apostle will be prepared, as in the past and the present, to remind his readers of the truths they know (some mss. have *ouk ameleso*, "I will not be negligent," KJV; cf., however, v. **15**. Field, in *Notes on the Translation of the NT*, suggests that the true reading is *meleso*, the future of *melo*, "to be a care, or an object of care"); in Rev. 3:2, RV, "were ready" (some texts have the present tense, as in the KJV). Elsewhere, where the KJV has the rendering to be ready, the RV gives renderings in accordance with the usual significance as follows: Luke 7:2, "was ... at the point of"; Acts 20:7, "intending"; Rev. 12:4, "about (to)."

Always *aei* (104), has two meanings: (a) "perpetually, incessantly," Acts 7:51; 2 Cor. 4:11; 6:10; Titus 1:12; Heb. 3:10; (b) "invariably, at any and every time," of successive occurrences, when some thing is to be repeated, according to the circumstances, 1 Pet. 3:15; **2 Pet. 1:12**.

Established *sterizo* (4741), "to fix, make fast, to set" (from *sterix*, "a prop"), is used of "establishing" or "stablishing" (i.e., the confirmation) of persons; the apostle Peter was called by the Lord to "establish" his brethren, Luke 22:32, translated "strengthen"; Paul desired to visit Rome that the saints might be "established," Rom. 1:11; cf. Acts 8:23; so with Timothy at Thessalonica, 1 Thess. 3:2; the "confirmation" of the saints is the work of God, Rom. 16:25, "to stablish (you)"; 1 Thess. 3:13, "stablish (your hearts)"; 2 Thess. 2:17, "stablish them (in every good work and word)"; 1 Pet. 5:10, "stablish"; the means used to eflect the "confirmation" is the ministry of the Word of God, **2 Pet. 1:12**, "are established (in the truth which is with you)"; James exhorts Christians to "stablish" their hearts, Jas. 5:8; cf. Rev. 3:2, RV. The character of this "confirmation" may be learned from its use in Luke 9:51, "steadfastly set"; 16:26, "fixed," and in the Sept. in Exod. 17:12, "stayed up" (also from its strengthened form *episterizo*, "to confirm," in Acts 14:22; 15:32, 41; in some mss. "to strengthen," in 18:23). Neither the laying on of hands nor the impartation of the Holy Spirit is mentioned in the NT in connection with either of these words, or with the synonymous verb *bebaioo* (see 1 Cor. 1:8; 2 Cor. 1:21, etc.).

Present *pareimi* (3918), signifies (a) "to be by, at hand or present," of persons, e.g., Luke 13:1; Acts 10:33; 24:19; 1 Cor. 5:3; 2 Cor. 10:2, 11; Gal. 4:18, 20; of things, John 7:6, of a particular season in the Lord's life on earth, "is (not yet) come," or "is not yet at hand"; Heb. 12:11, of chastening "(for the) present" (the neuter of the present participle, used as a noun); in 13:5 "such things as ye have" is, lit., "the things that are present"; **2 Pet. 1:12**, of the truth "(which) is with (you)" (not as KJV, "the present truth," as if of special doctrines applicable to a particular time); in v. **9** "he that lacketh" is lit., "to whom are not present"; (b) "to have arrived or come," Matt. 26:50, "thou art come," RV; John 11:28; Acts 10:21; Col. 1:6.

1:13 Yea, I think it meet, as long as I am in this tabernacle, to stir you up by putting *you* in remembrance;

Think *hegeomai* (2233), is rendered "to think" in Acts 26:2; 2 Cor. 9:5, "I thought"; Phil. 2:6, KJV (RV, "counted"); **2 Pet. 1:13**.

Meet *dikaios* (1342), "just, righteous, that which is in accordance with" *dike*, "rule, right, justice," is translated "right" in Matt. 20:4; v. 7, KJV only (RV omits, according to the most authentic mss., the clause having been inserted from v. 4, to the detriment of the narrative); Luke 12:57; Acts 4:19; Eph. 6:1; Phil. 1:7, RV (KJV, "meet"); **2 Pet. 1:13** (KJV, "meet").

Tabernacle *skenoma* (4638), "a booth," or "tent pitched," is used of the Temple as God's dwelling, as that which David desired to build, Acts 7:46 (RV, "habitation," KJV, "tabernacle"); metaphorically of the body as a temporary tabernacle, **2 Pet. 1:13, 14**.

Stir ... up *diegeiro* (1326), is used of "awaking from natural sleep," Matt. 1:24; Mark 4:38; of the act of the disciples in "awaking" the Lord, Luke 8:24 (cf. *egeiro*, in Matt. 8:25); metaphorically, "of arousing the mind," **2 Pet. 1:13; 3:1**.

Remembrance *hupomnesis* (5280), denotes "a reminding, a reminder"; in 2 Tim. 1:5 it is used with *lambano*, "to receive," lit., "having received a reminder," RV, "having been reminded" (KJV, "when I call to remembrance"); in **2 Pet. 1:13** and **3:1**, "remembrance."

1:14 Knowing that shortly I must put off *this* my tabernacle, even as our Lord Jesus Christ hath shewed me.

Shortly *tachinos* (5031) "of swift approach," is used in **2 Pet. 1:14**, RV, "swiftly" (KJV, "shortly"), lit., "(the putting off of my tabernacle is) swift," i.e., "imminent"; in **2:1**, "swift (destruction)." In the Sept., Prov. 1:16; Isa. 59:7; Hab. 1:6.

Must In **2 Pet. 1:14**, KJV, the verb "to be," with *apothesis*, "a putting off," is translated "I must put off," RV, "(the) putting off ... cometh," lit., "is (swift)."

Put *apothesis* (595), "a putting off or away" (akin to *apotithemi*), is used metaphorically in 1 Pet. 3:21, of the "putting" away of the filth of the flesh; in **2 Pet. 1:14**, RV, of "the putting off" of the body (as a tabernacle) at death (KJV, "I must put off").

Tabernacle *see 2 Peter 1:13*.

Shewed *deloo* (1213), "to make plain" (*delos*, "evident"), is translated "to signify" in 1 Cor. 1:11, RV, "it hath been signified" (KJV, "declared"); Heb. 9:8; 12:27; 1 Pet. 1:11, KJV (RV, "point unto"); **2 Pet. 1:14**, RV, "signified" (KJV, "hath showed").

1:15 Moreover I will endeavour that ye may be able after my decease to have these things always in remembrance.

Moreover *de* (1161), a particle signifying "and" or "but," is translated "moreover" in Matt. 18:15, KJV (RV, "and"); Acts 11:12 (RV, "and"); Rom. 5:20, KJV (RV, "but"); 8:30 ("and"); 1 Cor. 15:1 (RV, "now"); 2 Cor. 1:23 (RV, "but"); **2 Pet. 1:15** (RV, "yea").

Endeavour *spoudazo* (4704), "to make haste, to be zealous," and hence, "to be diligent," is rendered "endeavoring" in Eph. 4:3, KJV; RV, "giving diligence." In **2 Pet. 1:15**, KJV, "endeavor," RV, "give diligence." Both have "endeavored in 1 Thess. 2:17. *See also* **Diligence** at *2 Peter 1:10*.

Able *echo* (2192), "to have," is translated "your ability" in 2 Cor. 8:11, and "ye may be able" in **2 Pet. 1:15**, and is equivalent to the phrase "to have the means of."

Decease *exodos* (1841), (Eng., "exodus"), lit. signifies "a way out" (*ex*, "out," *hodos*, "a way"); hence, "a departure," especially from life, "a decease"; in Luke 9:31, of the Lord's death, "which He was about to accomplish"; in **2 Pet. 1:15**, of Peter's death (marg., "departure" in each case); "departure" in Heb. 11:22, RV.

Always *hekastote* (1539), from *hekastos*, "each," is used in **2 Pet. 1:15**, RV, "at every time" (KJV, "always").

Remembrance *mneme* (3420), denotes "a memory" (akin to *mnaomai*), "remembrance, mention," **2 Pet. 1:15**, "remembrance"; here, however, it is used with *poieo*, "to make" (middle voice), and some suggest that the meaning is "to make mention." *mneia* (3417), "remembrance, mention" (akin to *mimnesko*, "to remind, remember"), is always used in connection with prayer, and translated "mention" in Rom. 1:9; Eph. 1:16; 1 Thess. 1:2; Philem. 4, in each of which it is preceded by the verb to make; "remembrance" in Phil. 1:3; 1 Thess. 3:6; 2 Tim. 1:3. Some mss. have it in Rom. 12:13, instead of *chreiais*, necessities. Cf. *mneme*, "memory, remembrance," **2 Pet. 1:15**.

1:16 For we have not followed cunningly devised fables, when we made known unto you the power and coming of our Lord Jesus Christ, but were eyewitnesses of his majesty.

Followed *exakoloutheo* (1811), "to follow up, or out to the end," is used metaphorically, and only by the apostle Peter in his second epistle: in **1:16**, of cunningly devised fables; **2:2** of lascivious doings; **2:15**, of the way of Balaam. In the Sept., Job 31:9; Is. 56:11; Jer. 2:2; Amos 2:4.

Devised *sophizo* (4679), from *sophos*, "wise" (connected etymologically with *sophes*, "tasty"), in the active voice signifies "to make wise," 2 Tim. 3:15 (so in the Sept. of Ps. 19:7, e.g., "making babes wise"; in 119:98, "Thou hast made me wiser than mine enemies"). In the middle voice it means (a) "to become wise"; it is not used thus in the NT, but is so found in the Sept., e.g., in Eccles. 2:15, 19; 7:17; (b) "to play the sophist, to devise cleverly", it is used with this meaning in the passive voice in **2 Pet. 1:16**, "cunningly devised fables."

Fables *muthos* (3454), primarily signifies "speech, conversation." The first syllable comes from a root *mu*-, signifying "to close, keep secret, be dumb"; whence, *muo*, "to close" (eyes, mouth) and *musterion*, "a secret, a mystery"; hence, "a story, narrative, fable, fiction" (Eng., "myth"). The word is used of gnostic errors and of Jewish and profane fables and genealogies, in 1 Tim. 1:4; 4:7; 2 Tim. 4:4; Titus 1:14; of fiction, in **2 Pet. 1:16**. *Muthos* is to be contrasted with *aletheia*, "truth," and with *logos*, "a story, a narrative purporting to set forth facts," e.g., Matt. 28:15, a "saying" (i.e., an account, story, in which actually there is a falsification of facts); Luke 5:15, RV, "report."

Known *gnorizo* (1107), signifies (a) "to come to know, discover, know," Phil. 1:22, "I wot (not)," i.e., "I know not," "I have not come to know" (the RV, marg. renders it, as under (b), "I do not make known"); (b) "to make known," whether (I) communicating things before "unknown," Luke 2:15, 17; in the latter some mss. have the verb *diagnorizo* (hence the KJV, "made known abroad)"; John 15:15, "I have made known"; 17:26; Acts 2:28; 7:13 (1st part), see *Note* (3) below; Rom. 9:22, 23; 16:26 (passive voice); 2 Cor. 8:1, "we make known (to you)," RV, KJV, "we do (you) to wit"; Eph. 1:9; 3:3, 5, 10 (all three in the passive voice); 6:19, 21; Col. 1:27; 4:7, 9, "shall make known" (KJV, "shall declare"); **2 Pet. 1:16**; or (II) reasserting things already "known," 1 Cor. 12:3, "I give (you) to understand" (the apostle reaffirms what they knew); 15:1, of the gospel; Gal. 1:11 (he reminds them of what they well knew, the ground of his claim to apostleship); Phil. 4:6 (passive voice), of requests to God.

Coming *parousia* (3952), lit., "a presence," *para*, "with," and *ousia*, "being" (from *eimi*, "to be"), denotes both an "arrival" and a consequent "presence with." For instance, in a papyrus letter a lady speaks of the necessity of her parousia in a place in order to attend to matters relating to her property there. Paul speaks of his *parousia* in Philippi, Phil. 2:12 (in contrast to his *apousia*, "his absence") ... *Parousia* is used to describe the presence of Christ with His disciples on the Mount of Transfiguration, **2 Pet. 1:16**. When used of the return of Christ, at the rapture of the church, it signifies, not merely His momentary "coming" for His saints, but His presence with them from that moment until His revelation and manifestation to the world. In some passages the word gives prominence to the beginning of that period, the course of the period being implied, 1 Cor. 15:23; 1 Thess. 4:15; 5:23; 2 Thess. 2:1; Jas. 5:7-8; **2 Pet. 3:4**. In some, the course is prominent, Matt. 24:3, 37; 1 Thess. 3:13; 1 John 2:28; in others the conclusion of the period, Matt. 24:27; 2 Thess. 2:8. The word is also used of the Lawless One, the Man of Sin, his access to power and his doings in the world during his *parousia*, 2 Thess. 2:9. In addition to Phil. 2:12 (above), it is used in the same way of the apostle, or his companions, in 1 Cor. 16:17; 2 Cor. 7:6-7; 10:10; Phil. 1:26; of the Day of God, **2 Pet. 3:12**.

Eyewitnesses *epoptes* (2030), primarily "an overseer" (*epi*, "over"), then, a "spectator, an eyewitness" of anything, is used in **2 Pet. 1:16** of those who were present at the transfiguration of Christ. Among the Greeks the word was used of those who had attained to the third grade, the highest, of the Eleusinian mysteries, a religious cult at Eleusis, with its worship, rites, festival and pilgrimages; this brotherhood was open to all Greeks. In the Sept., Esth. 5:1, where it is used of God as the Overseer and Preserver of all things. Cf. *epopteuo*, "to behold," 1 Pet. 2:12 and 3:2.

His These translate (a) forms of pronouns under he (a frequent use: in 1 Pet. 2:24, "His own self"); the form *autou*, "his," becomes emphatic when placed between the article and the noun, e.g., 1 Thess. 2:19; Titus 3:5; Heb. 2:4; John 5:47; 9:28; 1 Cor. 10:28; 2 Cor. 8:9; 2 Tim. 2:26; Titus 3:7; **2 Pet. 1:16**; (b) *heautou*, "of himself, his own"; the RV rightly puts "his own," for the KJV, "his," in Luke 11:21; 14:26; Rom. 4:19; 5:8, "His own (love)"; 1 Cor. 7:37; Gal. 6:8; Eph. 5:28, 33; 1 Thess. 2:11, 12; 4:4; in Rev. 10:7 the change has not been made; it should read "his own servants"; (c) *idios*, "one's own," "his own," in the RV, in Matt. 22:5; John 5:18; **2 Pet. 2:16**; in Matt. 25:15, it is rendered "his several"; in John 19:27, "his own home," lit., "his own things"; in 1 Tim. 6:15, RV, "its own (times)," referring to the future appearing of Christ; in Heb. 4:10 (end of verse), both KJV and RV have "his," where it should be "his own"; so in Acts 24:23, for KJV and RV, "his"; in 1 Cor. 7:7, RV, "his own," KJV, "his proper"; (d) in Acts 17:28, the genitive case of the definite article, "His (offspring)," lit., "of the" (i.e., the one referred to, namely, God).

Majesty *megaleiotes* (3168), denotes "splendor, magnificence" (from *megaleios*, "magnificent," mighty," Acts 2:11, *megas*, "great"), translated "magnificence" in Acts 19:27, of the splendor of the goddess Diana. In Luke 9:43, RV (KJV, "mighty power"); in **2 Pet. 1:16**, "majesty." In the papyri writings it is frequent as a ceremonial title.

1:17 For he received from God the Father honour and glory, when there came such a voice to him from the excellent glory, This is my beloved Son, in whom I am well pleased.

Honour *time* (5092), primarily "a valuing," hence, objectively, (a) "a price paid or received," e.g., Matt. 27:6, 9; Acts 4:34; 5:2, 3; 7:16, RV, "price" (KJV, "sum"); 19:19; 1 Cor. 6:20; 7:23; (b) of "the preciousness of Christ" unto believers, 1 Pet. 2:7, RV, i.e., the honor and inestimable value of Christ as appropriated by believers, who are joined, as living stones, to Him the cornerstone; (c) in the sense of value, of human ordinances, valueless against the indulgence of the flesh, or, perhaps of no value in attempts at asceticism, Col. 2:23; (d) "honor, esteem," (1) used in ascriptions of worship to God, 1 Tim. 1:17; 6:16; Rev. 4:9, 11; 5:13; 7:12; to Christ, 5:12, 13; (2) bestowed upon Christ by the Father, Heb. 2:9; **2 Pet. 1:17**; (3) bestowed upon man, Heb. 2:7 ...

Glory *doxa* (1391), "glory" (from *dokeo*, "to seem"), primarily signifies an opinion, estimate, and hence, the honor resulting from a good opinion. It is used (I) (a) of the nature and acts of God in self-manifestation, i.e., what He essentially is and does, as exhibited in whatever way he reveals Himself in these respects, and particularly in the person of Christ, in whom essentially His "glory" has ever shone forth and ever will do, John 17:5, 24; Heb. 1:3; it was exhibited in the character and acts of Christ in the days of His flesh, John 1:14; John 2:11; at Cana both His grace and His power were manifested, and these constituted His "glory", so also in the resurrection of Lazarus 11:4, 40; the "glory" of God was exhibited in the resurrection of Christ, Rom. 6:4, and in His ascension and exaltation, 1 Pet. 1:21, likewise on the Mount of Transfiguration, **2 Pet. 1:17**. In Rom. 1:23 His "everlasting power and Divinity" are spoken of as His "glory," i.e., His attributes and power as revealed through creation; in Rom. 3:23 the word denotes the manifested perfection of His character, especially His righteousness, of which all men fall short; in Col. 1:11 "the might of His glory" signifies the might which is characteristic of His "glory"; in Eph. 1:6, 12, 14, "the praise of the glory of His grace" and "the praise of His glory" signify the due acknowledgement of the exhibition of His attributes and ways; in Eph. 1:17, "the Father of glory" describes Him as the source from whom all divine splendor and perfection proceed in their manifestation, and to whom they belong; (b) of the character and ways of God as exhibited through Christ to and through believers, 2 Cor. 3:18 and 4:6; (c) of the state of blessedness into which believers are to enter hereafter through being brought into the likeness of Christ, e.g., Rom. 8:18, 21; Phil. 3:21 (RV, "the body of His glory"); 1 Pet. 5:1, 10; Rev. 21:11; (d) brightness or splendor, (1) supernatural, emanating from God (as in the *shekinah* "glory," in the pillar of cloud and in the Holy of Holies, e.g., Exod. 16:10; 25:22), Luke 2:9; Acts 22:11; Rom. 9:4; 2 Cor. 3:7; Jas. 2:1; in Titus 2:13 it is used of Christ's return, "the appearing of the glory of our great God and Savior Jesus Christ" (RV); cf. Phil. 3:21, above; (2) natural, as of the heavenly bodies, 1 Cor. 15:40, 41; (II) of good reputation, praise, honor, Luke 14:10 (RV, "glory," for KJV, "worship"); John 5:41 (RV, "glory," for KJV, "honor"); 7:18; 8:50; 12:43 (RV, "glory," for KJV, "praise"); 2 Cor. 6:8 (RV, "glory," for KJV "honor"); Phil. 3:19; Heb. 3:3; in 1 Cor. 11:7, of man as representing the authority of God, and of woman as rendering conspicuous the authority of man; in 1 Thess. 2:6, "glory" probably stands, by metonymy, for material gifts, an honorarium, since in human estimation "glory" is usually expressed in things material. The word is used in ascriptions of praise to God, e.g., Luke 17:18; John 9:24, RV, "glory" (KJV, "praise"); Acts 12:23; as in doxologies (lit., "glory-words"), e.g., Luke 2:14; Rom. 11:36; 16:27; Gal. 1:5; Rev. 1:6.

Came *phero* (5342), "to bear, carry," is rendered "came," in the sense of being borne from a place, in **2 Pet. 1:17-18, 21**.

Voice *phone* (5456), "a sound," is used of the voice (a) of God, Matt. 3:17; John 5:37; 12:28, 30; Acts 7:31; 10:13, 15; 11:7, 9; Heb. 3:7, 15; 4:7; 12:19, 26; **2 Pet. 1:17, 18**; Rev. 18:4; 21:3; (b) of Christ, (1) in the days of His flesh, Matt. 12:19 (negatively); John 3:29; 5:25; 10:3, 4, 16, 27; 11:43; 18:37; (2) on the cross Matt. 27:46, and parallel passages; (3) from heaven, Acts 9:4, 7; 22:7, 9, 14; 26:14; Rev. 1:10, 12 (here, by metonymy, of the speaker), 15; 3:20; (4) at the resurrection "to life," John 5:28; 1 Thess. 4:16, where "the voice of the archangel" is, lit., "a voice of an archangel," and probably refers to the Lord's voice as being of an archangelic character; (5) at the resurrection to judgment, John 5:28 [not the same event as (4)]; (c) of human beings on earth, e.g., Matt. 2:18; 3:3; Luke 1:42, in some texts, KJV, "voice", and frequently in the Synoptists; (d) of angels, Rev. 5:11, and frequently in Revelation; (e) of the redeemed in heaven, e.g., Rev. 6:10; 18:22; 19:1, 5; (f) of a pagan god, Acts 12:22; (g) of things, e.g., wind, John 3:8, RV, "voice" (KJV, "sound").

Excellent *megaloprepes* (3169), signifies "magnificent, majestic, that which is becoming to a great man" (from *megas*, "great," and *prepo*, "to be fitting or becoming"), in **2 Pet. 1:17**, "excellent."

Pleased *eudokeo* (2106), signifies (a) "to be well pleased, to think it good" [*eu*, "well," and *dokeo*], not merely an understanding of what is right and good as in *dokeo*, but stressing the willingness and freedom of an intention or resolve regarding what is good, e.g., Luke 12:32, "it is (your Father's) good pleasure"; so Rom. 15:26, 27, RV; 1 Cor. 1:21; Gal. 1:15; Col. 1:19; 1 Thess. 2:8, RV, "we were well pleased" (KJV, "we were willing"); this meaning is frequently found in the papyri in legal documents; (b) "to be well pleased with," or "take pleasure in," e.g., Matt. 3:17; 12:18; 17:5; 1 Cor. 10:5; 2 Cor. 12:10; 2 Thess. 2:12; Heb. 10:6, 8, 38; **2 Pet. 1:17**.

1:18 And this voice which came from heaven we heard, when we were with him in the holy mount.

Voice *see 2 Peter 1:17.*

Mount *oros* (3735), is used (a) without specification, e.g., Luke 3:5 (distinct from *bounos*, "a hill"); John 4:20; (b) of "the Mount of Transfiguration," Matt. 17:1, 9; Mark 9:2, 9; Luke 9:28, 37 (KJV, "hill"); **2 Pet. 1:18**; (c) of "Zion," Heb. 12:22; Rev. 14:1; (d) of "Sinai," Acts 7:30, 38; Gal. 4:24, 25; Heb. 8:5; 12:20; (e) of "the Mount of Olives," Matt. 21:1; 24:3; Mark 11:1; 13:3; Luke 19:29, 37; 22:39; John 8:1; Acts 1:12; (f) of "the hill districts as distinct from the lowlands," especially of the hills above the Sea of Galilee, e.g., Matt. 5:1; 8:1; 18:12; Mark 5:5; (g) of "the mountains on the east of Jordan" and "those in the land of Ammon" and "the region of Petra," etc., Matt. 24:16; Mark 13:14; Luke 21:21; (h) proverbially, "of overcoming difficulties, or accomplishing great things," 1 Cor. 13:2; cf. Matt. 17:20; 21:21; Mark 11:23; (i) symbolically, of "a series of the imperial potentates of the Roman dominion, past and future," Rev. 17:9.

1:19 We have also a more sure word of prophecy; whereunto ye do well that ye take heed, as unto a light that shineth in a dark place, until the day dawn, and the day star arise in your hearts:

Sure *see 2 Peter 1:10.*

Prophecy *prophetikos* (4397), "of or relating to prophecy," or "proceeding from a prophet, prophetic," is used of the OT Scriptures, Rom. 16:26, "of the prophets," lit., "(by) prophetic (Scriptures)"; **2 Pet. 1:19**, "the word of prophecy (*made* more sure)," i.e., confirmed by the person and work of Christ (KJV, "a more sure, etc."), lit., "the prophetic word."

Heed *prosecho* (4337), lit., "to hold to," signifies "to turn to, turn one's attention to"; hence, "to give heed"; it is rendered "take heed" in Matt. 6:1; Luke 17:3; 21:34; Acts 5:35; 20:28; **2 Pet. 1:19**; to give heed to, in Acts 8:6, 10; in v. 11 (KJV, "had regard to"); 16:14 (KJV, "attended unto"); 1 Tim. 1:4; 4:1, 13 (KJV, "give attendance to"); Titus 1:14; Heb. 2:1, lit., "to give heed more earnestly."

Light *luchnos* (3088), frequently mistranslated "candle," is a portable "lamp" usually set on a stand; the word is used literally, Matt. 5:15; Mark 4:21; Luke 8:16; 11:33, 36; 15:8; Rev. 18:23; 22:5; (b) metaphorically, of Christ as the Lamb, Rev. 21:23, RV, "lamp" (KJV, "light"); of John the Baptist, John 5:35, RV, "the lamp" (KJV, "a ... light"); of the eye, Matt. 6:22, and Luke 11:34, RV, "lamp"; of spiritual readiness, Luke 12:35,rv, "lamps"; of "the word of prophecy," **2 Pet. 1:19**, RV, "lamp."

"In rendering *luchnos* and *lampas* our translators have scarcely made the most of the words at their command. Had they rendered *lampas* by 'torch' not once only (John 18:3), but always, this would have left 'lamp,' now wrongly appropriated by lampas, disengaged. Altogether dismissing 'candle,' they might then have rendered *luchnos* by 'lamp' wherever it occurs. At present there are so many occasions where 'candle' would manifestly be inappropriate, and where, therefore, they are obliged to fall back on 'light,' that the distinction between *phos* and *luchnos* nearly, if not quite, disappears in our Version. The advantages of such a re-distribution of the words would be many. In the first place, it would be more accurate. *Luchnos* is not a 'candle' ('*candela,*' from '*candeo,*' the white wax light, and then any kind of taper), but a hand-lamp, fed with oil. Neither is *lampas* a 'lamp,' but a 'torch'" (Trench *Syn.*, Sec.xlvi).

Shineth *phaino* (5316), "to cause to appear," denotes, in the active voice, "to give light, shine," John 1:5; 5:35; in Matt. 24:27, passive voice; so Phil. 2:15, RV, "ye are seen" (for KJV, "ye shine"); **2 Pet. 1:19** (active); so 1 John 2:8, Rev. 1:16; in 8:12 and 18:23 (passive); 21:23 (active).

Dark *auchmeros* (850), from *auchmos*, "drought produced by excessive heat," hence signifies "dry, murky, dark," **2 Pet. 1:19** (RV marg., "squalid"). *Skoteinos* signifies "darkness" produced by covering; *auchmeros*, "darkness" produced by being squalid or murky.

Day *hemera* (2250), "a day," is used of (a) the period of natural light, Gen. 1:5; Prov. 4:18; Mark 4:35; (b) the same, but figuratively, for a period of opportunity for service, John 9:4; Rom. 13:13; (c) one period of alternate light and darkness, Gen. 1:5; Mark 1:13; (d) a period of undefined length marked by certain characteristics, such as "the day of small things," Zech. 4:10; of perplexity and distress, Isa. 17:11; Obad. 12-14; of prosperity and of adversity, Ecc. 7:14; of trial or testing, Ps. 95:8; of salvation, Isa. 49:8; 2 Cor. 6:2; cf. Luke 19:42; of evil, Eph. 6:13; of wrath and revelation of the judgments of God, Rom. 2:5; (e) an appointed time, Ecc. 8:6; Eph. 4:30; (f) a notable defeat in battle, etc., Isa. 9:4; Psa.

137:7; Ezek. 30:9; Hos. 1:11; (g) by metonymy = "when," "at the time when"; (1), of the past, Gen. 2:4; Num. 3:13; Deut. 4:10, (2), of the future, Gen. 2:17; Ruth 4:5; Matt. 24:50; Luke 1:20; (h) a judgment or doom, Job 18:20. (i) of a time of life, Luke 1:17-18 ("years"). As the "day" throws light upon things that have been in darkness, the word is often associated with the passing of judgment upon circumstances. In 1 Cor. 4:3, "man's day," KJV, "man's judgement," RV, denotes mere human judgment upon matters ("man's" translates the adjective *anthropinos*, "human"), a judgment exercised in the present period of human rebellion against "God"; probably therefore "the Lord's Day," Rev. 1:10, or "the Day of the Lord" (where an adjective, *kuriakos*, is similarly used), is the day of His manifested judgment on the world. The phrases "the day of Christ," Phil. 1:10; 2:16; "the day of Jesus Christ," 1:6; "the day of the Lord Jesus," 1 Cor. 5:5; 2 Cor. 1:14; "the day of our Lord Jesus Christ," 1 Cor. 1:8, denote the time of the Parousia of Christ with His saints, subsequent to the Rapture, 1 Thess. 4:16-17. In **2 Pet. 1:19** this is spoken of simply as the day. From these the phrase "the day of the Lord" is to be distinguished; in the OT it had reference to a time of the victorious interposition by God for the overthrow of the foes of Israel, e.g., Isa. 2:12; Amos 5:18; if Israel transgressed in the pride of their hearts, the Day of the Lord would be a time of darkness and judgment. For their foes, however, there would come "a great and terrible day of the Lord," Joel 2:31; Mal. 4:5. That period, still future, will see the complete overthrow of gentile power and the establishment of Messiah's kingdom, Isa. 13:9-11; 34:8; Dan. 2:34, 44; Obad. 15; cf. Isa. 61:2; John 8:56. In the NT "the day of the Lord" is mentioned in 1 Thess. 5:2 and 2 Thess. 2:2, RV, where the apostle's warning is that the church at Thessalonica should not be deceived by thinking that "the Day of the Lord is now present." This period will not begin till the circumstances mentioned in verses 3 and 4 take place. For the eventual development of the divine purposes in relation to the human race see **2 Pet. 3:12**, "the Day of God."

Dawn *diaugazo* (1306), signifies "to shine through" (*dia*, "through," *auge*, "brightness"); it describes the breaking of daylight upon the darkness of night, metaphorically in **2 Pet. 1:19**, of the shining of spiritual light into the heart. A probable reference is to the day to be ushered in at the second coming of Christ: "until the Day gleam through the present darkness, and the Light-bringer dawn in your hearts."

Day star *phosphoros* (5459), (Eng., "phosphorus," lit., "light-bearing" *phos*, "light," *phero*, "to bear"), is used of the morning star, as the light-bringer, **2 Pet. 1:19**, where it indicates the arising of the light of Christ as the personal fulfillment, in the hearts of believers, of the prophetic Scriptures concerning His coming to receive them to Himself.

Arise *anatello* (393), "to arise," is used especially of things in the natural creation, e.g., "the rising" of the sun, moon and stars; metaphorically, of light, in Matt. 4:16, "did spring up"; of the sun, Matt. 5:45; 13:6 (RV); Mark 4:6; Jas. 1:11; in Mark 16:2 the RV has "when the sun was risen," keeping to the verb form, for the KJV, "at the rising of"; of a cloud, Luke 12:54; of the day-star, **2 Pet. 1:19**; in Heb. 7:14 metaphorically, of the Incarnation of Christ: "Our Lord hath sprung out of Judah," more lit., "Our Lord hath arisen out of Judah," as of the rising of the light of the sun.

1:20 Knowing this first, that no prophecy of the scripture is of any private interpretation.

Prophecy *propheteia* (4394), signifies "the speaking forth of the mind and counsel of God" (*pro*, "forth," *phemi*, "to speak"); in the NT it is used (a) of the gift, e.g., Rom. 12:6; 1 Cor. 12:10; 13:2; (b) either of the exercise of the gift or of that which is "prophesied," e.g., Matt. 13:14; 1 Cor. 13:8; 14:6, 22 and 1 Thess. 5:20, "prophesying(s)"; 1 Tim. 1:18; 4:14; **2 Pet. 1:20, 21**; Rev. 1:3; 11:6; 19:10; 22:7, 10, 18, 19.

"Though much of OT prophecy was purely predictive, see Micah 5:2, e.g., and cf. John 11:51, prophecy is not necessarily, nor even primarily, fore-telling. It is the declaration of that which cannot be known by natural means, Matt. 26:68, it is the forth-telling of the will of God, whether with reference to the past, the present, or the future, see Gen. 20:7; Deut. 18:18; Rev. 10:11; 11:3....

"In such passages as 1 Cor. 12:28; Eph. 2:20, the 'prophets' are placed after the 'Apostles,' since not the prophets of Israel are intended, but the 'gifts' of the ascended Lord, Eph. 4:8, 11; cf. Acts 13:1; ... ; the purpose of their ministry was to edify, to comfort, and to encourage the believers, 1 Cor. 14:3, while its effect upon unbelievers was to show that the secrets of a man's heart are known to God, to convict of sin, and to constrain to worship, vv. 24, 25. "With the completion of the canon of Scripture prophecy apparently passed away, 1 Cor. 13:8, 9. In his measure the teacher has taken the place of the prophet, cf. the significant change in **2 Pet. 2:1**. The difference is that, whereas the message of the prophet was a direct revelation of the mind of God for the occasion, the message of the teacher is gathered from the completed revelation contained in the Scriptures."

Scripture *graphe* (1124), akin to *grapho*, "to write" (Eng., "graph," "graphic," etc.), primarily denotes "a drawing, painting"; then "a writing," (a) of the OT Scriptures, (1) in the plural, the whole, e.g., Matt. 21:42; 22:29; John 5:39; Acts 17:11; 18:24; Rom. 1:2, where "the prophets" comprises the OT writers in general; 15:4; 16:26, lit., "prophetic writings," expressing the character of all the Scriptures; (2) in the singular in reference to a particular passage, e.g., Mark 12:10; Luke 4:21; John 2:22; 10:35 (though applicable to all); 19:24, 28, 36, 37; 20:9; Acts 1:16; 8:32, 35; Rom. 4:3; 9:17; 10:11; 11:2; Gal. 3:8, 22; 4:30; 1 Tim. 5:18, where the 2nd quotation is from Luke 10:7, from which it may be inferred that the apostle included Luke's Gospel as "Scripture" alike with Deuteronomy, from which the first quotation is taken; in reference to the whole, e.g. Jas. 4:5 (see RV, a separate rhetorical question from the one which follows); in **2 Pet. 1:20**, "no prophecy of Scripture," a description of all, with special application to the OT in the next verse; (b) of the OT Scriptures (those accepted by the Jews as canonical) and all those of the NT which were to be accepted by Christians as authoritative, 2 Tim. 3:16; these latter were to be discriminated from the many forged epistles and other religious "writings" already produced and circulated in Timothy's time. Such discrimination would be directed by the fact that "every Scripture," characterized by inspiration of God, would be profitable for the purposes mentioned; so the RV ...

Private *idios* (2398), one's own, is translated "private" in **2 Pet. 1:20**.

Interpretation *epilusis* (1955), from *epiluo*, "to loose, solve, explain," denotes "a solution, explanation," lit., "a release" (*epi*, "up," *luo*, "to loose"), **2 Pet. 1:20**, "(of private) interpretation"; i.e., the writers of Scripture did not put their own construction upon the "God-breathed" words they wrote.

1:21 For the prophecy came not in old time by the will of man: but holy men of God spake *as they were* moved by the Holy Ghost.

Prophecy *see 2 Peter 1:20.*

Came *see 2 Peter 1:17.*

Old time In 1 Pet. 3:5, KJV, the particle *pote*, "once, formerly, ever, sometime," is translated "in the old time" (RV, "aforetime"); in **2 Pet. 1:21**, "in old time" (RV, "ever"), KJV marg., "at any time."

Will *thelema* (2307), signifies (a) objectively, "that which is willed, of the will of God," e.g., Matt. 18:14; Mark 3:35, the fulfilling being a sign of spiritual relationship to the Lord, John 4:34; 5:30; 6:39, 40; Acts 13:22, plural, "my desires"; Rom. 2:18; 12:2, lit., "the will of God, the good and perfect and acceptable"; here the repeated article is probably resumptive, the adjectives describing the will, as in the Eng. versions; Gal. 1:4; Eph. 1:9; 5:17, "of the Lord"; Col. 1:9; 4:12; 1 Thess. 4:3; 5:18, where it means "the gracious design," rather than "the determined resolve"; 2 Tim. 2:26, which should read "which have been taken captive by him" [(*autou*), i.e., by the Devil; the RV, "by the Lord's servant" is an interpretation; it does not correspond to the Greek] unto His (*ekeinou*) will" (i.e., "God's will"; the different pronoun refers back to the subject of the sentence, viz., God); Heb. 10:10; Rev. 4:11, RV, "because of Thy will"; of human will, e.g., 1 Cor. 7:37; (b) subjectively, the "will" being spoken of as the emotion of being desirous, rather than as the thing "willed"; of the "will" of God, e.g., Rom. 1:10; 1 Cor. 1:1; 2 Cor. 1:1; 8:5; Eph. 1:1, 5, 11; Col. 1:1; 2 Tim. 1:1; Heb. 10:7, 9, 36; 1 John 2:17; 5:14; of human "will," e.g., John 1:13; Eph. 2:3, "the desires of the flesh"; 1 Pet. 4:3 (in some texts); **2 Pet. 1:21**.

Holy *hagios* (40), fundamentally signifies "separated" (among the Greeks, dedicated to the gods), and hence, in Scripture in its moral and spiritual significance, separated from sin and therefore consecrated to God, sacred.

(a) It is predicated of God (as the absolutely "Holy" One, in His purity, majesty and glory): of the Father, e.g., Luke 1:49; John 17:11; 1 Pet. 1:15, 16; Rev. 4:8; 6:10; of the Son, e.g., Luke 1:35; Acts 3:14; 4:27, 30; 1 John 2:20; of the Spirit, e.g., Matt. 1:18 and frequently in all the Gospels, Acts, Romans, 1 and 2 Cor., Eph., 1 Thess.; also in 2 Tim. 1:14; Titus 3:5; 1 Pet. 1:12; **2 Pet. 1:21**; Jude 20.

(b) It is used of men and things in so far as they are devoted to God. Indeed the quality, as attributed to God, is often presented in a way which involves divine demands upon the conduct of believers. These are called *hagioi*, "saints," i.e., "sanctified" or "holy" ones.

This sainthood is not an attainment, it is a state into which God in grace calls men; yet believers are called to sanctify themselves (consistently with their calling, 2 Tim. 1:9), cleansing themselves from all defilement, forsaking sin, living a "holy" manner of life, 1 Pet. 1:15; **2 Pet. 3:11**, and experiencing fellowship with God in His holiness. The saints are thus figuratively spoken of as "a holy temple", 1 Cor. 3:17 (a local church); Eph. 2:21 (the whole

"Be astounded that God should have written to us."

ANTONY OF EGYPT

Church), cp. 5:27; "a holy priesthood," 1 Pet. 2:5; "a holy nation," 2:9.

"It is evident that *hagios* and its kindred words ... express something more and higher than *hieros*, sacred, outwardly associated with God; ... something more than *semnos*, worthy, honorable; something more than *hagnos*, pure, free from defilement. *Hagios* is ... more comprehensive.... It is characteristically godlikeness" (G. B. Stevens, in Hastings' *Bib. Dic.*).

Moved *phero* (5342), "to bear, carry," is rendered "being moved" in **2 Pet. 1:21**, signifying that they were "borne along," or impelled, by the Holy Spirit's power, not acting according to their own wills, or simply expressing their own thoughts, but expressing the mind of God in words provided and ministered by Him.

Chapter 2

2:1 But there were false prophets also among the people, even as there shall be false teachers among you, who privily shall bring in damnable heresies, even denying the Lord that bought them, and bring upon themselves swift destruction.

False prophets *pseudoprophetes* (5578), "a false prophet," is used of such (a) in OT times, Luke 6:26; **2 Pet. 2:1**; (b) in the present period since Pentecost, Matt. 7:15; 24:11, 24; Mark 13:22; Acts 13:6; 1 John 4:1; (c) with reference to a false "prophet" destined to arise as the supporter of the "Beast" at the close of this age, Rev. 16:13; 19:20; 20:10 (himself described as "another beast," 13:11). *See also* **Prophecy** at *2 Peter 1:20*.

False teachers *pseudodidaskalos* (5572), "a false teacher," occurs in the plural in **2 Pet. 2:1**.

Bring *pareisago* (3919), "to bring in privily" (lit., "to bring in beside"), "to introduce secretly," **2 Pet. 2:1**.

Heresies *hairesis* (139), denotes (a) "a choosing, choice" (from *haireomai*, "to choose"); then, "that which is chosen," and hence, "an opinion," especially a self-willed opinion, which is substituted for submission to the power of truth, and leads to division and the formation of sects, Gal. 5:20 (marg., "parties"); such erroneous opinions are frequently the outcome of personal preference or the prospect of advantage; see **2 Pet. 2:1**, where "destructive" (RV) signifies leading to ruin; some assign even this to (b); in the papyri the prevalent meaning is "choice" (Moulton and Milligan, *Vocab.*); (b) "a sect"; this secondary meaning, resulting from (a), is the dominating significance in the NT, Acts 5:17; 15:5; 24:5, 14; 26:5; 28:22; "heresies" in 1 Cor. 11:19 (see marg.).

Denying *arneomai* (720), signifies (a) "to say ... not, to contradict," e.g., Mark 14:70; John 1:20; 18:25, 27; 1 John 2:22; (b) "to deny" by way of disowning a person, as, e.g., the Lord Jesus as master, e.g., Matt. 10:33; Luke 12:9; John 13:38 (in the best mss.); 2 Tim. 2:12; or, on the other hand, of Christ Himself, "denying" that a person is His follower, Matt. 10:33; 2 Tim. 2:12; or to "deny" the Father and the Son, by apostatizing and by disseminating pernicious teachings, to "deny" Jesus Christ as master and Lord by immorality under a cloak of religion, **2 Pet. 2:1**; Jude 4; (c) "to deny oneself," either in a good sense, by disregarding one's own interests, Luke 9:23, or in a bad sense, to prove false to oneself, to act quite unlike oneself, 2 Tim. 2:13; (d) to "abrogate, forsake, or renounce a thing," whether evil, Titus 2:12, or good, 1 Tim. 5:8; 2 Tim. 3:5; Rev. 2:13; 3:8; (e) "not to accept, to reject" something offered, Acts 3:14; 7:35, "refused"; Heb. 11:24 "refused."

Lord *despotes* (1203), "a master, lord, one who possesses supreme authority," is used in personal address to God in Luke 2:29; Acts 4:24; Rev. 6:10; with reference to Christ, **2 Pet. 2:1**; Jude 4; elsewhere it is translated "master," "masters," 1 Tim. 6:1, 2; 2 Tim. 2:21 (of Christ); Titus 2:9; 1 Pet. 2:18.

Bought *agorazo* (59), primarily, "to frequent the market-place," the *agora*, hence "to do business there, to buy or sell," is used lit., e.g., in Matt. 14:15. Figuratively Christ is spoken of as having bought His redeemed, making them His property at the price of His blood (i.e., His death through the shedding of His blood in expiation for their sins), 1 Cor. 6:20; 7:23; **2 Pet. 2:1**; see also Rev. 5:9; 14:3-4 (not as KJV, "redeemed"). *Agorazo* does not mean "to redeem."

Bring *epago* (1863), "to bring upon," Acts 5:28; **2 Pet. 2:1, 5**.

Swift *see* **Shortly** at *2 Peter 1:14*.

Destruction *apoleia* (684), indicating "loss of well-being, not of being," is used (a) of things, signifying their waste, or ruin; of ointment, Matt. 26:8; Mark 14:4; of money, Acts 8:20 ("perish"); (b) of persons, signifying their spiritual and eternal perdition, Matt. 7:13; John 17:12; 2 Thess. 2:3, where "son of perdition" signifies the proper destiny of the person mentioned; metaphorically of men persistent in evil, Rom. 9:22, where "fitted" is in the middle voice, indicating that the vessels of wrath fitted themselves for "destruction", of the adversaries of the Lord's people, Phil. 1:28 ("perdition"); of professing Christians, really enemies of the cross of Christ, Phil. 3:19 (RV, "perdition"); of those who are subjects of foolish and hurtful lusts, 1 Tim. 6:9; of professing Hebrew adherents who shrink back into unbelief, Heb. 10:39; of false teachers, **2 Pet. 2:1**, **3**; of ungodly men, **3:7**; of those who wrest the Scriptures, **3:16**; of the Beast, the final head of the revived Roman Empire, Rev. 17:8, 11; (c) of impersonal subjects, as heresies, **2 Pet. 2:1**, where "destructive heresies" (RV; KJV, "damnable") is, lit., "heresies of destruction" (marg., "sects of perdition"); in v. **2** the most authentic mss. have *aselgeiais*, "lascivious," instead of *apoleiais*.

2:2 And many shall follow their pernicious ways; by reason of whom the way of truth shall be evil spoken of.

Follow *see* **Followed** at *2 Peter 1:16*.

Pernicious *aselgeia* (766), denotes "excess, licentiousness, absence of restraint, indecency, wantonness"; "lasciviousness" in Mark 7:22, one of the evils that proceed from the heart; in 2 Cor. 12:21, one of the evils of which some in the church at Corinth had been guilty; in Gal. 5:19, classed among the works of the flesh; in Eph. 4:19, among the sins of the unregenerate who are "past feeling"; so in 1 Pet. 4:3; in Jude 4, of that into which the grace of God had been turned by ungodly men; it is translated "wantonness" in Rom. 13:13, one of the sins against which believers are warned; in **2 Pet. 2:2**, according to the best mss., "lascivious (doings)," RV (the KJV "pernicious ways" follows those texts which have *apoleiais*); in v. **7**, RV, "lascivious (life)," KJV, "filthy (conversation)," of the people of Sodom and Gomorrah; in **2:18**, RV, "lasciviousness" (KJV, "wantonness"), practiced by the same persons as mentioned in Jude. The prominent idea is shameless conduct. Some have derived the word from *a*, negative, and *selge*, "a city in Pisidia." Others, with similar improbability, trace it to *a*, negative, and *selgo*, or *thelgo*, "to charm." *See also* **Destruction** at *2 Peter 2:1*.

Ways *hodos* (3598), denotes (a) "a natural path, road, way," frequent in the Synoptic Gospels; elsewhere, e.g., Acts 8:26; 1 Thess. 3:11; Jas. 2:25; Rev. 16:12; (b) "a traveler's way"; (c) metaphorically, of "a course of conduct," or "way of thinking," e.g., of righteousness, Matt. 21:32; **2 Pet. 2:21**; of God, Matt. 22:16, and parallels, i.e., the "way" instructed and approved by God; so Acts 18:26 and Heb. 3:10, "My ways" (cf. Rev. 15:3); of the Lord, Acts 18:25; "that leadeth to destruction," Matt. 7:13; "... unto life," 7:14; of peace, Luke 1:79; Rom. 3:17; of Paul's "ways" in Christ, 1 Cor. 4:17 (plural); "more excellent" (of love), 1 Cor. 12:31; of truth, **2 Pet. 2:2**; of the right "way," **2:15**; of Balaam (*id.*), of Cain, Jude 11; of a "way" consisting in what is from God, e.g., of life, Acts 2:28 (plural); of salvation, Acts 16:17; personified, of Christ as the means of access to the Father, John 14:6; of the course followed and characterized by the followers of Christ, Acts 9:2; 19:9, 23; 24:22.

Evil spoken of *blasphemeo* (987), "to blaspheme, rail at or revile," is used (a) in a general way, of any contumelious speech, reviling, calumniating, railing at, etc., as of those who railed at Christ, e.g., Matt. 27:39; Mark 15:29; Luke 22:65 (RV, "reviling"); 23:39; (b) of those who speak contemptuously of God or of sacred things, e.g., Matt. 9:3; Mark 3:28; Rom. 2:24; 1 Tim. 1:20; 6:1; Rev. 13:6; 16:9, 11, 21; "hath spoken blasphemy," Matt. 26:65; "rail at," **2 Pet. 2:10**; Jude 8, 10; "railing," **2 Pet. 2:12**; "slanderously reported," Rom. 3:8; "be evil spoken of," Rom. 14:16; 1 Cor. 10:30; **2 Pet. 2:2**; "speak evil of," Titus 3:2; 1 Pet. 4:4; "being defamed," 1 Cor. 4:13. The verb (in the present participial form) is translated "blasphemers" in Acts 19:37; in Mark 2:7, "blasphemeth," RV, for KJV, "speaketh blasphemies." There is no noun in the original representing the English "blasphemer." This is expressed either by the verb, or by the adjective *blasphemos*.

2:3 And through covetousness shall they with feigned words make merchandise of you: whose judgment now of a long time lingereth not, and their damnation slumbereth not.

Covetousness *pleonexia* (4124), "covetousness," lit., "a desire to have more" (*pleon*, "more," *echo*, "to have"), always in a bad sense, is used in a general way in Mark 7:22 (plural, lit., "covetings," i.e., various ways in which "covetousness" shows itself); Rom. 1:29; Eph. 5:3; 1 Thess. 2:5. Elsewhere it is used, (a) of material possessions, Luke 12:15; **2 Pet. 2:3**; 2 Cor. 9:5 (RV, "extortion"), lit., "as (a matter of) extortion," i.e., a gift which betrays the giver's unwillingness to bestow what is due; (b) of sensuality, Eph.

4:19, "greediness"; Col. 3:5 (where it is called "idolatry"); **2 Pet. 2:14** (KJV, "covetous practices").

Feigned *plastos* (4112), primarily denotes "formed, molded" (from *plasso*, to mold; Eng., "plastic"); then, metaphorically, "made up, fabricated, feigned," **2 Pet. 2:3**. Cf. *plasma*, "that which is molded," Rom. 9:20.

Merchandise *emporeuomai* (1710), primarily signifies "to travel," especially for business; then, "to traffic, trade," Jas. 4:13; then, "to make a gain of, make merchandise of," **2 Pet. 2:3**. *kapeleuo* (2585), primarily signifies "to be a retailer, to peddle, to hucksterize" (from *kapelos*, "an inn-keeper, a petty retailer, especially of wine, a huckster, peddler," in contrast to *emporos*, "a merchant"); hence, "to get base gain by dealing in anything," and so, more generally, "to do anything for sordid personal advantage." It is found in 2 Cor. 2:17, with reference to the ministry of the gospel. The significance can be best ascertained by comparison and contrast with the verb *doloo* in 4:2 (likewise there only in the NT), "to handle deceitfully." The meanings are not identical. While both involve the deceitful dealing of adulterating the word of truth, *kapeleuo* has the broader significance of doing so in order to make dishonest gain. Those to whom the apostle refers in 2:17 are such as make merchandise of souls through covetousness (cf. Titus 1:11; **2 Pet. 2:3, 14-15**; Jude 11, 16; Ezek. 13:19); accordingly "hucksterizing" would be the most appropriate rendering in this passage, while "handling deceitfully" is the right meaning in 4:2. See Trench, *Syn.* Sec.lxii. In Isa. 1:22, the Sept. has "thy wine-merchants" (*kapeloi*, "hucksterizer").

Judgment *krima* (2917), "a judgment," a decision passed on the faults of others, is used especially of God's judgment upon men, and translated "sentence" in **2 Pet. 2:3**, RV (KJV, judgment).

Long time *ekpalai* (1597), "from of old, for a long time," occurs in **2 Pet. 2:3**, RV, "from of old" (KJV, "of a long time"); **3:5**.

Lingereth *argeo* (69), "to be idle, to linger" (akin to *argos*, "idle": see *kalargeo*), is used negatively regarding the judgment of the persons mentioned in **2 Pet. 2:3**. In the Sept., Ezra 4:24; Eccles. 12:3.

Damnation *see* Destruction at *2 Peter 2:1*.

Slumbereth *nustazo* (3573), denotes "to nod in sleep" (akin to *neuo*, "to nod"), "fall asleep," and is used (a) of natural slumber, Matt. 25:5; (b) metaphorically in **2 Pet. 2:3**, negatively, of the destruction awaiting false teachers.

2:4 For if God spared not the angels that sinned, but cast *them* down to hell, and delivered *them* into chains of darkness, to be reserved unto judgment;

Spared *pheidomai* (5339), "to spare," i.e., "to forego" the infliction of that evil or retribution which was designed, is used with a negative in Acts 20:29; Rom. 8:32; 11:21 (twice); 2 Cor. 13:2; **2 Pet. 2:4, 5**; positively, in 1 Cor. 7:28; 2 Cor. 1:3; rendered "forbear" in 2 Cor. 12:6.

Angels *angelos* (32), "a messenger" (from *angello*, "to deliver a message"), sent whether by God or by man or by Satan, "is also used of a guardian or representative in Rev. 1:20, cf. Matt. 18:10; Acts 12:15 (where it is better understood as 'ghost'), but most frequently of an order of created beings, superior to man, Heb. 2:7; Ps. 8:5, belonging to Heaven, Matt. 24:36; Mark 12:25, and to God, Luke 12:8, and engaged in His service, Ps. 103:20. "Angels" are spirits, Heb. 1:14, i.e., they have not material bodies as men have; they are either human in form, or can assume the human form when necessary, cf. Luke 24:4, with v. 23, Acts 10:3 with v. 30.

"They are called 'holy' in Mark 8:38, and 'elect,' 1 Tim. 5:21, in contrast with some of their original number, Matt. 25:41, who 'sinned,' **2 Pet. 2:4**, 'left their proper habitation,' Jude 6, *oiketerion*, a word which occurs again, in the NT, only in 2 Cor. 5:2. Angels are always spoken of in the masculine gender, the feminine form of the word does not occur."

Sinned *hamartano* (264), lit., "to miss the mark," is used in the NT (a) of "sinning" against God, (1) by angels, **2 Pet. 2:4**; (2) by man, Matt. 27:4; Luke 15:18, 21 (heaven standing, by metonymy, for God); John 5:14; 8:11; 9:2, 3; Rom. 2:12 (twice); 3:23; 5:12, 14, 16; 6:15; 1 Cor. 7:28 (twice), 36; 15:34; Eph. 4:26; 1 Tim. 5:20; Titus 3:11; Heb. 3:17; 10:26; 1 John 1:10; in 2:1 (twice), the aorist tense in each place, referring to an act of "sin"; on the contrary, in 3:6 (twice), 8, 9, the present tense indicates, not the committal of an act, but the continuous practice of "sin"; in 5:16 (twice) the present tense indicates the condition resulting from an act, "unto death" signifying "tending towards death"; (b) against Christ, 1 Cor. 8:12; (c) against man, (1) a brother, Matt. 18:15, RV, "sin" (KJV, "trespass"); v. 21; Luke 17:3, 4, RV, "sin" (KJV, "trespass"); 1 Cor. 8:12; (2) in Luke 15:18, 21, against the father by the Prodigal Son, "in thy sight" being suggestive of befitting reverence; (d) against Jewish law, the Temple, and Caesar, Acts 25:8,

RV, "sinned" (KJV, "offended"); (e) against one's own body, by fornication, 1 Cor. 6:18; (f) against earthly masters by servants, 1 Pet. 2:20, RV, "(when) ye sin (and are buffeted for it)," KJV, "(when ye be buffeted) for your faults," lit., "having sinned."

Cast down ... to hell The verb *tartaroo*, translated "cast down to hell" in **2 Pet. 2:4**, signifies to consign to Tartarus, which is neither Sheol nor hades nor hell, but the place where those angels whose special sin is referred to in that passage are confined "to be reserved unto judgment"; the region is described as "pits of darkness." RV

Delivered *paradidomi* (3860), "to give over," is often rendered by the verb "to commit," e.g., to prison, Acts 8:3; to the grace of God, Acts 14:26; to God, 1 Pet. 2:23; by God to pits of darkness, **2 Pet. 2:4**.

Chains Some ancient authorities have *seira*, "a cord, rope, band, chain," in **2 Pet. 2:4**, instead of *seiros*, "a cavern," RV, "pits."

Darkness *zophos* (2217), denotes "the gloom of the nether world", hence, "thick darkness, darkness that may be felt"; it is rendered "darkness" in Heb. 12:18; **2 Pet. 2:4** and Jude 6; in **2 Pet. 2:17**, RV, "blackness," KJV, "mists"; in Jude 13, RV and KJV, blackness.

Reserved *tereo* (5083), denotes (a) "to watch over, preserve, keep, watch," e.g., Acts 12:5, 6; 16:23; in 25:21, RV (1st part), "kept" (KJV, "reserved"); the present participle is translated "keepers" in Matt. 28:4, lit. "the keeping (ones)"; it is used of the "keeping" power of God the Father and Christ, exercised over His people, John 17:11, 12, 15; 1 Thess. 5:23, "preserved"; 1 John 5:18, where "He that was begotten of God," RV, is said of Christ as the Keeper ("keepeth him," RV, for KJV, "keepeth himself"); Jude 1, RV, "kept for Jesus Christ" (KJV, "preserved in Jesus Christ"), Rev. 3:10; of their inheritance, 1 Pet. 1:4 ("reserved"); of judicial reservation by God in view of future doom, **2 Pet. 2:4, 9, 17; 3:7**; Jude 6, 13; of "keeping" the faith, 2 Tim. 4:7; the unity of the Spirit, Eph. 4:3; oneself, 2 Cor. 11:9; 1 Tim. 5:22; Jas. 1:27; figuratively, one's garments, Rev. 16:15; (b) "to observe, to give heed to," as of keeping commandments, etc., e.g., Matt. 19:17; John 14:15; 15:10; 17:6; Jas. 2:10; 1 John 2:3, 4, 5; 3:22, 24; 5:2 (in some mss.), 3; Rev. 1:3; 2:26; 3:8, 10; 12:17; 14:12; 22:7, 9.

Judgment *krisis* (2920), (a) denotes "the process of investigation, the act of distinguishing and separating" (as distinct from *krima*); hence "a judging, a passing of judgment upon a person or thing"; it has a variety of meanings, such as judicial authority, John 5:22, 27; justice, Acts 8:33; Jas. 2:13; a tribunal, Matt. 5:21-22; a trial, John 5:24; **2 Pet. 2:4**; a judgment, **2 Pet. 2:11**; Jude 9; by metonymy, the standard of judgment, just dealing, Matt. 12:18, 20; 23:23; Luke 11:42; divine judgment executed, 2 Thess. 1:5; Rev. 16:7; (b) sometimes it has the meaning "condemnation," and is virtually equivalent to *krima* (a); see Matt. 23:33; John 3:19; Jas. 5:12, *hupo krisin*, "under judgment."

2:5 And spared not the old world, but saved Noah the eighth *person*, a preacher of righteousness, bringing in the flood upon the world of the ungodly;

Spared *see 2 Peter 2:4*.

Old *archaios* (744), "original, ancient" (from *arche*, "a beginning": Eng., "archaic," "archaeology," etc.), is used (a) of persons belonging to a former age, "(to) them of old time," Matt. 5:21, 33, RV; in some mss. v. 27; the RV rendering is right; not ancient teachers are in view; what was said to them of old time was "to be both recognized in its significance and estimated in its temporary limitations, Christ intending His words to be regarded not as an abrogation, but a deepening and fulfilling" (Cremer); of prophets, Luke 9:8, 19; (b) of time long gone by, Acts 15:21; (c) of days gone by in a person's experience, Acts 15:7, "a good while ago," lit., "from old (days)," i.e., from the first days onward in the sense of originality, not age; (d) of Mnason, "an early disciple," Acts 21:16, RV, not referring to age, but to his being one of the first who had accepted the gospel from the beginning of its proclamation; (e) of things which are "old" in relation to the new, earlier things in contrast to things present, 2 Cor. 5:17, i.e., of what characterized and conditioned the time previous to conversion in a believer's experience, RV, "they are become new," i.e., they have taken on a new complexion and are viewed in an entirely different way; (f) of the world (i.e., the inhabitants of the world) just previous to the Flood, **2 Pet. 2:5**; (g) of the Devil, as "that old serpent," Rev. 12:9; 20:2, "old," not in age, but as characterized for a long period by the evils indicated.

Saved *phulasso* (5442), "to guard, protect, preserve," is translated "preserved" in **2 Pet. 2:5**, RV (KJV, "saved").

Eighth *ogdoos* (3590), "eighth" (connected with the preceding), is used in Luke 1:59; Acts 7:8; **2 Pet. 2:5**; Rev. 17:11; 21:20.

Person In **2 Pet. 2:5**, KJV, *ogdoos*, "eighth," is translated "the (lit., 'an') eighth *person*" (RV, "with seven others"). (b) Various adjectives are used with the word "persons," e.g., "devout, perjured, profane."

Preacher *kerux* (2783), "a herald," is used (a) of the "preacher" of the gospel, 1 Tim. 2:7; 2 Tim. 1:11; (b) of Noah, as a "preacher" of righteousness, **2 Pet. 2:5**.

Bringing *see* **Bring** at *2 Peter 2:1*.

Flood *kataklusmos* (2627), "a deluge" (Eng., "cataclysm"), akin to *katakluzo*, "to inundate," **2 Pet. 3:6**, is used of the "flood" in Noah's time, Matt. 24:38, 39; Luke 17:27; **2 Pet. 2:5**.

Ungodly *asebes* (765), "impious, ungodly," "without reverence for God," not merely irreligious, but acting in contravention of God's demands, Rom. 4:5; 5:6; 1 Tim. 1:9; 1 Pet. 4:18; **2 Pet. 2:5** (v. **6** in some mss.); **3:7**; Jude 4, 15 (twice).

2:6 And turning the cities of Sodom and Gomorrha into ashes condemned *them* with an overthrow, making *them* an ensample unto those that after should live ungodly;

Ashes *tephroo* (5077),. "to turn to ashes," is found in **2 Pet. 2:6**, with reference to the destruction of Sodom and Gomorrah.

Condemned *katakrino* (2632) signifies "to give judgment against, pass sentence upon"; hence, "to condemn," implying (a) the fact of a crime, e.g., Rom. 2:1; 14:23; **2 Pet. 2:6**; some mss. have it in Jas. 5:9; (b) the imputation of a crime, as in the "condemnation" of Christ by the Jews, Matt. 20:18; Mark 14:64. It is used metaphorically of "condemning" by a good example, Matt. 12:41-42; Luke 11:31-32; Heb. 11:7. In Rom. 8:3, God's "condemnation" of sin is set forth in that Christ, His own Son, sent by Him to partake of human nature (sin apart) and to become an offering for sin, died under the judgment due to our sin.

Overthrow *katastrophe* (2692), lit., "a turning down" (*kata*, "down," *strophe*, "a turning"; Eng., "catastrophe"), is used (a) literally, **2 Pet. 2:6**, (b) metaphorically, 2 Tim. 2:14 "subverting," i.e., the "overthrowing" of faith. Cf. *kathairesis*, "a pulling down," 2 Cor. 10:4, 8; 13:10.

Making *tithemi* (5087), "to put," is used of "appointment" to any form of service. Christ used it of His followers, John 15:16 (RV, "appointed" for KJV, "ordained"). "I set you" would be more in keeping with the metaphor of grafting. The verb is used by Paul of his service in the ministry of the gospel, 1 Tim. 1:12 (RV, "appointing" for "putting"); 2:7 (RV, "appointed" for "ordained"); and 2 Tim. 1:11 (RV, "appointing" for "putting"); of the overseers, or bishops, in the local church at Ephesus, as those "appointed" by the Holy Ghost, to tend the church of God, Acts 20:28 ("hath made"); of the Son of God, as appointed Heir of all things, Heb. 1:2. It is also used of "appointment" to punishment, as of the unfaithful servant, Matt. 24:51; Luke 12:46; of unbelieving Israel, 1 Pet. 2:8. Cf. **2 Pet. 2:6**.

Ensample *hupodeigma* (5262), lit., "that which is shown" (from *hupo*, "under," and *deiknumi*, "to show"), hence, (a) "a figure, copy," Heb. 8:5, RV, "copy," for KJV, "example"; 9:23; (b) "an example," whether for imitation, John 13:15; Jas. 5:10, or for warning, Heb. 4:11; **2 Pet. 2:6**, RV, example.

Ungodly *asebeo* (764), signifies (a) "to be or live ungodly," **2 Pet. 2:6**; (b) "to commit ungodly deeds," Jude 15. *See also* ***2 Peter 2:5***.

2:7 And delivered just Lot, vexed with the filthy conversation of the wicked:

Just *dikaios* (1342), signifies "just," without prejudice or partiality, e.g., of the judgment of God, 2 Thess. 1:5, 6; of His judgments, Rev. 16:7; 19:2; of His character as Judge, 2 Tim. 4:8; Rev. 16:5; of His ways and doings, Rev. 15:3. In the following the RV substitutes "righteous" for the KJV "just"; Matt. 1:19; 13:49; 27:19, 24; Mark 6:20; Luke 2:25; 15:7; 20:20; 23:50; John 5:30; Acts 3:14; 7:52; 10:22; 22:14; Rom. 1:17; 7:12; Gal. 3:11; Heb. 10:38; Jas. 5:6; 1 Pet. 3:18; **2 Pet. 2:7**; 1 John 1:9; Rev. 15:3.

Vexed *kataponeo* (2669), primarily, "to tire down with toil, exhaust with labor" (*kata*, "down," *ponos*, "labor"), hence signifies "to afflict, oppress"; in the passive voice, "to be oppressed, much distressed"; it is translated "oppressed" in Acts 7:24, and "sore distressed" in **2 Pet. 2:7**, RV, (KJV, "vexed").

Filthy *aselgeia* (766), "wantonness, licentiousness, lasciviousness," is translated "filthy (conversation)," in **2 Pet. 2:7**, KJV; RV, lascivious (life). *See also* **Pernicious** at *2 Peter 2:2*.

Conversation *anastrophe* (391), lit., "a turning back," is translated "manner of life," "living," etc., in the RV, for KJV, "conversation," Gal. 1:13; Eph. 4:22; 1 Tim. 4:12; Heb. 13:7; Jas. 3:13; 1 Pet. 1:15, 18; 2:1 ("behavior"); 3:1, 2, 16 (ditto); **2 Pet. 2:7**; **3:11**.

Wicked *athesmos* (113), "lawless" (*a*, negative, *thesmos*, "law, custom"), "wicked," occurs in **2 Pet. 2:7**; **3:17**. An instance of the use of the word is found in the papyri, where a father breaks off his daughter's engagement because he learnt that her fiance was giving himself over to lawless deeds (Moulton and Milligan, *Vocab.*).

2:8 (For that righteous man dwelling among them, in seeing and hearing, vexed *his*

righteous soul from day to day with *their* unlawful deeds;)

Dwelling *enkatoikeo* (1460), "to dwell among," is used in **2 Pet. 2:8.**

Seeing *blemma* (990), primarily, "a look, a glance," denotes "sight," **2 Pet. 2:8**, rendered "seeing"; some interpret it as meaning "look"; Moulton and Milligan illustrate it thus from the papyri; it seems difficult, however to take the next word "hearing" (in the similar construction) in this way.

Hearing *akoe* (189), "hearing," akin to *akouo*, "to hear," denotes (a) the sense of "hearing," e.g., 1 Cor. 12:17; **2 Pet. 2:8**; (b) that which is "heard," a report, e.g., Matt. 4:24; (c) the physical organ, Mark 7:35, standing for the sense of "hearing"; so in Luke 7:1, RV, for KJV, "audience"; Acts 17:20; 2 Tim. 4:3-4 (in v. 3, lit., "being tickled as to the ears"); (d) a message or teaching, John 12:38; Rom. 10:16-17; Gal. 3:2, 5; 1 Thess. 2:13; Heb. 4:2, RV, "(the word) of hearing," for KJV, "(the word) preached."

Vexed *basanizo* (928), "to torment," is translated "vexed" in **2 Pet. 2:8.**

Soul *psuche* (5590), denotes "the breath, the breath of life," then "the soul," in its various meanings. The NT uses "may be analyzed approximately as follows: (a) the natural life of the body, Matt. 2:20; Luke 12:22; Acts 20:10; Rev. 8:9; 12:11; cf. Lev. 17:11; 2 Sam. 14:7; Esth. 8:11; (b) the immaterial, invisible part of man, Matt. 10:28; Acts 2:27; cf. 1 Kings 17:21; (c) the disembodied (or "unclothed" or "naked," 2 Cor. 5:3, 4) man, Rev. 6:9; (d) the seat of personality, Luke 9:24, explained as = "own self," v. 25; Heb. 6:19; 10:39; cf. Isa. 53:10 with 1 Tim. 2:6; (e) the seat of the sentient element in man, that by which he perceives, reflects, feels, desires, Matt. 11:29; Luke 1:46; 2:35; Acts 14:2, 22; cf. Ps. 84:2; 139:14; Isa. 26:9; (f) the seat of will and purpose, Matt. 22:37; Acts 4:32; Eph. 6:6; Phil. 1:27; Heb. 12:3; cf. Num. 21:4; Deut. 11:13; (g) the seat of appetite, Rev. 18:14; cf. Ps. 107:9; Prov. 6:30; Isa. 5:14 ("desire"); 29:8; (h) persons, individuals, Acts 2:41, 43; Rom. 2:9; Jas. 5:20; 1 Pet. 3:20; **2 Pet. 2:14**; cf. Gen. 12:5; 14:21 ("persons"); Lev. 4:2 ('any one'); Ezek. 27:13; of dead bodies, Num. 6:6, lit., "dead soul"; and of animals, Lev. 24:18, lit., "soul for soul"; (i) the equivalent of the personal pronoun, used for emphasis and effect: 1st person, John 10:24 ("us"); Heb. 10:38; cf. Gen. 12:13; Num. 23:10; Jud. 16:30; Ps. 120:2 ("me"); 2nd person, 2 Cor. 12:15; Heb. 13:17; Jas. 1:21; 1 Pet. 1:9; 2:25; cf. Lev. 17:11; 26:15; 1 Sam. 1:26; 3rd person, 1 Pet. 4:19; **2 Pet. 2:8**; cf. Exod. 30:12; Job 32:2, Heb. "soul," Sept. "self"; (j) an animate creature, human or other, 1 Cor. 15:45; Rev. 16:3; cf. Gen. 1:24; 2:7, 19; (k) "the inward man," the seat of the new life, Luke 21:19 (cf. Matt. 10:39); 1 Pet. 2:11; 3 John 2."

Day to day The following phrases contain the word *hemera*, "day," and are translated "daily" or otherwise: (a) *kath' hemeran*, lit., "according to, or for, (the) day, or throughout the day," "day by day," e.g., Luke 11:3; Acts 3:2; 16:5; 1 Cor. 15:31; Heb. 7:27; (b) *hemera kai hemera*, lit., "day and day," "day by day," 2 Cor. 4:16; (c) *hemeran ex hemeras*, lit., "day from day," "from day to day," **2 Pet. 2:8**; (d) *semeron*, "this day," or "today," used outside the Synoptists and the Acts, in 2 Cor. 3:14-15, eight times in Hebrews, and in Jas. 4:13; (e) *tessemeron hemeras*, "(unto) this very day," Rom. 11:8 (RV); (f) *tas hemeras*, Luke 21:37, RV, "every day," for KJV, "in the daytime"; (g) *pasan hemeran*, Acts 5:42, RV, "every day"; preceded by *kata* in Acts 17:17, RV, "every day"; (h) *kath' hekasten hemeran*, lit., "according to each day," Heb. 3:13, "day by day," RV.

Unlawful *anomos* (459), "without law," also denotes "lawless," and is so rendered in the RV of Acts 2:23, "lawless (men)," marg., "(men) without the law," KJV, "wicked (hands);" 2 Thess. 2:8, "the lawless one" (KJV, "that wicked"), of the man of sin (2 Thess. 2:4); in **2 Pet. 2:8**, of deeds (KJV, "unlawful"), where the thought is not simply that of doing what is unlawful, but of flagrant defiance of the known will of God.

2:9 The Lord knoweth how to deliver the godly out of temptations, and to reserve the unjust unto the day of judgment to be punished:

Knoweth *oida* (1492), from the same root as *eidon*, "to see," is a perfect tense with a present meaning, signifying, primarily, "to have seen or perceived"; hence, "to know, to have knowledge of," whether absolutely, as in divine knowledge, e.g., Matt. 6:8, 32; John 6:6, 64; 8:14; 11:42; 13:11; 18:4; 2 Cor. 11:31; **2 Pet. 2:9**; Rev. 2:2, 9, 13, 19; 3:1, 8, 15; or in the case of human "knowledge," to know from observation, e.g., 1 Thess. 1:4, 5; 2:1; 2 Thess. 3:7. The differences between *ginosko* and *oida* demand consideration: (a) *ginosko*, frequently suggests inception or progress in "knowledge," while *oida* suggests fullness of "knowledge," e.g., John 8:55, "ye have not known Him" (*ginosko*), i.e., begun to "know," "but I know Him" (*oida*), i.e., "know Him perfectly"; 13:7, "What I do thou knowest not now," i.e. Peter did not yet perceive (*oida*) its significance, "but thou shalt understand," i.e., "get to know (*ginosko*), hereafter"; 14:7, "If ye had known Me" (*ginosko*), i.e., "had definitely come to know Me," "ye would have known My Father also" (*oida*), i.e., "would have had perception of": "from henceforth ye know Him" (*ginosko*), i.e., having unconsciously been coming to the Father, as the One who was in Him, they would now consciously be in the constant and progressive experience of "knowing" Him; in Mark 4:13, "Know ye not (*oida*) this parable? and how shall ye know (*ginosko*) all the parables?" (RV), i.e., "Do ye not understand this parable? How shall ye come to perceive all ..." the intimation being that the first parable is a leading and testing one; (b) while *ginosko* frequently implies an active relation between the one who "knows" and the person or thing "known," *oida* expresses the fact that the object has simply come within the scope of the "knower's" perception; thus in Matt. 7:23 "I never knew you" (*ginosko*) suggests "I have never been in approving connection with you," whereas in 25:12, "I know you not" (*oida*) suggests "you stand in no relation to Me."

Deliver *rhuomai* (4506), "to rescue from, to preserve from," and so, "to deliver," the word by which it is regularly translated, is largely synonymous with *sozo*, "to save," though the idea of "rescue from" is predominant in *rhuomai* (see Matt. 27:43), that of "preservation from," in *sozo*. In Rom. 11:26 the present participle is used with the article, as a noun, "the Deliverer." This is the construction in 1 Thess. 1:10, where Christ is similarly spoken of. Here the KJV wrongly has "which delivered" (the tense is not past); RV, "which delivereth"; the translation might well be (as in Rom. 11:26), "our Deliverer," that is, from the retributive calamities with which God will visit men at the end of the present age. From that wrath believers are to be "delivered." The verb is used with *apo*, "away from," in Matt. 6:13; Luke 11:4 (in some mss.); so also in 11:4; Rom. 15:31; 2 Thess. 3:2; 2 Tim. 4:18; and with *ek*, "from, out of," in Luke 1:74; Rom. 7:24; 2 Cor. 1:10; Col. 1:13, from bondage; in **2 Pet. 2:9**, from temptation, in 2 Tim. 3:11, from persecution; but *ek* is used of ills impending, in 2 Cor. 1:10; in 2 Tim. 4:17, *ek* indicates that the danger was more imminent than in v. 18, where *apo* is used. Accordingly the meaning "out of the midst of" cannot be pressed in 1 Thess. 1:10.

Godly *eusebes* (2152), from *eu*, "well," *sebomai*, "to reverence," the root *seb-* signifying "sacred awe," describes "reverence" exhibited especially in actions, reverence or awe well directed. Among the Greeks it was used, e.g., of practical piety towards parents. In the NT it is used of a pious attitude towards God, Acts 10:2, 7; (in some mss. in 22:12); "godly," in **2 Pet. 2:9**. In the Sept., Prov. 12:12; Isa. 24:16; 26:7; 32:8; Mic. 7:2.

Temptations *peirasmos* (3986), is used of (1) "trials" with a beneficial purpose and effect, (a) of "trials" or "temptations," divinely permitted or sent, Luke 22:28; Acts 20:19; Jas. 1:2; 1 Pet. 1:6; 4:12, RV, "to prove," KJV, "to try"; **2 Pet. 2:9** (singular); Rev. 3:10, RV, "trial" (KJV, "temptation"); in Jas. 1:12, "temptation" apparently has meanings (1) and (2) combined, and is used in the widest sense; (b) with a good or neutral significance, Gal. 4:14, of Paul's physical infirmity, "a temptation" to the Galatian converts, of such a kind as to arouse feelings of natural repugnance; (c) of "trials" of a varied character, Matt. 6:13 and Luke 11:4, where believers are commanded to pray not to be led into such by forces beyond their own control; Matt. 26:41; Mark 14:38; Luke 22:40, 46, where they are commanded to watch and pray against entering into "temptations" by their own carelessness or disobedience; in all such cases God provides "the way of escape," 1 Cor. 10:13 (where *peirasmos* occurs twice). (2) Of "trial" definitely designed to lead to wrong doing, "temptation," Luke 4:13; 8:13; 1 Tim. 6:9; (3) of "trying" or challenging God, by men, Heb. 3:8.

Reserve *see* ***Reserved*** at ***2 Peter 2:4***.

Unjust *adikos* (94), not conforming to *dike*, "right," is translated "unrighteous" in Luke 16:10 (twice), RV, 11; Rom. 3:5; 1 Cor. 6:1, RV; 6:9; Heb. 6:10; 1 Pet. 3:18, RV; **2 Pet. 2:9**, RV.

Punished *kolazo* (2849), primarily denotes "to curtail, prune, dock" (from *kolos*, "docked"); then, "to check, restrain, punish"; it is used in the middle voice in Acts 4:21; passive voice in **2 Pet. 2:9**, KJV, "to be punished" (RV, "under punishment," lit., "being punished"), a futurative present tense.

2:10 But chiefly them that walk after the flesh in the lust of uncleanness, and despise government. Presumptuous *are they*, selfwilled, they are not afraid to speak evil of dignities.

Chiefly *malista* (3122), the superlative of *mala*, "very, very much," is rendered "chiefly" in **2 Pet. 2:10** and in the KJV of Phil. 4:22 (RV, especially).

Walk *poreuo* (4198), is used in the middle voice and rendered "to walk" in Luke 1:6, of the general activities of life; so in Luke 13:33, KJV, "walk" (RV, "go on My way"); Acts 9:31; 14:16; 1 Pet. 4:3; **2 Pet. 2:10**; Jude 16, 18.

Lust *epithumia* (1939), denotes "strong desire" of any kind, the various kinds being frequently specified by some adjective. The word is used of a good desire in Luke 22:15; Phil. 1:23, and 1 Thess. 2:17 only. Everywhere else it has a bad sense. In Rom. 6:12 the injunction against letting sin reign in our mortal body to obey the "lust" thereof, refers to those evil desires which are ready to express themselves in bodily activity. They are equally the "lusts" of the flesh, Rom. 13:14; Gal. 5:16, 24; Eph. 2:3; **2 Pet. 2:18**; 1 John 2:16, a phrase which describes the emotions of the soul, the natural tendency towards things evil. Such "lusts" are not necessarily base and immoral, they may be refined in character, but are evil if inconsistent with the will of God. Other descriptions besides those already mentioned are:—"of the mind," Eph. 2:3; "evil (desire)," Col. 3:5; "the passion of," 1 Thess. 4:5, RV; "foolish and hurtful," 1 Tim. 6:9; "youthful," 2 Tim. 2:22; "divers," 2 Tim. 3:6 and Titus 3:3; "their own," 2 Tim. 4:3; **2 Pet. 3:3**; Jude 16; "worldly," Titus 2:12; "his own," Jas. 1:14; "your former," 1 Pet. 1:14, RV; "fleshly," 2:11; "of men," 4:2; "of defilement," **2 Pet. 2:10**; "of the eyes," 1 John 2:16; of the world ("thereof"), v. 17; "their own ungodly," Jude 18. In Rev. 18:14 "(the fruits) which thy soul lusted after" is, lit., "of thy soul's lust."

Uncleanness *miasmos* (3394), primarily denotes "the act of defiling," the process, in contrast to the "defiling" thing. It is found in **2 Pet. 2:10** (KJV, "uncleanness," RV, "defilement.").

Despise *kataphroneo* (2706), lit., "to think down upon or against anyone" (*kata*, "down," *phren*, "the mind"), hence signifies "to think slightly of, to despise," Matt. 6:24; 18:10; Luke 16:13; Rom. 2:4; 1 Cor. 11:22; 1 Tim. 4:12; 6:2; Heb. 12:2; **2 Pet. 2:10**.

Government *kuriotes* (2963), denotes "lordship" (*kurios*, "a lord"), "power, dominion," whether angelic or human, Eph. 1:21; Col. 1:16; **2 Pet. 2:10** (RV, for KJV, "government"); Jude 8. In Eph. and Col. it indicates a grade in the angelic orders, in which it stands second.

Presumptious *tolmetes* (5113), "daring," is used in **2 Pet. 2:10**, RV, "daring" (KJV "presumptuous"), "shameless and irreverent daring."

Selfwilled *authades* (829), "self-pleasing" (*autos*, "self," *hedomai*, "to please"), denotes one who, dominated by self-interest, and inconsiderate of others, arrogantly asserts his own will, "self-willed," Titus 1:7; **2 Pet. 2:10** (the opposite of *epieikes*, "gentle," e.g., 1 Tim. 3:3), "one so far overvaluing any determination at which he has himself once arrived that he will not be removed from it" (Trench, who compares and contrasts *philautos*, "loving self, selfish"; *Syn.* Sec.xciii). In the Sept., Gen. 49:3, 7; Prov. 21:24.

Not afraid *tremo* (5141), "to tremble, especially with fear," is used in Mark 5:33; Luke 8:47 (Acts 9:6, in some mss.); **2 Pet. 2:10**, RV, "they tremble (not)," KJV, "they are (not) afraid."

Speak evil of *blasphemeo* (987), "to blaspheme, rail, revile," is translated "to rail at, or on," in Matt. 27:39, RV (KJV, "reviled"); Mark 15:29; Luke 23:39; **2 Pet. 2:10**, RV (KJV, "to speak evil of"); **2:12**, RV (KJV, "speak evil of"). Cf. *loidoreo*, "to revile." *See also* **Evil spoken of** at *2 Peter 2:2*.

Dignities *doxa* (1391), primarily denotes "an opinion, estimation, repute"; in the NT, always "good opinion, praise, honor, glory, an appearance commanding respect, magnificence, excellence, manifestation of glory"; hence, of angelic powers, in respect of their state as commanding recognition, "dignities," **2 Pet. 2:10**; Jude 8.

2:11 Whereas angels, which are greater in power and might, bring not railing accusation against them before the Lord.

Power *ischus* (2479), denotes "might, strength, power," (a) inherent and in action as used of God, Eph. 1:19, RV, "(the strength, *kratos*, of His) might," KJV, "(His mighty) power," i.e., power (over external things) exercised by strength; Eph. 6:10, "of His might"; 2 Thess. 1:9, RV, "(from the glory) of His might" (KJV "power"); Rev. 5:12, RV, "might" (KJV, "strength"); 7:12, "might"; (b) as an endowment, said (1) of angels, **2 Pet. 2:11**; here the order is *ischus* and *dunamis*, RV, "might and power," which better expresses the distinction than the KJV, "power and might"; in some mss. in Rev. 18:2 it is said of the voice of an angel; the most authentic mss. have the adjective *ischuros*, "mighty"; (2) of men, Mark 12:30, 33; Luke 10:27 (RV and KJV, "strength," in all three verses); 1 Pet. 4:11, RV, "strength" (KJV, "ability" this belongs rather to *dunamis*). Either "strength" or "might" expresses the true significance of *ischus*.

Might *dunamis* (1411), "power," (a) used relatively, denotes "inherent ability, capability, ability to perform anything," e.g., Matt. 25:15, "ability"; Acts 3:12, "power"; 2 Thess. 1:7, RV, "(angels) of His power" (KJV, "mighty"); Heb. 11:11, RV, "power" (KJV, "strength"); (b) used absolutely, denotes (1) "power to work, to carry something into effect," e.g.,

Luke 24:49; (2) "power in action," e.g., Rom. 1:16; 1 Cor. 1:18; it is translated "might" in the KJV of Eph. 1:21 (RV, "power"); so 3:16; Col. 1:11 (1st clause); **2 Pet. 2:11**; in Rom. 15:19, KJV, this noun is rendered "mighty"; RV, "(in the) power of signs." The RV consistently avoids the rendering "might" for *dunamis;* the usual rendering is "power." Under this heading comes the rendering "mighty works," e.g., Matt. 7:22, RV (KJV, "wonderful works"); 11:20-23; singular number in Mark 6:5; in Matt. 14:2 and Mark 6:14 the RV has "powers"; in 2 Cor. 12:12, RV, "mighty works" (KJV, "mighty deeds").

Railing *blasphemos* (989), "abusive, speaking evil," is translated "blasphemous," in Acts 6:11, 13; "a blasphemer," 1 Tim. 1:13; "railers," 2 Tim. 3:2, RV; "railing," **2 Pet. 2:11**.

Accusation *krisis,* which has been translated "accusation," in the KJV of **2 Pet. 2:11** and Jude 9 (RV, "judgement"), does not come under this category. It signifies "a judgment, a decision given concerning anything." *See also* **Judgment** at *2 Peter 2:4.*

2:12 But these, as natural brute beasts, made to be taken and destroyed, speak evil of the things that they understand not; and shall utterly perish in their own corruption;

Natural *phusikos* (5446), originally signifying "produced by nature, inborn," from *phusis,* "nature," cf. Eng., "physical," "physics," etc., denotes (a) "according to nature," Rom. 1:26, 27; (b) "governed by mere natural instincts," **2 Pet. 2:12**, RV, "(born) mere animals," KJV and RV marg., "natural (brute beasts)."

Brute *alogos* (249), translated "brute" in the KJV of **2 Pet. 2:12** and Jude 10, signifies "without reason," RV, though, as J. Hastings points out, "brute beasts" is not at all unsuitable, as "brute" is from Latin *brutus,* which means "dull, irrational"; in Acts 25:27 it is rendered "unreasonable".

Beasts *zoon* (2226), primarily denotes "a living being" (*zoe,* "life"). The Eng., "animal," is the equivalent, stressing the fact of life as the characteristic feature. In Heb. 13:11 the KJV and the RV translate it "beasts" ("animals" would be quite suitable). In **2 Pet. 2:12** and Jude 10, the KJV has "beasts," the RV "creatures." In Revelation, where the word is found some 20 times, and always of those beings which stand before the throne of God, who give glory and honor and thanks to Him, 4:6, and act in perfect harmony with His counsels, 5:14; 6:1-7, e.g., the word "beasts" is most unsuitable; the RV, "living creatures," should always be used; it gives to *zoon* its appropriate significance.

Made *gennao* (1080), "to beget," in the passive voice, "to be born," is chiefly used of men "begetting" children, Matt. 1:2-16; more rarely of women "begetting" children, Luke 1:13, 57, "brought forth"; 23:29; John 16:21, "is delivered of," and of the child, "is born." In Gal. 4:24, it is used allegorically, to contrast Jews under bondage to the Law, and spiritual Israel, KJV, "gendereth," RV, "bearing children," to contrast the natural birth of Ishmael and the supernatural birth of Isaac. In Matt. 1:20 it is used of conception, "that which is conceived in her." It is used of the act of God in the birth of Christ, Acts 13:33; Heb. 1:5; 5:5, quoted from Psalm 2:7, none of which indicate that Christ became the Son of God at His birth.

It is used metaphorically (a) in the writings of the apostle John, of the gracious act of God in conferring upon those who believe the nature and disposition of "children," imparting to them spiritual life, John 3:3, 5, 7; 1 John 2:29; 3:9; 4:7; 5:1, 4, 18; (b) of one who by means of preaching the gospel becomes the human instrument in the impartation of spiritual life, 1 Cor. 4:15; Philem. 10; (c) in **2 Pet. 2:12**, with reference to the evil men whom the apostle is describing, the RV rightly has "born mere animals" (KJV, "natural brute beasts"); (d) in the sense of gendering strife, 2 Tim. 2:23.

Taken In **2 Pet. 2:12** "to be taken" translates the phrase *eis halosin,* lit., "for capture" (*halosis,* "a taking").

Destroyed *phthora* (5356), denotes "the destruction that comes with corruption." In **2 Pet. 2:12** it is used twice; for the KJV, "made to be taken and destroyed ... shall utterly perish (*phtheiro*) in their own corruption," the RV has "to be taken and destroyed (lit., 'unto capture and destruction,' *phthora*) ... shall in their destroying (*phthora*) surely be destroyed," taking the noun in the last clause in the sense of their act of "destroying" others.

Speak evil of *see* **Evil spoken of** at *2 Peter 2:2. See also* ***2 Peter 2:10.***

Understand not *agnoeo* (50), signifies (a) "to be ignorant, not to know," either intransitively, 1 Cor. 14:38 (in the 2nd occurrence in this verse, the RV text translates the active voice, the margin the passive); 1 Tim. 1:13, lit., "being ignorant (I did it)"; Heb. 5:2, "ignorant"; or transitively, **2 Pet. 2:12**, KJV, "understand not," RV, "are ignorant (of)"; Acts 13:27, "knew (Him) not"; 17:23, RV, "(what ye worship) in ignorance," for KJV, "(whom ye) ignorantly (worship)," lit., "(what) not knowing (ye worship"; also rendered by the verb "to be ignorant that," or "to be ignorant of," Rom. 1:13; 10:3; 11:25; 1 Cor. 10:1; 12:1; 2 Cor. 1:8; 2:11; 1 Thess. 4:13; to know not, Rom. 2:4; 6:3; 7:1; to be unknown (passive voice), 2 Cor. 6:9; Gal. 1:22; (b) "not to understand," Mark 9:32; Luke 9:45.

Perish *phtheiro* (5351), signifies "to destroy by means of corrupting," and so "bringing into a worse state"; (a) with this significance it is used of the effect of evil company upon the manners of believers, and so of the effect of association with those who deny the truth and hold false doctrine, 1 Cor. 15:33 (this was a saying of the pagan poet Menander, which became a well known proverb); in 2 Cor. 7:2, of the effects of dishonorable dealing by bringing people to want (a charge made against the apostle); in 11:3, of the effects upon the minds (or thoughts) of believers by "corrupting" them "from the simplicity and the purity that is toward Christ"; in Eph. 4:22, intransitively, of the old nature in waxing "corrupt," "morally decaying, on the way to final ruin" (Moule), "after the lusts of deceit"; in Rev. 19:2, metaphorically, of the Babylonish harlot, in "corrupting" the inhabitants of the earth by her false religion.

(b) With the significance of destroying, it is used of marring a local church by leading it away from that condition of holiness of life and purity of doctrine in which it should abide, 1 Cor. 3:17 (KJV, "defile"), and of God's retributive destruction of the offender who is guilty of this sin (id.); of the effects of the work of false and abominable teachers upon themselves, **2 Pet. 2:12** (some texts have *kataphtheiro*; KJV, "shall utterly perish"), and Jude 10 (KJV, "corrupt themselves," RV, marg., "are corrupted").

Corruption *see 2 Peter 1:4.*

2:13 And shall receive the reward of unrighteousness, *as* they that count it pleasure to riot in the day time. Spots *they are* and blemishes, sporting themselves with their own deceivings while they feast with you;

Receive *adikeo* (91), "to do wrong," is used (a) intransitively, to act unrighteously, Acts 25:11, RV, "I am a wrongdoer" (KJV, "... an offender"); 1 Cor. 6:8; 2 Cor. 7:12 (1st part); Col. 3:25 (1st part); cf. Rev. 22:11; (b) transitively, "to wrong," Matt. 20:13; Acts 7:24 (passive voice), 26, 27; 25:10; 2 Cor. 7:2, v. 12 (2nd part; passive voice); Gal. 4:12, "ye did (me no) wrong," anticipating a possible suggestion that his vigorous language was due to some personal grievance; the occasion referred to was that of his first visit; Col. 3:25 (2nd part), lit., "what he did wrong," which brings consequences both in this life and at the judgment seat of Christ; Philem. 18; **2 Pet. 2:13** (1st part); in the middle or passive voice, "to take or suffer wrong, to suffer (oneself) to be wronged," 1 Cor. 6:7.

komizo (2865), denotes "to bear, carry," e.g., Luke 7:37; in the middle voice, "to bear for oneself," hence (a) "to receive," Heb. 10:36; 11:13 (in the best texts; some have *lambano*), 39; 1 Pet. 1:9; 5:4; in some texts in **2 Pet. 2:13** (in the best mss. *adikeomai*, "suffering wrong," RV); (b) "to receive back, recover," Matt. 25:27; Heb. 11:19; metaphorically, of requital, 2 Cor. 5:10; Col. 3:25, of "receiving back again" by the believer at the judgment seat of Christ hereafter, for wrong done in this life; Eph. 6:8, of "receiving," on the same occasion, "whatsoever good thing each one doeth," RV.

Reward *misthos* (3408), denotes (a) "wages, hire," Matt. 20:8; Luke 10:7; Jas. 5:4; in 1 Tim. 5:18; **2 Pet. 2:13**; Jude 11, RV, "hire" (KJV, "reward"); in **2 Pet. 2:15**, RV, "hire" (KJV, "wages").

Unrighteousness *adikia* (93), denotes (a) "injustice," Luke 18:6, lit., "the judge of injustice"; Rom. 9:14; (b) "unrighteousness, iniquity," e.g., Luke 16:8, lit., "the steward of unrighteousness," RV marg., i.e., characterized by "unrighteousness"; Rom. 1:18, 29; 2:8; 3:5; 6:13; 1 Cor. 13:6, RV, "unrighteousness"; 2 Thess. 2:10, "[with all (lit., 'in every) deceit'] of unrighteousness," i.e., deceit such as "unrighteousness" uses, and that in every variety; Antichrist and his ministers will not be restrained by any scruple from words or deeds calculated to deceive; 2 Thess. 2:12, of those who have pleasure in it, not an intellectual but a moral evil; distaste for truth is the precursor of the rejection of it; 2 Tim. 2:19, RV; 1 John 1:9, which includes (c); (c) "a deed or deeds violating law and justice" (virtually the same as *adikema*, "an unrighteous act"), e.g., Luke 13:27, "iniquity"; 2 Cor. 12:13, "wrong," the wrong of depriving another of what is his own, here ironically of a favor; Heb. 8:12, 1st clause, "iniquities," lit., "unrighteousnesses" (plural, not as KJV); **2 Pet. 2:13, 15**, RV, "wrongdoing," KJV, "unrighteousness"; 1 John 5:17.

Count *hegeomai* (2233), primarily, "to lead the way"; hence, "to lead before the mind, account," is found with this meaning in Phil. 2:3, RV (KJV, "esteem"); 2:6, RV (KJV, "thought"); 2:25 (KJV, "supposed"); Phil. 3:7-8; 2 Thess. 3:15; 1 Tim. 1:12; 6:1; Heb. 10:29; Jas. 1:2; Heb. 11:11 (KJV, "judged"); **2 Pet. 2:13; 3:9.**

Pleasure *hedone* (2237), "pleasure," is used of the gratification of the natural desire or sinful desires (akin to *hedormai*, "to be glad," and *hedeos*, "gladly"), Luke 8:14; Titus 3:3; Jas. 4:1, 3, RV, "pleasures" (KJV, "lusts"); in the singular, **2 Pet. 2:13**.

Riot *truphe* (5172), "luxuriousness, daintiness, reveling," is translated freely by the verb "to revel" in **2 Pet. 2:13**, RV (KJV, "to riot"), lit., "counting reveling in the daytime a pleasure." In Luke 7:25 it is used with *en*, "in," and translated "delicately."

Spots *spilos* (4696), "a spot or stain," is used metaphorically (a) of moral blemish, Eph. 5:27; (b) of lascivious and riotous persons, **2 Pet. 2:13**.

Blemishes *momos* (3470), akin to *momaomai*, signifies (a) "a blemish" (Sept. only); (b) "a shame, a moral disgrace," metaphorical of the licentious, **2 Pet. 2:13**.

Sporting *entruphao* (1792), occurs in **2 Pet. 2:13** (RV, "revel").

Deceivings In **2 Pet. 2:13**, the most authentic texts have "revelling in their love-feasts," RV (*agapais*), for KJV, "deceivings" (*apatais*). *agape* (26), is used in the plural in Jude 12, and in some mss. in **2 Pet. 2:13**; RV marg., "many ancient authorities read 'deceivings,'" (*apatais*); so the KJV. These love feasts arose from the common meals of the early churches (cf. 1 Cor. 11:21). They may have had this origin in the private meals of Jewish households, with the addition of the observance of the Lord's Supper. There were, however, similar common meals among the pagan religious brotherhoods. The evil dealt with at Corinth (l.c.) became enhanced by the presence of immoral persons, who degraded the feasts into wanton banquets, as mentioned in 2 Pet. and Jude. In later times the *agape* became detached from the Lord's Supper.

Feast with *suneuocheo* (4910), "to entertain sumptuously with," is used in the passive voice, denoting "to feast sumptuously with" (*sun*, "together," and *euochia*, "good cheer"), "to revel with," translated "feast with" in **2 Pet. 2:13** and Jude 12.

2:14 Having eyes full of adultery, and that cannot cease from sin; beguiling unstable souls: an heart they have exercised with covetous practices; cursed children:

Eyes *ophthalmos* (3788), akin to *opsis*, "sight," probably from a root signifying "penetration, sharpness" (Curtius, Gk. Etym.) (cf. Eng., "ophthalmia," etc.). is used (a) of the physical organ, e.g., Matt. 5:38; of restoring sight, e.g., Matt. 20:33; of God's power of vision, Heb. 4:13; 1 Pet. 3:12; of Christ in vision, Rev. 1:14; 2:18; 19:12; of the Holy Spirit in the unity of Godhood with Christ, Rev. 5:6; (b) metaphorically, of ethical qualities, evil, Matt. 6:23; Mark 7:22 (by metonymy, for envy); singleness of motive, Matt. 6:22; Luke 11:34; as the instrument of evil desire, "the principal avenue of temptation," 1 John 2:16; of adultery, **2 Pet. 2:14**; (c) metaphorically, of mental vision, Matt. 13:15; John 12:40; Rom. 11:8; Gal. 3:1, where the metaphor of the "evil eye" is altered to a different sense from that of bewitching (the posting up or placarding of an "eye" was used as a charm, to prevent mischief); by gospel-preaching Christ had been, so to speak, placarded before their "eyes"; the question may be paraphrased, "What evil teachers have been malignly fascinating you?"; Eph. 1:18, of the "eyes of the heart," as a means of knowledge.

Full *mestos* (3324), probably akin to a root signifying "to measure," hence conveys the sense of "having full measure," (a) of material things, a vessel, John 19:29; a net, 21:11; (b) metaphorically, of thoughts and feelings, exercised (1) in evil things, hypocrisy, Matt. 23:28; envy, murder, strife, deceit, malignity, Rom. 1:29; the utterances of the tongue, Jas. 3:8; adultery, **2 Pet. 2:14**; (2) in virtues, goodness, Rom. 15:14; mercy, etc., Jas. 3:17.

Adultery *moichalis* (3428), "an adulteress," is used (a) in the natural sense, **2 Pet. 2:14**; Rom. 7:3; (b) in the spiritual sense, Jas. 4:4; here the RV rightly omits the word "adulterers." It was added by a copyist. As in Israel the breach of their relationship with God through their idolatry, was described as "adultery" or "harlotry" (e.g., Ezek. 16:15, etc.; 23:43), so believers who cultivate friendship with the world, thus breaking their spiritual union with Christ, are spiritual "adulteresses," having been spiritually united to Him as wife to husband, Rom. 7:4. It is used adjectivally to describe the Jewish people in transferring their affections from God, Matt. 12:39; 16:4; Mark 8:38. In **2 Pet. 2:14**, the lit. translation is "full of an adulteress" (RV, marg.).

Cease *akatapaustos*, "incessant, not to be set at rest" (from *a*, negative, *kata*, "down," *pauo*, "to cease"), is used in **2 Pet. 2:14**, of those who "cannot cease" from sin, i.e., who cannot be restrained from sinning.

Beguiling *deleazo* (1185), originally meant "to catch by a bait" (from *delear*, "a bait"); hence "to beguile, entice by blandishments": in Jas. 1:14, "entice"; in **2 Pet. 2:14**, KJV, "beguile"; in v. **18**, KJV, "allure"; RV, "entice" in both.

Unstable *asteriktos* (793), *a*, negative, *sterizo*, "to fix," is used in **2 Pet. 2:14**; **3:16**, KJV, "unstable," RV, "unsteadfast."

Souls *see* **Soul** at *2 Peter 2:8*.

Heart *kardia* (2588), "the heart" (Eng., "cardiac," etc.), the chief organ of physical life ("for the life of the flesh is in the blood," Lev. 17:11), occupies the most important place in the human system. By an easy transition the word came to stand for man's entire mental and moral activity, both the rational and the emotional elements. In other words, the heart is used figuratively for the hidden springs of the personal life. "The Bible describes human depravity as in the 'heart,' because sin is a principle which has its seat in the center of man's inward life, and then 'defiles' the whole circuit of his action, Matt. 15:19, 20. On the other hand, Scripture regards the heart as the sphere of Divine influence, Rom. 2:15; Acts 15:9.... The heart, as lying deep within, contains 'the hidden man,' 1 Pet. 3:4, the real man. It represents the true character but conceals it" (**J. Laidlaw**, in *Hastings' Bible Dic.*). As to its usage in the NT it denotes (a) the seat of physical life, Acts 14:17; Jas. 5:5; (b) the seat of moral nature and spiritual life, the seat of grief, John 14:1; Rom. 9:2; 2 Cor. 2:4; joy, John 16:22; Eph. 5:19; the desires, Matt. 5:28; **2 Pet. 2:14**; the affections, Luke 24:32; Acts 21:13; the perceptions, John 12:40; Eph. 4:18; the thoughts, Matt. 9:4; Heb. 4:12; the understanding, Matt. 13:15; Rom. 1:21; the reasoning powers, Mark 2:6; Luke 24:38; the imagination, Luke 1:51; conscience, Acts 2:37; 1 John 3:20; the intentions, Heb. 4:12, cf. 1 Pet. 4:1; purpose, Acts 11:23; 2 Cor. 9:7; the will, Rom. 6:17; Col. 3:15; faith, Mark 11:23; Rom. 10:10; Heb. 3:12. The heart, in its moral significance in the OT, includes the emotions, the reason and the will.

Exercised *gumnazo* (1128), primarily signifies "to exercise naked" (from *gumnos*, "naked"); then, generally, "to exercise, to train the body or mind" (Eng., "gymnastic"), 1 Tim. 4:7, with a view to godliness; Heb. 5:14, of the senses, so as to discern good and evil; 12:11, of the effect of chastening, the spiritual "exercise producing the fruit of righteousness"; **2 Pet. 2:14**, of certain evil teachers with hearts "exercised in covetousness," RV.

Covetous *see* **Covetousness** at *2 Peter 2:3*.

Cursed *katara* (2671), denotes an "execration, imprecation, curse," uttered out of malevolence, Jas. 3:10; **2 Pet. 2:14**; or pronounced by God in His righteous judgment, as upon a land doomed to barrenness, Heb. 6:8; upon those who seek for justification by obedience, in part or completely, to the Law, Gal. 3:10, 13; in this 13th verse it is used concretely of Christ, as having "become a curse" for us, i.e., by voluntarily undergoing on the cross the appointed penalty of the "curse." He thus was identified, on our behalf, with the doom of sin. Here, not the verb in the Sept. of Deut. 21:23 is used, but the concrete noun.

Children *teknon* (5043), "a child" (akin to *tikto*, "to beget, bear"), is used in both the natural and the figurative senses. In contrast to *huios*, "son," it gives prominence to the fact of birth, whereas *huios* stresses the dignity and character of the relationship. Figuratively, *teknon* is used of "children" of (a) God, John 1:12; (b) light, Eph. 5:8; (c) obedience, 1 Pet. 1:14; (d) a promise, Rom. 9:8; Gal. 4:28; (e) the Devil, 1 John 3:10; (f) wrath, Eph. 2:3; (g) cursing, **2 Pet. 2:14**; (h) spiritual relationship, 2 Tim. 2:1; Philem. 10.

2:15 Which have forsaken the right way, and are gone astray, following the way of Balaam *the son* of Bosor, who loved the wages of unrighteousness;

Forsaken *kataleipo* (2641), a strengthened form of *leipo*, "to leave," signifies (a) "to leave, to leave behind," e.g., Matt. 4:13; (b) "to leave remaining, reserve," e.g., Luke 10:40; (c) "to forsake," in the sense of abandoning, translated "to forsake" in the RV of Luke 5:28 and Acts 6:2; in Heb. 11:27 and **2 Pet. 2:15**, KJV and RV. In this sense it is translated "to leave," in Mark 10:7; 14:52; Luke 15:4; Eph. 5:31.

Right *euthus* (2117), "straight," hence, metaphorically, "right," is so rendered in Acts 8:21, of the heart; 13:10, of the ways of the Lord; **2 Pet. 2:15**.

Way *see* **Ways** at *2 Peter 2:2*.

Following *see* **Followed** at *2 Peter 1:16*.

Wages *misthos* (3408), "hire," is rendered "wages" in John 4:36; in **2 Pet. 2:15**, KJV (RV, hire). *See also* **Reward** at *2 Peter 2:13*.

Unrighteousness *see 2 Peter 2:13*.

2:16 But was rebuked for his iniquity: the dumb ass speaking with man's voice forbad the madness of the prophet.

Rebuked *elenxis* (1649), denotes "rebuke"; in **2 Pet. 2:16**, it is used with *echo*, "to have," and translated "he was rebuked," lit., "he had rebuke." In the Sept., Job 21:4, "reproof"; 23:2, "pleading."

His *see 2 Peter 1:16*.

Iniquity *paranomia* (3892), "lawbreaking" (*para*, "against," *nomos*, "law"), denotes "transgression," so rendered in **2 Pet. 2:16**, for KJV, "iniquity."

Dumb *aphonos* (880), lit., "voiceless, or soundless" (*a*, negative, and *phone*, "a sound"), has reference to voice,

Acts 8:32; 1 Cor. 12:2; **2 Pet. 2:16**, while *alalos* has reference to words. In 1 Cor. 14:10 it is used metaphorically of the significance of voices or sounds, "without signification." In the Sept. Isa. 53:7.

Ass *hupozugion* (5268), lit., "under a yoke" (*hupo*, "under," *zugos*, "a yoke"), is used as an alternative description of the same animal, in Matt. 21:5, where both words are found together, "Behold, thy king cometh unto thee, meek and riding upon an ass (*onos*), and upon a colt the foal of an ass (*hupozugion*)." It was upon the colt that the Lord sat, John 12:14. In **2 Pet. 2:16**, it is used of Balaam's "ass."

Speaking *phthengomai* (5350), "to utter a sound or voice," is translated "to speak" in Acts 4:18; **2 Pet. 2:16**; in **2:18**, KJV, "speak" (RV, "utter").

Forbad *koluo* (2967), "to hinder, restrain, withhold, forbid" (akin to *kolos*, "docked, lopped, clipped"), is most usually translated "to forbid," often an inferior rendering to that of hindering or restraining, e.g., 1 Thess. 2:16; Luke 23:2; **2 Pet. 2:16**, where the RV has "stayed"; in Acts 10:47 "forbid." In Luke 6:29, the RV has "withhold not (thy coat also)."

Madness *paraphronia* (3913), "madness" (from *para*, "contrary to," and *phren*, "the mind"), is used in **2 Pet. 2:16**. Cf. *paraphroneo*, 2 Cor. 11:23, "I speak like one distraught."

2:17 These are wells without water, clouds that are carried with a tempest; to whom the mist of darkness is reserved for ever.

Wells *pege* (4077), "a spring or fountain," is used of (a) "an artificial well," fed by a spring, John 4:6; (b) metaphorically (in contrast to such a well), "the indwelling Spirit of God," 4:14; (c) "springs," metaphorically in **2 Pet. 2:17**, RV, for KJV, "wells"; (d) "natural fountains or springs," Jas. 3:11, 12; Rev. 8:10; 14:7; 16:4; (e) metaphorically, "eternal life and the future blessings accruing from it," Rev. 7:17; 21:6; (f) "a flow of blood," Mark 5:29.

Without water *anudros* (504), "waterless" (*a*, negative, *n*, euphonic, *hudor*, "water"), is rendered "dry" in Matt. 12:43, KJV, and Luke 11:24 (RV, "waterless"); "without water" in **2 Pet. 2:17** and Jude 12.

Clouds *homichle* (3658a), "a mist" (not so thick as *nephos* and *nephele*, "a cloud"), occurs in **2 Pet. 2:17** (1st part), RV, "mists"; some mss. have *nephelai*, "clouds" (KJV)." *nephele* (3507), "a definitely shaped cloud, or masses of clouds possessing definite form," is used, besides the physical element, (a) of the "cloud" on the mount of transfiguration, Matt. 17:5; (b) of the "cloud" which covered Israel in the Red Sea, 1 Cor. 10:1-2; (c), of "clouds" seen in the Apocalyptic visions, Rev. 1:7; 10:1; 11:12; 14:14-16; (d) metaphorically in **2 Pet. 2:17**, of the evil workers there mentioned; but RV, "and mists" (*homichle*), according to the most authentic mss. In 1 Thess. 4:17, the "clouds" referred to in connection with the rapture of the saints are probably the natural ones, as also in the case of those in connection with Christ's second advent to the earth. See Matt. 24:30; 26:64, and parallel passages. So at the Ascension, Acts 1:9.

Carried *elauno* (1643), signifies "to drive, impel, urge on." It is used of "rowing," Mark 6:48 and John 6:19; of the act of a demon upon a man, Luke 8:29; of the power of winds upon ships, Jas. 3:4; and of storms upon mists, **2 Pet. 2:17**, KJV, "carried," RV, "driven."

Tempest *lailaps* (2978), "a hurricane, whirlwind," is rendered "storm" in Mark 4:37; Luke 8:23; **2 Pet. 2:17**, RV (KJV, "tempest").

Mist *zophos* (2217), is rendered "mist" in the KJV of **2 Pet. 2:17** (2nd part), RV, "blackness"; "murkiness" would be a suitable rendering. For this and other synonymous terms see BLACKNESS, DARKNESS.

Darkness *skotos* (4655), a neuter noun frequent in the Sept., is used in the NT (a) of "physical darkness," Matt. 27:45; 2 Cor. 4:6; (b) of "intellectual darkness," Rom. 2:19; (c) of "blindness," Acts 13:11; (d) by metonymy, of the "place of punishment," e.g., Matt. 8:12; **2 Pet. 2:17**; Jude 13; (e) metaphorically, of "moral and spiritual darkness," e.g., Matt. 6:23; Luke 1:79; 11:35; John 3:19; Acts 26:18; 2 Cor. 6:14; Eph. 6:12; Col. 1:13; 1 Thess. 5:4-5; 1 Pet. 2:9; 1 John 1:6; (f) by metonymy, of "those who are in moral or spiritual darkness," Eph. 5:8; (g) of "evil works," Rom. 13:12; Eph. 5:11, (h) of the "evil powers that dominate the world," Luke 22:53; (i) "of secrecy." While *skotos* is used more than twice as many times as *skotia* in the NT, the apostle John uses *skotos* only once, 1 John 1:6, but *skotia* 15 times out of the 18. *See also 2 Peter 2:4*.

Reserved *see 2 Peter 2:4*.

2:18 For when they speak great swelling *words* of vanity, they allure through the lusts of the flesh, *through much* wantonness, those that were clean escaped from them who live in error.

Speak *see* **Speaking** at *2 Peter 2:16*.

Swelling *huperonkos* (5246), an adjective denoting "of excessive weight or size," is used metaphorically in the sense of "immoderate," especially of arrogant speech, in the neuter plural, virtually as a noun, **2 Pet. 2:18**; Jude 16, "great swelling words," doubtless with reference to gnostic phraseology.

Vanity *mataiotes* (3153), "emptiness as to results," akin to *mataios*, is used (a) of the creation, Rom. 8:20, as failing of the results designed, owing to sin; (b) of the mind which governs the manner of life of the Gentiles, Eph. 4:17; (c) of the "great swelling *words*" of false teachers, **2 Pet. 2:18**.

Allure *see* **Beguiling** at *2 Peter 2:14*.

Lusts *see* **Lust** at *2 Peter 2:10*.

Flesh *sarx* (4561) ... Its uses in the NT may be analyzed as follows: "(a) "the substance of the body," whether of beasts or of men, 1 Cor. 15:39; (b) "the human body," 2 Cor. 10:3a; Gal. 2:20; Phil. 1:22; (c) by synecdoche, of "mankind," in the totality of all that is essential to manhood, i.e., spirit, soul, and body, Matt. 24:22; John 1:13; Rom. 3:20; (d) by synecdoche, of "the holy humanity" of the Lord Jesus, in the totality of all that is essential to manhood, i.e., spirit, soul, and body John 1:14; 1 Tim. 3:16; 1 John 4:2; 2 John 7, in Heb. 5:7, "the days of His flesh," i.e., His past life on earth in distinction from His present life in resurrection; (e) by synecdoche, for "the complete person," John 6:51-57; 2 Cor. 7:5; Jas. 5:3; (f) "the weaker element in human nature," Matt. 26:41; Rom. 6:19; 8:3a; (g) "the unregenerate state of men," Rom. 7:5; 8:8, 9; (h) "the seat of sin in man" (but this is not the same thing as in the body), **2 Pet. 2:18**; 1 John 2:16; (i) "the lower and temporary element in the Christian," Gal. 3:3; 6:8, and in religious ordinances, Heb. 9:10; (j) "the natural attainments of men," 1 Cor. 1:26; 2 Cor. 10:2, 3b; (k) "circumstances," 1 Cor. 7:28; the externals of life, 2 Cor. 7:1; Eph. 6:5; Heb. 9:13; (l) by metonymy, "the outward and seeming," as contrasted with the spirit, the inward and real, John 6:63; 2 Cor. 5:16; (m) "natural relationship, consanguine," 1 Cor. 10:18; Gal. 4:23, or marital, Matt. 19:5."

Wantonness *aselgeia* (766), "lasciviousness, licentiousness," is rendered "wantonness" in **2 Pet. 2:18**, KJV. *See also* **Pernicious** at *2 Peter 2:2*.

Clean In **2 Pet. 2:18**, some inferior mss. have *ontos*, "certainly" (KJV, "clean"), for *oligos*, "scarcely" (RV, "just").

Escaped *see 2 Peter 1:4*.

Live *anastrepho* (390), used metaphorically, in the middle voice, "to conduct oneself, behave, live," is translated "to live," in Heb. 13:18 ("honestly"); in **2 Pet. 2:18** ("in error").

Error *plane* (4106), akin to *planao*, "a wandering, a forsaking of the right path," see Jas. 5:20, whether in doctrine, **2 Pet. 3:17**; 1 John 4:6, or in morals, Rom. 1:27; **2 Pet. 2:18**; Jude 11, though, in Scripture, doctrine and morals are never divided by any sharp line. See also Matt. 27:64, where it is equivalent to 'fraud.'" "Errors" in doctrine are not infrequently the effect of relaxed morality, and vice versa. In Eph. 4:14 the RV has "wiles of error," for KJV, "they lie in wait to deceive"; in 1 Thess. 2:3, RV, "error," for KJV, "deceit"; in 2 Thess. 2:11, RV, "a working of error," for KJV, "strong delusion." Cf. *planetes*, "a wandering," Jude 13, and the adjective *planos*, "leading astray, deceiving, a deceiver."

2:19 While they promise them liberty, they themselves are the servants of corruption: for of whom a man is overcome, of the same is he brought in bondage.

Promise *epangello* (1861), "to announce, proclaim," has in the NT the two meanings "to profess" and "to promise," each used in the middle voice; "to promise" (a) of "promises" of God, Acts 7:5; Rom. 4:21; in Gal. 3:19, passive voice; Titus 1:2; Heb. 6:13; 10:23; 11:11; 12:26; Jas. 1:12; 2:5; 1 John 2:25; (b) made by men, Mark 14:11; **2 Pet. 2:19**.

Servants *see* **Servant** at *2 Peter 1:1*.

Corruption *see 2 Peter 1:4*.

Overcome *hettaomai* (2274), "to be made inferior, be enslaved," is rendered "is (are) overcome," in **2 Pet. 2:19-20**.

Bondage *douloo* (1402), signifies "to make a slave of, to bring into bondage," Acts 7:6; 1 Cor. 9:19, RV; in the passive voice, "to be brought under bondage," **2 Pet. 2:19**; "to be held in bondage," Gal. 4:3 (lit., "were reduced to bondage"); Titus 2:3, "of being enslaved to wine"; Rom. 6:18, "of service to righteousness" (lit., "were made bondservants"). As with the purchased slave there were no limitations either in the kind or the time of service, so the life of the believer is to be lived in continuous obedience to God.

2:20 For if after they have escaped the pollutions of the world through the knowledge of the Lord and Saviour Jesus Christ, they are again entangled therein, and overcome, the latter end is worse with them than the beginning.

Escaped *see 2 Peter 1:4*.

Pollutions *miasma* (3393), whence the Eng. word, denotes "defilement," and is found in **2 Pet. 2:20**, KJV, "pollutions," RV, "defilements," the vices of the ungodly which contaminate a person in his intercourse with the world.

Knowledge *see 2 Peter 1:2.*

Saviour *see 2 Peter 1:1.*

Entangled *empleko* (1707), "to weave in" (*en*, "in," *pleko*, "to weave"), hence, metaphorically, to be involved, entangled in, is used in the passive voice in 2 Tim. 2:4, "entangleth himself;" **2 Pet. 2:20**, "are entangled." In the Sept., Prov. 28:18.

Overcome *see 2 Peter 2:19.*

Latter For "latter" (*husteros*) in the KJV of 1 Tim. 4:1 and for **2 Pet. 2:20**

End *eschatos* (2078), "last, utmost, extreme," is used as a noun (a) of time, rendered "end" in Heb. 1:2, RV, "at the "end" of these days," i.e., at the "end" of the period under the Law, for KJV, "in these last days"; so in 1 Pet. 1:20, "at the end of the times." In **2 Pet. 2:20**, the plural, *ta eschata*, lit., "the last things," is rendered "the latter end," KJV, (RV, "the last state"); the same phrase is used in Matt. 12:45; Luke 11:26; (b) of place, Acts 13:47, KJV, "ends (of the earth)," RV, "uttermost part.

Worse *cheiron* (5501), used as the comparative degree of *kakos*, "evil," describes (a) the condition of certain men, Matt. 12:45; Luke 11:26; **2 Pet. 2:20**; (b) evil men themselves and seducers, 2 Tim. 3:13; (c) indolent men who refuse to provide for their own households, and are worse than unbelievers, 1 Tim. 5:8, RV; (d) a rent in a garment, Matt. 9:16; Mark 2:21; (e) an error, Matt. 27:64; (f) a person suffering from a malady, Mark 5:26; (g) a possible physical affliction, John 5:14; (h) a punishment, Heb. 10:29, "sorer."

Beginning *protos* (4413), the superlative degree of *pro*, "before," is used (I) "of time or place," (a) as a noun, e.g., Luke 14:18; Rev. 1:17; opposite to "the last," in the neuter plural, Matt. 12:45; Luke 11:26; **2 Pet. 2:20**; in the neuter singular, opposite to "the second," Heb. 10:9; in 1 Cor. 15:3, *en protois*, lit., "in the first (things, or matters)" denotes "first of all"; (b) as an adjective, e.g., Mark 16:9, used with "day" understood, lit., "the first (day) of (i.e., after) the Sabbath," in which phrase the "of" is objective, not including the Sabbath, but following it; in John 20:4, 8; Rom. 10:19, e.g., equivalent to an English adverb; in John 1:15, lit., "first of me," i.e., "before me" (of superiority); (II) "of rank or dignity."

2:21 For it had been better for them not to have known the way of righteousness, than, after they have known *it*, to turn from the holy commandment delivered unto them.

Better *kreisson* (2909), from *kratos*, "strong" (which denotes power in activity and effect), serves as the comparative degree of *agathos*, "good" (good or fair, intrinsically). *Kreisson* is especially characteristic of the Epistle to the Hebrews, where it is used 12 times; it indicates what is (a) advantageous or useful, 1 Cor. 7:9, 38; 11:17; Heb. 11:40; 12:24; **2 Pet. 2:21**; Phil. 1:23, where it is coupled with *mallon*, "more," and *pollo*, "much, by far," "very far better" (RV); (b) excellent, Heb. 1:4; 6:9; 7:7, 19, 22; 8:6; 9:23; 10:34; 11:16, 35.

Way *see* Ways at *2 Peter 2:2.*

2:22 But it is happened unto them according to the true proverb, The dog *is* turned to his own vomit again; and the sow that was washed to her wallowing in the mire.

Happened *sumbaino* (4819), lit., "to go or come together" (*sun*, "with," *baino*, "to go"), signifies "to happen together," of things or events, Mark 10:32; Luke 24:14; Acts 3:10; 1 Cor. 10:11; 1 Pet. 4:12; **2 Pet. 2:22**; "befell" in Acts 20:19; in Acts 21:35, "so it was."

True *alethes* (227), primarily, "unconcealed, manifest" (*a*, negative, *letho*, "to forget," = *lanthano*, "to escape notice"), hence, actual, "true to fact," is used (a) of persons, "truthful," Matt. 22:16; Mark 12:14; John 3:33; 7:18; 8:26; Rom. 3:4; 2 Cor. 6:8; (b) of things, "true," conforming to reality, John 4:18, "truly," lit., "true"; 5:31, 32; in the best texts, 6:55 (twice), "indeed"; 8:13, 14 (v. 16 in some texts), 17; 10:41; 19:35; 21:24; Acts 12:9; Phil. 4:8; Titus 1:13; 1 Pet. 5:12; **2 Pet. 2:22**; 1 John 2:8, 27; 3 John 1:2.

Proverb *paroimia* (3942), denotes "a wayside saying" (from *paroimos*, "by the way"), "a byword," "maxim," or "problem," **2 Pet. 2:22**. The word is sometimes spoken of as a "parable," John 10:6, i.e., a figurative discourse (RV marg., "proverb"); see also 16:25, 29, where the word is rendered "proverbs" (marg. "parables") and "proverb."

Dog *kuon* (2965), is used in two senses, (a) natural, Matt. 7:6; Luke 16:21; **2 Pet. 2:22**; (b) metaphorical, Phil. 3:2; Rev. 22:15, of those whose moral impurity will exclude them from the New Jerusalem. The Jews used the term of Gentiles, under the idea of ceremonial impurity. Among the Greeks it was an epithet of impudence. Lat., *canis*, and Eng., "hound" are etymologically akin to it.

Vomit *exerama* (1829), "a vomit" (from *exerao*, "to disgorge"), occurs in **2 Pet. 2:22**.

Sow *hus* (5300), "swine" (masc. or fem.), is used in the fem. in **2 Pet. 2:22**.

Washed *louo* (3068), signifies "to bathe, to wash the body," (a) active voice, Acts 9:37; 16:33; (b) passive voice, John 13:10, RV, "bathed" (KJV, "washed"); Heb. 10:22, lit., "having been washed as to the body," metaphorical of the effect of the Word of God upon the activities of the believer; (c) middle voice, **2 Pet. 2:22.** Some inferior mss. have it instead of *luo*, "to loose," in Rev. 1:5 (see RV).

Wallowing *kulismos* (2946), "a rolling, wallowing," (some texts have *kulisma*), is used in **2 Pet. 2:22**, of the proverbial sow that had been washed.

Mire *borboros* (1004), "mud, filth," occurs in **2 Pet. 2:22.** In the Sept., Jer. 38:6 (twice), of the "mire" in the dungeon into which Jeremiah was cast.

Chapter 3

3:1 This second epistle, beloved, I now write unto you; in *both* which I stir up your pure minds by way of remembrance:

Stir up *see* **Stir ... up** at *2 Peter 1:13.*

Pure *eilikrines* (1506), signifies "unalloyed, pure"; (a) it was used of unmixed substances; (b) in the NT it is used of moral and ethical "purity," Phil. 1:10, "sincere"; so the RV in **2 Pet. 3:1** (KJV, "pure"). Some regard the etymological meaning as "tested by the sunlight" (Cremer).

Minds *dianoia* (1271), lit. "a thinking through, or over, a meditation, reflecting," signifies (a) "the faculty of knowing, understanding, or moral reflection," (1) with an evil significance, a consciousness characterized by a perverted moral impulse, Eph. 2:3 (plural); 4:18; (2) with a good significance, the faculty renewed by the Holy Spirit, Matt. 22:37; Mark 12:30; Luke 10:27; Heb. 8:10; 10:16; 1 Pet. 1:13; 1 John 5:20; (b) "sentiment, disposition" (not as a function but as a product); (1) in an evil sense, Luke 1:51, "imagination"; Col. 1:21; (2) in a good sense, **2 Pet. 3:1.**

Way In **2 Pet. 3:1**, the KJV translates *en* "by way of" ("by," RV).

Remembrance *see 2 Peter 1:13.*

3:2 That ye may be mindful of the words which were spoken before by the holy prophets, and of the commandment of us the apostles of the Lord and Saviour:

Mindful *mimnesko* (3403), from the older form *mnaomai*, in the active voice signifies "to remind"; in the middle voice, "to remind oneself of," hence, "to remember, to be mindful of"; the later form is found only in the present tense, in Heb. 2:6, "are mindful of," and 13:3, "remember"; the perfect tense in 1 Cor. 11:2 and in 2 Tim. 1:4 (RV, "remembering," KJV, "being mindful of"), is used with a present meaning. RV variations from the KJV are, in Luke 1:54, RV, "that He might remember" (KJV, "in remembrance of"); **2 Pet. 3:2**, "remember" (KJV, "be mindful of"); Rev. 16:19 (passive voice), "was remembered" (KJV, "came in remembrance"). The passive voice is used also in Acts 10:31, KJV and RV, "are had in remembrance."

Words *rhema* (4487), denotes "that which is spoken, what is uttered in speech or writing"; in the singular, "a word," e.g., Matt. 12:36; 27:14; 2 Cor. 12:4; 13:1; Heb. 12:19; in the plural, speech, discourse, e.g., John 3:34; 8:20; Acts 2:14; 6:11, 13; 11:14; 13:42; 26:25; Rom. 10:18; **2 Pet. 3:2**; Jude 17; it is used of the gospel in Rom. 10:8 (twice), 17, RV, "the word of Christ" (i.e., the "word" which preaches Christ); 10:18; 1 Pet. 1:25 (twice); of a statement, command, instruction, e.g., Matt. 26:75; Luke 1:37, RV, "(no) word (from God shall be void of power)", v. 38; Acts 11:16; Heb. 11:3. The significance of *rhema* (as distinct from *logos*) is exemplified in the injunction to take "the sword of the Spirit, which is the word of God," Eph. 6:17; here the reference is not to the whole Bible as such, but to the individual Scripture which the Spirit brings to our remembrance for use in time of need, a prerequisite being the regular storing of the mind with Scripture.

Spoken before *proeipon* (4302), and *proereo*, "to say before," used as aorist and future respectively of *prolego*, is used (a) of prophecy, e.g., Rom. 9:29; "to tell before," Matt. 24:25; Mark 13:23; "were spoken before," **2 Pet. 3:2**; Jude 17; (b) of "saying" before, 2 Cor. 7:3; 13:2, RV (KJV, "to tell before" and "foretell"); Gal. 1:9; 5:21; in 1 Thess. 4:6, "we forewarned," RV.

Saviour *see 2 Peter 1:1.*

3:3 Knowing this first, that there shall come in the last days scoffers, walking after their own lusts,

Scoffers *empaiktes* (1703), "a mocker," is used in **2 Pet. 3:3**, RV, "mockers". (KJV, "scoffers"); Jude 18, RV and KJV, "mockers." In the Sept., Isa. 3:4.

Lusts *see* **Lust** at *2 Peter 2:10.*

3:4 And saying, Where is the promise of his coming? for since the fathers fell asleep, all things continue as *they were* from the beginning of the creation.

Promise *epangelia* (1860), primarily a law term, denoting "a summons" (*epi*, "upon," *angello*, "to proclaim, announce"), also meant "an undertaking to do or give something, a promise." Except in Acts 23:21 it is used only of the "promises" of God. It frequently stands for the thing "promised," and so signifies a gift graciously bestowed, not a pledge secured by negotiation; thus, in Gal. 3:14, "the promise of the Spirit" denotes "the promised Spirit": cf. Luke 24:49; Acts 2:33 and Eph. 1:13; so in Heb. 9:15, "the promise of the eternal inheritance" is "the promised eternal inheritance." On the other hand, in Acts 1:4, "the promise of the Father," is the "promise" made by the Father. In Gal. 3:16, the plural "promises" is used because the one "promise" to Abraham was variously repeated (Gen. 12:1-3; 13:14-17; 15:18; 17:1-14; 22:15-18), and because it contained the germ of all subsequent "promises"; cf. Rom. 9:4; Heb. 6:12; 7:6; 8:6; 11:17; Gal. 3 is occupied with showing that the "promise" was conditional upon faith and not upon the fulfillment of the Law. The Law was later than, and inferior to, the "promise," and did not annul it, v. 21; cf. 4:23, 28. Again, in Eph. 2:12, "the covenants of the promise" does not indicate different covenants, but a covenant often renewed, all centering in Christ as the "promised" Messiah-Redeemer, and comprising the blessings to be bestowed through Him. In 2 Cor. 1:20 the plural is used of every "promise" made by God: cf. Heb. 11:33; in 7:6, of special "promises" mentioned. For other applications of the word, see, e.g., Eph. 6:2; 1 Tim. 4:8; 2 Tim. 1:1; Heb. 4:1; **2 Pet. 3:4**, **9**; in 1 John 1:5 some mss. have this word, instead of *angelia*, "message." The occurrences of the word in relation to Christ and what centers in Him, may be arranged under the headings (1) the contents of the "promise," e.g., Acts 26:6; Rom. 4:20; 1 John 2:25; (2) the heirs, e.g., Rom. 9:8; 15:8; Gal. 3:29; Heb. 11:9; (3) the conditions, e.g., Rom. 4:13, 14; Gal. 3:14-22; Heb. 10:36.

Coming *see* ***2 Peter 1:16***.

Fathers *pater* (3962), from a root signifying "a nourisher, protector, upholder" (Lat., *pater*, Eng., "father," are akin), is used (a) of the nearest ancestor, e.g., Matt. 2:22; (b) of a more remote ancestor, the progenitor of the people, a "forefather," e.g., Matt. 3:9; 23:30; 1 Cor. 10:1; the patriarchs, **2 Pet. 3:4**; (c) one advanced in the knowledge of Christ, 1 John 2:13; (d) metaphorically, of the originator of a family or company of persons animated by the same spirit as himself, as of Abraham, Rom. 4:11, 12, 16, 17, 18, or of Satan, John 8:38, 41, 44; (e) of one who, as a preacher of the gospel and a teacher, stands in a "father's" place, caring for his spiritual children, 1 Cor. 4:15 (not the same as a mere title of honor, which the Lord prohibited, Matt. 23:9); (f) of the members of the Sanhedrin, as of those who exercised religious authority over others, Acts 7:2; 22:1; (g) of God in relation to those who have been born anew (John 1:12, 13), and so are believers, Eph. 2:18; 4:6 (cf. 2 Cor. 6:18), and imitators of their "Father," Matt. 5:45, 48; 6:1, 4, 6, 8, 9, etc. Christ never associated Himself with them by using the personal pronoun "our"; He always used the singular, "My Father," His relationship being unoriginated and essential, whereas theirs is by grace and regeneration, e.g., Matt. 11:27; 25:34; John 20:17; Rev. 2:27; 3:5, 21; so the apostles spoke of God as the "Father" of the Lord Jesus Christ, e.g., Rom. 15:6; 2 Cor. 1:3; 11:31; Eph. 1:3; Heb. 1:5; 1 Pet. 1:3; Rev. 1:6; (h) of God, as the "Father" of lights, i.e., the Source or Giver of whatsoever provides illumination, physical and spiritual, Jas. 1:17; of mercies, 2 Cor. 1:3; of glory, Eph. 1:17; (i) of God, as Creator, Heb. 12:9 (cf. Zech. 12:1).

Asleep *koimaomai* (2837), is used of natural "sleep," Matt. 28:13; Luke 22:45; John 11:12; Acts 12:6; of the death of the body, but only of such as are Christ's; yet never of Christ Himself, though He is "the firstfruits of them that have fallen asleep," 1 Cor. 15:20, of saints who departed before Christ came, Matt. 27:52; Acts 13:36; of Lazarus, while Christ was yet upon the earth, John 11:11; of believers since the Ascension, 1 Thess. 4:13-15, and Acts 7:60; 1 Cor. 7:39; 11:30; 15:6, 18, 51; **2 Pet. 3:4**.

Continue *diameno* (1265), "to continue throughout," i.e., without interruption, is said of the dumbness of Zacharias, Luke 1:22, KJV, "remained"; of the "continuance" of the disciples with Christ, Luke 22:28; of the permanency of the truth of the gospel with churches, Gal. 2:5; of the unchanged course of things, **2 Pet. 3:4**; of the eternal permanency of Christ, Heb. 1:11.

3:5 For this they willingly are ignorant of, that by the word of God the heavens were of old, and the earth standing out of the water and in the water:

Willingly *thelo* (2309), "to will," used in the present participle in **2 Pet. 3:5**, is rendered "willfully (forget)" in the RV, KJV, "willingly (are ignorant of)," lit., "this escapes them (i.e., their notice) willing (i.e., of their own will)."

Ignorant *lanthano* (2990), "to escape notice," is translated "they (willfully) forget" in **2 Pet. 3:5**, RV, lit., "this escapes them (i.e., their notice, wilfully on their part)," KJV, "they willingly are ignorant of"; in v. **8**, RV, "forget not," lit., "let not this one thing escape you" (your notice), KJV, "be not ignorant of."

Of old *see* **Long time** at *2 Peter 2:3.*

Standing *sunistemi* (4921), and transitively *sunistao*, "to stand together" (*sun*, "with," *histemi*, "to stand"), is rendered "compacted," in **2 Pet. 3:5**, of the earth as formerly arranged by God in relation to the waters.

3:6 Whereby the world that then was, being overflowed with water, perished:

Whereby *dia* (1223), "by, by means of," when followed by the genitive case, is instrumental, e.g., **2 Pet. 3:6**, RV, "by which means" (KJV, "whereby").

Then *tote* (5119), a demonstrative adverb of time, denoting "at that time," is used (a) of concurrent events, e.g., Matt. 2:17; Gal. 4:8, "at that time"; v. 29, "then"; **2 Pet. 3:6**, "(the world) that then was," lit., "(the) then (world)"; (b) of consequent events, "then, thereupon," e.g., Matt. 2:7; Luke 11:26; 16:16, "[from (KJV, "since")] that time"; John 11:14; Acts 17:14; (c) of things future, e.g., Matt. 7:23; 24:30 (twice), 40; eight times in ch. 25; 1 Cor. 4:5; Gal. 6:4; 1 Thess. 5:3; 2 Thess. 2:8. It occurs 90 times in Matthew, more than in all the rest of the NT together.

Overflowed *katakluzo* (2626), "to inundate, deluge" (*kata*, "down," *kluzo*, "to wash" or "dash over," said, e.g., of the sea), is used in the passive voice in **2 Pet. 3:6**, of the Flood. *See also* **Flood** at *2 Peter 2:5.*

Perished *apollumi* (622), "to destroy," signifies, in the middle voice, "to perish," and is thus used (a) of things, e.g., Matt. 5:29, 30; Luke 5:37; Acts 27:34, RV, "perish" (in some texts *pipto*, "to fall," as KJV); Heb. 1:11; **2 Pet. 3:6**; Rev. 18:14 (2nd part), RV, "perished" (in some texts *aperchomai*, "to depart," as KJV); (b) of persons, e.g., Matt. 8:25; John 3:15), 16; 10:28; 17:12, RV, "perished" (KJV, "is lost"); Rom. 2:12; 1 Cor. 1:18, lit., "the perishing," where the perfective force of the verb implies the completion of the process of destruction (Moulton, *Proleg.*, p. 114); 8:11; 15:18; **2 Pet. 3:9**; Jude 11.

3:7 But the heavens and the earth, which are now, by the same word are kept in store, reserved unto fire against the day of judgment and perdition of ungodly men.

Heavens *ouranos* (3772), probably akin to *ornumi*, "to lift, to heave," is used in the NT (a) of "the aerial heavens," e.g., Matt. 6:26; 8:20; Acts 10:12; 11:6 (RV, "heaven," in each place, KJV, "air"); Jas. 5:18; (b) "the sidereal," e.g., Matt. 24:29, 35; Mark 13:25, 31; Heb. 11:12, RV, "heaven," KJV, "sky"; Rev. 6:14; 20:11; they, (a) and (b), were created by the Son of God, Heb. 1:10, as also by God the Father, Rev. 10:6; (c) "the eternal dwelling place of God," Matt. 5:16; 12 :50; Rev. 3:12; 11:13; 16:11; 20:9. From thence the Son of God descended to become incarnate, John 3:13, 31; 6:38, 42. In His ascension Christ "passed through the heavens," Heb. 4:14, RV; He "ascended far above all the heavens," Eph. 4:10, and was "made higher than the heavens," Heb. 7:26; He "sat down on the right hand of the throne of the Majesty in the heavens," Heb. 8:1; He is "on the right hand of God," having gone into heaven, 1 Pet. 3:22. Since His ascension it is the scene of His present life and activity, e.g., Rom. 8:34; Heb. 9:24. From thence the Holy Spirit descended at Pentecost, 1 Pet. 1:12. It is the abode of the angels, e.g., Matt. 18:10; 22:30; cf. Rev. 3:5. Thither Paul was "caught up," whether in the body or out of the body, he knew not, 2 Cor. 12:2. It is to be the eternal dwelling place of the saints in resurrection glory, 2 Cor. 5:1. From thence Christ will descend to the air to receive His saints at the Rapture, 1 Thess. 4:16; Phil. 3:20, 21, and will subsequently come with His saints and with His holy angels at His second advent, Matt. 24:30; 2 Thess. 1:7. In the present life "heaven" is the region of the spiritual citizenship of believers, Phil. 3:20. The present "heavens," with the earth, are to pass away, **2 Pet. 3:10**, "being on fire," v. **12** (see v. **7**); Rev. 20:11, and new "heavens" and earth are to be created, **2 Pet. 3:13**; Rev. 21:1, with Isa. 65:17, e.g.

Kept in store *thesaurizo* (2343), "to lay up, store up," is rendered "in store" (lit., "storing"), with a view to help a special case of need, 1 Cor. 16:2; said of the heavens and earth in **2 Pet. 3:7**, RV, "have been stored up (for fire)," marg., "stored (with fire)," KJV, "kept in store (reserved unto fire)."

Reserved *see 2 Peter 2:4.*

Judgment *see* **Destruction** at *2 Peter 2:1.*

Ungodly *see 2 Peter 2:5.*

3:8 But, beloved, be not ignorant of this one thing, that one day *is* with the Lord as a thousand years, and a thousand years as one day.

Ignorant *see 2 Peter 3:5.*

Thousand *chilioi* (5507), "a thousand," occurs in **2 Pet. 3:8**; Rev. 11:3; 12:6; 14:20; 20:2–7. 2. *chilias* (5505), "one thousand," is always used in the plural, *chiliades*, but translated in the sing. everywhere, except in the phrase "thousands of thousands," Rev. 5:11.

3:9 The Lord is not slack concerning his promise, as some men count slackness; but is longsuffering to us-ward, not willing that any should perish, but that all should come to repentance.

Slack *braduno* (1019), used intransitively signifies "to be slow, to tarry" (*bradus*, "slow"), said negatively of God, **2 Pet. 3:9**, "is (not) slack"; in 1 Tim. 3:15, translated "(if) I tarry." In the Sept., Gen. 43:10; Deut. 7:10; Isa. 46:13.

Promise *see* ***2 Peter 3:4***.

Count *see* ***2 Peter 2:13***.

Slackness *bradutes* (1022), "slowness," is rendered "slackness" in **2 Pet. 3:9**.

Longsuffering *makrothumeo* (3114), "to be patient, longsuffering, to bear with," lit., "to be long-tempered," is rendered by the verb "to be longsuffering" in Luke 18:7, RV (KJV, "bear long"); in 1 Thess. 5:14, RV (KJV, "be patient"); so in Jas. 5:7, 8; in **2 Pet. 3:9**, KJV and RV, "is longsuffering."

Willing *boulomai* (1014), is rendered "(if) Thou be willing" in Luke 22:42; in **2 Pet. 3:9**, KJV (RV, wishing).

Perish *apollumi* (622), a strengthened form of *ollumi*, signifies "to destroy utterly"; in middle voice, "to perish." The idea is not extinction but ruin, loss, not of being, but of wellbeing. This is clear from its use, as, e.g., of the marring of wine skins, Luke 5:37; of lost sheep, i.e., lost to the shepherd, metaphorical of spiritual destitution, Luke 15:4, 6, etc.; the lost son, 15:24; of the perishing of food, John 6:27; of gold, 1 Pet. 1:7. So of persons, Matt. 2:13, "destroy"; 8:25, "perish"; 22:7; 27:20; of the loss of well-being in the case of the unsaved hereafter, Matt. 10:28; Luke 13:3, 5; John 3:16 (v. 15 in some mss.); 10:28; 17:12; Rom. 2:12; 1 Cor. 15:18; 2 Cor. 2:15, "are perishing"; 4:3; 2 Thess. 2:10; Jas. 4:12; **2 Pet. 3:9**. *See also* **Perished** at *2 Peter 3:6*.

Come *choreo* (5562), lit., "to make room (*chora*, "a place") for another, and so to have place, receive," is rendered "come" (followed by "to repentance") in **2 Pet. 3:9**; the meaning strictly is "have room (i.e., space of time) for repentance."

3:10 But the day of the Lord will come as a thief in the night; in the which the heavens shall pass away with a great noise, and the elements shall melt with fervent heat, the earth also and the works that are therein shall be burned up.

Come *heko* (2240), means (a) "to come, to be present"; (b) "to come upon, of time and events," Matt. 24:14; John 2:4; **2 Pet. 3:10**; Rev. 18:8; (c) metaphorically, "to come upon one, of calamitous times, and evils," Matt. 23:36; Luke 19:43.

Thief *kleptes* (2812), is used (a) literally, Matt. 6:19, 20; 24:43; Luke 12:33, 39; John 10:1, 10; 12:6; 1 Cor. 6:10; 1 Pet. 4:15; (b) metaphorically of "false teachers," John 10:8; (c) figuratively, (1) of the personal coming of Christ, in a warning to a local church, with most of its members possessed of mere outward profession and defiled by the world, Rev. 3:3; in retributive intervention to overthrow the foes of God, 16:15; (2) of the Day of the Lord, in divine judgment upon the world, **2 Pet. 3:10** and 1 Thess. 5:2, 4; in v. 2, according to the order in the original "the word 'night' is not to be read with 'the day of the Lord,' but with 'thief,' i.e., there is no reference to the time of the coming, only to the manner of it. To avoid ambiguity the phrase may be paraphrased, 'so comes as a thief in the night comes.' The use of the present tense instead of the future emphasizes the certainty of the coming.... The unexpectedness of the coming of the thief, and the unpreparedness of those to whom he comes, are the essential elements in the figure; cf. the entirely different figure used in Matt. 25:1-13."

Heavens *see* ***2 Peter 3:7***.

Pass *parerchomai* (3928), from *para*, "by," *erchomai*, "to come" or "go," denotes (I) literally, "to pass, pass by," (a) of persons, Matt. 8:28; Mark 6:48; Luke 18:37; Acts 16:8; (b) of things, Matt. 26:39, 42; of time, Matt. 14:15; Mark 14:35; Acts 27:9, KJV, "past" (RV, "gone by"); 1 Pet. 4:3; (II) metaphorically, (a) "to pass away, to perish," Matt. 5:18; 24:34, 35; Mark 13:30, 31; Luke 16:17; 21:32, 33; 2 Cor. 5:17; Jas. 1:10; **2 Pet. 3:10**; (b) "to pass by, disregard, neglect, pass over," Luke 11:42; 15:29, "transgressed." For the meaning "to come forth or come," see Luke 12:37; 17:7, RV (Acts 24:7 in some mss.).

Noise *rhoizedon* (4500), from *rhoizos*, "the whistling of an arrow," signifies "with rushing sound," as of roaring flames, and is used in **2 Pet. 3:10**, of the future passing away of the heavens.

Elements *stoicheion* (4747), used in the plural, primarily signifies any first things from which others in a series, or a composite whole take their rise; the word denotes "an element, first principle" (from *stoichos*, "a row, rank, series"; cf. the verb *stoicheo*, "to walk or march in rank"); it was used of the letters of the alphabet, as elements of speech. In the NT it is used of (a) the substance of the material world, **2 Pet. 3:10**, **12**; (b) the delusive speculations of gentile cults and of Jewish theories, treated as elementary principles, "the rudiments of the world," Col. 2:8, spoken of as "philosophy and vain deceit"; these were presented as superior to faith in Christ; at Colosse the worship of angels, mentioned in v. 18, is explicable by the supposition, held by both Jews and Gentiles in that district, that the constellations were either themselves animated heavenly beings, or were governed by them; (c) the rudimentary principles of religion, Jewish or Gentile, also described as "the rudiments of the world," Col. 2:20, and as "weak and beggarly rudiments," Gal. 4:3, 9, RV, constituting a yoke of bondage; (d) the "elementary" principles (the A.B.C.) of the OT, as a revelation from God, Heb. 5:12, RV, "rudiments," lit., "the rudiments of the beginning of the oracles of God," such as are taught to spiritual babes.

Melt *luo* (3089), "to loose," is used of the future demolition of the elements or heavenly bodies, **2 Pet. 3:10-12**; in v. **10**, KJV, "shall melt," RV, "shall be dissolved"; in verses **11-12**, KJV and RV, "dissolved."

Heat *kausoo* (2741), was used as a medical term, of "a fever"; in the NT, "to burn with great heat," said of the future destruction of the natural elements, **2 Pet. 3:10**, **12**, "with fervent heat," passive voice, lit.. "being burned."

Burned *katakaio* (2618), signifies "to burn up, burn utterly," as of chaff, Matt. 3:12; Luke 3:17; tares, Matt. 13:30, 40; the earth and its works, **2 Pet. 3:10**; trees and grass, Rev. 8:7. This form should be noted in Acts 19:19; 1 Cor. 3:15; Heb. 13:11, Rev. 17:16. In each place the full rendering "burn utterly" might be used, as in Rev. 18:8.

3:11 *Seeing* then *that* all these things shall be dissolved, what manner *of persons* ought ye to be in *all* holy conversation and godliness,

Dissolved *see* **Melt** at *2 Peter 3:10*.

Manner *potapos* (4217), primarily, "from what country," then, "of what sort," is rendered "what manner of man." Matt. 8:27: so **2 Pet. 3:11**; Mark 13:1 (twice); Luke 1:29; 7:39; 1 John 3:1.

Holy *see 2 Peter 1:21*.

Conversation *see 2 Peter 2:7*.

Godliness *see 2 Peter 1:3*.

3:12 Looking for and hasting unto the coming of the day of God, wherein the heavens being on fire shall be dissolved, and the elements shall melt with fervent heat?

Looking for *prosdokao* (4328), "to await, expect" (*pros*, "to" or "towards," *dokeo*, "to think, be of opinion"), is translated "to look for," e.g., in Matt. 11:3; **2 Pet. 3:12**, **13**, **14**; the RV renders it by the verb "to expect, to be in expectation," in some instances, as does the KJV in Luke 3:15; Acts 3:5.

Hasting *speudo* (4692), denotes (a) intransitively, "to hasten," Luke 2:16, "with haste," lit., "(they came) hastening"; Luke 19:5, 6; Acts 20:16; 22:18; (b) transitively, "to desire earnestly," **2 Pet. 3:12**, RV, "earnestly desiring" (marg., "hastening"), KJV, "hasting" (the day of God), i.e., in our practical fellowship with God as those who are appointed by Him as instruments through prayer and service for the accomplishment of His purposes, purposes which will be unthwartably fulfilled both in time and manner of accomplishment. In this way the earnest desire will find its fulfillment.

Coming *see 2 Peter 1:16*.

Day *see 2 Peter 1:19*.

Heavens *see 2 Peter 3:7*.

On fire *puroomai* (4448), from *pur*, "fire, to glow with heat," is said of the feet of the Lord, in the vision in Rev. 1:15; it is translated "fiery" in Eph. 6:16 (of the darts of the evil one); used metaphorically of the emotions, in 1 Cor. 7:9; 2 Cor. 11:29; elsewhere literally, of the heavens, **2 Pet. 3:12**; of gold, Rev. 3:18 (RV, "refined").

Elements *see 2 Peter 3:10*.

Melt *teko* (5080), "to melt, melt down," is used in the passive voice in **2 Pet. 3:12**, "shall melt" (lit., "shall be melted"), of the elements (Eng., "thaw" is etymologically connected).

Heat *see 2 Peter 3:10*.

3:13 Nevertheless we, according to his promise, look for new heavens and a new earth, wherein dwelleth righteousness.

Promise *see 2 Peter 1:4*.

Look for *see* **Looking for** at *2 Peter 3:12*.

Heavens *see 2 Peter 3:7*.

Dwelleth *katoikeo* (2730), properly signifies "to settle down in a dwelling, to dwell fixedly in a place." Besides its literal sense, it is used of (a) the "indwelling" of the totality of the attributes and powers of the Godhead in Christ, Col. 1:19;

"He who loves the coming of the Lord is not he who affirms it is far off, nor is it he who says it is near. It is he who, whether it be far or near, awaits it with sincere faith, steadfast hope, and fervent love."

AUGUSTINE

2:9; (b) the "indwelling" of Christ in the hearts of believers ("may make a home in your hearts"), Eph. 3:17; (c) the "dwelling" of Satan in a locality, Rev. 2:13; (d) the future "indwelling" of righteousness in the new heavens and earth, **2 Pet. 3:13**. It is translated "dwellers" in Acts 1:19; 2:9; "inhabitants" in Rev. 17:2, KJV (RV, "they that dwell"), "inhabiters" in Rev. 8:13 and 12:12, KJV (RV, "them that dwell").

3:14 Wherefore, beloved, seeing that ye look for such things, be diligent that ye may be found of him in peace, without spot, and blameless.

Wherefore *see 2 Peter 1:10.*

Look for *see* **Looking for** at *2 Peter 3:12.*

Diligent *see* **Diligence** at *2 Peter 1:10.*

Without spot *aspilos* (784), "unspotted, unstained," is used of a lamb, 1 Pet. 1:19; metaphorically, of keeping a commandment without alteration and in the fulfillment of it, 1 Tim. 6:14; of the believer in regard to the world, Jas. 1:27, and free from all defilement in the sight of God, **2 Pet. 3:14.**

Blameless *amometos* (298), translated in Phil. 2:15 "without blemish" (KJV, "without rebuke"), is rendered "blameless" in **2 Pet. 3:14** (KJV and RV).

3:15 And account *that* the longsuffering of our Lord *is* salvation; even as our beloved brother Paul also according to the wisdom given unto him hath written unto you;

Account *hegeomai* (2233), primarily signifies "to lead"; then, "to consider"; it is translated "accounting" in Heb. 11:26, RV (KJV, "esteeming"); **2 Pet. 3:15**, "account."

Longsuffering *makrothumia* (3115), "forbearance, patience, longsuffering" (*makros*, "long," *thumos*, "temper"), is usually rendered "longsuffering," Rom. 2:4; 9:22; 2 Cor. 6:6; Gal. 5:22; Eph. 4:2; Col. 1:11; 3:12; 1 Tim. 1:16; 2 Tim. 3:10; 4:2; 1 Pet. 3:20; **2 Pet. 3:15**; "patience" in Heb. 6:12 and Jas. 5:10.

Salvation *soteria* (4991), denotes "deliverance, preservation, salvation." "Salvation" is used in the NT (a) of material and temporal deliverance from danger and apprehension, (1) national, Luke 1:69, 71; Acts 7:25, RV marg., "salvation" (text, "deliverance"); (2) personal, as from the sea, Acts 27:34; RV, "safety" (KJV, "health"); prison, Phil. 1:19; the flood, Heb. 11:7; (b) of the spiritual and eternal deliverance granted immediately by God to those who accept His conditions of repentance and faith in the Lord Jesus, in whom alone it is to be obtained, Acts 4:12, and upon confession of Him as Lord, Rom. 10:10; for this purpose the gospel is the saving instrument, Rom. 1:16; Eph. 1:13; (c) of the present experience of God's power to deliver from the bondage of sin, e.g., Phil. 2:12, where the special, though not the entire, reference is to the maintenance of peace and harmony; 1 Pet. 1:9; this present experience on the part of believers is virtually equivalent to sanctification; for this purpose, God is able to make them wise, 2 Tim. 3:15; they are not to neglect it, Heb. 2:3; (d) of the future deliverance of believers at the Parousia of Christ for His saints, a salvation which is the object of their confident hope, e.g., Rom. 13:11; 1 Thess. 5:8, and v. 9, where "salvation" is assured to them, as being deliverance from the wrath of God destined to be executed upon the ungodly at the end of this age (see 1 Thess. 1:10); 2 Thess. 2:13; Heb. 1:14; 9:28; 1 Pet. 1:5; **2 Pet. 3:15**; (e) of the deliverance of the nation of Israel at the second advent of Christ at the time of "the epiphany (or shining forth) of His Parousia" (2 Thess. 2:8); Luke 1:71; Rev. 12:10; (f) inclusively, to sum up all the blessings bestowed by God on men in Christ through the Holy Spirit, e.g., 2 Cor. 6:2; Heb. 5:9; 1 Pet. 1:9, 10; Jude 3; (g) occasionally, as standing virtually for the Savior, e.g., Luke 19:9; cf. John 4:22; (h) in ascriptions of praise to God, Rev. 7:10, and as that which it is His prerogative to bestow, 19:1 (RV).

Wisdom *sophia* (4678), is used with reference to (a) God, Rom. 11:33; 1 Cor. 1:21, 24; 2:7; Eph. 3:10; Rev. 7:12; (b) Christ, Matt. 13:54; Mark 6:2; Luke 2:40, 52; 1 Cor. 1:30; Col. 2:3; Rev. 5:12; (c) "wisdom" personified, Matt. 11:19; Luke 7:35; 11:49; (d) human "wisdom" (1) in spiritual things, Luke 21:15; Acts 6:3, 10; 7:10; 1 Cor. 2:6 (1st part); 12:8; Eph. 1:8, 17; Col. 1:9,

RV, "(spiritual) wisdom," 28; 3:16; 4:5; Jas. 1:5; 3:13, 17; **2 Pet. 3:15**; Rev. 13:18; 17:9; (2) in the natural sphere, Matt. 12:42; Luke 11:31; Acts 7:22; 1 Cor. 1:17, 19, 20, 21 (twice), 22; 2:1, 4, 5, 6 (2nd part), 13; 3:19; 2 Cor. 1:12; Col. 2:23; (3) in its most debased form, Jas. 3:15, "earthly, sensual, devilish" (marg., "demoniacal").

3:16 As also in all *his* epistles, speaking in them of these things; in which are some things hard to be understood, which they that are unlearned and unstable wrest, as *they do* also the other scriptures, unto their own destruction.

Epistles *epistole* (1992), primarily "a message" (from *epistello*, "to send to"), hence, "a letter, an epistle," is used in the singular, e.g., Acts 15:30; in the plural, e.g., Acts 9:2; 2 Cor. 10:10. "Epistle is a less common word for a letter. A letter affords a writer more freedom, both in subject and expression, than does a formal treatise. A letter is usually occasional, that is, it is written in consequence of some circumstance which requires to be dealt with promptly. The style of a letter depends largely on the occasion that calls it forth." "A broad line is to be drawn between the letter and the epistle. The one is essentially a spontaneous product dominated throughout by the image of the reader, his sympathies and interests, instinct also with the writer's own soul: it is virtually one half of an imaginary dialogue, the suppressed responses of the other party shaping the course of what is actually written.... the other has a general aim, addressing all and sundry whom it may concern: it is like a public speech and looks towards publication" (J. V. Bartlet, in *Hastings' Bib. Dic.*). In **2 Pet. 3:16** the apostle includes the Epistles of Paul as part of the God-breathed Scriptures.

Some The indefinite pronoun *tis* in its singular or plural forms, frequently means "some," "some one" (translated "some man," in the KJV, e.g., of Acts 8:31; 1 Cor. 15:35), or "somebody," Luke 8:46; the neuter plural denotes "some things" in **2 Pet. 3:16**; the singular denotes "something," e.g., Luke 11:54; John 13:29 (2nd part); Acts 3:5; 23:18; Gal. 6:3, where the meaning is "anything," as in 2:6, "somewhat." It is translated "somewhat," in the more indefinite sense, in Luke 7:40; Acts 23:20; 25:26; 2 Cor. 10:8; Heb. 8:3.

Understood *dusnoetos* (1425), "hard to be understood," occurs in **2 Pet. 3:16**.

Unlearned *amathes* (261), "unlearned" *manthano*, "to learn"), is translated "unlearned" in **2 Pet. 3:16**, KJV (RV, "ignorant").

Unstable *see 2 Peter 2:14.*

Wrest *strebloo* (4761), "to twist, to torture" (from *streble*, "a winch" or "instrument of torture," and akin to *strepho*, "to turn"), is used metaphorically in **2 Pet. 3:16**, of "wresting" the Scriptures on the part of the ignorant and unsteadfast. In the Sept., 2 Sam. 22:27.

Destruction *see 2 Peter 2:1.*

3:17 Ye therefore, beloved, seeing ye know *these things* before, beware lest ye also, being led away with the error of the wicked, fall from your own stedfastness.

Know *proginosko* (4267), "to know beforehand," is used (a) of the divine "foreknowledge" concerning believers, Rom. 8:29; Israel, 11:2; Christ as the Lamb of God, 1 Pet. 1:20, RV, "foreknown" (KJV, "foreordained"); (b) of human previous "knowledge," of a person, Acts 26:5, RV, "having knowledge of" (KJV, "which knew"); of facts, **2 Pet. 3:17**.

Beware *phulasso* (5442), "to guard, watch, keep," is used, in the middle voice, of being "on one's guard against" (the middle v. stressing personal interest in the action), Luke 12:15, "beware of," RV, "keep yourselves from," as in Acts 21:25; in 2 Tim. 4:15, "be thou ware"; in **2 Pet. 3:17**, "beware."

Led *sunapago* (4879), "to carry away with," is used in a bad sense, in Gal. 2:13 and **2 Pet. 3:17**, "being carried away with" (RV); in a good sense in Rom. 12:16; the RV marg. "be carried away with" is preferable to the text "condescend" (RV, and KJV), and to the KJV marg., "be contented (with mean things)." A suitable rendering would be "be led along with."

Error *see 2 Peter 2:18.*

Wicked *see 2 Peter 2:7.*

Fall *ekpipto* (1601), "to fall out of," "is used in the NT, literally, of flowers that wither in the course of nature, Jas. 1:11; 1 Pet. 1:24; of a ship not under control, Acts 27:17, 26, 29, 32; of shackles loosed from a prisoner's wrist, 12:7; figuratively, of the Word of God (the expression of His purpose), which cannot 'fall' away from the end to which it is set, Rom. 9:6; of the believer who is warned lest he 'fall' away from the course in which he has been confirmed by the Word of God, **2 Pet. 3:17**." So of those who seek to be justified by law, Gal. 5:4, "ye are fallen away from grace." Some mss. have this verb in Mark 13:25; so in Rev. 2:5.

Stedfastness *sterigmos* (4740), "a setting firmly, supporting," then "fixedness, steadfastness" (akin to *sterizo*, "to establish"), is used in **2 Pet. 3:17**.

"Measure your growth in grace by your sensitiveness to sin."

OSWALD CHAMBERS

3:18 But grow in grace, and *in* the knowledge of our Lord and Saviour Jesus Christ. To him *be* glory both now and for ever. Amen.

Grow *auxano* (837), "to grow or increase," of the growth of that which lives, naturally or spiritually, is used (a) transitively, signifying to make to increase, said of giving the increase, 1 Cor. 3:6, 7; 2 Cor. 9:10, the effect of the work of God, according to the analogy of His operations in nature; "to grow, become greater," e.g. of plants and fruit, Matt. 6:28; used in the passive voice in 13:32 and Mark 4:8, "increase"; in the active in Luke 12:27; 13:19; of the body, Luke 1:80; 2:40; of Christ, John 3:30, "increase"; of the work of the gospel of God, Acts 6:7, "increased"; 12:24; 19:20; of people, Acts 7:17; of faith, 2 Cor. 10:15 (passive voice), RV, "groweth" (KJV, "is increased"); of believers individually, Eph. 4:15; Col. 1:6, RV, 10 (passive voice), "increasing"; 1 Pet. 2:2; **2 Pet. 3:18**; of the church, Col. 2:19; of churches, Eph. 2:21.

Grace *charis* (5485), has various uses, (a) objective, that which bestows or occasions pleasure, delight, or causes favorable regard; it is applied, e.g., to beauty, or gracefulness of person, Luke 2:40; act, 2 Cor. 8:6, or speech, Luke 4:22, RV, "words of grace" (KJV, "gracious words"); Col. 4:6; (b) subjective, (1) on the part of the bestower, the friendly disposition from which the kindly act proceeds, graciousness, loving-kindness, goodwill generally, e.g., Acts 7:10; especially with reference to the divine favor or "grace," e.g., Acts 14:26; in this respect there is stress on its freeness and universality, its spontaneous character, as in the case of God's redemptive mercy, and the pleasure or joy He designs for the recipient; thus it is set in contrast with debt, Rom. 4:4, 16, with works, 11:6, and with law, John 1:17; see also, e.g., Rom. 6:14, 15; Gal. 5:4; (2) on the part of the receiver, a sense of the favor bestowed, a feeling of gratitude, e.g., Rom. 6:17 ("thanks"); in this respect it sometimes signifies "to be thankful," e.g., Luke 17:9 ("doth he thank the servant?" lit., "hath he thanks to"); 1 Tim. 1:12; (c) in another objective sense, the effect of "grace," the spiritual state of those who have experienced its exercise, whether (1) a state of "grace," e.g., Rom. 5:2; 1 Pet. 5:12; **2 Pet. 3:18**, or (2) a proof thereof in practical effects, deeds of "grace," e.g., 1 Cor. 16:3, RV, "bounty" (KJV, "liberality"); 2 Cor. 8:6, 19 (in 2 Cor. 9:8 it means the sum of earthly blessings); the power and equipment for ministry, e.g., Rom. 1:5; 12:6; 15:15; 1 Cor. 3:10; Gal. 2:9; Eph. 3:2, 7. To be in favor with is to find "grace" with, e.g., Acts 2:47; hence it appears in this sense at the beginning and the end of several epistles, where the writer desires "grace" from God for the readers, e.g., Rom. 1:7; 1 Cor. 1:3; in this respect it is connected with the imperative mood of the word *chairo*, "to rejoice," a mode of greeting among Greeks, e.g., Acts 15:23; Jas. 1:1 (marg.); 2 John 10, 11, RV, "greeting" (KJV, "God speed"). The fact that "grace" is received both from God the Father, 2 Cor. 1:12, and from Christ, Gal. 1:6; Rom. 5:15 (where both are mentioned), is a testimony to the deity of Christ. See also 2 Thess. 1:12, where the phrase "according to the grace of our God and the Lord Jesus Christ" is to be taken with each of the preceding clauses, "in you," "and ye in Him."

Knowledge *ginosko* (1097), signifies "to be taking in knowledge, to come to know, recognize, understand," or "to understand completely," e.g., Mark 13:28, 29; John 13:12; 15:18; 21:17; 2 Cor. 8:9; Heb. 10:34; 1 John 2:5; 4:2, 6 (twice), 7, 13; 5:2, 20; in its past tenses it frequently means "to know in the sense of realizing," the aorist or point tense usually indicating definiteness, Matt. 13:11; Mark 7:24; John 7:26; in 10:38 "that ye may know (aorist tense) and understand, (present tense)"; 19:4; Acts 1:7; 17:19; Rom. 1:21; 1 Cor. 2:11 (2nd part), 14; 2 Cor. 2:4; Eph. 3:19; 6:22; Phil. 2:19; 3:10; 1 Thess. 3:5; 2 Tim. 2:19; Jas. 2:20; 1 John 2:13 (twice), 14; 3:6; 4:8; 2 John 1; Rev. 2:24; 3:3, 9. In the passive voice, it often signifies "to become known," e.g., Matt. 10:26; Phil. 4:5. In the sense of complete and absolute understanding on God's part, it is used, e.g., in Luke 16:15; John 10:15 (of the Son as well as the Father); 1 Cor. 3:20. In Luke 12:46, KJV, it is rendered "he is ... aware."

In the NT *ginosko* frequently indicates a relation between the person "knowing" and the object known; in this respect, what is "known" is of value or importance to the one who knows, and hence the establishment of the relationship, e.g., especially of God's "knowledge," 1 Cor. 8:3, "if any man love God, the same is known of Him"; Gal. 4:9, "to be known of God"; here the "knowing" suggests approval and bears the meaning "to be approved"; so in 2 Tim. 2:19; cf. John 10:14, 27; Gen. 18:19; Nah. 1:7; the relationship implied may involve remedial chastisement, Amos 3:2. The same idea of appreciation as well as "knowledge" underlies several statements concerning the "knowledge" of God and His truth on the part of believers, e.g., John 8:32; 14:20, 31; 17:3; Gal. 4:9 (1st part); 1 John 2:3-13, 14; 4:6, 8, 16; 5:20; such "knowledge" is obtained, not by mere intellectual activity, but by operation of the Holy Spirit consequent upon acceptance of Christ. Nor is such "knowledge" marked by finality; see e.g., **2 Pet. 3:18**; Hos. 6:3, RV. The verb is also used to convey the thought of connection or union, as between man and woman, Matt. 1:25; Luke 1:34. *See also* ***2 Peter 1:5***.

Saviour *see* ***2 Peter 1:1***.

1 John

Chapter 1

1:1 That which was from the beginning, which we have heard, which we have seen with our eyes, which we have looked upon, and our hands have handled, of the Word of life;

Seen *theaomai* (2300), "to behold, view attentively, contemplate," had, in earlier Greek usage, the sense of a wondering regard. This idea was gradually lost. It signifies a more earnest contemplation than the ordinary verbs for "to see," "a careful and deliberate vision which interprets ... its object," and is more frequently rendered "behold" in the RV than the KJV. Both translate it by "behold" in Luke 23:55 (of the sepulchre); "we beheld," in John 1:14, of the glory of the Son of God; "beheld," RV, in John 1:32; Acts 1:11; **1 John 1:1** (more than merely seeing); **4:12, 14**.

Handled *pselaphao* (5584), "to feel, touch, handle," is rendered by the latter verb in Luke 24:39, in the Lord's invitation to the disciples to accept the evidence of His resurrection in His being bodily in their midst; in **1 John 1:1**, in the apostle's testimony (against the gnostic error that Christ had been merely a phantom) that he and his fellow apostles had handled Him.

Of In the following, *peri*, "concerning," is so translated in the RV (for KJV, "of"), e.g., Acts 5:24; 1 Cor. 1:11; **1 John 1:1** (the RV is important); cf. John 16:8.

Word *logos* (3056), denotes (I) "the expression of thought" – not the mere name of an object – (a) as embodying a conception or idea, e.g., Luke 7:7; 1 Cor. 14:9, 19; (b) a saying or statement, (1) by God, e.g., John 15:25; Rom. 9:9; 9:28, RV, "word" (KJV, "work"); Gal. 5:14; Heb. 4:12; (2) by Christ, e.g., Matt. 24:35 (plur.); John 2:22; 4:41; 14:23 (plur.); 15:20. In connection with (1) and (2) the phrase "the word of the Lord," i.e., the revealed will of God (very frequent in the OT), is used of a direct revelation given by Christ, 1 Thess. 4:15; of the gospel, Acts 8:25; 13:49; 15:35, 36; 16:32; 19:10; 1 Thess. 1:8; 2 Thess. 3:1; in this respect it is the message from the Lord, delivered with His authority and made effective by His power (cf. Acts 10:36); for other instances relating to the gospel see Acts 13:26; 14:3; 15:7; 1 Cor. 1:18, RV; 2 Cor. 2:17; 4:2; 5:19; 6:7; Gal. 6:6; Eph. 1:13; Phil. 2:16; Col. 1:5; Heb. 5:13; sometimes it is used as the sum of God's utterances, e.g., Mark 7:13; John 10:35; Rev. 1:2, 9; (c) discourse, speech, of instruction, etc., e.g., Acts 2:40; 1 Cor. 2:13; 12:8; 2 Cor. 1:18; 1 Thess. 1:5; 2 Thess. 2:15; Heb. 6:1, RV, marg.; doctrine, e.g., Matt. 13:20; Col. 3:16; 1 Tim. 4:6; 2 Tim. 1:13; Titus 1:9; **1 John 2:7**.

(II) "The Personal Word," a title of the Son of God; this identification is substantiated by the statements of doctrine in John 1:1-18, declaring in verses 1 and 2 (1) His distinct and superfinite Personality, (2) His relation in the Godhead (*pros*, "with," not mere company, but the most intimate communion), (3) His deity; in v. 3 His creative power; in v. 14 His incarnation ("became flesh," expressing His voluntary act; not as KJV, "was made"), the reality and totality of His human nature, and His glory "as of the only begotten from the Father," RV (marg., "an only begotten from a father"), the absence of the article in each place lending stress to the nature and character of the relationship; His was the *shekinah* glory in open manifestation; v. 18 consummates the identification: "the only-begotten Son (RV marg., many ancient authorities read "God only begotten,"), which is in the bosom of the Father, He hath declared Him," thus fulfilling the significance of the title "*Logos*," the "Word," the personal manifestation, not of a part of the divine nature, but of the whole deity.

The title is used also in **1 John 1**, "the Word of life" combining the two declarations in John 1:1 and 4 and Rev. 19:13.

1:2 (For the life was manifested, and we have seen *it*, and bear witness, and shew unto you that eternal life, which was with the Father, and was manifested unto us;)

Life *zoe* (2222), (Eng., "zoo," "zoology") is used in the NT "of life as a principle, life in the absolute sense, life as God has it, that which the Father has in Himself, and which He gave to the Incarnate Son to have in Himself, John 5:26, and which the Son manifested in the world, **1 John 1:2.** From this life man has become alienated in consequence of the Fall, Eph. 4:18, and of this life men become partakers through faith in the Lord Jesus Christ, John 3:15, who becomes its Author to all such as trust in Him, Acts 3:15, and who is therefore said to be 'the life' of the believer, Col. 3:4, for the life that He gives He maintains, John 6:35, 63. Eternal life is the present actual possession of the believer because of his relationship with Christ, John 5:24; **1 John 3:14**, and that it will one day extend its domain to the sphere of the body is assured by the Resurrection of Christ, 2 Cor. 5:4; 2 Tim. 1:10. This life is not merely a principle of power and mobility, however, for it has moral associations which are inseparable from it, as of holiness and righteousness. Death and sin, life and holiness, are frequently contrasted in the Scriptures.

"*Zoe* is also used of that which is the common possession of all animals and men by nature, Acts 17:25; **1 John 5:16**, and of the present sojourn of man upon the earth with reference to its duration, Luke 16:25; 1 Cor. 15:19; 1 Tim. 4:8; 1 Pet. 3:10. 'This life' is a term equivalent to 'the gospel,' 'the faith,' 'Christianity,' Acts 5:20." *See also **1 John 2:16**.*

Manifested, Shew *apangello* (518), signifies "to announce or report from a person or place" (*apo*, "from"); hence, "to declare, publish"; it is rendered "declare" in Luke 8:47; Heb. 2:12; **1 John 1:3.** It is very frequent in the Gospels and Acts; elsewhere, other than the last two places mentioned, only in 1 Thess. 1:9 and **1 John 1:2.**

Witness *martureo* (3140), denotes "to be a *martus*," or "to bear witness to," sometimes rendered "to testify"; it is used of the witness (a) of God the Father to Christ, John 5:32, 37; 8:18 (2nd part); **1 John 5:9, 10**; to others, Acts 13:22; 15:8; Heb. 11:2, 4 (twice), 5, 39; (b) of Christ, John 3:11, 32; 4:44; 5:31; 7:7; 8:13, 14, 18 (1st part); 13:21; 18:37; Acts 14:3; 1 Tim. 6:13; Rev. 22:18, 20; of the Holy Spirit, to Christ, John 15:26; Heb. 10:15; **1 John 5:7, 8**, RV, which rightly omits the latter part of v. **7** (it was a marginal gloss which crept into the original text); it finds no support in Scripture; (c) of the Scriptures, to Christ, John 5:39; Heb. 7:8, 17; (d) of the works of Christ, to Himself, and of the circumstances connected with His death, John 5:36; 10:25; **1 John 5:8**; (e) of prophets and apostles, to the righteousness of God, Rom. 3:21; to Christ, John 1:7, 8, 15, 32, 34; 3:26; 5:33, RV; 15:27; 19:35; 21:24; Acts 10:43; 23:11; 1 Cor. 15:15; **1 John 1:2; 4:14**; Rev. 1:2; to doctrine, Acts 26:22 (in some texts, so KJV); to the Word of God, Rev. 1:2; (f) of others, concerning Christ, Luke 4:22; John 4:39; 12:17; (g) of believers to one another, John 3:28; 2 Cor. 8:3; Gal. 4:15; Col. 4:13; 1 Thess. 2:11; 3 John 3, 6, 12 (2nd part); (h) of the apostle Paul concerning Israel, Rom. 10:2; (i) of an angel, to the churches, Rev. 22:16; (j) of unbelievers, concerning themselves, Matt. 23:31; concerning Christ, John 18:23; concerning others, John 2:25; Acts 22:5; 26:5. *See also **1 John 5:9**.*

1:3 That which we have seen and heard declare we unto you, that ye also may have fellowship with us: and truly our fellowship *is* with the Father, and with his Son Jesus Christ.

Declare *see* **Manifested, Shew** at *1 John 1:2*.

Fellowship *koinonia* (2842), "a having in common (*koinos*), partnership, fellowship", denotes (a) the share which one has in anything, a participation, fellowship recognized and enjoyed; thus it is used of the common experiences and interests of Christian men, Acts 2:42; Gal. 2:9; of participation in the knowledge of the Son of God, 1 Cor. 1:9; of sharing in the realization of the effects of the blood (i.e., the death) of Christ and the body of Christ, as set forth by the emblems in the Lord's Supper, 1 Cor. 10:16; of participation in what is derived from the Holy Spirit, 2 Cor. 13:14 (RV, "communion"); Phil. 2:1; of participation in the sufferings of Christ, Phil. 3:10; of sharing in the resurrection life possessed in Christ, and so of fellowship with the Father and the Son, **1 John 1:3, 6-7**; negatively, of the impossibility of "communion" between light and darkness, 2 Cor. 6:14; (b) fellowship manifested in acts, the practical effects of fellowship with God, wrought by the Holy Spirit in the lives of believers as the outcome of faith, Philem. 6, and finding expression in joint ministration to the needy, Rom. 15:26; 2 Cor. 8:4; 9:13; Heb. 13:16, and in the furtherance of the gospel by gifts, Phil. 1:5.

Our In Luke 24:22, "of our company" is, lit., "from among us." *Hemeteros*, a possessive pronoun, more emphatic than *hemeis*, is used in Luke 16:12, in the best mss. (some have *humeteros*, "your own"); Acts 2:11; 24:6, in some mss.; 26:5; 2 Tim. 4:15; Titus 3:14, "ours"; **1 John 1:3; 2:2**, "ours."

1:4 And these things write we unto you, that your joy may be full.

Full *pleroo* (4137), signifies (1) "to fill"; (2) "to fulfill, complete," (a) of time, e.g., Mark 1:15; Luke 21:24; John 7:8 (KJV, "full come"); Acts 7:23, RV, "he was wellnigh forty years old" (KJV, "was full," etc.), lit., "the time of forty years was fulfilled to him"; v. 30, KJV, "were expired"; 9:23; 24:27 (KJV, "after two years"; RV, "when two years were fulfilled"); (b) of number, Rev. 6:11; (c) of good pleasure, 2 Thess. 1:11; (d) of joy, Phil. 2:2; in the passive voice, "to be fulfilled," John 3:29 and 17:13; in the following the verb is rendered "fulfilled" in the RV, for the KJV, "full," John 15:11; 16:24; **1 John 1:4**; 2 John 12; (e) of obedience, 2 Cor. 10:6; (f) of works, Rev. 3:2; (g) of the future Passover, Luke 22:16; (h) of sayings, prophecies, etc., e.g., Matt. 1:22 (twelve times in Matt., two in Mark, four in Luke, eight in John, two in Acts); Jas. 2:23; in Col. 1:25 the word signifies to preach "fully," to complete the ministry of the gospel appointed.

1:5 This then is the message which we have heard of him, and declare unto you, that God is light, and in him is no darkness at all.

Message *angelia* (31), akin to *angello*, "to bring a message, proclaim," denotes a "message, proclamation, news," **1 John 1:5** [some mss. have *epangelia*]; **1 John 3:11**, where the word is more precisely defined (by being followed by the conjunction "that," expressing the purpose that we should love one another) as being virtually equivalent to an order. *Epangelia* (1860), "a promise," is found in some mss. in **1 John 1:5**, "message". The occurrences of the word in relation to Christ and what centers in Him, may be arranged under the headings (1) the contents of the "promise," e.g., Acts 26:6; Rom. 4:20; **1 John 2:25**; (2) the heirs, e.g., Rom. 9:8; 15:8; Gal. 3:29; Heb. 11:9; (3) the conditions, e.g., Rom. 4:13, 14; Gal. 3:14-22; Heb. 10:36.

Declare *anangello* (312), "to declare, announce" (*ana*, "up," *angello*, "to report"), is used especially of heavenly messages, and is translated "announced" in the RV of 1 Pet. 1:12, for KJV "reported," and in **1 John 1:5**, RV, "announce," for KJV, "declare."

God *theos* (2316) The word was appropriated by Jews and retained by Christians to denote "the one true God." In the Sept. *theos* translates (with few exceptions) the Hebrew words *Elohim* and *Jehovah*, the former indicating His power and preeminence, the latter His unoriginated, immutable, eternal and self-sustained existence. In the NT, these and all the other divine attributes are predicated of Him. To Him are ascribed, e.g., His unity, or monism, e.g., Mark 12:29; 1 Tim. 2:5; self-existence, John 5:26; immutability, Jas. 1:17; eternity, Rom. 1:20; universality, Matt. 10:29; Acts 17:26-28; almighty power, Matt. 19:26; infinite knowledge, Acts 2:23; 15:18; Rom. 11:33, creative power, Rom. 11:36; 1 Cor. 8:6; Eph. 3:9; Rev. 4:11; 10:6; absolute holiness, 1 Pet. 1:15; **1 John 1:5**; righteousness, John 17:25; faithfulness, 1 Cor. 1:9; 10:13; 1 Thess. 5:24; 2 Thess. 3:3; **1 John 1:9**; love, **1 John 4:8, 16**; mercy, Rom. 9:15, 18; truthfulness, Titus 1:2; Heb. 6:18.

(b) The divine attributes are likewise indicated or definitely predicated of Christ, e.g., Matt. 20:18-19; John 1:1-3; 1:18, RV, marg.; 5:22-29; 8:58; 14:6; 17:22-24; 20:28; Rom. 1:4; 9:5; Phil. 3:21; Col. 1:15; 2:3; Titus 2:13, RV; Heb. 1:3; 13:8; **1 John 5:20**; Rev. 22:12, 13.

(c) Also of the Holy Spirit, e.g., Matt. 28:19; Luke 1:35; John 14:16; 15:26; 16:7-14; Rom. 8:9, 26; 1 Cor. 12:11; 2 Cor. 13:14 ...

Light *phos* (5457), akin to *phao*, "to give light" (from roots *pha-* and *phan-*, expressing "light as seen by the eye," and, metaphorically, as "reaching the mind," whence *phaino*, "to make to appear," *phaneros*, "evident," etc.); cf. Eng., "phosphorus" (lit., "light-bearing"). "Primarily light is a luminous emanation, probably of force, from certain bodies, which enables the eye to discern form and color. Light requires an organ adapted for its reception (Matt. 6:22). Where the eye is absent, or where it has become impaired from any cause, light is useless. Man, naturally, is incapable of receiving spiritual light inasmuch as he lacks the capacity for spiritual things, 1 Cor. 2:14. Hence believers are called 'sons of light,' Luke 16:8, not merely because they have received a revelation from God, but because in the New Birth they have received the spiritual capacity for it.

"Apart from natural phenomena, light is used in Scripture of (a) the glory of God's dwellingplace, 1 Tim. 6:16; (b) the nature of God, **1 John 1:5**; (c) the impartiality of God, Jas. 1:17; (d) the favor of God, Ps. 4:6; of the King, Prov. 16:15; of an influential man, Job 29:24; (e) God, as the illuminator of His people, Isa. 60:19, 20; (f) the Lord Jesus as the illuminator of men, John 1:4, 5, 9; 3:19; 8:12; 9:5; 12:35, 36, 46; Acts 13:47;

(g) the illuminating power of the Scriptures, Ps. 119:105; and of the judgments and commandments of God, Isa. 51:4; Prov. 6:23, cf. Ps. 43:3; (h) the guidance of God Job 29:3; Ps. 112:4; Isa. 58:10; and, ironically, of the guidance of man, Rom. 2:19; (i) salvation, 1 Pet. 2:9; (j) righteousness, Rom. 13:12; 2 Cor. 11:14, 15; **1 John 2:9, 10**; (k) witness for God, Matt. 5:14, 16; John 5:35; (l) prosperity and general well-being, Esth. 8:16; Job 18:18; Isa. 58:8-10."

Darkness *skotia* (4653), is used (a) of physical darkness, "dark," John 6:17, lit., "darkness had come on," and 20:1, lit., "darkness still being"; (b) of secrecy, in general, whether what is done therein is good or evil, Matt. 10:27; Luke 12:3; (c) of spiritual or moral "darkness," emblematic of sin, as a condition of moral or spiritual depravity, Matt. 4:16; John 1:5; 8:12; 12:35, 46; **1 John 1:5; 2:8-9, 11.** *See also* ***1 John 1:6***.

1:6 If we say that we have fellowship with him, and walk in darkness, we lie, and do not the truth:

Fellowship *see* ***1 John 1:3***.

Darkness *skotos* (4655), a neuter noun frequent in the Sept., is used in the NT as the equivalent (a) of "physical darkness," Matt. 27:45; 2 Cor. 4:6; (b) of "intellectual darkness," Rom. 2:19; (c) of "blindness," Acts 13:11; (d) by metonymy, of the "place of punishment," e.g., Matt. 8:12; 2 Pet. 2:17; Jude 13; (e) metaphorically, of "moral and spiritual darkness," e.g., Matt. 6:23; Luke 1:79; 11:35; John 3:19; Acts 26:18; 2 Cor. 6:14; Eph. 6:12; Col. 1:13; 1 Thess. 5:4-5; 1 Pet. 2:9; **1 John 1:6**; (f) by metonymy, of "those who are in moral or spiritual darkness," Eph. 5:8; (g) of "evil works," Rom. 13:12; Eph. 5:11, (h) of the "evil powers that dominate the world," Luke 22:53; (i) "of secrecy". While *skotos* is used more than twice as many times as *skotia* in the NT, the apostle John uses *skotos* only once, **1 John 1:6**, but *skotia* 15 times out of the 18. *See also* ***1 John 1:5***.

Lie *pseudo* (5574), "to deceive by lies" (always in the middle voice in the NT), is used (a) absolutely, in Matt. 5:11, "falsely," lit., "lying" (v, marg.); Rom. 9:1; 2 Cor. 11:31; Gal. 1:20; Col. 3:9 (where the verb is followed by the preposition *eis*, "to"); 1 Tim. 2:7; Heb. 6:18; Jas. 3:14 (where it is followed by the preposition *kata*, "against"); **1 John 1:6**; Rev. 3:9; (b) transitively, with a direct object (without a preposition following), Acts 5:3 (with the accusative case) "to lie to (the Holy Ghost)," RV marg., "deceive"; v. 4 (with the dative case) "thou hast (not) lied (unto men, but unto God)." *See also* **Liar** at ***1 John 1:10;*** **Lie** at ***1 John 2:21***.

1:7 But if we walk in the light, as he is in the light, we have fellowship one with another, and the blood of Jesus Christ his Son cleanseth us from all sin.

Cleanseth *katharizo* (2511), signifies (1) "to make clean, to cleanse" (a) from physical stains and dirt, as in the case of utensils, Matt. 23:25 (figuratively in verse 26); from disease, as of leprosy, Matt. 8:2; (b) in a moral sense, from the defilement of sin, Acts 15:9; 2 Cor. 7:1; Heb. 9:14; Jas. 4:8, "cleanse" from the guilt of sin, Eph. 5:26; **1 John 1:7**; (2) "to pronounce clean in a Levitical sense," Mark 7:19, RV; Acts 10:15; 11:9; "to consecrate by cleansings," Heb. 9:22, 23; 10:2.

Sin *hamartia* (266), is, lit., "a missing of the mark," but this etymological meaning is largely lost sight of in the NT. It is the most comprehensive term for moral obliquity. It is used of "sin" as (a) a principle or source of action, or an inward element producing acts, e.g., Rom. 3:9; 5:12, 13, 20; 6:1, 2; 7:7 (abstract for concrete); 7:8 (twice), 9, 11, 13, "sin, that it might be shown to be sin," i.e., "sin became death to me, that it might be exposed in its heinous character": in the last clause, "sin might become exceeding sinful," i.e., through the holiness of the Law, the true nature of sin was designed to be manifested to the conscience;

(b) a governing principle or power, e.g., Rom. 6:6, "(the body) of sin," here "sin" is spoken of as an organized power, acting through the members of the body, though the seat of "sin" is in the will (the body is the organic instrument); in the next clause, and in other passages, as follows, this governing principle is personified, e.g., Rom. 5:21; 6:12, 14, 17; 7:11, 14, 17, 20, 23, 25; 8:2; 1 Cor. 15:56; Heb. 3:13; 11:25; 12:4; Jas. 1:15 (2nd part);

(c) a generic term; in Rom. 8:3, "God, sending His own Son in the likeness of sinful flesh," lit., "flesh of sin," the flesh stands for the body, the instrument of indwelling "sin" [Christ, preexistently the Son of God, assumed human flesh, "of the substance of the Virgin Mary"; the reality of incarnation was His, without taint of sin], and *as an offering* for sin," i.e., "a sin offering" (so the Sept., e.g., in Lev. 4:32; 5:6, 7, 8, 9), "condemned sin in the flesh," i.e., Christ, having taken human nature, "sin" apart (Heb. 4:15), and having lived a sinless life, died under the condemnation and judgment due to our "sin"; for the generic sense see further, e.g., Heb. 9:26; 10:6, 8, 18; 13:11; **1 John 1:7, 8; 3:4** (1st part; in the 2nd part, "sin" is defined as "lawlessness," RV), **8, 9**; in these verses the KJV use of the

"God does not want to punish you; He has provided for your forgiveness."

COLIN URQUHART

verb to commit is misleading; not the committal of an act is in view, but a continuous course of "sin," as indicated by the RV, "doeth." The apostle's use of the present tense of *poieo*, "to do," virtually expresses the meaning of *prasso*, "to practice," which John does not use (it is not infrequent in this sense in Paul's Epp., e.g., Rom. 1:32, RV; 2:1; Gal. 5:21; Phil. 4:9);1 Pet. 4:1 (singular in the best texts), lit., "has been made to cease from sin," i.e., as a result of suffering in the flesh, the mortifying of our members, and of obedience to a Savior who suffered in flesh. Such no longer lives in the flesh, "to the lusts of men, but to the will of God"; sometimes the word is used as virtually equivalent to a condition of "sin," e.g., John 1:29, "the sin (not sins) of the world"; 1 Cor. 15:17; or a course of "sin," characterized by continuous acts, e.g., 1 Thess. 2:16; in **1 John 5:16** (2nd part) the RV marg., is probably to be preferred, "there is sin unto death," not a special act of "sin," but the state or condition producing acts; in v. **17**, "all unrighteousness is sin" is not a definition of "sin" (as in **3:4**), it gives a specification of the term in its generic sense;

(d) a sinful deed, an act of "sin," e.g., Matt. 12:31; Acts 7:60; Jas. 1:15 (1st part); 2:9; 4:17; 5:15, 20; **1 John 5:16** (1st part).

See also **Sinned** at *1 John 1:10*.

1:8 If we say that we have no sin, we deceive ourselves, and the truth is not in us.

Sin *see 1 John 1:7*.

1:9 If we confess our sins, he is faithful and just to forgive us *our* sins, and to cleanse us from all unrighteousness.

Confess *homologeo* (3670), lit., "to speak the same thing" (*homos*, "same," *lego*, "to speak"), "to assent, accord, agree with," denotes, (a) "to confess, declare, admit," John 1:20; e.g., Acts 24:14; Heb. 11:13; (b) "to confess by way of admitting oneself guilty of what one is accused of, the result of inward conviction," **1 John 1:9**; (c) "to declare openly by way of speaking out freely, such confession being the effect of deep conviction of facts," Matt. 7:23; 10:32 (twice) and Luke 12:8 (see next par.); John 9:22; 12:42; Acts 23:8; Rom. 10:9-10 ("confession is made"); 1 Tim. 6:12 (RV); Titus 1:16; **1 John 2:23; 4:2, 15**; 2 John 7 (in John's epistle it is the necessary antithesis to Gnostic doceticism); Rev. 3:5, in the best mss.; (d) "to confess by way of celebrating with praise," Heb. 13:15; (e) "to promise," Matt. 14:7. In Matt. 10:32 and Luke 12:8 the construction of this verb with *en*, "in," followed by the dative case of the personal pronoun, has a special significance, namely, to "confess" in a person's name, the nature of the "confession" being determined by the context, the suggestion being to make a public "confession." Thus the statement, "every one ... who shall confess Me (lit. "in Me," i.e., in My case) before men, him (lit., "in him," i.e., in his case) will I also confess before My Father ... ," conveys the thought of "confessing" allegiance to Christ as one's Master and Lord, and, on the other hand, of acknowledgment, on His part, of the faithful one as being His worshipper and servant, His loyal follower; this is appropriate to the original idea in *homologeo* of being identified in thought or language.

He *see* God at *1 John 1:5*.

Faithful *pistos* (4103), a verbal adjective, akin to *peitho*, is used in two senses, (a) passive, "faithful, to be trusted, reliable," said of God, e.g., 1 Cor. 1:9; 10:13; 2 Cor. 1:18 (KJV, "true"); 2 Tim. 2:13; Heb. 10:23; 11:11; 1 Pet. 4:19; **1 John 1:9**; of Christ, e.g., 2 Thess. 3:3; Heb. 2:17; 3:2; Rev. 1:5; 3:14; 19:11; of the words of God, e.g., Acts 13:34, "sure"; 1 Tim. 1:15; 3:1 (KJV, "true"); 4:9; 2 Tim. 2:11; Titus 1:9; 3:8; Rev. 21:5; 22:6; of servants of the Lord, Matt. 24:45; 25:21, 23; Acts 16:15; 1 Cor. 4:2, 17; 7:25; Eph. 6:21; Col. 1:7; 4:7, 9; 1 Tim. 1:12; 3:11; 2 Tim. 2:2; Heb. 3:5; 1 Pet. 5:12; 3 John 5; Rev. 2:13; 17:14; of believers, Eph. 1:1; Col. 1:2; (b) active, signifying "believing, trusting, relying," e.g., Acts 16:1 (feminine); 2 Cor. 6:15; Gal. 3:9 seems best taken in this respect, as the context lays stress upon Abraham's "faith" in God, rather than upon his "faithfulness." In John 20:27 the context requires the active sense, as the Lord is reproaching Thomas for his want of "faith." With regard to believers, they are spoken of sometimes in the active sense, sometimes in the passive, i.e., sometimes as believers, sometimes as "faithful."

Just *dikaios* (1342), signifies "just," without prejudice or partiality, e.g., of the judgment of God, 2 Thess. 1:5, 6; of His judgments, Rev. 16:7; 19:2; of His character as Judge, 2 Tim. 4:8; Rev. 16:5; of His ways and doings, Rev. 15:3. In the following the RV substitutes "righteous" for the KJV "just"; Matt. 1:19; 13:49; 27:19, 24; Mark 6:20; Luke 2:25; 15:7; 20:20;

23:50; John 5:30; Acts 3:14; 7:52; 10:22; 22:14; Rom. 1:17; 7:12; Gal. 3:11; Heb. 10:38; Jas. 5:6; 1 Pet. 3:18; 2 Pet. 2:7; **1 John 1:9**; Rev. 15:3.

Forgive *aphiemi* (863), primarily, "to send forth, send away" (*apo*, "from," *hiemi*, "to send"), denotes, besides its other meanings, "to remit or forgive" (a) debts, Matt. 6:12; 18:27, 32, these being completely cancelled; (b) sins, e.g., Matt. 9:2, 5, 6; 12:31, 32; Acts 8:22 ("the thought of thine heart"); Rom. 4:7; Jas. 5:15; **1 John 1:9; 2:12**. In this latter respect the verb, like its corresponding noun (below), firstly signifies the remission of the punishment due to sinful conduct, the deliverance of the sinner from the penalty divinely, and therefore righteously, imposed; secondly, it involves the complete removal of the cause of offense; such remission is based upon the vicarious and propitiatory sacrifice of Christ. In the OT atoning sacrifice and "forgiveness" are often associated, e.g., Lev. 4:20, 26. The verb is used in the NT with reference to trespasses (*paraptoma*), e.g., Matt. 6:14, 15; sins (*hamartia*), e.g., Luke 5:20; debts (*opheilema*), Matt. 6:12; (*opheile*), 18:32; (*daneion*), 18:27; the thought (*dianoia*) of the heart, Acts 8:22. Cf. *kalupto*, "to cover," 1 Pet. 4:8; Jas. 5:20; and *epikalupto*, "to cover over," Rom. 4:7, representing the Hebrew words for "atonement." Human "forgiveness" is to be strictly analogous to divine "forgiveness," e.g., Matt. 6:12. If certain conditions are fulfilled, there is no limitation to Christ's law of "forgiveness," Matt. 18:21, 22. The conditions are repentance and confession, Matt. 18:15-17; Luke 17:3.

Unrighteousness *adikia* (93), denotes (a) "injustice," Luke 18:6, lit., "the judge of injustice"; Rom. 9:14; (b) "unrighteousness, iniquity," e.g., Luke 16:8, lit., "the steward of unrighteousness," RV marg., i.e., characterized by "unrighteousness"; Rom. 1:18, 29; 2:8; 3:5; 6:13; 1 Cor. 13:6, RV, "unrighteousness"; 2 Thess. 2:10, "[with all (lit., 'in every) deceit'] of unrighteousness," i.e., deceit such as "unrighteousness" uses, and that in every variety; Antichrist and his ministers will not be restrained by any scruple from words or deeds calculated to deceive; 2 Thess. 2:12, of those who have pleasure in it, not an intellectual but a moral evil; distaste for truth is the precursor of the rejection of it; 2 Tim. 2:19, RV; **1 John 1:9**, which includes (c); (c) "a deed or deeds violating law and justice" (virtually the same as *adikema*, "an unrighteous act"), e.g., Luke 13:27, "iniquity"; 2 Cor. 12:13, "wrong," the wrong of depriving another of what is his own, here ironically of a favor; Heb. 8:12, 1st clause, "iniquities," lit., "unrighteousnesses" (plural, not as KJV); 2 Pet. 2:13, 15, RV, "wrongdoing," KJV, "unrighteousness"; **1 John 5:17**.

1:10 If we say that we have not sinned, we make him a liar, and his word is not in us.

Sinned *hamartano* (264), lit., "to miss the mark," is used in the NT (a) of "sinning" against God, (1) by angels, 2 Pet. 2:4; (2) by man, Matt. 27:4; Luke 15:18, 21 (heaven standing, by metonymy, for God); John 5:14; 8:11; 9:2, 3; Rom. 2:12 (twice); 3:23; 5:12, 14, 16; 6:15; 1 Cor. 7:28 (twice), 36; 15:34; Eph. 4:26; 1 Tim. 5:20; Titus 3:11; Heb. 3:17; 10:26; **1 John 1:10**; in **2:1** (twice), the aorist tense in each place, referring to an act of "sin"; on the contrary, in **3:6** (twice), **8**, **9**, the present tense indicates, not the committal of an act, but the continuous practice of "sin"; in **5:16** (twice) the present tense indicates the condition resulting from an act, "unto death" signifying "tending towards death"; (b) against Christ, 1 Cor. 8:12; (c) against man, (1) a brother, Matt. 18:15, RV, "sin" (KJV, "trespass"); v. 21; Luke 17:3, 4, RV, "sin" (KJV, "trespass"); 1 Cor. 8:12; (2) in Luke 15:18, 21, against the father by the Prodigal Son, "in thy sight" being suggestive of befitting reverence; (d) against Jewish law, the Temple, and Caesar, Acts 25:8, RV, "sinned" (KJV, "offended"); (e) against one's own body, by fornication, 1 Cor. 6:18; (f) against earthly masters by servants, 1 Pet. 2:20, RV, "(when) ye sin (and are buffeted for it)," KJV, "(when ye be buffeted) for your faults," lit., "having sinned." *See also* **Sin** at *1 John 1:7*.

Make *poieo* (4160), "to do, to make," is used in the latter sense (a) of constructing or producing anything, of the creative acts of God, e.g., Matt. 19:4 (2nd part); Acts 17:24; of the acts of human beings, e.g., Matt. 17:4; Acts 9:39; (b) with nouns denoting a state or condition, to be the author of, to cause, e.g., peace, Eph. 2:15; Jas. 3:18; stumbling blocks, Rom. 16:17; (c) with nouns involving the idea of action (or of something accomplished by action), so as to express the idea of the verb more forcibly (the middle voice is commonly used in this respect, suggesting the action as being of special interest to the doer); for the active voice see, e.g., Mark 2:23, of "making" one's way, where the idea is not that the disciples "made" a path through the standing corn, but simply that they went, the phrase being equivalent to going, "(they began) as they went (to pluck the ears)"; other instances of the active are Rev. 13:13, 14; 16:14; 19:20; for the middle voice (the dynamic or subjective middle), see, e.g., John 14:23, "will make Our abode"; in Acts 20:24, "none of these things move me," lit., "I make account of none of these things"; 25:17, "I made no delay" RV, Rom. 15:26; Eph. 4:16; Heb. 1:2; 2 Pet. 1:10; (d) to "make" ready or prepare, e.g., a dinner, Luke 14:12; a supper, John 12:2; (e) to acquire, provide a thing for oneself, Matt. 25:16; Luke 19:18; (f) to render or "make" one or oneself anything, or cause a person or thing to become something, e.g., Matt. 4:19; 12:16, "make (Him known)"; John 5:11, 15, to "make" whole; 16:2, lit., "they shall make (you put out of the synagogue)"; Eph. 2:14; Heb. 1:7; to change one thing into another, Matt. 21:13; John 2:16; 4:46; 1 Cor. 6:15; (g) to constitute one anything, e.g., Acts 2:36, (h) to declare one or oneself anything, John 5:18, "making (Himself equal with God)"; 8:53; 10:33; 19:7, 12; **1 John 1:10**; **5:10**; (i) to "make" one do a thing, e.g., Luke 5:34; John 6:10; Rev. 3:9.

Liar *pseustes* (5583), "a liar," occurs in John 8:44, 55; Rom. 3:4; 1 Tim. 1:10; Titus 1:12; **1 John 1:10**; **2:4**, **22**; **4:20**; **5:10**. *See also* **Lie** at *1 John 1:6*.

Chapter 2

2:1 My little children, these things write I unto you, that ye sin not. And if any man sin, we have an advocate with the Father, Jesus Christ the righteous:

Children *teknion* (5040), "a little child," a diminutive, is used only figuratively in the NT, and always in the plural. It is found frequently in 1 John, see **2:1**, **12**, **28**; **3:7**, **18**; **4:4**; **5:21**; elsewhere, once in John's Gospel, 13:33, once in Paul's epistles, Gal. 4:19. It is a term of affection by a teacher to his disciples under circumstances requiring a tender appeal, e.g., of Christ to the Twelve just before His death; the apostle John used it in warning believers against spiritual dangers; Paul, because of the deadly errors of Judaism assailing the Galatian churches. Cf. his use of *teknon* in Gal. 4:28.

Sin *see* **Sinned** at *1 John 1:10*.

Advocate *parakletos* (3875), lit., "called to one's side," i.e., to one's aid, is primarily a verbal adjective, and suggests the capability or adaptability for giving aid. It was used in a court of justice to denote a legal assistant, counsel for the defense, an advocate; then, generally, one who pleads another's cause, an intercessor, advocate, as in **1 John 2:1**, of the Lord Jesus. In the widest sense, it signifies a "succorer, comforter." Christ was this to His disciples, by the implication of His word "another (*allos*, "another of the same sort," not *heteros*, "different") Comforter," when speaking of the Holy Spirit, John 14:16. In 14:26; 15:26; 16:7 He calls Him "the Comforter." "Comforter" or "Consoler" corresponds to the name "*Menahem*," given by the Hebrews to the Messiah.

Righteous *see* **Just** at *1 John 1:9*.

2:2 And he is the propitiation for our sins: and not for ours only, but also for *the sins of* the whole world.

Propitiation *hilasmos* (2434), akin to *hileos* ("merciful, propitious"), signifies "an expiation, a means whereby sin is covered and remitted." It is used in the NT of Christ Himself as "the propitiation," in **1 John 2:2** and **4:10**, signifying that He Himself, through the expiatory sacrifice of His death, is the personal means by whom God shows mercy to the sinner who believes on Christ as the One thus provided. In the former passage He is described as "the propitiation for our sins; and not for ours only, but also for the whole world." The italicized addition in the KJV, "*the sins of*," gives a wrong interpretation. What is indicated is that provision is made for the whole world, so that no one is, by divine predetermination, excluded from the scope of God's mercy; the efficacy of the "propitiation," however, is made actual for those who believe. In **4:10**, the fact that God "sent His Son to be the propitiation for our sins," is shown to be the great expression of God's love toward man, and the reason why Christians should love one another. In the Sept., Lev. 25:9; Num. 5:8; 1 Chron. 28:20; Ps. 130:4; Ezek. 44:27; Amos 8:14.

Our *see* **I** *John 1:3*.

Whole *holos* (3650), signifies "whole," (a) with a noun, e.g., Matt. 5:29, 30; Mark 8:36; 15:1, 16, 33; Luke 11:36 (1st part), though *holon* may here be used adverbially with *photeinon*, "wholly light" [as in the 2nd part, RV, "wholly (full of light)"]; John 11:50; 1 Cor. 12:17 (1st part); **1 John 2:2**; **5:19**; (b) absolutely, as a noun, e.g., Matt. 13:33; 1 Cor. 12:17 (2nd part).

2:3 And hereby we do know that we know him, if we keep his commandments.

Hereby This translates the phrase *en touto*, lit., "in this," 1 Cor. 4:4; **1 John 2:3**, **5**; **3:16**, **19**, **24**; **4:2**, **13**; **5:2** (RV, "hereby," KJV, "by this").

Know *ginosko* (1097), signifies "to be taking in knowledge, to come to know, recognize, understand," or "to understand completely," e.g., Mark 13:28, 29; John 13:12; 15:18; 21:17; 2 Cor. 8:9; Heb. 10:34; **1 John 2:5**; **4:2**, **6** (twice), **7**, **13**; **5:2**, **20**; in its past tenses it frequently means "to know in the sense of realizing," the aorist or point tense usually indicating definiteness, Matt. 13:11; Mark 7:24; John 7:26; in 10:38 "that ye may know (aorist tense) and understand, (present tense)"; 19:4; Acts 1:7; 17:19; Rom. 1:21; 1 Cor. 2:11 (2nd part), 14; 2 Cor. 2:4; Eph. 3:19; 6:22; Phil. 2:19; 3:10; 1 Thess. 3:5; 2 Tim. 2:19; Jas. 2:20; **1 John 2:13** (twice), **14**; **3:6**; **4:8**; 2 John 1; Rev. 2:24; 3:3, 9. In the passive voice, it often signifies "to become known," e.g., Matt. 10:26; Phil. 4:5. In the sense of complete and absolute understanding on God's part, it is used, e.g., in Luke 16:15; John 10:15 (of the Son as well as the Father); 1 Cor. 3:20. In Luke 12:46, KJV, it is rendered "he is ... aware." In the NT *ginosko* frequently indicates a relation between the person "knowing" and the object known; in this respect, what is "known" is of value or importance to the one who knows, and hence the establishment of the relationship, e.g., especially of God's "knowledge," 1 Cor. 8:3, "if any man love God, the same is known of Him"; Gal. 4:9, "to be known of God"; here the "knowing" suggests approval and bears the meaning "to be approved"; so in 2 Tim. 2:19; cf. John 10:14, 27; Gen. 18:19; Nah. 1:7; the relationship implied may involve remedial chastisement, Amos 3:2. The same idea of appreciation as well as "knowledge" underlies several statements concerning the "knowledge" of God and His truth on the part of believers, e.g., John 8:32; 14:20, 31; 17:3; Gal. 4:9 (1st part); **1 John 2:3-13**, **14**; **4:6**, **8**, **16**; **5:20**; such "knowledge" is obtained, not by mere intellectual activity, but by operation of the Holy Spirit consequent upon acceptance of Christ. Nor is such "knowledge" marked by finality; see e.g., 2 Pet. 3:18; Hos. 6:3, RV. The verb is also used to convey the thought of connection or union, as between man and woman, Matt. 1:25; Luke 1:34.

Keep *tereo* (5083), denotes (a) "to watch over, preserve, keep, watch," e.g., Acts 12:5, 6; 16:23; in 25:21, RV (1st part), "kept" (KJV, "reserved"); the present participle is translated "keepers" in Matt. 28:4, lit. "the keeping (ones)"; it is used of the "keeping" power of God the Father and Christ, exercised over His people, John 17:11, 12, 15; 1 Thess. 5:23, "preserved"; **1 John 5:18**, where "He that was begotten of God," RV, is said of Christ as the Keeper ("keepeth him," RV, for KJV, "keepeth himself"); Jude 1, RV, "kept for Jesus Christ" (KJV, "preserved in Jesus Christ"), Rev. 3:10; of their inheritance, 1 Pet. 1:4 ("reserved"); of judicial reservation by God in view of future doom, 2 Pet. 2:4, 9, 17; 3:7; Jude 6, 13; of "keeping" the faith, 2 Tim. 4:7; the unity of the Spirit, Eph. 4:3; oneself, 2 Cor. 11:9; 1 Tim. 5:22; Jas. 1:27; figuratively, one's garments, Rev. 16:15; (b) "to observe, to give heed to," as of keeping commandments, etc., e.g., Matt. 19:17; John 14:15; 15:10; 17:6; Jas. 2:10; **1 John 2:3**, **4**, **5**; **3:22**, **24**; **5:2** (in some mss.), 3; Rev. 1:3; 2:26; 3:8, 10; 12:17; 14:12; 22:7, 9.

2:4 He that saith, I know him, and keepeth not his commandments, is a liar, and the truth is not in him.

Keepeth *see* Keep at *1 John 2:3*.

Liar *see 1 John 1:10*.

2:5 But whoso keepeth his word, in him verily is the love of God perfected: hereby know we that we are in him.

Keepeth *see* Keep at *1 John 2:3*.

Verily *alethos* (230), "truly" (akin to *aletheia*, "truth"), is translated "verily" in **1 John 2:5**.

Love *agapao* (25), and the corresponding noun *agape* present "the characteristic word of Christianity, and since the Spirit of revelation has used it to express ideas previously unknown, inquiry into its use, whether in Greek literature or in the Septuagint, throws but little light upon its distinctive meaning in the NT. Cf, however, Lev. 19:18; Deut. 6:5.

"*Agape* and *agapao* are used in the NT (a) to describe the attitude of God toward His Son, John 17:26; the human race, generally, John 3:16; Rom. 5:8, and to such as believe on the Lord Jesus Christ particularly John 14:21; (b) to convey His will to His children concerning their attitude one toward another, John 13:34, and toward all men, 1 Thess. 3:12; 1 Cor. 16:14; 2 Pet. 1:7; (c) to express the essential nature of God, **1 John 4:8**. "Love can be known only from the actions it prompts. God's love is seen in the gift of His Son, **1 John 4:9**, **10**. But obviously this is not the love of complacency, or affection, that is, it was not drawn out by any excellency in its objects, Rom. 5:8. It was an exercise of the divine will in deliberate choice, made without assignable cause save that which lies in the nature of God Himself, Cf. Deut. 7:7, 8. Love had its perfect expression among men in the Lord Jesus Christ, 2 Cor. 5:14; Eph. 2:4; 3:19; 5:2; Christian love is the fruit of His Spirit in the Christian, Gal. 5:22. Christian love has God for its primary object, and expresses itself first of all in implicit obedience to His commandments, John 14:15, 21, 23; 15:10; **1 John 2:5**; **5:3**; 2 John 6. Selfwill, that is, self-pleasing, is the negation of love to God.

Christian love, whether exercised toward the brethren, or toward men generally, is not an impulse from the feelings, it does not always run with the natural inclinations, nor does it spend itself only upon those for whom some affinity is discovered. Love seeks the welfare of all, Rom. 15:2, and works no ill to any, 13:8-10; love seeks opportunity to do good to 'all men, and especially toward them that are of the household of the faith,' Gal. 6:10. See further 1 Cor. 13 and Col. 3:12-14."

In respect of *agapao* as used of God, it expresses the deep and constant "love" and interest of a perfect Being towards entirely unworthy objects, producing and fostering a reverential "love" in them towards the Giver, and a practical "love" towards those who are partakers of the same, and a desire to help others to seek the Giver.

See also **Loveth, Love** at *1 John 4:21*.

Of In addition to the rendering of a number of prepositions, "of" translates the genitive case of nouns, with various shades of meaning. Of these the subjective and objective are mentioned here, which need careful distinction. Thus the phrase "the love of God," e.g., in **1 John 2:5** and **3:16**, is subjective, signifying "God's love"; in **1 John 5:3**, it is objective, signifying our love to God. Again, "the witness of God," e.g., **1 John 5:9**, is subjective, signifying the witness which God Himself has given; in Rev. 1:2, 9, and 19:10, e.g., "the testimony of Jesus" is objective, signifying the testimony borne to Him. In the KJV "the faith of" is sometimes ambiguous; with reference to Christ it is objective, i.e., faith in Him, not His own faith, in the following passages in which the RV, "in" gives the correct meaning; Rom. 3:22; Gal. 2:16 (twice), 20, RV, "I live in faith, the faith which is in the Son of God"; 3:22; Eph. 3:12; Phil. 3:9 (cf. Col. 2:12, "faith in the working of God"). In Eph. 2:20, "the foundation of the apostles and prophets" is subjective, i.e., the foundation laid by the apostles and prophets ("other foundation can no man lay than ... Jesus Christ," 1 Cor. 3:11).

Perfected *teleioo* (5048), "to bring to an end by completing or perfecting," is used (I) of "accomplishing"; (II) of "bringing to completeness," (a) of persons: of Christ's assured completion of His earthly course, in the accomplishment of the Father's will, the successive stages culminating in His death, Luke 13:32; Heb. 2:10, to make Him "perfect," legally and officially, for all that He would be to His people on the ground of His sacrifice; cf. 5:9; 7:28, RV, "perfected" (KJV, "consecrated"); of His saints, John 17:23, RV, "perfected" (KJV, "made perfect"); Phil. 3:12; Heb. 10:14; 11:40 (of resurrection glory); 12:23 (of the departed saints); **1 John 4:18**, of former priests (negatively), Heb. 9:9; similarly of Israelites under the Aaronic priesthood, 10:1; (b) of things, Heb. 7:19 (of the ineffectiveness of the Law); Jas. 2:22 (of faith made "perfect" by works); **1 John 2:5**, of the love of God operating through him who keeps His word; **4:12**, of the love of God in the case of those who love one another; **4:17**, of the love of God as "made perfect with" (RV) those who abide in God, giving them to be possessed of the very character of God, by reason of which "as He is, even so are they in this world."

Hereby *see 1 John 2:3*.

Know *see 1 John 2:3*.

2:6 He that saith he abideth in him ought himself also so to walk, even as he walked.

Ought *opheilo* (3784), "to owe," is translated "ought," with various personal pronouns, in John 13:14; 19:7; Acts 17:29; Rom. 15:1; Heb. 5:3, KJV (RV, "he is bound"); 5:12; **1 John 3:16**; **4:11**; 3 John 8; with other subjects in 1 Cor. 11:7, 10; 2 Cor. 12:14; Eph. 5:28; **1 John 2:6**.

2:7 Brethren, I write no new commandment unto you, but an old commandment which ye had from the beginning. The old commandment is the word which ye have heard from the beginning.

Brethren *adelphos* (80), in **1 John 2:7**, KJV, "brethren" the RV has "beloved," according to the mss. which have *agapetos*.

Old *palaios* (3820), (Eng., "paleontology," etc.), "of what is of long duration, old in years," etc., a garment, wine (in contrast to *neos*), Matt. 9:16-17; Mark 2:21-22 (twice); Luke 5:36-37, 39 (twice); of the treasures of divine truth, Matt. 13:52 (compared with *kainos*); of what belongs to the past, e.g., the believer's former self before his conversion, his "old man," "old" because it has been superseded by that which is new, Rom. 6:6; Eph. 4:22 (in contrast to *kainos*); Col. 3:9 (in contrast to *neos*); of the covenant in connection with the Law, 2 Cor. 3:14; of leaven, metaphorical of moral evil, 1 Cor. 5:7, 8 (in contrast to *neos*); of that which was given long ago and remains in force, an "old" commandment, **1 John 2:7** (twice), that which was familiar and well known in contrast to that which is fresh (*kainos*).

Word *see 1 John 1:1*.

2:8 Again, a new commandment I write unto you, which thing is true in him and in you: because the darkness is past, and the true light now shineth.

Again *palin* (3825), the regular word for "again," is used chiefly in two senses, (a) with reference to repeated action; (b) rhetorically, in the sense of "moreover" or "further," indicating a statement to be added in the course of an argument, e.g., Matt. 5:33; or with the meaning "on the other hand, in turn," Luke 6:43; 1 Cor. 12:21; 2 Cor. 10:7; **1 John 2:8**. In the first chapter of Hebrews, v. 5, *palin* simply introduces an additional quotation; in v. 6 this is not so. There the RV rightly puts the word "again" in connection with "He bringeth in the firstborn into the world," "When He again bringeth, etc." That is to say, *palin* is here set in contrast to the time when God *first* brought His Son into the world. This statement, then, refers to the future second advent of Christ. The word is used far more frequently in the Gospel of John than in any other book in the New Testament.

True *alethes* (227), primarily, "unconcealed, manifest" (*a*, negative, *letho*, "to forget," = *lanthano*, "to escape notice"), hence, actual, "true to fact," is used (a) of persons, "truthful," Matt. 22:16; Mark 12:14; John 3:33; 7:18; 8:26; Rom. 3:4; 2 Cor. 6:8; (b) of things, "true," conforming to reality, John 4:18, "truly," lit., "true"; 5:31, 32; in the best texts, 6:55 (twice), "indeed"; 8:13, 14 (v. 16 in some texts), 17; 10:41; 19:35; 21:24; Acts 12:9; Phil. 4:8; Titus 1:13; 1 Pet. 5:12; 2 Pet. 2:22; **1 John 2:8, 27**; 3 John 1:2.

Darkness *see 1 John 1:5*.

Past *parago* (3855), "to pass by, pass away," in Matt. 9:9, RV, "passed by" (KJV, "forth"), is used in the middle voice in **1 John 2:8**, RV, "is passing away" (KJV, "is past"), of the "passing" of spiritual darkness through the light of the gospel, and in v. **17** of the world.

True *alethinos* (228), denotes "true" in the sense of real, ideal, genuine; it is used (a) of God, John 7:28; 17:3; 1 Thess. 1:9; Rev. 6:10; these declare that God fulfills the meaning of His Name; He is "very God," in distinction from all other gods, false gods; (b) of Christ, John 1:9; 6:32; 15:1; **1 John 2:8**; **5:20** (thrice); Rev. 3:7, 14; 19:11; His judgment, John 8:16 (in the best texts); (c) God's words, John 4:37; Rev. 19:9, 21:5; 22:6; (d) His ways, Rev. 15:3; (e) His judgments, Rev. 16:7; 19:2; (f) to His riches, Luke 16:11; (g) His worshipers, John 4:23; (h) their hearts, Heb. 10:22; (i) the witness of the apostle John, John 19:35; (j) the spiritual, antitypical tabernacle, Heb. 8:2; 9:24, not that the wilderness tabernacle was false, but that it was a weak and earthly copy of the heavenly.

Now *ede* (2235), is always used of time in the NT and means "now, at (or by) this time," sometimes in the sense of "already," i.e., without mentioning or insisting upon anything further, e.g., 1 Tim. 5:15. In 1 Cor. 4:8 and **1 John 2:8**, the RV corrects the KJV "now," and, in 2 Tim. 4:6, the KJV, "now ready to be," by the rendering "already." See also John 9:27 (KJV, "already," RV, "even now") and 1 Cor. 6:7 (KJV, "now," RV, "already").

Shineth *phaino* (5316), "to cause to appear," denotes, in the active voice, "to give light, shine," John 1:5; 5:35; in Matt. 24:27, passive voice; so Phil. 2:15, RV, "ye are seen" (for KJV, "ye shine"); 2 Pet. 1:19 (active); so **1 John 2:8**, Rev. 1:16; in 8:12 and 18:23 (passive); 21:23 (active).

2:9 He that saith he is in the light, and hateth his brother, is in darkness even until now.

Light *see 1 John 1:5*.

And *kai* In some passages *kai* has the meaning "and yet," e.g., Matt. 3:14, "and yet comest Thou to me?"; 6:26, "and yet (RV, 'and,' KJV, 'yet') your Heavenly Father feedeth them"; Luke 18:7, "and yet He is longsuffering"; John 3:19, "and yet men loved the darkness"; 4:20, "and yet we say"; 6:49, "and yet they died"; 1 Cor. 5:2, "and yet ye are puffed up"; **1 John 2:9**, "and yet hateth his brother." The same is probably the case in John 7:30, "and yet no man laid hands on Him", some rule this and similar cases out because of the negative in the sentence following the *kai*, but that seems hardly tenable.

Hateth *miseo* (3404), "to hate," is used especially (a) of malicious and unjustifiable feelings towards others, whether towards the innocent or by mutual animosity, e.g., Matt. 10:22; 24:10; Luke 6:22, 27; 19:14; John 3:20, of "hating" the light (metaphorically); 7:7; 15:18, 19, 23-25; Titus 3:3; **1 John 2:9, 11**; **3:13, 15**; **4:20**; Rev. 18:2, where "hateful" translates the perfect participle passive voice of the verb, lit., "hated," or "having been hated"; (b) of a right feeling of aversion from what is evil; said of wrongdoing, Rom. 7:15; iniquity, Heb. 1:9; "the garment (figurative) spotted by the flesh," Jude 23; "the works of the Nicolaitans," Rev. 2:6 (and v. 15, in some mss.; see the KJV); (c) of relative preference for one thing over another, by way of expressing either aversion from, or disregard for, the claims of one person or thing relatively to those of another, Matt. 6:24, and Luke 16:13, as to the impossibility of serving two masters; Luke 14:26, as to the claims of parents relatively to those of Christ; John 12:25, of disregard for one's life relatively to the claims of Christ; Eph. 5:29, negatively, of one's flesh, i.e. of one's own, and therefore a man's wife as one with him.

2:10 He that loveth his brother abideth in the light, and there is none occasion of stumbling in him.

Light *see 1 John 1:5.*

Stumbling *skandalon* (4625), originally was "the name of the part of a trap to which the bait is attached, hence, the trap or snare itself, as in Rom. 11:9, RV, 'stumblingblock,' quoted from Psa. 69:22, and in Rev. 2:14, for Balaam's device was rather a trap for Israel than a stumblingblock to them, and in Matt. 16:23, for in Peter's words the Lord perceived a snare laid for Him by Satan.

"In NT *skandalon* is always used metaphorically, and ordinarily of anything that arouses prejudice, or becomes a hindrance to others, or causes them to fall by the way. Sometimes the hindrance is in itself good, and those stumbled by it are the wicked."

Thus it is used (a) of Christ in Rom. 9:33, "(a rock) of offense"; so 1 Pet. 2:8; 1 Cor. 1:23 (KJV and RV, "stumblingblock"), and of His cross, Gal. 5:11 (RV, ditto); of the "table" provided by God for Israel, Rom. 11:9; (b) of that which is evil, e.g., Matt. 13:41, RV, "things that cause stumbling" (KJV, "things that offend"), lit., "all stumblingblocks"; 18:7, RV, "occasions of stumbling" and "occasion"; Luke 17:1 (ditto); Rom. 14:13, RV, "an occasion of falling" (KJV, "an occasion to fall"), said of such a use of Christian liberty as proves a hindrance to another; 16:17, RV, "occasions of stumbling," said of the teaching of things contrary to sound doctrine; **1 John 2:10**, "occasion of stumbling," of the absence of this in the case of one who loves his brother and thereby abides in the light. Love, then, is the best safeguard against the woes pronounced by the Lord upon those who cause others to stumble. Cf. the Sept. in Hos. 4:17, "Ephraim partaking with idols hath laid stumblingblocks in his own path."

2:11 But he that hateth his brother is in darkness, and walketh in darkness, and knoweth not whither he goeth, because that darkness hath blinded his eyes.

Hateth *see 1 John 2:9.*

Darkness *see 1 John 1:5.*

Goeth *hupago* (1517), "to go away or to go slowly away, to depart, withdraw oneself," often with the idea of going without noise or notice, is very frequent in the Gospels; elsewhere it is used in Jas. 2:16; **1 John 2:11**; Rev. 10:8; 13:10; 14:4; 16:1; 17:8, 11. It is frequently rendered "go your (thy) way."

Blinded *tuphloo* (5186), "to blind" (from a root *tuph-*, "to burn, smoke"; cf. *tuphos*, "smoke"), is used metaphorically, of the dulling of the intellect, John 12:40; 2 Cor. 4:4; **1 John 2:11**.

2:12 I write unto you, little children, because your sins are forgiven you for his name's sake.

Children *see 1 John 2:1.*

Forgiven *see* **Forgive** at *1 John 1:9.*

Name *onoma* (3686), is used ... for all that a "name" implies, of authority, character, rank, majesty, power, excellence, etc., of everything that the "name" covers: (a) of the "Name" of God as expressing His attributes, etc., e.g., Matt. 6:9; Luke 1:49; John 12:28; 17:6, 26; Rom. 15:9; 1 Tim. 6:1; Heb. 13:15; Rev. 13:6; (b) of the "Name" of Christ, e.g., Matt. 10:22; 19:29; John 1:12; 2:23; 3:18; Acts 26:9; Rom. 1:5; Jas. 2:7; **1 John 3:23**; 3 John 7; Rev. 2:13; 3:8; also the phrases rendered "in the name"; these may be analyzed as follows: (1) representing the authority of Christ, e.g., Matt. 18:5 (with *epi*, "on the ground of My authority"); so Matt. 24:5 (falsely) and parallel passages; as substantiated by the Father, John 14:26; 16:23 (last clause), RV; (2) in the power of (with *en*, "in"), e.g., Mark 16:17; Luke 10:17; Acts 3:6; 4:10; 16:18; Jas. 5:14; (3) in acknowledgement or confession of, e.g., Acts 4:12; 8:16; 9:27, 28; (4) in recognition of the authority of (sometimes combined with the thought of relying or resting on), Matt. 18:20; cf. 28:19; Acts 8:16; 9:2 (*eis*, "into"); John 14:13; 15:16; Eph. 5:20; Col. 3:17; (5) owing to the fact that one is called by Christ's "Name" or is identified with Him, e.g. 1 Pet. 4:14 (with *en*, "in"); with *heneken*, "for the sake of," e.g., Matt. 19:29; with *dia*, "on account of," Matt. 10:22; 24:9; Mark 13:13; Luke 21:17; John 15:21; **1 John 2:12**; Rev. 2:3.

2:13 I write unto you, fathers, because ye have known him *that is* from the beginning. I write unto you, young men, because ye have overcome the wicked one. I write unto you, little children, because ye have known the Father.

Fathers *pater* (3962), from a root signifying "a nourisher, protector, upholder" (Lat., *pater*, Eng., "father," are akin), is used (a) of the nearest ancestor, e.g., Matt. 2:22; (b) of a more remote ancestor, the progenitor of the people, a "forefather," e.g., Matt. 3:9; 23:30; 1 Cor. 10:1; the patriarchs, 2 Pet. 3:4; (c) one advanced in the knowledge of Christ, **1 John 2:13**; (d) metaphorically, of the originator of a family or company of persons animated by the same spirit as himself, as of Abraham, Rom. 4:11, 12, 16, 17, 18, or of Satan, John 8:38, 41, 44; (e) of one who, as a preacher of the gospel and a teacher, stands in a "father's" place, caring for his spiritual children, 1 Cor. 4:15 (not the same as a mere title of honor, which the Lord prohibited, Matt. 23:9); (f) of the members of the Sanhedrin, as of those who exercised religious authority over others, Acts 7:2; 22:1; (g) of God in relation to those who have been born anew (John 1:12, 13), and so are believers, Eph. 2:18; 4:6 (cf. 2 Cor. 6:18), and imitators of their "Father," Matt. 5:45, 48; 6:1, 4, 6, 8, 9, etc. Christ never associated Himself with them by using the personal pronoun "our"; He always used the singular, "My Father," His relationship being unoriginated and essential, whereas theirs is by grace and regeneration, e.g., Matt. 11:27; 25:34; John 20:17; Rev. 2:27; 3:5, 21; so the apostles spoke of God as the "Father" of the Lord Jesus Christ, e.g., Rom. 15:6; 2 Cor. 1:3; 11:31; Eph. 1:3; Heb. 1:5; 1 Pet. 1:3; Rev. 1:6; (h) of God, as the "Father" of lights, i.e., the Source or Giver of whatsoever provides illumination, physical and spiritual, Jas. 1:17; of mercies, 2 Cor. 1:3; of glory, Eph. 1:17; (i) of God, as Creator, Heb. 12:9 (cf. Zech. 12:1).

Known *see* **Know** at ***1 John 2:3***.

Young men *neaniskos* (3495), a diminutive of "a youth, a young man," occurs in Matt. 19:20, 22; Mark 14:51 (1st part; RV omits in 2nd part); 16:5; Luke 7:14; Acts 2:17; 5:10 (i.e., attendants); 23:18 (in the best texts), 22; **1 John 2:13, 14**, of the second branch of the spiritual family.

Overcome *nikao* (3528), is used (a) of God, Rom. 3:4 (a law term), RV, "mightest prevail"; (b) of Christ, John 16:33; Rev. 3:21; 5:5; 17:14; (c) of His followers, Rom. 12:21 (2nd part); **1 John 2:13-14**; **4:4**; **5:4-5**; Rev. 2:7, 11, 17, 26; 3:5, 12, 21; 12:11; 15:2; 21:7; (d) of faith, **1 John 5:4**; (e) of evil (passive voice), Rom. 12:21; (f) of predicted human potentates, Rev. 6:2; 11:7; 13:7.

Wicked *poneros* (4190), is translated "wicked" in the KJV and RV in Matt. 13:49; 18:32; 25:26; Luke 19:22; Acts 18:14; 1 Cor. 5:13; in the following the RV substitutes "evil" for KJV, "wicked": Matt. 12:45 (twice); 13:19; 16:4; Luke 11:26; Col. 1:21; 2 Thess. 3:2; and in the following, where Satan is mentioned as "the (or that) evil one": Matt. 13:38; Eph. 6:16; **1 John 2:13, 14; 3:12** (1st part); **5:18**; in v. **19** for KJV, "wickedness"; he is so called also in KJV and RV in John 17:15; 2 Thess. 3:3; KJV only in Luke 11:4; in 3 John 10, KJV, the word is translated "malicious," RV, "wicked."

Children *paidion* (3813), a diminutive of *pais*, signifies "a little or young child"; it is used of an infant just born, John 16:21, of a male child recently born, e.g., Matt. 2:8; Heb. 11:23; of a more advanced child, Mark 9:24; of a son, John 4:49; of a girl, Mark 5:39, 40, 41; in the plural, of "children," e.g., Matt. 14:21. It is used metaphorically of believers who are deficient in spiritual understanding, 1 Cor. 14:20, and in affectionate and familiar address by the Lord to His disciples, almost like the Eng., "lads," John 21:5; by the apostle John to the youngest believers in the family of God, **1 John 2:13, 18**; there it is to be distinguished from *teknia*, which term he uses in addressing all his readers (vv. **1, 12, 28**: see *teknia*). *See also **1 John 2:1***.

2:14 I have written unto you, fathers, because ye have known him *that is* from the beginning. I have written unto you, young men, because ye are strong, and the word of God abideth in you, and ye have overcome the wicked one.

Known *see* **Know** at ***1 John 2:3***.

Young men *see **1 John 2:13***.

Strong *ichuros* (2478), "strong, mighty," is used of (a) persons: (1) God, Rev. 18:8; (2) angels, Rev. 5:2; 10:1; 18:21; (3) men, Matt. 12:29 (twice) and parallel passages; Heb. 11:34, KJV, "valiant" (RV, "mighty"); Rev. 6:15 (in the best texts); 19:18, "mighty"; metaphorically, (4) the church at Corinth, 1 Cor. 4:10, where the apostle reproaches them ironically with their unspiritual and self-complacent condition; (5) of young men in Christ spiritually strong, through the Word of God, to overcome the evil one, **1 John 2:14**; of (b) things: (1) wind, Matt. 14:30 (in some mss.), "boisterous"; (2) famine, Luke 15:14; (3) things in the mere human estimate, 1 Cor. 1:27; (4) Paul's letters, 2 Cor. 10:10; (5) the Lord's crying and tears, Heb. 5:7; (6) consolation, 6:18; (7) the voice of an angel, Rev. 18:2 (in the best texts; some have *megas*, "great"); (8) Babylon, Rev. 18:10; (9) thunderings, Rev. 19:6.

Abideth *meno* (3306), used (a) of place, e.g., Matt. 10:11, metaphorically **1 John 2:19**, is said of God, **1 John 4:15**; Christ, John 6:56; 15:4, etc.; the Holy Spirit, John 1:32-33;

14:17; believers, John 6:56; 15:4; **1 John 4:15**, etc.; the Word of God, **1 John 2:14**; the truth, 2 John 2, etc.; (b) of time; it is said of believers, John 21:22-23; Phil. 1:25; **1 John 2:17**; Christ, John 12:34; Heb. 7:24; the Word of God, 1 Pet. 1:23; sin, John 9:41; cities, Matt. 11:23; Heb. 13:14; bonds and afflictions, Acts 20:23; (c) of qualities; faith, hope, love, 1 Cor. 13:13; Christ's love, John 15:10; afflictions, Acts 20:23; brotherly love, Heb. 13:1; the love of God, **1 John 3:17**; the truth, 2 John 2. The RV usually translates it by "abide," but "continue" in 1 Tim. 2:15; in the following, the RV substitutes "to abide" for the KJV, "to continue," John 2:12; 8:31; 15:9; 2 Tim. 3:14; Heb. 7:24; 13:14; **1 John 2:24**.

Wicked *see 1 John 2:13*.

2:15-16 Love not the world, neither the things *that are* in the world. If any man love the world, the love of the Father is not in him.

For all that *is* in the world, the lust of the flesh, and the lust of the eyes, and the pride of life, is not of the Father, but is of the world.

All *pas* (3956), signifies (1) with nouns without the article, (a) "every one" of the class denoted by the noun connected with *pas*, e.g., Matt. 3:10, "every tree"; Mark 9:49, "every sacrifice"; see also John 2:10; Acts 2:43; Rom. 2:9; Eph. 1:21; 3:15; 2 Thess. 2:4; 2 Tim. 3:16, RV; (b) "any and every, of every kind, all manner of," e.g., Matt. 4:23; "especially with nouns denoting virtues or vices, emotions, condition, indicating every mode in which a quality manifests itself; or any object to which the idea conveyed by the noun belongs" (GrimmThayer). This is often translated "all," e.g., Acts 27:20; Rom. 15:14; 2 Cor. 10:6; Eph. 4:19, 31; Col. 4:12, "all the will of God," i.e., everything God wills; (2) without a noun, "every one, everything, every man" (i.e., person), e.g., Luke 16:16; or with a negative, "not everyone," e.g., Mark 9:49; with a participle and the article, equivalent to a relative clause, everyone who, e.g., 1 Cor. 9:25; Gal. 3:10, 13; **1 John 2:29; 3:3-4, 6, 10, 15**, rendered "whosoever." So in the neuter, **1 John 2:16; 5:4**, often rendered "whatsoever"; governed by the preposition *en*, "in," without a noun following, it signifies "in every matter, or condition," Phil. 4:6; 1 Thess. 5:18; "in every way or particular," 2 Cor. 4:8, translated "on every side"; so 2 Cor. 7:5; "in everything," Eph. 5:24; Phil. 4:12, lit., "in everything and (perhaps "even") in all things."

Lust *epithumia* (1939), denotes "strong desire" of any kind, the various kinds being frequently specified by some adjective. The word is used of a good desire in Luke 22:15; Phil. 1:23, and 1 Thess. 2:17 only. Everywhere else it has a bad sense. In Rom. 6:12 the injunction against letting sin reign in our mortal body to obey the "lust" thereof, refers to those evil desires which are ready to express themselves in bodily activity. They are equally the "lusts" of the flesh, Rom. 13:14; Gal. 5:16, 24; Eph. 2:3; 2 Pet. 2:18; **1 John 2:16**, a phrase which describes the emotions of the soul, the natural tendency towards things evil. Such "lusts" are not necessarily base and immoral, they may be refined in character, but are evil if inconsistent with the will of God. Other descriptions besides those already mentioned are: "of the mind," Eph. 2:3; "evil (desire)," Col. 3:5; "the passion of," 1 Thess. 4:5, RV; "foolish and hurtful," 1 Tim. 6:9; "youthful," 2 Tim. 2:22; "divers," 2 Tim. 3:6 and Titus 3:3; "their own," 2 Tim. 4:3; 2 Pet. 3:3; Jude 16; "worldly," Titus 2:12; "his own," Jas. 1:14; "your former," 1 Pet. 1:14, RV; "fleshly," 2:11; "of men," 4:2; "of defilement," 2 Pet. 2:10; "of the eyes," **1 John 2:16**; of the world ("thereof"), v. **17**; "their own ungodly," Jude 18. In Rev. 18:14 "(the fruits) which thy soul lusted after" is, lit., "of thy soul's lust."

Flesh *sarx* (4561), has a wider range of meaning in the NT than in the OT. Its uses in the NT may be analyzed as follows:

"(a) "the substance of the body," whether of beasts or of men, 1 Cor. 15:39; (b) "the human body," 2 Cor. 10:3a; Gal. 2:20; Phil. 1:22; (c) by synecdoche, of "mankind," in the totality of all that is essential to manhood, i.e., spirit, soul, and body, Matt. 24:22; John 1:13; Rom. 3:20; (d) by synecdoche, of "the holy humanity" of the Lord Jesus, in the totality of all that is essential to manhood, i.e., spirit, soul, and body John 1:14; 1 Tim. 3:16; **1 John 4:2**; 2 John 7, in Heb. 5:7, "the days of His flesh," i.e., His past life on earth in distinction from His present life in resurrection; (e) by synecdoche, for "the complete person," John 6:51-57; 2 Cor. 7:5; Jas. 5:3; (f) "the weaker element in human nature," Matt. 26:41; Rom. 6:19; 8:3a; (g) "the unregenerate state of men," Rom. 7:5; 8:8, 9; (h) "the seat of sin in man" (but this is not the same thing as in the body), 2 Pet. 2:18; **1 John 2:16**; (i) "the lower and temporary element in the Christian," Gal. 3:3; 6:8, and in religious ordinances, Heb. 9:10; (j) "the natural attainments of men," 1 Cor. 1:26; 2 Cor. 10:2, 3b; (k) "circumstances," 1 Cor. 7:28; the externals of life, 2 Cor. 7:1; Eph. 6:5; Heb. 9:13; (l) by metonymy, "the outward and seeming," as contrasted with the spirit, the inward and real, John 6:63; 2 Cor. 5:16; (m) "natural relationship, consanguine," 1 Cor. 10:18; Gal. 4:23, or marital, Matt. 19:5."

Eyes *ophthalmos* (3788), akin to *opsis*, "sight," probably from a root signifying "penetration, sharpness" (Curtius, Gk. Etym.) (cf. Eng., "ophthalmia," etc.). is used (a) of the physical organ, e.g., Matt. 5:38; of restoring sight, e.g., Matt. 20:33; of God's power of vision, Heb. 4:13; 1 Pet. 3:12; of Christ in vision, Rev. 1:14; 2:18; 19:12; of the Holy Spirit in the unity of Godhood with Christ, Rev. 5:6; (b) metaphorically, of ethical qualities, evil, Matt. 6:23; Mark 7:22 (by metonymy, for envy); singleness of motive, Matt. 6:22; Luke 11:34; as the instrument of evil desire, "the principal avenue of temptation," **1 John 2:16**; of adultery, 2 Pet. 2:14; (c) metaphorically, of mental vision, Matt. 13:15; John 12:40; Rom. 11:8; Gal. 3:1, where the metaphor of the "evil eye" is altered to a different sense from that of bewitching (the posting up or placarding of an "eye" was used as a charm, to prevent mischief); by gospel-preaching Christ had been, so to speak, placarded before their "eyes"; the question may be paraphrased, "What evil teachers have been malignly fascinating you?"; Eph. 1:18, of the "eyes of the heart," as a means of knowledge.

Pride *alazoneia* (212), the practice of an *alazon*, denotes quackery; hence, "arrogant display, or boastings," Jas. 4:16, RV, "vauntings"; in **1 John 2:16**, RV, "vainglory"; KJV, "pride."

Life *bios* (979), (cf. Eng. words beginning with *bio*), is used in three respects (a) of "the period or duration of life," e.g., in the KJV of 1 Pet. 4:3, "the time past of our life" (the RV follows the mss. which omit "of our life"); Luke 8:14; 2 Tim. 2:4; (b) of "the manner of life, life in regard to its moral conduct," 1 Tim. 2:2; **1 John 2:16**; (c) of "the means of life, livelihood, maintenance, living," Mark 12:44; Luke 8:43; 15:12, 30; 21:4; **1 John 3:17**, "goods," RV (KJV, "good").

See also ***1 John 1:2***.

2:17 And the world passeth away, and the lust thereof: but he that doeth the will of God abideth for ever.

Passeth *see* **Past** at ***1 John 2:8***.

Lust *see* ***1 John 2:16***.

Will *thelema* (2307), signifies (a) objectively, "that which is willed, of the will of God," e.g., Matt. 18:14; Mark 3:35, the fulfilling being a sign of spiritual relationship to the Lord, John 4:34; 5:30; 6:39, 40; Acts 13:22, plural, "my desires"; Rom. 2:18; 12:2, lit., "the will of God, the good and perfect and acceptable"; here the repeated article is probably resumptive, the adjectives describing the will, as in the Eng. versions; Gal. 1:4; Eph. 1:9; 5:17, "of the Lord"; Col. 1:9; 4:12; 1 Thess. 4:3; 5:18, where it means "the gracious design," rather than "the determined resolve"; 2 Tim. 2:26, which should read "which have been taken captive by him" [(*autou*), i.e., by the Devil; the RV, "by the Lord's servant" is an interpretation; it does not correspond to the Greek] unto His (*ekeinou*) will" (i.e., "God's will"; the different pronoun refers back to the subject of the sentence, viz., God); Heb. 10:10; Rev. 4:11, RV, "because of Thy will"; of human will, e.g., 1 Cor. 7:37; (b) subjectively, the "will" being spoken of as the emotion of being desirous, rather than as the thing "willed"; of the "will" of God, e.g., Rom. 1:10; 1 Cor. 1:1; 2 Cor. 1:1; 8:5; Eph. 1:1, 5, 11; Col. 1:1; 2 Tim. 1:1; Heb. 10:7, 9, 36; **1 John 2:17**; **5:14**; of human "will," e.g., John 1:13; Eph. 2:3, "the desires of the flesh"; 1 Pet. 4:3 (in some texts); 2 Pet. 1:21.

Abideth *see* ***1 John 2:14***.

2:18 Little children, it is the last time: and as ye have heard that antichrist shall come, even now are there many antichrists; whereby we know that it is the last time.

Children *see* ***1 John 2:13***.

Last *eschatos* (2078), "last, utmost, extreme," is used (a) of place, e.g., Luke 14:9, 10, "lowest;" Acts 1:8 and 13:47, "uttermost part;" (b) of rank, e.g., Mark 9:35; (c) of time, relating either to persons or things, e.g., Matt. 5:26, "the last (farthing)," RV (KJV, "uttermost"); Matt. 20:8, 12, 14; Mark 12:6, 22; 1 Cor. 4:9, of apostles as "last" in the program of a spectacular display; 1 Cor. 15:45, "the last Adam"; Rev. 2:19; of the "last" state of persons, Matt. 12:45, neuter plural, lit., "the last (things)"; so Luke 11:26; 2 Pet. 2:20, RV, "the last state" (KJV, "the latter end"); of Christ as the Eternal One, Rev. 1:17 (in some mss. v. 11); 2:8; 22:13; in eschatological phrases as follows: (a) "the last day," a comprehensive term including both the time of the resurrection of the redeemed, John 6:39, 40, 44, 54 and 11:24, and the ulterior time of the judgment of the unregenerate, at the Great White Throne, John 12:48; (b) "the last days," Acts 2:17, a period relative to the supernatural manifestation of the Holy Spirit at Pentecost and the resumption of the divine interpositions in the affairs of the world at the end of the present age, before "the great and notable Day of the Lord," which will usher in the messianic kingdom; (c) in 2 Tim. 3:1, "the last days" refers to the close of the present age of world conditions; (d) in Jas. 5:3, the phrase "in the last days" (RV) refers both to the period preceding the Roman overthrow of the city and the land in AD 70, and to the closing part of the age in consummating acts of gentile persecution including "the time of Jacob's trouble" (cf. verses 7, 8); (e) in 1 Pet. 1:5, "the last time" refers to the time of the Lord's second advent; (f) in **1 John 2:18**, "the last hour" (RV) and, in Jude 18, "the last time" signify the present age previous to the Second Advent.

Time *hora* (5610), primarily, "any time or period fixed by nature," is translated "time" in Matt. 14:15; Luke 14:17; Rom. 13:11, "high time"; in the following the RV renders it "hour," for KJV, "time," Matt. 18:1; Luke 1:10; John 16:2, 4, 25; **1 John 2:18** (twice); Rev. 14:15; in Mark 6:35, RV, "day"; in 1 Thess. 2:17, RV, "a short (season)," lit., "(the season, KJV, 'time') of an hour."

Antichrist, Antichrists *antichristos* (500), can mean either "against Christ" or "instead of Christ," or perhaps, combining the two, "one who, assuming the guise of Christ, opposes Christ" (Westcott). The word is found only in John's epistles, (a) of the many "antichrists" who are forerunners of the "Antichrist" himself, **1 John 2:18, 22**; 2 John 7; (b) of the evil power which already operates anticipatively of the "Antichrist," **1 John 4:3**. What the apostle says of him so closely resembles what he says of the first beast in Rev. 13, and what the apostle Paul says of the Man of Sin in 2 Thess. 2, that the same person seems to be in view in all these passages, rather than the second beast in Rev. 13, the false prophet; for the latter supports the former in all his Antichristian assumptions.

2:19 They went out from us, but they were not of us; for if they had been of us, they would *no doubt* have continued with us: but *they went out*, that they might be made manifest that they were not all of us.

Continued *see* **Abideth** at *1 John 2:14*.

2:20 But ye have an unction from the Holy One, and ye know all things.

Ye These are most frequently the translations of various inflections of a verb; sometimes of the article before a nominative used as a vocative, e.g., Rev. 18:20, "ye saints, and ye apostles, and ye prophets" (lit., "the saints, etc."). When the 2nd person plural pronouns are used separately from a verb, they are usually one or other of the forms of *humeis*, the plural of *su*, "thou," and are frequently emphatic, especially when they are subjects of the verb, an emphasis always to be noticed, e.g., Matt. 5:13, 14, 48; 6:9, 19, 20; Mark 6:31, 37; John 15:27a; Rom. 1:6; 1 Cor. 3:17, 23; Gal. 3:28, 29a; Eph. 1:13a; 2:8; 2:11, 13; Phil. 2:18; Col. 3:4, 7a; 4:1; 1 Thess. 1:6; 2:10, 19, 20; 3:8; 2 Thess. 3:13; Jas. 5:8; 1 Pet. 2:9a; **1 John 2:20, 24** (1st and 3rd occurrences), **27a**; **4:4**; Jude 17, 20.

Unction *chrisma* (5545), signifies "an unguent, or an anointing." It was prepared from oil and aromatic herbs. It is used only metaphorically in the NT; by metonymy, of the Holy Spirit, **1 John 2:20, 27**, twice. The RV translates it "anointing" in all three places, instead of the KJV "unction" and "anointing." That believers have "an anointing from the Holy One" indicates that this anointing renders them holy, separating them to God. The passage teaches that the gift of the Holy Spirit is the all-efficient means of enabling believers to possess a knowledge of the truth. In the Sept., it is used of the oil for "anointing" the high priest, e.g., Exod. 29:7, lit., "Thou shalt take of the oil of the anointing." In Exod. 30:25, etc., it is spoken of as "a holy anointing oil." In Dan. 9:26 *chrisma* stands for the "anointed" one, "Christ," the noun standing by metonymy for the person Himself.

Holy *hagios* (40), fundamentally signifies "separated" (among the Greeks, dedicated to the gods), and hence, in Scripture in its moral and spiritual significance, separated from sin and therefore consecrated to God, sacred. It is predicated of God (as the absolutely "Holy" One, in His purity, majesty and glory): of the Father, e.g., Luke 1:49; John 17:11; 1 Pet. 1:15, 16; Rev. 4:8; 6:10; of the Son, e.g., Luke 1:35; Acts 3:14; 4:27, 30; **1 John 2:20**; of the Spirit, e.g., Matt. 1:18 and frequently in all the Gospels, Acts, Romans, 1 and 2 Cor., Eph., 1 Thess.; also in 2 Tim. 1:14; Titus 3:5; 1 Pet. 1:12; 2 Pet. 1:21; Jude 20.

2:21 I have not written unto you because ye know not the truth, but because ye know it, and that no lie is of the truth.

Lie *pseudos* (5579), "a falsehood, lie", is translated "lie" in John 8:44 (lit., "the lie"); Rom. 1:25, where it stands by metonymy for an idol, as, e.g., in Isa. 44:20; Jer. 10:14; 13:25; Amos 2:4 (plural); 2 Thess. 2:11, with special reference to the lie of v. 4, that man is God (cf. Gen. 3:5); **1 John 2:21, 27**; Rev. 21:27; 22:15; in Eph. 4:25, KJV "lying," RV, "falsehood," the practice; in Rev. 14:5, RV, "lie." (some mss. have *dolos*, "guile," KJV); 2 Thess. 2:9, where "lying wonders" is, lit., "wonders of falsehood," i.e., wonders calculated to deceive (cf. Rev. 13:13-15), the purpose being to deceive people into the acknowledgement of the spurious claim to deity on the part of the Man of Sin. *See also* *1 John 1:6*.

2:22 Who is a liar but he that denieth that Jesus is the Christ? He is antichrist, that denieth the Father and the Son.

Liar *see 1 John 1:10*.

Antichrist *see* Antichrist, Antichrists at *1 John 2:18*.

Denieth *arneomai* (720), signifies (a) "to say ... not, to contradict," e.g., Mark 14:70; John 1:20; 18:25, 27; **1 John 2:22**; (b) "to deny" by way of disowning a person, as, e.g., the Lord Jesus as master, e.g., Matt. 10:33; Luke 12:9; John 13:38 (in the best mss.); 2 Tim. 2:12; or, on the other hand, of Christ Himself, "denying" that a person is His follower, Matt. 10:33; 2 Tim. 2:12; or to "deny" the Father and the Son, by apostatizing and by disseminating pernicious teachings, to "deny" Jesus Christ as master and Lord by immorality under a cloak of religion, 2 Pet. 2:1; Jude 4; (c) "to deny oneself," either in a good sense, by disregarding one's own interests, Luke 9:23, or in a bad sense, to prove false to oneself, to act quite unlike oneself, 2 Tim. 2:13; (d) to "abrogate, forsake, or renounce a thing," whether evil, Titus 2:12, or good, 1 Tim. 5:8; 2 Tim. 3:5; Rev. 2:13; 3:8; (e) "not to accept, to reject" something offered, Acts 3:14; 7:35, "refused"; Heb. 11:24 "refused."

2:23 Whosoever denieth the Son, the same hath not the Father: [*but*] *he that acknowledgeth the Son hath the Father also*.

Acknowledgeth *see* Confess at *1 John 1:9*.

2:24 Let that therefore abide in you, which ye have heard from the beginning. If that which ye have heard from the beginning shall remain in you, ye also shall continue in the Son, and in the Father.

Abide *see* Abideth at *1 John 2:14*.

Ye *see 1 John 2:20*.

2:25 And this is the promise that he hath promised us, *even* eternal life.

Promise *see* Message at *1 John 1:5*.

Promised *epangello* (1861), "to announce, proclaim," has in the NT the two meanings "to profess" and "to promise," each used in the middle voice; "to promise" (a) of "promises" of God, Acts 7:5; Rom. 4:21; in Gal. 3:19, passive voice; Titus 1:2; Heb. 6:13; 10:23; 11:11; 12:26; Jas. 1:12; 2:5; **1 John 2:25**; (b) made by men, Mark 14:11; 2 Pet. 2:19.

2:26 These *things* have I written unto you concerning them that seduce you.

Seduce *planao* (4105), "to cause to wander, lead astray," is translated "to seduce" in **1 John 2:26**, KJV (RV, "lead ... astray"); in Rev. 2:20, "to seduce."

2:27 But the anointing which ye have received of him abideth in you, and ye need not that any man teach you: but as the same anointing teacheth you of all things, and is truth, and is no lie, and even as it hath taught you, ye shall abide in him.

Anointing *see* Unction at *1 John 2:20*.

Ye *see 1 John 2:20*.

Need *chreia* (5532), denotes "a need," in such expressions as "there is a need"; or "to have need of" something, e.g., Matt. 3:14; 6:8; 9:12, RV, "(have no) need," KJV, "need (not)," the RV adheres to the noun form; so in 14:16; Mark 14:63; Luke 5:31; 22:71; Eph. 4:28; 1 Thess. 4:9; in the following, however, both RV and KJV use the verb form, "to need" (whereas the original has the verb *echo*, "to have," with the noun *chreia* as the object, as in the instances just mentioned): Luke 15:7; John 2:25; 13:10; 16:30; 1 Thess. 1:8; **1 John 2:27**; Rev. 22:5; in all these the verb "to have" could well have been expressed in the translation. In Luke 10:42 it is translated "needful," where the "one thing" is surely not one dish, or one person, but is to be explained according to Matt. 6:33 and 16:26. In Eph. 4:29, for the KJV, "(to) the use (of edifying)," the RV more accurately has "(for edifying) as the need may be," marg., "the building up of the need," i.e., "to supply that which needed in each case"; so Westcott, who adds "The need represents a gap in the life which the wise word 'builds up,' fills up solidly and surely." In Phil. 4:19 the RV has "every need of yours" (KJV, "all your need"); in 1 Thess. 4:12, RV, "need" (KJV, "lack"); in Acts 28:10, RV, "(such things) as we needed" (KJV, "as were necessary"), lit., "the things for the needs (plural)."

Man The RV often substitutes "one" for "man," e.g., Matt. 17:8 (*oudeis*, "no one"); 1 Cor. 3:21 (i.e., "no person"); 1 Cor. 15:35; 1 Thess. 5:15; 2 Tim. 4:16; **1 John 2:27**; **3:3**.

Truth *see* True at *1 John 2:8*.

Lie *see 1 John 2:21*.

2:28 And now, little children, abide in him; that, when he shall appear, we may have confidence, and not be ashamed before him at his coming.

Children *see* *1 John 2:1.*

Appear *phaneroo* (5319), signifies, in the active voice, "to manifest"; in the passive voice, "to be manifested"; so, regularly, in the RV, instead of "to appear." See 2 Cor. 7:12; Col. 3:4; Heb. 9:26; 1 Pet. 5:4; **1 John 2:28**; **3:2**; Rev. 3:18. To be manifested, in the Scriptural sense of the word, is more than to "appear." A person may "appear" in a false guise or without a disclosure of what he truly is; to be manifested is to be revealed in one's true character; this is especially the meaning of *phaneroo*, see, e.g., John 3:21; 1 Cor. 4:5; 2 Cor. 5:10-11; Eph. 5:13.

Confidence *parrhesia* (3954), from *pas*, "all," *rhesis*, "speech," denotes (a), primarily, "freedom of speech, unreservedness of utterance," Acts 4:29, 31; 2 Cor. 3:12; 7:4; Philem. 8; or "to speak without ambiguity, plainly," John 10:24; or "without figures of speech," John 16:25; (b) "the absence of fear in speaking boldly; hence, confidence, cheerful courage, boldness, without any connection necessarily with speech"; the RV has "boldness" in the following; Acts 4:13; Eph. 3:12; 1 Tim. 3:13; Heb. 3:6; 4:16; 10:19, 35; **1 John 2:28**; **3:21**; **4:17**; **5:14**; (c) the deportment by which one becomes conspicuous, John 7:4; 11:54, acts openly, or secures publicity, Col. 2:15.

Ashamed *aischuno* (153), from *aischos*, "shame," always used in the passive voice, signifies (a) "to have a feeling of fear or shame which prevents a person from doing a thing," e.g., Luke 16:3; (b) "the feeling of shame arising from something that has been done," e.g., 2 Cor. 10:8; Phil. 1:20; **1 John 2:28**, of the possibility of being "ashamed" before the Lord Jesus at His judgment seat in His Parousia with His saints; in 1 Pet. 4:16, of being ashamed of suffering as a Christian.

Coming *parousia* (3952), lit., "a presence," *para*, "with," and *ousia*, "being" (from *eimi*, "to be"), denotes both an "arrival" and a consequent "presence with." For instance, in a papyrus letter a lady speaks of the necessity of her parousia in a place in order to attend to matters relating to her property there. Paul speaks of his *parousia* in Philippi, Phil. 2:12 (in contrast to his *apousia*, "his absence" Other words denote "the arrival" (see *eisodos* and *eleusis*, above). *Parousia* is used to describe the presence of Christ with His disciples on the Mount of Transfiguration, 2 Pet. 1:16. When used of the return of Christ, at the rapture of the church, it signifies, not merely His momentary "coming" for His saints, but His presence with them from that moment until His revelation and manifestation to the world. In some passages the word gives prominence to the beginning of that period, the course of the period being implied, 1 Cor. 15:23; 1 Thess. 4:15; 5:23; 2 Thess. 2:1; Jas. 5:7-8; 2 Pet. 3:4. In some, the course is prominent, Matt. 24:3, 37; 1 Thess. 3:13; **1 John 2:28**; in others the conclusion of the period, Matt. 24:27; 2 Thess. 2:8. The word is also used of the Lawless One, the Man of Sin, his access to power and his doings in the world during his *parousia*, 2 Thess. 2:9. In addition to Phil. 2:12 (above), it is used in the same way of the apostle, or his companions, in 1 Cor. 16:17; 2 Cor. 7:6-7; 10:10; Phil. 1:26; of the Day of God, 2 Pet. 3:12.

2:29 If ye know that he is righteous, ye know that every one that doeth righteousness is born of him.

Righteous *see* Just at *1 John 1:9.*

Every *see* All at *1 John 2:16.*

Born *gennao* (1080), "to beget," in the passive voice, "to be born," is chiefly used of men "begetting" children, Matt. 1:2-16; more rarely of women "begetting" children, Luke 1:13, 57, "brought forth"; 23:29; John 16:21, "is delivered of," and of the child, "is born." In Gal. 4:24, it is used allegorically, to contrast Jews under bondage to the Law, and spiritual Israel, KJV, "gendereth," RV, "bearing children," to contrast the natural birth of Ishmael and the supernatural birth of Isaac. In Matt. 1:20 it is used of conception, "that which is conceived in her." It is used of the act of God in the birth of Christ, Acts 13:33; Heb. 1:5; 5:5, quoted from Psalm 2:7, none of which indicate that Christ became the Son of God at His birth. It is used metaphorically (a) in the writings of the apostle John, of the gracious act of God in conferring upon those who believe the nature and disposition of "children," imparting to them spiritual life, John 3:3, 5, 7; **1 John 2:29**; **3:9**; **4:7**; **5:1**, **4**, **18**; (b) of one who by means of preaching the gospel becomes the human instrument in the impartation of spiritual life, 1 Cor. 4:15; Philem. 10; (c) in 2 Pet. 2:12, with reference to the evil men whom the apostle is describing, the RV rightly has "born mere animals" (KJV, "natural brute beasts"); (d) in the sense of gendering strife, 2 Tim. 2:23.

Chapter 3

3:1 Behold, what manner of love the Father hath bestowed upon us, that we should be called the sons of God: therefore the world knoweth us not, because it knew him not.

Manner *potapos* (4217), primarily, "from what country," then, "of what sort," is rendered "what manner of man." Matt. 8:27: so 2 Pet. 3:11; Mark 13:1 (twice); Luke 1:29; 7:39; **1 John 3:1**.

Bestowed *didomi* (1325), "to give," is rendered "bestow" in **1 John 3:1**, the implied idea being that of giving freely. The KJV has it in 2 Cor. 8:1; the RV adheres to the lit. rendering, "the grace of God which hath been given in the churches of Macedonia.

Sons *huios* (5207), primarily signifies the relation of offspring to parent (see John 9:18-20; Gal. 4:30). It is often used metaphorically of prominent moral characteristics. "It is used in the NT of (a) male offspring, Gal. 4:30; (b) legitimate, as opposed to illegitimate offspring, Heb. 12:8; (c) descendants, without reference to sex, Rom. 9:27; (d) friends attending a wedding, Matt. 9:15; (e) those who enjoy certain privileges, Acts 3:25; (f) those who act in a certain way, whether evil, Matt. 23:31, or good, Gal. 3:7; (g) those who manifest a certain character, whether evil, Acts 13:10; Eph. 2:2, or good, Luke 6:35; Acts 4:36; Rom. 8:14; (h) the destiny that corresponds with the character, whether evil, Matt. 23:15; John 17:12; 2 Thess. 2:3, or good, Luke 20:36; (i) the dignity of the relationship with God whereinto men are brought by the Holy Spirit when they believe on the Lord Jesus Christ, Rom. 8:19; Gal. 3:26....

"The Apostle John does not use *huios*, 'son,' of the believer, he reserves that title for the Lord; but he does use *teknon*, 'child,' as in his Gospel, 1:12; **1 John 3:1, 2**; Rev. 21:7 (*huios*) is a quotation from 2 Sam. 7:14. The Lord Jesus used *huios* in a very significant way, as in Matt. 5:9, 'Blessed are the peacemakers, for they shall be called the sons of God,' and vv. 44, 45, 'Love your enemies, and pray for them that persecute you; that ye may be (become) sons of your Father which is in heaven.' The disciples were to do these things, not in order that they might become children of God, but that, being children (note 'your Father' throughout), they might make the fact manifest in their character, might 'become sons.' See also 2 Cor. 6:17, 18. As to moral characteristics, the following phrases are used: (a) sons of God, Matt. 5:9, 45; Luke 6:35; (b) sons of the light, Luke 16:8; John 12:36; (c) sons of the day, 1 Thess. 5:5; (d) sons of peace, Luke 10:6; (e) sons of this world, Luke 16:8; (f) sons of disobedience, Eph. 2:2; (g) sons of the evil one, Matt. 13:38, cf. 'of the Devil,' Acts 13:10; (h) son of perdition, John 17:12; 2 Thess. 2:3. It is also used to describe characteristics other than moral, as: (i) sons of the resurrection, Luke 20:36; (j) sons of the Kingdom, Matt. 8:12; 13:38; (k) sons of the bridechamber, Mark 2:19; (l) sons of exhortation, Acts 4:36; (m) sons of thunder, Boanerges, Mark 3:17."

3:2 Beloved, now are we the sons of God, and it doth not yet appear what we shall be: but we know that, when he shall appear, we shall be like him; for we shall see him as he is.

Sons *see 1 John 3:1*.

Appear *see 1 John 2:28*.

Like *homoios* (3664), "like, resembling, such as, the same as," is used (a) of appearance or form John 9:9; Rev. 1:13, 15; 2:18; 4:3 (twice), 6, 7; 9:7 (twice), 10, 19; 11:1; 13:2, 11; 14:14; (b) of ability, condition, nature, Matt. 22:39; Acts 17:29; Gal. 5:21, "such like," lit., "and the (things) similar to these"; **1 John 3:2**; Rev. 13:4; 18:18; 21:11, 18; (c) of comparison in parables, Matt. 13:31, 33, 44, 45, 47; 20:1; Luke 13:18, 19, 21; (d) of action, thought, etc., Matt. 11:16; 13:52; Luke 6:47, 48, 49; 7:31, 32; 12:36; John 8:55; Jude 7.

3:3 And every man that hath this hope in him purifieth himself, even as he is pure.

Every *see* **All** at *1 John 2:16*.

Man *see 1 John 2:27*.

Hope *elpis* (1680), in the NT, "favorable and confident expectation" (contrast the Sept. in Isa. 28:19, "an evil hope"). It has to do with the unseen and the future, Rom. 8:24, 25. "Hope" describes (a) the happy anticipation of good (the most frequent significance), e.g., Titus 1:2; 1 Pet. 1:21; (b) the ground upon which "hope" is based, Acts 16:19; Col. 1:27, "Christ in you the hope of glory"; (c) the object upon which the "hope" is fixed, e.g., 1 Tim. 1:1. Various phrases are used with the word "hope," in Paul's epistles and speeches: (1) Acts 23:6, "the hope and resurrection of the dead"; this has been regarded as a hendiadys (one by means of two), i.e., the "hope" of the resurrection; but the *kai*, "and," is epexegetic, defining the "hope," namely, the resurrection; (2) Acts 26:6, 7, "the hope of the promise (i.e., the fulfillment of the promise) made unto the fathers"; (3) Gal. 5:5, "the hope of righteousness"; i.e., the believer's complete conformity to God's will, at the coming of Christ; (4) Col. 1:23, "the hope of the gospel," i.e., the "hope" of the fulfillment of all the promises presented in the gospel; cf. 1:5; (5) Rom. 5:2, "(the) hope of the glory of God," i.e., as in Titus 2:13, "the blessed hope and appearing of the glory of our great God and Savior Jesus Christ"; cf. Col. 1:27; (6) 1 Thess. 5:8, "the hope of salvation," i.e., of the rapture of believers, to take place at the opening of the Parousia of Christ; (7) Eph. 1:18, "the hope of His (God's) calling," i.e., the prospect before those who respond to His call in the gospel; (8) Eph. 4:4, "the hope of your calling," the same as (7), but regarded from the point of view of the called; (9) Titus 1:2, and 3:7, "the hope of eternal life," i.e., the full manifestation and realization of that life which is already the believer's possession; (10) Acts 28:20, "the hope of Israel," i.e., the expectation of the coming of the Messiah. See *Notes on Galatians* by Hogg and Vine, pp. 248, 249. In Eph. 1:18; 2:12 and 4:4, the "hope" is objective. The objective and subjective use of the word need to be distinguished, in Rom. 15:4, e.g., the use is subjective. In the NT three adjectives are descriptive of "hope": "good," 2 Thess. 2:16; "blessed," Titus 2:13; "living," 1 Pet. 1:3. To these may be added Heb. 7:19, "a better hope," i.e., additional to the commandment, which became disannulled (v. 18), a hope centered in a new priesthood. In Rom. 15:13 God is spoken of as "the God of hope," i.e., He is the author, not the subject, of it. "Hope" is a factor in salvation, Rom. 8:24; it finds its expression in endurance under trial, which is the effect of waiting for the coming of Christ, 1 Thess. 1:3; it is "an anchor of the soul," staying it amidst the storms of this life, Heb. 6:18, 19; it is a purifying power, "every one that hath this hope set on Him (Christ) purifieth himself, even as He is pure," **1 John 3:3**, RV (the apostle John's one mention of "hope"). The phrase "fullness of hope," Heb. 6:11, RV, expresses the completeness of its activity in the soul; cf. "fullness of faith," 10:22, and "of understanding," Col. 2:2 (RV, marg.).

Purifieth *hagnizo* (48), akin to *hagnos*, "pure", "to purify, cleanse from defilement," is used of "purifying" (a) ceremonially, John 11:55; Acts 21:24, 26; 24:18; (b) morally, the heart, Jas. 4:8; the soul, 1 Pet. 1:22; oneself, **1 John 3:3**.

He *ekeinos* (1565), denotes "that one, that person"; its use marks special distinction, favorable or unfavorable; this form of emphasis should always be noted; e.g., John 2:21 "(But) He (spake)"; 5:19, "(what things soever) He (doeth)"; 7:11; 2 Cor. 10:18, lit., "for not he that commendeth himself, he (*ekeinos*) is approved"; 2 Tim. 2:13, "He (in contrast to "we") abideth faithful"; **1 John 3:3**, "(even as) He (is pure)"; v. **5**, "He (was manifested)"; v. **7**, "He (is righteous)"; v. **16**, "He laid down"; **4:17**, "(as) He (is)."

Pure *hagnos* (53), signifies (a) "pure from every fault, immaculate," 2 Cor. 7:11 (KJV, "clear"); Phil. 4:8; 1 Tim. 5:22; Jas. 3:17; **1 John 3:3** (in all which the RV rendering is "pure"), and 1 Pet. 3:2, "chaste"; (b) "pure from carnality, modest," 2 Cor. 11:2, RV, "pure"; Titus 2:5, chaste.

3:4 Whosoever committeth sin transgresseth also the law: for sin is the transgression of the law.

Committeth *prasso* (4238), signifies "to practice," though this is not always to be pressed. The apostle John, in his epistles, uses the continuous tenses of *poieo*, to indicate a practice, the habit of doing something, e.g., **1 John 3:4** (the KJV, "committeth" and "commit" in **1 John 3:8** and **9**, e.g., is wrong; "doeth," RV, in the sense of practicing, is the meaning). He uses *prasso* twice in the Gospel, 3:20 and 5:29. The apostle Paul uses *prasso* in the sense of practicing, and the RV so renders the word in Rom. 1:32; 2:2, instead of KJV, "commit," though, strangely enough, the RV translates it "committed," instead of "practiced," in 2 Cor. 12:21. Generally speaking, in Paul's epistles *poieo* denotes "an action complete in itself," while *prasso* denotes "a habit." The difference is seen in Rom. 1:32, RV. Again, *poieo* stresses the accomplishment, e.g., "perform," in Rom. 4:21; *prasso* stresses the process leading to the accomplishment, e.g., "doer," in 2:25. In Rom. 2:3 he who does, *poieo*, the things mentioned, is warned against judging those who practice them, *prasso*. The distinction in John 3:20-21 is noticeable: "Every one that doeth (*prasso*, practiceth) ill ... he that doeth (*poieo*) the truth." While we cannot draw the regular distinction, that *prasso* speaks of doing evil things, and *poieo* of doing good things, yet very often "where the words assume an ethical tinge, there is a tendency to use the verbs with this distinction" (Trench, *Syn.*, Sec.xcvi). In **1 John 3:4**, **8**, **9**, the KJV wrongly has "commit" (an impossible meaning in v. **8**); the RV rightly has "doeth," i.e., of a continuous habit, equivalent to *prasso*, "to practice." The committal of an act is not in view in that passage.

Sin *see 1 John 1:7*.

Transgresseth ... law In **1 John 3:4** (1st part), KJV, *poieo*, "to do," with *anomia* (458), "lawlessness," is rendered "transgresseth ... the law"

(RV, "doeth ... lawlessness"); in the 2nd part *anomia* alone is rendered "transgression of the law," KJV (RV, "lawlessness").

3:5 And ye know that he was manifested to take away our sins; and in him is no sin.

He *see 1 John 3:3.*

Take *airo* (142), "to lift, carry, take up or away," occurs very frequently with its literal meanings. In John 1:29 it is used of Christ as "the Lamb of God, which taketh away the sin of the world," not the sins, but sin, that which has existed from the time of the Fall, and in regard to which God has had judicial dealings with the world; through the expiatory sacrifice of Christ the sin of the world will be replaced by everlasting righteousness; cf. the plural, "sins", in **1 John 3:5**. Righteous judgment was "taken away" from Christ at human tribunals, and His life, while voluntarily given by Himself (John 10:17, 18), was "taken (from the earth)," Acts 8:33 (quoted from the Sept. of Isa. 53:8). In John 15:2 it is used in the Lord's statement, "Every branch in Me that beareth not fruit, He taketh it away." This does not contemplate members of the "body" of Christ, but those who (just as a graft which being inserted, does not "abide" or "strike") are merely professed followers, giving only the appearance of being joined to the parent stem.

Sin Christ is predicated as having been without "sin" in every respect, e.g., (a), (b), (c) above, 2 Cor. 5:21 (1st part); **1 John 3:5**; John 14:30; (d) John 8:46; Heb. 4:15; 1 Pet. 2:22.

3:6 Whosoever abideth in him sinneth not: whosoever sinneth hath not seen him, neither known him.

Whosoever *see* **All** at *1 John 2:16.*

Sinneth *see* **Sinned** at *1 John 1:10.*

Known *see* **Know** at *1 John 2:3.*

3:7 Little children, let no man deceive you: he that doeth righteousness is righteous, even as he is righteous.

Children *see 1 John 2:1.*

Deceive *planao* (4105), (Eng., "planet"), in the passive form sometimes means "to go astray, wander," Matt. 18:12; 1 Pet. 2:25; Heb. 11:38; frequently active, "to deceive, by leading into error, to seduce," e.g., Matt. 24:4, 5, 11, 24; John 7:12, "leadeth astray," RV (cf. **1 John 3:7**). In Rev. 12:9 the present participle is used with the definite article, as a title of the Devil, "the Deceiver," lit., "the deceiving one." Often it has the sense of "deceiving oneself," e.g., 1 Cor. 6:9; 15:33; Gal. 6:7; Jas. 1:16, "be not deceived," RV, "do not err," KJV.

Righteous *see* **Just** at *1 John 1:9.*

He *see 1 John 3:3.*

3:8 He that committeth sin is of the devil; for the devil sinneth from the beginning. For this purpose the Son of God was manifested, that he might destroy the works of the devil.

Committeth *see 1 John 3:4.*

Sin *see 1 John 1:7.*

Devil *diabolos* (1228), "an accuser, a slanderer" (from *diaballo*, "to accuse, to malign"), is one of the names of Satan. From it the English word "Devil" is derived, and should be applied only to Satan, as a proper name. *Daimon*, "a demon," is frequently, but wrongly, translated "devil"; it should always be translated "demon," as in the RV margin. There is one "Devil," there are many demons. Being the malignant enemy of God and man, he accuses man to God, Job 1:6-11; 2:1-5; Rev. 12:9, 10, and God to man, Gen. 3. He afflicts men with physical sufferings, Acts 10:38. Being himself sinful, **1 John 3:8**, he instigated man to sin, Gen. 3, and tempts man to do evil, Eph. 4:27; 6:11, encouraging him thereto by deception, Eph. 2:2. Death having been brought into the world by sin, the "Devil" had the power of death, but Christ through His own death, has triumphed over him, and will bring him to nought, Heb. 2:14; his power over death is intimated in his struggle with Michael over the body of Moses, Jude 9. Judas, who gave himself over to the "Devil," was so identified with him, that the Lord described him as such, John 6:70 (see 13:2). As the "Devil" raised himself in pride against God and fell under condemnation, so believers are warned against similar sin, 1 Tim. 3:6; for them he lays snares, v. 7, seeking to devour them as a roaring lion, 1 Pet. 5:8; those who fall into his snare may be recovered therefrom unto the will of God, 2 Tim. 2:26, "having been taken captive by him (i.e., by the 'Devil')"; "by the Lord's servant" is an alternative, which some regard as confirmed by the use of *zogreo* ("to catch alive") in Luke 5:10; but the general use is that of taking captive in the usual way. If believers resist he will flee from them, Jas. 4:7. His fury and malignity will be especially exercised at the end of the present age, Rev. 12:12. His doom is the lake of fire, Matt. 25:41; Rev. 20:10. The noun is applied to slanderers, false accusers, 1 Tim. 3:11; 2 Tim. 3:3; Titus 2:3.

Purpose The following phrases are translated with the word "purpose": (a) *eis auto touto*, "for this same (or very) purpose," lit., "unto this same (thing)," Rom. 9:17; Eph. 6:22; Col. 4:8; (b) *eis touto*, "for this purpose," Acts 26:16, KJV (RV, "to this end"), lit., "unto this"; so **1 John 3:8**; (c) *eis ti*, "to what purpose," Matt. 26:8, lit., "unto what"; Mark 14:4, RV, "to what purpose" (KJV, "why").

Destroy *luo* (3089), "to loose, dissolve, sever, break, demolish," is translated "destroy," in **1 John 3:8**, of the works of the Devil.

Works *ergon* (2041), denotes (I) "work, employment, task," e.g., Mark 13:34; John 4:34; 17:4; Acts 13:2; Phil. 2:30; 1 Thess. 5:13; in Acts 5:38 with the idea of enterprise; (II) "a deed, act," (a) of God, e.g., John 6:28, 29; 9:3; 10:37; 14:10; Acts 13:41; Rom. 14:20; Heb. 1:10; 2:7; 3:9; 4:3, 4, 10; Rev. 15:3; (b) of Christ, e.g., Matt. 11:2; especially in John, 5:36; 7:3, 21; 10:25, 32, 33, 38; 14:11, 12; 15:24; Rev. 2:26; (c) of believers, e.g., Matt. 5:16; Mark 14:6; Acts 9:36; Rom. 13:3; Col. 1:10; 1 Thess. 1:3, "work of faith," here the initial act of faith at conversion (turning to God, v. 9); in 2 Thess. 1:11, "*every* work of faith," RV, denotes every activity undertaken for Christ's sake; 2:17; 1 Tim. 2:10; 5:10; 6:18; 2 Tim. 2:21; 3:17; Titus 2:7, 14; 3:1, 8, 14; Heb. 10:24; 13:21; frequent in James, as the effect of faith [in 1:25, KJV, "(a doer) of the work," RV, "(a doer) that worketh"]; 1 Pet. 2:12; Rev. 2:2 and in several other places in chs. 2 and 3; 14:13; (d) of unbelievers, e.g., Matt. 23:3, 5; John 7:7; Acts 7:41 (for idols); Rom. 13:12; Eph. 5:11; Col. 1:21; Titus 1:16 (1st part); **1 John 3:12**; Jude 15, RV; Rev. 2:6, RV; of those who seek justification by works, e.g., Rom. 9:32; Gal. 3:10; Eph. 2:9; described as the works of the law, e.g., Gal. 2:16; 3:2, 5; dead works, Heb. 6:1; 9:14; (e) of Babylon, Rev. 18:6; (f) of the Devil, John 8:41; **1 John 3:8**.

3:9 Whosoever is born of God doth not commit sin; for his seed remaineth in him: and he cannot sin, because he is born of God.

Born *see 1 John 2:29*.

Commit *see* **Committeth** at *1 John 3:4*.

Sin *see 1 John 1:7*.

Seed *sperma* (4690), akin to *speiro*, "to sow" (Eng., "sperm," "spermatic," etc.), has the following usages, (a) agricultural and botanical, e.g., Matt. 13:24, 27, 32; 1 Cor. 15:38; 2 Cor. 9:10; (b) physiological, Heb. 11:11; (c) metaphorical and by metonymy for "offspring, posterity," (1) of natural offspring, e.g., Matt. 22:24, 25, RV, "seed" (KJV, "issue"); John 7:42; 8:33, 37; Acts 3:25; Rom. 1:3; 4:13, 16, 18; 9:7 (twice), 8, 29; 11:1; 2 Cor. 11:22; Heb. 2:16; 11:18; Rev. 12:17; Gal. 3:16, 19, 29; in the 16th v., "He saith not, And to seeds, as of many; but as of one, And to thy seed, which is Christ," quoted from the Sept. of Gen. 13:15 and 17:7, 8, there is especial stress on the word "seed," as referring to an individual (here, Christ) in fulfillment of the promises to Abraham—a unique use of the singular. While the plural form "seeds," neither in Hebrew nor in Greek, would have been natural any more than in English (it is not so used in Scripture of human offspring; its plural occurrence is in 1 Sam. 8:15, of crops), yet if the divine intention had been to refer to Abraham's natural descendants, another word could have been chosen in the plural, such as "children"; all such words were, however, set aside, "seed" being selected as one that could be used in the singular, with the purpose of showing that the "seed" was Messiah. Some of the rabbis had even regarded "seed," e.g., in Gen. 4:25 and Isa. 53:10, as referring to the Coming One. Descendants were given to Abraham by other than natural means, so that through him Messiah might come, and the point of the apostle's argument is that since the fulfillment of the promises of God is secured alone by Christ, they only who are "in Christ" can receive them; (2) of spiritual offspring, Rom. 4:16, 18; 9:8; here "the children of the promise are reckoned for a seed" points, firstly, to Isaac's birth as being not according to the ordinary course of nature but by divine promise, and, secondly, by analogy, to the fact that all believers are children of God by spiritual birth; Gal. 3:29. As to **1 John 3:9**, "his seed abideth in him," it is possible to understand this as meaning that children of God (His "seed") abide in Him, and do not go on doing (practicing) sin (the verb "to commit" does not represent the original in this passage). Alternatively, the "seed" signifies the principle of spiritual life as imparted to the believer, which abides in him without possibility of removal or extinction; the child of God remains eternally related to Christ, he who lives in sin has never become so related, he has not the principle of life in him. This meaning suits the context and the general tenor of the Epistle.

Remaineth *meno* (3306), "to stay, abide," is frequently rendered "to remain," e.g., Matt. 11:23; Luke 10:7; John 1:33, KJV (RV, "abiding"); 9:41 (in 15:11, the best texts have the verb to be, see RV); 15:16, KJV (RV, "abide"); 19:31; Acts 5:4 (twice), RV, "whiles it remained, did it (not) remain (thine own)?"; 27:41; 1 Cor. 7:11; 15:6; 2 Cor. 3:11, 14; 9:9, KJV (RV, "abideth"); Heb. 12:27; **1 John 3:9**.

3:10 In this the children of God are manifest, and the children of the devil: whosoever doeth not righteousness is not of God, neither he that loveth not his brother.

Children *teknon* (5043), "a child" (akin to *tikto*, "to beget, bear"), is used in both the natural and the figurative senses. In contrast to *huios*, "son," it gives prominence to the fact of birth, whereas *huios* stresses the dignity and character of the relationship. Figuratively, *teknon* is used of "children" of (a) God, John 1:12; (b) light, Eph. 5:8; (c) obedience, 1 Pet. 1:14; (d) a promise, Rom. 9:8; Gal. 4:28; (e) the Devil, **1 John 3:10**; (f) wrath, Eph. 2:3; (g) cursing, 2 Pet. 2:14; (h) spiritual relationship, 2 Tim. 2:1; Philem. 10.

Manifest *phaneros* (5318), "open to sight, visible, manifest," is translated "manifest" in Luke 8:17; Acts 4:16; 7:13, RV (KJV, "known"); Rom. 1:19; 1 Cor. 3:13; 11:19; 14:25; Gal. 5:19; Phil. 1:13; 1 Tim. 4:15 (KJV "appear"); **1 John 3:10**.

Whosoever *see* All at *1 John 2:16*.

3:11 For this is the message that ye heard from the beginning, that we should love one another.

Message *see 1 John 1:5*.

3:12 Not as Cain, *who* was of that wicked one, and slew his brother. And wherefore slew he him? Because his own works were evil, and his brother's righteous.

Wicked *see 1 John 2:13*.

Slew *sphazo* or *sphatto* (4969), "to slay," especially of victims for sacrifice (akin to *sphage*), is used (a) of taking human life, **1 John 3:12** (twice); Rev. 6:4, RV, "slay" (KJV, "kill"); in 13:3, probably of assassination, RV, "smitten (unto death)," KJV, "wounded (to death)," RV marg., "slain;" 18:24; (b) of Christ, as the Lamb of sacrifice, Rev. 5:6, 9, 12; 6:9; 13:8.

Works *see 1 John 3:8*.

Evil *poneros* (4190), akin to *ponos*, "labor, toil," denotes "evil that causes labor, pain, sorrow, malignant evil"; it is used (a) with the meaning bad, worthless, in the physical sense, Matt. 7:17-18; in the moral or ethical sense, "evil," wicked; of persons, e.g., Matt. 7:11; Luke 6:45; Acts 17:5; 2 Thess. 3:2; 2 Tim. 3:13; of "evil" spirits, e.g., Matt. 12:45; Luke 7:21; Acts 19:12-13, 15-16; of a generation, Matt. 12:39, 45; 16:4; Luke 11:29; of things, e.g., Matt. 5:11; 6:23; 20:15; Mark 7:22; Luke 11:34; John 3:19; 7:7; Acts 18:14; Gal. 1:4; Col. 1:21; 1 Tim. 6:4; 2 Tim. 4:18; Heb. 3:12; 10:22; Jas. 2:4; 4:16; **1 John 3:12**; 2 John 11; 3 John 10; (b) with the meaning toilsome, painful, Eph. 5:16; 6:13; Rev. 16:2. Cf. *poneria*, "iniquity, wickedness."

Righteous *see* Just at *1 John 1:9*.

3:13 Marvel not, my brethren, if the world hate you.

Hate *see* Hateth at *1 John 2:9*.

3:14 We know that we have passed from death unto life, because we love the brethren. He that loveth not *his* brother abideth in death.

Passed *metabaino* (3327), "to pass over from one place to another" (*meta*, implying change), is translated "we have passed out of" (KJV, "from") in **1 John 3:14**, RV, as to the change from death to life.

Death *thanatos* (2288), "death," is used in Scripture of: (a) the separation of the soul (the spiritual part of man) from the body (the material part), the latter ceasing to function and turning to dust, e.g., John 11:13; Heb. 2:15; 5:7; 7:23. In Heb. 9:15, the KJV, "by means of death" is inadequate; the RV, "a death having taken place" is in keeping with the subject. In Rev. 13:3, 12, the RV, "death-stroke" (KJV, "deadly wound") is, lit., "the stroke of death." (b) the separation of man from God; Adam died on the day he disobeyed God, Gen. 2:17, and hence all mankind are born in the same spiritual condition, Rom. 5:12, 14, 17, 21, from which, however, those who believe in Christ are delivered, John 5:24; **1 John 3:14**. "Death" is the opposite of life; it never denotes nonexistence. As spiritual life is "conscious existence in communion with God," so spiritual "death" is "conscious existence in separation from God."

Life *see 1 John 1:2*.

3:15 Whosoever hateth his brother is a murderer: and ye know that no murderer hath eternal life abiding in him.

Whosoever *see* All at *1 John 2:16*.

Hateth *see 1 John 2:9*.

Murderer *anthropoktonos* (443), an adjective, lit., "manslaying," used as a noun, "a manslayer, murderer" (*anthropos*, "a man," *kteino*, "to slay"), is used of Satan, John 8:44; of one who hates his brother, and who, being a "murderer," has not eternal life, **1 John 3:15** (twice).

3:16 Hereby perceive we the love *of God*, because he laid down his life for us: and we ought to lay down *our* lives for the brethren.

Hereby *see 1 John 2:3*.

Perceive *ginosko* (1097), "to know by experience and observation," is translated "to perceive" in Matt. 12:15, RV (KJV, "knew"); 16:8; 21:45; 22:18; 26:10, RV, (KJV, "understood"); Mark 8:17; 12:12 and 15:10, RV (KJV, "knew"); so Luke 9:11; 18:34; in Luke 7:39, RV (KJV, "known"); 20:19; John 6:15; 8:27, RV (KJV, "understood"); 16:19, RV (KJV, "knew"); Acts 23:6; Gal. 2:9; in **1 John 3:16**, KJV, "perceive" (RV, "know," perfect tense, lit., "we have perceived," and therefore "know").

Of *see 1 John 2:5.*

He *see 1 John 3:3.*

Laid *tithemi* (5087), "to put, place, set," frequently signifies "to lay," and is used of (a) "laying" a corpse in a tomb, Matt. 27:60; Mark 6:29; 15:47; 16:6; Luke 23:53, 55; John 11:34; 19:41, 42; 20:2, 13, 15; Acts 7:16; 13:29; Rev. 11:9, RV, "to be laid" (KJV, "to be put"); in an upper chamber, Acts 9:37; (b) "laying" the sick in a place, Mark 6:56; Luke 5:18; Acts 3:2; 5:15; (c) "laying" money at the apostles' feet, Acts 4:35, 37; 5:2; (d) Christ's "laying" His hands upon children, Mark 10:16, RV, "laying" (KJV, "put"); upon John, Rev. 1:17 (in the best mss.); (e) "laying" down one's life, (1) of Christ, John 10:11, RV, "layeth down" (KJV, "giveth"); vv. 17, 18 (twice); **1 John 3:16**; (2) of Peter for Christ's sake, John 13:37, 38; (3) of Christ's followers, on behalf of others, **1 John 3:16**; (4) of anyone, for his friends, John 15:13; (f) "laying" up sayings in one's heart, Luke 1:66 (middle voice, in the sense of "for themselves"); in 9:44, of letting Christ's words "sink" (middle voice, in the sense of "for oneself"; KJV, "sink down") into the ears; (g) "laying" a foundation (1) literally, Luke 6:48; 14:29; (2) metaphorically, of Christ in relation to an assembly, 1 Cor. 3:10, 11; (h) in "laying" Christ as a "stone of stumbling" for Israel, Rom. 9:33; (i) Christ's "laying" aside His garments, John 13:4; (j) Christians, in "laying" money in store for the help of the needy, 1 Cor. 16:2 (lit., "let him put"); (k) "depositing" money, Luke 19:21, 22.

Ought *see 1 John 2:6.*

3:17 But whoso hath this world's good, and seeth his brother have need, and shutteth up his bowels *of compassion* from him, how dwelleth the love of God in him?

World *kosmos* (2889), primarily "order, arrangement, ornament, adornment," is used to denote (a) the "earth," e.g., Matt. 13:35; John 21:25; Acts 17:24; Rom. 1:20 (probably here the universe: it had this meaning among the Greeks, owing to the order observable in it); 1 Tim. 6:7; Heb. 4:3; 9:26; (b) the "earth" in contrast with Heaven, **1 John 3:17** (perhaps also Rom. 4:13); (c) by metonymy, the "human race, mankind," e.g., Matt. 5:14; John 1:9 [here "that cometh (RV, 'coming') into the world" is said of Christ, not of "every man"; by His coming into the world He was the light for all men]; v. 10; 3:16, 17 (thrice), 19; 4:42, and frequently in Rom., 1 Cor. and 1 John; (d) "Gentiles" as distinguished from Jews, e.g., Rom. 11:12, 15, where the meaning is that all who will may be reconciled (cf. 2 Cor. 5:19); (e) the "present condition of human affairs," in alienation from and opposition to God, e.g., John 7:7; 8:23; 14:30; 1 Cor. 2:12; Gal. 4:3; 6:14; Col. 2:8; Jas. 1:27; **1 John 4:5** (thrice); **5:19**; (f) the "sum of temporal possessions," Matt. 16:26; 1 Cor. 7:31 (1st part); (g) metaphorically, of the "tongue" as "a world (of iniquity)," Jas. 3:6, expressive of magnitude and variety.

Good *bios* (979), which denotes (a) "life, lifetime," (b) "livelihood, living, means of living," is translated "goods" in **1 John 3:17**, RV (KJV, "good"). *See also* **Life** at *1 John 2:16.*

Shutteth *kleio* (2808), is used (a) of things material, Matt. 6:6; 25:10; Luke 11:7; John 20:19, 26; Acts 5:23; 21:30; Rev. 20:3; figuratively, 21:25; (b) metaphorically, of the kingdom of heaven, Matt. 23:13; of heaven, with consequences of famine, Luke 4:25; Rev. 11:6; of compassion, **1 John 3:17**, RV (KJV, "bowels *of compassion*"); of the blessings accruing from the promises of God regarding David, Rev. 3:7; of a door for testimony, 3:8.

Bowels of compassion *splanchnon* (4698), always in the plural, properly denotes "the physical organs of the intestines," and is once used in this respect, Acts 1:18. The RV substitutes the following for the word "bowels": "affections," 2 Cor. 6:12; "affection," 2 Cor. 7:15; "tender mercies," Phil. 1:8; 2:1; "a heart (of compassion)," Col. 3:12; "heart," Philem. 12, 20; "hearts," Philem. 7; "compassion," **1 John 3:17**. The word is rendered "tender" in the KJV and RV of Luke 1:78, in connection with the word mercy.

Dwelleth *see* **Abideth** at *1 John 2:14.*

3:18 My little children, let us not love in word, neither in tongue; but in deed and in truth.

Children *see 1 John 2:1.*

Tongue *glossa* (1100), is used of (1) the "tongues ... like as of fire" which appeared at Pentecost; (2) "the tongue," as an organ of speech, e.g., Mark 7:33; Rom. 3:13; 14:11; 1 Cor. 14:9; Phil. 2:11; Jas. 1:26; 3:5, 6, 8; 1 Pet. 3:10; **1 John 3:18**; Rev. 16:10; (3) "a language," coupled with *phule*, "a tribe," *laos*, "a people," *ethnos*, "a nation," seven times in Revelation, 5:9; 7:9; 10:11; 11:9; 13:7; 14:6; 17:15 ...

Truth *aletheia* (225), "truth," is used (a) objectively, signifying "the reality lying at the basis of an appearance; the manifested, veritable essence of a matter" (Cremer), e.g., Rom. 9:1; 2 Cor. 11:10; especially of Christian doctrine, e.g., Gal. 2:5, where "the truth of the gospel" denotes the "true" teaching of the gospel, in contrast to perversions of it; Rom. 1:25, where "the truth of God" may be "the truth concerning God" or "God whose existence is a verity"; but in Rom. 15:8 "the truth of God" is indicative of His faithfulness in the fulfillment of His promises as exhibited in Christ; the word has an absolute force in John 14:6; 17:17; 18:37, 38; in Eph. 4:21, where the RV, "even as truth is in Jesus," gives the correct rendering, the meaning is not merely ethical "truth," but "truth" in all its fullness and scope, as embodied in Him; He was the perfect expression of the truth; this is virtually equivalent to His statement in John 14:6; (b) subjectively, "truthfulness," "truth," not merely verbal, but sincerity and integrity of character, John 8:44; 3 John 3, RV; (c) in phrases, e.g., "in truth" (*epi*, "on the basis of"), Mark 12:14; Luke 20:21; with *en*, "in," 2 Cor. 6:7; Col. 1:6; 1 Tim. 2:7, RV (KJV, "in ... verity"), **1 John 3:18**; 2 John 1, 3, 4.

3:19 And hereby we know that we are of the truth, and shall assure our hearts before him.

Hereby *see 1 John 2:3.*

Assure *peitho* (3782), "to persuade," is rendered "assure" in **1 John 3:19** (marg., "persuade"), where the meaning is that of confidence toward God consequent upon loving in deed and in truth.

3:20 For if our heart condemn us, God is greater than our heart, and knoweth all things.

Heart *kardia* (2588), "the heart" (Eng., "cardiac," etc.), the chief organ of physical life ("for the life of the flesh is in the blood," Lev. 17:11), occupies the most important place in the human system. By an easy transition the word came to stand for man's entire mental and moral activity, both the rational and the emotional elements. In other words, the heart is used figuratively for the hidden springs of the personal life. "The Bible describes human depravity as in the 'heart,' because sin is a principle which has its seat in the center of man's inward life, and then 'defiles' the whole circuit of his action, Matt. 15:19, 20. On the other hand, Scripture regards the heart as the sphere of Divine influence, Rom. 2:15; Acts 15:9.... The heart, as lying deep within, contains 'the hidden man,' 1 Pet. 3:4, the real man. It represents the true character but conceals it" (J. Laidlaw, in *Hastings' Bible Dic.*). As to its usage in the NT it denotes (a) the seat of physical life, Acts 14:17; Jas. 5:5; (b) the seat of moral nature and spiritual life, the seat of grief, John 14:1; Rom. 9:2; 2 Cor. 2:4; joy, John 16:22; Eph. 5:19; the desires, Matt. 5:28; 2 Pet. 2:14; the affections, Luke 24:32; Acts 21:13; the perceptions, John 12:40; Eph. 4:18; the thoughts, Matt. 9:4; Heb. 4:12; the understanding, Matt. 13:15; Rom. 1:21; the reasoning powers, Mark 2:6; Luke 24:38; the imagination, Luke 1:51; conscience, Acts 2:37; **1 John 3:20**; the intentions, Heb. 4:12, cf. 1 Pet. 4:1; purpose, Acts 11:23; 2 Cor. 9:7; the will, Rom. 6:17; Col. 3:15; faith, Mark 11:23; Rom. 10:10; Heb. 3:12. The heart, in its moral significance in the OT, includes the emotions, the reason and the will.

"Truth is given, not to be contemplated, but to be done. Life is an action, not a thought."

FREDERICK WILLIAM ROBERTSON

Condemn *kataginosko* (2607), "to know something against" (*kata*, "against," *ginosko*, "to know by experience"), hence, "to think ill of, to condemn," is said, in Gal. 2:11, of Peter's conduct (RV, "stood condemned"), he being "self-condemned" as the result of an exercised and enlightened conscience, and "condemned" in the sight of others; so of "self-condemnation" due to an exercise of heart, **1 John 3:20-21**.

3:21 Beloved, if our heart condemn us not, *then* have we confidence toward God.

Confidence *see 1 John 2:28.*

3:22 And whatsoever we ask, we receive of him, because we keep his commandments, and do those things that are pleasing in his sight.

Ask *aiteo* (154), "to ask," frequently suggests the attitude of a suppliant, the petition of one who is lesser in position than he to whom the petition is made; e.g., in the case of men in asking something from God, Matt. 7:7; a child from a parent, Matt. 7:9-10; a subject from a king, Acts 12:20; priests and people from Pilate, Luke 23:23 (RV, "asking" for KJV, "requiring"); a beggar from a passer by, Acts 3:2. With reference to petitioning God, this verb is found in Paul's epistles in Eph. 3:20 and Col. 1:9; in James four times, 1:5-6; 4:2-3; in 1 John, five times, **3:22; 5:14, 15** (twice), **16**.

Keep *see 1 John 2:3*.

Pleasing *arestos* (701), denotes "pleasing, agreeable," John 8:29, RV, "(the things that are) pleasing," KJV, "(those things that) please", KJV and RV in **1 John 3:22**; in Acts 6:2, "fit" (RV marg., "pleasing"); 12:3, "it pleased," lit., "it was pleasing."

3:23 And this is his commandment, That we should believe on the name of his Son Jesus Christ, and love one another, as he gave us commandment.

Name *see 1 John 2:12*.

3:24 And he that keepeth his commandments dwelleth in him, and he in him. And hereby we know that he abideth in us, by the Spirit which he hath given us.

Keepeth *see* Keep at *1 John 2:3*.

Hereby *see 1 John 2:3*.

Chapter 4

4:1 Beloved, believe not every spirit, but try the spirits whether they are of God: because many false prophets are gone out into the world.

Spirit *pneuma* (4151), primarily denotes "the wind" (akin to *pneo*, "to breathe, blow"); also "breath"; then, especially "the spirit," which, like the wind, is invisible, immaterial and powerful. The NT uses of the word may be analyzed approximately as follows:

"(a) the wind, John 3:8 (where marg. is, perhaps, to be preferred); Heb. 1:7; cf. Amos 4:13, Sept.; (b) the breath, 2 Thess. 2:8; Rev. 11:11; 13:15; cf. Job 12:10, Sept.; (c) the immaterial, invisible part of man, Luke 8:55; Acts 7:59; 1 Cor. 5:5; Jas. 2:26; cf. Eccl. 12:7, Sept.; (d) the disembodied (or 'unclothed,' or 'naked,' 2 Cor. 5:3, 4) man, Luke 24:37, 39; Heb. 12:23; 1 Pet. 4:6; (e) the resurrection body, 1 Cor. 15:45; 1 Tim. 3:16; 1 Pet. 3:18; (f) the sentient element in man, that by which he perceives, reflects, feels, desires, Matt. 5:3; 26:41; Mark 2:8; Luke 1:47, 80; Acts 17:16; 20:22; 1 Cor. 2:11; 5:3, 4; 14:4, 15; 2 Cor. 7:1; cf. Gen. 26:35; Isa. 26:9; Ezek. 13:3; Dan. 7:15; (g) purpose, aim, 2 Cor. 12:18; Phil. 1:27; Eph. 4:23; Rev. 19:10; cf. Ezra 1:5; Ps. 78:8; Dan. 5:12; (h) the equivalent of the personal pronoun, used for emphasis and effect: 1st person, 1 Cor. 16:18; cf. Gen. 6:3; 2nd person, 2 Tim. 4:22; Philem. 25; cf. Ps. 139:7; 3rd person, 2 Cor. 7:13; cf. Isa. 40:13; (i) character, Luke 1:17; Rom. 1:4; cf. Num. 14:24; (j) moral qualities and activities: bad, as of bondage, as of a slave, Rom. 8:15; cf. Isa. 61:3; stupor, Rom. 11:8; cf. Isa. 29:10; timidity, 2 Tim. 1:7; cf. Josh. 5:1; good, as of adoption, i.e., liberty as of a son, Rom. 8:15; cf. Ps. 51:12; meekness, 1 Cor. 4:21; cf. Prov. 16:19; faith, 2 Cor. 4:13; quietness, 1 Pet. 3:4; cf. Prov. 14:29; (k) the Holy Spirit, e.g., Matt. 4:1; Luke 4:18; (l) 'the inward man' (an expression used only of the believer, Rom. 7:22; 2 Cor. 4:16; Eph. 3:16); the new life, Rom. 8:4-6, 10, 16; Heb. 12:9; cf. Ps. 51:10; (m) unclean spirits, demons, Matt. 8:16; Luke 4:33; 1 Pet. 3:19; cf. 1 Sam. 18:10; (n) angels, Heb. 1:14; cf. Acts 12:15; (o) divine gift for service, 1 Cor. 14:12, 32; (p) by metonymy, those who claim to be depositories of these gifts, 2 Thess. 2:2; **1 John 4:1-3**; (q) the significance, as contrasted with the form, of words, or of a rite, John 6:63; Rom. 2:29; 7:6; 2 Cor. 3:6; (r) a vision, Rev. 1:10; 4:2; 17:3; 21:10."

Try *dokimazo* (1381), "to test, prove," with the expectation of approving, is translated "to prove" in Luke 14:19; Rom. 12:2; 1 Cor. 3:13, RV (KJV, "shall try"); 11:28, RV (KJV, "examine"); 2 Cor. 8:8, 22; 13:5; Gal. 6:4; Eph. 5:10; 1 Thess. 2:4 (2nd part), RV (KJV, "trieth"); 5:21; 1 Tim. 3:10; in some mss., Heb. 3:9 (the most authentic have the noun *dokimasia*, "a proving"); 1 Pet. 1:7, RV (KJV, "tried"); **1 John 4:1**, RV (KJV, "try").

False prophets *pseudoprophetes* (5578), "a false prophet," is used of such (a) in OT times, Luke 6:26; 2 Pet. 2:1; (b) in the present period since Pentecost, Matt. 7:15; 24:11, 24; Mark 13:22; Acts 13:6; **1 John 4:1**; (c) with reference to a false "prophet" destined to arise as the supporter of the "Beast" at the close of this age, Rev. 16:13; 19:20; 20:10 (himself described as "another beast," 13:11).

4:2 Hereby know ye the Spirit of God: Every spirit that confesseth that Jesus Christ is come in the flesh is of God:

Hereby *see 1 John 2:3*.

Know *see 1 John 2:3*.

Confesseth *see* Confess at *1 John 1:9*.

Flesh *see 1 John 2:16*.

4:3 And every spirit that confesseth not that Jesus Christ is come in the flesh is not of God: and this is that *spirit* of antichrist, whereof ye have heard that it should come; and even now already is it in the world.

Antichrist *see* Antichrist, Antichrists at *1 John 2:18*.

Even *kai* (2532), a conjunction, is usually a mere connective, meaning "and"; it frequently, however, has an ascensive or climactic use, signifying "even," the thing that is added being out of the ordinary, and producing a climax. The determination of this meaning depends on the context. Examples are Matt. 5:46-47; Mark 1:27; Luke 6:33 (RV); 10:17; John 12:42; Gal. 2:13, 17, where "also" should be "even"; Eph. 5:12. Examples where the RV corrects the KJV "and" or "also," by substituting "even," are Luke 7:49; Acts 17:28; Heb. 11:11; in **1 John 4:3** the RV rightly omits "even." When followed by "if" or "though," *kai* often signifies "even," e.g., Matt. 26:35; John 8:14. So sometimes when preceded by "if," e.g., 1 Cor. 7:11, where "but and if" should be "but even if." The epexegetic or explanatory use of *kai* followed by a noun in apposition, and meaning "namely," or "even" is comparatively rare. Winer's cautionary word needs heeding, that "this meaning has been introduced into too many passages" (Gram. of the NT, p. 546.). Some think it has this sense in John 3:5, "water, even the Spirit," and Gal. 6:16, "even the Israel of God."

4:4 Ye are of God, little children, and have overcome them: because greater is he that is in you, than he that is in the world.

Ye *see 1 John 2:20.*

Children *see 1 John 2:1.*

Overcome *see 1 John 2:13.*

4:5 They are of the world: therefore speak they of the world, and the world heareth them.

World *see 1 John 3:17.*

4:6 We are of God: he that knoweth God heareth us; he that is not of God heareth not us. Hereby know we the spirit of truth, and the spirit of error.

Knoweth, Know *see* Know at *1 John 2:3.*

Hereby In **1 John 4:6**, KJV, *ek toutou*, lit., "out of this," i.e., in consequence of this, is rendered "hereby" (RV, "by this").

Error *plane* (4106), akin to *planao*, "a wandering, a forsaking of the right path," see Jas. 5:20, whether in doctrine, 2 Pet. 3:17; **1 John 4:6**, or in morals, Rom. 1:27; 2 Pet. 2:18; Jude 11, though, in Scripture, doctrine and morals are never divided by any sharp line. See also Matt. 27:64, where it is equivalent to 'fraud.'" "Errors" in doctrine are not infrequently the effect of relaxed morality, and vice versa. In Eph. 4:14 the RV has "wiles of error," for KJV, "they lie in wait to deceive"; in 1 Thess. 2:3, RV, "error," for KJV, "deceit"; in 2 Thess. 2:11, RV, "a working of error," for KJV, "strong delusion." Cf. *planetes*, "a wandering," Jude 13, and the adjective *planos*, "leading astray, deceiving, a deceiver."

4:7 Beloved, let us love one another: for love is of God; and every one that loveth is born of God, and knoweth God.

Born *see 1 John 2:29.*

Knoweth *see* Know at *1 John 2:3.*

4:8 He that loveth not knoweth not God; for God is love.

Knoweth *see* Know at *1 John 2:3.*

God *see 1 John 1:5.*

Love In the two statements in **1 John 4:8** and **16**, "God is love," both are used to enjoin the exercise of "love" on the part of believers. While the former introduces a declaration of the mode in which God's love has been manifested (vv. **9**, **10**), the second introduces a statement of the identification of believers with God in character, and the issue at the Judgment Seat hereafter (v. **17**), an identification represented ideally in the sentence "as He is, so are we in this world." *See also 1 John 2:5.*

4:9 In this was manifested the love of God toward us, because that God sent his only begotten Son into the world, that we might live through him.

In this This translates the phrase *en touto*, "in this," in John 4:37; 9:30; 15:8; Acts 24:16; 2 Cor. 8:10; **1 John 4:9** (KJV, "in this"), **10**, **17**.

Love *see 1 John 2:5.*

Sent *apostello* (649), lit., "to send forth" (*apo*, "from"), akin to *apostolos*, "an apostle," denotes (a) "to send on service, or with a commission." (1) of persons; Christ, sent by the Father, Matt. 10:40; 15:24; 21:37; Mark 9:37; 12:6; Luke 4:18, 43; 9:48; 10:16; John 3:17; 5:36, 38; 6:29, 57; 7:29; 8:42; 10:36; 11:42; 17:3, 8, 18 (1st part), 21, 23, 25; 20:21; Acts 3:20 (future); 3:26; **1 John 4:9**, **10**, **14**; the Holy Spirit, Luke 24:49 (in some texts); 1 Pet. 1:12; Rev. 5:6; Moses, Acts 7:35; John the Baptist, John 1:6; 3:28; disciples and apostles, e.g., Matt. 10:16; Mark 11:1; Luke 22:8; John 4:38; 17:18 (2nd part); Acts 26:17; servants, e.g., Matt. 21:34; Luke 20:10; officers and officials, Mark 6:27; John 7:32; Acts 16:35; messengers, e.g., Acts 10:8, 17, 20; 15:27; evangelists, Rom. 10:15; angels, e.g., Matt. 24:31; Mark 13:27; Luke 1:19, 26; Heb. 1:14; Rev. 1:1; 22:6; demons, Mark 5:10; (2) of things, e.g., Matt. 21:3; Mark 4:29, RV, marg., "sendeth forth," text, "putteth forth" (KJV, "... in"); Acts 10:36; 11:30; 28:28; (b) "to send away, dismiss," e.g., Mark 8:26; 12:3; Luke 4:18, "to set (at liberty)."

Only begotten *monogenes* (3439), is used five times, all in the writings of the apostle John, of Christ as the

Son of God; it is translated "only begotten" in Heb. 11:17 of the relationship of Isaac to Abraham. With reference to Christ, the phrase "the only begotten from the Father," John 1:14, RV (see also the marg.), indicates that as the Son of God He was the sole representative of the Being and character of the One who sent Him. In the original the definite article is omitted both before "only begotten" and before "Father," and its absence in each case serves to lay stress upon the characteristics referred to in the terms used. The apostle's object is to demonstrate what sort of glory it was that he and his fellow apostles had seen. That he is not merely making a comparison with earthly relationships is indicated by *para*, "from." The glory was that of a unique relationship and the word "begotten" does not imply a beginning of His Sonship. It suggests relationship indeed, but must be distinguished from generation as applied to man. We can only rightly understand the term "the only begotten" when used of the Son, in the sense of unoriginated relationship. "The begetting is not an event of time, however remote, but a fact irrespective of time. The Christ did not *become*, but necessarily and eternally *is* the Son. He, a Person, possesses every attribute of pure Godhood. This necessitates eternity, absolute being; in this respect He is not 'after' the Father" (Moule). The expression also suggests the thought of the deepest affection, as in the case of the OT word *yachid*, variously rendered, "only one," Gen. 22:2, 12; "only son," Jer. 6:26; Amos 8:10; Zech. 12:10; "only beloved," Prov. 4:3, and "darling," Ps. 22:20; 35:17. In John 1:18 the clause "the only begotten son, which is in the bosom of the Father," expresses both His eternal union with the Father in the Godhead and the ineffable intimacy and love between them, the Son sharing all the Father's counsels and enjoying all His affections. Another reading is *monogenes Theos*, "God only-begotten." In John 3:16 the statement, "God so loved the world that He gave His only begotten son," must not be taken to mean that Christ became the only begotten son by incarnation. The value and the greatness of the gift lay in the Sonship of Him who was given. His Sonship was not the effect of His being given. In John 3:18 the phrase "the name of the only begotten son of God" lays stress upon the full revelation of God's character and will, His love and grace, as conveyed in the name of One who, being in a unique relationship to Him, was provided by Him as the object of faith. In **1 John 4:9** the statement "God hath sent His only begotten son into the world" does not mean that God sent out into the world one who at His birth in Bethlehem had become His Son. Cf. the parallel statement, "God sent forth the Spirit of His Son," Gal. 4:6, RV, which could not mean that God sent forth One who became His Spirit when He sent Him.

4:10 Herein is love, not that we loved God, but that he loved us, and sent his Son *to be* the propitiation for our sins.

Herein *see* **In this** at *1 John 4:9*.

Love *see 1 John 2:5*.

Sent *see 1 John 4:9*.

Propitiation *see 1 John 2:2*.

4:11 Beloved, if God so loved us, we ought also to love one another.

Ought *see 1 John 2:6*.

4:12 No man hath seen God at any time. If we love one another, God dwelleth in us, and his love is perfected in us.

Seen *see 1 John 1:1*.

Time *popote* (4455), "ever yet," is rendered "at any time" in John 1:18; 5:37; **1 John 4:12**. For Luke 15:29 see *Note* (14), below.

Perfected *see 1 John 2:5*.

4:13 Hereby know we that we dwell in him, and he in us, because he hath given us of his Spirit.

Hereby *see 1 John 2:3*.

Know *see 1 John 2:3*.

4:14 And we have seen and do testify that the Father sent the Son *to be* the Saviour of the world.

Seen *see 1 John 1:1*.

Testify *martureo* (3140), is frequently rendered "to bear witness, to witness," in the RV, where KJV renders it "to testify," John 2:25; 3:11, 32; 5:39; 15:26; 21:24; 1 Cor. 15:15; Heb. 7:17; 11:4; **1 John 4:14**; **5:9**; 3 John 3. In the following, however, the RV, like the KJV, has the rendering "to testify," John 4:39, 44; 7:7; 13:21; Acts 26:5; Rev. 22:16, 18, 20. *See also* **Witness** at *1 John 1:2*.

Sent *see 1 John 4:9*.

Saviour *soter* (4990), "a savior, deliverer, preserver," is used (a) of God, Luke 1:47; 1 Tim. 1:1; 2:3; 4:10 (in the sense of "preserver," since He gives "to all life and breath and all things"); Titus 1:3; 2:10; 3:4; Jude 25; (b) of Christ, Luke 2:11; John 4:42; Acts 5:31; 13:23 (of Israel); Eph. 5:23 (the sustainer and preserver of the church, His "body"); Phil. 3:20 (at His return to receive the Church to

Himself); 2 Tim. 1:10 (with reference to His incarnation, "the days of His flesh"); Titus 1:4 (a title shared, in the context, with God the Father); 2:13, RV, "our great God and Savior Jesus Christ," the pronoun "our," at the beginning of the whole clause, includes all the titles; Titus 3:6; 2 Pet. 1:1, "our God and Savior Jesus Christ; RV, where the pronoun "our," coming immediately in connection with "God," involves the inclusion of both titles as referring to Christ, just as in the parallel in v. 11, "our Lord and Savior Jesus Christ" (KJV and RV); these passages are therefore a testimony to His deity; 2 Pet. 2:20; 3:2, 18; **1 John 4:14**.

4:15 Whosoever shall confess that Jesus is the Son of God, God dwelleth in him, and he in God.

Confess *see 1 John 1:9.*

Dwelleth *see* **Abideth** at *1 John 2:14.*

4:16 And we have known and believed the love that God hath to us. God is love; and he that dwelleth in love dwelleth in God, and God in him.

Known *see* **Know** at *1 John 2:3.*

Love *see 1 John 4:8.*

God *see 1 John 1:5.*

4:17 Herein is our love made perfect, that we may have boldness in the day of judgment: because as he is, so are we in this world.

Herein *see* **In this** at *1 John 4:9.*

Our In **1 John 4:17**, the phrase *meta hemon*, rendered "our (love)" in the KJV, is accurately translated in the RV "(herein is love made perfect) with us," i.e., divine love in Christ finds its expression in "our" manifestation of it to others.

Love *see 1 John 4:8.*

Perfect *see* **Perfected** at *1 John 2:5.*

Boldness *see* **Confidence** at *1 John 2:28.*

He *see 1 John 3:3.*

4:18 There is no fear in love; but perfect love casteth out fear: because fear hath torment. He that feareth is not made perfect in love.

Fear *phobos* (5401), first had the meaning of "flight," that which is caused by being scared; then, "that which may cause flight," (a) "fear, dread, terror," always with this significance in the four Gospels; also e.g., in Acts 2:43; 19:17; 1 Cor. 2:3; 1 Tim. 5:20 (lit., "may have fear"); Heb. 2:15; **1 John 4:18**; Rev. 11:11; 18:10, 15; by metonymy, that which causes "fear," Rom. 13:3; 1 Pet. 3:14, RV, "(their) fear," KJV "(their) terror," an adaptation of the Sept. of Isa. 8:12, "fear not their fear"; hence some take it to mean, as there, "what they fear," but in view of Matt. 10:28, e.g., it seems best to understand it as that which is caused by the intimidation of adversaries; (b) "reverential fear," (1) of God, as a controlling motive of the life, in matters spiritual and moral, not a mere "fear" of His power and righteous retribution, but a wholesome dread of displeasing Him, a "fear" which banishes the terror that shrinks from His presence, Rom. 8:15, and which influences the disposition and attitude of one whose circumstances are guided by trust in God, through the indwelling Spirit of God, Acts 9:31; Rom. 3:18; 2 Cor. 7:1; Eph. 5:21 (RV, "the fear of Christ"); Phil. 2:12; 1 Pet. 1:17 (a comprehensive phrase: the reverential "fear" of God will inspire a constant carefulness in dealing with others in His "fear"); 3:2, 15; the association of "fear and trembling," as, e.g., in Phil. 2:12, has in the Sept. a much sterner import, e.g., Gen. 9:2; Exod. 15:16; Deut. 2:25; 11:25; Ps. 55:5; Isa. 19:16; (2) of superiors, e.g., Rom. 13:7; 1 Pet. 2:18.

Perfect *see* **Perfected** at *1 John 2:5.*

Hath *echo* (2192), the usual verb for "to have," is used with the following meanings: (a) "to hold, in the hand," etc., e.g., Rev. 1:16; 5:8; (b) "to hold fast, keep," Luke 19:20; metaphorically, of the mind and conduct, e.g., Mark 16:8; John 14:21; Rom. 1:28; 1 Tim. 3:9; 2 Tim. 1:13; (c) "to hold on, cling to, be next to," e.g., of accompaniment, Heb. 6:9, "things that accompany (salvation)," lit., "the things holding themselves of salvation" (RV, marg., "are near to"); of place, Mark 1:38, "next (towns)," lit., "towns holding nigh"; of time, e.g., Luke 13:33, "(the day) following," lit., "the holding (day)"; Acts 13:44; 20:15; 21:26; (d) "to hold, to count, consider, regard," e.g., Matt. 14:5; 21:46; Mark 11:32; Luke 14:18; Philem. 17; (e) "to involve," Heb. 10:35; Jas. 1:4; **1 John 4:18**; (f) "to wear," of clothing, arms, etc., e.g., Matt. 3:4; 22:12; John 18:10; (g) "to be with child," of a woman, Mark 13:17; Rom. 9:10 (lit., "having conception"); (h) "to possess," the most frequent use, e.g., Matt. 8:20; 19:22; Acts 9:14; 1 Thess. 3:6; (i) of complaints, disputes, Matt. 5:23; Mark 11:25; Acts 24:19; Rev. 2:4, 20; (j) of ability, power, e.g., Luke 12:4; Acts 4:14 (lit., "had nothing to say"); (k) of necessity, e.g., Luke 12:50; Acts 23:17-19; (l) "to be in a certain condition," as of readiness, Acts 21:12 (lit., "I have readily"); of illness, Matt. 4:24, "all that were sick" (lit., "that had themselves sickly"); Mark 5:23, "lieth (lit., "hath herself") at the point of death"; Mark 16:18 "they shall recover" (lit., "shall have themselves well"), John 4:52, "he began to amend" (lit., "he had himself

"He alone loves the Creator perfectly who manifests pure love for his neighbor."

THE VENERABLE BEDE

better"); of evil works, 1 Tim. 5:25, "they that are otherwise," (lit., "the things having otherwise"); to be so, e.g., Acts 7:1, "are these things so?" (lit., "have these things thus?"), of time, Acts 24:25, "for this time" (lit., "the thing having now").

Torment *kolasis* (2851), akin to *kolazo*, "punishment," is used in Matt. 25:46, "(eternal) punishment," and **1 John 4:18**, "(fear hath) punishment," RV (KJV, "torment"), which there describes a process, not merely an effect; this kind of fear is expelled by perfect love; where God's love is being perfected in us, it gives no room for the fear of meeting with His reprobation; the "punishment" referred to is the immediate consequence of the sense of sin, not a holy awe but a slavish fear, the negation of the enjoyment of love.

Perfect *teleios* (5049), signifies "having reached its end" (*telos*), "finished, complete, perfect." It is used (I) of persons, (a) primarily of physical development, then, with ethical import, "fully grown, mature," 1 Cor. 2:6; 14:20 ("men"; marg., "of full age"); Eph. 4:13; Phil. 3:15; Col. 1:28; 4:12; in Heb. 5:14, RV, "fullgrown" (marg., "perfect"), KJV, "of full age" (marg., "perfect"); (b) "complete," conveying the idea of goodness without necessary reference to maturity or what is expressed under (a) Matt. 5:48; 19:21; Jas. 1:4 (2nd part); 3:2. It is used thus of God in Matt. 5:48; (II) of "things, complete, perfect," Rom. 12:2; 1 Cor. 13:10 (referring to the complete revelation of God's will and ways, whether in the completed Scriptures or in the hereafter); Jas. 1:4 (of the work of patience); v. 25; **1 John 4:18**.

4:19-20 We love him, because he first loved us.

If a man say, I love God, and hateth his brother, he is a liar: for he that loveth not his brother whom he hath seen, how can he love God whom he hath not seen?

Man *tis* (5100), "some one, a certain one," is rendered "a man," "a certain man," e.g., in Matt. 22:24; Mark 8:4, KJV (RV, "one"); 12:19; John 3:3, 5; 6:50; 14:23; 15:6, 13; Acts 13:41, KJV (RV, "one"); 1 Cor. 4:2; 1 Tim. 1:8; 2 Tim. 2:5, 21; Jas. 2:14, 18; 1 Pet. 2:19; **1 John 4:20**.

Hateth *see 1 John 2:9.*

Liar *see 1 John 1:10.*

4:21 And this commandment have we from him, That he who loveth God love his brother also.

Loveth, Love *phileo* (5368), is to be distinguished from *agapao* in this, that *phileo* more nearly represents "tender affection." The two words are used for the "love" of the Father for the Son, John 3:35 (*agapao*), and 5:20 (*phileo*); for the believer, 14:21 (*agapao*) and 16:27 (*phileo*); both, of Christ's "love" for a certain disciple, 13:23 (*agapao*), and 20:2 (*phileo*). Yet the distinction between the two verbs remains, and they are never used indiscriminately in the same passage; if each is used with reference to the same objects, as just mentioned, each word retains its distinctive and essential character. *Phileo* is never used in a command to men to "love" God; it is, however, used as a warning in 1 Cor. 16:22; *agapao* is used instead, e.g., Matt. 22:37; Luke 10:27; Rom. 8:28; 1 Cor. 8:3; 1 Pet. 1:8; **1 John 4:21**. The distinction between the two verbs finds a conspicuous instance in the narrative of John 21:15-17. The context itself indicates that *agapao* in the first two questions suggests the "love" that values and esteems (cf. Rev. 12:11). It is an unselfish "love," ready to serve. The use of *phileo* in Peter's answers and the Lord's third question, conveys the thought of cherishing the Object above all else, of manifesting an affection characterized by constancy, from the motive of the highest veneration. See also Trench, *Syn.*, Sec.xii. Again, to "love" (*phileo*) life, from an undue desire to preserve it, forgetful of the real object of living, meets with the Lord's reproof, John 12:25. On the contrary, to "love" life (*agapao*) as used in 1 Pet. 3:10, is to consult the true interests of living. Here the word *phileo* would be quite inappropriate. *See also 1 John 2:5.*

Chapter 5

5:1 Whosoever believeth that Jesus is the Christ is born of God: and every one that loveth him that begat loveth him also that is begotten of him.

Born *see 1 John 2:29.*

5:2 By this we know that we love the children of God, when we love God, and keep his commandments.

By this *see* Hereby at *1 John 2:3.*

Know *see 1 John 2:3.*

Keep *see 1 John 2:3.*

5:3 For this is the love of God, that we keep his commandments: and his commandments are not grievous.

Love *see 1 John 2:5.*

Of *see 1 John 2:5.*

Grievous *barus* (926), denotes "heavy, burdensome"; it is always used metaphorically in the NT, and is translated "heavy" in Matt. 23:4, of Pharisaical ordinances; in the comparative degree "weightier," 23:23, of details of the law of God; "grievous," metaphorically of wolves, in Acts 20:29; of charges, 25:7; negatively of God's commandments, **1 John 5:3** (causing a burden on him who fulfills them); in 2 Cor. 10:10, "weighty," of Paul's letters.

5:4 For whatsoever is born of God overcometh the world: and this is the victory that overcometh the world, *even* our faith.

Whatsoever *see* All at *1 John 2:16.*

Born *see 1 John 2:29.*

Overcometh *see* Overcome at *1 John 2:13.*

Victory *nike* (3529), "victory," is used in **1 John 5:4**.

5:5-6 Who is he that overcometh the world, but he that believeth that Jesus is the Son of God?

This is he that came by water and blood, *even* Jesus Christ; not by water only, but by water and blood. And it is the Spirit that beareth witness, because the Spirit is truth.

Water *hudor* (5204), whence Eng. prefix, "hydro-," is used (a) of the natural element, frequently in the Gospels; in the plural especially in Revelation; elsewhere, e.g., Heb. 9:19; Jas. 3:12; in **1 John 5:6**, that Christ "came by water and blood," may refer either (1) to the elements that flowed from His side on the cross after His death, or, in view of the order of the words and the prepositions here used, (2) to His baptism in Jordan and His death on the cross. As to (1), the "water" would symbolize the moral and practical cleansing effected by the removal of defilement by our taking heed to the Word of God in heart, life and habit; cf. Lev. 14, as to the cleansing of the leper. As to (2), Jesus the Son of God came on His mission by, or through, "water" and blood, namely, at His baptism, when He publicly entered upon His mission and was declared to be the Son of God by the witness of the Father, and at the cross, when He publicly closed His witness; the apostle's statement thus counteracts the doctrine of the Gnostics that the divine *Logos* united Himself with the Man Jesus at His baptism, and left him at Gethsemane. On the contrary, He who was baptized and He who was crucified was the Son of God throughout in His combined deity and humanity. The word "water" is used symbolically in John 3:5, either (1) of the Word of God, as in 1 Pet. 1:23 (cf. the symbolic use in Eph. 5:26), or, in view of the preposition *ek*, "out of," (2) of the truth conveyed by baptism, this being the expression, not the medium, the symbol, not the cause, of the believer's identification with Christ in His death, burial and resurrection. So the New Birth is, in one sense, the setting aside of all that the believer was according to the flesh, for it is evident that there must be an entirely new beginning. Some regard the *kai*, "and," in John 3:5, as epexegetic, = "even," in which case the "water" would be emblematic of the Spirit, as in John 7:38 (cf. 4:10, 14), but not in **1 John 5:8**, where the Spirit and the "water" are distinguished. "The water of life," Rev. 21:6 and 22:1, 17, is emblematic of the maintenance of spiritual life in perpetuity. In Rev. 17:1 "the waters" are symbolic of nations, peoples, etc.

Christ *christos* (5547), "anointed," translates, in the Sept., the word "Messiah," a term applied to the priests who were anointed with the holy oil, particularly the high priest, e.g., Lev. 4:3, 5, 16. The prophets are called *hoi christoi Theou*, "the anointed of God," Ps. 105:15. A king of Israel was described upon occasion as *christos tou Kuriou*, "the anointed of the Lord," 1 Sam. 2:10, 35; 2 Sam. 1:14; Ps. 2:2; 18:50; Hab. 3:13; the term is used even of Cyrus, Isa. 45:1. The title *ho Christos*, "the Christ," is not used of Christ in the Sept. version of the inspired books of the OT. In the NT the word is frequently used with the article, of the Lord Jesus, as an appellative rather than a title, e.g., Matt. 2:4; Acts 2:31; without the article, Luke 2:11; 23:2; John 1:41. Three times the title was expressly accepted by the Lord Himself, Matt. 16:17; Mark 14:61-62; John 4:26. It is added as an appellative to the proper name "Jesus," e.g., John 17:3, the only time when the Lord so spoke of Himself; Acts 9:34; 1 Cor. 3:11; **1 John 5:6**. It is distinctly a proper name in many passages, whether with the article, e.g., Matt. 1:17; 11:2; Rom. 7:4, 9:5; 15:19; 1 Cor. 1:6, or without the article, Mark 9:41; Rom. 6:4; 8:9, 17; 1 Cor. 1:12; Gal. 2:16. The single title Christos is sometimes used without the article to signify the One who by His Holy Spirit and power indwells believers and molds their character in conformity to His likeness, Rom. 8:10; Gal. 2:20; 4:19; Eph. 3:17. As to the use or absence of the article, the title with the article specifies the Lord Jesus as "the Christ"; the title without the article stresses His character and His relationship with believers. Again, speaking generally, when the title is the subject of a sentence it has the article; when it forms part of the predicate the article is absent.

5:7 For there are three that bear record in heaven, the Father, the Word, and the Holy Ghost: and these three are one.

Three *treis* (5143), is regarded by many as a number sometimes symbolically indicating fullness of testimony or manifestation, as in the three persons in the Godhead, cf. 1 Tim. 5:19; Heb. 10:28; the mention in **1 John 5:7** is in a verse which forms no part of the original; no Greek ms. earlier than the 14th century contained it; no version earlier than the 5th cent. in any other language contains it, nor is it quoted by any of the Greek or Latin "Fathers" in their writings on the Trinity. That there are those who bear witness in Heaven is not borne out by any other Scripture. It must be regarded as the interpolation of a copyist. In Mark 9:31 and 10:34 the best texts have *meta treis hemeras*, "after three days," which idiomatically expresses the same thing as *te tritehemera*, "on the third day," which some texts have here, as, e.g., the phrase "the third day" in Matt. 17:23; 20:19; Luke 9:22; 18:33, where the repetition of the article lends stress to the number, lit., "the day the third"; 24:7, 46; Acts 10:40.

Record *see* Witness at *1 John 1:2*.

Word *see 1 John 1:1*.

5:8 And there are three that bear witness in earth, the Spirit, and the water, and the blood: and these three agree in one.

Witness *see 1 John 1:2*.

Water *see 1 John 5:6*.

One *heis* (1520), the first cardinal numeral, masculine (feminine and neuter nominative forms are *mia* and *hen*, respectively), is used to signify (1) (a) "one" in contrast to many, e.g., Matt. 25:15; Rom. 5:18, RV, "(through) one (trespass)," i.e., Adam's transgression, in contrast to the "one act of righteousness," i.e., the death of Christ (not as KJV, "the offense of one," and "the righteousness of one"); (b) metaphorically, "union" and "concord," e.g., John 10:30; 11:52; 17:11, 21-22; Rom. 12:4-5; Phil. 1:27; (2) emphatically, (a) a single ("one"), to the exclusion of others, e.g., Matt. 21:24; Rom. 3:10; 1 Cor. 9:24; 1 Tim. 2:5 (twice); (b) "one, alone," e.g., Mark 2:7, RV (KJV, "only"); 10:18; Luke 18:19; (c) "one and the same," e.g., Rom. 3:30, RV, "God is one," i.e., there is not "one" God for the Jew and one for the Gentile; cf. Gal. 3:20, which means that in a promise there is no other party; 1 Cor. 3:8; 11:5; 12:11; **1 John 5:8** (lit., "and the three are into one," i.e., united in "one" and the same witness); (3) a certain "one," in the same sense as the indefinite pronoun *tis*, e.g., Matt. 8:19, RV, "a (scribe)," marg., "one (scribe)," KJV, "a certain (scribe)"; 19:16, "one;" in Rev. 8:13, RV marg., "one (eagle)"; *heis tis* are used together in Luke 22:50; John 11:49; this occurs frequently in the papyri (Moulton, *Prol.*, p. 96); (4) distributively, with *hekastos*, "each," i.e., "every one," e.g., Luke 4:40; Acts 2:6, "every man" (lit., "every one"); in the sense of "one ... and one," e.g., John 20:12; or "one" ... followed by *allos* or *heteros*, "the other," e.g., Matt. 6:24; or by a second *heis*, e.g., Matt. 24:40, RV, "one"; John 20:12; in Rom. 12:5 *heis* is preceded by *kata* (*kath'* in the sense of "severally (members) one (of another)," RV (KJV, "every one ... one"); cf. Mark 14:19; in 1 Thess. 5:11 the phrase in the 2nd part, "each other," RV (KJV, "one another"), is, lit., "one the one"; (5) as an ordinal number, equivalent to *protos*, "first," in the phrase "the first day of the week," lit. and idiomatically, "one of sabbaths," signifying "the first day after the sabbath," e.g., Matt. 28:1; Mark 16:2; Acts 20:7; 1 Cor. 16:2. Moulton remarks on the tendency for certain cardinal numerals to replace ordinals (*Prol.*, p. 96).

5:9 If we receive the witness of men, the witness of God is greater: for this is the witness of God which he hath testified of his Son.

Witness *marturia* (3141), "testimony, a bearing witness," is translated "witness" in Mark 14:55, 56, 59; Luke 22:71; John 1:7, 19 (RV); 3:11, 32 and 33 (RV); 5:31, 32, 34 (RV), 36; RV in 8:13, 14, 17; 19:35; 21:24; KJV in Titus 1:13; KJV and RV in **1 John 5:9** (thrice), **10a**; RV in **10b**, **11**; 3 John 12. *See also 1 John 1:2*.

Of *see 1 John 2:5*.

Testified *see* Testify at *1 John 4:14*.

5:10 He that believeth on the Son of God hath the witness in himself: he that believeth not God hath made him a liar; because he believeth not the record that God gave of his Son.

Witness *see 1 John 5:9*.

Made *see* Make at *1 John 1:10*.

Liar *see 1 John 1:10*.

Record *marturia* (3141), "witness, evidence, testimony," is almost always rendered "witness" in the RV (for KJV, "testimony" in John 3:32, 33; 5:34; 8:17; 21:24, and always for KJV, "record," e.g., **1 John 5:10, 11**), except in Acts 22:18 and in Revelation, where both, with one exception, have "testimony," 1:2, 9; 6:9; 11:7; 12:11, 17; 19:10 (twice); 20:4 (KJV, "witness"). In 19:10, "the testimony of Jesus" is objective, the "testimony" or witness given to Him (cf. 1:2, 9; as to those who will bear it, see Rev. 12:17, RV). The statement "the testimony of Jesus is the spirit of prophecy," is to be understood in the light, e.g., of the "testimony" concerning Christ and Israel in the Psalms, which will be used by the godly Jewish remnant in the coming time of "Jacob's Trouble." All such "testimony" centers in and points to Christ.

5:11 And this is the record, that God hath given to us eternal life, and this life is in his Son.

Record *see 1 John 5:10. See also* Witness at *1 John 5:9.*

5:12-14 He that hath the Son hath life; *and* he that hath not the Son of God hath not life.

These things have I written unto you that believe on the name of the Son of God; that ye may know that ye have eternal life, and that ye may believe on the name of the Son of God.

And this is the confidence that we have in him, that, if we ask any thing according to his will, he heareth us:

Confidence *see 1 John 2:28.*

Ask *see 1 John 3:22.*

Will *see 1 John 2:17.*

Heareth *akouo* (191), the usual word denoting "to hear," is used (a) intransitively, e.g., Matt. 11:15; Mark 4:23; (b) transitively when the object is expressed, sometimes in the accusative case, sometimes in the genitive. Thus in Acts 9:7, "hearing the voice," the noun "voice" is in the partitive genitive case [i.e., hearing (something) of], whereas in 22:9, "they heard not the voice," the construction is with the accusative. This removes the idea of any contradiction. The former indicates a "hearing" of the sound, the latter indicates the meaning or message of the voice (this they did not hear). "The former denotes the sensational perception, the latter (the accusative case) the thing perceived" (Cremer). In John 5:25, 28, the genitive case is used, indicating a "sensational perception" that the Lord's voice is sounding; in 3:8, of "hearing" the wind, the accusative is used, stressing "the thing perceived."

That God "hears" prayer signifies that He answers prayer, e.g., John 9:31; **1 John 5:14, 15**. Sometimes the verb is used with *para* ("from beside"), e.g., John 1:40, "one of the two which heard John speak," lit., "heard from beside John," suggesting that he stood beside him; in John 8:26, 40, indicating the intimate fellowship of the Son with the Father; the same construction is used in Acts 10:22 and 2 Tim. 2:2, in the latter case, of the intimacy between Paul and Timothy.

5:15 And if we know that he hear us, whatsoever we ask, we know that we have the petitions that we desired of him.

Hear *see* Heareth at *1 John 5:14.*

Ask *see 1 John 3:22.*

Petitions *aitema* (155), denotes "that which has been asked for" (akin to *aiteo,* "to ask"); in Luke 23:24, RV, "what they asked for" (KJV, "as they required"), lit., "their request (should be done, *ginomai*)"; in Phil. 4:6, "requests"; in **1 John 5:15**, "petitions."

5:16 If any man see his brother sin a sin *which is* not unto death, he shall ask, and he shall give him life for them that sin not unto death. There is a sin unto death: I do not say that he shall pray for it.

Sin *see 1 John 1:7.*

Ask *see 1 John 3:22.*

Life *see 1 John 1:2.*

Pray *erotao* (2065), more frequently suggests that the petitioner is on a footing of equality or familiarity with the person whom he requests. It is used of a king in making request from another king, Luke 14:32; of the Pharisee who "desired" Christ that He would eat with him, an indication of the inferior conception he had of Christ, Luke 7:36; cf. 11:37; John 9:15; 18:19. In this respect it is significant that the Lord Jesus never used *aiteo* in the matter of making request to the Father. "The consciousness of His equal dignity, of His potent and prevailing intercession, speaks out in this, that as often as He asks, or declares that He will ask anything of the Father, it is always *erotao,* an asking, that is, upon equal terms, John 14:16; 16:26; 17:9, 15, 20, never *aiteo,* that He uses. Martha, on the contrary, plainly reveals her poor unworthy conception of His person, that ... she ascribes that *aiteo* to Him which He never ascribes to Himself, John 11:22" (Trench, *Syn.* Sec. xl). In passages where both words are used, the

"Whenever we take what God has done and put it in the place of himself, we become idolaters."

OSWALD CHAMBERS

distinction should be noticed, even if it cannot be adequately represented in English. In John 16:23, "in that day ye shall ask Me nothing," the verb is *erotao*, whereas in the latter part of the verse, in the sentence, "If ye shall ask anything of the Father," the verb is *aiteo*. The distinction is brought out in the RV margin, which renders the former clause "Ye shall ask Me no question," and this meaning is confirmed by the fact that the disciples had been desirous of "asking" Him a question (*erotao*, v. 19). If the Holy Spirit had been given, the time for "asking" questions from the Lord would have ceased. In John 14:14, where, not a question, but a request is made by the disciples, *aiteo*, is used. Both verbs are found in **1 John 5:16**: in the sentence "he shall ask, and God will give him life for them that sin not unto death," the verb is *aiteo*, but with regard to the sin unto death, in the sentence "not concerning this do I say that he shall make request," the verb is *erotao*. Later, the tendency was for *erotao* to approximate to *aiteo*.

5:17 All unrighteousness is sin: and there is a sin not unto death.

Unrighteousness *see 1 John 1:9*.

Sin *see 1 John 1:7*.

5:18 We know that whosoever is born of God sinneth not; but he that is begotten of God keepeth himself, and that wicked one toucheth him not.

Born, Begotten *see* **Born** at *1 John 2:29*.

Keepeth *see* **Keep** at *1 John 2:3*.

Wicked *see 1 John 2:13*.

Toucheth *hapto* (681), primarily, "to fasten to," hence, of fire, "to kindle," denotes, in the middle voice (a) "to touch," e.g., Matt. 8:3, 15; 9:20, 21, 29; (b) "to cling to, lay hold of," John 20:17; here the Lord's prohibition as to clinging to Him was indicative of the fact that communion with Him would, after His ascension, be by faith, through the Spirit; (c) "to have carnal intercourse with a woman," 1 Cor. 7:1; (d) "to have fellowship and association with unbelievers," 2 Cor. 6:17; (e) (negatively) "to adhere to certain Levitical and ceremonial ordinances," in order to avoid contracting external defilement, or to practice rigorous asceticism, all such abstentions being of "no value against the indulgence of the flesh," Col. 2:21, KJV (RV, "handle"); (f) "to assault," in order to sever the vital union between Christ and the believer, said of the attack of the Evil One, **1 John 5:18**.

5:19 *And* we know that we are of God, and the whole world lieth in wickedness.

Whole *see 1 John 2:2*.

World *see 1 John 3:17*.

Lieth *keimai* (2749), "to be laid, to lie," used as the passive voice of *tithemi*, "to lay", is said (a) of the Child Jesus, Luke 2:12, 16; (b) of the dead body of the Lord, Matt. 28:6; John 20:12; in Luke 23:53, "had ... lain," RV, KJV, "was laid," in the tomb as hitherto empty; (c) of the linen cloths, John 20:5, 6, 7; (d) figuratively of a veil as "lying" upon the hearts of the Jews, 2 Cor. 3:15, RV, "lieth" (KJV, "is"); (e) metaphorically, of the world as "lying" in the evil one, **1 John 5:19**, RV; (f) of the heavenly city, Rev. 21:16.

Wickedness *see* **Wicked** at *1 John 2:13*.

5:20 And we know that the Son of God is come, and hath given us an understanding, that we may know him that is true, and we are in him that is true, *even* in his Son Jesus Christ. This is the true God, and eternal life.

Know *see 1 John 2:3*.

God *see 1 John 1:5*.

Understanding *dianoia* (1271), is rendered "understanding" in Eph. 4:18; **1 John 5:20** (in some texts, Eph. 1:18, KJV, for *kardia*, "heart," RV).

True *see 1 John 2:8*.

5:21 Little children, keep yourselves from idols. Amen.

Children *see 1 John 2:1*.

Keep *phulasso* (5442), "to guard, watch, keep," is rendered by the verb "to guard" in the RV (KJV, "to keep") of Luke 11:21; John 17:12; Acts 12:4; 28:16; 2 Thess. 3:3; 1 Tim. 6:20; 2 Tim. 1:12, 14; **1 John 5:21**; Jude 24. In Luke 8:29, "was kept under guard," RV (KJV, kept).

Idols *eidolon* (1497), primarily "a phantom or likeness" (from *eidos*, "an appearance," lit., "that which is seen"), or "an idea, fancy," denotes in the NT (a) "an idol," an image to represent a false god, Acts 7:41; 1 Cor. 12:2; Rev. 9:20; (b) "the false god" worshipped in an image, Acts 15:20; Rom. 2:22; 1 Cor. 8:4, 7; 10:19; 2 Cor. 6:16; 1 Thess. 1:9; **1 John 5:21**.

"The corresponding Heb. word denotes 'vanity,' Jer. 14:22; 18:15; 'thing of nought,' Lev. 19:4, marg., cf. Eph. 4:17. Hence what represented a deity to the Gentiles, was to Paul a 'vain thing,' Acts 14:15; 'nothing in the world,' 1 Cor. 8:4; 10:19. Jeremiah calls the idol a 'scarecrow' ('pillar in a garden,' 10:5, marg.), and Isaiah, 44:9-20, etc., and Habakkuk, 2:18, 19 and the Psalmist, 115:4-8, etc., are all equally scathing. It is important to notice, however, that in each case the people of God are addressed. When he speaks to idolaters, Paul, knowing that no man is won by ridicule, adopts a different line, Acts 14:15-18; 17:16, 21-31."

2 John

1 The elder unto the elect lady and her children, whom I love in the truth; and not I only, but also all they that have known the truth;

Elect *eklektos* (1588), lit. signifies "picked out, chosen" (*ek*, "from," *lego*, "to gather, pick out"), and is used of (a) Christ, the "chosen" of God, as the Messiah, Luke 23:35, and metaphorically as a "living Stone," "a chief corner Stone," 1 Pet. 2:4, 6; some mss. have it in John 1:34, instead of *huios*, "Son"; (b) angels, 1 Tim. 5:21, as "chosen" to be of especially high rank in administrative association with God, or as His messengers to human beings, doubtless in contrast to fallen angels (see 2 Pet. 2:4 and Jude 6); (c) believers (Jews or Gentiles), Matt. 24:22, 24, 31; Mark 13:20, 22, 27; Luke 18:7; Rom. 8:33; Col. 3:12; 2 Tim. 2:10; Titus 1:1; 1 Pet. 1:1; 2:9 (as a spiritual race); Matt. 20:16; 22:14 and Rev. 17:14, "chosen"; individual believers are so mentioned in Rom. 16:13; **2 John 1, 13**. Believers were "chosen" "before the foundation of the world" (cf. "before times eternal," 2 Tim. 1:9), in Christ, Eph. 1:4, to adoption, Eph. 1:5; good works, 2:10; conformity to Christ, Rom. 8:29; salvation from the delusions of the Antichrist and the doom of the deluded, 2 Thess. 2:13; eternal glory, Rom. 9:23. The source of their "election" is God's grace, not human will, Eph. 1:4, 5; Rom. 9:11; 11:5. They are given by God the Father to Christ as the fruit of His death, all being foreknown and foreseen by God, John 17:6 and Rom. 8:29. While Christ's death was sufficient for all men, and is effective in the case of the "elect," yet men are treated as responsible, being capable of the will and power to choose. For the rendering "being chosen as firstfruits," an alternative reading in 2 Thess. 2:13.

Lady *kuria* (2959), is the person addressed in **2 John 1** and **5**. Not improbably it is a proper name (Eng., "Cyria"), in spite of the fact that the full form of address in v. **1** is not quite in accord, in the original, with those in v. **13** and in 3 John 1. The suggestion that the church is addressed is most unlikely. Possibly the person is one who had a special relation with the local church.

Truth *aletheia* (225), "truth," is used (a) objectively, signifying "the reality lying at the basis of an appearance; the manifested, veritable essence of a matter" (Cremer), e.g., Rom. 9:1; 2 Cor. 11:10; especially of Christian doctrine, e.g., Gal. 2:5, where "the truth of the gospel" denotes the "true" teaching of the gospel, in contrast to perversions of it; Rom. 1:25, where "the truth of God" may be "the truth concerning God" or "God whose existence is a verity"; but in Rom. 15:8 "the truth of God" is indicative of His faithfulness in the fulfillment of His promises as exhibited in Christ; the word has an absolute force in John 14:6; 17:17; 18:37, 38; in Eph. 4:21, where the RV, "even as truth is in Jesus," gives the correct rendering, the meaning is not merely ethical "truth," but "truth" in all its fullness and scope, as embodied in Him; He was the perfect expression of the truth; this is virtually equivalent to His statement in John 14:6; (b) subjectively, "truthfulness," "truth," not merely verbal, but sincerity and integrity of character, John 8:44; 3 John 3, RV; (c) in phrases, e.g., "in truth" (*epi*, "on the basis of"), Mark 12:14; Luke 20:21; with *en*, "in," 2 Cor. 6:7; Col. 1:6; 1 Tim. 2:7, RV (KJV, "in ... verity"), 1 John 3:18; **2 John 1, 3, 4**.

Only *monos* (3441), "alone, solitary," is translated "only," e.g., in Matt. 4:10; 12:4; 17:8; 1 Cor. 9:6; 14:36; Phil. 4:15; Col. 4:11; **2 John 1**; it is used as an attribute of God in John 5:44; 17:3; Rom. 16:27; 1 Tim. 1:17; 1 Tim. 6:15-16; Jude 4, 25; Rev. 15:4.

Known *ginosko* (1097), signifies "to be taking in knowledge, to come to know, recognize, understand," or "to understand completely," e.g., Mark 13:28, 29; John 13:12; 15:18; 21:17; 2 Cor. 8:9; Heb. 10:34; 1 John

2:5; 4:2, 6 (twice), 7, 13; 5:2, 20; in its past tenses it frequently means "to know in the sense of realizing," the aorist or point tense usually indicating definiteness, Matt. 13:11; Mark 7:24; John 7:26; in 10:38 "that ye may know (aorist tense) and understand, (present tense)"; 19:4; Acts 1:7; 17:19; Rom. 1:21; 1 Cor. 2:11 (2nd part), 14; 2 Cor. 2:4; Eph. 3:19; 6:22; Phil. 2:19; 3:10; 1 Thess. 3:5; 2 Tim. 2:19; Jas. 2:20; 1 John 2:13 (twice), 14; 3:6; 4:8; **2 John 1**; Rev. 2:24; 3:3, 9. In the passive voice, it often signifies "to become known," e.g., Matt. 10:26; Phil. 4:5. In the sense of complete and absolute understanding on God's part, it is used, e.g., in Luke 16:15; John 10:15 (of the Son as well as the Father); 1 Cor. 3:20. In Luke 12:46, KJV, it is rendered "he is ... aware."

2 For the truth's sake, which dwelleth in us, and shall be with us for ever.

Dwelleth *meno* (3306), used (a) of place, e.g., Matt. 10:11,metaphorically 1 John 2:19, is said of God, 1 John 4:15; Christ, John 6:56; 15:4, etc.; the Holy Spirit, John 1:32-33; 14:17; believers, John 6:56; 15:4; 1 John 4:15, etc.; the Word of God, 1 John 2:14; the truth, **2 John 2**, etc.; (b) of time; it is said of believers, John 21:22-23; Phil. 1:25; 1 John 2:17; Christ, John 12:34; Heb. 7:24; the Word of God, 1 Pet. 1:23; sin, John 9:41; cities, Matt. 11:23; Heb. 13:14; bonds and afflictions, Acts 20:23; (c) of qualities; faith, hope, love, 1 Cor. 13:13; Christ's love, John 15:10; afflictions, Acts 20:23; brotherly love, Heb. 13:1; the love of God, 1 John 3:17; the truth, **2 John 2**. The RV usually translates it by "abide," but "continue" in 1 Tim. 2:15; in the following, the RV substitutes "to abide" for the KJV, "to continue," John 2:12; 8:31; 15:9; 2 Tim. 3:14; Heb. 7:24; 13:14; 1 John 2:24.

3 Grace be with you, mercy, *and* peace, from God the Father, and from the Lord Jesus Christ, the Son of the Father, in truth and love.

Mercy *eleos* (1656), "is the outward manifestation of pity; it assumes need on the part of him who receives it, and resources adequate to meet the need on the part of him who shows it. It is used (a) of God, who is rich in mercy, Eph. 2:4, and who has provided salvation for all men, Titus 3:5, for Jews, Luke 1:72, and Gentiles, Rom. 15:9. He is merciful to those who fear him, Luke 1:50, for they also are compassed with infirmity, and He alone can succor them. Hence they are to pray boldly for mercy, Heb. 4:16, and if for themselves, it is seemly that they should ask for mercy for one another, Gal. 6:16; 1 Tim. 1:2. When God brings His salvation to its issue at the Coming of Christ, His people will obtain His mercy, 2 Tim. 1:16; Jude 21; (b) of men; for since God is merciful to them, He would have them show mercy to one another, Matt. 9:13; 12:7; 23:23; Luke 10:37; Jas. 2:13.

"Wherever the words mercy and peace are found together they occur in that order, except in Gal. 6:16. Mercy is the act of God, peace is the resulting experience in the heart of man. Grace describes God's attitude toward the lawbreaker and the rebel; mercy is His attitude toward those who are in distress."

"In the order of the manifestation of God's purposes of salvation grace must go before mercy ... only the forgiven may be blessed.... From this it follows that in each of the apostolic salutations where these words occur, grace precedes mercy, 1 Tim. 1:2; 2 Tim. 1:2; Titus 1:4 (in some mss.); **2 John 3**" (Trench, *Syn.* Sec.xlvii).

Truth *see 2 John 1.*

4 I rejoiced greatly that I found of thy children walking in truth, as we have received a commandment from the Father.

Rejoiced *chairo* (5463), "to rejoice," is most frequently so translated. As to this verb, the following are grounds and occasions for "rejoicing," on the part of believers: in the Lord, Phil. 3:1; 4:4; His incarnation, Luke 1:14; His power, Luke 13:17; His presence with the Father, John 14:28; His presence with them, John 16:22; 20:20; His ultimate triumph, 8:56; hearing the gospel, Acts 13:48; their salvation, Acts 8:39; receiving the Lord, Luke 19:6; their enrollment in Heaven, Luke 10:20; their liberty in Christ, Acts 15:31; their hope, Rom. 12:12 (cf. Rom. 5:2; Rev. 19:7); their prospect of reward, Matt. 5:12; the obedience and godly conduct of fellow believers, Rom. 16:19, RV, "I rejoice" (KJV, "I am glad"); 2 Cor. 7:7, 9; 13:9; Col. 2:5; 1 Thess. 3:9; **2 John 4**; 3 John 3; the proclamation of Christ, Phil. 1:18; the gospel harvest, John 4:36; suffering with Christ, Acts 5:41; 1 Pet. 4:13; suffering in the cause of the gospel, 2 Cor. 13:9 (1st part); Phil. 2:17 (1st part); Col. 1:24; in persecutions, trials and afflictions, Matt. 5:12; Luke 6:23; 2 Cor. 6:10; the manifestation of grace, Acts 11:23; meeting with fellow believers, 1 Cor. 16:17, RV, "I rejoice"; Phil. 2:28; receiving tokens of love and fellowship, Phil. 4:10; the "rejoicing" of others, Rom. 12:15; 2 Cor. 7:13; learning of the well-being of others, 2 Cor. 7:16.

Greatly *lian* (3029), "very, exceedingly," is rendered "greatly" in Matt. 27:14, of wonder 2 Tim. 4:15, of opposition; **2 John 4** and 3 John 3, of joy.

Walking *peripateo* (4043), is used (a) physically, in the Synoptic Gospels (except Mark 7:5); always in the Acts except in 21:21; never in the

Pauline Epistles, nor in those of John; (b) figuratively, "signifying the whole round of the activities of the individual life, whether of the unregenerate, Eph. 4:17, or of the believer, 1 Cor. 7:17; Col. 2:6. It is applied to the observance of religious ordinances, Acts 21:21; Heb. 13:9, marg., as well as to moral conduct. The Christian is to walk in newness of life, Rom. 6:4, after the spirit, 8:4, in honesty, 13:13, by faith, 2 Cor. 5:7, in good works, Eph. 2:10, in love, 5:2, in wisdom, Col. 4:5, in truth, **2 John 4**, after the commandments of the Lord, v. **6**. And, negatively, not after the flesh, Rom. 8:4; not after the manner of men, 1 Cor. 3:3; not in craftiness, 2 Cor. 4:2; not by sight, 5:7; not in the vanity of the mind, Eph. 4:17; not disorderly, 2 Thess. 3:6."

Truth *see* ***2 John 1***.

5 And now I beseech thee, lady, not as though I wrote a new commandment unto thee, but that which we had from the beginning, that we love one another.

Beseech *erotao* (2065), often translated by the verb "to beseech," in the Gospels, is elsewhere rendered "beseech" in 1 Thess. 4:1; 5:12; 2 Thess. 2:1; **2 John 5**.

Lady *see* ***2 John 1***.

6 And this is love, that we walk after his commandments. This is the commandment, That, as ye have heard from the beginning, ye should walk in it.

Love *agapao* (25), and the corresponding noun *agape* present "the characteristic word of Christianity, and since the Spirit of revelation has used it to express ideas previously unknown, inquiry into its use, whether in Greek literature or in the Septuagint, throws but little light upon its distinctive meaning in the NT. Cf, however, Lev. 19:18; Deut. 6:5.

"*Agape* and *agapao* are used in the NT (a) to describe the attitude of God toward His Son, John 17:26; the human race, generally, John 3:16; Rom. 5:8, and to such as believe on the Lord Jesus Christ particularly John 14:21; (b) to convey His will to His children concerning their attitude one toward another, John 13:34, and toward all men, 1 Thess. 3:12; 1 Cor. 16:14; 2 Pet. 1:7; (c) to express the essential nature of God, 1 John 4:8. Love can be known only from the actions it prompts. God's love is seen in the gift of His Son, 1 John 4:9, 10. But obviously this is not the love of complacency, or affection, that is, it was not drawn out by any excellency in its objects, Rom. 5:8. It was an exercise of the divine will in deliberate choice, made without assignable cause save that which lies in the nature of God Himself, Cf. Deut. 7:7, 8. Love had its perfect expression among men in the Lord Jesus Christ, 2 Cor. 5:14; Eph. 2:4; 3:19; 5:2: Christian love is the fruit of His Spirit in the Christian, Gal. 5:22. Christian love has God for its primary object, and expresses itself first of all in implicit obedience to His commandments, John 14:15, 21, 23; 15:10; 1 John 2:5; 5:3; **2 John 6**. Selfwill, that is, self-pleasing, is the negation of love to God. Christian love, whether exercised toward the brethren, or toward men generally, is not an impulse from the feelings, it does not always run with the natural inclinations, nor does it spend itself only upon those for whom some affinity is discovered. Love seeks the welfare of all, Rom. 15:2, and works no ill to any, 13:8-10; love seeks opportunity to do good to 'all men, and especially toward them that are of the household of the faith,' Gal. 6:10. See further 1 Cor. 13 and Col. 3:12-14."

Walk *see* **Walking** at ***2 John 4***.

7 For many deceivers are entered into the world, who confess not that Jesus Christ is come in the flesh. This is a deceiver and an antichrist.

Deceivers, Deceiver *planos* (4108), is, properly, an adjective, signifying "wandering, or leading astray, seducing," 1 Tim. 4:1, "seducing (spirits)", used as a noun, it denotes an impostor of the vagabond type, and so any kind of "deceiver" or corrupter, Matt. 27:63; 2 Cor. 6:8; **2 John 7** (twice), in the last of which the accompanying definite article necessitates the translation "the deceiver," RV.

Entered In **2 John 7**, the most authentic mss. have the verb *exerchomai*, "gone forth," RV, for KJV, "entered."

Confess *homologeo* (3670), lit., "to speak the same thing" (*homos*, "same," *lego*, "to speak"), "to assent, accord, agree with," denotes, (a) "to confess, declare, admit," John 1:20; e.g., Acts 24:14; Heb. 11:13; (b) "to confess by way of admitting oneself guilty of what one is accused of, the result of inward conviction," 1 John 1:9; (c) "to declare openly by way of speaking out freely, such confession being the effect of deep conviction of facts," Matt. 7:23; 10:32 (twice) and Luke 12:8 (see next par.); John 9:22; 12:42; Acts 23:8; Rom. 10:9-10 ("confession is made"); 1 Tim. 6:12 (RV); Titus 1:16; 1 John 2:23; 4:2, 15; **2 John 7** (in John's epistle it is the necessary antithesis to Gnostic doceticism); Rev. 3:5, in the best mss.; (d) "to confess by way of celebrating with praise," Heb. 13:15; (e) "to promise," Matt. 14:7.

Flesh *sarx* (4561), has a wider range of meaning in the NT than in the OT. Its uses in the NT may be analyzed as follows:

"(a) 'the substance of the body,' whether of beasts or of men, 1 Cor. 15:39; (b) 'the human body,' 2 Cor. 10:3a; Gal. 2:20; Phil. 1:22; (c) by synecdoche, of 'mankind,' in the totality of all that is essential to manhood, i.e., spirit, soul, and body, Matt. 24:22; John 1:13; Rom. 3:20; (d) by synecdoche, of 'the holy humanity' of the Lord Jesus, in the totality of all that is essential to manhood, i.e., spirit, soul, and body John 1:14; 1 Tim. 3:16; 1 John 4:2; **2 John 7**, in Heb. 5:7, 'the days of His flesh,' i.e., His past life on earth in distinction from His present life in resurrection; (e) by synecdoche, for 'the complete person,' John 6:51-57; 2 Cor. 7:5; Jas. 5:3; (f) 'the weaker element in human nature,' Matt. 26:41; Rom. 6:19; 8:3a; (g) 'the unregenerate state of men,' Rom. 7:5; 8:8, 9; (h) 'the seat of sin in man' (but this is not the same thing as in the body), 2 Pet. 2:18; 1 John 2:16; (i) 'the lower and temporary element in the Christian,' Gal. 3:3; 6:8, and in religious ordinances, Heb. 9:10; (j) 'the natural attainments of men,' 1 Cor. 1:26; 2 Cor. 10:2, 3b; (k) 'circumstances,' 1 Cor. 7:28; the externals of life, 2 Cor. 7:1; Eph. 6:5; Heb. 9:13; (l) by metonymy, 'the outward and seeming,' as contrasted with the spirit, the inward and real, John 6:63; 2 Cor. 5:16; (m) 'natural relationship, consanguine,' 1 Cor. 10:18; Gal. 4:23, or marital, Matt. 19:5."

Antichrist *antichristos* (500), can mean either "against Christ" or "instead of Christ," or perhaps, combining the two, "one who, assuming the guise of Christ, opposes Christ" (Westcott). The word is found only in John's epistles, (a) of the many "antichrists" who are forerunners of the "Antichrist" himself, 1 John 2:18, 22; **2 John 7**; (b) of the evil power which already operates anticipatively of the "Antichrist," 1 John 4:3. What the apostle says of him so closely resembles what he says of the first beast in Rev. 13, and what the apostle Paul says of the Man of Sin in 2 Thess. 2, that the same person seems to be in view in all these passages, rather than the second beast in Rev. 13, the false prophet; for the latter supports the former in all his anti-Christian assumptions.

8 Look to yourselves, that we lose not those things which we have wrought, but that we receive a full reward.

Look *blepo* (991), "to look", has the meaning of "taking heed, looking to oneself," in **2 John 8**.

Wrought *ergazomai* (2038), is used (I) intransitively, e.g., Matt. 21:28; John 5:17; 9:4 (2nd part); Rom. 4:4, 5; 1 Cor. 4:12; 9:6; 1 Thess. 2:9; 4:11; 2 Thess. 3:8, 10-12; (II) transitively, (a) "to work something, produce, perform," e.g., Matt. 26:10, "she hath wrought"; John 6:28, 30; 9:4 (1st part); Acts 10:35; 13:41; Rom. 2:10; 13:10; 1 Cor. 16:10; 2 Cor. 7:10a; Gal. 6:10, RV, "let us work"; Eph. 4:28; Heb. 11:33; **2 John 8**; (b) "to earn by working, work for," John 6:27, RV, "work" (KJV, "labor").

Receive *apolambano* (618), signifies "to receive from another," (a) to "receive" as one's due; Luke 23:41; Rom. 1:27; Col. 3:24; **2 John 8**; (b) without the indication of what is due, Luke 16:25; Gal. 4:5; (c) to receive back, Luke 6:34 (twice); 15:27. For its other meaning, "to take apart," Mark 7:33.

Full *pleres* (4134), denotes "full," (a) in the sense of "being filled," materially, Matt. 14:20; 15:37; Mark 8:19 (said of baskets "full" of bread crumbs); of leprosy, Luke 5:12; spiritually, of the Holy Spirit, Luke 4:1; Acts 6:3; 7:55; 11:24; grace and truth, John 1:14; faith, Acts 6:5; grace and power, 6:8; of the effects of spiritual life and qualities, seen in good works, Acts 9:36; in an evil sense, of guile and villany, Acts 13:10; wrath, 19:28; (b) in the sense of "being complete," "full corn in the ear," Mark 4:28; of a reward hereafter, **2 John 8**.

Reward *misthos* (3408), primarily "wages, hire," and then, generally, "reward," (a) received in this life, Matt. 5:46; 6:2, 5, 16; Rom. 4:4; 1 Cor. 9:17, 18; of evil "rewards," Acts 1:18; (b) to be received hereafter, Matt. 5:12; 10:41 (twice), 42; Mark 9:41; Luke 6:23, 35; 1 Cor. 3:8, 14; **2 John 8**; Rev. 11:18; 22:12.

9 Whosoever transgresseth, and abideth not in the doctrine of Christ, hath not God. He that abideth in the doctrine of Christ, he hath both the Father and the Son.

Transgresseth *proago* (4254), "to lead forth," used intransitively signifies "to go before," usually of locality, e.g., Matt. 2:9; figuratively, in 1 Tim. 1:18, "went before" (RV, marg., "led the way to"), of the exercise of the gifts of prophecy which pointed to Timothy as one chosen by God for the service to be committed to him; in 5:24, of sins "going before unto judgment." In **2 John 9**, where the best mss. have this verb (instead of *parabaino*, "to transgress," KJV), the RV renders it "goeth onward" (marg., "taketh the lead"), of not abiding in the doctrine of Christ. Cf. Mal. 4:4.

parabaino (3845), lit., "to go aside" (*para*), hence "to go beyond," is chiefly used metaphorically of "transgressing" the tradition of the elders, Matt. 15:2; the commandment of God, 15:3; in Acts 1:25, of Judas, KJV, "by transgression fell" (RV, "fell away"); in **2 John 9** some texts have this verb (KJV, "transgresseth"), the best have *proago*.

10 If there come any unto you, and bring not this doctrine, receive him not into *your* house, neither bid him God speed:

Receive *lambano* (2983), denotes either "to take" or "to receive," (I) literally, (a) without an object, in contrast to asking, e.g., Matt. 7:8; Mark 11:24, RV, "have received" (the original has no object); (b) in contrast to giving, e.g., Matt. 10:8; Acts 20:35; (c) with objects, whether things, e.g., Mark 10:30; Luke 18:30, in the best mss.; John 13:30; Acts 9:19, RV, "took" (KJV, "received"); 1 Cor. 9:25, RV, "receive" (KJV, "obtain"); or persons, e.g., John 6:21; 13:20; 16:14, RV, "take"; **2 John 10**; in Mark 14:65, RV, "received (Him with blows of their hands)"; this has been styled a vulgarism; (II) metaphorically, of the word of God, Matt. 13:20; Mark 4:16; the sayings of Christ, John 12:48; the witness of Christ, John 3:11; a hundredfold in this life, and eternal life in the world to come, Mark 10:30; mercy, Heb. 4:16, RV, "may receive" (KJV, "may obtain"); a person (*prosopon*), Luke 20:21, "acceptest," and Gal. 2:6, "accepteth," an expression used in the OT either in the sense of being gracious or kind to a person, e.g., Gen. 19:21; 32:20, or (negatively) in the sense of being impartial, e.g., Lev. 19:15; Deut. 10:17; this latter is the meaning in the two NT passages just mentioned. *Lambano* and *prosopon* are combined in the nouns *prosopolempsia*, "respect of persons," and *prosopolemptes*, "respecter of persons," and in the verb *prosopolempto*, "to have respect of persons".

House *oikia* (3614); in Attic law *oikos* denoted the whole estate, *oikia* stood for the dwelling only; this distinction was largely lost in later Greek. In the NT it denotes (a) "a house, a dwelling," e.g., Matt. 2:11; 5:15; 7:24-27; 2 Tim. 2:20; **2 John 10**; it is not used of the Tabernacle or the Temple; (b) metaphorically, the heavenly abode, spoken of by the Lord as "My Father's house," John 14:2, the eternal dwelling place of believers; the body as the dwelling place of the soul, 2 Cor. 5:1; similarly the resurrection body of believers (*id.*); property, e.g., Mark 12:40; by metonymy, the inhabitants of a house, a household, e.g., Matt. 12:25; John 4:53; 1 Cor. 16:15.

Bid *lego*, "to say," is translated "bid" and "biddeth" in the KJV of **2 John 10, 11**; RV, "give (him no greeting)," "giveth (him greeting).

God speed *chairo* (5463), "to rejoice," is thrice used as a formula of salutation in Acts 15:23, KJV, "send greeting," RV, "greeting"; so 23:26; Jas. 1:1. In **2 John 10, 11**, the RV substitutes the phrase (to give) "greeting," for the KJV (to bid) "God speed."

11 For he that biddeth him God speed is partaker of his evil deeds.

Biddeth *see* **Bid** at *2 John 10*.

God speed *see 2 John 10*.

Partaker *koinoneo* (2841), "to have a share of, to share with, take part in," is translated "to be partaker of" in 1 Tim. 5:22; Heb. 2:14 (1st part), KJV, "are partakers of," RV, "are sharers in"; 1 Pet. 4:13; **2 John 11**, RV, "partaketh in" (KJV, "is partaker of"); in the passive voice in Rom. 15:27.

Evil *poneros* (4190), akin to *ponos*, "labor, toil," denotes "evil that causes labor, pain, sorrow, malignant evil"; it is used (a) with the meaning bad, worthless, in the physical sense, Matt. 7:17-18; in the moral or ethical sense, "evil," wicked; of persons, e.g., Matt. 7:11; Luke 6:45; Acts 17:5; 2 Thess. 3:2; 2 Tim. 3:13; of "evil" spirits, e.g., Matt. 12:45; Luke 7:21; Acts 19:12-13, 15-16; of a generation, Matt. 12:39, 45; 16:4; Luke 11:29; of things, e.g., Matt. 5:11; 6:23; 20:15; Mark 7:22; Luke 11:34; John 3:19; 7:7; Acts 18:14; Gal. 1:4; Col. 1:21; 1 Tim. 6:4; 2 Tim. 4:18; Heb. 3:12; 10:22; Jas. 2:4; 4:16; 1 John 3:12; **2 John 11**; 3 John 10; (b) with the meaning toilsome, painful, Eph. 5:16; 6:13; Rev. 16:2. Cf. *poneria*, "iniquity, wickedness."

12 Having many things to write unto you, I would not *write* with paper and ink: but I trust to come unto you, and speak face to face, that our joy may be full.

Paper *chartes* (5489), "a sheet of paper made of strips of papyrus" (whence Eng., "paper"), Eng., "chart," "charter," etc.; the word is used in **2 John 12**. The papyrus reed grew in ancient times in great profusion in the Nile and was used as a material for writing. From Egypt its use spread to other countries and it was the universal material for writing in general in Greece and Italy during the most flourishing periods of their literature. The pith of the stem of the plant was cut into thin strips, placed side by side to form a sheath. Another layer was laid upon this at right angles to it. The two layers were united by moisture and pressure and frequently with the addition of glue. The sheets, after being dried and polished, were ready for use. Normally, the writing is on that side of the papyrus on which the fibers lie horizontally, parallel to the length of the roll, but where the material was scarce the writer used the other side also (cf. Rev. 5:1).

Papyrus continued to be used until the seventh cent. AD, when the conquest of Egypt by the Arabs led to the disuse of the material for literary purposes and the use of vellum till the 12th century.

Ink *melan* (3188), the neuter of the adjective *melas*, "black" (see Matt. 5:36; Rev. 6:5, 12), denotes "ink," 2 Cor. 3:3; **2 John 12**; 3 John 13.

Face to face *stoma* (4750), akin to *stomachos* (which originally meant "a throat, gullet"), is used (a) of "the mouth" of man, e.g., Matt. 15:11; of animals, e.g., Matt. 17:27; 2 Tim. 4:17 (figurative); Heb. 11:33; Jas. 3:3; Rev. 13:2 (2nd occurrence); (b) figuratively of "inanimate things," of the "edge" of a sword, Luke 21:24; Heb. 11:34; of the earth, Rev. 12:16; (c) figuratively, of the "mouth," as the organ of speech, (1) of Christ's words, e.g., Matt. 13:35; Luke 11:54; Acts 8:32; 22:14; 1 Pet. 2:22; (2) of human, e.g., Matt. 18:16; 21:16; Luke 1:64; Rev. 14:5; as emanating from the heart, Matt. 12:34; Rom. 10:8, 9; of prophetic ministry through the Holy Spirit, Luke 1:70; Acts 1:16; 3:18; 4:25; of the destructive policy of two world potentates at the end of this age, Rev. 13:2, 5, 6; 16:13 (twice); of shameful speaking, Eph. 4:29 and Col. 3:8; (3) of the Devil speaking as a dragon or serpent, Rev. 12:15, 16; 16:13; (d) figuratively, in the phrase *stoma pros stoma* "face to face" (lit., "mouth to mouth"), **2 John 12**; 3 John 14; (e) metaphorically, of "the utterances of the Lord, in judgment," 2 Thess. 2:8; Rev. 1:16; 2:16; 19:15, 21; of His judgment upon a local church for its lukewarmness, Rev. 3:16; (f) by metonymy, for "speech," Matt. 18:16; Luke 19:22; 21:15; 2 Cor. 13:1.

Full *pleroo* (4137), signifies (1) "to fill"; (2) "to fulfill, complete," (a) of time, e.g., Mark 1:15; Luke 21:24; John 7:8 (KJV, "full come"); Acts 7:23, RV, "he was wellnigh forty years old" (KJV, "was full," etc.), lit., "the time of forty years was fulfilled to him"; v. 30, KJV, "were expired"; 9:23; 24:27 (KJV, "after two years"; RV, "when two years were fulfilled"); (b) of number, Rev. 6:11; (c) of good pleasure, 2 Thess. 1:11; (d) of joy, Phil. 2:2; in the passive voice, "to be fulfilled," John 3:29 and 17:13; in the following the verb is rendered "fulfilled" in the RV, for the KJV, "full," John 15:11; 16:24; 1 John 1:4; **2 John 12**; (e) of obedience, 2 Cor. 10:6; (f) of works, Rev. 3:2; (g) of the future Passover, Luke 22:16; (h) of sayings, prophecies, etc., e.g., Matt. 1:22 (twelve times in Matt., two in Mark, four in Luke, eight in John, two in Acts); Jas. 2:23; in Col. 1:25 the word signifies to preach "fully," to complete the ministry of the gospel appointed.

13 The children of thy elect sister greet thee. Amen.

Elect *see 2 John 1.*

Sister *see* **Lady** at *2 John 1.*

Greet *aspazomai* (782), signifies "to greet welcome," or "salute." In the KJV it is chiefly rendered by either of the verbs "to greet" or "to salute." "There is little doubt that the revisers have done wisely in giving 'salute' ... in the passages where KJV has 'greet.' For the cursory reader is sure to imagine a difference of Greek and of meaning when he finds, e.g., in Phil. 4:21, 'Salute every saint in Christ Jesus. The brethren which are with me greet you,' or in 3 John 14, 'Our friends salute thee. Greet the friends by name'" (*Hastings' Bible Dic.*). In Acts 25:13 the meaning virtually is "to pay his respects to." In two passages the renderings vary otherwise; in Acts 20:1, of bidding farewell, KJV, "embraced them," RV, "took leave of them," or, as Ramsay translates it, "bade them farewell"; in Heb. 11:13, of welcoming promises, KJV, "embraced," RV, "greeted." The verb is used as a technical term for conveying "greetings" at the close of a letter, often by an amanuensis, e.g., Rom. 16:22, the only instance of the use of the first person in this respect in the NT; see also 1 Cor. 16:19, 20; 2 Cor. 13:13; Phil. 4:22; Col. 4:10-15; 1 Thess. 5:26; 2 Tim. 4:21; Titus 3:15; Philem. 23; Heb. 13:24; 1 Pet. 5:13, 14; **2 John 13**. This special use is largely illustrated in the papyri, one example of this showing how keenly the absence of the greeting was felt. The papyri also illustrate the use of the addition "by name," when several persons are included in the greeting, as in 3 John 14 (Moulton and Milligan, *Vocab*).

3 John

1 The elder unto the wellbeloved Gaius, whom I love in the truth.

Wellbeloved *agapetos* (27), from *agapao*, "to love," is used of Christ as loved by God, e.g., Matt. 3:17; of believers (ditto), e.g., Rom. 1:7; of believers, one of another, 1 Cor. 4:14; often, as a form of address, e.g., 1 Cor. 10:14. Whenever the KJV has "dearly beloved," the RV has "beloved"; so, "well beloved" in **3 John 1**; in 1 John 2:7, KJV, "brethren" (*adelphos*), the RV has "beloved," according to the mss. which have *agapetos*.

2 Beloved, I wish above all things that thou mayest prosper and be in health, even as thy soul prospereth.

Wish *euchomai* (2172), "to pray (to God)," is used with this meaning in 2 Cor. 13:7; v. 9, RV, "pray" (KJV, "wish"); Jas. 5:16; **3 John 2**, RV, "pray" (KJV, wish). Even when the RV and KJV translate by "I would," Acts 26:29, or "wished for," Acts 27:29 (RV, marg., "prayed"), or "could wish," Rom. 9:3 (RV, marg., "could pray"), the indication is that "prayer" is involved.

Prosper, Prospereth *euodoo* (2137), "to help on one's way" (*eu*, "well," *hodos*, "a way or journey"), is used in the passive voice signifying "to have a prosperous journey," Rom. 1:10; metaphorically, "to prosper, be prospered," 1 Cor. 16:2, RV, "(as) he may prosper," KJV, "(as God) hath prospered (him)," lit., "in whatever he may be prospered," i.e., in material things; the continuous tense suggests the successive circumstances of varying prosperity as week follows week; in **3 John 2**, of the "prosperity" of physical and spiritual health.

Health *hugianio* (5198), denotes "to be healthy, sound, in good health" (Eng., "hygiene"), rendered "mayest be in health," in **3 John 2**; rendered "safe and sound" in Luke 15:27.

Soul *psuche* (5590), denotes "the breath, the breath of life," then "the soul," in its various meanings. The NT uses "may be analyzed approximately as follows:

"(a) the natural life of the body, Matt. 2:20; Luke 12:22; Acts 20:10; Rev. 8:9; 12:11; cf. Lev. 17:11; 2 Sam. 14:7; Esth. 8:11; (b) the immaterial, invisible part of man, Matt. 10:28; Acts 2:27; cf. 1 Kings 17:21; (c) the disembodied (or "unclothed" or "naked," 2 Cor. 5:3, 4) man, Rev. 6:9; (d) the seat of personality, Luke 9:24, explained as = "own self," v. 25; Heb. 6:19; 10:39; cf. Isa. 53:10 with 1 Tim. 2:6; (e) the seat of the sentient element in man, that by which he perceives, reflects, feels, desires, Matt. 11:29; Luke 1:46; 2:35; Acts 14:2, 22; cf. Ps. 84:2; 139:14; Isa. 26:9; (f) the seat of will and purpose, Matt. 22:37; Acts 4:32; Eph. 6:6; Phil. 1:27; Heb. 12:3; cf. Num. 21:4; Deut. 11:13; (g) the seat of appetite, Rev. 18:14; cf. Ps. 107:9; Prov. 6:30; Isa. 5:14 ("desire"); 29:8; (h) persons, individuals, Acts 2:41, 43; Rom. 2:9; Jas. 5:20; 1 Pet. 3:20; 2 Pet. 2:14; cf. Gen. 12:5; 14:21 ("persons"); Lev. 4:2 ('any one'); Ezek. 27:13; of dead bodies, Num. 6:6, lit., "dead soul"; and of animals, Lev. 24:18, lit., "soul for soul"; (i) the equivalent of the personal pronoun, used for emphasis and effect: 1st person, John 10:24 ("us"); Heb. 10:38; cf. Gen. 12:13; Num. 23:10; Jud. 16:30; Ps. 120:2 ("me"); 2nd person, 2 Cor. 12:15; Heb. 13:17; Jas. 1:21; 1 Pet. 1:9; 2:25; cf. Lev. 17:11; 26:15; 1 Sam. 1:26; 3rd person, 1 Pet. 4:19; 2 Pet. 2:8; cf. Exod. 30:12; Job 32:2, Heb. "soul," Sept. "self"; (j) an animate creature, human or other, 1 Cor. 15:45; Rev. 16:3; cf. Gen. 1:24; 2:7, 19; (k) "the inward man," the seat of the new life, Luke 21:19 (cf. Matt. 10:39); 1 Pet. 2:11; **3 John 2**."

3 For I rejoiced greatly, when the brethren came and testified of the truth that is in thee, even as thou walkest in the truth.

Rejoiced *chairo* (5463), "to rejoice," is most frequently so translated. As to this verb, the following are grounds and occasions for "rejoicing," on the part of believers: in the Lord, Phil. 3:1; 4:4; His incarnation, Luke 1:14; His power, Luke 13:17; His presence with the Father, John 14:28; His presence with them, John 16:22; 20:20; His ultimate triumph, 8:56; hearing the gospel, Acts 13:48; their salvation, Acts 8:39; receiving the Lord, Luke 19:6; their enrollment in Heaven, Luke 10:20; their liberty in Christ, Acts 15:31; their hope, Rom. 12:12 (cf. Rom. 5:2; Rev. 19:7); their prospect of reward, Matt. 5:12; the obedience and godly conduct of fellow believers, Rom. 16:19, RV, "I rejoice" (KJV, "I am glad"); 2 Cor. 7:7, 9; 13:9; Col. 2:5; 1 Thess. 3:9; 2 John 4; **3 John 3**; the proclamation of Christ, Phil. 1:18; the gospel harvest, John 4:36; suffering with Christ, Acts 5:41; 1 Pet. 4:13; suffering in the cause of the gospel, 2 Cor. 13:9 (1st part); Phil. 2:17 (1st part); Col. 1:24; in persecutions, trials and afflictions, Matt. 5:12; Luke 6:23; 2 Cor. 6:10; the manifestation of grace, Acts 11:23; meeting with fellow believers, 1 Cor. 16:17, RV, "I rejoice"; Phil. 2:28; receiving tokens of love and fellowship, Phil. 4:10; the "rejoicing" of others, Rom. 12:15; 2 Cor. 7:13; learning of the well-being of others, 2 Cor. 7:16.

Greatly *lian* (3029), "very, exceedingly," is rendered "greatly" in Matt. 27:14, of wonder 2 Tim. 4:15, of opposition; 2 John 4 and **3 John 3**, of joy.

Testified *martureo* (3140), denotes (I) "to be a *martus*," or "to bear witness to," sometimes rendered "to testify"; it is used of the witness (a) of God the Father to Christ, John 5:32, 37; 8:18 (2nd part); 1 John 5:9, 10; to others, Acts 13:22; 15:8; Heb. 11:2, 4 (twice), 5, 39; (b) of Christ, John 3:11, 32; 4:44; 5:31; 7:7; 8:13, 14, 18 (1st part); 13:21; 18:37; Acts 14:3; 1 Tim. 6:13; Rev. 22:18, 20; of the Holy Spirit, to Christ, John 15:26; Heb. 10:15; 1 John 5:7, 8, RV, which rightly omits the latter part of v. 7 (it was a marginal gloss which crept into the original text); it finds no support in Scripture; (c) of the Scriptures, to Christ, John 5:39; Heb. 7:8, 17; (d) of the works of Christ, to Himself, and of the circumstances connected with His death, John 5:36; 10:25; 1 John 5:8; (e) of prophets and apostles, to the righteousness of God, Rom. 3:21; to Christ, John 1:7, 8, 15, 32, 34; 3:26; 5:33, RV; 15:27; 19:35; 21:24; Acts 10:43; 23:11; 1 Cor. 15:15; 1 John 1:2; 4:14; Rev. 1:2; to doctrine, Acts 26:22 (in some texts, so KJV); to the Word of God, Rev. 1:2; (f) of others, concerning Christ, Luke 4:22; John 4:39; 12:17; (g) of believers to one another, John 3:28; 2 Cor. 8:3; Gal. 4:15; Col. 4:13; 1 Thess. 2:11 (in some texts); **3 John 3, 6, 12** (2nd part); (h) of the apostle Paul concerning Israel, Rom. 10:2; (i) of an angel, to the churches, Rev. 22:16; (j) of unbelievers, concerning themselves, Matt. 23:31; concerning Christ, John 18:23; concerning others, John 2:25; Acts 22:5; 26:5; (II) "to give a good report, to approve of," Acts 6:3; 10:22; 16:2; 22:12; 1 Tim. 5:10; **3 John 12** (1st part); some would put Luke 4:22 here.

Truth *aletheia* (225), "truth," is used (a) objectively, signifying "the reality lying at the basis of an appearance; the manifested, veritable essence of a matter" (Cremer), e.g., Rom. 9:1; 2 Cor. 11:10; especially of Christian doctrine, e.g., Gal. 2:5, where "the truth of the gospel" denotes the "true" teaching of the gospel, in contrast to perversions of it; Rom. 1:25, where "the truth of God" may be "the truth concerning God" or "God whose existence is a verity"; but in Rom. 15:8 "the truth of God" is indicative of His faithfulness in the fulfillment of His promises as exhibited in Christ; the word has an absolute force in John 14:6; 17:17; 18:37, 38; in Eph. 4:21, where the RV, "even as truth is in Jesus," gives the correct rendering, the meaning is not merely ethical "truth," but "truth" in all its fullness and scope, as embodied in Him; He was the perfect expression of the truth; this is virtually equivalent to His statement in John 14:6; (b) subjectively, "truthfulness," "truth," not merely verbal, but sincerity and integrity of character, John 8:44; **3 John 3**, RV; (c) in phrases, e.g., "in truth" (*epi*, "on the basis of"), Mark 12:14; Luke 20:21; with *en*, "in," 2 Cor. 6:7; Col. 1:6; 1 Tim. 2:7, RV (KJV, "in ... verity"), 1 John 3:18; 2 John 1, 3, 4.

4 I have no greater joy than to hear that my children walk in truth.

Greater *meizoteros* (3186), a double comparative of *megas*, is used in **3 John 4**, of joy.

5 Beloved, thou doest faithfully whatsoever thou doest to the brethren, and to strangers;

Doest *ergazomai* (2038), denotes "to work" (*ergon*, "work"). In Gal. 6:10 the RV renders it "let us work," for KJV, "let us do"; in **3 John 5**, "thou doest."

Faithfully *pistos* (4103), a verbal adjective, akin to *peitho*, is used in two senses, (a) passive, "faithful, to be trusted, reliable," said of God, e.g., 1 Cor. 1:9; 10:13; 2 Cor. 1:18 (KJV, "true"); 2 Tim. 2:13; Heb. 10:23; 11:11; 1 Pet. 4:19; 1 John 1:9; of Christ, e.g., 2 Thess. 3:3; Heb. 2:17; 3:2; Rev. 1:5; 3:14; 19:11; of the words of God, e.g., Acts 13:34, "sure"; 1 Tim. 1:15; 3:1 (KJV, "true"); 4:9; 2 Tim. 2:11; Titus 1:9; 3:8; Rev. 21:5; 22:6; of servants of the Lord, Matt. 24:45; 25:21, 23; Acts 16:15; 1 Cor. 4:2, 17; 7:25; Eph. 6:21; Col. 1:7; 4:7, 9; 1 Tim. 1:12; 3:11; 2 Tim. 2:2; Heb. 3:5; 1 Pet. 5:12; **3 John 5**; Rev. 2:13; 17:14; of believers, Eph. 1:1; Col. 1:2; (b) active, signifying "believing, trusting, relying," e.g., Acts 16:1 (feminine); 2 Cor. 6:15; Gal. 3:9 seems best taken in this respect, as the context lays stress upon Abraham's "faith" in God, rather than upon his "faithfulness." In John 20:27 the context requires the active sense, as the Lord is reproaching Thomas for his want of "faith." With regard to believers, they are spoken of sometimes in the active sense, sometimes in the passive, i.e., sometimes as believers, sometimes as "faithful." See Lightfoot on Galatians, p. 155.

Strangers *xenos* (3581), "strange", denotes "a stranger, foreigner," Matt. 25:35, 38, 43, 44; 27:7; Acts 17:21; Eph. 2:12, 19; Heb. 11:13; **3 John 5**.

6 Which have borne witness of thy charity before the church: whom if thou bring forward on their journey after a godly sort, thou shalt do well:

Witness *see* **Testified** at *3 John 3*.

Bring *propempo* (4311), "to send forth, to bring on one's way," Acts 15:3; 20:38, RV; 21:5; Rom. 15:24; 1 Cor. 16:6, 11; 2 Cor. 1:16; Titus 3:13; **3 John 6**.

Journey *propempo* (4311), "to send before or forth" (*pro*, "before," *pempo*, "to send"), also means "to set forward on a journey, to escort"; in 1 Cor. 16:6, "may set (me) forward on my journey," RV [KJV, "may bring (me) etc."]; so Titus 3:13, and **3 John 6**.

Godly In **3 John 6**, where the KJV translates the adverb *axios*, with the noun *theos*, "after a godly sort," the RV rightly substitutes "worthily of God."

7 Because that for his name's sake they went forth, taking nothing of the Gentiles.

Name *onoma* (3686), is used (I) in general of the "name" by which a person or thing is called, e.g., Mark 3:16, 17, "(He) surnamed," lit., "(He added) the name"; 14:32, lit., "(of which) the name (was)"; Luke 1:63; John 18:10, sometimes translated "named," e.g., Luke 8:5, "named (Zacharias)," lit., "by name"; in the same verse, "named (Elizabeth)," lit., "the name of her," an elliptical phrase, with "was" understood; Acts 8:9, RV, "by name," 10:1; the "name" is put for the reality in Rev. 3:1; in Phil. 2:9, the "Name" represents "the title and dignity" of the Lord, as in Eph. 1:21 and Heb. 1:4;

(II) for all that a "name" implies, of authority, character, rank, majesty, power, excellence, etc., of everything that the "name" covers: (a) of the "Name" of God as expressing His attributes, etc., e.g., Matt. 6:9; Luke 1:49; John 12:28; 17:6, 26; Rom. 15:9; 1 Tim. 6:1; Heb. 13:15; Rev. 13:6; (b) of the "Name" of Christ, e.g., Matt. 10:22; 19:29; John 1:12; 2:23; 3:18; Acts 26:9; Rom. 1:5; Jas. 2:7; 1 John 3:23; **3 John 7**; Rev. 2:13; 3:8; also the phrases rendered "in the name"; these may be analyzed as follows: (1) representing the authority of Christ, e.g., Matt. 18:5 (with *epi*, "on the ground of My authority"); so Matt. 24:5 (falsely) and parallel passages; as substantiated by the Father, John 14:26; 16:23 (last clause), RV; (2) in the power of (with *en*, "in"), e.g., Mark 16:17; Luke 10:17; Acts 3:6; 4:10; 16:18; Jas. 5:14; (3) in acknowledgement or confession of, e.g., Acts 4:12; 8:16; 9:27, 28; (4) in recognition of the authority of (sometimes combined with the thought of relying or resting on), Matt. 18:20; cf. 28:19; Acts 8:16; 9:2 (*eis*, "into"); John 14:13; 15:16; Eph. 5:20; Col. 3:17; (5) owing to the fact that one is called by Christ's "Name" or is identified with Him, e.g. 1 Pet. 4:14 (with *en*, "in"); with *heneken*, "for the sake of," e.g., Matt. 19:29; with *dia*, "on account of," Matt. 10:22; 24:9; Mark 13:13; Luke 21:17; John 15:21; 1 John 2:12; Rev. 2:3.

Gentiles *ethnikos* (1482), is used as a noun, and translated "Gentiles" in the RV of Matt. 5:47; 6:7; "the Gentile" in 18:17 (KJV, "an heathen man"); "the Gentiles" in **3 John 7**, KJV and RV.

8 We therefore ought to receive such, that we might be fellowhelpers to the truth.

Ought *opheilo* (3784), "to owe," is translated "ought," with various personal pronouns, in John 13:14; 19:7; Acts 17:29; Rom. 15:1; Heb. 5:3, KJV (RV, "he is bound"); 5:12; 1 John 3:16; 4:11; **3 John 8**; with other subjects in 1 Cor. 11:7, 10; 2 Cor. 12:14; Eph. 5:28; 1 John 2:6.

Receive *hupolambano* (5274), "to take or bear up" (*hupo*, "under"), "to receive," is rendered "received" in Acts 1:9, of the cloud at the Ascension; in **3 John 8**, RV, "welcome" (KJV, "receive"); *apolambano* (618), in some mss. **3 John 8**.

Fellowhelpers *sunergos* (4904), an adjective, "a fellow worker," is translated "helper" in the KJV of Rom. 16:3, 9, RV, "fellow worker"; in 2 Cor. 1:24, KJV and RV, "helpers"; in 2 Cor. 8:23, KJV, "fellow helper," RV, "fellow worker"; so the plural in **3 John 8**.

9 I wrote unto the church: but Diotrephes, who loveth to have the preeminence among them, receiveth us not.

Preeminence *philoproteuo* (5383), lit., "to love to be preeminent" (*philos*, "loving"), "to strive to be first," is said of Diotrephes, **3 John 9**.

Receiveth *epidechomai* (1926), lit., "to accept besides" (*epi*, "upon"), "to accept" (found in the papyri, of accepting the terms of a lease), is used in the sense of accepting in **3 John 9**; in v. **10**, in the sense of "receiving" with hospitality, in each verse said negatively concerning Diotrephes.

10 Wherefore, if I come, I will remember his deeds which he doeth, prating against us with malicious words: and not content therewith, neither doth he himself receive the brethren, and forbiddeth them that would, and casteth *them* out of the church.

Wherefore Some phrases introduced by the preposition *dia*, "on account of," *dia touto*, "on account of this," e.g., Matt. 12:31; Rom. 5:12; Eph. 1:15; **3 John 10**; *dia hen* (the accusative feminine of *hos*, "who"), "on account of which" (*aitia*, "a cause," being understood), e.g., Acts 10:21 (with *aitia*, expressed, Titus 1:13; Heb. 2:11); *dia ti* "on account of what?" (sometimes as one word, *diati*) e.g., Luke 19:23; Rom. 9:32; 2 Cor. 11:11; Rev. 17:7.

Remember *hupomimnesko* (5279), signifies "to cause one to remember, put one in mind of," John 14:26, "shall ... bring ... to (your) remembrance"; 2 Tim. 2:14, "put ... in remembrance"; Titus 3:1, "put ... in mind"; **3 John 10**, RV, "I will bring to remembrance" (KJV, "I will remember"); Jude 5, "to put ... in remembrance." In Luke 22:61 it is used in the passive voice, "(Peter) remembered," lit., "was put in mind."

Prating *phluareo* (5396), signifies "to talk nonsense" (from *phluo*, "to babble"; cf. the adjective *phluaros*, "babbling, garrulous, tattlers," 1 Tim. 5:13), "to raise false accusations," **3 John 10**.

Malicious *poneros* (4190), is translated "wicked" in the KJV and RV in Matt. 13:49; 18:32; 25:26; Luke 19:22; Acts 18:14; 1 Cor. 5:13; in the following the RV substitutes "evil" for KJV, "wicked": Matt. 12:45 (twice); 13:19; 16:4; Luke 11:26; Col. 1:21; 2 Thess. 3:2; and in the following, where Satan is mentioned as "the (or that) evil one": Matt. 13:38; Eph. 6:16; 1 John 2:13, 14; 3:12 (1st part); 5:18; in v. 19 for KJV, "wickedness"; he is so called also in KJV and RV in John 17:15; 2 Thess. 3:3; KJV only in Luke 11:4; in **3 John 10**, KJV, the word is translated "malicious," RV, "wicked."

Content *arkeo* (174), primarily signifies "to be sufficient, to be possessed of sufficient strength, to be strong, to be enough for a thing"; hence, "to defend, ward off"; in the middle voice, "to be satisfied, contented with," Luke 3:14, with wages; 1 Tim. 6:8, with food and raiment; Heb. 13:5, with "such things as ye have"; negatively of Diotrephes, in **3 John 10**, "not content therewith."

Receive *see* **Receiveth** at *3 John 9*.

Casteth *ekballo* (1544), "to cast out of, from, forth," is very frequent in the Gospels and Acts; elsewhere, in Gal. 4:30; **3 John 10**; in Jas. 2:25, "sent out"; in Rev. 11:2, "leave out" (marg., "cast without").

11 Beloved, follow not that which is evil, but that which is good. He that doeth good is of God: but he that doeth evil hath not seen God.

Follow *mimeomai* (3401), "a mimic, an actor" (Eng., "mime," etc.), is always translated "to imitate" in the RV, for KJV, "to follow," (a) of imitating the conduct of missionaries, 2 Thess. 3:7, 9; the faith of spiritual guides, Heb. 13:7; (b) that which is good, **3 John 11**. The verb is always used in exhortations, and always in the continuous tense, suggesting a constant habit or practice.

Good *agathos* (18), describes that which, being "good" in its character or constitution, is beneficial in its effect; it is used (a) of things physical, e.g., a tree, Matt. 7:17; ground, Luke 8:8; (b) in a moral sense, frequently of persons and things. God is essentially, absolutely and consummately "good," Matt. 19:17; Mark 10:18; Luke 18:19. To certain persons the word is applied in Matt. 20:15; 25:21, 23; Luke 19:17; 23:50; John 7:12; Acts 11:24; Titus 2:5; in a general application, Matt. 5:45; 12:35; Luke 6:45; Rom. 5:7; 1 Pet. 2:18. The neuter of the adjective with the definite article signifies that which is "good," lit., "the good," as being morally honorable, pleasing to God, and therefore beneficial. Christians are to prove it, Rom. 12:2; to cleave to it, 12:9; to do it, 13:3; Gal. 6:10; 1 Pet. 3:11 (here, and here only, the article is absent); John 5:29 (here, the neuter plural is used, "the good things"); to work it, Rom. 2:10; Eph. 4:28; 6:8; to follow after it, 1 Thess. 5:15; to be zealous of it, 1 Pet. 3:13; to imitate it, **3 John 11**; to overcome evil with it, Rom. 12:21. Governmental authorities are ministers of "good," i.e., that which is salutary, suited to the course of human affairs, Rom. 13:4. In Philem. 14, "thy goodness," RV (lit., "thy good"), means "thy benefit." As to Matt. 19:17, "why askest thou Me concerning that which is good?" the RV follows the most ancient mss. The neuter plural is also used of

"Those who act selfishly do so because they have no fellowship with God."

G. CAMPBELL MORGAN

material "goods," riches, etc., Luke 1:53; 12:18, 19; 16:25; Gal. 6:6 (of temporal supplies); in Rom. 10:15; Heb. 9:11; 10:1, the "good" things are the benefits provided through the sacrifice of Christ, in regard both to those conferred through the gospel and to those of the coming messianic kingdom.

Doeth good *agathopoieo* (15), is used (a) in a general way, "to do well," 1 Pet. 2:15, 20; 3:6, 17; **3 John 11**; (b) with pointed reference "to the benefit of another," Luke 6:9, 33, 35; in Mark 3:4 the parts of the word are separated in some mss. Some mss. have it in Acts 14:17. Cf. the noun *agathopoiia*, "well-doing," 1 Pet. 4:19, and the adjective *agathopoios*, "doing well," 1 Pet. 2:14.

Doeth evil *kakopoieo* (2554), signifies "to do evil," Mark 3:4 (RV, "to do harm"); so, Luke 6:9; in **3 John 11**, "doeth evil"; in 1 Pet. 3:17, "evil doing."

12 Demetrius hath good report of all *men*, and of the truth itself: yea, and we *also* bear record; and ye know that our record is true.

Report *martureo* (3140), "to be a witness, bear witness, testify," signifies, in the passive voice, "to be well testified of, to have a good report," Acts 6:3, "of good (KJV, honest) report," lit., "being well testified of"; 10:22; 16:2; 22:12; 1 Tim. 5:10; in Heb. 11:2, 39, KJV, "obtained a good report" (RV, "had witness borne to them"); in **3 John 12**, KJV "hath good report" (RV, "hath the witness"), lit., "witness hath been borne."

Record *marturia* (3141), "testimony, a bearing witness," is translated "witness" in Mark 14:55, 56, 59; Luke 22:71; John 1:7, 19 (RV); 3:11, 32 and 33 (RV); 5:31, 32, 34 (RV), 36; RV in 8:13, 14, 17; 19:35; 21:24; KJV in Titus 1:13; KJV and RV in 1 John 5:9 (thrice), 10a; RV in 10b, 11; **3 John 12**. *See also* **Testified** at *3 John 3*.

13 I had many things to write, but I will not with ink and pen write unto thee:

Will not "I am unwilling" is the RV rendering of *thelo*, "to will," with the negative *ou*, in **3 John 13** (KJV, "I will not").

Ink *melan* (3188), the neuter of the adjective *melas*, "black" (see Matt. 5:36; Rev. 6:5, 12), denotes "ink," 2 Cor. 3:3; 2 John 12; **3 John 13**.

Pen *kalamos* (2563), "a reed, reed pipe, flute, staff, measuring rod," is used of a "writing-reed" or "pen" in **3 John 13**. This was used on papyrus. Different instruments were used on different materials; the *kalamos* may have been used also on leather. "Metal pens in the form of a reed or quill have been found in the so-called Grave of Aristotle at Eretria."

14 But I trust I shall shortly see thee, and we shall speak face to face. Peace *be* to thee. *Our* friends salute thee. Greet the friends by name.

Shortly *eutheos* (2112), "straightway, directly," is translated "shortly" in **3 John 14**. The general use of the word suggests something sooner than "shortly."

Face to face *stoma* (4750), akin to *stomachos* (which originally meant "a throat, gullet"), is used (a) of "the mouth" of man, e.g., Matt. 15:11; of animals, e.g., Matt. 17:27; 2 Tim. 4:17 (figurative); Heb. 11:33; Jas. 3:3; Rev. 13:2 (2nd occurrence); (b) figuratively of "inanimate things," of the "edge" of a sword, Luke 21:24; Heb. 11:34; of the earth, Rev. 12:16; (c) figuratively, of the "mouth," as the organ of speech, (1) of Christ's words, e.g., Matt. 13:35; Luke 11:54; Acts 8:32; 22:14; 1 Pet. 2:22; (2) of human, e.g., Matt. 18:16; 21:16; Luke 1:64; Rev. 14:5; as emanating from the heart, Matt. 12:34; Rom. 10:8, 9; of prophetic ministry through the Holy Spirit, Luke 1:70; Acts 1:16; 3:18; 4:25; of the destructive policy of two world potentates at the end of this age, Rev. 13:2, 5, 6; 16:13 (twice); of shameful speaking, Eph. 4:29 and Col. 3:8; (3) of the Devil speaking as a dragon or serpent, Rev. 12:15, 16; 16:13; (d) figuratively, in the phrase *stoma pros stoma*, "face to face" (lit., "mouth to mouth"), 2 John 12; **3 John 14**; (e) metaphorically, of "the utterances of the Lord, in judgment," 2 Thess. 2:8; Rev. 1:16; 2:16; 19:15, 21; of His judgment upon a local church for its lukewarmness, Rev. 3:16; (f) by metonymy, for "speech," Matt. 18:16; Luke 19:22; 21:15; 2 Cor. 13:1.

Friends *philos* (5384), primarily an adjective, denoting "loved, dear, or friendly," became used as a noun, (a) masculine, Matt. 11:19; fourteen times in Luke (once feminine, 15:9); six in John; three in Acts; two in James, 2:23, "the friend of God"; 4:4, "a friend of the world"; **3 John 14** (twice); (b) feminine, Luke 15:9, "her friends."

Salute, Greet *aspazomai* (782), signifies "to greet welcome," or "salute." In the KJV it is chiefly rendered by either of the verbs "to greet" or "to salute." "There is little doubt that the revisers have done wisely in giving 'salute' ... in the passages where KJV has 'greet.' For the cursory reader is sure to imagine a difference of Greek and of meaning when he finds, e.g., in Phil. 4:21, 'Salute every saint in Christ Jesus. The brethren which are with me greet you,' or in **3 John 14**, 'Our friends salute thee. Greet the friends by name'" (*Hastings' Bible Dic.*). In Acts 25:13 the meaning virtually is "to pay his respects to." In two passages the renderings vary otherwise; in Acts 20:1, of bidding farewell, KJV, "embraced them," RV, "took leave of them," or, as Ramsay translates it, "bade them farewell"; in Heb. 11:13, of welcoming promises, KJV, "embraced," RV, "greeted." The verb is used as a technical term for conveying "greetings" at the close of a letter, often by an amanuensis, e.g., Rom. 16:22, the only instance of the use of the first person in this respect in the NT; see also 1 Cor. 16:19, 20; 2 Cor. 13:13; Phil. 4:22; Col. 4:10-15; 1 Thess. 5:26; 2 Tim. 4:21; Titus 3:15; Philem. 23; Heb. 13:24; 1 Pet. 5:13, 14; 2 John 13. This special use is largely illustrated in the papyri, one example of this showing how keenly the absence of the greeting was felt. The papyri also illustrate the use of the addition "by name," when several persons are included in the greeting, as in **3 John 14** (Moulton and Milligan, *Vocab*).

Jude

1 Jude, the servant of Jesus Christ, and brother of James, to them that are sanctified by God the Father, and preserved in Jesus Christ, *and* called:

Servant *doulos* (1401), an adjective, signifying "in bondage," Rom. 6:19 (neuter plural, agreeing with *mele*, "members"), is used as a noun, and as the most common and general word for "servant," frequently indicating subjection without the idea of bondage; it is used (a) of natural conditions, e.g., Matt. 8:9; 1 Cor. 7:21, 22 (1st part); Eph. 6:5; Col. 4:1; 1 Tim. 6:1; frequently in the four Gospels; (b) metaphorically of spiritual, moral and ethical conditions: "servants" (1) of God, e.g., Acts 16:17; Titus 1:1; 1 Pet. 2:16; Rev. 7:3; 15:3; the perfect example being Christ Himself, Phil. 2:7; (2) of Christ, e.g., Rom. 1:1; 1 Cor. 7:22 (2nd part); Gal. 1:10; Eph. 6:6; Phil. 1:1; Col. 4:12; Jas. 1:1; 2 Pet. 1:1; **Jude 1**; (3) of sin, John 8:34 (RV, "bondservants"); Rom. 6:17, 20; (4) of corruption, 2 Pet. 2:19 (RV, "bondservants"); cf. the verb *douloo*.

Sanctified *hagiazo* (37); the KJV, "sanctified," **Jude 1**. The best texts (RV) have *agapao* (25), in its perfect participle passive form, translated "beloved" in Rom. 9:25; Eph. 1:6; Col. 3:12; 1 Thess. 1:4; 2 Thess. 2:13.

Preserved *tereo* (5083), denotes (a) "to watch over, preserve, keep, watch," e.g., Acts 12:5, 6; 16:23; in 25:21, RV (1st part), "kept" (KJV, "reserved"); the present participle is translated "keepers" in Matt. 28:4, lit. "the keeping (ones)"; it is used of the "keeping" power of God the Father and Christ, exercised over His people, John 17:11, 12, 15; 1 Thess. 5:23, "preserved"; 1 John 5:18, where "He that was begotten of God," RV, is said of Christ as the Keeper ("keepeth him," RV, for KJV, "keepeth himself"); **Jude 1**, RV, "kept for Jesus Christ" (KJV, "preserved in Jesus Christ"), Rev. 3:10; of their inheritance, 1 Pet. 1:4 ("reserved"); of judicial reservation by God in view of future doom, 2 Pet. 2:4, 9, 17; 3:7; **Jude 6, 13**; of "keeping" the faith, 2 Tim. 4:7; the unity of the Spirit, Eph. 4:3; oneself, 2 Cor. 11:9; 1 Tim. 5:22; Jas. 1:27; figuratively, one's garments, Rev. 16:15; (b) "to observe, to give heed to," as of keeping commandments, etc., e.g., Matt. 19:17; John 14:15; 15:10; 17:6; Jas. 2:10; 1 John 2:3, 4, 5; 3:22, 24; 5:2 (in some mss.), 3; Rev. 1:3; 2:26; 3:8, 10; 12:17; 14:12; 22:7, 9.

Called *kletos* (2822), "called, invited," is used, (a) "of the call of the gospel," Matt. 20:16; 22:14, not there "an effectual call," as in the Epistles, Rom. 1:1, 6-7; 8:28; 1 Cor. 1:2, 24; **Jude 1**; Rev. 17:14; in Rom. 1:7 and 1 Cor. 1:2 the meaning is "saints by calling"; (b) of "an appointment to apostleship," Rom. 1:1; 1 Cor. 1:1.

2 Mercy unto you, and peace, and love, be multiplied.

Multiplied *plethuno* (4129), used (a) transitively, denotes "to cause to increase, to multiply," 2 Cor. 9:10; Heb. 6:14 (twice); in the passive voice, "to be multiplied," Matt. 24:12, RV, "(iniquity) shall be multiplied" (KJV, "shall abound"); Acts 6:7; 7:17; 9:31; 12:24; 1 Pet. 1:2; 2 Pet. 1:2; **Jude 2**; (b) intransitively it denotes "to be multiplying," Acts 6:1, RV, "was multiplying" (KJV, "was multiplied").

3 Beloved, when I gave all diligence to write unto you of the common salvation, it was needful for me to write unto you, and exhort *you* that ye should earnestly contend for the faith which was once delivered unto the saints.

Gave *poieo* (4160), "to do," is used in **Jude 3** of "giving" diligence (the middle voice indicating Jude's especial interest in his task).

Diligence *spoude* (4710), "earnestness, zeal," or sometimes "the haste accompanying this," Mark 6:25; Luke 1:39, is translated "diligence" in Rom. 12:8; in v. 11, KJV, "business" (RV, "diligence"); in 2 Cor. 8:7, KJV, "diligence," RV, "earnestness"; both have "diligence" in Heb. 6:11; 2 Pet. 1:5; **Jude 3**; in 2 Cor. 7:11, 12, RV, "earnest care," KJV, "carefulness," and "care."

Common *koinos* (2834), denotes (a) "common, belonging to several" (Lat., *communis*), said of things had in common, Acts 2:44; 4:32; of faith, Titus 1:4; of salvation, **Jude 3**; it stands in contrast to *idios*, "one's own"; (b) "ordinary, belonging to the generality, as distinct from what is peculiar to the few", hence the application to religious practices of Gentiles in contrast with those of Jews; or of the ordinary people in contrast with those of the Pharisees; hence the meaning "unhallowed, profane," Levitically unclean (Lat., *profanus*), said of hands, Mark 7:2 (KJV, "defiled,") RV marg., "common"; of animals, ceremonially unclean, Acts 10:14; 11:8; of a man, 10:28; of meats, Rom. 14:14, "unclean"; of the blood of the covenant, as viewed by an apostate, Heb. 10:29, "unholy" (RV, marg., "common"); of everything unfit for the holy city, Rev. 21:27, RV, "unclean" (marg., "common"). Some mss. have the verb here.

Salvation *soteria* (4991), denotes "deliverance, preservation, salvation." "Salvation" is used in the NT (a) of material and temporal deliverance from danger and apprehension, (1) national, Luke 1:69, 71; Acts 7:25, RV marg., "salvation" (text, "deliverance"); (2) personal, as from the sea, Acts 27:34; RV, "safety" (KJV, "health"); prison, Phil. 1:19; the flood, Heb. 11:7; (b) of the spiritual and eternal deliverance granted immediately by God to those who accept His conditions of repentance and faith in the Lord Jesus, in whom alone it is to be obtained, Acts 4:12, and upon confession of Him as Lord, Rom. 10:10; for this purpose the gospel is the saving instrument, Rom. 1:16; Eph. 1:13; (c) of the present experience of God's power to deliver from the bondage of sin, e.g., Phil. 2:12, where the special, though not the entire, reference is to the maintenance of peace and harmony; 1 Pet. 1:9; this present experience on the part of believers is virtually equivalent to sanctification; for this purpose, God is able to make them wise, 2 Tim. 3:15; they are not to neglect it, Heb. 2:3; (d) of the future deliverance of believers at the Parousia of Christ for His saints, a salvation which is the object of their confident hope, e.g., Rom. 13:11; 1 Thess. 5:8, and v. 9, where "salvation" is assured to them, as being deliverance from the wrath of God destined to be executed upon the ungodly at the end of this age (see 1 Thess. 1:10); 2 Thess. 2:13; Heb. 1:14; 9:28; 1 Pet. 1:5; 2 Pet. 3:15; (e) of the deliverance of the nation of Israel at the second advent of Christ at the time of "the epiphany (or shining forth) of His Parousia" (2 Thess. 2:8); Luke 1:71; Rev. 12:10; (f) inclusively, to sum up all the blessings bestowed by God on men in Christ through the Holy Spirit, e.g., 2 Cor. 6:2; Heb. 5:9; 1 Pet. 1:9, 10; **Jude 3**; (g) occasionally, as standing virtually for the Savior, e.g., Luke 19:9; cf. John 4:22; (h) in ascriptions of praise to God, Rev. 7:10, and as that which it is His prerogative to bestow, 19:1 (RV).

Contend *epagonizomai* (1864), signifies "to contend about a thing, as a combatant" (*epi*, "upon or about," intensive, *agon*, "a contest"), "to contend earnestly," **Jude 3**. The word "earnestly" is added to convey the intensive force of the preposition.

Faith *pistis* (4102), primarily, "firm persuasion," a conviction based upon hearing (akin to *peitho*, "to persuade"), is used in the NT always of "faith in God or Christ, or things spiritual."

The word is used of (a) trust, e.g., Rom. 3:25; 1 Cor. 2:5; 15:14, 17; 2 Cor. 1:24; Gal. 3:23; Phil. 1:25; 2:17; 1 Thess. 3:2; 2 Thess. 1:3; 3:2; (b) trust-worthiness, e.g., Matt. 23:23; Rom. 3:3, RV, "the faithfulness of God"; Gal. 5:22 (RV, "faithfulness"); Titus 2:10, "fidelity"; (c) by metonymy, what is believed, the contents of belief, the "faith," Acts 6:7; 14:22; Gal. 1:23; 3:25 [contrast 3:23, under (a)]; 6:10; Phil. 1:27; 1 Thess. 3:10; **Jude 3, 20** (and perhaps 2 Thess. 3:2); (d) a ground for "faith," an assurance, Acts 17:31 (not as in KJV, marg., "offered faith"); (e) a pledge of fidelity, plighted "faith," 1 Tim. 5:12.

The main elements in "faith" in its relation to the invisible God, as distinct from "faith" in man, are especially brought out in the use of this noun and the corresponding verb, *pisteuo*; they are (1) a firm conviction, producing a full acknowledgement of God's revelation or truth, e.g., 2 Thess. 2:11-12; (2) a personal surrender to Him, John 1:12; (3) a conduct inspired by such surrender, 2 Cor. 5:7. Prominence is given to one or other of these elements according to the context. All this stands in contrast to belief in its purely natural exercise, which consists of an opinion held in good "faith" without necessary reference to its proof. The object of Abraham's "faith" was not God's promise (that was the occasion of its exercise); his "faith" rested on God Himself, Rom. 4:17, 20-21.

Needful The verb *echo*, "to have," with *ananke*, "a necessity," is translated "I was constrained," in **Jude 3**, RV (KJV, "it was needful").

Earnestly In **Jude 3**, *epagonizo*, "to contend earnestly," is so translated.

Once *hapax* (530), denotes (a) "once, one time," 2 Cor. 11:25; Heb. 9:7, 26-27; 12:26-27; in the phrase "once and again," lit., "once and twice," Phil. 4:16; 1 Thess. 2:18; (b) "once for all," of what is of perpetual validity, not requiring repetition, Heb. 6:4; 9:28; 10:2; 1 Pet. 3:18; **Jude 3**, RV, "once for all" (KJV, "once"); v. **5** (ditto); in some mss. 1 Pet. 3:20 (so the KJV).

4 For there are certain men crept in unawares, who were before of old ordained to this condemnation, ungodly men, turning the grace of our God into lasciviousness, and denying the only Lord God, and our Lord Jesus Christ.

Crept ... unawares *pareisduno* (391), "to enter in by the side" (*para*, "beside," *eis*, "in"), to insinuate oneself into, by stealth, to creep in stealthily, is used in **Jude 4**.

Old *palai* (3819), denotes "long ago, of old," Heb. 1:1, RV, "of old time" (KJV, "in time past"); in **Jude 4**, "of old"; it is used as an adjective in 2 Pet. 1:9, "(his) old (sins)," lit., "his sins of old."

Ordained *prographo* (4270), "to write before," is translated "were set forth (unto this condemnation)" in **Jude 4**, RV (KJV, "ordained"); the evil teachers were "designated of old for this judgment" (cf. 2 Pet. 2:3).

Condemnation *krima* (2917), denotes (a) "the sentence pronounced, a verdict, a condemnation, the decision resulting from an investigation," e.g., Mark 12:40; Luke 23:40; 1 Tim. 3:6; **Jude 4**; (b) "the process of judgment leading to a decision," 1 Pet. 4:17 ("judgment"), where *krisis* might be expected. In Luke 24:20, "to be condemned" translates the phrase *eis krima*, "unto condemnation" (i.e., unto the pronouncement of the sentence of "condemnation"). For the rendering "judgment," see, e.g., Rom. 11:33; 1 Cor. 11:34; Gal. 5:10; Jas. 3:1. In these (a) the process leading to a decision and (b) the pronouncement of the decision, the verdict, are to be distinguished. In 1 Cor. 6:7 the word means a matter for judgment, a lawsuit.

Ungodly *asebes* (765), "impious, ungodly," "without reverence for God," not merely irreligious, but acting in contravention of God's demands, Rom. 4:5; 5:6; 1 Tim. 1:9; 1 Pet. 4:18; 2 Pet. 2:5 (v. 6 in some mss.); 3:7; **Jude 4, 15** (twice).

Turning *metatithemi* (3346), "to change," is translated "turning (the grace of God)" in **Jude 4**.

Lasciviousness *aselgeia* (766), denotes "excess, licentiousness, absence of restraint, indecency, wantonness"; "lasciviousness" in Mark 7:22, one of the evils that proceed from the heart; in 2 Cor. 12:21, one of the evils of which some in the church at Corinth had been guilty; in Gal. 5:19, classed among the works of the flesh; in Eph. 4:19, among the sins of the unregenerate who are "past feeling"; so in 1 Pet. 4:3; in **Jude 4**, of that into which the grace of God had been turned by ungodly men; it is translated "wantonness" in Rom. 13:13, one of the sins against which believers are warned; in 2 Pet. 2:2, according to the best mss., "lascivious (doings)," RV (the KJV "pernicious ways" follows those texts which have *apoleiais*); in v. 7, RV, "lascivious (life)," KJV, "filthy (conversation)," of the people of Sodom and Gomorrah; in 2:18, RV, "lasciviousness" (KJV, "wantonness"), practiced by the same persons as mentioned in Jude. The prominent idea is shameless conduct. Some have derived the word from *a*, negative, and *selge*, "a city in Pisidia." Others, with similar improbability, trace it to *a*, negative, and *selgo*, or *thelgo*, "to charm."

Denying *arneomai* (720), signifies (a) "to say ... not, to contradict," e.g., Mark 14:70; John 1:20; 18:25, 27; 1 John 2:22; (b) "to deny" by way of disowning a person, as, e.g., the Lord Jesus as master, e.g., Matt. 10:33; Luke 12:9; John 13:38 (in the best mss.); 2 Tim. 2:12; or, on the other hand, of Christ Himself, "denying" that a person is His follower, Matt. 10:33; 2 Tim. 2:12; or to "deny" the Father and the Son, by apostatizing and by disseminating pernicious teachings, to "deny" Jesus Christ as master and Lord by immorality under a cloak of religion, 2 Pet. 2:1; **Jude 4**; (c) "to deny oneself," either in a good sense, by disregarding one's own interests, Luke 9:23, or in a bad sense, to prove false to oneself, to act quite unlike oneself, 2 Tim. 2:13; (d) to "abrogate, forsake, or renounce a thing," whether evil, Titus 2:12, or good, 1 Tim. 5:8; 2 Tim. 3:5; Rev. 2:13; 3:8; (e) "not to accept, to reject" something offered, Acts 3:14; 7:35, "refused"; Heb. 11:24 "refused."

Only *monos* (3441), "alone, solitary," is translated "only," e.g., in Matt. 4:10; 12:4; 17:8; 1 Cor. 9:6; 14:36; Phil. 4:15; Col. 4:11; 2 John 1; it is used as an attribute of God in John 5:44; 17:3; Rom. 16:27; 1 Tim. 1:17; 1 Tim. 6:15-16; **Jude 4, 25**; Rev. 15:4.

Lord *despotes* (1203), "a master, lord, one who possesses supreme authority," is used in personal address to God in Luke 2:29; Acts 4:24; Rev. 6:10; with reference to Christ, 2 Pet. 2:1; **Jude 4**; elsewhere it is translated "master," "masters,"

1 Tim. 6:1, 2; 2 Tim. 2:21 (of Christ); Titus 2:9; 1 Pet. 2:18.

Lord *kurios* (2962), properly an adjective, signifying "having power" (*kuros*) or "authority," is used as a noun, variously translated in the NT, " 'Lord,' 'master,' 'Master,' 'owner,' 'Sir,' a title of wide significance, occurring in each book of the NT save Titus and the Epistles of John. It is used (a) of an owner, as in Luke 19:33, cf. Matt. 20:8; Acts 16:16; Gal. 4:1; or of one who has the disposal of anything, as the Sabbath, Matt. 12:8; (b) of a master, i.e., one to whom service is due on any ground, Matt. 6:24; 24:50; Eph. 6:5; (c) of an Emperor or King, Acts 25:26; Rev. 17:14; (d) of idols, ironically, 1 Cor. 8:5, cf. Isa. 26:13; (e) as a title of respect addressed to a father, Matt. 21:30, a husband, 1 Pet. 3:6, a master, Matt. 13:27; Luke 13:8, a ruler, Matt. 27:63, an angel, Acts 10:4; Rev. 7:14; (f) as a title of courtesy addressed to a stranger, John 12:21; 20:15; Acts 16:30; from the outset of His ministry this was a common form of address to the Lord Jesus, alike by the people, Matt. 8:2; John 4:11, and by His disciples, Matt. 8:25; Luke 5:8; John 6:68; (g) *kurios* is the Sept. and NT representative of Heb. Jehovah ('LORD' in Eng. versions), see Matt. 4:7; Jas. 5:11, e.g., of *adon*, Lord, Matt. 22:44, and of *Adonay*, Lord, 1:22; it also occurs for *Elohim*, God, 1 Pet. 1:25.

"Thus the usage of the word in the NT follows two main lines: one, *a-f*, customary and general, the other, *g*, peculiar to the Jews, and drawn from the Greek translation of the OT.

"Christ Himself assumed the title, Matt. 7:21, 22; 9:38; 22:41-45; Mark 5:19 (cf. Ps. 66:16; the parallel passage, Luke 8:39, has 'God'); Luke 19:31; John 13:13, apparently intending it in the higher senses of its current use, and at the same time suggesting its OT associations. His purpose did not become clear to the disciples until after His resurrection, and the revelation of His Deity consequent thereon. Thomas, when he realized the significance of the presence of a mortal wound in the body of a living man, immediately joined with it the absolute title of Deity, saying, 'My Lord and my God,' John 20:28. Thereafter, except in Acts 10:4 and Rev. 7:14, there is no record that *kurios* was ever again used by believers in addressing any save God and the Lord Jesus; cf Acts 2:47 with 4:29, 30. How soon and how completely the lower meaning had been superseded is seen in Peter's declaration in his first sermon after the resurrection, 'God hath made Him – Lord,' Acts 2:36, and that in the house of Cornelius, 'He is Lord of all,' 10:36, cf. Deut. 10:14; Matt. 11:25; Acts 17:24. In his writings the implications of his early teaching are confirmed and developed. Thus Ps. 34:8, 'O taste and see that Jehovah is good,' is applied to the Lord Jesus, 1 Pet. 2:3, and 'Jehovah of Hosts, Him shall ye sanctify,' Isa. 8:13, becomes 'sanctify in your hearts Christ as Lord,' 3:15. So also James who uses *kurios* alike of God, 1:7 (cf. v. 5); 3:9; 4:15; 5:4, 10, 11, and of the Lord Jesus, 1:1 (where the possibility that *kai* is intended epexegetically, i.e. = even, cf. 1 Thess. 3:11, should not be overlooked); 2:1 (lit., 'our Lord Jesus Christ of glory,' cf. Ps. 24:7; 29:3; Acts 7:2; 1 Cor. 2:8); 5:7, 8, while the language of 4:10; 5:15, is equally applicable to either. Jude, v. **4**, speaks of 'our only – Lord, Jesus Christ,' and immediately, v. **5**, uses 'Lord' of God (see the remarkable marg. here), as he does later, vv. **9**, **14**.

5 I will therefore put you in remembrance, though ye once knew this, how that the Lord, having saved the people out of the land of Egypt, afterward destroyed them that believed not.

Will *boulomai* (1014), "to wish, to will deliberately," expresses more strongly than *thelo* the deliberate exercise of the will; it is translated "to desire" in the RV of the following: Acts 22:30; 23:28; 27:43; 28:18; 1 Tim. 2:8; 5:14; 6:9 and **Jude 5**.

Remembrance *hupomimnesko* (5279), signifies "to cause one to remember, put one in mind of," John 14:26, "shall ... bring ... to (your) remembrance"; 2 Tim. 2:14, "put ... in remembrance"; Titus 3:1, "put ... in mind"; 3 John 10, RV, "I will bring to remembrance" (KJV, "I will remember"); **Jude 5**, "to put ... in remembrance." In Luke 22:61 it is used in the passive voice, "(Peter) remembered," lit., "was put in mind."

Once *see* ***Jude* 3**.

Lord *see* ***Jude* 4**.

Saved *sozo* (4982), "to save," is used (as with the noun *soteria*, "salvation") (a) of material and temporal deliverance from danger, suffering, etc., e.g., Matt. 8:25; Mark 13:20; Luke 23:35; John 12:27; 1 Tim. 2:15; 2 Tim. 4:18 (KJV, "preserve"); **Jude 5**; from sickness, Matt. 9:22, "made ... whole" (RV, marg., "saved"); so Mark 5:34; Luke 8:48; Jas. 5:15; (b) of the spiritual and eternal salvation granted immediately by God to those who believe on the Lord Jesus Christ, e.g., Acts 2:47, RV "(those that) were being saved"; 16:31; Rom. 8:24, RV, "were we saved"; Eph. 2:5, 8; 1 Tim. 2:4; 2 Tim. 1:9; Titus 3:5; of human agency in this, Rom. 11:14; 1 Cor. 7:16; 9:22; (c) of the present experiences of

God's power to deliver from the bondage of sin, e.g., Matt. 1:21; Rom. 5:10; 1 Cor. 15:2; Heb. 7:25; Jas. 1:21; 1 Pet. 3:21; of human agency in this, 1 Tim. 4:16; (d) of the future deliverance of believers at the second coming of Christ for His saints, being deliverance from the wrath of God to be executed upon the ungodly at the close of this age and from eternal doom, e.g., Rom. 5:9; (e) of the deliverance of the nation of Israel at the second advent of Christ, e.g., Rom. 11:26; (f) inclusively for all the blessings bestowed by God on men in Christ, e.g., Luke 19:10; John 10:9; 1 Cor. 10:33; 1 Tim. 1:15; (g) of those who endure to the end of the time of the Great Tribulation, Matt. 10:22; Mark 13:13; (h) of the individual believer, who, though losing his reward at the judgment seat of Christ hereafter, will not lose his salvation, 1 Cor. 3:15; 5:5; (i) of the deliverance of the nations at the Millennium, Rev. 21:24 (in some mss.).

Land *ge* (1093), in one of its usages, denotes (a) "land" as distinct from sea or other water, e.g., Mark 4:1; 6:47; Luke 5:3; John 6:21; (b) "land" as subject to cultivation, e.g., Luke 14:35; (c) "land" as describing a country or region, e.g., Matt. 2:20, 21; 4:15; Luke 4:25; in 23:44, RV, "(the whole) land," KJV, "(all the) earth"; Acts 7:29; Heb. 11:9, RV, "a land (not his own)," KJV "a (strange) country;" **Jude 5**. In Acts 7:11 the KJV follows a reading of the noun with the definite article which necessitates the insertion of "land."

Afterward *deuteros* (1208), denotes "second in order" with or without the idea of time, e.g., Matt. 22:26, 39; 2 Cor. 1:15; Rev. 2:11; in Rev. 14:8, RV only ("a second angel"); it is used in the neuter, *deuteron*, adverbially, signifying a "second" time, e.g., John 3:4; 21:16; Acts 7:13; Rev. 19:3, RV (KJV, "again"); **Jude 5**, "afterward" (RV, marg., "the second time"); used with *ek* ("of") idiomatically, the preposition signifying "for (the second time)," Mark 14:72; John 9:24 and Acts 11:9, RV (KJV, "again"); Heb. 9:28; in 1 Cor. 12:28, KJV, "secondarily," RV, "secondly."

6 And the angels which kept not their first estate, but left their own habitation, he hath reserved in everlasting chains under darkness unto the judgment of the great day.

Angels *angelos* (32), "a messenger" (from *angello*, "to deliver a message"), sent whether by God or by man or by Satan, "is also used of a guardian or representative in Rev. 1:20, cf. Matt. 18:10; Acts 12:15 (where it is better understood as 'ghost'), but most frequently of an order of created beings, superior to man, Heb. 2:7; Ps. 8:5, belonging to Heaven, Matt. 24:36; Mark 12:25, and to God, Luke 12:8, and engaged in His service, Ps. 103:20. "Angels" are spirits, Heb. 1:14, i.e., they have not material bodies as men have; they are either human in form, or can assume the human form when necessary, cf. Luke 24:4, with v. 23, Acts 10:3 with v. 30. They are called 'holy' in Mark 8:38, and 'elect,' 1 Tim. 5:21, in contrast with some of their original number, Matt. 25:41, who 'sinned,' 2 Pet. 2:4, 'left their proper habitation,' **Jude 6**, *oiketerion*, a word which occurs again, in the NT, only in 2 Cor. 5:2. Angels are always spoken of in the masculine gender, the feminine form of the word does not occur."

Kept *see* **Preserved** at *Jude 1*.

Estate In **Jude 6** *arche*, "principality," RV, KJV has "first estate."

Left *apoleipo* (620), "to leave behind" (*apo*, "from"), is used (a) in the active voice, of "leaving" behind a cloak, 2 Tim. 4:3; a person, 2 Tim. 4:20; of "abandoning" a principality (by angels), **Jude 6**, RV; (b) in the passive voice, "to be reserved, to remain," Heb. 4:6, 9; 10:26.

Own In **Jude 6** (1st part), KJV, *heauton*, "of themselves," "their own" (RV), is rendered "their"; in the 2nd part, RV, *idios*, one's own, is translated "their proper" (KJV, "their own").

Habitation *oiketerion* (3613), "a habitation" (from *oiketer*, "an inhabitant," and *oikos*, "a dwelling"), is used in **Jude 6**, of the heavenly region appointed by God as the dwelling place of angels; in 2 Cor. 5:2, RV, "habitation," KJV, "house," figuratively of the spiritual bodies of believers when raised or changed at the return of the Lord.

Reserved *tereo* (5083), "to guard, keep, preserve, give heed to," is translated "to reserve," (a) with a happy issue, 1 Pet. 1:4; (b) with a retributive issue, 2 Pet. 2:4; v. 9, KJV (RV, "keep"); 2:17; 3:7; **Jude 6**, KJV (RV, "hath kept"); v. **13**; and referenced (c) the possibility either of deliverance or execution, Acts 25:21, KJV (RV, kept).

Everlasting *aidios* (126), denotes "everlasting" (from *aei*, "ever"), Rom. 1:20, RV, "everlasting," for KJV, "eternal"; **Jude 6**, KJV and RV "everlasting." *Aionios*, should always be translated "eternal" and *aidios*, "everlasting." "While *aionios* ... negatives the end either of a space of time or of unmeasured time, and is used chiefly where something future is spoken of, *aidios* excludes interruption and lays stress upon permanence and unchangeableness" (Cremer).

Chains In **Jude 6** the RV renders *desmos* by "bonds" (for the KJV "chains").

Darkness *zophos* (2217), denotes "the gloom of the nether world", hence, "thick darkness, darkness that may be felt"; it is rendered "darkness" in Heb. 12:18; 2 Pet. 2:4 and **Jude 6**; in 2 Pet. 2:17, RV, "blackness," KJV, "mists"; in **Jude 13**, RV and KJV, blackness.

7 Even as Sodom and Gomorrha, and the cities about them in like manner, giving themselves over to fornication, and going after strange flesh, are set forth for an example, suffering the vengeance of eternal fire.

Even *hos* (5613), "as," in comparative sentences, is sometimes translated "even as," Matt. 15:28; Mark 4:36; Eph. 5:33; 1 Pet. 3:6 (KJV only); **Jude 7**.

Like *homoios* (3664), "like, resembling, such as, the same as," is used (a) of appearance or form John 9:9; Rev. 1:13, 15; 2:18; 4:3 (twice), 6, 7; 9:7 (twice), 10, 19; 11:1; 13:2, 11; 14:14; (b) of ability, condition, nature, Matt. 22:39; Acts 17:29; Gal. 5:21, "such like," lit., "and the (things) similar to these"; 1 John 3:2; Rev. 13:4; 18:18; 21:11, 18; (c) of comparison in parables, Matt. 13:31, 33, 44, 45, 47; 20:1; Luke 13:18, 19, 21; (d) of action, thought, etc., Matt. 11:16; 13:52; Luke 6:47, 48, 49; 7:31, 32; 12:36; John 8:55; **Jude 7**.

Manner *tropos* (5158), "a turning, fashion, manner, character, way of life," is translated "manner" in Acts 1:11, with reference to the Lord's ascension and return, in **Jude 7**, of the similarity of the evil of those mentioned in vv. **6** and **7**.

Fornication *ekporneuo* (1608), a strengthened form (*ek*, used intensively), "to give oneself up to fornication," implying excessive indulgence, **Jude 7**.

Set *prokeimai* (4295), signifies (a) "to be set before," and is so rendered in Heb. 6:18 of the hope of the believer; 12:1, of the Christian race; v. 2, of the joy "set" before Christ in the days of His flesh and at His death; (b) "to be set forth," said of Sodom and Gomorrah, in **Jude 7**. It is used elsewhere in 2 Cor. 8:12, "to lie beforehand."

Example *deigma* (1164), primarily "a thing shown, a specimen" (akin to *deiknumi*, "to show"), denotes an "example" given as a warning, **Jude 7**.

Suffering *hupecho* (5254), "to hold under" (*hupo*, "under," *echo*, "to have or hold"), is used metaphorically in **Jude 7** of "suffering" punishment. In the Sept., Ps. 89:50; Lam. 5:7.

Vengeance *dike* (1349), "justice," or "the execution of a sentence," is translated "punishment" in **Jude 7**, RV (KJV, "vengeance").

Eternal *aionios* (166), "describes duration, either undefined but not endless, as in Rom. 16:25; 2 Tim. 1:9; Titus 1:2; or undefined because endless as in Rom. 16:26, and the other sixty-six places in the NT. The predominant meaning of *aionios*, that in which it is used everywhere in the NT, save the places noted above, may be seen in 2 Cor. 4:18, where it is set in contrast with *proskairos*, lit., 'for a season,' and in Philem. 15, where only in the NT it is used without a noun. Moreover it is used of persons and things which are in their nature endless, as, e.g., of God, Rom. 16:26; of His power, 1 Tim. 6:16, and of His glory, 1 Pet. 5:10; of the Holy Spirit, Heb. 9:14; of the redemption effected by Christ, Heb. 9:12, and of the consequent salvation of men, 5:9, as well as of His future rule, 2 Pet. 1:11, which is elsewhere declared to be without end, Luke 1:33; of the life received by those who believe in Christ, John 3:16, concerning whom He said, 'they shall never perish,' 10:28, and of the resurrection body, 2 Cor. 5:1, elsewhere said to be 'immortal,' 1 Cor. 15:53, in which that life will be finally realized, Matt. 25:46; Titus 1:2. *Àionios* is also used of the sin that 'hath never forgiveness,' Mark 3:29, and of the judgment of God, from which there is no appeal, Heb. 6:2, and of the fire, which is one of its instruments, Matt. 18:8; 25:41; **Jude 7**, and which is elsewhere said to be 'unquenchable,' Mark 9:43. The use of *aionios* here shows that the punishment referred to in 2 Thess. 1:9, is no temporary, but final, and, accordingly, the phraseology shows that its purpose is not remedial but retributive."

8 Likewise also these *filthy* dreamers defile the flesh, despise dominion, and speak evil of dignities.

Likewise *homoios* (3668), "in like manner" (from the adjective *homoios*), is rendered "likewise" in the KJV of Matt. 22:26; 27:41, Luke 10:32; 16:25; John 5:19; Jas. 2:25; 1 Pet. 3:1, 7; **Jude 8**; Rev. 8:12 (in all these the RV has "in like manner"); in the following, KJV and RV have "likewise"; Matt. 26:35; Luke 5:33; 6:31; 10:37; 17:28, 31; 22:36; John 6:11; 21:13; Rom. 1:27; 1 Pet. 5:5.

Dreamers *enupniazo* (1797), is used in Acts 2:17, in the passive voice in a phrase (according to the most authentic mss.) which means "shall be given up to dream by dreams," translated "shall dream dreams" metaphorically in **Jude 8**, of being given over to sensuous "dreamings," RV, KJV, "dreamers," and so defiling the flesh.

Defile *miaino* (3392), primarily, "to stain, to tinge or dye with another color," as in the staining of a glass, hence, "to pollute, contaminate, soil, defile," is used (a) of "ceremonial defilement," John 18:28; so in the Sept., in Lev. 22:5, 8; Num. 19:13, 20, etc.; (b) of "moral defilement," Titus 1:15 (twice); Heb. 12:15; "of moral and physical defilement," **Jude 8**.

Despise *atheteo* (114), signifies "to put as of no value" (*a*, negative, (*theton*, "what is placed," from *tithemi*, "to put, place"); hence, (a) "to act towards anything as though it were annulled"; e.g., to deprive a law of its force by opinions or acts contrary to it, Gal. 3:15, KJV, "disannulleth," RV, "maketh void"; (b) "to thwart the efficacy of anything, to nullify, to frustrate it," Luke 7:30, "rejected"; 1 Cor. 1:19, "will I reject"; to make void, Gal. 2:21; to set at nought, **Jude 8**, RV (KJV, "despised"); the parallel passage, in 2 Pet. 2:10, has *kataphroneo*. In Mark 6:26, the thought is that of breaking faith with.

Dominion *kuriotes* (2963), denotes "lordship" (*kurios*, "a lord"), "power, dominion," whether angelic or human, Eph. 1:21; Col. 1:16; 2 Pet. 2:10 (RV, for KJV, "government"); **Jude 8**. In Eph. and Col. it indicates a grade in the angelic orders, in which it stands second.

Speak evil of *blasphemeo* (987), "to blaspheme, rail at or revile," is used (a) in a general way, of any contumelious speech, reviling, calumniating, railing at, etc., as of those who railed at Christ, e.g., Matt. 27:39; Mark 15:29; Luke 22:65 (RV, "reviling"); 23:39; (b) of those who speak contemptuously of God or of sacred things, e.g., Matt. 9:3; Mark 3:28; Rom. 2:24; 1 Tim. 1:20; 6:1; Rev. 13:6; 16:9, 11, 21; "hath spoken blasphemy," Matt. 26:65; "rail at," 2 Pet. 2:10; **Jude 8, 10**; "railing," 2 Pet. 2:12; "slanderously reported," Rom. 3:8; "be evil spoken of," Rom. 14:16; 1 Cor. 10:30; 2 Pet. 2:2; "speak evil of," Titus 3:2; 1 Pet. 4:4; "being defamed," 1 Cor. 4:13. The verb (in the present participial form) is translated "blasphemers" in Acts 19:37; in Mark 2:7, "blasphemeth," RV, for KJV, "speaketh blasphemies."

There is no noun in the original representing the English "blasphemer." This is expressed either by the verb, or by the adjective *blasphemos*.

Dignities *doxa* (1391), primarily denotes "an opinion, estimation, repute"; in the NT, always "good opinion, praise, honor, glory, an appearance commanding respect, magnificence, excellence, manifestation of glory"; hence, of angelic powers, in respect of their state as commanding recognition, "dignities," 2 Pet. 2:10; **Jude 8**.

9 Yet Michael the archangel, when contending with the devil he disputed about the body of Moses, durst not bring against him a railing accusation, but said, The Lord rebuke thee.

Archangel *archangelos* (743), "is not found in the OT, and in the NT only in 1 Thess. 4:16 and **Jude 9**, where it is used of Michael, who in Daniel is called 'one of the chief princes,' and 'the great prince' (Sept., 'the great angel'), 10:13, 21; 12:1. Cf. also Rev. 12:7.... Whether there are other beings of this exalted rank in the heavenly hosts, Scripture does not say, though the description 'one of the chief princes' suggests that this may be the case; cf. also Rom. 8:38; Eph. 1:21; Col. 1:16, where the word translated 'principalities' is *arche*, the prefix in archangel." In 1 Thess. 4:16 the meaning seems to be that the voice of the Lord Jesus will be of the character of an "archangelic" shout.

Contending *diakrino* (1252), lit., "to separate throughout or wholly" (*dia*, "asunder," *krino*, "to judge," from a root *kri*, meaning "separation"), then, to distinguish, decide, signifies, in the middle voice, "to separate oneself from, or to contend with," as did the circumcisionists with Peter, Acts 11:2; as did Michael with Satan, **Jude 9**.

Devil *diabolos* (1228), "an accuser, a slanderer" (from *diaballo*, "to accuse, to malign"), is one of the names of Satan. From it the English word "Devil" is derived, and should be applied only to Satan, as a proper name. *Daimon*, "a demon," is frequently, but wrongly, translated "devil"; it should always be translated "demon," as in the RV margin. There is one "Devil," there are many demons. Being the malignant enemy of God and man, he accuses man to God, Job 1:6-11; 2:1-5; Rev. 12:9, 10, and God to man, Gen. 3. He afflicts men with physical sufferings, Acts 10:38. Being himself sinful, 1 John 3:8, he instigated man to sin, Gen. 3, and tempts man to do evil, Eph. 4:27; 6:11, encouraging him thereto by deception, Eph. 2:2. Death having been brought into the world by sin, the "Devil" had the power of death, but Christ through His own death, has triumphed over him, and will bring him to nought, Heb. 2:14; his power over death is intimated in his struggle with Michael over the body of Moses, **Jude 9**. Judas, who gave himself over to the "Devil," was so identified with him, that the Lord described him as such, John 6:70 (see 13:2). As the "Devil" raised himself in pride against God and fell under condemnation, so believers are warned against similar sin, 1 Tim. 3:6; for them he lays snares, v. 7, seeking to devour them as a roaring lion, 1 Pet. 5:8; those who fall into his snare may be recovered therefrom unto the will of God, 2 Tim. 2:26, "having been taken captive by him (i.e., by the 'Devil')"; "by the Lord's servant" is an alternative, which some regard as confirmed by the use of *zogreo* ("to catch alive") in Luke 5:10; but the general use is that of taking captive in the usual way. If believers resist he will flee from them, Jas. 4:7. His fury and malignity will be especially exercised at the end of the present age, Rev. 12:12. His doom is the lake of fire, Matt. 25:41; Rev. 20:10. The noun is applied to slanderers, false accusers, 1 Tim. 3:11; 2 Tim. 3:3; Titus 2:3.

Disputed *dialegomai* (1256), primarily signifies "to think different things with oneself, to ponder"; then, with other persons, "to converse, argue, dispute"; it is translated "to dispute" in Mark 9:34, the RV and KJV "had disputed" is somewhat unsuitable here, for the delinquency was not that they had wrangled, but that they had reasoned upon the subject at all; in Acts 17:17, KJV (RV, "reasoned," as in the KJV of 18:4, 19); in 19:8-9 (RV, "reasoning"); in 24:12, "disputing"; in **Jude 9**, "disputed."

Durst *tolmao* (5111), signifies "to dare," (a) in the sense of not dreading or shunning through fear, Matt. 22:46; Mark 12:34; Mark 15:43, "boldly," lit., "having dared, went in"; Luke 20:40; John 21:12; Acts 5:13; 7:32; Rom. 15:18; 2 Cor. 10:2, RV, "show courage," (KJV, "be bold"); 10:12, RV, "are (not) bold", 11:21; Phil. 1:14, "are bold"; **Jude 9**; (b) in the sense of bearing, enduring, bringing oneself to do a thing, Rom. 5:7; 1 Cor. 6:1. Cf. *apotolmao*, "to be very bold," Rom. 10:20.

Bring *epiphero* (2018), signifies (a) "to bring upon, or to bring against," **Jude 9**; (b) "to impose, inflict, visit upon," Rom. 3:5. Some mss. have it in Acts 25:18; some in Phil. 1:16 (RV, v. 17, "raise up," translating *egeiro*).

Railing *blasphemia* (988), is translated "railings" in Matt. 15:19, RV; 1 Tim. 6:4, KJV and RV; "railing" in Mark 7:22, RV; Col. 3:8, RV; **Jude 9**, KJV and RV, lit., "judgment of railing"; in Eph. 4:31, RV (KJV, "evil speaking").

Accusation *krisis* (2920), (a) denotes "the process of investigation, the act of distinguishing and separating" (as distinct from *krima*); hence "a judging, a passing of judgment upon a person or thing"; it has a variety of meanings, such as judicial authority, John 5:22, 27; justice, Acts 8:33; Jas. 2:13; a tribunal, Matt. 5:21-22; a trial, John 5:24; 2 Pet. 2:4; a judgment, 2 Pet. 2:11; **Jude 9**; by metonymy, the standard of judgment, just dealing, Matt. 12:18, 20; 23:23; Luke 11:42; divine judgment executed, 2 Thess. 1:5; Rev. 16:7; (b) sometimes it has the meaning "condemnation," and is virtually equivalent to *krima* (a); see Matt. 23:33; John 3:19; Jas. 5:12, *hupo krisin*, "under judgment."

Lord *see **Jude 4**.*

Rebuke *epitimao* (2008), primarily, "to put honor upon," then, "to adjudge," hence signifies "to rebuke." Except for 2 Tim. 4:2 and **Jude 9**, it is confined in the NT to the Synoptic Gospels, where it is frequently used of the Lord's rebukes to (a) evil spirits, e.g., Matt. 17:18; Mark 1:25; 9:25; Luke 4:35, 41; 9:42; (b) winds, Matt. 8:26; Mark 4:39; Luke 8:24; (c) fever, Luke 4:39; (d) disciples, Mark 8:33; Luke 9:55; contrast Luke 19:39. For rebukes by others see Matt. 16:22; 19:13; 20:31; Mark 8:32; 10:13; 10:48, RV, "rebuked" (KJV, "charged"); Luke 17:3; 18:15, 39; 23:40.

10 But these speak evil of those things which they know not: but what they know naturally, as brute beasts, in those things they corrupt themselves.

Speak evil of *see **Jude 8**.*

What Other words are (a) *hoios*, "of what kind," e.g., 2 Cor. 10:11, RV (KJV, "such as"); 1 Thess. 1:5, "what manner of men"; 2 Tim. 3:11 (twice), lit., "what sorts of things," "what sorts of persecutions"; (b) *poios*, "what sort of," e.g., Matt. 21:23, 24, 27; 24:42, 43; Luke 5:19; 6:32-34; 20:2, 8; 24:19; John 12:33, "what manner of"; so in 18:32; 21:19; Rom. 3:27; 1 Cor. 15:35; in Jas. 4:14, "what"; 1 Pet. 2:20 and Rev. 3:3 (ditto); 1 Pet. 1:11, "what manner of"; (c) *hopoios*, "what sort of," 1 Cor. 3:13; "what manner of," 1 Thess. 1:9; (d) *hosos*, "how great," Mark 6:30 (twice), RV, "whatsoever"; Acts 15:12; Rom. 3:19, "what things soever"; **Jude 10** (1st part), "what soever things," RV; (2nd part) "what"; (e) *posos*, "how great, how much," 2 Cor. 7:11, "what (earnest care)," RV (*posos* here stands for the repeated words in the Eng. versions, the adjective not being repeated in the original); (f) *hostis*, "what (things)," Phil. 3:7; (g) in Matt. 26:40, *houtos*, "thus, so," is used as an exclamatory expression, translated "What" (in a word immediately addressed by the Lord to Peter), lit., "So"; (h) for *potapos*, rendered "what" in Mark 13:1 (2nd part), KJV; (i) in 1 Cor. 6:16, 19, KJV, the particle *e*, "or" (RV), is rendered "What?"; in 1 Cor. 14:36, KJV and RV, "what?" (j) in 1 Cor. 11:22, *gar*, "in truth, indeed," has its exclamatory use "What."

Know *epistamai* (1987), "to know, know of, understand" (probably an old middle voice form of *ephistemi*, "to set over"), is used in Mark 14:68, "understand," which follows *oida* "I (neither) know"; most frequently in the Acts, 10:28; 15:7; 18:25; 19:15, 25; 20:18; 22:19; 24:10; 26:26; elsewhere, 1 Tim. 6:4; Heb. 11:8; Jas. 4:14; **Jude 10**.

Naturally *phusikos* (5447), "naturally, by nature," is used in **Jude 10**.

Brute *alogos* (249), translated "brute" in the KJV of 2 Pet. 2:12 and **Jude 10**, signifies "without reason," RV, though, as J. Hastings points out, "brute beasts" is not at all unsuitable, as "brute" is from Latin *brutus*, which means "dull, irrational"; in Acts 25:27 it is rendered "unreasonable".

Beasts *zoon* (2226), primarily denotes "a living being" (*zoe*, "life"). The Eng., "animal," is the equivalent, stressing the fact of life as the characteristic feature. In Heb. 13:11 the KJV and the RV translate it "beasts" ("animals" would be quite suitable). In 2 Pet. 2:12 and **Jude 10**, the KJV has "beasts," the RV "creatures." In Revelation, where the word is found some 20 times, and always of those beings which stand before the throne of God, who give glory and honor and thanks to Him, 4:6, and act in perfect harmony with His counsels, 5:14; 6:1-7, e.g., the word "beasts" is most unsuitable; the RV, "living creatures," should always be used; it gives to *zoon* its appropriate significance.

Corrupt *phtheiro* (5351), signifies "to destroy by means of corrupting," and so "bringing into a worse state"; (a) with this significance it is used of the effect of evil company upon the manners of believers, and so of the effect of association with those who deny the truth and hold false doctrine, 1 Cor. 15:33 (this was a saying of the pagan poet Menander, which became a well known proverb); in 2 Cor. 7:2, of the effects of dishonorable dealing by bringing people to want (a charge made against the apostle); in 11:3, of the effects upon the minds (or thoughts) of believers by "corrupting" them "from the simplicity and the purity that is toward Christ"; in Eph. 4:22, intransitively, of the old nature in waxing "corrupt," "morally decaying, on the way to final ruin" (Moule), "after the lusts of deceit"; in Rev. 19:2, metaphorically, of the Babylonish harlot, in "corrupting" the inhabitants of the earth by her false religion.

(b) With the significance of destroying, it is used of marring a local church by leading it away from that condition of holiness of life and purity of doctrine in which it should abide, 1 Cor. 3:17 (KJV, "defile"), and of God's retributive destruction of the offender who is guilty of this sin (id.); of the effects of the work of false and abominable teachers upon themselves, 2 Pet. 2:12 (some texts have *kataphtheiro*; KJV, "shall utterly perish"), and **Jude 10** (KJV, "corrupt themselves," RV, marg., "are corrupted").

11 Woe unto them! for they have gone in the way of Cain, and ran greedily after the error of Balaam for reward, and perished in the gainsaying of Core.

Woe *ouai* (3759), an interjection, is used (a) in denunciation, Matt. 11:21; 18:7 (twice); eight times in ch. 23; 24:19; 26:24; Mark 13:17; 14:21; Luke 6:24, 25 (twice), 26; 10:13; six times in ch. 11; 17:1; 21:23; 22:22; 1 Cor. 9:16; **Jude 11**; Rev. 8:13 (thrice); 12:12; as a noun, Rev. 9:12 (twice); 11:14 (twice); (b) in grief, "alas," Rev. 18:10, 16, 19 (twice in each).

Way *hodos* (3598), denotes (a) "a natural path, road, way," frequent in the Synoptic Gospels; elsewhere, e.g., Acts 8:26; 1 Thess. 3:11; Jas. 2:25; Rev. 16:12; (b) "a traveler's way"; (c) metaphorically, of "a course of conduct," or "way of thinking," e.g., of righteousness, Matt. 21:32; 2 Pet. 2:21; of God, Matt. 22:16, and parallels, i.e., the "way" instructed and approved by God; so Acts 18:26 and Heb. 3:10, "My ways" (cf. Rev. 15:3); of the Lord, Acts 18:25; "that leadeth to destruction," Matt. 7:13; "... unto life," 7:14; of peace, Luke 1:79; Rom. 3:17; of Paul's "ways" in Christ, 1 Cor. 4:17 (plural); "more excellent" (of love), 1 Cor. 12:31; of truth, 2 Pet. 2:2; of the right "way," 2:15; of Balaam (*id.*), of Cain, **Jude 11**; of a "way" consisting in what is from God, e.g., of life, Acts 2:28 (plural); of salvation, Acts 16:17; personified, of Christ as the means of access to the Father, John 14:6; of the course followed and characterized by the followers of Christ, Acts 9:2; 19:9, 23; 24:22.

Ran *ekchunno* or *ekchuno* (1632), "to shed," is translated "ran riotously" in **Jude 11**, RV (KJV, "ran greedily").

Error *plane* (4106), akin to *planao*, "a wandering, a forsaking of the right path," see Jas. 5:20, whether in doctrine, 2 Pet. 3:17; 1 John 4:6, or in morals, Rom. 1:27; 2 Pet. 2:18; **Jude 11**, though, in Scripture, doctrine and morals are never divided by any sharp line. See also Matt. 27:64, where it is equivalent to 'fraud.'" "Errors" in doctrine are not infrequently the effect of relaxed morality, and vice versa. In Eph. 4:14 the RV has "wiles of error," for KJV, "they lie in wait to deceive"; in 1 Thess. 2:3, RV, "error," for KJV, "deceit"; in 2 Thess. 2:11, RV, "a working of error," for KJV, "strong delusion." Cf. *planetes*, "a wandering," **Jude 13**, and the adjective *planos*, "leading astray, deceiving, a deceiver."

Perished *apollumi* (622), "to destroy," signifies, in the middle voice, "to perish," and is thus used (a) of things, e.g., Matt. 5:29, 30; Luke 5:37; Acts 27:34, RV, "perish" (in some texts *pipto*, "to fall," as KJV); Heb. 1:11; 2 Pet. 3:6; Rev. 18:14 (2nd part), RV, "perished" (in some texts *aperchomai*, "to depart," as KJV); (b) of persons, e.g., Matt. 8:25; John 3:15), 16; 10:28; 17:12, RV, "perished" (KJV, "is lost"); Rom. 2:12; 1 Cor. 1:18, lit., "the perishing," where the perfective force of the verb implies the completion of the process of destruction (Moulton, *Proleg.*, p. 114); 8:11; 15:18; 2 Pet. 3:9; **Jude 11**.

Gainsaying *antilogia* (485), is rendered "gainsaying," in Heb. 12:3, RV, and **Jude 11**. Opposition in act seems to be implied in these two places; though this sense has been questioned by some, it is confirmed by instances from the papyri (Moulton and Milligan, *Vocab.*).

Reward *misthos* (3408), denotes (a) "wages, hire," Matt. 20:8; Luke 10:7; Jas. 5:4; in 1 Tim. 5:18; 2 Pet. 2:13; **Jude 11**, RV, "hire" (KJV, "reward"); in 2 Pet. 2:15, RV, "hire" (KJV, "wages").

12 These are spots in your feasts of charity, when they feast with you, feeding themselves without fear: clouds *they are* without water, carried about of winds; trees whose fruit withereth, without fruit, twice dead, plucked up by the roots;

Spots *spilas* (4694), is rendered "spots" in **Jude 12**, KJV.

Feasts *agape* (26), "love," is used in the plural in **Jude 12**, signifying "love feasts," RV (KJV, "feasts of charity"); in the corresponding passage, 2 Pet. 2:13, the most authentic mss. have the word *apate*, in the plural, "deceivings."

Feast with *suneuocheo* (4910), "to entertain sumptuously with," is used in the passive voice, denoting "to feast sumptuously with" (*sun*, "together," and *euochia*, "good cheer"), "to revel with," translated "feast with" in 2 Pet. 2:13 and **Jude 12**.

Feeding *poimaino* (4165), "to act as a shepherd" (from *poimen*, "a shepherd"), is used (a) literally, Luke 17:7, RV, "keeping sheep," for KJV, "feeding cattle"; 1 Cor. 9:7, (b) metaphorically, "to tend, to shepherd"; said of Christ Matt. 2:6, RV, "shall be Shepherd of" (for KJV, "shall rule"); of those who act as spiritual shepherds under Him, John 21:16, RV, "tend" (for KJV "feed"), so 1 Pet. 5:2; Acts 20:28, "to feed" ("to tend" would have been a consistent rendering; a shepherd does not only "feed" his flock); of base shepherds, **Jude 12**.

Without fear *aphobos* (880), denotes "without fear," and is said of serving the Lord, Luke 1:74; of being among the Lord's people as His servant, 1 Cor. 16:10; of ministering the Word of God, Phil. 1:14; of the evil of false spiritual shepherds, **Jude 12**. In the Sept., Prov. 1:33.

Without water *anudros* (504), "waterless" (*a*, negative, *n*, euphonic, *hudor*, "water"), is rendered "dry" in Matt. 12:43, KJV, and Luke 11:24 (RV, "waterless"); "without water" in 2 Pet. 2:17 and **Jude 12**.

Carried *periphero* (4064), signifies "to carry about, or bear about," and is used literally, of carrying the sick Mark 6:55, or of physical sufferings endured in fellowship with Christ, 2 Cor. 4:10; metaphorically, of being "carried" about by different evil doctrines, Eph. 4:14; Heb. 13:9; **Jude 12**.

Trees *dendron* (1186), "a living, growing tree" (cf. Eng., "rhododendron," lit., "rose tree"), known by the fruit it produces, Matt. 12:33; Luke 6:44; certain qualities are mentioned in the NT; "a good tree," Matt. 7:17, 18; 12:33; Luke 6:43; "a corrupt tree" (ditto); in **Jude 12**, metaphorically, of evil teachers, "autumn trees (KJV, 'trees whose fruit withereth') without fruit, twice dead, plucked up by the roots," RV; in Luke 13:19 in some texts, "a great tree," KJV (RV, "a tree"); in Luke 21:29 "the fig tree" is illustrative of Israel, "all the trees" indicating gentile nations.

phthinoporinos (5352), an adjective signifying autumnal (from *phthinoporon*, "late autumn," from *phthino*, "to waste away," or "wane," and *opora*, "autumn"), is used in **Jude 12**, where unfruitful and worthless men are figuratively described as trees such as they are at the close of "autumn," fruitless and leafless (KJV, "trees whose fruit withereth").

Without fruit *akarpos* (175), "unfruitful," is used figuratively (a) of "the word of the Kingdom," rendered "unfruitful" in the case of those influenced by the cares of the world and the deceitfulness of riches, Matt. 13:22; Mark 4:19; (b) of the understanding of one praying with a "tongue," which effected no profit to the church without an interpretation of it, 1 Cor. 14:14; (c) of the works of darkness, Eph. 5:11; (d) of believers who fail "to maintain good works," indicating the earning of one's living so as to do good works to others, Titus 3:14; of the effects of failing to supply in one's faith the qualities of virtue, knowledge, temperance, patience, godliness, love of the brethren, and love, 2 Pet. 1:8. In **Jude 12** it is rendered "without fruit," of ungodly men, who oppose the gospel while pretending to uphold it, depicted as "autumn trees." In the Sept., Jer. 2:6.

Twice *dis* (1364), occurs in Mark 14:30, 72; Luke 18:12; **Jude 12**; combined with *muriades*, "ten thousand," in Rev. 9:16; rendered "again" in Phil. 4:16 and 1 Thess. 2:18.

Dead *apothnesko* (599), lit., "to die off or out," is used (a) of the separation of the soul from the body, i.e., the natural "death" of human beings, e.g., Matt. 9:24; Rom. 7:2; by reason of descent from Adam, 1 Cor. 15:22; or of violent "death," whether of men or animals; with regard to the latter it is once translated "perished," Matt. 8:32; of vegetation, **Jude 12**; of seeds, John 12:24; 1 Cor. 15:36; it is used of "death" as a punishment in Israel under the Law, in Heb. 10:28; (b) of the separation of man from God, all who are descended from Adam not only "die" physically, owing to sin, see (a) above, but are naturally in the state of separation from God, 2 Cor. 5:14. From this believers are freed both now and eternally, John 6:50; 11:26, through the "death" of Christ, Rom. 5:8, e.g.; unbelievers, who "die" physically as such, remain in eternal separation from God, John 8:24. Believers have spiritually "died" to the Law as a means of life, Gal. 2:19; Col. 2:20; to sin, Rom. 6:2, and in general to all spiritual association with the world and with that which pertained to their unregenerate state, Col. 3:3, because of their identification with the "death" of Christ, Rom. 6:8. As life never means mere existence, so "death," the opposite of life, never means nonexistence.

Plucked *ekrizoo* (1610), "to pluck up by the roots" (*ek*, "out," *rhiza*, "a root"), is so translated in **Jude 12** (figuratively), and in the KJV in Luke 17:6, RV, "rooted up"; "root up," Matt. 13:29; "shall be rooted up," 15:13.

13 Raging waves of the sea, foaming out their own shame; wandering stars, to whom is reserved the blackness of darkness for ever.

Raging *agrios* (66), denotes (a) "of or in fields" (*agros*, "a field"), hence, "not domestic," said of honey, Matt. 3:4; Mark 1:6; (b) "savage, fierce," **Jude 13**, RV, metaphorically, "wild (waves)," KJV, "raging." It is used in the papyri of a malignant wound.

Waves *kuma* (2949), from *kuo*, "to be pregnant, to swell," is used (a) literally in the plural, Matt. 8:24; 14:24; Mark 4:37 (Acts 27:41, in some mss.); (b) figuratively, **Jude 13**.

Sea *thalassa* (2281), is used (a) chiefly literally, e.g., "the Red Sea," Acts 7:36; 1 Cor. 10:1; Heb. 11:29; the "sea" of Galilee or Tiberias, Matt. 4:18; 15:29; Mark 6:48, 49, where the acts of Christ testified to His deity; John 6:1; 21:1; in general, e.g., Luke 17:2; Acts 4:24; Rom. 9:27; Rev. 16:3; 18:17; 20:8, 13; 21:1; (b) metaphorically, of "the ungodly men" described in **Jude 13** (cf. Isa. 57:20); (c) symbolically, in the apocalyptic vision of "a glassy sea like unto crystal," Rev. 4:6, emblematic of the fixed purity and holiness of all that appertains to the authority and judicial dealings of God; in 15:2, the same, "mingled with fire," and, standing by it (RV) or on it (KJV and RV marg.), those who had "come victorious from the beast" (ch. 13); of the wild and restless condition of nations, Rev. 13:1 (see 17:1, 15), where "he stood" (RV) refers to the dragon, not John (KJV); from the midst of this state arises the beast, symbolic of the final gentile power dominating the federated nations of the Roman world (see Dan., chs. 2, 7, etc.).

Foaming *epaphrizo* (1890), "to foam out, or up," is used metaphorically in **Jude 13**, of the impious libertines, who had crept in among the saints, and "foamed" out their own shame with swelling words. The metaphor is drawn from the refuse borne on the crest of waves and cast up on the beach.

Shame *aischune* (152), "shame," signifies (a) subjectively, the confusion of one who is "ashamed" of anything, a sense of "shame," Luke 14:9; those things which "shame" conceals, 2 Cor. 4:2; (b) objectively, ignominy, that which is visited on a person by the wicked, Heb. 12:2; that which should arise from guilt, Phil. 3:19; (c) concretely, a thing to be "ashamed" of, Rev. 3:18; **Jude 13**, where the word is in the plural, lit., "basenesses," "disgraces."

Wandering *planetes* (4107), "a wanderer" (Eng., "planet"), is used metaphorically in **Jude 13**, of the evil teachers there mentioned as "wandering (stars)." In the Sept., Hos. 9:17. *See also* **Error** at ***Jude 11***.

Stars *aster* (792), "a star," Matt. 2:2–10; 24:29; Mark 13:25; 1 Cor. 15:41; Rev. 6:13; 8:10-12; 9:1; 12:1, 4, is used metaphorically, (a) of Christ, as "the morning star," figurative of the approach of the day when He will appear as the "sun of righteousness," to govern the earth in peace, an event to be preceded by the rapture of the Church, Rev. 2:28; 22:16, the promise of the former to the overcomer being suggestive of some special personal interest in Himself and His authority; (b) of the angels of the seven churches, Rev. 1:16, 20; 2:1; 3:1; (c) of certain false teachers, described as "wandering stars," **Jude 13**, as if the "stars," intended for light and guidance, became the means of deceit by irregular movements.

Reserved *see* ***Jude 6***. *See also* **Preserved** at ***Jude 1***.

Blackness *see* **Darkness** at *Jude 6*.

Darkness *skotos* (4655), a neuter noun frequent in the Sept., is used in the NT (a) of "physical darkness," Matt. 27:45; 2 Cor. 4:6; (b) of "intellectual darkness," Rom. 2:19; (c) of "blindness," Acts 13:11; (d) by metonymy, of the "place of punishment," e.g., Matt. 8:12; 2 Pet. 2:17; **Jude 13**; (e) metaphorically, of "moral and spiritual darkness," e.g., Matt. 6:23; Luke 1:79; 11:35; John 3:19; Acts 26:18; 2 Cor. 6:14; Eph. 6:12; Col. 1:13; 1 Thess. 5:4-5; 1 Pet. 2:9; 1 John 1:6; (f) by metonymy, of "those who are in moral or spiritual darkness," Eph. 5:8; (g) of "evil works," Rom. 13:12; Eph. 5:11, (h) of the "evil powers that dominate the world," Luke 22:53; (i) "of secrecy." While *skotos* is used more than twice as many times as *skotia* in the NT, the apostle John uses *skotos* only once, 1 John 1:6, but *skotia* 15 times out of the 18.

"With the exception of the significance of secrecy, darkness is always used in a bad sense. Moreover the different forms of darkness are so closely allied, being either cause and effect, or else concurrent effects of the same cause, that they cannot always be distinguished; 1 John 1:5; 2:8, e.g., are passages in which both spiritual and moral darkness are intended." *See also* **Jude 6**.

14 And Enoch also, the seventh from Adam, prophesied of these, saying, Behold, the Lord cometh with ten thousands of his saints,

Seventh *hebdomos* (1442), occurs in John 4:52; Heb. 4:4 (twice); **Jude 14**; Rev. 8:1; 10:7; 11:15; 16:17; 21:20.

Prophesied *propheteuo* (4395), "to be a prophet, to prophesy," is used (a) with the primary meaning of telling forth the divine counsels, e.g., Matt. 7:22; 26:68; 1 Cor. 11:4, 5; 13:9; 14:1, 3-5, 24, 31, 39; Rev. 11:3; (b) of foretelling the future, e.g., Matt. 15:7; John 11:51; 1 Pet. 1:10; **Jude 14**.

Lord *see* **Jude 4**.

Thousands *murias*, "a myriad, a vast number," "many thousands," Luke 12:1, RV; Acts 21:20; it also denotes 10,000, Acts 19:19, lit., "five ten-thousands"; **Jude 14**, "ten thousands"; in Rev. 5:11 "ten thousand times ten thousand" is, lit., "myriads of myriads"; in Rev. 9:16 in the best texts, *dismuriades muriadon*, "twice ten thousand times ten thousand" RV (KJV, "two hundred thousand thousand").

Saints *hagios* (40), is used as a noun in the singular in Phil. 4:21, where *pas*, "every," is used with it. In the plural, as used of believers, it designates all such and is not applied merely to persons of exceptional holiness, or to those who, having died, were characterized by exceptional acts of "saintliness." See especially 2 Thess. 1:10, where "His saints" are also described as "them that believed," i.e., the whole number of the redeemed. They are called "holy ones" in **Jude 14**, RV.

15 To execute judgment upon all, and to convince all that are ungodly among them of all their ungodly deeds which they have ungodly committed, and of all their hard *speeches* which ungodly sinners have spoken against him.

Execute *poieo* (4160), "to do, to make," is thrice rendered "execute," of the Lord's authority and acts in "executing" judgment, (a) of His authority as the One to whom judgment is committed, John 5:27; (b) of the judgment which He will mete out to all transgressors at His second advent, **Jude 15**; (c) of the carrying out of His Word (not "work," as in the KJV) in the earth, especially regarding the nation of Israel, the mass being rejected, the remnant saved, Rom. 9:28. That He will "execute His Word finishing and cutting it short," is expressive of the summary and decisive character of His action.

Convince *exelencho* (1827), an intensive form, "to convict thoroughly," is used of the Lord's future "conviction" of the ungodly, **Jude 15**.

Ungodly *asebeia* (763), "impiety, ungodliness," is used of (a) general impiety, Rom. 1:18; 11:26; 2 Tim. 2:16; Titus 2:12; (b) "ungodly" deeds, **Jude 15**, RV, "works of ungodliness"; (c) of lusts or desires after evil things, **Jude 18**. It is the opposite of *eusebeia*, "godliness." *See also* **Jude 4**.

Deeds *ergon* (2041), denotes (I) "work, employment, task," e.g., Mark 13:34; John 4:34; 17:4; Acts 13:2; Phil. 2:30; 1 Thess. 5:13; in Acts 5:38 with the idea of enterprise; (II) "a deed, act," (a) of God, e.g., John 6:28, 29; 9:3; 10:37; 14:10; Acts 13:41; Rom. 14:20; Heb. 1:10; 2:7; 3:9; 4:3, 4, 10; Rev. 15:3; (b) of Christ, e.g., Matt. 11:2; especially in John, 5:36; 7:3, 21; 10:25, 32, 33, 38; 14:11, 12; 15:24; Rev. 2:26; (c) of believers, e.g., Matt. 5:16; Mark 14:6; Acts 9:36; Rom. 13:3; Col. 1:10; 1 Thess. 1:3, "work of faith," here the initial act of faith at conversion (turning to God, v. 9); in 2 Thess. 1:11, "*every* work of faith," RV, denotes every activity undertaken for Christ's sake; 2:17; 1 Tim. 2:10; 5:10; 6:18; 2 Tim. 2:21; 3:17; Titus 2:7, 14; 3:1, 8, 14; Heb. 10:24; 13:21; frequent in James, as the effect of faith [in 1:25, KJV, "(a doer) of the work," RV, "(a doer) that worketh"]; 1 Pet. 2:12; Rev. 2:2 and in several other places in chs. 2 and 3; 14:13; (d) of unbelievers, e.g., Matt. 23:3, 5; John 7:7; Acts 7:41 (for idols); Rom. 13:12; Eph. 5:11; Col. 1:21; Titus 1:16

(1st part); 1 John 3:12; **Jude 15**, RV; Rev. 2:6, RV; of those who seek justification by works, e.g., Rom. 9:32; Gal. 3:10; Eph. 2:9; described as the works of the law, e.g., Gal. 2:16; 3:2, 5; dead works, Heb. 6:1; 9:14; (e) of Babylon, Rev. 18:6; (f) of the Devil, John 8:41; 1 John 3:8.

Ungodly committed *asebeo* (764), signifies (a) "to be or live ungodly," 2 Pet. 2:6; (b) "to commit ungodly deeds," **Jude 15.**

Hard Synonymous with *austeros*, but to be distinguished from it, is *skleros* (from *skello*, "to be dry"). It was applied to that which lacks moisture, and so is rough and disageeable to the touch, and hence came to denote "harsh, stern, hard." It is used by Matthew to describe the unprofitable servant's remark concerning his master, in the parable corresponding to that in Luke 19 (see *austeros*, above). *Austeros* is derived from a word having to do with the taste, *skleros*, "with the touch." *Austeros* is not necessarily a term of reproach, whereas *skleros* is always so, and indicates a harsh, even inhuman character. *Austeros* is "rather the exaggeration of a virtue pushed too far, than an absolute vice" (Trench, *Syn.* Sec. xiv). *Skleros* is used of the character of a man, Matt. 25:24; of a saying, John 6:60; of the difficulty and pain of kicking against the ox-goads, Acts 9:5; 26:14; of rough winds, Jas. 3:4 and of harsh speeches, **Jude 15**. Cf. *sklerotes*, "hardness," *skleruno*, "to harden," *sklerokardia*, "hardness of heart," and *sklerotrachelos*, "stiff-necked."

16 These are murmurers, complainers, walking after their own lusts; and their mouth speaketh great swelling *words*, having men's persons in admiration because of advantage.

Murmurers *gongustes* (1113), "a murmurer" "one who complains," is used in **Jude 16**, especially perhaps of utterances against God.

Complainers *mempsimoiros* (3202), denotes "one who complains," lit., "complaining of one's lot" (*memphomai*, "to blame," *moira*, "a fate, lot"); hence, "discontented, querulous, repining"; it is rendered "complainers" in **Jude 16**.

Walking *poreuo* (4198), is used in the middle voice and rendered "to walk" in Luke 1:6, of the general activities of life; so in Luke 13:33, KJV, "walk" (RV, "go on My way"); Acts 9:31; 14:16; 1 Pet. 4:3; 2 Pet. 2:10; **Jude 16, 18.**

Lusts *epithumia* (1939), denotes "strong desire" of any kind, the various kinds being frequently specified by some adjective. The word is used of a good desire in Luke 22:15; Phil. 1:23, and 1 Thess. 2:17 only. Everywhere else it has a bad sense. In Rom. 6:12 the injunction against letting sin reign in our mortal body to obey the "lust" thereof, refers to those evil desires which are ready to express themselves in bodily activity. They are equally the "lusts" of the flesh, Rom. 13:14; Gal. 5:16, 24; Eph. 2:3; 2 Pet. 2:18; 1 John 2:16, a phrase which describes the emotions of the soul, the natural tendency towards things evil. Such "lusts" are not necessarily base and immoral, they may be refined in character, but are evil if inconsistent with the will of God. Other descriptions besides those already mentioned are: "of the mind," Eph. 2:3; "evil (desire)," Col. 3:5; "the passion of," 1 Thess. 4:5, RV; "foolish and hurtful," 1 Tim. 6:9; "youthful," 2 Tim. 2:22; "divers," 2 Tim. 3:6 and Titus 3:3; "their own," 2 Tim. 4:3; 2 Pet. 3:3; **Jude 16**; "worldly," Titus 2:12; "his own," Jas. 1:14; "your former," 1 Pet. 1:14, RV; "fleshly," 2:11; "of men," 4:2; "of defilement," 2 Pet. 2:10; "of the eyes," 1 John 2:16; of the world ("thereof"), v. 17; "their own ungodly," **Jude 18**. In Rev. 18:14 "(the fruits) which thy soul lusted after" is, lit., "of thy soul's lust."

Swelling *huperonkos* (5246), an adjective denoting "of excessive weight or size," is used metaphorically in the sense of "immoderate," especially of arrogant speech, in the neuter plural, virtually as a noun, 2 Pet. 2:18; **Jude 16**, "great swelling words," doubtless with reference to gnostic phraseology.

Persons *prosopon* (4383), denotes "the countenance," lit., "the part towards the eyes" (from *pros*, "towards," *ops*, "the eye"), and is used (a) of the "face," Matt. 6:16-17; 2 Cor. 3:7, 2nd part (KJV, "countenance"); in 2 Cor. 10:7, in the RV, "things that are before your face" (KJV, "outward appearance"), the phrase is figurative of superficial judgment; (b) of the look, i.e., the "face," which by its various movements affords an index of inward thoughts and feelings. e g., Luke 9:51, 53; 1 Pet. 3:12; (c) the presence of a person, the "face" being the noblest part, e.g., Acts 3:13, RV, "before the face of," KJV, "in the presence of"; 5:41, "presence"; 2 Cor. 2:10, "person"; 1 Thess. 2:17 (first part), "presence"; 2 Thess. 1:9, RV, "face," KJV, "presence"; Rev. 12:14, "face"; (d) the person himself, e.g., Gal. 1:22; 1 Thess. 2:17 (second part); (e) the appearance one presents by his wealth or poverty, his position or state, Matt. 22:16; Mark 12:14; Gal. 2:6; **Jude 16**; (f) the outward appearance of inanimate things, Matt. 16:3; Luke 12:56; 21:35; Acts 17:26.

Advantage *opheleia* (5622), is found in Rom. 3:1, "profit," and **Jude 16**, "advantage." (i.e., they shew respect of persons for the sake of what they may gain from them).

17 But, beloved, remember ye the words which were spoken before of the apostles of our Lord Jesus Christ;

Ye These are most frequently the translations of various inflections of a verb; sometimes of the article before a nominative used as a vocative, e.g., Rev. 18:20, "ye saints, and ye apostles, and ye prophets" (lit., "the saints, etc."). When the 2nd person plural pronouns are used separately from a verb, they are usually one or other of the forms of *humeis*, the plural of *su*, "thou," and are frequently emphatic, especially when they are subjects of the verb, an emphasis always to be noticed, e.g., Matt. 5:13, 14, 48; 6:9, 19, 20; Mark 6:31, 37; John 15:27a; Rom. 1:6; 1 Cor. 3:17, 23; Gal. 3:28, 29a; Eph. 1:13a; 2:8; 2:11, 13; Phil. 2:18; Col. 3:4, 7a; 4:1; 1 Thess. 1:6; 2:10, 19, 20; 3:8; 2 Thess. 3:13; Jas. 5:8; 1 Pet. 2:9a; 1 John 2:20, 24 (1st and 3rd occurrences), 27a; 4:4; **Jude 17, 20**.

Words *rhema* (4487), denotes "that which is spoken, what is uttered in speech or writing"; in the singular, "a word," e.g., Matt. 12:36; 27:14; 2 Cor. 12:4; 13:1; Heb. 12:19; in the plural, speech, discourse, e.g., John 3:34; 8:20; Acts 2:14; 6:11, 13; 11:14; 13:42; 26:25; Rom. 10:18; 2 Pet. 3:2; **Jude 17**; it is used of the gospel in Rom. 10:8 (twice), 17, RV, "the word of Christ" (i.e., the "word" which preaches Christ); 10:18; 1 Pet. 1:25 (twice); of a statement, command, instruction, e.g., Matt. 26:75; Luke 1:37, RV, "(no) word (from God shall be void of power)", v. 38; Acts 11:16; Heb. 11:3.

The significance of *rhema* (as distinct from *logos*) is exemplified in the injunction to take "the sword of the Spirit, which is the word of God," Eph. 6:17; here the reference is not to the whole Bible as such, but to the individual Scripture which the Spirit brings to our remembrance for use in time of need, a prerequisite being the regular storing of the mind with Scripture.

Spoken before *proeipon* (4302), and *proereo*, "to say before," used as aorist and future respectively of *prolego*, is used (a) of prophecy, e.g., Rom. 9:29; "to tell before," Matt. 24:25; Mark 13:23; "were spoken before," 2 Pet. 3:2; **Jude 17**; (b) of "saying" before, 2 Cor. 7:3; 13:2, RV (KJV, "to tell before" and "foretell"); Gal. 1:9; 5:21; in 1 Thess. 4:6, "we forewarned," RV.

18 How that they told you there should be mockers in the last time, who should walk after their own ungodly lusts.

Mockers *empaiktes* (1703), "a mocker," is used in 2 Pet. 3:3, RV, "mockers". (KJV, "scoffers"); **Jude 18**, RV and KJV, "mockers." In the Sept., Isa. 3:4.

Last *eschatos* (2078), "last, utmost, extreme," is used (a) of place, e.g., Luke 14:9, 10, "lowest;" Acts 1:8 and 13:47, "uttermost part;" (b) of rank, e.g., Mark 9:35; (c) of time, relating either to persons or things, e.g., Matt. 5:26, "the last (farthing)," RV (KJV, "uttermost"); Matt. 20:8, 12, 14; Mark 12:6, 22; 1 Cor. 4:9, of apostles as "last" in the program of a spectacular display; 1 Cor. 15:45, "the last Adam"; Rev. 2:19; of the "last" state of persons, Matt. 12:45, neuter plural, lit., "the last (things)"; so Luke 11:26; 2 Pet. 2:20, RV, "the last state" (KJV, "the latter end"); of Christ as the Eternal One, Rev. 1:17 (in some mss. v. 11); 2:8; 22:13; in eschatological phrases as follows: (a) "the last day," a comprehensive term including both the time of the resurrection of the redeemed, John 6:39, 40, 44, 54 and 11:24, and the ulterior time of the judgment of the unregenerate, at the Great White Throne, John 12:48; (b) "the last days," Acts 2:17, a period relative to the supernatural manifestation of the Holy Spirit at Pentecost and the resumption of the divine interpositions in the affairs of the world at the end of the present age, before "the great and notable Day of the Lord," which will usher in the messianic kingdom; (c) in 2 Tim. 3:1, "the last days" refers to the close of the present age of world conditions; (d) in Jas. 5:3, the phrase "in the last days" (RV) refers both to the period preceding the Roman overthrow of the city and the land in AD 70, and to the closing part of the age in consummating acts of gentile persecution including "the time of Jacob's

> *"Hypocrites in the church? Yes, and in the lodge, and at home. Don't hunt through the church for a hypocrite. Go home and look in the glass. Hypocrites? Yes. See that you make the number one less."*
>
> BILLY SUNDAY

trouble" (cf. verses 7, 8); (e) in 1 Pet. 1:5, "the last time" refers to the time of the Lord's second advent; (f) in 1 John 2:18, "the last hour" (RV) and, in **Jude 18**, "the last time" signify the present age previous to the Second Advent.

Walk *see* **Walking** at *Jude 16*.

Ungodly *see Jude 15*.

Lusts *see Jude 16*.

19 These be they who separate themselves, sensual, having not the Spirit.

Separate *apodiorizo* (592), "to mark off" (*apo*, "from," *dia*, "asunder," *horizo*, "to limit"), hence denotes metaphorically to make "separations," **Jude 19**, RV (KJV, "separate themselves"), of persons who make divisions (in contrast with v. **20**); there is no pronoun in the original representing "themselves."

Sensual *psuchikos* (5591), "belonging to the *psuche*, soul" (as the lower part of the immaterial in man), "natural, physical," describes the man in Adam and what pertains to him (set in contrast to *pneumatikos* "spiritual"), 1 Cor. 2:14; 15:44 (twice), 46 (in the latter used as a noun); Jas. 3:15, "sensual" (RV marg., "natural" or "animal"), here relating perhaps more especially to the mind, a wisdom in accordance with, or springing from, the corrupt desires and affections; so in **Jude 19**.

20 But ye, beloved, building up yourselves on your most holy faith, praying in the Holy Ghost,

Ye *see Jude 17*.

Building *epoikodomeo* (2026), signifies "to build upon" (*epi*, "upon"), 1 Cor. 3:10, 12, 14; Eph. 2:20; **Jude 20**; or up, Acts 20:32; Col. 2:7.

Yourselves The reflexive pronoun "yourselves" represents the various plural forms of the reflexive pronoun *heautou* (frequently governed by some preposition), e.g., Matt. 3:9; 16:8; 23:31; 25:9; Mark 9:50; Luke 3:8; 12:33, 57; 16:9; 21:30, "of your own selves"; 21:34; Acts 5:35; in Rom. 11:25, "in your own (conceits)," lit., "in (*en;* some texts have *para*, 'among') yourselves"; so 12:16 (with *para*); 1 Pet. 4:8; **Jude 20, 21**; in Eph. 5:19, RV, "one to another" (KJV, and RV marg., "to yourselves"). In 1 Thess. 5:11, KJV, *allelous*, "one another" (RV), is rendered "yourselves together."

Holy *hagios* (40), fundamentally signifies "separated" (among the Greeks, dedicated to the gods), and hence, in Scripture in its moral and spiritual significance, separated from sin and therefore consecrated to God, sacred.

(a) It is predicated of God (as the absolutely "Holy" One, in His purity, majesty and glory): of the Father, e.g., Luke 1:49; John 17:11; 1 Pet. 1:15, 16; Rev. 4:8; 6:10; of the Son, e.g., Luke 1:35; Acts 3:14; 4:27, 30; 1 John 2:20; of the Spirit, e.g., Matt. 1:18 and frequently in all the Gospels, Acts, Romans, 1 and 2 Cor., Eph., 1 Thess.; also in 2 Tim. 1:14; Titus 3:5; 1 Pet. 1:12; 2 Pet. 1:21; **Jude 20**.

(b) It is used of men and things in so far as they are devoted to God. Indeed the quality, as attributed to God, is often presented in a way which involves divine demands upon the conduct of believers. These are called *hagioi*, "saints," i.e., "sanctified" or "holy" ones ...

"It is evident that *hagios* and its kindred words ... express something more and higher than *hieros*, sacred, outwardly associated with God; ... something more than *semnos*, worthy, honorable; something more than *hagnos*, pure, free from defilement. *Hagios* is ... more comprehensive.... It is characteristically godlikeness" (G. B. Stevens, in *Hastings' Bib. Dic.*).

The adjective is also used of the outer part of the tabernacle, Heb. 9:2 (RV, "the holy place"); of the inner sanctuary, 9:3, RV, "the Holy of Holies"; 9:4, "a holy place," RV; v. 25 (plural), of the presence of God in heaven, where there are not two compartments as in the tabernacle, all being "the holy place"; 9:8, 12 (neuter plural); 10:19, "the holy place," RV (KJV, "the holiest," neut. plural); of the city of Jerusalem. Rev. 11:2; its temple, Acts 6:13; of the faith **Jude 20**; of the greetings of saints, 1 Cor. 16:20; of angels, e.g., Mark 8:38; of apostles and prophets, Eph. 3:5; of the future heavenly Jerusalem, Rev. 21:2, 10; 22:19.

Faith *see Jude 3*.

Praying *proseuchomai* (4336), "to pray," is always used of "prayer" to God, and is the most frequent word in this respect, especially in the Synoptists and Acts, once in Romans, 8:26; in Ephesians, 6:18; in Philippians, 1:9; in 1 Timothy, 2:8; in Hebrews, 13:18; in Jude, v. **20**. For the injunction in 1 Thess. 5:17.

"Prayer is properly addressed to God the Father Matt. 6:6; John 16:23; Eph. 1:17; 3:14, and the Son, Acts 7:59; 2 Cor. 12:8; but in no instance in the NT is prayer addressed to the Holy Spirit distinctively, for whereas the Father is in Heaven, Matt. 6:9, and the Son is at His right hand, Rom. 8:34, the Holy Spirit is in and with the believers, John 14:16, 17. Prayer is to be offered in the Name of the Lord Jesus, John 14:13, that is, the prayer must accord with His character, and must be presented in the same spirit of dependence and submission that marked Him, Matt. 11:26; Luke 22:42. The

Holy Spirit, being the sole interpreter of the needs of the human heart, makes His intercession therein; and inasmuch as prayer is impossible to man apart from His help, Rom. 8:26, believers are exhorted to pray at all seasons in the Spirit, Eph. 6:18; cf. **Jude 20**, and Jas. 5:16, the last clause of which should probably be read 'the inwrought [i.e., by the Holy Spirit] supplication of righteous man availeth much' (or 'greatly prevails' *ischuo*, as in Acts 19:16, 20). None the less on this account is the understanding to be engaged in prayer, 1 Cor. 14:15, and the will, Col. 4:12; Acts 12:5 (where 'earnestly' is, lit., 'stretched out') and so in Luke 22:44. Faith is essential to prayer, Matt. 21:22; Mark 11:24; Jas. 1:5-8, for faith is the recognition of, and the committal of ourselves and our matters to, the faithfulness of God. Where the Jews were numerous, as at Thessalonica, they had usually a Synagogue, Acts 17:1; where they were few, as at Philippi, they had merely a *proseuche*, or 'place of prayer,' of much smaller dimensions, and commonly built by a river for the sake of the water necessary to the preliminary ablutions prescribed by Rabbinic tradition, Acts 16:13, 16."

21 Keep yourselves in the love of God, looking for the mercy of our Lord Jesus Christ unto eternal life.

Yourselves *see* ***Jude 20***.

Looking for *prosdechomai* (4327), "to receive favorably," also means "to expect," and is rendered "to look for," e.g., in Luke 2:38; 23:51; Acts 24:15, RV (KJV, "allow"); Titus 2:13; **Jude 21**.

Mercy *eleos* (1656), "is the outward manifestation of pity; it assumes need on the part of him who receives it, and resources adequate to meet the need on the part of him who shows it. It is used (a) of God, who is rich in mercy, Eph. 2:4, and who has provided salvation for all men, Titus 3:5, for Jews, Luke 1:72, and Gentiles, Rom. 15:9. He is merciful to those who fear him, Luke 1:50, for they also are compassed with infirmity, and He alone can succor them. Hence they are to pray boldly for mercy, Heb. 4:16, and if for themselves, it is seemly that they should ask for mercy for one another, Gal. 6:16; 1 Tim. 1:2. When God brings His salvation to its issue at the Coming of Christ, His people will obtain His mercy, 2 Tim. 1:16; **Jude 21**; (b) of men; for since God is merciful to them, He would have them show mercy to one another, Matt. 9:13; 12:7; 23:23; Luke 10:37; Jas. 2:13."

22 And of some have compassion, making a difference:

Compassion *eleeo* (1653), signifies, in general, "to feel sympathy with the misery of another," and especially sympathy manifested in act, (a) in the active voice, "to have pity or mercy on, to show mercy" to, e.g., Matt. 9:27; 15:22; 17:15; 18:33; 20:30, 31 (three times in Mark, four in Luke); Rom. 9:15, 16, 18; 11:32; 12:8; Phil. 2:27; **Jude 22, 23**; (b) in the passive voice, "to have pity or mercy shown one, to obtain mercy," Matt. 5:7; Rom. 11:30, 31; 1 Cor. 7:25; 2 Cor. 4:1; 1 Tim. 1:13, 16; 1 Pet. 2:10.

Difference *diakrino* (1252), lit., "to separate throughout, to make a distinction," Acts 15:9, RV, is translated "to make to differ," in 1 Cor. 4:7. In **Jude 22**, where the middle voice is used, the KJV has "making a difference"; the RV, adopting the alternative reading, the accusative case, has "who are in doubt," a meaning found in Matt. 21:21; Mark 11:23; Acts 10:20; Rom. 14:23; Jas. 1:6; 2:4.

23 And others save with fear, pulling *them* out of the fire; hating even the garment spotted by the flesh.

Others The plural of the definite article is translated "others" in Acts 17:32; in **Jude 23**, KJV, "others" (RV, "some").

Save *see* **Compassion** at ***Jude 22***.

Pulling *harpazo* (726), "to snatch or catch away," is said of the act of the Spirit of the Lord in regard to Philip in Acts 8:39; of Paul in being "caught" up to paradise, 2 Cor. 12:2, 4; of the rapture of the saints at the return of the Lord, 1 Thess. 4:17; of the rapture of the man child in the vision of Rev. 12:5. This verb conveys the idea of force suddenly exercised, as in Matt. 11:12, "take (it) by force"; 12:29, "spoil" (some mss. have *diarpazo* here), in 13:19, RV, "snatcheth"; for forceful seizure, see also John 6:15; 10:12 28-29; Acts 23:10; in **Jude 23**, RV, "snatching."

Fire *pur* (4442), (akin to which are *pura*, and *puretos*, "a fever," Eng., "fire," etc.) is used (besides its ordinary natural significance):

(a) of the holiness of God, which consumes all that is inconsistent therewith, Heb. 10:27; 12:29; cf. Rev. 1:14; 2:18; 10:1; 15:2; 19:12; similarly of the holy angels as His ministers Heb. 1:7 in Rev. 3:18 it is symbolic of that which tries the faith of saints, producing what will glorify the Lord:

(b) of the divine judgment, testing the deeds of believers, at the judgment seat of Christ 1 Cor. 3:13 and 15:

(c) of the fire of divine judgment upon the rejectors of Christ, Matt. 3:11 (where a distinction is to be made between the baptism of the Holy Spirit at Pentecost and the "fire" of divine retribution; Acts 2:3 could not refer to baptism): Luke 3:16:

(d) of the judgments of God at the close of the present age previous to the establishment of the kingdom of Christ in the world, 2 Thess. 1:8; Rev. 18:8:

(e) of the "fire" of Hell, to be endured by the ungodly hereafter, Matt. 5:22; 13:42, 50; 18:8, 9; 25:41; Mark 9:43, 48; Luke 3:17:

(f) of human hostility both to the Jews and to Christ's followers, Luke 12:49:

(g) as illustrative of retributive judgment upon the luxurious and tyrannical rich, Jas. 5:3:

(h) of the future overthrow of the Babylonish religious system at the hands of the Beast and the nations under him, Rev. 17:16:

(i) of turning the heart of an enemy to repentance by repaying his unkindness by kindness, Rom. 12:20:

(j) of the tongue, as governed by a "fiery" disposition and as exercising a destructive influence over others, Jas. 3:6:

(k) as symbolic of the danger of destruction, **Jude 23**.

Hating *miseo* (3404), "to hate," is used especially (a) of malicious and unjustifiable feelings towards others, whether towards the innocent or by mutual animosity, e.g., Matt. 10:22; 24:10; Luke 6:22, 27; 19:14; John 3:20, of "hating" the light (metaphorically); 7:7; 15:18, 19, 23-25; Titus 3:3; 1 John 2:9, 11; 3:13, 15; 4:20; Rev. 18:2, where "hateful" translates the perfect participle passive voice of the verb, lit., "hated," or "having been hated"; (b) of a right feeling of aversion from what is evil; said of wrongdoing, Rom. 7:15; iniquity, Heb. 1:9; "the garment (figurative) spotted by the flesh," **Jude 23**; "the works of the Nicolaitans," Rev. 2:6 (and v. 15, in some mss.; see the KJV); (c) of relative preference for one thing over another, by way of expressing either aversion from, or disregard for, the claims of one person or thing relatively to those of another, Matt. 6:24, and Luke 16:13, as to the impossibility of serving two masters; Luke 14:26, as to the claims of parents relatively to those of Christ; John 12:25, of disregard for one's life relatively to the claims of Christ; Eph. 5:29, negatively, of one's flesh, i.e. of one's own, and therefore a man's wife as one with him.

Garment *chiton* (5509), denotes "the inner vest or undergarment," and is to be distinguished, as such, from the *himation*. The distinction is made, for instance, in the Lord's command in Matt. 5:40: "If any man would go to law with thee, and take away thy coat (*chiton*), (*himation*) also." The order is reversed in Luke 6:29, and the difference lies in this, that in Matt. 5:40 the Lord is referring to a legal process, so the claimant is supposed to claim the inner garment, the less costly. The defendant is to be willing to let him have the more valuable one too. In the passage in Luke an act of violence is in view, and there is no mention of going to law. So the outer garment is the first one which would be seized.

A person was said to be "naked" (*gumnos*), whether he was without clothing, or had thrown off his outer garment, e.g., his *ependutes*, and was clad in a light undergarment, as was the case with Peter, in John 21:7. The high priest, in rending his clothes after the reply the Lord gave him in answer to his challenge, rent his undergarments (*chiton*), the more forcibly to express his assumed horror and indignation, Mark 14:63. In **Jude 23**, "the garment spotted by the flesh" is the *chiton*, the metaphor of the undergarment being appropriate; for it would be that which was brought into touch with the pollution of the flesh.

Spotted *spiloo* (4695), "to make a stain or spot," and so "to defile," is used in Jas. 3:6 of the "defiling" effects of an evil use of the tongue; in **Jude 23**, "spotted," with reference to moral "defilement."

24 Now unto him that is able to keep you from falling, and to present *you* faultless before the presence of his glory with exceeding joy,

Keep *phulasso* (5442), "to guard, watch, keep," is rendered by the verb "to guard" in the RV (KJV, "to keep") of Luke 11:21; John 17:12; Acts 12:4; 28:16; 2 Thess. 3:3; 1 Tim. 6:20; 2 Tim. 1:12, 14; 1 John 5:21; **Jude 24**. In Luke 8:29, "was kept under guard," RV (KJV, kept).

Falling In **Jude 24** the adjective *aptaistos*, "without stumbling, sure footed" (*a*, negative, and *ptaio*, "to stumble"), is translated "from stumbling," RV, for KJV, "from falling."

Present *histemi* (2476), "to cause to stand," is translated "to set" in Matt. 4:5 (aorist tense in the best texts; some have the present, as in KJV); 18:2; 25:33; Mark 9:36; Luke 4:9; 9:47; John 8:3; Acts 4:7; 5:27; 6:6; v. 13, "set up"; 22:30; in **Jude 24**, RV, "to set" (KJV, "to present").

Faultless *amomos* (299), "without blemish"; is always so rendered in the RV, Eph. 1:4; 5:27; Phil. 2:15; Col. 1:22; Heb. 9:14; 1 Pet. 1:19; **Jude 24**; Rev. 14:5. This meaning is to be preferred to the various KJV renderings, "without blame," Eph. 1:4, "unblameable," Col. 1:22, "faultless," **Jude 24**, "without fault," Rev. 14:5. The most authentic mss.

have *amomos*, "without blemish," in Phil. 2:15, for *amometos*, "without rebuke." In the Sept., in reference to sacrifices, especially in Lev. and Num., the Psalms and Ezek., "of blamelessness in character and conduct."

Before *katenopion* (2714), signifies "right over against, opposite"; (a) of place, **Jude 24**; (b) before God as Judge, Eph. 1:4; Col. 1:22.

Presence *katenopion* (2714), "in the very presence of," is translated "before the presence of" in **Jude 24**.

Joy *agalliasis* (20), "exultation, exuberant joy," is translated "gladness" in Luke 1:14; Acts 2:6; Heb. 1:9; "joy" in Luke 1:44; "exceeding joy" in **Jude 24**. It indicates a more exultant "joy" than *chara*. In the Sept. this word is found chiefly in the Psalms, where it denotes "joy" in God's redemptive work, e.g., 30:5; 42:4; 45:7, 15.

25 To the only wise God our Saviour, *be* glory and majesty, dominion and power, both now and ever. Amen.

Only *see Jude 4.*

Wise *sophos* (4680), is used of (a) God, Rom. 16:27; in 1 Tim. 1:17 and **Jude 25** *sophos* is absent, in the best mss. (see the RV), the comparative degree, *sophoteros*, occurs in 1 Cor. 1:25, where "foolishness" is simply in the human estimate; (b) spiritual teachers in Israel, Matt. 23:34; (c) believers endowed with spiritual and practical wisdom, Rom. 16:19; 1 Cor. 3:10; 6:5; Eph. 5:15; Jas. 3:13; (d) Jewish teachers in the time of Christ, Matt. 11:25; Luke 10:21; (e) the naturally learned, Rom. 1:14, 22; 1 Cor. 1:19, 20, 26, 27; 3:15-20.

Saviour *soter* (4990), "a savior, deliverer, preserver," is used (a) of God, Luke 1:47; 1 Tim. 1:1; 2:3; 4:10 (in the sense of "preserver," since He gives "to all life and breath and all things"); Titus 1:3; 2:10; 3:4; **Jude 25**; (b) of Christ, Luke 2:11; John 4:42; Acts 5:31; 13:23 (of Israel); Eph. 5:23 (the sustainer and preserver of the church, His "body"); Phil. 3:20 (at His return to receive the Church to Himself); 2 Tim. 1:10 (with reference to His incarnation, "the days of His flesh"); Titus 1:4 (a title shared, in the context, with God the Father); 2:13, RV, "our great God and Savior Jesus Christ," the pronoun "our," at the beginning of the whole clause, includes all the titles; Titus 3:6; 2 Pet. 1:1, "our God and Savior Jesus Christ; RV, where the pronoun "our," coming immediately in connection with "God," involves the inclusion of both titles as referring to Christ, just as in the parallel in v. 11, "our Lord and Savior Jesus Christ" (KJV and RV); these passages are therefore a testimony to His deity; 2 Pet. 2:20; 3:2, 18; 1 John 4:14.

Majesty *megalosune* (3172), from *megas*, "great," denotes "greatness, majesty"; it is used of God the Father, signifying His greatness and dignity, in Heb. 1:3, "the Majesty (on high)," and 8:1, "the Majesty (in the Heavens)"; and in an ascription of praise acknowledging the attributes of God in **Jude 25**.

Dominion *kratos* (2904), "force, strength, might," more especially "manifested power," is derived from a root *kra-*, "to perfect, to complete": "creator" is probably connected. It also signifies "dominion," and is so rendered frequently in doxologies, 1 Pet. 4:11; 5:11; **Jude 25**; Rev. 1:6; 5:13 (RV); in 1 Tim. 6:16, and Heb. 2:14 it is translated "power."

Power *exousia* (1849), denotes "authority" (from the impersonal verb *exesti*, "it is lawful"). From the meaning of "leave or permission," or liberty of doing as one pleases, it passed to that of "the ability or strength with which one is endued," then to that of the "power of authority," the right to exercise power, e.g., Matt. 9:6; 21:23; 2 Cor. 10:8; or "the power of rule or government," the power of one whose will and commands must be obeyed by others, e.g., Matt. 28:18; John 17:2; **Jude 25**; Rev. 12:10; 17:13; more specifically of apostolic "authority," 2 Cor. 10:8; 13:10; the "power" of judicial decision, John 19:10; of "managing domestic affairs," Mark 13:34. By metonymy, or name-change (the substitution of a suggestive word for the name of the thing meant), it stands for "that which is subject to authority or rule," Luke 4:6 (RV, "authority," for the KJV "power"); or, as with the English "authority," "one who possesses authority, a ruler, magistrate," Rom. 13:1-3; Luke 12:11; Titus 3:1; or "a spiritual potentate," e.g., Eph. 3:10; 6:12; Col. 1:16; 2:10, 15; 1 Pet. 3:22. The RV usually translates it "authority."

Revelation

Chapter 1

1:1 The Revelation of Jesus Christ, which God gave unto him, to shew unto his servants things which must shortly come to pass; and he sent and signified *it* by his angel unto his servant John:

Revelation *apokalupsis* (602), "an uncovering" (akin to *apokalupto*), "is used in the NT of (a) the drawing away by Christ of the veil of darkness covering the Gentiles, Luke 2:32; cf. Isa. 25:7; (b) 'the mystery,' the purpose of God in this age, Rom. 16:25; Eph. 3:3; (c) the communication of the knowledge of God to the soul, Eph. 1:17; (d) an expression of the mind of God for the instruction of the church, 1 Cor. 14:6, 26, for the instruction of the Apostle Paul, 2 Cor. 12:1, 7; Gal. 1:12, and for his guidance, Gal. 2:2; (e) the Lord Jesus Christ, to the saints at His Parousia, 1 Cor. 1:7, RV (KJV, 'coming'); 1 Pet. 1:7, RV (KJV, 'appearing'), 13; 4:13; (f) the Lord Jesus Christ when He comes to dispense the judgments of God, 2 Thess. 1:7; cf. Rom. 2:5; (g) the saints, to the creation, in association with Christ in His glorious reign, Rom. 8:19, RV, 'revealing' (KJV, 'manifestation'); (h) the symbolic forecast of the final judgments of God, **Rev. 1:1** (hence the Greek title of the book, transliterated 'Apocalypse' and translated 'Revelation')."

Shew *deiknumi*, or *deiknuo* (1166), denotes (a) "to show, exhibit," e.g., Matt. 4:8; 8:4; John 5:20; 20:20; 1 Tim. 6:15; (b) "to show by making known," Matt. 16:21; Luke 24:40; John 14:8, 9; Acts 10:28; 1 Cor. 12:31; **Rev. 1:1**; **4:1**; **22:6**; (c) "to show by way of proving," Jas. 2:18; 3:13.

Come to pass *ginomai*, "to become, take place," is often translated "to come to pass"; frequently in the Synoptic Gospels and Acts (note the RV of Luke 24:21); elsewhere in John 13:19; 14:22, RV, "(what) is come to pass ...?" KJV, "(how) is it ...?"; 14:29 (twice); 1 Thess. 3:4; **Rev. 1:1**.

Sent *apostello* (649), lit., "to send forth" (*apo*, "from"), akin to *apostolos*, "an apostle," denotes (a) "to send on service, or with a commission." (1) of persons; Christ, sent by the Father, Matt. 10:40; 15:24; 21:37; Mark 9:37; 12:6; Luke 4:18, 43; 9:48; 10:16; John 3:17; 5:36, 38; 6:29, 57; 7:29; 8:42; 10:36; 11:42; 17:3, 8, 18 (1st part), 21, 23, 25; 20:21; Acts 3:20 (future); 3:26; 1 John 4:9, 10, 14; the Holy Spirit, Luke 24:49; 1 Pet. 1:12; **Rev. 5:6**; Moses, Acts 7:35; John the Baptist, John 1:6; 3:28; disciples and apostles, e.g., Matt. 10:16; Mark 11:1; Luke 22:8; John 4:38; 17:18 (2nd part); Acts 26:17; servants, e.g., Matt. 21:34; Luke 20:10; officers and officials, Mark 6:27; John 7:32; Acts 16:35; messengers, e.g., Acts 10:8, 17, 20; 15:27; evangelists, Rom. 10:15; angels, e.g., Matt. 24:31; Mark 13:27; Luke 1:19, 26; Heb. 1:14; **Rev. 1:1**; **22:6**; demons, Mark 5:10; (2) of things, e.g., Matt. 21:3; Mark 4:29, RV, marg., "sendeth forth," text, "putteth forth" (KJV, "... in"); Acts 10:36; 11:30; 28:28; (b) "to send away, dismiss," e.g., Mark 8:26; 12:3; Luke 4:18, "to set (at liberty)."

Signified *semaino* (4591), "to give a sign, indicate" (*sema*, "a sign"), "to signify," is so translated in John 12:33; 18:32; 21:19; Acts 11:28; 25:27; **Rev. 1:1**, where perhaps the suggestion is that of expressing by signs.

1:2 Who bare record of the word of God, and of the testimony of Jesus Christ, and of all things that he saw.

Record, Testimony *martureo* (3140), denotes (I) "to be a *martus*," or "to bear witness to," sometimes rendered "to testify"; it is used of the witness (a) of God the Father to Christ, John 5:32, 37; 8:18 (2nd part); 1 John 5:9, 10; to others, Acts 13:22; 15:8; Heb. 11:2, 4 (twice), 5, 39; (b) of Christ, John 3:11, 32; 4:44; 5:31; 7:7; 8:13, 14, 18 (1st part); 13:21; 18:37; Acts 14:3; 1 Tim. 6:13; **Rev. 22:18**,

20; of the Holy Spirit, to Christ, John 15:26; Heb. 10:15; 1 John 5:7, 8, RV, which rightly omits the latter part of v. 7 (it was a marginal gloss which crept into the original text); it finds no support in Scripture; (c) of the Scriptures, to Christ, John 5:39; Heb. 7:8, 17; (d) of the works of Christ, to Himself, and of the circumstances connected with His death, John 5:36; 10:25; 1 John 5:8; (e) of prophets and apostles, to the righteousness of God, Rom. 3:21; to Christ, John 1:7, 8, 15, 32, 34; 3:26; 5:33, RV; 15:27; 19:35; 21:24; Acts 10:43; 23:11; 1 Cor. 15:15; 1 John 1:2; 4:14; **Rev. 1:2**; to doctrine, Acts 26:22 (in some texts, so KJV); to the Word of God, **Rev. 1:2**; (f) of others, concerning Christ, Luke 4:22; John 4:39; 12:17; (g) of believers to one another, John 3:28; 2 Cor. 8:3; Gal. 4:15; Col. 4:13; 1 Thess. 2:11 (in some texts); 3 John 3, 6, 12 (2nd part); (h) of the apostle Paul concerning Israel, Rom. 10:2; (i) of an angel, to the churches, **Rev. 22:16**; (j) of unbelievers, concerning themselves, Matt. 23:31; concerning Christ, John 18:23; concerning others, John 2:25; Acts 22:5; 26:5; (II) "to give a good report, to approve of," Acts 6:3; 10:22; 16:2; 22:12; 1 Tim. 5:10; 3 John 12 (1st part); some would put Luke 4:22 here.

Word *logos* (3056), denotes (I) "the expression of thought"—not the mere name of an object—(a) as embodying a conception or idea, e.g., Luke 7:7; 1 Cor. 14:9, 19; (b) a saying or statement, (1) by God, e.g., John 15:25; Rom. 9:9; 9:28, RV, "word" (KJV, "work"); Gal. 5:14; Heb. 4:12; (2) by Christ, e.g., Matt. 24:35 (plur.); John 2:22; 4:41; 14:23 (plur.); 15:20. In connection with (1) and (2) the phrase "the word of the Lord," i.e., the revealed will of God (very frequent in the OT), is used of a direct revelation given by Christ, 1 Thess. 4:15; of the gospel, Acts 8:25; 13:49; 15:35, 36; 16:32; 19:10; 1 Thess. 1:8; 2 Thess. 3:1; in this respect it is the message from the Lord, delivered with His authority and made effective by His power (cf. Acts 10:36); for other instances relating to the gospel see Acts 13:26; 14:3; 15:7; 1 Cor. 1:18, RV; 2 Cor. 2:17; 4:2; 5:19; 6:7; Gal. 6:6; Eph. 1:13; Phil. 2:16; Col. 1:5; Heb. 5:13; sometimes it is used as the sum of God's utterances, e.g., Mark 7:13; John 10:35; **Rev. 1:2, 9**; (c) discourse, speech, of instruction, etc., e.g., Acts 2:40; 1 Cor. 2:13; 12:8; 2 Cor. 1:18; 1 Thess. 1:5; 2 Thess. 2:15; Heb. 6:1, RV, marg.; doctrine, e.g., Matt. 13:20; Col. 3:16; 1 Tim. 4:6; 2 Tim. 1:13; Titus 1:9; 1 John 2:7;

(II) "The Personal Word," a title of the Son of God; this identification is substantiated by the statements of doctrine in John 1:1-18, declaring in verses 1 and 2 (1) His distinct and superfinite Personality, (2) His relation in the Godhead (*pros*, "with," not mere company, but the most intimate communion), (3) His deity; in v. 3 His creative power; in v. 14 His incarnation ("became flesh," expressing His voluntary act; not as KJV, "was made"), the reality and totality of His human nature, and His glory "as of the only begotten from the Father," RV (marg., "an only begotten from a father"), the absence of the article in each place lending stress to the nature and character of the relationship; His was the *shekinah* glory in open manifestation; v. 18 consummates the identification: "the only-begotten Son (RV marg., many ancient authorities read "God only begotten,"), which is in the bosom of the Father, He hath declared Him," thus fulfilling the significance of the title "*Logos*," the "Word," the personal manifestation, not of a part of the divine nature, but of the whole deity. The title is used also in 1 John 1, "the Word of life" combining the two declarations in John 1:1 and 4 and **Rev. 19:13**.

Of In addition to the rendering of a number of prepositions, "of" translates the genitive case of nouns, with various shades of meaning. Of these the subjective and objective are mentioned here, which need careful distinction. Thus the phrase "the love of God," e.g., in 1 John 2:5 and 3:16, is subjective, signifying "God's love"; in 1 John 5:3, it is objective, signifying our love to God. Again, "the witness of God," e.g., 1 John 5:9, is subjective, signifying the witness which God Himself has given; in **Rev. 1:2, 9**, and **19:10**, e.g., "the testimony of Jesus" is objective, signifying the testimony borne to Him. In the KJV "the faith of" is sometimes ambiguous; with reference to Christ it is objective, i.e., faith in Him, not His own faith, in the following passages in which the RV, "in" gives the correct meaning; Rom. 3:22; Gal. 2:16 (twice), 20, RV, "I live in faith, the faith which is in the Son of God"; 3:22; Eph. 3:12; Phil. 3:9 (cf. Col. 2:12, "faith in the working of God"). In Eph. 2:20, "the foundation of the apostles and prophets" is subjective, i.e., the foundation laid by the apostles and prophets ("other foundation can no man lay than ... Jesus Christ," 1 Cor. 3:11).

1:3 Blessed *is* he that readeth, and they that hear the words of this prophecy, and keep those things which are written therein: for the time *is* at hand.

Blessed *makarios* (3107), is used in the beatitudes in Matt. 5 and Luke 6, is especially frequent in the Gospel of Luke, and is found seven times in Revelation, **1:3**; **14:13**; **16:15**; **19:9**; **20:6**; **22:7, 14**. It is said of God twice, 1 Tim. 1:11; 6:15. In the beatitudes the Lord indicates not only the characters that are "blessed," but the nature of that which is the highest good.

Readeth *anaginosko* (314), primarily, "to know certainly, to know again, recognize" (*ana*, "again," *ginosko*, "to know"), is used of "reading" written characters, e.g., Matt. 12:3, 5; 21:16; 24:15; of the private "reading" of Scripture, Acts 8:28, 30, 32; of the public "reading" of Scripture, Luke 4:16; Acts 13:27; 15:21; 2 Cor. 3:15; Col. 4:16 (thrice); 1 Thess. 5:27; **Rev. 1:3.**

Prophecy *propheteia* (4394), signifies "the speaking forth of the mind and counsel of God" (*pro*, "forth," *phemi*, "to speak"); in the NT it is used (a) of the gift, e.g., Rom. 12:6; 1 Cor. 12:10; 13:2; (b) either of the exercise of the gift or of that which is "prophesied," e.g., Matt. 13:14; 1 Cor. 13:8; 14:6, 22 and 1 Thess. 5:20, "prophesying(s)"; 1 Tim. 1:18; 4:14; 2 Pet. 1:20, 21; **Rev. 1:3**; **11:6**; **19:10**; **22:7**, **10**, **18**, **19**.

"Though much of OT prophecy was purely predictive, see Micah 5:2, e.g., and cf. John 11:51, prophecy is not necessarily, nor even primarily, fore-telling. It is the declaration of that which cannot be known by natural means, Matt. 26:68, it is the forth-telling of the will of God, whether with reference to the past, the present, or the future, see Gen. 20:7; Deut. 18:18; **Rev. 10:11**; **11:3**...."

Keep *tereo* (5083), denotes (a) "to watch over, preserve, keep, watch," e.g., Acts 12:5, 6; 16:23; in 25:21, RV (1st part), "kept" (KJV, "reserved"); the present participle is translated "keepers" in Matt. 28:4, lit. "the keeping (ones)"; it is used of the "keeping" power of God the Father and Christ, exercised over His people, John 17:11, 12, 15; 1 Thess. 5:23, "preserved"; 1 John 5:18, where "He that was begotten of God," RV, is said of Christ as the Keeper ("keepeth him," RV, for KJV, "keepeth himself"); Jude 1, RV, "kept for Jesus Christ" (KJV, "preserved in Jesus Christ"), **Rev. 3:10**; of their inheritance, 1 Pet. 1:4 ("reserved"); of judicial reservation by God in view of future doom, 2 Pet. 2:4, 9, 17; 3:7; Jude 6, 13; of "keeping" the faith, 2 Tim. 4:7; the unity of the Spirit, Eph. 4:3; oneself, 2 Cor. 11:9; 1 Tim. 5:22; Jas. 1:27; figuratively, one's garments, **Rev. 16:15**; (b) "to observe, to give heed to," as of keeping commandments, etc., e.g., Matt. 19:17; John 14:15; 15:10; 17:6; Jas. 2:10; 1 John 2:3, 4, 5; 3:22, 24; 5:2 (in some mss.), 3; **Rev. 1:3**; **2:26**; **3:8**, **10**; **12:17**; **14:12**; **22:7**, **9**.

At hand *engus* (1451), "near, nigh," frequently rendered "at hand," is used (a) of place, e.g., of the Lord's sepulchre, John 19:42, "nigh at hand"; (b) of time, e.g., Matt. 26:18; Luke 21:30, 31, RV, "nigh," KJV, "nigh at hand"; in Phil. 4:5, "the Lord is at hand," it is possible to regard the meaning as that either of (a) or (b); the following reasons may point to (b): (1) the subject of the preceding context has been the return of Christ, 3:20, 21; (2) the phrase is a translation of the Aramaic "Maranatha," 1 Cor. 16:22, a Christian watchword, and the use of the title "the Lord" is appropriate; (3) the similar use of the adverb in **Rev. 1:3** and **22:10**; (4) the similar use of the corresponding verb in Rom. 13:12; Heb. 10:25, "drawing nigh," RV; Jas. 5:8; cf. 1 Pet. 4:7.

1:4 John to the seven churches which are in Asia: Grace *be* unto you, and peace, from him which is, and which was, and which is to come; and from the seven Spirits which are before his throne;

Which In the triple title of God in **Rev. 1:4**, **8**; **4:8**, "which" is the translation, firstly, of the article with the present participle of *eimi*, to be, lit., "the (One) being," secondly, of the article with the imperfect tense of *eimi* (impossible of lit. translation, the title not being subject to grammatical change), thirdly, of the article with the present participle of *erchomai*, to come, lit., "the coming (One)"; in **11:17** and **16:5** the wording of the KJV and RV differs; in **11:17** the KJV follows the inferior mss. by adding "and art to come" (RV omits); in **16:5**, the KJV, "and shalt be," represents *kai* ("and") followed by the article and the future participle of *eimi*, "to be," lit., "and the (One) about to be"; the RV substitutes the superior reading "Thou Holy One," lit., "the holy (One)".

Before *enopion* (1799), from *en*, "in," and *ops*, "the eye," is the neuter of the adjective *enopios*, and is used prepositionally, (a) of place, that which is before or opposite a person, "towards which he turns his eyes," e.g., Luke 1:19; Acts 4:10; 6:6; **Rev. 1:4**; **4-10**; **7:15**; (b) in metaphorical phrases after verbs of motion, Luke 1:17; 12:9; Acts 9:15, etc.; signifying "in the mind or soul of persons," Luke 12:6; Acts 10:31; **Rev. 16:19**; (c) "in one's sight or hearing," Luke 24:43; John 20:30; 1 Tim. 6:12; metaphorically, Rom. 14:22; especially in Gal. 1:20; 1 Tim. 5:21; 6:13; 2 Tim. 2:14; 4:1; before, as "having a person present to the mind," Acts 2:25; Jas. 4:10; "in the judgment of a person," Luke 16:15; 24:11, RV, "in their sight," for KJV, "to"; Acts 4:19; Rom. 3:20; 12:17; 2 Cor. 8:21; 1 Tim. 2:3; "in the approving sight of God," Luke 1:75; Acts 7:46; 10:33; 2 Cor. 4:2; 7:12.

Throne *thronos* (2362), "a throne, a seat of authority," is used of the "throne" (a) of God, e.g., Heb.

4:16, "the throne of grace," i.e., from which grace proceeds; 8:1; 12:2; **Rev. 1:4**; **3:21** (2nd part); **4:2** (twice); **5:1**; frequently in Rev.; in **20:12**, in the best texts, "the throne" (some have *Theos*, "God," KJV); cf. **21:3**; Matt. 5:34; 23:22; Acts 7:49; (b) of Christ, e.g. Heb. 1:8; **Rev. 3:21** (1st part); **22:3**; His seat of authority in the Millennium, Matt. 19:28 (1st part); (c) by metonymy for angelic powers, Col. 1:16; (d) of the Apostles in millennial authority, Matt. 19:28 (2nd part); Luke 22:30; (e) of the elders in the heavenly vision, **Rev. 4:4** (2nd and 3rd parts), RV, "thrones" (KJV, "seats"); so **11:16**; (f) of David, Luke 1:32; Acts 2:30; (g) of Satan, **Rev. 2:13**, RV, "throne" (KJV, "seat"); (h) of "the beast," the final and federal head of the revived Roman Empire, **Rev. 13:2**; **16:10**.

1:5 And from Jesus Christ, *who is* the faithful witness, *and* the first begotten of the dead, and the prince of the kings of the earth. Unto him that loved us, and washed us from our sins in his own blood,

Faithful *pistos* (4103), a verbal adjective, akin to *peitho*, is used in two senses, (a) passive, "faithful, to be trusted, reliable," said of God, e.g., 1 Cor. 1:9; 10:13; 2 Cor. 1:18 (KJV, "true"); 2 Tim. 2:13; Heb. 10:23; 11:11; 1 Pet. 4:19; 1 John 1:9; of Christ, e.g., 2 Thess. 3:3; Heb. 2:17; 3:2; **Rev. 1:5**; **3:14**; **19:11**; of the words of God, e.g., Acts 13:34, "sure"; 1 Tim. 1:15; 3:1 (KJV, "true"); 4:9; 2 Tim. 2:11; Titus 1:9; 3:8; **Rev. 21:5**; **22:6**; of servants of the Lord, Matt. 24:45; 25:21, 23; Acts 16:15; 1 Cor. 4:2, 17; 7:25; Eph. 6:21; Col. 1:7; 4:7, 9; 1 Tim. 1:12; 3:11; 2 Tim. 2:2; Heb. 3:5; 1 Pet. 5:12; 3 John 5; **Rev. 2:13**; **17:14**; of believers, Eph. 1:1; Col. 1:2; (b) active, signifying "believing, trusting, relying," e.g., Acts 16:1 (feminine); 2 Cor. 6:15; Gal. 3:9 seems best taken in this respect, as the context lays stress upon Abraham's "faith" in God, rather than upon his "faithfulness." In John 20:27 the context requires the active sense, as the Lord is reproaching Thomas for his want of "faith." With regard to believers, they are spoken of sometimes in the active sense, sometimes in the passive, i.e., sometimes as believers, sometimes as "faithful."

Witness *martus* or *martur* (3144), (whence Eng., "martyr," one who bears "witness" by his death) denotes "one who can or does aver what he has seen or heard or knows"; it is used (a) of God, Rom. 1:9; 2 Cor. 1:23; Phil. 1:8; 1 Thess. 2:5, 10 (2nd part); (b) of Christ, **Rev. 1:5**; **3:14**; (c) of those who "witness" for Christ by their death, Acts 22:20; **Rev. 2:13**; **Rev. 17:6**; (d) of the interpreters of God's counsels, yet to "witness" in Jerusalem in the times of the Antichrist, **Rev. 11:3**; (e) in a forensic sense, Matt. 18:16; 26:65; Mark 14:63; Acts 6:13; 7:58; 2 Cor. 13:1; 1 Tim. 5:19; Heb. 10:28; (f) in a historical sense, Luke 11:48; 24:48; Acts 1:8, 22; 2:32; 3:15; 5:32; 10:39, 41; 13:31; 22:15; 26:16; 1 Thess. 2:10 (1st part); 1 Tim. 6:12; 2 Tim. 2:2; Heb. 12:1, "(a cloud) of witnesses," those whose lives and actions testified to the worth and effect of faith, and whose faith received "witness" in Scripture; 1 Pet. 5:1.

First begotten *prototokos* (4416), "firstborn" (from *protos*, "first," and *tikto*, "to beget"), is used of Christ as born of the Virgin Mary, Luke 2:7; further, in His relationship to the Father, expressing His priority to, and preeminence over, creation, not in the sense of being the "first" to be born. It is used occasionally of superiority of position in the OT, see Exod. 4:22; Deut. 21:16, 17, the prohibition being against the evil of assigning the privileged position of the "firstborn" to one born subsequently to the "first" child. The five passages in the NT relating to Christ may be set forth chronologically thus: (a) Col. 1:15, where His eternal relationship with the Father is in view, and the clause means both that He was the "Firstborn" before all creation and that He Himself produced creation (the genitive case being objective, as v. 16 makes clear); (b) Col. 1:18 and **Rev. 1:5**, in reference to His resurrection; (c) Rom. 8:29, His position in relationship to the church; (d) Heb. 1:6, RV, His second advent (the RV "when He again bringeth in," puts "again" in the right place, the contrast to His first advent, at His birth, being implied); cf. Ps. 89:27. The word is used in the plural, in Heb. 11:28, of the firstborn sons in the families of the Egyptians, and in 12:23, of the members of the Church.

Prince *archon* (758), the present participle of the verb *archo*, "to rule"; denotes "a ruler, a prince." It is used as follows ("p" denoting "prince," or "princes"; "r," "ruler" or "rulers"): (a) of Christ, as "the Ruler (KJV, Prince) of the kings of the earth," **Rev. 1:5**; (b) of rulers of nations, Matt. 20:25, RV, "r," KJV, "p"; Acts 4:26, "r"; 7:27, "r"; 7:35, "r" (twice); (c) of judges and magistrates, Acts 16:19, "r"; Rom. 13:3, "r"; (d) of members of the Sanhedrin, Luke 14:1, RV, "r" (KJV, "chief"); 23:13, 35, "r"; so 24:20, John 3:1; 7:26, 48; 12:42, RV, "r" (KJV, "chief r."); "r" in Acts 3:17; 4:5, 8; 13:27; 14:5; (e) of rulers of synagogues, Matt. 9:18, 23, "r"; so Luke 8:41; 18:18; (f) of the Devil, as "prince" of this world, John 12:31; 14:30; 16:11; of the power of the air, Eph. 2:2, "the air" being that sphere in which the inhabitants of the world live and which, through the rebellious and godless condition of humanity, constitutes the seat of his authority; (g) of Beelzebub, the "prince" of the demons, Matt. 9:24; 12:24; Mark 3:22; Luke 11:15.

Washed *louo* (3068), signifies "to bathe, to wash the body," (a) active voice, Acts 9:37; 16:33; (b) passive voice, John 13:10, RV, "bathed" (KJV, "washed"); Heb. 10:22, lit., "having been washed as to the body," metaphorical of the effect of the Word of God upon the activities of the believer; (c) middle voice, 2 Pet. 2:22. Some inferior mss. have it instead of *luo*, "to loose," in **Rev. 1:5** (see RV). *See also* **Loose** at *Revelation 5:2.*

1:6 And hath made us kings and priests unto God and his Father; to him *be* glory and dominion for ever and ever. Amen.

Kings In **Rev. 1:6** and **5:10**, the most authentic mss. have the word *basileia*, "kingdom," instead of the plural of *basileus*, KJV, "kings;" RV, "a kingdom (to be priests)," and "a kingdom (and priests)." The kingdom was conditionally offered by God to Israel, that they should be to Him "a kingdom of priests," Exod. 19:6, the entire nation fulfilling priestly worship and service. Their failure to fulfill His covenant resulted in the selection of the Aaronic priesthood. The bringing in of the new and better covenant of grace has constituted all believers a spiritual kingdom, a holy and royal priesthood, 1 Pet. 2:5, 9.

Priests *hiereus* (2409), "one who offers sacrifice and has the charge of things pertaining thereto," is used (a) of a "priest" of the pagan god Zeus, Acts 14:13; (b) of Jewish "priests," e.g., Matt. 8:4; 12:4, 5; Luke 1:5, where allusion is made to the 24 courses of "priests" appointed for service in the Temple (cf. 1 Chron. 24:4ff.); John 1:19; Heb. 8:4; (c) of believers, **Rev. 1:6; 5:10; 20:6.** Israel was primarily designed as a nation to be a kingdom of "priests," offering service to God, e.g., Ex. 19:6, the Israelites having renounced their obligations, Ex. 20:19, the Aaronic priesthood was selected for the purpose, till Christ came to fulfil His ministry in offering up Himself; since then the Jewish priesthood has been abrogated, to be resumed nationally, on behalf of Gentiles, in the millennial kingdom, Is. 61:6; 66:21. Meanwhile all believers, from Jews and Gentiles, are constituted "a kingdom of priests," **Rev. 1:6**, "a holy priesthood," 1 Pet. 2:5, and "royal," v. 9. The NT knows nothing of a sacerdotal class in contrast to the laity; all believers are commanded to offer the sacrifices mentioned in Rom. 12:1; Phil. 2:17; 4:18; Heb. 13:15, 16; 1 Pet. 2:5; (d) of Christ, Heb. 5:6; 7:11, 15, 17, 21; 8:4 (negatively); (e) of Melchizedek, as the foreshadower of Christ, Heb. 7:1, 3.

Father *pater* (3962), from a root signifying "a nourisher, protector, upholder" (Lat., *pater*, Eng., "father," are akin), is used (a) of the nearest ancestor, e.g., Matt. 2:22; (b) of a more remote ancestor, the progenitor of the people, a "forefather," e.g., Matt. 3:9; 23:30; 1 Cor. 10:1; the patriarchs, 2 Pet. 3:4; (c) one advanced in the knowledge of Christ, 1 John 2:13; (d) metaphorically, of the originator of a family or company of persons animated by the same spirit as himself, as of Abraham, Rom. 4:11, 12, 16, 17, 18, or of Satan, John 8:38, 41, 44; (e) of one who, as a preacher of the gospel and a teacher, stands in a "father's" place, caring for his spiritual children, 1 Cor. 4:15 (not the same as a mere title of honor, which the Lord prohibited, Matt. 23:9); (f) of the members of the Sanhedrin, as of those who exercised religious authority over others, Acts 7:2; 22:1; (g) of God in relation to those who have been born anew (John 1:12, 13), and so are believers, Eph. 2:18; 4:6 (cf. 2 Cor. 6:18), and imitators of their "Father," Matt. 5:45, 48; 6:1, 4, 6, 8, 9, etc. Christ never associated Himself with them by using the personal pronoun "our"; He always used the singular, "My Father," His relationship being unoriginated and essential, whereas theirs is by grace and regeneration, e.g., Matt. 11:27; 25:34; John 20:17; **Rev. 2:27; 3:5, 21**; so the apostles spoke of God as the "Father" of the Lord Jesus Christ, e.g., Rom. 15:6; 2 Cor. 1:3; 11:31; Eph. 1:3; Heb. 1:5; 1 Pet. 1:3; **Rev. 1:6**; (h) of God, as the "Father" of lights, i.e., the Source or Giver of whatsoever provides illumination, physical and spiritual, Jas. 1:17; of mercies, 2 Cor. 1:3; of glory, Eph. 1:17; (i) of God, as Creator, Heb. 12:9 (cf. Zech. 12:1).

Glory *doxa* (1391), "glory" (from *dokeo*, "to seem"), primarily signifies an opinion, estimate, and hence, the honor resulting from a good opinion. It is used (I) (a) of the nature and acts of God in self-manifestation, i.e., what He essentially is and does, as exhibited in whatever way he reveals Himself in these respects, and particularly in the person of Christ, in whom essentially His "glory" has ever shone forth and ever will do, John 17:5, 24; Heb. 1:3; it was exhibited in the character and acts of Christ in the days of His flesh, John 1:14; John 2:11; at Cana both His grace and His power were manifested, and these constituted His "glory", so also in the resurrection of Lazarus

11:4, 40; the "glory" of God was exhibited in the resurrection of Christ, Rom. 6:4, and in His ascension and exaltation, 1 Pet. 1:21, likewise on the Mount of Transfiguration, 2 Pet. 1:17. In Rom. 1:23 His "everlasting power and Divinity" are spoken of as His "glory," i.e., His attributes and power as revealed through creation; in Rom. 3:23 the word denotes the manifested perfection of His character, especially His righteousness, of which all men fall short; in Col. 1:11 "the might of His glory" signifies the might which is characteristic of His "glory"; in Eph. 1:6, 12, 14, "the praise of the glory of His grace" and "the praise of His glory" signify the due acknowledgement of the exhibition of His attributes and ways; in Eph. 1:17, "the Father of glory" describes Him as the source from whom all divine splendor and perfection proceed in their manifestation, and to whom they belong; (b) of the character and ways of God as exhibited through Christ to and through believers, 2 Cor. 3:18 and 4:6; (c) of the state of blessedness into which believers are to enter hereafter through being brought into the likeness of Christ, e.g., Rom. 8:18, 21; Phil. 3:21 (RV, "the body of His glory"); 1 Pet. 5:1, 10; **Rev. 21:11**; (d) brightness or splendor, (1) supernatural, emanating from God (as in the *shekinah* "glory," in the pillar of cloud and in the Holy of Holies, e.g., Exod. 16:10; 25:22), Luke 2:9; Acts 22:11; Rom. 9:4; 2 Cor. 3:7; Jas. 2:1; in Titus 2:13 it is used of Christ's return, "the appearing of the glory of our great God and Savior Jesus Christ" (RV); cf. Phil. 3:21, above; (2) natural, as of the heavenly bodies, 1 Cor. 15:40, 41; (II) of good reputation, praise, honor, Luke 14:10 (RV, "glory," for KJV, "worship"); John 5:41 (RV, "glory," for KJV, "honor"); 7:18; 8:50; 12:43 (RV, "glory," for KJV, "praise"); 2 Cor. 6:8 (RV, "glory," for KJV "honor"); Phil. 3:19; Heb. 3:3; in 1 Cor. 11:7, of man as representing the authority of God, and of woman as rendering conspicuous the authority of man; in 1 Thess. 2:6, "glory" probably stands, by metonymy, for material gifts, an honorarium, since in human estimation "glory" is usually expressed in things material. The word is used in ascriptions of praise to God, e.g., Luke 17:18; John 9:24, RV, "glory" (KJV, "praise"); Acts 12:23; as in doxologies (lit., "glory-words"), e.g., Luke 2:14; Rom. 11:36; 16:27; Gal. 1:5; **Rev. 1:6**.

Dominion *kratos* (2904), "force, strength, might," more especially "manifested power," is derived from a root *kra-*, "to perfect, to complete": "creator" is probably connected. It also signifies "dominion," and is so rendered frequently in doxologies, 1 Pet. 4:11; 5:11; Jude 25; **Rev. 1:6; 5:13** (RV); in 1 Tim. 6:16, and Heb. 2:14 it is translated "power."

1:7 Behold, he cometh with clouds; and every eye shall see him, and they *also* which pierced him: and all kindreds of the earth shall wail because of him. Even so, Amen.

Clouds *nephele* (3507), "a definitely shaped cloud, or masses of clouds possessing definite form," is used, besides the physical element, (a) of the "cloud" on the mount of transfiguration, Matt. 17:5; (b) of the "cloud" which covered Israel in the Red Sea, 1 Cor. 10:1-2; (c), of "clouds" seen in the Apocalyptic visions, **Rev. 1:7; 10:1; 11:12; 14:14-16**; (d) metaphorically in 2 Pet. 2:17, of the evil workers there mentioned; but RV, "and mists" (*homichle*), according to the most authentic mss. In 1 Thess. 4:17, the "clouds" referred to in connection with the rapture of the saints are probably the natural ones, as also in the case of those in connection with Christ's second advent to the earth. See Matt. 24:30; 26:64, and parallel passages. So at the Ascension, Acts 1:9.

Pierced *ekkenteo* (1574), primarily, "to prick out" (*ek*, "out," *kenteo*, "to prick"), signifies "to pierce," John 19:37; **Rev. 1:7**.

Kindreds *phule* (5443), "a company of people united by kinship or habitation, a clan, tribe," is used (a) of the peoples of the earth, Matt. 24:30; in the following the RV has "tribe(-s)" for KJV, "kindred(-s)," **Rev. 1:7; 5:9; 7:9; 11:9; 13:7; 14:6**; (b) of the "tribes" of Israel, Matt. 19:28; Luke 2:36; 22:30; Acts 13:21; Rom. 11:1; Phil. 3:5; Heb. 7:13, 14; Jas. 1:1; **Rev. 5:5; 7:4-8; 21:12**.

Wail *kopto* (2875), primarily, "to beat, smite"; then, "to cut off," Matt. 21:8; Mark 11:8, is used in the middle voice, of beating oneself, beating the breast, as a token of grief; hence, "to bewail," Matt. 11:17 (RV, "mourn," for KJV, "lament"); 24:30, "mourn"; **Rev. 1:7** (RV, "mourn"; KJV, "wail"); in Luke 8:52; 23:27 "bewail"; in **Rev. 18:9**, "wail" (for KJV, "lament"). Cf. *kopetos*, "lamentation," Acts 8:2.

Even so *nai* (3483), a particle of affirmation, is used (a) in answer to a question, Matt. 9:28; 11:9; 13:51; 17:25; 21:16; Luke 7:26; John 11:27; 21:15, 16; Acts 5:8; 22:27; Rom. 3:29; (b) in assent to an assertion, Matt. 15:27, RV (KJV, "truth"); Mark 7:28; **Rev. 14:13; 16:7**, RV (KJV, "even so"); (c) in confirmation of an assertion, Matt. 11:26 and Luke 10:21, RV (KJV, "even so"); Luke 11:51, RV (KJV, "verily"); 12:5; Phil. 4:3 (in the best texts); Philem. 20; (d) in solemn asseveration, **Rev.**

1:7 (KJV and RV, "even so"); **22:20**, RV (KJV, "surely"); (e) in repetition for emphasis, Matt. 5:37; 2 Cor. 1:17; Jas. 5:12; (f) singly in contrast to *ou*, "nay," 2 Cor. 1:18, 19 (twice), 20, "(the) yea," RV.

1:8 I am Alpha and Omega, the beginning and the ending, saith the Lord, which is, and which was, and which is to come, the Almighty.

Ending *telos* (5056), signifies (a) "the limit," either at which a person or thing ceases to be what he or it was up to that point, or at which previous activities were ceased, 2 Cor. 3:13; 1 Pet. 4:7; (b) "the final issue or result" of a state or process, e.g., Luke 1:33; in Rom. 10:4, Christ is described as "the end of the Law unto righteousness to everyone that believeth"; this is best explained by Gal. 3:23-26; cf. Jas. 5:11; the following more especially point to the issue or fate of a thing, Matt. 26:58; Rom. 6:21; 2 Cor. 11:15; Phil. 3:19; Heb. 6:8; 1 Pet. 1:9; (c) "a fulfillment," Luke 22:37, KJV, "(have) an end"; (d) "the utmost degree" of an act, as of the love of Christ towards His disciples, John 13:1; (e) "the aim or purpose" of a thing, 1 Tim. 1:5; (f) "the last" in a succession or series **Rev. 1:8** (KJV, only, "ending"); **21:6**; **22:13**.

Which *see Revelation 1:4.*

1:9 I John, who also am your brother, and companion in tribulation, and in the kingdom and patience of Jesus Christ, was in the isle that is called Patmos, for the word of God, and for the testimony of Jesus Christ.

Companion *sunkoinonos* (4791), denotes "partaking jointly with" (*sun*, and *koinonos*), Rom. 11:17, RV, "(didst become) partaker with them" (KJV, "partakest"); 1 Cor. 9:23, RV, "a joint partaker," i.e., with the gospel, as cooperating in its activity; the KJV misplaces the "with" by attaching it to the superfluous italicized pronoun "*you*"; Phil. 1:7, "partakers with (me of grace)," RV, and KJV marg.; not as KJV text, "partakers (of my grace)"; **Rev. 1:9**, "partaker with (you in the tribulation, etc.)," KJV, "companion."

Tribulation *thlipsis* (2347), is translated "tribulation" in the RV (for KJV, "affliction") in Mark 4:17; 13:19; plural in 2 Thess. 1:4, KJV, "tribulations," RV, "afflictions"; in Acts 14:22 "many tribulations" (KJV, "much tribulation"); in Matt. 24:9, "unto tribulation" (KJV, "to be afflicted"); in 2 Cor. 1:4; 7:4; 2 Thess. 1:6, KJV, "tribulation" for RV, "affliction"; RV and KJV, "tribulation(-s)," e.g., in Rom. 2:9; 5:3 (twice); 8:35; 12:12; Eph. 3:13; **Rev. 1:9**; **2:9**, **10**, **22**. In **Rev. 7:14**, "the great tribulation," RV, lit., "the tribulation, the great one" (not as KJV, without the article), is not that in which all saints share; it indicates a definite period spoken of by the Lord in Matt. 24:21, 29; Mark 13:19, 24, where the time is mentioned as preceding His second advent, and as a period in which the Jewish nation, restored to Palestine in unbelief by gentile instrumentality, will suffer an unprecedented outburst of fury on the part of the antichristian powers confederate under the Man of Sin (2 Thess. 2:10-12; cf. **Rev. 12:13-17**); in this tribulation gentile witnesses for God will share (**Rev. 7:9**), but it will be distinctly "the time of Jacob's trouble" (Jer. 30:7); its beginning is signalized by the setting up of the "abomination of desolation" (Matt. 24:15; Mark 13:14, with Dan. 11:31; 12:11).

Kingdom *basileia* (932), is primarily an abstract noun, denoting "sovereignty, royal power, dominion," e.g., **Rev. 17:18**, translated "(which) reigneth," lit., "hath a kingdom" (RV marg.); then, by metonymy, a concrete noun, denoting the territory or people over whom a king rules, e.g., Matt. 4:8; Mark 3:24. It is used especially of the "kingdom" of God and of Christ.

"The Kingdom of God is (a) the sphere of God's rule, Ps. 22:28; 145:13; Dan. 4:25; Luke 1:52; Rom. 13:1, 2. Since, however, this earth is the scene of universal rebellion against God, e.g., Luke 4:5, 6; 1 John 5:19; **Rev. 11:15-18**, the "kingdom" of God is (b) the sphere in which, at any given time, His rule is acknowledged. God has not relinquished His sovereignty in the face of rebellion, demoniac and human, but has declared His purpose to establish it, Dan. 2:44; 7:14; 1 Cor. 15:24, 25. Meantime, seeking willing obedience, He gave His law to a nation and appointed kings to administer His "kingdom" over it, 1 Chron. 28:5. Israel, however, though declaring still a nominal allegiance shared in the common rebellion, Isa. 1:2-4, and, after they had rejected the Son of God, John 1:11 (cf. Matt. 21:33-43), were "cast away," Rom. 11:15, 20, 25. Henceforth God calls upon men everywhere, without distinction of race or nationality, to submit voluntarily to His rule. Thus the "kingdom" is said to be "in mystery" now, Mark 4:11, that is, it does not come within the range of the natural powers of observation, Luke 17:20, but is spiritually discerned, John 3:3 (cf. 1 Cor. 2:14). When, hereafter, God asserts His rule universally, then the "kingdom" will be in glory, that is, it will be manifest to all; cf. Matt. 25:31-34; Phil. 2:9-11; 2 Tim. 4:1, 18. Thus, speaking generally, references to the Kingdom fall into two classes, the first, in which it is viewed as present and involving suffering for those who enter it, 2 Thess. 1:5; the second, in which it is viewed as future and is associated with reward, Matt. 25:34, and glory, 13:43. See also Acts 14:22. The fundamental principle of the Kingdom is declared in the words of the Lord spoken in the midst of a company of Pharisees, "the Kingdom of God is in the midst of you," Luke 17:21, marg., that is, where the King is, there is the Kingdom. Thus at the present time and so far as this earth is concerned, where the King is and where His rule is acknowledged, is, first, in the heart of the individual believer, Acts 4:19; Eph. 3:17; 1 Pet. 3:15; and then in the churches of God, 1 Cor. 12:3, 5, 11; 14:37; cf. Col. 1:27, where for "in" read "among." Now, the King and His rule being refused, those who enter the Kingdom of God are brought into conflict with all who disown its allegiance, as well as with the desire for ease, and the dislike of suffering and unpopularity, natural to all. On the other hand, subjects of the Kingdom are the objects of the care of God, Matt. 6:33, and of the rejected King, Heb. 13:5. Entrance into the Kingdom of God is by the new birth, Matt. 18:3; John 3:5, for nothing that a man may be by nature, or can attain to by any form of self-culture, avails in the spiritual realm. And as the new nature, received in the new birth, is made evident by obedience, it is further said that only such as do the will of God shall enter into His Kingdom, Matt. 7:21, where, however, the context shows that the reference is to the future, as in 2 Pet. 1:10, 11. Cf. also 1 Cor. 6:9, 10; Gal. 5:21; Eph. 5:5. The expression 'Kingdom of God' occurs four times in Matthew, 'Kingdom of the Heavens' usually taking its place. The latter (cf. Dan. 4:26) does not occur elsewhere in NT, but see 2 Tim. 4:18, "His heavenly Kingdom." ... This Kingdom is identical with the Kingdom of the Father (cf. Matt. 26:29 with Mark 14:25), and with the Kingdom of the Son (cf. Luke 22:30). Thus there is but one Kingdom, variously described: of the Son of Man, Matt. 13:41; of Jesus, **Rev. 1:9**; of Christ Jesus, 2 Tim. 4:1; "of Christ and God," Eph. 5:5; "of our Lord, and of His Christ," **Rev. 11:15**; "of our God, and the authority of His Christ," **12:10**; "of the Son of His love," Col. 1:13. Concerning the future, the Lord taught His disciples to pray, "Thy Kingdom come," Matt. 6:10, where the verb is in the point tense, precluding the notion of gradual progress and development, and implying a sudden catastrophe as declared in 2 Thess. 2:8. Concerning the present, that a man is of the Kingdom of God is not shown in the punctilious observance of ordinances, which are external and material, but in the deeper matters of the heart, which are spiritual and essential, viz., "righteousness, and peace, and joy in the Holy Spirit," Rom. 14:17."

"With regard to the expressions "the Kingdom of God" and the "Kingdom of the Heavens," while they are often used interchangeably, it does not follow that in every case they mean exactly the same and are quite identical. The Apostle Paul often speaks of the Kingdom of God, not dispensationally but morally, e.g., in Rom. 14:17; 1 Cor. 4:20, but never so of the Kingdom of Heaven. 'God' is not the equivalent of 'the heavens.' He is everywhere and above all dispensations, whereas 'the heavens' are distinguished from the earth, until the Kingdom comes in judgment and power and glory (**Rev. 11:15**, RV) when rule in heaven and on earth will be one. While, then, the sphere of the Kingdom of God and the Kingdom of Heaven are at times identical, yet the one term cannot be used indiscriminately for the other. In the 'Kingdom of Heaven' (32 times in Matt.), heaven is in antithesis to earth, and the phrase is limited to the Kingdom in its earthly aspect for the time being, and is used only dispensationally and in connection with Israel. In the 'Kingdom of God', in its broader aspect, God is in antithesis to 'man' or 'the world,' and the term signifies the entire sphere of God's rule and action in relation to the world. It has a moral and spiritual force and is a general term for the Kingdom at any time. The Kingdom of Heaven is always the Kingdom of God, but the Kingdom of God is not limited to the Kingdom of Heaven, until in their final form, they become identical, e.g., **Rev. 11:15**, RV; John 3:5; **Rev. 12:10**."

Patience *hupomone* (5281), lit., "an abiding under" (*hupo*, "under," *meno*, "to abide"), is almost invariably rendered "patience." "Patience, which grows only in trial, Jas. 1:3 may be passive, i.e., = "endurance," as, (a) in trials, generally, Luke 21:19 (which is to be understood by Matt. 24:13), cf. Rom. 12:12; Jas. 1:12; (b) in trials incident to service in the gospel, 2 Cor. 6:4; 12:12; 2 Tim. 3:10; (c) under chastisement, which is trial viewed as coming from the hand of God our Father, Heb. 12:7; (d) under undeserved affliction, 1 Pet. 2:20; or active, i.e. = "persistence, perseverance," as (e) in well doing, Rom. 2:7 (KJV, "patient continuance"); (f) in fruit bearing, Luke 8:15; (g) in running the appointed race, Heb. 12:1. Patience perfects Christian character, Jas. 1:4, and fellowship in the patience of Christ is therefore the condition upon which believers are to be admitted to reign with Him, 2 Tim. 2:12; **Rev. 1:9**. For this patience believers are 'strengthened with all power,' Col. 1:11, 'through His Spirit in the inward man,' Eph. 3:16. In 2 Thess. 3:5, the phrase 'the patience of Christ,' RV, is possible of three interpretations, (a) the patient waiting for Christ, so KJV paraphrases the words, (b) that they might be patient in their sufferings as Christ was in His, see Heb. 12:2, (c) that since Christ is 'expecting till His enemies be made the footstool of His feet,' Heb. 10:13, so they might be patient also in their hopes of His triumph and their deliverance. While a too rigid exegesis is to be avoided it may, perhaps, be permissible to paraphrase: 'the Lord teach and enable you to love as God loves, and to be patient as Christ is patient.'" In **Rev. 3:10**, "the word of My patience" is the word which tells of Christ's patience, and its effects in producing "patience" on the part of those who are His.

Of *see* ***Revelation 1:2***.

Jesus *iesous* (2424), is a transliteration of the Heb. "Joshua," meaning "Jehovah is salvation," i.e., "is the Savior," "a common name among the Jews, e.g., Ex. 17:9; Luke 3:29 (RV); Col. 4:11. It was given to the Son of God in Incarnation as His personal name, in obedience to the command of an angel to Joseph, the husband of His Mother, Mary, shortly before He was born, Matt. 1:21. By it He is spoken of throughout the Gospel narratives generally, but not without exception, as in Mark 16:19, 20; Luke 7:13, and a dozen other places in that Gospel, and a few in John.

" 'Jesus Christ' occurs only in Matt. 1:1, 18; 16:21, marg.; Mark 1:1; John 1:17; 17:3. In Acts the name 'Jesus' is found frequently. 'Lord Jesus' is the normal usage, as in Acts 8:16; 19:5, 17; see also the reports of the words of Stephen, 7:59, of Ananias, 9:17, and of Paul, 16:31; though both Peter, 10:36, and Paul, 16:18, also used 'Jesus Christ.' In the Epistles of James, Peter, John and Jude, the personal name is not once found alone, but in Rev. eight times (RV), **1:9**; **12:17**; **14:12**; **17:6**; **19:10** (twice); **20:4**; **22:16**. In the Epistles of Paul 'Jesus' appears alone just thirteen times, and in the Hebrews eight times; in the latter the title 'Lord' is added once only, at 13:20. In the Epistles of James, Peter, John, and Jude, men who had companied with the Lord in the days of His flesh, 'Jesus Christ' is the invariable order (in the RV) of the Name and Title, for this was the order of their experience; as 'Jesus' they knew Him first, that He was Messiah they learnt finally in His resurrection. But Paul came to know Him first in the glory of heaven, Acts 9:1-6, and his experience being thus the reverse of theirs, the reverse order, 'Christ Jesus,' is of frequent occurrence in his letters, but, with the exception of Acts 24:24, does not occur elsewhere in the RV. In Paul's letters the order is always in harmony with the context. Thus 'Christ Jesus' describes the Exalted One who emptied Himself, Phil. 2:5, and testifies to His pre-existence; 'Jesus Christ' describes the despised and rejected One Who was afterwards glorified, Phil. 2:11, and testifies to His resurrection. 'Christ Jesus' suggests His grace, 'Jesus Christ' suggests His glory."

Isle *nesos* (3520), "an island," occurs in Acts 13:6; 27:26; 28:1, 7, 9, 11; **Rev. 1:9**; **6:14**; **16:20**.

Word *see* ***Revelation 1:2***.

1:10 I was in the Spirit on the Lord's day, and heard behind me a great voice, as of a trumpet,

Spirit *pneuma* (4151), primarily denotes "the wind" (akin to *pneo*, "to breathe, blow"); also "breath"; then, especially "the spirit," which, like the wind, is invisible, immaterial and powerful. The NT uses of the word may be analyzed approximately as follows: "(a) the wind, John 3:8 (where marg. is, perhaps, to be preferred); Heb. 1:7; cf. Amos 4:13, Sept.; (b) the breath, 2 Thess. 2:8; **Rev. 11:11**; **13:15**; cf. Job 12:10, Sept.; (c) the immaterial, invisible part of man, Luke 8:55; Acts 7:59; 1 Cor. 5:5; Jas. 2:26; cf. Eccl. 12:7, Sept.; (d) the disembodied (or 'unclothed,' or 'naked,' 2 Cor. 5:3, 4) man, Luke 24:37, 39; Heb. 12:23; 1 Pet. 4:6; (e) the resurrection body, 1 Cor. 15:45; 1 Tim. 3:16; 1 Pet. 3:18; (f) the sentient element in man, that by which he perceives, reflects, feels, desires, Matt. 5:3; 26:41; Mark 2:8; Luke 1:47, 80; Acts 17:16; 20:22; 1 Cor. 2:11; 5:3, 4; 14:4, 15; 2 Cor. 7:1; cf. Gen. 26:35; Isa. 26:9; Ezek. 13:3; Dan. 7:15; (g) purpose, aim, 2 Cor. 12:18; Phil. 1:27; Eph. 4:23; **Rev. 19:10**; cf. Ezra 1:5; Ps. 78:8; Dan. 5:12; (h) the equivalent of the personal pronoun, used for emphasis and effect: 1st person, 1 Cor. 16:18; cf. Gen. 6:3; 2nd person, 2 Tim. 4:22; Philem. 25; cf. Ps. 139:7; 3rd person, 2 Cor. 7:13; cf. Isa. 40:13; (i) character, Luke 1:17; Rom. 1:4; cf. Num. 14:24; (j) moral qualities and activities: bad, as of bondage, as of a slave, Rom. 8:15; cf. Isa. 61:3; stupor, Rom. 11:8; cf. Isa. 29:10; timidity, 2 Tim. 1:7; cf. Josh. 5:1; good, as of adoption, i.e., liberty as of a son, Rom. 8:15; cf. Ps. 51:12; meekness, 1 Cor. 4:21; cf. Prov. 16:19; faith, 2 Cor. 4:13; quietness, 1 Pet. 3:4; cf. Prov. 14:29; (k) the Holy Spirit, e.g.,

Matt. 4:1; Luke 4:18; (l) 'the inward man' (an expression used only of the believer, Rom. 7:22; 2 Cor. 4:16; Eph. 3:16); the new life, Rom. 8:4-6, 10, 16; Heb. 12:9; cf. Ps. 51:10; (m) unclean spirits, demons, Matt. 8:16; Luke 4:33; 1 Pet. 3:19; cf. 1 Sam. 18:10; (n) angels, Heb. 1:14; cf. Acts 12:15; (o) divine gift for service, 1 Cor. 14:12, 32; (p) by metonymy, those who claim to be depositories of these gifts, 2 Thess. 2:2; 1 John 4:1-3; (q) the significance, as contrasted with the form, of words, or of a rite, John 6:63; Rom. 2:29; 7:6; 2 Cor. 3:6; (r) a vision, **Rev. 1:10; 4:2; 17:3; 21:10.**"

Lord's *kuriakos* (2960), from *kurios*, signifies "pertaining to a lord or master"; "lordly" is not a legitimate rendering for its use in the NT, where it is used only of Christ; in 1 Cor. 11:20, of the Lord's Supper, or the Supper of the Lord; in **Rev. 1:10**, of the Day of the Lord.

Day *hemera* (2250), "a day," is used of (a) the period of natural light, Gen. 1:5; Prov. 4:18; Mark 4:35; (b) the same, but figuratively, for a period of opportunity for service, John 9:4; Rom. 13:13; (c) one period of alternate light and darkness, Gen. 1:5; Mark 1:13; (d) a period of undefined length marked by certain characteristics, such as "the day of small things," Zech. 4:10; of perplexity and distress, Isa. 17:11; Obad. 12-14; of prosperity and of adversity, Ecc. 7:14; of trial or testing, Ps. 95:8; of salvation, Isa. 49:8; 2 Cor. 6:2; cf. Luke 19:42; of evil, Eph. 6:13; of wrath and revelation of the judgments of God, Rom. 2:5; (e) an appointed time, Ecc. 8:6; Eph. 4:30; (f) a notable defeat in battle, etc., Isa. 9:4; Psa. 137:7; Ezek. 30:9; Hos. 1:11; (g) by metonymy = "when," "at the time when"; (1), of the past, Gen. 2:4; Num. 3:13; Deut. 4:10, (2), of the future, Gen. 2:17; Ruth 4:5; Matt. 24:50; Luke 1:20; (h) a judgment or doom, Job 18:20. (i) of a time of life, Luke 1:17-18 ("years"). As the "day" throws light upon things that have been in darkness, the word is often associated with the passing of judgment upon circumstances. In 1 Cor. 4:3, "man's day," KJV, "man's judgement," RV, denotes mere human judgment upon matters ("man's" translates the adjective *anthropinos*, "human"), a judgment exercised in the present period of human rebellion against "God"; probably therefore "the Lord's Day," **Rev. 1:10**, or "the Day of the Lord" (where an adjective, *kuriakos*, is similarly used), is the day of His manifested judgment on the world. The phrases "the day of Christ," Phil. 1:10; 2:16; "the day of Jesus Christ," 1:6; "the day of the Lord Jesus," 1 Cor. 5:5; 2 Cor. 1:14; "the day of our Lord Jesus Christ," 1 Cor. 1:8, denote the time of the Parousia of Christ with His saints, subsequent to the Rapture, 1 Thess. 4:16-17. In 2 Pet. 1:19 this is spoken of simply as the day. From these the phrase "the day of the Lord" is to be distinguished; in the OT it had reference to a time of the victorious interposition by God for the overthrow of the foes of Israel, e.g., Isa. 2:12; Amos 5:18; if Israel transgressed in the pride of their hearts, the Day of the Lord would be a time of darkness and judgment. For their foes, however, there would come "a great and terrible day of the Lord," Joel 2:31; Mal. 4:5. That period, still future, will see the complete overthrow of gentile power and the establishment of Messiah's kingdom, Isa. 13:9-11; 34:8; Dan. 2:34, 44; Obad. 15; cf. Isa. 61:2; John 8:56. In the NT "the day of the Lord" is mentioned in 1 Thess. 5:2 and 2 Thess. 2:2, RV, where the apostle's warning is that the church at Thessalonica should not be deceived by thinking that "the Day of the Lord is now present." This period will not begin till the circumstances mentioned in verses 3 and 4 take place. For the eventual development of the divine purposes in relation to the human race see 2 Pet. 3:12, "the Day of God."

Voice *phone* (5456), "a sound," is used of the voice (a) of God, Matt. 3:17; John 5:37; 12:28, 30; Acts 7:31; 10:13, 15; 11:7, 9; Heb. 3:7, 15; 4:7; 12:19, 26; 2 Pet. 1:17, 18; **Rev. 18:4; 21:3**; (b) of Christ, (1) in the days of His flesh, Matt. 12:19 (negatively); John 3:29; 5:25; 10:3, 4, 16, 27; 11:43; 18:37; (2) on the cross Matt. 27:46, and parallel passages; (3) from heaven, Acts 9:4, 7; 22:7, 9, 14; 26:14; **Rev. 1:10, 12** (here, by metonymy, of the speaker), 15; 3:20; (4) at the resurrection "to life," John 5:28; 1 Thess. 4:16, where "the voice of the archangel" is, lit., "a voice of an archangel," and probably refers to the Lord's voice as being of an archangelic character; (5) at the resurrection to judgment, John 5:28 [not the same event as (4)]; (c) of human beings on earth, e.g., Matt. 2:18; 3:3; Luke 1:42, in some texts, KJV, "voice", and frequently in the Synoptists; (d) of angels, **Rev. 5:11**, and frequently in Revelation; (e) of the redeemed in heaven, e.g., **Rev. 6:10; 18:22; 19:1, 5**; (f) of a pagan god, Acts 12:22; (g) of things, e.g., wind, John 3:8, RV, "voice" (KJV, "sound").

Trumpet *salpinx* (4536), is used (1) of the natural instrument, 1 Cor. 14:8; (2) of the supernatural accompaniment of divine interpositions, (a) at Sinai, Heb. 12:19; (b) of the acts of angels at the second advent of Christ, Matt. 24:31; (c) of their acts in the period of divine judgments preceding this, **Rev. 8:2, 6, 13; 9:14**; (d) of a summons to John to the

"To worship God is to realize the purpose for which God created us."

HERBERT M. CARSON

presence of God, **Rev. 1:10**; **4:1**; (e) of the act of the Lord in raising from the dead the saints who have fallen asleep and changing the bodies of those who are living, at the Rapture of all to meet Him in the air, 1 Cor. 15:52, where "the last trump" is a military allusion, familiar to Greek readers, and has no connection with the series in **Rev. 8:6** to **11:15**; there is a possible allusion to Num. 10:2-6, with reference to the same event, 1 Thess. 4:16, "the (lit., a) trump of God" (the absence of the article suggests the meaning "a trumpet such as is used in God's service").

1:11 Saying, I am Alpha and Omega, the first and the last: and, What thou seest, write in a book, and send *it* unto the seven churches which are in Asia; unto Ephesus, and unto Smyrna, and unto Pergamos, and unto Thyatira, and unto Sardis, and unto Philadelphia, and unto Laodicea.

Last *eschatos* (2078), "last, utmost, extreme," is used (a) of place, e.g., Luke 14:9, 10, "lowest;" Acts 1:8 and 13:47, "uttermost part;" (b) of rank, e.g., Mark 9:35; (c) of time, relating either to persons or things, e.g., Matt. 5:26, "the last (farthing)," RV (KJV, "uttermost"); Matt. 20:8, 12, 14; Mark 12:6, 22; 1 Cor. 4:9, of apostles as "last" in the program of a spectacular display; 1 Cor. 15:45, "the last Adam"; **Rev. 2:19**; of the "last" state of persons, Matt. 12:45, neuter plural, lit., "the last (things)"; so Luke 11:26; 2 Pet. 2:20, RV, "the last state" (KJV, "the latter end"); of Christ as the Eternal One, **Rev. 1:17** (in some mss. v. **11**); **2:8**; **22:13**; in eschatological phrases as follows: (a) "the last day," a comprehensive term including both the time of the resurrection of the redeemed, John 6:39, 40, 44, 54 and 11:24, and the ulterior time of the judgment of the unregenerate, at the Great White Throne, John 12:48; (b) "the last days," Acts 2:17, a period relative to the supernatural manifestation of the Holy Spirit at Pentecost and the resumption of the divine interpositions in the affairs of the world at the end of the present age, before "the great and notable Day of the Lord," which will usher in the messianic kingdom; (c) in 2 Tim. 3:1, "the last days" refers to the close of the present age of world conditions; (d) in Jas. 5:3, the phrase "in the last days" (RV) refers both to the period preceding the Roman overthrow of the city and the land in AD 70, and to the closing part of the age in consummating acts of gentile persecution including "the time of Jacob's trouble" (cf. verses 7, 8); (e) in 1 Pet. 1:5, "the last time" refers to the time of the Lord's second advent; (f) in 1 John 2:18, "the last hour" (RV) and, in Jude 18, "the last time" signify the present age previous to the Second Advent.

Book *biblion* (975), had in Hellenistic Greek almost lost its diminutive force and was ousting *biblos* in ordinary use; it denotes "a scroll or a small book." It is used in Luke 4:17, 20, of the "book" of Isaiah; in John 20:30, of the Gospel of John; in Gal. 3:10 and Heb. 10:7, of the whole of the OT; in Heb. 9:19, of the "book" of Exodus; in **Rev. 1:11**; **22:7, 9-10, 18** (twice), **19**, of Revelation; in John 21:25 and 2 Tim. 4:13, of "books" in general; in **Rev. 13:8**; **17:8**; **20:12**; **21:27**, of the "Book" of Life; in **Rev. 20:12**, of other "books" to be opened in the Day of Judgment, containing, it would seem, the record of human deeds. In **Rev. 5:1- 9** the "Book" represents the revelation of God's purposes and counsels concerning the world. So with the "little book" in **Rev. 10:8**. In **6:14** it is used of a scroll, the rolling up of which illustrates the removal of the heaven. In Matt. 19:7 and Mark 10:4 the word is used of a bill of divorcement.

Send *pempo* (3992), "to send," is used (a) of persons: Christ, by the Father, Luke 20:13; John 4:34; 5:23, 24, 30, 37; 6:38, 39, (40), 44; 7:16, 18, 28, 33; 8:16, 18, 26, 29; 9:4; 12:44, 45, 49; 13:20 (2nd part); 14:24; 15:21; 16:5; Rom. 8:3; the Holy Spirit, John 14:26; 15:26; 16:7; Elijah, Luke 4:26; John the Baptist, John 1:33; disciples and apostles, e.g., Matt. 11:2; John 20:21; servants, e.g., Luke 20:11, 12; officials, Matt. 14:10; messengers, e.g., Acts 10:5, 32, 33; 15:22, 25; 2 Cor. 9:3, Eph. 6:22; Phil. 2:19, 23, 25; 1 Thess. 3:2, 5; Titus 3:12; a prisoner, Acts 25:25, 27; potentates, by God, 1 Pet. 2:14; an angel, **Rev. 22:16**, demons, Mark 5:12; (b) of things, Acts 11:29; Phil. 4:16; 2 Thess. 2:11; **Rev. 1:11**; **11:10**; **14:15, 18**, RV, "send forth" (KJV, "thrust in").

1:12 And I turned to see the voice that spake with me. And being turned, I saw seven golden candlesticks;

Voice *see Revelation 1:10*.

Candlesticks *luchnia* (3087), is mistranslated "candlestick" in every occurrence in the KJV and in certain places in the RV; the RV has "stand" in Matt. 5:15; Mark 4:21; Luke 8:16; 11:33; "candlestick" in Heb. 9:2; **Rev. 1:12, 13, 20** (twice); **2:1, 5; 11:4**; the RV marg., gives "lampstands" in the passages in Rev., but not in Heb. 9:2.

1:13 And in the midst of the seven candlesticks *one* like unto the Son of man, clothed with a garment down to the foot, and girt about the paps with a golden girdle.

Candlesticks *see Revelation 1:12.*

Like unto *homoios* (3664), "like, resembling, such as, the same as," is used (a) of appearance or form John 9:9; **Rev. 1:13, 15; 2:18; 4:3** (twice), **6, 7; 9:7** (twice), **10, 19; 11:1; 13:2, 11; 14:14**; (b) of ability, condition, nature, Matt. 22:39; Acts 17:29; Gal. 5:21, "such like," lit., "and the (things) similar to these"; 1 John 3:2; **Rev. 13:4; 18:18; 21:11, 18**; (c) of comparison in parables, Matt. 13:31, 33, 44, 45, 47; 20:1; Luke 13:18, 19, 21; (d) of action, thought, etc., Matt. 11:16; 13:52; Luke 6:47, 48, 49; 7:31, 32; 12:36; John 8:55; Jude 7.

Son. *The Son of God* In this title the word "Son" is used sometimes (a) of relationship, sometimes (b) of the expression of character. "Thus, e.g., when the disciples so addressed Him, Matt. 14:33; 16:16; John 1:49, when the centurion so spoke of Him, Matt. 27:54, they probably meant that (b) He was a manifestation of God in human form. But in such passages as Luke 1:32, 35; Acts 13:33, which refer to the humanity of the Lord Jesus, ... the word is used in sense (a).

"The Lord Jesus Himself used the full title on occasion, John 5:25; 9:35 [some mss. have 'the Son of Man'; see RV marg.]; 11:4, and on the more frequent occasions on which He spoke of Himself as 'the Son,' the words are to be understood as an abbreviation of 'the Son of God,' not of 'The Son of Man'; this latter He always expressed in full; see Luke 10:22; John 5:19, etc.

"John uses both the longer and shorter forms of the title in his Gospel, see 3:16-18; 20:31, e.g., and in his Epistles; cf. **Rev. 2:18**. So does the writer of Hebrews, 1:2; 4:14; 6:6, etc. An eternal relation subsisting between the Son and the Father in the Godhead is to be understood. That is to say, the Son of God, in His eternal relationship with the Father, is not so entitled because He at any time began to derive His being from the Father (in which case He could not be co-eternal with the Father), but because He is and ever has been the expression of what the Father is; cf. John 14:9, 'he that hath seen Me hath seen the Father.' The words of Heb. 1:3, 'Who being the effulgence of His (God's) glory, and the very image of His (God's) substance' are a definition of what is meant by 'Son of God.' Thus absolute Godhead, not Godhead in a secondary or derived sense, is intended in the title."

Other titles of Christ as the "Son of God" are: "His Son," 1 Thess. 1:10 (in Acts 13:13, 26, RV, *pais* is rendered "servant"); "His own Son," Rom. 8:32; "My beloved Son," Matt. 3:17; "His Only Begotten Son," John 3:16; "the Son of His love," Col. 1:13.

"The Son is the eternal object of the Father's love, John 17:24, and the sole Revealer of the Father's character, John 1:14; Heb. 1:3. The words, 'Father' and 'Son,' are never in the NT so used as to suggest that the Father existed before the Son; the Prologue to the Gospel according to John distinctly asserts that the Word existed 'in the beginning,' and that this Word is the Son, Who 'became flesh and dwelt among us.'"

Son of Man In the NT this is a designation of Christ, almost entirely confined to the Gospels. Elsewhere it is found in Acts 7:56, the only occasion where a disciple applied it to the Lord and in **Rev. 1:13; 14:14.** "Son of Man" is the title Christ used of Himself; John 12:34 is not an exception, for the quotation by the multitude was from His own statement. The title is found especially in the Synoptic Gospels. The occurrences in John's Gospel, 1:51; 3:13, 14; 5:27; 6:27, 53, 62; 8:28 (9:35 in some texts); 12:23, 34 (twice); 13:31, are not parallel to those in the Synoptic Gospels. In the latter the use of the title falls into two groups, (a) those in which it refers to Christ's humanity, His earthly work, sufferings and death, e.g., Matt. 8:20; 11:19; 12:40; 26:2, 24; (b) those which refer to His glory in resurrection and to that of His future advent, e.g., Matt. 10:23; 13:41; 16:27, 28; 17:9; 24:27, 30 (twice), 37, 39, 44. While it is a messianic title it is evident that the Lord applied it to Himself in a distinctive way, for it indicates more than Messiahship, even universal headship on the part of One who is Man. It therefore stresses His manhood, manhood of a unique order in comparison with all other men, for He is declared to be of heaven, 1 Cor. 15:47, and even while here below, was "the Son of Man, which is in Heaven," John 3:13. As the "Son of Man" He must be appropriated spiritually as a condition of possessing eternal life, John 6:53. In His death, as in His life, the glory of His Manhood was displayed in the absolute obedience and submission to the will of the Father (12:23; 13:31), and, in view of this, all judgment has been committed to Him, who will judge in full understanding experimentally of human conditions, sin apart, and will exercise the judgment as sharing the nature of those judged, John 5:22, 27. Not only is He man, but He is "Son of Man," not by human generation but, according to the Semitic usage of the expression, partaking of the characteristics (sin apart) of manhood belonging to the category of mankind. Twice in Revelation, 1:13 and 14:14, He is described as "One like unto a Son of man," RV (KJV, "... the Son of Man"), cf. Dan. 7:13. He who was thus seen was indeed the "Son of Man," but the absence of the article in the original serves to stress what morally characterizes Him as such. Accordingly in these passages He is revealed, not as the Person known by the title, but as the One who is qualified to act as the Judge of all men. He is the same Person as in the days of His flesh, still continuing His humanity with His Deity. The phrase "like unto" serves to distinguish Him as there seen in His glory and majesty in contrast to the days of His humiliation.

Clothed *enduo* (1746), (Eng., "endue"), signifies "to enter into, get into," as into clothes, "to put on," e.g., Mark 1:6; Luke 8:27 (in the best mss.); 24:49 (KJV, "endued"); 2 Cor. 5:3; **Rev. 1:13**; **19:14**.

Garment *poderes* (4158), signifies "reaching to the feet," from *pous*, and *aro*, "to fit," and is said of a garment, **Rev. 1:13**. In the Sept. it is used of the high priest's garment, e.g., Ex. 28:4. 2. *pezos* (3978), an adjective, "on foot," is used in one of its forms as an adverb in Matt. 14:3, and Mark 6:33, in each place signifying "by land," in contrast to by sea. Cf. *pezeuo*, "to go on foot," Acts 20:3, RV, "to go by land" (marg., "on foot").

Girt *perizonnumi* (4024), "to gird around or about," is used (a) literally, of "girding" oneself for service, Luke 12:37; 17:8; for rapidity of movement, Acts 12:8; (b) figuratively, of the condition for service on the part of the followers of Christ, Luke 12:35; Eph. 6:14; (c) emblematically, of Christ's priesthood, **Rev. 1:13**, indicative of majesty of attitude and action, the middle voice suggesting the particular interest taken by Christ in "girding" Himself thus; so of the action of the angels mentioned in **15:6**.

Paps *mastos* (3149), used in the plural, "paps," Luke 11:27; 23:29; **Rev. 1:13**, KJV, is preferably rendered "breasts," in the RV.

Girdle *zone* (2223), Eng., "zone," denotes "a belt or girdle," Matt. 3:4; Mark 1:6; Acts 21:11; **Rev. 1:13**; **15:6**; it was often hollow, and hence served as a purse, Matt. 10:9; Mark 6:8.

1:14 His head and *his* hairs *were* white like wool, as white as snow; and his eyes *were* as a flame of fire;

Hairs *thrix* (2359), denotes the "hair," whether of beast, as of the camel's "hair" which formed the raiment of John the Baptist, Matt. 3:4; Mark 1:6; or of man. Regarding the latter (a) it is used to signify the minutest detail, as that which illustrates the exceeding care and protection bestowed by God upon His children, Matt. 10:30; Luke 12:7; 21:18; Acts 27:34; (b) as the Jews swore by the "hair," the Lord used the natural inability to make one "hair" white or black, as one of the reasons for abstinence from oaths, Matt. 5:36; (c) while long "hair" is a glory to a woman, and to wear it loose or dishevelled is a dishonor, yet the woman who wiped Christ's feet with her "hair" (in place of the towel which Simon the Pharisee omitted to provide), despised the shame in her penitent devotion to the Lord (slaves were accustomed to wipe their masters' feet), Luke 7:38, 44 (RV, "hair"); see also John 11:2; 12:3; (d) the dazzling whiteness of the head and "hair" of the Son of Man in the vision of **Rev. 1** (v. **14**) is suggestive of the holiness and wisdom of "the Ancient of Days"; (e) the long "hair" of the spirit-beings described as locusts in **Rev. 9:8** is perhaps indicative of their subjection to their satanic master (cf. 1 Cor. 11:10, RV); (f) Christian women are exhorted to refrain from adorning their "hair" for outward show, 1 Pet. 3:3.

White *leukos* (3022), is used of (a) clothing (sometimes in the sense of "bright"), Matt. 17:2; 28:3; Mark 9:3; 16:5; Luke 9:29; John 20:12; Acts 1:10; symbolically, **Rev. 3:4**, **5**, **18**; **4:4**; **6:11**; **7:9**, **13**; **19:14** (2nd part); (b) hair, Matt. 5:36; Christ's head and hair (in a vision; cf. Dan. 7:9), **Rev. 1:14** (twice); ripened grain, John 4:35; a stone, **Rev. 2:17**, an expression of the Lord's special delight in the overcomer, the new name on it being indicative of a secret communication of love and joy; a horse (in a vision), **6:2**; **19:11-14** (1st part); a cloud, **14:14**; the throne of God, **20:11**.

Like In the following the most authentic mss. have *hos*, "as," for *hosei*, "like," in the KJV; Mark 1:10; Luke 3:22; John 1:32; **Rev. 1:14**.

Wool *erion* (2053), occurs in Heb. 9:19; **Rev. 1:14**.

Snow *chion* (5510), occurs in Matt. 28:3; **Rev. 1:14**. Some mss. have it in Mark 9:3 (KJV).

Eyes *ophthalmos* (3788), akin to *opsis*, "sight," probably from a root signifying "penetration, sharpness" (Curtius, Gk. Etym.) (cf. Eng., "ophthalmia," etc.), is used (a) of the physical organ, e.g., Matt. 5:38; of restoring sight, e.g., Matt. 20:33; of God's power of vision, Heb. 4:13; 1 Pet. 3:12; of Christ in vision, **Rev. 1:14**; **2:18**; **19:12**; of the Holy Spirit in the unity of Godhood with Christ, **Rev. 5:6**; (b) metaphorically, of ethical qualities, evil, Matt. 6:23; Mark 7:22 (by metonymy, for envy); singleness of motive, Matt. 6:22; Luke 11:34; as the instrument of evil desire, "the principal avenue of temptation," 1 John 2:16; of adultery, 2 Pet. 2:14; (c) metaphorically, of mental vision, Matt. 13:15; John 12:40; Rom. 11:8; Gal. 3:1, where the metaphor of the "evil eye" is altered to a different sense from that of bewitching (the posting up or placarding of an "eye" was used as a charm, to prevent mischief); by gospel-preaching Christ had been, so to speak, placarded before their "eyes"; the question may be paraphrased, "What evil teachers have been malignly fascinating you?"; Eph. 1:18, of the "eyes of the heart," as a means of knowledge.

Flame *phlox* (5395), akin to Lat. *fulgeo*, "to shine," is used apart from *pur*, "fire," in Luke 16:24; with *pur*, it signifies "a fiery flame," lit., "a flame of fire," Acts 7:30; 2 Thess. 1:8, where the fire is to be understood as the instrument of divine judgment; Heb. 1:7, where the meaning probably is that God makes His angels as active and powerful as a "flame" of fire; in **Rev. 1:14**; **2:18**; **19:12**, of the eyes of the Lord Jesus as emblematic of penetrating judgment, searching out evil.

Fire *pur* (4442), (akin to which are *pura*, and *puretos*, "a fever," Eng., "fire," etc.) is used (besides its ordinary natural significance): (a) of the holiness of God, which consumes all that is inconsistent therewith, Heb. 10:27; 12:29; cf. **Rev. 1:14**; **2:18**; **10:1**; **15:2**; **19:12**; similarly of the holy angels as His ministers Heb. 1:7 in **Rev. 3:18** it is symbolic of that which tries the faith of saints, producing what will glorify the Lord. (b) of the divine judgment, testing the deeds of believers, at the judgment seat of Christ 1 Cor. 3:13 and 15. (c) of the fire of divine judgment upon the rejectors of Christ, Matt. 3:11 (where a distinction is to be made between the baptism of the Holy Spirit at Pentecost and the "fire" of divine retribution; Acts 2:3 could not refer to baptism): Luke 3:16. (d) of the judgments of God at the close of the present age previous to the establishment of the kingdom of Christ in the world, 2 Thess. 1:8; **Rev. 18:8**. (e) of the "fire" of Hell, to be endured by the ungodly hereafter, Matt. 5:22; 13:42, 50; 18:8, 9; 25:41; Mark 9:43, 48; Luke 3:17. (f) of human hostility both to the Jews and to Christ's followers, Luke 12:49. (g) as illustrative of retributive judgment upon the luxurious and tyrannical rich, Jas. 5:3. (h) of the future overthrow of the Babylonish religious system at the hands of the Beast and the nations under him, **Rev. 17:16**. (i) of turning the heart of an enemy to repentance by repaying his unkindness by kindness, Rom. 12:20. (j) of the tongue, as governed by a "fiery" disposition and as exercising a destructive influence over others, Jas. 3:6. (k) as symbolic of the danger of destruction, Jude 23.

1:15 And his feet like unto fine brass, as if they burned in a furnace; and his voice as the sound of many waters.

Like unto *see Revelation 1:13.*

Brass *chalkolibanon* (5474), is used of "white or shining copper or bronze," and describes the feet of the Lord, in **Rev. 1:15** and **2:18**.

Burned *puroomai* (4448), from *pur*, "fire, to glow with heat," is said of the feet of the Lord, in the vision in **Rev. 1:15**; it is translated "fiery" in Eph. 6:16 (of the darts of the evil one); used metaphorically of the emotions, in 1 Cor. 7:9; 2 Cor. 11:29; elsewhere literally, of the heavens, 2 Pet. 3:12; of gold, **Rev. 3:18** (RV, "refined").

Furnace *kaminos* (2575), "an oven, furnace, kiln" (whence Lat. *caminus*, Eng., chimney), used for smelting, or for burning earthenware, occurs in Matt. 13:42, 50; **Rev. 1:15**; **9:2**.

Sound *phone* (5456), most frequently "a voice," is translated "sound" in Matt. 24:31 (KJV marg., "voice"); John 3:8, KJV (RV, "voice"); so 1 Cor. 14:7 (1st part), 8; **Rev. 1:15**; **18:22** (2nd part, RV, "voice"); KJV and RV in **9:9** (twice); in Acts 2:6, RV, "(this) sound (was heard)," KJV, "(this) was noised abroad."

Many *polus* (4183), "much, many great," is used especially of number when its significance is "many," e.g., Matt. 8:30; 9:10; 13:17; so the RV of Matt. 12:15, where some mss. follow the word by *ochloi*, "multitudes"; 1 Cor. 12:12; **Rev. 1:15**; it is more frequently used as a noun, "many (persons)," e.g., Matt. 3:7; 7:22; 22:14; with the article, "the many," e.g., Matt. 24:12, RV; Mark 9:26, RV, "the more part" (KJV "many"); Rom. 5:15, 19 (twice), RV; 12:5; 1 Cor. 10:17; v. 33, RV; so 2 Cor. 2:17; in 1 Cor. 11:30, RV, "not a few." In Luke 12:47 it is translated "many stripes," the noun being understood.

1:16 And he had in his right hand seven stars: and out of his mouth went a sharp twoedged sword: and his countenance *was* as the sun shineth in his strength.

Had *echo* (2192), the usual verb for "to have," is used with the following meanings: (a) "to hold, in the hand," etc., e.g., **Rev. 1:16; 5:8**; (b) "to hold fast, keep," Luke 19:20; metaphorically, of the mind and conduct, e.g., Mark 16:8; John 14:21; Rom. 1:28; 1 Tim. 3:9; 2 Tim. 1:13; (c) "to hold on, cling to, be next to," e.g., of accompaniment, Heb. 6:9, "things that accompany (salvation)," lit., "the things holding themselves of salvation" (RV, marg., "are near to"); of place, Mark 1:38, "next (towns)," lit., "towns holding nigh"; of time, e.g., Luke 13:33, "(the day) following," lit., "the holding (day)"; Acts 13:44; 20:15; 21:26; (d) "to hold, to count, consider, regard," e.g., Matt. 14:5; 21:46; Mark 11:32; Luke 14:18; Philem. 17; (e) "to involve," Heb. 10:35; Jas. 1:4; 1 John 4:18; (f) "to wear," of clothing, arms, etc., e.g., Matt. 3:4; 22:12; John 18:10; (g) "to be with child," of a woman, Mark 13:17; Rom. 9:10 (lit., "having conception"); (h) "to possess," the most frequent use, e.g., Matt. 8:20; 19:22; Acts 9:14; 1 Thess. 3:6; (i) of complaints, disputes, Matt. 5:23; Mark 11:25; Acts 24:19; **Rev. 2:4, 20**.

Stars *aster* (792), "a star," Matt. 2:2–10; 24:29; Mark 13:25; 1 Cor. 15:41; **Rev. 6:13; 8:10-12; 9:1; 12:1, 4**, is used metaphorically, (a) of Christ, as "the morning star," figurative of the approach of the day when He will appear as the "sun of righteousness," to govern the earth in peace, an event to be preceded by the rapture of the Church, **Rev. 2:28; 22:16**, the promise of the former to the overcomer being suggestive of some special personal interest in Himself and His authority; (b) of the angels of the seven churches, **Rev. 1:16, 20; 2:1; 3:1**; (c) of certain false teachers, described as "wandering stars," Jude 13, as if the "stars," intended for light and guidance, became the means of deceit by irregular movements.

Mouth *stoma* (4750), akin to *stomachos* (which originally meant "a throat, gullet"), is used (a) of "the mouth" of man, e.g., Matt. 15:11; of animals, e.g., Matt. 17:27; 2 Tim. 4:17 (figurative); Heb. 11:33; Jas. 3:3; **Rev. 13:2** (2nd occurrence); (b) figuratively of "inanimate things," of the "edge" of a sword, Luke 21:24; Heb. 11:34; of the earth, **Rev. 12:16**; (c) figuratively, of the "mouth," as the organ of speech, (1) of Christ's words, e.g., Matt. 13:35; Luke 11:54; Acts 8:32; 22:14; 1 Pet. 2:22; (2) of human, e.g., Matt. 18:16; 21:16; Luke 1:64; **Rev. 14:5**; as emanating from the heart, Matt. 12:34; Rom. 10:8, 9; of prophetic ministry through the Holy Spirit, Luke 1:70; Acts 1:16; 3:18; 4:25; of the destructive policy of two world potentates at the end of this age, **Rev. 13:2, 5, 6; 16:13** (twice); of shameful speaking, Eph. 4:29 and Col. 3:8; (3) of the Devil speaking as a dragon or serpent, **Rev. 12:15, 16; 16:13**; (d) figuratively, in the phrase "face to face" (lit., "mouth to mouth"), 2 John 12; 3 John 14; (e) metaphorically, of "the utterances of the Lord, in judgment," 2 Thess. 2:8; **Rev. 1:16; 2:16; 19:15, 21**; of His judgment upon a local church for its lukewarmness, **Rev. 3:16**; (f) by metonymy, for "speech," Matt. 18:16; Luke 19:22; 21:15; 2 Cor. 13:1.

Went *ekporeuomai* (1607), "to go forth," is translated "to proceed out of" in Matt. 4:4; 15:11, RV; 15:18; Mark 7:15, RV; 7:20, RV; 7:21; 7:23, RV; Luke 4:22; John 15:26; Eph. 4:29; **Rev. 1:16**, RV; **4:5; 9:17, 18**, RV (KJV, "issued"); **11:5; 19:15**, RV; **19:21**, KJV (RV, "came forth"); **22:1**.

Sharp *oxus* (3691), denotes (a) "sharp" (Eng., "oxy-)," said of a sword, **Rev. 1:16; 2:12; 19:15**; of a sickle, **14:14, 17, 18** (twice); (b) of motion, "swift," Rom. 3:15.

Twoedged *distomos* (1366), lit., "two-mouthed" (*dis*, and *stoma*, "a mouth"), was used of rivers and branching roads; in the NT of swords, Heb. 4:12; **Rev. 1:16; 2:12**, RV, "two-edged" (KJV, "with two edges"). In the Sept., Judg. 3:16; Ps. 149:6; Prov. 5:4.

Sword *rhomphaia* (4501), a word of somewhat doubtful origin, denoted "a Thracian weapon of large size," whether a sword or spear is not certain; it occurs (a) literally in **Rev. 6:8**; (b) metaphorically, as the instrument of anguish, Luke 2:35; of judgment, **Rev. 1:16; 2:12, 16; 19:15, 21**, probably figurative of the Lord's judicial utterances.

Countenance *opsis* (3799), is primarily "the act of seeing"; then, (a) "the face"; of the body of Lazarus, John 11:44; of the "countenance" of Christ in a vision, **Rev. 1:16**; (b) the "outward appearance" of a person or thing, John 7:24.

Sun *helios* (2246), whence Eng. prefix "helio-," is used (a) as a means of the natural benefits of light and heat, e.g., Matt. 5:45, and power, **Rev. 1:16**; (b) of its qualities of brightness and glory, e.g., Matt. 13:43; 17:2; Acts 26:13; 1 Cor. 15:41; **Rev. 10:1; 12:1**; (c) as a means of destruction, e.g., Matt. 13:6; Jas. 1:11; of physical misery, **Rev. 7:16**; (d) as a means of judgment, e.g., Matt. 24:29; Mark 13:24; Luke 21:25; 23:45; Acts 2:20; **Rev. 6:12; 8:12; 9:2; 16:8**.

Shineth *phaino* (5316), "to cause to appear," denotes, in the active voice, "to give light, shine," John 1:5; 5:35; in Matt. 24:27, passive voice; so Phil. 2:15, RV, "ye are seen" (for KJV, "ye shine"); 2 Pet. 1:19

(active); so 1 John 2:8, **Rev. 1:16**; in **8:12** and **18:23** (passive); **21:23** (active).

Strength *dunamis* (1411), is rendered "strength" in the RV and KJV of **Rev. 1:16**; elsewhere the RV gives the word its more appropriate meaning "power," for KJV, "strength," 1 Cor. 15:56; 2 Cor. 1:8; 12:9; Heb. 11:11; **Rev. 3:8**; **12:10**.

1:17 And when I saw him, I fell at his feet as dead. And he laid his right hand upon me, saying unto me, Fear not; I am the first and the last:

Fell *pipto* (4098), "to fall," is used (a) of descent, to "fall" down from, e.g., Matt. 10:29; 13:4; (b) of a lot, Acts 1:26; (c) of "falling" under judgment, Jas. 5:12 (cf. **Rev. 18:2**, RV); (d) of persons in the act of prostration, to prostrate oneself, e.g., Matt. 17:6; John 18:6; **Rev. 1:17**; in homage and worship, e.g., Matt. 2:11; Mark 5:22; **Rev. 5:14**; **19:4**; (e) of things, "falling" into ruin, or failing, e.g., Matt. 7:25; Luke 16:17, RV, "fall," for KJV, "fail"; Heb. 11:30; (f), of "falling" in judgment upon persons, as of the sun's heat, **Rev. 7:16**, RV, "strike," KJV, "light"; of a mist and darkness, Acts 13:11 (some mss. have *epipipto*); (g) of persons, in "falling" morally or spiritually, Rom. 14:4; 1 Cor. 10:8, 12; **Rev. 2:5**.

Laid *tithemi* (5087), "to put, place, set," frequently signifies "to lay," and is used of (a) "laying" a corpse in a tomb, Matt. 27:60; Mark 6:29; 15:47; 16:6; Luke 23:53, 55; John 11:34; 19:41, 42; 20:2, 13, 15; Acts 7:16; 13:29; **Rev. 11:9**, RV, "to be laid" (KJV, "to be put"); in an upper chamber, Acts 9:37; (b) "laying" the sick in a place, Mark 6:56; Luke 5:18; Acts 3:2; 5:15; (c) "laying" money at the apostles' feet, Acts 4:35, 37; 5:2; (d) Christ's "laying" His hands upon children, Mark 10:16, RV, "laying" (KJV, "put"); upon John, **Rev. 1:17** (in the best mss.).

First *protos* (4413), the superlative degree of *pro*, "before," is used (I) "of time or place," (a) as a noun, e.g., Luke 14:18; **Rev. 1:17**; opposite to "the last," in the neuter plural, Matt. 12:45; Luke 11:26; 2 Pet. 2:20; in the neuter singular, opposite to "the second," Heb. 10:9; in 1 Cor. 15:3, *en protois*, lit., "in the first (things, or matters)" denotes "first of all"; (b) as an adjective, e.g., Mark 16:9, used with "day" understood, lit., "the first (day) of (i.e., after) the Sabbath," in which phrase the "of" is objective, not including the Sabbath, but following it; in John 20:4, 8; Rom. 10:19, e.g., equivalent to an English adverb; in John 1:15, lit., "first of me," i.e., "before me" (of superiority); (II) "of rank or dignity."

Last *see* ***Revelation 1:11***.

1:18 I *am* he that liveth, and was dead; and, behold, I am alive for evermore, Amen; and have the keys of hell and of death.

Keys *kleis* (2807), "a key," is used metaphorically (a) of "the keys of the kingdom of heaven," which the Lord committed to Peter, Matt. 16:19, by which he would open the door of faith, as he did to Jews at Pentecost, and to Gentiles in the person of Cornelius, acting as one commissioned by Christ, through the power of the Holy Spirit; he had precedence over his fellow disciples, not in authority, but in the matter of time, on the ground of his confession of Christ (v. 16); equal authority was committed to them (18:18); (b) of "the key of knowledge," Luke 11:52, i.e., knowledge of the revealed will of God, by which men entered into the life that pleases God; this the religious leaders of the Jews had presumptuously "taken away," so that they neither entered in themselves, nor permitted their hearers to do so; (c) of "the keys of death and of Hades," **Rev. 1:18**, RV, indicative of the authority of the Lord over the bodies and souls of men; (d) of "the key of David," **Rev. 3:7**, a reference to Isa. 22:22, speaking of the deposition of Shebna and the investiture of Eliakim, in terms evidently messianic, the metaphor being that of the right of entrance upon administrative authority; the mention of David is symbolic of complete sovereignty; (e) of "the key of the pit of the abyss," **Rev. 9:1**; here the symbolism is that of competent authority; the pit represents a shaft or deep entrance into the region, from whence issued smoke, symbolic of blinding delusion; (f) of "the key of the abyss," **Rev. 20:1**; this is to be distinguished from (e): the symbolism is that of the complete supremacy of God over the region of the lost, in which, by angelic agency, Satan is destined to be confined for a thousand years.

Hell *hades* (86), "the region of departed spirits of the lost" (but including the blessed dead in periods preceding the ascension of Christ). It has been thought by some that the word etymologically meant "the unseen" (from *a*, negative, and *eido*, "to see"), but this derivation is questionable; a more probable derivation is from *hado*, signifying "all-receiving." It corresponds to "Sheol" in the OT. In the KJV of the OT and NT; it has been unhappily rendered "hell," e.g., Ps. 16:10; or "the grave," e.g., Gen. 37:35; or "the pit," Num. 16:30, 33; in the NT the revisers have always used the rendering "hades"; in the OT, they have not been uniform in the translation, e.g. in Isa. 14:15 "hell" (marg., "Sheol"); usually they have "Sheol" in the text and "the grave" in the margin. It never denotes the grave, nor is it the permanent region of the lost; in point of time it is, for such, intermediate between decease and the doom of Gehenna. For the condition, see Luke 16:23-31. The word is used four times in the Gospels, and always by the Lord, Matt. 11:23; 16:18; Luke 10:15; 16:23; it is used with reference to the soul of Christ, Acts 2:27, 31; Christ declares that He has the keys of it, **Rev. 1:18**; in **Rev. 6:8** it is personified, with the signification of the temporary destiny of the doomed; it is to give up those who are therein, **20:13**, and is to be cast into the lake of fire, v. **14**.

1:19 Write the things which thou hast seen, and the things which are, and the things which shall be hereafter;

Shall *mello* (3195), "to be about (to be or do)," is used of purpose, certainty, compulsion or necessity. It is rendered simply by "shall" or "should" (which frequently represent elsewhere part of the future tense of the verb) in the following (the RV sometimes translates differently, as noted): Matt. 16:27 (1st part), lit., "is about to come"; 17:12, 22; 20:22, RV, "am about"; 24:6; Mark 13:4 (2nd part), RV, "are about"; Luke 9:44; 21:7 (2nd part), RV, "are about"; v. 36; Acts 23:3; 24:15; 26:2, RV, "I am (to)"; Rom. 4:24; 8:13 (1st part), RV, "must"; v. 18; 2 Tim. 4:1; Heb. 1:14; 10:27; Jas. 2:12, RV "are to"; 1 Pet. 5:1; **Rev. 1:19**; **2:10** (1st and 2nd parts), RV, "art about," "is about"; **3:10**, RV, "is (to)"; **17:8** (1st part), RV, "is about."

Hereafter This adverb translates the phrase *meta tauta*, lit., "after these things," John 13:7; **Rev. 1:19**, and frequently in Revelation, see **4:1** (twice); **7:9**; **9:12**; **15:5**; **18:1**; **19:1**; **20:3**.

1:20 The mystery of the seven stars which thou sawest in my right hand, and the seven golden candlesticks. The seven stars are the angels of the seven churches: and the seven candlesticks which thou sawest are the seven churches.

Mystery *musterion* (3466), primarily that which is known to the *mustes*, "the initiated" (from *mueo*, "to initiate into the mysteries"; cf. Phil. 4:12, *mueomai*, "I have learned the secret," RV). In the NT it denotes, not the mysterious (as with the Eng. word), but that which, being outside the range of unassisted natural apprehension, can be made known only by divine revelation, and is made known in a manner and at a time appointed by God, and to those only who are illumined by His Spirit. In the ordinary sense a "mystery" implies knowledge withheld; its Scriptural significance is truth revealed. Hence the terms especially associated with the subject are "made known," "manifested," "revealed," "preached," "understand," "dispensation." The definition given above may be best illustrated by the following passage: "the mystery which hath been hid from all ages and generations: but now hath it been manifested to His saints" (Col. 1:26, RV). "It is used of:

"(a) spiritual truth generally, as revealed in the gospel, 1 Cor. 13:2; 14:2 [cf. 1 Tim. 3:9]. Among the ancient Greeks 'the mysteries' were religious rites and ceremonies practiced by secret societies into which any one who so desired might be received. Those who were initiated into these 'mysteries' became possessors of certain knowledge, which was not imparted to the uninitiated, and were called 'the perfected,' cf. 1 Cor. 2:6-16 where the Apostle has these 'mysteries' in mind and presents the gospel in contrast thereto; here 'the perfected' are, of course the believers, who alone can perceive the things revealed; (b) Christ, who is God Himself revealed under the conditions of human life, Col. 2:2; 4:3, and submitting even to death, 1 Cor. 2:1 [in some mss., for *marturion*, testimony], 7, but raised from among the dead, 1 Tim. 3:16, that the will of God to coordinate the universe in Him, and subject it to Him, might in due time be accomplished, Eph. 1:9 (cf. **Rev. 10:7**), as is declared in the gospel Rom. 16:25; Eph. 6:19; (c) the Church, which is Christ's Body, i.e., the union of redeemed men with God in Christ, Eph. 5:32 [cf. Col. 1:27]; (d) the rapture into the presence of Christ of those members of the Church which is His Body who shall be alive on the earth at His Parousia, 1 Cor. 15:51; (e) the operation of those hidden forces that either retard or accelerate the Kingdom of Heaven (i.e., of God), Matt. 13:11; Mark 4:11; (f) the cause of the present condition of Israel, Rom. 11:25; (g) the spirit of disobedience to God, 2 Thess. 2:7; **Rev. 17:5**, **7**, cf. Eph. 2:2."

To these may be added (h) the seven local churches, and their angels, seen in symbolism, **Rev. 1:20**; (i) the ways of God in grace, Eph. 3:9. The word is used in a comprehensive way in 1 Cor. 4:1.

Stars *see* ***Revelation 1:16.***

Candlesticks *see* ***Revelation 1:12.***

Angels *angelos* (32), "a messenger" (from *angello*, "to deliver a message"), sent whether by God or by man or by Satan, "is also used of a guardian or representative in **Rev. 1:20**, cf. Matt. 18:10; Acts 12:15 (where it is better understood as 'ghost'), but most frequently of an order of created beings, superior to man, Heb. 2:7; Ps. 8:5, belonging to Heaven, Matt. 24:36; Mark 12:25, and to God, Luke 12:8, and engaged in His service, Ps. 103:20. "Angels" are spirits, Heb. 1:14, i.e., they have not material bodies as men have; they are either human in form, or can assume the human form when necessary, cf. Luke 24:4, with v. 23, Acts 10:3 with v. 30.

Chapter 2

2:1 Unto the angel of the church of Ephesus write; These things saith he that holdeth the seven stars in his right hand, who walketh in the midst of the seven golden candlesticks;

Holdeth *krateo* (2902), "to be strong, mighty, to prevail," (1) is most frequently rendered "to lay or take hold on," (a) literally, e.g., Matt. 12:11; 14:3; 18:28 and 21:46, RV (KJV, "laid hands on"); 22:6, RV (KJV, "took"); 26:55, KJV (RV, "took"); 28:9, RV, "took hold of" (KJV, "held by"); Mark 3:21; 6:17; 12:12; 14:51; Act 24:6, RV (KJV, "took"); **Rev. 20:2**; (b) metaphorically, of "laying hold of the hope of the Lord's return," Heb. 6:18; (2) also signifies "to hold" or "hold fast," i.e., firmly, (a), literally, Matt. 26:48, KJV (RV, "take"); Acts 3:11; **Rev. 2:1**; (b) metaphorically, of "holding fast a tradition or teaching," in an evil sense, Mark 7:3, 4, 8; **Rev. 2:14, 15**; in a good sense, 2 Thess. 2:15; **Rev. 2:25**; **3:11**; of "holding" Christ, i.e., practically apprehending Him, as the head of His church, Col. 2:19; a confession, Heb. 4:14; the name of Christ, i.e., abiding by all that His name implies, **Rev. 2:13**; of restraint, Luke 24:16, "(their eyes) were holden"; of the winds, **Rev. 7:1**; of the impossibility of Christ's being "holden" of death, Acts 2:24.

Stars *see* ***Revelation 1:16.***

Candlesticks *see* ***Revelation 1:12.***

2:2 I know thy works, and thy labour, and thy patience, and how thou canst not bear them which are evil: and thou hast tried them which say they are apostles, and are not, and hast found them liars:

Know *oida* (1492), from the same root as *eidon*, "to see," is a perfect tense with a present meaning, signifying, primarily, "to have seen or perceived"; hence, "to know, to have knowledge of," whether absolutely, as in divine knowledge, e.g., Matt. 6:8, 32; John 6:6, 64; 8:14; 11:42; 13:11; 18:4; 2 Cor. 11:31; 2 Pet. 2:9; **Rev. 2:2, 9, 13, 19**; **3:1, 8, 15**; or in the case of human "knowledge," to know from observation, e.g., 1 Thess. 1:4, 5; 2:1; 2 Thess. 3:7. The differences between *ginosko* and *oida* demand consideration: (a) *ginosko*, frequently suggests inception or progress in "knowledge," while *oida* suggests fullness of "knowledge," e.g., John 8:55, "ye have not known Him" (*ginosko*), i.e., begun to "know," "but I know Him" (*oida*), i.e., "know Him perfectly"; 13:7, "What I do thou knowest not now," i.e. Peter did not yet perceive (*oida*) its significance, "but thou shalt understand," i.e., "get to know (*ginosko*), hereafter"; 14:7, "If ye had known Me" (*ginosko*), i.e., "had definitely come to know Me," "ye would have known My Father also" (*oida*), i.e., "would have had perception of": "from henceforth ye know Him" (*ginosko*), i.e., having unconsciously been coming to the Father, as the One who was in Him, they would now consciously be in the constant and progressive experience of "knowing" Him; in Mark 4:13, "Know ye not (*oida*) this parable? and how shall ye know (*ginosko*) all the parables?" (RV), i.e., "Do ye not understand this parable? How shall ye come to perceive all ..." the intimation being that the first parable is a leading and testing one; (b) while *ginosko* frequently implies an active relation between the one who "knows" and the person or thing "known," *oida* expresses the fact that the object has simply come within the scope of the "knower's" perception; thus in Matt. 7:23 "I never knew you" (*ginosko*) suggests "I have never been in approving connection with you," whereas in 25:12, "I know you not" (*oida*) suggests "you stand in no relation to Me."

Works *ergon* (2041), denotes (I) "work, employment, task," e.g., Mark 13:34; John 4:34; 17:4; Acts 13:2; Phil. 2:30; 1 Thess. 5:13; in Acts 5:38 with the idea of enterprise; (II) "a deed, act," (a) of God, e.g., John 6:28, 29; 9:3; 10:37; 14:10; Acts 13:41; Rom. 14:20; Heb. 1:10; 2:7; 3:9; 4:3, 4, 10; **Rev. 15:3**; (b) of Christ, e.g., Matt. 11:2; especially in John, 5:36; 7:3, 21; 10:25, 32, 33, 38; 14:11, 12; 15:24; **Rev. 2:26**; (c) of believers, e.g., Matt. 5:16; Mark 14:6; Acts 9:36; Rom. 13:3; Col. 1:10; 1 Thess. 1:3, "work of faith," here the initial act of faith at conversion (turning to God, v. 9); in 2 Thess. 1:11, "*every* work of faith," RV, denotes every activity undertaken for Christ's sake; 2:17; 1 Tim. 2:10; 5:10; 6:18; 2 Tim. 2:21; 3:17; Titus 2:7, 14; 3:1, 8, 14; Heb. 10:24; 13:21; frequent in James, as the effect of faith [in 1:25, KJV, "(a doer) of the work," RV, "(a doer) that worketh"]; 1 Pet. 2:12; **Rev. 2:2** and in several other places in chs. **2** and **3**; **14:13**; (d) of unbelievers, e.g., Matt. 23:3, 5; John 7:7; Acts 7:41 (for idols); Rom. 13:12; Eph. 5:11; Col. 1:21; Titus 1:16 (1st part); 1 John 3:12; Jude 15, RV; **Rev. 2:6**, RV; of those who seek justification by works, e.g., Rom. 9:32; Gal. 3:10; Eph. 2:9; described as the works of the law, e.g., Gal. 2:16; 3:2, 5; dead works, Heb. 6:1; 9:14; (e) of Babylon, **Rev. 18:6**; (f) of the Devil, John 8:41; 1 John 3:8.

Labour *kopos* (2873), primarily denotes "a striking, beating" (akin to *kopto*, "to strike, cut"), then, "toil resulting in weariness, laborious toil, trouble"; it is translated "labor" or "labors" in John 4:38; 1 Cor. 3:8; 15:58; 2 Cor. 6:5; 10:15; 11:23, 27, RV, "labor" (KJV, "weariness"); 1 Thess. 1:3; 2:9; 3:5; 2 Thess. 3:8; (in some mss., Heb. 6:10); **Rev. 2:2** (RV "toil"); **14:13**. In the following the noun is used as the object of the verb *parecho*, "to afford, give, cause," the phrase being rendered "to trouble," lit., "to cause toil or trouble," to embarrass a person by giving occasion for anxiety, as some disciples did to the woman with the ointment, perturbing her spirit by their criticisms, Matt. 26:10; Mark 14:6; or by distracting attention or disturbing a person's rest, as the importunate friend did, Luke 11:7; 18:5; in Gal. 6:17, "let no man trouble me," the apostle refuses, in the form of a peremptory prohibition, to allow himself to be distracted further by the Judaizers, through their proclamation of a false gospel and by their malicious attacks upon himself.

Bear *bastazo* (941), signifies "to support as a burden." It is used with the meaning (a) "to take up," as in picking up anything stones, John 10:31; (b) "to carry" something, Matt. 3:11; Mark 14:13; Luke 7:14; 22:10; Acts 3:2; 21:35; **Rev. 17:7**; "to carry" on one's person, Luke 10:4; Gal. 6:17; in one's body, Luke 11:27; "to bear" a name in testimony, Acts 9:15; metaphorically, of a root "bearing" branches, Rom. 11:18; (c) "to bear" a burden, whether physically, as of the cross, John 19:17, or metaphorically in respect of sufferings endured in the cause of Christ, Luke 14:27; **Rev. 2:3**; it is said of physical endurance, Matt. 20:12; of sufferings "borne" on behalf of others, Matt. 8:17; Rom. 15:1; Gal. 6:2; of spiritual truths not able to be "borne," John 16:12; of the refusal to endure evil men, **Rev. 2:2**; of religious regulations imposed on others, Acts 15:10; of the burden of the sentence of God to be executed in due time, Gal. 5:10; of the effect at the judgment seat of Christ, to be "borne" by the believer for failure in the matter of discharging the obligations of discipleship, Gal. 6:5; (d) to "bear" by way of carrying off, John 12:6; 20:15.

Evil *kakos* (2556), stands for "whatever is evil in character, base," in distinction (wherever the distinction is observable) from *poneros*, which indicates "what is evil in influence and effect, malignant." *Kakos* is the wider term and often covers the meaning of *poneros*. *Kakos* is antithetic to *kalos*, "fair, advisable, good in character," and to *agathos*, "beneficial, useful, good in act"; hence it denotes what is useless, incapable, bad; *poneros* is essentially antithetic to *chrestos*, "kind, gracious, serviceable"; hence it denotes what is destructive, injurious, evil. As evidence that *poneros* and *kakos* have much in common, though still not interchangeable, each is used of thoughts, cf. Matt. 15:19 with Mark 7:21; of speech, Matt. 5:11 with 1 Pet. 3:10; of actions, 2 Tim. 4:18 with 1 Thess. 5:15; of man, Matt. 18:32 with 24:48. The use of *kakos* may be broadly divided as follows: (a) of what is morally or ethically "evil," whether of persons, e.g., Matt. 21:41; 24:48; Phil. 3:2; **Rev. 2:2**, or qualities, emotions, passions, deeds, e.g., Mark 7:21; John 18:23, 30; Rom. 1:30; 3:8; 7:19, 21; 13:4; 14:20; 16:19; 1 Cor. 13:5; 2 Cor. 13:7; 1 Thess. 5:15; 1 Tim. 6:10; 2 Tim. 4:14; 1 Pet. 3:9, 12; (b) of what is injurious, destructive, baneful, pernicious, e.g., Luke 16:25; Acts 16:28; 28:5; Titus 1:12; Jas. 3:8; **Rev. 16:2**, where *kakos* and *poneros* come in that order, "noisome and grievous."

Tried *peirazo* (3985), is rendered "to try" in Heb. 11:17; **Rev. 2:2, 10; 3:10**. In Acts 16:7 it is rendered "assayed"; in 24:6, RV, "assayed" (KJV, "hath gone about").

Say *lego* (3004), "to speak," is used of all kinds of oral communication, e.g. "to call, to call by name," to surname, Matt. 1:16; 26:36; John 4:5; 11:54; 15:15; **Rev. 2:2**, RV, "call themselves," etc.

Liars *pseudes* (5571), "lying, false" (Eng. "pseudo-"), rendered "false" in Acts 6:13 and in the RV of **Rev. 2:2** (KJV, "liars"), is used as a noun, "liars," in **Rev. 21:8**.

2:3 And hast borne, and hast patience, and for my name's sake hast laboured, and hast not fainted.

Borne *see* **Bear** at *Revelation 2:2*.

Name *onoma* (3686), is used (I) in general of the "name" by which a person or thing is called, e.g., Mark 3:16, 17, "(He) surnamed," lit., "(He added) the name"; 14:32, lit., "(of which) the name (was)"; Luke 1:63; John 18:10, sometimes translated "named," e.g., Luke 8:5, "named (Zacharias)," lit., "by name"; in the same verse, "named (Elizabeth)," lit., "the name of her," an elliptical phrase, with "was" understood; Acts 8:9, RV, "by name," 10:1; the "name" is put for the reality in **Rev. 3:1**; in Phil. 2:9, the "Name" represents "the title and dignity" of the Lord, as in Eph. 1:21 and Heb. 1:4; (II) for all that a "name" implies, of authority, character, rank, majesty, power, excellence, etc., of everything that the "name" covers: (a) of the "Name" of God as expressing His attributes, etc., e.g., Matt. 6:9; Luke 1:49; John 12:28; 17:6, 26; Rom. 15:9; 1 Tim. 6:1; Heb. 13:15; **Rev. 13:6**; (b) of the "Name" of Christ, e.g., Matt. 10:22; 19:29; John 1:12; 2:23; 3:18; Acts 26:9; Rom. 1:5; Jas. 2:7; 1 John 3:23; 3 John 7; **Rev. 2:13**; **3:8**; also the phrases rendered "in the name"; these may be analyzed as follows: (1) representing the authority of Christ, e.g., Matt. 18:5 (with *epi*, "on the ground of My authority"); so Matt. 24:5 (falsely) and parallel passages; as substantiated by the Father, John 14:26; 16:23 (last clause), RV; (2) in the power of (with *en*, "in"), e.g., Mark 16:17; Luke 10:17; Acts 3:6; 4:10; 16:18; Jas. 5:14; (3) in acknowledgement or confession of, e.g., Acts 4:12; 8:16; 9:27, 28; (4) in recognition of the authority of (sometimes combined with the thought of relying or resting on), Matt. 18:20; cf. 28:19; Acts 8:16; 9:2 (*eis*, "into"); John 14:13; 15:16; Eph. 5:20; Col. 3:17; (5) owing to the fact that one is called by Christ's "Name" or is identified with Him, e.g. 1 Pet. 4:14 (with *en*, "in"); with *heneken*, "for the sake of," e.g., Matt. 19:29; with *dia*, "on account of," Matt. 10:22; 24:9; Mark 13:13; Luke 21:17; John 15:21; 1 John 2:12; **Rev. 2:3**; (III) as standing, by metonymy, for "persons," Acts 1:15; **Rev. 3:4**; **11:13** (RV, "persons").

Laboured *kopiao* (2872), has the two different meanings (a) "growing weary," (b) "toiling"; it is sometimes translated "to bestow labor". It is translated by the verb "to labor" in Matt. 11:28; John 4:38 (2nd part); Acts 20:35; Rom. 16:12 (twice); 1 Cor. 15:10; 16:16; Eph. 4:28; Phil. 2:16; Col. 1:29; 1 Thess. 5:12; 1 Tim. 4:10; 5:17; 2 Tim. 2:6; **Rev. 2:3**; 1 Cor. 4:12, RV, "toil" (KJV, "labor").

Fainted *kamno* (2577), primarily signified "to work"; then, as the effect of continued labor, "to be weary"; it is used in Heb. 12:3, of becoming "weary," RV, "wax not weary"; in Jas. 5:15, of sickness; some mss. have it in **Rev. 2:3**, KJV, "hast (not) fainted," RV, "grown weary."

2:4 Nevertheless I have *somewhat* against thee, because thou hast left thy first love.

Have *see* **Had** at ***Revelation 1:16***.

Left *aphiemi* (863), *apo*, "from," and *hiemi*, "to send," has three chief meanings, (a) "to send forth, let go, forgive"; (b) "to let, suffer, permit"; (c) "to leave, leave alone, forsake, neglect." It is translated by the verb "to leave" (c), in Matt. 4:11; 4:20, 22, and parallel passages; 5:24; 8:15, and parallel passages; 8:22, RV, "leave (the dead)," KJV, "let," and the parallel passage; 13:36, RV, "left (the multitude)," KJV, "sent ... away"; 18:12; 19:27, and parallel passages, RV, "we have left" (KJV, "we have forsaken"), so v. 29; 22:22, 25; 23:23, RV, "have left undone" (KJV, "have omitted," in the 1st part, "leave undone" in the second); 23:38, and the parallel passage; 24:2, 40, 41, and parallel passages; 26:56, RV, "left"; Mark 1:18, "left"; 1:31; 7:8, RV, "ye leave"; 8:13; 10:28, 29; 12:12, 19-22; 13:34; Luke 10:30; 11:42 (in some mss.); Luke 12:39, RV "have left," KJV "have suffered"; John 4:3, 28, 52; 8:29; 10:12; 14:18, 27; 16:28, 32; Rom. 1:27; 1 Cor. 7:11, RV, "leave" (KJV "put away"); 7:13 (KJV and RV); Heb. 2:8; 6:1; **Rev. 2:4**.

> *"A man's spiritual health is exactly proportional to his love for God."*
>
> C. S. LEWIS

2:5 Remember therefore from whence thou art fallen, and repent, and do the first works; or else I will come unto thee quickly, and will remove thy candlestick out of his place, except thou repent.

Remember *mnemoneuo* (3421), signifies "to call to mind, remember"; it is used absolutely in Mark 8:18; everywhere else it has an object, (a) persons, Luke 17:32; Gal. 2:10; 2 Tim. 2:8, where the RV rightly has "remember Jesus Christ, risen from the dead"; Paul was not reminding Timothy (nor did he need to) that Christ was raised from the dead (KJV), what was needful for him was to "remember" (to keep in mind) the One who rose, the Source and Supplier of all his requirements; (b) things, e.g., Matt. 16:9; John 15:20; 16:21; Acts 20:35; Col. 4:18; 1 Thess. 1:3; 2:9; Heb. 11:15, "had been mindful of"; 13:7; **Rev. 18:5**; (c) a clause, representing a circumstance, etc., John 16:4; Acts 20:31; Eph. 2:11; 2 Thess. 2:5; **Rev. 2:5**; **3:3**; in Heb. 11:22 it signifies "to make mention of."

Fallen *ekpipto* (1601), "to fall out of," is used in the NT, literally, of flowers that wither in the course of nature, Jas. 1:11; 1 Pet. 1:24; of a ship not under control, Acts 27:17, 26, 29, 32; of shackles loosed from a prisoner's wrist, 12:7; figuratively, of the Word of God (the expression of His purpose), which cannot "fall" away from the end to which it is set, Rom. 9:6; of the believer who is warned lest he "fall" away from the course in which he has been confirmed by the Word of God, 2 Pet. 3:17." So of those who seek to be justified by law, Gal. 5:4, "ye are fallen away from grace." Some mss. have this verb in Mark 13:25; so in **Rev. 2:5**. *See also* **Fell** at ***Revelation 1:17***.

Repent *metanoeo* (3340), lit., "to perceive afterwards" (*meta*, "after," implying "change," *noeo*, "to perceive"; *nous*, "the mind, the seat of moral reflection"), in contrast to *pronoeo*, "to perceive beforehand," hence signifies "to change one's mind or purpose," always, in the NT, involving a change for the better, an amendment, and always, except in Luke 17:3, 4, of "repentance" from sin. The word is found in the Synoptic Gospels (in Luke, nine times), in Acts five times, in Revelation twelve times, eight in the messages to the churches, **2:5** (twice), **16**, **21** (twice), RV, "she willeth not to repent" (2nd part); **3:3**, **19** (the only churches in those chapters which contain no exhortation in this respect are those at Smyrna and Philadelphia); elsewhere only in 2 Cor. 12:21.

Quickly *tachu* (5035), the neuter of *tachus*, "swift, quick," signifies "quickly," Matt. 5:25; 28:7, 8; Mark 9:39, RV (KJV, "lightly"); Luke 15:22; John 11:29; **Rev. 2:16** (v. **5** in some mss.); **3:11**; **11:14**; **22:7**, **12**, **20**.

Remove *kineo* (2795), "to set in motion, move" (hence, e.g., Eng. "kinematics," "kinetics," "cinema"), is used (a) of wagging the head, Matt. 27:39; Mark 15:29; (b) of the general activity of the human being, Acts 17:28; (c) of the "moving" of mountains, **Rev. 6:14**, in the sense of removing, as in **Rev. 2:5**, of removing a lampstand (there figuratively of causing a local church to be discontinued); (d) figuratively, of exciting, stirring up feelings and passions, Acts 21:30 (passive voice); 24:5, "a mover"; (e) of "moving burdens," Matt. 23:4. Cf. *sunkineo*, "to stir up," Acts 6:12.

Candlestick *see* **Candlesticks** at ***Revelation 1:12***.

Place *topos* (5117), (Eng., "topic," "topography," etc.) is used of "a region" or "locality," frequently in the Gospels and Acts, in Luke 2:7 and 14:22, "room"; of a place which a person or thing occupies, a couch at table, e.g., Luke 14:9, 10, RV, "place" (KJV, "room"); of the destiny of Judas Iscariot, Acts 1:25; of the condition of the "unlearned" or nongifted in a church gathering, 1 Cor. 14:16, RV, "place"; the sheath of a sword, Matt. 26:52; a place in a book, Luke 4:17; see also **Rev. 2:5**; **6:14**; **12:8**; metaphorically, of "condition, occasion, opportunity" Acts 25:16, RV, "opportunity" (KJV, "license"); Rom. 12:19; Eph. 4:27.

2:6 But this thou hast, that thou hatest the deeds of the Nicolaitans, which I also hate.

Hatest, Hate *miseo* (3404), "to hate," is used especially (a) of malicious and unjustifiable feelings towards others, whether towards the innocent or by mutual animosity, e.g., Matt. 10:22; 24:10; Luke 6:22, 27; 19:14; John 3:20, of "hating" the light (metaphorically); 7:7; 15:18, 19, 23-25; Titus 3:3; 1 John 2:9, 11; 3:13, 15; 4:20; **Rev. 18:2**, where "hateful" translates the perfect participle passive voice of the verb, lit., "hated," or "having been hated"; (b) of a right feeling of aversion from what is evil; said of wrongdoing, Rom. 7:15; iniquity, Heb. 1:9; "the garment (figurative) spotted by the flesh," Jude 23; "the works of the Nicolaitans," **Rev. 2:6** (and v. **15**, in some mss.; see the KJV); (c) of relative preference for one thing over another, by way of expressing either aversion from, or disregard for, the claims of one person or thing relatively to those of another, Matt. 6:24, and Luke 16:13, as to the impossibility of serving two masters; Luke 14:26, as to the claims of parents relatively to those of Christ; John 12:25, of disregard for one's life relatively to the claims of Christ; Eph. 5:29, negatively, of one's flesh, i.e. of one's own, and therefore a man's wife as one with him.

Deeds *see* **Works** at ***Revelation 2:2***.

2:7 He that hath an ear, let him hear what the Spirit saith unto the churches; To him that overcometh will I give to eat of the tree of life, which is in the midst of the paradise of God.

Ear *ous* (3775), Latin *auris*, is used (a) of the physical organ, e.g., Luke 4:21; Acts 7:57; in Acts 11:22, in the plural with *akouo*, "to hear," lit., "was heard into the ears of someone," i.e., came to the knowledge of, similarly, in the singular, Matt. 10:27, in familiar private conversation; in Jas. 5:4 the phrase is used with *eiserchomai*, "to enter into"; in Luke 1:44, with *ginomai*, "to become, to come"; in Luke 12:3, with *lalein*, "to speak" and *pros*, "to", (b) metaphorically, of the faculty of perceiving with the mind, understanding and knowing, Matt. 13:16; frequently with *akouo*, "to hear," e.g., Matt. 11:15; 13:9, 43; **Rev. 2** and **3**, at the close of each of the messages to the churches, in Matt. 13:15 and Acts 28:27, with *bareos*, "heavily," of being slow to understand and obey; with a negative in Mark 8:18; Rom. 11:8; in Luke 9:44 the lit. meaning is "put those words into your ears," i.e., take them into your mind and keep them there, in Acts 7:51 it is used with *aperitmetos*, "uncircumcised." As seeing is metaphorically associated with conviction, so hearing is with obedience (*hupakoe*, lit., "hearing under"; the Eng., "obedience" is etymologically "hearing over against," i.e., with response in the hearer).

Overcometh *nikao* (3528), is used (a) of God, Rom. 3:4 (a law term), RV, "mightest prevail"; (b) of Christ, John 16:33; **Rev. 3:21**; **5:5**; **17:14**; (c) of His followers, Rom. 12:21 (2nd part); 1 John 2:13-14; 4:4; 5:4-5; **Rev. 2:7, 11, 17, 26**; **3:5, 12, 21**; **12:11**; **15:2**; **21:7**; (d) of faith, 1 John 5:4; (e) of evil (passive voice), Rom. 12:21; (f) of predicted human potentates, **Rev. 6:2**; **11:7**; **13:7**.

Tree *xulon* (3586), "wood, a piece of wood, anything made of wood", is used, with the rendering "tree," (a) in Luke 23:31, where "the green tree" refers either to Christ, figuratively of all His living power and excellencies, or to the life of the Jewish people while still inhabiting their land, in contrast to "the dry," a figure fulfilled in the horrors of the Roman massacre and devastation in AD 70 (cf. the Lord's parable in Luke 13:6–9; see Ezek. 20:47, and cf. 21:3); (b) of "the cross," the tree being the *stauros*, the upright pale or stake to which Romans nailed those who were thus to be executed, Acts 5:30; 10:39; 13:29; Gal. 3:13; 1 Pet. 2:24; (c) of "the tree of life," **Rev. 2:7**; **22:2** (twice), 14, 19, RV, KJV, "book."

Paradise *paradeisos* (3857), is an Oriental word, first used by the historian Xenophon, denoting "the parks of Persian kings and nobles." It is of Persian origin (Old Pers. *pairidaeza*, akin to Gk. *peri*, "around," and *teichos*, "a wall") whence it passed into Greek. See the Sept., e.g., in Neh. 2:8; Eccl. 2:5; Song of Sol. 4:13. The Sept. translators used it of the garden of Eden, Gen. 2:8, and in other respects, e.g., Num. 24:6; Isa. 1:30; Jer. 29:5; Ezek. 31:8-9. In Luke 23:43, the promise of the Lord to the repentant robber was fulfilled the same day; Christ, at His death, having committed His spirit to the Father, went in spirit immediately into Heaven itself, the dwelling place of God (the Lord's mention of the place as "paradise" must have been a great comfort to the malefactor; to the oriental mind it expressed the sum total of blessedness). Thither the apostle Paul was caught up, 2 Cor. 12:4, spoken of as "the third heaven" (v. 3 does not introduce a different vision), beyond the heavens of the natural creation (see Heb. 4:14, RV, with reference to the Ascension). The same region is mentioned in **Rev. 2:7**, where the "tree of life," the figurative antitype of that in Eden, held out to the overcomer, is spoken of as being in "the Paradise of God" (RV), marg., "garden," as in Gen. 2:8.

2:8 And unto the angel of the church in Smyrna write; These things saith the first and the last, which was dead, and is alive;

Last *see Revelation 1:11.*

2:9 I know thy works, and tribulation, and poverty, (but thou art rich) and *I know* the blasphemy of them which say they are Jews, and are not, but *are* the synagogue of Satan.

Know *see Revelation 2:2.*

Tribulation *see Revelation 1:9.*

Poverty *ptocheia* (4432), "destitution" is used of the "poverty" which Christ voluntarily experienced on our behalf, 2 Cor. 8:9; of the destitute condition of saints in Judea, v. 2; of the condition of the church in Smyrna, **Rev. 2:9**, where the word is used in a general sense.

Rich *plousios* (4145), "rich, wealthy," is used (I) literally, (a) adjectivally (with a noun expressed separately) in Matt. 27:57; Luke 12:16; 14:12; 16:1, 19; (without a noun), 18:23; 19:2; (b) as a noun, singular, a "rich" man (the noun not being expressed), Matt. 19:23, 24; Mark 10:25; 12:41; Luke 16:21, 22; 18:25; Jas. 1:10, 11, "the rich," "the rich (man)"; plural, Mark 12:41, lit., "rich (ones)"; Luke 6:24 (ditto); 21:1; 1 Tim. 6:17, "(them that are) rich," lit., "(the) rich"; Jas. 2:6, RV, "the rich"; 5:1, RV, "ye rich"; **Rev. 6:15** and **13:16**, RV, "the rich"; (II) metaphorically, of God, Eph. 2:4 ("in mercy"); of Christ, 2 Cor. 8:9; of believers, Jas. 2:5, RV, "(*to be*) rich (in faith)"; **Rev. 2:9**, of spiritual "enrichment" generally; **3:17**, of a false sense of "enrichment."

Synagogue *sunagoge* (4864), properly "a bringing together" (*sun*, "together," *ago*, "to bring"), denoted (a) "a gathering of things, a collection," then, of "persons, an assembling, of Jewish religious gatherings," e.g., Acts 9:2; an assembly of Christian Jews, Jas. 2:2, RV, "synagogue" (KJV, marg.; text, "assembly"); a company dominated by the power and activity of Satan, **Rev. 2:9**; **3:9**; (b) by metonymy, "the building" in which the gathering is held, e.g. Matt. 6:2; Mark 1:21. The origin of the Jewish "synagogue" is probably to be assigned to the time of the Babylonian exile. Having no temple, the Jews assembled on the

Sabbath to hear the Law read, and the practice continued in various buildings after the return. Cf. Ps. 74:8.

Satan *satanas* (4567), a Greek form derived from the Aramaic (Heb., *Satan*), "an adversary," is used (a) of an angel of Jehovah in Num. 22:22 (the first occurrence of the Word in the OT); (b) of men, e.g., 1 Sam. 29:4; Ps. 38:20; 71:13; four in Ps. 109; (c) of "Satan," the Devil, some seventeen or eighteen times in the OT; in Zech. 3:1, where the name receives its interpretation, "to be (his) adversary," RV (see marg.; KJV, "to resist him").

In the NT the word is always used of "Satan," the adversary (a) of God and Christ, e.g., Matt. 4:10; 12:26; Mark 1:13; 3:23, 26; 4:15; Luke 4:8 (in some mss.); 11:18; 22:3; John 13:27; (b) of His people, e.g., Luke 22:31; Acts 5:3; Rom. 16:20; 1 Cor. 5:5; 7:5; 2 Cor. 2:11; 11:14; 12:7; 1 Thess. 2:18; 1 Tim. 1:20; 5:15; **Rev. 2:9**, **13** (twice), **24**; **3:9**; (c) of mankind, Luke 13:16; Acts 26:18; 2 Thess. 2:9; **Rev. 12:9**; **20:7**. His doom, sealed at the Cross, is foretold in its stages in Luke 10:18; **Rev. 20:2**, **10**. Believers are assured of victory over him, Rom. 16:20. The appellation was given by the Lord to Peter, as a "Satan-like" man, on the occasion when he endeavored to dissuade Him from death, Matt. 16:23; Mark 8:33.

"Satan" is not simply the personification of evil influences in the heart, for he tempted Christ, in whose heart no evil thought could ever have arisen (John 14:30; 2 Cor. 5:21; Heb. 4:15); moreover his personality is asserted in both the OT and the NT, and especially in the latter, whereas if the OT language was intended to be figurative, the NT would have made this evident.

2:10 Fear none of those things which thou shalt suffer: behold, the devil shall cast *some* of you into prison, that ye may be tried; and ye shall have tribulation ten days: be thou faithful unto death, and I will give thee a crown of life.

Shalt, Shall *see* **Shall** at *Revelation 1:19*.

Suffer *pascho* (3958), "to suffer," is used (I) of the "sufferings" of Christ (a) at the hands of men, e.g., Matt. 16:21; 17:12; 1 Pet. 2:23; (b) in His expiatory and vicarious sacrifice for sin, Heb. 9:26; 13:12; 1 Pet. 2:21; 3:18; 4:1; (c) including both (a) and (b), Luke 22:15; 24:26, 46; Acts 1:3, "passion"; 3:18; 17:3; Heb. 5:8; (d) by the antagonism of the evil one, Heb. 2:18; (II) of human "suffering" (a) of followers of Christ, Acts 9:16; 2 Cor. 1:6; Gal. 3:4; Phil. 1:29; 1 Thess. 2:14; 2 Thess. 1:5; 2 Tim. 1:12; 1 Pet. 3:14, 17; 5:10; **Rev. 2:10**; in identification with Christ in His crucifixion, as the spiritual ideal to be realized, 1 Pet. 4:1; in a wrong way, 4:15; (b) of others, physically, as the result of demoniacal power, Matt. 17:15, RV, "suffereth (grievously)," KJV, "is (sore) vexed"; cf. Mark 5:26; in a dream, Matt. 27:19; through maltreatment, Luke 13:2; 1 Pet. 2:19, 20; by a serpent (negatively), Acts 28:5, RV, "took" (KJV, "felt"); (c) of the effect upon the whole body through the "suffering" of one member, 1 Cor. 12:26, with application to a church.

Prison *phulake* (5438), denotes a "prison," e.g., Matt. 14:10; Mark 6:17; Acts 5:19; 2 Cor. 11:23; in 2 Cor. 6:5 and Heb. 11:36 it stands for the condition of imprisonment; in **Rev. 2:10**; **18:2**, "hold" (twice, RV, marg., "prison"; in the 2nd case, KJV, "cage"); **20:7**.

Tried *see Revelation 2:2*.

Tribulation *see Revelation 1:9*.

Ten *deka* (1176), whence the Eng. prefix "deca-," is regarded by some as the measure of human responsibility, e.g., Luke 19:13, 17; **Rev. 2:10**; it is used in a figurative setting in **Rev. 12:3**; **13:1**; **17:3**, **7**, **12**, **16**.

Crown *stephanos* (4735), primarily, "that which surrounds, as a wall or crowd" (from *stepho*, "to encircle"), denotes (a) "the victor's crown," the symbol of triumph in the games or some such contest; hence, by metonymy, a reward or prize; (b) "a token of public honor" for distinguished service, military prowess, etc., or of nuptial joy, or festal gladness, especially at the parousia of kings. It was woven as a garland of oak, ivy, parsley, myrtle, or olive, or in imitation of these in gold. In some passages the reference to the games is clear, 1 Cor. 9:25; 2 Tim. 4:8 ("crown of righteousness"); it may be so in 1 Pet. 5:4, where the fadeless character of "the crown of glory" is set in contrast to the garlands of earth. In other passages it stands as an emblem of life, joy, reward and glory, Phil. 4:1; 1 Thess. 2:19; Jas. 1:12 ("crown of life "); **Rev. 2:10** (ditto); **3:11**; **4:4**, **10**: of triumph, **6:2**; **9:7**; **12:1**; **14:14**. It is used of "the crown of thorns" which the soldiers plaited and put on Christ's head, Matt. 27:29; Mark 15:17; John 19:2, 5. At first sight this might be taken as an alternative for *diadema*, "a kingly crown," but considering the blasphemous character of that masquerade, and the materials used, obviously *diadema* would be quite unfitting and the only alternative was *stephanos*.

2:11 He that hath an ear, let him hear what the Spirit saith unto the churches; He that overcometh shall not be hurt of the second death.

Overcometh *see Revelation 2:7.*

Hurt *adikeo* (91), signifies, intransitively, "to do wrong, do hurt, act unjustly" (*a*, negative, and *dike*, "justice"), transitively, "to wrong, hurt or injure a person." It is translated "to hurt" in the following: (a), intransitively, **Rev. 9:19**; (b) transitively, Luke 10:19; **Rev. 2:11** (passive); **6:6; 7:2, 3; 9:4, 10; 11:5.**

Second *deuteros* (1208), denotes "second in order" with or without the idea of time, e.g., Matt. 22:26, 39; 2 Cor. 1:15; **Rev. 2:11**; in **Rev. 14:8**, RV only ("a second angel"); it is used in the neuter, *deuteron*, adverbially, signifying a "second" time, e.g., John 3:4; 21:16; Acts 7:13; **Rev. 19:3**, RV (KJV, "again"); Jude 5, "afterward" (RV, marg., "the second time"); used with *ek* ("of") idiomatically, the preposition signifying "for (the second time)," Mark 14:72; John 9:24 and Acts 11:9, RV (KJV, "again"); Heb. 9:28; in 1 Cor. 12:28, KJV, "secondarily," RV, "secondly."

2:12 And to the angel of the church in Pergamos write; These things saith he which hath the sharp sword with two edges;

Sharp *see Revelation 1:16.*

Sword *see Revelation 1:16.*

Two edges *see* **Twoedged** at *Revelation 1:16.*

2:13 I know thy works, and where thou dwellest, *even* where Satan's seat *is*: and thou holdest fast my name, and hast not denied my faith, even in those days wherein Antipas *was* my faithful martyr, who was slain among you, where Satan dwelleth.

Know *see Revelation 2:2.*

Dwellest *katoikeo* (2730), the most frequent verb with this meaning, properly signifies "to settle down in a dwelling, to dwell fixedly in a place." Besides its literal sense, it is used of (a) the "indwelling" of the totality of the attributes and powers of the Godhead in Christ, Col. 1:19; 2:9; (b) the "indwelling" of Christ in the hearts of believers ("may make a home in your hearts"), Eph. 3:17; (c) the "dwelling" of Satan in a locality, **Rev. 2:13**; (d) the future "indwelling" of righteousness in the new heavens and earth, 2 Pet. 3:13. It is translated "dwellers" in Acts 1:19; 2:9; "inhabitants" in **Rev. 17:2**, KJV (RV, "they that dwell"), "inhabiters" in **Rev. 8:13** and **12:12**, KJV (RV, "them that dwell"). Cf. the nouns *katoikesis* (below), *katoikia*, "habitation," Acts 17:26; *katoiketerion*, "a habitation," Eph. 2:22; **Rev. 18:2**. Contrast *paroikeo*, "to sojourn," the latter being temporary, the former permanent.

Satan *see Revelation 2:9.*

Seat *see* **Throne** at *Revelation 1:4.*

Holdest *see* **Holdeth** at *Revelation 2:1.*

Name *see Revelation 2:3.*

Denied *arneomai* (720), signifies (a) "to say ... not, to contradict," e.g., Mark 14:70; John 1:20; 18:25, 27; 1 John 2:22; (b) "to deny" by way of disowning a person, as, e.g., the Lord Jesus as master, e.g., Matt. 10:33; Luke 12:9; John 13:38 (in the best mss.); 2 Tim. 2:12; or, on the other hand, of Christ Himself, "denying" that a person is His follower, Matt. 10:33; 2 Tim. 2:12; or to "deny" the Father and the Son, by apostatizing and by disseminating pernicious teachings, to "deny" Jesus Christ as master and Lord by immorality under a cloak of religion, 2 Pet. 2:1; Jude 4; (c) "to deny oneself," either in a good sense, by disregarding one's own interests, Luke 9:23, or in a bad sense, to prove false to oneself, to act quite unlike oneself, 2 Tim. 2:13; (d) to "abrogate, forsake, or renounce a thing," whether evil, Titus 2:12, or good, 1 Tim. 5:8; 2 Tim. 3:5; **Rev. 2:13; 3:8**; (e) "not to accept, to reject" something offered, Acts 3:14; 7:35, "refused"; Heb. 11:24 "refused."

Faithful *see Revelation 1:5.*

Martyr *see* **Witness** at *Revelation 1:5.*

Slain *apokteino* (615), the usual word for "to kill," is so translated in the RV wherever possible (e.g., for KJV, "to slay," in Luke 11:49; Acts 7:52; **Rev. 2:13; 9:15; 11:13; 19:21**); in the following the verb "to kill" would not be appropriate, Rom. 7:11, "slew," metaphorically of sin, as using the commandment; Eph. 2:16, "having slain," said metaphorically of the enmity between Jew and Gentile.

2:14 But I have a few things against thee, because thou hast there them that hold the doctrine of Balaam, who taught Balac to cast a stumblingblock before the children of Israel, to eat things sacrificed unto idols, and to commit fornication.

Few *oligos* (3641), used of number quantity, and size, denotes "few, little, small, slight," e.g., Matt. 7:14; 9:37; 15:34; 20:16; neuter plural, "a few things," Matt. 25:21, 23; **Rev. 2:14** (**20** in some mss.); in Eph. 3:3, the phrase *en oligo*, in brief, is translated "in a few words."

"It is better to be faithful than famous."

THEODORE ROOSEVELT

Hold *see* **Holdeth** at *Revelation 2:1*.

Doctrine *didache* (1322), denotes "teaching," either (a) that which is taught, e.g., Matt. 7:28, KJV, "doctrine," RV, "teaching"; Titus 1:9, RV; **Rev. 2:14- 15, 24**, or (b) the act of teaching, instruction, e.g., Mark 4:2, KJV, "doctrine," RV, "teaching" the RV has "the doctrine" in Rom. 16:17.

Taught *didasko* (1321), is used (a) absolutely, "to give instruction," e.g., Matt. 4:23; 9:35; Rom. 12:7; 1 Cor. 4:17; 1 Tim. 2:12; 4:11; (b) transitively, with an object, whether persons, e.g., Matt. 5:2; 7:29, and frequently in the Gospels and Acts, or things "taught," e.g., Matt. 15:9; 22:16; Acts 15:35; 18:11; both persons and things, e.g., John 14:26; **Rev. 2:14, 20**.

Stumblingblock *skandalon* (4625), originally was "the name of the part of a trap to which the bait is attached, hence, the trap or snare itself, as in Rom. 11:9, RV, 'stumblingblock,' quoted from Psa. 69:22, and in **Rev. 2:14**, for Balaam's device was rather a trap for Israel than a stumblingblock to them, and in Matt. 16:23, for in Peter's words the Lord perceived a snare laid for Him by Satan.

"In NT *skandalon* is always used metaphorically, and ordinarily of anything that arouses prejudice, or becomes a hindrance to others, or causes them to fall by the way. Sometimes the hindrance is in itself good, and those stumbled by it are the wicked."

Thus it is used (a) of Christ in Rom. 9:33, "(a rock) of offense"; so 1 Pet. 2:8; 1 Cor. 1:23 (KJV and RV, "stumblingblock"), and of His cross, Gal. 5:11 (RV, ditto); of the "table" provided by God for Israel, Rom. 11:9; (b) of that which is evil, e.g., Matt. 13:41, RV, "things that cause stumbling" (KJV, "things that offend"), lit., "all stumblingblocks"; 18:7, RV, "occasions of stumbling" and "occasion"; Luke 17:1 (ditto); Rom. 14:13, RV, "an occasion of falling" (KJV, "an occasion to fall"), said of such a use of Christian liberty as proves a hindrance to another; 16:17, RV, "occasions of stumbling," said of the teaching of things contrary to sound doctrine; 1 John 2:10, "occasion of stumbling," of the absence of this in the case of one who loves his brother and thereby abides in the light. Love, then, is the best safeguard against the woes pronounced by the Lord upon those who cause others to stumble. Cf. the Sept. in Hos. 4:17, "Ephraim partaking with idols hath laid stumblingblocks in his own path."

Idols *eidolothutos* (1494), is an adjective signifying "sacrificed to idols" (*eidolon*, as above, and *thuo*, "to sacrifice"), Acts 15:29; 21:25; 1 Cor. 8:1, 4, 7, 10; 10:19 (in all these the RV substitutes "sacrificed" for the KJV); **Rev. 2:14, 20** (in these the RV and KJV both have "sacrificed"). The flesh of the victims, after sacrifice, was eaten or sold.

Fornication *porneuo* (4203), "to commit fornication," is used (a) literally, Mark 10:19; 1 Cor. 6:18; 10:8; **Rev. 2:14, 20**; (b) metaphorically, **Rev. 17:2; 18:3, 9**. *See also* ***Revelation 2:21***.

2:15 So hast thou also them that hold the doctrine of the Nicolaitans, which thing I hate.

Hold *see* **Holdeth** at *Revelation 2:1*.

Hate *see* **Hatest, Hate** at *Revelation 2:6*.

2:16 Repent; or else I will come unto thee quickly, and will fight against them with the sword of my mouth.

Repent *see Revelation 2:5*.

Quickly *see Revelation 2:5*.

Fight *polemeo* (4170), (Eng., "polemics"), "to fight, to make war," is used (a) literally, **Rev. 12:7** (twice), RV; **13:4; 17:14; 19:11**; (b) metaphorically, **Rev. 2:16**, RV; (c) hyperbolically, Jas. 4:2.

Sword *see Revelation 1:16*.

Mouth *see Revelation 1:16*.

2:17 He that hath an ear, let him hear what the Spirit saith unto the churches; To him that overcometh will I give to eat of the hidden manna, and will give him a white stone, and in the stone a new name written, which no man knoweth saving he that receiveth *it*.

Overcometh *see Revelation 2:7*.

Manna *manna* (3131), the supernaturally provided food for Israel during their wilderness journey (for details see Exod. 16 and Num. 11). The Hebrew equivalent is given in Exod. 16:15, RV marg., "*man hu*." The translations are, RV, "what is it?"; KJV and RV marg., "it is manna." It is described in Ps. 78:24, 25 as "the corn of heaven" and "the bread of the mighty," RV text and KJV marg. ("angels' food," KJV text), and in 1 Cor. 10:3, as "spiritual meat." The vessel appointed to contain it as a perpetual memorial, was of gold, Heb. 9:4, with Exod. 16:33. The Lord speaks of it as being typical of Himself, the true Bread from Heaven, imparting eternal life and sustenance to those who by faith partake spiritually of Him, John 6:31-35. The "hidden manna" is promised as one of the rewards of the overcomer, **Rev. 2:17**; it is thus suggestive of the moral excellence of Christ in His life on earth, hid from the eyes of men, by whom He was "despised and rejected"; the path of the overcomer is a reflex of His life. None of the natural substances called "manna" is to be identified with that which God provided for Israel.

White *see Revelation 1:14.*

Stone *psephos* (5586), "a smooth stone, a pebble," worn smooth as by water, or polished (akin to *psao*, "to rub"), denotes (a) by metonymy, a vote (from the use of "pebbles" for this purpose; cf. *psephizo*, "to count"), Acts 26:10, RV (KJV, "voice"); (b) a (white) "stone" to be given to the overcomer in the church at Pergamum, **Rev. 2:17** (twice); a white "stone" was often used in the social life and judicial customs of the ancients; festal days were noted by a white "stone," days of calamity by a black; in the courts a white "stone" indicated acquittal, a black condemnation. A host's appreciation of a special guest was indicated by a white "stone" with the name or a message written on it; this is probably the allusion here.

New *kainos* (2537), denotes "new," of that which is unaccustomed or unused, not "new" in time, recent, but "new" as to form or quality, of different nature from what is contrasted as old. " 'The new tongues,' kainos, of Mark 16:17 are the 'other tongues,' heteros, of Acts 2:4. These languages, however, were 'new' and 'different,' not in the sense that they had never been heard before, or that they were new to the hearers, for it is plain from v. 8 that this is not the case; they were new languages to the speakers, different from those in which they were accustomed to speak. The new things that the Gospel brings for present obedience and realization are: a new covenant, Matt. 26:28 in some texts; a new commandment, John 13:34; a new creative act, Gal. 6:15; a new creation, 2 Cor. 5:17; a new man, i.e., a new character of manhood, spiritual and moral, after the pattern of Christ, Eph. 4:24; a new man, i.e., 'the Church which is His (Christ's) body,' Eph. 2:15. The new things that are to be received and enjoyed hereafter are: a new name, the believer's, **Rev. 2:17**; a new name, the Lord's, **Rev. 3:12**; a new song, **Rev. 5:9**; a new Heaven and a new Earth, **Rev. 21:1**; the new Jerusalem, **Rev. 3:12; 21:2**; 'And He that sitteth on the Throne said, Behold, I make all things new,' **Rev. 21:5**."

Saving In Luke 4:27 and **Rev. 2:17**, KJV, *ei me* (lit., "if not"), is translated "saving" (RV, "but only" and "but").

2:18 And unto the angel of the church in Thyatira write; These things saith the Son of God, who hath his eyes like unto a flame of fire, and his feet *are* like fine brass;

Son *see Revelation 1:13.*

Eyes *see Revelation 1:14.*

Like unto *hos* (5613), used as a relative adverb of manner, means "as, like as," etc., and is translated "like," e.g., in Matt. 6:29; Mark 4:31; Luke 12:27; in Acts 3:22 and 7:37 (see RV, marg.); in 8:32 (2nd part), RV, "as" (KJV, "like"); **Rev. 2:18**, RV (the rendering should have been "as" here); **18:21**, RV, "as it were" (KJV, "like"); **21:11**, 2nd part (ditto). *See also Revelation 1:13.*

Flame *see Revelation 1:14.*

Fire *see Revelation 1:14.*

Brass *see Revelation 1:15.*

2:19 I know thy works, and charity, and service, and faith, and thy patience, and thy works; and the last *to be* more than the first.

Know *see Revelation 2:2.*

Service *diakonua* (1248), "the office and work of a *diakonos*", "service, ministry," is used (a) of domestic duties, Luke 10:40; (b) of religious and spiritual "ministration," (1) of apostolic "ministry," e.g., Acts 1:17, 25; 6:4; 12:25; 21:19; Rom. 11:13, RV (KJV, "office"); (2) of the service of believers, e.g., Acts 6:1; Rom. 12:7; 1 Cor. 12:5, RV, "ministrations" (KJV, "administrations"); 1 Cor. 16:15; 2 Cor. 8:4; 9:1, 12, RV, "ministration"; v. 13; Eph. 4:12, RV, "ministering" (KJV, "the ministry," not in the sense of an ecclesiastical function); 2 Tim. 4:11, RV, "(for) ministering"; collectively of a local church, Acts 11:29, "relief" (RV marg. "for ministry"); **Rev. 2:19**, RV, "ministry" (KJV, "service"); of Paul's service on behalf of poor saints, Rom. 15:31; (3) of the "ministry" of the Holy Spirit in the gospel, 2 Cor. 3:8; (4) of the "ministry" of angels, Heb. 1:14, RV, "to do service" (KJV, "to minister"); (5) of the work of the gospel, in general, e.g., 2 Cor. 3:9, "of righteousness;" 5:18, "of reconciliation"; (6) of the general "ministry" of a servant of the Lord in preaching and teaching, Acts 20:24; 2 Cor. 4:1; 6:3; 11:8; 1 Tim. 1:12, RV, "(to His) service"; 2 Tim. 4:5; undefined in Col. 4:17; (7) of the Law, as a "ministration" of death, 2 Cor. 3:7; of condemnation, 3:9.

Last *see Revelation 1:11.*

2:20 Notwithstanding I have a few things against thee, because thou sufferest that woman Jezebel, which calleth herself a prophetess, to teach and to seduce my servants to commit fornication, and to eat things sacrificed unto idols.

Notwithstanding *alla*, "but," in **Rev. 2:20** (RV, "but").

Have *see* **Had** at **Revelation** *1:16*.

Few *see* ***Revelation 2:14***.

Prophetess *prophetis* (4398), the feminine of *prophetes*, is used of Anna, Luke 2:36; of the self-assumed title of "the woman Jezebel" in **Rev. 2:20**.

Teach *see* **Taught** at ***Revelation 2:14***.

Seduce *planao* (4105), "to cause to wander, lead astray," is translated "to seduce" in 1 John 2:26, KJV (RV, "lead ... astray"); in **Rev. 2:20**, "to seduce."

Fornication *see* ***Revelation 2:14***.

Idols *see* ***Revelation 2:14*** **Idols**.

2:21 And I gave her space to repent of her fornication; and she repented not.

Space In Acts 15:33 and **Rev. 2:21**, KJV, *chronos*, "time" (RV), is translated "space."

Repent, Repented *see* **Repent** at *Revelation 2:5*.

Fornication *porneia* (4202), is used (a) of "illicit sexual intercourse," in John 8:41; Acts 15:20, 29; 21:25; 1 Cor. 5:1; 6:13, 18; 2 Cor. 12:21; Gal. 5:19; Eph. 5:3; Col. 3:5; 1 Thess. 4:3; **Rev. 2:21**; **9:21**; in the plural in 1 Cor. 7:2; in Matt. 5:32 and 19:9 it stands for, or includes, adultery; it is distinguished from it in 15:19 and Mark 7:21; (b) metaphorically, of "the association of pagan idolatry with doctrines of, and professed adherence to, the Christian faith," **Rev. 14:8**; **17:2**, **4**; **18:3**; **19:2**; some suggest this as the sense in **2:21**.

2:22 Behold, I will cast her into a bed, and them that commit adultery with her into great tribulation, except they repent of their deeds.

Bed *kline* (2825), akin to *klino*, "to lean" (Eng., "recline, incline," etc.), "a bed," e.g., Mark 7:30, also denotes a "couch" for reclining at meals, Mark 4:21, or a "couch" for carrying the sick, Matt. 9:2, 6. The metaphorical phrase "to cast into a bed," **Rev. 2:22**, signifies to afflict with disease (or possibly, to lay on a bier). In Mark 7:4 the KJV curiously translates the word "tables" (marg., "beds"), RV, marg. only, "couches."

Adultery *moicheuo* (3431), is used in Matt. 5:27-28, 32; 19:18; Mark 10:19; Luke 16:18; 18:20; John 8:4; Rom. 2:22; 13:9; Jas. 2:11; in **Rev. 2:22**, metaphorically, of those who are by a Jezebel's solicitations drawn away to idolatry.

Tribulation *see* ***Revelation 1:9***.

Repent *see* ***Revelation 2:5***.

2:23 And I will kill her children with death; and all the churches shall know that I am he which searcheth the reins and hearts: and I will give unto every one of you according to your works.

Searcheth *eraunao* or *ereunao, an earlier form,* (2045), "to search, examine," is used (a) of God, as "searching" the heart, Rom. 8:27; (b) of Christ, similarly, **Rev. 2:23**; (c) of the Holy Spirit, as "searching" all things, 1 Cor. 2:10, acting in the spirit of the believer; (d) of the OT prophets, as "searching" their own writings concerning matters foretold of Christ, testified by the Spirit of Christ in them, 1 Pet. 1:11; (e) of the Jews, as commanded by the Lord to "search" the Scriptures, John 5:39, KJV, and RV marg., "search," RV text, "ye search," either is possible grammatically; (f) of Nicodemus as commanded similarly by the chief priests and Pharisees, John 7:52.

Reins *nephros* (3510), "a kidney" (Eng., "nephritis," etc.), usually in the plural, is used metaphorically of "the will and the affections," **Rev. 2:23**, "reins" (cf. Ps. 7:9; Jer. 11:20; 17:10; 20:12). The feelings and emotions were regarded as having their seat in the "kidneys."

2:24 But unto you I say, and unto the rest in Thyatira, as many as have not this doctrine, and which have not known the depths of Satan, as they speak; I will put upon you none other burden.

Doctrine *see* ***Revelation 2:14***.

Which This is the translation of (a) the article with nouns, adjectives, numerals, participles, etc., e.g., "that which," etc.; (b) the relative pronoun *hos*, "who," in one of its forms (a frequent use); (c) *hostis*, "whoever," differing from *hos* by referring to a subject in general, as one of a class, e.g., Rom. 2:15; Gal. 4:24 (twice); 5:19; **Rev. 2:24**; **20:4**; (d) the interrogative pronoun *tis*, "who? which?," e.g., Matt. 6:27; John 8:46; (e) *hoios*, "of what kind," e.g., Phil. 1:30; (f) *poios*, the interrogative of (e), e.g., John 10:32; (g) *hosos*, "whatsoever," etc.; plural, how many, translated "which" in Acts 9:39.

Known *ginosko* (1097), signifies "to be taking in knowledge, to come to know, recognize, understand," or "to understand completely," e.g., Mark 13:28, 29; John 13:12; 15:18; 21:17; 2 Cor. 8:9; Heb. 10:34; 1 John 2:5; 4:2, 6 (twice), 7, 13; 5:2, 20; in its past tenses it frequently means "to know in the sense of realizing," the aorist or point tense usually indicating definiteness, Matt. 13:11; Mark 7:24; John 7:26; in 10:38 "that ye may know (aorist tense) and understand, (present tense)"; 19:4; Acts 1:7; 17:19; Rom. 1:21; 1 Cor. 2:11 (2nd part), 14; 2 Cor. 2:4; Eph. 3:19; 6:22; Phil. 2:19; 3:10; 1 Thess. 3:5; 2 Tim. 2:19; Jas. 2:20; 1 John

2:13 (twice), 14; 3:6; 4:8; 2 John 1; **Rev. 2:24**; **3:3**, **9**. In the passive voice, it often signifies "to become known," e.g., Matt. 10:26; Phil. 4:5. In the sense of complete and absolute understanding on God's part, it is used, e.g., in Luke 16:15; John 10:15 (of the Son as well as the Father); 1 Cor. 3:20. In Luke 12:46, KJV, it is rendered "he is ... aware." In the NT *ginosko* frequently indicates a relation between the person "knowing" and the object known; in this respect, what is "known" is of value or importance to the one who knows, and hence the establishment of the relationship, e.g., especially of God's "knowledge," 1 Cor. 8:3, "if any man love God, the same is known of Him"; Gal. 4:9, "to be known of God"; here the "knowing" suggests approval and bears the meaning "to be approved"; so in 2 Tim. 2:19; cf. John 10:14, 27; Gen. 18:19; Nah. 1:7; the relationship implied may involve remedial chastisement, Amos 3:2. The same idea of appreciation as well as "knowledge" underlies several statements concerning the "knowledge" of God and His truth on the part of believers, e.g., John 8:32; 14:20, 31; 17:3; Gal. 4:9 (1st part); 1 John 2:3-13, 14; 4:6, 8, 16; 5:20; such "knowledge" is obtained, not by mere intellectual activity, but by operation of the Holy Spirit consequent upon acceptance of Christ. Nor is such "knowledge" marked by finality; see e.g., 2 Pet. 3:18; Hos. 6:3, RV. The verb is also used to convey the thought of connection or union, as between man and woman, Matt. 1:25; Luke 1:34.

Depths *bathos* (899), is used (a) naturally, in Matt. 13:5, "deepness"; Mark 4:5, KJV, "depth," RV, "deepness"; Luke 5:4, of "deep" water; Rom. 8:39 (contrasted with *hupsoma*, "height"); (b) metaphorically, in Rom. 11:33, of God's wisdom and knowledge; in 1 Cor. 2:10, of God's counsels; in Eph. 3:18, of the dimensions of the sphere of the activities of God's counsels, and of the love of Christ which occupies that sphere; in 2 Cor. 8:2, of "deep" poverty; some mss. have it in **Rev. 2:24**.

Satan *see Revelation 2:9.*

Put *ballo* (906), "to throw, cast, put," is translated "to put," in Matt. 9:17 (twice); 25:27; 27:6; Mark 2:22; 7:33; Luke 5:37; John 5:7; 12:6; 13:2 (of "putting" into the heart by the Devil); 18:11 (of "putting" up a sword); 20:25 (RV twice, KJV, "put" and "thrust"); v. 27, RV; Jas, 3:3; **Rev. 2:24** (RV, "cast").

Burden *baros* (922), denotes "a weight, anything pressing on one physically," Matt. 20:12, or "that makes a demand on one's resources," whether material, 1 Thess. 2:6 (to be burdensome), or spiritual, Gal. 6:2; **Rev. 2:24**, or religious, Acts 15:28. In one place it metaphorically describes the future state of believers as "an eternal weight of glory," 2 Cor. 4:17.

2:25 But that which ye have *already* hold fast till I come.

Hold *see* **Holdeth** at *Revelation 2:1.*

2:26 And he that overcometh, and keepeth my works unto the end, to him will I give power over the nations:

Overcometh *see Revelation 2:7.*

Keepeth *see* **Keep** at *Revelation 1:3.*

Works *see Revelation 2:2.*

End The following phrases contain *telos* (the word itself coming under one or other of the above): *eis telos*, "unto the end," e.g., Matt. 10:22; 24:13; Luke 18:5, "continual"; John 13:1; 2 Cor. 3:13, "on the end" (RV); *heos telous*, "unto the end," 1 Cor. 1:8; 2 Cor. 1:13; *achri telous*, "even to the end" (a stronger expression than the preceding); Heb. 6:11; **Rev. 2:26** (where "even" might well have been added); *mechri telous*, with much the same meaning as *achri telous*, Heb. 3:6, 14.

2:27 And he shall rule them with a rod of iron; as the vessels of a potter shall they be broken to shivers: even as I received of my Father.

Rule *poimaino* (4165), "to act as a shepherd, tend flocks," is translated "to rule" in **Rev. 2:27**; **12:5**; **19:15**, all indicating that the governing power exercised by the Shepherd is to be of a firm character; in Matt. 2:6, KJV, "shall rule" (RV, "shall be shepherd of").

Rod *rhabdos* (4464), "a staff, rod, scepter," is used (a) of Aaron's "rod," Heb. 9:4; (b) a staff used on a journey, Matt. 10:10, RV, "staff" (KJV, "staves"); so Luke 9:3; Mark 6:8, "staff"; Heb. 11:21, "staff"; (c) a ruler's staff, a "scepter," Heb. 1:8 (twice); elsewhere a "rod," **Rev. 2:27**; **12:5**; **19:15**; (d) a "rod" for chastisement (figuratively), 1 Cor. 4:21; (e) a measuring rod, **Rev. 11:1**.

Iron *sidereos* (4603), "of iron," occurs in Acts 12:10, of an iron gate; "of iron," **Rev. 2:27**; **9:9**; **12:5**; **19:15**.

Vessels *skeuos* (4632), is used (a) of "a vessel or implement" of various kinds, Mark 11:16; Luke 8:16; John 19:29; Acts 10:11, 16; 11:5; 27:17 (a sail); Rom. 9:21; 2 Tim. 2:20; Heb. 9:21; **Rev. 2:27**; **18:12**; (b) of "goods or household stuff," Matt. 12:29 and Mark 3:27, "goods"; Luke 17:31, RV, "goods" (KJV, "stuff"); (c) of "persons," (1) for the service of God, Acts 9:15, "a (chosen) vessel"; 2 Tim. 2:21, "a vessel (unto honor)"; (2) the "subjects" of divine wrath, Rom.

9:22; (3) the "subjects" of divine mercy, Rom. 9:23; (4) the human frame, 2 Cor. 4:7; perhaps 1 Thess. 4:4; (5) a husband and wife, 1 Pet. 3:7; of the wife, probably, 1 Thess. 4:4; while the exhortation to each one "to possess himself of his own vessel in sanctification and honor" is regarded by some as referring to the believer's body [cf. Rom. 6:13; 1 Cor. 9:27], the view that the "vessel" signifies the wife, and that the reference is to the sanctified maintenance of the married state, is supported by the facts that in 1 Pet. 3:7 the same word *time*, "honor," is used with regard to the wife, again in Heb. 13:4, *timios*, "honorable" (RV, "in honor") is used in regard to marriage; further, the preceding command in 1 Thess. 4 is against fornication, and the succeeding one (v. 6) is against adultery. In Ruth 4:10, Sept., *ktaomai*, "to possess," is used of a wife.

Potter *keramikos* (2764), denotes "of (or made by) a potter" (Eng., "ceramic"), "earthen," **Rev. 2:27**.

Broken *suntribo* (4937), lit., "to rub together," and so "to shatter, shiver, break in pieces by crushing," is said of the bruising of a reed, Matt. 12:20; the "breaking" of fetters in pieces, Mark 5:4; the "breaking" of an alabaster cruse, Mark 14:3; an earthenware vessel, **Rev. 2:27**; of the physical bruising of a person possessed by a demon, Luke 9:39; concerning Christ, "a bone of Him shall not be broken," John 19:36; metaphorically of the crushed condition of a "broken-hearted" person, Luke 4:18 (KJV only); of the eventual crushing of Satan, Rom. 16:20. This verb is frequent in the Sept. in the passive voice, e.g., Ps. 51:17; Isa. 57:15, of a contrite heart, perhaps a figure of stones made smooth by being rubbed together in streams. Cf. *suntrimma*, "destruction."

Even as *kago*, for *kai ego*, means either "even I" or "even so I" or "I also." In John 10:15, the RV has "and I" for the KJV, "even so ... I"; in 17:18 and 20:21, KJV and RV, "even so I"; in the following, *kago* is preceded by *hos*, or *kathos*, "even as I, "1 Cor. 7:8; 10:33; "even as I also," 11:1; "as I also," **Rev. 2:27**.

Father *see* ***Revelation 1:6***.

2:28 And I will give him the morning star.

Morning *proinos* (4407), qualifies *aster*, "star," in **Rev. 2:28** and **22:16**. That Christ will give to the overcomer "the morning star" indicates a special interest for such in Himself, as He thus describes Himself in the later passage. For Israel He will appear as "the sun of righteousness"; as the "morning" Star which precedes He will appear for the rapture of the church.

Star *see* **Stars** at **Revelation** ***1:16***.

2:29 He that hath an ear, let him hear what the Spirit saith unto the churches.

Chapter 3

3:1 And unto the angel of the church in Sardis write; These things saith he that hath the seven Spirits of God, and the seven stars; I know thy works, that thou hast a name that thou livest, and art dead.

Stars *see* ***Revelation 1:16***.

Know *see* ***Revelation 2:2***.

Works *see* ***Revelation 2:2***.

Name *see* ***Revelation 2:3***.

Dead *nekros* (3498), is used of (a) the death of the body, cf. Jas. 2:26, its most frequent sense: (b) the actual spiritual condition of unsaved men, Matt. 8:22; John 5:25; Eph. 2:1, 5; 5:14; Phil. 3:11; Col. 2:13; cf. Luke 15:24: (c) the ideal spiritual condition of believers in regard to sin, Rom. 6:11: (d) a church in declension, inasmuch as in that state it is inactive and barren, **Rev. 3:1**: (e) sin, which apart from law cannot produce a sense of guilt, Rom. 7:8: (f) the body of the believer in contrast to his spirit, Rom. 8:10: (g) the works of the Law, inasmuch as, however good in themselves, Rom. 7:13, they cannot produce life, Heb. 6:1; 9:14: (h) the faith that does not produce works, Jas. 2:17, 26; cf. v. 20.

3:2 Be watchful, and strengthen the things which remain, that are ready to die: for I have not found thy works perfect before God.

Watchful *gregoreo* (1127), "to watch," is used (a) of "keeping awake," e.g., Matt. 24:43; 26:38, 40, 41; (b) of "spiritual alertness," e.g., Acts 20:31; 1 Cor. 16:13; Col. 4:2; 1 Thess. 5:6, 10; 1 Pet. 5:8, RV, "be watchful" (KJV, "be vigilant"); **Rev. 3:2, 3; 16:15**.

Strengthen *sterizo* (4741), "to fix, make fast, to set" (from *sterix*, "a prop"), is used of "establishing" or "stablishing" (i.e., the confirmation) of persons; the apostle Peter was called by the Lord to "establish" his brethren, Luke 22:32, translated "strengthen"; Paul desired to visit Rome that the saints might be "established," Rom. 1:11; cf. Acts 8:23; so with Timothy at Thessalonica, 1 Thess. 3:2; the "confirmation" of the saints is the work of God, Rom. 16:25, "to stablish (you)"; 1 Thess. 3:13, "stablish (your hearts)"; 2 Thess. 2:17, "stablish them (in every good work and word)"; 1 Pet. 5:10, "stablish"; the means used to effect the "confirmation" is the ministry of the Word of God, 2 Pet. 1:12, "are established (in the truth which is with you)"; James exhorts Christians to "stablish" their hearts, Jas. 5:8; cf. **Rev. 3:2**, RV. The character of this "confirmation" may be learned from its use in Luke 9:51, "steadfastly set"; 16:26, "fixed," and in the Sept. in Exod. 17:12, "stayed up" (also from its strengthened form *episterizo*, "to confirm," in Acts 14:22; 15:32, 41; in some mss. "to strengthen," in 18:23). Neither the laying on of hands nor the impartation of the Holy Spirit is mentioned in the NT in connection with either of these words, or with the synonymous verb *bebaioo* (see 1 Cor. 1:8; 2 Cor. 1:21, etc.).

Remain In 1 Cor. 7:29, KJV, *to loipon*, lit., "(as to) what is left," "(as for) the rest," is translated "it remaineth" (RV, "henceforth"); in **Rev. 3:2**, *ta loipa*, the plural, "the things that remain."

Ready *mello* (3195), "to be about to," is translated "to be ready" in 2 Pet. 1:12, RV, where the future indicates that the apostle will be prepared, as in the past and the present, to remind his readers of the truths they know (some mss. have *ouk ameleso*, "I will not be negligent," KJV; cf., however, v. 15. Field, in *Notes on the Translation of the NT*, suggests that the true reading is *meleso*, the future of *melo*, "to be a care, or an object of care"); in **Rev. 3:2**, RV, "were ready" (some texts have the present tense, as in the KJV). Elsewhere, where the KJV has the rendering to be ready, the RV gives renderings in accordance with the usual significance as follows: Luke 7:2, "was ... at the point of"; Acts 20:7, "intending"; **Rev. 12:4**, "about (to)."

Perfect *pleroo* (4137), signifies (1) "to fill"; (2) "to fulfill, complete," (a) of time, e.g., Mark 1:15; Luke 21:24; John 7:8 (KJV, "full come"); Acts 7:23, RV, "he was wellnigh forty years old" (KJV, "was full," etc.), lit., "the time of forty years was fulfilled to him"; v. 30, KJV, "were expired"; 9:23; 24:27 (KJV, "after two years"; RV, "when two years were fulfilled"); (b) of number, **Rev. 6:11**; (c) of good pleasure, 2 Thess. 1:11; (d) of joy, Phil. 2:2; in the passive voice, "to be fulfilled," John 3:29 and 17:13; in the following the verb is rendered "fulfilled" in the RV, for the KJV, "full," John 15:11; 16:24; 1 John 1:4; 2 John 12; (e) of obedience, 2 Cor. 10:6; (f) of works, **Rev. 3:2**; (g) of the future Passover, Luke 22:16; (h) of sayings, prophecies, etc., e.g., Matt. 1:22 (twelve times in Matt., two in Mark, four in Luke, eight in John, two in Acts); Jas. 2:23; in Col. 1:25 the word signifies to preach "fully," to complete the ministry of the gospel appointed.

3:3 Remember therefore how thou hast received and heard, and hold fast, and repent. If therefore thou shalt not watch, I will come on thee as a thief, and thou shalt not know what hour I will come upon thee.

Remember *see Revelation 2:5.*

Hold fast *tereo* (5083), "to watch over, keep, give heed to, observe," is rendered "hold fast" in **Rev. 3:3**, KJV (RV, "keep").

Repent *see Revelation 2:5.*

Watch *see* **Watchful** at *Revelation 3:2.*

Thief *kleptes* (2812), is used (a) literally, Matt. 6:19, 20; 24:43; Luke 12:33, 39; John 10:1, 10; 12:6; 1 Cor. 6:10; 1 Pet. 4:15; (b) metaphorically of "false teachers," John 10:8; (c) figuratively, (1) of the personal coming of Christ, in a warning to a local church, with most of its members possessed of mere outward profession and defiled by the world, **Rev. 3:3**; in retributive intervention to overthrow the foes of God, **16:15**; (2) of the Day of the Lord, in divine judgment upon the world, 2 Pet. 3:10 and 1 Thess. 5:2, 4; in v. 2, according to the order in the original "the word 'night' is not to be read with 'the day of the Lord,' but with 'thief,' i.e., there is no reference to the time of the coming, only to the manner of it. To avoid ambiguity the phrase may be paraphrased, 'so comes as a thief in the night comes.' The use of the present tense instead of the future emphasizes the certainty of the coming.... The unexpectedness of the coming of the thief, and the unpreparedness of those to whom he comes, are the essential elements in the figure; cf. the entirely different figure used in Matt. 25:1-13."

Know *see* **Known** at *Revelation 2:24.*

What *poios*, "what sort of," e.g., Matt. 21:23, 24, 27; 24:42, 43; Luke 5:19; 6:32-34; 20:2, 8; 24:19; John 12:33, "what manner of"; so in 18:32; 21:19; Rom. 3:27; 1 Cor. 15:35; in Jas. 4:14, "what"; 1 Pet. 2:20 and **Rev. 3:3** (ditto); 1 Pet. 1:11, "what manner of."

Hour *hora* (5610), whence Lat., *hora*, Eng., "hour," primarily denoted any time or period, expecially a season. In the NT it is used to denote (a) "a part of the day," especially a twelfth part of day or night, an "hour," e.g., Matt. 8:13; Acts 10:3, 9; 23:23; **Rev. 9:15**; in 1 Cor. 15:30, "every hour" stands for "all the time"; in some passages it expresses duration, e.g., Matt. 20:12; 26:40; Luke 22:59; inexactly, in such phrases as "for a season," John 5:35; 2 Cor. 7:8; "for an hour," Gal. 2:5; "for a short season," 1 Thess. 2:17, RV (KJV, "for a short time," lit., "for the time of an hour"); (b) "a period more or less extended," e.g., 1 John 2:18, "it is the last hour," RV; (c) "a definite point of time," e.g., Matt. 26:45, "the hour is at hand"; Luke 1:10; 10:21; 14:17, lit., "at the hour of supper"; Acts 16:18; 22:13; **Rev. 3:3; 11:13; 14:7;** a point of time when an appointed action is to begin, **Rev. 14:15**; in Rom. 13:11, "it is high time," lit., "it is already an hour," indicating that a point of time has come later than would have been the case had responsibility been realized. In 1 Cor. 4:11, it indicates a point of time previous to which certain circumstances have existed.

3:4 Thou hast a few names even in Sardis which have not defiled their garments; and they shall walk with me in white: for they are worthy.

Names *see* **Name** at *Revelation 2:3*.

Defiled *moluno* (3435), properly denotes "to besmear," as with mud or filth, "to befoul." It is used in the figurative sense, of a conscience "defiled" by sin, 1 Cor. 8:7; of believers who have kept themselves (their "garments") from "defilement," **Rev. 3:4**, and of those who have not "soiled" themselves by adultery or fornication, **Rev. 14:4**.

White *see Revelation 1:14*.

Worthy *axios* (514), "of weight, worth, worthy," is said of persons and their deeds: (a) in a good sense, e.g., Matt. 10:10, 11, 13 (twice), 37 (twice), 38; 22:8; Luke 7:4; 10:7; 15:19, 21; John 1:27; Acts 13:25; 1 Tim. 5:18; 6:1; Heb. 11:38; **Rev. 3:4; 4:11; 5:2, 4, 9, 12**; (b) in a bad sense, Luke 12:48; 23:15; Acts 23:29; 25:11, 25; 26:31; Rom. 1:32; **Rev. 16:6**.

3:5 He that overcometh, the same shall be clothed in white raiment; and I will not blot out his name out of the book of life, but I will confess his name before my Father, and before his angels.

Overcometh *see Revelation 2:7*.

White *see Revelation 1:14*.

Raiment For *himation*, rendered "raiment" in Matt. 17:2, KJV (RV, "garments"), so Matt. 27:31; Mark 9:3; Luke 23:34; John 19:24; Acts 22:20; **Rev. 3:5, 18; 4:4**; KJV and RV, Acts 18:6.

Blot out *exaleipho* (1813), from *ek*, "out," used intensively, and *aleipho*, "to wipe," signifies "to wash, or to smear completely." Hence, metaphorically, in the sense of removal, "to wipe away, wipe off, obliterate"; Acts 3:19, of sins; Col. 2:14, of writing; **Rev. 3:5**, of a name in a book; **Rev. 7:17; 21:4**, of tears.

Book *biblos* (976), (Eng. "Bible") was the inner part, or rather the cellular substance, of the stem of the papyrus (Eng. "paper"). It came to denote the paper made from this bark in Egypt, and then a written "book," roll, or volume. It is used in referring to "books" of Scripture, the "book," or scroll, of Matthew's Gospel, Matt. 1:1; the Pentateuch, as the "book" of Moses, Mark 12:26; Isaiah, as "the book of the words of Isaiah," Luke 3:4; the Psalms, Luke 20:42 and Acts 1:20; "the prophets," Acts 7:42; to "the Book of Life," Phil. 4:3; **Rev. 3:5; 20:15**. Once only it is used of secular writings, Acts 19:19.

Confess *homologeo* (3670), lit., "to speak the same thing" (*homos*, "same," *lego*, "to speak"), "to assent, accord, agree with," denotes, (a) "to confess, declare, admit," John 1:20; e.g., Acts 24:14; Heb. 11:13; (b) "to confess by way of admitting oneself guilty of what one is accused of, the result of inward conviction," 1 John 1:9; (c) "to declare openly by way of speaking out freely, such confession being the effect of deep conviction of facts," Matt. 7:23; 10:32 (twice) and Luke 12:8 (see next par.); John 9:22; 12:42; Acts 23:8; Rom. 10:9-10 ("confession is made"); 1 Tim. 6:12 (RV); Titus 1:16; 1 John 2:23; 4:2, 15; 2 John 7 (in John's epistle it is the necessary antithesis to Gnostic doceticism); **Rev. 3:5**, in the best mss. (some mss. have *exomologeo* (1843) in **Rev. 3:5**); (d) "to confess by way of celebrating with praise," Heb. 13:15; (e) "to promise," Matt. 14:7. In Matt. 10:32 and Luke 12:8 the construction of this verb with *en*, "in," followed by the dative case of the personal pronoun, has a special significance, namely, to "confess" in a person's name, the nature of the "confession" being determined by the context, the suggestion being to make a public "confession." Thus the statement, "every one ... who shall confess Me (lit. "in Me," i.e., in My case) before men, him (lit., "in him," i.e., in his case) will I also confess before My Father ... ," conveys the thought of "confessing" allegiance to Christ as one's Master and Lord, and, on the other hand, of acknowledgment, on His part, of the faithful one as being His worshipper and servant, His loyal follower; this is appropriate to the original idea in *homologeo* of being identified in thought or language.

Father *see Revelation 1:6*.

3:6-7 He that hath an ear, let him hear what the Spirit saith unto the churches.

And to the angel of the church in Philadelphia write; These things saith he that is holy, he that is true, he that hath the key of David, he that openeth, and no man shutteth; and shutteth, and no man openeth;

True *alethinos* (228), denotes "true" in the sense of real, ideal, genuine; it is used (a) of God, John 7:28; 17:3; 1 Thess. 1:9; **Rev. 6:10**; these declare that God fulfills the meaning of His Name; He is "very God," in distinction from all other gods, false gods; (b) of Christ, John 1:9; 6:32; 15:1; 1 John 2:8; 5:20 (thrice); **Rev. 3:7, 14; 19:11**; His judgment, John 8:16; (c) God's words, John 4:37; **Rev. 19:9, 21:5; 22:6**; the last three are equivalent to *alethes*; (d) His ways, **Rev. 15:3**; (e) His judgments, **Rev. 16:7; 19:2**; (f) to His riches, Luke 16:11; (g) His worshipers, John 4:23; (h) their hearts, Heb. 10:22; (i) the witness of the apostle John, John 19:35; (j) the spiritual, antitypical tabernacle, Heb. 8:2; 9:24, not that the wilderness tabernacle was false, but that it was a weak and earthly copy of the heavenly.

Key *see* **Keys** at **Revelation** *1:18.*

Openeth *anoigo* (455), is used (1) transitively, (a) literally, of "a door or gate," e.g., Acts 5:19; graves, Matt. 27:52; a sepulchre, Rom. 3:13; a book, e.g., Luke 4:17; **Rev. 5:2-5; 10:8**; the seals of a roll, e.g., **Rev. 5:9; 6:1**; the eyes, Acts 9:40; the mouth of a fish, Matt. 17:27; "the pit of the abyss," **Rev. 9:2**, RV; heaven and the heavens, Matt. 3:16; Luke 3:21; Acts 10:11; **Rev. 19:11**; "the temple of the tabernacle of the testimony in heaven," **Rev. 15:5**; by metonymy, for that which contained treasures, Matt. 2:11; (b) metaphorically, e.g., Matt. 7:7-8; 25:11; **Rev. 3:7**; Hebraistically, "to open the mouth," of beginning to speak, e.g., Matt. 5:2; 13:35; Acts 8:32, 35; 10:34; 18:14; **Rev. 13:6** (cf., e.g., Num. 22:28; Job. 3:1; Isa. 50:5); and of recovering speech, Luke 1:64; of the earth "opening," **Rev. 12:16**; of the "opening" of the eyes, Acts 26:18; the ears, Mark 7:35 (in the best mss.); (2) intransitively (perfect tense, active, in the Greek), (a) literally, of "the heaven," John 1:51, RV, "opened;" (b) metaphorically, of "speaking freely," 2 Cor. 6:11.

Shutteth *kleio* (2808), is used (a) of things material, Matt. 6:6; 25:10; Luke 11:7; John 20:19, 26; Acts 5:23; 21:30; **Rev. 20:3**; figuratively, **21:25**; (b) metaphorically, of the kingdom of heaven, Matt. 23:13; of heaven, with consequences of famine, Luke 4:25; **Rev. 11:6**; of compassion, 1 John 3:17, RV (KJV, "bowels *of compassion*"); of the blessings accruing from the promises of God regarding David, **Rev. 3:7**; of a door for testimony, **3:8.**

3:8 I know thy works: behold, I have set before thee an open door, and no man can shut it: for thou hast a little strength, and hast kept my word, and hast not denied my name.

Know *see Revelation 2:2.*

Set *didomi* (1325), "to give," is translated "I have set before" in **Rev. 3:8** (RV marg., "given").

Door *thura* (2374), "a door, gate" (Eng., "door" is connected), is used (a) literally, e.g., Matt. 6:6; 27:60; (b) metaphorically, of Christ, John 10:7, 9; of faith, by acceptance of the gospel, Acts 14:27; of "openings" for preaching and teaching the Word of God, 1 Cor. 16:9; 2 Cor. 2:12; Col. 4:3; **Rev. 3:8**; of "entrance" into the Kingdom of God, Matt. 25:10; Luke 13:24-25; of Christ's "entrance" into a repentant believer's heart, **Rev. 3:20**; of the nearness of Christ's second advent, Matt. 24:33; Mark 13:29; cf. Jas. 5:9; of "access" to behold visions relative to the purposes of God, **Rev. 4:1.**

Shut *see* **Shutteth** at *Revelation 3:7.*

Little *mikros* (3398), "little, small" (the opposite of *megos*, "great"), is used (a) of persons, with regard to (1) station, or age, in the singular, Mark 15:40, of James "the less" (RV marg., "little"), possibly referring to age; Luke 19:3; in the plural,

> *"Repentance is an ongoing process. One must be forever repentant. It is not enough to once feel sorrow over sin. True repentance affects the whole man and alters the entire life style."*
>
> RICHARD OWEN ROBERTS

"little" ones, Matt. 18:6, 10, 14; Mark 9:42; (2) rank or influence, e.g., Matt. 10:42 (see context); Acts 8:10; 26:22, "small," as in **Rev. 11:18; 13:16; 19:5, 18; 20:12**; (b) of things, with regard to (1) size, e.g., Jas. 3:5; (2) quantity, Luke 12:32; 1 Cor. 5:6; Gal. 5:9; **Rev. 3:8**; (3) time, John 7:33; 12:35; **Rev. 6:11; 20:3.**

Strength *see Revelation 1:16.*

Kept *see* **Keep** at *Revelation 1:3.*

Denied *see Revelation 2:13.*

Name *see Revelation 2:3.*

3:9 Behold, I will make them of the synagogue of Satan, which say they are Jews, and are not, but do lie; behold, I will make them to come and worship before thy feet, and to know that I have loved thee.

Make *didomi* (1325), "to give," is used in 2 Thess. 3:9 "to make (ourselves an ensample)"; in **Rev. 3:9** (1st part), RV, "I will give," the sense is virtually the same as *poieo* in the 2nd part of the verse.

Synagogue *see Revelation 2:9*.

Satan *see Revelation 2:9*.

Lie *pseudo* (5574), "to deceive by lies" (always in the middle voice in the NT), is used (a) absolutely, in Matt. 5:11, "falsely," lit., "lying" (v, marg.); Rom. 9:1; 2 Cor. 11:31; Gal. 1:20; Col. 3:9 (where the verb is followed by the preposition *eis*, "to"); 1 Tim. 2:7; Heb. 6:18; Jas. 3:14 (where it is followed by the preposition *kata*, "against"); 1 John 1:6; **Rev. 3:9**; (b) transitively, with a direct object (without a preposition following), Acts 5:3 (with the accusative case) "to lie to (the Holy Ghost)," RV marg., "deceive"; v. 4 (with the dative case) "thou hast (not) lied (unto men, but unto God)."

Make *poieo* (4160), "to do, to make," is used in the latter sense (a) of constructing or producing anything, of the creative acts of God, e.g., Matt. 19:4 (2nd part); Acts 17:24; of the acts of human beings, e.g., Matt. 17:4; Acts 9:39; (b) with nouns denoting a state or condition, to be the author of, to cause, e.g., peace, Eph. 2:15; Jas. 3:18; stumbling blocks, Rom. 16:17; (c) with nouns involving the idea of action (or of something accomplished by action), so as to express the idea of the verb more forcibly (the middle voice is commonly used in this respect, suggesting the action as being of special interest to the doer); for the active voice see, e.g., Mark 2:23, of "making" one's way, where the idea is not that the disciples "made" a path through the standing corn, but simply that they went, the phrase being equivalent to going, "(they began) as they went (to pluck the ears)"; other instances of the active are **Rev. 13:13, 14; 16:14; 19:20**; for the middle voice (the dynamic or subjective middle), see, e.g., John 14:23, "will make Our abode"; in Acts 20:24, "none of these things move me," lit., "I make account of none of these things"; 25:17, "I made no delay" RV, Rom. 15:26; Eph. 4:16; Heb. 1:2; 2 Pet. 1:10; (d) to "make" ready or prepare, e.g., a dinner, Luke 14:12; a supper, John 12:2; (e) to acquire, provide a thing for oneself, Matt. 25:16; Luke 19:18; (f) to render or "make" one or oneself anything, or cause a person or thing to become something, e.g., Matt. 4:19; 12:16, "make (Him known)"; John 5:11, 15, to "make" whole; 16:2, lit., "they shall make (you put out of the synagogue)"; Eph. 2:14; Heb. 1:7; to change one thing into another, Matt. 21:13; John 2:16; 4:46; 1 Cor. 6:15; (g) to constitute one anything, e.g., Acts 2:36, (h) to declare one or oneself anything, John 5:18, "making (Himself equal with God)"; 8:53; 10:33; 19:7, 12; 1 John 1:10; 5:10; (i) to "make" one do a thing, e.g., Luke 5:34; John 6:10; **Rev. 3:9**.

Know *see* **Known** at *Revelation 2:24*.

3:10 Because thou hast kept the word of my patience, I also will keep thee from the hour of temptation, which shall come upon all the world, to try them that dwell upon the earth.

Kept, Keep *see* **Keep** at *Revelation 1:3*.

Patience *see Revelation 1:9*.

Temptation *peirasmos* (3986), is used of (1) "trials" with a beneficial purpose and effect, (a) of "trials" or "temptations," divinely permitted or sent, Luke 22:28; Acts 20:19; Jas. 1:2; 1 Pet. 1:6; 4:12, RV, "to prove," KJV, "to try"; 2 Pet. 2:9 (singular); **Rev. 3:10**, RV, "trial" (KJV, "temptation"); in Jas. 1:12, "temptation" apparently has meanings (1) and (2) combined, and is used in the widest sense; (b) with a good or neutral significance, Gal. 4:14, of Paul's physical infirmity, "a temptation" to the Galatian converts, of such a kind as to arouse feelings of natural repugnance; (c) of "trials" of a varied character, Matt. 6:13 and Luke 11:4, where believers are commanded to pray not to be led into such by forces beyond their own control; Matt. 26:41; Mark 14:38; Luke 22:40, 46, where they are commanded to watch and pray against entering into "temptations" by their own carelessness or disobedience; in all such cases God provides "the way of escape," 1 Cor. 10:13 (where *peirasmos* occurs twice). (2) Of "trial" definitely designed to lead to wrong doing, "temptation," Luke 4:13; 8:13; 1 Tim. 6:9; (3) of "trying" or challenging God, by men, Heb. 3:8.

Shall *see Revelation 1:19*.

World *oikoumene* (3625), "the inhabited earth", is used (a) of the whole inhabited world, Matt. 24:14; Luke 4:5; 21:26; Rom. 10:18; Heb. 1:6; **Rev. 3:10; 16:14**; by metonymy, of its inhabitants, Acts 17:31; **Rev. 12:9**; (b) of the Roman Empire, the world as viewed by the writer or speaker, Luke 2:1; Acts 11:28; 24:5; by metonymy, of its inhabitants, Acts 17:6; 19:27; (c) the inhabited world in a coming age, Heb. 2:5.

Try *see* **Tried** at *Revelation 2:2*.

3:11 Behold, I come quickly: hold that fast which thou hast, that no man take thy crown.

Quickly *see Revelation 2:5*.

Hold *see* **Holdeth** at *Revelation 2:1*.

Crown *see Revelation 2:10*.

3:12 Him that overcometh will I make a pillar in the temple of my God, and he shall go no more out: and I will write upon

him the name of my God, and the name of the city of my God, *which is* new Jerusalem, which cometh down out of heaven from my God: and *I will write upon him* my new name.

Overcometh *see Revelation 2:7.*

Pillar *stulos* (4769), "a column supporting the weight of a building," is used (a) metaphorically, of those who bear responsibility in the churches, as of the elders in the church at Jerusalem, Gal. 2:9; of a local church as to its responsibility, in a collective capacity, to maintain the doctrines of the faith by teaching and practice, 1 Tim. 3:15; some would attach this and the next words to the statement in v. 16; the connection in the Eng. versions seems preferable; (b) figuratively in **Rev. 3:12**, indicating a firm and permanent position in the spiritual, heavenly and eternal Temple of God; (c) illustratively, of the feet of the angel in the vision in **Rev. 10:1**, seen as flames rising like columns of fire indicative of holiness and consuming power, and thus reflecting the glory of Christ as depicted in **1:15**; cf. Ezek. 1:7.

Temple *naos* (3485), "a shrine or sanctuary," was used (a) among the heathen, to denote the shrine containing the idol, Acts 17:24; 19:24 (in the latter, miniatures); (b) among the Jews, the sanctuary in the "Temple," into which only the priests could lawfully enter, e.g., Luke 1:9, 21, 22; Christ, as being of the tribe of Judah, and thus not being a priest while upon the earth (Heb. 7:13, 14; 8:4), did not enter the *naos*; (c) by Christ metaphorically, of His own physical body, John 2:19, 21; (d) in apostolic teaching, metaphorically, (1) of the church, the mystical body of Christ, Eph. 2:21; (2) of a local church, 1 Cor. 3:16, 17; 2 Cor. 6:16; (3) of the present body of the individual believer, 1 Cor. 6:19; (4) of the "Temple" seen in visions in Revelation, **3:12; 7:15; 11:19; 14:15, 17; 15:5, 6, 8; 16:1, 17**; (5) of the Lord God Almighty and the Lamb, as the "Temple" of the new and heavenly Jerusalem, **Rev. 21:22**.

No more *eti* (2089), "yet, as yet, still," used of degree is translated "more" in Matt. 18:16, "(one or two) more"; Heb. 8:12 and 10:17, "(will I remember no) more"; 10:2, "(no) more (conscience)"; 11:32, "(what shall I) more (say)?" **Rev. 3:12**, "(he shall go out thence no) more"; **7:16**, "(no) more" and "any more;" **9:12**, KJV "more" (RV, "hereafter"); **18:21-23**, "(no) more" "any more" (5 times); **20:3**, "(no) more"; **21:1, 4** (twice); **22:3**.

City *polis* (4172), primarily "a town enclosed with a wall" (perhaps from a root *ple-*, signifying "fullness," whence also the Latin *pleo*, "to fill," Eng., "polite, polish, politic, etc."), is used also of the heavenly Jerusalem, the abode and community of the redeemed, Heb. 11:10, 16; 12:22; 13:14. In Revelation it signifies the visible capital of the heavenly kingdom, as destined to descend to earth in a coming age, e.g., **Rev. 3:12; 21:2, 14, 19**. By metonymy the word stands for the inhabitants, as in the English use, e.g., Matt. 8:34; 12:25; 21:10; Mark 1:33; Acts 13:44.

Heaven *ouranos* (3772), probably akin to *ornumi*, "to lift, to heave," is used in the NT (a) of "the aerial heavens," e.g., Matt. 6:26; 8:20; Acts 10:12; 11:6 (RV, "heaven," in each place, KJV, "air"); Jas. 5:18; (b) "the sidereal," e.g., Matt. 24:29, 35; Mark 13:25, 31; Heb. 11:12, RV, "heaven," KJV, "sky"; **Rev. 6:14; 20:11**; they, (a) and (b), were created by the Son of God, Heb. 1:10, as also by God the Father, **Rev. 10:6**; (c) "the eternal dwelling place of God," Matt. 5:16; 12 :50; **Rev. 3:12; 11:13; 16:11; 20:9**. From thence the Son of God descended to become incarnate, John 3:13, 31; 6:38, 42. In His ascension Christ "passed through the heavens," Heb. 4:14, RV; He "ascended far above all the heavens," Eph. 4:10, and was "made higher than the heavens," Heb. 7:26; He "sat down on the right hand of the throne of the Majesty in the heavens," Heb. 8:1; He is "on the right hand of God," having gone into heaven, 1 Pet. 3:22. Since His ascension it is the scene of His present life and activity, e.g., Rom. 8:34; Heb. 9:24. From thence the Holy Spirit descended at Pentecost, 1 Pet. 1:12. It is the abode of the angels, e.g., Matt. 18:10; 22:30; cf. **Rev. 3:5**. Thither Paul was "caught up," whether in the body or out of the body, he knew not, 2 Cor. 12:2. It is to be the eternal dwelling place of the saints in resurrection glory, 2 Cor. 5:1. From thence Christ will descend to the air to receive His saints at the Rapture, 1 Thess. 4:16; Phil. 3:20, 21, and will subsequently come with His saints and with His holy angels at His second advent, Matt. 24:30; 2 Thess. 1:7. In the present life "heaven" is the region of the spiritual citizenship of believers, Phil. 3:20. The present "heavens," with the earth, are to pass away, 2 Pet. 3:10, "being on fire," v. 12 (see v. 7); **Rev. 20:11**, and new "heavens" and earth are to be created, 2 Pet. 3:13; **Rev. 21:1**, with Isa. 65:17, e.g. In Luke 15:18, 21, "heaven" is used, by metonymy, for God.

New *see Revelation 2:17.*

3:13-14 He that hath an ear, let him hear what the Spirit saith unto the churches.

And unto the angel of the church of the Laodiceans write; These things saith the Amen, the faithful and true witness, the beginning of the creation of God;

Amen *amen* (281), is transliterated from Hebrew into both Greek and English. "Its meanings may be seen in such passages as Deut. 7:9, 'the faithful (the Amen) God,' Isa. 49:7, 'Jehovah that is faithful.' 65:16, 'the God of truth,' marg., 'the God of Amen.' And if God is faithful His testimonies and precepts are "sure (*amen*)," Ps. 19:7; 111:7, as are also His warnings, Hos. 5:9, and promises, Isa. 33:16; 55:3. 'Amen' is used of men also, e.g., Prov. 25:13.

"Once in the NT 'Amen' is a title of Christ, **Rev. 3:14**, because through Him the purposes of God are established, 2 Cor. 1:20. The early Christian churches followed the example of Israel in associating themselves audibly with the prayers and thanksgivings offered on their behalf, 1 Cor. 14:16, where the article 'the' points to a common practice. Moreover this custom conforms to the pattern of things in the Heavens, see **Rev. 5:14**, etc. The individual also said 'Amen' to express his 'let it be so' in response to the Divine 'thus it shall be,' **Rev. 22:20**. Frequently the speaker adds 'Amen' to his own prayers and doxologies, as is the case at Eph. 3:21, e.g. The Lord Jesus often used 'Amen,' translated 'verily,' to introduce new revelations of the mind of God. In John's Gospel it is always repeated, 'Amen, Amen,' but not elsewhere. Luke does not use it at all, but where Matthew, 16:28, and Mark, 9:1, have 'Amen,' Luke has 'of a truth'; thus by varying the translation of what the Lord said, Luke throws light on His meaning."

Faithful *see Revelation 1:5.*

True *see Revelation 3:7.*

Witness *see Revelation 1:5.*

3:15 I know thy works, that thou art neither cold nor hot: I would thou wert cold or hot.

Know *see Revelation 2:2.*

Cold *psuchros* (5593), "cool, fresh, cold, chilly" (fuller in expression than *psuchos*), is used in the natural sense in Matt. 10:42, "cold water"; metaphorically in **Rev. 3:15-16**.

Hot *zestos* (2200), "boiling hot" (from *zeo*, "to boil, be hot, fervent"; cf. Eng., "zest"), is used, metaphorically, in **Rev. 3:15, 16**.

Would *ophelon* (the 2nd aorist tense of *opheilo*, "to owe") expresses a wish, "I would that," either impracticable, 1 Cor. 4:8, RV (KJV, "would to God"); or possible, 2 Cor. 11:1; Gal. 5:12; **Rev. 3:15**.

3:16 So then because thou art lukewarm, and neither cold nor hot, I will spue thee out of my mouth.

Lukewarm *chliaros* (5513), "tepid, warm" (akin to *chlio*, "to become warm," not found in the NT or Sept.), is used metaphorically in **Rev. 3:16**, of the state of the Laodicean church, which afforded no refreshment to the Lord, such as is ministered naturally by either cold or hot water.

Hot *see Revelation 3:15.*

Mouth *see Revelation 1:16.*

Will *mello* (3195), "to be about to," is translated "will" in Matt. 2:13 and John 7:35 (twice); "wilt," John 14:22; "will," Acts 17:31; "wouldest," 23:20; "will," 27:10 and **Rev. 3:16**.

Spue *emeo* (1692), "to vomit" (cf. Eng., "emetic"), is used in **Rev. 3:16**, figuratively of the Lord's utter abhorrence of the condition of the church at Laodicea. In the Sept., Isa. 19:14.

3:17 Because thou sayest, I am rich, and increased with goods, and have need of nothing; and knowest not that thou art wretched, and miserable, and poor, and blind, and naked:

Rich *see Revelation 2:9.*

Increased with goods *plouteo* (4147), "to be rich," in the aorist or point tense, "to become rich," is used (a) literally, Luke 1:53, "the rich," present participle, lit., "(ones or those) being rich"; 1 Tim. 6:9, 18; **Rev. 18:3, 15, 19** (all three in the aorist tense); (b) metaphorically, of Christ, Rom. 10:12 (the passage stresses the fact that Christ is Lord; see v. 9, and the RV); of the "enrichment" of believers through His poverty, 2 Cor. 8:9 (the aorist tense expressing completeness, with permanent results); so in **Rev. 3:18**, where the spiritual "enrichment" is conditional upon righteousness of life and conduct; of a false sense of "enrichment," 1 Cor. 4:8 (aorist), RV, "ye are become rich" (KJV, "ye are rich"); **Rev. 3:17** (perfect tense, RV, "I ... have gotten riches," KJV, "I am ... increased with goods").

Wretched *talaiporia* (5004), "hardship, suffering, distress" (akin to *talaiporos*, "wretched," Rom. 7:24; **Rev. 3:17**, and to *talaiporeo*, in the middle voice, "to afflict oneself," in Jas. 4:9, "be afflicted"), is used as an abstract noun, "misery," in Rom. 3:16; as a concrete noun, "miseries," in Jas. 5:1.

Miserable *eleeinos* (1652), "pitiable, miserable" (from *eleos*, "mercy, pity"), is used in **Rev. 3:17**, in the Lord's description of the church at Laodicea; here the idea is probably that of a combination of "misery" and pitiableness.

Poor *ptochos* (4434), has the broad sense of "poor," (a) literally, e.g., Matt. 11:5; 26:9, 11; Luke 21:3 (with stress on the word, "a conspicuously poor widow"); John 12:5, 6, 8; 13:29; Jas. 2:2, 3, 6; the "poor" are constantly the subjects of injunctions to assist them, Matt. 19:21; Mark 10:21; Luke 14:13, 21; 18:22; Rom. 15:26; Gal. 2:10; (b) metaphorically, Matt. 5:3; Luke 6:20; **Rev. 3:17**.

Blind *tuphlos* (5185), "blind," is used both physically and metaphorically, chiefly in the Gospels; elsewhere four times; physically, Acts 13:11; metaphorically, Rom. 2:19; 2 Pet. 1:9; **Rev. 3:17**. The word is frequently used as a noun, signifying "a blind man."

Naked *gumnos* (1131), signifies (a) "unclothed," Mark 14:52; in v. 51 it is used as a noun (*"his"* and *"body"* being italicized); (b) "scantily or poorly clad," Matt. 25:36, 38, 43, 44; Acts 19:16 (with torn garments); Jas. 2:15; (c) "clad in the undergarment only" (the outer being laid aside), John 21:7; (d) metaphorically, (1) of "a bare seed," 1 Cor. 15:37; (2) of "the soul without the body," 2 Cor. 5:3; (3) of "things exposed to the allseeing eye of God," Heb. 4:13; (4) of "the carnal condition of a local church," **Rev. 3:17**; (5) of "the similar state of an individual," **16:15**; (6) of "the desolation of religious Babylon," **17:16**.

3:18 I counsel thee to buy of me gold tried in the fire, that thou mayest be rich; and white raiment, that thou mayest be clothed, and *that* the shame of thy nakedness do not appear; and anoint thine eyes with eyesalve, that thou mayest see.

Counsel *sumbouleuo* (4823), in the active voice, "to advise, to counsel," John 18:14, "gave counsel"; in **Rev. 3:18**, "I counsel"; in the middle voice, "to take counsel, consult," Matt. 26:4, RV, "took counsel together," for KJV, "consulted"; Acts 9:23, "took counsel" (RV adds "together"); in some mss. John 11:53.

Gold *chrusion* (5553), is used (a) of "coin," Acts 3:6; 20:33; 1 Pet. 1:18; (b) of "ornaments," 1 Pet. 3:3, and the following, 1 Tim. 2:9; **Rev. 17:4; 18:16**; (c) of "the metal in general," Heb. 9:4; 1 Pet. 1:7; **Rev. 21:18, 21**; metaphorically, (d) of "sound doctrine and its effects," 1 Cor. 3:12; (e) of "righteousness of life and conduct," **Rev. 3:18**.

Tried In **Rev. 3:18**, KJV, *puroo*, in the passive voice, "to be purified by fire" (RV, "refined"), is rendered "tried." *See also* **Burned** at ***Revelation 1:15***.

Fire *see* ***Revelation 1:14***.

Rich *see* **Increased with goods** at ***Revelation 3:17***.

White *see* ***Revelation 1:14***.

Raiment *see* ***Revelation 3:5***.

Shame *aischune* (152), "shame," signifies (a) subjectively, the confusion of one who is "ashamed" of anything, a sense of "shame," Luke 14:9; those things which "shame" conceals, 2 Cor. 4:2; (b) objectively, ignominy, that which is visited on a person by the wicked, Heb. 12:2; that which should arise from guilt, Phil. 3:19; (c) concretely, a thing to be "ashamed" of, **Rev. 3:18**; Jude 13, where the word is in the plural, lit., "basenesses," "disgraces."

Nakedness *gumnotes* (1132), "nakedness," is used (a) of "want of sufficient clothing," Rom. 8:35; 2 Cor. 11:27; (b) metaphorically, of "the nakedness of the body," said of the condition of a local church, **Rev. 3:18**.

Appear *phaneroo* (5319), signifies, in the active voice, "to manifest"; in the passive voice, "to be manifested"; so, regularly, in the RV, instead of "to appear." See 2 Cor. 7:12; Col. 3:4; Heb. 9:26; 1 Pet. 5:4; 1 John 2:28; 3:2; **Rev. 3:18**. To be manifested, in the Scriptural sense of the word, is more than to "appear." A person may "appear" in a false guise or without a disclosure of what he truly is; to be manifested is to be revealed in one's true character; this is especially the meaning of *phaneroo*, see, e.g., John 3:21; 1 Cor. 4:5; 2 Cor. 5:10-11; Eph. 5:13.

Anoint *enchrio* (1472), primarily, "to rub in," hence, "to besmear, to anoint," is used metaphorically in the command to the church in Laodicea to "anoint" their eyes with eyesalve, **Rev. 3:18**. In the Sept., Jer. 4:30, it is used of the "anointing" of the eyes with a view to beautifying them.

Eyesalve *kollourion* (2854), primarily a diminutive of *kollura*, and denoting "a coarse bread roll" (as in the Sept. of 1 Kings 12: after v. 24, lines 30, 32, 39; Eng. version, 14:3), hence an "eye-salve," shaped like a roll, **Rev. 3:18**, of the true knowledge of one's condition and of the claims of Christ. The word is doubtless an allusion to the Phrygian powder used by oculists in the famous medical school at Laodicea.

3:19 As many as I love, I rebuke and chasten: be zealous therefore, and repent.

Rebuke *elencho* (1651), "to convict, refute, reprove," is translated "to rebuke" in the KJV of the following (the RV always has the verb "to reprove"): 1 Tim. 5:20; Titus 1:13; 2:15; Heb. 12:5; **Rev. 3:19**.

Chasten *paideuo* (3811), primarily denotes "to train children," suggesting the broad idea of education (*pais*, "a child"), Acts 7:22; 22:3; see also Titus 2:12, "instructing" (RV), here of a training gracious and firm; grace, which brings salvation, employs means to give us full possession of it, hence, "to chastise," this being part of the training, whether (a) by correcting with words, reproving, and admonishing, 1 Tim. 1:20 (RV, "be taught"); 2 Tim. 2:25, or (b) by "chastening" by the infliction of evils and calamities, 1 Cor. 11:32; 2 Cor. 6:9; Heb. 12:6-7, 10; **Rev. 3:19**. The verb also has the meaning "to chastise with blows, to scourge," said of the command of a judge, Luke 23:16, 22.

Zealous *zeloo* (2206), "to be jealous," also signifies "to seek or desire eagerly"; in Gal. 4:17, RV, "they zealously seek (you)," in the sense of taking a very warm interest in, so in v. 18, passive voice, "to be zealously sought" (KJV, "to be zealously affected"), i.e., to be the object of warm interest on the part of others; some texts have this verb in **Rev. 3:19**.

Repent *see* ***Revelation 2:5.***

3:20 Behold, I stand at the door, and knock: if any man hear my voice, and open the door, I will come in to him, and will sup with him, and he with me.

Door *see* ***Revelation 3:8.***

Knock *krouo* (2925), "to strike, knock," is used in the NT of "knocking" at a door, (a) literally, Luke 12:36; Acts 12:13, 16; (b) figuratively, Matt. 7:7, 8; Luke 11:9, 10 (of importunity in dealing with God); 13:25; **Rev. 3:20**.

Sup *deipneo* (1172), "to sup" (said of taking the chief meal of the day), occurs in Luke 17:8; 22:20 (in the best texts), lit., "(the) supping"; so 1 Cor. 11:25; metaphorically in **Rev. 3:20**, of spiritual communion between Christ and the faithful believer.

3:21-22 To him that overcometh will I grant to sit with me in my throne, even as I also overcame, and am set down with my Father in his throne.

He that hath an ear, let him hear what the Spirit saith unto the churches.

Overcometh *see* ***Revelation 2:7.***

Sit *kathizo* (2523), is used (a) transitively, "to make sit down," Acts 2:30; (b) intransitively, "to sit down," e.g., Matt. 5:1, RV, "when (He) had sat down" (KJV, "was set"); 19:28; 20:21, 23; 23:2; 25:31; 26:36; Mark 11:2, 7; 12:41; Luke 14:28, 31; 16:6; John 19:13; Acts 2:3 (of the tongues of fire); 8:31; 1 Cor. 10:7; 2 Thess. 2:4, "he sitteth," aorist tense, i.e., "he takes his seat" (as, e.g., in Mark 16:19); **Rev. 3:21** (twice), RV, "to sit down" and "sat down"; **20:4**.

Throne *see* ***Revelation 1:4.***

Set In Heb. 8:1, *kathizo* is used intransitively, RV, "sat down" (KJV, "is set"); so in 12:2, RV, "hath sat down" (KJV, "is set down"); **Rev. 3:21**, RV, "I ... sat down" (KJV, "am set down"). So *epikathizo* in Matt. 21:7 (last part), RV, "He sat" [some mss. have the plural in a transitive sense, KJV, "they set (Him)]."

Father *see* ***Revelation 1:6.***

Chapter 4

4:1 After this I looked, and, behold, a door *was* opened in heaven: and the first voice which I heard *was* as it were of a trumpet talking with me; which said, Come up hither, and I will shew thee things which must be hereafter.

Looked *eidon* (3708), used as the aorist tense of *horao*, "to see," in various senses, is translated "to look," in the KJV of John 7:52, RV, "see;" **Rev. 4:1** (RV, "I saw"); so in **6:8**; **14:1**, **14** (as in KJV of v. **6**), and **15:5**. *See also* **Before** at ***Revelation 1:4.***

Door *see* ***Revelation 3:8.***

Trumpet *see* ***Revelation 1:10.***

Talking *laleo* (2980), "to speak, say," is always translated "to speak" in the RV, where the KJV renders it by "to talk," Matt. 12:46; Mark 6:50; Luke 24:32; John 4:27 (twice); 9:37; 14:30; Acts 26:31; **Rev. 4:1**; **17:1**; **21:9**, **15**. The RV rendering is preferable; the idea of "chat" or "chatter" is entirely foreign to the NT, and should never be regarded as the meaning in 1 Cor. 14:34, 35.

Shew *see* ***Revelation 1:1.***

Hereafter *see* ***Revelation 1:19.***

4:2 And immediately I was in the spirit: and, behold, a throne was set in heaven, and *one* sat on the throne.

Spirit *see* ***Revelation 1:10.***

Throne *see* ***Revelation 1:4.***

Set *keimai* (2749), "to lie, to be laid" (used as the passive voice of *tithemi*), is translated "to be set," e.g., in Matt. 5:14 (of a city); Luke 2:34 (of Christ); John 2:6 (of waterpots); 19:29 (of a vessel of vinegar); Phil. 1:16, RV (v. 17, KJV) (of the apostle Paul); **Rev. 4:2** (of the throne in heaven).

4:3 And he that sat was to look upon like a jasper and a sardine stone: and *there was* a rainbow round about the throne, in sight like unto an emerald.

Look upon, Sight *horasis* (3706), denotes (a) a vision (so the associated noun *horama*, e.g., Acts 7:31; *horasis* signifies especially the act of seeing, *horama* that which is seen),

Acts 2:17; **Rev. 9:17**; (b) an appearance, **Rev. 4:3**, translated "to look upon" (twice in the RV; in the second instance the KJV has "in sight").

Jasper *iaspis* (2393), a Phoenician word (cf. Heb. *uash'pheh*, e.g., Exod. 28:20; 39:16), seems to have denoted a translucent stone of various colors, especially that of fire, **Rev. 4:3; 21:11, 18, 19**. The sardius and the jasper, of similar color, were the first and last stones on the breastplate of the high priest, Ex. 28:17, 20.

Sardine *sardion* or *sardinos* (4555), denotes "the sardian stone." *Sardius* is the word in the best texts in **Rev. 4:3** (RV, "a sardius"), where it formed part of the symbolic appearance of the Lord on His throne, setting forth His glory and majesty in view of the judgment to follow. There are two special varieties, one a yellowish brown, the other a transparent red (like a cornelian). The beauty of the stone, its transparent brilliance, the high polish of which it is susceptible, made it a favorite among the ancients. It forms the sixth foundation of the wall of the heavenly Jerusalem, **Rev. 21:20**.

Stone *lithos* (3037), is used (I) literally, of (a) the "stones" of the ground, e.g., Matt. 4:3, 6; 7:9; (b) "tombstones," e.g., Matt. 27:60, 66; (c) "building stones," e.g., Matt. 21:42; (d) "a millstone," Luke 17:2; cf. **Rev. 18:21**; (e) the "tables (or tablets)" of the Law, 2 Cor. 3:7; (f) "idol images," Acts 17:29; (g) the "treasures" of commercial Babylon, **Rev. 18:12, 16**; (II) metaphorically, of (a) Christ, Rom. 9:33; 1 Pet. 2:4, 6, 8; (b) believers, 1 Pet. 2:5; (c) spiritual edification by scriptural teaching, 1 Cor. 3:12; (d) the adornment of the foundations of the wall of the spiritual and heavenly Jerusalem, **Rev. 21:19**; (e) the adornment of the seven angels in **Rev. 15:6**, RV (so the best texts; some have *linon*, "linen," KJV); (f) the adornment of religious Babylon, **Rev. 17:4**; (III) figuratively, of Christ, **Rev. 4:3; 21:11**, where "light" stands for "Light-giver" (*phoster*).

Rainbow *iris* (2463), whence Eng., "iris," the flower, describes the "rainbow" seen in the heavenly vision, "round about the throne, like an emerald to look upon," **Rev. 4:3**, emblematic of the fact that, in the exercise of God's absolute sovereignty and perfect counsels, He will remember His covenant concerning the earth (Gen. 9:9-17); in **Rev. 10:1**, "the rainbow," RV, the definite article suggests a connection with the scene in **4:3**; here it rests upon the head of an angel who declares that "there shall be delay no longer" (v. **6**, RV marg., the actual meaning); the mercy to be shown to the earth must be preceded by the execution of divine judgments upon the nations who defy God and His Christ. Cf. Ezek. 1:28.

Round about *kuklothen* (2943), from *kuklos*, "a circle, ring" (Eng., "cycle," etc.), occurs in **Rev. 4:3, 4**; in v. **8**, RV, "round about," with reference to the eyes.

Like unto *see Revelation 1:13.*

Emerald *smaragdinos* (4664), "emerald in character," descriptive of the rainbow round about the throne in **Rev. 4:3**, is used in the papyri to denote emerald green.

4:4 And round about the throne *were* four and twenty seats: and upon the seats I saw four and twenty elders sitting, clothed in white raiment; and they had on their heads crowns of gold.

Round about *see Revelation 4:3.*

Throne *see Revelation 1:4.*

Twenty *eikosi* (1501), occurs in Luke 14:31; John 6:19; Acts 1:15; 27:28; 1 Cor. 10:8; of the "four and twenty" elders, in **Rev. 4:4** (twice), 10; 5:8; 11:16; 19:4 (combined in one numeral with *tessares*, "four," in some mss.).

Elders *presbuteros* (4245), an adjective, the comparative degree of *presbus*, "an old man, an elder," is used (a) of age, whether of the "elder" of two persons, Luke 15:25, or more, John 8:9, "the eldest", or of a person advanced in life, a senior, Acts 2:17; in Heb. 11:2, the "elders" are the forefathers in Israel so in Matt. 15:2; Mark 7:3, 5 the feminine of the adjective is used of "elder" women in the churches, 1 Tim. 5:2, not in respect of position but in seniority of age; (b) of rank or positions of responsibility, (1) among Gentiles, as in the Sept. of Gen. 50:7; Num. 22:7, (2) in the Jewish nation, firstly, those who were the heads or leaders of the tribes and families, as of the seventy who assisted Moses, Num. 11:16; Deut. 27:1, and those assembled by Solomon; secondly, members of the Sanhedrin, consisting of the chief priests, "elders" and scribes, learned in Jewish law, e.g., Matt. 16:21; 26:47; thirdly, those who managed public affairs in the various cities, Luke 7:3; (3) in the Christian churches those who, being raised up and qualified by the work of the Holy Spirit, were appointed to have the spiritual care of, and to exercise oversight over, the churches. To these the term "bishops," *episkopoi*, or "overseers," is applied (see Acts 20, v. 17 with v. 28, and Titus 1:5 and 7), the latter term indicating the nature of their work *presbuteroi* their maturity of spiritual experience. The divine arrangement seen throughout the NT was for a plurality of these to be appointed in each church, Acts 14:23; 20:17; Phil. 1:1; 1 Tim. 5:17; Titus 1:5. The duty of "elders" is described by the verb *episkopeo*. They were appointed according as they had given evidence of fulfilling the divine qualifications, Titus 1:6 to 9; cf. 1 Tim. 3:1-7 and 1 Pet. 5:2; (4) the twenty-four "elders" enthroned in heaven around the throne of God, **Rev. 4:4, 10; 5:5-14; 7:11, 13; 11:16; 14:3; 19:4**. The number twenty-four is representative of earthly conditions. The word "elder" is nowhere applied to angels.

White *see* ***Revelation 1:14***.

Raiment *see* ***Revelation 3:5***.

Crowns *see* **Crown** at ***Revelation 2:10***.

4:5 And out of the throne proceeded lightnings and thunderings and voices: and *there were* seven lamps of fire burning before the throne, which are the seven Spirits of God.

Proceeded *see* **Went** at ***Revelation 1:16***.

Lightnings *astrape* (796), denotes (a) "lightning," Matt. 24:27; 28:3; Luke 10:18; 17:24; in the plural, **Rev. 4:5; 8:5; 11:19; 16:18**; (b) "bright shining," or "shining brightness," Luke 11:36.

Thunderings *bronte* (1027), in Mark 3:17 "sons of thunder" is the interpretation of Boanerges, the name applied by the Lord to James and John; their fiery disposition is seen in 9:38 and Luke 9:54; perhaps in the case of James it led to his execution. The name and its interpretation have caused much difficulty; some suggest the meaning "the twins." It is however most probably the equivalent of the Aramaic *bene regesh*, "sons of tumult"; the latter of the two words was no doubt used of "thunder" in Palestinian Aramaic; hence the meaning "the sons of thunder"; the cognate Hebrew word *ragash*, "to rage," is used in Ps. 2:1 and there only. In John 12:29 *bronte* is used with *ginomai*, "to take place," and rendered "it had thundered"; lit., "there was thunder"; elsewhere, **Rev. 4:5; 6:1; 8:5; 10:3, 4; 11:19; 14:2; 16:18; 19:6**.

Lamps *lampas* (2985), denotes "a torch" (akin to *lampo*, "to shine"), frequently fed, like a "lamp," with oil from a little vessel used for the purpose (the *angeion* of Matt. 25:4); they held little oil and would frequently need replenishing. Rutherford (*The New Phrynichus*) points out that it became used as the equivalent of *luchnos*, as in the parable of the ten virgins, Matt. 25:1, 3, 4, 7, 8; John 18:3, "torches"; Acts 20:8, "lights"; **Rev. 4:5; 8:10** (RV, "torch," KJV, "lamp"). Cf. *phanos*, "a torch," John 18:3 (translated "lanterns").

Burning *kaio* (2545), "to set fire to, to light"; in the passive voice, "to be lighted, to burn," Matt. 5:15; John 15:6; Heb. 12:18; **Rev. 4:5; 8:8, 10; 19:20; 21:8**; 1 Cor. 13:3, is used metaphorically of the heart, Luke 24:32; of spiritual light, Luke 12:35; John 5:35.

4:6 And before the throne *there was* a sea of glass like unto crystal: and in the midst of the throne, and round about the throne, *were* four beasts full of eyes before and behind.

Before *emprocthen* (1715), is used of place or position only; adverbially, signifying "in front," Luke 19:28; Phil. 3:13; **Rev. 4:6**; as a preposition, e.g., Matt. 5:24; John 10:4; with the meaning "in the sight of a person," e.g., Matt. 5:16; 6:1; 17:2; Luke 19:27; John 12:37; 1 Thess. 2:19, RV, "before"; KJV, "in the presence of"; **Rev. 19:10**, RV, "before," especially in phrases signifying in the sight of God, as God wills, Matt. 11:26; 18:14 (lit., "a thing willed before your Father," RV, marg.); Luke 10:21; in the sense of "priority of rank or position or dignity," John 1:15, 30 (in some texts, v. 27); in an antagonistic sense, "against," Matt. 23:13 (RV, marg., "before").

Sea *thalassa* (2281), is used (a) chiefly literally, e.g., "the Red Sea," Acts 7:36; 1 Cor. 10:1; Heb. 11:29; the "sea" of Galilee or Tiberias, Matt. 4:18; 15:29; Mark 6:48, 49, where the acts of Christ testified to His deity; John 6:1; 21:1; in general, e.g., Luke 17:2; Acts 4:24; Rom. 9:27; **Rev. 16:3; 18:17; 20:8, 13; 21:1**; Matt. 18:6; (b) metaphorically, of "the ungodly men" described in Jude 13 (cf. Isa. 57:20); (c) symbolically, in the apocalyptic vision of "a glassy sea like unto crystal," **Rev. 4:6**, emblematic of the fixed purity and holiness of all that appertains to the authority and judicial dealings of God; in **15:2**, the same, "mingled with fire," and, standing by it (RV) or on it (KJV and RV marg.), those who had "come victorious from the beast" (ch. **13**); of the wild and restless condition of nations, **Rev. 13:1** (see **17:1, 15**), where "he stood" (RV) refers to the dragon, not John (KJV); from the midst of this state arises the beast, symbolic of the final gentile power dominating the federated nations of the Roman world (see Dan., chs. 2, 7, etc.).

Glass *hualinos* (5193), signifies "glassy, made of glass," **Rev. 4:6; 15:2** (twice), RV, "glassy."

Like unto *see* ***Revelation 1:13***.

Crystal *krustallos* (2930), from *kruos*, "ice," and hence properly anything congealed and transparent, denotes "crystal," a kind of precious stone, **Rev. 4:6; 22:1**. Rock crystal is pure quartz; it crystallizes in hexagonal prisms, each with a pyramidical apex.

Round about *kuklo* (2945), the dative case of *kuklos*, means "round about," lit., "in a circle." It is used in Mark 3:34; 6:6, 36; Luke 9:12; Rom. 15:19; **Rev. 4:6; 5:11; 7:11.**

Beasts *zoon* (2226), primarily denotes "a living being" (*zoe*, "life"). The Eng., "animal," is the equivalent, stressing the fact of life as the characteristic feature. In Heb. 13:11 the KJV and the RV translate it "beasts" ("animals" would be quite suitable). In 2 Pet. 2:12 and Jude 10, the KJV has "beasts," the RV "creatures." In Revelation, where the word is found some 20 times, and always of those beings which stand before the throne of God, who give glory and honor and thanks to Him, **4:6**, and act in perfect harmony with His counsels, **5:14; 6:1-7**, e.g., the word "beasts" is most unsuitable; the RV, "living creatures," should always be used; it gives to *zoon* its appropriate significance.

Full *gemo* (1073), "to be full, to be heavily laden with," was primarily used of a ship; it is chiefly used in the NT of evil contents, such as extortion and excess, Matt. 23:25; dead men's bones, v. 27; extortion and wickedness, Luke 11:39; cursing, Rom. 3:14; blasphemy, **Rev. 17:3**; abominations, v. **4**; of divine judgments **15:7; 21:9**; (RV, "laden," KJV, "full"); of good things, **4:6, 8; 5:8.**

4:7 And the first beast *was* like a lion, and the second beast like a calf, and the third beast had a face as a man, and the fourth beast *was* like a flying eagle.

Like *see* **Like unto** at *Revelation 1:13.*

Lion *leon* (3023), occurs in 2 Tim. 4:17, probably figurative of the imminent peril of death, the figure being represented by the whole phrase, not by the word "lion" alone; some suppose the reference to be to the lions of the amphitheater; the Greek commentators regarded the "lion" as Nero; others understand it to be Satan. The language not improbably recalls that of Ps. 22:21, and Dan. 6:20. The word is used metaphorically, too, in **Rev. 5:5**, where Christ is called "the Lion of the tribe of Judah." Elsewhere it has the literal meaning, Heb. 11:33; 1 Pet. 5:8; **Rev. 4:7; 9:8, 17; 10:3; 13:2.** Taking the OT and NT occurrences the allusions are to the three great features of the "lion," (1) its majesty and strength, indicative of royalty, e.g., Prov. 30:30, (2) its courage, e.g., Prov. 28:1, (3) its cruelty, e.g., Ps. 22:13.

Calf *moschos* (3448), primarily denotes "anything young," whether plants or the offspring of men or animals, the idea being that which is tender and delicate; hence "a calf, young bull, heifer," Luke 15:23, 27, 30; Heb. 9:12, 19; **Rev. 4:7.**

Flying *petomai* (4072), "to fly" (the root of which is seen in *pteron* and *pterux*, "a wing," *ptilon*, "a feather," etc.), is confined to Revelation, **4:7; 8:13; 12:14; 14:6; 19:17.** Some mss. have the verb *petaomai*, a frequentative form.

Eagle *aetos* (105), "an eagle" (also a vulture), is perhaps connected with *aemi*, "to blow," as of the wind, on account of its windlike flight. In Matt. 24:28 and Luke 17:37 the vultures are probably intended. The meaning seems to be that, as these birds of prey gather where the carcass is, so the judgments of God will descend upon the corrupt state of humanity. The figure of the "eagle" is used in Ezek. 17 to represent the great powers of Egypt and Babylon, as being employed to punish corrupt and faithless Israel. Cf. Job 39:30; Prov. 30:17. The "eagle" is mentioned elsewhere in the NT in **Rev. 4:7; 8:13** (RV); **12:14.** There are eight species in Palestine.

4:8 And the four beasts had each of them six wings about *him*; and *they were* full of eyes within: and they rest not day and night, saying, Holy, holy, holy, Lord God Almighty, which was, and is, and is to come.

Each *ana* (303), used with numerals or measures of quantity with a distributive force, is translated "apiece" in Luke 9:3, "two coats apiece," KJV; in John 2:6, "two or three firkins apiece." In Matt. 20:9-10, "every man a penny," is a free rendering for "a penny apiece"; in Luke 9:14, the RV adds "each" to translate the *ana*, in 10:1, *ana duo* is "two by two." See **Rev. 4:8**, "each."

Six *hex* (1803), whence Eng. prefix, "hex"-, is used separately from other numerals in Matt. 17:1; Mark 9:2; Luke 4:25; 13:14; John 2:6; 12:1; Acts 11:12; 18:11; Jas. 5:17; **Rev. 4:8.** It sometimes suggests incompleteness, in comparison with the perfect number seven.

Wings *pterux* (4420), is used of birds, Matt. 23:37; Luke 13:34; symbolically in **Rev. 12:14**, RV, "the two wings of the great eagle" (KJV, "two wings of a great eagle"), suggesting the definiteness of the action, the "wings" indicating rapidity and protection, an allusion, perhaps, to Exod. 19:4 and Deut. 32:11, 12; of the "living creatures" in a vision, **Rev. 4:8; 9:9.** Cf. *pterugion*, "a pinnacle."

About *see* **Round about** at **Revelation** *4:3.*

Full *see Revelation 4:6.*

Within This is a translation of (a) *entos*; in Luke 17:21 the RV marg., "in the midst of," is to be preferred;

the kingdom of God was not in the hearts of the Pharisees; (b) *en*, "of thinking or saying within oneself," e.g., Luke 7:39, 49 (marg., "among"); locally, e.g., Luke 19:44; (c) *esothen*, 2 Cor. 7:5; **Rev. 4:8**; **5:1**; "from within," Mark 7:21, 23; Luke 11:7; "within," Matt. 23:25; Luke 11:40, RV, "inside"; in Matt. 23:27, 28, RV, "inwardly"; (d) *eso*, John 20:26; Acts 5:23; 1 Cor. 5:12 (i.e., "within" the church); (e) *pros*, to, or with, in Mark 14:4, KJV, "within" (RV, "among"); (f) *dia*, "through," rendered "within (three days)" in Mark 14:58, KJV (RV, "in," looking through the time to the event, and in keeping with the metaphor of building); (g) *esoteros*, Heb. 6:19, the comparative degree of *eso*, used with the article translated "that within," lit., "the inner (part of the veil)," i.e., "inside"; (h) in Luke 11:41, RV, *eneimi*, "to be in," is rendered "are within" (KJV, "ye have").

Rest *anapausis* (372), "cessation, refreshment, rest" (*ana*, "up," *pauo*, "to make to cease"), the constant word in the Sept. for the Sabbath "rest," is used in Matt. 11:29; here the contrast seems to be to the burdens imposed by the Pharisees. Christ's "rest" is not a "rest" from work, but in work, "not the rest of inactivity but of the harmonious working of all the faculties and affections – of will, heart, imagination, conscience – because each has found in God the ideal sphere for its satisfaction and development" (J. Patrick, in *Hastings Bib. Dic.*); it occurs also in Matt. 12:43; Luke 11:24; **Rev. 4:8**, RV, "(they have no) rest" [KJV, "(they) rest (not)"], where the noun is the object of the verb *echo*, "to have"; so in **14:11**.

Night *nux* (3571), is used (I) literally, (a) of "the alternating natural period to that of the day," e.g., Matt. 4:2; 12:40; 2 Tim. 1:3; **Rev. 4:8**; (b) of "the period of the absence of light," the time in which something takes place, e.g., Matt. 2:14 (27:64), in some mss.); Luke 2:8; John 3:2 (7:50, in some mss.); Acts 5:19; 9:25; (c) of "point of time," e.g., Matt. 14:27 (in some mss.), 30; Luke 12:20; Acts 27:23; (d) of "duration of time," e.g., Luke 2:37; 5:5; Acts 20:31; 26:7 (note the difference in the phrase in Mark 4:27); (II) metaphorically, (a) of "the period of man's alienation from God," Rom. 13:12; 1 Thess. 5:5, lit., "not of night," where "of" means 'belonging to;' cf. "of the Way," Acts 9:2; "of shrinking back" and "of faith," Heb. 10:39, marg.; (b) of "death," as the time when work ceases, John 9:4.

Holy *hagios* (40), from the same root as *hagnos* (found in *hazo*, "to venerate"), fundamentally signifies "separated" (among the Greeks, dedicated to the gods), and hence, in Scripture in its moral and spiritual significance, separated from sin and therefore consecrated to God, sacred.

(a) It is predicated of God (as the absolutely "Holy" One, in His purity, majesty and glory): of the Father, e.g., Luke 1:49; John 17:11; 1 Pet. 1:15, 16; **Rev. 4:8**; **6:10**; of the Son, e.g., Luke 1:35; Acts 3:14; 4:27, 30; 1 John 2:20; of the Spirit, e.g., Matt. 1:18 and frequently in all the Gospels, Acts, Romans, 1 and 2 Cor., Eph., 1 Thess.; also in 2 Tim. 1:14; Titus 3:5; 1 Pet. 1:12; 2 Pet. 1:21; Jude 20.

(b) It is used of men and things in so far as they are devoted to God. Indeed the quality, as attributed to God, is often presented in a way which involves divine demands upon the conduct of believers. These are called *hagioi*, "saints," i.e., "sanctified" or "holy" ones. This sainthood is not an attainment, it is a state into which God in grace calls men; yet believers are called to sanctify themselves (consistently with their calling, 2 Tim. 1:9), cleansing themselves from all defilement, forsaking sin, living a "holy" manner of life, 1 Pet. 1:15; 2 Pet. 3:11, and experiencing fellowship with God in His holiness. The saints are thus figuratively spoken of as "a holy temple", 1 Cor. 3:17 (a local church); Eph. 2:21 (the whole Church), cp. 5:27; "a holy priesthood," 1 Pet. 2:5; "a holy nation," 2:9. "It is evident that *hagios* and its kindred words ... express something more and higher than *hieros*, sacred, outwardly associated with God; ... something more than *semnos*, worthy, honorable; something more than *hagnos*, pure, free from defilement. *Hagios* is ... more comprehensive.... It is characteristically godlikeness" (G. B. Stevens, in Hastings' *Bib. Dic.*).

The adjective is also used of the outer part of the tabernacle, Heb. 9:2 (RV, "the holy place"); of the inner sanctuary, 9:3, RV, "the Holy of Holies"; 9:4, "a holy place," RV; v. 25 (plural), of the presence of God in heaven, where there are not two compartments as in the tabernacle, all being "the holy place"; 9:8, 12 (neuter plural); 10:19, "the holy place," RV (KJV, "the holiest," neut. plural); of the city of Jerusalem. **Rev. 11:2**; its temple, Acts 6:13; of the faith. Jude 20; of the greetings of saints, 1 Cor. 16:20; of angels, e.g., Mark 8:38; of apostles and prophets, Eph. 3:5; of the future heavenly Jerusalem, **Rev. 21:2**, **10**; **22:19**.

Which *see Revelation 1:4*.

4:9 And when those beasts give glory and honour and thanks to him that sat on the throne, who liveth for ever and ever,

Honour *time* (5092), primarily "a valuing," hence, objectively, (a) "a price paid or received," e.g., Matt. 27:6, 9; Acts 4:34; 5:2, 3; 7:16, RV, "price" (KJV, "sum"); 19:19; 1 Cor.

6:20; 7:23; (b) of "the preciousness of Christ" unto believers, 1 Pet. 2:7, RV, i.e., the honor and inestimable value of Christ as appropriated by believers, who are joined, as living stones, to Him the cornerstone; (c) in the sense of value, of human ordinances, valueless against the indulgence of the flesh, or, perhaps of no value in attempts at asceticism, Col. 2:23; (d) "honor, esteem," (1) used in ascriptions of worship to God, 1 Tim. 1:17; 6:16; **Rev. 4:9, 11**; **5:13**; **7:12**; to Christ, **5:12, 13**; (2) bestowed upon Christ by the Father, Heb. 2:9; 2 Pet. 1:17; (3) bestowed upon man, Heb. 2:7; (4) bestowed upon Aaronic priests, Heb. 5:4; (5) to be the reward hereafter of "the proof of faith" on the part of tried saints, 1 Pet. 1:7, RV; (6) used of the believer who as a vessel is "meet for the Master's use," 2 Tim. 2:21 ... (18) of the festive honor to be possessed by nations, and brought into the Holy City, the heavenly Jerusalem, **Rev. 21:26** (in some mss., v. **24**).

Thanks *eucharistia* (2169), *eu*, "well," *charizomai*, "to give freely" (Eng., "eucharist"), denotes (a) "gratitude," "thankfulness," Acts 24:3; (b) "giving of thanks, thanksgiving," 1 Cor. 14:16; 2 Cor. 4:15; 9:11, 12 (plur.); Eph. 5:4; Phil. 4:6; Col. 2:7; 4:2; 1 Thess. 3:9 ("thanks"); 1 Tim. 2:1 (plur.); 4:3, 4; **Rev. 4:9**, "thanks"; **7:12**.

4:10 The four and twenty elders fall down before him that sat on the throne, and worship him that liveth for ever and ever, and cast their crowns before the throne, saying,

Elders *see Revelation 4:4.*

Worship *proskuneo* (4352), "to make obeisance, do reverence to" (from *pros*, "towards," and *kuneo*, "to kiss"), is the most frequent word rendered "to worship." It is used of an act of homage or reverence (a) to God, e.g., Matt. 4:10; John 4:21-24; 1 Cor. 14:25; **Rev. 4:10**; **5:14**; **7:11**; **11:16**; **19:10** (2nd part) and **22:9**; (b) to Christ, e.g., Matt. 2:2, 8, 11; 8:2; 9:18; 14:33; 15:25; 20:20; 28:9, 17; John 9:38; Heb. 1:6, in a quotation from the Sept. of Deut. 32:43, referring to Christ's second advent; (c) to a man, Matt. 18:26; (d) to the Dragon, by men, **Rev. 13:4**; (e) to the Beast, his human instrument, **Rev. 13:4, 8, 12**; **14:9, 11**; (f) the image of the Beast, **13:15**; **14:11**; **16:2**; (g) to demons, **Rev. 9:20**; (h) to idols, Acts 7:43.

Crowns *see* **Crown** at *Revelation 2:10.*

4:11 Thou art worthy, O Lord, to receive glory and honour and power: for thou hast created all things, and for thy pleasure they are and were created.

Worthy *see Revelation 3:4.*

Honour *see Revelation 4:9.*

Created *ktizo* (2936), used among the Greeks to mean the founding of a place, a city or colony, signifies, in Scripture, "to create," always of the act of God, whether (a) in the natural creation, Mark 13:19; Rom. 1:25 (where the title "The Creator" translates the article with the aorist participle of the verb); 1 Cor. 11:9; Eph. 3:9; Col. 1:16; 1 Tim. 4:3; **Rev. 4:11**; **10:6**, or (b) in the spiritual creation, Eph. 2:10, 15; 4:24; Col. 3:10.

Pleasure *thelema* (2307), signifies (a) objectively, "that which is willed, of the will of God," e.g., Matt. 18:14; Mark 3:35, the fulfilling being a sign of spiritual relationship to the Lord, John 4:34; 5:30; 6:39, 40; Acts 13:22, plural, "my desires"; Rom. 2:18; 12:2, lit., "the will of God, the good and perfect and acceptable"; here the repeated article is probably resumptive, the adjectives describing the will, as in the Eng. versions; Gal. 1:4; Eph. 1:9; 5:17, "of the Lord"; Col. 1:9; 4:12; 1 Thess. 4:3; 5:18, where it means "the gracious design," rather than "the determined resolve"; 2 Tim. 2:26, which should read "which have been taken captive by him" [(*autou*), i.e., by the Devil; the RV, "by the Lord's servant" is an interpretation; it does not correspond to the Greek] "unto His (*ekeinou*) will" (i.e., "God's will"; the different pronoun refers back to the subject of the sentence, viz., God); Heb. 10:10; **Rev. 4:11**, RV, "because of Thy will"; of human will, e.g., 1 Cor. 7:37; (b) subjectively, the "will" being spoken of as the emotion of being desirous, rather than as the thing "willed"; of the "will" of God, e.g., Rom. 1:10; 1 Cor. 1:1; 2 Cor. 1:1; 8:5; Eph. 1:1, 5, 11; Col. 1:1; 2 Tim. 1:1; Heb. 10:7, 9, 36; 1 John 2:17; 5:14; of human "will," e.g., John 1:13; Eph. 2:3, "the desires of the flesh"; 1 Pet. 4:3 (in some texts); 2 Pet. 1:21.

"Finish then Thy new creation, / Pure and spotless may we be; / Let us see Thy great salvation, / Perfectly restored in Thee; / Changed from glory into glory, / Till in heaven we take our place, / Till we cast our crowns before Thee, / Lost in wonder, love, and praise."

CHARLES WESLEY

Chapter 5

5:1 And I saw in the right hand of him that sat on the throne a book written within and on the backside, sealed with seven seals.

Throne *see Revelation 1:4.*

Book *see Revelation 1:11.*

Within *see Revelation 4:8.*

Backside *opisthen* (3693), "behind," is used only of place, e.g., Matt. 9:20; Mark 5:27; Luke 8:44; **Rev. 4:6**; as a preposition, Matt. 15:23 ("after"), and Luke 23:26; in **Rev. 5:1**, RV, "on the back"; KJV, "backside."

Sealed *katosphragizo* (2696), intensive, is used of the "book" seen in the vision in **Rev. 5:1**, RV, "close sealed (with seven seals)," the successive opening of which discloses the events destined to take place throughout the period covered by chapters **6** to **19**. In the Sept., Job 9:7; 37:7.

Seals *sphragis* (4973), denotes (a) "a seal" or "signet," **Rev. 7:2**, "the seal of the living God," an emblem of ownership and security, here combined with that of destination (as in Ezek. 9:4), the persons to be "sealed" being secured from destruction and marked for reward; (b) "the impression" of a "seal" or signet, (1) literal, a "seal" on a book or roll, combining with the ideas of security and destination those of secrecy and postponement of disclosures, **Rev. 5:1, 2, 5, 9; 6:1, 3, 5, 7, 9, 12; 8:1**; (2) metaphorical, Rom. 4:11, said of "circumcision," as an authentication of the righteousness of Abraham's faith, and an external attestation of the covenant made with him by God; the rabbis called circumcision "the seal of Abraham"; in 1 Cor. 9:2, of converts as a "seal" or authentication of Paul's apostleship; in 2 Tim. 2:19, "the firm foundation of God standeth, having this seal, The Lord knoweth them that are His," RV, indicating ownership, authentication, security and destination, "and, Let every one that nameth the Name of the Lord depart from unrighteousness," indicating a ratification on the part of the believer of the determining counsel of God concerning him; **Rev. 9:4** distinguishes those who will be found without the "seal" of God on their foreheads.

5:2 And I saw a strong angel proclaiming with a loud voice, Who is worthy to open the book, and to loose the seals thereof?

Strong *ichuros* (2478), "strong, mighty," is used of (a) persons: (1) God, **Rev. 18:8**; (2) angels, **Rev. 5:2; 10:1; 18:21**; (3) men, Matt. 12:29 (twice) and parallel passages; Heb. 11:34, KJV, "valiant" (RV, "mighty"); **Rev. 6:15** (in the best texts; some have *dunatos*); **19:18**, "mighty"; metaphorically, (4) the church at Corinth, 1 Cor. 4:10, where the apostle reproaches them ironically with their unspiritual and self-complacent condition; (5) of young men in Christ spiritually strong, through the Word of God, to overcome the evil one, 1 John 2:14; of (b) things: (1) wind, Matt. 14:30 (in some mss.), "boisterous"; (2) famine, Luke 15:14; (3) things in the mere human estimate, 1 Cor. 1:27; (4) Paul's letters, 2 Cor. 10 :10; (5) the Lord's crying and tears, Heb. 5:7; (6) consolation, 6:18; (7) the voice of an angel, **Rev. 18:2** (in the best texts; some have *megas*, "great"); (8) Babylon, **Rev. 18:10**; (9) thunderings, **Rev. 19:6**.

Proclaiming *kerusso* (2784), signifies (a) "to be a herald," or, in general, "to proclaim," e.g., Matt. 3:1; Mark 1:45, "publish"; in Luke 4:18, RV, "to proclaim," KJV, "to preach"; so verse 19; Luke 12:3; Acts 10:37; Rom. 2:21; **Rev. 5:2**. In 1 Pet. 3:19 the probable reference is, not to glad tidings (which there is no real evidence that Noah preached, nor is there evidence that the spirits of antediluvian people are actually "in prison"), but to the act of Christ after His resurrection in proclaiming His victory to fallen angelic spirits; (b) "to preach the gospel as a herald," e.g., Matt. 24:14; Mark 13:10, RV, "be preached" (KJV, "be published"); 14:9; 16:15, 20; Luke 8:1; 9:2; 24:47; Acts 8:5; 19:13; 28:31; Rom. 10:14, present participle, lit., "(one) preaching," "a preacher"; 10:15 (1st part); 1 Cor. 1:23; 15:11, 12; 2 Cor. 1:19; 4:5; 11:4; Gal. 2:2; Phil. 1:15; Col. 1:23; 1 Thess. 2:9; 1 Tim. 3:16; (c) "to preach the word," 2 Tim. 4:2 (of the ministry of the Scriptures, with special reference to the gospel).

Loud *megas* (3173), is used (a) of external form, size, measure, e.g., of a stone, Matt. 27:60; fish, John 21:11; (b) of degree and intensity, e.g., of fear, Mark 4:41; wind, John 6:18; **Rev. 6:13**, RV, "great" (KJV, "mighty"); of a circumstance, 1 Cor. 9:11; 2 Cor. 11:15; it is also used, besides other meanings, of intensity, as, e.g., of the force of a voice, e.g., Matt. 27:46, 50; in the following the RV has "great" for the KJV, "loud," **Rev. 5:2, 12; 6:10; 7:2, 10; 8:13; 10:3; 12:10; 14:7, 9, 15, 18.**

Worthy *see Revelation 3:4.*

Open *see* **Openeth** at *Revelation 3:7.*

Loose *luo* (3089), denotes (a) "to loose, unbind, release," (1) of things, e.g., in Acts 7:33, RV, "loose (the shoes)," KJV, "put off"; Mark 1:7; (2) of animals, e.g., Matt. 21:2; (3) of persons, e.g., John 11:44; Acts 22:30; (4) of Satan, **Rev. 20:3, 7,** and angels, **Rev. 9:14, 15**; (5) metaphorically, of one diseased, Luke 13:16; of the marriage tie, 1 Cor. 7:27; of release from sins, **Rev. 1:5** (in the most authentic mss.); (b) "to loosen, break up, dismiss, dissolve, destroy"; in this sense it is translated "to loose" in Acts 2:24, of the pains of death; in **Rev. 5:2**, of the seals of a roll.

Seals *see Revelation 5:1.*

5:3 And no man in heaven, nor in earth, neither under the earth, was able to open the book, neither to look thereon.

Under *hupokato* (5270), an adverb signifying "under," is used as a preposition and rendered "under" in Mark 6:11; 7:28; Luke 8:16; Heb. 2:8; **Rev. 5:3, 13; 6:9; 12:1**; "underneath" in Matt. 22:44, RV (Mark 12:36 in some mss.); John 1:50, RV (KJV, "under").

5:4 And I wept much, because no man was found worthy to open and to read the book, neither to look thereon.

Much *polus* (4183), is used (a) as an adjective of degree, e.g., Matt. 13:5, "much (earth)"; Acts 26:24, "much (learning)"; in v. 29, in the answer to Agrippa's "with but little persuasion," some texts have *pollo* (some *megalo*, "with great"), RV, "(whether with little or) with much"; of number, e.g., Mark 5:24, RV, "a great (multitude)," KJV, "much (people)"; so Luke 7:11; John 12:12; **Rev. 19:1**, etc.; (b) in the neuter singular form (*polu*), as a noun, e.g., Luke 16:10 (twice); in the plural (*polla*), e.g., Rom. 16:6, 12, "(labored) much," lit., "many things"; (c) adverbially, in the neuter singular, e.g., Acts 18:27; James 5:16; Matt. 26:9 (a genitive of price); in the plural, e.g., Mark 5:43, RV, "much" (KJV, "straitly"); Mark 9:26, RV, "much" (KJV, "sore"); John 14:30; and with the article, Acts 26:24; Rom. 15:22; 1 Cor. 16:19; **Rev. 5:4**.

Found *heurisko* (2147), denotes (a) "to find," either with previous search, e.g., Matt. 7:7, 8, or without, e.g., Matt. 27:32; in the passive voice, of Enoch's disappearance, Heb. 11:5; of mountains, **Rev. 16:20**; of Babylon and its occupants, **18:21, 22**; (b) metaphorically, "to find out by enquiry," or "to learn, discover," e.g., Luke 19:48; John 18:38; 19:4, 6; Acts 4:21; 13:28; Rom. 7:10; Gal. 2:17, which indicates "the surprise of the Jew" who learned for the first time that before God he had no moral superiority over the Gentiles whom he superciliously dubbed "sinners," while he esteemed himself to be "righteous"; 1 Pet. 1:7; **Rev. 5:4**; (c) in the middle voice, "to find for oneself, gain, procure, obtain," e.g. Matt. 10:39; 11:29, "ye shall find (rest)"; Luke 1:30; Acts 7:46; 2 Tim. 1:18.

Worthy *see Revelation 3:4.*

5:5 And one of the elders saith unto me, Weep not: behold, the Lion of the tribe of Juda, the Root of David, hath prevailed to open the book, and to loose the seven seals thereof.

Elders *see Revelation 4:4.*

Weep *klaio* (2799), is used of "any loud expression of grief," especially in mourning for the dead, Matt. 2:18; Mark 5:38, 39; 16:10; Luke 7:13; 8:52 (twice); John 11:31, 33 (twice); 20:11 (twice), 13, 15; Acts 9:39; otherwise, e.g., in exhortations, Luke 23:28; Rom. 12:15; Jas. 4:9; 5:1; negatively, "weep not," Luke 7:13; 8:52; 23:28; **Rev. 5:5** (cf. Acts 21:13); in 18:9, RV, "shall weep" (KJV, "bewail").

Lion *see Revelation 4:7.*

Tribe *see* **Kindreds** at *Revelation 1:7.*

Root *rhiza* (4491), is used (a) in the natural sense, Matt. 3:10; 13:6, 21; Mark 4:6, 17, 11:20; Luke 3:9; 8:13; (b) metaphorically (1) of "cause, origin, source," said of persons, ancestors, Rom. 11:16, 17, 18 (twice); of things, evils, 1 Tim. 6:10, RV, of the love of money as a "root" of all "kinds of evil" (marg., "evils", KJV, "evil"); bitterness, Heb. 12:15; (2) of that which springs from a "root," a shoot, said of offspring, Rom. 15:12; **Rev. 5:5; 22:16**.

Prevailed *nikao* (3528), "to conquer, prevail," is used as a law term in Rom. 3:4, "(that) Thou ... mightest prevail [KJV, 'overcome'] (when Thou comest into judgment)"; that the righteousness of the judge's verdict compels an acknowledgement on the part of the accused, is inevitable where God is the judge. God's promises to Israel provided no guarantee that an unrepentant Jew would escape doom. In **Rev. 5:5**, KJV, "hath prevailed" (RV, "hath overcome"). See also **Overcometh** at *Revelation 2:7.*

Seals *see Revelation 5:1.*

5:6 And I beheld, and, lo, in the midst of the throne and of the four beasts, and in the midst of the elders, stood a Lamb as it had been slain, having seven horns and seven eyes, which are the seven Spirits of God sent forth into all the earth.

Lamb *arnion* (721), is a diminutive in form, but the diminutive force is not to be pressed. The general tendency in the vernacular was to use nouns in *-ion* freely, apart from their diminutive significance. It is used only by the apostle John, (a) in the plural, in the Lord's command to Peter, John 21:15, with symbolic reference to young converts; (b) elsewhere, in the singular, in Revelation, some 28 times, of Christ as the "Lamb" of God, the symbolism having reference to His character and His vicarious Sacrifice, as the basis both of redemption and of divine vengeance. He is seen in the position of sovereign glory and honor, e.g., **7:17**, which He shares equally with the Father, **22:1**, **3**, the center of angelic beings and of the redeemed and the object of their veneration, e.g. **5:6**, **8**, **12**, **13**; **15:3**, the Leader and Shepherd of His saints, e.g., **7:17**; **14:4**, the Head of his spiritual bride, e.g., **21:9**, the luminary of the heavenly and eternal city, **21:23**, the One to whom all judgment is committed, e.g., **6:1**, **16**; **13:8**, the Conqueror of the foes of God and His people, **17:14**; the song that celebrates the triumph of those who "gain the victory over the Beast," is the song of Moses ... and the song of the Lamb **15:3**. His sacrifice, the efficacy of which avails for those who accept the salvation thereby provided, forms the ground of the execution of divine wrath for the rejector, and the defier of God, **14:10**; (c) in the description of the second "Beast," **Rev. 13:11**, seen in the vision "like a lamb," suggestive of his acting in the capacity of a false messiah, a travesty of the true.

Slain *sphazo* or *sphatto* (4969), "to slay," especially of victims for sacrifice (akin to *sphage*), is used (a) of taking human life, 1 John 3:12 (twice); **Rev. 6:4**, RV, "slay" (KJV, "kill"); in **13:3**, probably of assassination, RV, "smitten (unto death)," KJV, "wounded (to death)," RV marg., "slain;" **18:24**; (b) of Christ, as the Lamb of sacrifice, **Rev. 5:6**, **9**, **12**; **6:9**; **13:8**.

Horns *keras* (2768), "a horn," is used in the plural, as the symbol of strength, (a) in the apocalyptic visions; (1) on the head of the Lamb as symbolic of Christ, **Rev. 5:6**; (2) on the heads of beasts as symbolic of national potentates, **Rev. 12:3**; **13:1**, **11**; **17:3**, **7**, **12**, **16** (cf. Dan. 7:8; 8:9; Zech. 1:18, etc.); (3) at the corners of the golden altar, **Rev. 9:13** (cf. Exod. 30:2; the horns were of one piece with the altar, as in the case of the brazen altar, 27:2, and were emblematic of the efficacy of the ministry connected with it); (b) metaphorically, in the singular, "a horn of salvation," Luke 1:69 (a frequent metaphor in the OT, e.g., Ps. 18:2; cf. 1 Sam. 2:10; Lam. 2:3).

Eyes *see Revelation 1:14.*

Sent *see Revelation 1:1.*

5:7-8 And he came and took the book out of the right hand of him that sat upon the throne.

And when he had taken the book, the four beasts and four *and* twenty elders fell down before the Lamb, having every one of them harps, and golden vials full of odours, which are the prayers of saints.

Lamb *see Revelation 5:6.*

Having *see* **Had** at *Revelation 1:16.*

Harps *kithara* (2788), whence Eng., "guitar," denotes "a lyre" or "harp"; it is described by Josephus as an instrument of ten strings, played by a plectrum (a smaller instrument was played by the hand); it is mentioned in 1 Cor. 14:7; **Rev. 5:8**; **14:2**; **15:2**.

Vials *phiale* (5357), (Eng., "phial") denotes "a bowl"; so the RV, for KJV, "vial," in **Rev. 5:8**; **15:7**; **16:1-4**, **8**, **10**, **12**, **17**; **17:1**; **21:9**; the word is suggestive of rapidity in the emptying of the contents. While the seals (ch. 6) give a general view of the events of the last "week" or "hebdomad," in the vision given to Daniel, Dan. 9:23-27, the "trumpets" refer to the judgments which, in a more or less extended period, are destined to fall especially, though not only, upon apostate Christendom and apostate Jews. The emptying of the "bowls" betokens the final series of judgments in which this exercise of the wrath of God is "finished" (**Rev. 15:1**, RV). These are introduced by the 7th trumpet. See **Rev. 11:15** and the successive order in v. **18**, "the nations were wroth, and Thy wrath came ..."; see also **6:17**; **14:19**, **20**; **19:11-12**.

Full *see Revelation 4:6.*

Odours *thumiama* (2368), denotes "fragrant stuff for burning, incense" (from *thuo*, "to offer in sacrifice"), Luke 1:10, 11; in the plural, **Rev. 5:8** and **18:13**, RV (KJV, "odors"); **8:3**, **4**, signifying "frankincense" here. In connection with the tabernacle, the "incense" was to be prepared from stacte, onycha, and galbanum, with pure frankincense, an equal weight of each; imitation for private use was forbidden, Exod. 30:34-38. Cf. *thumiaterion*, "a censer," Heb. 9:4, and *libanos*, "frankincense," **Rev. 18:13**.

5:9 And they sung a new song, saying, Thou art worthy to take the book, and to open the seals thereof: for thou wast slain, and hast redeemed us to God by thy blood out of every kindred, and tongue, and people, and nation;

Sung *ado* (103), is used always of "praise to God," (a) intransitively, Eph. 5:19; Col. 3:16; (b) transitively, **Rev. 5:9**; **14:3**; **15:3**.

New *see Revelation 2:17.*

Song *ode* (5603), "an ode, song," is always used in the NT (as in the Sept.), in praise of God or Christ; in Eph. 5:19 and Col. 3:16 the adjective "spiritual" is added, because the word in itself is generic and might be used of songs anything but spiritual; in **Rev. 5:9** and **14:3** (1st part) the descriptive word is "new" (*kainos*, "new," in reference to character and form), a "song," the significance of which was confined to those mentioned (v. **3**, and 2nd part); in **15:3** (twice), "the song of Moses ... and the song of the Lamb," the former as celebrating the deliverance of God's people by His power, the latter as celebrating redemption by atoning sacrifice.

Worthy *see Revelation 3:4.*

Open *see* **Openeth** at *Revelation 3:7.*

Seals *see Revelation 5:1.*

Slain *see Revelation 5:6.*

Redeemed *agorazo* (59), primarily, "to frequent the market-place," the *agora*, hence "to do business there, to buy or sell," is used lit., e.g., in Matt. 14:15. Figuratively Christ is spoken of as having bought His redeemed, making them His property at the price of His blood (i.e., His death through the shedding of His blood in expiation for their sins), 1 Cor. 6:20; 7:23; 2 Pet. 2:1; see also **Rev. 5:9**; **14:3-4** (not as KJV, "redeemed"). *Agorazo* does not mean "to redeem."

Kindred *see* **Kindreds** at *Revelation 1:7.*

Tongue *glossa* (1100), is used of (1) the "tongues ... like as of fire" which appeared at Pentecost; (2) "the tongue," as an organ of speech, e.g., Mark 7:33; Rom. 3:13; 14:11; 1 Cor. 14:9; Phil. 2:11; Jas. 1:26; 3:5, 6, 8; 1 Pet. 3:10; 1 John 3:18; **Rev. 16:10**; (3) "a language," coupled with *phule*, "a tribe," *laos*, "a people," *ethnos*, "a nation," seven times in Revelation, **5:9**; **7:9**; **10:11**; **11:9**; **13:7**; **14:6**; **17:15**.

People *laos* (2992), is used of (a) "the people at large," especially of people assembled, e.g., Matt. 27:25; Luke 1:21; 3:15; Acts 4:27; (b) "a people of the same race and language," e.g., **Rev. 5:9**; in the plural, e.g., Luke 2:31; Rom. 15:11; **Rev. 7:9**; **11:9**; especially of Israel, e.g., Matt. 2:6; 4:23; John 11:50; Acts 4:8; Heb. 2:17; in distinction from their rulers and priests, e.g., Matt. 26:5; Luke 20:19; Heb. 5:3; in distinction from Gentiles, e.g., Acts 26:17, 23; Rom. 15:10; (c) of Christians as the people of God, e.g., Acts 15:14; Titus 2:14; Heb. 4:9; 1 Pet. 2:9.

5:10 And hast made us unto our God kings and priests: and we shall reign on the earth.

Kings *see Revelation 1:6.*

Priests *see Revelation 1:6.*

Reign *basileuo* (936), "to reign," is used (I) literally, (a) of God, **Rev. 11:17**; **19:6**, in each of which the aorist tense (in the latter, translated "reigneth") is "ingressive," stressing the point of entrance; (b) of Christ, Luke 1:33; 1 Cor. 15:25; **Rev. 11:15**; as rejected by the Jews, Luke 19:14, 27; (c) of the saints, hereafter, 1 Cor. 4:8 (2nd part), where the apostle, casting a reflection upon the untimely exercise of authority on the part of the church at Corinth, anticipates the due time for it in the future; **Rev. 5:10**; **20:4**, where the aorist tense is not simply of a "point" character, but "constative," that is, regarding a whole action as having occurred, without distinguishing any steps in its progress (in this instance the aspect is future); v. **6**; **22:5**; (d) of earthly potentates, Matt. 2:22; 1 Tim. 6:15, where "kings" is, lit., "them that reign"; (II), metaphorically, (a) of believers, Rom. 5:17, where "shall reign in life" indicates the activity of life in fellowship with Christ in His sovereign power, reaching its fullness hereafter; 1 Cor. 4:8 (1st part), of the carnal pride that laid claim to a power not to be exercised until hereafter; (b) of divine grace, Rom. 5:21; (c) of sin, Rom. 5:21; 6:12; (d) of death, Rom. 5:14, 17.

5:11 And I beheld, and I heard the voice of many angels round about the throne and the beasts and the elders: and the number of them was ten thousand times ten thousand, and thousands of thousands;

Voice *see Revelation 1:10.*

Round about *see Revelation 4:6.*

Ten thousand *murias* (3461), denotes either "ten thousand," or, "indefinitely, a myriad, a numberless host," in the plural, Acts 19:19; lit. "five ten-thousands," **Rev. 5:11**; **9:16**; in the following, used of vast numbers, Luke 12:1, KJV, "an innumerable multitude," RV, "the many thousands" (RV marg., "the myriads"); Acts 21:20, "thousands"; Heb. 12:22, "innumerable hosts"; Jude 14, "ten thousands" (RV, marg., in each place, "myriads"). Cf. the adjective *murios*, "ten thousand," Matt. 18:24; 1 Cor. 4:15; 14:19.

Thousands *chilioi* (5507), "a thousand," occurs in 2 Pet. 3:8; **Rev. 11:3**; **12:6**; **14:20**; **20:2–7**. 2. *chilias* (5505), "one thousand," is always used in the plural, *chiliades*, but translated in the sing. everywhere, except in the phrase "thousands of thousands," **Rev. 5:11**. In **Rev. 9:16** in the best texts, *dismuriades muriadon*, "twice ten thousand times ten thousand" RV (KJV, "two hundred thousand thousand").

5:12 Saying with a loud voice, Worthy is the Lamb that was slain to receive power, and riches, and wisdom, and strength, and honour, and glory, and blessing.

Loud *see Revelation 5:2.*

Worthy *see Revelation 3:4.*

Lamb *see Revelation 5:6.*

Slain *see Revelation 5:6.*

Riches *ploutos* (4149), is used in the singular (I) of material "riches," used evilly, Matt. 13:22: Mark 4:19; Luke 8:14; 1 Tim. 6:17; Jas. 5:2; **Rev. 18:17**; (II) of spiritual and moral "riches," (a) possessed by God and exercised towards men, Rom. 2:4, "of His goodness and forbearance and longsuffering"; 9:23 and Eph. 3:16, "of His glory" (i.e., of its manifestation in grace towards believers); Rom. 11:33, of His wisdom and knowledge; Eph. 1:7 and 2:7, "of His grace"; 1:18, "of the glory of His inheritance in the saints"; 3:8, "of Christ"; Phil. 4:19, "in glory in Christ Jesus," RV; Col. 1:27, "of the glory of this mystery ... Christ in you, the hope of glory"; (b) to be ascribed to Christ, **Rev. 5:12**; (c) of the effects of the gospel upon the Gentiles, Rom. 11:12 (twice); (d) of the full assurance of understanding in regard to the mystery of God, even Christ, Col. 2:2, RV; (e) of the liberality of the churches of Macedonia, 2 Cor. 8:2 (where "the riches" stands for the spiritual and moral value of their liberality); (f) of "the reproach of Christ" in contrast to this world's treasures, Heb. 11:26.

Wisdom *sophia* (4678), is used with reference to (a) God, Rom. 11:33; 1 Cor. 1:21, 24; 2:7; Eph. 3:10; **Rev. 7:12**; (b) Christ, Matt. 13:54; Mark 6:2; Luke 2:40, 52; 1 Cor. 1:30; Col. 2:3; **Rev. 5:12**; (c) "wisdom" personified, Matt. 11:19; Luke 7:35; 11:49; (d) human "wisdom" (1) in spiritual things, Luke 21:15; Acts 6:3, 10; 7:10; 1 Cor. 2:6 (1st part); 12:8; Eph. 1:8, 17; Col. 1:9, RV, "(spiritual) wisdom," 28; 3:16; 4:5; Jas. 1:5; 3:13, 17; 2 Pet. 3:15; **Rev. 13:18**; **17:9**; (2) in the natural sphere, Matt. 12:42; Luke 11:31; Acts 7:22; 1 Cor. 1:17, 19, 20, 21 (twice), 22; 2:1, 4, 5, 6 (2nd part), 13; 3:19; 2 Cor. 1:12; Col. 2:23; (3) in its most debased form, Jas. 3:15, "earthly, sensual, devilish" (marg., "demoniacal").

Strength *ischus* (2479), denotes "might, strength, power," (a) inherent and in action as used of God, Eph. 1:19, RV, "(the strength, *kratos*, of His) might," KJV, "(His mighty) power," i.e., power (over external things) exercised by strength; Eph. 6:10, "of His might"; 2 Thess. 1:9, RV, "(from the glory) of His might" (KJV "power"); **Rev. 5:12**, RV, "might" (KJV, "strength"); **7:12**, "might"; (b) as an endowment, said (1) of angels, 2 Pet. 2:11; here the order is, RV, "might and power," which better expresses the distinction than the KJV, "power and might"; in some mss. in **Rev. 18:2** it is said of the voice of an angel; the most authentic mss. have the adjective *ischuros*, "mighty"; (2) of men, Mark 12:30, 33; Luke 10:27 (RV and KJV, "strength," in all three verses); 1 Pet. 4:11, RV, "strength" (KJV, "ability"). Either "strength" or "might" expresses the true significance of *ischus*. *See also* **Strong** at *Revelation 5:2.*

Honour *see Revelation 4:9.*

Blessing *eulogia* (2129), lit., "good speaking, praise," is used of (a) God and Christ, **Rev. 5:12-13**; **7:12**; (b) the invocation of blessings, benediction, Heb. 12:17; Jas. 3:10; (c) the giving of thanks, 1 Cor. 10:16; (d) a blessing, a benefit bestowed, Rom. 15:29; Gal. 3:14; Eph. 1:3; Heb. 6:7; of a monetary gift sent to needy believers, 2 Cor. 9:5-6; (e) in a bad sense, of fair speech, Rom. 16:18, RV, where it is joined with *chrestologia*, "smooth speech," the latter relating to the substance, *eulogia* to the expression.

5:13 And every creature which is in heaven, and on the earth, and under the earth, and such as are in the sea, and all that are in them, heard I saying, Blessing, and honour, and glory, and power, *be* unto him that sitteth upon the throne, and unto the Lamb for ever and ever.

Creature *ktistma* (2938), has the concrete sense, "the created thing, the creature, the product of the creative act," 1 Tim. 4:4; Jas. 1:18; **Rev. 5:13**; **8:9**.

Under *see Revelation 5:3.*

Honour *see Revelation 4:9.*

Power *see* **Dominion** at *Revelation 1:6.*

Lamb *see Revelation 5:6.*

5:14 And the four beasts said, Amen. And the four *and* twenty elders fell down and worshipped him that liveth for ever and ever.

Beasts *see Revelation 4:6.*

Amen *see Revelation 3:14.*

Fell *see Revelation 1:17.*

Worshipped *see* **Worship** at *Revelation 4:10.*

Chapter 6

6:1 And I saw when the Lamb opened one of the seals, and I heard, as it were the noise of thunder, one of the four beasts saying, Come and see.

Lamb *see Revelation 5:6.*

Opened *see* **Openeth** at *Revelation 3:7.*

Seals *see Revelation 5:1.*

Noise In **Rev. 6:1**, KJV, *phone*, "a voice" or "sound," is translated "noise"

(RV, "voice") it is used with *ginomai* in Acts 2:6, KJV, "(this) was noised abroad," RV, "(this) sound was heard."

Thunder *see* Thunderings at *Revelation 4:5*.

Beasts *see Revelation 4:6*.

6:2 And I saw, and behold a white horse: and he that sat on him had a bow; and a crown was given unto him: and he went forth conquering, and to conquer.

White *see Revelation 1:14*.

Horse *hippos* (2462), apart from the fifteen occurrences in Revelation, occurs only in Jas. 3:3; in Revelation "horses" are seen in visions in **6:2, 4, 5, 8; 9:7, 9, 17** (twice); **14:20; 19:11, 14, 19, 21**; otherwise in **18:13; 19:18**.

Bow *toxon* (5115), "a bow," is used in **Rev. 6:2**. Cf. Hab. 3:8-9. The instrument is frequently mentioned in the Sept., especially in the Psalms.

Crown *see Revelation*

Conquering, Conquer *nikao* (3528), "to overcome" (its usual meaning), is translated "conquering" and "to conquer" in **Rev. 6:2**. See also **Overcometh** at *Revelation 2:7*.

6:3 And when he had opened the second seal, I heard the second beast say, Come and see.

Seal *see* Seals at *Revelation 5:1*.

6:4 And there went out another horse *that was* red: and *power* was given to him that sat thereon to take peace from the earth, and that they should kill one another: and there was given unto him a great sword.

Horse *see Revelation 6:2*.

Red *purrhos* (4450), denotes "firecolored" (*pur*, "fire"), hence, "fiery red," **Rev. 6:4; 12:3**, in the latter passage said of the Dragon, indicative of the cruelty of the Devil.

Take *lambano* (2983), "to take, lay hold of," besides its literal sense, e.g., Matt. 5:40; 26:26, 27, is used metaphorically, of fear, in "taking" hold of people, Luke 7:16, RV (KJV, "came ... on"); of sin in "finding (occasion)," RV (KJV, "taking"), Rom. 7:8, 11, where sin is viewed as the corrupt source of action, an inward element using the commandment to produce evil effects; of the power of temptation, 1 Cor. 10:13; of "taking" an example, Jas. 5:10; of "taking" peace from the earth, **Rev. 6:4**; of Christ in "taking" the form of a servant, Phil. 2:7; of "taking" rightful power (by the Lord, hereafter), **Rev. 11:17**.

Peace *eirene* (1515), "occurs in each of the books of the NT, save 1 John and save in Acts 7:26 ['(at) one again'] it is translated "peace" in the RV. It describes (a) harmonious relationships between men, Matt. 10:34; Rom. 14:19; (b) between nations, Luke 14:32; Acts 12:20; **Rev. 6:4**; (c) friendliness, Acts 15:33; 1 Cor. 16:11; Heb. 11:31; (d) freedom from molestation, Luke 11:21; 19:42; Acts 9:31 (RV, 'peace,' KJV, 'rest'); 16:36; (e) order, in the State, Acts 24:2 (RV, 'peace,' KJV, 'quietness'); in the churches, 1 Cor. 14:33; (f) the harmonized relationships between God and man, accomplished through the gospel, Acts 10:36; Eph. 2:17; (g) the sense of rest and contentment consequent thereon, Matt. 10:13; Mark 5:34; Luke 1:79; 2:29; John 14:27; Rom. 1:7; 3:17; 8:6; in certain passages this idea is not distinguishable from the last, Rom. 5:1."

Kill *sphazo*, or *sphatto* (4969), "to slay, to slaughter," especially victims for sacrifice, is most frequently translated by the verb "to slay"; so the RV in **Rev. 6:4** (KJV, "should kill"), in **13:3**, RV, "smitten unto death" (KJV, "wounded"). Cf. *katasphazo*, "to kill off," Luke 19:27; *sphage*, "slaughter," e.g., Acts 8:32, and *sphagion*, "a victim for slaughter," Acts 7:42. *See also* Slain at *Revelation 5:6*.

6:5 And when he had opened the third seal, I heard the third beast say, Come and see. And I beheld, and lo a black horse; and he that sat on him had a pair of balances in his hand.

Seal *see* Seals at *Revelation 5:1*.

Black *melan* (3188), the neuter of the adjective *melas*, "black" (see Matt. 5:36; **Rev. 6:5, 12**), denotes "ink," 2 Cor. 3:3; 2 John 12; 3 John 13.

Horse *see Revelation 6:2*.

Balances *zugos* (2218), "a yoke," serving to couple two things together, is used (1) metaphorically, (a) of submission to authority, Matt. 11:29, 30, of Christ's "yoke," not simply imparted by Him but shared with Him; (b) of bondage, Acts 15:10 and Gal. 5:1, of bondage to the Law as a supposed means of salvation; (c) of bond service to masters, 1 Tim. 6:1; (2) to denote "a balance," **Rev. 6:5**.

6:6 And I heard a voice in the midst of the four beasts say, A measure of wheat for a penny, and three measures of barley for a penny; and *see* thou hurt not the oil and the wine.

Measure, Measures *choinix* (5518), a dry "measure" of rather less than a quart, about "as much as would support a person of moderate appetite for a day," occurs in **Rev.**

6:6 (twice). Usually eight *choenixes* could be bought for a *denarius* (about 9 1/2d.); this passage predicts circumstances in which the *denarius* is the price of one *choenix*. In the Sept., Ezek. 45:10, 11, where it represents the Heb. *ephah* and *bath*.

Wheat *sitos* (4621), "wheat, corn"; in the plural, "grain," is translated "corn" in Mark 4:28; "wheat," Matt. 3:12; 13:25, 29-30; Luke 3:17; 12:18 (some mss. have *genemata*, "fruits," here); 16:7; 22:31; John 12:24; Acts 27:38; 1 Cor. 15:37; **Rev. 6:6**; **18:13**.

Penny *denarion* (1220), a Roman coin, a *denarius*, a little less than the value of the Greek *drachme*, now estimated as amounting to about 9 1/2d. in the time of our Lord, occurs in the singular, e.g., Matt. 20:2; 22:19; Mark 12:15; **Rev. 6:6**; in the plural, e.g., Matt. 18:28; Mark 14:5; Luke 7:41; 10:35; John 12:5; "pennyworth" in Mark 6:37 and John 6:7, lit., "(loaves of two hundred) pence." Considering the actual value, "shilling" would have been a more accurate translation, as proposed by the American translators, retaining "penny" for the *as*, and "farthing" for the *quadrans*.

Barley *krithe* (2915), "barley," is used in the plural in **Rev. 6:6**.

Hurt *see* ***Revelation 2:11***.

Oil *elaion* (1637), "olive oil," is mentioned over 200 times in the Bible. Different kinds were known in Palestine. The "pure," RV (KJV, beaten), mentioned in Exod. 27:20; 29:40; Lev. 24:2; Num. 28:5 (now known as virgin oil), extracted by pressure, without heat, is called "golden" in Zech. 4:12. There were also inferior kinds. In the NT the uses mentioned were (a) for lamps, in which the "oil" is a symbol of the Holy Spirit, Matt. 25:3-4, 8; (b) as a medicinal agent, for healing, Luke 10:34; (c) for anointing at feasts, Luke 7:46; (d) on festive occasions, Heb. 1:9, where the reference is probably to the consecration of kings; (e) as an accompaniment of miraculous power, Mark 6:13, or of the prayer of faith, Jas. 5:14. For its general use in commerce, see Luke 16:6; **Rev. 6:6**; **18:13**.

6:7 And when he had opened the fourth seal, I heard the voice of the fourth beast say, Come and see.

Seal *see* **Seals** at ***Revelation 5:1***.

6:8 And I looked, and behold a pale horse: and his name that sat on him was Death, and Hell followed with him. And power was given unto them over the fourth part of the earth, to kill with sword, and with hunger, and with death, and with the beasts of the earth.

Looked *see* ***Revelation 4:1***.

Pale *chloros* (5515), akin to *chloe*, "tender foliage" (cf. the name "Chloe," 1 Cor. 1:11, and Eng., "chlorine"), denotes (a) "pale green," the color of young grass, Mark 6:39; **Rev. 8:7**; **9:4**, "green thing"; hence, (b) "pale," **Rev. 6:8**, the color of the horse whose rider's name is Death.

Horse *see* ***Revelation 6:2***.

Hell *see* ***Revelation 1:18***.

Part In **Rev. 6:8**, *tetartos*, "a fourth," is rendered "the fourth part."

Sword *see* ***Revelation 1:16***.

Hunger *limos* (3042), is translated "hunger" in Luke 15:17; 2 Cor. 11:27; elsewhere it signifies "a famine," and is so translated in each place in the RV; the KJV has the word "dearth" in Acts 7:11 and 11:28, and "hunger" in **Rev. 6:8**; the RV "famine" is preferable there; see Matt. 24:7; Mark 13:8; Luke 4:25; 15:14; 21:11; Rom. 8:35; **Rev. 18:8**.

Beasts In **Rev. 6:8** the RV renders *therion* (plural) "wild beasts" (KJV, "beasts").

6:9 And when he had opened the fifth seal, I saw under the altar the souls of them that were slain for the word of God, and for the testimony which they held:

Fifth *pemptos* (3991), akin to *pente*, "five," is found only in Revelation, **6:9**; **9:1**; **16:10**; **21:20**.

Seal *see* **Seals** at ***Revelation 5:1***.

Under *see* ***Revelation 5:3***.

Souls *psuche* (5590), denotes "the breath, the breath of life," then "the soul," in its various meanings. The NT uses "may be analyzed approximately as follows:

"(a) the natural life of the body, Matt. 2:20; Luke 12:22; Acts 20:10; **Rev. 8:9**; **12:11**; cf. Lev. 17:11; 2 Sam. 14:7; Esth. 8:11; (b) the immaterial, invisible part of man, Matt. 10:28; Acts 2:27; cf. 1 Kings 17:21; (c) the disembodied (or "unclothed" or "naked," 2 Cor. 5:3, 4) man, **Rev. 6:9**; (d) the seat of personality, Luke 9:24, explained as = "own self," v. 25; Heb. 6:19; 10:39; cf. Isa. 53:10 with 1 Tim. 2:6; (e) the seat of the sentient element in man, that by which he perceives, reflects, feels, desires, Matt. 11:29; Luke 1:46; 2:35; Acts 14:2, 22; cf. Ps. 84:2; 139:14; Isa. 26:9; (f) the seat of will and purpose, Matt. 22:37; Acts 4:32; Eph. 6:6; Phil. 1:27; Heb. 12:3; cf. Num. 21:4; Deut. 11:13; (g) the seat of appetite, **Rev. 18:14**; cf. Ps. 107:9; Prov. 6:30; Isa. 5:14 ("desire"); 29:8; (h) persons, individuals, Acts 2:41, 43; Rom. 2:9; Jas. 5:20; 1 Pet. 3:20; 2 Pet. 2:14; cf. Gen. 12:5;

14:21 ("persons"); Lev. 4:2 ('any one'); Ezek. 27:13; of dead bodies, Num. 6:6, lit., "dead soul"; and of animals, Lev. 24:18, lit., "soul for soul"; (i) the equivalent of the personal pronoun, used for emphasis and effect:—1st person, John 10:24 ("us"); Heb. 10:38; cf. Gen. 12:13; Num. 23:10; Jud. 16:30; Ps. 120:2 ("me"); 2nd person, 2 Cor. 12:15; Heb. 13:17; Jas. 1:21; 1 Pet. 1:9; 2:25; cf. Lev. 17:11; 26:15; 1 Sam. 1:26; 3rd person, 1 Pet. 4:19; 2 Pet. 2:8; cf. Exod. 30:12; Job 32:2, Heb. "soul," Sept. "self"; (j) an animate creature, human or other, 1 Cor. 15:45; **Rev. 16:3**; cf. Gen. 1:24; 2:7, 19; (k) "the inward man," the seat of the new life, Luke 21:19 (cf. Matt. 10:39); 1 Pet. 2:11; 3 John 2."

Slain *see Revelation 5:6.*

6:10 And they cried with a loud voice, saying, How long, O Lord, holy and true, dost thou not judge and avenge our blood on them that dwell on the earth?

Loud *see Revelation 5:2.*

Voice *see Revelation 1:10.*

Lord *despotes* (1203), "a master, lord, one who possesses supreme authority," is used in personal address to God in Luke 2:29; Acts 4:24; **Rev. 6:10**; with reference to Christ, 2 Pet. 2:1; Jude 4; elsewhere it is translated "master," "masters," 1 Tim. 6:1, 2; 2 Tim. 2:21 (of Christ); Titus 2:9; 1 Pet. 2:18.

Holy *see Revelation 4:8.*

True *see Revelation 3:7.*

Avenge *ekdikeo* (1556), *ek*, "from," *dike*, "justice," i.e., that which proceeds from justice, means (a) "to vindicate a person's right," (b) "to avenge a thing." With the meaning (a), it is used in the parable of the unjust judge, Luke 18:3, 5, of the "vindication" of the rights of the widow; with the meaning (b) it is used in **Rev. 6:10** and **19:2**, of the act of God in "avenging" the blood of the saints; in 2 Cor. 10:6, of the apostle's readiness to use his apostolic authority in punishing disobedience on the part of his readers; here the RV substitutes "avenge" for the KJV, "revenge"; in Rom. 12:19 of "avenging" oneself, against which the believer is warned.

6:11 And white robes were given unto every one of them; and it was said unto them, that they should rest yet for a little season, until their fellowservants also and their brethren, that should be killed as they *were*, should be fulfilled.

White *see Revelation 1:14.*

Robes *stole* (4749), (Eng., "stole"), denotes any "stately robe," a long garment reaching to the feet or with a train behind. It is used of the long clothing in which the scribes walked, making themselves conspicuous in the eyes of men, Mark 12:38; Luke 20:46; of the robe worn by the young man in the Lord's tomb, Mark 16:5; of the best or, rather, the chief robe, which was brought out for the returned prodigal, Luke 15:22; five times in Revelation, as to glorified saints, **6:11**; **7:9, 13-14**; **22:14**. In the Sept. it is used of the holy garments of the priests, e.g., Exod. 28:2; 29:21; 31:10.

Every *hekastos* (1538), "each" or "every," is used of any number separately, either (a) as an adjective qualifying a noun, e.g., Luke 6:44; John 19:23; Heb. 3:13, where "day by day," is, lit., "according to each day"; or, more emphatically with *heis*, "one," in Matt. 26:22; Luke 4:40; 16:5; Acts 2:3, 6, 20:31; 1 Cor. 12:18; Eph. 4:7, 16, RV, "each (several)," for KJV, "every"; Col. 4:6; 1 Thess. 2:11; 2 Thess. 1:3; (b) as a distributive pronoun, e.g., Acts 4:35; Rom. 2:6; Gal. 6:4; in Phil. 2:4, it is used in the plural; some mss. have it thus in **Rev. 6:11**. The repetition in Heb. 8:11 is noticeable "every man" (i.e., everyone). Prefixed by the preposition *ana*, "apiece" (a colloquialism), it is used, with stress on the individuality, in **Rev. 21:21**, of the gates of the heavenly city, "each one of the several," RV; in Eph. 5:33, preceded by *kath' hena*, "by one," it signifies "each (one) his own."

Said *eiro* (3004), an obsolete verb, has the future tense *ereo*, used, e.g., in Matt. 7:4; Luke 4:23 (2nd part); 13:25 (last part); Rom. 3:5; 4:1; 6:1; 7:7 (1st part); 8:31; 9:14, 19, 20, 30; 11:19; 1 Cor. 15:35; 2 Cor. 12:6; Jas. 2:18. The perfect is used, e.g., in John 12:50. The 1st aorist passive, "it was said," is used in Rom. 9:12, 26; **Rev. 6:11**.

Should *mello* (3195), "to be about to," e.g., Mark 10:32, RV, "were to"; Luke 19:11, RV, "was to"; "should" in 22:23; 24:21; John 6:71; 7:39, RV, "were to"; 11:51; 12:4, 33; 18:32; Acts 11:28; 23:27, RV, "was about (to be slain)"; 1 Thess. 3:4, RV, "are to"; **Rev. 6:11**.

Rest *anapauo* (373), in the active voice, signifies "to give intermission from labor, to give rest, to refresh," Matt. 11:28; 1 Cor. 16:18, "have refreshed"; Philem. 20, "refresh"; passive voice, "to be rested, refreshed," 2 Cor. 7:13, "was refreshed"; Philem. 7, "are refreshed"; in the middle voice, "to take or enjoy rest," Matt. 26:45; Mark 6:31; 14:41; Luke 12:19, "take thine ease"; 1 Pet. 4:14; **Rev. 6:11**; **14:13**. In the papyri it is found as an agricultural term, e.g., of giving land "rest" by sowing light crops upon it. In inscriptions it is found on gravestones of Christians, followed by the date of death (Moulton and Milligan).

Little *see* ***Revelation 3:8.***

Season *chronos* (5550), whence Eng. words beginning with "chron", denotes "a space of time," whether long or short: (a) it implies duration, whether longer, e.g., Acts 1:21, "(all the) time"; Acts 13:18; 20:18, RV, "(all the) time" (KJV, "at all seasons"); or shorter, e.g., Luke 4:5; (b) it sometimes refers to the date of an occurrence, whether past, e.g., Matt. 2:7, or future, e.g., Acts 3:21; 7:17. Broadly speaking, *chronos* expresses the duration of a period, *kairos* stresses it as marked by certain features; thus in Acts 1:7, "the Father has set within His own authority" both the times (*chronos*), the lengths of the periods, and the "seasons" (*kairos*), epochs characterized by certain events; in 1 Thess. 5:1, "times" refers to the length of the interval before the Parousia takes place (the presence of Christ with the saints when He comes to receive them to Himself at the Rapture), and to the length of time the Parousia will occupy; "seasons" refers to the special features of the period before, during, and after the Parousia. *Chronos* marks quantity, *kairos*, quality. Sometimes the distinction between the two words is not sharply defined as, e.g., in 2 Tim. 4:6, though even here the apostle's "departure" signalizes the time (*kairos*). The words occur together in the Sept. only in Dan. 2:21 and Eccl. 3:1. *Chronos* is rendered "season" in Acts 19:22, KJV (RV, "a while); 20:18 (RV, "all the time,"); **Rev. 6:11**, KJV (RV, "time"); so **20:3**. In Luke 23:8 it is used with *hikanos* in the plural, RV, "(of a long) time," more lit., "(for a sufficient number) of times." In **Rev. 10:6** *chronos* has the meaning "delay" (RV, marg.), an important rendering for the understanding of the passage (the word being akin to *chronizo*, "to take time, to linger, delay," Matt. 24:48; Luke 12:45).

Fellowservants *sundoulos* (4889), "a fellow servant," is used (a) of natural conditions, Matt. 18:28, 29, 31, 33; 24:49; (b) of "servants" of the same divine Lord, Col. 1:7; 4:7; **Rev. 6:11**; of angels, **Rev. 19:10**; **22:9**.

Fulfilled *see* **Perfect** at ***Revelation 3:2.***

6:12 And I beheld when he had opened the sixth seal, and, lo, there was a great earthquake; and the sun became black as sackcloth of hair, and the moon became as blood;

Sixth *hektos* (1623), is used (a) of a month, Luke 1:26, 36; (b) an hour, Matt. 20:5; 27:45 and parallel passages; John 4:6; (c) an angel, **Rev. 9:13**, **14**; **16:12**; (d) a seal of a roll, in vision, **Rev. 6:12**; (e) of the "sixth" precious stone, the sardius, in the foundations of the wall of the heavenly Jerusalem, **Rev. 21:20**.

Seal *see* **Seals** at ***Revelation 5:1.***

Earthquake *seismos* (4578), "a shaking, a shock," from *seio*, "to move to and fro, to shake," chiefly with the idea of concussion (Eng., "seismic," "seismology," "seismometry"), is used (a) of a "tempest" in the sea, Matt. 8:24; (b) of "earthquakes," Matt. 24:7; 27:54; 28:2; Mark 13:8; Luke 21:11; Acts 16:26; **Rev. 6:12**; **8:5**; **11:13** (twice), **19**; **16:18** (twice).

Sun *see* ***Revelation 1:16.***

Black *see* ***Revelation 6:5.***

Sackcloth *sakkos* (4526), "a warm material woven from goat's or camel's hair," and hence of a dark color, **Rev. 6:12**; Jerome renders it *saccus cilicinus* (being made from the hair of the black goat of Cilicia; the Romans called it *cilicium*); cf. Isa. 50:3; it was also used for saddlecloths, Josh. 9:4; also for making sacks, e.g., Gen. 42:25, and for garments worn as expressing mourning or penitence, Matt. 11:21; Luke 10:13, or for purposes of prophetic testimony, **Rev. 11:3**.

Hair *trichinos* (5155), signifies "hairy, made of hair," **Rev. 6:12**, lit., "hairy sackcloth."

Moon *selene* (4582), from *selas*, "brightness" (the Heb. words are *yareach*, "wandering," and *lebanah*, "white"), occurs in Matt. 24:29; Mark 13:24; Luke 21:25; Acts 2:20; 1 Cor. 15:41; **Rev. 6:12**; **8:12**; **12:1**; **21:23**. In **Rev. 12:1**, "the moon under her feet" is suggestive of derived authority, just as her being clothed with the sun is suggestive of supreme authority, everything in the symbolism of the passage centers in Israel. In **6:12** the similar symbolism of the sun and "moon" is suggestive of the supreme authority over the world, and of derived authority, at the time of the execution of divine judgments upon nations at the close of the present age.

6:13 And the stars of heaven fell unto the earth, even as a fig tree casteth her untimely figs, when she is shaken of a mighty wind.

Stars *see* ***Revelation 1:16.***

Fig tree *suke* or *sukea* (4808), "a fig tree," is found in Matt. 21:19, 20, 21; 24:32; Mark 11:13, 20, 21; 13:28; Luke 13:6, 7; 21:29; John 1:48, 50, Jas. 3:12; **Rev. 6:13**.

Figs *olunthos* (3653), denotes "an unripe fig," which grows in winter and usually falls off in the spring, **Rev. 6:13**. In the Sept. Song of Sol., 2:13.

Shaken *seio* (4579), "to shake, move to and fro," usually of violent concussion (Eng., "seismic," "seismograph," "seismology"), is said (a) of the earth as destined to be shaken by God, Heb. 12:26; (b) of a local convulsion of the earth, at the death of Christ, Matt. 27:51, "did quake"; (c) of a fig tree, **Rev. 6:13**; (d) metaphorically, to stir up with fear or some other emotion, Matt. 21:10, of the people of a city; 28:4, of the keepers or watchers, at the Lord's tomb, RV, "did quake" (KJV, "did shake").

Mighty In **Rev. 6:13**, KJV, *megas*, "great," is translated "mighty" (RV, "great"), of a wind. *See also* **Strong** at *Revelation 5:2*.

6:14 And the heaven departed as a scroll when it is rolled together; and every mountain and island were moved out of their places.

Heaven *see Revelation 3:12*.

Departed *apochorizo* (673), signifies "to separate off" (*apo*); in the middle voice, "to depart from," Acts 15:39, KJV, "departed asunder"; RV, "parted asunder"; **Rev. 6:14**, RV, "was removed."

Scroll *biblion* (975), the diminutive of *biblos*, "a book," is used in **Rev. 6:14**, of "a scroll," the rolling up of which illustrates the removal of the heaven. *See also* **Book** at *Revelation 1:11*.

Rolled *heilisso*, or *helisso* (1507), "to roll," or "roll up," is used (a) of the "rolling" up of a mantle, illustratively of the heavens, Heb. 1:12, RV; (b) of the "rolling" up of a scroll, **Rev. 6:14**, illustratively of the removing of the heaven.

Island *see* **Isle** at *Revelation 1:9*.

Moved *apochorizo* (673), "to separate, part asunder," is used in the passive voice in **Rev. 6:14**, "(the heaven) was removed," RV (KJV, "departed"). *See also* **Remove** at *Revelation 2:5*.

Places *see* **Place** at *Revelation 2:5*.

6:15 And the kings of the earth, and the great men, and the rich men, and the chief captains, and the mighty men, and every bondman, and every free man, hid themselves in the dens and in the rocks of the mountains;

Great men *megistan* (3175), akin to *megistos*, "greatest," the superlative degree of *megas*, "great," denotes "chief men, nobles," it is rendered "lords" in Mark 6:21, of nobles in Herod's entourage; "princes" in **Rev. 6:15** and **18:23**, RV (KJV, "great men").

Rich *see Revelation 2:9*.

Captains *chiliarchos* (5506), denoting "a commander of 1000 soldiers" (from *chilios*, "a thousand," and *archo*, "to rule"), was the Greek word for the Persian vizier, and for the Roman military tribune, the commander of a Roman cohort, e.g., John 18:12; Acts 21:31-33, 37. One such commander was constantly in charge of the Roman garrison in Jerusalem. The word became used also for any military commander, e.g., a "captain" or "chief captain," Mark 6:21; **Rev. 6:15**; **19:18**.

Mighty *ischuros* (2478), "strong, mighty," is usually translated "strong"; "mighty" in Luke 15:14 (of a famine); **Rev. 19:6** (of thunders); **19:18** (of men): in the following, where the KJV has "mighty," the RV substitutes "strong," 1 Cor. 1:27; **Rev. 6:15** (KJV, "mighty men"); **18:10, 21**; Heb. 11:34, RV, "(waxed) mighty" (KJV, "valiant"). *See also* **Strong** at *Revelation 5:2*.

Free man *eleutheros* (1658), primarily of "freedom to go wherever one likes," is used (a) of "freedom from restraint and obligation" in general, Matt. 17:26; Rom. 7:3; 1 Cor. 7:39, RV, "free," of the second marriage of a woman; 9:1, 19; 1 Pet. 2:16; from the Law, Gal. 4:26; from sin, John 8:36; with regard to righteousness, Rom. 6:20 (i.e., righteousness laid no sort of bond upon them, they had no relation to it); (b) in a civil sense, "free" from bondage or slavery, John 8:33; 1 Cor. 7:21, 22, 2nd part; 12:13; Gal. 3:28; Eph. 6:8; **Rev. 13:16**; **19:18**; as a noun, "freeman," Col. 3:11, RV; **Rev. 6:15**; "freewoman," Gal. 4:22, 23, 30, and v. 31, RV.

Dens *spelaion* (4693), "a grotto, cavern, den" (Lat., *spelunca*), "cave," John 11:38, is said of the grave of Lazarus; in the RV in Heb. 11:38 and **Rev. 6:15** (KJV, "dens"); in the Lord's rebuke concerning the defilement of the Temple, Matt. 21:13; Mark 11:17; Luke 19:46, "den" is used.

Rocks *petra* (4073), denotes "a mass of rock," as distinct from *petros*, "a detached stone or boulder," or a stone that might be thrown or easily moved. For the nature of *petra*, see Matt. 7:24, 25; 27:51, 60; Mark 15:46; Luke 6:48 (twice), a type of a sure foundation (here the true reading is as in the RV, "because it had been well builded"); **Rev. 6:15, 16** (cf. Isa. 2:19ff.; Hos. 10:8); Luke 8:6, 13, used illustratively; 1 Cor. 10:4 (twice), figuratively, of Christ; in Rom. 9:33 and 1 Pet. 2:8, metaphorically, of Christ; in Matt. 16:18, metaphorically, of Christ and the testimony concerning Him; here the distinction between *petra*, concerning the Lord Himself, and *Petros*, the apostle, is clear.

6:16 And said to the mountains and rocks, Fall on us, and hide us from the face of him that sitteth on the throne, and from the wrath of the Lamb:

"The blood of the martyrs is the seed of the Church."

QUINTUS TERTULLIAN

Rocks *see Revelation 6:15.*

Lamb *see Revelation 5:6.*

6:17 For the great day of his wrath is come; and who shall be able to stand?

Come In **Rev. 15:1**, KJV, *teleo*, "to finish, complete," is incorrectly rendered "filled up" (RV, "finished"); the contents of the seven bowls are not the sum total of the divine judgments; they form the termination of them; there are many which precede, which are likewise comprised under "the wrath of God," to be executed at the closing period of the present age, e.g., **6:17**; **11:18**; **14:10**, **19**.

Chapter 7

7:1 And after these things I saw four angels standing on the four corners of the earth, holding the four winds of the earth, that the wind should not blow on the earth, nor on the sea, nor on any tree.

Corners *gonia* (1137), "an angle" (Eng., "coign"), signifies (a) "an external angle," as of the "corner" of a street, Matt. 6:5; or of a building, 21:42; Mark 12:10; Luke 20:17; Acts 4:11; 1 Pet. 2:7, "the corner stone or head-stone of the corner"; or the four extreme limits of the earth, **Rev. 7:1**; **20:8**; (b) "an internal corner," a secret place, Acts 26:26.

Holding *see* Holdeth at *Revelation 2:1.*

Winds *anemos* (417), besides its literal meaning, is used metaphorically in Eph. 4:14, of variable teaching. In Matt. 24:31 and Mark 13:27 the four "winds" stand for the four cardinal points of the compass; so in **Rev. 7:1**, "the four winds of the earth" (cf. Jer. 49:36; Dan. 7:2); the contexts indicate that these are connected with the execution of divine judgments. Deissmann (*Bible Studies*) and Moulton and Milligan (*Vocab.*) illustrate the phrase from the papyri.

7:2 And I saw another angel ascending from the east, having the seal of the living God: and he cried with a loud voice to the four angels, to whom it was given to hurt the earth and the sea,

East *anatole* (395), primarily "a rising," as of the sun and stars, corresponds to *anatello*, "to make to rise," or, intransitively, "to arise," which is also used of the sunlight, as well as of other objects in nature. In Luke 1:78 it is used metaphorically of Christ as "the Dayspring," the One through whom light came into the world, shining immediately into Israel, to dispel the darkness which was upon all nations. Cf. Mal. 4:2. Elsewhere it denotes the "east," as the quarter of the sun's rising, Matt. 2:1-2, 9; 8:11; 24:27; Luke 13:29; **Rev. 7:2**; **16:12**; **21:13**. The "east" in general stands for that side of things upon which the rising of the sun gives light. In the heavenly city itself, **Rev. 21:13**, the reference to the "east" gate points to the outgoing of the influence of the city "eastward."

Seal *see* Seals at Revelation *5:1.*

Loud *see Revelation 5:2.*

Hurt *see Revelation 2:11.*

7:3 Saying, Hurt not the earth, neither the sea, nor the trees, till we have sealed the servants of our God in their foreheads.

Hurt *see Revelation 2:11.*

Sealed *sphragizo* (4972), "to seal," is used to indicate (a) security and permanency (attempted but impossible), Matt. 27:66; on the contrary, of the doom of Satan, fixed and certain, **Rev. 20:3**, RV, "sealed it over"; (b) in Rom. 15:28, "when ... I have ... sealed to them this fruit," the formal ratification of the ministry of the churches of the Gentiles in Greece and Galatia to needy saints in Judea, by Paul's faithful delivery of the gifts to them; this material help was the fruit of his spiritual ministry to the Gentiles, who on their part were bringing forth the fruit of their having shared with them in spiritual things; the metaphor stresses the sacred formalities of the transaction ; (c) secrecy and security and the postponement of disclosure, **Rev. 10:4**; in a negative command **22:10**; (d) ownership and security, together with destination, **Rev. 7:3**, **4**, **5**; the same three indications are conveyed in Eph. 1:13, in the metaphor of the "sealing" of believers by the gift of the Holy Spirit, upon believing (i.e., at the time of their regeneration, not after a lapse of time in their spiritual life, "having also believed" – not as KJV, "after that ye believed"; the aorist participle marks the definiteness and completeness of the act of faith); the idea of destination is stressed by the phrase "the Holy Spirit of promise" (see also v. 14); so 4:30, "ye were sealed unto the day of redemption"; so in 2 Cor. 1:22, where the middle voice intimates the special interest of the Sealer in His act; (e) authentication by the believer (by receiving the witness of the Son) of the fact that "God is true," John 3:33; authentication by God in sealing the Son as the Giver of eternal life (with perhaps a figurative allusion to the impress of a mark upon loaves), 6:27.

Servants *doulos* (1401), an adjective, signifying "in bondage," Rom. 6:19 (neuter plural, agreeing with *mele*, "members"), is used as a noun, and as the most common and general word for "servant," frequently indicating subjection without the idea of bondage; it is used (a) of natural conditions, e.g., Matt. 8:9; 1 Cor. 7:21, 22 (1st part); Eph. 6:5; Col. 4:1; 1 Tim. 6:1; frequently in the four Gospels; (b) metaphorically of spiritual, moral and ethical conditions: "servants" (1) of God, e.g., Acts 16:17; Titus 1:1; 1 Pet. 2:16; **Rev. 7:3**; **15:3**; the perfect example being Christ Himself, Phil. 2:7; (2) of Christ, e.g., Rom. 1:1; 1 Cor. 7:22 (2nd part); Gal. 1:10; Eph. 6:6; Phil. 1:1; Col. 4:12; Jas. 1:1; 2 Pet. 1:1; Jude 1; (3) of sin, John 8:34 (RV, "bondservants"); Rom. 6:17, 20; (4) of corruption, 2 Pet. 2:19 (RV, "bondservants"); cf. the verb *douloo*.

Foreheads *metopon* (3359), from *meta*, "with," and *ops*, "an eye," occurs only in Revelation, **7:3**; **9:4**; **13:16**; **14:1, 9**; **17:5**; **20:4**; **22:4**.

7:4 And I heard the number of them which were sealed: *and there were* sealed an hundred *and* forty *and* four thousand of all the tribes of the children of Israel.

Sealed *see Revelation 7:3.*

Hundred *hekaton* (1540), an indeclinable numeral, denotes "a hundred," e.g., Matt. 18:12, 28; it also signifies "a hundredfold," Matt. 13:8, 23, and the RV in the corresponding passage, Mark 4:8, 20 (for KJV, "hundred"), signifying the complete productiveness of sown seed. In the passage in Mark the phrase is, lit., "in thirty and in sixty and in a hundred." In Mark 6:40 it is used with the preposition *kata*, in the phrase "by hundreds." It is followed by other numerals in John 21:11; Acts 1:15; **Rev. 7:4**; **14:1, 3**; **21:17**.

Tribes *see* **Kindreds** at *Revelation 1:7.*

7:5 Of the tribe of Juda *were* sealed twelve thousand. Of the tribe of Reuben *were* sealed twelve thousand. Of the tribe of Gad *were* sealed twelve thousand.

Sealed *see Revelation 7:3.*

Twelve *dodeka* (1427), is used frequently in the Gospels for the twelve apostles, and in Acts 6:2; 1 Cor. 15:5; **Rev. 21:14b**; of the tribes of Israel, Matt. 19:28; Luke 22:30; Jas. 1:1; **Rev. 21:12c** (cf. **7:5-8**; **12:1**); in various details relating to the heavenly Jerusalem, **Rev. 21:12-21**; **22:2**. The number in general is regarded as suggestive of divine administration.

7:6-8 Of the tribe of Aser *were* sealed twelve thousand. Of the tribe of Nepthalim *were* sealed twelve thousand. Of the tribe of Manasses *were* sealed twelve thousand.

Of the tribe of Simeon *were* sealed twelve thousand. Of the tribe of Levi *were* sealed twelve thousand. Of the tribe of Issachar *were* sealed twelve thousand.

Of the tribe of Zabulon *were* sealed twelve thousand. Of the tribe of Joseph *were* sealed twelve thousand. Of the tribe of Benjamin *were* sealed twelve thousand.

Sealed *See Revelation 7:3.* In **Rev. 7**, after the 5th verse (first part) the original does not repeat the mention of the "sealing" except in v. **8** (last part) (hence the omission in the RV).

7:9 After this I beheld, and, lo, a great multitude, which no man could number, of all nations, and kindreds, and people, and tongues, stood before the throne, and before the Lamb, clothed with white robes, and palms in their hands;

After this *see* **Hereafter** at *Revelation 1:19.*

Multitude *ochlos* (3793), is used frequently in the four Gospels and the Acts; elsewhere only in **Rev. 7:9**; **17:15**; **19:1, 6**; it denotes (a) "a crowd or multitude of persons, a throng," e.g., Matt. 14:14, 15; 15:33; often in the plural, e.g., Matt. 4:25; 5:1; with *polus*, "much" or "great," it signifies "a great multitude," e.g., Matt. 20:29, or "the common people," Mark 12:37, perhaps preferably "the mass of the people." Field supports the meaning in the text, but either rendering is suitable. The mass of the people was attracted to Him (for the statement "heard Him gladly" cf. what is said in Mark 6:20 of Herod Antipas concerning John the Baptist); in John 12:9, "the common people," RV, stands in contrast with their leaders (v. 10); Acts 24:12, RV, "crowd"; (b) "the populace, an unorganized multitude," in contrast to *demos*, "the people as a body politic," e.g., Matt. 14:5; 21:26; John 7:12 (2nd part); (c) in a more general sense, "a multitude or company," e.g., Luke 6:17, RV, "a (great) multitude (of His disciples)," KJV, "the company"; Acts 1:15, "a multitude (of persons)," RV, KJV, "the number (of names)"; Acts 24:18, RV, "crowd" (KJV, "multitude").

Number *arithmeo* (705), is found in Matt. 10:30; Luke 12:7; **Rev. 7:9**.

All nations *see* **Tribulation** at *Revelation 1:9*.

Kindreds *see Revelation 1:7*.

People *see Revelation 5:9*.

Tongues *see* **Tongue** at *Revelation 5:9*.

White *see Revelation 1:14*.

Robes *see Revelation 6:11*.

Palms *phoinix* (5404), denotes "the date palm"; it is used of "palm" trees in John 12:13, from which branches were taken; of the branches themselves in **Rev. 7:9**. The "palm" gave its name to Phoenicia and to Phoenix in Crete, Acts 27:12, RV. Jericho was the city of "palm trees," Deut. 34:3; Judg. 1:16; 3:13; 2 Chron. 28:15. They were plentiful there in the time of Christ.

7:10 And cried with a loud voice, saying, Salvation to our God which sitteth upon the throne, and unto the Lamb.

Loud *see Revelation 5:2*.

Salvation *soteria* (4991), denotes "deliverance, preservation, salvation." "Salvation" is used in the NT (a) of material and temporal deliverance from danger and apprehension, (1) national, Luke 1:69, 71; Acts 7:25, RV marg., "salvation" (text, "deliverance"); (2) personal, as from the sea, Acts 27:34; RV, "safety" (KJV, "health"); prison, Phil. 1:19; the flood, Heb. 11:7; (b) of the spiritual and eternal deliverance granted immediately by God to those who accept His conditions of repentance and faith in the Lord Jesus, in whom alone it is to be obtained, Acts 4:12, and upon confession of Him as Lord, Rom. 10:10; for this purpose the gospel is the saving instrument, Rom. 1:16; Eph. 1:13; (c) of the present experience of God's power to deliver from the bondage of sin, e.g., Phil. 2:12, where the special, though not the entire, reference is to the maintenance of peace and harmony; 1 Pet. 1:9; this present experience on the part of believers is virtually equivalent to sanctification; for this purpose, God is able to make them wise, 2 Tim. 3:15; they are not to neglect it, Heb. 2:3; (d) of the future deliverance of believers at the Parousia of Christ for His saints, a salvation which is the object of their confident hope, e.g., Rom. 13:11; 1 Thess. 5:8, and v. 9, where "salvation" is assured to them, as being deliverance from the wrath of God destined to be executed upon the ungodly at the end of this age (see 1 Thess. 1:10); 2 Thess. 2:13; Heb. 1:14; 9:28; 1 Pet. 1:5; 2 Pet. 3:15; (e) of the deliverance of the nation of Israel at the second advent of Christ at the time of "the epiphany (or shining forth) of His Parousia" (2 Thess. 2:8); Luke 1:71; **Rev. 12:10**; (f) inclusively, to sum up all the blessings bestowed by God on men in Christ through the Holy Spirit, e.g., 2 Cor. 6:2; Heb. 5:9; 1 Pet. 1:9, 10; Jude 3; (g) occasionally, as standing virtually for the Savior, e.g., Luke 19:9; cf. John 4:22; (h) in ascriptions of praise to God, **Rev. 7:10**, and as that which it is His prerogative to bestow, **19:1** (RV).

7:11 And all the angels stood round about the throne, and *about* the elders and the four beasts, and fell before the throne on their faces, and worshipped God,

Round about *see Revelation 4:6*.

Elders *see Revelation 4:4*.

Worshipped *see* **Worship** at *Revelation 4:10*.

7:12 Saying, Amen: Blessing, and glory, and wisdom, and thanksgiving, and honour, and power, and might, *be* unto our God for ever and ever. Amen.

Blessing *see Revelation 5:12*.

Wisdom *see Revelation 5:12*.

Thanksgiving *see* **Thanks** at *Revelation 4:9*.

Honour *see Revelation 4:9*.

Power *see Revelation 5:12*.

7:13 And one of the elders answered, saying unto me, What are these which are arrayed in white robes? and whence came they?

Elders *see Revelation 4:4*.

White *see Revelation 1:14*.

Robes *see Revelation 6:11*.

7:14 And I said unto him, Sir, thou knowest. And he said to me, These are they which came out of great tribulation, and have washed their robes, and made them white in the blood of the Lamb.

Sir *kurios* (2962), properly an adjective, signifying "having power" (*kuros*) or "authority," is used as a noun, variously translated in the NT, " 'Lord,' 'master,' 'Master,' 'owner,' 'Sir,' a title of wide significance, occurring in each book of the NT save Titus and the Epistles of John. It is used (a) of an owner, as in Luke 19:33, cf. Matt. 20:8; Acts 16:16; Gal. 4:1; or of one who has the disposal of anything, as the Sabbath, Matt. 12:8; (b) of a master, i.e., one to whom service is due on any ground, Matt. 6:24; 24:50; Eph. 6:5; (c) of an Emperor or King, Acts 25:26; **Rev. 17:14**; (d) of idols, ironically, 1 Cor. 8:5, cf. Isa. 26:13; (e) as a title of respect addressed to a father, Matt. 21:30, a husband, 1 Pet. 3:6, a master, Matt. 13:27; Luke 13:8, a ruler, Matt. 27:63, an angel, Acts 10:4; **Rev. 7:14**; (f) as a title of courtesy addressed to a stranger, John 12:21; 20:15; Acts 16:30; from the outset of His ministry this was a common form of address to the Lord Jesus, alike by the people, Matt. 8:2; John 4:11, and by His disciples, Matt. 8:25; Luke 5:8; John 6:68; (g) *kurios* is the Sept. and NT representative of Heb. Jehovah ('LORD' in Eng. versions), see Matt. 4:7; Jas. 5:11, e.g., of *adon*, Lord, Matt. 22:44, and of *Adonay*, Lord, 1:22; it also occurs for *Elohim*, God, 1 Pet. 1:25.

"Thus the usage of the word in the NT follows two main lines: one, *a-f*, customary and general, the other, *g*, peculiar to the Jews, and drawn from the Greek translation of the OT. Christ Himself assumed the title, Matt. 7:21, 22; 9:38; 22:41-45; Mark 5:19 (cf. Ps. 66:16; the parallel passage, Luke 8:39, has 'God'); Luke 19:31; John 13:13, apparently intending it in the higher senses of its current use, and at the same time suggesting its OT associations. His purpose did not become clear to the disciples until after His resurrection, and the revelation of His Deity consequent thereon. Thomas, when he realized the significance of the presence of a mortal wound in the body of a living man, immediately joined with it the absolute title of Deity, saying, 'My Lord and my God,' John 20:28. Thereafter, except in Acts 10:4 and **Rev. 7:14**, there is no record that *kurios* was ever again used by believers in addressing any save God and the Lord Jesus; cf Acts 2:47 with 4:29, 30. How soon and how completely the lower meaning had been superseded is seen in Peter's declaration in his first sermon after the resurrection, 'God hath made Him—Lord,' Acts 2:36, and that in the house of Cornelius, 'He is Lord of all,' 10:36, cf. Deut. 10:14; Matt. 11:25; Acts 17:24. In his writings the implications of his early teaching are confirmed and developed. Thus Ps. 34:8, 'O taste and see that Jehovah is good,' is applied to the Lord Jesus, 1 Pet. 2:3, and 'Jehovah of Hosts, Him shall ye sanctify,' Isa. 8:13, becomes 'sanctify in your hearts Christ as Lord,' 3:15. So also James who uses *kurios* alike of God, 1:7 (cf. v. 5); 3:9; 4:15; 5:4, 10, 11, and of the Lord Jesus, 1:1 (where the possibility that *kai* is intended epexegetically, i.e. = even, cf. 1 Thess. 3:11, should not be overlooked); 2:1 (lit., 'our Lord Jesus Christ of glory,' cf. Ps. 24:7; 29:3; Acts 7:2; 1 Cor. 2:8); 5:7, 8, while the language of 4:10; 5:15, is equally applicable to either. Jude, v. 4, speaks of 'our only – Lord, Jesus Christ,' and immediately, v. 5, uses 'Lord' of God (see the remarkable marg. here), as he does later, vv. 9, 14. Paul ordinarily uses *kurios* of the Lord Jesus, 1 Cor. 1:3, e.g., but also on occasion, of God, in quotations from the OT, 1 Cor. 3:20, e.g., and in his own words, 1 Cor. 3:5, cf. v. 10. It is equally appropriate to either in 1 Cor. 7:25; 2 Cor. 3:16; 8:21; 1 Thess. 4:6, and if 1 Cor. 11:32 is to be interpreted by 10:21, 22, the Lord Jesus is intended, but if by Heb. 12:5-9, then *kurios* here also = God. 1 Tim. 6:15, 16 is probably to be understood of the Lord Jesus, cf. **Rev. 17:14**. Though John does not use 'Lord' in his Epistles, and though, like the other Evangelists, he ordinarily uses the personal Name in his narrative, yet he occasionally speaks of Him as 'the Lord,' John 4:1; 6:23; 11:2; 20:20; 21:12. The full significance of this association of Jesus with God under the one appellation, 'Lord,' is seen when it is remembered that these men belonged to the only monotheistic race in the world. To associate with the Creator one known to be a creature, however exalted, though possible to Pagan philosophers, was quite impossible to a Jew. It is not recorded that in the days of His flesh any of His disciples either addressed the Lord, or spoke of Him, by His personal Name. Where Paul has occasion to refer to the facts of the gospel history he speaks of what the Lord Jesus said, Acts 20:35, and did, 1 Cor. 11:23, and suffered, 1 Thess. 2:15; 5:9, 10. It is our Lord Jesus who is coming, 1 Thess. 2:19, etc. In prayer also the title is given, 3:11; Eph. 1:3; the sinner is invited to believe on the Lord Jesus, Acts 16:31; 20:21, and the saint to look to the Lord Jesus for deliverance, Rom. 7:24, 25, and in the few exceptional cases in which the personal Name stands alone a reason is always discernible in the immediate context. The title 'Lord,' as given to the Savior, in its full significance rests upon the resurrection, Acts 2:36; Rom. 10:9; 14:9, and is realized only in the Holy Spirit, 1 Cor. 12:3."

Tribulation *see Revelation 1:9*.

Washed *pluno* (4150), is used of "washing inanimate objects," e.g., "nets," Luke 5:2 (some texts have *apopluno*); of "garments," figuratively, **Rev. 7:14**; **22:14** (in the best texts; the KJV translates those which have the verb *poieo*, "to do," followed by *tas entolas autou*, "His commandments").

White *leukaino* (3021), "to whiten, make white," is used in Mark 9:3; figuratively in **Rev. 7:14**.

7:15 Therefore are they before the throne of God, and serve him day and night in his temple: and he that sitteth on the throne shall dwell among them.

Before *see Revelation 1:4*.

Serve *latreuo* (3000), primarily "to work for hire" (akin to *latris*, "a hired servant"), signifies (1) to worship, (2) to "serve"; in the latter sense it is used of service (a) to God, Matt. 4:10; Luke 1:74 ("without fear"); 4:8; Acts 7:7; 24:14, RV, "serve" (KJV, "worship"); 26:7; 27:23; Rom. 1:9 ("with my spirit"); 2 Tim. 1:3; Heb. 9:14; 12:28, KJV, "we may serve," RV, "we may offer service"; **Rev. 7:15**; (b) to God and Christ ("the Lamb"), **Rev. 22:3**; (c) in the tabernacle, Heb. 8:5, RV; 13:10; (d) to "the host of heaven," Acts 7:42, RV, "to serve" (KJV, "to worship"); (e) to "the creature," instead of the Creator, Rom. 1:25, of idolatry.

Temple *see Revelation 3:12.*

Dwell *skenoo* (4637), "to pitch a tent" (*skene*), "to tabernacle," is translated "dwelt," in John 1:14, KJV, RV marg., "tabernacled"; in **Rev. 7:15**, KJV, "shall dwell," RV, "shall spread (His) tabernacle"; in **Rev. 12:12**; **13:6**; **21:3**, dwell.

7:16 They shall hunger no more, neither thirst any more; neither shall the sun light on them, nor any heat.

Hunger *peinao* (3983), "to hunger, be hungry, hungered," is used (a) literally, e.g., Matt. 4:2; 12:1; 21:18; Rom. 12:20; 1 Cor. 11:21, 34; Phil. 4:12; **Rev. 7:16**; Christ identifies Himself with His saints in speaking of Himself as suffering in their sufferings in this and other respects, Matt. 25:35, 42; (b) metaphorically, Matt. 5:6; Luke 6:21, 25; John 6:35.

No more *see Revelation 3:12.*

Thirst *dipsao* (1372), is used (a) in the natural sense, e.g., Matt. 25:35, 37, 42; in v. 44, "athirst" (lit., "thirsting"); John 4:13, 15; 19:28; Rom. 12:20; 1 Cor. 4:11; **Rev. 7:16**; (b) figuratively, of spiritual "thirst," Matt. 5:6; John 4:14; 6:35; 7:37; in **Rev. 21:6** and **22:17**, "that is athirst."

Sun *see Revelation 1:16.*

Light *see* **Fell** at *Revelation 1:17.*

Heat *kauma* (2738), "heat," signifies "the result of burning," or "the heat produced," **Rev. 7:16**; **16:9**; cf. *kaumatizo*, "to scorch," *kausis*, "burning," *kauteriazomai*, "to brand, sear."

7:17 For the Lamb which is in the midst of the throne shall feed them, and shall lead them unto living fountains of waters: and God shall wipe away all tears from their eyes.

Lamb *see Revelation 5:6.*

Midst *mesos* (3319), an adjective denoting "middle, in the middle or midst," is used in the following, in which the English requires a phrase, and the adjectival rendering must be avoided: Luke 22:55, "Peter sat in the midst of them," lit., "a middle one of (them)"; Luke 23:45, of the rending of the veil "in the midst"; here the adjective idiomatically belongs to the verb "was rent," and is not to be taken literally, as if it meant "the middle veil"; John 1:26, "in the midst of you (standeth One)," RV (lit., "a middle One"); Acts 1:18, where the necessity of avoiding the lit. rendering is obvious. Cf. the phrases "at midday," "at midnight." *Mesos* is used adverbially, in prepositional phrases, (a) *ana mesos*, e.g., 1 Cor. 6:5, "between"; Matt. 13:25, "among"; **Rev. 7:17**, "in the midst"; (b) *dia mesos*, e.g., Luke 4:30; 17:11, "through the midst"; (c) *en mesos*, Luke 10:3, RV, "in the midst," KJV, "among"; so 22:27; 1 Thess. 2:7; with the article after *en*, e.g., Matt. 14:6, RV, "in the midst," KJV, "before"; (d) *eis mesos*, Mark 14:60, "in the midst"; with the article, e.g., Mark 3:3, "forth" (lit., "into the midst"); (e) *ek mesos*, "out of the way," lit., "out of the midst," Col. 2:14; 2 Thess. 2:7, where, however, removal is not necessarily in view; there is no accompanying verb signifying removal, as in each of the other occurrences of the phrase; with the article, e.g., 1 Cor. 5:2; 2 Cor. 6:17; (f) *kata mesos*, Acts 27:27, "about mid(night)."

Lead *hodegeo* (3594), "to lead the way," is used (a) literally, RV, "guide" (KJV, "lead"), of "guiding" the blind, in Matt. 15:14; Luke 6:39; of "guiding" unto fountains of waters of life, **Rev. 7:17**; (b) figuratively, in John 16:13, of "guidance" into the truth by the Holy Spirit; in Acts 8:31, of the interpretation of Scripture.

Fountains *pege* (4077), "a spring or fountain," is used of (a) "an artificial well," fed by a spring, John 4:6; (b) metaphorically (in contrast to such a well), "the indwelling Spirit of God," 4:14; (c) "springs," metaphorically in 2 Pet. 2:17, RV, for KJV, "wells"; (d) "natural fountains or springs," Jas. 3:11, 12; **Rev. 8:10**; **14:7**; **16:4**; (e) metaphorically, "eternal life and the future blessings accruing from it," **Rev. 7:17**; **21:6**; (f) "a flow of blood," Mark 5:29.

Wipe *exaleipho* (1813), "to wipe out or away" (*ek*, or *ex*, "out," *aleipho*, "to anoint"), is used metaphorically of "wiping" away tears from the eyes, **Rev. 7:17**; **21:4**. *See also* **Blot out** at *Revelation 3:5*.

Tears *dakruon* or *dakru* (1144), akin to *dakruo*, "to weep," is used in the plural, Mark 9:24; Luke 7:38, 44 (with the sense of washing therewith the Lord's feet); Acts 20:19, 31; 2 Cor. 2:4; 2 Tim. 1:4; Heb. 5:7; 12:17; **Rev. 7:17**; **21:4**.

Chapter 8

8:1 And when he had opened the seventh seal, there was silence in heaven about the space of half an hour.

Seventh *hebdomos* (1442), occurs in John 4:52; Heb. 4:4 (twice); Jude 14; **Rev. 8:1**; **10:7**; **11:15**; **16:17**; **21:20**.

Seal *see* **Seals** at *Revelation 5:1*.

Silence *sige* (4602), occurs in Acts 21:40; **Rev. 8:1**, where the "silence" is introductory to the judgments following the opening of the seventh seal.

About *hos* (5613), usually means "as." Used with numerals it signifies "about," e.g., Mark 5:13; 8:9; John 1:40; 6:19; 11:18; Acts 1:15; **Rev. 8:1**.

Hour In **Rev. 8:1**, *hemioron*, "half an hour" (*hemi*, "half," and *hora*), is used with *hos*, "about," of a period of silence in Heaven after the opening of the 7th seal, a period corresponding to the time customarily spent in silent worship in the Temple during the burning of incense.

8:2 And I saw the seven angels which stood before God; and to them were given seven trumpets.

Trumpets *see* Trumpet at *Revelation 1:10*.

8:3 And another angel came and stood at the altar, having a golden censer; and there was given unto him much incense, that he should offer *it* with the prayers of all saints upon the golden altar which was before the throne.

Censer *libanotos* (3031), denotes "frankincense," the gum of the *libanos*, "the frankincense tree"; in a secondary sense, "a vessel in which to burn incense," **Rev. 8:3, 5**.

Incense *libanos* (2030), from a Semitic verb signifying "to be white," is a vegetable resin, bitter and glittering, obtained by incisions in the bark of the *arbor thuris*, "the incense tree," and especially imported through Arabia; it was used for fumigation at sacrifices, Exod. 30:7, etc., or for perfume, Song of Sol., 3:6. The Indian variety is called *looban*. It was among the offerings brought by the wise men, Matt. 2:11. In **Rev. 18:13** it is listed among the commodities of Babylon. The "incense" of **Rev. 8:3** should be "frankincense." *See also* **Odours** at *Revelation 5:8*.

Offer *didomi* (1325), to give, is translated "to offer" in Luke 2:24; in **Rev. 8:3**, KJV, "offer" (RV, "add;" marg., "give").

8:4 And the smoke of the incense, *which came* with the prayers of the saints, ascended up before God out of the angel's hand.

Smoke *see Revelation 9:2*.

Incense *see* **Odours** at *Revelation 5:8*.

8:5 And the angel took the censer, and filled it with fire of the altar, and cast *it* into the earth: and there were voices, and thunderings, and lightnings, and an earthquake.

Censer *see Revelation 8:3*.

Filled *gemizo* (1072), "to fill or load full," is used of a boat, Mark 4:37 (RV, "was filling"); a sponge, Mark 15:36, a house, Luke 14:23; the belly, Luke 15:16; waterpots, John 2:1; baskets, 6:13; bowls, with fire, **Rev. 8:5**; the temple, with smoke, **15:8**. Cf. *gemo*, "to be full."

"More spiritual progress can be made in one short moment of speechless silence in the awesome presence of God than in years of mere study."

A. W. TOZER

Thunderings *see Revelation 4:5*.

Lightnings *see Revelation 4:5*.

Earthquake *see Revelation 6:12*.

8:6 And the seven angels which had the seven trumpets prepared themselves to sound.

Trumpets *see* **Trumpet** at *Revelation 1:10*.

Prepared *hetoimazo* (2090), "to prepare, make ready," is used (I) absolutely, e.g., Mark 14:15; Luke 9:52; (II) with an object, e.g., (a) of those things which are ordained (1) by God, such as future positions of authority, Matt. 20:23; the coming Kingdom, 25:34; salvation personified in Christ, Luke 2:31; future blessings, 1 Cor. 2:9; a city, Heb. 11:16; a place of refuge for the Jewish remnant, **Rev. 12:6**; Divine judgments on the world, **Rev. 8:6**; **9:7**, **15**; **16:12**; eternal fire, for the Devil and his angels, Matt. 25:41; (2) by Christ: a place in Heaven for His followers, John 14:2, 3; (b) of human "preparation" for the Lord, e.g., Matt. 3:3; 26:17, 19; Luke 1:17 ("make ready"), 76; 3:4, KJV (RV, "make ye ready"); 9:52 ("to make ready"); 23:56; **Rev. 19:7; 21:2**; in 2 Tim. 2:21, of "preparation" of oneself for "every good work"; (c) of human "preparations" for human objects, e.g., Luke 12:20, RV, "thou hast prepared" (KJV, "provided"); Acts 23:23; Philem. 22.

Sound *salpizo* (4537), "to sound a trumpet" (*salpinx*), occurs in Matt. 6:2; 1 Cor. 15:52, "the trumpet shall sound"; **Rev. 8:6-8, 10, 12, 13; 9:1, 13; 10:7; 11:15.**

8:7 The first angel sounded, and there followed hail and fire mingled with blood, and they were cast upon the earth: and the third part of trees was burnt up, and all green grass was burnt up.

Sounded *see* **Sound** at *Revelation 8:6.*

Followed *ginomai* (1096), "to become, to come into existence," is used in **Rev. 8:7; 11:15, 19**, in the sense of taking place after translated "there followed."

Hail *chalaza* (5464), akin to *chalao*, "to let loose, let fall," is always used as an instrument of divine judgment, and is found in the NT in **Rev. 8:7; 11:19; 16:21.**

Mingled *mignumi* (3396), "to mix, mingle" (from a root *mik*; Eng., "mix" is akin), is always in the NT translated "to mingle," Matt. 27:34; Luke 13:1; **Rev. 8:7; 15:2.**

Third *tritos* (5154), is used (a) as a noun, e.g., Luke 20:12, 31; in **Rev. 8:7-12** and **9:15, 18**, "the third part," lit., "the third"; (b) as an adverb, with the article, "the third time," e.g., Mark 14:41; John 21:17 (twice); without the article, lit., "a third time," e.g., John 21:14; 2 Cor. 12:14; 13:1; in enumerations, in Matt. 26:44, with *ek*, "from," lit., "from the third time" (the *ek* indicates the point of departure, especially in a succession of events, cf. John 9:24; 2 Pet. 2:8); absolutely, in the accusative neuter, in 1 Cor. 12:28, "thirdly"; (c) as an adjective (its primary use), e.g., in the phrase the third heaven, 2 Cor. 12:2; in the phrase "the third hour," Matt. 20:3; Mark 15:25; Acts 2:15 ("... of the day"); 23:23 ("... of the night"); in a phrase with *hemera*, "a day," "on the third day" (i.e., "the next day but one"), e.g., Matt. 16:21; Luke 24:46; Acts 10:40; in this connection the idiom "three days and three nights," Matt. 12:40, is explained by ref to 1 Sam. 30:12, 13, and Esth. 4:16 with 5:1; in Mark 9:31 and 10:34, the RV, "after three days," follows the texts which have this phrase, the KJV, "the third day," those which have the same phrase as in Matt. 16:21, etc.

Green *see* **Pale** at *Revelation 6:8.*

Grass *chortos* (5528), primarily denoted "a feeding enclosure" (whence Latin *hortus*, "a garden"; Eng.. "yard," and "garden"); then, "food," especially grass for feeding cattle; it is translated "grass" in Matt. 6:30; 14:19; Mark 6:39 (where "the green grass" is the first evidence of early spring); Luke 12:28; John 6:10; Jas. 1:10, 11; 1 Pet. 1:24; **Rev. 8:7; 9:4**; "blade" in Matt. 13:26; Mark 4:28; "hay" in 1 Cor. 3:12, used figuratively. In Palestine or Syria there are 90 genera and 243 species of grass.

Burnt *katakaio* (2618), from *kata*, "down" (intensive), signifies "to burn up, burn utterly," as of chaff, Matt. 3:12; Luke 3:17; tares, Matt. 13:30, 40; the earth and its works, 2 Pet. 3:10; trees and grass, **Rev. 8:7.** This form should be noted in Acts 19:19; 1 Cor. 3:15; Heb. 13:11, **Rev. 17:16.** In each place the full rendering "burn utterly" might be used, as in **Rev. 18:8.**

8:8 And the second angel sounded, and as it were a great mountain burning with fire was cast into the sea: and the third part of the sea became blood;

Burning *see Revelation 4:5.*

8:9 And the third part of the creatures which were in the sea, and had life, died; and the third part of the ships were destroyed.

Creatures *see* **Creature** at *Revelation 5:13.*

Life *psuche* (5590), besides its meanings, "heart, mind, soul," denotes "life" in two chief respects, (a) "breath of life, the natural life," e.g., Matt. 2:20; 6:25; Mark 10:45; Luke 12:22; Acts 20:10; **Rev. 8:9; 12:11** (cf. Lev. 17:11; Esth. 8:11); (b) "the seat of personality," e.g., Luke 9:24, explained in v. 25 as "own self." *See also* **Souls** at *Revelation 6:9.*

Ships *ploion* (4143), akin to *pleo*, "to sail," a boat or a ship, always rendered appropriately "boat" in the RV in the Gospels; "ship" in the Acts; elsewhere, Jas. 3:4; **Rev. 8:9; 18:17** (in some mss.), **19.**

Destroyed *diaphtheiro* (1311), "to corrupt utterly, through and through," is said of men "corrupted in mind," whose wranglings result from the doctrines of false teachers, 1 Tim. 6:5 (the KJV wrongly renders it as an adjective, "corrupt"). It is translated "destroyeth" instead of "corrupteth," in the RV of Luke 12:33, of the work of a moth, in **Rev. 8:9**, of the effect of divine judgments hereafter upon navigation; in **11:18**, of the divine retribution of destruction upon those who have destroyed the earth; in 2 Cor. 4:16 it is translated "is decaying," said of the human body.

8:10 And the third angel sounded, and there fell a great star from heaven, burning as it were a lamp, and it fell upon the third part of the rivers, and upon the fountains of waters;

Sounded *see* **Sound** at *Revelation 8:6.*

Star *see* **Stars** at *Revelation 1:16.*

Burning *see Revelation 4:5.*

Lamp *lampas* (2985), "a torch," is used in the plur. and translated "torches" in John 18:3; in **Rev. 8:10**, RV, "torch" (KJV, "lamp"). *See also* **Lamps** at *Revelation 4:5.*

Rivers *potamos* (4215), denotes (a) "a stream," Luke 6:48, 49; (b) "a flood or floods," Matt. 7:25, 27; (c) "a river," natural, Matt. 3:6, RV; Mark 1:5; Acts 16:13; 2 Cor. 11:26, RV (KJV, "waters"); **Rev. 8:10; 9:14; 16:4, 12**; symbolical, **Rev. 12:15** (1st part), RV, "river" (KJV, "flood"); so v. **16; 22:1, 2** (cf. Gen. 2:10; Ezek. 47); figuratively, John 7:38, "the effects of the operation of the Holy Spirit in and through the believer."

Fountains *see Revelation 7:17.*

8:11 And the name of the star is called Wormwood: and the third part of the waters became wormwood; and many men died of the waters, because they were made bitter.

Wormwood *apsinthos* (894), (Eng., "absinthe"), a plant both bitter and deleterious, and growing in desolate places, figuratively suggestive of "calamity" (Lam. 3:15) and injustice (Amos 5:7), is used in **Rev. 8:11** (twice; in the 1st part as a proper name).

Bitter *pikraino* (4087), signifies, in the active voice, "to be bitter," Col. 3:19, or "to embitter, irritate, or to make bitter," **Rev. 10:9**; the passive voice, "to be made bitter," is used in **Rev. 8:11; 10:10.**

8:12 And the fourth angel sounded, and the third part of the sun was smitten, and the third part of the moon, and the third part of the stars; so as the third part of them was darkened, and the day shone not for a third part of it, and the night likewise.

Sounded *see* **Sound** at *Revelation 8:6.*

Sun *see Revelation 1:16.*

Smitten *plesso* (4141), akin to *plege,* "a plague, stripe, wound," is used figuratively of the effect upon sun, moon and stars, after the sounding of the trumpet by the fourth angel, in the series of divine judgments upon the world hereafter, **Rev. 8:12.**

Moon *see Revelation 6:12.*

Darkened *skotizo* (4654), "to deprive of light, to make dark," is used in the NT in the passive voice only, (a) of the heavenly bodies Matt. 24:29; Mark 13:24; **Rev. 8:12**; (b) metaphorically, of the mind, Rom. 1:21; 11:10; (some mss. have it in Luke 23:45).

Shone *see* **Shineth** at *Revelation 1:16.*

Likewise *homoios* (3668), "in like manner," is rendered "likewise" in the KJV of Matt. 22:26; 27:41, Luke 10:32; 16:25; John 5:19; Jas. 2:25; 1 Pet. 3:1, 7; Jude 8; **Rev. 8:12** (in all these the RV has "in like manner"); in the following, KJV and RV have "likewise"; Matt. 26:35; Luke 5:33; 6:31; 10:37; 17:28, 31; 22:36; John 6:11; 21:13; Rom. 1:27; 1 Pet. 5:5.

8:13 And I beheld, and heard an angel flying through the midst of heaven, saying with a loud voice, Woe, woe, woe, to the inhabiters of the earth by reason of the other voices of the trumpet of the three angels, which are yet to sound!

Flying *see Revelation 4:7.*

Heaven *mesouranema* (3321), denotes "mid-heaven," or the midst of the heavens, **Rev. 8:13; 14:6; 19:17.**

Loud *see Revelation 5:2.*

Woe *ouai* (3759), an interjection, is used (a) in denunciation, Matt. 11:21; 18:7 (twice); eight times in ch. 23; 24:19; 26:24; Mark 13:17; 14:21; Luke 6:24, 25 (twice), 26; 10:13; six times in ch. 11; 17:1; 21:23; 22:22; 1 Cor. 9:16; Jude 11; **Rev. 8:13** (thrice); **12:12**; as a noun, **Rev. 9:12** (twice); **11:14** (twice); (b) in grief, "alas," **Rev. 18:10, 16, 19** (twice in each).

Inhabiters *see* **Dwellest** at *Revelation 2:13.*

Trumpet *see Revelation 1:10.*

Yet *mello,* "to be about to," "are yet," **Rev. 8:13.**

Sound *see Revelation 8:6.*

Chapter 9

9:1 And the fifth angel sounded, and I saw a star fall from heaven unto the earth: and to him was given the key of the bottomless pit.

Fifth *see Revelation 6:9.*

Sounded *see* **Sound** at *Revelation 8:6.*

Star *see* **Stars** at **Revelation** *1:16.*

Key *see* **Keys** at *Revelation 1:18.*

Bottomless *abussos* (12), "bottomless" (from *a,* intensive, and *bussos,* "a depth"; akin to *bathus,* "deep"; Eng., "bath"), is used as a noun denoting the abyss (KJV, "bottomless pit"). It describes an immeasurable depth, the underworld, the lower regions, the abyss of Sheol. In Rom. 10:7, quoted from Deut. 30:13, the abyss (the abode of the lost dead) is substituted for the sea (the change in the quotation is due to the facts of the death and resurrection of Christ); the KJV has "deep" here and in Luke 8:31; the reference is to the lower regions as the abode of demons, out of which they can be let loose, **Rev. 11:7; 17:8**, it is found seven times in Revelation, **9:1-2, 11; 11:7; 17:8; 20:1, 3**; in **9:1, 2** the RV has "the pit of the abyss."

Pit *phrear* (5421), "a well, dug for water" (distinct from *pege*, "a fountain"), denotes "a pit" in **Rev. 9:1, 2**, RV, "the pit (of the abyss)," "the pit," i.e., the shaft leading down to the abyss, KJV, "(bottomless) pit"; in Luke 14:5, RV, well (KJV, "pit"); in John 4:11, 12, "well."

9:2 And he opened the bottomless pit; and there arose a smoke out of the pit, as the smoke of a great furnace; and the sun and the air were darkened by reason of the smoke of the pit.

Opened *see* **Openeth** at *Revelation 3:7*.

Bottomless *see Revelation 9:1*.

Pit *see Revelation 9:1*.

Smoke *kapnos* (2586), "smoke," occurs in Acts 2:19 and 12 times in Revelation (**8:4; 9:2** (three times); **9:3, 17-18; 14:11; 15:8; 18:9, 18; 19:3**.

Furnace *see Revelation 1:15*.

Sun *see Revelation 1:16*.

Air *aer* (109), Eng., "air," signifies "the atmosphere," certainly in five of the seven occurrences Acts 22:23; 1 Cor. 9:26; 14:9; **Rev. 9:2; 16:11**, and almost certainly in the other two, Eph. 2:2 and 1 Thess. 4:17.

Darkened *skotoo* (4656), "to darken," is used (a) of the heavenly bodies, **Rev. 9:2; 16:10**; (b) metaphorically, of the mind, Eph. 4:18.

9:3 And there came out of the smoke locusts upon the earth: and unto them was given power, as the scorpions of the earth have power.

Smoke *see Revelation 9:2*.

Locusts *akris* (200), occurs in Matt. 3:4 and Mark 1:6, of the animals themselves, as forming part of the diet of John the Baptist; they are used as food; the Arabs stew them with butter, after removing the head, legs and wings. In **Rev. 9:3, 7**, they appear as monsters representing satanic agencies, let loose by divine judgments inflicted upon men for five months, the time of the natural life of the "locust." For the character of the judgment see the whole passage.

Scorpions *skorpios* (4651), akin to *skorpizo*, "to scatter" (which see), is a small animal (the largest of the several species is 6 in. long) like a lobster, but with a long tail, at the end of which is its venomous sting; the pain, the position of the sting, and the effect are mentioned in **Rev. 9:3, 5, 10**. The Lord's rhetorical question as to the provision of a "scorpion" instead of an egg, Luke 11:12, is, firstly, an allusion to the egg-like shape of the creature when at rest; secondly, an indication of the abhorrence with which it is regarded. In Luke 10:19, the Lord's assurance to the disciples of the authority given them by Him to tread upon serpents and scorpions conveys the thought of victory over spiritually antagonistic forces, the powers of darkness, as is shown by His reference to the "power of the enemy" and by the context in vv. 17, 20.

9:4 And it was commanded them that they should not hurt the grass of the earth, neither any green thing, neither any tree; but only those men which have not the seal of God in their foreheads.

Commanded In **Rev. 9:4**, *rheo*, "to speak," is translated "said" in the RV (KJV, "commanded").

Hurt *see Revelation 2:11*.

Grass *see Revelation 8:7*.

Green *see* **Pale** at **Revelation** *6:8*.

Seal *see* **Seals** at *Revelation 5:1*.

Foreheads *see Revelation 7:3*.

9:5 And to them it was given that they should not kill them, but that they should be tormented five months: and their torment *was* as the torment of a scorpion, when he striketh a man.

Tormented *basanizo* (928), is translated "to torment," (a) of sickness, Matt. 8:6; (b) of the doom of evil spirits, Mark 5:7; Luke 8:28; (c) of retributive judgments upon impenitent mankind at the close of this age, **Rev. 9:5; 11:10**; (d) upon those who worship the Beast and his image and receive the mark of his name, **14:10**; (e) of the doom of Satan and his agents, **20:10**.

Months *men* (3376), connected with *mene*, "the moon," akin to a Sanskrit root *ma*–, "to measure" (the Sanskrit *masa* denotes both moon and month, cf, e.g., Lat. *mensis*, Eng., "moon" and "month," the moon being in early times the measure of the "month"). The interval between the 17th day of the second "month" (Gen. 7:11) and the 17th day of the seventh "month," is said to be 150 days (8:3, 4), i.e., five months of 30 days each; hence the year would be 360 days (cf. Dan. 7:25; 9:27; 12:7 with **Rev. 11:2-3; 12:6, 14; 13:5**; whence we conclude that 3 ½ years or 42 months = 1260 days, i.e., one year = 60 days); this was the length of the old Egyptian year; later, five days were added to correspond to the solar year. The Hebrew year was as nearly solar as was compatible with its commencement, coinciding with the new moon, or first day of the "month." This was a regular feast day, Num. 10:10; 28:11-14; the Passover coincided with the full moon (the 14th of the month Abib). Except in Gal. 4:10; Jas. 5:17; **Rev. 9:5, 10, 15; 11:2; 13:5; 22:2**, the word is found only in Luke's writings, Luke 1:24, 26, 36, 56; 4:25; Acts 7:20; 18:11; 19:8; 20:3; 28:11, examples of Luke's care as to accuracy of detail.

Torment *basanismos* (929), akin to *basanizo*, is used of divine judgments in **Rev. 9:5; 14:11; 18:7, 10, 15**.

Scorpion *see* **Scorpions** at *Revelation 9:3*.

Striketh *paio* (3817), signifies "to strike or smite" (a) with the hand or fist, Matt. 26:68; Luke 22:64; (b) with a sword, Mark 14:47; John 18:10, KJV (RV, "struck"); (c) with a sting, **Rev. 9:5**, "striketh."

9:6 And in those days shall men seek death, and shall not find it; and shall desire to die, and death shall flee from them.

Desire *epithumeo* (1937), has the same twofold meaning as the noun, namely (a) "to desire," used of the Holy Spirit against the flesh, Gal. 5:17; of the Lord Jesus, Luke 22:15, "I have desired;" of the holy angels, 1 Pet. 1:12; of good men, for good things, Matt. 13:17; 1 Tim. 3:1; Heb. 6:11; of men, for things without moral quality, Luke 15:16; 16:21; 17:22; **Rev. 9:6**; (b) of "evil desires," in respect of which it is translated "to lust" in Matt. 5:28; 1 Cor. 10:6; Gal. 5:17; Jas. 4:2; to covet, Acts 20:23; Rom. 7:7; 13:9.

Flee *pheugo* (5343), "to flee from or away" (Lat., *fugio;* Eng., "fugitive," etc.), besides its literal significance, is used metaphorically, (a) transitively, of "fleeing" fornication, 1 Cor. 6:18; idolatry, 10:14; evil doctrine, questionings, disputes of words, envy, strife, railings, evil surmisings, wranglings, and the love of money, 1 Tim. 6:11; youthful lusts, 2 Tim. 2:22; (b) intransitively, of the "flight" of physical matter, **Rev. 16:20; 20:11**; of death, **9:6**.

9:7 And the shapes of the locusts *were* like unto horses prepared unto battle; and on their heads *were* as it were crowns like gold, and their faces *were* as the faces of men.

Shapes *homoioma* (3667), denotes "that which is made like something, a resemblance," (a) in the concrete sense, **Rev. 9:7**, "shapes" (RV, marg., "likenesses"); (b) in the abstract sense, Rom. 1:23, RV, "(for) the likeness (of an image)"; the KJV translates it as a verb, "(into an image) made like to"; the association here of the two words *homoioma* and *eikon* serves to enhance the contrast between the idol and "the glory of the incorruptible God," and is expressive of contempt; in 5:14, "(the) likeness of Adam's transgression" (KJV, "similitude"); in 6:5, "(the) likeness (of His death); in 8:3, "(the) likeness (of sinful flesh); in Phil. 2:7, "the likeness of men." "The expression 'likeness of men' does not of itself imply, still less does it exclude or diminish, the reality of the nature which Christ assumed. That ... is declared in the words 'form of a servant.' 'Paul justly says *in the likeness of men*, because, in fact, Christ, although certainly perfect Man (Rom. 5:15; 1 Cor. 15:21; 1 Tim. 2:5), was, by reason of the Divine nature present in Him, not simply and merely man ... but the Incarnate Son of God'" (Gifford, quoting Meyer).

Locusts *see Revelation 9:3*.

Like unto *see Revelation 1:13*.

Horses *see* **Horse** at *Revelation 6:2*.

Prepared *see Revelation 8:6*.

Battle *polemos* (4171), "war," is so translated in the RV, for KJV, "battle," 1 Cor. 14:8; **Rev. 9:7, 9; 16:14; 20:8**; for KJV, "fight," Heb. 11:34; KJV and RV in Jas. 4:1, hyperbolically of private "quarrels"; elsewhere, literally, e.g., Matt. 24:6; **Rev. 11:7**.

Crowns *see* **Crown** at *Revelation 2:10*.

Gold *chrusos* (5557), is used (a) of "coin," Matt. 10:9; Jas. 5:3; (b) of "ornaments," Matt. 23:16, 17; Jas. 5:3 (perhaps both coin and ornaments); **Rev. 18:12**; (c) of "images," Acts 17:29; (d) of "the metal in general," Matt. 2:11; **Rev. 9:7** (some mss. have it in **Rev. 18:16**).

9:8 And they had hair as the hair of women, and their teeth were as *the teeth* of lions.

Hair *see Revelation 1:14*.

Teeth *odous* (3599), is used in the sing. in Matt. 5:38 (twice); elsewhere in the plural, of "the gnashing of teeth," the gnashing being expressive of anguish and indignation, Matt. 8:12; 13:42, 50; 22:13; 24:51; 25:30; Mark 9:18; Luke 13:28; Acts 7:54; in **Rev. 9:8**, of the beings seen in a vision and described as locusts.

Lions *see* **Lion** at *Revelation 4:7*.

9:9 And they had breastplates, as it were breastplates of iron; and the sound of their wings *was* as the sound of chariots of many horses running to battle.

Breastplates *thorax* (2382), primarily, "the breast," denotes "a breastplate or corselet," consisting of two parts and protecting the body on both sides, from the neck to the middle. It is used metaphorically of righteousness, Eph. 6:14; of faith and love, 1 Thess. 5:8, with perhaps a suggestion of the two parts, front and back, which formed the coat of mail (an alternative term for the word in the NT sense); elsewhere in **Rev. 9:9, 17**.

Iron *see Revelation 2:27.*

Sound *see Revelation 1:15.*

Wings *see Revelation 4:8.*

Chariots *harma* (716), akin to *ararisko*, "to join," denotes "a war chariot with two wheels," Acts 8:28, 29, 38; **Rev. 9:9**.

Horses *see* **Horse** at *Revelation 6:2.*

Running *trecho* (5143), "to run," is used (a) literally, e.g., Matt. 27:48 (*dramon*, an aorist participle, from an obsolete verb *dramo*, but supplying certain forms absent from *trecho*, lit., "having run, running," expressive of the decisiveness of the act); the same form in the indicative mood is used, e.g., in Matt. 28:8; in the Gospels the literal meaning alone is used; elsewhere in 1 Cor. 9:24 (twice in 1st part); **Rev. 9:9**, KJV, "running" (RV, "rushing"); (b) metaphorically, from the illustration of "runners" in a race, of either swiftness or effort to attain an end, Rom. 9:16, indicating that salvation is not due to human effort, but to God's sovereign right to exercise mercy; 1 Cor. 9:24 (2nd part), and v. 26, of persevering activity in the Christian course with a view to obtaining the reward; so Heb. 12:1; in Gal. 2:2 (1st part), RV, "(lest) I should be running," continuous present tense referring to the activity of the special service of his mission to Jerusalem; (2nd part), "had run," aorist tense, expressive of the continuous past, referring to the activity of his antagonism to the Judaizing teachers at Antioch, and his consent to submit the case to the judgment of the church in Jerusalem; in 5:7 of the erstwhile faithful course doctrinally of the Galatian believers; in Phil. 2:16, of the apostle's manner of life among the Philippian believers; in 2 Thess. 3:1, of the free and rapid progress of "the word of the Lord."

Battle *see Revelation 9:7.*

9:10 And they had tails like unto scorpions, and there were stings in their tails: and their power *was* to hurt men five months.

Tails *oura* (3769), "the tail of an animal," occurs in **Rev. 9:10** (twice), **19**; **12:4**.

Like unto *see Revelation 1:13.*

Scorpions *see Revelation 9:3.*

Stings *kentron* (2759), from *kenteo*, "to prick," denotes (a) "a sting," **Rev. 9:10**; metaphorically, of sin as the "sting" of death, 1 Cor. 15:55, 56; (b) "a goad," Acts 26:14, RV, "goad" (marg., "goads"), for KJV, "pricks" (in some mss. also in 9:5), said of the promptings and misgivings which Saul of Tarsus had resisted before conversion.

Hurt *see Revelation 2:11.*

Months *see Revelation 9:5.*

9:11 And they had a king over them, *which is* the angel of the bottomless pit, whose name in the Hebrew tongue *is* Abaddon, but in the Greek tongue hath *his* name Apollyon.

Bottomless *see Revelation 9:1.*

Tongue *hebraisti* (or *ebraisti, Westcott and Hort)* (1447), denotes (a) "in Hebrew," **Rev. 9:11**, RV (KJV, "in the Hebrew tongue"); so **16:16**; (b) in the Aramaic vernacular of Palestine, John 5:2, KJV, "in the Hebrew tongue" (RV, "in Hebrew"); in 19:13, 17, KJV, "in the Hebrew" (RV, "in Hebrew"); in v. 20, KJV and RV, "in Hebrew"; in 20:16, RV only, "in Hebrew (Rabboni)."

Apollyon For the construction in Heb. 11:28, "the destroyer." Cf. *apolluon*, in **Rev. 9:11**, the present participle of *apollumi*, used as a proper noun.

9:12 One woe is past; *and*, behold, there come two woes more hereafter.

Woe *see Revelation 8:13.*

Past *aperchomai* (565), "to go away," is rendered "to pass" in **Rev. 9:12**; **11:14**; "passed away" in **Rev. 21:4**.

More *see* **No more** at *Revelation 3:12.*

Hereafter *see Revelation 1:19.*

9:13 And the sixth angel sounded, and I heard a voice from the four horns of the golden altar which is before God,

Sixth *see Revelation 6:12.*

Sounded *see* **Sound** at *Revelation 8:6.*

Horns *see Revelation 5:6.*

9:14 Saying to the sixth angel which had the trumpet, Loose the four angels which are bound in the great river Euphrates.

Sixth *see Revelation 6:12.*

Trumpet *see Revelation 1:10.*

Loose *see Revelation 5:2.*

River *see* **Rivers** at Revelation *8:10.*

9:15 And the four angels were loosed, which were prepared for an hour, and a day, and a month, and a year, for to slay the third part of men.

Loosed *see* Loose at *Revelation 5:2.*

Prepared *see Revelation 8:6.*

Hour *see Revelation 3:3.*

Month *see* Months at *Revelation 9:5.*

Year *eniautos* (1763), originally "a cycle of time," is used (a) of a particular time marked by an event, e.g., Luke 4:19; John 11:49, 51; 18:13; Gal. 4:10; **Rev. 9:15**; (b) to mark a space of time, Acts 11:26; 18:11; Jas. 4:13; 5:17; (c) of that which takes place every year, Heb. 9:7; with *kata,* Heb. 9:25; 10:1, 3.

Slay *see* Slain at *Revelation 2:13.*

Third *see Revelation 8:7.*

9:16 And the number of the army of the horsemen *were* two hundred thousand thousand: and I heard the number of them.

Army *strateuma* (4753), denotes (a) "an army" of any size, large or small, Matt. 22:7; **Rev. 9:16**; **19:14**, **19** (twice); (b) "a company of soldiers," such as Herod's bodyguard, Luke 23:11 (RV, "soldiers"), or the soldiers of a garrison, Acts 23:10, 27 (RV, "the soldiers," for KJV, "an army").

Horsemen *hippikos* (2461), an adjective signifying "of a horse" or "of horsemen, equestrian," is used as a noun denoting "cavalry," in **Rev. 9:16**, "horsemen," numbering "twice ten thousand times ten thousand," RV.

Two hundred thousand thousand *see* Thousands at *Revelation 5:11.*

9:17 And thus I saw the horses in the vision, and them that sat on them, having breastplates of fire, and of jacinth, and brimstone: and the heads of the horses *were* as the heads of lions; and out of their mouths issued fire and smoke and brimstone.

Horses *see* Horse at *Revelation 6:2.*

Vision *horasis* (3706), "sense of sight," is rendered "visions" in Acts 2:17; **Rev. 9:17**.

Breastplates *see Revelation 9:9.*

Fire *purinos* (4447), "fiery," is translated "of fire" in **Rev. 9:17**. In the Sept., Ezek. 28:14, 16.

Jacinth *huakinthinos* (5191), signifies "hyacinthine," perhaps primarily having the color of the hyacinth. Some regard its color as that of the martagon lily, a dusky red. According to Swete, the word in **Rev. 9:17** is "doubtless meant to describe the blue smoke of a sulphurous flame."

Brimstone *theion* (2303), originally denoted "fire from heaven." It is connected with sulphur. Places touched by lightning were called *theia,* and, as lightning leaves a sulphurous smell, and sulphur was used in pagan purifications, it received the name of *theion* Luke 17:29; **Rev. 9:17-18**; **14:10**; **19:20**; **20:10**; **21:8**.

Lions *see* Lion at *Revelation 4:7.*

Issued *ekporeuo* (1607), "to cause to go forth" (*ek,* "out," *poreuo,* "to cause to go"), is used in the middle voice in **Rev. 9:17**, **18**, of the coming forth of fire, smoke and brimstone from the mouths of the symbolic horses in a vision, KJV, "issued" (the RV renders it by the verb "to proceed"). *See also* Went at *Revelation 1:16.*

Smoke *see Revelation 9:2.*

9:18 By these three was the third part of men killed, by the fire, and by the smoke, and by the brimstone, which issued out of their mouths.

Third *see Revelation 8:7.*

Smoke *see Revelation 9:2.*

Issued *see Revelation 9:17. See also* Went at *Revelation 1:16.*

9:19 For their power is in their mouth, and in their tails: for their tails *were* like unto serpents, and had heads, and with them they do hurt.

Tails *see Revelation 9:10.*

Like unto *see Revelation 1:13.*

Serpents *ophis* (3789), the characteristics of the "serpent" as alluded to in Scripture are mostly evil (though Matt. 10:16 refers to its caution in avoiding danger); its treachery, Gen. 49:17; 2 Cor. 11:3; its venom, Ps. 58:4; 1 Cor. 10:9; **Rev. 9:19**; its skulking, Job 26:13; its murderous proclivities, e.g., Ps. 58:4; Prov. 23:32; Eccl. 10:8, 11; Amos 5:19; Mark 16:18; Luke 10:19; the Lord used the word metaphorically of the scribes and Pharisees, Matt. 23:33 (cf. *echidna,* "viper," in Matt. 3:7; 12:34). The general aspects of its evil character are intimated in the Lord's rhetorical question in Matt. 7:10 and Luke 11:11. Its characteristics are concentrated in the archadversary of God and man, the Devil, metaphorically described as the serpent, 2 Cor. 11:3; **Rev. 12:9**, **14**, **15**; **20:2**. The brazen "serpent" lifted up by Moses was symbolical of the means of salvation provided by God, in Christ and His vicarious death under the divine judgment upon sin, John 3:14. While the living "serpent" symbolizes sin in its origin, hatefulness, and deadly effect, the brazen "serpent" symbolized the bearing away of the curse and the judgment of sin; the metal was itself figurative of the righteousness of God's judgment.

Hurt *see Revelation 2:11*.

9:20 And the rest of the men which were not killed by these plagues yet repented not of the works of their hands, that they should not worship devils, and idols of gold, and silver, and brass, and stone, and of wood: which neither can see, nor hear, nor walk:

Men In **Rev. 9:20**, the RV translates the genitive plural of *anthropos* with the article, "mankind" (KJV, "the men"); it might have been rendered "(the rest) of men."

Plagues *plege* (4127), "a stripe, wound" (akin to *plesso*, "to smite"), is used metaphorically of a calamity, "a plague," **Rev. 9:20**; **11:6**; **15:1, 6, 8**; **16:9, 21** (twice); **18:4, 8**; **21:9**; **22:18**.

Repented *see* **Repent** at *Revelation 2:5*.

Worship *see Revelation 4:10*.

Devils *daimonion* (1140), not a diminutive of *daimon*, but the neuter of the adjective *daimonios*, pertaining to a demon, is also mistranslated "devil," "devils." In Acts 17:18, it denotes an inferior pagan deity. "Demons" are the spiritual agents acting in all idolatry. The idol itself is nothing, but every idol has a "demon" associated with it who induces idolatry, with its worship and sacrifices, 1 Cor. 10:20-21; **Rev. 9:20**; cf. Deut. 32:17; Isa. 13:21; 34:14; 65:3, 11. They disseminate errors among men, and seek to seduce believers, 1 Tim. 4:1. As seducing spirits they deceive men into the supposition that through mediums (those who have "familiar spirits," Lev. 20:6, 27, e.g.) they can converse with deceased human beings. Hence the destructive deception of spiritism, forbidden in Scripture, Lev. 19:31; Deut. 18:11; Isa. 8:19. "Demons" tremble before God, Jas. 2:19; they recognized Christ as Lord and as their future Judge, Matt. 8:29; Luke 4:41. Christ cast them out of human beings by His own power. His disciples did so in His name, and by exercising faith, e.g., Matt. 17:20. Acting under Satan (cf. **Rev. 16:13-14**), "demons" are permitted to afflict with bodily disease, Luke 13:16. Being unclean they tempt human beings with unclean thoughts, Matt. 10:1; Mark 5:2; 7:25; Luke 8:27-29; **Rev. 16:13**; **18:2**, e.g. They differ in degrees of wickedness, Matt. 12:45. They will instigate the rulers of the nations at the end of this age to make war against God and His Christ, **Rev. 16:14**.

Idols *eidolon* (1497), primarily "a phantom or likeness" (from *eidos*, "an appearance," lit., "that which is seen"), or "an idea, fancy," denotes in the NT (a) "an idol," an image to represent a false god, Acts 7:41; 1 Cor. 12:2; **Rev. 9:20**; (b) "the false god" worshipped in an image, Acts 15:20; Rom. 2:22; 1 Cor. 8:4, 7; 10:19; 2 Cor. 6:16; 1 Thess. 1:9; 1 John 5:21.

Silver *argureos* (693), signifies "made of silver," Acts 19:24; 2 Tim. 2:20; **Rev. 9:20**.

Brass *chalkeos* (5470), "made of brass or bronze," is used of idols, **Rev. 9:20**.

Stone *lithinos* (3035), "of stone," occurs in John 2:6; 2 Cor. 3:3; **Rev. 9:20**.

9:21 Neither repented they of their murders, nor of their sorceries, nor of their fornication, nor of their thefts.

Repented *see* **Repent** at *Revelation 2:5*.

Murders *phonos* (5408), is used (a) of a special act, Mark 15:7; Luke 23:19, 25; (b) in the plural, of "murders" in general, Matt. 15:19; Mark 7:21 (Gal. 5:21, in some inferior mss.); **Rev. 9:21**; in the singular, Rom. 1:29; (c) in the sense of "slaughter," Heb. 11:37, "they were slain with the sword," lit., "(they died by) slaughter (of the sword)"; in Acts 9:1, "slaughter."

Sorceries *pharmakia* (or *-eia*) (5331), (Eng., "pharmacy," etc.) primarily signified "the use of medicine, drugs, spells"; then, "poisoning"; then, "sorcery," Gal. 5:20, RV, "sorcery" (KJV, "witchcraft"), mentioned as one of "the works of the flesh." See also **Rev. 9:21**; **18:23**. In the Sept., Ex. 7:11, 22; 8:7, 18; Isa. 47:9, 12. In "sorcery," the use of drugs, whether simple or potent, was generally accompanied by incantations and appeals to occult powers, with the provision of various charms, amulets, etc., professedly designed to keep the applicant or patient from the attention and power of demons, but actually to impress the applicant with the mysterious resources and powers of the sorcerer.

Fornication *see Revelation 2:21*.

Thefts *klemma* (2809), "a thing stolen," and so, "a theft," is used in the plural in **Rev. 9:21**. In the Sept., Gen. 31:39; Ex. 22:3, 4.

Chapter 10

10:1 And I saw another mighty angel come down from heaven, clothed with a cloud: and a rainbow *was* upon his head, and his face *was* as it were the sun, and his feet as pillars of fire:

Mighty *see* Strong at *Revelation 5:2*.

Cloud *see* Clouds at *Revelation 1:7*.

Rainbow *see Revelation 4:3*.

Sun *see Revelation 1:16*.

Pillars *see* Pillar at *Revelation 3:12*.

Fire *see Revelation 1:14*.

10:2 And he had in his hand a little book open: and he set his right foot upon the sea, and *his* left *foot* on the earth,

Book *biblaridion* (974), is always rendered "little book," in **Rev. 10:2, 9-10**. Some texts have it also in verse **8**, instead of *biblion*.

Set *tithemi* (5087), "to put, to place," is translated "to set" in Acts 1:7, of times and seasons (KJV, "put"); Acts 13:47; **Rev. 10:2**; "setteth on" (of wine) in John 2:10, RV (KJV, "doth set forth"); in the KJV of Mark 4:21 (2nd part) and in Luke 8:16 it is rendered "set" (RV, "put"), of a lamp. In Mark 4:30 it is used of "setting" forth by parable the teaching concerning the kingdom of God, RV, "shall we set (it) forth" (KJV, "compare").

Left *euonumos* (2176), lit., "of good name," or "omen" (*eu*, "well," *onoma*, "a name"), a word adopted to avoid the ill-omen attaching to the "left" (omens from the "left" being unlucky, but a good name being desired for them, cf. *aristeros*, lit., "better of two," euphemistic for the ill-omened *laios* and *skaios*; cf, too, the Eng., "sinister," from the Latin word meaning "left"), is used euphemistically, either (a) simply as an adjective in **Rev. 10:2**, of the "left" foot; in Acts 21:3, "on the left" (lit., "left"); or (b) with the preposition *ex* (for *ek*), signifying "on the left hand," Matt. 20:21, 23; 25:33, 41; 27:38; Mark 10:40; 15:27.

10:3 And cried with a loud voice, as *when* a lion roareth: and when he had cried, seven thunders uttered their voices.

Loud *see Revelation 5:2*.

Lion *see Revelation 4:7*.

Roareth *mukaomai* (3455), properly of oxen, an onomatopoeic word, "to low, bellow," is used of a lion, **Rev. 10:3**.

Thunders *see* Thunderings at *Revelation 4:5*.

Uttered *laleo* (2980), "to speak," is rendered "to utter" in 2 Cor. 12:4 and **Rev. 10:3, 4** (twice).

10:4 And when the seven thunders had uttered their voices, I was about to write: and I heard a voice from heaven saying unto me, Seal up those things which the seven thunders uttered, and write them not.

Thunders *see* Thunderings at *Revelation 4:5*.

Uttered *see Revelation 10:3*.

Seal *see Revelation 7:2*.

10:5 And the angel which I saw stand upon the sea and upon the earth lifted up his hand to heaven,

Lifted *airo* (142), signifies (a) "to raise take up, lift, draw up," (b) "to bear, carry," (c) "to take or carry away." It is used of "lifting" up the voice, Luke 17:13; Acts 4:24; eyes, John 11:41; hand, **Rev. 10:5**.

10:6 And sware by him that liveth for ever and ever, who created heaven, and the things that therein are, and the earth, and the things that therein are, and the sea, and the things which are therein, that there should be time no longer:

Sware *omnumi or omnuo* (3660), is used of "affirming or denying by an oath," e.g., Matt. 26:74; Mark 6:23; Luke 1:73; Heb. 3:11, 18; 4:3; 7:21; accompanied by that by which one swears, e.g., Matt. 5:34, 36; 23:16; Heb. 6:13, 16; Jas. 5:12; **Rev. 10:6**.

Created *see Revelation 4:11*.

Heaven *see Revelation 3:12*.

Time *see* Season at *Revelation 6:11*. In **Rev. 10:6**, *chronos* is translated "delay" in RV marg., and is to be taken as the true meaning.

10:7 But in the days of the voice of the seventh angel, when he shall begin to sound, the mystery of God should be finished, as he hath declared to his servants the prophets.

Seventh *see Revelation 8:1*.

Begin *mello* (3195), "to be about to," is rendered "begin" in the KJV of **Rev. 10:7**; RV suitably, "when he is about to sound."

Sound *see Revelation 8:6*.

Mystery *see Revelation 1:20*.

Declared *euangelizo* (2097), "to bring or announce glad tidings" (Eng., "evangelize"), is used (a) in the active voice in **Rev. 10:7** ("declared") and **14:6** ("to proclaim," RV, KJV, "to preach"); (b) in the passive voice, of matters to be proclaimed as "glad tidings," Luke 16:16; Gal. 1:11; 1 Pet. 1:25; of persons to whom the proclamation is made, Matt. 11:5; Luke 7:22; Heb. 4:2, 6; 1 Pet. 4:6; (c) in the middle voice, especially of the message of salvation, with a personal object, either of the person preached, e.g., Acts 5:42; 11:20; Gal. 1:16, or, with a preposition, of the persons evangelized, e.g., Acts 13:32, "declare glad tidings"; Rom. 1:15; Gal. 1:8; with an impersonal object, e.g., "the word," Acts 8:4; "good tidings," 8:12; "the word of the Lord," 15:35; "the gospel," 1 Cor. 15:1; 2 Cor. 11:7; "the faith," Gal. 1:23; "peace," Eph. 2:17; "the unsearchable riches of Christ, 3:8.

Finished *teleo* (5055), "to finish, to bring to an end" (*telos*, "an end"), frequently signifies, not merely to terminate a thing, but to carry out a thing to the full. It is used especially in Revelation, where it occurs eight times, and is rendered "finish" in **10:7**; **11:7**, and in the RV of **15:1**, which rightly translates it "(in them) is finished (the wrath of God)." So in v. **8**; in **17:17**, RV, "accomplish," and "finish" in **20:3**, **5**, **7**; in Luke 2:39, RV, "accomplish," for KJV, performed.

His These translate (a) forms of pronouns under he, (a frequent use: in 1 Pet. 2:24, "His own self"); the form *autou*, "his," becomes emphatic when placed between the article and the noun, e.g., 1 Thess. 2:19; Titus 3:5; Heb. 2:4; also, e.g., John 5:47; 9:28; 1 Cor. 10:28; 2 Cor. 8:9; 2 Tim. 2:26; Titus 3:7; 2 Pet. 1:16; (b) *heautou*, "of himself, his own"; the RV rightly puts "his own," for the KJV, "his," in Luke 11:21; 14:26; Rom. 4:19; 5:8, "His own (love)"; 1 Cor. 7:37; Gal. 6:8; Eph. 5:28, 33; 1 Thess. 2:11, 12; 4:4; in **Rev. 10:7** the change has not been made; it should read "his own servants"; (c) *idios*, "one's own," "his own," in the RV, in Matt. 22:5; John 5:18; 2 Pet. 2:16; in Matt. 25:15, it is rendered "his several"; in John 19:27, "his own home," lit., "his own things"; in 1 Tim. 6:15, RV, "its own (times)," referring to the future appearing of Christ; in Heb. 4:10 (end of verse), both KJV and RV have "his," where it should be "his own"; so in Acts 24:23, for KJV and RV, "his"; in 1 Cor. 7:7, RV, "his own," KJV, "his proper"; (d) in Acts 17:28, the genitive case of the definite article, "His (offspring)," lit., "of the" (i.e., the one referred to, namely, God).

10:8 And the voice which I heard from heaven spake unto me again, and said, Go *and* take the little book which is open in the hand of the angel which standeth upon the sea and upon the earth.

Go *hupago* (1517), "to go away or to go slowly away, to depart, withdraw oneself," often with the idea of going without noise or notice, is very frequent in the Gospels; elsewhere it is used in Jas. 2:16; 1 John 2:11; **Rev. 10:8**; **13:10**; **14:4**; **16:1**; **17:8**, **11**. It is frequently rendered "go your (thy) way."

Book *see Revelation 1:11.*

Open *see* Openeth at *Revelation 3:7.*

10:9 And I went unto the angel, and said unto him, Give me the little book. And he said unto me, Take *it*, and eat it up; and it shall make thy belly bitter, but it shall be in thy mouth sweet as honey.

Book *see Revelation 10:2.*

Eat *katesthio* and *kataphago* (2719), signifies (a) "to consume by eating, to devour," said of birds, Matt. 13:4; Mark 4:4; Luke 8:5; of the Dragon, **Rev. 12:4**; of a prophet, "eating" up a book, suggestive of spiritually "eating" and digesting its contents, **Rev. 10:9** (cf. Ezek. 2:8; 3:1-3; Jer. 15:16); (b) metaphorically, "to squander, to waste," Luke 15:30; "to consume" one's physical powers by emotion, John 2:17; "to devour" by forcible appropriation, as of widows' property, Matt. 23:14 (KJV only); Mark 12:40; "to demand maintenance," as false apostles did to the church at Corinth, 2 Cor. 11:20; "to exploit or prey on one another," Gal. 5:15, where "bite ... devour ... consume" form a climax, the first two describing a process, the last the act of swallowing down; to "destroy" by fire, **Rev. 11:5**; **20:9**.

Bitter *see Revelation 8:11.*

Sweet *glukus* (1099), (cf. Eng., "glycerine," "glucose"), occurs in Jas. 3:11, 12 (KJV, "fresh" in this verse); **Rev. 10:9**, **10**.

Honey *meli* (3192), occurs with the adjective *agrios*, "wild," in Matt. 3:4; Mark 1:6; in **Rev. 10:9**, **10**, as an example of sweetness. As "honey" is liable to ferment, it was precluded from offerings to God, Lev. 2:11. The liquid "honey" mentioned in Ps. 19:10 and Prov. 16:24 is regarded as the best; a cruse of it was part of the present brought to Ahijah by Jeroboam's wife, 1 Kings 14:3.

10:10 And I took the little book out of the angel's hand, and ate it up; and it was in my mouth sweet as honey: and as soon as I had eaten it, my belly was bitter.

Sweet *see Revelation 10:9.*

Honey *see Revelation 10:9.*

Bitter *see Revelation 8:11.*

10:11 And he said unto me, Thou must prophesy again before many peoples, and nations, and tongues, and kings.

Prophesy *see* Prophecy at *Revelation 1:3.*

Tongues *see* Tongue at Revelation 5:9.

Chapter 11

11:1 And there was given me a reed like unto a rod: and the angel stood, saying, Rise, and measure the temple of God, and the altar, and them that worship therein.

Reed *kalamos* (2563), denotes (a) "the reed" mentioned in Matt. 11:7; 12:20; Luke 7:24, the same as the Heb., *qaneh* (among the various reeds in the OT), e.g., Isa. 42:3, from which Matt. 12:20 is quoted (cf. Job 40:21; Ezek. 29:6, "a reed with jointed, hollow stalk"); (b) "a reed staff, staff," Matt. 27:29, 30, 48; Mark 15:19, 36 (cf. *rhabdos*, "a rod"; in 2 Kings 18:21, *rhabdos kalamine*); (c) "a measuring reed or rod," **Rev. 11:1; 21:15, 16**; (d) "a writing reed, a pen," 3 John 13.

Like unto *see* ***Revelation 1:13.***

Rod *see* ***Revelation 2:27.***

Rise *egeiro* (1453), is frequently used in the NT in the sense of "raising" (active voice), or "rising" (middle and passive voices): (a) from sitting, lying, sickness, e.g., Matt. 2:14; 9:5, 7, 19; Jas. 5:15; **Rev. 11:1**; (b) of causing to appear, or, in the passive, appearing, or raising up so as to occupy a place in the midst of people, Matt. 3:9; 11:11; Mark 13:22; Acts 13:22. It is thus said of Christ in Acts 13:23; (c) of rousing, stirring up, or "rising" against, Matt. 24:7; Mark 13:8; (d) of "raising buildings," John 2:19-20; (e) of "raising or rising" from the dead; (1) of Christ, Matt. 16:21; and frequently elsewhere (but not in Phil., 2 Thess., 1 Tim., Titus, Jas., 2 Pet., 1, 2, 3 John, and Jude); (2) of Christ's "raising" the dead, Matt. 11:5; Mark 5:41; Luke 7:14; John 12:1, 9, 17; (3) of the act of the disciples, Matt. 10:8; (4) of the resurrection of believers, Matt. 27:52; John 5:21; 1 Cor. 15:15-16, 29, 32, 35, 42-44 52; 2 Cor. 1:9; 4:14; of unbelievers, Matt. 12:42. *Egeiro* stands in contrast to *anistemi* (when used with reference to resurrection) in this respect, that *egeiro* is frequently used both in the transitive sense of "raising up" and the intransitive of "rising," whereas *anistemi* is comparatively infrequent in the transitive use.

Measure *metreo* (3354), "to measure," is used (a) of space, number, value, etc., **Rev. 11:1, 2; 21:15, 16, 17**; metaphorically, 2 Cor. 10:12; (b) in the sense of "measuring" out, giving by "measure," Matt. 7:2, "ye mete"; Mark 4:24; in some mss. in Luke 6:38.

11:2 But the court which is without the temple leave out, and measure it not; for it is given unto the Gentiles: and the holy city shall they tread under foot forty *and* two months.

Court *aule* (833), primarily, "an uncovered space around a house, enclosed by a wall, where the stables were," hence was used to describe (a) "the courtyard of a house"; in the OT it is used of the "courts" of the tabernacle and Temple; in this sense it is found in the NT in **Rev. 11:2**; (b) "the courts in the dwellings of well-to-do folk," which usually had two, one exterior, between the door and the street (called the *proaulion*, or "porch," Mark 14:68.), the other, interior, surrounded by the buildings of the dwellings, as in Matt. 26:69 (in contrast to the room where the judges were sitting); Mark 14:66; Luke 22:55; KJV, "hall"; RV "court" gives the proper significance, Matt. 26:3, 58; Mark 14:54; 15:16 (RV, "Praetorium"); Luke 11:21; John 18:15. It is here to be distinguished from the Praetorium, translated "palace." For the other meaning "sheepfold," John 10:1, 16.

Without This is a translation of *exothen*, "from without," or "without," e.g., Mark 7:15, 18; Luke 11:40; 2 Cor. 7:5; 1 Tim. 3:7; as a preposition, **Rev. 11:2**.

Leave *ekballo* (1544), "to cast out" (*ek*, "from," *ballo*, "to cast"), "to drive out," is used in the sense of "rejecting" or "leaving out," in **Rev. 11:2**, as to the measuring of the court of the Temple (marg., "cast without").

Measure *see* ***Revelation 11:1.***

Holy *see* ***Revelation 4:8.***

Tread *pateo* (3961), is used (a) intransitively and figuratively, of "treading" upon serpents, Luke 10:19; (b) transitively, of "treading" on, down or under, of the desecration of Jerusalem by its foes, Luke 21:24; **Rev. 11:2**; of the avenging, by the Lord in Person hereafter, of this desecration and of the persecution of the Jews, in divine retribution, metaphorically spoken of as the "treading" of the winepress of God's wrath, **Rev. 14:20; 19:15** (cf. Isa. 63:2, 3).

Months *see* ***Revelation 9:5.***

11:3 And I will give *power* unto my two witnesses, and they shall prophesy a thousand two hundred *and* threescore days, clothed in sackcloth.

Witnesses *see* **Witness** at ***Revelation 1:5.***

Prophesy *propheteuo* (4395), "to be a prophet, to prophesy," is used (a) with the primary meaning of telling forth the divine counsels, e.g., Matt. 7:22; 26:68; 1 Cor. 11:4, 5; 13:9; 14:1, 3-5, 24, 31, 39; **Rev. 11:3**; (b) of foretelling the future, e.g., Matt. 15:7; John 11:51; 1 Pet. 1:10; Jude 14. *See also* **Prophecy** at ***Revelation 1:3.***

Thousand *see* **Thousands** at ***Revelation 5:11.***

Two hundred *diakosioi* (1250), occurs in Mark 6:37; John 6:7; 21:8; Acts 23:23 (twice); 27:37, "two hundred (threescore and sixteen)"; **Rev. 11:3**, "(a thousand) two hundred (and threescore)"; so **12:6**.

Threescore *hexekonta* (1835), occurs in Matt. 13:8, RV (KJV, "sixty-fold"); 13:23; Mark 4:8, where the RV and KJV reverse the translation, as in Matt. 13:8, while in Mark 4:20 the RV has "sixtyfold," KJV, "sixty"; in **Rev. 13:18**, RV, "sixty" (KJV, "threescore"). It is rendered "threescore" in Luke 24:13; 1 Tim. 5:9; **Rev. 11:3; 12:6**.

Sackcloth *see Revelation 6:12*.

11:4 These are the two olive trees, and the two candlesticks standing before the God of the earth.

Olive trees *elaia* (1636), denotes (a) "an olive tree," Rom. 11:17, 24; **Rev. 11:4** (plural); the Mount of Olives was so called from the numerous olive trees there, and indicates the importance attached to such; the Mount is mentioned in the NT in connection only with the Lord's life on earth, Matt. 21:1; 24:3; 26:30; Mark 11:1; 13:3; 14:26; Luke 19:37; 22:39; John 8:1; (b) "an olive," Jas. 3:12, RV (KJV, "olive berries").

Candlesticks *see Revelation 1:12*.

11:5 And if any man will hurt them, fire proceedeth out of their mouth, and devoureth their enemies: and if any man will hurt them, he must in this manner be killed.

Hurt *see Revelation 2:11*.

Proceedeth *see* **Went** at *Revelation 1:16*.

Devoureth *see* **Eat** at *Revelation 10:9*.

Enemies *echthros* (2190), an adjective, primarily denoting "hated" or "hateful" (akin to *echthos*, "hate"; perhaps associated with *ekos*, "outside"), hence, in the active sense, denotes "hating, hostile"; it is used as a noun signifying an "enemy," adversary, and is said (a) of the Devil, Matt. 13:39; Luke 10:19; (b) of death, 1 Cor. 15:26; (c) of the professing believer who would be a friend of the world, thus making himself an enemy of God, Jas. 4:4; (d) of men who are opposed to Christ, Matt. 13:25, 28; 22:44; Mark 12:36; Luke 19:27; 20:43; Acts 2:35; Rom. 11:28; Phil. 3:18; Heb. 1:13; 10:13; or to His servants, **Rev. 11:5, 12**; to the nation of Israel, Luke 1:71, 74; 19:43; (e) of one who is opposed to righteousness, Acts 13:10; (f) of Israel in its alienation from God, Rom. 11:28; (g) of the unregenerate in their attitude toward God, Rom. 5:10; Col. 1:21; (h) of believers in their former state, 2 Thess. 3:15; (i) of foes, Matt. 5:43-44; 10:36; Luke 6:27, 35; Rom. 12:20; 1 Cor. 15:25; of the apostle Paul because he told converts "the truth," Gal. 4:16. Cf. *echthra*, "enmity".

Manner *houtos* or *houto* (3779), "thus, in this way," is rendered "after this manner" in Matt. 6:9; 1 Pet. 3:5; **Rev. 11:5**.

11:6 These have power to shut heaven, that it rain not in the days of their prophecy: and have power over waters to turn them to blood, and to smite the earth with all plagues, as often as they will.

Shut *see* **Shutteth** at *Revelation 3:7*.

Rain *huetos* (5205), from *huo*, "to rain," is used especially, but not entirely, of "showers," and is found in Acts 14:17; 28:2; Heb. 6:7; Jas. 5:7; 5:18; **Rev. 11:6**. *Brecho* (1026), signifies (a) "to wet," Luke 7:38, 44, RV (KJV, "to wash); (b) "to send rain," Matt. 5:45; to rain, Luke 17:29 (of fire and brimstone); Jas. 5:17, used impersonally (twice); **Rev. 11:6**, where *huetos* is used as the subject, lit., "(that) rain rain (not)."

Prophecy *see Revelation 1:3*.

Turn *strepho* (4762), denotes (1) in the active voice, (a) "to turn" (something), Matt. 5:39; (b) "to bring back," Matt. 27:3 (in the best texts); (c) reflexively, "to turn oneself, to turn the back to people," said of God, Acts 7:42; (d) "to turn one thing into another," **Rev. 11:6** (the only place where this word occurs after the Acts); (2) in the passive voice, (a) used reflexively, "to turn oneself," e.g. Matt. 7:6; John 20:14, 16; (b) metaphorically, Matt. 18:3, RV, "(except) ye turn" (KJV, "... be converted"); John 12:40 (in the best texts).

Smite *patasso* (3960), "to strike, smite," is used (I) literally, of giving a blow with the hand, or fist or a weapon, Matt. 26:51, RV, "smote" (KJV, "struck"); Luke 22:49, 50; Acts 7:24; 12:7; (II) metaphorically, (a) of judgment meted out to Christ, Matt. 26:31; Mark 14:27; (b) of the infliction of disease, by an angel, Acts 12:23; of plagues to be inflicted upon men by two divinely appointed witnesses, **Rev. 11:6**; (c) of judgment to be executed by Christ upon the nations, **Rev. 19:15**, the instrument being His Word, described as a sword.

Plagues *see Revelation 9:20*.

Often *hosakis* (3740), a relative adverb, "as often" (or oft) as, 1 Cor. 11:25-26; **Rev. 11:6**.

11:7 And when they shall have finished their testimony, the beast that ascendeth out of the bottomless pit shall make war against them, and shall overcome them, and kill them.

Finished *see Revelation 10:7.*

Beast *therion* (2342), to be distinguished from *zoon*, almost invariably denotes "a wild beast." In Acts 28:4, "venomous beast" is used of the viper which fastened on Paul's hand. *Zoon* stresses the vital element, *therion* the bestial. The idea of a "beast" of prey is not always present. Once, in Heb. 12:20, it is used of the animals in the camp of Israel, such, e.g., as were appointed for sacrifice: But in the Sept. *therion* is never used of sacrificial animals; the word *ktenos* is reserved for these. *Therion*, in the sense of wild "beast," is used in Revelation for the two antichristian potentates who are destined to control the affairs of the nations with Satanic power in the closing period of the present era, **11:7; 13:1-18; 14:9, 11; 15:2; 16:2, 10, 13; 17:3-17; 19:19-20; 20:4, 10.**

Bottomless *see Revelation 9:1.*

War *see* **Battle** at *Revelation 9:7.*

Overcome *see* **Overcometh at** *Revelation 2:7.*

11:8 And their dead bodies *shall lie* in the street of the great city, which spiritually is called Sodom and Egypt, where also our Lord was crucified.

Bodies *ptoma* (4430), denotes, lit., "a fall" (akin to *pipto*, "to fall"); hence, "that which is fallen, a corpse," Matt. 14:12; 24:28, "carcase"; Mark 6:29; 15:45, "corpse"; **Rev. 11:8-9**, "dead bodies" (Gk., "carcase," but plural in the 2nd part of v. **9**).

Street *plateia* (4113), grammatically the feminine of *platus*, "broad," is used as a noun (*hodos*, "a way," being understood, i.e., "a broad way"), "a street," Matt. 6:5; 12:19 (in some texts, Mark 6:56); Luke 10:10; 13:26; 14:21; Acts 5:15; **Rev. 11:8; 21:21; 22:2.**

Spiritually *pneumatikos* (4153), "spiritually," occurs in 1 Cor. 2:14, and **Rev. 11:8**. Some mss. have it in 1 Cor. 2:13.

11:9 And they of the people and kindreds and tongues and nations shall see their dead bodies three days and an half, and shall not suffer their dead bodies to be put in graves.

People *see Revelation 5:9.*

Kindreds *see Revelation 1:7.*

Tongues *see* **Tongue** at *Revelation 5:9.*

See *blepo* (991), primarily, "to have sight, to see," then, "observe, discern, perceive," frequently implying special contemplation, is rendered by the verb "to look" in Luke 9:62, "looking (back)"; John 13:22 "(the disciples) looked (one on another)"; Acts 1:9, RV, "were looking" (KJV, "beheld"); 3:4, "look (on us)"; 27:12, RV, "looking," KJV, "that lieth (towards)," of the haven Phenix; Eph. 5:15, RV, "look (therefore carefully how ye walk)," KJV, "see (that ye walk circumspectly)"; **Rev. 11:9** and **18:9**, RV, "look upon" (KJV, "shall see").

Bodies *see Revelation 11:8.*

Half *hemisus* (2255), an adjective, is used (a) as such in the neuter plural, in Luke 19:8, lit., "the halves (of my goods)"; (b) as a noun, in the neuter sing., "the half," Mark 6:23; "half (a time)," **Rev. 12:14**; "a half," **11:9, 11**, RV.

Suffer *aphiemi* (863), "to send away," signifies "to permit, suffer," in Matt. 3:15 (twice); Matt. 19:14; 23:13; Mark 1:34; 5:19, 37; 10:14; 11:16; Luke 8:51; 12:39, KJV (RV, "left"); 18:16; John 12:7, RV, KJV and RV marg., "let (her) alone"; **Rev. 11:9.**

Put *tithemi* (5087), "to place, lay, set, put," is translated "to put" in Matt. 5:15; 12:18; in Matt. 22:44, RV, "put (underneath Thy feet)"; Mark 4:21 (1st part), in the 2nd part, RV, "put" (in some texts, KJV, "set"); 10:16, KJV (RV, "laying"); Luke 8:16 (1st part); 2nd part, RV (KJV, "setteth"); 11:33; John 19:19; Acts 1:7, KJV (RV, "set"); 4:3; 5:18, 25; 12:4; Rom. 14:13; 1 Cor. 15:25; 2 Cor. 3:13; 1 Tim. 1:12, KJV (RV, "appointing"); **Rev. 11:9**, KJV (RV, "laid"). *See also* **Laid** at *Revelation 1:17.*

Graves *mnema* (3418), signified "a memorial" or "record of a thing or a dead person," then "a sepulchral monument," and hence "a tomb"; it is rendered "graves" in the KJV of **Rev. 11:9** (RV, "a tomb"); "tomb" or "tombs," Mark 5:3, 5; and 16:2 (KJV, "sepulchre"); Luke 8:27; Acts 2:29 and 7:16 (KJV, "sepulchre").

11:10 And they that dwell upon the earth shall rejoice over them, and make merry, and shall send gifts one to another; because these two prophets tormented them that dwelt on the earth.

Send *see Revelation 1:11.*

Merry *euphraino* (2165), in the active voice, "to cheer, make glad," 2 Cor. 2:2, is used everywhere else in the passive voice, signifying, "to be happy, rejoice, make merry," and translated "to be merry" in Luke 12:19; 15:23, 24, 29, 32; in 16:19, "fared (sumptuously)"; in **Rev. 11:10**, make merry.

Gifts *doron* (1435), akin to *didomi*, "to give," is used (a) of "gifts" presented as an expression of honor, Matt. 2:11; (b) of "gifts" for the support of the temple and the needs of the poor, Matt. 15:5; Mark 7:11; Luke 21:1, 4; (c) of "gifts" offered to God, Matt. 5:23, 24; 8:4; 23:18, 19; Heb. 5:1; 8:3, 4; 9:9; 11:4; (d) of salvation by grace as the "gift" of God, Eph.

2:8; (e) of "presents" for mutual celebration of an occasion, **Rev. 11:10.**

Prophets *prophetes* (4396), "one who speaks forth or openly", "a proclaimer of a divine message," denoted among the Greeks an interpreter of the oracles of the gods. In the Sept. it is the translation of the word *roeh*, "a seer"; 1 Sam. 9:9, indicating that the "prophet" was one who had immediate intercourse with God. It also translates the word *nabhi*, meaning "either one in whom the message from God springs forth" or "one to whom anything is secretly communicated." Hence, in general, "the prophet" was one upon whom the Spirit of God rested, Num. 11:17-29, one, to whom and through whom God speaks, Num. 12:2; Amos 3:7, 8. In the case of the OT prophets their messages were very largely the proclamation of the divine purposes of salvation and glory to be accomplished in the future; the "prophesying" of the NT "prophets" was both a preaching of the divine counsels of grace already accomplished and the foretelling of the purposes of God in the future. In the NT the word is used (a) of "the OT prophets," e.g., Matt. 5:12; Mark 6:15; Luke 4:27; John 8:52; Rom. 11:3; (b) of "prophets in general," e.g., Matt. 10:41; 21:46; Mark 6:4; (c) of "John the Baptist," Matt. 21:26; Luke 1:76; (d) of "prophets in the churches," e.g., Acts 13:1; 15:32; 21:10; 1 Cor. 12:28, 29; 14:29, 32, 37; Eph. 2:20; 3:5; 4:11; (e) of "Christ, as the aforepromised Prophet," e.g., John 1:21; 6:14; 7:40; Acts 3:22; 7:37, or, without the article, and, without reference to the Old Testament, Mark 6:15; Luke 7:16; in Luke 24:19 it is used with *aner*, "a man"; John 4:19; 9:17; (f) of "two witnesses" yet to be raised up for special purposes, **Rev. 11:10, 18**; (g) of "the Cretan poet Epimenides," Titus 1:12; (h) by metonymy, of "the writings of prophets," e.g., Luke 24:27; Acts 8:28.

Tormented *see Revelation 9:5.*

11:11 And after three days and an half the Spirit of life from God entered into them, and they stood upon their feet; and great fear fell upon them which saw them.

Half *see Revelation 11:9.*

Spirit *pneuma* (4151), "spirit," also denotes "breath," **Rev. 11:11** and **13:15**, RV. In 2 Thess. 2:8, the KJV has "spirit" for RV, breath. *See also Revelation 1:10.*

Fear *phobos* (5401), first had the meaning of "flight," that which is caused by being scared; then, "that which may cause flight," (a) "fear, dread, terror," always with this significance in the four Gospels; also, e.g., in Acts 2:43; 19:17; 1 Cor. 2:3; 1 Tim. 5:20 (lit., "may have fear"); Heb. 2:15; 1 John 4:18; **Rev. 11:11; 18:10, 15**; by metonymy, that which causes "fear," Rom. 13:3; 1 Pet. 3:14, RV, "(their) fear," KJV "(their) terror," an adaptation of the Sept. of Isa. 8:12, "fear not their fear"; hence some take it to mean, as there, "what they fear," but in view of Matt. 10:28, e.g., it seems best to understand it as that which is caused by the intimidation of adversaries; (b) "reverential fear," (1) of God, as a controlling motive of the life, in matters spiritual and moral, not a mere "fear" of His power and righteous retribution, but a wholesome dread of displeasing Him, a "fear" which banishes the terror that shrinks from His presence, Rom. 8:15, and which influences the disposition and attitude of one whose circumstances are guided by trust in God, through the indwelling Spirit of God, Acts 9:31; Rom. 3:18; 2 Cor. 7:1; Eph. 5:21 (RV, "the fear of Christ"); Phil. 2:12; 1 Pet. 1:17 (a comprehensive phrase: the reverential "fear" of God will inspire a constant carefulness in dealing with others in His "fear"); 3:2, 15; the association of "fear and trembling," as, e.g., in Phil. 2:12, has in the Sept. a much sterner import, e.g., Gen. 9:2; Exod. 15:16; Deut. 2:25; 11:25; Ps. 55:5; Isa. 19:16; (2) of superiors, e.g., Rom. 13:7; 1 Pet. 2:18.

Fell *epipipto* (1968), "to fall upon," is used (a) literally, Mark 3:10, "pressed upon"; Acts 20:10, 37; (b) metaphorically, of fear, Luke 1:12; Acts 19:17; **Rev. 11:11**; reproaches, Rom. 15:3; of the Holy Spirit, Acts 8:16; 10:44; 11:15.

11:12 And they heard a great voice from heaven saying unto them, Come up hither. And they ascended up to heaven in a cloud; and their enemies beheld them.

Cloud *see* **Clouds** at *Revelation 1:7.*

Enemies *see Revelation 11:5.*

11:13 And the same hour was there a great earthquake, and the tenth part of the city fell, and in the earthquake were slain of men seven thousand: and the remnant were affrighted, and gave glory to the God of heaven.

Hour *see Revelation 3:3.*

Earthquake *see Revelation 6:12.*

Tenth *dekatos* (1182), an adjective from *deka*, "ten," occurs in John 1:39; **Rev. 11:13; 21:20.**

Slain *see Revelation 2:13.*

Men *anthropos* (444), a generic name for man, is translated "persons" in **Rev. 11:13**, RV (KJV, "men").

Remnant *loipos* (3062), an adjective (akin to *leipo*, "to leave") signifying "remaining," is used as a noun and translated "the rest" in the RV, where the KJV has "the remnant," Matt. 22:6; **Rev. 11:13**; **12:17**; **19:21**.

Affrighted *emphobos* (1719), lit., "in fear" (*en*, "in," *phobos*, "fear"), means "affrighted," Luke 24:5, RV (KJV "afraid"); 24:37; Acts 10:4, RV (KJV, "afraid"); **Rev. 11:13**. The RV omits it in Acts 22:9.

Heaven *see Revelation 3:12.*

11:14 The second woe is past; *and*, behold, the third woe cometh quickly.

Woe *see Revelation 8:13.*

Past *see Revelation 9:12.*

Quickly *see Revelation 2:5.*

11:15 And the seventh angel sounded; and there were great voices in heaven, saying, The kingdoms of this world are become *the kingdoms* of our Lord, and of his Christ; and he shall reign for ever and ever.

Seventh *see Revelation 8:1.*

Sounded *see* Sound at *Revelation 8:6.*

Kingdoms *see* Kingdom at *Revelation 1:9.*

Reign *see Revelation 5:10.*

11:16 And the four and twenty elders, which sat before God on their seats, fell upon their faces, and worshipped God,

Elders *see Revelation 4:4.*

Seats *see* Throne at *Revelation 1:4.*

Worshipped *see* Worship at *Revelation 4:10.*

11:17 Saying, We give thee thanks, O Lord God Almighty, which art, and wast, and art to come; because thou hast taken to thee thy great power, and hast reigned.

Thanks *eucharisteo* (2168), "to give thanks," (a) is said of Christ, Matt. 15:36; 26:27; Mark 8:6; 14:23; Luke 22:17, 19; John 6:11, 23; 11:41; 1 Cor. 11:24; (b) of the Pharisee in Luke 18:11 in his selfcomplacent prayer; (c) is used by Paul at the beginning of all his epistles, except 2 Cor. (see, however, *eulogetos* in 1:3), Gal., 1 Tim., 2 Tim. (see, however, *charin echo*, 1:3), and Titus, (1) for his readers, Rom. 1:8; Eph. 1:16; Col. 1:3; 1 Thess. 1:2; 2 Thess. 1:3 (cf. 2:13); virtually so in Philem. 4; (2) for fellowship shown, Phil. 1:3; (3) for God's gifts to them, 1 Cor. 1:4; (d) is recorded (1) of Paul elsewhere, Acts 27:35; 28:15; Rom. 7:25; 1 Cor. 1:14; 14:18; (2) of Paul and others, Rom. 16:4; 1 Thess. 2:13; of himself, representatively, as a practice, 1 Cor. 10:30; (3) of others, Luke 17:16; Rom. 14:6 (twice); 1 Cor. 14:17; **Rev. 11:17**; (e) is used in admonitions to the saints, the Name of the Lord Jesus suggesting His character and example, Eph. 5:20; Col. 1:12; 3:17; 1 Thess. 5:18; (f) as the expression of a purpose, 2 Cor. 1:11, RV; (g) negatively of the ungodly, Rom. 1:21. "Thanksgiving" is the expression of joy Godward, and is therefore the fruit of the Spirit (Gal. 5:22); believers are encouraged to abound in it (e.g., Col. 2:7).

Which *see Revelation 1:4.*

Taken *see* Take at *Revelation 6:4.*

Reigned *see* Reign at *Revelation 5:10.*

11:18 And the nations were angry, and thy wrath is come, and the time of the dead, that they should be judged, and that thou shouldest give reward unto thy servants the prophets, and to the saints, and them that fear thy name, small and great; and shouldest destroy them which destroy the earth.

> *"If you do not wish for His kingdom, don't pray for it. But if you do, you must do more than pray for it; you must work for it."*
>
> JOHN RUSKIN

Angry *orgizo* (3710), "to provoke, to arouse to anger," always in the middle or passive voice in the NT, is rendered "was (were) wroth" in Matt. 18:34; 22:7; **Rev. 11:18**, RV, (KJV, were angry); **12:17**, RV, "waxed wroth."

Reward *misthos* (3408), primarily "wages, hire," and then, generally, "reward," (a) received in this life, Matt. 5:46; 6:2, 5, 16; Rom. 4:4; 1 Cor. 9:17, 18; of evil "rewards," Acts 1:18; (b) to be received hereafter, Matt. 5:12; 10:41 (twice), 42; Mark 9:41; Luke 6:23, 35; 1 Cor. 3:8, 14; 2 John 8; **Rev. 11:18**; **22:12**.

Prophets *see Revelation 11:10.*

Small *mikros* (3398), "little, small" (of age, quantity, size, space), is translated "small" in Acts 26:22; **Rev. 11:18**; **13:16**; **19:5**, **18**; **20:12**. *See also* Little at *Revelation 3:8.*

Destroy *see* Destroyed at *Revelation 8:9.*

11:19 And the temple of God was opened in heaven, and there was seen in his temple the ark of his testament: and there were lightnings, and

voices, and thunderings, and an earthquake, and great hail.

Temple *see Revelation 3:12.*

Ark *kibotos* (2787), "a wooden box, a chest," is used of (a) Noah's vessel, Matt. 24:38; Luke 17:27; Heb. 11:7; 1 Pet. 3:20; (b) the "ark" of the covenant in the tabernacle, Heb. 9:4; (c) the "ark" seen in vision in the heavenly temple, **Rev. 11:19**.

Testament *diatheke* (1242), primarily signifies "a disposition of property by will or otherwise."

"The NT uses of the word may be analyzed as follows: (a) a promise or undertaking, human or divine, Gal. 3:15; (b) a promise or undertaking on the part of God, Luke 1:72; Acts 3:25; Rom. 9:4; 11:27; Gal. 3:17Eph. 2:12; Heb. 7:22; 8:6, 8, 10; 10:16; (c) an agreement, a mutual undertaking, between God and Israel, see Deut. 29-30 (described as a 'commandment,' Heb. 7:18, cf. v. 22); Heb. 8:9; 9:20; (d) by metonymy, the token of the covenant, or promise, made to Abraham, Acts 7:8, (e) by metonymy, the record of the covenant, 2 Cor. 3:14; Heb. 9:4; cf. **Rev. 11:19**; (f) the basis, established by the death of Christ, on which the salvation of men is secured, Matt. 26:28; Mark 14:24; Luke 22:20; 1 Cor. 11:25; 2 Cor. 3:6; Heb. 10:29; 12:24; 13:20. This covenant is called the 'new,' Heb. 9:15, the 'second,' 8:7, the 'better,' 7:22. In Heb. 9:16-17, the translation is much disputed. There does not seem to be any sufficient reason for departing in these verses from the word used everywhere else. The English word 'Testament' is taken from the titles prefixed to the Latin Versions."

Lightnings *see Revelation 4:5.*

Thunderings *see Revelation 4:5.*

Earthquake *see Revelation 6:12.*

Hail *see Revelation 8:7.*

Chapter 12

12:1 And there appeared a great wonder in heaven; a woman clothed with the sun, and the moon under her feet, and upon her head a crown of twelve stars:

Wonder *semeion* (4592), "a sign, mark, indication, token," is used (a) of that which distinguished a person or thing from others, e.g., Matt. 26:48; Luke 2:12; Rom. 4:11; 2 Cor. 12:12 (1st part); 2 Thess. 3:17, "token," i.e., his autograph attesting the authenticity of his letters; (b) of a "sign" as a warning or admonition, e.g., Matt. 12:39, "the sign of (i.e., consisting of) the prophet Jonas"; 16:4; Luke 2:34; 11:29, 30; (c) of miraculous acts (1) as tokens of divine authority and power, e.g., Matt. 12:38, 39 (1st part); John 2:11, RV, "signs"; 3:2 (ditto); 4:54, "(the second) sign," RV; 10:41 (ditto); 20:30; in 1 Cor. 1:22, "the Jews ask for signs," RV, indicates that the Apostles were met with the same demand from Jews as Christ had been: "signs were vouchsafed in plenty, signs of God's power and love, but these were not the signs which they sought.... They wanted signs of an outward Messianic Kingdom, of temporal triumph, of material greatness for the chosen people.... With such cravings the Gospel of a 'crucified Messiah' was to them a stumbling-block indeed" (Lightfoot); 1 Cor. 14:22; (2) by demons, **Rev. 16:14**; (3) by false teachers or prophets, indications of assumed authority, e.g., Matt. 24:24; Mark 13:22; (4) by Satan through his special agents, 2 Thess. 2:9; **Rev. 13:13, 14; 19:20**; (d) of tokens portending future events, e.g., Matt. 24:3, where "the sign of the Son of Man" signifies, subjectively, that the Son of Man is Himself the "sign" of what He is about to do; Mark 13:4; Luke 21:7, 11, 25; Acts 2:19; **Rev. 12:1**, RV; **12:3**, RV; **15:1**. "Signs" confirmatory of what God had accomplished in the atoning sacrifice of Christ, His resurrection and ascension, and of the sending of the Holy Spirit, were given to the Jews for their recognition, as at Pentecost, and supernatural acts by apostolic ministry, as well as by the supernatural operations in the churches, such as the gift of tongues and prophesyings; there is no record of the continuance of these latter after the circumstances recorded in Acts 19:1-20.

Sun *see Revelation 1:16.*

Moon *see Revelation 6:12.*

Under *see Revelation 5:3.*

Crown *see Revelation 2:10.*

Twelve *see Revelation 7:5.*

Stars *see Revelation 1:16.*

12:2 And she being with child cried, travailing in birth, and pained to be delivered.

Travailing *odino* (5605), is used negatively in Gal. 4:27, "(thou) that travailest (not)," quoted from Isa. 54:1; the apostle applies the circumstances of Sarah and Hagar (which doubtless Isaiah was recalling) to show that, whereas the promise by grace had temporarily been replaced by the works of the Law (see Gal. 3:17), this was now reversed, and, in the fulfillment of the promise to Abraham, the number of those saved by the gospel would far exceed those who owned allegiance to the Law. Isa. 54 has primary reference to the future prosperity of Israel restored to God's favor, but frequently the principles underlying events recorded in the OT extend beyond their immediate application. In 4:19 the apostle uses it metaphorically of a second travailing on his part regarding the churches of Galatia; his first was for their deliverance from idolatry (v. 8), now it was for their deliverance from bondage to Judaism. There is no suggestion here of a second regeneration necessitated by defection. There is a hint of reproach, as if he was enquiring whether they had ever heard of a mother experiencing second birth pangs for her children. In **Rev. 12:2** the woman is figurative of Israel; the circumstances of her birth pangs are mentioned in Isa. 66:7 (see also Micah 5:2, 3). Historically the natural order is reversed. The Manchild, Christ, was brought forth at His first advent; the travail is destined to take place in "the time of Jacob's trouble," the "great tribulation," Matt. 24:21; **Rev. 7:14.** The object in **12:2** in referring to the birth of Christ is to connect Him with His earthly people Israel in their future time of trouble, from which the godly remnant, the nucleus of the restored nation, is to be delivered (Jer. 30:7).

Pained *bosanizo* (928), primarily signifies "to rub on the touchstone, to put to the test" (from *basanos*, "a touchstone," a dark stone used in testing metals); hence, "to examine by torture," and, in general, "to distress"; in **Rev. 12:2**, "in pain," RV (KJV, "pained"), in connection with parturition. (In the Sept., 1 Sam. 5:3.).

Delivered *tikto* (5088), "to bring forth," Luke 1:57; John 16:21; Heb. 11:11; **Rev. 12:2, 4**, or, "to be born," said of the Child, Matt. 2:2; Luke 2:11, is used metaphorically in Jas. 1:15, of lust as bringing forth sin.

12:3 And there appeared another wonder in heaven; and behold a great red dragon, having seven heads and ten horns, and seven crowns upon his heads.

Wonder *see Revelation 12:1.*

Red *see Revelation 6:4.*

Dragon *drakon* (1404), denoted "a mythical monster, a dragon"; also a large serpent, so called because of its keen power of sight (from a root *derk-*, signifying "to see"). Twelve times in Revelation it is used of the Devil **12:3-4, 7, 9, 13, 16-17; 13:2, 4, 11; 16:13; 20:2.**

Ten *see Revelation 2:10.*

Horns *see Revelation 5:6.*

Crowns *diadema* (1238), is never used as *stephanos* is; it is always the symbol of kingly or imperial dignity, and is translated "diadem" instead of "crown" in the RV, of the claims of the Dragon, **Rev. 12:3; 13:1; 19:12.**

12:4 And his tail drew the third part of the stars of heaven, and did cast them to the earth: and the dragon stood before the woman which was ready to be delivered, for to devour her child as soon as it was born.

Tail *see* Tails at *Revelation 9:10.*

Drew *suro* (4951), "to draw, drag, haul," is used of a net, John 21:8; of violently "dragging" persons along, Acts 8:3, "haling"; 14:19, RV, "dragged," KJV, "drew"; 17:6 (ditto); **Rev. 12:4**, KJV, "drew," RV, "draweth."

Stars *see Revelation 1:16.*

Dragon *see Revelation 12:3.*

Stood *steko* (4739), a late present tense from *hesteka*, the perfect of *histemi*, is used (a) literally, Mark 3:31; 11:25; John 1:26, in the best texts (in some texts **Rev. 12:4**); (b) figuratively, Rom. 14:4, where the context indicates the meaning "standeth upright" rather than that of acquittal; of "standing fast," 1 Cor. 16:13, "in the faith," i.e., by adherence to it; Gal. 5:1, in freedom from legal bondage; Phil. 1:27, "in one spirit"; Phil. 4:1 and 1 Thess. 3:8, "in the Lord," i.e., in the willing subjection to His authority; 2 Thess. 2:15, in the apostle's teaching; some mss. have it in John 8:44, the most authentic have *histemi*, RV, "stood" (KJV, "abode").

Ready *see Revelation 3:2* y.

Delivered *see Revelation 12:2.*

Devour *see* Eat at *Revelation 10:9.*

12:5 And she brought forth a man child, who was to rule all nations with a rod of iron: and her child was caught up unto God, and *to* his throne.

Brought *tikto* (5088), "to beget, bring forth," Matt. 1:21, 23, 25; Jas. 1:15 (first part of verse, according to the best mss.); **Rev. 12:5** (RV, "was delivered of").

Man child *arsen* or *arren* (730), is translated "men" in Rom. 1:27 (three times); "man child" in **Rev. 12:5** (v. **13** in some mss.); "male" in Matt. 19:4; Mark 10:6; Luke 2:23; Gal. 3:28, "(there can be no) male (and female)," RV, i.e. sex distinction does not obtain in Christ; sex is no barrier either to salvation or the development of Christian graces.

Rule *see Revelation 2:27.*

Rod *see Revelation 2:27.*

Iron *see Revelation 2:27.*

Caught *harpazo* (726), "to snatch or catch away," is said of the act of the Spirit of the Lord in regard to Philip in Acts 8:39; of Paul in being "caught" up to paradise, 2 Cor. 12:2,

"You are but a poor soldier of Christ if you think you can overcome without fighting, and suppose you can have the crown without the conflict."

ST. JOHN CHRYSOSTOM

4; of the rapture of the saints at the return of the Lord, 1 Thess. 4:17; of the rapture of the man child in the vision of **Rev. 12:5**. This verb conveys the idea of force suddenly exercised, as in Matt. 11:12, "take (it) by force"; 12:29, "spoil" (some mss. have *diarpazo* here), in 13:19, RV, "snatcheth"; for forceful seizure, see also John 6:15; 10:12 28-29; Acts 23:10; in Jude 23, RV, "snatching."

12:6 And the woman fled into the wilderness, where she hath a place prepared of God, that they should feed her there a thousand two hundred *and* threescore days.

Prepared *see Revelation 8:6.*

Feed *trepho* (5142), signifies (a) "to make to grow, bring up, rear," Luke 4:16, "brought up"; (b) "to nourish, feed," Matt. 6:26; 25:37; Luke 12:24; Acts 12:20; **Rev. 12:6, 14**; of a mother, "to give suck," Luke 23:29 (some mss. here have *thelazo,* "to suckle"); "to fatten," as of fattening animals, Jas. 5:5, "ye have nourished (your hearts)."

Thousand *see* **Thousands** at *Revelation 5:11.*

Two hundred *see Revelation 11:3.*

Threescore *see Revelation 11:3.*

Days *see* **Months** at *Revelation 9:5.*

12:7 And there was war in heaven: Michael and his angels fought against the dragon; and the dragon fought and his angels,

Dragon *see Revelation 12:3.*

Fought *see* **Fight** at *Revelation 2:16.*

12:8 And prevailed not; neither was their place found any more in heaven.

Prevailed *ischuo* (2480), signifies (a) "to be strong in body, to be robust, in sound health," Matt. 9:12; Mark 2:17; (b) "to have power," as of the gospel, Acts 19:20; to prevail against, said of spiritual enemies, **Rev. 12:8**; of an evil spirit against exorcists, Acts 19:16; (c) "to be of force, to be effective, capable of producing results," Matt. 5:13 ("it is good for nothing"; lit., "it availeth nothing"); Gal. 5:6; in Heb. 9:17 it apparently has the meaning "to be valid" (RV, "for doth it ever avail ...?", for KJV, "it is of no strength"). It is translated "avail" with reference to prayer, in Jas. 5:16; cf. the strengthened form *exischuo* in Eph. 3:18.

Place *see Revelation 2:5.*

12:9 And the great dragon was cast out, that old serpent, called the Devil, and Satan, which deceiveth the whole world: he was cast out into the earth, and his angels were cast out with him.

Dragon *see Revelation 12:3.*

Old *archaios* (744), "original, ancient" (from *arche,* "a beginning": Eng., "archaic," "archaeology," etc.), is used (a) of persons belonging to a former age, "(to) them of old time," Matt. 5:21, 33, RV; in some mss. v. 27; the RV rendering is right; not ancient teachers are in view; what was said to them of old time was "to be both recognized in its significance and estimated in its temporary limitations, Christ intending His words to be regarded not as an abrogation, but a deepening and fulfilling" (Cremer); of prophets, Luke 9:8, 19; (b) of time long gone by, Acts 15:21; (c) of days gone by in a person's experience, Acts 15:7, "a good while ago," lit., "from old (days)," i.e., from the first days onward in the sense of originality, not age; (d) of Mnason, "an early disciple," Acts 21:16, RV, not referring to age, but to his being one of the first who had accepted the gospel from the beginning of its proclamation; (e) of things which are "old" in relation to the new, earlier things in contrast to things present, 2 Cor. 5:17, i.e., of what characterized and conditioned the time previous to conversion in a believer's experience, RV, "they are become new," i.e., they have taken on a new complexion and are viewed in an entirely different way; (f) of the world (i.e., the inhabitants of the world) just previous to the Flood, 2 Pet. 2:5; (g) of the Devil, as "that old serpent," **Rev. 12:9**; **20:2**, "old," not in age, but as characterized for a long period by the evils indicated.

Serpent *see* **Serpents** at *Revelation 9:19.*

Devil *diabolos* (1228), "an accuser, a slanderer" (from *diaballo,* "to accuse, to malign"), is one of the names of Satan. From it the English word "Devil" is derived, and should be applied only to Satan, as a proper name. *Daimon,* "a demon," is frequently, but wrongly, translated "devil"; it should always be translated "demon," as in the RV margin. There is one "Devil," there are many demons. Being the malignant enemy of God and man, he accuses man to God, Job 1:6-11; 2:1-5; **Rev. 12:9**, **10**, and God to man, Gen. 3. He afflicts men with physical sufferings, Acts 10:38. Being himself sinful, 1 John 3:8, he instigated man to sin, Gen. 3, and tempts man to do evil, Eph. 4:27; 6:11, encouraging him thereto by deception, Eph. 2:2. Death having been brought into the world by sin, the "Devil" had the power of death, but Christ through His own death, has triumphed over him, and will bring him to nought, Heb. 2:14; his power over death is intimated in his struggle with Michael over the body of Moses, Jude 9. Judas, who gave himself over to the "Devil," was so identified with him, that the Lord described him as such, John 6:70 (see 13:2). As the "Devil" raised himself in pride against God and fell under condemnation, so believers are warned against similar sin, 1 Tim. 3:6; for them he lays snares, v. 7, seeking to devour them as a roaring lion, 1 Pet. 5:8; those who fall into his snare may be recovered therefrom unto the will of God, 2 Tim. 2:26, "having been taken captive by him (i.e., by the 'Devil')"; "by the Lord's servant" is an alternative, which some regard as confirmed by the use of *zogreo* ("to catch alive") in Luke 5:10; but the general use is that of taking captive in the usual way. If believers resist he will flee from them, Jas. 4:7. His fury and malignity will be especially exercised at the end of the present age, **Rev. 12:12**. His doom is the lake of fire, Matt. 25:41; **Rev. 20:10**. The noun is applied to slanderers, false accusers, 1 Tim. 3:11; 2 Tim. 3:3; Titus 2:3.

Satan *see* ***Revelation 2:9.***

Deceiveth *planao* (4105), akin to *plane*, (Eng., "planet"), in the passive form sometimes means "to go astray, wander," Matt. 18:12; 1 Pet. 2:25; Heb. 11:38; frequently active, "to deceive, by leading into error, to seduce," e.g., Matt. 24:4, 5, 11, 24; John 7:12, "leadeth astray," RV (cf. 1 John 3:7). In **Rev. 12:9** the present participle is used with the definite article, as a title of the Devil, "the Deceiver," lit., "the deceiving one." Often it has the sense of "deceiving oneself," e.g., 1 Cor. 6:9; 15:33; Gal. 6:7; Jas. 1:16, "be not deceived," RV, "do not err," KJV.

World *see* ***Revelation 3:10.***

12:10 And I heard a loud voice saying in heaven, Now is come salvation, and strength, and the kingdom of our God, and the power of his Christ: for the accuser of our brethren is cast down, which accused them before our God day and night.

Loud *see* ***Revelation 5:2.***

Now *arti* (737), expressing "coincidence," and denoting "strictly present time," signifies "just now, this moment," in contrast (a) to the past, e.g., Matt. 11:12; John 2:10; 9:19, 25; 13:33; Gal. 1:9-10; (b) to the future, e.g., John 13:37; 16:12, 31; 1 Cor. 13:12; 2 Thess. 2:7; 1 Pet. 1:6, 8; (c) sometimes without necessary reference to either, e.g., Matt. 3:15; 9:18; 26:53; Gal. 4:20; **Rev. 12:10**.

Salvation *see* ***Revelation 7:10.***

Strength *see* ***Revelation 1:16.***

Kingdom *see* ***Revelation 1:9.***

Power *exousia* (1849), denotes "authority" (from the impersonal verb *exesti*, "it is lawful"). From the meaning of "leave or permission," or liberty of doing as one pleases, it passed to that of "the ability or strength with which one is endued," then to that of the "power of authority," the right to exercise power, e.g., Matt. 9:6; 21:23; 2 Cor. 10:8; or "the power of rule or government," the power of one whose will and commands must be obeyed by others, e.g., Matt. 28:18; John 17:2; Jude 25; **Rev. 12:10**; **17:13**; more specifically of apostolic "authority," 2 Cor. 10:8; 13:10; the "power" of judicial decision, John 19:10; of "managing domestic affairs," Mark 13:34. By metonymy, or name-change (the substitution of a suggestive word for the name of the thing meant), it stands for "that which is subject to authority or rule," Luke 4:6 (RV, "authority," for the KJV "power"); or, as with the English "authority," "one who possesses authority, a ruler, magistrate," Rom. 13:1-3; Luke 12:11; Titus 3:1; or "a spiritual potentate," e.g., Eph. 3:10; 6:12; Col. 1:16; 2:10, 15; 1 Pet. 3:22. The RV usually translates it "authority." In 1 Cor. 11:10 it is used of the veil with which a woman is required to cover herself in an assembly or church, as a sign of the Lord's "authority" over the church.

Accuser *kategoros* (2725), "an accuser," is used in John 8:10; Acts 23:30, 35; 24:8; 25:16, 18. In **Rev. 12:10**, it is used of Satan. In the Sept., Prov. 18:17. *See also* **Devil** at ***Revelation 12:9.***

Cast *kataballo* (2598), signifies "to cast down," 2 Cor. 4:9, KJV, "cast down," RV, "smitten down"; Heb. 6:1, "laying." Some mss. have this verb in **Rev. 12:10** (for *ballo*).

Accused *kategoreo* (2723), "to speak against, accuse," is used (a) in a general way, "to accuse," e.g., Luke 6:7, RV, "how to accuse"; Rom. 2:15;

Rev. 12:10; (b) before a judge, e.g., Matt. 12:10; Mark 15:4 (RV, "witness against"); Acts 22:30; 25:16. In Acts 24:19, RV renders it "make accusation," for the KJV, "object."

12:11 And they overcame him by the blood of the Lamb, and by the word of their testimony; and they loved not their lives unto the death.

Overcame *see* Overcometh at *Revelation 2:7*.

Loved *phileo* (5368), is to be distinguished from *agapao* in this, that *phileo* more nearly represents "tender affection." The two words are used for the "love" of the Father for the Son, John 3:35 (*agapao*), and 5:20 (*phileo*); for the believer, 14:21 (*agapao*) and 16:27 (*phileo*); both, of Christ's "love" for a certain disciple, 13:23 (*agapao*), and 20:2 (*phileo*). Yet the distinction between the two verbs remains, and they are never used indiscriminately in the same passage; if each is used with reference to the same objects, as just mentioned, each word retains its distinctive and essential character. *Phileo* is never used in a command to men to "love" God; it is, however, used as a warning in 1 Cor. 16:22; *agapao* is used instead, e.g., Matt. 22:37; Luke 10:27; Rom. 8:28; 1 Cor. 8:3; 1 Pet. 1:8; 1 John 4:21. The distinction between the two verbs finds a conspicuous instance in the narrative of John 21:15-17. The context itself indicates that *agapao* in the first two questions suggests the "love" that values and esteems (cf. **Rev. 12:11**). It is an unselfish "love," ready to serve. The use of *phileo* in Peter's answers and the Lord's third question, conveys the thought of cherishing the Object above all else, of manifesting an affection characterized by constancy, from the motive of the highest veneration. Again, to "love" (*phileo*) life, from an undue desire to preserve it, forgetful of the real object of living, meets with the Lord's reproof, John 12:25. On the contrary, to "love" life (*agapao*) as used in 1 Pet. 3:10, is to consult the true interests of living. Here the word *phileo* would be quite inappropriate.

Lives *see* Life at *Revelation 8:9*.

12:12 Therefore rejoice, *ye* heavens, and ye that dwell in them. Woe to the inhabiters of the earth and of the sea! for the devil is come down unto you, having great wrath, because he knoweth that he hath but a short time.

Rejoice *euphraino* (2165), in the active voice, "to cheer, gladden" (*eu*, "well," *phren*, "the mind"), signifies in the passive voice "to rejoice, make merry"; it is translated "to rejoice" in Acts 2:26, RV, "was glad," KJV, "did ... rejoice," of the heart of Christ as foretold in Ps. 16:9; in Acts 7:41, of Israel's idolatry; in Rom. 15:10 (quoted from the Sept. of Deut. 32:43, where it is a command to the Gentiles to "rejoice" with the Jews in their future deliverance by Christ from all their foes, at the establishment of the messianic kingdom) the apostle applies it to the effects of the gospel; in Gal. 4:27 (touching the barrenness of Sarah as referred to in Isa. 54:1, and there pointing to the ultimate restoration of Israel to God's favor, cf. 51:2), the word is applied to the effects of the gospel, in that the progeny of grace would greatly exceed the number of those who had acknowledged allegiance to the Law; grace and faith are fruitful, law and works are barren as a means of salvation; in **Rev. 12:12**, it is used in a call to the heavens to "rejoice" at the casting out of Satan and the inauguration of the Kingdom of God in manifestation and the authority of His Christ; in **18:20**, of a call to heaven, saints, apostles, prophets, to "rejoice" in the destruction of Babylon.

Dwell *see* Dwellest at *Revelation 2:13*.

Woe *see Revelation 8:13*.

Devil *see Revelation 12:9*.

Wrath *thumos* (2372), "hot anger, passion," is translated "wrath" in Luke 4:28; Acts 19:28; Rom. 2:8, RV; Gal. 5:20; Eph. 4:31; Col. 3:8; Heb. 11:27; **Rev. 12:12; 14:8, 10, 19; 15:1, 7; 16:1; 18:3**; "wraths" in 2 Cor. 12:20; "fierceness" in **Rev. 16:19; 19:15**.

Short *oligos* (3641), "little, few" (the opposite of *polus*, "much"), is translated "short" in **Rev. 12:12**; in the neut. sing., e.g., 2 Cor. 8:15.

Time *kairos* (2540), primarily, "due measure, fitness, proportion," is used in the NT to signify "a season, a time, a period" possessed of certain characteristics, frequently rendered "time" or "times"; in the following the RV substitutes "season" for the KJV "time," thus distinguishing the meaning from *chronos*: Matt. 11:25; 12:1; 14:1; 21:34; Mark 11:13; Acts 3:19; 7:20; 17:26; Rom. 3:26; 5:6; 9:9; 13:11; 1 Cor. 7:5; Gal. 4:10; 1 Thess. 2:17, lit., "for a season (of an hour)", 2 Thess. 2:6; in Eph. 6:18, "at all seasons" (KJV, "always"); in Titus 1:3, "His own seasons" (marg., "its"; KJV, "in due times"); in the preceding clause *chronos* is used. The characteristics of a period are exemplified in the use of the term with regard, e.g. to harvest, Matt. 13:30; reaping, Gal. 6:9; punishment, Matt. 8:29; discharging duties, Luke 12:42; opportunity for doing anything, whether good, e.g., Matt. 26:18; Gal. 6:10 ("opportunity"); Eph. 5:16; or evil, e.g., **Rev. 12:12**; the fulfillment of prophecy,

Luke 1:20; Acts 3:19; 1 Pet. 1:11; a time suitable for a purpose, Luke 4:13, lit., "until a season"; 2 Cor. 6:2.

12:13 And when the dragon saw that he was cast unto the earth, he persecuted the woman which brought forth the man *child*.

Dragon *see Revelation 12:3.*

Persecuted *dioko* (1377), has the meanings (a) "to put to flight, drive away," (b) "to pursue," whence the meaning "to persecute," Matt. 5:10-12, 44; 10:23; 23:34; Luke 11:49; 21:12; John 5:16; 15:20 (twice); Acts 7:52; 9:4, 5, and similar passages; Rom. 12:14; 1 Cor. 4:12; 15:9; 2 Cor. 4:9, KJV (RV, "pursued"); Gal. 1:13, 23; 4:29; Gal. 5:11, RV, "am ... persecuted" (KJV, "suffer persecution"); so 6:12; Phil. 3:6; 2 Tim. 3:12, "shall suffer persecution"; **Rev. 12:13**. *See also* **Tribulation** at *Revelation 1:9.*

Man child *see Revelation 12:5.*

12:14 And to the woman were given two wings of a great eagle, that she might fly into the wilderness, into her place, where she is nourished for a time, and times, and half a time, from the face of the serpent.

Wings *see Revelation 4:8.*

Eagle *see Revelation 4:7.*

Fly *see* **Flying** at *Revelation 4:7.*

Nourished *see* **Feed** at *Revelation 12:6.*

Half *see Revelation 11:9.*

Time, Times *see* **Months** at *Revelation 9:5.*

Face *prosopon* (4383), denotes "the countenance," lit., "the part towards the eyes" (from *pros*, "towards," *ops*, "the eye"), and is used (a) of the "face," Matt. 6:16-17; 2 Cor. 3:7, 2nd part (KJV, "countenance"); in 2 Cor. 10:7, in the RV, "things that are before your face" (KJV, "outward appearance"), the phrase is figurative of superficial judgment; (b) of the look, i.e., the "face," which by its various movements affords an index of inward thoughts and feelings. e g., Luke 9:51, 53; 1 Pet. 3:12; (c) the presence of a person, the "face" being the noblest part, e.g., Acts 3:13, RV, "before the face of," KJV, "in the presence of"; 5:41, "presence"; 2 Cor. 2:10, "person"; 1 Thess. 2:17 (first part), "presence"; 2 Thess. 1:9, RV, "face," KJV, "presence"; **Rev. 12:14**, "face"; (d) the person himself, e.g., Gal. 1:22; 1 Thess. 2:17 (second part); (e) the appearance one presents by his wealth or poverty, his position or state, Matt. 22:16; Mark 12:14; Gal. 2:6; Jude 16; (f) the outward appearance of inanimate things, Matt. 16:3; Luke 12:56; 21:35; Acts 17:26. "To spit in a person's face" was an expression of the utmost scorn and aversion, e.g., Matt. 26:67 (cf. 27:30; Mark 10:34; Luke 18:32).

Serpent *see* **Serpents** at *Revelation 9:19.*

12:15 And the serpent cast out of his mouth water as a flood after the woman, that he might cause her to be carried away of the flood.

Serpent *see* **Serpents** at *Revelation 9:19.*

Mouth *see Revelation 1:16.*

Flood *potamos* (4215), "a river, stream, torrent," is translated "flood" in Matt. 7:25, 27; in **Rev. 12:15, 16**, KJV, flood, RV, "river. *See also* **Rivers** at *Revelation 8:10.*

Carried away *potamophoretos* (4216), signifies "carried away by a stream or river," **Rev. 12:15**, RV, "carried away by the stream" (KJV, "of the flood").

12:16 And the earth helped the woman, and the earth opened her mouth, and swallowed up the flood which the dragon cast out of his mouth.

Helped *boetheo* (997), "to come to the aid of anyone, to succor," is used in Matt. 15:25; Mark 9:22, 24; Acts 16:9; 21:28; 2 Cor. 6:2, "did I succour"; Heb. 2:18, "to succour"; **Rev. 12:16.**

Opened *see* **Openeth** at *Revelation 3:7.*

Mouth *see Revelation 1:16.*

Swallowed *katapino* (2666), "to drink down" (*kata*, and *pino*, "to drink"), "to swallow," is used with this meaning (a) physically, but figuratively, Matt. 23:24; **Rev. 12:16**; (b) metaphorically, in the passive voice, of death (by victory), 1 Cor. 15:54; of being overwhelmed by sorrow, 2 Cor. 2:7; of the mortal body (by life), 5:4.

Flood *see Revelation 12:15.*

Dragon *see Revelation 12:3.*

12:17 And the dragon was wroth with the woman, and went to make war with the remnant of her seed, which keep the commandments of God, and have the testimony of Jesus Christ.

Dragon *see Revelation 12:3.*

Wroth *see* **Angry** at *Revelation 11:18.*

Remnant *see Revelation 11:13.*

Seed *sperma* (4690), akin to *speiro*, "to sow" (Eng., "sperm," "spermatic," etc.), has the following usages, (a) agricultural and botanical, e.g., Matt. 13:24, 27, 32; 1 Cor. 15:38; 2 Cor. 9:10; (b) physiological, Heb. 11:11; (c) metaphorical and by metonymy for "offspring, posterity," (1) of natural offspring, e.g., Matt.

22:24, 25, RV, "seed" (KJV, "issue"); John 7:42; 8:33, 37; Acts 3:25; Rom. 1:3; 4:13, 16, 18; 9:7 (twice), 8, 29; 11:1; 2 Cor. 11:22; Heb. 2:16; 11:18; **Rev. 12:17**; Gal. 3:16, 19, 29; in the 16th v., "He saith not, And to seeds, as of many; but as of one, And to thy seed, which is Christ," quoted from the Sept. of Gen. 13:15 and 17:7, 8, there is especial stress on the word "seed," as referring to an individual (here, Christ) in fulfillment of the promises to Abraham—a unique use of the singular. While the plural form "seeds," neither in Hebrew nor in Greek, would have been natural any more than in English (it is not so used in Scripture of human offspring; its plural occurrence is in 1 Sam. 8:15, of crops), yet if the divine intention had been to refer to Abraham's natural descendants, another word could have been chosen in the plural, such as "children"; all such words were, however, set aside, "seed" being selected as one that could be used in the singular, with the purpose of showing that the "seed" was Messiah. Some of the rabbis had even regarded "seed," e.g., in Gen. 4:25 and Isa. 53:10, as referring to the Coming One. Descendants were given to Abraham by other than natural means, so that through him Messiah might come, and the point of the apostle's argument is that since the fulfillment of the promises of God is secured alone by Christ, they only who are "in Christ" can receive them; (2) of spiritual offspring, Rom. 4:16, 18; 9:8; here "the children of the promise are reckoned for a seed" points, firstly, to Isaac's birth as being not according to the ordinary course of nature but by divine promise, and, secondly, by analogy, to the fact that all believers are children of God by spiritual birth; Gal. 3:29.

Keep *see Revelation 1:3*.

Testimony *marturia* (3141), "witness, evidence, testimony," is almost always rendered "witness" in the RV (for KJV, "testimony" in John 3:32, 33; 5:34; 8:17; 21:24, and always for KJV, "record," e.g., 1 John 5:10, 11), except in Acts 22:18 and in Revelation, where both, with one exception, have "testimony," 1:2, 9; 6:9; 11:7; 12:11, 17; 19:10 (twice); 20:4 (KJV, "witness"). In 19:10, "the testimony of Jesus" is objective, the "testimony" or witness given to Him (cf. 1:2, 9; as to those who will bear it, see **Rev. 12:17**, RV). The statement "the testimony of Jesus is the spirit of prophecy," is to be understood in the light, e.g., of the "testimony" concerning Christ and Israel in the Psalms, which will be used by the godly Jewish remnant in the coming time of "Jacob's Trouble." All such "testimony" centers in and points to Christ.

Jesus *see Revelation 1:9*.

Chapter 13

13:1 And I stood upon the sand of the sea, and saw a beast rise up out of the sea, having seven heads and ten horns, and upon his horns ten crowns, and upon his heads the name of blasphemy.

Stood *histemi* (2476), (a) transitively, denotes "to cause to stand, to set"; in the passive voice, "to be made to stand," e.g., Matt. 2:9, lit., "was made to stand"; so Luke 11:18; 19:8 (Col. 4:12 in some mss.); in **Rev. 13:1** the RV follows the best texts, "he stood" (not as KJV, "I stood"); the reference is to the Dragon. In the middle voice, "to take one's stand, place oneself," e.g., **Rev. 18:15**; (b) intransitively, in the 2nd aorist and perfect active, "to stand, stand by, stand still," e.g., Matt. 6:5; 20:32, "stood still"; in Luke 6:8, "stand forth" and "stood forth"; metaphorically, "to stand firm," John 8:44 (negatively), in the truth; Rom. 5:2, in grace; 1 Cor. 15:1, in the gospel; Rom. 11:20, "by thy faith," RV; 2 Cor. 1:24, "by faith" (marg., "by your faith"); of steadfastness, 1 Cor. 7:37; Eph. 6:11, 13, 14; Col. 4:12 [some mss. have the passive, see (a)].

Sand *ammos* (285), "sand" or "sandy ground," describes (a) an insecure foundation, Matt. 7:26; (b) numberlessness, vastness, Rom. 9:27; Heb. 11:12; **Rev. 20:8**; (c) symbolically in **Rev. 13:1**, RV, the position taken up by the Dragon (not, as in the KJV, by John), in view of the rising of the Beast out of the sea (emblematic of the restless condition of nations).

Sea *see Revelation 4:6*.

Beast *see Revelation 11:7*.

Rise *anabaino* (305), "to go up, to ascend," is once rendered "arise" in the RV, Luke 24:38, of reasonings in the heart; in **Rev. 13:1**, RV, "coming up," for KJV, "rise up," with reference to the beast; in **17:8**, KJV, "ascend," for RV, "to come up"; in **19:3**, RV, "goeth up," for KJV, "rose up.

Heads *kephale* (2776), besides its natural significance, is used (a) figuratively in Rom. 12:20, of heaping coals of fire on a "head"; in Acts 18:6, "Your blood be upon your own heads," i.e., "your blood-guiltiness rest upon your own persons," a mode of expression frequent in the OT, and perhaps here directly connected with Ezek. 3:18, 20; 33:6, 8; see also Lev. 20:16; 2 Sam. 1:16; 1 Kings 2:37; (b) metaphorically, of the authority or direction of God in relation to Christ, of Christ in relation to believing men, of the husband in relation to the wife, 1 Cor. 11:3; of Christ in relation to the Church, Eph. 1:22; 4:15; 5:23; Col. 1:18; 2:19; of Christ in relation to principalities and powers, Col. 2:10. As to 1 Cor. 11:10, taken in connection with the context, the word "authority" probably stands, by metonymy, for a sign of authority (RV), the angels being witnesses of the preeminent relationship as established by God in the creation of man as just mentioned, with the spiritual significance regarding the position of Christ in relation to the Church; cf. Eph. 3:10; it is used of Christ as the foundation of the spiritual building set forth by the Temple, with its "corner stone," Matt. 21:42; symbolically also of the imperial rulers of the Roman power, as seen in the apocalyptic visions, **Rev. 13:1, 3; 17:3, 7, 9.**

Ten *see Revelation 2:10.*

Horns *see Revelation 5:6.*

Crowns *see Revelation 12:3.*

13:2 And the beast which I saw was like unto a leopard, and his feet were as *the feet* of a bear, and his mouth as the mouth of a lion: and the dragon gave him his power, and his seat, and great authority.

Like unto *see Revelation 1:13.*

Leopard *pardalis* (3917), denotes "a leopard or a panther," an animal characterized by swiftness of movement and sudden spring, in Dan. 7:6 symbolic of the activities of Alexander the Great, and the formation of the Grecian kingdom, the third seen in the vision there recorded. In **Rev. 13:2** the imperial power, described there also as a "beast," is seen to concentrate in himself the characteristics of those mentioned in Dan. 7.

Bear *ark(t)os* (715), "a bear," occurs in **Rev. 13:2.**

Mouth *see Revelation 1:16.*

Lion *see Revelation 4:7.*

Dragon *see Revelation 12:3.*

Seat *see* **Throne** at *Revelation 1:4.*

13:3 And I saw one of his heads as it were wounded to death; and his deadly wound was healed: and all the world wondered after the beast.

Heads *see Revelation 13:1.*

Wounded to death *sphazo* (4969), "to slay," is translated "smitten unto death" in **Rev. 13:3.** In **Rev. 13:3, 12,** *plege* is used with the genitive case of *thanatos,* "death," lit., "stroke of death," RV, "death stroke" (KJV, "deadly wound"); the rendering "wound" does not accurately give the meaning; in v. **14,** with the genitive of *machaira,* "a sword," KJV, "wound" (RV, "stroke"). See also **Slain** at *Revelation 5:6.*

Deadly *thanatos* (2288), "death," is used in Scripture of: (a) the separation of the soul (the spiritual part of man) from the body (the material part), the latter ceasing to function and turning to dust, e.g., John 11:13; Heb. 2:15; 5:7; 7:23. In Heb. 9:15, the KJV, "by means of death" is inadequate; the RV, "a death having taken place" is in keeping with the subject. In **Rev. 13:3, 12,** the RV, "death-stroke" (KJV, "deadly wound") is, lit., "the stroke of death." (b) the separation of man from God; Adam died on the day he disobeyed God, Gen. 2:17, and hence all mankind are born in the same spiritual condition, Rom. 5:12, 14, 17, 21, from which, however, those who believe in Christ are delivered, John 5:24; 1 John 3:14. "Death" is the opposite of life; it never denotes nonexistence. As spiritual life is "conscious existence in communion with God," so spiritual "death" is "conscious existence in separation from God."

"Death, in whichever of the above-mentioned senses it is used, is always, in Scripture, viewed as the penal consequence of sin, and since sinners alone are subject to death, Rom. 5:12, it was as the Bearer of sin that the Lord Jesus submitted thereto on the Cross, 1 Pet. 2:24. And while the physical death of the Lord Jesus was of the essence of His sacrifice, it was not the whole. The darkness symbolized, and His cry expressed, the fact that He was left alone in the Universe, He was 'forsaken;' cf. Matt. 27:45-46."

Healed *therapeuo* (2323), primarily signifies "to serve as a *therapon,* an attendant"; then, "to care for the sick, to treat, cure, heal" (Eng., "therapeutics"). It is chiefly used in Matthew and Luke, once in John (5:10), and, after the Acts, only **Rev. 13:3** and **12.**

World In **Rev. 13:3,** KJV, *ge,* "the earth" (RV), is translated "world."

13:4 And they worshipped the dragon which gave power unto the beast: and they worshipped the beast, saying, Who *is* like unto the beast? who is able to make war with him?

Worshipped *see* **Worship** at *Revelation 4:10.*

Dragon *see Revelation 12:3.*

Like unto *see Revelation 1:13.*

Make war *see* **Fight** at *Revelation 2:16.*

13:5 And there was given unto him a mouth speaking great things and blasphemies; and power was given unto him to continue forty *and* two months.

Mouth *see Revelation 1:16.*

Continue *poieo* (4160), "to do, make," is used of spending a time or tarrying, in a place, Acts 15:33; 20:3; in 2 Cor. 11:25 it is rendered "I have been (a night and a day)"; a preferable translation is "I have spent," as in Jas. 4:13, "spend a year" (RV). So in Matt. 20:12. Cf., the English idiom "did one hour"; in **Rev. 13:5** "continue" is perhaps the best rendering.

Months *see Revelation 9:5.*

13:6 And he opened his mouth in blasphemy against God, to blaspheme his name, and his tabernacle, and them that dwell in heaven.

Opened *see* **Openeth** at *Revelation 3:7.*

Mouth *see Revelation 1:16.*

Blasphemy, Blaspheme *blasphemeo* (987), "to blaspheme, rail at or revile," is used (a) in a general way, of any contumelious speech, reviling, calumniating, railing at, etc., as of those who railed at Christ, e.g., Matt. 27:39; Mark 15:29; Luke 22:65 (RV, "reviling"); 23:39; (b) of those who speak contemptuously of God or of sacred things, e.g., Matt. 9:3; Mark 3:28; Rom. 2:24; 1 Tim. 1:20; 6:1; **Rev. 13:6; 16:9, 11, 21**; "hath spoken blasphemy," Matt. 26:65; "rail at," 2 Pet. 2:10; Jude 8, 10; "railing," 2 Pet. 2:12; "slanderously reported," Rom. 3:8; "be evil spoken of," Rom. 14:16; 1 Cor. 10:30; 2 Pet. 2:2; "speak evil of," Titus 3:2; 1 Pet. 4:4; "being defamed," 1 Cor. 4:13. The verb (in the present participial form) is translated "blasphemers" in Acts 19:37; in Mark 2:7, "blasphemeth," RV, for KJV, "speaketh blasphemies." There is no noun in the original representing the English "blasphemer." This is expressed either by the verb, or by the adjective *blasphemos*.

Name *see Revelation 2:3.*

Tabernacle *skene* (4633), "a tent, booth, tabernacle," is used of (a) tents as dwellings, Matt. 17:4; Mark 9:5; Luke 9:33; Heb. 11:9, KJV, "tabernacles" (RV, "tents"); (b) the Mosaic tabernacle, Acts 7:44; Heb. 8:5; 9:1 (in some mss.); 9:8, 21, termed "the tent of meeting," RV (i.e., where the people were called to meet God), a preferable description to "the tabernacle of the congregation," as in the KJV in the OT; the outer part 9:2, 6; the inner sanctuary, 9:3; (c) the heavenly prototype, Heb. 8:2; 9:11; **Rev. 13:6; 15:5; 21:3** (of its future descent); (d) the eternal abodes of the saints, Luke 16:9, RV, "tabernacles" (KJV, "habitations"); (e) the Temple in Jerusalem, as continuing the service of the tabernacle, Heb. 13:10; (f) the house of David, i.e., metaphorically of his people, Acts 15:16; (g) the portable shrine of the god Moloch, Acts 7:43.

Dwell *see Revelation 7:15.*

13:7 And it was given unto him to make war with the saints, and to overcome them: and power was given him over all kindreds, and tongues, and nations.

Overcome *see* **Overcometh** at *Revelation 2:7.*

Kindreds *see Revelation 1:7.*

Tongues *see* **Tongue** at *Revelation 5:9.*

13:8 And all that dwell upon the earth shall worship him, whose names are not written in the book of life of the Lamb slain from the foundation of the world.

Earth *ge* (1093), denotes (a) "earth as arable land," e.g., Matt. 13:5, 8, 23; in 1 Cor. 15:47 it is said of the "earthly" material of which "the first man" was made, suggestive of frailty; (b) "the earth as a whole, the world," in contrast, whether to the heavens, e.g., Matt. 5:18, 35, or to heaven, the abode of God, e.g., Matt. 6:19, where the context suggests the "earth" as a place characterized by mutability and weakness; in Col. 3:2 the same contrast is presented by the word "above"; in John 3:31 (RV, "of the earth," for KJV, "earthly") it describes one whose origin and nature are "earthly" and whose speech is characterized thereby, in contrast with Christ as the One from heaven; in Col. 3:5 the physical members are said to be "upon the earth," as a sphere where, as potential instruments of moral evils, they are, by metonymy, spoken of as the evils themselves; (c) "the inhabited earth," e.g., Luke 21:35; Acts 1:8; 8:33; 10:12; 11:6; 17:26; 22:22; Heb. 11:13; **Rev. 13:8**. In the following the phrase "on the earth" signifies "among men," Luke 12:49; 18:8; John 17:4, (d) "a country, territory," e.g. Luke 4:25; John 3:22; (e) "the ground," e.g., Matt. 10:29; Mark 4:26, RV, "(upon the) earth," for KJV, "(into the) ground"; (f) "land," e.g., Mark 4:1; John 21:8-9, 11. Cf. Eng. words beginning with *ge-*, e.g., "geodetic," "geodesy," "geology," "geometry," "geography."

Worship *see Revelation 4:10.*

Book *see Revelation 1:11.*

Lamb *see Revelation 5:6.*

Slain *see Revelation 5:6.*

Foundation *katabole* (2602), lit., "a casting down," is used (a) of "conceiving seed," Heb. 11:11; (b) of "a foundation," as that which is laid down, or in the sense of founding; metaphorically, of "the foundation of the world"; in this respect two phrases are used, (1) "from the foundation of the world," Matt.

25:34 (in the most authentic mss. in 13:35 there is no phrase representing "of the world"); Luke 11:50; Heb. 4:3; 9:26; **Rev. 13:8**; **17:8**; (2) "before the foundation of the world," John 17:24; Eph. 1:4; 1 Pet. 1:20. The latter phrase looks back to the past eternity.

13:9-10 If any man have an ear, let him hear.

He that leadeth into captivity shall go into captivity: he that killeth with the sword must be killed with the sword. Here is the patience and the faith of the saints.

He that In **Rev. 13:10**, *ei tis*, "if any-one," is rendered "if any man" in the RV, for KJV, "he that."

Leadeth *sunago* (4863), "to assemble" (*sun*, "together," *ago*, "to bring"), is used of the "gathering together" of people or things; in Luke 12:17-18, "bestow," with reference to the act of "gathering" one's goods; so in Luke 15:13, suggesting that the Prodigal, having "gathered" all his goods together, sold them off; in John 6:12, of "gathering" up fragments; in John 18:2, "resorted," with reference to the "assembling" of Christ with His disciples in the garden of Gethsemane, there in the passive voice (unsuitable, however, in an English translation). In Acts 11:26, the RV has "were gathered together (with the church)," for KJV, "assembled themselves" (possibly "they were hospitably entertained by"). The verb is not found in the most authentic mss. in **Rev. 13:10**.

Captivity *aichmalosia* (161), "captivity," the abstract noun. The concrete is found in **Rev. 13:10** and Eph. 4:8, where "He led captivity captive" (marg., "a multitude of captives") seems to be an allusion to the triumphal procession by which a victory was celebrated, the "captives" taken forming part of the procession. See Judg. 5:12. The quotation is from Ps. 68:18, and probably is a forceful expression for Christ's victory, through His death, over the hostile powers of darkness. An alternative suggestion is that at His ascension Christ transferred the redeemed Old Testament saints from Sheol to His own presence in glory.

Go *see Revelation 10:8.*

Here *hode* (5602), an adverb signifying (a) "here" (of place), e.g., Matt. 12:6; Mark 9:1; used with the neuter plural of the article, Col. 4:9, "(all) things (that are done) here," lit., "(all) the (things) here"; in Matt. 24:23, *hode* is used in both parts, hence the RV, "Lo, here (is the Christ, or) Here"; in Mark 13:21 *hode* is followed by *ekei*, "there." The word is used metaphorically in the sense of "in this circumstance," or connection, in 1 Cor. 4:2; **Rev. 13:10, 18**; **14:12**; **17:9**.

13:11 And I beheld another beast coming up out of the earth; and he had two horns like a lamb, and he spake as a dragon.

Beast *pseudoprophetes* (5578), "a false prophet," is used of such (a) in OT times, Luke 6:26; 2 Pet. 2:1; (b) in the present period since Pentecost, Matt. 7:15; 24:11, 24; Mark 13:22; Acts 13:6; 1 John 4:1; (c) with reference to a false "prophet" destined to arise as the supporter of the "Beast" at the close of this age, **Rev. 16:13**; **19:20**; **20:10** (himself described as "another beast," **13:11**).

Horns *see Revelation 5:6.*

Like *see* **Like unto** at *Revelation 1:13.*

Lamb *see Revelation 5:6.*

Dragon *see Revelation 12:3.*

13:12 And he exerciseth all the power of the first beast before him, and causeth the earth and them which dwell therein to worship the first beast, whose deadly wound was healed.

Exerciseth *poieo* (4160), "to do," is translated "exerciseth" in **Rev. 13:12**, said of the authority of the second "Beast."

Before *enopion* (1799), is translated "in the sight of" in the RV (for KJV, "before") in Luke 12:6; 15:18; 16:15; Acts 7:46; 10:33; 19:19; 1 Tim. 5:4, 21; 2 Tim. 2:14; 4:1; **Rev. 13:12.** The RV is more appropriate in most passages, as giving the real significance of the word.

Causeth In Matt. 5:32 the RV translates *poieo* "maketh (her an adulteress)": in **Rev. 13:12**, RV, "maketh," for KJV, "causeth."

Worship *see Revelation 4:10.*

Deadly *see Revelation 13:3.*

Wound *see Revelation 13:3.*

Healed *see Revelation 13:3.*

13:13 And he doeth great wonders, so that he maketh fire come down from heaven on the earth in the sight of men,

Wonders *see* **Wonder** at *Revelation 12:1.*

Maketh *see* **Make** at *Revelation 3:9.*

13:14 And deceiveth them that dwell on the earth by *the means of* those miracles which he had power to do in the sight of the beast; saying to them that dwell on the earth, that they should make an image to the beast, which had the wound by a sword, and did live.

Deceiveth *apate* (539), "deceit or deceitfulness" (akin to *apatao*, "to cheat, deceive, beguile"), that which gives a false impression, whether by appearance, statement or influence, is said of riches, Matt. 13:22; Mark 4:19; of sin, Heb. 3:13. The phrase in Eph. 4:22, "deceitful lusts," KJV, "lusts of deceit," RV, signifies lusts excited by "deceit," of which "deceit" is the source of strength, not lusts "deceitful" in themselves. In 2 Thess. 2:10, "all deceit of unrighteousness," RV, signifies all manner of unscrupulous words and deeds designed to "deceive" (see **Rev. 13:13-15**). In Col. 2:8, "vain deceit" suggests that "deceit" is void of anything profitable.

Means In **Rev. 13:14**, RV, *dia*, followed by the accusative case, is rightly translated "by reason of," i.e., "on account of" (KJV, wrongly, "by *the means of*").

Miracles *semeion* (4592), "a sign, mark, token" (akin to *semaino*, "to give a sign"; *sema*, "a sign"), is used of "miracles" and wonders as signs of divine authority; it is translated "miracles" in the RV and KJV of Luke 23:8; Acts 4:16, 22; most usually it is given its more appropriate meaning "sign," "signs," e.g., Matt. 12:38, 39, and in every occurrence in the Synoptists, except Luke 23:8; in the following passages in John's Gospel the RV substitutes "sign" or "signs" for the KJV "miracle or miracles"; 2:11, 23; 3:2; 4:54; 6:2, 14, 26; 7:31; 9:16; 10:41; 11:47; 12:18, 37; the KJV also has "signs" elsewhere in this Gospel; in Acts, RV, "signs," KJV, "miracles," in 6:8; 8:6; 15:12; elsewhere only in **Rev. 13:14; 16:14; 19:20**. *See also* **Wonder** at *Revelation 12:1.*

"No matter how many pleasures Satan offers you, his ultimate intention is to ruin you. Your destruction is his highest priority."

ERWIN W. LUTZER

Power In **Rev. 13:14, 15**, KJV, *didomi*, "to give," is translated "(he) had power"; RV, "it was given (him)" and "it was given *unto him*"; the KJV misses the force of the permissive will of God in the actings of the Beast.

Make *see Revelation 3:9.*

Image *eikon* (1504), denotes "an image"; the word involves the two ideas of representation and manifestation. "The idea of perfection does not lie in the word itself, but must be sought from the context" (Lightfoot); the following instances clearly show any distinction between the imperfect and the perfect likeness. The word is used of an "image" or a coin (not a mere likeness), Matt. 22:20; Mark 12:16; Luke 20:24; so of a statue or similar representation (more than a resemblance), Rom. 1:23; **Rev. 13:14, 15** (thrice); **14:9, 11; 15:2; 16:2; 19:20; 20:4**; of the descendants of Adam as bearing his image, 1 Cor. 15:49, each a representation derived from the prototype.

Wound *see* **Wounded to death** at *Revelation 13:3.*

13:15 And he had power to give life unto the image of the beast, that the image of the beast should both speak, and cause that as many as would not worship the image of the beast should be killed.

Power *see Revelation 13:14.*

Life *see* **Spirit** at *Revelation 11:11.*

Image *see Revelation 13:14.*

Worship *see Revelation 4:10.*

Cause *poieo* (4160), "to do," is translated by the verb "to cause" in John 11:37; Acts 15:3; Rom. 16:17; Col. 4:16; **Rev. 13:15-16**.

13:16 And he causeth all, both small and great, rich and poor, free and bond, to receive a mark in their right hand, or in their foreheads:

Small *see Revelation 11:18. See also* **Little** at *Revelation 3:8.*

Rich *see Revelation 2:9.*

Free *see Revelation 6:15.*

Receive In **Rev. 13:16**, KJV, *didomi* is translated "to receive" (marg., "to give them"), RV, "(that) there be given (them)."

Mark *charagma* (5480), from *charasso*, "to engrave" (akin to *charakter*, "an impress," RV, marg., of Heb. 1:3), denotes (a) "a mark" or "stamp," e.g., **Rev. 13:16, 17; 14:9, 11; 16:2; 19:20; 20:4; 15:2** in some mss.; (b) "a thing graven," Acts 17:29.

Foreheads *see Revelation 7:3.*

13:17 And that no man might buy or sell, save he that had the mark, or the name of the beast, or the number of his name.

No man In some mss. the negative *me* and the indefinite pronoun *tis*, "some one, anyone," appear as one word, *metis* (always separated in the best mss.), e.g., Matt. 8:28, "no man"; so in 1 Cor. 16:11; 2 Cor. 11:16; 2 Thess. 2:3. The words are separated also in Matt. 24:4; 2 Cor. 8:20 (RV, "any man," after "avoiding"); **Rev. 13:17**. These instances represent either impossibility or prohibition; contrast *ouch* (i.e., *ou*) ... *tis* in Heb. 5:4, "no man (taketh)," where a direct negative statement is made.

Might *dunamai* (1410), "to be able, have power," whether by personal ability, permission, or opportunity, is sometimes rendered "may" or "might," e.g., Matt. 26:9; Mark 14:5; Acts 17:19; 1 Thess. 2:6. In the following the RV substitutes "can," "canst," "couldst," for the KJV, e.g., Matt. 26:42; Mark 4:32; 14:7; Luke 16:2; Acts 24:11; 25:11; 27:12; 1 Cor. 7:21; 14:31 (here the alteration is especially important, as not permission for all to prophesy, but ability to do so, is the meaning); Eph. 3:4. In the following the RV substitutes the verb "to be able," Acts 19:40; 24:8; **Rev. 13:17.**

Sell *poleo* (4453), "to exchange or barter, to sell," is used in the latter sense in the NT; six times in Matthew, three in Mark, six in Luke; in John only in connection with the cleansing of the Temple by the Lord, 2:14, 16; in Acts only in connection with the disposing of property for distribution among the community of believers, 4:34, 37; 5:1; elsewhere, 1 Cor. 10:25; **Rev. 13:17.**

Mark *see Revelation 13:16.*

13:18 Here is wisdom. Let him that hath understanding count the number of the beast: for it is the number of a man; and his number *is* Six hundred threescore *and* six.

Here *see Revelation 13:10.*

Wisdom *see Revelation 5:12.*

Understanding *nous* (3563), "mind," denotes, speaking generally, the seat of reflective consciousness, comprising the faculties of perception and understanding, and those of feeling, judging and determining. Its use in the NT may be analyzed as follows: it denotes (a) the faculty of knowing, the seat of the understanding, Luke 24:45; Rom. 1:28; 14:5; 1 Cor. 14:15, 19; Eph. 4:17; Phil. 4:7; Col. 2:18; 1 Tim. 6:5; 2 Tim. 3:8; Titus 1:15; **Rev. 13:18; 17:9**; (b) counsels, purpose, Rom. 11:34 (of the "mind" of God); 12:2; 1 Cor. 1:10; 2:16, twice (1) of the thoughts and counsels of God, (2) of Christ, a testimony to His Godhood; Eph. 4:23; (c) the new nature, which belongs to the believer by reason of the new birth, Rom. 7:23, 25, where it is contrasted with "the flesh," the principle of evil which dominates fallen man. Under (b) may come 2 Thess. 2:2, where it stands for the determination to be steadfast amidst afflictions, through the confident expectation of the day of rest and recompense mentioned in the first chapter.

Count *psephizo* (5585), akin to *psephos*, "a stone," used in voting, occurs in Luke 14:28; **Rev. 13:18.**

Six It forms the first syllable of *hexekonta*, "sixty" and *hexakosioi*, "six hundred," **Rev. 13:18; 14:20.**

Threescore In **Rev. 13:18**, the number of the "Beast," the human potentate destined to rule with satanic power the ten-kingdom league at the end of this age, is given as "six hundred and sixty and six" (RV), and described as "the number of (a) man." The number is suggestive of the acme of the pride of fallen man, the fullest development of man under direct satanic control, and standing in contrast to "seven" as the number of completeness and perfection. *See also Revelation 11:3.*

Chapter 14

14:1 And I looked, and, lo, a Lamb stood on the mount Sion, and with him an hundred forty *and* four thousand, having his Father's name written in their foreheads.

Looked *see Revelation 4:1.*

Mount *oros* (3735), is used (a) without specification, e.g., Luke 3:5 (distinct from *bounos*, "a hill"); John 4:20; (b) of "the Mount of Transfiguration," Matt. 17:1, 9; Mark 9:2, 9; Luke 9:28, 37 (KJV, "hill"); 2 Pet. 1:18; (c) of "Zion," Heb. 12:22; **Rev. 14:1**; (d) of "Sinai," Acts 7:30, 38; Gal. 4:24, 25; Heb. 8:5; 12:20; (e) of "the Mount of Olives," Matt. 21:1; 24:3; Mark 11:1; 13:3; Luke 19:29, 37; 22:39; John 8:1; Acts 1:12; (f) of "the hill districts as distinct from the lowlands," especially of the hills above the Sea of Galilee, e.g., Matt. 5:1; 8:1; 18:12; Mark 5:5; (g) of "the mountains on the east of Jordan" and "those in the land of Ammon" and "the region of Petra," etc., Matt. 24:16; Mark 13:14; Luke 21:21; (h) proverbially, "of overcoming difficulties, or accomplishing great things," 1 Cor. 13:2; cf. Matt. 17:20; 21:21; Mark 11:23; (i) symbolically, of "a series of the imperial potentates of the Roman dominion, past and future," **Rev. 17:9.**

Hundred *see Revelation 7:4.*

Foreheads *see Revelation 7:3.*

14:2 And I heard a voice from heaven, as the voice of many waters, and as the voice of a great thunder: and I heard the voice of harpers harping with their harps:

Thunder *see* Thunderings at *Revelation 4:5.*

Harpers *kitharodos* (2790), denotes "one who plays and sings to the lyre" (from *kithara*, "a lyre," and *aoidos*, "a singer"), **Rev. 14:2; 18:22.**

Harping *kitharizo* (2789), signifies "to play on the harp," 1 Cor. 14:7; **Rev. 14:2.** In the Sept., Isa. 23:16.

Harps *see* ***Revelation 5:8.***

14:3 And they sung as it were a new song before the throne, and before the four beasts, and the elders: and no man could learn that song but the hundred *and* forty *and* four thousand, which were redeemed from the earth.

Sung *see* ***Revelation 5:9.***

Song *see* ***Revelation 5:9.***

Elders *see* ***Revelation 4:4.***

Learn *manthano* (3129), denotes (a) "to learn" (akin to *mathetes*, "a disciple"), "to increase one's knowledge," or "be increased in knowledge," frequently "to learn by inquiry, or observation," e.g., Matt. 9:13; 11:29; 24:32; Mark 13:28; John 7:15; Rom. 16:17; 1 Cor. 4:6; 14:35; Phil. 4:9; 2 Tim. 3:14; **Rev. 14:3**; said of "learning" Christ, Eph. 4:20, not simply the doctrine of Christ, but Christ Himself, a process not merely of getting to know the person but of so applying the knowledge as to walk differently from the rest of the Gentiles; (b) "to ascertain," Acts 23:27, RV, "learned" (KJV, "understood"); Gal. 3:2, "This only would I learn from you," perhaps with a tinge of irony in the enquiry, the answer to which would settle the question of the validity of the new Judaistic gospel they were receiving; (c) "to learn by use and practice, to acquire the habit of, be accustomed to," e.g., Phil. 4:11; 1 Tim. 5:4, 13; Titus 3:14; Heb. 5:8.

Hundred *see* ***Revelation 7:4.***

Redeemed *see* ***Revelation 5:9.***

14:4 These are they which were not defiled with women; for they are virgins. These are they which follow the Lamb whithersoever he goeth. These were redeemed from among men, *being* the firstfruits unto God and to the Lamb.

Defiled *see* ***Revelation 3:4.***

Virgins *parthenos* (3933), is used (a) of "the Virgin Mary," Matt. 1:23; Luke 1:27; (b) of the ten "virgins" in the parable, Matt. 25:1, 7, 11; (c) of the "daughters" of Philip the evangelist, Acts 21:9; (d) those concerning whom the apostle Paul gives instructions regarding marriage, 1 Cor. 7:25, 28, 34; in vv. 36, 37, 38, the subject passes to that of "virgin *daughters*" (RV), which almost certainly formed one of the subjects upon which the church at Corinth sent for instructions from the apostle; one difficulty was relative to the discredit which might be brought upon a father (or guardian), if he allowed his daughter or ward to grow old unmarried. The interpretation that this passage refers to a man and woman already in some kind of relation by way of a spiritual marriage and living together in a vow of virginity and celibacy, is untenable if only in view of the phraseology of the passage; (e) figuratively, of "a local church" in its relation to Christ, 2 Cor. 11:2; (f) metaphorically of "chaste persons," **Rev. 14:4.**

Lamb *see* ***Revelation 5:6.***

Goeth *see* **Go** at ***Revelation 10:8.***

Redeemed *see* ***Revelation 5:9.***

Firstfruits *aparche* (536), denotes, primarily, "an offering of firstfruits" (akin to *aparchomai*, "to make a beginning"; in sacrifices, "to offer firstfruits"). "Though the English word is plural in each of its occurrences save Rom. 11:16, the Greek word is always singular. Two Hebrew words are thus translated, one meaning the "chief" or "principal part," e.g., Num. 18:12; Prov. 3:9; the other, "the earliest ripe of the crop or of the tree," e.g., Exod. 23:16; Neh. 10:35; they are found together, e.g., in Exod. 23:19, "the first of the firstfruits." "The term is applied in things spiritual, (a) to the presence of the Holy Spirit with the believer as the firstfruits of the full harvest of the Cross, Rom. 8:23; (b) to Christ Himself in resurrection in relation to all believers who have fallen asleep, 1 Cor. 15:20, 23; (c) to the earliest believers in a country in relation to those of their countrymen subsequently converted, Rom. 16:5; 1 Cor. 16:15; (d) to the believers of this age in relation to the whole of the redeemed, 2 Thess. 2:13 and Jas. 1:18. Cf. **Rev. 14:4.**

14:5 And in their mouth was found no guile: for they are without fault before the throne of God.

Mouth *see* ***Revelation 1:16.***

Guile *pseudos* (5579), "a falsehood, lie", is translated "lie" in John 8:44 (lit., "the lie"); Rom. 1:25, where it stands by metonymy for an idol, as, e.g., in Isa. 44:20; Jer. 10:14; 13:25; Amos 2:4 (plural); 2 Thess. 2:11, with special reference to the lie of v. 4, that man is God (cf. Gen. 3:5); 1 John 2:21, 27; **Rev. 21:27; 22:15**; in Eph. 4:25, KJV "lying," RV, "falsehood," the practice; in **Rev. 14:5**, RV, "lie." (some mss. have *dolos*, "guile," KJV); 2 Thess. 2:9, where "lying wonders" is, lit., "wonders of falsehood," i.e., wonders calculated to deceive (cf. **Rev. 13:13-15**), the purpose being to deceive people into the acknowledgement of the spurious claim to deity on the part of the Man of Sin.

Fault *amomos* (299), "without blemish"; is always so rendered in the RV, Eph. 1:4; 5:27; Phil. 2:15; Col. 1:22; Heb. 9:14; 1 Pet. 1:19; Jude 24; **Rev. 14:5**. This meaning is to be preferred to the various KJV renderings, "without blame," Eph. 1:4, "unblameable," Col. 1:22, "faultless," Jude 24, "without fault," **Rev. 14:5**. The most authentic mss. have *amomos*, "without blemish," in Phil. 2:15, for *amometos*, "without rebuke." In the Sept., in reference to sacrifices, especially in Lev. and Num., the Psalms and Ezek., "of blamelessness in character and conduct."

14:6 And I saw another angel fly in the midst of heaven, having the everlasting gospel to preach unto them that dwell on the earth, and to every nation, and kindred, and tongue, and people,

Saw *see* **Looked** at *Revelation 4:1*.

Fly *see* **Flying** at *Revelation 4:7*.

Heaven *see Revelation 8:13*.

Gospel *euangelion* (2098), originally denoted a reward for good tidings; later, the idea of reward dropped, and the word stood for "the good news" itself. The Eng. word "gospel," i.e. "good message," is the equivalent of *euangelion* (Eng., "evangel"). In the NT it denotes the "good tidings" of the kingdom of God and of salvation through Christ, to be received by faith, on the basis of His expiatory death, His burial, resurrection, and ascension, e.g., Acts 15:7; 20:24; 1 Pet. 4:17. Apart from those references and those in the Gospels of Matthew and Mark, and **Rev. 14:6**, the noun is confined to Paul's epistles. The apostle uses it of two associated yet distinct things, (a) of the basic facts of the death, burial and resurrection of Christ, e.g., 1 Cor. 15:1-3; (b) of the interpretation of these facts, e.g., Rom. 2:16; Gal. 1:7, 11; 2:2; in (a) the "gospel" is viewed historically, in (b) doctrinally, with reference to the interpretation of the facts, as is sometimes indicated by the context. The following phrases describe the subjects or nature or purport of the message; it is the "gospel" of God, Mark 1:14; Rom. 1:1; 15:16; 2 Cor. 11:7; 1 Thess. 2:2, 9; 1 Pet. 4:17; God, concerning His Son, Rom. 1:1-3; His Son, Rom. 1:9; Jesus Christ, the Son of God, Mark 1:1; our Lord Jesus, 2 Thess. 1:8; Christ, Rom. 15:19, etc.; the glory of Christ, 2 Cor. 4:4; the grace of God, Acts 20:24; the glory of the blessed God, 1 Tim. 1:11; your salvation, Eph. 1:13; peace, Eph. 6:15. Cf. also "the gospel of the Kingdom," Matt. 4:23; 9:35; 24:14; "an eternal gospel," **Rev. 14:6**.

Preach *see* **Declared** at *Revelation 10:7*.

Dwell *kathemai* (2521), is used (a) of the natural posture, e.g., Matt. 9:9, most frequently in Revelation, some 32 times; frequently in the Gospels and Acts; elsewhere only in 1 Cor. 14:30; Jas. 2:3 (twice); and of Christ's position of authority on the throne of God, Col. 3:1, KJV, "sitteth" (RV, "is, seated"); Heb. 1:13 (cf. Matt. 22:44; 26:64 and parallel passages in Mark and Luke, and Acts 2:34); often as antecedent or successive to, or accompanying, another act (in no case a superfluous expression), e.g., Matt. 15:29; 27:36; Mark 2:14; 4:1; (b) metaphorically in Matt. 4:16 (twice); Luke 1:79; of inhabiting a place (translated "dwell"), Luke 21:35; **Rev. 14:6**, RV marg., "sit" (in the best texts: some have *katoikeo*, "to dwell").

Kindred *see* **Kindreds** at *Revelation 1:7*.

Tongue *see Revelation 5:9*.

14:7 Saying with a loud voice, Fear God, and give glory to him; for the hour of his judgment is come: and worship him that made heaven, and earth, and the sea, and the fountains of waters.

Loud *see Revelation 5:2*.

Fear *phobeo* (5399), in earlier Greek, "to put to flight," in the NT is always in the passive voice, with the meanings either (a) "to fear, be afraid," its most frequent use, e.g., Acts 23:10, according to the best mss.; or (b) "to show reverential fear," (1) of men, Mark 6:20; Eph. 5:33, RV, "fear," for KJV, "reverence"; (2) of God, e.g., Acts 10:2, 22; 13:16, 26; Col. 3:22 (RV, "the Lord"); 1 Pet. 2:17; **Rev. 14:7; 15:4; 19:5**; (a) and (b) are combined in Luke 12:4, 5, where Christ warns His followers not to be afraid of men, but to "fear" God.

Hour *see Revelation 3:3*.

Fountains *see Revelation 7:17*.

14:8 And there followed another angel, saying, Babylon is fallen, is fallen, that great city, because she made all nations drink of the wine of the wrath of her fornication.

Another *see* **Second** at *Revelation 2:11*.

Drink *potizo* (4222), "to give to drink, to make to drink," is used (a) in the material sense, in Matt. 10:42, 25:35, 37, 42 (here of "ministering" to those who belong to Christ and thus doing so virtually to Him); 27:48;

Mark 9:41; 15:36; Luke 13:15 ("to watering"); Rom. 12:20; 1 Cor. 3:7-8; (b) figuratively, with reference to "teaching" of an elementary character, 1 Cor. 3:2, "I fed (you with milk)"; of "spiritual watering by teaching" the Word of God, 3:6; of being "provided" and "satisfied" by the power and blessing of the Spirit of God, 1 Cor. 12:13; of the effect upon the nations of "partaking" of the abominable mixture, provided by Babylon, of paganism with details of the Christian faith **Rev. 14:8**.

Wine *oinos* (3631), is the general word for "wine." The mention of the bursting of the wineskins, Matt. 9:17; Mark 2:22; Luke 5:37, implies fermentation. See also Eph. 5:18 (cf. John 2:10; 1 Tim. 3:8; Titus 2:3). In Matt. 27:34, the RV has "wine" (KJV, "vinegar," translating the inferior reading *oxos*). The drinking of "wine" could be a stumbling block and the apostle enjoins abstinence in this respect, as in others, so as to avoid giving an occasion of stumbling to a brother, Rom. 14:21. Contrast 1 Tim. 5:23, which has an entirely different connection. The word is used metaphorically (a) of the evils ministered to the nations by religious Babylon, **14:8; 17:2; 18:3**; (b) of the contents of the cup of divine wrath upon the nations and Babylon, **Rev. 14:10; 16:19; 19:15**.

Wrath *see* ***Revelation 12:12.***

Fornication *see* ***Revelation 2:21.***

14:9 And the third angel followed them, saying with a loud voice, If any man worship the beast and his image, and receive *his* mark in his forehead, or in his hand,

Loud *see* ***Revelation 5:2.***

Worship *see* ***Revelation 4:10.***

Beast *see* ***Revelation 11:7.***

Image *see* ***Revelation 13:14.***

Mark *see* ***Revelation 13:16.***

Forehead *see* **Foreheads** at ***Revelation 7:3.***

14:10 The same shall drink of the wine of the wrath of God, which is poured out without mixture into the cup of his indignation; and he shall be tormented with fire and brimstone in the presence of the holy angels, and in the presence of the Lamb:

Drink *pino* (4095), "to drink," is used chiefly in the Gospels and in 1 Cor., whether literally (most frequently), or figuratively, (a) of "drinking" of the blood of Christ, in the sense of receiving eternal life, through His death, John 6:53-54, 56; (b) of "receiving" spiritually that which refreshes, strengthens and nourishes the soul, John 7:37; (c) of "deriving" spiritual life from Christ, John 4:14, as Israel did typically 1 Cor. 10:4; (d) of "sharing" in the sufferings of Christ humanly inflicted, Matt. 20:22-23; Mark 10:38-39; (e) of "participating" in the abominations imparted by the corrupt religious and commercial systems emanating from Babylon, **Rev. 18:3**; (f) of "receiving" divine judgment, through partaking unworthily of the Lord's Supper, 1 Cor. 11:29; (g) of "experiencing" the wrath of God, **Rev. 14:10; 16:6**; (h) of the earth's "receiving" the benefits of rain, Heb. 6:7.

Wine *see* ***Revelation 14:8.***

Wrath *see* ***Revelation 12:12.***

Without mixture *kerannumi* (2767), "to mix, to mingle," chiefly of the diluting of wine, implies "a mixing of two things, so that they are blended and form a compound, as in wine and water, whereas *mignumi* implies a mixing without such composition, as in two sorts of grain" (Liddell and Scott, *Lex.*). It is used in **Rev. 18:6** (twice); in **14:10**, RV, "prepared" (marg., "mingled"; KJV, "poured out"), lit., "mingled," followed by *akratos*, "unmixed, pure" (*a*, negative, and *kratos*, an adjective, from this verb *kerannumi*), the two together forming an oxymoron, the combination in one phrase of two terms that are ordinarily contradictory.

Cup *poterion* (4221), a diminutive of *poter*, denotes, primarily, a "drinking vessel"; hence, "a cup" (a) literal, as, e.g., in Matt. 10:42. The "cup" of blessing, 1 Cor. 10:16, is so named from the third (the fourth according to Edersheim) "cup" in the Jewish Passover feast, over which thanks and praise were given to God. This connection is not to be rejected on the ground that the church at Corinth was unfamiliar with Jewish customs. That the contrary was the case, see 5:7; (b) figurative, of one's lot or experience, joyous or sorrowful (frequent in the Psalms; cf. Ps. 116:18, "cup of salvation"); in the NT it is used most frequently of the sufferings of Christ, Matt. 20:22-23; 26:39; Mark 10:38-39; 14:36; Luke 22:42; John 18:11; also of the evil deeds of Babylon, **Rev. 17:4; 18:6**; of divine punishments to be inflicted, **Rev. 14:10; 16:19**. Cf. Ps. 11:6; 75:8; Isa. 51:17; Jer. 25:15; Ezek. 23:32-34; Zech. 12:2.

Indignation *orge*, "wrath," is translated "indignation" in **Rev. 14:10**, KJV; RV, "anger."

Tormented *see* ***Revelation 9:5.***

Brimstone *see* ***Revelation 9:17.***

Presence *enopion* (1799), is translated "in the presence of" in Luke 1:19; 13:26; 14:10; 15:10; John 20:30; **Rev. 14:10** (twice); in 1 Cor. 1:29 KJV, "in His presence" (RV, "before God").

Lamb *see* ***Revelation 5:6.***

14:11 And the smoke of their torment ascendeth up for ever and ever: and they have no rest day nor night, who worship the beast and his image, and whosoever receiveth the mark of his name.

Smoke *see Revelation 9:2.*

Torment *see Revelation 9:5.*

Rest *see Revelation 4:8.*

Worship *see Revelation 4:10.*

Beast *see Revelation 11:7.*

Image *see Revelation 13:14* e.

Mark *see Revelation 13:16.*

14:12 Here is the patience of the saints: here *are* they that keep the commandments of God, and the faith of Jesus.

Here *see Revelation 13:10.*

Keep *see Revelation 1:3.*

Jesus *see Revelation 1:9.*

14:13 And I heard a voice from heaven saying unto me, Write, Blessed *are* the dead which die in the Lord from henceforth: Yea, saith the Spirit, that they may rest from their labours; and their works do follow them.

Blessed *see Revelation 1:3.*

Henceforth *aparti* (534), positively, "henceforth" stands for the following: (a) *ap' arti* (i.e., *apo arti*), lit., "from now," e.g., Matt. 26:64; Luke 22:69; John 13:19, RV, and KJV marg., "from henceforth"; **Rev. 14:13** (where *aparti* is found as one word in the best mss.); (b) *to loipon*, lit., "(for) the remaining (time)," Heb. 10:13; *tou loipou*, Gal. 6:17; (c) *apo tou nun*, lit., "from the now," e.g., Luke 1:48; 5:10; 12:52; Acts 18:6; 2 Cor. 5:16 (1st part).

Yea *see* Even so at *Revelation 1:7.*

Rest *see Revelation 6:11.*

Labours *see* Labour at *Revelation 2:2.*

Works *see Revelation 2:2.*

14:14 And I looked, and behold a white cloud, and upon the cloud *one* sat like unto the Son of man, having on his head a golden crown, and in his hand a sharp sickle.

Looked *see Revelation 4:1.*

White *see Revelation 1:14.*

Cloud *see* Clouds at *Revelation 1:7.*

Like unto *see Revelation 1:13.*

Son *see Revelation 1:13.*

Crown *see Revelation 2:10.*

Sharp *see Revelation 1:16.*

Sickle *drepanon* (1407), "a pruning hook, a sickle" (akin to *drepo*, "to pluck"), occurs in Mark 4:29; **Rev. 14:14, 15, 16, 17, 18** (twice), 19.

14:15 And another angel came out of the temple, crying with a loud voice to him that sat on the cloud, Thrust in thy sickle, and reap: for the time is come for thee to reap; for the harvest of the earth is ripe.

Temple *see Revelation 3:12.*

Loud *see Revelation 5:2.*

Thrust In **Rev. 14:15, 18**, KJV, *pempo*, to send (RV, "send forth"), is translated "thrust in." *See also* **Send** at *Revelation 1:11.*

Sickle *see Revelation 14:14.*

Reap *therizo* (2325), "to reap" (akin to *theros*, "summer, harvest"), is used (a) literally, Matt. 6:26; 25:24, 26; Luke 12:24; 19:21, 22; Jas. 5:4 (2nd part), KJV, "have reaped"; (b) figuratively or in proverbial expressions, John 4:36 (twice), 37, 38, with immediate reference to bringing Samaritans into the kingdom of God, in regard to which the disciples would enjoy the fruits of what Christ Himself had been doing in Samaria; the Lord's words are, however, of a general application in respect of such service; in 1 Cor. 9:11, with reference to the right of the apostle and his fellow missionaries to receive material assistance from the church, a right which he forbore to exercise; in 2 Cor. 9:6 (twice), with reference to rendering material help to the needy, either "sparingly" or "bountifully," the "reaping" being proportionate to the sowing; in Gal. 6:7, 8 (twice), of "reaping" corruption, with special reference, according to the context, to that which is naturally shortlived transient (though the statement applies to every form of sowing to the flesh), and of "reaping" eternal life (characteristics and moral qualities being in view), as a result of sowing "to the Spirit," the reference probably being to the new nature of the believer, which is, however, under the controlling power of the Holy Spirit, v. 9, the "reaping" (the effect of well doing) being accomplished, to a limited extent, in this life, but in complete fulfillment at and beyond the judgment seat of Christ; diligence or laxity here will then produce proportionate results; in **Rev. 14:15** (twice), **16**, figurative of the discriminating judgment divinely to be fulfilled at the close of this age, when the wheat will be separated from the tares (see Matt. 13:30).

Time *hora* (5610), primarily, "any time or period fixed by nature," is translated "time" in Matt. 14:15; Luke 14:17; Rom. 13:11, "high time"; in the following the RV renders it "hour," for KJV, "time," Matt. 18:1; Luke 1:10; John 16:2, 4, 25; 1 John 2:18 (twice); **Rev. 14:15**; in Mark 6:35, RV, "day"; in 1 Thess. 2:17, RV, "a short (season)," lit., "(the season, KJV, 'time') of an hour." *See also* **Hour** at *Revelation 3:3*.

Harvest *therismos* (2326), akin to *therizo*, "to reap," is used (a) of "the act of harvesting," John 4:35; (b) "the time of harvest," figuratively, Matt. 13:30, 39; Mark 4:29; (c) "the crop," figuratively, Matt. 9:37, 38; Luke 10:2; **Rev. 14:15**. The beginning of "harvest" varied according to natural conditions, but took place on the average about the middle of April in the eastern lowlands of Palestine, in the latter part of the month in the coast plains and a little later in high districts. Barley "harvest" usually came first and then wheat. "Harvesting" lasted about seven weeks, and was the occasion of festivities.

Ripe *xeraino* (3583), "to dry up, wither," is used of "ripened" crops in **Rev. 14:15**, RV, "overripe," KJV, "ripe" (marg., "dried").

14:16 And he that sat on the cloud thrust in his sickle on the earth; and the earth was reaped.

Thrust *ballo* (906), is rendered "to thrust" in John 20:25, 27, KJV (RV, put); Acts 16:24, KJV (RV, "cast"); so **Rev. 14:16, 19**.

Sickle *see Revelation 14:14*.

Reaped *see* **Reap at** *Revelation 14:15*.

14:17 And another angel came out of the temple which is in heaven, he also having a sharp sickle.

Temple *see Revelation 3:12*.

Sharp *see Revelation 1:16*.

Sickle *see Revelation 14:14*.

14:18 And another angel came out from the altar, which had power over fire; and cried with a loud cry to him that had the sharp sickle, saying, Thrust in thy sharp sickle, and gather the clusters of the vine of the earth; for her grapes are fully ripe.

Cried *phoneo* (5455), "to utter a loud sound or cry," whether of animals, e.g., Matt. 26:34; or persons, Luke 8:8; 16:24; this is the word which Luke uses to describe the "cry" of the Lord at the close of His sufferings on the cross, Luke 23:46 (see under *anaboao* and *krazo*, above); also, e.g., Acts 16:28; **Rev. 14:18**.

Loud *see Revelation 5:2*.

Cry *krauge* (2906), an onomatopoeic word, is used in Matt. 25:6; Luke 1:42 (some mss. have *phone*); Acts 23:9, RV, "clamor"; Eph. 4:31, "clamor"; Heb. 5:7; **Rev. 21:4**, "crying." Some mss. have it in **Rev. 14:18** (the most authentic have *phone*).

Sharp *see Revelation 1:16*.

Sickle *see Revelation 14:14*.

Thrust *see Revelation 14:15*. *See also* **Send** at *Revelation 1:11*.

Gather *trugao* (5166), signifies "to gather in," of harvest, vintage, ripe fruits (*truge* denotes "fruit," etc., gathered in autumn), Luke 6:44, of grapes; metaphorically, of the clusters of "the vine of the earth," **Rev. 14:18**; of that from which they are "gathered," v. **19**.

Clusters *botrus* (1009), "a cluster, or bunch, bunch of grapes," is found in **Rev. 14:18**.

Vine *ampelos* (288), is used (a) lit., e.g., Matt. 26:29 and parallel passages; Jas. 3:12; (b) figuratively, (1) of Christ, John 15:1, 4, 5; (2) of His enemies, **Rev. 14:18, 19**, "the vine of the earth" (RV, "vintage" in v. **19**), probably figurative of the remaining mass of apostate Christendom.

Grapes *staphule* (4718), denotes "a bunch of grapes, or a grape," Matt. 7:16; Luke 6:44; **Rev. 14:18**. It is to be distinguished from *omphax*, "an unripe grape" (not in NT), e.g., in the Sept. of Job 15:33, and from *botrus*, "a cluster," used together with *staphule* in **Rev. 14:18**.

Ripe *akmazo* (187), "to be at the prime" (akin to *akme*, "a point"), "to be ripe," is translated "are fully ripe" in **Rev. 14:18**.

14:19 And the angel thrust in his sickle into the earth, and gathered the vine of the earth, and cast *it* into the great winepress of the wrath of God.

Thrust *see Revelation 14:16*.

Gathered *see* **Gather** at *Revelation 14:18*.

Vine *see Revelation 14:18*.

Winepress *lenos* (3025), denotes "a trough or vat," used especially for the treading of grapes, Matt. 21:33. Not infrequently they were dug out in the soil or excavated in a rock, as in the rock vats in Palestine today. In **Rev. 14:19, 20** (twice) and **19:15** (where *oinos* is added, lit., "the winepress of the wine") the word is used metaphorically with reference to the execution of divine judgment upon the gathered foes of the Jews at the close of this age preliminary to the establishment of the millennial kingdom.

Wrath *see Revelation 12:12*.

14:20 And the winepress was trodden without the city, and blood came out of the winepress, even unto the horse bridles, by the space of a thousand *and* six hundred furlongs.

Winepress *see Revelation 14:19.*

Trodden *see* **Tread** at *Revelation 11:2.*

Horse *see Revelation 6:2.*

Bridles *chalinos* (5469), "a bridle," is used in Jas. 3:3 (KJV, "bits"), and **Rev. 14:20**. "The primitive bridle was simply a loop on the halter-cord passed round the lower jaw of the horse. Hence in Ps. 32:9 the meaning is bridle and halter" (Hastings, *Bib. Dic.*).

By the space of In **Rev. 14:20**, KJV, *apo*, "away from," is translated "by the space of" (RV, "as far as").

Thousand *see Revelation 5:11.*

Six *see Revelation 13:18.*

Furlongs *stoion* (4712), denotes (a) "a stadium," i.e., a measure of length, 600 Greek feet, or one-eighth of a Roman mile, Matt. 14:24 (in the best mss.); Luke 24:13; John 6:19; 11:18; **Rev. 14:20**; **21:16**; (b) "a race course," the length of the Olympic course, 1 Cor. 9:24.

Chapter 15

15:1 And I saw another sign in heaven, great and marvellous, seven angels having the seven last plagues; for in them is filled up the wrath of God.

Sign *see* **Wonder** at *Revelation 12:1.*

Marvellous *thaumastos* (2298), "marvelous," is said (a) of the Lord's doing in making the rejected Stone the Head of the corner, Matt. 21:42; Mark 12:11; (b) of the erstwhile blind man's astonishment that the Pharisees knew not from whence Christ had come, and yet He had given him sight, John 9:30, RV, "the marvel," KJV, "a marvellous thing"; (c) of the spiritual light into which believers are brought, 1 Pet. 2:9; (d) of the vision of the seven angels having the seven last plagues, **Rev. 15:1**; (e) of the works of God, **15:3**.

Plagues *see Revelation 9:20.*

Filled up In regard to this word in **Rev. 15:1** and **8**, the RV, "finished," corrects the KJV, "filled up," and "fulfilled," as the judgments there indicated finish the whole series of those consisting of the wrath of God; so in **20:3**, of the thousand years of the Millennium (cf. vv. **5**, **7**). *See also* **Finished** at *Revelation 10:7.*

Wrath *see Revelation 12:12.*

15:2 And I saw as it were a sea of glass mingled with fire: and them that had gotten the victory over the beast, and over his image, and over his mark, *and* over the number of his name, stand on the sea of glass, having the harps of God.

Sea *see Revelation 4:6.*

Glass *see Revelation 4:6.*

Mingled *see Revelation 8:7.*

Fire *see Revelation 1:14.*

Gotten In **Rev. 15:2**, KJV, *nikao*, "to conquer, prevail over," is translated "had gotten the victory" (RV, "come victorious").

Victory *nikao* (3528), "to conquer, overcome," is translated "(them) that come victorious (from)" in **Rev. 15:2**, RV (KJV, "that had gotten the victory"). *See also* **Overcometh** at *Revelation 2:7.*

Beast *see Revelation 11:7.*

Image *see Revelation 13:14.*

Mark *see Revelation 13:16.*

Harps *see Revelation 5:8.*

15:3 And they sing the song of Moses the servant of God, and the song of the Lamb, saying, Great and marvellous *are* thy works, Lord God Almighty; just and true *are* thy ways, thou King of saints.

Sing *see Revelation 5:9.*

Song *see Revelation 5:9.*

Servant *see* **Servants** at *Revelation 7:3.*

Lamb *see Revelation 5:6.*

Marvellous *see Revelation 15:1.*

Works *see Revelation 2:2.*

Just *dikaios* (1342), signifies "just," without prejudice or partiality, e.g., of the judgment of God, 2 Thess. 1:5, 6; of His judgments, **Rev. 16:7**; **19:2**; of His character as Judge, 2 Tim. 4:8; **Rev. 16:5**; of His ways and doings, **Rev. 15:3**. In the following the RV substitutes "righteous" for the KJV "just"; Matt. 1:19; 13:49; 27:19, 24; Mark 6:20; Luke 2:25; 15:7; 20:20; 23:50; John 5:30; Acts 3:14; 7:52; 10:22; 22:14; Rom. 1:17; 7:12; Gal. 3:11; Heb. 10:38; Jas. 5:6; 1 Pet. 3:18; 2 Pet. 2:7; 1 John 1:9; **Rev. 15:3**.

True *see Revelation 3:7.*

Ways *hodos* (3598), denotes (a) "a natural path, road, way," frequent in the Synoptic Gospels; elsewhere, e.g., Acts 8:26; 1 Thess. 3:11; Jas. 2:25; **Rev. 16:12**; (b) "a traveler's way"; (c) metaphorically, of "a course of conduct," or "way of thinking," e.g., of righteousness, Matt. 21:32; 2 Pet. 2:21; of God, Matt. 22:16, and parallels, i.e., the "way" instructed and approved by God; so Acts 18:26 and Heb. 3:10, "My ways" (cf. **Rev. 15:3**); of the Lord, Acts 18:25; "that leadeth to destruction," Matt. 7:13; "... unto life," 7:14; of peace, Luke 1:79; Rom. 3:17; of Paul's "ways" in Christ, 1 Cor. 4:17

(plural); "more excellent" (of love), 1 Cor. 12:31; of truth, 2 Pet. 2:2; of the right "way," 2:15; of Balaam (*id.*), of Cain, Jude 11; of a "way" consisting in what is from God, e.g., of life, Acts 2:28 (plural); of salvation, Acts 16:17; personified, of Christ as the means of access to the Father, John 14:6; of the course followed and characterized by the followers of Christ, Acts 9:2; 19:9, 23; 24:22.

King *basileus* (935), "a king" (cf. Eng., "Basil"), e.g., Matt. 1:6, is used of the Roman emperor in 1 Pet. 2:13, 17 (a command of general application); this reference to the emperor is illustrated frequently in the *Koine*; of Herod the Tetrarch (used by courtesy), Matt. 14:9; of Christ, as the "King" of the Jews, e.g., Matt, 2:2; 27:11, 29, 37; as the "King" of Israel, Mark 15:32; John 1:49; 12:13; as "King of kings," **Rev. 17:14; 19:16**; as "the King" in judging nations and men at the establishment of the millennial kingdom, Matt. 25:34, 40; of God, "the great King," Matt. 5:35; "the King eternal, incorruptible, invisible," 1 Tim. 1:17; "King of kings," 1 Tim. 6:15; "King of the ages," **Rev. 15:3**, RV (KJV, "saints"). Christ's "kingship" was predicted in the OT, e.g., Ps. 2:6, and in the NT, e.g., Luke 1:32, 33; He came as such, e.g., Matt. 2:2; John 18:37; was rejected and died as such, Luke 19:14; Matt. 27:37; is now a "King" Priest, after the order of Melchizedek, Heb. 5:6; 7:1, 17; and will reign for ever and ever, **Rev. 11:15**.

Saints In **Rev. 15:3** the RV follows those texts which have *aionon*, "ages," and assigns the reading *ethnon*, "nations," to the margin; the KJV translates those which have the inferior reading *hagion*, "saints," and puts "nations" and "ages" in the margin.

15:4 Who shall not fear thee, O Lord, and glorify thy name? for *thou* only *art* holy: for all nations shall come and worship before thee; for thy judgments are made manifest.

Fear *see* ***Revelation 14:7***.

Glorify *doxazo* (1392), primarily denotes "to suppose" (from *doxa*, "an opinion"); in the NT (a) "to magnify, extol, praise," especially of "glorifying"; God, i.e., ascribing honor to Him, acknowledging Him as to His being, attributes and acts, i.e., His glory, e.g., Matt. 5:16; 9:8; 15:31; Rom. 15:6, 9; Gal. 1:24; 1 Pet. 4:16; the Word of the Lord, Acts 13:48; the Name of the Lord, **Rev. 15:4**; also of "glorifying" oneself, John 8:54; **Rev. 18:7**; (b) "to do honor to, to make glorious," e.g., Rom. 8:30; 2 Cor. 3:10; 1 Pet. 1:8, "full of glory," passive voice (lit., "glorified"); said of Christ, e.g., John 7:39; 8:54, RV, "glorifieth," for KJV, "honor" and "honoreth" (which would translate *timao*, "to honor"); of the Father, e.g., John 13:31, 32; 21:19; 1 Pet. 4:11; of "glorifying" one's ministry, Rom. 11:13, RV, "glorify" (KJV, "magnify"); of a member of the body, 1 Cor. 12:26, "be honored" (RV marg., "be glorified").

Only *monos* (3441), "alone, solitary," is translated "only," e.g., in Matt. 4:10; 12:4; 17:8; 1 Cor. 9:6; 14:36; Phil. 4:15; Col. 4:11; 2 John 1; it is used as an attribute of God in John 5:44; 17:3; Rom. 16:27; 1 Tim. 1:17; 1 Tim. 6:15-16; Jude 4, 25; **Rev. 15:4**.

Holy *hosios* (3741), signifies "religiously right, holy," as opposed to what is unrighteous or polluted. It is commonly associated with righteousness. It is used "of God, **Rev. 15:4**; **16:5**; and of the body of the Lord Jesus, Acts 2:27; 13:35, citations from Ps. 16:10, Sept.; Heb. 7:26; and of certain promises made to David, which could be fulfilled only in the resurrection of the Lord Jesus, Acts 13:34. In 1 Tim. 2:8 and Titus 1:8, it is used of the character of Christians.... In the Sept., *hosios* frequently represents the Hebrew word *chasid*, which varies in meaning between 'holy' and 'gracious,' or 'merciful;' cf. Ps. 16:10 with 145:17." *See also* ***Revelation 4:8***.

Judgments *dikaioma* (1345), has three distinct meanings, and seems best described comprehensively as "a concrete expression of righteousness"; it is a declaration that a person or thing is righteous, and hence, broadly speaking, it represents the expression and effect of *dikaiosis*. It signifies (a) "an ordinance," Luke 1:6; Rom. 1:32, RV, "ordinance," i.e., what God has declared to be right, referring to His decree of retribution (KJV, "judgment"); Rom. 2:26, RV, "ordinances of the Law" (i.e., righteous requirements enjoined by the Law); so 8:4, "ordinance of the Law," i.e., collectively, the precepts of the Law, all that it demands as right; in Heb. 9:1, 10, ordinances connected with the tabernacle ritual; (b) "a sentence of acquittal," by which God acquits men of their guilt, on the conditions (1) of His grace in Christ, through His expiatory sacrifice, (2) the acceptance of Christ by faith, Rom. 5:16; (c) "a righteous act," Rom. 5:18, "(through one) act of righteousness," RV, not the act of "justification," nor the righteous character of Christ (as suggested by the KJV: *dikaioma* does not signify character, as does *dikaiosune*, righteousness), but the death of Christ, as an act accomplished consistently with God's character and counsels; this is clear as being in antithesis to the "one trespass" in the preceding statement. Some take the word here as meaning a decree of righteousness, as in v. 16; the death of Christ could indeed be regarded as fulfilling such a decree, but as the apostle's argument proceeds, the word, as is frequently the case, passes from one shade of meaning to another, and here stands not for a decree, but an act; so in **Rev. 15:4**, RV, "righteous acts" (KJV, "judgments"), and **19:8**, "righteous acts (of the saints)" (KJV, "righteousness").

15:5 And after that I looked, and, behold, the temple of the tabernacle of the testimony in heaven was opened:

After *see* Hereafter at *Revelation 1:19.*

Looked *see Revelation 4:1.*

Temple *see Revelation 3:12.*

Tabernacle *see Revelation 13:6.*

Testimony *marturion* (3142), "a testimony, witness," is almost entirely translated "testimony" in both KJV and RV. The only place where both have "witness" is Acts 4:33. In Acts 7:44 and Jas. 5:3, the RV has "testimony" (KJV, "witness"). In 2 Thess. 1:10, "our testimony unto you," RV, refers to the fact that the missionaries, besides proclaiming the truths of the gospel, had borne witness to the power of these truths. *Kerugma*, "the thing preached, the message," is objective, having especially to do with the effect on the hearers; *marturion* is mainly subjective, having to do especially with the preacher's personal experience. In 1 Tim. 2:6 the RV is important, "the testimony (i.e., of the gospel) *to be borne* in its own times," i.e., in the times divinely appointed for it, namely, the present age, from Pentecost till the church is complete. In **Rev. 15:5**, in the phrase, "the temple of the tabernacle of the testimony in Heaven," the "testimony" is the witness to the rights of God, denied and refused on earth, but about to be vindicated by the exercise of the judgments under the pouring forth of the seven bowls or vials of divine retribution.

Opened *see* Openeth at *Revelation 3:7.*

15:6 And the seven angels came out of the temple, having the seven plagues, clothed in pure and white linen, and having their breasts girded with golden girdles.

Temple *see Revelation 3:12.*

Plagues *see Revelation 9:20.*

Pure *katharos* (2513), "free from impure admixture, without blemish, spotless," is used (a) physically, e.g., Matt. 23:26; 27:59; John 13:10 (where the Lord, speaking figuratively, teaches that one who has been entirely "cleansed," needs not radical renewal, but only to be "cleansed" from every sin into which he may fall); 15:3; Heb. 10:22; **Rev. 15:6**; **19:8**, **14**; **21:18**, **21**; (b) in a Levitical sense, Rom. 14:20; Titus 1:15, "pure"; (c) ethically, with the significance free from corrupt desire, from guilt, Matt. 5:8; John 13:10-11; Acts 20:26; 1 Tim. 1:5; 3:9; 2 Tim. 1:3; 2:22; Titus 1:15; Jas. 1:27; blameless, innocent (a rare meaning for this word), Acts 18:6; (d) in a combined Levitical and ethical sense ceremonially, Luke 11:41, "all things are clean unto you."

White *lampros* (2986), "shining, brilliant, bright," is used of the clothing of an angel, Acts 10:30 and **Rev. 15:6**; symbolically, of the clothing of the saints in glory, **Rev. 19:8**, RV, in the best texts (KJV, "white"); of Christ as the Morning Star, **22:16**; of the water of life, **22:1**, KJV, "clear."

Linen *linon* (3043), denotes (a) "flax," Matt. 12:20; (b) "linen," in **Rev. 15:6**, KJV; the best texts have *lithos*, "stone," RV.

Breasts *stethos* (4738), connected with *histemi*, "to stand," i.e., that which stands out, is used of mourners in smiting the "breast," Luke 18:13; 23:48; of John in reclining on the "breast" of Christ, John 13:25; 21:20; of the "breasts" of the angels in **Rev. 15:6**.

Girded *see* Girt at *Revelation 1:13.*

Girdles *see* Girdle at *Revelation 1:13.*

15:7 And one of the four beasts gave unto the seven angels seven golden vials full of the wrath of God, who liveth for ever and ever.

Vials *see Revelation 5:8.*

Full *see Revelation 4:6.*

Wrath *see Revelation 12:12.*

15:8 And the temple was filled with smoke from the glory of God, and from his power; and no man was able to enter into the temple, till the seven plagues of the seven angels were fulfilled.

Temple *see Revelation 3:12.*

Filled *see Revelation 8:5.*

Smoke *see Revelation 9:2.*

Plagues *see Revelation 9:20.*

Fulfilled *see* Filled up at *Revelation 15:1. See also* Finished at *Revelation 10:7.*

Chapter 16

16:1 And I heard a great voice out of the temple saying to the seven angels, Go your ways, and pour out the vials of the wrath of God upon the earth.

Temple *see Revelation 3:12.*

Go *see Revelation 10:8.*

Pour *ekcheo* (1632), "to pour out" (*ek*, "out"), is used (a) of Christ's act as to the changers' money, John 2:15; (b) of the Holy Spirit, Acts 2:17, 18, 33, RV, "He hath poured forth" (KJV, "... shed forth"); Titus 3:6, RV, "poured out" (KJV, "shed"); (c) of the emptying of the contents of the bowls (KJV, "vials") of divine wrath, **Rev. 16:1-4, 8, 10, 12, 17**; (d) of the shedding of the blood of saints by the foes of God, **Rev. 16:6**, RV, "poured out" (KJV, "shed"); some mss. have it in Acts 22:20.

Vials *see Revelation 5:8.*

Wrath *see Revelation 12:12.*

16:2 And the first went, and poured out his vial upon the earth; and there fell a noisome and grievous sore upon the men which had the mark of the beast, and *upon* them which worshipped his image.

Fell In **Rev. 16:2**, *ginomai*, "to become," is translated "it became," RV, for KJV, "there fell."

Noisome *kakos* (2556), "evil," is translated "noisome" in **Rev. 16:2**. *See also* Evil at *Revelation 2:2.*

Grievous *poneros* (4190), "painful, bad," is translated "grievous" in **Rev. 16:2**, of a sore inflicted retributively.

Sore *helkos* (1668), "a sore" or "ulcer" (primarily a wound), occurs in Luke 16:21; **Rev. 16:2, 11.**

Mark *see Revelation 13:16.*

Beast *see Revelation 11:7.*

Worshipped *see* Worship at *Revelation 4:10.*

Image *see Revelation 13:14.*

16:3 And the second angel poured out his vial upon the sea; and it became as the blood of a dead *man*: and every living soul died in the sea.

Sea *see Revelation 4:6.*

Soul *see* Souls at *Revelation 6:9.*

16:4 And the third angel poured out his vial upon the rivers and fountains of waters; and they became blood.

Rivers *see Revelation 8:10.*

Fountains *see Revelation 7:17.*

16:5 And I heard the angel of the waters say, Thou art righteous, O Lord, which art, and wast, and shalt be, because thou hast judged thus.

Righteous *see Revelation 15:3.*

Which *see Revelation 1:4.*

16:6 For they have shed the blood of saints and prophets, and thou hast given them blood to drink; for they are worthy.

Shed *see* Pour at *Revelation 16:1.*

Drink *see Revelation 14:10.*

Worthy *see Revelation 3:4.*

16:7 And I heard another out of the altar say, Even so, Lord God Almighty, true and righteous *are* thy judgments.

Even so *see Revelation 1:7.*

True *see Revelation 3:7.*

Righteous *see Revelation 15:3.*

Judgments *krisis* (2920), (a) denotes "the process of investigation, the act of distinguishing and separating"; hence "a judging, a passing of judgment upon a person or thing"; it has a variety of meanings, such as judicial authority, John 5:22, 27; justice, Acts 8:33; Jas. 2:13; a tribunal, Matt. 5:21-22; a trial, John 5:24; 2 Pet. 2:4; a judgment, 2 Pet. 2:11; Jude 9; by metonymy, the standard of judgment, just dealing, Matt. 12:18, 20; 23:23; Luke 11:42; divine judgment executed, 2 Thess. 1:5; **Rev. 16:7**; (b) sometimes it has the meaning "condemnation," and is virtually equivalent to *krima* (a); see Matt. 23:33; John 3:19; Jas. 5:12, *hupo krisin*, "under judgment."

16:8 And the fourth angel poured out his vial upon the sun; and power was given unto him to scorch men with fire.

Vial *see* Vials at *Revelation 5:8.*

Poured *see* Pour at *Revelation 16:1.*

Sun *see Revelation 1:16.*

Scorch *kaumatizo* (2739), "to scorch" (from *kauma*, "heat"), is used (a) of seed that had not much earth, Matt. 13:6; Mark 4:6; (b) of men, stricken retributively by the sun's heat, **Rev. 16:8, 9.**

16:9 And men were scorched with great heat, and blasphemed the name of God, which hath power over these plagues: and they repented not to give him glory.

Scorched *see* Scorch at *Revelation 16:8.*

Heat *see Revelation 7:16.*

Blasphemed *see* Blasphemy, Blaspheme at *Revelation 13:6.*

Plagues *see Revelation 9:20.*

Repented *see* Repent at *Revelation 2:5.*

16:10 And the fifth angel poured out his vial upon the seat of the beast; and his kingdom was full of darkness; and they gnawed their tongues for pain,

Fifth *see Revelation 6:9.*

Poured *see* Pour at *Revelation 16:1.*

Vial *see* Vials at *Revelation 5:8.*

Seat *see* Throne at *Revelation 1:4.*

Beast *see Revelation 11:7.*

Darkness *see* Darkened at *Revelation 9:2.*

Gnawed *masaomai* or *massaomai* (3145), denotes "to bite or chew," **Rev. 16:10.** In the Sept., Job. 30:4.

Tongues *see* Tongue at *Revelation 5:9.*

Pain *ponos* (4192), is translated "pain" in **Rev. 16:10; 21:4;** "pains" in **16:11.**

16:11 And blasphemed the God of heaven because of their pains and their sores, and repented not of their deeds.

Blasphemed *see* Blasphemy, Blaspheme at *Revelation 13:6.*

Heaven *see Revelation 3:12. See also* Air at *Revelation 9:2.*

Pains *see* Pain at *Revelation 16:10.*

Sores *see* Sore at *Revelation 16:2.*

Repented *see* Repent at *Revelation 2:5.*

16:12 And the sixth angel poured out his vial upon the great river Euphrates; and the water thereof was dried up, that the way of the kings of the east might be prepared.

Sixth *see Revelation 6:12.*

Poured *see* Pour at *Revelation 16:1.*

Vial *see* Vials at *Revelation 5:8.*

River *see* Rivers at *Revelation 8:10.*

Dried *see* Ripe at *Revelation 14:15.*

Way *see* Ways at *Revelation 15:3.*

East *see Revelation 7:2.*

Prepared *see Revelation 8:6.*

16:13 And I saw three unclean spirits like frogs *come* out of the mouth of the dragon, and out of the mouth of the beast, and out of the mouth of the false prophet.

Unclean *akathartos* (169), "unclean, impure" (*a*, negative, *kathairo*, "to purify"), is used (a) of "unclean" spirits, frequently in the Synoptists, not in John's Gospel; in Acts 5:16; 8:7; **Rev. 16:13; 18:2a** (in the 2nd clause the birds are apparently figurative of destructive satanic agencies); (b) ceremonially, Acts 10:14, 28; 11:8; 1 Cor. 7:14; (c) morally, 2 Cor. 6:17, including (b), RV; "no unclean thing"; Eph. 5:5; **Rev. 17:4,** RV, "the unclean things" (KJV follows the text which have the noun *akathartes*, "the filthiness").

Spirits *see* Devils at *Revelation 9:20.*

Frogs *batrachos* (944), is mentioned in **Rev. 16:13.** Quacks were represented as "frogs" and were associated metaphorically with serpents.

Mouth *see Revelation 1:16.*

Dragon *see Revelation 12:3.*

Beast *see Revelation 11:7.*

Prophet *see* Beast at *Revelation 13:11.*

16:14 For they are the spirits of devils, working miracles, *which* go forth unto the kings of the earth and of the whole world, to gather them to the battle of that great day of God Almighty.

Devils *see Revelation 9:20.*

"Do not rejoice in earthly reality, rejoice in Christ, rejoice in his word, rejoice in his law ... There will be peace and tranquility in the Christian heart; but only as long as our faith is watchful; if, however, our faith sleeps, we are in danger."

ST. AUGUSTINE

Working *poieo* (4160), "to do," is rendered "to work" in Matt. 20:12, KJV (RV, "spent"); Acts 15:12, "had wrought"; 19:11; 21:19; Heb. 13:21; **Rev. 16:14; 19:20; 21:27,** KJV (RV, "maketh"; marg., "doeth"). *See also* Make at *Revelation 3:9.*

Miracles *see Revelation 13:14. See also* Wonder at *Revelation 12:1.*

World *see Revelation 3:10.*

Battle *see Revelation 9:7.*

16:15 Behold, I come as a thief. Blessed *is* he that watcheth, and keepeth his garments, lest he walk naked, and they see his shame.

Thief *see Revelation 3:3.*

Blessed *see Revelation 1:3.*

Watcheth *see* Watchful at *Revelation 3:2.*

Keepeth *see* Keep at *Revelation 1:3*.

Naked *see Revelation 3:17*.

Shame *aschemosune* (808), denotes (a) "unseemliness," Rom. 1:27, RV (KJV, "that which is unseemly"); (b) "shame, nakedness," **Rev. 16:15**, a euphemism for *aischune*. *See also Revelation 3:18*.

16:16 And he gathered them together into a place called in the Hebrew tongue Armageddon.

Tongue *see Revelation 9:11*.

16:17 And the seventh angel poured out his vial into the air; and there came a great voice out of the temple of heaven, from the throne, saying, It is done.

Seventh *see Revelation 8:1*.

Poured *see* Pour at *Revelation 16:1*.

Vial *see* Vials at *Revelation 5:8*.

Temple *see Revelation 3:12*.

16:18 And there were voices, and thunders, and lightnings; and there was a great earthquake, such as was not since men were upon the earth, so mighty an earthquake, *and* so great.

Thunders *see* Thunderings at *Revelation 4:5*.

Lightnings *see Revelation 4:5*.

Earthquake *see Revelation 6:12*.

So *houtos* or *houto* (3779), "in this way, so, thus," is used (a) with reference to what precedes, e.g., Luke 1:25; 2:48; (b) with reference to what follows, e.g., Luke 19:31, rendered "on this wise," in Matt. 1:18; John 21:1, and before quotations, Acts 7:6; 13:34; Rom. 10:6, KJV (RV, "thus"); Heb. 4:4; (c) marking intensity, rendered "so," e.g., Gal. 1:6; Heb. 12:21; **Rev. 16:18**; (d) in comparisons, rendered "so," e.g., Luke 11:30; Rom. 5:15.

Mighty *telikoutos* (5082), "so great," is used in the NT of things only, a death, 2 Cor. 1:10; salvation, Heb. 2:3; ships, Jas. 3:4; an earthquake, **Rev. 16:18**, KJV, "so mighty," corrected in the RV to "so great."

16:19 And the great city was divided into three parts, and the cities of the nations fell: and great Babylon came in remembrance before God, to give unto her the cup of the wine of the fierceness of his wrath.

Divided *ginomai* (1096), "to become," is translated "was divided" in **Rev. 16:19** (of "the great city"), lit., "became into three parts."

Parts *meros* (3313), denotes (a) "a part, portion," of the whole, e.g., John 13:8; **Rev. 20:6**; **22:19**; hence, "a lot" or "destiny," e.g., **Rev. 21:8**; in Matt. 24:51 and Luke 12:46, "portion"; (b) "a part" as opposite to the whole, e.g., Luke 11:36; John 19:23; 21:6, "side"; Acts 5:2; 23:6; Eph. 4:16; **Rev. 16:19**; a party, Acts 23:9; the divisions of a province, e.g., Matt. 2:22; Acts 2:10; the regions belonging to a city, e.g., Matt. 15:21, RV, "parts" (KJV, "coasts"); 16:13 (ditto); Mark 8:10, KJV and RV, "parts"; "the lower parts of the earth," Eph. 4:9; this phrase means the regions beneath the earth; (c) "a class," or "category" (with *en*, in, "in respect of"), Col. 2:16; "in this respect," 2 Cor. 3:10; 9:3, RV (KJV, "in this behalf").

Remembrance *mimnesko* (3403), from the older form *mnaomai*, in the active voice signifies "to remind"; in the middle voice, "to remind oneself of," hence, "to remember, to be mindful of"; the later form is found only in the present tense, in Heb. 2:6, "are mindful of," and 13:3, "remember"; the perfect tense in 1 Cor. 11:2 and in 2 Tim. 1:4 (RV, "remembering," KJV, "being mindful of"), is used with a present meaning. RV variations from the KJV are, in Luke 1:54, RV, "that He might remember" (KJV, "in remembrance of"); 2 Pet. 3:2, "remember" (KJV, "be mindful of"); **Rev. 16:19** (passive voice), "was remembered" (KJV, "came in remembrance"). The passive voice is used also in Acts 10:31, KJV and RV, "are had in remembrance."

Before *see Revelation 1:4*.

Cup *see Revelation 14:10*.

Wine *see Revelation 14:8*.

Fierceness *thumos* (2372), "hot anger, wrath," is rendered "fierceness" in **Rev. 16:19**; **19:15**, of the wrath of God.

Wrath *see Revelation 12:12*.

16:20 And every island fled away, and the mountains were not found.

Island *see* Isle at *Revelation 1:9*.

Fled *see* Flee at *Revelation 9:6*.

Found *see Revelation 5:4*.

16:21 And there fell upon men a great hail out of heaven, *every stone* about the weight of a talent: and men blasphemed God because of the plague of the hail; for the plague thereof was exceeding great.

Fell *katabaino* (2597), denotes "to come (or fall) down," Luke 22:44; in **Rev. 16:21**, "cometh down," RV.

Hail *see Revelation 8:7*.

Talent *alantiaios* (5006), denotes "of a talent's weight," **Rev. 16:21**.

Blasphemed *see* **Blasphemy, Blaspheme** at *Revelation 13:6*.

Plague *see* **Plagues** at *Revelation 9:20*.

Exceeding *sphodra* (4970), properly the neuter plural of *sphodros*, "excessive, violent" (from a root indicating restlessness), signifies "very, very much, exceedingly," Matt. 2:10; 17:6, "sore"; 17:23; 18:31, RV, "exceeding," for KJV, "very"; 19:25; 26:22; 27:54, RV, "exceedingly" for KJV, "greatly"; Mark 16:4, "very"; Luke 18:23 (ditto); Acts 6:7, RV, "exceedingly," for KJV, greatly; **Rev. 16:21**.

Chapter 17

17:1 And there came one of the seven angels which had the seven vials, and talked with me, saying unto me, Come hither; I will shew unto thee the judgment of the great whore that sitteth upon many waters:

Vials *see Revelation 5:8*.

Talked *see* **Talking** at *Revelation 4:1*.

Come *deuro*, "hither, here," is used (sometimes with verbs of motion) in the singular number, in calling a person to come, Matt. 19:21; Mark 10:21; Luke 18:22; John 11:43; Acts 7:3, 34; **Rev. 17:1**; **21:9**. It has a plural, *deute*, frequent in the Gospels; elsewhere in **Rev. 19:17**.

Whore *porne* (4204), "a prostitute, harlot" (from *pernemi*, "to sell"), is used (a) literally, in Matt. 21:31, 32, of those who were the objects of the mercy shown by Christ; in Luke 15:30, of the life of the Prodigal; in 1 Cor. 6:15, 16, in a warning to the Corinthian church against the prevailing licentiousness which had made Corinth a byword; in Heb. 11:31 and Jas. 2:25, of Rahab; (b) metaphorically, of mystic Babylon, **Rev. 17:1**, **5** (KJV, "harlots"), **15**, **16**; **19:2**, RV, for KJV, "whore."

Waters *hudor* (5204), whence Eng. prefix, "hydro-," is used (a) of the natural element, frequently in the Gospels; in the plural especially in Revelation; elsewhere, e.g., Heb. 9:19; Jas. 3:12; in 1 John 5:6, that Christ "came by water and blood," may refer either (1) to the elements that flowed from His side on the cross after His death, or, in view of the order of the words and the prepositions here used, (2) to His baptism in Jordan and His death on the cross. As to (1), the "water" would symbolize the moral and practical cleansing effected by the removal of defilement by our taking heed to the Word of God in heart, life and habit; cf. Lev. 14, as to the cleansing of the leper. As to (2), Jesus the Son of God came on His mission by, or through, "water" and blood, namely, at His baptism, when He publicly entered upon His mission and was declared to be the Son of God by the witness of the Father, and at the cross, when He publicly closed His witness; the apostle's statement thus counteracts the doctrine of the Gnostics that the divine *Logos* united Himself with the Man Jesus at His baptism, and left him at Gethsemane. On the contrary, He who was baptized and He who was crucified was the Son of God throughout in His combined deity and humanity. The word "water" is used symbolically in John 3:5, either (1) of the Word of God, as in 1 Pet. 1:23 (cf. the symbolic use in Eph. 5:26), or, in view of the preposition *ek*, "out of," (2) of the truth conveyed by baptism, this being the expression, not the medium, the symbol, not the cause, of the believer's identification with Christ in His death, burial and resurrection. So the New Birth is, in one sense, the setting aside of all that the believer was according to the flesh, for it is evident that there must be an entirely new beginning. Some regard the *kai*, "and," in John 3:5, as epexegetic, = "even," in which case the "water" would be emblematic of the Spirit, as in John 7:38 (cf. 4:10, 14), but not in 1 John 5:8. where the Spirit and the "water" are distinguished. "The water of life," **Rev. 21:6** and **22:1**, **17**, is emblematic of the maintenance of spiritual life in perpetuity. In **Rev. 17:1** "the waters" are symbolic of nations, peoples, etc. *See also* **Sea** at *Revelation 4:6*.

17:2 With whom the kings of the earth have committed fornication, and the inhabitants of the earth have been made drunk with the wine of her fornication.

Inhabitants *see* **Dwellest** at *Revelation 2:13*.

Drunk *methuo* (3184), signifies "to be drunk with wine" (from *methu*, "mulled wine"; hence Eng., "mead, honey-wine"); originally it denoted simply "a pleasant drink." The verb is used of "being intoxicated" in Matt. 24:49; Acts 2:15; 1 Cor. 11:21; 1 Thess. 5:7*b*; metaphorically, of the effect upon men of partaking of the abominations of the Babylonish system, **Rev. 17:2**; of being in a state of mental "intoxication," through the shedding of men's blood profusely, v. **6**.

Wine *see Revelation 14:8* e.

Fornication *see Revelation 2:21*.

17:3 So he carried me away in the spirit into the wilderness: and I saw a woman sit upon a scarlet coloured beast, full of

names of blasphemy, having seven heads and ten horns.

Spirit *see Revelation 1:10.*

Scarlet *kokkinos* (2847), is derived from *kokkos*, used of the "berries" (clusters of the eggs of an insect) collected from the *ilex coccifera;* the color, however, is obtained from the cochineal insect, which attaches itself to the leaves and twigs of the coccifera oak; another species is raised on the leaves of the *cactus ficus*. The Arabic name for this insect is *qirmiz*, whence the word "crimson." It is used (a) of "scarlet" wool, Heb. 9:19; cf. in connection with the cleansing of a leper, Lev. 14:4, 6, "scarlet"; with the offering of the red heifer, Num. 19:6; (b) of the robe put on Christ by the soldiers, Matt. 27:28; (c) of the "beast" seen in symbolic vision in **Rev. 17:3**, "scarlet-colored"; (d) of the clothing of the "woman" as seen sitting on the "beast," **17:4**; (e) of part of the merchandise of Babylon, **18:12**; (f) figuratively, of the glory of the city itself, **18:16**; the neuter is used in the last three instances.

Beast *see Revelation 11:7.*

Full *see Revelation 4:6.*

Heads *see Revelation 13:1.*

Ten *see Revelation 2:10.*

Horns *see Revelation 5:6.*

17:4 And the woman was arrayed in purple and scarlet colour, and decked with gold and precious stones and pearls, having a golden cup in her hand full of abominations and filthiness of her fornication:

Purple *porphureos* (4210), "purple, a reddish purple," is used of the robe put in mockery on Christ, John 19:2, 5; in **Rev. 17:4** (in the best texts); **18:16**, as a noun (with *himation*, "a garment," understood).

Scarlet *see Revelation 17:3.*

Decked *chrusoo* (5558), lit., "to gild with gold" (*chrusos*, "gold"), is used in **Rev. 17:4; 18:16**.

Gold *see Revelation 3:18.*

Precious *timios* (5093), from *time*, "honor, price," signifies (a), primarily, "accounted as of great price, precious, costly," 1 Cor. 3:12; **Rev. 17:4; 18:12, 16; 21:19**, and in the superlative degree, **18:12; 21:11**; the comparative degree is found in 1 Pet. 1:7 (*polutimoteros*, in the most authentic mss., "much more precious"); (b) in the metaphorical sense, "held in honor, esteemed, very dear," Acts 5:34, "had in honor," RV (KJV, "had in reputation"); so in Heb. 13:4, RV, "let marriage be had in honor"; KJV, "is honorable"; Acts 20:24, "dear," negatively of Paul's estimate of his life; Jas. 5:7, "precious" (of fruit); 1 Pet. 1:19, "precious" (of the blood of Christ); 2 Pet. 1:4 (of God's promises). Cf. *timiotes*, preciousness, **Rev. 18:19**.

Stones *see* **Stone** at *Revelation 4:3.*

Pearls *margarites* (3135), "a pearl" (Eng., Margaret), occurs in Matt. 7:6 (proverbially and figuratively); 13:45, 46; 1 Tim. 2:9; **Rev. 17:4; 18:12, 16; 21:21** (twice).

Cup *see Revelation 14:10.*

Full *see Revelation 4:6.*

Abominations *bdelugma* (946), denotes an "object of disgust, an abomination." This is said of the image to be set up by Antichrist, Matt. 24:15; Mark 13:14; of that which is highly esteemed amongst men, in contrast to its real character in the sight of God, Luke 16:15. The constant association with idolatry suggests that what is highly esteemed among men constitutes an idol in the human heart. In **Rev. 21:27**, entrance is forbidden into the Holy City on the part of the unclean, or one who "maketh an abomination and a lie." It is also used of the contents of the golden cup in the hand of the evil woman described in **Rev. 17:4**, and of the name ascribed to her in the following verse.

Filthiness In **Rev. 17:4** the best mss. have this word in the plural, RV. "the unclean things" (*akathartes*, "filthiness," in some mss.). See also **Unclean** at *Revelation 16:13.*

Fornication *see Revelation 2:21.*

17:5 And upon her forehead *was* a name written, MYSTERY, BABYLON THE GREAT, THE MOTHER OF HARLOTS AND ABOMINATIONS OF THE EARTH.

Forehead *see* **Foreheads** at *Revelation 7:3.*

Mystery *see Revelation 1:20.*

Mother *meter* (3384), is used (a) of the natural relationship, e.g., Matt. 1:18; 2 Tim. 1:5; (b) figuratively, (1) of "one who takes the place of a mother," Matt. 12:49, 50; Mark 3:34, 35; John 19:27; Rom. 16:13; 1 Tim. 5:2; (2) of "the heavenly and spiritual Jerusalem," Gal. 4:26, which is "free" (not bound by law imposed externally, as under the Law of Moses), "which is our mother" (RV), i.e., of Christians, the metropolis, mother-city, used allegorically, just as the capital of a country is "the seat of its government, the center of its activities, and the place where the national characteristics are most fully expressed"; (3) symbolically, of "Babylon," **Rev. 17:5**, as the source from which has proceeded the religious harlotry of mingling pagan rites and doctrines with the Christian faith.

Harlots *see* Whore at *Revelation 17:1*.

17:6 And I saw the woman drunken with the blood of the saints, and with the blood of the martyrs of Jesus: and when I saw her, I wondered with great admiration.

Drunken *see* Drunk at *Revelation 17:2*.

Blood *haima* (129), (hence Eng., prefix *haem-*), besides its natural meaning, stands, (a) in conjunction with *sarx*, "flesh," "flesh and blood," Matt. 16:17; 1 Cor. 15:50; Gal. 1:16; the original has the opposite order, blood and flesh, in Eph. 6:12 and Heb. 2:14; this phrase signifies, by *synecdoche*, "man, human beings." It stresses the limitations of humanity; the two are essential elements in man's physical being; "the life of the flesh is in the blood," Lev. 17:11; (b) for human generation, John 1:13; (c) for "blood" shed by violence, e.g., Matt. 23:35; **Rev. 17:6**; (d) for the "blood" of sacrificial victims, e.g., Heb. 9:7; of the "blood" of Christ, which betokens His death by the shedding of His "blood" in expiatory sacrifice; to drink His "blood" is to appropriate the saving effects of His expiatory death, John 6:53. As "the life of the flesh is in the blood," Lev. 17:11, and was forfeited by sin, life eternal can be imparted only by the expiation made, in the giving up of the life by the sinless Savior.

Martyrs *see* Witness at *Revelation 1:5*.

Jesus *see* *Revelation 1:9*.

Wondered *thauma* (2295), "a wonder" (akin to *theaomai*, "to gaze in wonder"), is found in the most authentic mss. in 2 Cor. 11:14 (some mss. have the adjective *thaumastos*), "(no) marvel"; in **Rev. 17:6**, RV, "wonder" (KJV, "admiration"), said of John's astonishment at the vision of the woman described as Babylon the Great. In the Sept., Job 17:8; 18:20; in some mss., 20:8 and 21:5. Cf. *teras*, "a wonder"; *semeion*, "a sign"; *thambos*, "wonder"; *ekstasis*, "amazement."

17:7 And the angel said unto me, Wherefore didst thou marvel? I will tell thee the mystery of the woman, and of the beast that carrieth her, which hath the seven heads and ten horns.

Wherefore Some phrases introduced by the preposition *dia*, "on account of," *dia touto*, "on account of this," e.g., Matt. 12:31; Rom. 5:12; Eph. 1:15; 3 John 10; *dia hen* (the accusative feminine of *hos*, "who"), "on account of which" (*aitia*, "a cause," being understood), e.g., Acts 10:21 (with *aitia*, expressed, Titus 1:13; Heb. 2:11); *dia ti* "on account of what?" (sometimes as one word, *diati*), e.g., Luke 19:23; Rom. 9:32; 2 Cor. 11:11; **Rev. 17:7**.

Tell *eiro* (3004), is rendered "to tell" in Matt. 21:24; Mark 11:29; John 14:29; **Rev. 17:7**.

Mystery *see* *Revelation 1:20*.

Carrieth *see* Bear at *Revelation 2:2*.

Heads *see* *Revelation 13:1*.

Ten *see* *Revelation 2:10*.

Horns *see* *Revelation 5:6*.

17:8 The beast that thou sawest was, and is not; and shall ascend out of the bottomless pit, and go into perdition: and they that dwell on the earth shall wonder, whose names were not written in the book of life from the foundation of the world, when they behold the beast that was, and is not, and yet is.

Shall *see* *Revelation 1:19*.

Ascend *see* Rise at *Revelation 13:1*.

Bottomless *see* *Revelation 9:1*.

Go *see* *Revelation 10:8*.

Perdition *apoleia* (684), indicating "loss of well-being, not of being," is used (a) of things, signifying their waste, or ruin; of ointment, Matt. 26:8; Mark 14:4; of money, Acts 8:20 ("perish"); (b) of persons, signifying their spiritual and eternal perdition, Matt. 7:13; John 17:12; 2 Thess. 2:3, where "son of perdition" signifies the proper destiny of the person mentioned; metaphorically of men persistent in evil, Rom. 9:22, where "fitted" is in the middle voice, indicating that the vessels of wrath fitted themselves for "destruction", of the adversaries of the Lord's people, Phil. 1:28 ("perdition"); of professing Christians, really enemies of the cross of Christ, Phil. 3:19 (RV, "perdition"); of those who are subjects of foolish and hurtful lusts, 1 Tim. 6:9; of professing Hebrew adherents who shrink back into unbelief, Heb. 10:39; of false teachers, 2 Pet. 2:1, 3; of ungodly men, 3:7; of those who wrest the Scriptures, 3:16; of the Beast, the final head of the revived Roman Empire, **Rev. 17:8, 11**; (c) of impersonal subjects, as heresies, 2 Pet. 2:1, where "destructive heresies" (RV; KJV, "damnable") is, lit., "heresies of destruction" (marg., "sects of perdition"); in v. 2 the most authentic mss. have *aselgeiais*, "lascivious," instead of *apoleiais*.

Book *see* *Revelation 1:11*.

Foundation *see* *Revelation 13:8*.

17:9 And here *is* the mind which hath wisdom. The seven heads are seven mountains, on which the woman sitteth.

Here *see Revelation 13:10.*

Mind *see* Understanding at *Revelation 13:18.*

Wisdom *see Revelation 5:12.*

Heads *see Revelation 13:1.*

Mountains *see* Mount at *Revelation 14:1.*

17:10 And there are seven kings: five are fallen, and one is, *and* the other is not yet come; and when he cometh, he must continue a short space.

Short space *oligon* (3641), is used adverbially of time, Mark 6:31, "a while;" 1 Pet. 1:6, RV, "a little while (KJV, "a season"); 5:10, RV, "a little while" (KJV, "a while"); **Rev. 17:10**, RV, "a little while" (KJV, "a short space").

17:11 And the beast that was, and is not, even he is the eighth, and is of the seven, and goeth into perdition.

Eighth *ogdoos* (3590), "eighth" (connected with the preceding), is used in Luke 1:59; Acts 7:8; 2 Pet. 2:5; **Rev. 17:11**; **21:20**.

Goeth *see* Go at *Revelation 10:8.*

Perdition *see Revelation 17:8.*

17:12 And the ten horns which thou sawest are ten kings, which have received no kingdom as yet; but receive power as kings one hour with the beast.

Ten *see Revelation 2:10.*

Horns *see Revelation 5:6.*

17:13 These have one mind, and shall give their power and strength unto the beast.

Mind *gnome* (1106), primarily "a means of knowing" (akin to *ginosko*, "to know"), came to denote "a mind, understanding"; hence (a) "a purpose," Acts 20:3, lit., "(it was his) purpose"; (b) "a royal purpose, a decree," **Rev. 17:17**, RV, "mind" (KJV, "will"); (c) "judgment, opinion," 1 Cor. 1:10, "(in the same) judgment"; **Rev. 17:13**, "mind"; (d) "counsel, advice," 1 Cor. 7:25, "(I give my) judgment;" 7:40, "(after my) judgment"; Philem. 14, mind.

Give *diadidomi* (1239), lit., "to give through," (*dia*, "through," *didomi*, "to give"), as from one to another, "to deal out," is said of "distributing" to the poor, Luke 18:22; Acts 4:35, "distribution was made," or to a company of people, John 6:11. It is translated "divideth" in Luke 11:22. In **Rev. 17:13** the most authentic mss. have the verb *didomi*, to give, instead of the longer form.

Power *see Revelation 12:10.*

Strength In **Rev. 17:13**, KJV, *exousia*, "freedom of action," is rendered "strength" (RV, "authority").

17:14 These shall make war with the Lamb, and the Lamb shall overcome them: for he is Lord of lords, and King of kings: and they that are with him *are* called, and chosen, and faithful.

War *see* Fight at *Revelation 2:16.*

Lamb *see Revelation 5:6.*

Overcome *see* Overcometh at *Revelation 2:7.*

Lord *see* Sir at *Revelation 7:14.*

King *see Revelation 15:3.*

Called *kletos* (2822), "called, invited," is used, (a) "of the call of the gospel," Matt. 20:16; 22:14, not there "an effectual call," as in the Epistles, Rom. 1:1, 6-7; 8:28; 1 Cor. 1:2, 24; Jude 1; **Rev. 17:14**; in Rom. 1:7 and 1 Cor. 1:2 the meaning is "saints by calling"; (b) of "an appointment to apostleship," Rom. 1:1; 1 Cor. 1:1.

Chosen *eklektos* (1588), signifies "chosen out, select," e.g., Matt. 22:14; Luke 23:35; Rom. 16:13 (perhaps in the sense of "eminent"), **Rev. 17:14**. In 1 Pet. 2:4, 9, the RV translates it "elect."

Faithful *see Revelation 1:5.*

17:15 And he saith unto me, The waters which thou sawest, where the whore sitteth, are peoples, and multitudes, and nations, and tongues.

Waters *see* Sea at *Revelation 4:6.*

Whore *see Revelation 17:1.*

Multitudes *see* Multitude at *Revelation 7:9.*

Tongues *see* Tongue at *Revelation 5:9.*

17:16 And the ten horns which thou sawest upon the beast, these shall hate the whore, and shall make her desolate and naked, and shall eat her flesh, and burn her with fire.

Ten *see Revelation 2:10.*

Horns *see Revelation 5:6.*

Whore *see Revelation 17:1.*

Desolate *eremoo* (2049), signifies "to make desolate, lay waste." From the primary sense of "making quiet" comes that of "making lonely." It is used only in the passive voice in the NT; in **Rev. 17:16**, "shall make desolate" is, lit., "shall make her desolated"; in **18:17**, **19**, "is made desolate"; in Matt. 12:25 and Luke 11:17, "is brought to desolation."

Naked *see Revelation 3:17.*

Burn *see* **Burnt** at *Revelation 8:7.*

Fire *see Revelation 1:14.*

17:17 For God hath put in their hearts to fulfil his will, and to agree, and give their kingdom unto the beast, until the words of God shall be fulfilled.

Put *didomi* (1325), "to give," is rendered "to put" in Luke 15:22, of the ring on the returned Prodigal's finger; 2 Cor. 8:16 and **Rev. 17:17**, of "putting" into the heart by God; Heb. 8:10, of laws into the mind (KJV, marg., "give"); 10:16, of laws on (RV; KJV, "into") the heart.

Fulfil *poieo,* "to do," is so rendered in the RV, for KJV "fulfill," in Acts 13:22; Eph. 2:3; **Rev. 17:17**.

Will In **Rev. 17:17**, KJV, *gnome,* "an opinion," RV, "mind," is translated "will." *See also* **Mind** at *Revelation 17:13.*

Agree *gnome* (1106), "mind, will," is used with *poieo,* "to make," in the sense of "to agree," **Rev. 17:17** (twice), lit., "to do His mind, and to make one mind"; RV, "to come to one mind," KJV, "to agree.

Fulfilled In **17:17**, the RV has "should be accomplished," for KJV, "shall be fulfilled." *See also* **Finished** at *Revelation 10:7.*

17:18 And the woman which thou sawest is that great city, which reigneth over the kings of the earth.

Reigneth In **Rev. 17:18**, *echo,* "to have," with *basileia,* "a kingdom," is translated "reigneth," lit., "hath a kingdom," suggestive of a distinction between the sovereignty of mystic Babylon and that of ordinary sovereigns.

Chapter 18

18:1 And after these things I saw another angel come down from heaven, having great power; and the earth was lightened with his glory.

After *see* **Hereafter** at *Revelation 1:19.*

Lightened *photizo* (5461), used (a) intransitively, signifies "to shine, give light," **Rev. 22:5**; (b) transitively, (1) "to illumine, to light, enlighten, to be lightened," Luke 11:36; **Rev. 21:23**; in the passive voice, **Rev. 18:1**; metaphorically, of spiritual enlightenment, John 1:9; Eph. 1:18; 3:9, "to make ... see;" Heb. 6:4; 10:32, "ye were enlightened," RV (KJV, "... illuminated"); (2) "to bring to light," 1 Cor. 4:5 (of God's act in the future); 2 Tim. 1:10 (of God's act in the past).

18:2 And he cried mightily with a strong voice, saying, Babylon the great is fallen, is fallen, and is become the habitation of devils, and the hold of every foul spirit, and a cage of every unclean and hateful bird.

Mightily *see* **Power** at *Revelation 5:12.*

Strong *see Revelation 5:2.*

Fallen *see* **Fell** at *Revelation 1:17.*

Habitation *katoiketerion* (2732), implying permanency, is used in Eph. 2:22 of the church as the dwelling place of the Holy Spirit; in **Rev. 18:2** of Babylon, figuratively, as the dwelling place of demons. *See also* **Dwellest** at *Revelation 2:13.*

Devils *see Revelation 9:20.*

Hold, Cage *phulake* (5438), "a guarding" or "guard" (akin to *phulasso,* "to guard or watch"), also denotes "a prison, a hold," **Rev. 18:2** (twice), RV, "hold" in both places, KJV, "cage," in the second (RV, marg., "prison," in both). *See also* **Prison** at *Revelation 2:10.*

Foul *akathartos* (169), denotes "unclean, impure" (*a,* negative, and *kathairo,* "to purify"), (a) ceremonially, e g., Acts 10:14, 28; (b) morally, always, in the Gospels, of unclean spirits; it is translated "foul" in the KJV of Mark 9:25 and **Rev. 18:2**, but always "unclean" in the RV. Since the word primarily had a ceremonial significance, the moral significance is less prominent as applied to a spirit, than when *poneros,* "wicked," is so applied. Cf. *akatharsia,* "uncleanness."

Unclean *see Revelation 16:13.*

Hateful *see* **Hatest, Hate** at *Revelation 2:6.*

Bird *orneon* (3732), is probably connected with a word signifying "to perceive, to hear"; **Rev. 18:2**; **19:17, 21**. Cf. *ornis,* a hen.

18:3 For all nations have drunk of the wine of the wrath of her fornication, and the kings of the earth have committed fornication with her, and the merchants of the earth are waxed rich through the abundance of her delicacies.

Drunk *see* **Drink** at *Revelation 14:10.*

Wine *see Revelation 14:8.*

Wrath *see Revelation 12:12.*

Fornication *see Revelation 2:21.*

Merchants *emporos* (1713), denotes "a person on a journey" (*poros,* "a journey"), "a passenger on shipboard"; then, "a merchant," Matt. 13:45; **Rev. 18:3, 11, 15, 23**.

Rich *see Revelation 3:17.*

Abundance *dunamis,* "power," is translated "abundance" in the KJV of **Rev. 18:3** (RV and KJV marg., "power").

Delicacies *strenos* (4764), "insolent luxury," is rendered "wantonness" in **Rev. 18:3**, RV (marg., "luxury"; KJV, "delicacies," not a sufficiently strong rendering).

18:4 And I heard another voice from heaven, saying, Come out of her, my people, that ye be not partakers of her sins, and that ye receive not of her plagues.

Voice *see Revelation 1:10.*

Partakers *sunkoinoneo* (4790), "to share together with," is translated "communicated with" in Phil. 4:14; "have fellowship with," Eph. 5:11; "be ... partakers of," **Rev. 18:4** (RV, "have fellowship"). The thought is that of sharing with others what one has, in order to meet their needs.

Plagues *see Revelation 9:20.*

18:5 For her sins have reached unto heaven, and God hath remembered her iniquities.

Reached *akoloutheo* (190), "to follow," is translated "have reached," in **Rev. 18:5**, of the sins of Babylon. Some mss. have the verb *kollaomai*, "to cleave together," RV, marg.

Remembered *see* **Remember** at *Revelation 2:5.*

Iniquities *adikema* (92), denotes "a wrong, injury, misdeed" (from *adikeo*, "to do wrong"), the concrete act, in contrast to the general meaning of *adikia*, and translated "a matter of wrong," in Acts 18:14; "wrongdoing," 24:20 (KJV, "evil-doing"); "iniquities," **Rev. 18:5**.

18:6 Reward her even as she rewarded you, and double unto her double according to her works: in the cup which she hath filled fill to her double.

Reward, Rewarded *apodidomi* (591), to give up or back," is translated "to render," (a) of righteous acts, (1) human, Matt. 21:41; 22:21; Mark 12:17; Luke 16:2, RV (KJV, "give"); Luke 20:25; Rom. 13:7, 1 Cor. 7:3; (2) divine, Matt. 16:27, RV, "shall render" (KJV, "shall reward"), an important RV change; Rom. 2:6; 2 Tim. 4:14, RV (KJV, "reward"); **Rev. 18:6** (ditto); **22:12**, RV (KJV, "give"); (b) of unrighteous acts. Rom. 12:17, RV (KJV, "recompense"); 1 Thess. 5:15; 1 Pet. 3:9.

Double *diploo* (1363), signifies "to double, to repay or render twofold," **Rev. 18:6**.

Double *diplous* (1362), denotes "twofold, double," 1 Tim. 5:17; **Rev. 18:6** (twice). The comparative degree *diploteron* (neuter) is used adverbially in Matt. 23:15, "twofold more."

Works *see Revelation 2:2.*

Cup *see Revelation 14:10.*

Filled fill In **Rev. 18:6**, KJV, *kerannumi*, "to mix," is incorrectly rendered "to fill full" (RV, to mingle). *See also* **Without mixture** at *Revelation 14:10.*

18:7 How much she hath glorified herself, and lived deliciously, so much torment and sorrow give her: for she saith in her heart, I sit a queen, and am no widow, and shall see no sorrow.

Much The adjective *tosoutos*, "so great, so much," is translated "so much (bread)," in Matt. 15:33, plural, RV, "so many (loaves)"; in the genitive case, of price, in Acts 5:8, "for so much"; in the dative case, of degree, in Heb. 1:4, RV, "by so much" (KJV, "so much"); so in Heb. 10:25; in Heb. 7:22 "by so much" translates the phrase *kata tosouto;* in **Rev. 18:7**, "so much."

Glorified *see* **Glorify** at *Revelation 15:4.*

Deliciously *streniao* (4763), "to run riot," translated "lived deliciously," in **Rev. 18:7, 9**, KJV (RV, "waxed wanton" and "lived wantonly"), and "lived wantonly" in v. **8**.

Torment *see Revelation 9:5.*

Sorrow *penthos* (3997), "mourning," is used in Jas. 4:9; **Rev. 18:7** (twice), RV, "mourning" (KJV, "sorrow"); v. **8**, "mourning"; **21:4**, RV, "mourning" (KJV, "sorrow").

Queen *basilissa* (938), the feminine of *basileus*, "a king," is used (a) of the "Queen of Sheba," Matt. 12:42; Luke 11:31; of "Candace," Acts 8:27; (b) metaphorically, of "Babylon," **Rev. 18:7**.

Widow *chera* (5503), Matt. 28:13 (in some texts); Mark 12:40, 42, 43; Luke 2:37; 4:25, 26, lit., "a woman a widow"; 7:12; 18:3, 5; 20:47; 21:2, 3; Acts 6:1; 9:39, 41; 1 Tim. 5:3 (twice), 4, 5, 11, 16 (twice); Jas. 1:27; 1 Tim. 5:9 refers to elderly "widows" (not an ecclesiastical "order"), recognized, for relief or maintenance by the church (cf. vv. 3, 16), as those who had fulfilled the conditions mentioned; where relief could be ministered by those who had relatives that were "widows" (a likely circumstance in large families), the church was not to be responsible; there is an intimation of the tendency to shelve individual responsibility at the expense of church funds. In **Rev. 18:7**, it is used figuratively of a city forsaken.

18:8 Therefore shall her plagues come in one day, death, and mourning, and famine; and she shall be utterly burned with fire: for strong *is* the Lord God who judgeth her.

Plagues *see Revelation 9:20.*

Come *heko* (2240), means (a) "to come, to be present"; (b) "to come upon, of time and events," Matt. 24:14; John 2:4; 2 Pet. 3:10; **Rev. 18:8**; (c) metaphorically, "to come upon one, of calamitous times, and evils," Matt. 23:36; Luke 19:43.

Mourning *see* Sorrow at *Revelation 18:7.*

Famine *see* Hunger at *Revelation 6:8.*

Burned *see* Burnt at *Revelation 8:7.*

Fire *see Revelation 1:14.*

Strong *see Revelation 5:2.*

18:9 And the kings of the earth, who have committed fornication and lived deliciously with her, shall bewail her, and lament for her, when they shall see the smoke of her burning,

Fornication *see Revelation 2:14.*

Deliciously *see Revelation 18:7.*

Bewail *klaio* (2799), "to wail," whether with tears or any external expression of grief, is regularly translated "weep" in the RV; once in the KJV it is rendered "bewail," **Rev. 18:9**. *See also* Wail at *Revelation 1:7.*

See *see Revelation 11:9.*

Smoke *see Revelation 9:2.*

Burning *purosis* (4451), is used literally in **Rev. 18:9, 18**; metaphorically in 1 Pet. 4:12, "fiery trial."

18:10 Standing afar off for the fear of her torment, saying, Alas, alas, that great city Babylon, that mighty city! for in one hour is thy judgment come.

Afar *makrothen* (3113), also from *makros*, signifies "afar off, from far," Matt. 26:58; 27:55, etc. It is used with *apo*, "from," in Mark 5:6; 14:54; 15:40, etc.; outside the Synoptists, three times, **Rev. 18:10, 15, 17**.

Fear *see Revelation 11:11.*

Torment *see Revelation 9:5.*

Alas *see* Woe at *Revelation 8:13.*

Great *see* Strong at *Revelation 5:2.*

Mighty *see Revelation 6:15.*

18:11 And the merchants of the earth shall weep and mourn over her; for no man buyeth their merchandise any more:

Merchants *see Revelation 18:3.*

Mourn *pentheo* (3996), "to mourn for, lament," is used (a) of mourning in general, Matt. 5:4; 9:15; Luke 6:25; (b) of sorrow for the death of a loved one, Mark 16:10; (c) of "mourning" for the overthrow of Babylon and the Babylonish system, **Rev. 18:11, 15**, RV, "mourning" (KJV, "wailing"); v. **19** (ditto); (d) of sorrow for sin or for condoning it, Jas. 4:9; 1 Cor. 5:2; (e) of grief for those in a local church who show no repentance for evil committed, 2 Cor. 12:21, RV, "mourn" (KJV, "bewail").

Merchandise *gomos* (1117), from a root *gem-*, signifying "full, or heavy," seen in *gemo*, "to be full," *gemizo*, "to fill," Lat. *gemo*, "to groan," denotes "the lading of freight of a ship," Acts 21:3, or "merchandise conveyed in a ship," and so "merchandise in general," **Rev. 18:11-12**.

Any more *ouketi* (3765), a negative adverb of time, signifies "no longer, no more" (*ou*, "not," *k*, euphonic, *eti* "longer"), denying absolutely and directly, e.g., Matt. 19:6; John 4:42, "now ... not"; 6:66; Acts 20:25, 38; 2 Cor. 1:23, KJV, "not as yet"; Eph. 2:19; with another negative, to strengthen the negation, e.g., Matt. 22:46; Mark 14:25; 15:5, RV, "no more (anything)," KJV, "yet ... no (thing)"; Acts 8:39; **Rev. 18:11, 14**.

18:12 The merchandise of gold, and silver, and precious stones, and of pearls, and fine linen, and purple, and silk, and scarlet, and all thyinewood, and all manner vessels of ivory, and all manner vessels of most precious wood, and of brass, and iron, and marble,

Merchandise *see Revelation 18:11.*

Gold *see Revelation 9:7.*

Silver *arguros* (696), akin to *argos*, "shining," denotes "silver." In each occurrence in the NT it follows the mention of gold, Matt. 10:9; Acts 17:29; Jas. 5:3; **Rev. 18:12**.

Precious *see Revelation 17:4.*

Stones *see* Stone at *Revelation 4:3.*

Pearls *see Revelation 17:4.*

Fine linen *bussinos* (1039), denoting "made of fine linen." This is used of the clothing of the mystic Babylon, **Rev. 18:12; 16**, and of the suitable attire of the Lamb's wife, **19:8, 14**, figuratively describing "the righteous acts of the saints." The presumption of Babylon is conspicuous in that she arrays herself in that which alone befits the bride of Christ.

Purple *porphura* (4209), originally denoted the "purple fish," then, "purple dye" (extracted from certain shell fish): hence, "a purple garment," Mark 15:17, 20; Luke 16:19; **Rev. 18:12**.

Silk *serikos* or *sirikos* (4596), "silken," an adjective derived from the *Seres*, a people of India, who seem to have produced "silk" originally as a marketable commodity, is used as a noun with the article, denoting "silken fabric," **Rev. 18:12**.

Scarlet *see Revelation 17:3.*

Thyinewood *thuinos* (2367), is akin to *thuia*, or *thua*, an African aromatic and coniferous tree; in **Rev.**

18:12 it describes a wood which formed part of the merchandise of Babylon; it was valued by Greeks and Romans for tables, being hard, durable and fragrant (KJV marg., "sweet").

Wood *xulon* (3586), denotes "timber, wood for any use" 1 Cor. 3:12; **Rev. 18:12** (twice).

Manner In Matt. 12:31; Luke 11:42; **Rev. 18:12**, KJV, *pas*, "every" (so RV), is translated "all manner."

Vessels *see* ***Revelation 2:27***.

Ivory *elephantinos* (1661), an adjective from *elephas* (whence Eng., elephant), signifies "of ivory," **Rev. 18:12**.

Brass *chalkos* (5475), primarily, "copper," became used for metals in general, later was applied to bronze, a mixture of copper and tin, then, by metonymy, to any article made of these metals, e.g., money, Matt. 10:9; Mark 6:8; 12:41, or a sounding instrument, 1 Cor. 13:1, figurative of a person destitute of love. See **Rev. 18:12**.

Iron *sideros* (4604), "iron," occurs in **Rev. 18:12**.

Marble *marmaros* (3139), primarily denoted any "glistering stone" (from *maraino*, "to glisten"); hence, "marble," **Rev. 18:12**.

18:13 And cinnamon, and odours, and ointments, and frankincense, and wine, and oil, and fine flour, and wheat, and beasts, and sheep, and horses, and chariots, and slaves, and souls of men.

Cinnamon *kinnamomon* (2792), is derived from an Arabic word signifying "to emit a smell"; the substance was an ingredient in the holy oil for anointing, Ex. 30:23. See also Prov. 7:17 and Song of Sol. 4:14. In the NT it is found in **Rev. 18:13**. The cinnamon of the present day is the inner bark of an aromatic tree called *canella zeylanica*.

Odours *amomon* (298a), *amomum*, probably a word of Semitic origin, a fragrant plant of India, is translated "spice" in **Rev. 18:13**, RV (KJV, "odors"). *See also* ***Revelation 5:8***.

Ointments *muron* (3464), a word derived by the ancients from *muro*, "to flow," or from *murra*, "myrrh-oil" (it is probably of foreign origin). The "ointment" is mentioned in the NT in connection with the anointing of the Lord on the occasions recorded in Matt. 26:7, 9, 12; Mark 14:3-4; Luke 7:37-38, 46; John 11:2; 12:3 (twice), 5. The alabaster cruse mentioned in the passages in Matthew, Mark and Luke was the best of its kind, and the spikenard was one of the costliest of perfumes. "Ointments" were used in preparing a body for burial, Luke 23:56 ("ointments"). Of the act of the woman mentioned in Matt. 26:6-13, the Lord said, "she did it to prepare Me for burial"; her devotion led her to antedate the customary ritual after death, by showing both her affection and her understanding of what was impending. For the use of the various kinds of "ointments" as articles of commerce, see **Rev. 18:13**.

Frankincense *see* **Incense** at ***Revelation 8:3***.

Oil *see* ***Revelation 6:6***.

Flour *semidalis* (4585), denotes the "finest wheaten flour," **Rev. 18:13**.

Wheat *see* ***Revelation 6:6***.

Beasts *ktenos* (2934), primarily denotes "property" (the connected verb *ktaomai* means "to possess"); then, "property in flocks and herds." In Scripture it signifies, (a) a "beast" of burden, Luke 10:34; Acts 23:24, (b) "beasts" of any sort, apart from those signified by *therion*, 1 Cor. 15:39; **Rev. 18:13**, (c) animals for slaughter; this meaning is not found in the NT, but is very frequent in the Sept.

Horses *see* **Horse** at ***Revelation 6:2***.

Chariots *rhede* (4480), "a wagon with four wheels," was chiefly used for traveling purposes, **Rev. 18:13**.

Slaves *soma* (4983), is "the body as a whole, the instrument of life," whether of man living, e.g., Matt. 6:22, or dead, Matt. 27:52; or in resurrection, 1 Cor. 15:44; or of beasts, Heb. 13:11; of grain, 1 Cor. 15:37-38; of the heavenly hosts, 1 Cor. 15:40. In **Rev. 18:13** it is translated "slaves." In its figurative uses the essential idea is preserved. Sometimes the word stands, by *synecdoche*, for "the complete man," Matt. 5:29; 6:22; Rom. 12:1; Jas. 3:6; **Rev. 18:13**. Sometimes the person is identified with his or her "body," Acts 9:37; 13:36, and this is so even of the Lord Jesus, John 19:40 with 42. The "body" is not the man, for he himself can exist apart from his "body," 2 Cor. 12:2-3. The "body" is an essential part of the man and therefore the redeemed are not perfected till the resurrection, Heb. 11:40; no man in his final state will be without his "body," John 5:28-29; **Rev. 20:13**.

18:14 And the fruits that thy soul lusted after are departed from thee, and all things which were dainty and goodly are departed from thee, and thou shalt find them no more at all.

Fruits *opora* (3703), primarily denotes "late summer or early autumn," i.e., late July, all August and early September. Since that is the time of "fruit-bearing," the word was used, by metonymy, for the "fruits" themselves, **Rev. 18:14**.

Soul *see* Souls at *Revelation 6:9*.

Lusted *epithumia* (1939), denotes "strong desire" of any kind, the various kinds being frequently specified by some adjective. The word is used of a good desire in Luke 22:15; Phil. 1:23, and 1 Thess. 2:17 only. Everywhere else it has a bad sense. In Rom. 6:12 the injunction against letting sin reign in our mortal body to obey the "lust" thereof, refers to those evil desires which are ready to express themselves in bodily activity. They are equally the "lusts" of the flesh, Rom. 13:14; Gal. 5:16, 24; Eph. 2:3; 2 Pet. 2:18; 1 John 2:16, a phrase which describes the emotions of the soul, the natural tendency towards things evil. Such "lusts" are not necessarily base and immoral, they may be refined in character, but are evil if inconsistent with the will of God. Other descriptions besides those already mentioned are:—"of the mind," Eph. 2:3; "evil (desire)," Col. 3:5; "the passion of," 1 Thess. 4:5, RV; "foolish and hurtful," 1 Tim. 6:9; "youthful," 2 Tim. 2:22; "divers," 2 Tim. 3:6 and Titus 3:3; "their own," 2 Tim. 4:3; 2 Pet. 3:3; Jude 16; "worldly," Titus 2:12; "his own," Jas. 1:14; "your former," 1 Pet. 1:14, RV; "fleshly," 2:11; "of men," 4:2; "of defilement," 2 Pet. 2:10; "of the eyes," 1 John 2:16; of the world ("thereof"), v. 17; "their own ungodly," Jude 18. In **Rev. 18:14** "(the fruits) which thy soul lusted after" is, lit., "of thy soul's lust."

Departed *aperchomai* (565), lit., "to come or go away" (*apo*), hence, "to set off, depart," e.g., Matt. 8:18, is frequent in the Gospels and Acts; **Rev. 18:14**, RV, "are gone."

Dainty *liparos* (3045), properly signifies "oily, or anointed with oil" (from *lipos*, "grease," connected with *aleipho*, "to anoint"); it is said of things which pertain to delicate and sumptuous living; hence, "dainty," **Rev. 18:14**. In the Sept., Judg. 3:29; Neh. 9:35; Isa. 30:23.

Goodly *lampros* (2986), "bright," is rendered "sumptuous" in **Rev. 18:14**, RV.

Departed *apollumi* (622), "to destroy," signifies, in the middle voice, "to perish," and is thus used (a) of things, e.g., Matt. 5:29, 30; Luke 5:37; Acts 27:34, RV, "perish" (in some texts *pipto*, "to fall," as KJV); Heb. 1:11; 2 Pet. 3:6; **Rev. 18:14** (2nd part), RV, "perished" (in some texts *aperchomai*, "to depart," as KJV); (b) of persons, e.g., Matt. 8:25; John 3:15), 16; 10:28; 17:12, RV, "perished" (KJV, "is lost"); Rom. 2:12; 1 Cor. 1:18, lit., "the perishing," where the perfective force of the verb implies the completion of the process of destruction (Moulton, *Proleg.*, p. 114); 8:11; 15:18; 2 Pet. 3:9; Jude 11.

No more *see* Any more at *Revelation 18:11*.

18:15 The merchants of these things, which were made rich by her, shall stand afar off for the fear of her torment, weeping and wailing,

Merchants *see Revelation 18:3*.

Rich *see Revelation 3:17*.

Stand *see* Stood at *Revelation 13:1*.

Afar *see Revelation 18:10*.

Fear *see Revelation 11:11*.

Torment *see Revelation 9:5*.

Wailing For *pentheo*, rendered "to wail" in **Rev. 18:15, 19**, KJV. *See also* Mourn at *Revelation 18:11*.

18:16 And saying, Alas, alas, that great city, that was clothed in fine linen, and purple, and scarlet, and decked with gold, and precious stones, and pearls!

Alas *see* Woe at *Revelation 8:13*.

Purple *see Revelation 17:4*.

Scarlet *see Revelation 17:3*.

Decked *see Revelation 17:4*.

Gold *see Revelation 9:7*.

Precious *see Revelation 17:4*.

Stones *see* Stone at *Revelation 4:3*.

Pearls *see Revelation 17:4*.

18:17 For in one hour so great riches is come to nought. And every shipmaster, and all the company in ships, and sailors, and as many as trade by sea, stood afar off,

Great *tosoutos* (5118), "so great, so many, so much," of quantity, size, etc., is rendered "so great," in Matt. 8:10, and Luke 7:9, of faith; Matt. 15:33, of a multitude; Heb. 12:1, of a cloud of witnesses; **Rev. 18:17**, of riches.

Riches *see Revelation 5:12*.

Nought **Rev. 18:17**, KJV, *eremoo*, "to make desolate," is translated "is come to nought" (RV, "is made desolate"). *See also* **Desolate** at *Revelation 17:16*.

Shipmaster *kubernetes* (2942), "the pilot or steersman of a ship," or, metaphorically, "a guide or governor" (akin to *kubernao*, "to guide": Eng., "govern" is connected; cf. *kubernesis*, "a steering, pilotage," 1 Cor. 12:28, "governments"), is translated "master" in Acts 27:11; "shipmaster" in **Rev. 18:17**. In the Sept., Prov. 23:34; Ezek. 27:8, 27-28.

Company *homilos* (3658), "a throng or crowd," is found, in some mss., in **Rev. 18:17**, "all the company in ships," KJV. *Homilos* denotes the concrete; *homilia* is chiefly an abstract noun.

Ships *see Revelation 8:9*.

Sailors *nautes* (3492), "a seaman, mariner, sailor" (from *naus*, "a ship," Eng., "nautical"), is translated "sailors" in Acts 27:27, 30, RV (KJV, "shipmen"); in **Rev. 18:17**, RV, "mariners" (KJV, "sailors").

Trade *ergazomai* (2038), "to work," is rendered "traded" in Matt. 25:16; in **Rev. 18:17**, KJV, "trade," RV, "gain their living."

Sea *see Revelation 4:6*.

Afar *see Revelation 18:10*.

18:18 And cried when they saw the smoke of her burning, saying, What *city is* like unto this great city!

Smoke *see Revelation 9:2*.

Burning *see Revelation 18:9*.

Like unto *see Revelation 1:13*.

18:19 And they cast dust on their heads, and cried, weeping and wailing, saying, Alas, alas, that great city, wherein were made rich all that had ships in the sea by reason of her costliness! for in one hour is she made desolate.

Dust *chous*, or *choos* (5522), from *cheo*, "to pour," primarily, "earth dug out, an earth heap," then, "loose earth or dust," is used in Mark 6:11 and **Rev. 18:19**.

Wailing *see Revelation 18:15. See also* **Mourn** at *Revelation 18:11*.

Alas *see* **Woe** at *Revelation 8:13*.

Rich *see Revelation 3:17*.

Ships *see Revelation 8:9*.

Costliness *timiotes* (5094), "costliness" (from *timios*, "valued at great price, precious" connected with *time*, "honor, price," and used in **Rev. 18:19**, in reference to Babylon. *See also* **Precious** at *Revelation 17:4*.

Desolate *see Revelation 17:16*.

18:20 Rejoice over her, *thou* heaven, and *ye* holy apostles and prophets; for God hath avenged you on her.

Rejoice *see Revelation 12:12*.

Ye These are most frequently the translations of various inflections of a verb; sometimes of the article before a nominative used as a vocative, e.g., **Rev. 18:20**, "ye saints, and ye apostles, and ye prophets" (lit., "the saints, etc."). When the 2nd person plural pronouns are used separately from a verb, they are usually one or other of the forms of *humeis*, the plural of *su*, "thou," and are frequently emphatic, especially when they are subjects of the verb, an emphasis always to be noticed, e.g., Matt. 5:13, 14, 48; 6:9, 19, 20; Mark 6:31, 37; John 15:27a; Rom. 1:6; 1 Cor. 3:17, 23; Gal. 3:28, 29a; Eph. 1:13a; 2:8; 2:11, 13; Phil. 2:18; Col. 3:4, 7a; 4:1; 1 Thess. 1:6; 2:10, 19, 20; 3:8; 2 Thess. 3:13; Jas. 5:8; 1 Pet. 2:9a; 1 John 2:20, 24 (1st and 3rd occurrences), 27a; 4:4; Jude 17, 20.

Apostles In **Rev. 18:20**, the best texts have *hagioi* and *apostoloi*, each with the article, each being preceeded by *kai*, "and," RV, "and ye saints, and ye apostles"; the KJV, "and ye holy apostles" follows those mss. from which the 2nd *kai* and the article are absent.

Avenged In **Rev. 18:20**, the KJV mistranslates *krino* and *krima* "hath avenged you"; RV, "hath judged your judgment."

18:21 And a mighty angel took up a stone like a great millstone, and cast *it* into the sea, saying, Thus with violence shall that great city Babylon be thrown down, and shall be found no more at all.

Mighty *see Revelation 6:15. See also* **Strong** at *Revelation 5:2*.

Stone *see Revelation 4:3*.

Like *see* **Like unto** at *Revelation 2:18*.

Millstone *mulos* (3458), denotes "a handmill," consisting of two circular stones, one above the other, the lower being fixed. From the center of the lower a wooden pin passes through a hole in the upper, into which the grain is thrown, escaping as flour between the stones and falling on a prepared material below them. The handle is inserted into the upper stone near the circumference. Small stones could be turned by one woman (millgrinding was a work deemed fit only for women and slaves; cf. Judg. 16:21); larger ones were turned by two (cf. Matt. 24:41), or more. Still larger ones were turned by an ass (*onikos*), Matt. 18:6, RV, "a great millstone" (marg., "a millstone turned by an ass"), indicating the immediate and overwhelming drowning of one who causes one young believer to stumble; Mark 9:42 (where some mss. have *lithos mulikos*, "a stone of a mill," as in Luke 17:2); **Rev. 18:22** (some mss. have it in v. **21**).

Cast *ballo* (906), "to cast, to throw," is rendered "to throw" in Mark 12:42, KJV (RV, "cast"); so Acts 22:23 (2nd part); "to throw down," **Rev. 18:21** (2nd part), KJV (RV, "cast down").

Violence *hormema* (3731), "a rush" (akin to *hormao*, "to urge on, to rush"), is used of the fall of Babylon, **Rev. 18:21**, KJV, "violence," RV, "mighty fall."

Found *see Revelation 5:4.*

More *see Revelation 3:12.*

18:22 And the voice of harpers, and musicians, and of pipers, and trumpeters, shall be heard no more at all in thee; and no craftsman, of whatsoever craft *he be*, shall be found any more in thee; and the sound of a millstone shall be heard no more at all in thee;

Voice *see Revelation 1:10.*

Harpers *see Revelation 14:2.*

Musicians *mousikos* (3451), is found in **Rev. 18:22**, RV, "minstrels" (KJV, "musicians"); inasmuch as other instrumentalists are mentioned, some word like "minstrels" is necessary to make the distinction, hence the RV; Bengel and others translate it "singers." Primarily the word denoted "devoted to the Muses" (the nine goddesses who presided over the principal departments of letters), and was used of anyone devoted to or skilled in arts and sciences, or "learned."

Pipers *auletes* (834), "a flute-player" (from *auleo*, "to play the flute"), occurs in Matt. 9:23 (KJV, "minstrel"), and **Rev. 18:22** (KJV "pipers"). In the papyri writings of the time the word is chiefly associated with religious matters (Moulton and Milligan, *Vocab.*).

Trumpeters *salpistes* (4538), occurs in **Rev. 18:22**.

Craftsman *technites* (5079), "an artificer, artisan, craftsman," is translated "craftsman" in Acts 19:24, 38 and **Rev. 18:22**. It is found elsewhere in Heb. 11:10 "builder"; but this is practically the same as "maker." Trench, *Syn.* Sec.qv., suggests that *technites* brings out the artistic side of creation, viewing God as "moulding and fashioning ... the materials which He called into existence." This agrees with the usage of the word in the Sept.

Craft *techne* (5078), "an art, handicraft, trade," is used in Acts 17:29, of the plastic art; in Acts 18:3, of a trade or craft (KJV, "occupation," RV, "trade"); in **Rev. 18:22**, "craft" (cf. *technites*, "a craftsman," Eng., "technical").

Found *see Revelation 5:4.*

Sound *see Revelation 1:15.*

Millstone *see Revelation 18:21.*

18:23 And the light of a candle shall shine no more at all in thee; and the voice of the bridegroom and of the bride shall be heard no more at all in thee: for thy merchants were the great men of the earth; for by thy sorceries were all nations deceived.

Candle *luchnos* (3088), frequently mistranslated "candle," is a portable "lamp" usually set on a stand; the word is used (a) literally, Matt. 5:15; Mark 4:21; Luke 8:16; 11:33, 36; 15:8; **Rev. 18:23**; **22:5**; (b) metaphorically, of Christ as the Lamb, **Rev. 21:23**, RV, "lamp" (KJV, "light"); of John the Baptist, John 5:35, RV, "the lamp" (KJV, "a ... light"); of the eye, Matt. 6:22, and Luke 11:34, RV, "lamp"; of spiritual readiness, Luke 12:35,RV, "lamps"; of "the word of prophecy," 2 Pet. 1:19, RV, "lamp."

"In rendering *luchnos* and *lampas* our translators have scarcely made the most of the words at their command. Had they rendered *lampas* by 'torch' not once only (John 18:3), but always, this would have left 'lamp,' now wrongly appropriated by lampas, disengaged. Altogether dismissing 'candle,' they might then have rendered *luchnos* by 'lamp' wherever it occurs. At present there are so many occasions where 'candle' would manifestly be inappropriate, and where, therefore, they are obliged to fall back on 'light,' that the distinction between *phos* and *luchnos* nearly, if not quite, disappears in our Version. The advantages of such a re-distribution of the words would be many. In the first place, it would be more accurate. *Luchnos* is not a 'candle' ('*candela*,' from '*candeo*,' the white wax light, and then any kind of taper), but a hand-lamp, fed with oil. Neither is *lampas* a 'lamp,' but a 'torch'" (Trench *Syn.*, Sec.xlvi).

Shine *see* **Shineth** at *Revelation 1:16.*

Bridegroom *numphios* (3566), "a bridegroom," occurs fourteen times in the Gospels, and in **Rev. 18:23**. "The friend of the bridegroom," John 3:29, is distinct from "the sons of the bridechamber" who were numerous. When John the Baptist speaks of "the friend of the Bridegroom," he uses language according to the customs of the Jews.

Bride *numphe* (3565), (Eng. "nymph") "a bride, or young wife," John 3:29; **Rev. 18:23**; **21:2**, **9**; **22:17**, is probably connected with the Latin *nubo*, "to veil"; the "bride" was often adorned with embroidery and jewels (see **Rev. 21:2**), and was led veiled from her home to the "bridegroom." Hence the secondary meaning of "daughter-in-law," Matt. 10:35; Luke 12:53. For the relationship between Christ and a local church, under this figure, see 2 Cor. 11:2; regarding the whole church, Eph. 5:23-32; **Rev. 22:17**.

Merchants *see Revelation 18:3.*

Great *see Revelation 6:15.*

Sorceries *see Revelation 9:21.*

18:24 And in her was found the blood of prophets, and of saints, and of all that were slain upon the earth.

Slain *see Revelation 5:6.*

Chapter 19

19:1 And after these things I heard a great voice of much people in heaven, saying, Alleluia; Salvation, and glory, and honour, and power, unto the Lord our God:

After *see* Hereafter at *Revelation 1:19.*

Voice *see Revelation 1:10.*

Much *see Revelation 5:4.*

People *see* Multitude at *Revelation 7:9.*

Alleluia *hallelouia* (239), signifies "Praise ye Jah." It occurs as a short doxology in the Psalms, usually at the beginning, e.g., 111, 112, or the end, e.g., 104, 105, or both, e.g., 106, 135 (where it is also used in v. 3), 146-150. In the NT it is found in **Rev. 19:1, 3, 4, 6**, as the keynote in the song of the great multitude in heaven. "Alleluia," without the initial "H," is a misspelling.

Salvation *see Revelation 7:10.*

19:2 For true and righteous *are* his judgments: for he hath judged the great whore, which did corrupt the earth with her fornication, and hath avenged the blood of his servants at her hand.

True *see Revelation 3:7.*

Righteous *see* Just at *Revelation 15:3.*

"Be not afraid of saying too much in the praises of God; all the danger is of saying too little."

MATTHEW HENRY

Whore *see Revelation 17:1.*

Corrupt *phtheiro* (5351), signifies "to destroy by means of corrupting," and so "bringing into a worse state"; (a) with this significance it is used of the effect of evil company upon the manners of believers, and so of the effect of association with those who deny the truth and hold false doctrine, 1 Cor. 15:33 (this was a saying of the pagan poet Menander, which became a well-known proverb); in 2 Cor. 7:2, of the effects of dishonorable dealing by bringing people to want (a charge made against the apostle); in 11:3, of the effects upon the minds (or thoughts) of believers by "corrupting" them "from the simplicity and the purity that is toward Christ"; in Eph. 4:22, intransitively, of the old nature in waxing "corrupt," "morally decaying, on the way to final ruin" (Moule), "after the lusts of deceit"; in **Rev. 19:2**, metaphorically, of the Babylonish harlot, in "corrupting" the inhabitants of the earth by her false religion. (b) With the significance of destroying, it is used of marring a local church by leading it away from that condition of holiness of life and purity of doctrine in which it should abide, 1 Cor. 3:17 (KJV, "defile"), and of God's retributive destruction of the offender who is guilty of this sin (id.); of the effects of the work of false and abominable teachers upon themselves, 2 Pet. 2:12 (some texts have *kataphtheiro*; KJV, "shall utterly perish"), and Jude 10 (KJV, "corrupt themselves." RV, marg., "are corrupted").

Fornication *see Revelation 2:21.*

Avenged *see* Avenge at *Revelation 6:10.*

Hand *cheir* (5495), "the hand" (cf. Eng., "chiropody"), is used, besides its ordinary significance, (a) in the idiomatic phrases, "by the hand of," "at the hand of," etc., to signify "by the agency of," Acts 5:12; 7:35; 17:25; 14:3; Gal. 3:19 (cf. Lev. 26:46); **Rev. 19:2**; (b) metaphorically, for the power of God, e.g., Luke 1:66; 23:46; John 10:28, 29; Acts 11:21; 13:11; Heb. 1:10; 2:7; 10:31; (c) by metonymy, for power, e.g., Matt. 17:22; Luke 24:7; John 10:39; Acts 12:11.

19:3 And again they said, Alleluia. And her smoke rose up for ever and ever.

Again *see* Second at *Revelation 2:11.*

Alleluia *see Revelation 19:1.*

Smoke *see Revelation 9:2.*

Rose *see* Rise at *Revelation 13:1.*

19:4 And the four and twenty elders and the four beasts fell down and worshipped God that sat on the throne, saying, Amen; Alleluia.

Elders *see Revelation 4:4.*

Fell *see Revelation 1:17.*

Alleluia *see Revelation 19:1.*

19:5 And a voice came out of the throne, saying, Praise our God, all ye his servants, and ye that fear him, both small and great.

Voice *see Revelation 1:10.*

Praise *aineo* (134), "to speak in praise of, to praise," is always used of "praise" to God, (a) by angels, Luke 2:13; (b) by men, Luke 2:?; 19:37; 24:53; Acts 2:20, 47; 3:8, 9; Rom. 15:11; **Rev. 19:5**.

Fear *see Revelation 14:7.*

Small *see Revelation 11:18. See also* Little at *Revelation 3:8.*

19:6 And I heard as it were the voice of a great multitude, and as the voice of many waters, and as the voice of mighty thunderings, saying, Alleluia: for the Lord God omnipotent reigneth.

Multitude *see* ***Revelation 7:9.***

Mighty *see* ***Revelation 6:15.*** *See also* **Strong** at ***Revelation 5:2.***

Thunderings *see* ***Revelation 4:5.***

Alleluia *see* ***Revelation 19:1.***

Omnipotent *pantokrator* (3841), "almighty, or ruler of all" (*pas,* "all," *krateo,* "to hold, or to have strength"), is used of God only, and is found, in the Epistles, only in 2 Cor. 6:18, where the title is suggestive in connection with the context; elsewhere only in Revelation, nine times. In one place, **19:6**, the KJV has "omnipotent"; RV, "(the Lord our God) the Almighty." The word is introduced in the Sept. as a translation of "Lord (or God) of hosts," e.g., Jer. 5:14 and Amos 4:13.

Reigneth *see* **Reign** at ***Revelation 5:10.***

19:7 Let us be glad and rejoice, and give honour to him: for the marriage of the Lamb is come, and his wife hath made herself ready.

Be glad *agalliao* (21), "to rejoice greatly, to exult," is used, (I) in the active voice, of "rejoicing" in God, Luke 1:47; in faith in Christ, 1 Pet. 1:8, RV (middle voice in some mss.), "ye rejoice greatly"; in the event of the marriage of the Lamb, **Rev. 19:7**, "be exceeding glad," RV; (II) in the middle voice, (a) of "rejoicing" in persecutions, Matt. 5:12 (2nd part); in the light of testimony for God, John 5:35; in salvation received through the gospel, Acts 16:34, "he rejoiced greatly," RV; in salvation ready to be revealed, 1 Pet. 1:6; at the revelation of His glory, 1 Pet. 4:13, "with exceeding joy," lit., "ye may rejoice exulting"; (b) of Christ's "rejoicing" (greatly) "in the Holy Spirit," Luke 10:21, RV; said of His praise, as foretold in Ps. 16:9, quoted in Acts 2:26 (which follows the Sept., "My tongue"); (c) of Abraham's "rejoicing," by faith, to see Christ's day, John 8:56.

Rejoice *chairo* (5463), is the usual word for "rejoicing, being glad"; it is rendered by the verb "to be glad" in Mark 14:11; Luke 15:32; 22:5; 23:8; John 8:56; 11:15; 20:20; Acts 11:23; 13:48; in the following the RV has "to rejoice" for KJV, "to be glad," Rom. 16:19; 1 Cor. 16:17; 2 Cor. 13:9; 1 Pet. 4:13; **Rev. 19:7**.

Honour *doxa* (1391), "glory," is translated "honor" in the KJV of John 5:41, 44 (twice); 8:54; 2 Cor. 6:8, and **Rev. 19:7**; the RV keeps to the word "glory," as the KJV everywhere else.

Marriage *gamos* (1062), "a wedding," especially a wedding "feast" (akin to *gameo,* "to marry"); it is used in the plural in the following passages (the RV rightly has "marriage feast" for the KJV, "marriage," or "wedding"), Matt. 22:2, 3, 4, 9 (in verses 11, 12, it is used in the singular, in connection with the wedding garment); 25:10; Luke 12:36; 14:8; in the following it signifies a wedding itself, John 2:1, 2; Heb. 13:4; and figuratively in **Rev. 19:7**, of the marriage of the Lamb; in v. **9** it is used in connection with the supper, the wedding supper (or what in English is termed "breakfast"), not the wedding itself, as in v. **7**.

Made ready *see* **Prepared** at ***Revelation 8:6.***

19:8 And to her was granted that she should be arrayed in fine linen, clean and white: for the fine linen is the righteousness of saints.

Fine linen *see* ***Revelation 18:2.***

Clean *see* **Pure** at ***Revelation 15:6.***

White *see* ***Revelation 15:6.***

Righteousness *see* **Judgments** at ***Revelation 15:4.***

19:9 And he saith unto me, Write, Blessed *are* they which are called unto the marriage supper of the Lamb. And he saith unto me, These are the true sayings of God.

Blessed *see* ***Revelation 1:3.***

Called *kaleo* (2564), "to call," often means "to bid," in the sense of "invite," e.g., Matt. 22:3-4, 8, 9; Luke 14:7-10, 13, RV; **Rev. 19:9**, RV.

Marriage *see* ***Revelation 19:7.***

Supper *deipnon* (1173), denotes (a) "the chief meal of the day," dinner or supper, taken at or towards evening; in the plural "feasts," Matt. 23:6; Mark 6:21; 12:39; Luke 20:46; otherwise translated "supper," Luke 14:12, 16, 17, 24; John 12:2; 13:2, 4; 21:20; 1 Cor. 11:21 (of a social meal); (b) "the Lord's Supper," 1 Cor. 11:20; (c) "the supper or feast" which will celebrate the marriage of Christ with His spiritual Bride, at the inauguration of His Kingdom, **Rev. 19:9**; (d) figuratively, of that to which the birds of prey will be summoned after the overthrow of the enemies of the Lord at the termination of the war of Armageddon, **19:17** (cf. Ezek. 39:4, 17-20).

True *see* ***Revelation 3:7.***

Sayings *logos* (3056), "a word," as embodying a conception or idea, denotes among its various meanings, "a saying, statement or declaration," uttered (a) by God; RV, "word" or "words" (KJV, "saying"), e.g., in John 8:55; Rom. 3:4; **Rev.**

19:9; 22:6, 7, 9, 10; (b) by Christ, e.g., Mark 8:32; 9:10; 10:22; Luke 9:28; John 6:60; 21:23; the RV appropriately substitutes "word" or "words" for KJV, "saying" or "sayings," especially in John's Gospel, e.g. 7:36, 40; 8:51, 52; 10:19; 14:24; 15:20; 18:9, 32; 19:13; (c) by an angel, Luke 1:29; (d) by OT prophets, John 12:38 (RV, "word") Rom. 13:9 (ditto); 1 Cor. 15:54; (e) by the apostle Paul in the Pastoral Epp., 1 Tim. 1:15; 3:1; 4:9; 2 Tim. 2:11; Titus 3:8; (f) by other men, Mark 7:29; Acts 7:29; John 4:37 (in general).

19:10 And I fell at his feet to worship him. And he said unto me, See *thou do it* not: I am thy fellowservant, and of thy brethren that have the testimony of Jesus: worship God: for the testimony of Jesus is the spirit of prophecy.

Worship *see Revelation 4:10.*

Fellowservant *see* Fellowservants at *Revelation 6:11.*

Of *see Revelation 1:2.*

Brethren Believers, apart from sex, Matt. 23:8; Acts 1:15; Rom. 1:13; 1 Thess. 1:4; **Rev. 19:10** (the word "sisters" is used of believers, only in 1 Tim. 5:2).

Jesus *see Revelation 1:9.*

Spirit *see Revelation 1:10.*

Prophecy *see Revelation 1:3.*

19:11 And I saw heaven opened, and behold a white horse; and he that sat upon him *was* called Faithful and True, and in righteousness he doth judge and make war.

Opened *see* Openeth at *Revelation 3:7.*

White *see Revelation 1:14.*

Horse *see Revelation 6:2.*

Faithful *see Revelation 1:5.*

True *see Revelation 3:7.*

War *see* Fight at *Revelation 2:16.*

19:12 His eyes *were* as a flame of fire, and on his head *were* many crowns; and he had a name written, that no man knew, but he himself.

Eyes *see Revelation 1:14.*

Fire *see Revelation 1:14.*

Flame *see Revelation 1:14.*

Crowns *see Revelation 12:3.*

19:13 And he *was* clothed with a vesture dipped in blood: and his name is called The Word of God.

Vesture *himation* (2440), "an outer garment," is rendered "vesture" in **Rev. 19:13, 16**, KJV (RV, "garment").

Dipped *bapto* (911), "to immerse, dip" (derived from a root signifying "deep"), also signified "to dye," which is suggested in **Rev. 19:13**, of the Lord's garment "dipped (i.e. dyed) in blood" (RV, "sprinkled" translates the verb *rhantizo*. It is elsewhere translated "to dip," Luke 16:24; John 13:26. Cf the longer form *baptizo* (primarily a frequentative form).

Word *see Revelation 1:2.*

19:14 And the armies *which were* in heaven followed him upon white horses, clothed in fine linen, white and clean.

Armies *see* Army at *Revelation 9:16.*

White *see Revelation 1:14.*

Horses *see* Horse at *Revelation 6:2.*

Clothed *see Revelation 1:13.*

Fine linen *see Revelation 18:12.*

Clean *see* Pure at *Revelation 15:6.*

19:15 And out of his mouth goeth a sharp sword, that with it he should smite the nations: and he shall rule them with a rod of iron: and he treadeth the winepress of the fierceness and wrath of Almighty God.

Mouth *see Revelation 1:16.*

Goeth *see* Went at *Revelation 1:16.*

Sharp *see Revelation 1:16.*

Sword *see Revelation 1:16.*

Smite *see Revelation 11:6.*

Rule *see Revelation 2:27.*

Rod *see Revelation 2:27.*

Iron *see Revelation 2:27.*

Treadeth *see* Tread at *Revelation 11:2.*

Winepress *see Revelation 14:19.*

Fierceness *see Revelation 16:19.*

Wrath *see Revelation 12:12.*

19:16 And he hath on *his* vesture and on his thigh a name written, KING OF KINGS, AND LORD OF LORDS.

Vesture *see Revelation 19:13.*

Thigh *meros* (3382), occurs in **Rev. 19:16**; Christ appears there in the manifestation of His judicial capacity and action hereafter as the executor of divine vengeance upon the foes of God; His name is spoken of figuratively as being upon His "thigh" (where the sword would be worn; cf. Ps. 45:3), emblematic of His strength to tread down His foes, His action being the exhibition of His divine attributes of righteousness and power.

King, Kings *see* King at *Revelation 15:3.*

19:17 And I saw an angel standing in the sun; and he cried with a loud voice, saying to all the fowls that fly in the midst of heaven, Come and gather yourselves together unto the supper of the great God;

Fowls *see* Bird at *Revelation 18:2*.

Fly *see* Flying at *Revelation 4:7*.

Heaven *see Revelation 8:13*.

Come *see Revelation 17:1*.

Supper *see Revelation 19:9*.

19:18 That ye may eat the flesh of kings, and the flesh of captains, and the flesh of mighty men, and the flesh of horses, and of them that sit on them, and the flesh of all *men, both* free and bond, both small and great.

Captains *see Revelation 6:15*.

Mighty *see Revelation 6:15*. *See also* Strong at *Revelation 5:2*.

Horses *see* Horse at *Revelation 6:2*.

Free *see Revelation 6:15*.

Small *see Revelation 11:18*. *See also* Little at *Revelation 3:8*.

19:19 And I saw the beast, and the kings of the earth, and their armies, gathered together to make war against him that sat on the horse, and against his army.

Beast *see Revelation 11:7*.

Horse *see Revelation 6:2*.

Army *see Revelation 9:16*.

19:20 And the beast was taken, and with him the false prophet that wrought miracles before him, with which he deceived them that had received the mark of the beast, and them that worshipped his image. These both were cast alive into a lake of fire burning with brimstone.

Taken *piazo* (4084), "to lay hold of," with the suggestion of firm pressure or force, is used in the Gospels only in John, six times of efforts to seize Christ and is always rendered "take" in the RV, 7:30, 32, 44; 8:20; 10:39; 11:57. The KJV has "laid hands on" in 8:20. In Acts 12:4 and 2 Cor. 11:32 (KJV), it is translated respectively "apprehended" and "apprehend" (RV, "had taken," and "take"). In **Rev. 19:20** it is used of the seizure of the Beast and the False Prophet. In John 21:3, 10 it is used of catching fish. Elsewhere in Acts 3:7. In the Sept., Song of Sol. 2:15.

Prophet *see* Beast at *Revelation 13:11*.

Wrought *see* Working at *Revelation 16:14*. *See also* Make at *Revelation 3:9*.

Miracles *see Revelation 13:14*. *See also* Wonder at *Revelation 12:1*.

Mark *see Revelation 13:16*.

Image *see Revelation 13:14*.

Both *duo* (1417), is rendered "twain" in Matt. 5:41; 19:5, 6; 21:31; 27:21, 51; Mark 10:8 (twice); 15:38; in 1 Cor. 6:16 and Eph. 5:31, RV (KJV, "two"); Eph. 2:15; in **Rev. 19:20**, RV (KJV, "both").

Lake *limne* (3041), "a lake," is used (a) in the Gospels, only by Luke, of the Sea of Galilee, Luke 5:2; 8:22, 23, 33, called Gennesaret in 5:1 (Matthew and Mark use *thalassa*, "a sea"); (b) of the "lake" of fire, **Rev. 19:20; 20:10, 14, 15; 21:8**.

Burning *see Revelation 4:5*.

Brimstone *see Revelation 9:17*.

19:21 And the remnant were slain with the sword of him that sat upon the horse, which *sword* proceeded out of his mouth: and all the fowls were filled with their flesh.

Remnant *see Revelation 11:13*.

Slain *see Revelation 2:13*.

Sword *see Revelation 1:16*.

Horse *see Revelation 6:2*.

Proceeded *see* Went at *Revelation 1:16*.

Mouth *see Revelation 1:16*.

Fowls *see* Bird at *Revelation 18:2*.

Filled *chortazo* (5526), "to feed, to fatten," is used (a) primarily of animals, **Rev. 19:21**; (b) of persons, to fill or satisfy with food. It is usually translated by the verb "to fill," but is once rendered "to be fed," in Luke 16:21, of Lazarus, in his desire for the crumbs (he could be well supplied with them) that fell from the rich man's table, a fact which throws light upon the utter waste that went on at the table of the latter. The crumbs that fell would provide no small meal.

Chapter 20

20:1 And I saw an angel come down from heaven, having the key of the bottomless pit and a great chain in his hand.

Key *see* Keys at *Revelation 1:18*.

Bottomless *see Revelation 9:1*.

Chain *halusis* (254), denotes "a chain or bond for binding the body, or any part of it (the hands or feet)." Some derive the word from *a*, negative, and *luo*, "to loose," i.e., "not to be loosed"; others from a root connected with a word signifying "to restrain." It is used in Mark 5:3-4; Luke 8:29; Acts 12:6-7; 21:33; 28:20; Eph. 6:20; 2 Tim. 1:16; **Rev. 20:1**.

20:2 And he laid hold on the dragon, that old serpent, which is the Devil, and Satan, and bound him a thousand years,

Hold *see* Holdeth at *Revelation 2:1*.

Dragon *see Revelation 12:3*.

Old *see Revelation 12:9*.

Serpent *see* Serpents at *Revelation 9:19*.

Satan *see Revelation 2:9*.

Thousand *see Revelation 5:11*.

Years *etos* (2094), is used (a) to mark a point of time at or from which events take place, e.g., Luke 3:1 (dates were frequently reckoned from the time when a monarch began to reign); in Gal. 3:17 the time of the giving of the Law is stated as 430 "years" after the covenant of promise given to Abraham; there is no real discrepancy between this and Ex. 12:40; the apostle is not concerned with the exact duration of the interval, it certainly was not less than 430 "years"; the point of the argument is that the period was very considerable; Gal. 1:18 and 2:1 mark events in Paul's life; as to the former the point is that three "years" elapsed before he saw any of the apostles; in 2:1 the 14 "years" may date either from his conversion or from his visit to Peter mentioned in 1:18; the latter seems the more natural; (b) to mark a space of time, e.g., Matt. 9:20; Luke 12:19; 13:11; John 2:20; Acts 7:6, where the 400 "years" mark not merely the time that Israel was in bondage in Egypt, but the time that they sojourned or were strangers there (the RV puts a comma after the word "evil"); the Genevan Version renders Gen. 15:13 "thy posterity shall inhabit a strange land for 400 years"; Heb. 3:17; **Rev. 20:2-7**; (c) to date an event from one's birth, e.g., Mark 5:42; Luke 2:42; 3:23; John 8:57; Acts 4:22; 1 Tim. 5:9; (d) to mark recurring events, Luke 2:41 (with *kata*, used distributively); 13:7; (e) of an unlimited number, Heb. 1:12.

20:3 And cast him into the bottomless pit, and shut him up, and set a seal upon him, that he should deceive the nations no more, till the thousand years should be fulfilled: and after that he must be loosed a little season.

Shut *see* Shutteth at *Revelation 3:7*.

Seal *see Revelation 7:2*.

More *see Revelation 3:12*. *See also* Hereafter at *Revelation 1:19*.

Fulfilled *see* Filled up at *Revelation 15:1*. *See also* Finished at *Revelation 10:7*.

Loosed *see* Loose at *Revelation 5:2*.

Little *see Revelation 3:8*.

Season *see Revelation 6:11*.

20:4 And I saw thrones, and they sat upon them, and judgment was given unto them: and *I saw* the souls of them that were beheaded for the witness of Jesus, and for the word of God, and which had not worshipped the beast, neither his image, neither had received *his* mark upon their foreheads, or in their hands; and they lived and reigned with Christ a thousand years.

Sat *see* Sit at *Revelation 3:21*.

Judgment *krima* (2917), denotes the result of the action signified by the verb *krino*, "to judge"; it is used (a) of a decision passed on the faults of others, Matt. 7:2; (b) of "judgment" by man upon Christ, Luke 24:20; (c) of God's "judgment" upon men, e.g., Rom. 2:2, 3; 3:8; 5:16; 11:33; 13:2; 1 Cor. 11:29; Gal. 5:10; Heb. 6:2; Jas. 3:1; through Christ, e.g., John 9:39; (d) of the right of "judgment," **Rev. 20:4**; (e) of a lawsuit, 1 Cor. 6:7.

Beheaded *pelekizo* (3990), denotes "to cut with an axe" (from *pelekus*, "an axe"), **Rev. 20:4**.

Jesus *see Revelation 1:9*.

Which *see Revelation 2:24*.

Beast *see Revelation 11:7*.

Image *see Revelation 13:14*.

Mark *see Revelation 13:16*.

Foreheads *see Revelation 7:3*.

Lived *zao* (2198), "to live, be alive," is used in the NT of "(a) God, Matt. 16:16; John 6:57; Rom. 14:11; (b) the Son in Incarnation, John 6:57; (c) the Son in Resurrection, John 14:19; Acts 1:3; Rom. 6:10; 2 Cor. 13:4; Heb. 7:8; (d) spiritual life, John 6:57; Rom. 1:17; 8:13b; Gal. 2:19, 20; Heb. 12:9; (e) the present state of departed saints, Luke 20:38; 1 Pet. 4:6; (f) the hope of resurrection, 1 Pet. 1:3; (g) the resurrection of believers, 1 Thess. 5:10; John 5:25; **Rev. 20:4**, and of unbelievers, v. **5**, cf. v. **13**; (h) the way of access to God through the Lord Jesus Christ, Heb. 10:20; (i) the manifestation of divine power in support of divine authority, 2 Cor. 13:4b; cf. 12:10, and 1 Cor. 5:5; (j) bread, figurative of the Lord Jesus, John 6:51; (k) a stone, figurative of the Lord Jesus, 1 Pet. 2:4; (l) water, figurative of the Holy Spirit, John 4:10; 7:38; (m) a sacrifice, figurative of the believer, Rom. 12:1; (n) stones, figurative of the believer, 1 Pet. 2:5; (o) the oracles, *logion*, Acts 7:38, and word, *logos*, Heb. 4:12; 1 Pet. 1:23, of God; (p) the physical life of men, 1 Thess.

4:15; Matt. 27:63; Acts 25:24; Rom. 14:9; Phil. 1:21 (in the infinitive mood used as a noun with the article, 'living'), 22; 1 Pet. 4:5; (q) the maintenance of physical life, Matt. 4:4; 1 Cor. 9:14; (r) the duration of physical life, Heb. 2:15; (s) the enjoyment of physical life, 1 Thess. 3:8; (t) the recovery of physical life from the power of disease, Mark 5:23; John 4:50; (u) the recovery of physical life from the power of death, Matt. 9:18; Acts 9:41; **Rev. 20:5**; (v) the course, conduct, and character of men, (1) good, Acts 26:5; 2 Tim. 3:12; Titus 2:12; (2) evil, Luke 15:13; Rom. 6:2; 8:13a; 2 Cor. 5:15b; Col. 3:7; (3) undefined, Rom. 7:9; 14:7; Gal. 2:14; (w) restoration after alienation, Luke 15:32."

Reigned *see* **Reign** at *Revelation 5:10*.

20:5 But the rest of the dead lived not again until the thousand years were finished. This *is* the first resurrection.

Lived *see Revelation 20:4*.

Finished *see Revelation 10:7*. *See also* **Filled up** at *Revelation 15:1*.

Resurrection *anastasis* (386), denotes (I) "a raising up," or "rising" (*ana*, "up," and *histemi*, "to cause to stand"), Luke 2:34, "the rising up"; the KJV "again" obscures the meaning; the Child would be like a stone against which many in Israel would stumble while many others would find in its strength and firmness a means of their salvation and spiritual life; (II) of "resurrection" from the dead, (a) of Christ, Acts 1:22; 2:31; 4:33; Rom. 1:4; 6:5; Phil. 3:10; 1 Pet. 1:3; 3:21; by metonymy, of Christ as the Author of "resurrection," John 11:25; (b) of those who are Christ's at His Parousia, Luke 14:14, "the resurrection of the just"; Luke 20:33, 35, 36; John 5:29 (1st part), "the resurrection of life"; 11:24; Acts 23:6; 24:15 (1st part); 1 Cor. 15:21, 42; 2 Tim. 2:18; Heb. 11:35 (2nd part); **Rev. 20:5**, "the first resurrection"; hence the insertion of "is" stands for the completion of this "resurrection," of which Christ was "the firstfruits"; **20:6**; (c) of "the rest of the dead," after the Millennium (cf. **Rev. 20:5**); John 5:29 (2nd part), "the resurrection of judgment"; Acts 24:15 (2nd part), "of the unjust"; (d) of those who were raised in more immediate connection with Christ's "resurrection," and thus had part already in the first "resurrection," Acts 26:23 and Rom. 1:4 (in each of which "dead" is plural; see Matt. 27:52); (e) of the "resurrection" spoken of in general terms, Matt. 22:23; Mark 12:18; Luke 20:27; Acts 4:2; 17:18; 23:8; 24:21; 1 Cor. 15:12, 13; Heb. 6:2; (f) of those who were raised in OT times, to die again, Heb. 11:35 (1st part), lit., "out of resurrection."

20:6 Blessed and holy *is* he that hath part in the first resurrection: on such the second death hath no power, but they shall be priests of God and of Christ, and shall reign with him a thousand years.

Blessed *see Revelation 1:3*.

Part *see* **Parts** at *Revelation 16:19*.

Resurrection *see Revelation 20:5*.

Second *see Revelation 2:11*.

Priests *see Revelation 1:6*.

Reign *sunbasileuo* (4821), "to reign together with," is used of the future "reign" of believers together and with Christ in the kingdom of God in manifestation, 1 Cor. 4:8 (3rd part); of those who endure 2 Tim. 2:12. cf. **Rev. 20:6**. *See also Revelation 5:10*.

20:7 And when the thousand years are expired, Satan shall be loosed out of his prison,

Expired *see* **Finished** at *Revelation 10:7*. *See also* **Filled up** at *Revelation 15:1*.

Loosed *see* **Loose** at *Revelation 5:2*.

Satan *see Revelation 2:9*.

Prison *see Revelation 2:10*.

20:8 And shall go out to deceive the nations which are in the four quarters of the earth, Gog and Magog, to gather them together to battle: the number of whom *is* as the sand of the sea.

Quarters In **Rev. 20:8**, KJV, *gonia*, "an angle, corner," is rendered "quarter" (RV, "corner"). *See also* **Corners** at *Revelation 7:1*.

Battle *see* **Fight** at *Revelation 9:7*.

Sand *see Revelation 13:1*.

Sea *see Revelation 4:6*.

20:9 And they went up on the breadth of the earth, and compassed the camp of the saints about, and the beloved city: and fire came down from God out of heaven, and devoured them.

Breadth *platos* (4114), denotes "breadth," Eph. 3:18; **Rev. 20:9**; **21:16** (twice).

Compassed *kukleuo* (2944), denotes "to encircle, surround," and is found in the best texts in John 10:24, "came round about," and **Rev. 20:9**, of a camp surrounded by foes.

Camp *parembole* (3925), lit., "a casting in among, an insertion" (*para*, "among," *ballo*, "to throw"), in the Macedonian dialect, was a military term. In the NT it denotes the distribution of troops in army formation, "armies," Heb. 11:34; a camp, as of the Israelites, Exod. 19:17; 29:14; 32:17; hence, in Heb. 13:11, 13, of

"The Lord is King! child of the dust, / The Judge of all the earth is just: / Holy and true are all His ways; / Let every creature speak His praise."

JOSIAH CONDER

Jerusalem, since the city was to the Jews what the camp in the wilderness had been to the Israelites; in **Rev. 20:9**, the "armies" or camp of the saints, at the close of the Millennium. It also denoted a castle or barracks, Acts 21:34, 37; 22:24; 23:10, 16, 32.

Heaven *see Revelation 3:12.*

Devoured *see* Eat at *Revelation 10:9.*

20:10 And the devil that deceived them was cast into the lake of fire and brimstone, where the beast and the false prophet *are*, and shall be tormented day and night for ever and ever.

Devil *see Revelation 12:9. See also* Satan at *Revelation 2:9.*

Lake *see Revelation 19:20.*

Brimstone *see Revelation 9:17.*

Beast *see Revelation 11:7.*

False prophet *see* Beast at *Revelation 13:11.*

Tormented *see Revelation 9:5.*

20:11 And I saw a great white throne, and him that sat on it, from whose face the earth and the heaven fled away; and there was found no place for them.

White *see Revelation 1:14.*

Heaven *see Revelation 3:12.*

Fled *see* Flee at *Revelation 9:6.*

20:12 And I saw the dead, small and great, stand before God; and the books were opened: and another book was opened, which is *the book* of life: and the dead were judged out of those things which were written in the books, according to their works.

Small *see Revelation 11:18. See also* Little at *Revelation 3:8.*

Books, Book *see* Book at *Revelation 1:11.*

20:13 And the sea gave up the dead which were in it; and death and hell delivered up the dead which were in them: and they were judged every man according to their works.

Sea *see Revelation 4:6.*

Hell *see Revelation 1:18.*

20:14 And death and hell were cast into the lake of fire. This is the second death.

Hell *see Revelation 1:18.*

Lake *see Revelation 19:20.*

Second *see Revelation 2:11.*

20:15 And whosoever was not found written in the book of life was cast into the lake of fire.

Book *see Revelation 3:5.*

Lake *see Revelation 19:20.*

Chapter 21

21:1 And I saw a new heaven and a new earth: for the first heaven and the first earth were passed away; and there was no more sea.

New *see Revelation 2:17.*

Heaven *see Revelation 3:12.*

More *see Revelation 3:12.*

Sea *see Revelation 4:6.*

21:2 And I John saw the holy city, new Jerusalem, coming down from God out of heaven, prepared as a bride adorned for her husband.

Holy *see Revelation 4:8.*

City *see Revelation 3:12.*

New *see Revelation 2:17.*

Prepared *see Revelation 8:6.*

Bride *see Revelation 18:23.*

Adorned *kosmeo* (2885), primarily "to arrange, to put in order" (Eng., "cosmetic"), is used of furnishing a room, Matt. 12:44; Luke 11:25, and of trimming lamps, Matt. 25:7. Hence, "to adorn, to ornament," as of garnishing tombs, Matt. 23:29; buildings, Luke 21:5; **Rev. 21:19**; one's person, 1 Tim. 2:9; 1 Pet. 3:5; **Rev. 21:2**; metaphorically, of "adorning a doctrine," Titus 2:10.

21:3 And I heard a great voice out of heaven saying, Behold, the tabernacle of God *is* with men, and he will dwell with them, and they shall be his people, and God himself shall be with them, *and be* their God.

Voice *see Revelation 1:10.*

Tabernacle *see Revelation 13:6.*

Dwell *see Revelation 7:15.*

21:4 And God shall wipe away all tears from their eyes; and there shall be no more death, neither sorrow, nor crying, neither shall there be any more pain: for the former things are passed away.

Wipe *see Revelation 7:17. See also* Blot out at *Revelation 3:5.*

Tears *see Revelation 7:17.*

More *see Revelation 3:12.*

Sorrow *see Revelation 18:7.*

Crying *see* Cry at *Revelation 14:18.*

Pain *see Revelation 16:10.*

Former *protos* (4413), "first," is translated "former" in Acts 1:1, of Luke's first treatise; in **Rev. 21:4**, RV, "first" (KJV, "former").

Passed *see* Past at *Revelation 9:12.*

21:5 And he that sat upon the throne said, Behold, I make all things new. And he said unto me, Write: for these words are true and faithful.

New *see Revelation 2:17.*

True *see Revelation 3:7.*

Faithful *see Revelation 1:5.*

21:6 And he said unto me, It is done. I am Alpha and Omega, the beginning and the end. I will give unto him that is athirst of the fountain of the water of life freely.

End *see* Ending at *Revelation 1:8.*

Athirst *see* Thirst at *Revelation 7:16.*

Fountain *see* Fountains at *Revelation 7:17.*

Water *see* Waters at *Revelation 17:1.*

Freely *dorean* (1432), from *dorea,* "a gift" is used as an adverb in the sense "freely," in Matt. 10:8; Rom. 3:24; 2 Cor. 11:7 (RV, "for nought"); **Rev. 21:6; 22:17**. Here the prominent thought is the grace of the Giver.

21:7 He that overcometh shall inherit all things; and I will be his God, and he shall be my son.

Overcometh *see Revelation 2:7.*

Inherit *kleronomeo* (2816), strictly means "to receive by lot" (*kleros,* "a lot," *nemomai,* "to possess"); then, in a more general sense, "to possess oneself of, to receive as one's own, to obtain." The following list shows how in the NT the idea of inheriting broadens out to include all spiritual good provided through and in Christ, and particularly all that is contained in the hope grounded on the promises of God. The verb is used of the following objects: "(a) birthright, that into the possession of which one enters in virtue of sonship, not because of a price paid or of a task accomplished, Gal. 4:30; Heb. 1:4; 12:17; (b) that which is received as a gift, in contrast with that which is received as the reward of law-keeping, Heb. 1:14; 6:12 ("through," i.e., 'through experiences that called for the exercise of faith and patience,' but not 'on the ground of the exercise of faith and patience.'); (c) that which is received on condition of obedience to certain precepts, 1 Pet. 3:9, and of faithfulness to God amidst opposition, **Rev. 21:7**; (d) the reward of that condition of soul which forbears retaliation and self-vindication, and expresses itself in gentleness of behavior.... Matt. 5:5. The phrase "inherit the earth," or "land," occur several times in OT. See especially Ps. 37:11, 22; (e) the reward (in the coming age, Mark 10:30) of the acknowledgment of the paramountcy of the claims of Christ, Matt. 19:29. (f) the reward of those who have shown kindness to the "brethren" of the Lord in their distress, Matt. 25:34; (g) the kingdom of God, which the morally corrupt cannot "inherit," 1 Cor. 6:9, 10, the "inheritance" of which is likewise impossible to the present physical constitution of man, 1 Cor. 15:50; (h) incorruption, impossible of "inheritance" by corruption, 1 Cor. 15:50."

"When I get to heaven, I shall see three wonders there – the first wonder will be to see many people there whom I did not expect to see; the second wonder will be to miss many people whom I did expect to see; and the third and greatest wonder of all will be to find myself there."

JOHN NEWTON

Son *huios* (5207), primarily signifies the relation of offspring to parent (see John 9:18-20; Gal. 4:30). It is often used metaphorically of prominent moral characteristics. "It is used in the NT of (a) male offspring, Gal. 4:30; (b) legitimate, as opposed to illegitimate offspring, Heb. 12:8; (c) descendants, without reference to sex, Rom. 9:27; (d) friends attending a wedding, Matt. 9:15; (e) those who enjoy certain privileges, Acts 3:25; (f) those who act in a certain way, whether evil, Matt. 23:31, or good, Gal. 3:7; (g) those who manifest a certain character, whether evil, Acts 13:10; Eph. 2:2, or good, Luke 6:35; Acts 4:36; Rom. 8:14; (h) the destiny that corresponds with the character, whether evil, Matt. 23:15; John 17:12; 2 Thess. 2:3, or good, Luke 20:36; (i) the dignity of the relationship with God whereinto men are brought by the Holy Spirit when they believe on the Lord Jesus Christ, Rom. 8:19; Gal. 3:26....

"The Apostle John does not use *huios*, 'son,' of the believer, he reserves that title for the Lord; but he does use *teknon*, 'child,' as in his Gospel, 1:12; 1 John 3:1, 2; **Rev. 21:7** (*huios*) is a quotation from 2 Sam. 7:14.

21:8 But the fearful, and unbelieving, and the abominable, and murderers, and whoremongers, and sorcerers, and idolaters, and all liars, shall have their part in the lake which burneth with fire and brimstone: which is the second death.

Fearful *deilos* (1169), "cowardly," "timid," is used in Matt. 8:26; Mark 4:40; **Rev. 21:8** (here "the fearful" are first in the list of the transgressors).

Unbelieving *apistos* (571), is used with meanings somewhat parallel to *pistos*; (a) "untrustworthy" (*a*, negative, and *pistos*), not worthy of confidence or belief, is said of things "incredible," Acts 26:8 (b) "unbelieving, distrustful," used as a noun, "unbeliever," Luke 12:46; 1 Tim. 5:8 (RV, for KJV, "infidel"); in Titus 1:15 and **Rev. 21:8**, "unbelieving"; "faithless" in Matt. 17:17; Mark 9:19; Luke 9:41; John 20:27. The word is most frequent in 1 and 2 Corinthians. (In the Sept., Prov. 17:6; 28:25; Isa. 17:10.).

Abominable *bdelusso* (948), "to render foul" (from *bdeo*, "to stink"), "to cause to be abhorred" (in the Sept. in Exod. 5:21; Lev. 11:43; 20:25, etc.), is used in the middle voice, signifying "to turn oneself away from" (as if from a stench); hence, "to detest," Rom. 2:22. In **Rev. 21:8** it denotes "to be abominable."

Murderers *phoneus* (5406), akin to *phoneuo* and *phonos*, is used (a) in a general sense, in the singular, 1 Pet. 4:15; in the plural, **Rev. 21:8**; **22:15**; (b) of those guilty of particular acts, Matt. 22:7; Acts 3:14, lit. "a man (*aner*), a murderer"; 7:52; 28:4.

Whoremongers *pornos* (4205), denotes "a man who indulges in fornication, a fornicator," 1 Cor. 5:9, 10, 11; 6:9; Eph. 5:5, RV; 1 Tim. 1:10, RV; Heb. 12:16; 13:4, RV; **Rev. 21:8** and **22:15**, RV (KJV, "whoremonger").

Sorcerers *pharmakos* (5333), an adjective signifying "devoted to magical arts," is used as a noun, "a sorcerer," especially one who uses drugs, potions, spells, enchantments, **Rev. 21:8**, in the best texts (some have *pharmakeus*), and **22:15**.

Idolaters *eidololatres* (1496), an "idolater" (from *eidolon*, and *latris*, "a hireling"), is found in 1 Cor. 5:10, 11; 6:9; 10:7; the warning is to believers against turning away from God to idolatry, whether "openly or secretly, consciously or unconsciously" (Cremer); Eph. 5:5; **Rev. 21:8**; **22:15**.

Liars *see Revelation 2:2*.

Part *see* **Parts** at *Revelation 16:19*.

Lake *see Revelation 19:20*.

Burneth *see* **Burning** at *Revelation 4:5*.

Brimstone *see Revelation 9:17*.

Second *see Revelation 2:11*.

21:9 And there came unto me one of the seven angels which had the seven vials full of the seven last plagues, and talked with me, saying, Come hither, I will shew thee the bride, the Lamb's wife.

Vials *see Revelation 5:8*.

Full *gemo* (1073), "to be full," is translated "laden" in **Rev. 21:9**, RV. *See also Revelation 4:6*.

Plagues *see Revelation 9:20*.

Talked *see* **Talking** at *Revelation 4:1*.

Come *see Revelation 17:1*.

Bride *see Revelation 18:23*.

Lamb's *see* **Lamb** at *Revelation 5:6*.

21:10 And he carried me away in the spirit to a great and high mountain, and shewed me that great city, the holy Jerusalem, descending out of heaven from God,

Spirit *see Revelation 1:10*.

Great In **Rev. 21:10**, the most authentic mss. omit "that great" [RV, "the holy (city)"].

High *hupselos* (5308), "high, lofty," is used (a) naturally, of mountains, Matt. 4:8; 17:1; Mark 9:2; **Rev. 21:10**; of a wall, **Rev. 21:12**; (b) figuratively, of the arm of God, Acts 13:17; of heaven, "on high," plural, lit., "in high (places)," Heb. 1:3; (c) metaphorically, Luke 16:15, RV, "exalted" (KJV, "highly esteemed"); Rom. 11:20, in the best texts, "high-minded" [lit., "mind (not) high things"]; 12:16.

Holy *see Revelation 4:8*.

Descending *katabaino* (2597), "to go down" (*kata*, "down," *baino*, "to go"), used for various kinds of motion on the ground (e.g., going, walking, stepping), is usually translated "to descend." The RV uses the verb "to come down," for KJV, "descend," in Mark 15:32; Acts 24:1; **Rev. 21:10**.

21:11 Having the glory of God: and her light *was* like unto a stone most precious, even like a jasper stone, clear as crystal;

Glory *see Revelation 1:6.*

Light *phoster* (5458), denotes "a luminary, light," or "light-giver"; it is used figuratively of believers, as shining in the spiritual darkness of the world, Phil. 2:15; in **Rev. 21:11** it is used of Christ as the "Light" reflected in and shining through the heavenly city (cf. v. **23**). In the Sept., Gen. 1:14, 16.

Like unto *see Revelation 1:13.*

Stone *see Revelation 4:3.*

Precious *see Revelation 17:4.*

Jasper *see Revelation 4:3.*

Clear as crystal *krustallizo* (2929), "to shine like crystal, to be of crystalline brightness, or transparency," is found in **Rev. 21:11**, "clear as crystal." The verb may, however, have a transitive force, signifying "to crystallize or cause to become like crystal." In that case it would speak of Christ (since He is the "Lightgiver," see the preceding part of the verse), as the One who causes the saints to shine in His own likeness.

21:12 And had a wall great and high, *and* had twelve gates, and at the gates twelve angels, and names written thereon, which are *the names* of the twelve tribes of the children of Israel:

Wall *teichos* (5038), "a wall," especially one around a town, is used (a) literally, Acts 9:25; 2 Cor. 11:33; Heb. 11:30; (b) figuratively, of the "wall" of the heavenly city, **Rev. 21:12, 14, 15, 17, 18, 19**.

High *see Revelation 21:10.*

Twelve *see Revelation 7:5.*

Gates *pulon* (4440), primarily signifies "a porch or vestibule," e.g., Matt. 26:71; Luke 16:20; Acts 10:17; 12:13, 14; then, the "gateway" or "gate tower" of a walled town, Acts 14:13; **Rev. 21:12, 13, 15, 21, 25; 22:14**.

Tribes *see* **Kindreds** at *Revelation 1:7.*

Written *epigrapho* (1924), is rendered "to write over or upon" (*epi*) in Mark 15:26; figuratively, on the heart, Heb. 8:10; 10:16; on the gates of the heavenly Jerusalem, **Rev. 21:12**.

21:13 On the east three gates; on the north three gates; on the south three gates; and on the west three gates.

East *see Revelation 7:2.*

Gates *see Revelation 21:12.*

North *borras* (1005), primarily Boreas, the North Wind, came to denote the "north" (cf. "Borealis"), Luke 13:29; **Rev. 21:13**.

South *notos* (3558), denotes (a) "the south wind," Luke 12:55; Acts 27:13; 28:13; (b) "south," as a direction, Luke 13:29; **Rev. 21:13**; (c) "the South," as a region, Matt. 12:42; Luke 11:31.

West *dusme* (1424), "the quarter of the sun-setting" (*dusis*, "a sinking, setting"; *duno*, "to sink"), hence, "the west," occurs in Matt. 8:11; 24:27; Luke 12:54 (some regard this as the sunset); 13:29; **Rev. 21:13**.

21:14 And the wall of the city had twelve foundations, and in them the names of the twelve apostles of the Lamb.

Wall *see Revelation 21:12.*

City *see Revelation 3:12.*

Twelve *see Revelation 7:5.*

Foundations *themelios*, or *themelion* (2310), is properly an adjective denoting "belonging to a foundation" (connected with *tithemi*, "to place"). It is used (1) as a noun, with *lithos*, "a stone," understood, in Luke 6:48, 49; 14:29; Heb. 11:10; **Rev. 21:14, 19**; (2) as a neuter noun in Acts 16:26, and metaphorically, (a) of "the ministry of the gospel and the doctrines of the faith," Rom. 15:20; 1 Cor. 3:10, 11, 12; Eph. 2:20, where the "of" is not subjective (i.e., consisting of the apostles and prophets), but objective (i.e., laid by the apostles, etc.); so in 2 Tim. 2:19, where "the foundation of God" is "the foundation laid by God,"—not the Church (which is not a "foundation"), but Christ Himself, upon whom the saints are built; Heb. 6:1; (b) "of good works," 1 Tim. 6:19.

21:15 And he that talked with me had a golden reed to measure the city, and the gates thereof, and the wall thereof.

Talked *see* **Talking** at *Revelation 4:1.*

Reed *see Revelation 11:1.*

Measure *see Revelation 11:1.*

Gates *see Revelation 21:12.*

Wall *see Revelation 21:12.*

21:16 And the city lieth foursquare, and the length is as large as the breadth: and he measured the city with the reed, twelve thousand furlongs. The length and the breadth and the height of it are equal.

Lieth *keimai* (2749), "to be laid, to lie," used as the passive voice of *tithemi*, "to lay", is said (a) of the Child Jesus, Luke 2:12, 16; (b) of the dead body of the Lord, Matt. 28:6; John 20:12; in Luke 23:53, "had ... lain," RV, KJV, "was laid," in the tomb as hitherto empty; (c) of the linen cloths, John 20:5, 6, 7; (d) figuratively of a veil as "lying" upon the hearts of the Jews, 2 Cor. 3:15, RV, "lieth" (KJV, "is"); (e) metaphorically, of the world as "lying" in the evil one, 1 John 5:19, RV; (f) of the heavenly city, **Rev. 21:16**.

Foursquare *tetragonos* (5068), "four-cornered" (from *tetra*, and *gonia*, "a corner, or angle"), is found in **Rev. 21:16**.

Length *mekos* (3372), "length," from the same root as *makros*, "long", occurs in Eph. 3:18 and **Rev. 21:16** (twice).

Large *hosos* (3745), "how much, how many," is used in the neuter plural to signify how great things, Mark 5:19, 20; Luke 8:39 (twice); Acts 9:16, KJV (RV, "how many things"); in **Rev. 21:16** (in the best mss.), "as great as," RV (KJV, "as large as," said of length).

Breadth *see Revelation 20:9*.

Measured *see* **Measure** at *Revelation 11:1*.

Reed *see Revelation 11:1*.

Furlongs *see Revelation 14:20*.

Height *hupsos* (5311), "a summit, top," is translated "height" in Eph. 3:18, where it may refer either to "the love of Christ" or to "the fullness of God"; the two are really inseparable, for they who are filled into the fullness of God thereby enter appreciatively into the love of Christ, which "surpasseth knowledge"; in **Rev. 21:16**, of the measurement of the heavenly Jerusalem.

21:17 And he measured the wall thereof, an hundred *and* forty *and* four cubits, *according to* the measure of a man, that is, of the angel.

Measured, Measure *see* **Measure** at *Revelation 11:1*.

Wall *see Revelation 21:12*.

Hundred *see Revelation 7:4*.

Cubits *pechus* (4083), denotes the forearm, i.e., the part between the hand and the elbowjoint; hence, "a measure of length," not from the wrist to the elbow, but from the tip of the middle finger to the elbow joint, i.e., about a foot and a half, or a little less than two feet, Matt. 6:27; Luke 12:25; John 21:8; **Rev. 21:17**.

21:18 And the building of the wall of it was *of* jasper: and the city *was* pure gold, like unto clear glass.

Building *endomesis* (1739), "a thing built, structure" (*en*, "in," *domao*, "to build"), is used of the wall of the heavenly city, **Rev. 21:18** (some suggest that the word means "a fabric"; others, "a roofing or coping"; these interpretations are questionable; the probable significance is "a building").

Wall *see Revelation 21:12*.

Jasper *see Revelation 4:3*.

Pure *see Revelation 15:6*.

Gold *see Revelation 3:18*.

Like unto *see Revelation 1:13*.

Clear In **Rev. 21:18**, *katharos*, ("pure," RV) is rendered "clear," in the KJV.

Glass *hualos* (5194), primarily denoted anything transparent, e.g., a transparent stone or gem, hence, "a lens of crystal, a glass," **Rev. 21:18, 21**.

21:19 And the foundations of the wall of the city *were* garnished with all manner of precious stones. The first foundation *was* jasper; the second, sapphire; the third, a chalcedony; the fourth, an emerald;

Foundations, Foundation *see Revelation 21:14*.

Wall *see Revelation 21:12*.

City *see Revelation 3:12*.

Garnished *kosmeo* (2885), is translated by the verb "to garnish" in Matt. 12:44; 23:29; Luke 11:25; and in the KJV of **Rev. 21:19**. *See also* **Adorned** at *Revelation 21:2*.

Precious *see Revelation 17:4*.

Stones *see* **Stone** at *Revelation 4:3*.

Jasper *see Revelation 4:3*.

Sapphire *sappheiros* (4552), is mentioned in **Rev. 21:19** (RV, marg., "*lapis lazuli*") as the second of the foundations of the wall of the heavenly Jerusalem (cf. Isa. 54:11). It was one of the stones in the high priest's breastplate, Exod. 28:18; 39:11; as an intimation of its value see Job 28:16; Ezek. 28:13. See also Exod. 24:10; Ezek. 1:26; 10:1. The "sapphire" has various shades of blue and ranks next in hardness to the diamond.

Chalcedony *chalkedon* (5472), the name of a gem, including several varieties, one of which resembles a cornelian, is "supposed to denote a green silicate of copper found in the mines near Chalcedon" (*Swete, on the Apocalypse*), **Rev. 21:19**.

Emerald *smaragdos* (4665), is a transparent stone of a light green color, occupying the first place in the second row on the high priest's breastplate, Exod. 28:18. Tyre imported it from Syria, Ezek. 27:16. It is one of the foundations of the heavenly Jerusalem, **Rev. 21:19**. The name was applied to other stones of a similar character, such as the carbuncle.

21:20 The fifth, sardonyx; the sixth, sardius; the seventh, chrysolite; the eighth, beryl; the ninth, a topaz; the tenth, a chrysoprasus; the eleventh, a jacinth; the twelfth, an amethyst.

Fifth *see Revelation 6:9.*

Sardonyx *sardonux* (4557), a name which indicates the formation of the gem, a layer of sard, and a layer of onyx, marked by the red of the sard and the white of the onyx. It was used among the Romans both for cameos and for signets. It forms the fifth foundation of the wall of the heavenly Jerusalem, **Rev. 21:20**.

Sixth *see Revelation 6:12.*

Sardius *see* **Sardine** at *Revelation 4:3.*

Seventh *see Revelation 8:1.*

Chrysolite *chrusolithos* (5555), lit., "a gold stone" (*chrusos*, "gold," *lithos*, "a stone"), is the name of a precious stone of a gold color, now called "a topaz," **Rev. 21:20** (see also Exod. 28:20 and Ezek. 28:13).

Eighth *see Revelation 17:11.*

Beryl *berullos* (969), "beryl," is a precious stone of a sea-green color, **Rev. 21:20** (cf. Exod. 28:20).

Ninth *enatos*, or *enn-* (1766), is found in reference (a) to "the ninth hour" (3 o'clock, p.m.) in Matt. 20:5; 27:45-46; Mark 15:33-34; Luke 23:44; Acts 3:1; 10:3, 30; (b) to "the topaz" as the "ninth" foundation of the city wall in the symbolic vision in **Rev. 21** (v. **20**).

Topaz *topazion* (5116), is mentioned in **Rev. 21:20**, as the ninth of the foundation stones of the wall of the heavenly Jerusalem; the stone is of a yellow color (though there are topazes of other colors) and is almost as hard as the diamond. It has the power of double refraction, and when heated or rubbed becomes electric. In the Sept., Ex. 28:17; 39:10; Job 28:19; Ps. 119:127, "(gold and) topaz"; Ezek. 28:13.

Tenth *see Revelation 11:13.*

Chrysoprasus *chrusoprasos* (5556), from (*chrusos*, "gold," and *prasos*, "a leek"), is a precious stone like a leek in color, a translucent, golden green. Pliny reckons it among the beryls. The word occurs in **Rev. 21:20.**

Eleventh *hendekatos* (1734), an adjective derived from the above, is found in Matt. 20:6, 9; **Rev. 21:20.**

Jacinth *huakinthos* (5192), primarily denoted "a hyacinth," probably the dark blue iris; then, "a precious stone," most likely the sapphire, **Rev. 21:20.**

Twelfth *dodekatos* (1428), occurs in **Rev. 21:20.**

Amethyst *amethustos* (271), primarily meaning "not drunken" (*a*, negative, and *methu* "wine"), became used as a noun, being regarded as possessing a remedial virtue against drunkenness. Pliny, however, says that the reason for its name lay in the fact that in color it nearly approached that of wine, but did not actually do so, **Rev. 21:20.**

21:21 And the twelve gates *were* twelve pearls; every several gate was of one pearl: and the street of the city *was* pure gold, as it were transparent glass.

Gates, Gate *see Revelation 21:12.*

Pearls, Pearl *see Revelation 17:4.*

Every *hekastos* (1538). It is used with *heis*, "one," in Acts 2:6, "every man," and in Eph. 4:16, "each several (part)," for KJV, "every (part)." In **Rev. 22:2** the most authentic mss. omit the numeral in the phrase "every month." It is preceded by *kath hena* (*kata*, "according to," *hena*, "one"), a strengthened phrase, in Eph. 5:33, KJV, "everyone ... in particular," RV, "severally, each one." The same kind of phrase with *ana*, "each," before the numeral, is used in **Rev. 21:21**, RV, "each one of the several (gates)," for KJV, "every several (gate)." *See also Revelation 6:11.*

Street *see Revelation 11:8.*

Pure *see Revelation 15:6.*

Gold *see Revelation 3:18.*

Transparent Cf. *diauges*, "translucent, transparent," **Rev. 21:21** (some texts have *diaphanes*, "transparent").

Glass *see Revelation 21:18.*

21:22 And I saw no temple therein: for the Lord God Almighty and the Lamb are the temple of it.

Temple *see Revelation 3:12.*

21:23 And the city had no need of the sun, neither of the moon, to shine in it: for the glory of God did lighten it, and the Lamb *is* the light thereof.

Moon *see Revelation 6:12.*

Shine *see* **Shineth** at *Revelation 1:16.*

Lighten *see* **Light** at *Revelation 21:11.*

Lamb *see Revelation 5:6.*

Lamp *see* **Candle** at *Revelation 18:23.*

21:24 And the nations of them which are saved shall walk in the light of it: and the kings of the earth do bring their glory and honour into it.

Saved *sozo* (4982), "to save," is used (as with the noun *soteria*, "salvation") (a) of material and temporal deliverance from danger, suffering, etc., e.g., Matt. 8:25; Mark 13:20; Luke 23:35; John 12:27; 1 Tim. 2:15; 2 Tim. 4:18 (KJV, "preserve"); Jude 5; from sickness, Matt. 9:22, "made ... whole" (RV, marg., "saved"); so Mark 5:34; Luke 8:48; Jas. 5:15; (b) of the spiritual and eternal salvation granted immediately by God to those who believe on the Lord Jesus Christ, e.g., Acts 2:47, RV "(those that) were being saved"; 16:31; Rom. 8:24, RV, "were we saved"; Eph. 2:5, 8; 1 Tim. 2:4; 2 Tim. 1:9; Titus 3:5; of human agency in this, Rom. 11:14; 1 Cor. 7:16; 9:22; (c) of the present experiences of God's power to deliver from the bondage of sin, e.g., Matt. 1:21; Rom. 5:10; 1 Cor. 15:2; Heb. 7:25; Jas. 1:21; 1 Pet. 3:21; of human agency in this, 1 Tim. 4:16; (d) of the future deliverance of believers at the second coming of Christ for His saints, being deliverance from the wrath of God to be executed upon the ungodly at the close of this age and from eternal doom, e.g., Rom. 5:9; (e) of the deliverance of the nation of Israel at the second advent of Christ, e.g., Rom. 11:26; (f) inclusively for all the blessings bestowed by God on men in Christ, e.g., Luke 19:10; John 10:9; 1 Cor. 10:33; 1 Tim. 1:15; (g) of those who endure to the end of the time of the Great Tribulation, Matt. 10:22; Mark 13:13; (h) of the individual believer, who, though losing his reward at the judgment seat of Christ hereafter, will not lose his salvation, 1 Cor. 3:15; 5:5; (i) of the deliverance of the nations at the Millennium, **Rev. 21:24** (in some mss.).

Honour *see Revelation 4:9.*

21:25 And the gates of it shall not be shut at all by day: for there shall be no night there.

Gates *see Revelation 21:12.*

Shut *see* Shutteth at *Revelation 3:7.*

21:26 And they shall bring the glory and honour of the nations into it.

Honour *see Revelation 4:9.*

21:27 And there shall in no wise enter into it any thing that defileth, neither *whatsoever* worketh abomination, or *maketh* a lie: but they which are written in the Lamb's book of life.

Defileth *koinos* (2839), "common," is translated "unclean" in Rom. 14:14 (thrice); in **Rev. 21:27**, RV (KJV, "that defileth," follows the inferior texts which have the verb *koinoo*).

Worketh *see* Working at *Revelation 16:14.*

Abomination *see* Abominations at *Revelation 17:4.*

Lie *see* Guile at *Revelation 14:5.*

Book *see Revelation 1:11.*

Chapter 22

22:1 And he shewed me a pure river of water of life, clear as crystal, proceeding out of the throne of God and of the Lamb.

Pure *see Revelation 15:6.*

River *see* Rivers at *Revelation 8:10.*

Water *see* Waters at *Revelation 17:1.*

Clear *lampros* (2986), is said of crystal, **Rev. 22:1**, KJV, clear, RV, bright.

Crystal *see Revelation 4:6.*

Proceeding *see* Went at *Revelation 1:16.*

Lamb *see Revelation 5:6.*

22:2 In the midst of the street of it, and on either side of the river, *was there* the tree of life, which bare twelve *manner of* fruits, *and* yielded her fruit every month: and the leaves of the tree *were* for the healing of the nations.

Street *see Revelation 11:8.*

Either side *enteuthen* (1782), is used (a) of place, "hence," or "from hence," Luke 4:9; 13:31; John 2:16; 7:3; 14:31; 18:36; in John 19:18, "on either side (one)," lit., "hence and hence"; in **Rev. 22:2**, it is contrasted with *ekeithen*, "thence," RV, "on this side ... on that" (KJV, "on either side"), lit. "hence ... thence"; (b) causal; Jas. 4:1, "(come they not) hence," i.e., "owing to."

River *see* Rivers at *Revelation 8:10.*

Tree *see Revelation 2:7.*

Bare *poieo* (4160), "to do," sometimes means "to produce, bear," Luke 8:8; 13:9; Jas. 3:12 (KJV, "bear," RV, "yield"); **Rev. 22:2.**

Twelve *see Revelation 7:5.*

Yielded *apodidomi* (591), "to give up or back," is translated "to yield" in Heb. 12:11; **Rev. 22:2** (in each case, of bearing fruit).

Every *see Revelation 21:21.*

Month *see* Months at *Revelation 9:5.*

Leaves *phullon* (5444), "a leaf" (originally *phulion*, Lat., *folium*, Eng., "folio," "foliaceous," "foliage," "foliate," "folious," etc.), is found in Matt. 21:19; 24:32; Mark 11:13 (twice); 13:28; **Rev. 22:2.**

Healing *therapeia* (2322), primarily denotes "care, attention," Luke 12:42; then, "medical service, healing" (Eng., "therapy"), Luke 9:11; **Rev. 22:2**, of the effects of the leaves of the tree of life, perhaps here with the meaning "health."

22:3 And there shall be no more curse: but the throne of God and of the Lamb shall be in it; and his servants shall serve him:

More *see Revelation 3:12.*

Curse *katathema* (2652), or, as in some mss., the longer form *katanathema,* denotes, by metonymy, "an accursed thing" (the object "cursed" being put for the "curse" pronounced), **Rev. 22:3.**

Throne *see Revelation 1:4.*

Lamb *see Revelation 5:6.*

Serve *see Revelation 7:15.*

22:4 And they shall see his face; and his name *shall be* in their foreheads.

Foreheads *see Revelation 7:3.*

22:5 And there shall be no night there; and they need no candle, neither light of the sun; for the Lord God giveth them light: and they shall reign for ever and ever.

Need *chreia* (5532), denotes "a need," in such expressions as "there is a need"; or "to have need of" something, e.g., Matt. 3:14; 6:8; 9:12, RV, "(have no) need," KJV, "need (not)," the RV adheres to the noun form; so in 14:16; Mark 14:63; Luke 5:31; 22:71; Eph. 4:28; 1 Thess. 4:9; in the following, however, both RV and KJV use the verb form, "to need" (whereas the original has the verb *echo,* "to have," with the noun *chreia* as the object, as in the instances just mentioned): Luke 15:7; John 2:25; 13:10; 16:30; 1 Thess. 1:8; 1 John 2:27; **Rev. 22:5**; in all these the verb "to have" could well have been expressed in the translation.

Candle *see Revelation 18:23.*

Light *see* Lightened at *Revelation 18:1.*

Giveth ... light *photizo* (5461), from *phos,* "light," (a), used intransitively, signifies "to give light, shine," **Rev. 22:5**; (b), used transitively, "to enlighten, illumine," is rendered "enlighten" in Eph. 1:18, metaphorically of spiritual "enlightenment"; so John 1:9, i.e., "lighting every man" (by reason of His coming); Eph. 3:9, "to make (all men) see" (RV marg., "to bring to light"); Heb. 6:4, "were enlightened"; 10:32, RV, "enlightened," KJV, "illuminated." Cf. *photismos,* "light," and *photeinos,* "full of light."

Reign *see Revelation 5:10.*

22:6 And he said unto me, These sayings *are* faithful and true: and the Lord God of the holy prophets sent his angel to shew unto his servants the things which must shortly be done.

Sayings *see Revelation 19:9.*

Faithful *see Revelation 1:5.*

True *see Revelation 3:7.*

Sent *see Revelation 1:1.*

Shew *see Revelation 1:1.*

22:7 Behold, I come quickly: blessed *is* he that keepeth the sayings of the prophecy of this book.

Quickly *see Revelation 2:5.*

Blessed *see Revelation 1:3.*

Keepeth *see* Keep at *Revelation 1:3.*

Sayings *see Revelation 19:9.*

Prophecy *see Revelation 1:3.*

Book *see Revelation 1:11.*

22:8-9 And I John saw these things, and heard *them*. And when I had heard and seen, I fell down to worship before the feet of the angel which shewed me these things. Then saith he unto me, See *thou do it* not: for I am thy fellowservant, and of thy brethren the prophets, and of them which keep the sayings of this book: worship God.

Fellowservant *see* Fellowservants at *Revelation 6:11.*

Keep *see Revelation 1:3.*

Sayings *see Revelation 19:9.*

Book *see Revelation 1:11.*

Worship *see Revelation 4:10.*

22:10 And he saith unto me, Seal not the sayings of the prophecy of this book: for the time is at hand.

Seal *see Revelation 7:2.*

Sayings *see Revelation 19:9.*

Prophecy *see Revelation 1:3.*

At hand *see Revelation 1:3.*

22:11 He that is unjust, let him be unjust still: and he which is filthy, let him be filthy still: and he that is righteous, let him be righteous still: and he that is holy, let him be holy still.

Unjust *adikeo* (91), "to do wrong," is used (a) intransitively, to act unrighteously, Acts 25:11, RV, "I am a wrongdoer" (KJV, "... an offender"); 1 Cor. 6:8; 2 Cor. 7:12 (1st part); Col. 3:25 (1st part); cf. **Rev. 22:11**; (b) transitively, "to wrong," Matt. 20:13; Acts 7:24 (passive voice), 26, 27; 25:10; 2 Cor. 7:2, v. 12 (2nd part; passive voice); Gal. 4:12, "ye did (me no) wrong," anticipating a possible suggestion that his vigorous language was due to some personal grievance; the occasion referred to was that of his first visit; Col. 3:25 (2nd part), lit., "what he did wrong," which brings consequences both in this life and at the judgment seat of

"The anguish of hell is the anguish of knowing – eternally – that you could have chosen differently, but didn't."

JOHN WHITE

Christ; Philem. 18; 2 Pet. 2:13 (1st part); in the middle or passive voice, "to take or suffer wrong, to suffer (oneself) to be wronged," 1 Cor.6:7.

Still *eti* (2089), "yet, as yet, still," is translated "still" in the RV in 1 Cor. 12:31; 2 Cor. 1:10; Gal. 1:10 and 5:11; KJV and RV in **Rev. 22:11** (four times), where the word indicates the permanent character, condition and destiny of the unrighteous and the filthy, the righteous and the holy (for the verbs see the RV); in John 11:30, the best mss. have the word; so RV (KJV omits).

Filthy *rhuparos* (4508), "dirty," is said of shabby clothing, Jas. 2:2: metaphorically, of moral "defilement," **Rev. 22:11** (in the best mss.).

Righteous In **Rev. 22:11** the best texts have *dikaiosune*, "righteousness," with *poieo*, "to do," RV, "let him do righteousness"; the KJV follows those which have the passive voice of *dikaioo* and renders it "let him be righteous," lit., "let him be made righteous."

Holy *hagiazo* (37), "to hallow, sanctify," in the passive voice, "to be made holy, be sanctified," is translated "let him be made holy" in **Rev. 22:11**, the aorist or point tense expressing the definiteness and completeness of the divine act; elsewhere it is rendered by the verb "to sanctify."

22:12 And, behold, I come quickly; and my reward *is* with me, to give every man according as his work shall be.

Quickly *see Revelation 2:5*.

Reward *see Revelation 11:18*.

Give *see* **Reward** at *Revelation 18:6*.

According as *hos* (5613), is sometimes rendered "according as," e.g., **Rev. 22:12**; in 2 Pet. 1:3, the RV has "seeing that," for the KJV "according as."

22:13 I am Alpha and Omega, the beginning and the end, the first and the last.

End *see Revelation 1:8*.

Last *see Revelation 1:11*.

22:14 Blessed *are* they that do his commandments, that they may have right to the tree of life, and may enter in through the gates into the city.

Blessed *see Revelation 1:3*.

Commandments In **Rev. 22:14** the RV, "wash their robes" (for KJV, "do His commandments") follows the most authentic mss. *See also* **Wash** at *Revelation 7:14*.

Right *exousia* (1849), "authority, power," is translated "right" in the RV, for KJV, "power," in John 1:12; Rom. 9:21; 1 Cor. 9:4, 5, 6, 12 (twice), 18; 2 Thess. 3:9, where the "right" is that of being maintained by those among whom the ministers of the gospel had labored, a "right" possessed in virtue of the "authority" given them by Christ, Heb. 13:10; **Rev. 22:14**. *Exousia* first denotes "freedom to act" and then "authority for the action." This is first true of God, Acts 1:7. It was exercised by the Son of God, as from, and in conjunction with, the Father when the Lord was upon earth, in the days of His flesh, Matt. 9:6; John 10:18, as well as in resurrection, Matt. 28:18; John 17:2. All others hold their freedom to act from God (though some of them have abused it), whether angels, Eph. 1:21, or human potentates, Rom. 13:1. Satan offered to delegate his authority over earthly kingdoms to Christ, Luke 4:6, who, though conscious of His "right" to it, refused, awaiting the divinely appointed time.

Gates *see Revelation 21:12*.

22:15 For without *are* dogs, and sorcerers, and whoremongers, and murderers, and idolaters, and whosoever loveth and maketh a lie.

Dogs *kuon* (2965), is used in two senses, (a) natural, Matt. 7:6; Luke 16:21; 2 Pet. 2:22; (b) metaphorical, Phil. 3:2; **Rev. 22:15**, of those whose moral impurity will exclude them from the New Jerusalem. The Jews used the term of Gentiles, under the idea of ceremonial impurity. Among the Greeks it was an epithet of impudence. Lat., *canis*, and Eng., "hound" are etymologically akin to it.

Sorcerers *see Revelation 21:8*.

Whoremongers *see Revelation 21:8*.

Murderers *see Revelation 21:8*.

Idolaters *see Revelation 21:8*.

Lie *see* **Guile** at *Revelation 14:5*.

22:16 I Jesus have sent mine angel to testify unto you these things in the churches. I am the root and the offspring of David, *and* the bright and morning star.

Jesus *see Revelation 1:9*.

Sent *see* **Send** at *Revelation 1:11*.

Testify *martureo* (3140), is frequently rendered "to bear witness, to witness," in the RV, where KJV renders it "to testify," John 2:25; 3:11, 32; 5:39; 15:26; 21:24; 1 Cor. 15:15; Heb. 7:17; 11:4; 1 John 4:14; 5:9; 3 John 3. In the following, however, the RV, like the KJV, has the rendering "to testify," John 4:39, 44; 7:7; 13:21; Acts 26:5; **Rev. 22:16, 18, 20.** *See* also **Record, Testimony** at *Revelation 1:2.*

Root *see Revelation 5:5.*

Offspring *genos* (1085), "a race, family" (akin to *ginomai*, "to become"), denotes "an offspring," Acts 17:28, 29; **Rev. 22:16.**

Bright *see* **White** at *Revelation 15:6.*

Morning *orthrinos* or *orthrios* (3721), "pertaining to dawn or morning," in some mss. in **Rev. 22:16**. *See also Revelation 2:28.*

Star *see* **Stars** at *Revelation 1:16.*

22:17 And the Spirit and the bride say, Come. And let him that heareth say, Come. And let him that is athirst come. And whosoever will, let him take the water of life freely.

Bride *see Revelation 18:23.*

Athirst *see* **Thirst** at *Revelation 7:16.*

Water *see* **Waters** at Revelation *17:1.*

Freely *see Revelation 21:6.*

22:18 For I testify unto every man that heareth the words of the prophecy of this book, If any man shall add unto these things, God shall add unto him the plagues that are written in this book:

Testify *see Revelation 22:16.* In **Rev. 22:18** some texts have *summartureo*, "to bear witness with." *See also* **Record, Testimony** at *Revelation 1:2.*

Prophecy *see Revelation 1:3.*

Book *see Revelation 1:11.*

Add *epitithemi* (2007), lit., "to put upon" (*epi* "upon," *tithemi*, "to put"), has a secondary and somewhat infrequent meaning, "to add to," and is found in this sense in Mark 3:16-17, lit., "He added the name Peter to Simon," "He added to them the name Boanerges," and **Rev. 22:18**, where the word is set in contrast to "take away from" (v. **19**).

Plagues *see Revelation 9:20.*

22:19 And if any man shall take away from the words of the book of this prophecy, God shall take away his part out of the book of life, and out of the holy city, and *from* the things which are written in this book.

Take *aphaireo* (851), "to take away" (*apo*), is used with this meaning in Luke 1:25; 10:42; 16:3; Rom. 11:27, of the "removal" of the sins of Israel; Heb. 10:4, of the impossibility of the "removal" of sins by offerings under the Law; in **Rev. 22:19** (twice).

Prophecy *see Revelation 1:3.*

Part *see* **Parts** at *Revelation 16:19.*

Book *see Revelation 1:11.* In **Rev. 22:19**, the most authentic mss. have *xulon*, "tree (of life)," instead of "*biblion*."

Holy *see Revelation 4:8.*

22:20 He which testifieth these things saith, Surely I come quickly. Amen. Even so, come, Lord Jesus.

Testifieth *see* **Testify** at *Revelation 22:16. See also* **Record, Testimony** at *Revelation 1:2.*

Surely In the KJV of Matt. 26:73; Mark 14:70; John 17:8, *alethos*, "truly," is rendered "surely" (RV, "of a truth"); so *pantos*, "at all events, altogether," in Luke 4:23 (RV, "doubtless"), and *nai*, "yea," in **Rev. 22:20** (RV, "yea").

Quickly *see Revelation 2:5.*

Amen *see Revelation 3:14.*

Even so *see Revelation 1:7.*

22:21 The grace of our Lord Jesus Christ *be* with you all. Amen.

All In **Rev. 22:21**, the RV follows those mss. which have *hagion*, with the article, "(with) the saints"; the KJV those which simply have *panton*, "all," but adds "you" (RV, marg., "with all").

CPSIA information can be obtained
at www.ICGtesting.com
Printed in the USA
LVHW091212221122
733520LV00013B/80